STUDY GUIDE
to accompany
McConnell and Brue
ECONOMICS

About the Authors

William B. Walstad is a professor of economics at the University of Nebraska–Lincoln, where he directs the National Center for Research in Economic Education. He received his Ph.D. degree from the University of Minnesota. Professor Walstad has been honored with a Distinguished Teaching Award at Nebraska. He also received the Henry H. Villard Research Award for his published research in economic education. He is the chair of the Committee on Economic Education of the American Economic Association. He coedited *Teaching Undergraduate Economics: A Handbook for Instructors* (McGraw-Hill) and serves as an associate editor of the *Journal of Economic Education*.

Robert C. Bingham was an undergraduate student at DePauw University and obtained M.A. and Ph.D. degrees from Northwestern University. He taught at the University of Nebraska–Lincoln, where he was a colleague of Professor McConnell before moving to Kent State University, from which he retired in 1985. He was the author of several other study guides and supplements for the principles of economics courses.

To
Tammie, Laura, Kristin, Eileen, Clara, and Martha

Contents

How to Use the Study Guide to Learn Economics   xi

An Introduction to Economics and the Economy

1   The Nature and Method of Economics   1
2   The Economizing Problem   17
3   Individual Markets: Demand and Supply   27
3 Web Applications and Extensions of Supply
       and Demand Analysis
       www.mcconnell16.com   39
4   The Market System   49
5   The U.S. Economy: Private and
       Public Sectors   57
6   The United States in the Global Economy   67

Macroeconomic Measurement and Basic Concepts

7   Measuring Domestic Output and
       National Income   77
8   Introduction to Economic Growth and
       Instability   89
9   Basic Macroeconomic Relationships   99

Macroeconomic Models and Fiscal Policy

10   The Aggregate Expenditures Model   109
11   Aggregate Demand and Aggregate Supply   121
12   Fiscal Policy   135

Money, Banking, and Monetary Policy

13   Money and Banking   147
14   How Banks and Thrifts Create Money   157
15   Monetary Policy   167

Long-Run Perspectives and Macroeconomic Debates

16   Extending the Analysis of Aggregate
       Supply   179
17   Economic Growth   191
18   Deficits, Surpluses, and the Public Debt   201
19   Disputes over Macro Theory and Policy   211

Microeconomics of Product Markets

20   Elasticity of Demand and Supply   221
21   Consumer Behavior and Utility
       Maximization   231

22   The Costs of Production   247
23   Pure Competition   259
24   Pure Monopoly   273
25   Monopolistic Competition and Oligopoly   285
26   Technology, R&D, and Efficiency   299

Microeconomics of Resource Markets

27   The Demand for Resources   309
28   Wage Determination   319
29   Rent, Interest, and Profit   331

Microeconomics of Government

30   Government and Market Failure   341
31   Public Choice Theory and the
       Economics of Taxation   353

Microeconomic Issues and Policies

32   Antitrust Policy and Regulation   363
33   Agriculture: Economics and Policy   373
34   Income Inequality and Poverty   383
35   Labor Market Institutions and Issues:
       Unionism, Discrimination, Immigration   395
36   The Economics of Health Care   407

International Economics and the World Economy

37   International Trade   417
38   Exchange Rates, the Balance of
       Payments, and Trade Deficit   429
39 Web The Economics of Developing Countries
       www.mcconnell16.com   441
40 Web Transition Economies: Russia and China
       www.mcconnell16.com   451

Glossary   463

Answers to Key Questions   489

How to Use the Study Guide to Learn Economics

This *Study Guide* is designed to help you read and understand Campbell R. McConnell and Stanley L. Brue's textbook, *Economics,* sixteenth edition. If used properly, a study guide can be a great aid to you for what is probably your first course in economics.

No one pretends that the study of economics is easy, but it can be made easier. Of course, a study guide will not do your work for you, and its use is no substitute for reading the text. You must be willing to read the text, spend time on the subject, and work at learning if you wish to understand economics.

Many students do read their text and work hard on their economics course and still fail to learn the subject. This occurs because principles of economics is a new subject for these students, and they have had no previous experience in learning economics. They want to learn but do not know just how to go about it. Here is where the *Study Guide* can help. Let's first see what the *Study Guide* contains and then how to use it.

■ WHAT THE STUDY GUIDE IS

This *Study Guide* contains 38 chapters to support your learning of each of the 38 textbook chapters in *Economics.* There are also three more *Study Guide* chapters that support the three **Bonus Web Chapters** for *Economics.* In addition, the *Study Guide* has a **glossary** and answers to each end-of-chapter **Key Question** in your textbook. This *Study Guide* should give you a complete set of resources to advance your learning of principles of economics.

Each *Study Guide* chapter has 11 sections to give you complete coverage of the textbook material in each chapter. The first five sections identify and explain the basic content and concepts in each chapter.

1. An **introduction** explains what is in the chapter of the text and how it is related to material in earlier and later chapters. It points out topics to which you should give special attention and reemphasizes difficult or important principles and facts.

2. A **checklist** tells you the things you should be able to do when you have finished the chapter.

3. A **chapter outline** shows how the chapter is organized and summarizes briefly the essential points made in the chapter.

4. Selected **hints and tips** for each chapter help you master the material and make connections with any previous discussion of a topic.

5. A list of the **important terms** in the chapter points out what you must be able to define in order to understand the material in the chapter. A definition of each term is in the glossary at the end of the *Study Guide.*

The next six sections of the *Study Guide* allow you to **self-test** your understanding of the chapter material.

6. Fill-in questions (short-answer and list questions) help you learn and remember the important generalizations and facts in the chapter.

7. True–false questions test your understanding of the material in the chapter.

8. Multiple-choice questions also give you a chance to check your knowledge of the chapter content and prepare for this type of course examination.

9. Problems help you learn and understand economic concepts by requiring different skills—drawing a graph, completing a table, or finding relationships—to solve the problems.

10. Short answer and **essay questions** can be used as a self-test, to identify important questions in the chapter and to prepare for examinations.

11. Answers to fill-in questions, problems and projects, true–false questions, and multiple-choice questions are found at the end of each chapter. References to the specific pages in the textbook for each true–false, multiple-choice, and short answer or essay question are also provided.

■ HOW TO STUDY AND LEARN WITH THE HELP OF THE *STUDY GUIDE*

1. *Read and outline.* For best results, quickly read the introduction, outline, list of terms, and checklist in the *Study Guide* before you read the chapter in *Economics.* Then read the chapter in the text slowly, keeping one eye on the *Study Guide* outline and the list of terms. Highlight the chapter as you read it by identifying the *major and minor* points and by placing *Study Guide* outline numbers or letters (such as I or A or 1 or a) in the margins. When you have completed the chapter, you will have the chapter highlighted, and the *Study Guide* outline will serve as a handy set of notes on the chapter.

2. *Review and reread.* After you have read the chapter in the text once, return to the introduction, outline, and list of terms in the *Study Guide.* Reread the introduction and outline. Does everything there make sense? If not, go back to the text and reread the topics that you do not remember well or that still confuse you. Look at the outline. Try to recall each of the minor topics or points that were contained in the text under each of the major points in the outline. When you come to the list of terms, go over them one by one. *Define or explain each to yourself and then look for the definition of the term either in the text chapter or in the gloss*ary. Compare your own definition or explanation with that in the *text or glossary.* The quick way to find the definition of a term in the text is to look in the text index for the page(s) in which that term or concept is mentioned. Make any necessary correction or change in your own definition or explanation.

3. *Test and check answers.* When you have done the above reading and review, you will have a good idea of what is in the text chapter. Now complete the self-test sections of the *Study Guide* to check your understanding.

In doing the self-test, start with the *fill-in, true–false, multiple-choice,* and *problems* sections. Tackle each of these four sections one at a time, using the following procedures: (1) answer as many self-test items as you can without looking in the text or in the answer section of the *Study Guide*; (2) check the text for whatever help you need in answering the items; and (3) consult the answer section of the *Study Guide* for the correct answers and reread any section of the text for which you missed items.

The self-test items in these four sections are not equally difficult. Some will be easy to answer and others will be harder. Do not expect to get them all correct the first time. Some are designed to pinpoint material of importance that you will probably miss the first time you read the text and answering them will get you to read the text again with more insight and understanding.

The *short answer and essay questions* cover the major points in the chapter. For some of the easier questions, all you may do is mentally outline your answer. For the more difficult questions, you may want to write out a brief outline of the answer or a full answer. Do not avoid the difficult questions just because they are more work. Answering these questions is often the most valuable work you can do toward acquiring an understanding of economic relationships and principles.

Although no answers are given in the *Study Guide* to the short answer and essay questions, the answer section does list text page references for each question. You are *strongly* encouraged to read those text pages for an explanation of the question or for better insight into the question content.

4. *Double check.* Before you turn to the next chapter in the text and *Study Guide,* return to the checklist. If you cannot honestly check off each item in the list, you have not learned what the authors of the text and of this *Study Guide* hoped you would learn.

■ BONUS WEB CHAPTERS FOR *ECONOMICS*

The *Study Guide* includes chapters to cover the textbook material in the three web-based chapters for *Economics*: Applications and Extensions of Supply and Demand Analysis (Chapter 3W); The Economics of Developing Countries (Chapter 39W); and Transition Economies: Russia and China (Chapter 40W). These chapters are available for students at www.mcconnell16.com.

■ GLOSSARY

All of the important terms and concepts in *Economics* are defined and described in the glossary. It is included in the *Study Guide* for easy reference when you see a term or concept you do not know. It will also aid your work on self-test items in the *Study Guide.*

■ ANSWERS TO KEY QUESTIONS IN *ECONOMICS*

Your textbook has end-of-chapter questions that you can work on to further your understanding of economics. Some of these questions are designated as **Key Questions** because they cover important material. The answer to each Key Question is provided in the final part of the *Study Guide.* It is highly recommended that you try to complete these questions for each textbook chapter and then check the correct answers in the *Study Guide.*

■ SOME FINAL WORDS

Perhaps the method of using the *Study Guide* outlined above seems like a lot of work. It is! Study and learning necessarily entail work on your part. This is a fact you must accept if you are to learn economics.

After you have used the *Study Guide* to study three or four chapters, you will find that some sections are more valuable to you than others. Let your own experience determine how you will use it. But do not discontinue use of the *Study Guide* after three or four chapters merely because you are not sure whether it is helping you. **Stick with it.**

■ ACKNOWLEDGMENTS

The late Professor Robert Bingham prepared the first 10 editions of the *Study Guide* to serve as a valuable instructional aid for students. Although Professor Bingham did not participate directly in this revision, his work remains a major contribution.

I also want to acknowledge the other help I received. Campbell McConnell and Stanley Brue offered many insightful comments on the *Study Guide* and encouraged my work. I have also received valuable suggestions and help over the years from Kevin Clark, Loretta Fairchild, Joyce Gleason, Richard Harmstone, Ralph Lewis, Peter Kerr, Ken Rebeck, Dave Rosenbaum, Casey Snyder, Mary Stevenson, and Joshua Stull. Students in my principles of economics classes at the University of Nebraska–Lincoln continue to give me feedback that has improved the *Study Guide* with each edition. Sharon Nemeth has been of invaluable assistance in preparing and proofing the manuscript. Lucille Sutton and Erin Strathmann at McGraw-Hill provided great editorial and production support. In spite of the contributions from others, all responsibility for errors and omissions are mine. And as one final note, users of the *Study Guide* are encouraged to send me comments or suggestions at any time.

William B. Walstad

STUDY GUIDE
to accompany
McConnell and Brue
ECONOMICS

CHAPTER 1

The Nature and Method of Economics

Chapter 1 introduces you to economics—the study of how people decide how to use scarce productive resources to satisfy material wants. The purpose of this chapter is to explain the nature of the subject and to describe the methods that economists use to study economic questions.

The first section of the chapter describes the three key features of the **economic perspective.** This perspective first recognizes that all choices involve costs and that these costs must be involved in an economic decision. The economic perspective also incorporates the view that to achieve a goal, people make decisions that reflect their rational self-interest. The third feature considers that people compare marginal benefits against marginal costs when making decisions and will choose the situation where the marginal benefit is greater than the marginal cost. You will develop a better understanding of these features and the meaning of the economic perspective as you read about the economic issues in this book.

As you begin your study of economics, you might be wondering if the work you will do to learn the chapter material is worthwhile. It most certainly is. Knowledge of economics is important because it is essential for well-informed citizenship and has many practical applications to professional and personal decisions.

Economics relies heavily on the scientific method to develop theories and principles to explain the likely effects from human events and behavior. A central part of the economic methodology section focuses on **theoretical economics.** It involves gathering data, creating models, and making generalizations. In essence, economic theories and principles (and related terms such as hypotheses, laws, and models) are generalizations. They are imprecise statements and subject to exceptions because economists cannot easily conduct controlled laboratory experiments to test the validity of the generalizations. Economic theories and principles are simplifications—approximations of a complex world—for analyzing problems and for finding solutions to these problems.

Policy economics develops recommended actions (policies) for addressing an economic problem or advancing an economic goal. It involves stating the goal, considering the policy options, and evaluating the likely outcome. The analysis is based on economic theories and principles, but the choice of an economic policy often depends on the value judgments and weights given to different economic goals. In making a policy recommendation, we move from **economic theory** and **positive economics,** which investigates what is, to **normative economics,** which incorporates subjective views of what ought to be. Many of the apparent disagreements among economists are over normative policy issues and involve deciding which economic goals for our economy are most important in making the case for a policy solution.

Both theoretical economics and policy economics are conducted at two levels. Studies in **macroeconomics** focus on the whole economy, or large segments of it, and investigate such issues as how to increase economic growth, control inflation, or maintain full employment. Studies in **microeconomics** target specific units in the economy, and conduct research on such questions as how prices and output are determined for particular products and how consumers will react to price changes.

Clear thinking about economic questions requires that beginning students avoid many pitfalls. Errors of commission and omission can occur from bias, loaded terminology, imprecise definitions, fallacies of composition, and causation fallacies. Awareness of these pitfalls will help you think more objectively about the economic issues you will read about throughout this book.

■ CHECKLIST

When you have studied this chapter you should be able to

☐ Write a formal definition of economics.
☐ Describe the three key features of the economic perspective.
☐ Give applications of the economic perspective.
☐ Give two good reasons for studying economics.
☐ Identify the elements of the scientific method.
☐ Describe theoretical economics.
☐ Distinguish among hypotheses, theories, principles, laws, and models.
☐ Discuss how economic principles are generalizations and abstractions.
☐ Explain the "other things equal" (*ceteris paribus*) assumption and its use in economics.
☐ Define policy economics.
☐ List three steps in economic policymaking.
☐ Identify eight economic goals widely accepted in the United States and many other nations.
☐ Discuss the conflicting or complementary nature of economic goals.
☐ Distinguish between macroeconomics and microeconomics.

☐ Give examples of positive and normative economics.
☐ Identify the five pitfalls to objective thinking when given examples.

■ CHAPTER OUTLINE

1. Economics is concerned with the efficient use of limited productive resources to achieve the maximum satisfaction of economic wants.

2. The *economic perspective* has three interrelated features.

a. It recognizes that scarcity requires choice and all choices entail a cost.
b. It views people as rational decision makers who make choices based on their self-interests.
c. It uses marginal analysis to assess how the marginal costs of a decision compare with the marginal benefits.

3. Citizens in a democracy must understand elementary economics to comprehend the present-day problems of their society and to make intelligent decisions when they vote. Economics is an academic rather than a vocational subject, but a knowledge of it is valuable to business executives, consumers, and workers.

4. Economic methodology relies on the scientific method and includes both theoretical economics and policy economics.

a. *Theoretical economics* is the gathering and analysis of relevant facts to derive economic principles.
(1) Hypotheses are propositions that are tested and used to develop economic theories. Highly reliable theories are called principles or laws. Theories, principles, and laws are meaningful statements about economic behavior or the economy that can be used to predict the likely outcome from an economic action or event. Models are created when several economic principles are used to explain or describe reality.
(2) Each principle or theory is a generalization that shows a tendency or average effect.
(3) The "other-things-equal" (*ceteris paribus*) assumption is used to limit the influence of other factors when making a generalization.
(4) Economic principles and theories are abstractions from reality.
(5) Many economic principles or models can be illustrated graphically.
b. *Policy economics* is the use of economic principles to develop a course of action to solve economic problems.
(1) The three steps in creating economic policy are stating the goal, considering the options, and evaluating the results.
(2) Eight major economic goals are considered important in the United States and many other nations: economic growth, full employment, economic efficiency, price-level stability, economic freedom, eco-

nomic security, an equitable distribution of income, and a balance of trade. Economic goals can be complementary, or they can conflict and require tradeoffs. The interpretation of economic goals and the setting of priorities can be difficult and cause problems in economic policymaking.

5. Economic analysis is conducted at two levels, and might be positive or normative.

a. *Macroeconomics* looks at the entire economy or its major aggregates or sectors, such as households, businesses, or government.
b. *Microeconomics* studies the economic behavior of individuals, particular markets, firms, or industries.
c. *Positive economics* focuses on facts and is concerned with what is, or the scientific analysis of economic behavior.
d. *Normative economics* suggests what ought to be and answers policy questions based on value judgments. Most disagreements among economists involve normative economics.

6. Sound reasoning in the study and use of economic principles requires strict application of the rules of logic, in which personal emotions are irrelevant, if not detrimental. The pitfalls beginning students encounter when studying and applying economic principles include the following:

a. Bias of preconceived beliefs not warranted by facts.
b. Loaded terminology or the use of terms in a way that appeals to emotion and leads to a nonobjective analysis of the issues.
c. The definition of terms by economists in ways that may not be the same as the ways in which these terms are more commonly used.
d. The fallacy of composition or the assumption that what is true of the part is necessarily true of the whole.
e. Two causation fallacies confuse cause and effect.
(1) The "after this, therefore because of this fallacy" (*post hoc, ergo propter hoc*) is the mistaken belief that when one event precedes another, the first event is the cause of the second.
(2) The other fallacy is to confuse correlation with causation. Two factors may be related, but that does not mean that one factor caused the other.

■ HINTS AND TIPS

1. The economic perspective presented in the first section of the chapter has three features related to decision making: scarcity and the necessity of choice, rational self-interest in decision making, and marginal analysis of the costs and benefits of decisions. Although these features may seem strange to you at first, they are central to the economic thinking used to examine decisions and problems throughout the book.

2. The chapter introduces important pairs of terms: theoretical economics and policy economics; microeconomics and macroeconomics; and positive economics and normative economics. Make sure you understand what each pair means.

3. Sound reasoning about economic problems is difficult and requires that you be able to recognize the major pitfalls—loaded terminology, inaccurate definitions, fallacy of composition, *post hoc* fallacy, and confusing correlation with causation. One way to remember these pitfalls is to associate each one with a practical example.

■ **IMPORTANT TERMS**

Note: See Glossary in the back of the book for definitions of terms.

economics

economic perspective

utility

marginal analysis

scientific method

theoretical economics

principles

generalizations

"other-things-equal" assumption (*ceteris paribus*)

policy economics

tradeoffs

macroeconomics

aggregate

microeconomics

positive economics

normative economics

fallacy of composition

"after this, therefore because of this" fallacy (*post hoc, ergo propter hoc*)

SELF-TEST

■ **FILL-IN QUESTIONS**

1. Economics is the study of the efficient use of (unlimited, limited) __limited__ resources to achieve (minimum, maximum) __maximum__ satisfaction of economic wants.

2. The economic perspective recognizes that (resources, scarcity) __Scarcity__ requires choice and that choice has an opportunity (benefit, cost) __cost__. "There is no such thing as a free lunch" in economics because scarce resources have (unlimited, alternative) __alternative__ uses.

3. The economic perspective also assumes that people make choices based on their self-interest and that they are (irrational, rational) __rational__. It also is based on comparisons of the (extreme, marginal) __marginal__ costs and benefits of an economic decision.

4. An understanding of economics is essential if we are to be well-informed (citizens, technicians) __citizens__, and such an understanding has many personal and professional applications even though it is (a vocational, an academic) __academic__ and not __vocational__ subject.

5. Economics relies on the (model, scientific) __Scientific__ method. It involves the gathering of

(facts, theories) __facts__, and the formulation of (data, hypotheses) __hypotheses__. These are then tested to develop (facts, theories) __theories__.

6. The systematic arranging of facts, the interpretation of them, and the drawing of conclusions based on them is called (policy, theoretical) _____ economics.

7. Statements about economic behavior that enable the prediction of the likely effects of certain actions are economic (facts, theories) __theories__. The most reliable of these, those with strong predictive accuracy, are called (hypotheses, principles) __Principles__. Sometimes they are also called (policies, laws) __laws__. Simplified representations of how markets or the economy works based on combinations of economic principles are called (policies, models) __models__.

8. Economic principles are often imprecise quantitative statements or (fallacies, generalizations) __generalizations__ about people's economic behavior, and they necessarily involve (abstractions, distractions) __abstractions__ from reality to simplify complex situations.

9. When economists assume that other factors are held constant and do not change when studying an economic relationship, they are using the (*post hoc*, other-things-equal) _____ assumption.

10. The formulation of recommended solutions or remedies for economic problems is referred to as (theoretical, policy) __Policy__ economics.

11. The three steps in the formulation of economic policy are (1) stating the economic (theory, goal) __Goal__, (2) determining the policy (results, options) __options__, and (3) implementing and evaluating policy (assumptions, effectiveness) __effectiveness__

12. Eight widely accepted economic goals in the United States and many nations are

a. __economic growth__

b. __Full employment__

c. __Economic efficiency__

d. __Price level stability__

e. __Economic freedom__

f. __Equitable distribution of income__

g. __Economic security__

h. __Balance of trade__

13. Increases in economic growth that promote full employment would be an example of a set of (conflicting, complementary) _Complementary_ economic goals. Efforts to achieve an equitable distribution of income that at the same time reduce economic efficiency would be an example of a set of (conflicting, complementary) _Conflicting_ economic goals, indicating that there are (tradeoffs, laws) _tradeoffs_ among economic goals.

14. The study of the total output of the economy or the general level of prices is the subject of (microeconomics, macroeconomics) _Macro_, whereas the study of output in a particular industry or of a particular product is the subject of _micro_.

15. The collection of specific units that are being added and treated as if they were one unit is an (assumption, aggregate) _____.

16. Two different types of statements can be made about economic topics. A (positive, normative) _____ statement explains what is, by offering a scientific proposition about economic behavior that is based on economic theory and facts, but a _____ statement includes a value judgment about an economic policy or the economy that suggests what ought to be. Many of the reported disagreements among economists usually involve (positive, normative) _____ statements.

17. Holding a preconceived notion, such as thinking that corporate profits are always excessive, is an example of (an aggregate, a bias) _____ pitfall in sound economic thinking.

18. Pitfalls to sound economic thinking can also occur because terminology is (theoretical, loaded) _____ and definitions used by the public are based on (common, scientific) _____ usage.

19. The statement that "What is good for the individual is also good for the group" may not be correct because of the fallacy of (complexity, composition) _____.

20. The person who believes that "washing a car will cause it to rain tomorrow" is expressing an ("other-things-equal," "after this, therefore because of this") _____ fallacy.

■ **TRUE–FALSE QUESTIONS**

Circle T if the statement is true, F if it is false.

1. Economics is the social science concerned with the efficient use of scarce resources to achieve the maximum satisfaction of economic wants. **T** F

2. From the economic perspective, "there is no such thing as a free lunch." **T** F

3. Rational self-interest is the same thing as being selfish. **T** F

4. The economic perspective views individuals or institutions as making rational choices based on the marginal analysis of the costs and benefits of decisions. **T** F

5. Economics is academic and of little value because it does not teach the student how to earn a living. **T** F

6. The scientific method involves the observation of real-world data, the formulation of hypotheses based on the data, and the testing of those hypotheses to develop theories. **T** F

7. Systematically arranging facts, interpreting them, and using them to derive economic principles is called economic analysis. **T** F

8. Economic principles enable us to predict the economic consequences of many human actions. T **F**

9. The most reliable economic theories are often called economic principles or laws. **T** F

10. An economic model is simply an adding up of economic facts about an economic event. **T** F

11. The "other-things-equal" or *ceteris paribus* assumption is made to simplify the reasoning process. T **F**

12. Economic principles, or theories, are abstractions. **T** F

13. The first step in the formulation of an economic policy, the statement of goals, may be occasion for disagreement because different people may have different and conflicting goals to be achieved. T **F**

14. Determining the policy options requires a detailed assessment of the benefits, costs, and political feasibility of alternative policies. T **F**

15. One of the widely (although not universally) accepted economic goals of people in the United States is an equitable distribution of income. **T** F

16. A tradeoff is a situation in which some of one economic goal is sacrificed to obtain some of another economic goal. **T** F

17. Macroeconomic analysis is concerned with the economic activity of specific firms or industries. T **F**

18. Microeconomic analysis is concerned with the performance of the economy as a whole or its major aggregates. **T** F

19. The statement that "the legal minimum wage should be raised to give working people a decent income" is an example of a normative statement. T **F**

20. When value judgments are made about the economy or economic policy, this is called positive economics. **T** F

21. The belief that lending money is always superior to borrowing money is an example of a bias in sound reasoning about economic issues. T F

22. The fallacy of composition would be calling profits "excessive" or an unemployed worker "lazy." T F

23. If you speak of "capital" to most people, they understand that you are referring to money. The economist, therefore, is obligated to use the term "capital" to mean money. **T F**

24. The *post hoc, ergo propter hoc* fallacy is the belief that "what is true for the individual or part of a group is necessarily true for the group or whole." **T F**

25. A person who concludes that more education increases income may be confusing correlation with causation. **T F**

■ **MULTIPLE-CHOICE QUESTIONS**

Circle the letter that corresponds to the best answer.

1. What statement would best complete a short definition of economics? "Economics is the study of
(a) how businesses produce goods and services"
(b) the efficient use of scarce productive resources"
(c) the equitable distribution of society's income and wealth"
(d) the printing and circulation of money throughout the economy"

2. The idea in economics that "there is no such thing as a free lunch" means that
(a) the marginal benefit of such a lunch is greater than its marginal cost
(b) businesses cannot increase their market share by offering free lunches
(c) scarce resources have alternative uses or opportunity costs
(d) consumers are irrational when they ask for a free lunch

3. A major feature of the economic perspective is
(a) equating rational self-interest with selfishness
(b) comparing marginal benefits with marginal costs
(c) the validity of normative economics for decision making
(d) the recognition of the abundance of economic resources

4. From the economic perspective, when a business decides to employ more workers, the business decision maker has most likely concluded that the marginal
(a) costs of employing more workers have decreased
(b) benefits of employing more workers have increased
(c) benefits of employing more workers are greater than the marginal costs
(d) costs of employing more workers are not opportunity costs for the business because more workers are needed to increase production

5. Economic analysis that derives economic principles about how individuals behave or institutions act is called
(a) policy economics
(b) macroeconomics
(c) normative economics
(d) theoretical economics

6. The combination of economic theories or principles into a simplified representation of reality is referred to as an economic
(a) fact
(b) law
(c) model
(d) hypothesis

7. From the perspective of economists, which of the following would offer the highest degree of confidence for explaining economic behavior
(a) an assumption
(b) a speculation
(c) a correlation
(d) a principle

8. When economists state that "consumer spending rises when personal income increases," this is an example of
(a) a generalization
(b) loaded terminology
(c) a normative statement
(d) a fallacy of composition

9. Another term for the assumption that "other things equal" is
(a) *ceteris paribus*
(b) the correlation fallacy
(c) the fallacy of composition
(d) *post hoc, ergo propter hoc*

10. An economic principle states that the lower the price of a product, the greater the quantity consumers will wish to purchase. This principle is based on the critical assumption that
(a) economic analysis is normative
(b) the whole is not greater than the sum of the parts
(c) economic goals are complementary and not conflicting
(d) there are no other important changes affecting the demand for the product

11. The three basic steps in economic policymaking are
(a) gather facts, make abstractions, show findings
(b) state the goal, determine the options, evaluate results
(c) create the theory, analyze assumptions, derive conclusions
(d) form hypotheses, simplify the model, assume other things are equal

12. The production of more goods and services and the development of a higher standard of living would be associated with what economic goal?
(a) economic security
(b) economic freedom
(c) economic growth
(d) full employment

13. Which economic goal is associated with the idea that we want to get the maximum benefit at the minimum cost from the limited productive resources available?
(a) economic security
(b) economic freedom
(c) economic growth
(d) economic efficiency

14. Which economic goal would be most abstract and difficult to measure?
- **(a)** full employment
- **(b)** economic efficiency
- **(c)** economic freedom
- **(d)** price-level stability

15. To say that two economic goals are conflicting means
- **(a)** it is impossible to quantify both goals
- **(b)** there is a tradeoff in the achievement of the two goals
- **(c)** the two goals are not fully accepted as important economic goals
- **(d)** the attainment of one goal also results in the attainment of the other goal

16. If economic growth tends to produce a more equitable distribution of income among people in a nation, this relationship between the two economic goals appears to be
- **(a)** deductive
- **(b)** conflicting
- **(c)** complementary
- **(d)** mutually exclusive

17. When we look at the whole economy or its major aggregates, our analysis would be at the level of
- **(a)** microeconomics
- **(b)** macroeconomics
- **(c)** positive economics
- **(d)** normative economics

18. Which would be studied in microeconomics?
- **(a)** the output of the entire U.S. economy
- **(b)** the general level of prices in the U.S. economy
- **(c)** the output and price of wheat in the United States
- **(d)** the total number of workers employed in the United States

19. Which is a normative economic statement?
- **(a)** The consumer price index rose 1.2% last month.
- **(b)** The unemployment rate of 6.8% is too high.
- **(c)** The average rate of interest on loans is 4.6%.
- **(d)** The economy grew at an annual rate of 3.6%.

20. Sandra states that "there is a high correlation between consumption and income." Arthur replies that the correlation occurs because "people consume too much of their income and don't save enough."
- **(a)** Both Sandra's and Arthur's statements are positive.
- **(b)** Both Sandra's and Arthur's statements are normative.
- **(c)** Sandra's statement is positive and Arthur's statement is normative.
- **(d)** Sandra's statement is normative and Arthur's statement is positive.

21. What pitfall to sound reasoning is reflected in a person's view that corporate profits are always excessive?
- **(a)** bias
- **(b)** definition
- **(c)** the fallacy of composition
- **(d)** confusing correlation and causation

22. During World War II, the United States used price controls to prevent inflation; some people said this was "a fascist and arbitrary restriction of economic freedom," while others said it was "a necessary and democratic means of preventing ruinous inflation." Both labels are examples of
- **(a)** economic bias
- **(b)** loaded terminology
- **(c)** the fallacy of composition
- **(d)** the misuse of commonsense definitions

23. If a farmer grows a larger crop one year, he or she will likely receive more income. Therefore, to reason that if all farmers grew larger crops one year they will likely receive more income is an example of
- **(a)** the after this, therefore because of this fallacy
- **(b)** the fallacy of composition
- **(c)** using loaded terminology
- **(d)** economic bias

24. The government increases its expenditures for road construction equipment, and later the average price of this equipment falls. The belief that the lowered price was the result of the increase in government expenditures is an example of
- **(a)** the after this, therefore because of this fallacy
- **(b)** the fallacy of composition
- **(c)** using loaded terminology
- **(d)** imprecise definition

25. You observe that more education is associated with more income and conclude that more income leads to more education. This would be an example of
- **(a)** the fallacy of composition
- **(b)** confusing correlation and causation
- **(c)** using the other-things-equal assumption
- **(d)** the after this, therefore because of this fallacy

■ **PROBLEMS**

1. Use the appropriate number to match the terms with the phrase.

1. economics	**5. microeconomics**
2. theoretical economics	**6. positive economics**
3. policy economics	**7. normative economics**
4. macroeconomics	**8. marginal analysis**

a. The formulation of courses of action to bring about desired economic outcomes or to prevent undesired occurrences. _____

b. The attempt to establish scientific statements about economic behavior; a concern with "what is" rather than "what ought to be." _____

c. Part of economics that involves value judgments about what the economy should be like or the way the economic world should be. _____

d. Social science concerned with the efficient use of scarce resources to achieve maximum satisfaction of human material wants. _____

e. Part of economics concerned with the whole economy or its major sectors. _____

f. The comparison of additional benefits and additional costs. _____

g. Deriving economic principles from relevant economic facts. _____

h. Part of economics concerned with the economic behavior of individual units such as households, firms, and industries (particular markets). _____

2. ***News report:*** "The worldwide demand for wheat from the United States increased and caused the price of wheat in the United States to rise." This is a *specific* instance of a more *general* economic principle. Of which economic *generalization* is this a particular example? _____

_____

_____

3. Following is a list of economic statements. Indicate in the space to the right of each statement whether it is positive (**P**) or normative (**N**). Then, in the last four lines below, write two of your own examples of positive economic statements and two examples of normative economic statements.

a. New York City should control the rental price of apartments. _____

b. Consumer prices rose at an annual rate of 2% last year. _____

c. Most people who are unemployed are just too lazy to work. _____

d. Generally, if you lower the price of a product, people will buy more of that product. _____

e. The profits of drug companies are too large and ought to be used to conduct research on new medicines. _____

f. Government should do more to help the poor. _____

g. _____ P

h. _____ P

i. _____ N

j. _____ N

4. Following are five statements. Each is an example of one of the pitfalls frequently encountered in the study of economics. Indicate in the space following each statement the type of pitfall involved.

a. "Investment in stocks and bonds is the only way to build real capital assets." _____

b. "An unemployed worker can find a job if the worker looks diligently and conscientiously for employment; therefore, all unemployed workers can find employment if they are diligent and conscientious in looking for a job."

_____

c. ***McConnell:*** "Regulation of public utilities in the United States is an immoral and unconscionable interference with the divine right of private property and, as you know, there is no private property in the socialist nations." ***Brue:*** "It is far from that. You know perfectly well that it is an attempt to limit the unmitigated avarice of mammoth corporations in order, as the Constitution commands, to promote the general welfare of a democratic America." _____

_____

d. "The stock market crash of 1929 was followed by and resulted in 10 years of depression." _____

_____

e. "Be neither a borrower nor lender of money." _____

_____

■ SHORT ANSWER AND ESSAY QUESTIONS

1. Define economics in both a less and a more sophisticated way. In your latter definition, explain the meaning of "resources" and "wants."

2. What are the three interrelated features of the economic perspective?

3. What is the economic meaning of the statement "There is no such thing as a free lunch"?

4. What is the difference between rational self-interest and selfishness?

5. How do economists use marginal analysis?

6. What are the principal reasons for studying economics?

7. What are the elements of the scientific method?

8. Define and explain the relationships between economic theory and policy economics.

9. What are the differences and similarities between hypotheses, theories, principles, laws, and models?

10. What is a "laboratory experiment under controlled conditions"? Does the science of economics have any kind of laboratory? Why do economists use the "other-things-equal" assumption?

11. Why are economic principles and models necessarily generalized and abstract?

12. What does it mean to say that economic principles can be used for prediction?

13. What procedure should be followed in formulating sound economic policies?

14. Of the eight economic goals listed in the text, which one would you rank first, second, third, and so on? Would you add any other goals to this list? If the goals of full employment and price-level stability were conflicting, which goal would you prefer? Why? If goals of economic growth and an equitable distribution of income were conflicting, which would you prefer? Why?

15. How can the concept "tradeoffs" be applied to the discussion of economic goals? Give an example.

16. Explain the difference between macroeconomics and microeconomics.

17. Why do economists disagree?

18. What are some current examples of positive economic statements and normative economic statements?

19. Explain each of the following terms:
- **(a)** fallacy of composition
- **(b)** loaded terminology
- **(c)** the *post hoc, ergo propter hoc* fallacy

20. Use an example to describe how correlation differs from causation.

ANSWERS

Chapter 1 The Nature and Method of Economics

FILL-IN QUESTIONS

1. limited, maximum
2. scarcity, cost, alternative
3. rational, marginal
4. citizens, an academic, a vocational
5. scientific, facts, hypotheses, theories
6. theoretical
7. theories, principles, laws, models
8. generalizations, abstractions
9. other-things-equal (or *ceteris paribus*)
10. policy
11. goal, options, effectiveness
12. *a.* economic growth; *b.* full employment; *c.* economic efficiency; *d.* price stability; *e.* economic freedom; *f.* equitable distribution of income; *g.* economic security; *h.* balance of trade (*any order for a–h*)
13. complementary, conflicting, tradeoffs
14. macroeconomics, microeconomics
15. aggregate
16. positive, normative, normative
17. bias
18. loaded, common
19. composition
20. "after this, therefore because of this"

TRUE–FALSE QUESTIONS

1. T, p. 3	**8.** T, pp. 6–7	**15.** T, p. 9	**22.** F, p. 11
2. T, p. 3	**9.** T, pp. 6–7	**16.** T, p. 9	**23.** F, p. 11
3. F, p. 4	**10.** F, pp. 6–7	**17.** F, pp. 9–10	**24.** F, p. 11
4. T, pp. 4–5	**11.** T, pp. 7–8	**18.** F, pp. 9–10	**25.** T, pp. 11–12
5. F, p. 5	**12.** T, p. 8	**19.** T, p. 10	
6. T, p. 6	**13.** T, pp. 8–9	**20.** F, p. 10	
7. F, p. 6	**14.** T, p. 8	**21.** T, p. 10	

MULTIPLE-CHOICE QUESTIONS

1. b, p. 3	**8.** a, p. 7	**15.** b, p. 9	**22.** b, p. 10–11
2. c, pp. 3–4	**9.** a, pp. 7–8	**16.** c, p. 9	**23.** b, p. 11
3. b, pp. 4–5	**10.** d, pp. 7–8	**17.** b, p. 9	**24.** a, p. 11
4. c, pp. 4–5	**11.** b, p. 8	**18.** c, p. 9–10	**25.** b, pp. 11–12
5. d, p. 6	**12.** c, p. 8	**19.** b, p. 10	
6. c, p. 7	**13.** d, p. 9	**20.** c, p. 10	
7. d, p. 7	**14.** c, p. 9	**21.** a, pp. 10–11	

PROBLEMS

1. *a.* 3; *b.* 6; *c.* 7; *d.* 1; *e.* 4; *f.* 8; *g.* 2; *h.* 5
2. An increase in the demand for an economic good will cause the price of that good to rise.
3. *a.* N; *b.* P; *c.* N; *d.* P; *e.* N; *f.* N
4. *a.* definitions; *b.* the fallacy of composition; *c.* loaded terminology; *d.* the after this, therefore because of this fallacy; *e.* bias

SHORT ANSWER AND ESSAY QUESTIONS

1. p. 3	**6.** pp. 5–6	**11.** pp. 7–8	**16.** pp. 9–10
2. pp. 3–4	**7.** p. 6	**12.** pp. 7–8	**17.** p. 10
3. pp. 3–4	**8.** pp. 6–9	**13.** pp. 8–9	**18.** p. 10
4. p. 4	**9.** pp. 6–8	**14.** pp. 8–9	**19.** pp. 10–11
5. p. 4	**10.** pp. 7–8	**15.** p. 9	**20.** pp. 11–12

APPENDIX TO CHAPTER 1

Graphs and Their Meaning

This appendix introduces graphing in economics. Graphs help illustrate and simplify the economic theories and models presented throughout this book. The old saying that "a picture is worth 1000 words" applies to economics; graphs are the way that economists "picture" relationships between economic variables.

You must master the basics of graphing if these "pictures" are to be of any help to you. This appendix explains how to achieve that mastery. It shows you how to construct a graph from a table with data of two variables, such as income and consumption.

Economists usually, but not always, place the **independent variable** (income) on the horizontal axis and the **dependent variable** (consumption) on the vertical axis of the graph. Once the data points are plotted and a line drawn to connect the plotted points, you can determine whether there is a **direct** or an **inverse relationship** between the variables. Identifying direct and inverse relationships between variables is an essential skill used repeatedly in this book.

Information from data in graphs and tables can be written in an equation. This work involves determining the **slope** and **intercept** from a straight line in a graph or data in a table. Using values for the slope and intercept, you can write a **linear equation** that will enable you to calculate what the dependent variable would be for a given level of the independent variable.

Some graphs used in the book are *nonlinear*. With **nonlinear curves,** the slope of the line is no longer constant throughout but varies as one moves along the curve. This slope can be estimated at a point by determining the slope of a straight line that is drawn tangent to the curve at that point. Similar calculations can be made for other points to see how the slope changes along the curve.

■ APPENDIX CHECKLIST

After you have studied this appendix you should be able to

☐ Explain why economists use graphs.
☐ Construct a graph of two variables using the numerical data from a table.
☐ Make a table with two variables from data on a graph.
☐ Distinguish between a direct and an inverse relationship when given data on two variables.
☐ Identify dependent and independent variables in economic examples and graphs.
☐ Describe how economists use the other-things-equal (*ceteris paribus*) assumption in graphing two variables.

☐ Calculate the slope of a straight line between two points when given the tabular data, and indicate whether the slope is positive or negative.
☐ Describe how slopes are affected by the choice of the units of measurement for either variable.
☐ Explain how slopes are related to marginal analysis.
☐ Graph infinite or zero slopes and explain their meaning.
☐ Determine the vertical intercept for a straight line in a graph with two variables.
☐ Write a linear equation using the slope of a line and the vertical intercept; when given a value for the independent variable, determine a value for the dependent variable.
☐ Estimate the slope of a nonlinear curve at a point using a line that is tangent to the curve at that point.

■ APPENDIX OUTLINE

1. Graphs illustrate the relationship between variables and give economists and students another way, in addition to verbal explanation, of understanding economic phenomena. Graphs are aids in describing economic theories and models.

2. The construction of a simple graph involves plotting the numerical data of two variables from a table.

  a. Each graph has a **horizontal axis** and a **vertical axis** that can be labeled for each variable and then scaled for the range of the data points that will be measured on the axis.

  b. Data points are plotted on the graph by drawing perpendiculars from the scaled points on the two axes to the place on the graph where the perpendiculars intersect.

  c. A line or curve can then be drawn to connect the points plotted on the graph. If the graph is a straight line, it is *linear*.

3. A graph provides information about relationships between variables.

  a. An upward-sloping line to the right on a graph indicates that there is a positive or **direct relationship** between two variables: an increase in one is associated with an increase in the other; a decrease in one is associated with a decrease in the other.

  b. A downward-sloping line to the right means that there is a negative or **inverse relationship** between the two variables: an increase in one is associated with a decrease in the other; a decrease in one is associated with an increase in the other.

4. Economists are often concerned with determining cause and effect in economic events.

    a. A ***dependent variable*** changes (increases or decreases) because of a change in another variable.

    b. An ***independent variable*** produces or "causes" the change in the dependent variable.

    c. In a graph, mathematicians place an independent variable on the horizontal axis and a dependent variable on the vertical axis; economists are more arbitrary about which variable is placed on an axis.

5. Economic graphs are simplifications of economic relationships. When graphs are plotted, usually an implicit assumption is made that all other factors are being held constant. This "other-things-equal" or *ceteris paribus* assumption is used to simplify the analysis so the study can focus on the two variables of interest.

6. The ***slope of a straight line*** in a two-variable graph is the ratio of the vertical change to the horizontal change between two points.

    a. A *positive* slope indicates that the relationship between the two variables is *direct*.

    b. A *negative* slope indicates that there is an *inverse* relationship between the two variables.

    c. Slopes are affected by the *measurement units* for either variable.

    d. Slopes measure *marginal* changes.

    e. Slopes can be *infinite* (line parallel to vertical axis) or *zero* (line parallel to horizontal axis).

7. The ***vertical intercept*** of a straight line in a two-variable graph is the point where the line intersects the vertical axis of the graph.

8. The slope and intercept of a straight line can be expressed in the form of a *linear equation,* which is written as $y = a + bx$. Once the values for the intercept (a) and the slope (b) are calculated, then given any value of the independent variable (x), the value of the dependent variable (y) can be determined.

9. The slope of a straight line is constant, but the slope of a ***nonlinear curve*** changes throughout. To estimate the slope of a nonlinear curve at a point, the slope of a line tangent to the curve at that point is calculated.

■ HINTS AND TIPS

1. This appendix will help you understand the graphs and problems presented throughout the book. Do not skip reading the appendix or working on the self-test questions and problems in this *Study Guide.* The time you invest now will pay off in improved understanding in later chapters. Graphing is a basic skill for economic analysis.

2. Positive and negative relationships in graphs often confuse students. To overcome this confusion, draw a two-variable graph with a positive slope and another two-variable graph with a negative slope. In each graph, show what happens to the value of one variable when there is a change in the value of the other variable.

3. A straight line in a two-variable graph can be expressed in an equation. Make sure you know how to interpret each part of the linear equation.

■ IMPORTANT TERMS

vertical axis	independent variable
horizontal axis	slope of a straight line
direct (positive) relationship	vertical intercept
inverse (negative) relationship	nonlinear curve
dependent variable	tangent

SELF-TEST

■ FILL-IN QUESTIONS

1. The relationship between two economic variables can be visualized with the aid of a two-dimensional (graph, matrix) _____, which has (a horizontal, an inverse) _____ axis and a (vertical, direct) _____ axis.

2. Customarily, the (dependent, independent) _____ variable is placed on the horizontal axis and the _____ is placed on the vertical axis. The _____ variable is said to change because of a change in the _____ variables.

3. The vertical and horizontal (scales, ranges) _____ of the graph are calibrated to reflect the _____ of values in the table of data points on which the graph is based.

4. The graph of a straight line that slopes downward to the right indicates that there is (a direct, an inverse) _____ relationship between the two variables. A graph of a straight line that slopes upward to the right tells us that the relationship is (direct, inverse) _____. When the value of one variable increases and the value of the other variable increases, then the relationship is _____; when the value of one increases, while the other decreases, the relationship is _____.

5. When interpreting an economic graph, the "cause" or the "source" is the (dependent, independent) _____ variable and the "effect" or "outcome" is the _____ variable.

6. Other variables, beyond the two in a two-dimensional graph, that might affect the economic relationship are assumed to be (changing, held constant) _____. This assumption is also referred to as the "other-things-equal" assumption or as (*post hoc, ceteris paribus*) _____.

7. The slope of a straight line between two points is defined as the ratio of the (vertical, horizontal) _____ change to the _____ change.

8. When two variables move in the same direction, the slope will be (negative, positive) _____; when the variables move in opposite directions, the slope will be _____.

9. The slope of a line will be affected by the (units of measurement, vertical intercept) _____.

10. The concept of a slope is important to economists because it reflects the (marginal, total) _____ change in one variable on another variable.

11. A graph of a line with an infinite slope is (horizontal, vertical) _____, while a graph of a line with a zero slope is _____.

12. The point at which the slope of the line meets the vertical axis is called the vertical (tangent, intercept) _____.

13. We can express the graph of a straight line with a linear equation that can be written as $y = a + bx$.

   a. a is the (slope, intercept) _____ and b is the _____.

   b. y is the (dependent, independent) _____ variable and x is the _____ variable.

   c. If a were 2, b were 4, and x were 5, then y would be _____. If the value of x changed to 7, then y would be _____. If the value of x changed to 3, then y would be _____.

14. The slope of a (straight line, nonlinear curve) _____ is constant throughout; the slope of a _____ varies from point to point.

15. An estimate of the slope of a nonlinear curve at a certain point can be made by calculating the slope of a straight line that is (tangent, perpendicular) _____ to the point on the curve.

■ **TRUE–FALSE QUESTIONS**

Circle T if the statement is true, F if it is false.

1. Economists design graphs to confuse people. **T F**

2. If the straight line on a two-variable graph slopes downward to the right, then there is a positive relationship between the two variables. **T F**

3. A variable that changes as a consequence of a change in another variable is considered a dependent variable. **T F**

4. Economists always put the independent variable on the horizontal axis and the dependent variable on the vertical axis of a two-variable graph. **T F**

5. *Ceteris paribus* means that other variables are changing at the same time. **T F**

6. In the ratio for the calculation of the slope of a straight line, the vertical change is in the numerator and the horizontal change is in the denominator. **T F**

7. If the slope of the linear relationship between consumption and income was .90, then it tells us that for every $1 increase in income there will be a $.90 increase in consumption. **T F**

8. The slope of a straight line in a two-variable graph will *not* be affected by the choice of the units for either variable. **T F**

9. The slopes of lines measure marginal changes. **T F**

10. Assume in a graph that price is on the vertical axis and quantity is on the horizontal axis. The absence of a relationship between price and quantity would be a straight line parallel to the horizontal axis. **T F**

11. A line with an infinite slope in a two-variable graph is parallel to the horizontal axis. **T F**

12. In a two-variable graph, income is graphed on the vertical axis and the quantity of snow is graphed on the horizontal axis. If income was independent of the quantity of snow, then this independence would be represented by a line parallel to the horizontal axis. **T F**

13. If a linear equation is $y = 10 + 5x$, the vertical intercept is 5. **T F**

14. When a line is tangent to a nonlinear curve, then it intersects the curve at a particular point. **T F**

15. If the slope of a straight line on a two-variable (x, y) graph were .5 and the vertical intercept were 5, then a value of 10 for x would mean that y is also 10. **T F**

16. A slope of -4 for a straight line in a two-variable graph indicates that there is an inverse relationship between the two variables. **T F**

17. If x is an independent variable and y is a dependent variable, then a change in y results in a change in x. **T F**

18. An upward slope for a straight line that is tangent to a nonlinear curve indicates that the slope of the nonlinear curve at that point is positive. **T F**

19. If one pair of x, y points was (13, 10) and the other pair was (8, 20), then the slope of the straight line between the two sets of points in the two-variable graph, with x on the horizontal axis and y on the vertical axis, would be 2. **T F**

20. When the value of **x** is 2, a value of 10 for **y** would be calculated from a linear equation of $y = -2 + 6x$.

T   F

■ MULTIPLE-CHOICE QUESTIONS

Circle the letter that corresponds to the best answer.

1. If an increase in one variable is associated with a decrease in another variable, then we can conclude that the variables are
- **(a)** nonlinear
- **(b)** directly related
- **(c)** inversely related
- **(d)** positively related

2. The ratio of the absolute vertical change to the absolute horizontal change between two points of a straight line is the
- **(a)** slope
- **(b)** vertical intercept
- **(c)** horizontal intercept
- **(d)** point of tangency

3. There are two sets of **x, y** points on a straight line in a two-variable graph, with **y** on the vertical axis and **x** on the horizontal axis. If one set of points was (0, 5) and the other set (5, 20), the linear equation for the line would be
- **(a)** $y = 5x$
- **(b)** $y = 5 + 3x$
- **(c)** $y = 5 + 15x$
- **(d)** $y = 5 + .33x$

4. In a two-variable graph of data on the price and quantity of a product, economists place
- **(a)** price on the horizontal axis because it is the independent variable and quantity on the vertical axis because it is the dependent variable
- **(b)** price on the vertical axis because it is the dependent variable and quantity on the horizontal axis because it is the independent variable
- **(c)** price on the vertical axis even though it is the independent variable and quantity on the horizontal axis even though it is the dependent variable
- **(d)** price on the horizontal axis even though it is the dependent variable and quantity on the vertical axis even though it is the independent variable

5. In a two-dimensional graph of the relationship between two economic variables, an assumption is usually made that
- **(a)** both variables are linear
- **(b)** both variables are nonlinear
- **(c)** other variables are held constant
- **(d)** other variables are permitted to change

6. If the slope of a straight line is zero, then the straight line is
- **(a)** vertical
- **(b)** horizontal
- **(c)** upward sloping
- **(d)** downward sloping

Questions 7, 8, 9, and 10 are based on the following four data sets. In each set, the independent variable is in the left column and the dependent variable is in the right column.

(1)		(2)		(3)		(4)	
A	B	C	D	E	F	G	H
0	1	0	12	4	5	0	4
3	2	5	8	6	10	1	3
6	3	10	4	8	15	2	2
9	4	15	0	10	20	3	1

7. There is an inverse relationship between the independent and dependent variable in data sets
- **(a)** 1 and 4
- **(b)** 2 and 3
- **(c)** 1 and 3
- **(d)** 2 and 4

8. The vertical intercept is 4 in data set
- **(a)** 1
- **(b)** 2
- **(c)** 3
- **(d)** 4

9. The linear equation for data set 1 is
- **(a)** $B = 3A$
- **(b)** $B = 1 + 3A$
- **(c)** $B = 1 + .33A$
- **(d)** $A = 1 + .33B$

10. The linear equation for data set 2 is
- **(a)** $C = 12 - 1.25D$
- **(b)** $D = 12 + 1.25C$
- **(c)** $D = 12 - .80C$
- **(d)** $C = 12 - .80D$

Answer Questions 11, 12, 13, and 14 on the basis of the following diagram.

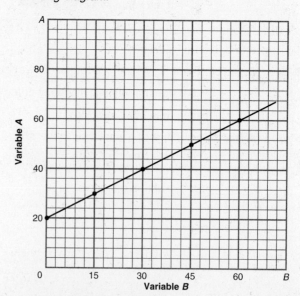

11. The variables **A** and **B** are:
- **(a)** positively related
- **(b)** negatively related
- **(c)** indirectly related
- **(d)** nonlinear

12. The slope of the line is
   (a) .33
   (b) .67
   (c) 1.50
   (d) 3.00

13. The vertical intercept is
   (a) 80
   (b) 60
   (c) 40
   (d) 20

14. The linear equation for the slope of the line is
   (a) $A = 20 + .33B$
   (b) $B = 20 + .33A$
   (c) $A = 20 + .67B$
   (d) $B = 20 + .67A$

Answer Questions 15, 16, and 17 on the basis of the following diagram.

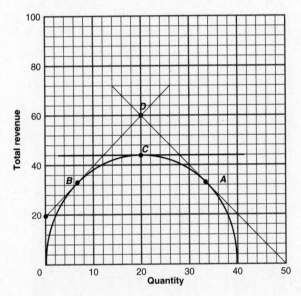

15. The slope of the line tangent to the curve at point **A** is
   (a) 2
   (b) −2
   (c) −1.5
   (d) −0.5

16. The slope of the line tangent to the curve at point **B** is
   (a) −2
   (b) 2
   (c) 3
   (d) 0.5

17. The slope of the line tangent to the curve at point **C** is
   (a) −1
   (b) 1
   (c) 0
   (d) undefined

18. Assume that the relationship between concert ticket prices and attendance is expressed in the equation $P =$ $25 - 1.25Q$, where **P** equals ticket price and **Q** equals concert attendance in thousands of people. On the basis of this equation, it can be said that
   (a) more people will attend the concert when the price is high compared to when the price is low
   (b) if 12,000 people attended the concert, then the ticket price was $10
   (c) if 18,000 people attended the concert, then entry into the concert was free
   (d) an increase in ticket price by $5 reduces concert attendance by 1000 people

19. If you know that the equation relating consumption (**C**) to income (**Y**) is $C = \$7,500 + .2Y$, then
   (a) consumption is inversely related to income
   (b) consumption is the independent variable and income is the dependent variable
   (c) if income is $15,000, then consumption is $10,500
   (d) if consumption is $30,000, then income is $10,000

20. If the dependent variable changes by 22 units when the independent variable changes by 12 units, then the slope of the line is
   (a) 0.56
   (b) 1.83
   (c) 2.00
   (d) 3.27

■ **PROBLEMS**

1. Following are three tables for making graphs. On the graphs, plot the economic relationships contained in each table. Be sure to label each axis of the graph and indicate the unit measurement and scale used on each axis.
   a. Use the table at the top of the next page to graph national income on the horizontal axis and consumption expenditures on the vertical axis below; connect the seven points and label the curve "Consumption." The relationship between income and consumption is (a direct, an inverse) _____ one and the consumption curve is (an up-, a down-) _____ sloping curve.

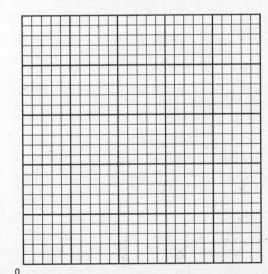

National income, billions of dollars	Consumption expenditures, billions of dollars
$ 600	$ 600
700	640
800	780
900	870
1000	960
1100	1050
1200	1140

b. Use the next table to graph investment expenditures on the horizontal axis and the rate of interest on the vertical axis; connect the seven points and label the curve "Investment." The relationship between the rate of interest and investment expenditures is (a direct, an inverse) _____ one and the investment curve is (an up-, a down-) _____ sloping curve.

Rate of interest, %	Investment expenditures, billions of dollars
8	$220
7	280
6	330
5	370
4	400
3	420
2	430

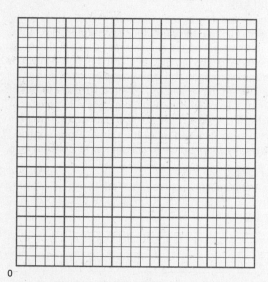

0

c. Use the next table to graph average salary on the horizontal axis and wine consumption on the vertical axis; connect the seven points.

Average salary, U.S. college professors	Annual per capita wine consumption in liters
$62,000	11.5
63,000	11.6
64,000	11.7
65,000	11.8
66,000	11.9
67,000	22.0
68,000	22.1

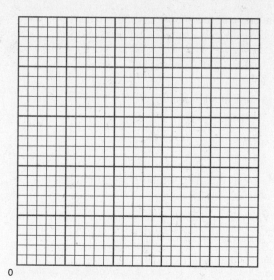

0

(1) The average salary of a college professor and wine consumption (are, are not) _____ *correlated.* The higher average salary (is, is not) _____ the *cause* of the greater consumption of wine.

(2) The relationship between the two variables may be purely (coincidental, planned) _____; or, both the higher salaries and the greater consumption of wine may be the result of the higher (taxes, incomes) _____.

2. This question is based on the following graph.

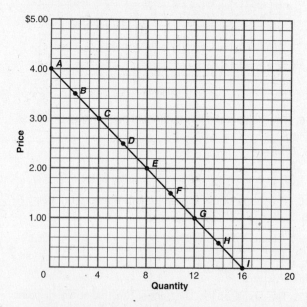

a. Construct a table for points **A–I** from the data shown in the graph.
b. According to economists, price is the (independent, dependent) _____ variable and quantity is the _____ variable.
c. Write a linear equation that summarizes the data.

3. The following three sets of data each show the relationship between an independent variable and a dependent variable. For each set, the independent variable is in the left column and the dependent variable is in the right column.

(1)		(2)		(3)	
A	**B**	**C**	**D**	**E**	**F**
00	10	0	100	0	20
10	30	10	75	50	40
20	50	20	50	100	60
30	70	30	25	150	80
40	90	40	0	200	100

a. Write an equation that summarizes the data for each of the sets (1), (2), and (3).
b. State whether each data set shows a positive or an inverse relationship between the two variables.
c. Plot data sets 1 and 2 on the following graph. Use the same horizontal scale for both sets of independent variables and the same vertical scale for both sets of dependent variables.

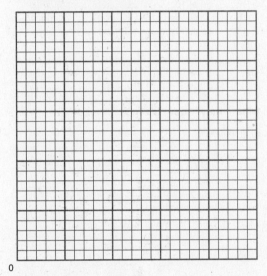

0

4. This problem is based on the following graph.

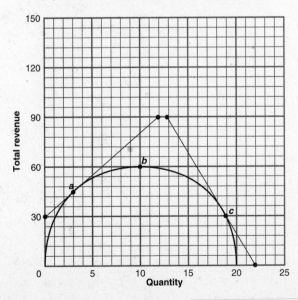

a. The slope of the straight line through point **a** is?
b. The slope of the straight line through point **b** is?
c. The slope of the straight line through point **c** is?

■ SHORT ANSWER AND ESSAY QUESTIONS

1. Why do economists use graphs in their work?

2. Give two examples of a graph that illustrates the relationship between two economic variables.

3. What does the slope tell you about a straight line? How would you interpret a slope of 4? A slope of −2? A slope of .5? A slope of −.25?

4. If the vertical intercept increases in value but the slope of a straight line stays the same, what happens to the graph of the line? If the vertical intercept decreases in value, what will happen to the line?

5. How do you interpret a vertical line on a two-variable graph? How do you interpret a horizontal line?

6. When you know that the price and quantity of a product are inversely related, what does this tell you about the slope of a line? What do you know about the slope when the two variables are positively related?

7. Which variable is the dependent and which is the independent in the following economic statement: "A decrease in business taxes had a positive effect on investment spending."

8. How do you tell the difference between a dependent and independent variable when examining economic relationships?

9. Why is an assumption made that all other variables are held constant when we construct a two-variable graph of the price and quantity of a product?

10. How do mathematicians and economists differ at times in how they construct two-dimensional graphs? Give an example.

11. How is the slope of a straight line in a two-variable graph affected by the choice of the units for either variable? Explain and give an example.

12. What is the relationship between the slopes of lines and marginal analysis?

13. Describe a case in which a straight line in a two-variable graph would have an infinite slope and a case in which the slope of a line would be zero.

14. If you know that the equation relating consumption (C) to income (Y) is $C = 10,000 + 5Y$, then what would consumption be when income is $5000? Construct an income-consumption table for five different levels of income.

15. How do the slopes of a straight line and a nonlinear curve differ? How do you estimate the slope of a nonlinear curve?

ANSWERS

Appendix to Chapter 1 Graphs and Their Meaning

FILL-IN QUESTIONS

1. graph, a horizontal, vertical
2. independent, dependent, dependent, independent
3. scales, ranges
4. an inverse, direct, direct, inverse
5. independent, dependent
6. held constant, *ceteris paribus*
7. vertical, horizontal
8. positive, negative
9. units of measurement
10. marginal
11. vertical, horizontal
12. intercept
13. *a.* intercept, slope; *b.* dependent, independent; *c.* 22, 30, 14
14. straight line, nonlinear curve
15. tangent

TRUE–FALSE QUESTIONS

1. F, p. 15   6. T, p. 17   11. F, pp. 17–18 16. T, p. 17
2. F, p. 16   7. T, pp. 17–18 12. T, pp. 17–18 17. F, pp. 16–17
3. T, p. 16   8. F, p. 17   13. F, p. 18   18. T, pp. 18–19
4. F, p. 16   9. T, p. 17   14. F, p. 19   19. F, p. 17
5. F, p. 17   10. T, pp. 17–18 15. T, p. 18   20. T, p. 18

MULTIPLE-CHOICE QUESTIONS

1. c, p. 16   6. b, pp. 17–18 11. a, p. 16   16. b, pp. 18–19
2. a, p. 17   7. d, p. 16   12. b, p. 17   17. c, pp. 18–19
3. b, p. 18   8. d, p. 18   13. d, p. 18   18. b, p. 18
4. c, p. 16   9. c, p. 18   14. c, p. 18   19. c, p. 18
5. c, p. 17   10. c, p. 18   15. b, pp. 18–19 20. b, p. 17

PROBLEMS

1. *a.* direct, up-; *b.* inverse, down-; *c.* (1) are, is not; (2) coincidental, incomes (standard of living, or similar answer)
2. *a.* table below; *b.* independent, dependent; *c.* $P = 4.00 - .25Q$

Point	Price	Quantity
A	$4.00	0
B	3.50	2
C	3.00	4
D	2.50	6
E	2.00	8
F	1.50	10
G	1.00	12
H	.50	14
I	.00	16

3. *a.* (1) $B = 10 + 2A$; (2) $D = 100 - 2.5C$; (3) $F = 20 + .4E$; *b.* (1) positive; (2) inverse; (3) positive
4. *a.* 5; *b.* 0; *c.* −10

SHORT ANSWER AND ESSAY QUESTIONS

1. p. 15   5. pp. 17–18 9. p. 17   13. pp. 17–18
2. pp. 15–16 6. p. 16   10. p. 16   14. p. 18
3. pp. 17–18 7. p. 16   11. p. 17   15. pp. 18–19
4. pp. 17–18 8. p. 16   12. p. 17

CHAPTER 2

The Economizing Problem

Chapter 2 explains that the central problem of economics is based on two fundamental facts. First, individuals and institutions have unlimited economic wants. The main purpose of economic activity is to satisfy these wants. Second, economic resources are limited or scarce. It is these resources—land, capital, labor, and entrepreneurial ability—that are used to produce the goods and services that ultimately satisfy these economic wants. The *economizing problem* for both individuals and institutions arises from this continual struggle to decide how best to use limited productive resources to satisfy insatiable economic wants.

Economics is called the science of efficiency. To understand what efficiency means, however, you must first define its two characteristics: *full employment* and *full production.* Full employment means that all productive resources available to the economy are being used. Full production requires that two types of efficiency—allocative and productive—are being achieved. *Allocative efficiency* means that resources are being devoted to the production of the goods and services society most highly values. *Productive efficiency* entails producing this optimal product mix in the least costly way.

The *production possibilities curve* is used in this chapter's tables and graphs to discuss the major concerns of economics. The production possibilities model is a valuable device for illustrating the meaning of many concepts defined in the chapter—scarcity, choice, tradeoffs, opportunity cost, allocative and productive efficiency, unemployment, economic growth, and international trade. It can also be applied to many real economic situations, as you will learn from the examples in the text. This basic economic model is the first and one of the most important ones presented in the text that you will be using to understand the economic world.

Every economy needs to develop an *economic system* to respond to the economizing problem of limited resources and unlimited wants. The two basic types of systems are the *market system* and the *command system.* In the market system there is extensive private ownership of resources and the use of markets and prices to coordinate and direct economic activity. In the command system, there is extensive public ownership of resources and the use of central planning for most economic decision making in the economy. Chapters 3 through 6 explain in greater detail how the U.S. economy uses the market system to respond to the economizing problem.

The *circular flow model* (or diagram) is a device that illustrates for a capitalistic economy the relationship between households and businesses, the flow of money and economic goods and services between households and businesses, their dual role as buyers and sellers, and the two basic types of markets essential to the capitalistic process.

■ CHECKLIST

When you have studied this chapter you should be able to

☐ Explain the economizing problem in terms of economic wants and resources.

☐ Identify four types of economic resources.

☐ Describe the resource payments made in return for each economic resource.

☐ Write a definition of economics that incorporates the relationship between resources and wants.

☐ Explain why full employment and full production are necessary for the efficient use of resources.

☐ Distinguish between allocative efficiency and productive efficiency.

☐ State the four assumptions made when a production possibilities table or curve is constructed.

☐ Construct a production possibilities curve when you are given the appropriate data.

☐ Define opportunity cost and utilize a production possibilities curve to explain the concept.

☐ Show how the law of increasing opportunity cost is reflected in the shape of the production possibilities curve.

☐ Explain the economic rationale for the law of increasing opportunity cost.

☐ Use marginal analysis to define allocative efficiency.

☐ Explain how allocative efficiency determines the optimal point on a production possibilities curve.

☐ Use a production possibilities curve to illustrate unemployment and productive inefficiency.

☐ Use the production possibilities curve to illustrate economic growth.

☐ Explain how international trade affects a nation's production possibilities curve.

☐ Give examples and applications of the production possibilities model.

☐ Compare and contrast the market system (capitalism) with the command system (socialism).

☐ Draw the circular flow model, correctly labeling the two markets and the real and money flows between the two sectors in this simplified economy.

■ **CHAPTER OUTLINE**

1. The study of economics rests on the bases of two facts:

a. Society's material wants are unlimited.

b. The economic resources that are the ultimate means of satisfying these wants are scarce in relation to the wants.

(1) Economic resources are classified as land, capital, labor, and entrepreneurial ability. They are called *factors of production*.

(2) The payments received by those who provide the economy with these four resources are in the form of rental income, interest income, wages, and profits, respectively.

(3) Because these resources are scarce (or limited), the output that the economy is able to produce is also limited.

2. Economics, then, is the study of how society's scarce resources are used (administered) to obtain the greatest satisfaction of its economic wants. To be efficient in the use of its resources, an economy must achieve both full employment and full production.

a. *Full employment* means that the economy is using all available resources.

b. *Full production* means that all resources used for production should contribute to the maximum satisfaction of society's economic wants. Full production implies that there is

(1) *productive efficiency,* in which the goods and services society desires are being produced in the least costly way.

(2) *allocative efficiency,* in which resources are devoted to the production of goods and services society most highly values.

c. The **production possibilities table** indicates the alternative combinations of goods and services an economy is capable of producing when it has achieved full employment and productive efficiency.

(1) The four assumptions usually made when a production possibilities table is constructed are that full employment and productive efficiency, fixed resources, fixed technology, and two products are being considered.

(2) The table illustrates the fundamental choice every economy must make: what quantity of each good it must sacrifice to obtain more of another good.

d. The data in the production possibilities table can be plotted on a graph to obtain a production possibilities curve.

e. The opportunity cost of producing an additional unit of one product is the amount of other products that are sacrificed. The **law of increasing opportunity costs** reflects that the opportunity cost of producing an additional unit of a product (the marginal opportunity cost) increases as more of that product is produced.

(1) The law of increasing opportunity costs results in a production possibilities curve that is concave (from the origin).

(2) The opportunity cost of producing an additional unit of a product increases as more of the product is pro-

duced because resources are not completely adaptable to alternative uses.

f. Allocative efficiency means that resources are devoted to the optimal product mix for society. This optimal mix is determined by assessing marginal costs and benefits.

(1) The marginal-cost curve for a product rises because of the law of increasing opportunity costs; the marginal-benefit curve falls because the consumption of a product yields less and less satisfaction.

(2) There will be *underallocation* of resources to production of a product when the marginal benefit is greater than the marginal cost, and *overallocation* when the marginal cost is greater than the marginal benefit.

(3) Allocative efficiency is achieved when the marginal cost of a product equals the marginal benefit of a product.

3. Different outcomes will occur when assumptions underlying the production possibilities model are relaxed.

a. *Unemployment.* The economy may be operating at a point inside the production possibilities curve if the assumption of full employment and productive efficiency no longer holds. In this case, there will be an unemployment of resources and production will not occur in the least costly way.

b. *Economic Growth.* The production possibilities curve can move outward if the assumption of fixed resources or the assumption of no technological change is dropped.

(1) Economic growth can occur when there is an expansion in the quantity and quality of resources.

(2) It can increase when there is technological advancement.

(3) The combination of goods and services an economy chooses to produce today helps determine its production possibilities in the future.

c. *Trade.* International specialization and trade allow a nation to obtain more goods and services than is indicated by its production possibilities curve. The effect on production possibilities is similar to an increase in economic growth.

4. There are many real-world examples and applications of the production possibilities model.

a. Events leading to unemployment and productive inefficiency may cause nations to operate inside their production possibilities curves. Examples would be the Great Depression in the United States, recessions in different nations, and policies of racial, ethnic, or religious discrimination.

b. It illustrates tradeoffs and opportunity costs. Controversies over the use of land (for wilderness or production) or decisions over how public funds should be spent (for more criminal justice or more education) are two applications.

c. The curves can shift. The increase in the number of women in the workforce over the past four decades and their increased productivity have shifted the curve outward for the United States. Similarly, recent advances in technology have shifted the curve outward for the United States.

5. An *economic system* is a set of institutions and a co-ordinating mechanism to respond to the economizing problem.

a. The *market system* (capitalism) has extensive private ownership of resources and uses markets and prices to coordinate and direct economic activity. In pure (*laissez-faire*) capitalism there is a limited government role in the economy. In a capitalist economy such as the United States, government plays a large role, but the two characteristics of the market system—private property and markets—dominate.

b. The *command system* (also called *socialism* or *communism*) is based primarily on extensive public ownership of resources and the use of central planning for most economic decision making. There used to be many examples of command economies (e.g., Soviet Union), but today there are few (e.g., Cuba, North Korea). Most former socialistic nations have been or are being transformed into capitalistic and market-oriented economies.

6. The circular flow model is a device used to clarify the relationships between households and business firms in a market economy. In resource markets, households sell and firms buy resources, and in product markets, the firms sell and households buy products. Households use the incomes they obtain from selling resources to purchase the goods and services produced by the firms, and in the economy there is a real flow of resources and products and a money flow of incomes and expenditures.

■ **HINTS AND TIPS**

1. Chapter 2 presents many economic definitions and classifications. Spend time learning these definitions now because they will be used in later chapters, and you must know them if you are to understand what follows.

2. The production possibilities graph is a simple and extremely useful economic model. Practice your understanding of it by using it to explain the following economic concepts: scarcity, choice, opportunity cost, the law of increasing opportunity costs, full employment, full production, productive efficiency, allocative efficiency, unemployment, and economic growth.

3. Opportunity cost is always measured in terms of a forgone alternative. From a production possibilities table, you can easily calculate how many units of one product you forgo when you get another unit of a product.

4. In the section on the law of increasing opportunity costs, note the distinction made between two types. The *marginal* opportunity cost measures what is given up to obtain an additional unit. Note too that the size of one unit can vary (e.g., 2 to 3 or 200 to 300). The *total* opportunity cost measures what is given up to obtain a specific number of units (e.g., 3 or 300 units). Review Quick Quiz 2–1 in the text.

■ **IMPORTANT TERMS**

economizing problem

economic resources

land

capital

investment

labor

entrepreneurial ability

factors of production

full employment

full production

productive efficiency

allocative efficiency

consumer goods

capital goods

production possibilities table

production possibilities curve

opportunity cost

law of increasing opportunity costs

economic growth

economic system

market system

capitalism

command system

resource market

product market

circular flow model

SELF-TEST

■ **FILL-IN QUESTIONS**

1. The economizing problem arises because society's economic wants are (limited, unlimited) _____ and its economic resources are _____.

2. Consumers want to obtain goods and services that provide satisfaction, or what economists call (resources, utility) "_____." Some wants that meet this objective are considered (capital goods, necessities) _____, while others are considered (investment goods, luxuries) _____.

3. The four types of resources are

a. _____

b. _____

c. _____

d. _____

4. Both consumer goods and capital goods satisfy human economic wants. The consumer goods satisfy these wants (directly, indirectly) _____, and the capital goods satisfy them _____.

5. The income individuals receive from supplying land or natural resources is (interest, rental) _____ income, whereas the income received from supplying capital goods is _____ income. The income received by individuals who supply labor is (wage, profit) _____ income; the income received from entrepreneurial ability is _____ income.

6. Economics is the social science concerned with the problem of using (unlimited, scarce) _____ resources to attain the maximum fulfillment of society's _____ economic wants.

7. Economic efficiency requires full (employment, allocation) _____ so that all available resources can be used and that there be full (production, distribution) _____ so that the employed resources contribute to the maximum satisfaction of material wants.

8. Full production implies that two types of efficiency are achieved: Resources are devoted to the production of the mix of goods and services society most wants, or there is (allocative, productive) _____ efficiency, and the goods and services will be produced in the least costly way, or there will be _____ efficiency.

9. When a production possibilities table or curve is constructed, four assumptions are made:

a. _____

b. _____

c. _____

d. _____

10. In a two-product world, the quantity of the other good or service an economy must give up to produce more housing is the opportunity (benefit, cost) _____ of producing the additional housing.

11. The law of increasing opportunity costs explains why the production possibilities curve is (convex, concave) _____ from the origin. The economic rationale for the law is that economic resources (are, are not) _____ completely adaptable to alternative uses.

12. Allocative efficiency is determined by assessing the marginal costs and benefits of the output from the allocation of resources to production.

a. The marginal cost curve for a product rises because of increasing (satisfaction, opportunity costs) _____, and the marginal benefit curve falls because of less _____ from the additional consumption of a product.

b. When the marginal benefit is greater than the marginal cost, there will be (over, under) _____-allocation of resources to the production of a product, but when the marginal cost is greater than the marginal benefit, there will be an _____-allocation.

c. Optimal allocation of resources occurs when the marginal costs of the product output are (greater than, less than, equal to) _____ the marginal benefits.

13. Following is a production possibilities curve for capital goods and consumer goods.

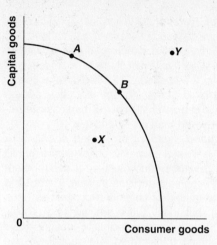

a. If the economy moves from point **A** to point **B,** it will produce (more, fewer) _____ capital goods and (more, fewer) _____ consumer goods.

b. If the economy is producing at point **X,** some resources in the economy are either (not available, unemployed) _____ or (underemployed, overemployed) _____.

c. If the economy moves from point **X** to point **B** (more, fewer) _____ capital goods and (more, fewer) _____ consumer goods will be produced.

d. If the economy is to produce at point **Y,** there must be (unemployment, economic growth) _____. This can occur because of a resource supply (decrease, increase) _____ or a technological (decline, improvement) _____.

14. Technological advances can shift a nation's production possibilities curve (inward, outward) _____ because the effects lead to (economic growth, unemployment) _____.

15. The more an economy consumes its current production, the (more, less) _____ it will be capable of producing in future years if other things are equal.

16. International specialization and trade enable a nation to obtain (more, less) _____ of a desired good at _____ sacrifice of some other good. The output gains from greater international specialization and trade are the equivalent to economic (growth, decline) _____.

17. The institutional arrangements and coordinating mechanisms used to respond to the economic problem are called (*laissez-faire* capitalism, an economic system) _____.

18. In capitalism, property resources are primarily (publicly, privately) _____ owned. The means used to direct and coordinate economic activity (is central planning, are markets and prices) _____.

19. In a command economy, property resources are primarily (publicly, privately) _____ owned. The coordinating device(s) in this economic system (is central planning, are markets and prices) _____.

20. In the circular flow model,
   a. Households are buyers and businesses are sellers in (product, resource) _____ markets, and businesses are buyers and households are sellers in _____ markets.
   b. The flow of economic resources and finished goods and services is the (money, real) _____ flow, and the flow of income and expenditures is the _____ flow.

■ **TRUE–FALSE QUESTIONS**

Circle T if the statement is true, F if it is false.

1. The conflict between the scarce economic wants of society and its unlimited economic resources gives rise to the economizing problem.   **T F**

2. The wants with which economics is concerned include only those wants that can be satisfied by goods and services.   **T F**

3. Money is a resource and is classified as "capital."   **T F**

4. From the economist's perspective, investment refers to the production and purchase of capital goods.   **T F**

5. The payment to entrepreneurial ability is interest income.   **T F**

6. Resources are scarce because society's material wants are unlimited and productive resources are limited.   **T F**

7. Economic efficiency requires that there be both full employment of resources and full production.   **T F**

8. Allocative efficiency means that goods and services are being produced by society in the least costly way.   **T F**

9. Only allocative efficiency is necessary for there to be full production.   **T F**

10. Given full employment and full production, it is not possible for an economy capable of producing just two goods to increase its production of both at any one point in time.   **T F**

11. The opportunity cost of producing antipollution devices is the other goods and services the economy is unable to produce because it has decided to produce these devices.   **T F**

12. The opportunity cost of producing a good tends to increase as more of it is produced because resources less suitable to its production must be employed.   **T F**

13. Drawing a production possibilities curve concave to the origin is the geometric way of stating the law of increasing opportunity costs.   **T F**

14. Economic rationale for the law of increasing opportunity cost is that economic resources are fully adaptable to alternative uses.   **T F**

15. Allocative efficiency is determined by assessing the marginal costs and benefits of the output from the allocation of resources to production.   **T F**

16. The marginal-cost curve for a product rises because of increasing satisfaction from the consumption of the product.   **T F**

17. Economic growth means an increase in the production of goods and services, and is shown by a movement of the production possibilities curve outward and to the right.   **T F**

18. The more capital goods an economy produces today, the greater will be the total output of all goods it can produce in the future, other things being equal.   **T F**

19. International specialization and trade permit an economy to overcome the limits imposed by domestic production possibilities and have the same effect on the economy as having more and better resources.   **T F**

20. The elimination of widespread discrimination based on race, ethnicity, or religion in an economy would move it from a point inside its production possibilities curve toward a point on its curve.   **T F**

21. Pure capitalism is also called *laissez-faire* capitalism.   **T F**

22. A command economy is characterized by the private ownership of resources and the use of markets and prices to coordinate and direct economic activity.   **T F**

23. Russia and most nations in Eastern Europe have been transforming their economies from a command to market system since the demise of the former Soviet Union.   **T F**

24. In the circular flow model, households function on the buying side of the resource and product markets.   **T F**

25. In the circular flow model, there is a *real flow* of economic resources and finished goods and services and a *money flow* of income and consumption expenditures.   **T F**

■ **MULTIPLE-CHOICE QUESTIONS**

Circle the letter that corresponds to the best answer.

1. Which is the correct match of an economic resource and payment for that resource?
   (a) land and wages

(b) labor and interest income
(c) capital and rental income
(d) entrepreneurial ability and profit

2. An "innovator" is defined as an entrepreneur who
(a) makes basic policy decisions in a business firm
(b) combines factors of production to produce a good or service
(c) invents a new product or process for producing a product
(d) introduces new products on the market or employs a new method to produce a product

3. An economy is efficient when it has achieved
(a) full employment
(b) full production
(c) either full employment or full production
(d) both full employment and full production

4. Allocative and productive efficiency are conditions that best characterize
(a) full employment
(b) full production
(c) traditional economies
(d) command economies

5. When a production possibilities schedule is written (or a production possibilities curve is drawn) in this chapter, four assumptions are made. Which is one of those assumptions?
(a) More than two products are produced.
(b) The state of technology changes.
(c) The economy has both full employment and full production.
(d) The quantities of all resources available to the economy are variable, not fixed.

Answer Questions 6, 7, 8, and 9 based on the following graph for an economy.

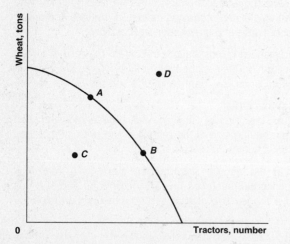

6. At point **A** on the production possibilities curve in the above illustration,
(a) wheat production is inefficient
(b) tractor production is inefficient
(c) the economy is employing all its resources
(d) the economy is not employing all its resources

7. Unemployment and productive inefficiency would best be represented in the graph by point
(a) *A*
(b) *B*
(c) *C*
(d) *D*

8. The choice of point **B** over point **A** as the optimal product mix for society would be based on
(a) productive efficiency
(b) full employment of resources
(c) the law of increasing opportunity costs
(d) a comparison of marginal costs and benefits

9. Economic growth could be represented by
(a) a movement from point **A** to point **B**
(b) a movement from point **B** to point **A**
(c) a shift in the production possibilities curve out to point **C**
(d) a shift in the production possibilities curve out to point **D**

10. The production possibilities curve is
(a) concave
(b) convex
(c) linear
(d) positive

11. What is the economic rationale for the law of increasing opportunity cost?
(a) Full production and full employment of resources have not been achieved.
(b) Economic resources are not completely adaptable to alternative uses.
(c) Economic growth is being limited by the pace of technological advancement.
(d) An economy's present choice of output is determined by fixed technology and fixed resources.

12. If there is an increase in the resources available within the economy,
(a) more goods and services will be produced in the economy
(b) the economy will be capable of producing more goods and services
(c) the standard of living in the economy will rise
(d) the technological efficiency of the economy will improve

13. If the production possibilities curve *on the next page* moves from position **A** to position **B,** then
(a) the economy has increased the efficiency with which it produces wheat
(b) the economy has increased the efficiency with which it produces tractors
(c) the economy has put previously idle resources to work
(d) the economy has gone from full employment to less than full employment

Wheat, tons / Tractors, number

14. Which would be the best example of allocative efficiency? When society devoted resources to the production of
  (a) slide rules instead of handheld calculators
  (b) horse-drawn carriages instead of automobiles
  (c) computers with word processors instead of typewriters
  (d) long-playing records instead of compact discs

15. Which situation would most likely shift the production possibilities curve for a nation in an outward direction?
  (a) deterioration in product quality
  (b) reductions in the supply of resources
  (c) increases in technological advances
  (d) rising levels of discrimination

16. The opportunity cost of a new public stadium is the
  (a) money cost of hiring guards and staff for the new stadium
  (b) cost of constructing the new stadium in a future year
  (c) change in the real estate tax rate to pay off the new stadium
  (d) other goods and services that must be sacrificed to construct the new stadium

17. Which situation would most likely cause a nation's production possibilities curve to shift inward?
  (a) investing more resources in new plants and equipment
  (b) eliminating discrimination based on race and ethnic background
  (c) increasing international trade or incurring a trade deficit
  (d) going to war with another nation and suffering a major defeat

18. The combination of products in society's production possibilities table that is the most valued or optimal is determined
  (a) at the midpoint of the production possibilities table
  (b) at the endpoint of the production possibilities table
  (c) where the marginal benefits equal marginal costs
  (d) where the opportunity costs are maximized

19. The underallocation of resources by society to the production of a product means that the
  (a) marginal benefit is greater than the marginal cost
  (b) marginal benefit is less than the marginal cost
  (c) opportunity cost of production is rising
  (d) consumption of the product is falling

Answer Questions 20, 21, and 22 on the basis of the data given in the following production possibilities table.

	Production possibilities (alternatives)					
	A	B	C	D	E	F
Capital goods	100	95	85	70	50	0
Consumer goods	0	100	180	240	280	300

20. The choice of alternative **B** compared with alternative **D** would tend to promote
  (a) a slower rate of economic growth
  (b) a faster rate of economic growth
  (c) increased consumption in the present
  (d) central economic planning

21. If the economy is producing at production alternative **D**, the opportunity cost of 40 more units of consumer goods is about
  (a) 5 units of capital goods
  (b) 10 units of capital goods
  (c) 15 units of capital goods
  (d) 20 units of capital goods

22. In the table, the law of increasing opportunity costs is suggested by the fact that
  (a) greater and greater quantities of consumer goods must be given up to get more capital goods
  (b) smaller and smaller quantities of consumer goods must be given up to get more capital goods
  (c) capital goods are relatively more scarce than consumer goods
  (d) the production possibilities curve will eventually shift outward as the economy expands

23. The private ownership of property resources and use of markets and prices to direct and coordinate economic activity is characteristic of
  (a) capitalism
  (b) communism
  (c) socialism
  (d) a command economy

24. The two kinds of markets found in the circular flow model are
  (a) real and money markets
  (b) real and socialist markets
  (c) money and command markets
  (d) product and resource markets

25. In the circular flow model, businesses
  (a) buy products and resources
  (b) sell products and resources
  (c) buy products and sell resources
  (d) sell products and buy resources

■ PROBLEMS

1. Following is a list of resources. Indicate in the space to the right of each whether the resource is land (**LD**), capital (**C**), labor (**LR**), entrepreneurial ability (**EA**), or some combination of these resources.

   a. Fishing grounds in the North Atlantic   _____

   b. A computer in a retail store   _____

   c. Uranium deposits in Canada   _____

   d. An irrigation ditch in Nebraska   _____

   e. Bill Gates in his work in starting Microsoft   _____

   f. The oxygen breathed by human beings   _____

   g. An IBM plant in Rochester, Minnesota   _____

   h. The food on the shelf of a grocery store   _____

   i. A machine in an auto plant   _____

   j. A person who creates new computer software and uses it to start a successful business   _____

   k. A carpenter building a house   _____

2. Following is a production possibilities table for two products, corn and cars. The table is constructed using the usual assumptions. Corn is measured in units of 100,000 bushels and cars in units of 100,000.

Combination	Corn	Cars
A	0	7
B	7	6
C	13	5
D	18	4
E	22	3
F	25	2
G	27	1
H	28	0

   a. Follow the general rules for making graphs (see the appendix to Chapter 1); plot the data from the table on the graph in the next column to obtain a production possibilities curve. Place corn on the vertical axis and cars on the horizontal axis.

   b. Fill in the following table showing the opportunity cost per unit of producing the 1st through the 7th car unit in terms of corn units.

Cars	Cost of production
1st	_____
2nd	_____
3rd	_____
4th	_____
5th	_____
6th	_____
7th	_____

   c. What is the *marginal* opportunity cost of the 3rd car unit in terms of units of corn? _____

   d. What is the *total* opportunity cost of producing 6 car units in terms of units of corn? _____

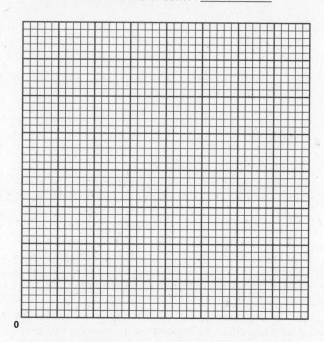

0

3. The following graph is a production possibilities curve. Draw on this graph

   a. a production possibilities curve that indicates greater efficiency in the production of good **A**

   b. a production possibilities curve that indicates greater efficiency in the production of good **B**

   c. a production possibilities curve that indicates an increase in the resources available to the economy

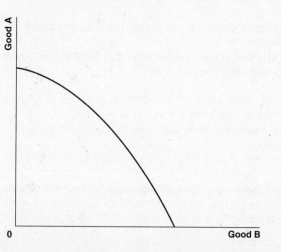

4. Following is a list of 12 economic goods. Indicate in the space to the right of each good whether it is a consumer good (**CON**), a capital good (**CAP**), or that it depends (**DEP**) on who is using it and for what purpose.

   a. An automobile   _____

   b. A tractor   _____

c. A taxicab _____

d. A house _____

e. A factory building _____

f. An office building _____

g. An ironing board _____

h. A refrigerator _____

i. A telephone _____

j. A quart of a soft drink _____

k. A cash register _____

l. A screwdriver _____

5. In the circular flow diagram below, the upper pair of flows (*a* and *b*) represents the resource market and the lower pair (*c* and *d*) the product market.

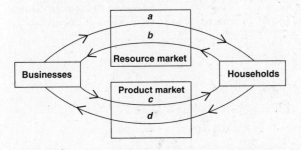

Supply labels or explanations for each of the four flows:

a. _____

b. _____

c. _____

d. _____

■ **SHORT ANSWER AND ESSAY QUESTIONS**

1. Explain what the term "economizing problem" means. Why are resources scarce?

2. In what sense are economic wants satiable or insatiable?

3. What are the four economic resources? How is each resource defined?

4. What is the income each economic resource earns?

5. When is a society economically efficient? What does "full production" mean, and how does it differ from "full employment"?

6. Explain why full production implies both allocative efficiency and productive efficiency.

7. What four assumptions are made in drawing a production possibilities curve or schedule?

8. What is opportunity cost? Give an example.

9. What is the law of increasing opportunity cost? Why do costs increase?

10. What determines the optimal product mix for society's production possibilities?

11. How can unemployment be illustrated with the production possibilities curve?

12. What will be the effect of increasing resource supplies on production possibilities?

13. Describe how technological advances will affect the production possibilities curve.

14. Explain the tradeoff between goods for the present and goods for the future and the effect of this tradeoff on economic growth.

15. What qualification does international specialization and trade make for the interpretation of production possibilities?

16. Give examples of how tradeoffs and opportunity costs can be illustrated by the production possibilities curve.

17. Give examples of shifts in the production possibilities curve.

18. The market system and the command system differ in two important ways. Compare and contrast the two economic systems.

19. In the circular flow model, what are the two markets? What roles do households play and what roles do businesses play in each market?

20. In the circular flow model, what are the income flows? What are the expenditure flows?

ANSWERS

Chapter 2 The Economizing Problem

FILL-IN QUESTIONS

1. unlimited, limited
2. utility, necessities, luxuries
3 *a.* land or natural resources, *b.* capital, *c.* labor, *d.* entrepreneurial ability
4. directly, indirectly
5. rental, interest, wage, profit
6. scarce, unlimited
7. employment, production
8. allocative, productive
9. *a.* there is full employment and productive efficiency; *b.* the available supplies of the factors of production are fixed; *c.* technology does not change during the course of the analysis; *d.* the economy produces only two products (any order for *a–d*)
10. cost
11. concave, are not
12. *a.* opportunity costs, satisfaction; *b.* under, over; *c.* equal to
13. *a.* fewer, more; *b.* unemployed, underemployed; *c.* more, more; *d.* economic growth, increase, improvement
14. outward, economic growth
15. less
16. more, less, growth
17. an economic system
18. privately, are markets and prices
19. publicly, is central planning
20. *a.* product, resource; *b.* real, money

TRUE–FALSE QUESTIONS

1. F, pp. 22–23 **8.** F, p. 24 **15.** T, pp. 27–28 **22.** F, pp. 33–34
2. T, pp. 22–23 **9.** F, p. 24 **16.** F, pp. 27–28 **23.** T, pp. 33–34
3. F, p. 23 **10.** T, pp. 25–27 **17.** T, pp. 29–30 **24.** F, pp. 34–35
4. T, p. 23 **11.** T, p. 27 **18.** T, pp. 30–31 **25.** T, pp. 34–35
5. F, pp. 23–24 **12.** T, p. 27 **19.** T, p. 31
6. T, p. 24 **13.** T, p. 27 **20.** T, p. 32
7. T, p. 24 **14.** F, p. 27 **21.** T, p. 33

MULTIPLE-CHOICE QUESTIONS

1. d, pp. 23–24 **8.** d, pp. 27–28 **15.** c, pp. 29–30 **22.** a, p. 27
2. d, pp. 23–24 **9.** d, pp. 29–30 **16.** d, p. 27 **23.** a, p. 33
3. d, p. 24 **10.** a, p. 27 **17.** d, pp. 32–33 **24.** d, pp. 34–35
4. b, p. 24 **11.** b, p. 27 **18.** c, pp. 27–28 **25.** d, pp. 34–35
5. c, p. 25 **12.** b, p. 29 **19.** a, pp. 27–28
6. c, pp. 26–27 **13.** b, pp. 29–31 **20.** b, pp. 30–31
7. c, p. 29 **14.** c, pp. 27–28 **21.** d, p. 27

PROBLEMS

1. *a.* LD; *b.* C; *c.* LD; *d.* C; *e.* EA; *f.* LD; *g.* C; *h.* C; *i.* C; *j.* EA; *k.* LR
2. *b.* 1, 2, 3, 4, 5, 6, 7 units of corn; *c.* 3; *d.* 21
3. *a.* curve will shift outward along good A axis but stay at the same point on good B axis; *b.* curve will shift outward along good B axis but stay at the same point on good A axis; *c.* entire curve will shift outward
4. *a.* DEP; *b.* CAP; *c.* CAP; *d.* DEP; *e.* CAP; *f.* CAP; *g.* DEP; *h.* DEP; *i.* DEP; *j.* DEP; *k.* CAP; *l.* DEP
5. *a.* money income payments (wages, rent, interest, and profit); *b.* services or resources (land, labor, capital, and entrepreneurial ability); *c.* goods and services; *d.* expenditures for goods and services

SHORT ANSWER AND ESSAY QUESTIONS

1. pp. 22–24 **6.** p. 24 **11.** p. 29 **16.** p. 32
2. pp. 22–23 **7.** p. 25 **12.** p. 29 **17.** pp. 32–33
3. p. 23 **8.** p. 27 **13.** pp. 29–30 **18.** pp. 33–34
4. p. 24 **9.** p. 27 **14.** pp. 30–31 **19.** pp. 34–35
5. p. 24 **10.** pp. 27–28 **15.** p. 31 **20.** pp. 34–35

CHAPTER 3

Individual Markets: Demand and Supply

Chapter 3 introduces you to the most fundamental tools of economic analysis: demand and supply. To progress successfully into the later chapters, it is essential that you understand what is meant by demand and supply and how to use these powerful tools.

Demand and supply are simply "boxes" or categories into which all the forces and factors that affect the price and the quantity of a good bought and sold in a competitive market are placed. Demand and supply determine price and quantity exchange, and it is necessary to see *why* and *how* they do this.

Many students never learn to *define* demand and supply. They never learn (1) what an increase or decrease in demand or supply means, (2) the important distinctions between "demand" and "quantity demanded" and between "supply" and "quantity supplied," and (3) the equally important distinctions between a change in demand and a change in quantity demanded, and between a change in supply and a change in quantity supplied.

Having learned these, however, it is no great trick to comprehend the so-called laws of demand and supply. The equilibrium price—that is, the price that will tend to prevail in the market as long as demand and supply do not change—is simply the price at which **quantity demanded** and **quantity supplied** are equal. The quantity bought and sold in the market (the equilibrium quantity) is the quantity demanded and supplied at the equilibrium price. If you can determine the equilibrium price and quantity under one set of demand and supply conditions, you can determine them under any other set.

This chapter includes a brief examination of the factors that determine demand and supply and the ways in which changes in these determinants will affect and cause changes in demand and supply. A graphic method is used in this analysis to illustrate demand and supply, equilibrium price and quantity, changes in demand and supply, and the resulting changes in equilibrium price and quantity. The **demand curve** and the **supply curve** are graphic (or geometric) representations of the same data contained in the schedules of demand and supply.

The application section at the end of the chapter explains government-set prices. When the government sets a legal price in a competitive market, it creates a **price ceiling** or **price floor.** This prevents supply and demand from determining the equilibrium price and quantity of a product that will be provided by a competitive market. As you will learn, the economic consequence of a price ceiling is that it will result in a persistent shortage of the product. An example of a price ceiling would be price controls on apartment rents. A price floor will result in a persistent surplus of a product, and the example given for it is price supports for an agricultural product.

You will use supply and demand over and over. It will turn out to be as important to you in economics as jet propulsion is to the pilot of an airplane: You can't get off the ground without it.

■ CHECKLIST

When you have studied this chapter you should be able to

☐ Define a market.
☐ Define demand and state the law of demand.
☐ Graph the demand curve when you are given a demand schedule.
☐ Explain the difference between individual demand and market demand.
☐ List the major determinants of demand and explain how each one shifts the demand curve.
☐ Distinguish between change in demand and change in the quantity demanded.
☐ Define supply and state the law of supply.
☐ Graph the supply curve when you are given a supply schedule.
☐ List the major determinants of supply and explain how each shifts the supply curve.
☐ Distinguish between change in supply and change in the quantity supplied.
☐ Define surplus and shortage.
☐ Describe how the equilibrium price and quantity are determined in a competitive market.
☐ Determine, when you are given the demand for and the supply of a good, the equilibrium price and the equilibrium quantity.
☐ Predict the effects of changes in demand and supply on equilibrium price and equilibrium quantity and on the prices of substitute and complementary goods.
☐ Explain the meaning of the rationing function of prices.
☐ Explain why violations of the "other-things-equal" assumption may cause confusion about the validity of the laws of demand and supply.
☐ Explain the economic effects of a government-set price ceiling on product price and quantity in a competitive market and give an example.
☐ Describe the economic consequences of a government-set price floor on product price and quantity in a competitive market and supply an example.

■ **CHAPTER OUTLINE**

1. A market is any institution or mechanism that brings together buyers ("demanders") and sellers ("suppliers") of a particular good or service. This chapter assumes that markets are highly competitive.

2. *Demand* is a schedule of prices and the quantities that buyers would purchase at each of these prices during a selected period of time.

a. As price rises, other things being equal, buyers will purchase smaller quantities, and as price falls they will purchase larger quantities; this is the law of demand.

b. The demand curve is a graphic representation of demand and the law of demand.

c. Market (or total) demand for a good is a summation of the demands of all individuals in the market for that good.

d. The demand for a good depends on the tastes, income, and expectations of buyers; the number of buyers in the market; and the prices of related goods.

e. A change (increase or decrease) in the entire demand schedule and the demand curve is referred to as a *change in demand.* It is the result of a change in one or more of the determinants of demand. For example, an *increase* in the demand for a good may result from an increase in:

(1) *tastes or preferences* for the good;

(2) *the number of buyers* (for the good);

(3) *income* if it is a normal good, but if it is a normal good, it may result from a decrease in income;

(4) *the price of a related good*, but if they are complements, it may result from a decrease in the price of a related good; and

(5) *expectations* of a price increase or a rise in income.

f. A change in demand and a change in the quantity demanded are *not* the same thing.

3. *Supply* is a schedule of prices and the quantities that sellers will sell at each of these prices during some period of time.

a. The supply schedule shows, other things equal, that as the price of the good rises, larger quantities will be offered for sale, and as the price of the good falls, smaller quantities will be offered for sale.

b. The supply curve is a graphic representation of supply and the law of supply; the market supply of a good is the sum of the supplies of all sellers of the good.

c. The supply of a good depends on the techniques used to produce it, the prices of the resources employed in its production, the extent to which it is taxed or subsidized, the prices of other goods that might be produced, the price expectations of sellers, and the number of sellers of the product.

d. A change (increase or decrease) in the entire supply schedule and the supply curve is referred to as a *change in supply.* It is the result of a change in one or more of the determinants of supply. For example, an increase in supply for a good may result from:

(1) a decrease in the *prices of resources* used to make it;

(2) an improvement in the *technology* to produce it;

(3) a fall in *taxes* on it, or an increase in *subsidies* for it;

(4) a decline in the *prices of other goods* that could be produced by firms making it;

(5) an increase or decrease (depending on the market in question) in *expectations* of its higher future prices; and

(6) an increase in the number of sellers of it.

e. A change in supply must be distinguished from a change in quantity supplied.

4. The *market* or *equilibrium price* of a product is that price at which quantity demanded and quantity supplied are equal; the quantity exchanged in the market (the equilibrium quantity) is equal to the quantity demanded and supplied at the equilibrium price.

a. If the price of a product is above the market equilibrium price, there will be a *surplus* or *excess supply.* In this case, the quantity demanded is less than the quantity supplied at that price.

b. If the price of a product is below the market equilibrium price, there will be a *shortage* or *excess demand.* In this case, the quantity demanded is greater than the quantity supplied at that price.

c. The rationing function of prices is the elimination of surpluses and shortages of a product.

d. A change in demand, supply, or both changes both the equilibrium price and the equilibrium quantity in specific ways. (See #4 in "Hints and Tips" section.)

e. When demand and supply schedules (or curves) are drawn up, it is assumed that all the nonprice determinants of demand and supply remain unchanged. This assumption is often stated as "other-things-equal."

5. Supply and demand analysis has many important applications to *government-set prices.*

a. A price ceiling set by government prevents price from performing its rationing function in a market system. It creates a shortage (quantity demanded is greater than the quantity supplied) at the government-set price.

(1) Another rationing method must be found, so government often steps in and establishes one. But all rationing systems have problems because they exclude someone.

(2) Also, a government-set price creates an illegal *black market* for those who want to buy and sell above the government-set price.

(3) One example of a legal price ceiling that creates a shortage would be rent control established in some cities to restrain apartment rents.

b. A *price floor* is a minimum price set by government for the sale of a product or resource. It creates a surplus (quantity supplied is greater than the quantity demanded) at the fixed price. The surplus may induce the government to increase demand or decrease supply to eliminate the surplus. The use of price floors has often been applied to several agricultural products.

■ HINTS AND TIPS

1. This chapter is the most important one in the book. Make sure you spend extra time on it and master the material. If you do, your long-term payoff will be a much easier understanding of the applications in later chapters.

2. One mistake students often make is to confuse *change in demand* with *change in quantity demanded.* A change in demand causes the entire demand curve to *shift,* whereas a change in quantity demanded is simply a *movement* along an existing demand curve.

3. It is strongly recommended that you draw supply and demand graphs as you work on supply and demand problems so you can see a picture of what happens when demand shifts, supply shifts, or both demand and supply shift.

4. Make a chart and related graphs that show the eight possible outcomes from changes in demand and supply. Figure 3–6 in the text illustrates the *four single shift* outcomes:

(1) *D*↑: *P*↑, *Q*↑ (3) *S*↑: *P*↓, *Q*↑
(2) *D*↓: *P*↓, *Q*↓ (4) *S*↓: *P*↑, *Q*↓

Four shift combinations are described in Table 3–9 of the text. Make a figure to illustrate each combination.

(1) *S*↑, *D*↓: *P*↓, *Q*? (3) *S*↑, *D*↑: *P*?, *Q*↑
(2) *S*↓, *D*↑: *P*↑, *Q*? (4) *S*↓, *D*↓: *P*?, *Q*↓

5. Make sure you understand the "other-things-equal" assumption described at the end of the chapter. It will help you understand why the law of demand is not violated even if the price and quantity of a product increase over time.

6. Practice always helps in understanding graphs. Without looking at the textbook, draw a supply and demand graph with a *price ceiling* below the equilibrium price and show the resulting shortage in the market for a product. Then, draw a supply and demand graph with a *price floor* above the equilibrium price and show the resulting surplus. Explain to yourself what the graphs show. Check your graphs and your explanations by referring to textbook Figures 3–7 and 3–8 and the related explanations.

■ IMPORTANT TERMS

market	change in quantity demanded
demand	quantity demanded
demand schedule	individual demand
law of demand	total or market demand
diminishing marginal utility	supply
income effect	supply schedule
substitution effect	law of supply
demand curve	quantity supplied
determinants of demand	supply curve
normal good	determinants of supply
inferior good	change in supply
substitute goods	change in quantity supplied
complementary goods	surplus
change in demand	shortage

equilibrium price	price ceiling
equilibrium quantity	price floor
rationing function of prices	

SELF-TEST

■ FILL-IN QUESTIONS

1. A market is the institution or mechanism that brings together buyers or (demanders, suppliers) _____ and sellers or _____ of a particular good or service.

2. The relationship between price and quantity in the demand schedule is (a direct, an inverse) _____ relationship; in the supply schedule the relationship is _____ one.

3. The added satisfaction or pleasure a consumer obtains from additional units of a product decreases as the consumer's consumption of the product increases. This phenomenon is called diminishing marginal (equilibrium, utility) _____.

4. A consumer tends to buy more of a product as its price falls because
   a. The purchasing power of the consumer is increased and the consumer tends to buy more of this product (and of other products); this is called the (income, substitution) _____ effect;
   b. The product becomes less expensive relative to similar products and the consumer tends to buy more of the original product and less of the similar products, which is called the _____ effect.

5. When demand or supply is graphed, price is placed on the (horizontal, vertical) _____ axis and quantity on the _____ axis.

6. The change from an individual to a market demand schedule involves (adding, multiplying) _____ the quantities demanded by each consumer at the various possible (incomes, prices) _____.

7. When the price of one product and the demand for another product are directly related, the two products are called (substitutes, complements) _____; however, when the price of one product and the demand for another product are inversely related, the two products are called _____.

8. When a consumer demand schedule or curve is drawn up, it is assumed that five factors that determine demand are fixed and constant. These five determinants of consumer demand are

   a. _____

   b. _____

c. _____

d. _____

e. _____

9. A decrease in demand means that consumers will buy (larger, smaller) _____ quantities at every price, or will pay (more, less) _____ for the same quantities.

10. A change in income or in the price of another product will result in a change in the (demand for, quantity demanded of) _____ the given product, while a change in the price of the given product will result in a change in the _____ the given product.

11. An increase in supply means that producers will make and be willing to sell (larger, smaller) _____ quantities at every price, or will accept (more, less) _____ for the same quantities.

12. A change in resource prices or the prices of other goods that could be produced will result in a change in the (supply, quantity supplied) _____ of the given product, but a change in the price of the given product will result in a change in the _____.

13. The fundamental factors that determine the supply of any commodity in the product market are

a. _____

b. _____

c. _____

d. _____

e. _____

f. _____

14. If quantity demanded is greater than quantity supplied, price is (above, below) _____ the equilibrium price, and the (shortage, surplus) _____ will cause the price to (rise, fall) _____. If quantity demanded is less than the quantity supplied, price is (above, below) _____ the equilibrium price, and the (shortage, surplus) _____ will cause the price to (rise, fall) _____.

15. The equilibrium price of a product is the price at which quantity demanded is (greater than, equal to) _____ quantity supplied, and there (is, is not) _____ a surplus or a shortage at that price.

16. In the space next to **a–h,** indicate the effect [*increase* (+), *decrease* (−), or *indeterminate* (?)] on equilibrium price (**P**) and equilibrium quantity (**Q**) of each of these changes in demand and/or supply.

                                                     P   **Q**

a. Increase in demand, supply constant ____ ____

b. Increase in supply, demand constant ____ ____

c. Decrease in demand, supply constant ____ ____

d. Decrease in supply, demand constant ____ ____

e. Increase in demand, increase in supply ____ ____

f. Increase in demand, decrease in supply ____ ____

g. Decrease in demand, decrease in supply ____ ____

h. Decrease in demand, increase in supply ____ ____

17. If supply and demand establish a price for a good so that there is no shortage or surplus of the product, then price is successfully performing its (utility, rationing) _____ function. The price that is set is a market-(changing, clearing) _____ price.

18. To assume that all the determinants of demand and supply do not change is to employ the (marginal utility, other-things-equal) _____ assumption.

19. A price ceiling is the (minimum, maximum) _____ legal price a seller may charge for a product or service, whereas a price floor is the _____ legal price set by government.

20. If a price ceiling is below the market equilibrium price, a (surplus, shortage) _____ will arise in a competitive market, and if a price floor is above the market equilibrium price, a (surplus, shortage) _____ will arise in a competitive market.

■ **TRUE–FALSE QUESTIONS**

Circle T if the statement is true, F if it is false.

1. A market is any arrangement that brings together the buyers and sellers of a particular good or service.
      T F

2. Demand is the amount of a good or service that a buyer will purchase at a particular price.   **T F**

3. The law of demand states that as price increases, other things being equal, the quantity of the product demanded increases.   **T F**

4. The law of diminishing marginal utility is one explanation of why there is an inverse relationship between price and quantity demanded.   **T F**

5. The substitution effect suggests that, at a lower price, you have the incentive to substitute the more expensive product for similar products which are relatively less expensive. **T F**

6. There is no difference between individual demand schedules and the market demand schedule for a product. **T F**

7. In graphing supply and demand schedules, supply is put on the horizontal axis and demand on the vertical axis. **T F**

8. If price falls, there will be an increase in demand. **T F**

9. If consumer tastes or preferences for a product decrease, the demand for the product will tend to decrease. **T F**

10. An increase in income will tend to increase the demand for a product. **T F**

11. When two products are substitute goods, the price of one and the demand for the other will tend to move in the same direction. **T F**

12. If two goods are complementary, an increase in the price of one will tend to increase the demand for the other. **T F**

13. A change in the quantity demanded means that there has been a change in demand. **T F**

14. Supply is a schedule that shows the amounts of a product a producer can make in a limited time period. **T F**

15. An increase in resource prices will tend to decrease supply. **T F**

16. A government subsidy for the production of a product will tend to decrease supply. **T F**

17. An increase in the prices of other goods that could be made by producers will tend to decrease the supply of the current good that the producer is making. **T F**

18. A change in supply means that there is a movement along an existing supply curve. **T F**

19. A surplus indicates that the quantity demanded is less than the quantity supplied at that price. **T F**

20. If the market price of a product is below its equilibrium price, the market price will tend to rise because demand will decrease and supply will increase. **T F**

21. The rationing function of prices is the elimination of shortages and surpluses. **T F**

22. If the supply of a product increases and demand decreases, the equilibrium price and quantity will increase. **T F**

23. If the demand for a product increases and the supply of the product decreases, the equilibrium price will increase and equilibrium quantity will be indeterminant. **T F**

24. Economists often make the assumption of other things equal to hold constant the effects of other factors when examining the relationship between prices and quantities demanded and supplied. **T F**

25. A price ceiling set by government below the competitive market price of a product will result in a surplus. **T F**

■ **MULTIPLE-CHOICE QUESTIONS**

Circle the letter that corresponds to the best answer.

1. The markets examined in this chapter
   (a) sell nonstandard or differentiated products
   (b) have buyers cooperating to determine prices
   (c) are controlled by a single producer
   (d) are highly competitive

2. A schedule that shows the various amounts of a product consumers are willing and able to purchase at each price in a series of possible prices during a specified period of time is called
   (a) supply
   (b) demand
   (c) quantity supplied
   (d) quantity demanded

3. The reason for the law of demand can best be explained in terms of
   (a) supply
   (b) complementary goods
   (c) the rationing function of prices
   (d) diminishing marginal utility

4. Assume that the price of video game players falls. What will most likely happen to the equilibrium price and quantity of video games, assuming this market is competitive?
   (a) Price will increase; quantity will decrease.
   (b) Price will decrease; quantity will increase.
   (c) Price will decrease; quantity will decrease.
   (d) Price will increase; quantity will increase.

5. Given the following individuals' demand schedules for product X, and assuming these are the only three consumers of X, which set of prices and output levels below will be on the market demand curve for this product?

Price X	Consumer 1 Q_{dx}	Consumer 2 Q_{dx}	Consumer 3 Q_{dx}
$5	1	2	0
4	2	4	0
3	3	6	1
2	4	8	2
1	5	10	3

   (a) ($5, 2); ($1, 10)
   (b) ($5, 3); ($1, 18)
   (c) ($4, 6); ($2, 12)
   (d) ($4, 0); ($1, 3)

6. Which factor will decrease the demand for a product?
  (a) a favorable change in consumer tastes
  (b) an increase in the price of a substitute good
  (c) a decrease in the price of a complementary good
  (d) a decrease in the number of buyers

7. The income of a consumer decreases and the consumer's demand for a particular good increases. It can be concluded that the good is
  (a) normal
  (b) inferior
  (c) a substitute
  (d) a complement

8. Which of the following could cause a decrease in consumer demand for product X?
  (a) a decrease in consumer income
  (b) an increase in the prices of goods that are good substitutes for product X
  (c) an increase in the price that consumers expect will prevail for product X in the future
  (d) a decrease in the supply of product X

9. If two goods are substitutes for each other, an increase in the price of one will necessarily
  (a) decrease the demand for the other
  (b) increase the demand for the other
  (c) decrease the quantity demanded of the other
  (d) increase the quantity demanded of the other

10. If two products, A and B, are complements, then
  (a) an increase in the price of A will decrease the demand for B
  (b) an increase in the price of A will increase the demand for B
  (c) an increase in the price of A will have no significant effect on the price of B
  (d) a decrease in the price of A will decrease the demand for B

11. If two products, X and Y, are independent goods, then
  (a) an increase in the price of X will significantly increase the demand for Y
  (b) an increase in the price of Y will significantly increase the demand for X
  (c) an increase in the price of Y will have no significant effect on the demand for X
  (d) a decrease in the price of X will significantly increase the demand for Y

12. The law of supply states that, other things being constant, as price increases
  (a) supply increases
  (b) supply decreases
  (c) quantity supplied increases
  (d) quantity supplied decreases

13. If the supply curve moves from S_1 to S_2 on the graph in the next column, there has been
  (a) an increase in supply
  (b) a decrease in supply
  (c) an increase in quantity supplied
  (d) a decrease in quantity supplied

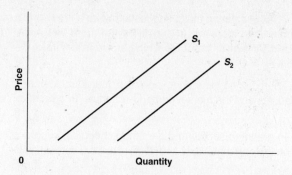

14. A decrease in the supply of a product would most likely be caused by
  (a) an increase in business taxes
  (b) an increase in consumer incomes
  (c) a decrease in resource costs for production
  (d) a decrease in the price of a complementary good

15. If the quantity supplied of a product is greater than the quantity demanded for a product, then
  (a) there is a shortage of the product
  (b) there is a surplus of the product
  (c) the product is a normal good
  (d) the product is an inferior good

16. If the price of a product is below the equilibrium price, the result will be
  (a) a surplus of the good
  (b) a shortage of the good
  (c) a decrease in the supply of the good
  (d) an increase in the demand for the good

Answer Questions 17, 18, and 19 on the basis of the data in the the following table. Consider the following supply and demand schedules for bushels of corn.

Price	Quantity demanded	Quantity supplied
$20	395	200
22	375	250
24	350	290
26	320	320
28	280	345
30	235	365

17. The equilibrium price in this market is
  (a) $22
  (b) $24
  (c) $26
  (d) $28

18. An increase in the cost of labor lowers the quantity supplied by 65 bushels at each price. The new equilibrium price would be
  (a) $22
  (b) $24
  (c) $26
  (d) $28

19. If the quantity demanded at each price increases by 130 bushels, then the new equilibrium quantity will be
  (a) 290
  (b) 320
  (c) 345
  (d) 365

20. A decrease in supply and a decrease in demand will
(a) increase price and decrease the quantity exchanged
(b) decrease price and increase the quantity exchanged
(c) increase price and affect the quantity exchanged in an indeterminate way
(d) affect price in an indeterminate way and decrease the quantity exchanged

21. An increase in demand and a decrease in supply will
(a) increase price and increase the quantity exchanged
(b) decrease price and decrease the quantity exchanged
(c) increase price and the effect upon quantity exchanged will be indeterminate
(d) decrease price and the effect upon quantity exchanged will be indeterminate

22. An increase in supply and an increase in demand will
(a) increase price and increase the quantity exchanged
(b) decrease price and increase the quantity exchanged
(c) affect price in an indeterminate way and decrease the quantity exchanged
(d) affect price in an indeterminate way and increase the quantity exchanged

23. A cold spell in Florida devastates the orange crop. As a result, California oranges command a higher price. Which of the following statements best explains the situation?
(a) The supply of Florida oranges decreases, causing the supply of California oranges to increase and their price to increase.
(b) The supply of Florida oranges decreases, causing their price to increase and the demand for California oranges to increase.
(c) The supply of Florida oranges decreases, causing the supply of California oranges to decrease and their price to increase.
(d) The demand for Florida oranges decreases, causing a greater demand for California oranges and an increase in their price.

Answer Questions 24, 25, 26, and 27 based on the following graph showing the market supply and demand for a product.

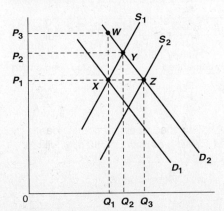

24. Assume that the market is initially in equilibrium where D_1 and S_1 intersect. If there is an increase in the number of buyers, then the new equilibrium would most likely be at point
(a) **W**
(b) **X**
(c) **Y**
(d) **Z**

25. Assume that the equilibrium price and quantity in the market are P_2 and Q_2. Which factor would cause the equilibrium price and quantity to shift to P_1 and Q_3?
(a) an increase in product price
(b) an increase in demand
(c) an increase in supply
(d) a decrease in quantity

26. What would cause a shift in the equilibrium price and quantity from point **Z** to point **X**?
(a) a decrease in production costs and more favorable consumer tastes for the product
(b) an increase in the number of suppliers and an increase in consumer incomes
(c) an increase in production costs and decrease in consumer incomes
(d) an improvement in production technology and decrease in the price of a substitute good

27. Assume that the market is initially in equilibrium where D_1 and S_1 intersect. If consumer incomes increased and the technology for making the product improved, then new equilibrium would most likely be at
(a) P_1 and Q_1
(b) P_2 and Q_2
(c) P_1 and Q_3
(d) P_3 and Q_1

28. The demand curve and its inverse relationship between price and quantity demanded is based on the assumption of
(a) other things equal
(b) changing expectations
(c) complementary goods
(d) increasing marginal utility

Questions 29 and 30 relate to the following table that shows a hypothetical supply and demand schedule for a product.

Quantity demanded (pounds)	Price (per pound)	Quantity supplied (pounds)
200	$4.40	800
250	4.20	700
300	4.00	600
350	3.80	500
400	3.60	400
450	3.40	300
500	3.20	200

29. A shortage of 150 pounds of the product will occur if a government-set price is established at
(a) $3.20
(b) $3.40
(c) $3.80
(d) $4.00

30. If a price floor set by the government is established at $4.20, there will be a
  (a) surplus of 300 pounds
  (b) shortage of 300 pounds
  (c) surplus of 450 pounds
  (d) shortage of 450 pounds

■ PROBLEMS

1. Using the demand schedule that follows, plot the demand curve on the graph below the schedule. Label the axes and indicate for each axis the units being used to measure price and quantity.

Price	Quantity demanded, 1000 bushels of soybeans
$7.20	10
7.00	15
6.80	20
6.60	25
6.40	30
6.20	35

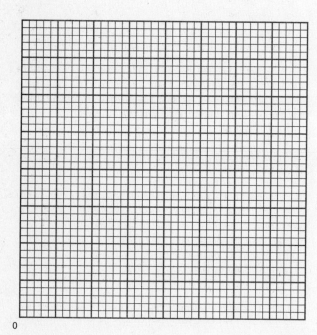

0

a. Plot the following supply schedule on the same graph.

Price	Quantity supplied, 1000 bushels of soybeans
$7.20	40
7.00	35
6.80	30
6.60	25
6.40	20
6.20	15

b. The equilibrium price of soybeans will be $_____.
c. How many thousand bushels of soybeans will be exchanged at this price? _____

d. Indicate clearly on the graph the equilibrium price and quantity by drawing lines from the intersection of the supply and demand curves to the price and quantity axes.
e. If the Federal government supported a price of $7.00 per bushel there would be a (shortage, surplus) _____ of _____ bushels of soybeans.

2. The demand schedules of three individuals (Ellie, Sam, and Lynn) for loaves of bread are shown in the following table. Assuming there are only three buyers of bread, determine and graph the total or market demand schedule for bread.

	Quantity demanded, loaves of bread			
Price	Ellie	Sam	Lynn	Total
$1.50	1	4	0	____
1.40	3	5	1	____
1.30	6	6	5	____
1.20	10	7	10	____
1.10	15	8	16	____

3. Following is a demand schedule for bushels of apples. In columns 3 and 4 insert *any* new figures for quantity that represent in column 3 an increase in demand and in column 4 a decrease in demand.

(1) Price	(2) Quantity demanded	(3) Demand increases	(4) Demand decreases
$6.00	400	____	____
5.90	500	____	____
5.80	600	____	____
5.70	700	____	____
5.60	800	____	____
5.50	900	____	____

4. Assume that O'Rourke has, when his income is $100 per week, the demand schedule for good A shown in columns 1 and 2 of the following table and the demand schedule for good B shown in columns 4 and 5. Assume that the prices of A and B are $.80 and $5, respectively.

Demand for A (per week)			Demand for B (per week)		
(1) Price	(2) Quantity demanded	(3) Quantity demanded	(4) Price	(5) Quantity demanded	(6) Quantity demanded
$.90	10	0	$5.00	4	7
.85	20	10	4.50	5	8
.80	30	20	4.00	6	9
.75	40	30	3.50	7	10
.70	50	40	3.00	8	11
.65	60	50	2.50	9	12
.60	70	60	2.00	10	13

a. How much A will O'Rourke buy? _____

How much B? _____

b. Suppose that as a consequence of a $10 increase in O'Rourke's weekly income, the quantities demanded of A become those shown in column 3 and the quantities demanded of B become those shown in column 6.
(1) How much A will he now buy? _____

How much B? _____
(2) Good A is (normal, inferior) _____.
(3) Good B is _____.

5. The market demand for good X is shown in columns 1 and 2 of the following table. Assume the price of X to be $2 and constant.

(1) Price	(2) Quantity demanded	(3) Quantity demanded	(4) Quantity demanded
$2.40	1,600	1,500	1,700
2.30	1,650	1,550	1,750
2.20	1,750	1,650	1,850
2.10	1,900	1,800	2,000
2.00	2,100	2,000	2,200
1.90	2,350	2,250	2,450
1.80	2,650	2,550	2,750

a. If as the price of good Y rises from $1.25 to $1.35, the quantities demanded of good X become those shown in column 3, it can be concluded that X and Y are (substitute, complementary) _____ goods.

b. If as the price of good Y rises from $1.25 to $1.35, the quantities of good X become those shown in column 4, it can be concluded that X and Y are _____ _____ goods.

6. In a local market for hamburger on a given date, each of 300 identical sellers of hamburger has the following supply schedule.

(1) Price	(2) Quantity supplied— one seller, lbs	(3) Quantity supplied— all sellers, lbs
$2.05	150	_____
2.00	110	_____
1.95	75	_____
1.90	45	_____
1.85	20	_____
1.80	0	_____

a. In column 3 construct the market supply schedule for hamburger.
b. Following is the market demand schedule for hamburger on the same date and in the same local market as that given above.

Price	Quantity demanded, lbs
$2.05	28,000
2.00	31,000
1.95	36,000
1.90	42,000
1.85	49,000
1.80	57,000

If the Federal government sets a price on hamburger of $1.90 a pound, the result would be a (shortage, surplus) _____ of _____ pounds of hamburger in this market.

7. Each of the following events would tend to increase or decrease either the demand for or the supply of computer games and, as a result, will increase or decrease the price of these games. In the first blank indicate the effect on demand or supply (increase, decrease); in the second blank, indicate the effect on price (increase, decrease). Assume that the market for computer games is a competitive one.

a. It becomes known that an electronics store is going to have a sale on these games 3 months from now. _____ ;

_____

b. The workers who produce the games go on strike for over 2 months. _____ ; _____

c. The workers in the industry receive a $2 an hour wage increase. _____ ; _____

d. The average price of movie tickets (a substitute) increases. _____ ; _____

e. The price of business software, a product also supplied by the computer software producers, rises. _____ ; _____

f. It is announced by a private research institute that children who play computer games also improve their grades in school. _____ ; _____

g. Because of the use of mass production techniques, the amount of labor necessary to produce a game decreases. _____ ; _____

h. The price of computers decreases. _____ ;

i. The average consumer believes that a shortage of games is developing in the economy. _____ ;

j. The Federal government imposes a $5 tax per game on the manufacturers of computer games. _____ ; _____

■ **SHORT ANSWER AND ESSAY QUESTIONS**

1. Define demand and the law of demand.

2. Use the diminishing marginal utility concept to explain why the quantity demanded of a product will tend to rise when the price of the product falls.

3. In past decades, the price of coffee in the United States rose significantly as a result of bad weather in coffee-producing regions. Use the income effect and the substitution effect concepts to explain why the quantity of coffee demanded in the United States significantly decreased.

4. What is the difference between individual demand and market demand? What is the relationship between these two types of demand?

5. Explain the difference between an increase in demand and an increase in the quantity demanded.

6. What are the factors that cause a change in demand? Use supply and demand graphs to illustrate what happens to price and quantity when demand increases.

7. How are inferior and normal (or superior) goods defined? What is the relationship between these goods and changes in income?

8. Why does the effect of a change in the price of related goods depend on whether a good is a substitute or complement? What are substitutes and complements?

9. A newspaper reports that "Blue jeans have become even more popular and are now the standard clothing that people wear for both play and work." How will this change affect the demand for blue jeans? What will happen to the price and quantity of blue jeans sold in the market? Explain and use a supply and demand graph to illustrate your answer.

10. Compare and contrast the supply schedule with the demand schedule.

11. Supply does not remain constant for long because the factors that determine supply change. What are these factors? How do changes in them affect supply?

12. Explain the difference between an increase in supply and an increase in the quantity supplied.

13. Describe and illustrate with a supply and demand graph the effect of an increase in supply on price and quantity. Do the same for a decrease in supply.

14. The U.S. Congress passes a law that raises the excise tax on gasoline by $1 per gallon. What effect will this change have on the demand and supply of gasoline? What will happen to gasoline prices and quantity? Explain and use a supply and demand graph to illustrate your answer.

15. What is the relationship between the price of a product and a shortage of the product? What is the relationship between the price of a product and a surplus of the product?

16. Given the demand for and the supply of a commodity, what price will be the equilibrium price of this commodity? Explain why this price will tend to prevail in the market and why higher (lower) prices, if they do exist temporarily, will tend to fall (rise).

17. Analyze the following quotation and explain the fallacies contained in it: "An increase in demand will cause price to rise; with a rise in price, supply will increase and the increase in supply will push price down. Therefore, an increase in demand results in little change in price because supply will increase also."

18. Suppose an industry sells 2000 units of a product at $10 per unit one year, 3000 units at $12 the next year, and 4000 units at $14 the third year. Is this evidence that the law of demand is violated? Explain.

19. What are the consequences of a price ceiling for a product if it is set below the equilibrium price? Illustrate your answer with a graph.

20. What are the economic problems with price floors? How have they been used by government?

ANSWERS

Chapter 3 Individual Markets: Demand and Supply

FILL-IN QUESTIONS

1. demanders, suppliers
2. an inverse, a direct
3. utility
4. *a.* income; *b.* substitution
5. vertical, horizontal
6. adding, prices
7. substitutes, complements
8. *a.* the tastes or preferences of consumers; *b.* the number of consumers in the market; *c.* the money income of consumers; *d.* the prices of related goods; *e.* consumer expectations with respect to future prices, product availability, and income (any order for *a–e*)
9. smaller, less
10. demand for, quantity demanded of
11. larger, less
12. supply, quantity supplied
13. *a.* the technology of production; *b.* resource prices; *c.* taxes and subsidies; *d.* prices of other goods; *e.* price expectations; *f.* the number of sellers in the market (any order for *a–f*)
14. below, shortage, rise, above, surplus, fall
15. equal to, is not
16. *a.* +, +; *b.* –, +; *c.* –, –; *d.* +, –; *e.* ?, +; *f.* +, ?; *g.* ?, –; *h.* –, ?
17. rationing, clearing
18. other-things-equal
19. maximum, minimum
20. shortage, surplus

TRUE–FALSE QUESTIONS

1. T, p. 39	10. T, p. 43	19. T, p. 48
2. F, pp. 40; 44–45	11. T, p. 44	20. F, pp. 48–49
3. F, p. 40	12. F, p. 44	21. T, p. 50
4. T, p. 40	13. F, pp. 44–45	22. F, pp. 50–52
5. F, pp. 40–41	14. F, p. 45	23. T, pp. 50–52
6. F, pp. 41–42	15. T, pp. 46–47	24. T, p. 52
7. F, p. 42	16. F, p. 47	25. F, pp. 52–53
8. F, pp. 42–44	17. T, p. 47	
9. T, p. 43	18. F, pp. 47–48	

MULTIPLE-CHOICE QUESTIONS

1. d, p. 39	**11.** c, p. 44	**21.** c, p. 51
2. b, p. 40	**12.** c, p. 45	**22.** d, p. 52
3. d, pp. 40–41	**13.** a, p. 46	**23.** b, p. 51
4. d, pp. 44; 50	**14.** a, pp. 46–47	**24.** c, pp. 43; 50
5. b, pp. 41–42	**15.** b, p. 48	**25.** c, p. 50
6. d, pp. 43–44	**16.** b, p. 48	**26.** c, pp. 43–44; 46–47; 51
7. b, p. 43	**17.** c, p. 49	**27.** c, pp. 43–44; 46–47; 52
8. a, p. 44	**18.** d, pp. 47; 50	**28.** a, p. 52
9. b, p. 44	**19.** d, pp. 45; 50	**29.** b, p. 53
10. a, p. 44	**20.** d, p. 52	**30.** c, p. 54

PROBLEMS

1. *a.* graph; *b.* 6.60; *c.* 25,000; *d.* graph; *e.* surplus, 20,000
2. Total: 5, 9, 17, 27, 39
3. Each quantity in column 3 is greater than in column 2, and each quantity in column 4 is less than in column 2.
4. *a.* 30, 4; *b.* (1) 20, 7; (2) inferior; (3) normal (superior)

5. *a.* complementary; *b.* substitute
6. *a.* 45,000; 33,000; 22,500; 13,500; 6,000; 0; *b.* shortage, 28,500
7. *a.* decrease demand, decrease price; *b.* decrease supply, increase price; *c.* decrease supply, increase price; *d.* increase demand, increase price; *e.* decrease supply, increase price; *f.* increase demand, increase price; *g.* increase supply, decrease price; *h.* increase demand, increase price; *i.* increase demand, increase price; *j.* decrease supply, increase price

SHORT ANSWER AND ESSAY QUESTIONS

1. p. 40	**8.** p. 44	**15.** p. 48
2. p. 40	**9.** pp. 43; 50	**16.** pp. 48–50
3. p. 41	**10.** pp. 40; 45	**17.** pp. 50–51
4. pp. 41–42	**11.** pp. 46–47	**18.** pp. 50–51
5. pp. 44–45	**12.** pp. 47–48	**19.** pp. 52–53
6. pp. 43–44	**13.** pp. 46; 50–51	**20.** pp. 54–55
7. p. 43	**14.** pp. 47; 50–51	

Applications and Extensions of Supply and Demand Analysis

Note: This bonus web chapter is available at the textbook website: www.mcconnell16.com. Go to Chapter 3W at the Student Center.

Chapter 3 Web has two basic purposes. It offers you numerous real-world applications of supply and demand analysis. It also uses supply and demand analysis to provide new insights into the allocation of common resources and economic efficiency.

The first section of the chapter gives you more examples of the effects of **changes in supply and demand** on price and quantity. You will first read about simple changes in which either the demand curve changes or the supply curve changes, but not both. These simple changes result in predictable effects on the price and quantity of a product, such as lettuce or American flags. Then you are given examples, using pink salmon, gasoline, and sushi, of complex changes. In these cases, there is a simultaneous shift in supply and demand. Here the effect of changes in supply and demand on price and quantity will be less certain and will depend on the direction and extent of the changes.

The chapter then extends your understanding of what happens in markets if **pre-set prices** are above or below the equilibrium price. You have already learned that when the government intervenes in a competitive market and sets the price below equilibrium (a price ceiling), it creates a shortage of a product. Similarly, when government sets a price above the equilibrium price (a price floor), it will result in a surplus. As you will learn, shortages and surpluses can also occur in competitive markets when sellers set the price in advance of sales and that pre-set price turns out to be below or above the equilibrium or actual price. The examples given in the text are ticket prices for sporting events that are priced too low or too high by the sellers, resulting in shortages and surpluses.

The third section of the chapter introduces you to a new concept, **nonpriced goods.** These goods or resources are ones that are owned in common by society, such as wildlife, fish, public water, and public land. Although there are no competitive markets or prices, supply and demand analysis can provide insights about the effective use and management of these resources. As you will read, this analysis can explain the plight of buffalo since the 1800s. The text also discusses the alternative methods government uses to ration scarce resources that do not have a market price.

Supply and demand analysis is also used to enhance your understanding of **economic efficiency** in the fourth section of the chapter. This extension requires an explanation of the concepts of **consumer and producer surplus.** Consumer surplus is the difference between the maximum price consumers are willing to pay for a product and the actual price. Producer surplus is the difference between the minimum price producers are willing to accept for a product and the actual price. The chapter also revisits the concept of **allocative efficiency** and explains that it is achieved when the combination of consumer and producer surplus is at a maximum.

Supply and demand analysis is one of the most important means for improving your understanding of the economic world. If you master its use, it will help you explain many events and outcomes in everyday life. This chapter helps you achieve that mastery and understanding.

■ **CHECKLIST**

When you have studied this chapter you should be able to

☐ Explain and graph the effect of an increase in the supply of a product (lettuce) on its equilibrium price and quantity.

☐ Describe and graph the effect of an increase in the demand for a product (American flags) on its equilibrium price and quantity.

☐ Discuss and graph the effects of an increase in the supply of and a decrease in demand for a product (pink salmon) on its equilibrium price and quantity.

☐ Predict and graph the effects of a decrease in the supply of and an increase in the demand for a product (gasoline) on its equilibrium price and quantity.

☐ Explain and graph the effects of an equal increase in the supply of and demand for a product (sushi) on its equilibrium price and quantity.

☐ Discuss and graph how a seller price for a service (Olympic figure skating finals) that is set below the equilibrium price will result in a shortage.

☐ Describe and graph how a seller price for a service (Olympic curling preliminaries) that is set above the equilibrium price will result in a surplus.

☐ Define and give examples of nonpriced goods.

☐ Describe and graph the supply and demand conditions that will result in a shortage of a nonpriced good.

☐ Explain and graph the supply and demand conditions that will result in a surplus of a nonpriced good.

☐ Define consumer surplus and give a graphical example.

☐ Define producer surplus and give a graphical example.

☐ Use consumer surplus and producer surplus to explain how allocative efficiency is achieved in a competitive market.

☐ List the three conditions for achieving allocative efficiency at a quantity level in a competitive market.

☐ Use a supply and demand graph to illustrate efficiency losses when the quantity is greater or less than its equilibrium in a competitive market.

■ **CHAPTER OUTLINE**

1. **Changes in supply and demand** result in changes in the equilibrium price and quantity. The simplest cases are ones where demand changes and supply remains constant, or where supply changes and demand remains constant. More complex cases involve simultaneous changes in supply and demand.

   a. *Supply increase.* In a competitive market for lettuce, if a severe freeze destroys a portion of the lettuce crop, then the supply of lettuce will decrease. The decrease in the supply of lettuce, with demand constant, will increase the equilibrium price and decrease the equilibrium quantity.

   b. *Demand increase.* In a competitive market for American flags, an increase in patriotism will increase the demand for flags. This increase in demand, with supply remaining the same, will increase the equilibrium price and quantity of flags.

   c. *Supply increase and demand decrease.* Over the years, improved fishing techniques and technology contributed to an increase in the supply of pink salmon. Also, an increase in consumer incomes and a lowering of the price of substitute fish contributed to reducing the demand for pink salmon. As a result the price of pink salmon fell. The equilibrium quantity could have increased, decreased, or stayed the same. In this case, the increase in supply was greater than the decrease in demand, so the equilibrium quantity increased.

   d. *Demand increase and supply decrease.* An increase in the price of oil, a resource used to produce gasoline, resulted in a decrease in the supply of gasoline. At the same time, rising incomes and a stronger economy created a greater demand for gasoline. This decrease in supply and increase in demand increased the equilibrium price. The equilibrium quantity could have increased, decreased, or stayed the same. In this case, the decrease in supply was less than the increase in demand, so the equilibrium quantity increased.

   e. *Demand increase and supply increase.* An increase in the taste for sushi among U.S. consumers resulted in an increase in the demand for this product. At the same time, there was an increase in the number of sushi bars and other food outlets that provide sushi, thus increasing its supply. This increase in both demand and supply increased the equilibrium quantity of sushi. The equilibrium price could have increased, decreased, or stayed the same. In this case, the increase in demand was the same as the increase in supply, so the equilibrium price remained the same.

2. **Pre-set prices** that are set by the seller below or above the equilibrium price can produce shortages and surpluses.

   a. If a price is set below the equilibrium price by a seller, then at that pre-set price the quantity demanded is greater than the quantity supplied, resulting in a **shortage.** This situation is typical of the market for tickets to Olympic figure skating finals. The shortage of tickets at the pre-set price creates a secondary market (*black market*) for tickets in which buyers bid for tickets held by the initial purchaser. The ticket scalping drives up the price of tickets.

   b. If a price is set above the equilibrium price by a seller, then at that pre-set price the quantity demanded is less than the quantity supplied, resulting in a **surplus.** This situation is typical of the market for tickets to Olympic curling preliminaries at which there are many empty seats.

3. **Nonpriced goods** (or resources) are ones that are owned in common by society and available for public use. The prices of these goods are essentially zero because they are not bought and sold in markets. Yet, supply and demand analysis can be applied to explain events and situations involving these nonpriced goods.

   a. When the demand for a nonpriced good is less than the supply of the good at each and every price across the demand and supply curves, the price of the good will be zero. In this case, the demand and supply curves do not intersect at any positive price. This situation occurred with the buffalo in the pre-railroad era in the United States.

   b. With the advent of the railroad and greater hunting of buffalo, the demand for buffalo increased. In graphical terms, the demand curve now intersected the supply curve at a positive equilibrium price, and this price for buffalo would have prevailed if there had been a market. But buffalo was a nonpriced good, so it had a zero price, and at this price a shortage arose. This shortage grew progressively worse as the supply curve shifted left because the buffalo population could not be sustained. Nonpriced goods often get overused.

   c. When price is not used as a rationing device, other types of rationing allocate scarce resources. In the case of nonpriced goods such as wildlife or fish sought by hunters or fishers, licenses or quantity limits are used to decrease demand so that it is balanced with the sustainable supply. In some cases, nonpriced goods such as buffalo are being converted to privately owned goods that can be bought and sold in competitive markets.

4. In market transactions, consumers can obtain a beneficial surplus and so can producers.

   a. **Consumer surplus** is the difference between the maximum price consumers are willing to pay for a product and the actual (equilibrium) price paid. Graphically, it is the triangular area bounded by the portion of the vertical axis between the equilibrium price and the demand curve intersection, the portion of the demand curve above the equilibrium price, and the horizontal line at the equilibrium price from the vertical axis to the demand curve. Price and consumer surplus are inversely (negatively) related: Higher prices reduce it and lower prices increase it.

b. *Producer surplus* is the difference between the minimum price producers are willing to accept for a product and the actual (equilibrium) price received. Graphically, it is the triangular area bounded by the portion of the vertical axis between the equilibrium price and the supply curve intersection, the portion of the supply curve below the equilibrium price, and the horizontal line at the equilibrium price from the vertical axis to the supply curve. Price and producer surplus are directly (positively) related: Higher prices increase it and lower prices decrease it.

c. The equilibrium quantity shown by the intersection of demand and supply curves reflects *economic efficiency*.

(1) *Productive efficiency* is achieved because production costs are minimized at each quantity level of output.

(2) *Allocative efficiency* is achieved at the equilibrium quantity of output because three conditions are satisfied: Marginal benefit equals marginal cost; maximum willingness to pay equals minimum acceptable price; and the combination of the consumer and producer surplus is at a maximum.

d. If quantity is less than or greater than the equilibrium or most efficient level, there are **efficiency losses.** The efficiency losses reduce the maximum possible size of the combined consumer and producer surplus.

■ HINTS AND TIPS

1. This web chapter offers applications and extensions of Chapter 3 in the textbook, so check your understanding of the corresponding text and web sections: (a) Review the text Chapter 3 section on "Changes in Supply, Demand, and Equilibrium" (pp. 50–52) before reading the web Chapter 3 section on "Changes in Supply and Demand"; and (b) review the text Chapter 3 section on "Application: Government-Set Prices" (pp. 52–55) before reading the web Chapter 3 section on "Pre-Set Prices."

2. Correct terminology is important for mastering supply and demand analysis. You must remember the distinction between a change in demand and a change in quantity demanded or a change in supply and a change in quantity supplied. Consider the case of a single shift in demand with supply staying the same. As the demand curve increases along the existing supply curve, it increases the quantity supplied, but it does not increase supply (which would be a shift in the entire supply curve).

3. The newest concepts in the chapter are those related to consumer surplus and producer surplus. The term "surplus" should not be confused with the previous use related to pre-set prices (when quantity supplied is greater than quantity demanded at a pre-set price). What the consumer surplus refers to is the extra utility or satisfaction that consumers get when they do not have to pay the price they were willing to pay and pay the lower equilibrium price. The producer surplus arises when producers receive an equilibrium price that is above the minimum price that they consider acceptable to selling the product.

4. The concept of allocative efficiency using marginal benefit and marginal cost was first presented in the text, Chapter 2 (pp. 27–28). Review your understanding of this concept in Chapter 2 before reading the web Chapter 3 section on "Efficiency Revisited."

■ IMPORTANT TERMS

nonpriced goods	**producer surplus**
consumer surplus	**efficiency losses**

SELF-TEST

■ FILL-IN QUESTIONS

1. A decrease in the supply of lettuce will result in an equilibrium price that (increases, decreases) _____ and an equilibrium quantity that _____.

2. An increase in the demand for American flags will result in an equilibrium price that (increases, decreases) _____ and an equilibrium quantity that _____.

3. An increase in the supply of pink salmon that is greater than the decrease in the demand for pink salmon will result in an equilibrium price that (increases, decreases, stays the same) _____ and an equilibrium quantity that _____.

4. An increase in the demand for gasoline that is greater than the decrease in the supply of gasoline will result in an equilibrium price that (increases, decreases, stays the same) _____ and an equilibrium quantity that _____.

5. An increase in the demand for sushi that is equal to the increase in the supply of sushi will result in an equilibrium price that (increases, decreases, stays the same) _____ and an equilibrium quantity that _____.

6. If government sets a legal price for a product, a shortage would arise from a price (ceiling, floor) _____ and a surplus would arise from a price _____.

7. If a pre-set price is set by the seller below the equilibrium price it will create a (surplus, shortage) _____, but if a pre-set price is set by the seller above the equilibrium price it will create a _____.

8. A market for tickets to popular sporting events in which buyers bid for tickets held by initial purchasers is referred to as a (primary, secondary) _____ market. In these markets, ticket (destruction, scalping) _____ occurs.

9. Nonpriced goods are resources that are (privately owned, owned in common) _____ and available for taking on (private, public) _____ lands.

10. At a zero price for a nonpriced good, where the quantity available (quantity supplied) is greater than the quantity demanded, there will be a (shortage, surplus) _____, but when the quantity available (quantity supplied) is less than the quantity demanded, there will be a _____.

11. A significant increase in the demand for a nonpriced good will lead to (under-, over-) _____ consumption of the good and (an increase, a decrease) _____ in the sustainable supply of the good.

12. The alternative to using prices and markets to ration nonpriced goods such as fish and game on public lands is to use (scalping, licenses) _____ or set (bonuses, limits) _____ on the number that can be taken.

13. A consumer surplus is the difference between the actual price and the (minimum, maximum) _____ price a consumer is (or consumers are) willing to pay for a product. In most markets, consumers individually or collectively gain more total utility or satisfaction when the actual or equilibrium price they have to pay for a product is (less, more) _____ than what they would have been willing to pay to obtain the product.

14. Consumer surplus and price are (positively, negatively) _____ related. This means that higher prices (increase, decrease) _____ consumer surplus and lower prices _____ it.

15. A producer surplus is the difference between the actual or equilibrium price and the (minimum, maximum) _____ acceptable price a producer is (or producers are) willing to accept in exchange for a product. In most markets, sellers individually or collectively benefit when they sell their product at an actual or equilibrium price that is (less, more) _____ than what they would have been willing to receive in exchange for the product.

16. Producer surplus and price are (positively, negatively) _____ related. This means that higher prices (increase, decrease) _____ producer surplus and lower prices _____ it.

17. When competition forces producers to use the best techniques and combinations of resources to make a product, then (allocative, productive) _____ efficiency is being achieved. When the correct or optimal quantity of output of a product is being produced relative to the other goods and services, then _____ efficiency is being achieved.

18. Points on the demand curve measure the marginal (cost, benefit) _____ of a product whereas points on the supply curve measure the marginal _____ of a product.

19. Allocative efficiency occurs at quantity levels where marginal benefit is (greater than, less than, equal to) _____ marginal cost, maximum willingness to pay by consumers is _____ the minimum acceptable price for producers, and the combined consumer and producer surplus is at a (minimum, maximum) _____.

20. When there is overproduction of a product, there are efficiency (gains, losses) _____ and when there is underproduction there are efficiency _____. In both cases, the combined consumer and producer surplus is (greater than, less than) _____ the maximum that would occur at the efficient quantity of output.

■ **TRUE–FALSE QUESTIONS**

Circle T if the statement is true, F if it is false.

1. An increase in the supply of lettuce decreases its equilibrium price and increases its equilibrium quantity. **T F**

2. A decrease in the demand for an American flag increases its equilibrium price and decreases its equilibrium quantity. **T F**

3. When demand for American flags increases, there is an increase in the quantity supplied as the equilibrium price rises, but no increase in supply. **T F**

4. In the market for pink salmon, the reason that the equilibrium quantity increased was that the increase in supply was greater than the decrease in demand. **T F**

5. In the market for gasoline, the reason that the equilibrium quantity increased was that the increase in demand was less than the decrease in supply. **T F**

6. In the market for sushi, an equal increase in supply and demand will increase the equilibrium price, but have no effect on the equilibrium quantity. **T F**

7. If the government sets a price ceiling below what would be the competitive market price of a product, a shortage of the product will develop. **T F**

8. A price floor set by government will increase the equilibrium price and quantity in a market. **T F**

9. If a seller pre-sets a price that turns out to be below the actual equilibrium price, a shortage will develop in the market. **T F**

10. Ticket scalping often occurs in markets where there is a surplus of tickets. **T F**

11. If a sporting event is not sold out, this indicates that the ticket prices for the event were pre-set above the actual equilibrium price. **T F**

12. A nonpriced good is one that is owned in common by society and available for the taking on public lands. **T F**

13. An example of a nonpriced good is cattle that are raised on a cattle ranch. **T F**

14. A nonpriced good has a zero price because demand is less than supply regardless of the price. **T F**

15. Assume that a downsloping demand curve intersects a vertical supply curve. A leftward shift in the supply curve will result in a surplus of a product. **T F**

16. Ways that government rations nonpriced goods are to use licenses and set quantity limits. **T F**

17. Consumer surplus is the difference between the minimum and maximum price a consumer is willing to pay for a good. **T F**

18. Consumer surplus is a utility surplus that reflects a gain in total utility or satisfaction. **T F**

19. Consumer surplus and price are directly or positively related. **T F**

20. The higher the equilibrium price, the greater the amount of consumer surplus. **T F**

21. Producer surplus is the difference between the actual price a producer receives for a product and the minimum price the producer would have been willing to accept for the product. **T F**

22. The higher the actual price, the less the amount of producer surplus. **T F**

23. Competitive markets produce equilibrium prices and quantities that minimize the sum of consumer and producer surpluses. **T F**

24. One of the three conditions for allocative efficiency is that the maximum willingness to pay by consumers is equal to the minimum acceptable price for producers. **T F**

25. Efficiency losses are increases in the combined consumer and producer surplus. **T F**

■ **MULTIPLE-CHOICE QUESTIONS**

Circle the letter that corresponds to the best answer.

1. Bad weather in coffee-producing regions of the world devastated the coffee crop. As a result, coffee prices increased worldwide. Which of the following statements best explains the situation?
 (a) the demand for coffee increased
 (b) the supply of coffee decreased
 (c) the demand for coffee increased and the supply of coffee increased
 (d) the demand for coffee decreased and the supply of coffee decreased

2. Assume that the supply of tomatoes in a competitive market increases. What will most likely happen to the equilibrium price and quantity of tomatoes?
 (a) price will increase; quantity will decrease
 (b) price will decrease; quantity will increase
 (c) price will decrease; quantity will decrease
 (d) price will increase; quantity will increase

3. Assume that the demand for security services increases in a competitive market. What will most likely happen to the equilibrium price and quantity of security services?
 (a) price will increase; quantity will decrease
 (b) price will decrease; quantity will increase
 (c) price will decrease; quantity will decrease
 (d) price will increase; quantity will increase

4. A decrease in the demand for hamburger is more than offset by an increase in its supply. As a result the equilibrium price will
 (a) increase and the equilibrium quantity will decrease
 (b) increase and the equilibrium quantity will increase
 (c) decrease and the equilibrium quantity will decrease
 (d) decrease and the equilibrium quantity will increase

5. A decrease in the supply of oil is more than offset by an increase in its demand. As a result, the equilibrium price will
 (a) increase and the equilibrium quantity will decrease
 (b) increase and the equilibrium quantity will increase
 (c) decrease and the equilibrium quantity will decrease
 (d) decrease and the equilibrium quantity will increase

6. What will happen to the equilibrium quantity and price of a product in a competitive market when there is an equal increase in demand and supply?
 (a) equilibrium quantity and price will both increase
 (b) equilibrium quantity and price will both decrease
 (c) equilibrium quantity will increase and equilibrium price will stay the same
 (d) equilibrium quantity will stay the same and equilibrium price will increase

7. What will happen to the equilibrium quantity and price of a product in a competitive market when the decrease in demand exactly offsets the increase in supply?
 (a) equilibrium quantity will increase and equilibrium price will decrease

(b) equilibrium quantity will decrease and equilibrium price will increase

(c) equilibrium quantity will increase and equilibrium price will stay the same

(d) equilibrium quantity will stay the same and equilibrium price will decrease

8. Which of the following is a correct statement?
  (a) price ceilings increase supply
  (b) price ceilings create shortages
  (c) price floors create shortages
  (d) price floors increase demand

9. If a seller sets a price for a product that turns out to be below the equilibrium price, then there will be a
  (a) shortage of the product
  (b) surplus of the product
  (c) price floor for a product
  (d) a zero price for the product

10. A surplus means that
  (a) demand for a product is greater than the supply
  (b) supply of the product is greater than the demand
  (c) quantity demanded is less than the quantity supplied at that price
  (d) quantity demanded is greater than the quantity supplied at that price

Answer Questions 11, 12, and 13 based on the following graph showing the market supply and demand for a product.

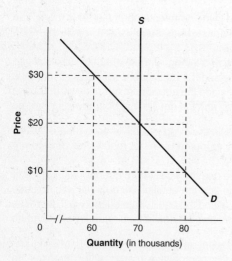

11. Given this market, if a seller pre-sets the price at $10, then this action results in a
  (a) surplus of 10,000 units
  (b) surplus of 80,000 units
  (c) shortage of 10,000 units
  (d) shortage of 80,000 units

12. Given this market, if a seller pre-sets the price at $30, then this action results in a
  (a) surplus of 10,000 units
  (b) surplus of 60,000 units
  (c) surplus of 70,000 units
  (d) shortage of 10,000 units

13. What price will eliminate a surplus or shortage in this market?
  (a) $0
  (b) $10
  (c) $20
  (d) $30

14. A market for tickets in which buyers bid for tickets held by initial purchasers rather than the original seller is a
  (a) primary market
  (b) secondary market
  (c) pre-set market
  (d) surplus market

15. What are resources called that are owned in common by society and available for the taking on public land?
  (a) consumer surplus
  (b) producer surplus
  (c) nonpriced goods
  (d) priced goods

16. A supply and demand graph of the "market" for buffalo in the pre-railroad era would show that
  (a) quantity demanded equaled quantity supplied
  (b) quantity demanded was greater than quantity supplied
  (c) demand was less than supply, so there was a zero price
  (d) supply was less than demand, so there was a zero price

17. A supply and demand graph of the "market" for buffalo in the post-railroad era would show that at a zero price
  (a) the supply curve was horizontal
  (b) the demand curve was vertical
  (c) quantity demanded was less than quantity supplied
  (d) quantity demanded was greater than quantity supplied

18. Why does government often ration the use of public resources such as fishing and hunting by using licenses and setting limits on quantities or seasons?
  (a) to increase the supply of these nonpriced goods
  (b) to increase the demand for these nonpriced goods
  (c) to decrease the demand for these nonpriced goods
  (d) to decrease the supply of these nonpriced goods

19. The difference between the maximum price a consumer is (or consumers are) willing to pay for a product and the actual price is consumer
  (a) sovereignty
  (b) demand
  (c) surplus
  (d) utility

20. Katie is willing to pay $50 for a product and Tom is willing to pay $40. The actual price that they have to pay is $30. What is the amount of the consumer surplus for Katie and Tom combined?
  (a) $30
  (b) $40
  (c) $50
  (d) $60

21. Given the demand curve, the consumer surplus is
   (a) increased by higher prices and decreased by lower prices
   (b) decreased by higher prices and increased by lower prices
   (c) increased by higher prices but not affected by lower prices
   (d) decreased by lower prices, but not affected by higher prices

22. The difference between the actual price that a producer receives (or producers receive) and the minimum acceptable price is producer
   (a) cost
   (b) wealth
   (c) surplus
   (d) investment

23. The minimum acceptable price for a product that Juan is willing to receive is $20. It is $15 for Carlos. The actual price they receive is $25. What is the amount of the producer surplus for Juan and Carlos combined?
   (a) $10
   (b) $15
   (c) $20
   (d) $25

24. When the combined consumer and producer surplus is at a maximum for a product,
   (a) the quantity supplied is greater than the quantity demanded
   (b) the market finds alternative ways to ration the product
   (c) the market is allocatively efficient
   (d) the product is a nonpriced good

25. When the output is greater than the optimal level of output for a product there are efficiency
   (a) gains from the underproduction of the product
   (b) losses from the underproduction of the product
   (c) gains from the overproduction of the product
   (d) losses from the overproduction of the product

■ **PROBLEMS**

1. The existing demand and supply schedules are given in columns 1, 2, and 3 of the following table.

Demand and Supply Schedules			New Demand and Supply Schedules		
(1)	**(2)**	**(3)**	**(4)**	**(5)**	**(6)**
	Quantity	**Quantity**		**Quantity**	**Quantity**
Price	**demanded**	**supplied**	**Price**	**demanded**	**supplied**
$5.00	10	50	$5.00	___	___
4.00	20	40	4.00	___	___
3.00	30	30	3.00	___	___
2.00	40	20	2.00	___	___
1.00	50	10	1.00	___	___

   a. Now the demand *increases* by 10 units at each price and supply *decreases* by 10 units. Enter the new amounts for quantity demanded and quantity supplied in columns 5 and 6.

   b. What was the old equilibrium price? _____
   What will be the new equilibrium price? _____

   c. What was the old equilibrium quantity? _____
   What will be the new equilibrium quantity? _____

2. The demand and supply schedules for a certain product are those given in the following table. Answer the related questions.

Quantity demanded	Price	Quantity supplied
12,000	$10	18,000
13,000	9	17,000
14,000	8	16,000
15,000	7	15,000
16,000	6	14,000
17,000	5	13,000
18,000	4	12,000

   a. The equilibrium price of the product is $_____
   and the equilibrium quantity is _____.

   b. If a seller established a pre-set price of $5 on this product, there would be a (shortage, surplus) _____ of _____ units.

   c. If a seller established a pre-set price of $8, there would be a (shortage, surplus) _____ of _____ units.

3. Given the following information, calculate the consumer surplus for each individual A to F.

(1)	(2)	(3)	(4)
	Maximum	**Actual price**	
	price willing	**(equilibrium**	**Consumer**
Person	**to pay**	**price)**	**surplus**
A	$25	$12	$_____
B	23	12	_____
C	18	12	_____
D	16	12	_____
E	13	12	_____
F	12	12	_____

4. Given the following information, calculate the producer surplus for each producer A to F.

(1)	(2)	(3)	(4)
	Maximum	**Actual price**	
	acceptable	**(equilibrium**	**Producer**
Person	**price**	**price)**	**surplus**
A	$4	$12	$_____
B	5	12	_____
C	7	12	_____
D	9	12	_____
E	10	12	_____
F	12	12	_____

5. Answer this question based on the following graph showing the market supply and demand for a product. Assume that the output level is Q_1.

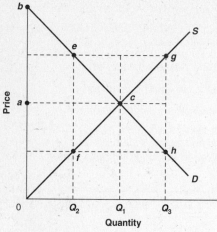

a. The area of consumer surplus would be shown by the area _____.

b. The area of producer surplus would be shown by the area _____.

c. The area that maximizes the combined consumer and producer surplus is _____.

d. If the output level is now Q_2, then there are efficiency losses shown by area _____.

e. If the output level is now Q_3, then there are efficiency losses shown by area _____.

■ **SHORT ANSWER AND ESSAY QUESTIONS**

1. Explain, using a supply and demand graph, how a freeze in a vegetable crop will affect the equilibrium price and quantity.

2. In a competitive market, if the supply of a product decreases and demand remains the same, what happens to the quantity demanded?

3. When there are single shifts in the supply or demand curve, you can predict the effects on both equilibrium price and quantity. When there are simultaneous shifts in demand and supply you can make only one prediction of the effects with any certainty. Why?

4. You observe that the equilibrium price has decreased and the equilibrium quantity has increased. What supply and demand conditions would best explain this outcome?

5. If the increase in the demand for gasoline outweighs the decrease in the supply of gasoline, what is the most likely effect on the equilibrium price and quantity? Explain and show your answer with a graph.

6. You observe that the equilibrium quantity has increased but the equilibrium price has stayed the same. What supply and demand conditions would best explain this outcome?

7. What are price ceilings and price floors?

8. What are the consequences if a seller sets a price below the actual equilibrium price?

9. Why do secondary markets arise? Give examples of such markets.

10. Explain, using a supply and demand graph, the situation that arises when there are many unsold tickets to an event. Why does this occur?

11. What are the differences in the characteristics of nonpriced and market goods? Give examples of each type.

12. Discuss the plight of the American bison since the 1800s using supply and demand analysis. How did the conditions for the buffalo change from the pre-railroad era to the post-railroad era?

13. What rationing mechanisms are typically used by society to limit consumption of nonpriced goods?

14. Explain using an example how a nonpriced good could be converted to a positively priced good in a private market.

15. How is the consumer surplus related to utility or satisfaction? Explain, using a supply and demand graph.

16. What is the nature of the relationship between prices and consumer surplus?

17. Define, using a supply and demand graph, the meaning of producer surplus.

18. Compare and contrast the relationship between price and consumer surplus and price and producer surplus.

19. Explain the three conditions that exist when there is allocative efficiency.

20. Use consumer and producer surplus to describe efficiency losses in a competitive market. Provide a supply and demand graph to show such losses.

ANSWERS

Chapter 3 Web: Applications and Extensions of Supply and Demand Analysis

FILL-IN QUESTIONS

1. increases, decreases
2. increases, increases
3. decreases, increases
4. increases, increases
5. stays the same, increases
6. ceiling, floor
7. shortage, surplus
8. secondary, scalping
9. owned in common, public
10. surplus, shortage
11. over-, a decrease
12. licenses, limits
13. maximum, less
14. negatively, decrease, increase
15. minimum, more
16. positively, increase, decrease
17. productive, allocative

18. benefit, cost
19. equal to, equal to, maximum
20. losses, losses, less than
Note: Page numbers refer to Chapter 3 Web of the textbook that is available at www.mcconnell16.com.

TRUE–FALSE QUESTIONS

1. T, pp. 2–3	**8.** F, p. 5	**15.** F, p. 7	**22.** F, p. 10
2. F, p. 3	**9.** T, p. 5	**16.** T, p. 8	**23.** F, p. 10
3. T, p. 3	**10.** F, p. 5	**17.** F, p. 8	**24.** T, p. 10
4. T, pp. 3–4	**11.** T, pp. 5–6	**18.** T, pp. 8–9	**25.** F, pp. 10–11
5. F, p. 4	**12.** T, p. 7	**19.** F, p. 9	
6. F, pp. 4–5	**13.** F, pp. 7–8	**20.** F, p. 9	
7. T, p. 5	**14.** T, p. 7	**21.** T, p. 9	

MULTIPLE-CHOICE QUESTIONS

1. b, p. 2	**8.** b, p. 5	**15.** c, p. 7	**22.** c, pp. 9–10
2. b, pp. 2–3	**9.** a, p. 5	**16.** c, p. 7	**23.** b, p. 10
3. d, p. 3	**10.** c, p. 5	**17.** d, pp. 7–8	**24.** c, p. 11
4. d, pp. 3–4	**11.** c, p. 5	**18.** c, p. 8	**25.** d, pp. 11–12
5. b, p. 4	**12.** a, pp. 5–6	**19.** c, pp. 8–9	
6. c, pp. 4–5	**13.** c, pp. 5–6	**20.** a, p. 9	
7. d, pp. 4–5	**14.** b, p. 5	**21.** b, p. 9	

PROBLEMS

1. *a.* column 5 (quantity demanded): 20, 30, 40, 50, 60; column 6 (quantity supplied): 40, 30, 20, 10, 0; *b.* $3.00, $4.00; *c.* 30, 30
2. *a.* $7, 15,000; *b.* shortage, 4000; *c.* surplus, 2000
3. 13, 11, 6, 4, 1, 0
4. 8, 7, 5, 3, 2, 0
5. *a.* abc; *b.* 0ac; *c.* 0bc; *d.* efc; *e.* ghc

SHORT ANSWER AND ESSAY QUESTIONS

1. p. 2	**6.** pp. 4–5	**11.** p. 7	**16.** p. 9
2. p. 2	**7.** p. 5	**12.** pp. 7–8	**17.** p. 9
3. pp. 3–5	**8.** p. 5	**13.** p. 8	**18.** pp. 9–10
4. pp. 3–4	**9.** p. 5	**14.** p. 8	**19.** pp. 10–11
5. p. 4	**10.** p. 6	**15.** pp. 8–9	**20.** pp. 11–12

CHAPTER 4

The Market System

Chapter 4 describes the major characteristics of the market system and offers a detailed explanation of how it works. The first part describes the *ideological* and *institutional* characteristics of the market system. In this system, most of the resources are owned as private property by citizens, who are free to use them as they wish in their own self-interest. Prices and markets express the self-interests of resource owners, consumers, and business firms. Competition regulates self-interest—to prevent the self-interest of any person or any group from working to the disadvantage of the economy and to make self-interests work for the benefit of the entire economy. Government plays an active, but limited, role in a market economy.

Three other characteristics are also found in a market economy. They are the employment of large amounts of *capital goods,* the development of *specialization,* and the *use of money.* Economies use capital goods and engage in specialization because this is a more efficient use of their resources; it results in larger total output and the greater satisfaction of wants. When workers, business firms, and regions within an economy specialize, they become dependent on each other for the goods and services they do not produce for themselves and they must engage in trade. Trade is made more convenient by using money as a medium of exchange.

The second part of Chapter 4 describes the operation of the market system. There are *Four Fundamental Questions* that any economic system must answer in its attempt to use its scarce resources to satisfy its material wants. The four questions or problems are: (1) What will be produced? (2) How will the output be produced? (3) Who is to receive the output? (4) Can the system adapt to change?

The explanation of how the market system finds answers to the Four Fundamental Questions is only an approximation—a simplified version or model—of the methods actually employed by the U.S. economy and other market economies. Yet this simple model, like all good models, contains enough realism to be truthful and is general enough to be understandable. If the aims of this chapter are accomplished, you can begin to understand the market system and methods our economy uses to solve the economizing problem presented in Chapter 2.

■ CHECKLIST

When you have studied this chapter you should be able to

☐ Identify the nine important characteristics of the market system.

☐ Describe the significance of property rights in the market system.

☐ Distinguish between freedom of enterprise and freedom of choice.

☐ Explain why self-interest is a driving force of the market system.

☐ Identify two features of competition.

☐ Explain the roles of markets and prices.

☐ Explain why the market system relies on technology and capital goods, and also why the production of capital goods entails roundabout production.

☐ Discuss how two types of specialization improve efficiency in the market system.

☐ Describe the advantages of money over barter for the exchange of goods and services in a market economy.

☐ Describe the size and role of government in the market system.

☐ List the Four Fundamental Questions to answer about the operation of a market economy.

☐ Explain how a market system determines what goods and services will be produced.

☐ Distinguish between normal profit and economic profit.

☐ Predict what will happen to the price charged by and the output of an expanding and a declining industry, and explain why these events will occur.

☐ Explain how consumer sovereignty and dollar votes work in a market economy.

☐ Describe market restraints on economic freedom.

☐ Explain how goods and services will be produced in a market system.

☐ Find the least costly combination of resources needed for production when given the technological data and the prices of the resources.

☐ Explain how a market system determines who will get the goods and services it produces.

☐ Describe the guiding function of prices to accommodate change in the market system.

☐ Explain how the market system initiates change by fostering technological advances and capital accumulation.
☐ State how the "invisible hand" in the market system tends to promote public or social interests.
☐ List three virtues of the market system.

■ **CHAPTER OUTLINE**

1. The market system has the following nine characteristics:

a. Private individuals and organizations own and control their property resources by means of the institution of private property.

b. These individuals and organizations possess both the freedom of enterprise and the freedom of choice.

c. Each of them is motivated largely by self-interest.

d. Competition is based on the independent actions of buyers and sellers. They have the freedom to enter or leave markets. This competition spreads economic power and limits its potential abuse.

e. Markets and prices are used to communicate and coordinate the decisions of buyers and sellers.

f. The market system employs complicated and advanced methods of production, new technology, and large amounts of capital equipment to produce goods and services efficiently.

g. It is a highly specialized economy. Human and geographic specializations increase the productive efficiency of the economy.

h. It uses money exclusively to facilitate trade and specialization.

i. Government has an active but limited role.

2. The system of prices and markets and households' and business firms' choices furnish the market economy with answers to **Four Fundamental Questions.**

a. *What goods and services will be produced?* The demands of consumers for products and the desires of business firms to maximize their profits determine what and how much of each product is produced and its price.

b. *How will the goods and services be produced?* The desires of business firms to maximize profits by keeping their costs of production as low as possible guide them to use the most efficient techniques of production and determine their demands for various resources; competition forces them to use the most efficient techniques and ensures that only the most efficient will be able to stay in business.

c. *Who will get the goods and services that are produced?* With resource prices determined, the money income of each household is determined; and with product prices determined, the quantity of goods and services these money incomes will buy is determined.

d. *How will the market system accommodate change?* The market system is able to accommodate itself to changes in consumer tastes, technology, and resource supplies.

(1) The desires of business firms for maximum profits and competition lead the economy to make the appropriate adjustments in the way it uses its resources.

(2) Competition and the desire to increase profits promote better techniques of production and capital accumulation.

3. Competition in the economy compels firms seeking to promote their own interests to promote (as though led by an "invisible hand") the best interests of society as a whole.

a. Competition results in an allocation of resources appropriate to consumer wants, production by the most efficient means, and the lowest possible prices.

b. Three noteworthy merits of the market system are
(1) The *efficient* use of resources
(2) The *incentive* the system provides for productive activity
(3) The personal *freedom* allowed participants as consumers, producers, workers, or investors.

■ **HINTS AND TIPS**

1. The first section of the chapter describes nine characteristics and institutions of a market system. After reading the section, check your understanding by listing the nine points and writing a short explanation of each one.

2. The section on the "Market System at Work" is both the most important and the most difficult part of the chapter. A market economy must answer *Four Fundamental Questions*. Detailed answers to the four questions are given in this section of the chapter. If you examine each one individually and in the order in which it is presented, you will more easily understand how the market system works. (Actually, the market system finds the answers simultaneously, but make your learning easier for now by considering them one by one.)

3. Be sure to understand the *importance* and *role* of each of the following in the operation of the market system: (1) the guiding function of prices, (2) the profit motive of business firms, (3) the entry into and exodus of firms from industries, (4) the meaning of competition, and (5) consumer sovereignty.

■ **IMPORTANT TERMS**

private property	**economic cost**
freedom of choice	**normal profit**
freedom of enterprise	**economic profit**
self-interest	**expanding industry**
competition	**declining industry**
roundabout production	**consumer sovereignty**
specialization	**dollar votes**
division of labor	**derived demand**
medium of exchange	**guiding function of prices**
barter	**creative destruction**
money	**"invisible hand"**
Four Fundamental Questions	

_____

SELF-TEST

■ **FILL-IN QUESTIONS**

1. The ownership of property resources by private individuals and organizations is the institution of private (resources, property) _____. The freedom of private businesses to obtain resources and use them to produce goods and services is the freedom of (choice, enterprise) _____, while the freedom to dispose of property or money as a person sees fit is the freedom of _____.

2. Self-interest means that each economic unit attempts to do what is best for itself, but this might lead to an abuse of power in a market economy if it were not directed and constrained by (government, competition) _____. Self-interest and selfishness (are, are not) _____ the same thing in a market economy.

3. Broadly defined, competition is present if two conditions prevail; these two conditions are

    a. _____
    _____

    b. _____
    _____

4. In a capitalist economy, individual buyers communicate their demands and individual sellers communicate their supplies in the system of (markets, prices) _____, and the outcomes from economic decisions are a set of product and resource _____ that are determined by demand and supply.

5. Market economies make extensive use of capital goods and engage in roundabout production because it is more (efficient, inefficient) _____ than direct production; they practice specialization and the division of labor because the self-sufficient producer or worker tends to be an _____ one.

6. In market economies money functions chiefly as a medium of (commerce, exchange) _____. Barter between two individuals will take place only if there is a coincidence of (resources, wants) _____.

7. In a market system, government is active, but is assigned (a limited, an extensive) _____ role.

8. List the Four Fundamental Questions every economy must answer.

    a. _____
    b. _____

    c. _____
    d. _____

9. A *normal profit* (is, is not) _____ an economic cost because it is a payment that (must, need not) _____ be paid to (workers, entrepreneurs) _____, but an *economic profit* (is, is not) _____ an economic cost because it (must, need not) _____ be paid to them to secure and retain the resources needed by the firm.

10. Pure or economic profit is equal to the total (revenue, cost) _____ of a firm less its total _____.

11. Business firms tend to produce those products from which they can obtain at least a(n) (economic, normal) _____ profit and a maximum _____ profit.

12. If firms in an industry are obtaining economic profits, firms will (enter, leave) _____ the industry; the price of the industry's product will (rise, fall) _____; the industry will employ (more, fewer) _____ resources and produce a (larger, smaller) _____ output; and the industry's economic profits will (increase, decrease) _____ until they are equal to (zero, infinity) _____.

13. Consumers vote with their dollars for the production of a good or service when they (sell, buy) _____ it, and because of this, consumers are said to be (dependent, sovereign) _____ in a market economy. The buying decisions of consumers (restrain, expand) _____ the freedom of firms and resource suppliers.

14. Firms are interested in obtaining the largest economic profits possible, so they try to produce a product in the (most, least) _____ costly way. The most efficient production techniques depend on the available (income, technology) _____ and the (prices, quotas) _____ of needed resources.

15. The market system determines how the total output of the economy will be distributed among its households by determining the (incomes, expenditures) _____ of each household and by determining the (prices, quality) _____ for each good and service produced.

16. In market economies, change is almost continuous in consumer (preferences, resources)

_____, in the supplies of _____, and in technology. To make the appropriate adjustments to these changes, a market economy allows price to perform its (monopoly, guiding) _____ function.

17. The market system fosters technological change. The incentive for a firm to be the first to use a new and improved technique of production or to produce a new and better product is a greater economic (profit, loss) _____, and the incentive for other firms to follow its lead is the avoidance of _____.

18. Technological advance will require additional (capital, consumer) _____ goods, so the entrepreneur uses profit obtained from the sale of _____ goods to acquire (capital, consumer) _____ goods.

19. A market system promotes (unity, disunity) _____ between private and public interests. Firms and resource suppliers seem to be guided by (a visible, an invisible) _____ hand to allocate the economy's resources efficiently.

20. The two *economic* arguments for a market system are that it promotes (public, efficient) _____ use of resources and that it uses (incentives, government) _____ for directing economic activity. The major *noneconomic* argument for the market system is that it allows for personal (wealth, freedom) _____.

■ **TRUE–FALSE QUESTIONS**

Circle T if the statement is true, F if it is false.

1. In a market system, the government owns most of the property resources (land and capital).   **T F**

2. Property rights encourage investment, innovation, exchange, maintenance of property, and economic growth.   **T F**

3. The freedom of business firms to produce a particular consumer good is always limited by the desires of consumers for that good.   **T F**

4. The pursuit of economic self-interest is the same thing as selfishness.   **T F**

5. When a market is competitive, the individual sellers of a product are unable to reduce the supply of the product and control its price.   **T F**

6. The market system is an organizing mechanism and also a communication network.   **T F**

7. The employment of capital to produce goods and services requires that there be "roundabout" production and it is more efficient than "direct" production.   **T F**

8. Increasing the amount of specialization in an economy generally leads to the more efficient use of its resources.   **T F**

9. One way human specialization can be achieved is through a division of labor in productive activity.   **T F**

10. Money is a device for facilitating the exchange of goods and services.   **T F**

11. "Coincidence of wants" means that two persons want to acquire the same good or service.   **T F**

12. Shells may serve as money if sellers are generally willing to accept them as money.   **T F**

13. One of the Four Fundamental Questions is who will control the output.   **T F**

14. Business firms try to maximize their normal profits.   **T F**

15. Industries in which economic profits are earned by the firms in the industry will attract the entry of new firms.   **T F**

16. If firms have sufficient time to enter industries, the economic profits of an industry will tend to disappear.   **T F**

17. Business firms are only free to produce whatever they want in any way they wish if they do not want to maximize profits or to minimize losses.   **T F**

18. The derived demand of a resource depends on the demands for the products the resource produces.   **T F**

19. Resources will tend to be used in those industries capable of earning normal or economic profits.   **T F**

20. Economic efficiency requires that a given output of a good or service be produced in the least costly way.   **T F**

21. If the market price of resource A decreases, firms will tend to employ smaller quantities of resource A.   **T F**

22. Changes in the tastes of consumers are reflected in changes in consumer demand for products.   **T F**

23. The incentive that the market system provides to induce technological improvement is the opportunity for economic profits.   **T F**

24. The tendency for individuals pursuing their own self-interests to bring about results that are in the best interest of society as a whole is often called the "invisible hand."   **T F**

25. A basic economic argument for the market system is that it promotes an efficient use of resources.   **T F**

■ **MULTIPLE-CHOICE QUESTIONS**

Circle the letter that corresponds to the best answer.

1. Which is one of the main characteristics of the market system?
  (a) central economic planning

(b) limits on freedom of choice

(c) the right to own private property

(d) an expanded role for government in the economy

2. In the market system, freedom of enterprise means that

(a) businesses are free to produce products that consumers want

(b) consumers are free to buy goods and services that they want

(c) resources are distributed freely to businesses that want them

(d) government is free to direct the actions of businesses

3. The maximization of profit tends to be the driving force in the economic decision making of

(a) entrepreneurs

(b) workers

(c) consumers

(d) legislators

4. How do consumers typically express self-interest?

(a) by minimizing their economic losses

(b) by maximizing their economic profits

(c) by seeking the lowest price for a product

(d) by seeking jobs with the highest wages and benefits

5. Which is a characteristic of competition as economists see it?

(a) a few sellers of all products

(b) the widespread diffusion of economic power

(c) a small number of buyers in product markets

(d) the relatively difficult entry into and exit from industries by producers

6. To decide how to use its scarce resources to satisfy economic wants, capitalism relies on

(a) central planning

(b) monopoly power

(c) markets and prices

(d) command and control

7. The market system is a method of

(a) communicating and coordinating the decisions of consumers, producers, and resource suppliers

(b) making economic decisions by central planning

(c) promoting productive efficiency, but not allocative efficiency

(d) promoting allocative efficiency, but not productive efficiency

8. What is roundabout production?

(a) the division of labor that results from specialization in the production of a good or service

(b) the production and use of capital goods to help make consumer goods

(c) the production of a good and service and the payment for it with money

(d) the production of a consumer good and its sale to consumers

9. When workers specialize in various tasks to produce a commodity, the situation is referred to as

(a) a coincidence of wants

(b) roundabout production

(c) freedom of choice

(d) division of labor

10. In what way does human specialization contribute to an economy's output?

(a) It serves as consumer sovereignty.

(b) It is a process of creative destruction.

(c) It acts like an "invisible hand."

(d) It fosters learning by doing.

11. Which is a prerequisite of specialization?

(a) having a convenient means of exchanging goods

(b) letting government create a plan for the economy

(c) deciding who will get the goods and services in an economy

(d) market restraints on freedom

12. In the market system, the role of government is best described as

(a) nonexistent

(b) significant

(c) extensive

(d) limited

13. Which best defines economic costs?

(a) the difference between economic profit and normal profit

(b) total payments made to secure and retain needed resources

(c) the demand for resources minus the supply of resources

(d) the total revenue plus the total losses of the firm

14. If a business's total economic cost of producing 10,000 units of a product is $750,000 and this output is sold to consumers for $1,000,000, then the firm would earn

(a) a normal profit of $750,000

(b) an economic profit of $750,000

(c) an economic profit of $250,000

(d) a normal profit of $1,750,000

15. If less-than-normal profits are being earned by the firms in an industry, the consequences will be that

(a) lower-priced resources will be drawn into the industry

(b) firms will leave the industry, causing the price of the industry's product to fall

(c) firms will leave the industry, causing the price of the industry's product to rise

(d) the price of the industry's product will fall and thereby cause the demand for the product to increase

16. Which would necessarily result, sooner or later, from a decrease in consumer demand for a product?

(a) a decrease in the profits of firms in the industry

(b) an increase in the output of the industry

(c) an increase in the supply of the product

(d) an increase in the prices of resources employed by the firms in the industry

17. The demand for resources is
(a) increased when the price of resources falls
(b) most influenced by the size of government in a capitalist economy
(c) derived from the demand for the products made with the resources
(d) decreased when the product that the resources produce becomes popular

Answer Questions 18, 19, and 20 on the basis of the following information.

Suppose 50 units of product X can be produced by employing just labor and capital in the four ways shown below. Assume the prices of labor and capital are $5 and $4, respectively.

	A	B	C	D
Labor	1	2	3	4
Capital	5	3	2	1

18. Which technique is economically most efficient in producing product X?
(a) A
(b) B
(c) C
(d) D

19. If the price of product X is $1, the firm will realize
(a) an economic profit of $28
(b) an economic profit of $27
(c) an economic profit of $26
(d) an economic profit of $25

20. Now assume that the price of labor falls to $3 and the price of capital rises to $5. Which technique is economically most efficient in producing product X?
(a) A
(b) B
(c) C
(d) D

21. Which is the primary factor determining the share of the total output of the economy received by a household?
(a) the tastes of the household
(b) the medium of exchange used by the household
(c) the prices at which the household sells its resources
(d) ethical considerations in the operation of a market economy

22. If an increase in the demand for a product and a rise in its price cause an increase in the quantity supplied, the size of the industry, and the resources used for production, price is successfully performing its
(a) guiding function
(b) roundabout function
(c) division-of-labor function
(d) medium-of-exchange function

23. The advent of personal computers and word processing software that eliminated the market for electric typewriters would be an example of

(a) creative destruction
(b) the "invisible hand"
(c) derived demand
(d) specialization

24. In the market system, if one firm introduces a new and better method of production that enhances the firm's economic profits, other firms will be forced to adopt the new method to
(a) increase derived demand
(b) follow rules for roundabout production
(c) avoid economic losses or bankruptcy
(d) specialize and divide the labor in an efficient way

25. The chief economic virtue of the competitive market system is that it
(a) allows extensive personal freedom
(b) efficiently allocates resources
(c) provides an equitable distribution of income
(d) eliminates the need for decision making

■ PROBLEMS

1. Use the appropriate number to match the term with the phrase.

1. invisible hand	**5. consumer sovereignty**
2. coincidence of wants	**6. derived demand**
3. division of labor	**7. specialization**
4. guiding function of prices	**8. roundabout production**

a. The construction and use of capital goods to aid in the production of consumer goods. _____

b. The ability of price changes to bring about changes in the quantities of products and resources demanded and supplied. _____

c. Using the resources of an individual, a firm, a region, or a nation to produce one (or a few) goods and services. _____

d. The tendency of firms and resource suppliers seeking to further their own self-interest while also promoting the interests of society in a market economy. _____

e. The demand for a resource that depends on the demand for the product it can be used to produce. _____

f. Splitting the work required to produce a product into a number of different tasks that are performed by different workers. _____

g. A situation in which the product the first trader wants to sell is the same as that the second trader wants to buy, and the product the second trader wants to sell is the same as the product the first trader wants to buy. _____

h. Determination by consumers of the types and quantities of goods and services that will be produced in a market economy. _____

2. Assume that a firm can produce product A, product B, *or* product C with the resources it currently employs.

These resources cost the firm a total of $50 per week. Assume, for the purposes of the problem, that the firm's employment of resources cannot be changed. Their market prices, and the quantities of A, B, and C these resources will produce per week are given below. Compute the firm's profit when it produces A, B, or C, and enter these profits in the table below.

Product	Market price	Output	Economic profit
A	$7.00	8	$_____
B	4.50	10	_____
C	.25	240	_____

a. Which product will the firm produce? _____

b. If the price of A rose to $8, the firm would _____

_____

(Hint: You will have to recompute the firm's profit from the production of A.)
c. If the firm were producing A and selling it at a price of $8, what would tend to happen to the number of

firms producing A? _____

_____

3. Suppose that a firm can produce 100 units of product X by combining labor, land, capital, and entrepreneurial ability in three different ways. If it can hire labor at $2 per unit, land at $3 per unit, capital at $5 per unit, and entrepreneurship at $10 per unit, and if the amounts of the resources required by the three methods of producing 100 units of product X are indicated in the table, answer the following questions.

Resource	Method 1	2	3
Labor	8	13	10
Land	4	3	3
Capital	4	2	4
Entrepreneurship	1	1	1

a. Which method is the least expensive way of producing 100 units of X? _____
b. If X sells for 70 cents per unit, what is the economic

profit of the firm? $_____
c. If the price of labor should rise from $2 to $3 per unit and if the price of X is 70 cents,
(1) the firm's use of

labor would change from _____ to _____

land would change from _____ to _____

capital would change from _____ to _____
entrepreneurship would not change
(2) the firm's economic profit would change from

$_____ to $_____

■ SHORT ANSWER AND ESSAY QUESTIONS

1. Explain the major characteristics — institutions and assumptions — embodied in a market system.

2. What do each of the following seek if they pursue their own self-interest: consumers, resource owners, and business firms?

3. Explain what economists mean by competition. For a market to be competitive, why is it important that there be buyers and sellers and easy entry and exit?

4. What are the advantages of indirect or roundabout production?

5. How does an economy benefit from specialization and the division of labor?

6. Give an example of how specialization can benefit two separate and diversely endowed geographic regions.

7. What is money? What important function does it perform? Explain how money performs this function and how it overcomes the disadvantages associated with barter.

8. For an item to be useful as money, what is its necessary major characteristic? Can you think of other characteristics that might be favorable?

9. What are the Four Fundamental Questions?

10. In what way do the desires of entrepreneurs to obtain economic profits and avoid losses make consumer sovereignty effective?

11. Why is the ability of firms to enter industries that are prosperous important to the effective functioning of competition?

12. Explain in detail how an increase in the consumer demand for a product will result in more of the product being produced and more resources being allocated to its production.

13. To what extent are firms "free" to produce what they wish by methods that they choose? Do resource owners have freedom to use their resources as they wish?

14. How can the market system adapt to change? How is it done?

15. What is the guiding function of price? Explain how it works.

16. Explain how the market system provides a strong incentive for technological advance.

17. What is "creative destruction"? Give some examples of it.

18. Who "votes" for the production of capital goods, why do they "vote" for capital goods production, and where do they obtain the dollars needed to cast these "votes"?

19. An "invisible hand operates to identify private and public interests." What are private interests and what is the public interest? What is it that leads the economy to operate as if it were directed by an invisible hand?

20. Describe three virtues of the market system.

ANSWERS

Chapter 4 The Market System

FILL-IN QUESTIONS

1. property, enterprise, choice
2. competition, are not
3. *a.* independently acting buyers and sellers operating in markets; *b.* freedom of buyers and sellers to enter or leave these markets
4. markets, prices
5. efficient, inefficient
6. exchange, wants
7. a limited
8. *a.* What goods and services will be produced? *b.* How will the goods and services be produced? *c.* Who will get the goods and services? *d.* How will the system accommodate change?
9. is, must, entrepreneurs, is not, need not
10. revenue, cost
11. normal, economic
12. enter, fall, more, larger, decrease, zero
13. buy, sovereign, restrain
14. least, technology, prices
15. incomes, prices
16. preferences, resources, guiding
17. profit, losses
18. capital, consumer, capital
19. unity, an invisible
20. efficient, incentives, freedom

TRUE–FALSE QUESTIONS

1. F, p. 60	**8.** T, p. 63	**15.** T, pp. 65–66	**22.** T, pp. 67–68
2. T, p. 60	**9.** T, p. 63	**16.** T, pp. 65–66	**23.** T, pp. 68–69
3. T, p. 61	**10.** T, pp. 63–64	**17.** T, pp. 66–67	**24.** T, p. 69
4. F, p. 61	**11.** F, p. 63	**18.** T, pp. 66–67	**25.** T, p. 69
5. T, p. 62	**12.** T, pp. 63–64	**19.** T, pp. 66–67	
6. T, p. 62	**13.** F, p. 65	**20.** T, p. 67	
7. T, pp. 62–63	**14.** F, p. 65	**21.** F, pp. 67–68	

MULTIPLE-CHOICE QUESTIONS

1. c, p. 60	**8.** b, p. 63	**15.** c, p. 66	**22.** a, p. 68
2. a, p. 61	**9.** d, p. 63	**16.** a, p. 66	**23.** a, pp. 68–69
3. a, p. 61	**10.** d, p. 63	**17.** c, pp. 66–67	**24.** c, pp. 68–69
4. c, p. 61	**11.** a, p. 63	**18.** b, p. 67	**25.** b, p. 69
5. b, p. 62	**12.** d, p. 64	**19.** a, pp. 65; 67	
6. c, p. 62	**13.** b, p. 65	**20.** d, p. 67	
7. a, p. 62	**14.** c, p. 65	**21.** c, pp. 67–68	

PROBLEMS

1. *a.* 8; *b.* 4; *c.* 7; *d.* 1; *e.* 6; *f.* 3; *g.* 2; *h.* 5
2. $6, −$5, $10; *a.* C; *b.* produce A and have an economic profit of $14; *c.* it would increase
3. *a.* method 2; *b.* 15; *c.* (1) 13, 8; 3, 4; 2, 4; (2) 15, 4

SHORT ANSWER AND ESSAY QUESTIONS

1. pp. 60–64	**6.** p. 63	**11.** pp. 65–66	**16.** pp. 68–69
2. p. 61	**7.** pp. 63–64	**12.** p. 66	**17.** pp. 68–69
3. p. 62	**8.** pp. 63–64	**13.** pp. 66–67	**18.** p. 69
4. pp. 62–63	**9.** p. 65	**14.** pp. 68–69	**19.** p. 69
5. p. 63	**10.** pp. 65–66	**15.** p. 68	**20.** p. 69

CHAPTER 5

The U.S. Economy: Private and Public Sectors

The U.S. economy is divided into a private sector and a public sector. The first half of Chapter 5 discusses the private sector—the characteristics of millions of households and business firms. The second half of Chapter 5 describes the public sector—the functions and financing of the Federal, state, and local governments. Learning about these two sectors will give you the basic facts and framework you need for understanding the U.S. economy.

Chapter 5 begins with an examination of the **households** of the economy. Two different distributions of household income are examined. The way in which the total personal income received by all U.S. households is divided among the five types of earned income is called the *functional distribution of income*. The way in which the total personal income received by all households is distributed among the various income classes is called the *personal distribution of income*. Households dispose of the income they receive by spending money on *personal consumption expenditures,* paying *personal taxes,* or allocating funds to *personal saving*.

Businesses in the United States are also a focus of the chapter. It is apparent that what most characterizes U.S. businesses is the differences among firms in size and legal form, as well as in the products they produce. You should note the distinctions between a *proprietorship,* a *partnership,* and a *corporation* and the major advantages and disadvantages of each business form. You will also learn about the principal–agent problem with corporations that can arise from the separation of ownership (the principals) and management (the agents).

Chapter 5 also introduces you to the five basic functions performed by the **government** in the U.S. economy. The chapter does not attempt to list all the specific ways in which government affects the behavior of the economy: Instead, it provides a general classification of the five functions that government performs.

The chapter also returns to the **circular flow model** first presented in Chapter 2. The model has now been modified to include government along with business and household sectors. This addition changes the real and monetary flows in the model.

The facts of **government finance** in the United States are presented in the final sections of Chapter 5. The organization of the discussion is relatively simple. First, the trends for taxes collected and expenditures made by all levels of government—Federal, state, and local—are examined. Second, an explanation is given for the major items on which the Federal government spends its income, the principal taxes it levies to obtain its income,

and the relative importance of these taxes. Third, the chapter closes with a look at the major expenditures and taxes of the state and local governments.

■ **CHECKLIST**

When you have studied this chapter you should be able to

☐ Define and distinguish between a functional and a personal distribution of income.
☐ State the five sources of personal income in the functional distribution.
☐ List the three uses to which households put their personal incomes and state the relative size of each.
☐ Distinguish among durable goods, nondurable goods, and services in personal consumption expenditures.
☐ Give definitions for a plant, a firm, and an industry.
☐ List the three legal forms of business enterprise.
☐ Report the relative importance of each of the legal forms of business enterprise in the U.S. economy.
☐ State the advantages and disadvantages of the three legal forms of business enterprise.
☐ Identify two hybrid structures for corporations.
☐ Explain the principal–agent problem as it applies to corporations.
☐ List the five economic functions of government in the United States.
☐ Give examples of how government provides the legal framework for the economy.
☐ Define monopoly and explain why government wishes to prevent monopoly and to maintain competition in the economy.
☐ Explain why government redistributes income and list the three principal policies it uses for this purpose.
☐ Define spillover cost and spillover benefit.
☐ Explain why a competitive market fails to allocate resources efficiently when there are spillover costs and benefits.
☐ List two actions government can take to reduce spillover costs.
☐ List three actions government can take to encourage spillover benefits.
☐ Give definitions of a public good and a quasi-public good.
☐ Explain how the government reallocates resources from the production of private goods to the production of public or quasi-public goods.
☐ Describe the stabilization role of government and the two main economic problems it is designed to address.

☐ Explain the qualifications to government's role in the economy.

☐ Draw the circular flow model that includes businesses, households, and government, labeling all the flows and illustrating the role of government.

☐ Explain the difference between government purchases and transfer payments and the effect of each on the composition of national output.

☐ Identify the four largest categories of Federal expenditures.

☐ List the three main sources of Federal tax revenues.

☐ Define and explain the differences between marginal and average tax rates.

☐ Identify the major expenditures by state and local governments.

☐ Describe how state and local governments raise tax revenue.

■ **CHAPTER OUTLINE**

1. *Households* play a dual role in the economy. They supply the economy with resources, and they purchase the greatest share of the goods and services produced by the economy. They obtain their personal incomes in exchange for the resources they furnish the economy and from the transfer payments they receive from government.

   a. The *functional distribution* of income indicates the way in which total personal income is divided among the five sources of earned income (wages and salaries, proprietors' income, corporate profits, interest, and rents).

   b. The *personal distribution* of income indicates the way in which total personal income is divided among households in different income classes.

2. Households use their incomes to purchase consumer goods, pay taxes, and accumulate savings.

   a. *Personal taxes* constitute a deduction from a household's personal income; what remains after taxes can be either saved or spent.

   b. *Saving* is what a household does not spend of its after-tax income.

   c. Households make *personal consumption expenditures* for durable goods, nondurable goods, and services.

3. The *businesses* of the U.S. economy consist of three major types of entities. A *plant* is a physical structure that produces a product. A *business firm* is an organization that owns and operates plants. (Multiplant firms may be horizontally or vertically integrated, or they may be conglomerates.) An *industry* is a group of firms producing the same or similar goods or services.

4. The three principal *legal forms* of business firms are the *proprietorship, partnership,* and *corporation.*

   a. Each has special characteristics and advantages and disadvantages.

   (1) The *proprietorship* is easy to form, lets the owner be boss, and allows for great freedom. Disadvantages are lack of access to large amounts of financial capital, difficulty of managerial specialization, and the owner's *unlimited liability.*

   (2) The *partnership* is also easy to form and allows for more access to financial capital and permits more managerial specialization. Potential disadvantages are that partners may disagree, there are still limits to financial capital or managerial specialization, continuity of the firm over time is a problem, and partners face unlimited liability.

   (3) The *corporation* can raise financial capital through the sale of stocks and bonds, has *limited liability* for owners, can become large in size, and has an independent life. Chief disadvantages of the corporation are the double taxation of some corporate income, potential for abuse of this legal entity, and legal or regulatory expenses.

   (4) There are also "hybrid" business structures such as the *limited liability company* (LLC) or the *S corporation* that give the advantage of corporations to one or relatively few owners.

   b. Large corporations are a major feature of the U.S. economy. They are also subject to a *principal–agent problem* that arises from the separation of ownership (by stockholders) and control (by corporate executives). This problem can sometimes be overcome by aligning the interests of executives with those of stockholders through stock payment plans.

5. *Government* performs five economic functions.

   a. The first of these functions is to provide the *legal framework and services* that contribute to the effective operation of the market economy.

   b. The second function of government is to *maintain competition* and the control of *monopoly* through regulation and antitrust laws.

   c. Government performs its third function when it *redistributes income* to reduce income inequality. The policies and programs it uses to achieve this objective are transfer payments, market interventions (changing market prices), and taxation.

   d. When government *reallocates resources* it performs its fourth function.

   (1) It reallocates resources to take into account spillovers or externalities.

      (a) Spillover costs are production or consumption costs paid for by a third party without compensation.

      (b) Spillover costs can be discouraged by legislation or specific taxes.

      (c) Spillover benefits are outcomes that benefit third parties without these parties paying for the benefits.

      (d) Spillover benefits can be encouraged by subsidizing consumers, subsidizing producers, or by having government provide the goods (when the benefits are extremely large).

   (2) Government also provides public goods. These goods have the characteristic of *nonrivalry* (benefits are not reduced by consumption) and *nonexcludability* (people cannot be excluded from the benefits).

   (3) Quasi-public goods (e.g., education) are divisible and subject to the exclusion principle, but they often have large spillover benefits, so they are provided by government.

(4) Government levies taxes and uses tax revenues to reallocate income and resources from private uses to public ones (for providing public and quasi-public goods).

e. The fifth function of government is **stabilization** of the economy by controlling inflation and reducing unemployment.

f. The economic role of government is conducted in the context of politics. This process can lead to imperfect and inefficient outcomes.

6. *A circular flow model* that includes the public sector as well as business firms and households in the private sector of the economy reveals that government purchases public goods from private businesses, collects taxes from and makes transfer payments to these firms, purchases labor services from households, collects taxes from and makes transfer payments to these households, and can alter the distribution of income, reallocate resources, and change the level of economic activity by affecting the real and monetary flows in the diagram.

7. *Government finance* is important in the economy. Government spending consists of *purchases* of goods and services and *transfer payments,* but they have different effects on the economy. Purchases are exhaustive because they directly use the economy's resources, while transfers are nonexhaustive. Total government spending is equal to about one-third of domestic output.

8. For the *Federal government,*
a. most spending goes for pensions and income security, national defense, health care, or interest on the public debt.
b. the major sources of revenue are personal income taxes, payroll taxes, and corporate income taxes.

9. For other levels of government,
a. *state governments* depend largely on sales, excise, and personal income taxes, and they spend their revenues on public welfare, education, health care, and highways.
b. *local governments* rely heavily on property taxes; they spend much of the revenue on education.

■ HINTS AND TIPS

1. This chapter is a long one, so do not try to learn everything at once. Break the chapter into its three natural parts and work on each one separately. The first part describes features of the private sector. The second part explains the functions of government. The third part looks at government finance.

2. There are many descriptive statistics about the private and public sectors. Avoid memorizing these statistics. Instead, look for the trends and generalizations that these statistics illustrate about the private or public sector. For example, the discussion of government finance describes recent trends in government expenditures and taxes and indicates the relative importance of taxes and expenditures at each level of government.

■ IMPORTANT TERMS

functional distribution of income	double taxation
personal distribution of income	principal–agent problem
personal taxes	monopoly
personal saving	spillover costs
personal consumption	spillover benefits
expenditures	public goods
durable good	free-rider problem
nondurable good	quasi-public goods
services	government purchases
plant	transfer payment
firm	personal income tax
industry	marginal tax rate
sole proprietorship	average tax rate
partnership	payroll tax
corporation	corporate income tax
stocks	sales tax
bonds	excise tax
limited liability	property tax

SELF-TEST

■ FILL-IN QUESTIONS

1. There are approximately 109 million (businesses, households) _**housholds**_ in the United States. They play a dual role in the economy because they (sell, buy) _**sell**_ their resources and _**buy**_ most of the total output of the economy.

2. The largest single source of income in the United States is (corporate profits, wages and salaries) _**wages and salaries**_. It is equal to about (30, 70) _**70**_ % of total income.

3. In the United States the poorest (1, 20) _**20**_ % of all families receive about 4% of total personal income, and the richest (1, 20) _**20**_ % of these families receive about 50% of total personal income.

4. The total income of households is disposed of in three ways: personal _**Consumption**_, personal _**Saving**_, and personal _**taxes**_.

5. Households use about 13% of their total income to pay for personal (taxes, consumption expenditures) _**taxes**_ and about 84% for personal _**Consumption expenditures**_

6. If a product has an expected life of 3 years or more it is a (durable, nondurable) _**durable**_ good, whereas if it has an expected life of less than 3 years it is a _**nonurable**_ good.

7. There are millions of business (firms, industries) ___firms___ in the United States. The legal form of the great majority of them is the (sole proprietorship, partnership, corporation) _Sole proprietoship_, but the legal form that produces almost 90% of the sales of the U.S. economy is the _Corporation_.

8. Shares of ownership of corporations are called (stocks, bonds) _Stocks_, whereas promises by corporations to repay a loan, usually at a fixed rate of interest, are _bonds_.

9. The liabilities of a sole proprietor and of partners are (limited, unlimited) _Unlimited_, but the liabilities of stockholders in a corporation are _limited_.

10. The separation of ownership and control in a corporation may create a (free-rider, principal–agent) _Principal agent_ problem. In this case, stockholders would be the (riders, principals, agents) _Principal_ and managers would be the _agents_.

11. List the five economic functions of government.

a. _Provide legal foundation_
b. _Maintain Competition_
c. _redistribute income_
d. _reallocate resources_
e. _Stabilize the economy_

12. To control monopoly, the U.S. government has created commissions to (tax, regulate) _regulate_ natural monopolies, and in cases at the local level, government has become an (agent, owner) _owner_. Government has also enacted (trust, antitrust) _antitrust_ laws to maintain competition.

13. The market system, because it is an impersonal mechanism, results in an (equal, unequal) _____ distribution of income. To redistribute income from the upper- to the lower-income groups, the government has provided (transfer, tax) _____ payments, engaged in (military, market) _____ intervention, and used the (income, sales) _____ tax to raise much of its revenues.

14. Government frequently reallocates resources when it finds instances of (market, public) _____ failure. The two major cases of such failure occur when the competitive market system either

a. _Produces the wrong goods & services_
b. _fails to allocate any resources_ _to the production_

15. Competitive markets bring about an efficient allocation of resources only if there are no (private, spillover) _____ costs or benefits in the consumption and production of a good or service.

16. There is an externality whenever some of the costs of producing a product accrue to people other than the (seller, buyer) _____ or some of the benefits from consuming a product accrue to people other than the _____.

17. a. What two things can government do to make the market reflect spillover costs?

(1) _enact legislation_
(2) _Pass Special taxes_

b. What three things can government do to make the market reflect spillover benefits?

(1) _Subsidize Consumer_
(2) _Subsidize Suppliers_
(3) _government Financing_

18. One characteristic of a public good is (rivalry, nonrivalry) _nonivarly_ and the other characteristic of a public good is (excludability, nonexcludability) _____. A private firm will not find it profitable to produce a public good because there is a (free-rider, principal–agent) _____ problem.

19. To reallocate resources from the production of private to the production of public and quasi-public goods, government reduces the demand for private goods by (taxing, subsidizing) _____ consumers and then uses the (profits, tax revenue) _____ to buy public or quasi-public goods.

20. To stabilize the economy with less than full employment, government may try to increase total spending by (increasing, decreasing) _____ its expenditures for public goods and services by (increasing, decreasing) _____ taxes, or by (raising, lowering) _____ interest rates. When there are inflationary pressures, the government may try to decrease total spending by (decreasing, increasing) _____ its expenditures for public goods and services, by _____ taxes, or by (raising, lowering) _____ interest rates.

21. An examination of government finance reveals that **a.** since 1960 government *purchases* of goods and services as a percentage of total output (increased, decreased) _____,

b. but government *transfer payments* as a percentage of domestic output since 1960 has (increased, decreased) _____,

c. and the tax revenues required to finance total government spending (purchases plus transfer payments) are today about (30, 70) _____% of domestic output.

d. Government transfer payments are (exhaustive, nonexhaustive) _____, whereas government purchases of goods and services are _____ because they absorb resources.

22. The most important source of revenue for the Federal government is the (personal income, payroll) _____ tax; next in importance is the _____ tax. The three largest categories of Federal expenditures ranked by budget size are (health, national defense, pensions and income security) _____,

_____, and _____.

23. Federal income tax rates are progressive, which means that people with (lower, higher) _higher_ incomes pay a larger percentage of that income as taxes than do persons with _lower_ incomes. The tax rate paid on an additional unit of income is the (average, marginal) _Marginal_ tax rate, while the total tax paid divided by the total taxable income is the _Average_ tax rate.

24. Many state governments rely primarily on (property, sales and excise) _____ taxes and (personal, corporate) _____ income taxes for their revenue, which they spend mostly on (national defense, public welfare) _____ and (interest, education) _____.

25. At local levels of government the single most important source of revenue is the (income, property) _____ tax and the single most important expenditure is for (public safety, education) _____.

■ **TRUE–FALSE QUESTIONS**

Circle T if the statement is true, F if it is false.

1. The personal distribution of income describes the manner in which society's total personal income is divided among wages and salaries, corporate profits, proprietors' income, interest, and rents. T (F)

2. Personal taxes have risen in relative terms since World War II. (T) F

3. Most of the personal saving in the U.S. economy is done by those households in the top 10% of its income receivers. (T) F

4. *Dissaving* means that personal consumption expenditures exceed after-tax income. (T) F

5. A durable good is defined as a good that has an expected life of 3 years or more. (T) F

6. A plant is defined as a group of firms under a single management. T (F)

7. An industry is a group of firms that produce the same or nearly the same products. (T) F

8. Limited liability refers to the fact that all members of a partnership are liable for the debts incurred by one another. T (F)

9. The corporate form of organization is the least used by firms in the United States. T (F)

10. The corporation in the United States has a tax advantage over other legal forms of business organization. T (F)

11. Whether a business firm should incorporate or not depends chiefly on the amount of money capital it must have to finance the enterprise. (T) F

12. A limited liability company is like an ordinary partnership for tax purposes, but like a corporation in matters of liability. (T) F

13. Bonds are shares of ownership in a corporation. T (F)

14. When the interests of the principals are the same as those of agents, there is a free-rider problem. T (F)

15. When the Federal government provides for a monetary system, it is doing so primarily to maintain competition. T (F)

16. Transfer payments are one means government uses to redistribute income. (T) F

17. If demand and supply reflected all the benefits and costs of producing a product, there would be efficient resource use. (T) F

18. When there are spillover costs, more resources are allocated to the production of the product and more is produced than is efficient. (T) F

19. One way for government to correct for spillover costs from a product is to increase its demand. T (F)

20. When there are spillover benefits from a product, there will be an overallocation of resources for its production. T (F)

21. One way for government to correct spillover benefits from a product is to subsidize consumers of the product. (T) F

22. Nonexcludability means government provides public goods so as to exclude private businesses from providing them. T (F)

23. Obtaining the benefits of private goods requires that they be purchased; obtaining benefits from public goods requires only that they be produced. **(T)** F

24. Government provides homeland defense services because these services have public benefits and because private producers of such services experience the free-rider problem. **(T)** F

25. When the Federal government takes actions to control unemployment or inflation it is performing the allocative function of government. T **(F)**

26. Government purchases of goods and services are called nonexhaustive expenditures and government transfer payments are called exhaustive expenditures. T **(F)**

27. When a government levies taxes and uses the tax revenue to make transfer payments, it shifts resources from the production of private goods to the production of public goods. T **(F)**

28. The chief source of revenue for the Federal government is the corporate income tax. T **(F)**

29. If the marginal tax rate is higher than the average tax rate, the average tax rate will fall as income rises. T **(F)**

30. Property taxes are the largest percentage of the total revenues of local governments. **(T)** F

■ **MULTIPLE-CHOICE QUESTIONS**

Circle the letter that corresponds to the best answer.

1. The functional distribution for the United States shows that the largest part of the nation's income is
(a) wages and salaries
(b) proprietors' income
(c) corporate profits
(d) interest and rents

2. The part of after-tax income which is not consumed is defined as
(a) saving
(b) capital investment
(c) wages and salaries
(d) nondurable goods expenditure

3. If personal consumption expenditures were 80% of income and personal taxes were 8% of income, then personal savings would be
(a) 8% of income
(b) 10% of income
(c) 12% of income
(d) 88% of income

4. Consumer products that have expected lives of three years or more are
(a) durable goods
(b) nondurable goods
(c) quasi-public goods
(d) services

5. A firm owns and operates a farm growing wheat, a flour-milling plant, and a plant that bakes and sells bakery products. This firm would best be described as
(a) a horizontally integrated firm
(b) a vertically integrated firm
(c) a conglomerate
(d) a monopoly

6. Limited liability is associated with
(a) sole proprietorships
(b) partnerships
(c) free-riders
(d) corporations

7. Which form of business can most effectively raise money capital?
(a) corporation
(b) partnership
(c) proprietorship
(d) households

8. The separation of ownership and control in a corporation may create
(a) a principal–agent problem
(b) a free-rider problem
(c) a monopoly
(d) limited liability

9. One major means that government uses to deal with a monopoly is to
(a) increase the demand for its product
(b) decrease the supply of its product
(c) stabilize incomes
(d) regulate the firm

10. Government redistributes income through
(a) limited liability
(b) conglomerates
(c) transfer payments
(d) sole proprietorships

11. To redistribute income from high-income to low-income households, government might
(a) increase transfer payments to high-income and decrease transfer payments to low-income households
(b) increase the taxes paid by high-income and increase the transfer payments to low-income households
(c) increase the taxes paid by low-income and decrease the taxes paid by high-income households
(d) decrease the taxes paid by high-income and decrease the transfer payments to low-income households

12. Which is the best example of a good or service providing the economy with a spillover cost?
(a) a textbook
(b) an automobile
(c) a business suit
(d) an audit of a business firm's books

13. Which economic situation would result in overallocation of resources to the production of a good?
(a) spillover benefits
(b) spillover costs

(c) a free-rider program
(d) inflation

14. How does government correct for spillover benefits?
(a) by taxing consumers
(b) by taxing producers
(c) by subsidizing producers
(d) by separating ownership from control

15. Which is characteristic of public goods?
(a) nonrivalry
(b) excludability
(c) limited liability
(d) spillover costs

16. There is a free-rider problem when people
(a) are willing to pay for what they want
(b) are not willing to pay for what they want
(c) benefit from a good without paying for its cost
(d) want to buy more than is available for purchase in the market

17. Quasi-public goods are goods and services
(a) that are indivisible
(b) that have large spillover costs
(c) that have large spillover benefits
(d) that would not be produced by private producers through the market system

18. In the circular flow model, government provides goods and services and receives net taxes from
(a) colleges and universities
(b) businesses and households
(c) resource and product markets
(d) foreign nations and corporations

19. Which accounts for the largest percentage of all Federal expenditures?
(a) income security
(b) national defense
(c) interest on the public debt
(d) veterans' services

20. Which is the largest source of the tax revenues of the Federal government?
(a) sales and excise taxes
(b) property taxes
(c) payroll taxes
(d) personal income taxes

21. A tax that would most likely alter consumer expenditures on a particular product would be
(a) an excise tax
(b) a payroll tax
(c) a personal income tax
(d) a corporate income tax

22. Which pair represents the chief source of income and the most important type of expenditure of *state* governments?
(a) personal income tax and expenditures for hospitals
(b) personal income tax and expenditures for highways
(c) sales and excise taxes and expenditures for education
(d) sales and excise taxes and expenditures for public safety

23. Which pair represents the chief source of income and the most important type of expenditure of local governments?
(a) property tax and expenditures for highways
(b) property tax and expenditures for education
(c) sales and excise taxes and expenditures for public welfare
(d) sales and excise taxes and expenditures for police, fire, safety, and general government

Questions 24 and 25 are based on the tax table given below. [Note: total tax is for the highest income in that tax bracket.]

Taxable income	Total tax
$ 0	$ 0
30,000	5,000
70,000	15,000
150,000	42,000

24. The marginal tax rate at the $70,000 level of taxable income is
(a) 16.6%
(b) 21.4
(c) 25.0
(d) 28.0

25. The average tax rate at the $150,000 level of taxable income is
(a) 21.4%
(b) 28.0
(c) 31.5
(d) 33.8

■ **PROBLEMS**

1. The following table shows the functional distribution of total income in the United States in a recent year.

	Billions of dollars
Wages and salaries	$4,703
Proprietors' income	545
Corporate profits	804
Interest	450
Rents	148
Total income	6,650

Of the total income about _____% were wages and salaries, and about _____% were corporate profits.

2. Indicate in the space to the right of **a–i** whether these business characteristics are associated with the proprietorship (**PRO**), partnership (**PART**), corporation (**CORP**), two of these, or all three of these legal forms.
a. Red tape and legal expense in obtaining a charter for the firm ___Corp___
b. Unlimited liability ___Pro-Part___
c. No specialized management _____
d. Has a life independent of its owner(s) _____
e. Double taxation of income _____

f. Greatest ability to acquire funds for the expansion of the firm _____

g. Permits some but not a great degree of specialized management _____

h. Possibility of an unresolved disagreement among several owners of the firm over courses of action

_____

i. The potential for the separation of ownership and control of the business _____

3. Following is a list of various government activities. Indicate in the space to the right of each into which of the five classes of government functions the activity falls. If it falls under more than one of the functions, indicate this.

a. Maintaining an army _____

b. Providing for a system of unemployment compensation _____

c. Establishment of the Federal Reserve Banks _____

d. Providing medical care for government employees _____

e. Establishment of an Antitrust Division in the Department of Justice _____

f. Making it a crime to sell stocks and bonds under false pretenses _____

g. Providing low-cost lunches to school children _____

h. Taxation of beer and wine _____

i. Regulation of organized stock, bond, and commodity markets _____

j. Setting tax *rates* higher for larger incomes than for smaller ones _____

4. The following circular flow diagram includes business firms, households, and the government (the public sector). Also shown are the product and resource markets.

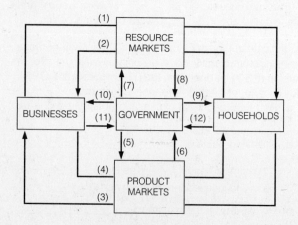

a. Supply a label or an explanation for each of the 12 flows in the model:

(1) _____

(2) _____

(3) _____

(4) _____

(5) _____

(6) _____

(7) _____

(8) _____

(9) _____

(10) _____

(11) _____

(12) _____

b. If government wished to

(1) expand output and employment in the economy, it would increase expenditure flows _____ or _____, decrease net tax flows _____ or _____, or do both;

(2) increase the production of public goods and decrease the production of private goods in the economy, it would increase flows _____ and _____ or _____;

(3) redistribute income from high-income to low-income households, it would (increase, decrease) _____ the net taxes (taxes minus transfers) paid by the former and _____ the net taxes paid by the latter in flow _____.

5. In the following table are several levels of taxable income and hypothetical marginal tax rates for each $1000 increase in income.

Taxable income	Marginal tax rate, %	Tax	Average tax rate, %
$1500		$300	20
2500	22	520	20.8
3500	25	___	___
4500	29	___	___
5500	34	___	___
6500	40	___	___

a. At the four income levels compute the tax and the average tax rate.

b. As the marginal tax rate

(1) increases, the average tax rate (increases, decreases, remains constant) _____.

(2) decreases, the average tax rate _____.

c. This tax is (progressive, regressive) _____ because the average tax rate increases as income (decreases, increases) _____.

■ **SHORT ANSWER AND ESSAY QUESTIONS**

1. Explain the difference between a functional and a personal distribution of income. Rank the five types of earned income in the order of their size.

2. Describe how saving and personal consumption vary across income levels. Which group is most likely to *dissave*?

3. The purchase of what type of consumer goods is largely postponable? Why is this? How is it possible for a family's personal consumption expenditures to exceed its after-tax income?

4. What is the difference between a plant and a firm? Between a firm and an industry?

5. What are the principal advantages and disadvantages of each type of the three legal forms of business organization?

6. Which of the disadvantages of the proprietorship and partnership accounts for the formation of corporations? Explain why it is important.

7. Describe the two different hybrid structures for business.

8. Explain what "separation of ownership and control" of the modern corporation means. What problem does this separation create for stockholders and managers?

9. How does government provide a legal framework and services for the effective operation of the economy?

10. What does the government do to maintain competition?

11. Why does the market system provide some people with lower incomes than it provides others?

12. What is meant by a spillover in general and by a spillover cost and a spillover benefit in particular?

13. How does the existence of spillover costs and benefits affect the allocation of resources and the prices of products?

14. What methods does government use to
(a) redistribute income?
(b) reallocate resources to take account of spillover costs?
(c) reallocate resources to take account of spillover benefits?

15. Distinguish between a private and a public good. Include in your answer an explanation of rivalry, excludability, and the free-rider problem.

16. What basic method does government in the United States use to reallocate resources away from the production of private goods and toward the production of public and quasi-public goods?

17. What is the stability function of government? What are the two economic problems that this function addresses?

18. How does politics affect the economic role of government in the economy?

19. In a circular flow diagram that includes not only business firms and households but also government (or the public sector), what are the four flows of money into or out of the government sector of the economy? Using this diagram, explain how government redistributes income, reallocates resources from the private to the public sector, and stabilizes the economy.

20. What is the present size of government spending and taxation in the U.S. economy?

21. Government expenditures fall into two broad classes: expenditures for goods and services and transfer payments. Explain the difference between these, and give examples of expenditures that fall into each of the two classes.

22. Explain precisely the difference between the marginal tax rate and the average tax rate.

23. Explain how the Federal personal income tax enables the Federal government to perform some of its economic functions.

24. Explain in detail the differences that exist among Federal and state governments in the taxes on which they primarily rely for their revenues and the major purposes for which they use these revenues.

25. What are tax revenue sources and expenditures at the local level?

ANSWERS

Chapter 5 The U.S. Economy: Private and Public Sectors

FILL-IN QUESTIONS

1. households, sell, buy
2. wages and salaries, 70
3. 20, 20
4. consumption, saving, taxes (any order)
5. taxes, consumption expenditures
6. durable, nondurable
7. firms, sole proprietorship, corporation
8. stocks, bonds
9. unlimited, limited
10. principal–agent, principals, agents
11. *a.* provide legal foundation; *b.* maintain competition; *c.* redistribute income; *d.* reallocate resources; *e.* stabilize the economy (any order for *a–e*)
12. regulate, owner, antitrust
13. unequal, transfer, market, income
14. market; *a.* produces the "wrong" amounts of certain goods and services; *b.* fails to allocate any resources to the production of certain goods and services whose production is economically justified
15. spillover
16. seller, buyer

17. *a.* (1) enact legislation, (2) pass special taxes; *b.* (1) subsidize consumers, (2) subsidize suppliers, (3) government financing or production of the product
18. nonrivalry, excludability, free-rider
19. taxing, tax revenue
20. increasing, decreasing, lowering, decreasing, increasing, raising
21. *a.* decreased; *b.* increased; *c.* 30; *d.* nonexhaustive, exhaustive
22. personal income, payroll, pensions and income security, national defense, health
23. higher, lower, marginal, average
24. sales and excise, personal, public welfare, education
25. property, education

TRUE–FALSE QUESTIONS

1. F, pp. 73–74	**9.** F, pp. 76–77	**17.** T, p. 80	**25.** F, pp. 82–83
2. T, p. 74	**10.** F, pp. 77–78	**18.** T, p. 80	**26.** F, p. 84
3. T, p. 74	**11.** T, pp. 77–78	**19.** F, pp. 80–81	**27.** F, pp. 84–85
4. T, p. 74	**12.** T, pp. 77–78	**20.** F, p. 81	**28.** F, pp. 85–86
5. T, p. 75	**13.** F, p. 77	**21.** T, p. 81	**29.** F, p. 86
6. F, p. 75	**14.** F, p. 78	**22.** F, p. 81	**30.** T, p. 87
7. T, p. 76	**15.** F, p. 79	**23.** T, p. 81	
8. F, p. 77	**16.** T, pp. 79–80	**24.** T, p. 81	

MULTIPLE-CHOICE QUESTIONS

1. a, p. 73	**8.** a, p. 78	**15.** a, p. 81	**22.** c, p. 87
2. a, p. 74	**9.** d, p. 79	**16.** c, pp. 81–82	**23.** b, p. 87
3. c, pp. 74–75	**10.** c, pp. 79–80	**17.** c, p. 82	**24.** c, p. 86
4. a, p. 75	**11.** b, pp. 79–80	**18.** b, pp. 83–84	**25.** b, p. 86
5. b, p. 76	**12.** b, p. 80	**19.** a, pp. 85–86	
6. d, p. 77	**13.** b, pp. 80–81	**20.** d, p. 86	
7. a, pp. 77–78	**14.** c, p. 81	**21.** a, p. 87	

PROBLEMS

1. 71, 12
2. *a.* CORP; *b.* PRO and PART; *c.* PRO; *d.* CORP; *e.* CORP; *f.* CORP; *g.* PART; *h.* PART; *i.* CORP
3. *a.* reallocates resources; *b.* redistributes income; *c.* provides a legal foundation and stabilizes the economy; *d.* reallocates resources; *e.* maintains competition; *f.* provides a legal foundation and maintains competition; *g.* redistributes income; *h.* reallocates resources; *i.* provides a legal foundation; *j.* redistributes income
4. *a.* (1) businesses pay costs for resources that become money income for households; (2) households provide resources to businesses; (3) household expenditures become receipts for businesses; (4) businesses provide goods and services to households; (5) government spends money in product market; (6) government receives goods and services from product market; (7) government spends money in resource market; (8) government receives resources from resource market; (9) government provides goods and services to households; (10) government provides goods and services to businesses; (11) businesses pay net taxes to government; (12) households pay net taxes to government; *b.* (1) 5, 7 (either order), 11, 12 (either order); (2) 9, 10, 11 (any order); (3) increase, decrease, 12
5. *a.* tax: $770, 1,060, 1,400, 1,800; average tax rate: 22%, 23.6%, 25.5%, 27.7%; *b.* (1) increases, (2) decreases; *c.* progressive, increases

SHORT ANSWER AND ESSAY QUESTIONS

1. pp. 73–74	**8.** p. 78	**15.** p. 81	**22.** p. 86
2. pp. 74–75	**9.** p. 79	**16.** pp. 81–82	**23.** pp. 85–86
3. p. 75	**10.** p. 79	**17.** pp. 82–83	**24.** pp. 85–87
4. pp. 76–77	**11.** pp. 79–80	**18.** p. 83	**25.** p. 87
5. pp. 76–78	**12.** pp. 80–81	**19.** p. 83	
6. pp. 76–78	**13.** pp. 80–81	**20.** pp. 84–85	
7. p. 78	**14.** pp. 79–80	**21.** p. 84	

CHAPTER 6

The United States in the Global Economy

The United States is linked to the global economy in many ways. As you will learn in the first section of Chapter 6, there are four types of **economic flows** among nations: trade; resource; information and technology; and financial.

The second section explains **why international trade is important** to the United States. In *relative* terms, other nations have exports and imports that are a larger percentage of their GDPs because they often have a small domestic market and a limited resource base. By contrast, the exports and imports of the United States account for a smaller percentage of its GDP because it has a larger domestic market and a more abundant resource base. In *absolute* terms, however, the United States is the world's largest trading nation. Most of the trade is with other industrially advanced nations such as Canada, Japan, and Germany. This volume of trade has grown over the years with expansion of the global economy, the rise of multinational corporations, and the emergence of new trading nations.

In the third section, you learn about the principle of **comparative advantage,** which is the basis for all trade between individuals, regions, and nations. A nation, for example, will specialize in the production of a product for which it has a lower domestic opportunity cost and trade to obtain those products for which its domestic opportunity cost is higher. Thus, specialization and trade increase productivity within a nation and increase a nation's output and standard of living.

Trading in a global economy requires a **foreign exchange market** in which national currencies are exchanged, as you discover in the fourth section. This market is competitive, so the principles of supply and demand that you read about in Chapter 3 apply to it. Changes in supply and demand for currency will affect the price of a national currency. When the U.S. dollar price of another currency has increased, the value of the U.S. dollar has *depreciated* relative to the other currency. Conversely, when the U.S. dollar price of another currency has decreased, the value of the U.S. dollar has *appreciated* in value relative to the other currency.

Government can affect international trade in many ways, as you learn in the fifth section. Governments can impose protective tariffs, import quotas, and nontariff barriers, or they can foster exports through subsidies. The reasons for the interventions are difficult to explain given the strong economic rationale for free trade based on the principle of comparative advantage. Nevertheless, public misunderstanding of the gains from trade, or political considerations designed to protect domestic industries, often lead to government policies that create trade barriers and distort the free flow of products between nations, thus increasing costs for society.

The sixth section discusses **multilateral agreements** among nations and the creation of **free-trade zones** that have been designed to reduce trade barriers and increase world trade. In the United States, the process of gradual tariff reduction began with the Reciprocal Trade Agreements Act of 1934. Since 1947, worldwide multilateral negotiations to reduce trade barriers have been conducted through the General Agreement on Tariffs and Trade (GATT). The Uruguay Round of GATT negotiations established the World Trade Organization (WTO) as GATT's successor. Trade negotiations under the WTO continue in the Doha Round that began in 2001.

The other major development has been the formation of free-trade zones. The European Union (EU), which was originally started in 1958 as the Common Market, is now a trading bloc of 25 European nations. A major accomplishment of the EU, in addition to the reduction of trade barriers among member nations, was the establishment of a common currency (the **euro**) that in 2003 was used by 12 nations. The United States, Canada, and Mexico also established a free-trade zone in 1993 through the North American Free Trade Agreement (NAFTA).

The final section of the chapter briefly explores the issue of the effects of **increased competition in the global economy.** Global competition has certainly changed production practices and employment in U.S. industry. Many U.S. firms have adapted to the changes by increasing productivity to reduce costs, improving product quality, and expanding export markets. Although some firms have failed and domestic jobs have been lost, the benefits of free trade to the economy in the form of lower prices, greater economic efficiency, and a wider variety of products far outweigh any losses.

■ **CHECKLIST**

When you have studied this chapter you should be able to

☐ Identify the four main categories of economic flows linking nations.

☐ Explain the importance of international trade to the U.S. economy in terms of volume, dependence, trade patterns, and financial linkages.

☐ Describe several factors that have facilitated the rapid growth of international trade since World War II.

☐ Identify the key participating nations in international trade.

☐ Explain the basic principle of comparative advantage based on an individual example.

☐ Compute the comparative costs of production from production possibilities data when you are given an example with cost data for two countries.

☐ Determine which of two countries has a comparative advantage in an example.

☐ Indicate the range in which the terms of trade will be found in an example.

☐ Show the gains from specialization and trade in an example.

☐ Define the main characteristics of the foreign exchange market.

☐ Demonstrate how supply and demand analysis applies to the foreign exchange market.

☐ Distinguish between the appreciation and depreciation of a currency.

☐ Identify four means by which governments interfere with free trade.

☐ Discuss two reasons why governments intervene in international trade.

☐ Give estimates of the cost to society from trade restrictions.

☐ List the major features of the Reciprocal Trade Agreements Act and the General Agreement on Tariffs and Trade (GATT).

☐ Identify the major provisions of the Uruguay round of GATT negotiations.

☐ Describe the World Trade Organization (WTO).

☐ Describe the history, goals, and results from the European Union (EU).

☐ Explain what the euro is and expectations for it.

☐ Explain the features and significance of the North American Free Trade Agreement (NAFTA).

☐ Discuss the effects on increased competition in the global economy on U.S. firms, workers, and consumers.

■ CHAPTER OUTLINE

1. Four main categories of *economic flows* link nations: goods and services flows, capital and labor flows, information and technology flows, and financial flows.

2. *Trade is important* and thus warrants special attention.

a. Although the relative importance of international trade to the United States is less than it is for other nations, it is still vital.

(1) Exports and imports are about 11–16% of GDP, and the United States is the largest trading nation in the world.

(2) The U.S. economy depends on international trade for vital raw materials and a variety of finished products.

(3) There are some patterns in U.S. trade: Most are with industrially advanced nations, with Canada being the largest trade partner; overall imports exceed exports, but the deficits are greatest with Japan, China, and OPEC countries.

(4) International trade must be financed, and, in the case of the United States, large trade deficits have required the selling of business ownership (securities) to companies in other nations.

b. Factors facilitating trade since World War II include improvements in transportation and communications technology, and a general decline in tariffs.

c. The major participants in international trade are the United States, Japan, and the nations of western Europe. Newer participants include many Asian economies—Hong Kong (now part of China), Singapore, South Korea, Taiwan, Malaysia, and Indonesia. China has also emerged as a major trading nation in this region. The collapse of communism in the former Soviet Union and the nations of Eastern Europe significantly changed trade patterns in that region, opened these nations to market forces, and increased international trade.

3. International trade policies have changed over the years with the development of *multilateral agreements* and *free-trade* zones.

a. United States trade policy has been significantly affected by the *Reciprocal Trade Agreements Act* of 1934. Until 1934, the United States steadily increased tariff rates to protect private interest groups, but since the passage of the 1934 act, tariff rates have been substantially reduced. This act gave the President the authority to negotiate with foreign nations and included *most-favored-nation (MFN) status* clauses.

b. The *General Agreement on Tariffs and Trade* (GATT) began in 1947. GATT provided equal treatment of all member nations and sought to reduce tariffs and eliminate import quotas by multilateral negotiations. The Uruguay Round of GATT negotiations started in 1986 and was completed in 1993. The major provisions, which will be phased in through 2005, reduce tariffs on products, cut restrictive rules applying to services, phase out quotas on textiles and apparel, and decrease subsidies for agriculture.

c. The *World Trade Organization* (WTO) was the successor to GATT. It oversees trade agreements and provides a forum for trade negotiations, the latest of which is the *Doha Round*. The WTO works to expand trade and reduce protectionism, but the outcomes can be controversial.

d. The *European Union* (EU) is an example of a regional free-trade zone or trade bloc among 25 western European nations. It abolished tariffs among member nations and developed common policies on various economic issues, such as the tariffs on goods to and from nonmember nations. The EU has produced freer trade and increased economies of scale for production in its member nations, but such a trading bloc creates trade frictions with nonmember nations like the United States. Many of the EU nations share a common currency–the *euro*.

e. In 1993, *The North American Free Trade Agreement* (NAFTA) created a free-trade zone covering the United States, Mexico, and Canada. Critics of this agreement fear job losses and the potential for abuse by other nations using Mexico as a base for production. Defenders cite the mutual advantages from freer trade and the fact that increased worldwide investment in Mexico will stimulate growth in that nation and trade with the United States.

4. Increased international trade has resulted in more *global competition.* Most U.S. firms have been able to meet the competitive challenge by lowering production costs, improving products, or using new technology. Some firms and industries have had difficulty remaining competitive and continue to lose market share and employment. Overall, increased trade has produced substantial benefits for U.S. consumers (lower prices and more products) and enabled the nation to make more efficient use of its scarce resources.

■ HINTS AND TIPS

1. Comparative advantage is directly related to the opportunity cost concept and production possibilities you learned about in Chapter 2.

    a. A nation has a comparative advantage in the production of a product when it can produce the product at a lower domestic opportunity cost than can a trading partner. A nation will specialize in the production of a product for which it is the low (opportunity) cost producer.

    b. When production possibilities schedules for two nations that trade two products have a constant cost ratio, you can reduce the complicated production possibilities schedules to a 2 × 2 table. Put the two products in the two columns and the two nations in the two rows of the matrix. In each cell of the matrix put the *maximum* of each product that can be produced by that row's nation. Then for each nation, divide the maximum of one product into the maximum amount of the other product to get the domestic opportunity cost of one product in terms of the other.

    c. This last point can be illustrated with an example from problem 2 in this study guide chapter. Lilliput can produce a *maximum* of 40 pounds of apples or 20 pounds of bananas. Brobdingnag can produce a *maximum* of 75 pounds of apples or 25 pounds of bananas. The 2 × 2 matrix would look like this:

	Apples	Bananas
Lilliput	40	20
Brobdingnag	75	25

For Lilliput, the domestic opportunity cost of producing 1 pound of apples is .5 pound of bananas. In Brobdingnag, the domestic opportunity cost of producing 1 pound of apples is .33 pound of bananas. Brobdingnag is the lower (opportunity) cost producer of apples and will specialize in the production of that product. Lilliput is the lower (opportunity) cost producer of bananas, because producing 1 pound of bananas requires giving up 2 pounds of apples, whereas in Brobdingnag producing 1 pound of bananas requires giving up 3 pounds of apples.

2. Foreign exchange rates often confuse students because they can be expressed in two ways: the U.S. dollar price of a unit of foreign currency ($1.56 for 1 British pound), or the amount of foreign currency that can be purchased by one U.S. dollar ($1 can purchase .64 British pound). If you know the exchange rate in one way, you can easily calculate it the other way. Using the information from the first way, dividing $1.56 into 1 British pound gives you the British pound price for 1 U.S. dollar (1/1.56 = .64 of a British pound). Using information from the second way, dividing .64 of a British pound into 1 U.S. dollar gives you the dollar price of a British pound (1/.64 = 1.56). Both ways may be used, although one way may be used more often than the other. Rates for British pounds or Canadian dollars are usually expressed the first way, in terms of U.S. dollars. Rates for the Swiss franc, Japanese yen, or European euro are expressed the second way, per U.S. dollar.

■ IMPORTANT TERMS

multinational corporations	**most-favored-nation clauses**
comparative advantage	**General Agreement on Tariffs and Trade (GATT)**
terms of trade	
foreign exchange market	**World Trade Organization (WTO)**
exchange rates	
depreciation	**European Union (EU)**
appreciation	**trade bloc**
protective tariffs	**euro**
import quotas	**North American Free Trade Agreement (NAFTA)**
nontariff barriers	
export subsidies	
Smoot-Hawley Tariff Act	
Reciprocal Trade Agreements Act	

SELF-TEST

■ FILL-IN QUESTIONS

1. List the four major economic flows among nations.

    a. _trade flows_

    b. _resource flows_

    c. _info and technology flow_

    d. _finance flows_

2. The importance of international trade varies by nation. Nations in which exports account for a relatively high percentage of GDP tend to have a (limited, diversified) _limited_ resource base and domestic market, whereas nations in which exports account for a lower percentage of GDP tend to have a _diversified_ resource base and domestic market. An example of a higher exporting nation would be the (United States, Netherlands) _Netherlands_, and a lower exporting nation would be the _USA_ .

3. In relative terms, the imports and exports of the United States amounted to about (11–16, 31–36) _11–16_ % of the economy's GDP in 2002. In absolute terms, the United States is the world's (smallest, largest) ____largest____ trading nation.

4. The bulk of the trade of the United States is with (less-developed, industrially advanced) _____ nations. The largest trading partner for the United States is (Canada, Japan) _____. The United States has a large trade deficit with (Canada, Japan) _____.

5. Factors that have helped increase the growth of world trade since World War II include improvement in _transportation_ and _communication_ technology and a general decline in ____tariffs____.

6. The top participants in international trade include the _U.S._, _Japan_, and the nations of western Europe. These participants serve as the headquarters for most (national, multinational) _____ corporations and dominate world trade. The economies of Singapore, South Korea, and Taiwan have (increased, decreased) _____ their share of the world trade in recent decades. Another major trading nation in Asia is (China, Thailand) _____.

7. Specialization and trade (increase, decrease) _____ the productivity of a nation's resources and _increase_ total output more than would be the case without them.

8. When one nation has a lower opportunity cost of producing a product relative to another nation it has a (nontariff barrier, comparative advantage) _____. The amount of one product that must be given up to obtain 1 unit of another product is the (foreign exchange, opportunity cost) _____.

9. When the dollar price of foreign currency increases, there has been a(n) (appreciation, depreciation) _dep_ in the the value of the dollar. When the dollar price of foreign currency decreases, there has been a(n) _Ap_ in the value of the dollar. For example, if the dollar price of a euro decreases from $1.00 = 1 euro to $0.90 = 1 euro, then it means that there has been a(n) (appreciation, depreciation) _ap_ in the value of the dollar; but if the dollar price of a euro increases from $0.95 = 1 euro to $1.05 = 1 euro, then it means that there has been a(n) _dep_ in the value of the dollar.

10. In the market for Japanese yen, an increase in the (demand for, supply of) _supply of_ yen will

decrease the dollar price of yen, while an increase in the ____demand of____ yen will increase the dollar price of yen. If the dollar price of the yen increases, then Japanese goods imported into the United States will be (more, less) _____ expensive.

11. The major government policies that restrict trade include
a. excise taxes or duties on imported goods that are called _____,
b. limits on the quantities or total value of specific items that may be imported, referred to as _____,
c. licensing requirements, unreasonable standards, and red tape for a product, which are _____,
d. government payments to domestic producers of export goods, known as _____.

12. Governments may intervene in trade between nations because they mistakenly think of (exports, imports) _____ as helpful and _____ as harmful for a national economy. In fact, there are important gains from trade in the form of the extra output obtained from abroad. Trade makes it possible to obtain (exports, imports) _____ at a lower cost than would be the case if they were produced using domestic resources, and the earnings from _____ help a nation pay for these lower cost (exports, imports) _____.

13. Another reason why governments interfere with free trade is based on (private, political) _____ considerations. Groups and industries seek protection from foreign competition through (GATT, tariffs) _____ and import (quotas, subsidies) _____, or other kinds of trade restrictions. The costs of trade protectionism are (clear to, hidden from) _____ consumers in the protected product so there is little opposition to demands for protectionism.

14. Tariffs and quotas (benefit, cost) _____ domestic firms in the protected industries, but _____ domestic consumers in the form of (lower, higher) _____ prices than would be the case if there were free trade. They also (benefit, cost) _____ domestic firms that use the protected goods as inputs in their production processes.

15. Until 1934, the trend of tariff rates in the United States was (upward, downward) _____. The trend has been (upward, downward) _____ since the 1934 passage of the (Smoot-Hawley Tariff, Reciprocal Trade Agreements) _____ Act. This act empowered the President to lower (tariffs, quotas) _____ by up to 50% in return for a reduction in foreign restrictions on U.S. goods and incorporated (quotas, most-favored-nation) _____ clauses in U.S. trade agreements.

16. The three cardinal principles established in the General Agreement on Tariffs and Trade of 1947 are

a. _____

b. _____

c. _____

17. The major provisions of the Uruguay Round of (NAFTA, GATT) _____ negotiations include (exchange rate, tariff) _____ reductions, coverage of legal, financial, and other (goods, services) _____ cuts in agricultural (import quotas, subsidies) _____, and protection of (collective, intellectual) _____ property against piracy. It also created the successor to GATT, called the (Reciprocal, World) _____ Trade Organization.

18. An example of a free-trade zone or trade bloc is the (Western, European) _____ Union.

a. The specific aims of the EU were the abolition of (capital and labor, tariffs and quotas) _____, the establishment of (common, different) _____ tariffs on goods imported from outside the EU, the (restricted, free) _____ movement of capital and labor within the EU, and common policies on other matters.

b. The EU created (small, large) _____ markets and stimulated production that has allowed industries to achieve (higher, lower) _____ costs. The economic effects of the EU on nonmember nations such as the United States are mixed because economic growth in the EU causes U.S. exports to the EU to (decrease, increase) _____ while the tariff barriers cause U.S. exports to _____.

c. The common currency of many of the member nations of the EU is called the (peso, euro) _____.

19. The North American Free Trade Agreement (NAFTA) formed a trade (barrier, bloc) _____ among the United States, Canada, and Mexico. This agreement eliminated (terms of trade, tariffs) _____ among the nations. Critics in the United States said that it would (increase, decrease) _____ jobs, but the evidence shows a(n) _____ in jobs and total output since its passage.

20. Many U.S. firms can (monopolize, compete) _____ and be successful in the global economy; however, some firms that benefited from past trade protection may find it difficult to adjust to global (control, competition) _____ and may go out of business.

■ **TRUE–FALSE QUESTIONS**

Circle T if the statement is true, F if it is false.

1. For the United States, the volume of international trade has been increasing relatively but not absolutely. **T F**

2. The U.S. economy's share of world trade has decreased since 1950. **T F**

3. The United States exports and imports goods and services with a dollar value greater than any other nation in the world. **T F**

4. The United States is dependent on trade for certain commodities that cannot be obtained in domestic markets. **T F**

5. Canada is the most important trading partner for the United States in terms of the volume of exports and imports. **T F**

6. If a person, firm, or region has a comparative advantage in the production of a particular commodity, it should specialize in the production of that commodity. **T F**

7. If one nation has a comparative advantage in the production of a commodity over another nation, then it has a higher opportunity cost of production relative to the other nation. **T F**

8. The economic effects of specialization and trade between nations are similar to increasing the quantity of resources or to achieving technological progress. **T F**

9. The interaction of the demand for, and supply of, Japanese yen will establish the dollar price of Japanese yen. **T F**

10. An increase in incomes in the United States would tend to cause the dollar price of the Japanese yen to fall. **T F**

11. When the dollar price of another nation's currency increases, there has been an appreciation in the value of the dollar. **T F**

12. When the dollar depreciates relative to the value of the currencies of the trading partners of the United States, then goods imported into the United States will tend to become more expensive. **T F**

13. Export subsidies are government payments to reduce the price of a product to buyers from other nations. **T F**

14. Nontariff barriers include excise taxes or duties placed on imported goods. **T F**

15. Through world trade, an economy can reach a point beyond its domestic production possibilities curve. **T F**

16. One reason that trade restrictions get public support is that the alleged benefits of the restrictions are often immediate and clear-cut, but the adverse affects are often obscure and dispersed over the economy. **T F**

17. Tariffs and quotas benefit domestic firms in the protected industries and also help domestic consumers by lowering the prices for those products. **T F**

18. The Smoot-Hawley Tariff Act of 1930 reduced tariffs in the United States to the lowest level ever in an attempt to pull the nation out of the Great Depression. **T F**

19. If the United States concludes a tariff agreement that lowers the tariff rates on goods imported from another nation, the lower tariff rates are then applied to those goods when they are imported from other nations with most-favored-nation (MFN) status. **T F**

20. The World Trade Organization (WTO) is the world's major advocate for trade protectionism. **T F**

21. The members of the European Union (EU) have experienced freer trade since it was formed. **T F**

22. The economic integration of nations creates larger markets for firms within the nations that integrate and makes it possible for these firms and their customers to benefit from the economies of large-scale (mass) production. **T F**

23. The formation of the European Union (EU) may make it more difficult for U.S. firms to compete for European customers with firms located within the Union. **T F**

24. The 1993 North American Free Trade Agreement (NAFTA) includes all Central American nations. **T F**

25. Major U.S. firms are unable to compete in global markets without significant protection from foreign competition. **T F**

■ **MULTIPLE-CHOICE QUESTIONS**

Circle the letter that corresponds to the best answer.

1. Which nation is the world's leading trading nation in terms of absolute volumes of imports and exports?
(a) Japan
(b) China
(c) Germany
(d) United States

2. Which nation is our most important trading partner in terms of the quantity of trade volume?
(a) Japan
(b) Canada
(c) Germany
(d) United Kingdom

3. Which of the following is true?
(a) Exports as a percentage of GDP are greatest in the United States.

(b) The United States is almost totally dependent on other nations for aircraft, machine tools, and coal.
(c) Most of the exports and imports trade of the United States is with industrially advanced nations.
(d) The United States has a trade surplus with Japan.

4. How is most of the trade deficit financed by a nation such as the United States?
(a) by buying securities or assets from other nations
(b) by selling securities or assets to other nations
(c) by borrowing from the Federal government
(d) by lending to the Federal government

5. Which is one way the United States finances its trade deficit?
(a) by lending to foreigners
(b) by selling real assets to foreigners
(c) by purchasing real assets from foreigners
(d) by passing protective tariffs on foreign products

6. Which factor has greatly facilitated international trade since World War II?
(a) greater import quotas
(b) expanded export subsidies
(c) increased nontariff barriers
(d) improved communications

7. Which industrializing nation would be considered one of the new participants in international trade?
(a) Canada
(b) Sweden
(c) Japan
(d) China

8. Why do nations specialize and engage in trade?
(a) to protect multinational corporations
(b) to increase output and income
(c) to improve communications
(d) to control other nations

Answer Questions 9, 10, 11, and 12 on the basis of the data given for two regions, Slobovia and Utopia, which have the following production possibilities tables.

SLOBOVIA PRODUCTION POSSIBILITIES TABLE

Product	Production alternatives					
	A	B	C	D	E	F
Cams	1,500	1,200	900	600	300	0
Widgets	0	100	200	300	400	500

UTOPIA PRODUCTION POSSIBILITIES TABLE

Product	Production alternatives				
	A	B	C	D	E
Cams	4,000	3,000	2,000	1,000	0
Widgets	0	200	400	600	800

9. In Slobovia, the comparative cost of
(a) 1 cam is 3 widgets
(b) 1 widget is .33 of a cam
(c) 1 cam is .33 of a widget
(d) 3 widgets is 1 cam

10. Which of the following statements is *not* true?

(a) Slobovia should specialize in the production of widgets.

(b) Slobovia has a comparative advantage in the production of widgets.

(c) Utopia should specialize in the production of widgets.

(d) Utopia has a comparative advantage in the production of cams.

11. The terms of trade will be

(a) greater than 7 cams for 1 widget

(b) between 7 cams for 1 widget and 5 cams for 1 widget

(c) between 5 cams for 1 widget and 3 cams for 1 widget

(d) less than 3 cams for 1 widget

12. Assume that if Slobovia did not specialize it would produce alternative C and that if Utopia did not specialize it would select alternative B. The gains from specialization are

(a) 100 cams and 100 widgets

(b) 200 cams and 200 widgets

(c) 400 cams and 500 widgets

(d) 500 cams and 400 widgets

13. If the dollar–yen exchange rate is $1 for 110 yen, then a Sony VCR priced at 27,500 yen would cost a U.S. consumer

(a) $200

(b) $250

(c) $275

(d) $300

14. If the equilibrium exchange rate changes so that the dollar price of Japanese yen increases

(a) the dollar has appreciated in value

(b) the dollar has depreciated in value

(c) U.S. citizens will be able to buy more Japanese goods

(d) Japanese citizens will be able to buy fewer U.S. goods

15. A decrease in the United States demand for Japanese goods will

(a) increase the demand for Japanese yen and increase the dollar price of yen

(b) increase the demand for Japanese yen but decrease the dollar price of yen

(c) decrease the demand for Japanese yen and decrease the dollar price of yen

(d) decrease the demand for Japanese yen but increase the dollar price of yen

16. If the exchange rate for one United States dollar changes from 1.0 euro to 1.1 euros, then there has been

(a) an appreciation in the value of the euro

(b) a depreciation in the value of the dollar

(c) a depreciation in the value of the euro

(d) an increase in the price of the euro

17. Which of the following is designed to restrict trade?

(a) GATT

(b) NAFTA

(c) import quotas

(d) multinational corporations

18. Why do governments often intervene in international trade?

(a) to expand a nation's production possibilities

(b) to improve the position of multinational corporations

(c) to protect domestic industries from foreign competition

(d) to increase revenue from tariff duties and excise taxes

19. Tariffs and quotas in a nation benefit domestic

(a) consumers and foreign producers of the protected product

(b) consumers and producers of the protected product

(c) producers of the protected product, but harm domestic consumers of the product

(d) producers and foreign producers of the product

20. Which one of the following specifically empowered the President of the United States to reduce tariff rates up to 50% if other nations would reduce their tariffs on American goods?

(a) the Smoot-Hawley Tariff Act of 1930

(b) the Reciprocal Trade Agreements Act of 1934

(c) the General Agreement on Tariffs and Trade of 1947

(d) North American Free Trade Agreement of 1993

21. Which of the following is characteristic of the General Agreement on Tariffs and Trade? Nations signing the agreement were committed to

(a) the expansion of import quotas

(b) the establishment of a world customs union

(c) the reciprocal increase in tariffs by negotiation

(d) the nondiscriminatory treatment of all member nations

22. One important outcome from the Uruguay Round of GATT was

(a) an increase in tariff barriers on services

(b) establishment of the World Trade Organization

(c) removal of voluntary export restraints in manufacturing

(d) abolishment of patent, copyright, and trademark protection

23. One of the potential problems with the European Union is that

(a) an unregulated free flow of labor and capital may reduce productivity

(b) economies of large-scale production may increase consumer prices

(c) tariffs may reduce trade with nonmember nations

(d) governments may have difficulty covering the shortfall from the elimination of duties and taxes

24. An example of the formation of a trade bloc would be the

(a) Smoot-Hawley Tariff Act

(b) North American Free Trade Agreement

(c) Reciprocal Trade Agreements Act

(d) General Agreement on Tariffs and Trade

25. The increase in global competition has resulted in:
(a) greater inefficiency among U.S. producers
(b) lower quality in the production of goods
(c) the inability of most U.S. firms to compete
(d) lower prices for many consumer goods and services

■ PROBLEMS

1. The following problem will help you understand the principle of comparative advantage and the benefits of specialization. A tailor named Hart has the production possibilities table for trousers and jackets as given. He chooses production alternative D.

HART'S PRODUCTION POSSIBILITIES TABLE

Product	Production alternatives					
	A	B	C	D	E	F
Trousers	75	60	45	30	15	0
Jackets	0	10	20	30	40	50

Another tailor, Schaffner, has the following production possibilities table and produces production alternative E.

SCHAFFNER'S PRODUCTION POSSIBILITIES TABLE

Product	Production alternatives						
	A	B	C	D	E	F	G
Trousers	60	50	40	30	20	10	0
Jackets	0	5	10	15	20	25	30

a. To Hart,

(1) the cost of one pair of trousers is _____ jackets

(2) the cost of one jacket is ____ pairs of trousers

b. To Schaffner,

(1) the cost of one pair of trousers is ____ jackets

(2) the cost of one jacket is ____ pairs of trousers

c. If Hart and Schaffner were to form a partnership to make suits,

(1) _____ should specialize in the making of trousers because he can make a pair of trousers at the cost of _____ of a jacket while it costs his partner _____ of a jacket to make a pair of trousers.

(2) _____ should specialize in the making of jackets because he can make a jacket at the cost of _____ pairs of trousers while it costs his partner _____ pairs of trousers to make a jacket.

d. Without specialization, Hart and Schaffner were able to make 50 pairs of trousers and 50 jackets. If each specializes completely in the item in the production in which he has a comparative advantage, their combined production will be _____ pairs of trousers and _____ jackets. Thus the gain from specialization is _____

_____.

e. When Hart and Schaffner come to divide the income of the partnership between them, the manufacture of a pair of trousers should be treated as the equivalent of from _____ to _____ jackets (or a jacket should be treated as the equivalent of from _____ to _____ pairs of trousers).

2. The countries of Lilliput and Brobdingnag have the production possibilities tables for apples and bananas shown below.

Note that the costs of producing apples and bananas are constant in both countries.

LILLIPUT PRODUCTION POSSIBILITIES TABLE

Product (lbs)	Production alternatives					
	A	B	C	D	E	F
Apples	40	32	24	16	8	0
Bananas	0	4	8	12	16	20

BROBDINGNAG PRODUCTION POSSIBILITIES TABLE

Product (lbs)	Production alternatives					
	A	B	C	D	E	F
Apples	75	60	45	30	15	0
Bananas	0	5	10	15	20	25

a. In Lilliput the cost of producing

(1) 8 apples is _____ bananas

(2) 1 apple is _____ bananas

b. In Brobdingnag the cost of producing

(1) 15 apples is _____ bananas

(2) 1 apple is _____ bananas

c. In Lilliput the cost of producing

(1) 4 bananas is _____ apples

(2) 1 banana is _____ apples

d. In Brobdingnag the cost of producing

(1) 5 bananas is _____ apples

(2) 1 banana is _____ apples

e. The cost of producing 1 apple is lower in the country of _____ and the cost of producing 1 banana is lower in the country of _____.

f. Lilliput has a comparative advantage in the production of _____ and Brobdingnag has a comparative advantage in the production of

_____.

g. The information in this problem is not sufficient to determine the exact terms of trade, but the terms of trade will be greater than _____ apples for 1 banana and less than _____ apples for 1 banana. Put another way, the terms of trade will be between _____ bananas for 1 apple and _____ bananas for 1 apple.

h. If neither nation could specialize, each would produce production alternative C. The combined production of apples in the two countries would be _____ apples and the combined production of bananas would be _____ bananas.

(1) If each nation specializes in producing the fruit for which it has a comparative advantage, their combined production will be _____ apples and _____ bananas.

(2) Their gain from specialization will be _____ apples and _____ bananas.

3. Use the following table that shows 10 different currencies and how much of each currency can be purchased with a U.S. dollar.

Currency per U.S. $				
Country	Currency	Year 1	Year 2	A or D
Brazil	Real	0.85	0.91	_____
Britain	Pound	0.65	0.59	_____
Canada	Dollar	1.41	1.51	_____
Switzerland	Franc	1.33	1.19	_____
Germany	Euro	1.58	1.69	_____
India	Rupee	31.39	34.55	_____
Japan	Yen	100.15	110.23	_____
Mexico	Peso	4.65	5.09	_____
Norway	Krone	6.88	6.49	_____
Thailand	Bhat	25.12	23.22	_____

a. In the far right column of the table, indicate whether the U.S. dollar has appreciated (**A**) or depreciated (**D**) from year 1 to year 2.

b. In year 1, a U.S. dollar would purchase _____ Swiss francs, but in year 2, it would purchase _____ Swiss francs. The U.S. dollar has (appreciated, depreciated) _____ against the Swiss franc from year 1 to year 2.

c. In year 1, a U.S. dollar would purchase _____ Japanese yen, but in year 2, it would purchase _____ Japanese yen. The U.S. dollar has (appreciated, depreciated) _____ against the Japanese yen from year 1 to year 2.

4. This problem asks you to calculate prices based on exchange rates. Use the data in the table for Problem 3 to answer the following items.

a. Using the exchange rates shown for year 1, what would be the U.S. dollar cost for the following products?

(1) Japanese television costing 30,000 yen.

$_____

(2) Swiss scarf costing 200 francs. $_____

(3) Thai artwork costing 3,768 bhats. $_____

(4) German auto costing 79,000 euros. $_____

(5) Mexican silver bracelet costing 1,376 pesos.

$_____

b. Using the exchange rates shown for year 2, what would be the U.S. dollar cost of the following products?
(1) Japanese television costing 30,000 yen.

$_____

(2) Swiss scarf costing 200 francs. $_____

(3) Thai artwork costing 3,768 bhats. $_____

(4) German auto costing 79,000 euros. $_____

(5) Mexican silver bracelet costing 1,376 pesos.

$_____

c. Indicate whether the U.S. dollar cost of each product in 4b has increased (+) or decreased (−) from year 1 to year 2. _____ _____ _____ _____ _____

d. What is the relationship between your answers in 4c to the ones you gave for the corresponding nations in 3a?

(1) When the U.S. dollar *appreciates* in value against a foreign currency, the U.S. dollar cost of a product from that nation will (increase, decrease) _____.

(2) When the U.S. dollar *depreciates* in value against a foreign currency, the U.S. dollar cost of a product from that nation will (increase, decrease) _____.

■ SHORT ANSWER AND ESSAY QUESTIONS

1. Describe the four major economic flows that link the United States to other nations.

2. In relative and absolute terms, how large is the volume of the international trade of the United States? What has happened to these figures over the past 40 or so years?

3. What are the principal exports and imports of the U.S. economy? What commodities used in the economy come almost entirely from abroad, and what American industries sell large percentages of their outputs abroad?

4. Which nations are the principal trading partners of the United States? How much of this trade is with the industrially advanced nations and how much of it is with the developing nations of the world?

5. Give several factors that have facilitated trade since World War II.

6. Who are the major participants in international trade? Describe the relative influence of the key players.

7. Use an example of two individuals to describe the basic principle of comparative advantage.

8. What is meant by comparative cost and comparative advantage?

9. Explain how comparative advantage determines the terms of trade between nations.

10. What is the gain for a nation that results from specialization in the production of products for which there is a comparative advantage?

11. Describe the characteristics of a foreign exchange market and of exchange rates. Why is an exchange rate an unusual price?

12. Illustrate with a supply and demand graph how equilibrium is determined in a dollar–yen market. Be sure to label axes and curves.

13. Why might an appreciation of the value of the U.S. dollar relative to the Japanese yen depress the U.S. economy and stimulate the Japanese economy? Why might a government intervene in the foreign exchange market and try to increase or decrease the value of its currency?

14. What are the major trade impediments and subsidies? How do they restrict international trade?

15. Why do governments intervene in international trade and develop restrictive trade policies?

16. What is the cost to society from trade protectionism? Who benefits and who is hurt by trade protectionism?

17. What was the Smoot-Hawley Tariff Act of 1930? What international trade problems are illustrated by this act?

18. Explain the basic provisions of the Reciprocal Trade Agreements Act of 1934.

19. What were the cardinal principles contained in the General Agreement on Tariffs and Trade (GATT)? What were the basic provisions and important results of the Uruguay Round of GATT negotiations?

20. Describe the purpose of the World Trade Organization (WTO). Why is it controversial?

21. What is the European Union? What has it achieved?

22. Discuss the potential effects of the European Union on the trade of the United States.

23. What is the euro and what are its likely economic effects?

24. What is the North American Free Trade Agreement (NAFTA)? What do its critics and defenders say about the agreement?

25. Evaluate the effects of increased global competition on U.S. firms, workers, and consumers.

ANSWERS

Chapter 6 The United States in the Global Economy

FILL-IN QUESTIONS

1. *a.* goods and services flows (trade flows); *b.* capital and labor flows (resource flows); *c.* information and technology flows; *d.* financial flows (any order for *a–d*)
2. limited, diversified, Netherlands, United States
3. 11–16, largest
4. industrially advanced, Canada, Japan
5. transportation, communications (any order), tariffs
6. United States, Japan (any order), multinational, increased, China
7. increase, increase
8. comparative advantage, opportunity cost

9. depreciation, appreciation, appreciation, depreciation
10. supply of, demand for, more
11. *a.* protective tariffs; *b.* import quotas; *c.* nontariff barriers; *d.* export subsidies
12. exports, imports, imports, exports, imports
13. political, tariffs, quotas, hidden from
14. benefit, cost, higher, cost
15. upward, downward, Reciprocal Trade Agreements, tariffs, most-favored-nation
16. *a.* equal, nondiscriminatory treatment of all member nations; *b.* reduction of tariffs by multilateral negotiations; *c.* elimination of import quotas
17. GATT, tariff, services, subsidies, intellectual, World
18. European; *a.* tariffs and quotas, common, free; *b.* large, lower, increase, decrease; *c.* euro
19. bloc, tariffs, decrease, increase
20. compete, competition

TRUE–FALSE QUESTIONS

1. F, p. 92	**10.** F, pp. 100–101	**19.** T, pp. 103–104
2. T, p. 92	**11.** F, pp. 100–101	**20.** F, p. 104
3. T, p. 92	**12.** T, pp. 100–101	**21.** T, pp. 104–105
4. T, pp. 92–93	**13.** T, p. 102	**22.** T, p. 105
5. T, p. 94	**14.** F, p. 102	**23.** T, p. 105
6. T, pp. 97–99	**15.** T, p. 102	**24.** F, p. 105
7. F, pp. 97–99	**16.** T, p. 102	**25.** F, pp. 106–107
8. T, pp. 98–99	**17.** F, pp. 102–103	
9. T, pp. 99–100	**18.** F, p. 103	

MULTIPLE-CHOICE QUESTIONS

1. d, p. 92	**10.** c, pp. 97–98	**19.** c, pp. 101–102
2. b, p. 94	**11.** c, p. 98	**20.** b, pp. 103–104
3. c, p. 94	**12.** a, pp. 98–99	**21.** d, p. 104
4. b, p. 94	**13.** b, p. 99	**22.** b, p. 104
5. b, p. 94	**14.** b, pp. 100–101	**23.** c, p. 105
6. d, pp. 95–96	**15.** c, pp. 100–101	**24.** b, p. 105
7. d, p. 95	**16.** c, pp. 100–101	**25.** d, pp. 106–107
8. b, p. 96	**17.** c, p. 102	
9. c, pp. 97–98	**18.** c, p. 102	

PROBLEMS

1. *a.* (1) .67, (2) 1.5; *b.* (1) .5, (2) 2; *c.* (1) Schaffner, .5, .67; (2) Hart, 1.5, 2; *d.* 60, 50, 10 pairs of trousers; *e.* .5, .67, 1.5, 2
2. *a.* (1) 4, (2) .5; *b.* (1) 5, (2) .33; *c.* (1) 8, (2) 2; *d.* (1) 15, (2) 3; *e.* Brobdingnag, Lilliput; *f.* bananas, apples; *g.* 2, 3, .33, .5; *h.* 69, 18, (1) 75, 20, (2) 6, 2
3. *a.* A, D, A, D, A, A, A, A, D, D; *b.* 1.33, 1.19, depreciated; *c.* 100.15, 110.23, appreciated
4. *a.* (1) 299.55 (2) 150.38 (3) 150 (4) 50,000 (5) 295.91; *b.* (1) 272.16 (2) 168.07 (3) 162.27 (4) 46,745.56 (5) 270.33; *c.* (1) − (2) + (3) + (4) − (5)−; *d.* (1) decrease (2) increase

SHORT ANSWER AND ESSAY QUESTIONS

1. pp. 91–92	**10.** pp. 98–99	**19.** p. 104
2. p. 92	**11.** pp. 99–100	**20.** p. 104
3. pp. 92–93	**12.** pp. 100–101	**21.** pp. 104–105
4. p. 94	**13.** pp. 100–101	**22.** p. 105
5. p. 95	**14.** pp. 101–102	**23.** p. 105
6. pp. 95–96	**15.** p. 102	**24.** p. 105
7. pp. 96–97	**16.** pp. 102–103	**25.** pp. 106–107
8. pp. 97–98	**17.** p. 103	
9. p. 98	**18.** pp. 103–104	

CHAPTER 7

Measuring Domestic Output and National Income

The subject of Chapter 7 is **national income accounting.** The first measure that you will learn about in the chapter is the **gross domestic product** (GDP). The GDP is an important economic statistic because it provides the best estimate of the total market value of all final goods and services produced by our economy in one year. You will also discover why GDP is a monetary measure that counts only the value of final goods and services and excludes nonproductive transactions such as secondhand sales.

National income accounting involves estimating output, or income, for the nation's society as a whole, rather than for an individual business firm or family. Note that the terms *"output"* and *"income"* are interchangeable because the nation's domestic output and its income are identical. The value of the nation's output equals the total expenditures for this output, and these expenditures become the income of those who have produced this output. Consequently, there are two equally acceptable methods—expenditures or income—for determining GDP.

From an *expenditure* perspective, GDP is composed of four expenditure categories: personal consumption expenditures (**C**), gross private domestic investment (I_g), government purchases (**G**), and net exports (X_n). These expenditures become income for people when they are paid out in the form of employee compensation, rents, interest, proprietors' income, and corporate profits, with adjustments made for indirect business taxes, depreciation, and net foreign factor income earned in the United States. In national income accounting, the amount spent to purchase this year's total output is equal to money income derived from production of this year's output.

This chapter also explains the relationship of GDP to other national accounts. These accounts include *net domestic product* (NDP), *national income* (NI) as derived from NDP, *personal income* (PI), and *disposable income* (DI). The relationship between GDP, NDP, NI, PI, and DI is shown in Table 7.4 of the text. The circular flow using the expenditures and income approaches to GDP are illustrated in Figure 7.3 of the text.

The next to the last section of the chapter shows you how to calculate *real* GDP from *nominal GDP*. This adjustment is important because nominal GDP is measured in monetary units, so if accurate comparisons are to be made for GDP over time, these monetary measures must be adjusted to take account of changes in the price level. A simple example is presented to show how a GDP price index is constructed. The index is then used to adjust *nominal GDP* to obtain *real GDP* and make correct GDP comparisons from one year to the next. The text also provides data for the U.S. economy so you can see why the calculation of real GDP is necessary and how it is used.

The last section of the chapter looks at the shortcomings of GDP as a measure of total output and economic well-being. You will learn about economic factors that are excluded from GDP measurement—nonmarket or illegal transactions, changes in leisure and product quality, differences in the composition and distribution of output, and the environmental effects of GDP production—and how their exclusion can lead to an under- or overstatement of economic well-being. Although national income accounts are not perfect measures of all economic conditions, they are still reasonably accurate and useful indicators of the performance of the national economy.

Chapter 7 is the essential background for Parts 2 and 3 of the text, which explain the history of and the factors that determine the level of domestic output and income in the economy. Chapter 7 is important because it explains the several methods used to measure the performance of the economy in a given year and to make the adjustments necessary to ensure accurate measurements of performance over time.

■ CHECKLIST

When you have studied this chapter you should be able to

☐ Identify three ways national income accounting can be used for economic decision making.
☐ Give a definition of the gross domestic product (GDP).
☐ Explain why GDP is a monetary measure.
☐ Describe how GDP measures value added and avoids multiple counting.
☐ Give examples of two types of nonproduction transactions that are excluded from GDP.
☐ Describe the relationship between the expenditures and income approaches to GDP accounting.
☐ List the three types of expenditures included in personal consumption expenditures (*C*).
☐ Identify three items included in gross private domestic investment (I_g).
☐ Explain why changes in inventories are an investment.
☐ Distinguish between gross and net investment.
☐ Discuss how differences in the amount of net investment affect the production capacity of the economy.
☐ List two components included in government purchases (*G*).

☐ Describe the meaning and calculation of net exports (X_n).

☐ Compute GDP using the expenditures approach when given national income accounting data.

☐ Identify the five income items that make up U.S. national income.

☐ List three things that can happen to corporate profits.

☐ Explain the adjustment of indirect business taxes to national income accounts.

☐ Define consumption of fixed capital and discuss how it affects national income accounts.

☐ Describe the effect of net foreign factor income on national income accounts.

☐ Compute GDP using the income approach when given national income accounting data.

☐ Define net domestic product (NDP).

☐ Show how to derive U.S. national income (NI) from net domestic product (NDP).

☐ Define personal income (PI) in national income accounts.

☐ Explain how to obtain disposable income (DI) from personal income (PI).

☐ Use Figure 7.3 in the text to describe the circular flow model for GDP.

☐ Distinguish between nominal and real GDP.

☐ Construct a price index when given the necessary price and quantity data.

☐ Obtain a price index when given data on nominal and real GDP.

☐ Discuss some real-world factors that affect the GDP price index.

☐ List seven shortcomings of GDP as a measure of total output and economic well-being.

■ **CHAPTER OUTLINE**

1. *National income accounting* consists of concepts that enable those who use them to measure the economy's output, to compare it with past outputs, to explain its size and the reasons for changes in its size, and to formulate policies designed to increase it.

2. The market value of all final goods and services produced in the economy during the year is measured by the *gross domestic product* (GDP).

    a. GDP is a *monetary measure* that is calculated in dollar terms rather than in terms of physical units of output.

    b. To avoid multiple counting, GDP includes only *final* goods and services (goods and services that will not be processed further during the *current* year).

    c. Nonproduction transactions are not included in GDP; purely financial transactions and secondhand sales are therefore excluded.

    d. Measurement of GDP can be accomplished by either the expenditures or the income method, but the same result is obtained by the two methods.

3. Computation of the GDP by the *expenditures approach* requires the summation of the total amounts of the four types of spending for final goods and services.

    a. *Personal consumption expenditures (C)* are the expenditures of households for *durable goods* and *nondurable goods* and for *services*.

    b. *Gross private domestic investment (I_g)* is the sum of the spending by business firms for machinery, equipment, and tools; spending by firms and households for new buildings; and the changes in the inventories of business firms.

    (1) A change in inventories is included in investment because it is the part of the output of the economy that was not sold during the year.

    (2) Investment does not include expenditures for stocks or bonds or for secondhand capital goods.

    (3) Gross investment exceeds net investment by the value of the capital goods worn out during the year. An economy in which net investment is positive is one with an expanding production capacity.

    c. *Government purchases (G)* are the expenditures made by all governments in the economy for products produced by business firms and for resource services from households. They include expenditures the government makes for products and services to provide public services, and spending for social capital (goods with a long lifetime such as highways).

    d. *Net exports (X_n)* in an economy equal the expenditures made by foreigners for goods and services produced in the economy less the expenditures made by the consumers, governments, and investors of the economy for goods and services produced in foreign nations.

    e. In equation form, $C + I_g + G + X_n = GDP$

4. Computation of GDP by the *income approach* requires adding the income derived from the production and sales of final goods and services. The five income items are

    a. Compensation of employees (the sum of wages and salaries *and* wage and salary supplements).

    b. Rents.

    c. Interest (only the interest payments made by business firms are included, and interest payments made by government are excluded).

    d. Proprietors' income (the profits or net income of unincorporated firms).

    e. Corporate profits which are subdivided into

    (1) Corporate income taxes

    (2) Dividends

    (3) Undistributed corporate profits.

    f. Three additions are made to the income side to balance it with expenditures.

    (1) Indirect business taxes are added because they are initially income that later gets paid to government.

    (2) Depreciation, or the consumption of fixed capital, is added because it is initially income to businesses that later gets deducted in calculating profits.

    (3) Net foreign factor income is added because it reflects income from all domestic output regardless of the foreign or domestic ownership of domestic resources.

5. In addition to GDP, *four other national income measures* are important in evaluating the performance of the economy. Each has a distinct definition and can be com-

puted by making additions to or deductions from another measure.

    a. NDP is the annual output of final goods and services over and above the capital goods worn out during the year. It is equal to the GDP minus depreciation (consumption of fixed capital).

    b. NI is the total income *earned* by U.S. owners of land and capital and by the U.S. suppliers of labor and entrepreneurial ability during the year. It equals NDP *minus* net foreign factor income earned in the United States and *minus* indirect business taxes.

    c. PI is the total income *received*—whether it is earned or unearned—by the households of the economy before the payment of personal taxes. It is found by *adding* transfer payments to and *subtracting* social security contributions, corporate income taxes, and undistributed corporate profits from the NI.

    d. DI is the total income available to households after the payment of personal taxes. It is equal to PI less personal taxes and also equal to personal consumption expenditures plus personal saving.

    e. The relations among the five income–output measures are summarized in Table 7.4.

    f. Figure 7.3 is a more realistic and complex circular flow diagram that shows the flows of expenditures and incomes among the households, business firms, and governments in the economy.

6. *Nominal GDP* is the total output of final goods and services produced by an economy in one year multiplied by the market prices when they were produced. Prices, however, change each year. To compare total output over time, nominal GDP is converted to **real GDP** to account for these price changes.

    a. There are two methods for deriving *real GDP* from *nominal GDP*. The first method involves computing a **price index.**

    (1) This index is a ratio of the price of a market basket in a given year to the price of the same market basket in a base year, with the ratio multiplied by 100.

    (2) To obtain real GDP, divide nominal GDP by the price index expressed in hundredths.

    b. In the second method, nominal GDP is broken down into prices and quantities for each year. Real GDP is found by using base-year prices and multiplying them by each year's physical quantities. The GDP price index for a particular year is the ratio of nominal to real GDP for that year.

    c. In the real world, complex methods are used to calculate the GDP price index. The price index is useful for calculating real GDP. The price index number for a reference period is arbitrarily set at 100.

    (1) For years when the price index is below 100, dividing nominal GDP by the price index (in hundredths) inflates nominal GDP to obtain real GDP.

    (2) For years when the price index is greater than 100, dividing nominal GDP by the price index (in hundredths) deflates nominal GDP to obtain real GDP.

7. GDP has shortcomings as a measure of total output and economic well-being.

    a. It excludes the value of final goods and services not bought and sold in the markets of the economy.

    b. It excludes the amount of leisure the citizens of the economy are able to have.

    c. It does not record the improvements in the quality of products that occur over the years.

    d. It does not measure the market value of the final goods and services produced in the underground sector of the economy.

    e. It does not record the pollution costs to the environment of producing final goods and services.

    f. It does not measure changes in the composition and the distribution of the domestic output.

    g. It does not measure noneconomic sources of well-being.

■ HINTS AND TIPS

1. Read through the chapter several times. A careful reading will enable you to avoid the necessity of memorizing. Begin by making sure you know precisely what GDP means and what is included in and excluded from its measurement.

2. Accounting is essentially an adding-up process. This chapter explains in detail and lists the items that must be added to obtain GDP by the *expenditures approach* or *income approach.* It is up to you to learn what to add on the expenditure side and what to add on the income side. Figure 7.1 is an important accounting reference for this task.

3. Changes in the price level have a significant effect on the measurement of GDP. Practice converting nominal GDP to real GDP using a price index. Problems 4 and 5 in this *Study Guide* should help you understand nominal and real GDP and the conversion process.

4. GDP is a good measure of the market value of the output of final goods and services that are produced in an economy in 1 year; however, the measure is not perfect, so you should be aware of its limitations, which are noted at the end of the chapter.

■ IMPORTANT TERMS

national income accounting	government purchases (*G*)
price level	net exports (*X_n*)
gross domestic product (GDP)	national income (NI)
intermediate goods	indirect business taxes
final goods	consumption of fixed capital (depreciation)
multiple counting	
value added	net domestic product (NDP)
expenditures approach	
income approach	personal income (PI)
personal consumption expenditures (*C*)	disposable income (DI)
gross private domestic investment (*I_g*)	nominal GDP
	real GDP
net private domestic investment	price index

SELF-TEST

■ **FILL-IN QUESTIONS**

1. National income accounting is valuable because it provides a means of keeping track of the level of (unemployment, production) _____ in the economy and the course it has followed over the long run and the information needed to make public (policies, payments) _____ that will improve the performance of the economy.

2. Gross domestic product (GDP) measures the total (market, nonmarket) _____ value of all (intermediate, final) _____ goods and services produced in a country (in 1 year, over 2 years) _____.

3. GDP for a country includes goods and services produced (within, outside) _____ its geographic boundaries and (does, does not) _____ treat resources supplied by U.S. citizens differently from resources supplied by citizens of other countries.

4. GDP is a (monetary, nonmonetary) _____ measure that permits comparison of the (relative, absolute) _____ worth of goods and services.

5. In measuring GDP, only (intermediate, final) _____ goods and services are included; if _____ goods and services were included, the accountant would be (over-, under-) _____ stating GDP, or (single, multiple) _____ counting.

6. A firm buys materials for $2000 from other firms in the economy and produces from them a product that sells for $3015. The value added by the firm is ($1015, $2000, $3015) _____.

7. GDP accounting excludes (production, nonproduction) _____ transactions. These include (financial, nonfinancial) _____ transactions such as public or private transfer payments or the sale of securities, and (first-, second-) _____ hand sales.

8. Personal consumption expenditures are the expenditures of households for goods such as automobiles, which are (durable, nondurable) _____, and goods such as food, which are _____, plus expenditures for (housing, services) _____.

9. Gross private domestic investment basically includes the final purchases of (capital, consumer) _____ goods by businesses, all (construction of new, sales of existing) _____ buildings and houses, and changes in (services, inventories) _____.

10. The difference between gross and net private domestic investment is equal to (depreciation, net exports) _____, or the (production, consumption) _____ of fixed capital.

11. If gross private domestic investment is greater than depreciation, net private domestic investment is (positive, negative) _____ and the production capacity of the economy is (declining, expanding) _____.

12. An economy's *net* exports equal its exports (minus, plus) _____ its imports. If exports are less than imports, net exports are (positive, negative) _____, but if exports are greater than imports, net exports are _____.

13. Using the expenditure approach, the GDP equation equals ($NDP + NI + PI, C + I_g + G + X_n$) _____.

14. The compensation of employees in the system of social accounting consists of actual wages and salaries (plus, minus) _____ wage and salary supplements. Salary supplements are the payments employers make to social security or (public, private) _____ insurance programs and to _____ pension, health, and welfare funds.

15. Corporate profits are disposed of in three ways: corporate income (taxes, interest) _____, (depreciation, dividends) _____, and undistributed corporate (taxes, profits) _____.

16. Three adjustments are added to national income to obtain (GDP, DI) _____. They are (direct, indirect) _____ business taxes, the consumption of (variable, fixed) _____ capital, and (gross, net) _____ foreign factor income earned in the United States.

17. Gross domestic product overstates the economy's production because it fails to make allowance for (multiple counting, depreciation) _____ or the need to replace (consumer, capital) _____ goods. When this adjustment is made, the calculations produce (net domestic product, national income) _____.

18. National income is equal to net domestic product (plus, minus) _____ indirect business taxes plus (gross, net) _____ foreign factor income earned in the United States.

19. Personal income equals national income (plus, minus)

_____ transfer payments _____ the sum of social security contributions, corporate income taxes, and undistributed corporate profits.

20. Disposable income equals (national, personal) _____ income (plus, minus) _____ personal taxes.

21. A GDP that reflects the prices prevailing when the output is produced is called unadjusted or (nominal, real) _____ GDP, but a GDP figure that is deflated or inflated for price level changes is called adjusted or _____ GDP.

22. To calculate a price index in a given year, the combined price of a market basket of goods and services in that year is (divided, multiplied) _____ by the combined price of the market basket in the base year. The result is then _____ by 100.

23. Real GDP is calculated by dividing (the price index, nominal GDP) _____ by _____.

24. The price index expressed in hundredths is calculated by dividing (real, nominal) _____ GDP by _____ GDP.

25. For several reasons, GDP has shortcomings as a measure of total output or economic well-being.
  a. It does not include the (market, nonmarket) _____ transactions that result in the production of goods and services or the amount of (work, leisure) _____ of participants in the economy.
  b. It fails to record improvements in the (quantity, quality) _____ of the products produced, or the changes in the (level, composition) _____, and distribution of the economy's total output.
  c. It does not take into account the undesirable effects of GDP production on the (government, environment) _____ or the goods and services produced in the (market, underground) _____ economy.

■ **TRUE–FALSE QUESTIONS**

Circle T if the statement is true, F if it is false.

1. National income accounting allows us to assess the performance of the economy and make policies to improve that performance. **T F**

2. Gross domestic product measures at their market values the total output of all goods and services produced in the economy during a year. **T F**

3. GDP is simply a count of the quantity of output and is not a monetary measure. **T F**

4. The total market value of the wine produced in the United States during a year is equal to the number of bottles of wine produced in that year multiplied by the (average) price at which a bottle sold during that year. **T F**

5. GDP includes the sale of intermediate goods and excludes the sale of final goods. **T F**

6. The total value added to a product and the value of the final product are equal. **T F**

7. Social security payments and other public transfer payments are counted as part of GDP. **T F**

8. The sale of stocks and bonds is excluded from GDP. **T F**

9. In computing gross domestic product, private transfer payments are excluded because they do not represent payments for currently produced goods and services. **T F**

10. The two approaches to the measurement of the gross domestic product yield identical results because one approach measures the total amount spent on the products produced by business firms during a year while the second approach measures the total income of business firms during the year. **T F**

11. Personal consumption expenditures only include expenditures for durable and nondurable goods. **T F**

12. The expenditure made by a household to have a new home built is a personal consumption expenditure. **T F**

13. In national income accounting, any increase in the inventories of business firms is included in gross private domestic investment. **T F**

14. If gross private domestic investment is greater than depreciation during a given year, the economy's production capacity has declined during that year. **T F**

15. Government purchases include spending by all units of government on the finished products of business, but exclude all direct purchases of resources such as labor. **T F**

16. The net exports of an economy equal its exports of goods and services less its imports of goods and services. **T F**

17. The income approach to GDP includes compensation of employees, rents, interest income, proprietors' income, and corporate profits. **T F**

18. Indirect business taxes are the difference between gross private domestic investment and net private domestic investment. **T F**

19. Net foreign factor income is the difference between the earnings of foreign-owned resources in the United States and the earnings from U.S.-supplied resources abroad. **T F**

20. A GDP that has been deflated or inflated to reflect changes in the price level is called real GDP. **T F**

21. To adjust nominal GDP for a given year to obtain real GDP, it is necessary to multiply nominal GDP by the price index (expressed in hundredths) for that year. **T F**

22. If nominal GDP for an economy is $11,000 billion and the price index is 110, then real GDP is $10,000 billion. **T F**

23. GDP is a precise measure of the economic well-being of society. **T F**

24. The productive services of a homemaker are included in GDP. **T F**

25. The spillover costs from pollution and other activities associated with the production of the GDP are deducted from total output. **T F**

■ **MULTIPLE-CHOICE QUESTIONS**

Circle the letter that corresponds to the best answer.

1. Which is a primary use for national income accounting?
(a) It provides a basis for assessing the performance of the economy.
(b) It measures economic efficiency in specific industries.
(c) It estimates expenditures on nonproduction transactions.
(d) It analyzes the cost of pollution to the economy.

2. Gross domestic product (GDP) is defined as
(a) personal consumption expenditures and gross private domestic investment
(b) the sum of wage and salary compensation of employees, corporate profits, and interest income
(c) the market value of final goods and services produced within a country in 1 year
(d) the market value of all final and intermediate goods and services produced by the economy in 1 year

3. GDP provides an indication of society's valuation of the relative worth of goods and services because it
(a) provides an estimate of the value of secondhand sales
(b) gives increased weight to security transactions
(c) is an estimate of income received
(d) is a monetary measure

4. To include the value of the parts used in producing the automobiles turned out during a year in gross domestic product for that year would be an example of
(a) including a nonmarket transaction
(b) including a nonproduction transaction
(c) including a noninvestment transaction
(d) multiple counting

5. Which of the following is a public transfer payment?
(a) the sale of a used (secondhand) toy house at a garage sale
(b) the sale of shares of stock in Microsoft Corporation
(c) the Social Security benefits sent to a retired worker
(d) the birthday gift of a check for $50 sent by a grandmother to her grandchild

6. The sale in year 2 of an automobile produced in year 1 would not be included in the gross domestic product for year 2; doing so would involve
(a) including a nonmarket transaction
(b) including a nonproduction transaction
(c) including a noninvestment transaction
(d) public transfer payments

7. The service a babysitter performs when she stays at home with her baby brother while her parents are out and for which she receives no payment is not included in the gross domestic product because
(a) this is a nonmarket transaction
(b) this is a nonproduction transaction
(c) this is a noninvestment transaction
(d) multiple counting would be involved

8. According to national income accounting, money income derived from the production of this year's output is equal to
(a) corporate profits and indirect business taxes
(b) the amount spent to purchase this year's total output
(c) the sum of interest income and the compensation of employees
(d) gross private domestic investment less the consumption of fixed capital

9. Which would be considered an investment according to economists?
(a) the purchase of newly issued shares of stock in Microsoft
(b) the construction of a new computer chip factory by Intel
(c) the resale of stock originally issued by the General Motors Corporation
(d) the sale of a retail department store building by Sears to JCPenney

10. A refrigerator was produced by its manufacturer in year 1, sold to a retailer in year 1, and sold by the retailer to a final consumer in year 2. The refrigerator was
(a) counted as consumption in year 1
(b) counted as savings in year 1
(c) counted as investment in year 1
(d) not included in the gross domestic product of year 1

11. If gross private domestic investment is greater than depreciation, the economy will most likely be
(a) static
(b) expanding
(c) declining
(d) experiencing inflation

12. The annual charge that estimates the amount of capital equipment used up in each year's production is called
(a) indirect business taxes
(b) inventory reduction
(c) depreciation
(d) investment

13. GDP in an economy is $3452 billion. Consumer expenditures are $2343 billion, government purchases are $865 billion, and gross investment is $379 billion. Net exports are
(a) +$93 billion
(b) +$123 billion
(c) −$45 billion
(d) −$135 billion

14. The income approach to GDP sums the total income earned by U.S. resource suppliers, adds net foreign factor income earned in the United States, and also adds two adjustments:
(a) net investment and the consumption of fixed capital
(b) the consumption of fixed capital and indirect business taxes
(c) indirect business taxes and undistributed corporate profits
(d) undistributed corporate profits and financial transactions

15. What can happen to the allocation of corporate profits?
(a) It is paid to proprietors as income.
(b) It is paid to to stockholders as dividends.
(c) It is paid to the government as interest income.
(d) It is retained by the corporation as rents.

Questions 16 through 22 use the national income accounting data given in the following table.

	Billions of dollars
Net private domestic investment	$ 32
Personal taxes	39
Transfer payments	19
Indirect business taxes	8
Corporate income taxes	11
Personal consumption expenditures	217
Consumption of fixed capital	7
U.S. exports	15
Dividends	15
Government purchases	51
Net foreign factor income earned in the U.S.	0
Undistributed corporate profits	10
Social Security contributions	4
U.S. imports	17

16. Gross private domestic investment is equal to
(a) $32 billion
(b) $39 billion
(c) $45 billion
(d) $56 billion

17. Net exports are equal to
(a) −$2 billion
(b) $2 billion
(c) −$32 billion
(d) $32 billion

18. The gross domestic product is equal to
(a) $298 billion
(b) $302 billion
(c) $317 billion
(d) $305 billion

19. Corporate profits are equal to
(a) $15 billion
(b) $25 billion
(c) $26 billion
(d) $36 billion

20. The net domestic product is equal to
(a) $298 billion
(b) $302 billion
(c) $317 billion
(d) $321 billion

21. National income is equal to
(a) $245 billion
(b) $278 billion
(c) $290 billion
(d) $310 billion

22. Personal income is equal to
(a) $266 billion
(b) $284 billion
(c) $290 billion
(d) $315 billion

23. If both nominal gross domestic product and the level of prices are rising, it is evident that
(a) real GDP is constant
(b) real GDP is rising but not so rapidly as prices
(c) real GDP is declining
(d) no conclusion can be drawn concerning the real GDP of the economy on the basis of this information

24. Suppose nominal GDP rose from $500 billion to $600 billion while the GDP price index increased from 125 to 150. The real GDP
(a) remained constant
(b) increased
(c) decreased
(d) cannot be calculated from these figures

25. In an economy, the total expenditure for a market basket of goods in year 1 (the base year) was $4000 billion. In year 2, the total expenditure for the same market basket of goods was $4500 billion. What was the GDP price index for the economy in year 2?
(a) .88
(b) 1.13
(c) 188
(d) 113

26. Nominal GDP is less than real GDP in an economy in year 1. In year 2, nominal GDP is equal to real GDP. In year 3, nominal GDP is slightly greater than real GDP. In year 4, nominal GDP is significantly greater than real GDP. Which year is most likely to be the base year that is being used to calculate the price index for this economy?
(a) 1
(b) 2
(c) 3
(d) 4

27. Nominal GDP was $3774 billion in year 1 and the GDP deflator was 108 and nominal GDP was $3989 in year 2 and the GDP deflator that year was 112. What was real GDP in years 1 and 2, respectively?

(a) $3494 billion and $3562 billion
(b) $3339 billion and $3695 billion
(c) $3595 billion and $3725 billion
(d) $3643 billion and $3854 billion

28. A price index one year was 145, and the next year it was 167. What is the approximate percentage change in the price level from one year to the next as measured by that index?

(a) 12%
(b) 13%
(c) 14%
(d) 15%

29. GDP accounting includes

(a) the goods and services produced in the underground economy
(b) expenditures for equipment to reduce the pollution of the environment
(c) the value of the leisure enjoyed by citizens
(d) the goods and services produced but not bought and sold in the markets of the economy

30. Which is a major reason why GDP is *not* an accurate index of society's economic well-being?

(a) It includes changes in the value of leisure.
(b) It excludes many improvements in product quality.
(c) It includes transactions from the underground economy.
(d) It excludes transactions from the buying and selling of stocks.

■ **PROBLEMS**

1. Following are national income accounting figures for the United States.

	Billions of dollars
Exports	$ 367
Dividends	60
Consumption of fixed capital	307
Compensation of employees	1722
Government purchases	577
Rents	33
Indirect business taxes	255
Gross private domestic investment	437
Corporate income taxes	88
Transfer payments	320
Interest	201
Proprietors' income	132
Personal consumption expenditures	1810
Imports	338
Social Security contributions	148
Undistributed corporate profits	55
Personal taxes	372
Net foreign factor income earned in the U.S.	0

a. In the following table, use any of these figures to prepare an income statement for the economy similar to the one found in Table 7.3 of the text.

Receipts: Expenditures approach		Allocations: Income approach	
Item	Amount	Item	Amount
_____	$_____	_____	$_____
_____	$_____	_____	$_____
_____	$_____	_____	$_____
_____	$_____	_____	$_____
		_____	$_____
		_____	$_____
		_____	$_____
		National income	$_____
		_____	$_____
		_____	$_____
		_____	$_____
Gross domestic product	$_____	Gross domestic product	$_____

b. Use the other national accounts to find

(1) Net domestic product is $_____

(2) National income is $_____

(3) Personal income is $_____

(4) Disposable income is $_____

2. A farmer owns a plot of ground and sells the right to pump crude oil from his land to a crude oil producer. The crude oil producer agrees to pay the farmer $20 a barrel for every barrel pumped from the farmer's land.

a. During one year 10,000 barrels are pumped.

(1) The farmer receives a payment of $_____ from the crude oil producer.

(2) The value added by the farmer is $_____.

b. The crude oil producer sells the 10,000 barrels pumped to a petroleum refiner at a price of $25 a barrel.

(1) The crude oil producer receives a payment of

$_____ from the refiner.

(2) The value added by the crude oil producer is

$_____.

c. The refiner employs a pipeline company to transport the crude oil from the farmer's land to the refinery and pays the pipeline company a fee of $1 a barrel for the oil transported.

(1) The pipeline company receives a payment of

$_____ from the refiner.

(2) The value added by the company is $_____.

d. From the 10,000 barrels of crude oil, the refiner produces 315,000 gallons of gasoline and various by-products which are sold to distributors and gasoline service stations at an average price of $1 per gallon.

(1) The total payment received by the refiner from its

customers is $_____.

(2) The value added by the refiner is $_____ .

e. The distributors and service stations sell the 315,000 gallons of gasoline and by-products to consumers at an average price of $1.30 a gallon.

(1) The total payment received by distributors and service stations is $_____ .

(2) The value added by them is $_____ .

f. The total value added by the farmer, crude oil producer, pipeline company, refiner, and distributors and service stations is $_____ , and the market value of the gasoline and by-products (the final good) is $_____ .

3. Following is a list of items which may or may not be included in the five income—output measures of the national income accounts (**GDP, NDP, NI, PI, DI**). Indicate in the space to the right of each which of the income—output measures includes this item; it is possible for the item to be included in none, one, two, three, four, or all of the measures. If the item is included in none of the measures, indicate why it is not included.

a. Interest on the national debt _____

_____

b. The sale of a used computer _____
c. The production of shoes that are not sold by the manufacturer _____

d. The income of a dealer in illegal drugs _____
e. The purchase of a share of common stock on the New York Stock Exchange _____
f. The interest paid on the bonds of the General Motors Corporation _____

g. The labor performed by a homemaker _____

h. The labor performed by a paid babysitter _____
i. The monthly check received by a college student from her parents _____

j. The purchase of a new tractor by a farmer _____

k. The labor performed by an assembly line worker in repapering his own kitchen _____

l. The services of a lawyer _____

m. The purchase of shoes from the manufacturer by a shoe retailer _____

n. The monthly check received from the Social Security Administration by a college student whose parents have died _____

o. The rent a homeowner would receive if she did not live in her own home _____

4. Following is hypothetical data for a market basket of goods in year 1 and year 2 for an economy.
a. Compute the expenditures for year 1.

MARKET BASKET FOR YEAR 1 (BASE YEAR)

Products	Quantity	Price	Expenditures
Toys	3	$10	$_____
Pencils	5	2	$_____
Books	7	5	$_____
Total			$_____

b. Compute the expenditures for year 2.

MARKET BASKET FOR YEAR 2

Products	Quantity	Price	Expenditures
Toys	3	$11	$_____
Pencils	5	3	$_____
Books	7	6	$_____
Total			$_____

c. In the space below, show how you computed the GDP price index for year 2.

_____

5. The following table shows nominal GDP figures for 3 years and the price indices for each of the 3 years. (The GDP figures are in billions.)

Year	Nominal GDP	Price index	Real GDP
1929	$104	121	$_____
1933	56	91	$_____
1939	91	100	$_____

a. Use the price indices to compute the real GDP in each year. (You may round your answers to the nearest billion dollars.) Write answers in the table.
b. Which of the 3 years appears to be the base year?

_____
c. Between
(1) 1929 and 1933 the economy experienced (inflation, deflation) _____ .

(2) 1933 and 1939 it experienced _____ .
d. The nominal GDP figure
(1) for 1929 was (deflated, inflated, neither) _____

_____

(2) for 1933 was _____ .

(3) for 1939 was _____ .
e. The price level

(1) fell by _____ % from 1929 to 1933.

(2) rose by _____ % from 1933 to 1939.

■ **SHORT ANSWER AND ESSAY QUESTIONS**

1. Of what use is national income accounting to economists and policymakers?

2. What is the definition of GDP? How are the values of output produced at a U.S.-owned factory in the United

States and a foreign-owned factory in the United States treated in GDP accounting?

3. Why is GDP a monetary measure?

4. How does GDP accounting avoid multiple counting and exaggeration of the value of GDP?

5. Why does GDP accounting exclude nonproduction transactions?

6. What are the two principal types of nonproduction transactions? List examples of each type.

7. What are the two sides to GDP accounting? What are the meaning and relationship between the two sides?

8. What would be included in personal consumption expenditures by households?

9. How is gross private domestic investment defined?

10. Is residential construction counted as investment or consumption? Explain.

11. Why is a change in inventories an investment?

12. How do you define an expanding production capacity using the concepts of gross private domestic investment and depreciation?

13. What do government purchases include and what do they exclude?

14. How are imports and exports handled in GDP accounting?

15. What are five income components of GDP that add up to national income? Define and explain the characteristics of each component.

16. What are three adjustments made to the income approach to GDP accounting to get it to balance with expenditures? Define and explain the characteristics of each one.

17. Explain how to calculate net domestic product (NDP), national income (NI), personal income (PI), and disposable income (DI).

18. What is the difference between real and nominal GDP? Describe two methods economists use to determine real GDP. Illustrate each method with an example.

19. Describe the real-world relationship between nominal and real GDP in the United States. Explain why nominal GDP may be greater or less than real GDP depending on the year or period selected.

20. Why might GDP not be considered an accurate measure of total output and the economic well-being of society? identify seven shortcomings of GDP.

ANSWERS

Chapter 7 Measuring Domestic Output and National Income

FILL-IN QUESTIONS

1. production, policies
2. market, final, in one year
3. within, does not
4. monetary, relative
5. final, intermediate, over, multiple
6. $1015
7. nonproduction, financial, second
8. durable, nondurable, services
9. capital, construction of new, inventories
10. depreciation, consumption
11. positive, expanding
12. minus, negative, positive
13. $C + I_g + G + X_n$
14. plus, public, private
15. taxes, dividends, profits
16. GDP, indirect, fixed, net
17. depreciation, capital, net domestic product
18. minus, net
19. plus, minus
20. personal, minus
21. nominal, real
22. divided, multiplied
23. nominal GDP, the price index
24. nominal, real
25. *a.* nonmarket, leisure; *b.* quality, composition; *c.* environment, underground

TRUE–FALSE QUESTIONS

1. T, p. 112	11. F, p. 115	21. F, pp. 124–125
2. F, pp. 112–113	12. F, pp. 115–116	22. T, pp. 124–125
3. F, p. 113	13. T, pp. 115–116	23. F, pp. 124–126
4. T, p. 113	14. F, p. 116	24. F, p. 125
5. F, p. 113	15. F, pp. 116–117	25. F, p. 126
6. T, p. 113	16. T, p. 117	
7. F, pp. 113–114	17. T, pp. 117–118	
8. T, p. 114	18. F, p. 119	
9. T, p. 114	19. T, p. 119	
10. F, pp. 114–115	20. T, pp. 123–124	

MULTIPLE-CHOICE QUESTIONS

1. a, p. 112	11. b, p. 116	21. c, p. 120
2. c, pp. 112–113	12. c, p. 116	22. b, pp. 120–121
3. d, p. 113	13. d, p. 117	23. d, pp. 124–125
4. d, p. 113	14. b, pp. 117–118	24. a, pp. 124–125
5. c, p. 114	15. b, p. 118	25. d, pp. 123–124
6. b, p. 114	16. b, pp. 115–117	26. b, pp. 124–125
7. a, pp. 114, 125	17. a, p. 117	27. a, pp. 124–125
8. b, p. 115	18. d, pp. 115–117	28. d, p. 124
9. b, pp. 115–116	19. d, p. 118	29. b, pp. 125–126
10. c, pp. 115–116	20. a, p. 120	30. b, pp. 125–126

PROBLEMS

1. *a.* See the following table; *b.* (1) 2546, (2) 2291, (3) 2320, (4) 1948

Receipts: Expenditures approach		Allocations: Income approach	
Personal consumption expenditures	$1810	Compensation of employees	$1722
Gross private domestic investment	437	Rents	33
		Interest	201
		Proprietors' income	132
Government purchases	577	Corporate income taxes	88
Net exports	29	Dividends	60
		Undistributed corporate profit	55
		National income	$2291
		Indirect business taxes	255
		Consumption of fixed capital	307
		Net foreign factor income earned in the U.S.	0
Gross domestic product	$2853	Gross domestic product	$2853

2. *a.* (1) 200,000, (2) 200,000; *b.* (1) 250,000, (2) 50,000; *c.* (1) 10,000, (2) 10,000; *d.* (1) 315,000, (2) 55,000; *e.* (1) 409,500, (2) 94,500; *f.* 409,500, 409,500

3. *a.* personal income and disposable income, a public transfer payment; *b.* none, a secondhand sale; *c.* all, represents investment (additions to inventories); *d.* none, illegal production and incomes are not included if not reported; *e.* none, a purely financial transaction; *f.* all; *g.* none, a nonmarket transaction; *h.* all if reported as income, none if not reported; *i.* none, a private transfer payment; *j.* all; *k.* none, a nonmarket transaction; *l.* all; *m.* all, represents additions to the inventory of the retailer; *n.* personal income and disposable income, a public transfer payment; *o.* all, estimate of rental value of owner-occupied homes is included in rents as if it were income and in personal consumption expenditures as if it were payment for a service

4. *a.* 30, 10, 35, 75; *b.* 33, 15, 42, 90; *c.* ($90/$75) 100 = 120

5. *a.* 86, 62, 91; *b.* 1939; *c.* (1) deflation, (2) inflation; *d.* (1) deflated, (2) inflated, (3) neither; *e.* (1) 24.8 (2) 9.9

SHORT ANSWER AND ESSAY QUESTIONS

1. p. 112
2. pp. 112–113
3. p. 113
4. p. 113
5. pp. 113–114
6. pp. 113–114
7. pp. 114–115
8. p. 115
9. pp. 115–116
10. pp. 115–116
11. pp. 115–116
12. p. 116
13. p. 116
14. p. 117
15. p. 118
16. p. 119
17. pp. 120–121
18. pp. 123–124
19. pp. 124–125
20. pp. 125–126

CHAPTER 8

Introduction to Economic Growth and Instability

The economic health of a nation relies on **economic growth** because it reduces the burden of scarcity. Small differences in real growth rates result in large differences in the standards of living in nations. The first short section of the chapter introduces you to this important concept and identifies the two main sources of growth. It also presents data on the long-term growth record of the United States.

This record has been interrupted by periods of economic instability, a topic that is the major focus of the chapter. The second section of the chapter discusses the **business cycle:** the ups and downs in the employment of labor and real output of the economy that occur over the years. What may not be immediately evident to you, but will become clear as you read this chapter, is that these alternating periods of prosperity and hard times have taken place over a long period in which the trends in real output, employment, and the standard of living have been upward. During this long history booms and busts have occurred quite irregularly; their duration and intensity have been so varied that it is better to think of them as economic instability rather than regular business cycles.

Two principal problems result from the instability of the economy. The first problem is described in the third section of the chapter. Here you will find an examination of the **unemployment** that accompanies a downturn in the level of economic activity in the economy. You will first learn how economists measure the unemployment rate in the economy and the problems they encounter. You will also discover that there are three different kinds of unemployment, and that full employment means that less than 100% of the labor force is employed. You will also find out how unemployment imposes an economic cost on the economy and this cost is unequally distributed among different groups in our society.

The second major problem that results from economic instability is **inflation.** It is examined in the fourth section of the chapter, and also in the following two sections. Inflation is an increase in the general (or average) level of prices in an economy. It does not have a unique cause: It may result from increases in demand, from increases in costs, or from both sources.

Regardless of its cause, inflation may impose a real hardship on different groups in our society as you will learn in the fifth section of the chapter. **Inflation arbitrarily redistributes real income and wealth** in the economy. Unanticipated inflation hurts those on fixed incomes, those who save money, and those who lend money. If inflation is anticipated some of its burden can be reduced, but that depends on whether a group can protect their income with cost-of-living or interest rate adjustments.

Finally, inflation has redistribution effects on the real output of the economy as described in the last section of the chapter. **Cost-push inflation** and **demand-pull inflation** have different effects on output and employment that vary with the severity of the inflation. In the extreme, an economy can experience very high rates of inflation—**hyperinflation**—that can result in its breakdown.

Understanding the basics of economic growth and the twin problems of unemployment and inflation are important because it prepares you for later chapters and the explanations of how the macroeconomy works.

■ **CHECKLIST**

When you have studied this chapter you should be able to

☐ Define economic growth in two different ways.
☐ Explain why economic growth is an important goal.
☐ Describe how different growth rates affect real domestic output over time.
☐ Identify the two main sources of economic growth and indicate their relative importance.
☐ Describe the growth record of the U.S. economy since 1940, its rates of economic growth since 1950, and several qualifications to this record.
☐ Explain what the business cycle means.
☐ Describe the four phases of a generalized business cycle.
☐ Identify the immediate case of the cyclical changes in the levels of real output and employment.
☐ Explain differences in the way cyclical fluctuations affect industries producing capital and consumer durable goods, and how they affect those producing consumer nondurable goods and services.
☐ Describe how the Bureau of Labor Statistics (BLS) measures the rate of unemployment, and list the two criticisms of their survey data.
☐ Distinguish among frictional, structural, and cyclical types of unemployment, and explain the causes of these three kinds of unemployment.
☐ Define full employment and the full-employment unemployment rate (the natural rate of unemployment).
☐ Identify the economic and noneconomic costs of unemployment.
☐ Define the GDP gap and state Okun's law.
☐ Discuss the unequal burdens of unemployment.

☐ Define inflation and the rate of inflation.

☐ Explain how inflation is measured with the Consumer Price Index.

☐ Make international comparisons of inflation rate and unemployment rate data.

☐ Define demand-pull inflation.

☐ Define cost-push inflation and its relation to per-unit production costs.

☐ Describe the complexities involved in distinguishing between demand-pull and cost-push inflation.

☐ Distinguish between real and nominal income and calculate real income when given data on nominal income and the price level.

☐ List groups that are hurt by and groups that are unaffected or benefit from unanticipated inflation.

☐ Describe how the redistributive effects of inflation are changed when it is anticipated.

☐ Explain the difference between the real and the nominal interest rates.

☐ Make three final points about the redistribution effects of inflation.

☐ Describe the effect of cost-push inflation on real output.

☐ Explain the contrasting views on the effects of demand-pull inflation.

☐ Define hyperinflation and explain its effects on prices and real output.

■ **CHAPTER OUTLINE**

1. *Economic growth* can be defined as an increase in real GDP over some time period. It can also be defined as an increase in real GDP per capita over some time period. This second definition takes into account the size of the population. With either definition, economic growth is calculated as a percentage rate of growth per year.

a. Economic growth is important because it lessens the burden of scarcity; it provides the means of satisfying economic wants more fully and fulfilling new wants.

b. One or two percentage point differences in the rate of growth result in substantial differences in annual increases in the economy's output.

c. Economic growth can be increased by increasing the inputs of resources and by increasing the ***productivity*** of those inputs. In the United States about one-third of growth comes from more inputs and two-thirds comes from improved productivity.

d. Over the past 50 years the U.S. economy has an impressive record of economic growth. The growth record may be understated because it does not take into account improvements in product quality or increases in leisure time. The effects of growth on the environment or quality of life could be negative *or* positive.

e. The growth record of the United States over the past 50 years lagged behind other major nations, but in the past decade it has surged ahead of those nations.

2. Economic growth in the U.S. economy has been interrupted by periods of inflation, recession, or both.

a. The ***business cycle*** means alternating periods of prosperity and recession. These recurrent periods of

ups and downs in employment, output, and prices are irregular in their duration and intensity, but the typical pattern is ***peak, recession, trough,*** and ***recovery,*** to another peak.

b. Most economists think that changes in the levels of output and employment are largely the result of changes in the level of ***total spending*** in the economy.

c. The business cycle affects almost the entire economy, but it does not affect all parts in the same way and to the same degree: The production of capital and consumer durable goods fluctuates more than the production of consumer nondurable goods and services during the cycle, because the purchase of capital and consumer durable goods can be postponed.

3. One of the twin problems arising from economic instability is ***unemployment.***

a. The ***unemployment rate*** is calculated by dividing the number of persons in the ***labor force*** who are unemployed by the total number of persons in the labor force. Unemployment data have been criticized for at least two reasons:

(1) Part-time workers are considered fully employed.

(2) ***Discouraged workers*** who have left the labor force are not counted as unemployed.

b. Full employment does not mean that all workers in the labor force are employed and there is no unemployment; some unemployment is normal. There are at least three types of unemployment.

(1) ***Frictional unemployment*** is due to workers searching for new jobs or waiting to take new jobs; this type of unemployment is generally desirable.

(2) ***Structural unemployment*** is due to the changes in technology and in the types of goods and services consumers wish to buy; these changes affect the total demand for labor in particular industries or regions.

(3) ***Cyclical unemployment*** is due to insufficient total spending in the economy; this type of unemployment arises during the recession phase of the business cycle.

c. "Full employment" is less than 100% because some frictional and structural unemployment is unavoidable, The ***full-employment unemployment rate*** or the ***natural rate of unemployment*** (NRU) is the sum of frictional and structural unemployment, and is achieved when cyclical unemployment is zero (the real output of the economy is equal to its potential output). The natural rate is about 4 to 5% of the labor force. It is not automatically achieved and changes over time.

d. Unemployment has an economic cost.

(1) The **GDP** gap is a measure of that cost. It is the difference between actual and potential GDP. When the difference is negative, it means that the economy is underperforming relative to its potential. ***Okun's law*** predicts that for every 1% the actual unemployment rate exceeds the natural rate of unemployment, there is a negative GDP gap of about 2%.

(2) This cost is unequally distributed among different groups of workers in the labor force.

e. Unemployment also has noneconomic costs in the form of social and psychological problems.

f. Unemployment rates differ across nations because of differences in phases of the business cycle and natural rates of unemployment.

4. Over its history, the U.S. economy has experienced not only periods of unemployment but periods of ***inflation.***

   a. Inflation is an increase in the general level of prices in the economy; a decline in the level of prices is deflation.

   b. The primary measure of inflation in the United States is the **Consumer Price Index** (CPI). It compares the prices of a "market basket" of consumer goods in a particular year to the prices for that market basket in a base period, to produce a price index. The rate of inflation from one year to the next is equal to the percentage change in the CPI between the current year and the preceding year. ***The rule of 70*** can be used to calculate the number of years it will take for the price level to double at any given rate of inflation.

   c. The United States has experienced both inflation and deflation, but the past half-century has been a period of inflation. Other industrial nations also experienced inflation.

   d. There are at least two causes of inflation. These may operate separately or simultaneously to raise the price level.

   (1) ***Demand-pull inflation*** is the result of excess total spending in the economy.

   (2) ***Cost-push inflation*** is the result of factors that raise ***per-unit production costs.*** This average cost is found by dividing the total cost of the resource inputs by the amount of output produced. With cost-push inflation, output and employment decline as the price level rises. The major source of this inflation has been supply shock from an increase in the prices of resource inputs.

   e. It is difficult to distinguish between demand-pull and cost-push inflation in the real world.

5. Inflation arbitrarily redistributes real income and wealth. It benefits some groups and hurts other groups in the economy.

   a. Whether someone benefits or is hurt by inflation is measured by what happens to real income. Inflation injures those whose real income falls and benefits those whose real income rises.

   (1) ***Real income*** is determined by dividing ***nominal income*** by the price level expressed in hundredths.

   (2) The percentage change in real income can be approximated by subtracting the percentage change in the price level from the percentage change in nominal income.

   (3) The redistribution effects of inflation depend on whether it is anticipated or unanticipated.

   b. ***Unanticipated inflation*** hurts *fixed-income receivers, savers,* and *creditors* because it lowers the real value of their assets.

   c. Unanticipated inflation may not affect or may help *flexible-income receivers.* It helps *debtors* because it lowers the real value of debts to be repaid.

   d. When there is ***anticipated inflation*** people can adjust their nominal incomes to reflect the expected rise in the price level, and the redistribution of income and

wealth is lessened. To reduce the effects of inflation on a nominal interest rate, an inflation premium (the expected rate of inflation) is added to the ***real interest rate.***

6. Inflation also has an effect on ***real output*** that varies by the type of inflation and its severity.

   a. Cost-push inflation reduces real output, employment, and income.

   b. Views of mild demand-pull inflation vary. It may reduce real output, or it may be a necessary by-product of economic growth.

   c. *Hyperinflation*—extremely high rates of inflation— can lead to a breakdown of the economy by redistributing income and reducing real output and employment.

■ HINTS AND TIPS

1. Some students get confused by the seemingly contradictory term *full-employment unemployment rate* and related unemployment concepts. Full employment does not mean that everyone who wants to work has a job; it means that the economy is achieving its potential output and has a natural rate of unemployment. Remember that there are three types of unemployment: frictional, structural, and cyclical. There will always be some unemployment arising from frictional reasons (e.g., people searching for jobs) or structural reasons (e.g., changes in industry demand), and these two types of unemployment are "natural" for an economy. When there is cyclical unemployment because of a downturn in the business cycle, the economy is not producing its potential output. Thus, full-employment unemployment rate means that there are no cyclical reasons causing unemployment, only frictional or structural reasons.

2. To verify your understanding of how to calculate the unemployment rate, GDP gap, or inflation rate, do Problems 3, 4, and 5 in this *Study Guide* chapter.

3. Inflation is a rise in the *general* level of prices, not just a rise in the prices of a few products. An increase in product price is caused by supply or demand factors. You now know why the prices for many products rise in an economy. The macroeconomic reasons given in Chapter 8 for the increase in the general level of prices are different from the microeconomic reasons for a price increase that you learned about in Chapter 3.

■ IMPORTANT TERMS

economic growth	**labor force**
real GDP per capita	**unemployment rate**
rule of 70	**discouraged workers**
productivity	**frictional unemployment**
business cycle	**structural unemployment**
peak	**cyclical unemployment**
recession	**full-employment rate of**
trough	**unemployment**
recovery	

natural rate of
  unemployment (NRU)

potential output

GDP gap

Okun's law

inflation

Consumer Price Index (CPI)

demand-pull inflation

cost-push inflation

per-unit production costs

nominal income

real income

anticipated inflation

unanticipated inflation

cost-of-living adjustments
  (COLAs)

real interest rate

nominal interest rate

deflation

hyperinflation

SELF-TEST

■ FILL-IN QUESTIONS

1. Economic growth is best measured either by an increase in (nominal, real) _____ GDP over a time period or by an increase in _____ GDP per capita over a time period.

2. A rise in real output per capita (increases, decreases) _____ the standard of living and _____ the burden of scarcity in the economy.

3. Assume an economy has a real GDP of $3600 billion. If the growth rate is 5%, real GDP will increase by ($360, $180) _____ billion next year; but if the rate of growth is only 3%, the annual increase in real GDP will be ($54, $108)_____ billion. A two percentage point difference in the growth rate results in a ($72, $254) _____ billion difference in the annual increase in real GDP.

4. The two main ways that society can increase its real output and income are by increasing outputs of (products, resources) _____ and by increasing the (consumption, productivity) _____ of these inputs.

5. Since 1940, real GDP has increased (fourfold, sixfold) _____ and real GDP per capita has increased almost _____. These figures do not fully account for (better, worse) _____ products and services and (more, less) _____ leisure.

6. The business cycle is a term that encompasses the recurrent ups, or (decreases, increases) _____, and downs, or _____, in the level of business activity in the economy. The order of the four phases of a typical business cycle are peak, (recovery, trough, recession) _____, _____, and _____.

7. Expansion and contraction of the economy affect to a greater extent the production and employment in the consumer (durables, nondurables) _____ and (capital, consumer) _____ goods industries than they do (durable, nondurable) _____ goods and service industries.

8. The unemployment rate is found by dividing the number of (employed, unemployed) _____ persons by the (population, labor force) _____ and (multiplying, dividing)_____ by 100.

9. When workers are searching for new jobs or waiting to start new jobs, this type of unemployment is called (structural, frictional, cyclical) _____, but when workers are laid off because of changes in the consumer demand and technology in industries or regions, this unemployment is called _____; when workers are unemployed because of insufficient total spending in the economy, this type of unemployment is called _____.

10. The full-employment unemployment rate is called the (Okun, natural) _____ rate of unemployment. It is equal to the total of (frictional and structural, cyclical and frictional) _____ unemployment in the economy. It is realized when the (frictional, cyclical) _____ unemployment in the economy is equal to zero and when the actual output of the economy is (less than, equal to) _____ its potential output. When the economy achieves its natural rate of unemployment, the number of job seekers is (greater than, equal to) _____ the number of job vacancies.

11. The GDP gap is equal to the actual GDP (minus, plus) _____ the potential GDP. For every percentage point the unemployment rate rises above the natural rate, there will be a GDP gap of (2, 5) ____%.

12. The burdens of unemployment are borne more heavily by (black, white) _____, (adult, teenage) _____, and (white-collar, blue-collar) _____ workers, and the percentage of the labor force unemployed for 15 or more weeks is much (higher, lower) _____ than the overall unemployment rate.

13. Inflation means (an increase, a decrease) _____ in the general level of (unemployment, prices) _____ in the economy. To calculate the rate of inflation from year 1 to year 2, subtract the price index for year 1 from year 2, then (multiply, divide) _____ the result by the price index for year 1, and _____ by 100.

14. To find the approximate number of years it takes the price level to double, (multiply, divide) _____ 70 by the percentage annual increase in the rate of inflation. This approximation is called (Okun's law, rule of 70) _____ .

15. The basic cause of demand-pull inflation is (an increase, a decrease) _____ in total spending beyond the full employment output rate in the economy. Cost-push inflation is explained in terms of factors that raise per-unit (inflation, production) _____ costs. In practice, it is (easy, difficult) _____ to distinguish between the two types of inflation.

16. The amount of goods and services one's nominal income can buy is called (variable, real) _____ income. If one's nominal income rises by 10% and the price level by 7%, the percentage of increase in (variable, real) _____ income would be (1, 2, 3) _____. If nominal income was $60,000 and the price index, expressed in hundredths, was 1.06, then (variable, real) _____ income would be ($56,604, $63,600) _____ .

17. Unanticipated inflation hurts those whose nominal incomes are relatively (fixed, flexible) _____ , penalizes (savers, borrowers) _____ , and hurts (creditors, debtors) _____ .

18. The redistributive effects of inflation are less severe when it is (anticipated, unanticipated) _____ . Clauses in labor contracts that call for automatic adjustments of workers' incomes from the effects of inflation are called (unemployment benefits, cost-of-living) _____ adjustments.

19. The percentage increase in purchasing power that the lender receives from the borrower is the (real, nominal) _____ rate of interest; the percentage increase in money that the lender receives is the _____ rate of interest. If the nominal rate of interest is 8% and the real interest rate is 5%, then the inflation premium is (8, 5, 3) _____%.

20. Cost-push inflation (increases, decreases) _____ real output. The output effects of demand-pull inflation are (more, less) _____ certain. Some economists argue that mild demand-pull inflation (increases, decreases) _____ real output while others argue that it _____ real output. Economists generally agree that there may be an economic collapse from (hyperproduction, hyperinflation) _____ .

■ **TRUE–FALSE QUESTIONS**

Circle T if the statement is true, F if it is false.

1. The more useful of the two definitions of economic growth for comparing living standards across economies is an increase in real GDP per capita.   **T   F**

2. Suppose two economies both have GDPs of $500 billion. If the GDPs grow at annual rates of 3% in the first economy and 5% in the second economy, the difference in their amounts of growth in one year is $10 billion. **T   F**

3. Increased labor productivity has been more important than increased labor inputs in the growth of the U.S. economy.   **T   F**

4. Growth rate estimates generally attempt to take into account changes in the quality of goods produced and changes in the amount of leisure members of the economy enjoy.   **T   F**

5. The U.S. economy has always experienced steady economic growth, price stability, and full employment. **T   F**

6. The business cycle is best defined as alternating periods of increases and decreases in the rate of inflation in the economy.   **T   F**

7. Individual business cycles tend to be of roughly equal duration and intensity.   **T   F**

8. The unemployment rate is equal to the number of people in the labor force divided by the number of people who are unemployed.   **T   F**

9. Frictional unemployment is not only inevitable but also partly desirable so that people can voluntarily move to better jobs.   **T   F**

10. The essential difference between frictionally and structurally unemployed workers is that the former *do not have* and the latter *do have* salable skills.   **T   F**

11. When the number of people seeking employment is less than the number of job vacancies in the economy, the actual rate of unemployment is less than the natural rate of unemployment, and the price level will tend to rise.   **T   F**

12. If unemployment in the economy is at its natural rate, the actual and potential outputs of the economy are equal.   **T   F**

13. An economy cannot produce an actual real GDP that exceeds its potential real GDP.   **T   F**

14. Unemployment imposes equal burdens on different groups in the economy.   **T   F**

15. The economy's GDP gap is measured by subtracting its potential GDP from its actual GDP.   **T   F**

16. The economic cost of cyclical unemployment is the goods and services that are not produced.   **T   F**

17. Inflation is defined as an increase in the total output of an economy.   **T   F**

18. From one year to the next, the Consumer Price Index rose from 154.5 to 160.5. The rate of inflation was therefore 6.6%.   **T   F**

19. If the price level increases by 10% each year, the price level will double every 10 years.   **T   F**

20. The essence of demand-pull inflation is "too much spending chasing too few goods."   **T   F**

21. Cost-push inflation explains rising prices in terms of factors that increase per-unit production cost.   **T   F**

22. A person's real income is the amount of goods and services that the person's nominal (or money) income will enable him or her to purchase.   **T   F**

23. Whether inflation is anticipated or unanticipated, the effects of inflation on the distribution of income are the same.   **T   F**

24. Borrowers are hurt by unanticipated inflation.   **T   F**

25. Hyperinflation may cause economic collapse in an economy by encouraging speculation, hoarding, and decisions based largely on inflationary expectations. **T   F**

■ **MULTIPLE-CHOICE QUESTIONS**

Circle the letter that corresponds to the best answer.

1. Which is a benefit of real economic growth to a society?
 (a) The society is less able to satisfy new wants.
 (b) Everyone enjoys a greater nominal income.
 (c) The burden of scarcity increases.
 (d) The standard of living increases.

2. If the real output of an economy were to increase from $2000 billion to $2100 billion in 1 year, the rate of growth of real output during that year would be
 (a) 1%
 (b) 5%
 (c) 10%
 (d) 50%

3. Which is one of the four phases of a business cycle?
 (a) inflation
 (b) recession
 (c) unemployment
 (d) hyperinflation

4. Most economists believe that the immediate determinant of the levels of domestic output and employment is
 (a) the price level
 (b) the level of total spending
 (c) the size of the civilian labor force
 (d) the nation's stock of capital goods

5. Production and employment would be least affected by a severe depression in which type of industry?
 (a) nondurable consumer goods
 (b) durable consumer goods
 (c) capital goods
 (d) labor goods

6. The unemployment rate in an economy is 8%. The total population of the economy is 250 million, and the size of the civilian labor force is 150 million. The number of employed workers in this economy is
 (a) 12 million
 (b) 20 million
 (c) 138 million
 (d) 140 million

7. The labor force includes those who are
 (a) less than 16 years of age
 (b) in mental institutions
 (c) not seeking work
 (d) employed

8. The unemployment data collected by the Bureau of Labor Statistics have been criticized because
 (a) part-time workers are not counted in the number of workers employed
 (b) discouraged workers are not considered a part of the labor force
 (c) it covers frictional unemployment, but not cyclical unemployment, which inflates unemployment figures
 (d) the underground economy may understate unemployment

9. A worker who loses a job at a petroleum refinery because consumers and business firms switch from the use of oil to the burning of coal is an example of
 (a) frictional unemployment
 (b) structural unemployment
 (c) cyclical unemployment
 (d) disguised unemployment

10. A worker who has quit one job and is taking 2 weeks off before reporting to a new job is an example of
 (a) frictional unemployment
 (b) structural unemployment
 (c) cyclical unemployment
 (d) disguised unemployment

11. Insufficient total spending in the economy results in
 (a) frictional unemployment
 (b) structural unemployment
 (c) cyclical unemployment
 (d) disguised unemployment

12. The full-employment unemployment rate in the economy has been achieved when
 (a) frictional unemployment is zero
 (b) structural unemployment is zero
 (c) cyclical unemployment is zero
 (d) the natural rate of unemployment is zero

13. Which has helped decrease the natural rate of unemployment in the United States in recent years?
 (a) a smaller proportion of young workers in the labor force
 (b) the increased size of benefits for the unemployed
 (c) less competition in product and labor markets
 (d) more workers covered by unemployment programs

14. Okun's law predicts that when the actual unemployment rate exceeds the natural rate of unemployment by

two percentage points, there will be a negative GDP gap of about
- (a) 2% of the potential GDP
- (b) 3% of the potential GDP
- (c) 4% of the potential GDP
- (d) 5% of the potential GDP

15. If the negative GDP gap were equal to 6% of the potential GDP, the actual unemployment rate would exceed the natural rate of unemployment by
- (a) two percentage points
- (b) three percentage points
- (c) four percentage points
- (d) five percentage points

16. The burden of unemployment is *least* felt by
- (a) white-collar workers
- (b) teenagers
- (c) blacks
- (d) males

17. If the Consumer Price Index was 110 in one year and 117 in the next year, then the rate of inflation from one year to the next was
- (a) 3.5%
- (b) 4.7%
- (c) 6.4%
- (d) 7.1%

18. The price of a good has doubled in about 14 years. The approximate annual percentage rate of increase in the price level over this period has been
- (a) 2%
- (b) 3%
- (c) 4%
- (d) 5%

19. Only two resources, capital and labor, are used in an economy to produce an output of 300 million units. If the total cost of capital resources is $150 million and the total cost of labor resources is $50 million, then the per-unit production costs in this economy are
- (a) $0.67 million
- (b) $1.50 million
- (c) $2.00 million
- (d) $3.00 million

20. If a person's nominal income increases by 8% while the price level increases by 10%, the person's real income
- (a) increases by 2%
- (b) increases by 18%
- (c) decreases by 18%
- (d) decreases by 2%

21. If the average level of nominal income is $21,000 and the price level index is 154, the average real income would be about
- (a) $12,546
- (b) $13,636
- (c) $15,299
- (d) $17,823

22. Who would be hurt by *unanticipated* inflation?
- (a) those living on incomes with cost-of-living adjustments

- (b) those who find prices rising less rapidly than their nominal incomes
- (c) those who lent money at a fixed interest rate
- (d) those who became debtors when prices were lower

23. With no inflation, a bank would be willing to lend a business firm $10 million at an annual interest rate of 8%. But, if the rate of inflation was anticipated to be 6%, the bank would charge the firm an annual interest rate of
- (a) 2%
- (b) 6%
- (c) 8%
- (d) 14%

24. Which contributes to cost-push inflation?
- (a) an increase in employment and output
- (b) an increase in per-unit production costs
- (c) a decrease in resource prices
- (d) an increase in unemployment

25. If an economy has experienced an inflation rate of over 1000% per year for several years, this economic condition would best be described as
- (a) a cost-of-living adjustment
- (b) cost-push inflation
- (c) hyperinflation
- (d) GDP gap

■ PROBLEMS

1. Given the hypothetical data in the table below, calculate the annual rates of growth in real GDP and real per capita GDP over the period given. The numbers of real GDP are in billions.

Year	Real GDP	Annual growth in %	Real GDP per capita	Annual growth in %
1	$2,416		$11,785	
2	2,472	_____	11,950	_____
3	2,563	_____	12,213	_____
4	2,632	_____	12,421	_____
5	2,724	_____	12,719	_____
6	2,850	_____	12,948	_____

2. Suppose the real GDP and the population of an economy in seven different years were those shown in the following table.

Year	Population, million	Real GDP, billions of dollars	Per capita real GDP
1	30	$ 9	$ 300
2	60	24	_____
3	90	45	_____
4	120	66	_____
5	150	90	_____
6	180	99	_____
7	210	105	_____

a. How large would the real per capita GDP of the economy be in each of the other six years? Put your figures in the table.

b. What would have been the size of the optimum population of this economy?_____

c. What was the *amount* of growth in real GDP between year 1 and year 2? _____

d. What was the rate of growth in real GDP between year 3 and year 4? _____%

3. The following table gives statistics on the labor force and total employment during year 1 and year 5. Make the computations necessary to complete the table. (Numbers of persons are in thousands.)

	Year 1	Year 5
Labor force	84,889	95,453
Employed	80,796	87,524
Unemployed	_____	_____
Unemployment rate	_____	_____

a. How is it possible that *both* employment and unemployment increased? _____

_____

b. In relative terms, if unemployment increases, employment will decrease. Why? _____

_____

_____

c. Would you say that year 5 was a year of full employment? _____

_____

d. Why is the task of maintaining full employment over the years more than just a problem of finding jobs for those who happen to be unemployed at any given time?

_____

_____

4. Suppose that in year 1 an economy is at full employment, has a potential and actual real GDP of $3000 billion, and has an unemployment rate of 5.5%.

a. Compute the GDP gap in year 1 and enter it in the table that follows.

Year	Actual GDP	Potential GDP	GDP gap
1	$3000.0	$3000	$_____
2	3724.0	3800	_____
3	3712.5	4125	_____

b. The actual and potential real GDPs in years 2 and 3 are also shown in the table. Compute and enter into the table the GDP gaps in these 2 years.

c. In year 2, the actual real GDP is _____% of the potential real GDP. (Hint: Divide the actual real GDP by the potential real GDP and multiply by 100.)

(1) The actual real GDP is _____% less than the potential real GDP.

(2) Using Okun's law, the unemployment rate will rise from 5.5% in year 1 and be _____% in year 2.

d. In year 3 the actual real GDP is _____% of the potential real GDP.

(1) The actual real GDP is _____% less than the potential real GDP.

(2) The unemployment rate, according to Okun's law, will be _____%.

5. The following table shows the price index in the economy at the end of four different years.

Year	Price index	Rate of inflation
1	100.00	
2	112.00	_____%
3	123.20	_____
4	129.36	_____

a. Compute and enter in the table the rates of inflation in years 2, 3, and 4.

b. Employing the rule of 70, how many years would it take for the price level to double at each of these three inflation rates? _____

_____

c. If nominal income increased by 15% from year 1 to year 2, what was the approximate percentage change in real income? _____

d. If nominal income increased by 7% from year 2 to year 3, what was the approximate percentage change in real income? _____

e. If nominal income was $25,000 in year 2, what was real income that year? _____

f. If nominal income was $25,000 in year 3, what was real income that year? _____

g. If the nominal interest rate was 14% to borrow money from year 1 to year 2, what was the approximate real rate of interest over that period? _____

h. If the nominal interest rate was 8% to borrow money from year 3 to year 4, what was the approximate real rate of interest over that period? _____

6. Indicate in the space below each of the following the most likely effect—beneficial **(B)**, detrimental **(D)**, or indeterminate **(I)**—of unanticipated inflation on these persons:

a. A retired business executive who now lives each month by spending a part of the amount that was saved and deposited in a fixed-rate savings account for a long term. _____

b. A retired private-school teacher who lives on the dividends received from shares of stock owned.

_____

c. A farmer who borrowed $500,000 from a bank at a fixed rate; the loan must be repaid in the next 10 years. _____

d. A retired couple whose sole source of income is the pension they receive from a former employer.

_____

e. A widow whose income consists entirely of interest received from the corporate bonds she owns.

_____

f. A public school teacher. _____

g. A member of a union who works for a firm that produces computers. _____

■ SHORT ANSWER AND ESSAY QUESTIONS

1. What two ways are used to measure economic growth? Why should the citizens of the United States be concerned with economic growth?

2. What is the relationship between real GDP produced in a year and the quantity of resource inputs and the productivity of those inputs?

3. Describe the growth record of the U.S. economy over the past half century and in the past decade. Compare recent U.S. growth rates with those in other nations.

4. Define the business cycle. Why do some economists prefer the term "business fluctuations" to "business cycle"? Describe the four phases of a business cycle.

5. In the opinion of most economists, what is the immediate determinant or cause of the fluctuations in the levels of output and employment in the economy?

6. Compare the manner in which the business cycle affects output and employment in the industries producing capital and durable goods with the way it affects industries producing nondurable goods and services. What causes these differences?

7. How is the unemployment rate measured in the United States? What criticisms have been made of the method the Bureau of Labor Statistics uses to determine the unemployment rate?

8. Distinguish among frictional, structural, and cyclical unemployment.

9. When is there full employment in the U.S. economy? (Answer in terms of the unemployment rate, the actual and potential output of the economy, and the markets for labor.)

10. What is the natural rate of unemployment? Will the economy always operate at the natural rate? Why is the natural rate subject to revision?

11. What is the economic cost of unemployment, and how is this cost measured? What is the quantitative relationship (called Okun's law) between the unemployment rate and the cost of unemployment?

12. What groups in the economy tend to bear the burdens of unemployment? How are women affected by unemployment, and how is the percentage of the labor force unemployed 15 or more weeks related to the unemployment rate in the economy?

13. How does the unemployment rate in the United States compare with the rates for other industrialized nations in recent years?

14. What is inflation, and how is the rate of inflation measured?

15. What has been the experience of the United States with inflation since the 1920s? How does the inflation rate in the United States compare with those of other industrialized nations in recent years?

16. Compare and contrast demand-pull and cost-push types of inflation.

17. What groups benefit from and what groups are hurt by inflation?

18. What is the difference between the effects of unanticipated inflation and the effects of anticipated inflation on the redistribution of real incomes in the economy?

19. What are the effects of cost-push and demand-pull inflation on real output? Are economists in agreement about these effects? Discuss.

20. Explain how the type and severity of inflation influence domestic output.

ANSWERS

Chapter 8 Introduction to Economic Growth and Instability

FILL-IN QUESTIONS

1. real, real
2. increases, decreases
3. $180, $108, $72
4. resources, productivity
5. sixfold, fourfold, better, more
6. increases, decreases, recession, trough, recovery
7. durables, capital, nondurable
8. unemployed, labor force, multiplying
9. frictional, structural, cyclical
10. natural, frictional and structural, cyclical, equal to, equal to
11. minus, 2
12. black, teenage, blue-collar, lower
13. an increase, prices, divide, multiply
14. divide, rule of 70
15. an increase, production, difficult
16. real, real, 3, real, $56,604
17. fixed, savers, creditors
18. anticipated, cost-of-living
19. real, nominal, 3
20. increases, less, increases, decreases, hyperinflation.

TRUE–FALSE QUESTIONS

1. T, p. 132	**10.** F, pp. 136–137	**19.** F, pp. 141–142
2. T, pp. 131–132	**11.** T, pp. 137–138	**20.** T, p. 142
3. T, p. 132	**12.** T, pp. 137–138	**21.** T, p. 143
4. F, p. 133	**13.** F, p. 138	**22.** T, p. 144
5. F, p. 133	**14.** F, pp. 138–139	**23.** F, pp. 145–146
6. F, pp. 133–134	**15.** T, p. 138	**24.** F, pp. 145–146
7. F, pp. 133–134	**16.** T, p. 138	**25.** T, p. 148
8. F, pp. 135–136	**17.** F, p. 141	
9. T, pp. 136–137	**18.** F, pp. 141–142	

MULTIPLE-CHOICE QUESTIONS

1. d, p. 132	**10.** a, pp. 136–137	**19.** a, p. 143
2. b, pp. 131–132	**11.** c, p. 137	**20.** d, p. 144
3. b, p. 134	**12.** c, pp. 137–138	**21.** b, p. 144
4. b, p. 135	**13.** a, p. 138	**22.** c, pp. 144–145
5. a, p. 135	**14.** c, p. 138	**23.** d, p. 146
6. c, p. 136	**15.** b, p. 138	**24.** b, p. 147
7. d, p. 136	**16.** a, pp. 138–140	**25.** c, p. 148
8. b, p. 136	**17.** c, p. 141	
9. b, pp. 136–137	**18.** d, pp. 141–142	

PROBLEMS

1. *real GDP*: years 1–2 (2.3%); years 2–3 (3.7%); years 3–4 (2.7%); years 4–5 (3.5%); years 5–6 (4.6%); *real GDP per capita*: years 1–2 (1.4%); years 2–3 (2.2%); years 3–4 (1.7%); years 4–5 (2.4%); years 5–6 (1.8%)

2. *a.* 400, 500, 550, 600, 550, 500; *b.* 150 million; *c.* $15 billion; *d.* 46.7%

3. year 1: 4,093, 4.8; year 5: 7,929, 8.3; *a.* the labor force increased more than employment increased; *b.* because unemployment and employment in relative terms are percentages of the labor force and *always* add to 100%, and if one increases the other must decrease; *c.* no economist would argue that the full-employment unemployment rate is as high as 8.3% and year 5 was not a year of full employment; *d.* the number of people looking for work expands

4. *a.* 0; *b.* 76, 412.5; *c.* 98, (1) 2, (2) 6.5; *d.* 90, (1) 10, (2) 10.5

5. *a.* 12, 10, 5; *b.* 5.8, 7, 14; *c.* 3; *d.* −3; *e.* $22,321; *f.* $20,292; *g.* 2; *h.* 3

6. *a.* D; *b.* I; *c.* B; *d.* D; *e.* D; *f.* I; *g.* I

SHORT ANSWER AND ESSAY QUESTIONS

1. pp. 131–132	**8.** pp. 136–137	**15.** p. 142
2. p. 132	**9.** pp. 137–138	**16.** pp. 142–143
3. p. 133	**10.** pp. 137–138	**17.** pp. 144–146
4. pp. 133–134	**11.** pp. 138–139	**18.** pp. 144–146
5. p. 135	**12.** pp. 138–140	**19.** pp. 147–148
6. p. 135	**13.** p. 140	**20.** pp. 147–148
7. pp. 135–136	**14.** p. 141	

CHAPTER 9

Basic Macro Relationships

This chapter introduces you to three basic relationships in the economy: income and consumption, the interest rate and investment, and changes in spending and changes in output. The relationships between these economic "aggregates" are essential building blocks for understanding the macro models that will be presented in the next two chapters.

The first section of Chapter 9 describes the relationship between the largest aggregate in the economy— *consumption.* An explanation of consumption, however, also entails a study of saving because saving is simply the part of disposable income that is not consumed. This section develops the consumption and saving schedules and describes their main characteristics. Other key concepts are also presented: average propensities to consume (APC), and save (APS), marginal propensities to consume (MPC), and save (MPS), and the nonincome determinants of consumption and saving.

Investment is the subject of the next section of the chapter. The purchase of capital goods depends on the rate of return that business firms expect to earn from an investment and on the real rate of interest they have to pay for the use of money. Because firms are anxious to make profitable investments and to avoid unprofitable ones, they undertake all investments that have an expected rate of return greater than (or equal to) the real rate of interest and do not undertake an investment when the expected rate of return is less than the real interest rate. This relationship between the real interest rate and the level of investment spending is an inverse one: the lower the interest rate, the greater the investment spending. It is illustrated by a downsloping *investment demand curve.* As you will learn, this curve can be shifted by five factors that can change the expected rate of return on investment. You will also learn that investment, unlike consumption, is quite volatile and is the most unstable component of total spending in the economy.

The third section of the chapter introduces you to the concept of the *multiplier.* It shows how an initial change in spending for consumption or investment changes real GDP by an amount that is larger than the initial stimulus. You will also learn about the rationale for the multiplier and how to interpret it. The multiplier can be derived from the marginal propensity to consume and the marginal propensity to save. You will have learned about these marginal propensities at the beginning of the chapter and now they are put to further use as you end the chapter.

■ CHECKLIST

When you have studied this chapter you should be able to

☐ Explain how consumption and saving are related to disposable income.

☐ Draw a graph to illustrate the relationship among consumption, saving, and disposable income.

☐ Construct a hypothetical consumption schedule.

☐ Construct a hypothetical saving schedule, and identify the level of break-even income.

☐ Compute the four propensities (APC, APS, MPC, and MPS) when given the necessary data.

☐ State the relationship between the APC and the APS as income increases.

☐ Demonstrate that the MPC is the slope of the consumption schedule and the MPS is the slope of the saving schedule.

☐ Explain each of the five nonincome determinants of consumption and saving.

☐ Explain the difference between a change in the amount consumed (or saved) and a change in the consumption (or saving) schedule.

☐ Explain how the expected rate of return affects investment decisions.

☐ Describe the influence of the real interest rate on an investment decision.

☐ Draw a graph of an investment demand curve for the business sector and explain what it shows.

☐ Explain how each of the five noninterest determinants of investment will shift the investment demand curve.

☐ Give four reasons why investment spending tends to be unstable.

☐ Define the multiplier effect in words, with a ratio, and using an equation.

☐ Make three clarifying points about the multiplier.

☐ Cite two facts on which the rationale for the multiplier is based.

☐ Discuss the relationship between the multiplier and the marginal propensities.

☐ Find the value of the multiplier when you are given the necessary information.

☐ Explain the significance of the multiplier.

☐ Discuss the reasons for the difference between the textbook example for the multiplier and the actual multiplier for the U.S. economy.

■ CHAPTER OUTLINE

1. There is a positive or direct relationship between **consumption** and disposable income (after-tax income) because as disposable income increases so does consumption. **Saving** is disposable income not spent for consumer goods. Disposable income is the most important determinant of both consumption and saving. The relationship among disposable income, consumption, and saving can be shown by a graph with consumption on the vertical axis and disposable income on the horizontal axis. The 45-degree line on the graph would show where consumption would equal disposable income. If consumption is less than disposable income, the difference is saving.

   a. The **consumption schedule** shows the amounts that households plan to spend for consumer goods at various levels of income, given a price level.

   b. The **saving schedule** indicates the amounts households plan to save at different income levels, given a price level.

   c. The average propensity to consume (**APC**) and the average propensity to save (**APS**) and the marginal propensity to consume (**MPC**) and the marginal propensity to save (**MPS**) can be computed from the consumption and saving schedules.

   (1) The APC and the APS are, respectively, the percentages of income spent for consumption and saved, and they sum to 1.

   (2) The MPC and the MPS are, respectively, the percentages of additional income spent for consumption and saved; and they sum to 1.

   (3) The MPC is the slope of the consumption schedule, and the MPS is the slope of the saving schedule when the two schedules are graphed.

   d. In addition to income, there are several other important determinants of consumption and saving. Changes in these nonincome determinants will cause the consumption and saving schedules to change. An increase in spending will shift the consumption schedule upward and a decrease in spending will shift it downward. Similarly, an increase in saving will shift the saving schedule upward and a decrease in saving will shift it downward.

   (1) The amount that households spend and save depends on their amount of *wealth*. If household wealth increases, people will spend more because they think they are wealthier (the wealth effect), and they will save less.

   (2) *Expectations* about the future affect spending and saving decisions. If prices are expected to rise in the future, people will spend more today and save less.

   (3) *Real interest rates* change spending and saving decisions. When real interest rates fall, households tend to consume more, borrow more, and save less.

   (4) The level of *household debt* influences consumption. Increasing debt will increase consumption, but if the debt level gets too high it will decrease consumption, because households have to spend money to pay off loans.

   (5) *Taxation* affects spending and saving. The higher taxes reduce both consumption and saving.

   e. Three other considerations need to be noted:

   (1) A change in the amount consumed (or saved) is not the same thing as a change in the consumption (or saving) schedule.

   (2) Changes in wealth, expectations, and household debt shift consumption and saving schedules in opposite directions; tax changes shift the consumption and saving schedules in the same direction.

   (3) Both consumption and saving schedules tend to be stable over time.

2. The investment decision is a marginal benefit and marginal cost decision that depends on the expected rate of return (r) from the purchase of additional capital goods and the real rate of interest (i) that must be paid for borrowed funds.

   a. The **expected rate of return** is directly related to the net profits (revenues less operating costs) that are expected to result from an investment. It is the marginal benefit of investment for a business.

   b. The **real rate of interest** is the price paid for the use of money. It is the marginal cost of investment for a business. When the expected real rate of return is greater (less) than the real rate of interest, a business will (will not) invest because the investment will be profitable (unprofitable).

   c. For this reason, the lower (higher) the real rate of interest, the greater (smaller) will be the level of investment spending in the economy; the **investment demand curve** shows this inverse relationship between the real rate of interest and the level of spending for capital goods. The amount of investment by the business sector is determined at the point where the marginal benefit of investment (r) equals the marginal cost (i).

   d. There are at least five noninterest determinants of investment demand, and a change in any of these determinants will shift the investment demand curve.

   (1) If the *acquisition, maintenance, and operating costs* for capital goods change, then this change in costs will change investment demand. Rising costs decrease investment demand and declining costs increase it.

   (2) Changes in *business taxes* are like a change in costs so they have a similar effect on investment demand as the previous item.

   (3) *An increase in technological progress* will stimulate investment and increase investment demand.

   (4) *The stock of existing capital goods* will influence investment decisions. If the economy is overstocked, there will be a decrease in investment demand, and if the economy is understocked there will be an increase in investment demand.

   (5) *Expectations* of the future are important. If expectations are positive because of more expected sales or profits, there is likely to be an increase in investment demand. Negative expectations will have an opposite effect on investment demand.

   e. Unlike consumption and saving, investment is inherently unstable. Four factors explain this instability.

(1) *Capital goods are durable,* so when they get replaced may depend on the optimism or pessimism of business owners. If owners are more optimistic about the future they will likely spend more to obtain new capital goods.

(2) *Innovation is not regular,* which means that technological progress is highly variable and contributes to instability in investment spending decisions.

(3) *Profit expectations* influence the investment spending of businesses, but profits are highly variable.

(4) *Other expectations* concerning such factors as exchange rates, the state of the economy, and the stock market can create positive or negative expectations that change investment spending.

3. There is a direct relationship between changes in spending and changes in real GDP. The initial change in spending, however, results in an increase in real GDP that is greater than the initial change in spending. This outcome is called the ***multiplier effect.*** The multiplier is the ratio of the change in the real GDP to the initial change in spending. The initial change in spending typically comes from investment spending, but changes in consumption, net exports, or government spending can also have multiplier effects.

   a. The multiplier effect occurs because a change in the dollars spent by one person alters the income of another person in the same direction, and because any change in the income of one person will change the person's consumption and saving in the same direction by a fraction of the change in income. For example, assuming a marginal propensity to consume (MPC) of .75, a change in investment spending of $5.00 will cause a change in consumption of $3.75. The change in consumption ($3.75) will become someone else's income in the second round. The process will continue through successive rounds, but the amount of income in each round will diminish by 25 percent because that is the amount saved from each change in income. After all rounds are completed the initial change of $5 in investment spending produces a total of $20 change because the multiplier was 4 (see Table 9.3 in the text).

   b. There is a formula for calculating the multiplier. The multiplier is directly related to the marginal propensity to consume (MPC) and inversely related to the marginal propensity to save (MPS). The multiplier is equal to [1/(1 − MPC)]. It is also equal to [1/MPS]. The significance of the multiplier is that relatively small changes in the spending plans of business firms or households bring about large changes in the equilibrium real GDP.

   c. The simple multiplier that has been described differs from the actual multiplier for the economy. In the simple case the only factor that reduced income in successive rounds was the fraction that went to savings. For the domestic economy, there are other leakages from consumption besides saving such as spending on imports and payment of taxes. These factors reduce the value of the multiplier. For the U.S. economy the multiplier is estimated to be about 2.

■ HINTS AND TIPS

1. An important graph in the chapter is the ***consumption schedule*** (see Key Graph 9.2). Know how to interpret it. There are two lines on the graph. The 45-degree reference line shows all points where disposable income equals consumption (there is no saving). The consumption schedule line shows the total amount of disposable income spent on consumption at each and every income level. Where the two lines *intersect,* all disposable income is spent (consumed). At all income levels to the right of the intersection, the consumption line lies below the 45-degree line, and not all disposable income is spent (there is saving). To the left of the intersection, the consumption line lies above the 45-degree line and consumption exceeds disposable income (there is dissaving).

2. Always remember that ***marginal propensities*** sum to 1 (MPC + MPS = 1). The same is true for average propensities (APC + APS = 1). Thus, if you know the value of one marginal propensity (e.g., MPC), you can always figure out the other (e.g., 1 − MPC = MPS).

3. The ***multiplier*** effect is a key concept in this chapter and in the ones that follow, so make sure you understand how it works.

   a. The multiplier is simply the ratio of the change in real GDP to the *initial* changes in spending. Multiplying the *initial* change in spending by the *multiplier* gives you the amount of change in real GDP.

   b. The multiplier effect works in both positive and negative directions. An *initial* decrease in spending will result in a larger decrease in real GDP, or an *initial* increase in spending will create a larger increase in real GDP.

   c. The multiplier is directly related to the marginal propensities. The multiplier equals 1/MPS. The multiplier also equals 1/(1 − MPC).

   d. The main reason for the multiplier effect is that the *initial* change in income (spending) induces additional rounds of income (spending) that add progressively less each round as some of the income (spending) gets saved because of the marginal propensity to save (see Table 9.3 of the text).

■ IMPORTANT TERMS

45° (degree) line	marginal propensity to consume (MPC)
consumption schedule	
saving schedule	marginal propensity to save (MPS)
break-even income	
average propensity to consume (APC)	wealth effect
	expected rate of return
average propensity to save (APS)	investment demand curve
	multiplier

SELF-TEST

■ FILL-IN QUESTIONS

   1. The consumption schedule shows the various amounts that households plan to (save, consume)

_____ at various levels of disposable income, while the saving schedule shows the various amounts that households plan to _____.

2. Both consumption and saving are (directly, indirectly) _____ related to the level of disposable income. At lower levels of disposable income, households tend to spend a (smaller, larger) _____ proportion of this income and save a _____ proportion, but at higher levels of disposable income, they tend to spend a (smaller, larger) _____ proportion of this income and save a _____ proportion. At the break-even income, consumption is (greater than, less than, equal to) _____ disposable income.

3. As disposable income falls, the average propensity to consume (APC) will (rise, fall) _____ and the average propensity to save (APS) will _____.

4. The sum of APC and APS is equal to (0, 1) _____. If the APC is .90, then the APS is (.10, 1) _____.

5. The marginal propensity to consume (MPC) is the change in (consumption, income) _____ divided by the change in _____.

6. The marginal propensity to save (MPS) is the change in (saving, income) _____ divided by the change in _____.

7. The sum of MPC and MPS is equal to (0, 1) _____. If the MPC is .75, then the MPS is (0, .25) _____.

8. The MPC is the numerical value of the slope of the (consumption, saving) _____ schedule, and the MPS is the numerical value of the slope of the _____ schedule.

9. The most important determinants of consumption spending, other than the level of income, are

a. _____

b. _____

c. _____

d. _____

e. _____

10. An increase in the consumption schedule means that the consumption schedule shifts (upward, downward) _____ and a decrease in the consumption schedule means that it will shift _____, and these shifts occur because of a change in one of the non-income determinants. An increase in the amount consumed occurs because of an increase in (income, stability) _____.

11. The investment spending decision depends on the expected rate of (interest, return) _____ and the real rate of _____.

12. The expected rate of return is the marginal (cost, benefit) _____ of investment and the real rate of return is the marginal _____ of investment.

13. If the expected rate of return on an investment is greater than the real rate of interest for the use of money, a business firm will (increase, decrease) _____ its investment spending, but if the expected rate of return is less than the real rate of interest, the firm will _____ its investment spending.

14. The relationship between the real rate of interest and the total amount of investment in the economy is (direct, inverse) _____ and is shown in the investment (supply, demand) _____ curve. This curve shows that if the real rate of interest rises, the quantity of investment will (increase, decrease) _____, but if the real rate of interest falls, the quantity of investment will _____.

15. Five noninterest determinants of investment demand are

a. _____

b. _____

c. _____

d. _____

e. _____

16. The demand for new capital goods tends to be unstable because of the (durability, nondurability) _____ of capital goods, the (regularity, irregularity) _____ of innovation, the (stability, variability) _____ of current and expected profits, and the _____ of expectations.

17. The multiplier is the change in real GDP (multiplied, divided) _____ by an initial change in spending. When the initial change in spending is _____ by the multiplier, the result equals the change in real GDP.

18. The multiplier means that an increase in initial spending may create a multiple (increase, decrease) _____ in real GDP, and also that a decrease in initial spending may create a multiple _____ in real GDP.

19. The multiplier has a value equal to 1 divided by the marginal propensity to (consume, save) _____,

which is the same thing as 1 divided by the quantity of 1 minus the marginal propensity to _____.

20. The higher the value of the marginal propensity to consume, the (larger, smaller) _____ the value of the multiplier, but the larger the value of the marginal propensity to save, the _____ the value of the multiplier.

■ TRUE–FALSE QUESTIONS

Circle T if the statement is true, F if it is false.

1. Consumption equals disposable income plus saving.　　　　　　　　　　　　　　　　　　　　**T F**

2. The most significant determinant of the level of consumer spending is disposable income.　　**T F**

3. Historical data suggest that the level of consumption expenditures is directly related to the level of disposable income.　　　　　　　　　　　　　　　　　　　　**T F**

4. Consumption rises and saving falls when disposable income increases.　　　　　　　　　　　　**T F**

5. Empirical data suggest that households tend to spend a similar proportion of a small disposable income than of a larger disposable income.　　　　　　　　　**T F**

6. The break-even income is the income level at which business begins to make a profit.　　　　　**T F**

7. The average propensity to save is equal to the level of saving divided by the level of consumption.　**T F**

8. The marginal propensity to consume is the change in consumption divided by the change in income.　**T F**

9. The slope of the saving schedule is equal to the average propensity to save.　　　　　　　　　　**T F**

10. An increase in wealth will increase the consumption schedule (shift the consumption curve upward).　**T F**

11. An increase in the taxes paid by consumers will decrease both the amount they spend for consumption and the amount they save.　　　　　　　　　　**T F**

12. Both the consumption schedule and the saving schedule tend to be relatively stable over time.　**T F**

13. The real interest rate is the nominal interest rate minus the rate of inflation.　　　　　　　　　　**T F**

14. A business firm will purchase additional capital goods if the real rate of interest it must pay exceeds the expected rate of return from the investment.　　　　　**T F**

15. An increase in the stock of capital goods on hand will decrease the investment-demand curve.　　**T F**

16. The relationship between the rate of interest and the level of investment spending is called the interest schedule.　　　　　　　　　　　　　　　**T F**

17. Investment tends to be relatively stable over time.　　　　　　　　　　　　　　　　　　　**T F**

18. The irregularity of innovations and the variability of business profits contribute to the instability of investment expenditures.　　　　　　　　　　　　　　**T F**

19. The multiplier is equal to the change in real GDP multiplied by the initial change in spending.　　**T F**

20. The initial change in spending for the multiplier is usually associated with investment spending because of investment's volatility.　　　　　　　　　　　**T F**

21. The multiplier effect works only in a positive direction in changing GDP.　　　　　　　　　　**T F**

22. The multiplier is based on the idea that any change in income will cause both consumption and saving to vary in the same direction as a change in income and by a fraction of that change in income.　　　　　**T F**

23. The higher the marginal propensity to consume, the larger the size of the multiplier.　　　　　**T F**

24. When it is computed as 1/MPS, the multiplier reflects only the leakage of income into saving.　　**T F**

25. The value of the actual multiplier for the economy will usually be greater than the value of a textbook multiplier because the actual multiplier is based only on the marginal propensity to save.　　　　　　　　**T F**

■ MULTIPLE-CHOICE QUESTIONS

Circle the letter that corresponds to the best answer.

1. Saving equals
  (a) investment plus consumption
  (b) investment minus consumption
  (c) disposable income minus consumption
  (d) disposable income plus consumption

2. As disposable income decreases, *ceteris paribus,*
  (a) both consumption and saving increase
  (b) consumption increases and saving decreases
  (c) consumption decreases and saving increases
  (d) both consumption and saving decrease

3. Households tend to spend a larger portion of
  (a) a small disposable income than a large disposable income
  (b) a large disposable income than a small disposable income
  (c) their disposable income on saving when the rate of return is high
  (d) their saving than their disposable income when the rate of return is low

4. If consumption spending increases from $358 to $367 billion when disposable income increases from $412 to $427 billion, it can be concluded that the marginal propensity to consume is
  (a) 0.4
  (b) 0.6
  (c) 0.8
  (d) 0.9

5. If disposable income is $375 billion when the average propensity to consume is 0.8, it can be concluded that
  (a) the marginal propensity to consume is also 0.8
  (b) the marginal propensity to save is 0.2
  (c) consumption is $325 billion
  (d) saving is $75 billion

6. As the disposable income of the economy increases
  (a) both the APC and the APS rise
  (b) the APC rises and the APS falls
  (c) the APC falls and the APS rises
  (d) both the APC and the APS fall

7. The slope of the consumption schedule or line for a given economy is the
  (a) marginal propensity to consume
  (b) average propensity to consume
  (c) marginal propensity to save
  (d) average propensity to save

Answer Questions 8 and 9 on the basis of the following graph.

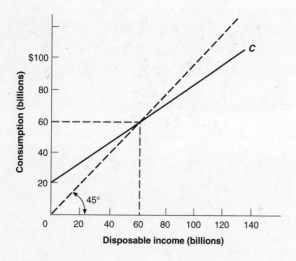

8. This graph indicates that
  (a) consumption decreases after the $60 billion level of disposable income
  (b) the marginal propensity to consume decreases after the $60 billion level of disposable income
  (c) consumption decreases as a percentage of disposable income as disposable income increases
  (d) consumption increases as disposable income decreases

9. If the relevant saving schedule were constructed, one would find that
  (a) the marginal propensity to save is negative up to the $60 billion level of disposable income
  (b) the marginal propensity to save increases after the $60 billion level of disposable income
  (c) saving is zero at the $60 billion level of disposable income
  (d) saving is $20 billion at the $0 level of disposable income

*Answer Questions 10, 11, and 12 on the basis of the following disposable income (**DI**) and consumption (**C**) schedules for a private, closed economy. All figures are in billions of dollars.*

DI	C
$ 0	$ 4
40	40
80	76
120	112
160	148
200	184

10. If plotted on a graph, the slope of the consumption schedule would be
  (a) 0.6
  (b) 0.7
  (c) 0.8
  (d) 0.9

11. At the $160 billion level of disposable income, the average propensity to save is
  (a) 0.015
  (b) 0.075
  (c) 0.335
  (d) 0.925

12. If consumption increases by $5 billion at each level of disposable income, then the marginal propensity to consume will
  (a) change, but the average propensity to consume will not change
  (b) change, and the average propensity to consume will change
  (c) not change, but the average propensity to consume will change
  (d) not change, and the average propensity to consume will not change

13. If the slope of a linear saving schedule decreases, then it can be concluded that
  (a) the MPS has decreased
  (b) the MPC has decreased
  (c) income has decreased
  (d) income has increased

14. An increase in wealth shifts the consumption schedule
  (a) downward and the saving schedule upward
  (b) upward and the saving schedule downward
  (c) downward and the saving schedule downward
  (d) upward and the saving schedule upward

15. Expectations of a recession are likely to lead households to
  (a) increase consumption and saving
  (b) decrease consumption and saving
  (c) decrease consumption and increase saving
  (d) increase consumption and decrease saving

16. Higher real interest rates are likely to
  (a) increase consumption and saving
  (b) decrease consumption and saving
  (c) decrease consumption and increase saving
  (d) increase consumption and decrease saving

17. An increase in taxes shifts the consumption schedule
  (a) downward and the saving schedule upward
  (b) upward and the saving schedule downward
  (c) downward and the saving schedule downward
  (d) upward and the saving schedule upward

18. Which relationship is an inverse one?
  (a) consumption and disposable income
  (b) investment spending and the rate of interest
  (c) saving and disposable income
  (d) investment spending and GDP

19. A decrease in investment demand would be a consequence of a decline in
  (a) the rate of interest
  (b) the level of wages paid
  (c) business taxes
  (d) expected future sales

20. Which would increase investment demand?
  (a) an increase in business taxes
  (b) an increase in the cost of acquiring capital goods
  (c) a decrease in the rate of technological change
  (d) a decrease in the stock of capital goods on hand

21. Which best explains the variability of investment?
  (a) the predictable useful life of capital goods
  (b) constancy or regularities in business innovations
  (c) instabilities in the level of profits
  (d) business pessimism about the future

22. If there was a change in investment spending of $10 and the marginal propensity to save was .25, then real GDP would increase by
  (a) $10
  (b) $20
  (c) $25
  (d) $40

23. If the value of the marginal propensity to consume is 0.6 and real GDP falls by $25, this was caused by a decrease in initial spending of
  (a) $10.00
  (b) $15.00
  (c) $16.67
  (d) $20.00

24. If the marginal propensity to consume is 0.67 and initial spending increases by $25, real GDP will
  (a) increase by $75
  (b) decrease by $75
  (c) increase by $25
  (d) decrease by $25

25. If in an economy a $150 billion increase in investment spending creates $150 billion of new income in the first round of the multiplier process and $105 billion in the second round, the multiplier and the marginal propensity to consume will be, respectively,
  (a) 5.00 and 0.80
  (b) 4.00 and 0.75
  (c) 3.33 and 0.70
  (d) 2.50 and 0.40

■ **PROBLEMS**

1. The following table is a consumption schedule. Assume taxes and transfer payments are zero and that all saving is personal saving.

(GDP = DI)	C	S	APC	APS
$1500	$1540	$_____	1.027	−.027
1600	1620	_____	1.013	−.013
1700	1700	_____	_____	
1800	1780	_____	.989	.011
1900	1860	_____	.979	.021
2000	1940	_____	_____	
2100	2020		.962	.038
2200	2100	_____	_____	_____

a. Compute saving at each of the eight levels of disposable income and the missing average propensities to consume and to save.
b. The break-even level of disposable income is $_____.
c. As disposable income rises, the marginal propensity to consume remains constant. Between each two GDPs the MPC can be found by dividing $_____ by $_____, and is equal to _____.
d. The marginal propensity to save also remains constant when the GDP rises. Between each two GDPs the MPS is equal to $_____ divided by $_____, or to _____.
e. Plot the consumption schedule, the saving schedule, and the 45-degree line on the graph on the next page.
(1) The numerical value of the slope of the consumption schedule is _____, and the term that is used to describe it is the _____.
(2) If the relevant saving schedule were constructed, the numerical value of the slope of the saving schedule would be _____, and the term that is used to describe it would be the _____.

2. Indicate in the space to the right of each of the following events whether the event will tend to increase (+) or decrease (−) the saving schedule.
a. Development of consumer expectations that prices will be higher in the future _____
b. Gradual shrinkage in the quantity of real assets owned by consumers _____
c. Increase in the volume of consumer indebtedness _____
d. Growing belief that disposable income will be lower in the future _____
e. Expectations that there will be a current shortage of consumer goods _____

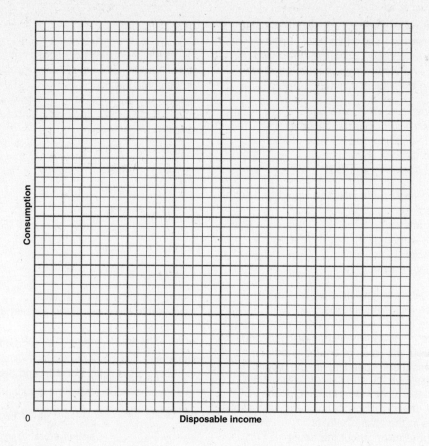

0   **Disposable income**

f. Rise in the actual level of disposable income _____

g. An increase in the financial assets owned by consumers _____

h. Development of a belief by consumers that the Federal government can and will prevent recessions in the future _____

3. The following schedule has eight different expected rates of return, and the dollar amounts of the investment projects expected to have each of these return rates.

Expected rate of return	Investment projects (billions)
18%	$ 0
16	10
14	20
12	30
10	40
8	50
6	60
4	70

a. If the real rate of interest in the economy were 18%, business firms would plan to spend $_____ billion for investment, but if the real interest rate were 16%, they would plan to spend $_____ for investment.

b. Should the real interest rate be 14%, they would still wish to make the investments they were willing to make at real interest rates of 18% and 16%, they would plan to spend an additional $_____ billion for investment, and their total investment would be $_____ billion.

c. If the real rate of interest were 12%, they would make all the investments they had planned to make at higher real interest rates plus an additional $_____ billion, and their total investment spending would be $_____ billion.

d. Complete the following table by computing the amount of planned investment at the four remaining real interest rates.

Real rate of interest	Amount of investment (billions)
18%	$ 0
16	10
14	30
12	60
10	____
8	____
6	____
4	____

e. Graph the schedule you completed on the following graph. Plot the real rate of interest on the vertical axis and the amount of investment planned at each real rate of interest on the horizontal axis.

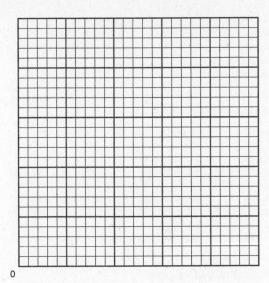

0

i. A recent period of a high level of investment spending, which has resulted in productive capacity in excess

of the current demand for goods and services _____

5. Assume the marginal propensity to consume is 0.8 and the change in investment is $10. Complete the following table modeled after Table 9.3 in the textbook.

	Change in income	Change in consumption	Change in saving
Increase in gross investment of $10	$ + 10	$_____	$_____
Second round	_____	_____	_____
Third round	_____	_____	_____
Fourth round	_____	_____	_____
Fifth round	_____	_____	_____
All other rounds	16.38	13.10	3.28
Totals	_____	_____	_____

■ **SHORT ANSWER AND ESSAY QUESTIONS**

1. What is the most important determinant of consumer spending and personal saving? What is the relationship between consumer spending and personal saving?

2. Use a graph to illustrate the historical relationship between consumption and disposable income in the U.S. economy. Explain why the slope of the consumption line will be less than the 45-degree reference line.

3. Describe the relationship between consumption and disposable income, called the consumption schedule. Draw a graph of this schedule.

4. Describe the relationship between saving and disposable income, called the saving schedule. Draw a graph of this schedule.

5. Define the two average propensities and the two marginal propensities.

6. Explain briefly how the average propensity to consume and the average propensity to save vary as disposable income varies. Why do APC and APS behave this way? What happens to consumption and saving as disposable income varies?

7. Why do the sum of the APC and the APS and the sum of the MPC and the MPS always equal exactly 1?

8. What is the relationship between MPC and MPS and the slopes of the consumption schedule and saving schedule?

9. Explain briefly and explicitly *how* changes in the five nonincome determinants will affect the consumption schedule and the saving schedule and *why* such changes will affect consumption and saving in the way you have indicated.

10. Which of the five nonincome determinants of consumption will shift the consumption schedule one way and the saving schedule the other way? Which one will shift both the consumption and saving schedules in the same direction?

f. Both the graph and the table show that the relationship between the real rate of interest and the amount of investment spending in the economy is

_____. This means that when the real rate of interest
(1) increases, investment will (increase, decrease)

_____.

(2) decreases, investment will _____.
g. It also means that should we wish to
(1) increase investment, we would need to

_____ the real rate of interest.
(2) decrease investment, we would have to

_____ the real rate of interest.

h. This graph (or table) is the _____ curve.

4. Indicate in the space to the right of the following events whether the event would tend to increase (+) or decrease (−) investment spending.

a. Rising stock market prices   _____
b. Development of expectations by business executives that business taxes will be higher in the future

_____
c. Step-up in the rates at which new products and new

production processes are being introduced   _____
d. Business beliefs that wage rates may be lower in the future and labor and capital are complementary

resources   _____

e. An expectation of a recession   _____
f. A belief that business is "too good" and the economy

is due for a period of "slow" consumer demand _____
g. Rising costs in the construction industry   _____
h. A rapid increase in the size of the economy's pop-

ulation   _____

11. What is the difference between a change in the amount consumed and a change in the consumption schedule? Explain your answer using a graph.

12. Are consumption and saving schedules relatively stable? Explain.

13. Discuss the marginal cost and marginal benefit of an investment decision. How are the marginal cost and the marginal benefit of investment measured?

14. Draw an investment demand curve. Use it to explain why investment spending tends to rise when the real rate of interest falls, and vice versa.

15. Identify and explain how five noninterest determinants of investment spending can increase or decrease the amount of investment. Illustrate the changes with a graph.

16. Why does the level of investment spending tend to be highly unstable? State four reasons.

17. What is the multiplier effect?

18. Give a rationale for the multiplier effect.

19. How is the multiplier effect related to the marginal propensities? Explain in words and equations.

20. How large is the actual multiplier effect? Explain the reasons for the difference between the textbook example of the multiplier and actual multiplier for the economy.

ANSWERS

Chapter 9 Basic Macro Relationships

FILL-IN QUESTIONS

1. consume, save
2. directly, larger, smaller, smaller, larger, equal to
3. rise, fall
4. 1, .10
5. consumption, income
6. saving, income
7. 1, .25
8. consumption, saving
9. *a.* wealth; *b.* expectations; *c.* real interest rate; *d.* level of household debt; *e.* taxation (any order for *a–e*)
10. upward, downward, income
11. return, interest
12. benefit, cost
13. increase, decrease
14. inverse, demand, decrease, increase
15. *a.* the cost of acquiring, maintaining, and operating capital goods; *b.* business taxes; *c.* technological change; *d.* the stock of capital goods on hand; *e.* expectations

16. durability, irregularity, variability, variability
17. divided, multiplied
18. increase, decrease
19. save, consume
20. larger, smaller

TRUE–FALSE QUESTIONS

1. F, p. 152	**10.** T, pp. 156–157	**19.** F, p. 164
2. T, p. 152	**11.** T, p. 157	**20.** T, p. 164
3. T, p. 152	**12.** T, p. 158	**21.** F, p. 164
4. F, pp. 153–154	**13.** T, p. 159	**22.** T, pp. 164–166
5. F, pp. 153–154	**14.** F, pp. 159–160	**23.** T, p. 166
6. F, p. 154	**15.** T, p. 162	**24.** T, pp. 166–167
7. F, pp. 154–156	**16.** F, pp. 160–161	**25.** F, pp. 166–167
8. T, p. 156	**17.** F, pp. 162–164	
9. F, p. 156	**18.** T, pp. 162–164	

MULTIPLE-CHOICE QUESTIONS

1. c, p. 152	**10.** d, pp. 155–156	**19.** d, p. 162
2. d, pp. 152–153	**11.** b, p. 154	**20.** d, p. 162
3. a, pp. 152–153	**12.** c, p. 156	**21.** c, p. 164
4. b, p. 156	**13.** a, p. 156	**22.** d, pp. 164–166
5. d, p. 154	**14.** b, p. 157	**23.** a, pp. 164–166
6. c, p. 154	**15.** c, p. 157	**24.** b, pp. 164–166
7. a, p. 156	**16.** c, p. 157	**25.** c, pp. 164–166
8. c, pp. 155–156	**17.** c, p. 157	
9. c, pp. 155–156	**18.** b, pp. 160–161	

PROBLEMS

1. *a.* S: −40, −20, 0, 20, 40, 60, 80, 100; APC: 1.000, 0.970, 0.955; APS: 0.000, 0.030, 0.045; *b.* 1700; *c.* 80, 100, .8; *d.* 20, 100, .20; *e.* (1) .8, MPC, (2) .2, MPS
2. *a.* −; *b.* +; *c.* −; *d.* +; *e.* −; *f.* none; *g.* −; *h.* −
3. *a.* 0, 10; *b.* 20, 30; *c.* 30, 60; *d.* 100, 150, 210, 280; *f.* inverse, (1) decrease, (2) increase; *g.* (1) lower, (2) raise; *h.* investment-demand
4. *a.* +; *b.* −; *c.* +; *d.* +; *e.* −; *f.* −; *g.* −; *h.* +; *i.* −
5. Change in income: 8.00, 6.40, 5.12, 4.10, 50; Change in consumption: 8.00, 6.40, 5.12, 4.10, 3.28, 40.00; Change in saving: 2.00, 1.60, 1.28, 1.02, 0.82, 10.00

SHORT ANSWER AND ESSAY QUESTIONS

1. p. 152	**8.** p. 156	**15.** pp. 161–162
2. p. 153	**9.** pp. 156–157	**16.** pp. 162–164
3. pp. 153–155	**10.** pp. 157–158	**17.** p. 164
4. pp. 153–155	**11.** pp. 157–158	**18.** pp. 164–165
5. pp. 154–156	**12.** p. 158	**19.** p. 166
6. p. 154	**13.** p. 159	**20.** pp. 166–167
7. pp. 154–156	**14.** pp. 160–161	

CHAPTER 10

The Aggregate Expenditures Model

This chapter develops the first macroeconomic model of the economy presented in the textbook—the **aggregate expenditures model.** You will find out what determines the demand for real domestic output (real GDP) and how an economy achieves an equilibrium level of output.

The chapter begins with some simplifying assumptions and then explains how the investment decisions of individual firms can be used to construct an **investment schedule.** The investment schedule is then combined with the consumption schedule to form an aggregate expenditures schedule that shows the various amounts that will be spent in a private closed economy at each possible output or income level. These aggregate expenditures in tabular or graphical form can be used to find **equilibrium GDP** for this economy. It will be important for you to understand how equilibrium GDP is determined and why this level of output will be produced when you are given information about consumption and investment schedules.

Two other features of this simplified aggregate expenditures model are worth noting. Saving and *actual* investment are always equal because they are defined in exactly the same way: the output of the economy minus its consumption. **Saving** and **planned investment,** however, are equal only when real GDP is at its equilibrium level. When real GDP is *not* at its equilibrium level, saving and planned investment are *not* equal and there are **unplanned changes in inventories.** Equilibrium real GDP is achieved when saving and *planned* investment are equal and there are no unplanned changes in inventories.

From Chapter 10 you will also learn **what causes real GDP to rise and fall** based on changes or additions to aggregate expenditures. The first change that will be discussed is the effect of a change in investment spending on equilibrium real GDP in a closed private economy. The initial change in investment will increase equilibrium real GDP by more than the initial investment stimulus because of the multiplier effect.

The methods used to find the equilibrium real GDP in an open economy (one that exports and imports) is the same one as for a closed economy. The economy will tend to produce a real GDP that is equal to aggregate expenditures. The only difference is that now the aggregate expenditures include not only consumption and investment but also the **net exports** (exports minus imports). An increase in net exports, like an increase in investment, will increase the equilibrium real GDP. A change in net exports also has a multiplier effect on real GDP just like a change in investment.

The section on "Adding the Public Sector" introduces **government taxing and spending** into the analysis of equilibrium real GDP. Government purchases of goods and services add to aggregate expenditures, and taxation reduces the disposable income of consumers, thereby reducing both the amount of consumption and the amount of saving that will take place at any level of real GDP. You will need to know the level of real GDP that will be produced and why.

It is important to be aware that the equilibrium real GDP is not necessarily the real GDP at which full employment is achieved. Aggregate expenditures may be greater or less than the full-employment real GDP. If they are greater, there is an **inflationary gap.** If they are less, there exists a **recessionary gap.** The chapter explains how to measure the size of each gap: the amount by which the aggregate expenditures schedule must change to bring the economy to its full-employment real GDP. Several historical examples are given to help you see the application of recessionary and inflationary gaps.

The aggregate expenditures model is a valuable tool for explaining such economic events as recession, inflation, and economic growth. The model also has limitations. The last section of the chapter describes the major shortcomings and how later chapters in the textbook will address them.

■ **CHECKLIST**

When you have studied this chapter you should be able to

☐ Describe the simplifying assumptions in this chapter.
☐ Construct an investment schedule showing the relationship between planned investment and GDP.
☐ Combine the consumption and investment schedule to form an aggregate expenditures schedule to explain the equilibrium levels of output, income, and employment in a private closed economy.
☐ Explain why the economy will tend to produce its equilibrium GDP rather than some smaller or larger level of real GDP.
☐ Illustrate graphically equilibrium in an aggregate expenditure model with consumption and investment components.
☐ Explain the relationship between saving and planned investment at equilibrium GDP.

☐ State the conditions for changes in inventories at equilibrium GDP.

☐ Discuss why equilibrium real GDP changes when the aggregate expenditure schedule shifts upward due to an increase in investment spending.

☐ Use the concept of net exports to define aggregate expenditures in an open economy.

☐ Describe the net export schedule and its relationship to real GDP.

☐ Explain what the equilibrium real GDP in an open economy will be when net exports are positive and when net exports are negative.

☐ Find the equilibrium real GDP in an open economy when given the tabular or graphical data.

☐ Give three examples of how circumstances or policies abroad can affect domestic GDP.

☐ List three simplifying assumptions used to add the public sector to the aggregate expenditures model.

☐ Find the equilibrium real GDP in an economy in which the government purchases goods and services when given the tabular or graphical data.

☐ Determine the effect on the equilibrium real GDP when lump-sum taxes are included in the aggregate expenditures model.

☐ Describe the conditions for leakages and injections and unplanned changes in inventories at the equilibrium level of GDP.

☐ Distinguish between the equilibrium real GDP and the full-employment real GDP.

☐ Find the recessionary and the inflationary gaps when you are provided the relevant data.

☐ Apply the concepts of recessionary and inflationary gaps to two historical events in the United States.

☐ Explain five shortcomings of the aggregate expenditures model.

■ CHAPTER OUTLINE

1. To simplify the explanation of the *aggregate expenditures model,* it is first assumed that the economy is private and closed, which means there is no international trade or government spending (or taxes). It is also assumed that: Output or income measures are equal (real GDP = disposable income, DI); aggregate output and employment are directly related to aggregate expenditures; and the economy has excess production capacity and unemployed labor, so the price level is constant.

2. The investment decisions of businesses in an economy can be aggregated to form an *investment schedule* that shows the amounts business firms collectively plan to invest at each possible level of GDP. A simplifying assumption is made that investment is independent of disposable income or real GDP.

3. In the aggregate expenditures model, the *equilibrium GDP* is the real GDP at which

   a. aggregate expenditures (consumption plus planned investment) equal real GDP, or

   b. in graphical terms, the aggregate expenditures curve crosses the 45-degree line. The slope of this curve is equal to the marginal propensity to consume.

4. The *investment schedule* indicates what investors plan to do. Actual investment consists of both planned and unplanned investment (unplanned changes in inventories).

   a. At above equilibrium levels of GDP, *saving* is greater than *planned investment,* and there will be unintended or unplanned investment through increases in inventories. At below equilibrium levels of GDP, planned investment is greater than saving, and there will be unintended or unplanned disinvestment through a decrease in inventories.

   b. Equilibrium is achieved when planned investment equals saving and there are no *unplanned changes in inventories.*

5. Changes in investment (or consumption) will cause the equilibrium real GDP to change in the same direction by an amount greater than the initial change in investment (or consumption). The reason for this greater change is due to the *multiplier effect.*

6. In an *open economy* there are *net exports* (X_n), which are defined as exports (X) minus imports (M).

   a. The equilibrium real GDP in an open economy means real GDP is equal to consumption plus investment plus net exports.

   b. The net export schedule will be positive when exports are greater than imports, and negative when imports are greater than exports.

   c. Any increase in X_n will increase the equilibrium real GDP with a multiplier effect. A decrease in X_n will do just the opposite.

   d. In an open economy model, circumstances and policies abroad can affect the U.S. GDP. There can be changes in:

   (1) the level of national incomes abroad;

   (2) tariffs or quotas; and

   (3) exchange rates.

7. Changes in *government spending and tax rates* can affect equilibrium real GDP. This simplified analysis assumes that government purchases do not affect investment or consumption, that taxes are purely personal taxes, and that a fixed amount of taxes are collected regardless of the level of GDP.

   a. *Government purchases* of goods and services add to the aggregate expenditures schedule and increase equilibrium real GDP; an increase in these purchases has a multiplier effect on equilibrium real GDP.

   b. *Taxes* decrease consumption and the aggregate expenditures schedule by the amount of the tax times the *MPC.* They decrease saving by the amount of the tax times the *MPS.* An increase in taxes has a negative multiplier effect on the equilibrium real GDP.

   (1) When government both taxes and purchases goods and services, the equilibrium GDP is the real GDP at which aggregate expenditures (*consumption + investment + net exports + government purchases of goods and services*) equals real GDP.

   (2) Or from a leakages and injections perspective, the equilibrium GDP is the real GDP at which leakages (*saving + imports + taxes*) equals injections (*investment + exports + government purchases*).

(3) At equilibrium real GDP, there are no unplanned changes in inventories.

8. The *equilibrium level of real GDP* may turn out to be an equilibrium that is at less than full employment, at full employment, or at full employment with inflation.

   a. If the equilibrium real GDP is less than the real GDP consistent with full-employment real GDP, there exists a *recessionary gap.* Aggregate expenditures are less than what is needed to achieve full-employment real GDP. The size of the recessionary gap equals the amount by which the aggregate expenditures schedule must increase (shift upward) to increase the real GDP to its full-employment level.

   b. The U.S. recession of 2001 is an example of a recessionary gap as investment spending declined, thus reducing aggregate expenditures.

   c. If aggregate expenditures are *greater* than those consistent with full-employment real GDP, then there is an *inflationary gap.* This gap results from excess spending and will increase the price level, creating demand-pull inflation. The size of the inflationary gap equals the amount by which the aggregate expenditures schedule must decrease (shift downward) if the economy is to achieve full-employment real GDP.

   d. The example of the inflationary gap is the U.S. inflation in the late 1980s during which the economy moved beyond its full-employment output and the price level rose.

9. There are *five limitations* of the aggregate expenditures model: an inability to measure price-level changes or the rate of inflation; no explanation for why demand-pull inflation can occur before the economy reaches its full-employment level of output; no insights into why the economy can expand beyond its full-employment level of real GDP; no coverage of cost-push inflation; and it does not permit "self-correction."

■ **HINTS AND TIPS**

1. Do not confuse the *investment demand curve* for the business sector with the *investment schedule* for an economy. The former shows the inverse relationship between the real interest rate and the amount of total investment by the business sector, whereas the latter shows the collective investment intentions of business firms at each possible level of disposable income or real GDP.

2. The distinction between *actual investment, planned investment,* and *unplanned investment* is important for determining the equilibrium level of real GDP. Actual investment includes both planned and unplanned investment. At any level of real GDP, saving and actual investment will always be equal by definition, but saving and planned investment may not equal real GDP because there may be unplanned investment (unplanned changes in inventories). Only at the equilibrium level of real GDP will saving and planned investment be equal (there is no unplanned investment).

3. There is an important difference between *equilibrium and full-employment real GDP* in the aggregate expenditures model. Equilibrium means no tendency for the economy to change its output (or employment) level. Thus, an economy can experience a low level of output and high unemployment and still be at equilibrium. The *recessionary gap* shows how much aggregate expenditures need to increase, so that when this increase is multiplied by the multiplier, it will shift the economy to a higher equilibrium and to the full-employment level of real GDP. Remember that you multiply the needed increase in aggregate expenditures (the recessionary gap) by the multiplier to calculate the change in real GDP that moves the economy from below to full-employment equilibrium.

■ **IMPORTANT TERMS**

planned investment	**unplanned changes in inventories**
investment schedule	
aggregate expenditures schedule	**net exports**
	lump-sum tax
equilibrium GDP	**recessionary gap**
leakage	**inflationary gap**
injection	

──────────────────────
SELF-TEST
──────────────────────

■ **FILL-IN QUESTIONS**

1. Some simplifying assumptions used in the first part of the chapter are that the economy is (an open, a closed) _____ economy, the economy is (private, public) _____, that real GDP equals disposable (consumption, income) _____, and that an increase in aggregate expenditures will (increase, decrease) _____ real output and employment, but not raise the price level.

2. A schedule showing the amounts business firms collectively intend to invest at each possible level of GDP is the (consumption, investment) _____ schedule. For this schedule, it is assumed that planned (saving, investment) _____ is independent of the level of current disposable income or real output.

3. Assuming a private and closed economy, the equilibrium level of real GDP is determined where aggregate expenditures are (greater than, less than, equal to) _____ real domestic output, consumption plus investment is _____ real domestic output, and the aggregate expenditures schedule or curve intersects the (90-degree, 45-degree) _____ line.

4. A leakage is (an addition to, a withdrawal from) _____ the income expenditure stream, whereas an injection is _____ the income expenditure stream. In this chapter, an example of a leakage is (investment, saving) _____, and an example of an injection is _____.

5. If aggregate expenditures are greater than the real domestic output, saving is (greater than, less than) _____ planned investment, there are unplanned (increases, decreases) _____ in inventories, and real GDP will (rise, fall) _____.

6. If aggregate expenditures are less than the real domestic output, saving is (greater than, less than) _____ planned investment, there are unplanned (increases, decreases) _____ in inventories, and real GDP will (rise, fall) _____.

7. If aggregate expenditures are equal to the real domestic output, saving is (greater than, less than, equal to) _____ planned investment, unplanned changes in inventories are (negative, positive, zero) _____, and real GDP will neither rise nor fall.

8. An upshift in the aggregate expenditures schedule will (increase, decrease) _____ the equilibrium GDP. The upshift in the aggregate expenditures schedule can result from (an increase, a decrease) _____ in the consumption schedule or _____ in the investment schedule.

9. When investment spending increases, the equilibrium real GDP (increases, decreases) _____, and when investment spending decreases, the equilibrium real GDP _____. The changes in the equilibrium real GDP are (greater, less) _____ than the initial changes in investment spending because of the (lump-sum tax, multiplier) _____.

10. In an open economy, a nation's net exports are equal to its exports (plus, minus) _____ its imports. In the open economy, aggregate expenditures are equal to consumption (plus, minus) _____ investment (plus, minus) _____ net exports.

11. What would be the effect, an increase (+) or a decrease (−), of each of the following on an open economy's equilibrium real GDP?

   a. an increase in imports _____

   b. an increase in exports _____

   c. a decrease in imports _____

   d. a decrease in exports _____

   e. an increasing level of national income among trading partners _____

   f. an increase in trade barriers imposed by trading partners _____

   g. a depreciation in the value of the economy's currency _____

12. Increases in public spending will (decrease, increase) _____ the aggregate expenditures schedule and equilibrium real GDP, but decreases in public spending will _____ the aggregate expenditures schedule and equilibrium real GDP.

13. A tax yielding the same amount of tax revenue at each level of GDP is a (lump-sum, constant) _____ tax.

14. Taxes tend to reduce consumption at each level of real GDP by an amount equal to the taxes multiplied by the marginal propensity to (consume, save) _____; saving will decrease by an amount equal to the taxes multiplied by the marginal propensity to _____.

15. In an economy in which government both taxes and purchases goods and services, the equilibrium level of real GDP is the real GDP at which aggregate (output, expenditures) _____ equal(s) real domestic _____, and at which real GDP is equal to consumption (plus, minus) _____ investment (plus, minus) _____ net exports (plus, minus) _____ purchases of goods and services by government.

16. When the public sector is added to the model, the equation for the leakages and injections shows (consumption, investment) _____ plus (imports, exports) _____, plus purchases of goods and services by government equals (consumption, saving) _____ plus (exports, imports) _____ plus taxes.

17. A recessionary gap exists when equilibrium real GDP is (greater, less) _____ than the full-employment real GDP. To bring real GDP to the full-employment level, the aggregate expenditures schedule must (increase, decrease) _____ by an amount equal to the difference between the equilibrium and the full-employment real GDP (multiplied, divided) _____ by the multiplier.

18. The amount by which aggregate spending at the full-employment GDP exceeds the full-employment level of real GDP is (a recessionary, an inflationary)

_____ gap. To eliminate this gap, the aggregate expenditures schedule must (increase, decrease)

_____ .

19. One limitation of the aggregate expenditures model is that it can explain (cost-push, demand-pull)

_____ inflation but not _____ inflation. Another problem is that the model also has no way of measuring the rate of (interest, inflation)

_____ because there is no price level.

20. Three other limitations of the aggregate expenditures model are its inability to explain premature (demand-pull,

cost-push) _____ inflation, how the economy

can expand (to, beyond) _____ the full-employment level of output, and how the economy "self-

(inflates," corrects") _____ .

■ **TRUE–FALSE QUESTIONS**

Circle T if the statement is true, F if it is false.

1. The basic premise of the aggregate expenditures model is that the amount of goods and services produced and the level of employment depend directly on the level of total spending.   **T   F**

2. In the aggregate expenditures model of the economy, the price level is assumed to be constant.   **T   F**

3. The investment schedule is a schedule of planned investment rather than a schedule of actual investment.   **T   F**

4. The equilibrium level of GDP is that GDP level corresponding to the intersection of the aggregate expenditures schedule with the 45-degree line.   **T   F**

5. At levels of GDP below equilibrium, the economy wants to spend at higher levels than the levels of GDP the economy is producing.   **T   F**

6. At levels of GDP below equilibrium, aggregate expenditures are less than GDP, which causes inventories to rise and production to fall.   **T   F**

7. Saving is an injection into and investment is a leakage from the income expenditures stream.   **T   F**

8. Saving and actual investment are always equal. **T   F**

9. Saving at any level of real GDP equals planned investment plus unplanned changes in inventories. **T   F**

10. The equilibrium level of GDP will change in response to changes in the investment schedule or the consumption schedule.   **T   F**

11. If there is a decrease in the investment schedule, there will be an upshift in the aggregate expenditures schedule.   **T   F**

12. Through the multiplier effect, an initial change in investment spending can cause a magnified change in domestic output and income.   **T   F**

13. The net exports of an economy equal the sum of its exports and imports of goods and services.   **T   F**

14. An increase in the volume of a nation's exports, other things being equal, will expand the nation's real GDP.   **T   F**

15. An increase in the imports of a nation will increase the exports of other nations.   **T   F**

16. A falling level of real output and income among U.S. trading partners enables the United States to sell more goods abroad.   **T   F**

17. An appreciation of the dollar will increase net exports.   **T   F**

18. If the MPS were 0.3 and taxes were levied by the government so that consumers paid $20 in taxes at each level of real GDP, consumption expenditures at each level of real GDP would be $14 less.   **T   F**

19. Equal changes in government spending and taxes do not have equivalent effects on real GDP.   **T   F**

20. At equilibrium, the sum of leakages equals the sum of injections.   **T   F**

21. The equilibrium real GDP is the real GDP at which there is full employment in the economy.   **T   F**

22. The existence of a recessionary gap in the economy is characterized by the full employment of labor.   **T   F**

23. An inflationary gap is the amount by which the economy's aggregate expenditures schedule must shift downward to eliminate demand-pull inflation and still achieve the full-employment GDP.   **T   F**

24. The aggregate expenditures model is valuable because it indicates how much the price level will rise when aggregate expenditures are excessive relative to the economy's capacity.   **T   F**

25. The aggregate expenditures model provides a good explanation for cost-push inflation.   **T   F**

■ **MULTIPLE-CHOICE QUESTIONS**

Circle the letter that corresponds to the best answer.

1. The premise of the model in this chapter is that the amount of goods and services produced, and therefore the level of employment, depends
   (a) directly on the rate of interest
   (b) directly on the level of total expenditures
   (c) inversely on the level of disposable income
   (d) inversely on the quantity of resources available

2. If the economy is private, closed to international trade, and government neither taxes nor spends, then real GDP equals
   (a) saving
   (b) consumption
   (c) disposable income
   (d) investment spending

Question 3 is based on the following consumption schedule.

Real GDP	C
$200	$200
240	228
280	256
320	284
360	312
400	340
440	368
480	396

3. If the investment schedule is $60 at each level of output, the equilibrium level of real GDP will be
(a) $320
(b) $360
(c) $400
(d) $440

4. If real GDP is $275 billion, consumption is $250 billion, and investment is $30 billion, real GDP
(a) will tend to decrease
(b) will tend to increase
(c) will tend to remain constant
(d) equals aggregate expenditures

5. On a graph, the equilibrium real GDP is found at the intersection of the 45-degree line and the
(a) saving curve
(b) consumption curve
(c) investment demand curve
(d) aggregate expenditures curve

6. Which is an injection of spending into the income expenditures stream?
(a) investment
(b) imports
(c) saving
(d) taxes

7. When the economy's real GDP exceeds its equilibrium real GDP,
(a) leakages equal injections
(b) planned investment exceeds saving
(c) there is unplanned investment in the economy
(d) aggregate expenditures exceed the real domestic output

8. If saving is greater than planned investment
(a) saving will tend to increase
(b) businesses will be motivated to increase their investments
(c) real GDP will be greater than planned investment plus consumption
(d) aggregate expenditures will be greater than the real domestic output

9. At the equilibrium level of GDP,
(a) actual investment is zero
(b) unplanned changes in inventories are zero
(c) saving is greater than planned investment
(d) saving is less than planned investment

Answer Questions 10 and 11 on the basis of the following table for a private, closed economy. All figures are in billions of dollars.

Real rate of return	Investment	Consumption	GDP
10%	$ 0	$200	$200
8	50	250	300
6	100	300	400
4	150	350	500
2	200	400	600
0	250	450	700

10. If the real rate of interest is 4%, then the equilibrium level of GDP will be
(a) $300 billion
(b) $400 billion
(c) $500 billion
(d) $600 billion

11. An *increase* in the real interest rate by 4% will
(a) increase the equilibrium level of GDP by $200 billion
(b) decrease the equilibrium level of GDP by $200 billion
(c) decrease the equilibrium level of GDP by $100 billion
(d) increase the equilibrium level of GDP by $100 billion

12. Compared with a closed economy, aggregate expenditures and GDP will
(a) increase when net exports are positive
(b) decrease when net exports are positive
(c) increase when net exports are negative
(d) decrease when net exports are zero

Use the data in the following table to answer Questions 13 and 14.

Real GDP	C + I_g	Net exports
$ 900	$ 913	$3
920	929	3
940	945	3
960	961	3
980	977	3
1,000	993	3
1,020	1,009	3

13. The equilibrium real GDP is
(a) $960
(b) $980
(c) $1000
(d) $1020

14. If net exports are increased by $4 billion at each level of GDP, the equilibrium real GDP would be
(a) $960
(b) $980
(c) $1000
(d) $1020

15. An increase in the real GDP of an economy will, other things remaining constant,

(a) increase its imports and the real GDPs in other economies

(b) decrease its imports and the real GDPs in other economies

(c) increase its imports and decrease the real GDPs in other economies

(d) decrease its imports and increase the real GDPs in other economies

16. Other things remaining constant, which would increase an economy's real GDP and employment?

(a) an increase in the exchange rate for foreign currencies

(b) the imposition of tariffs on goods imported from abroad

(c) an appreciation of the dollar relative to foreign currencies

(d) an increase in the level of national income among the trading partners for this economy

17. The economy is operating at the full-employment level of output. A depreciation of the dollar will most likely result in

(a) a decrease in exports

(b) an increase in imports

(c) a decrease in real GDP

(d) an increase in the price level

Answer Questions 18 and 19 on the basis of the following diagram.

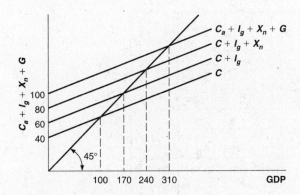

18. If this were an open economy without a government sector, the level of GDP would be

(a) $100

(b) $170

(c) $240

(d) $310

19. In this graph it is assumed that investment, net exports, and government expenditures

(a) vary directly with GDP

(b) vary inversely with GDP

(c) are independent of GDP

(d) are all negative

Questions 20 and 21 are based on the following consumption schedule.

Real GDP	C
$300	$290
310	298
320	306
330	314
340	322
350	330
360	338

20. If taxes were zero, government purchases of goods and services $10, planned investment $6, and net exports zero, equilibrium real GDP would be

(a) $310

(b) $320

(c) $330

(d) $340

21. If taxes were $5, government purchases of goods and services $10, planned investment $6, and net exports zero, equilibrium real GDP would be

(a) $300

(b) $310

(c) $320

(d) $330

22. The amount by which an economy's aggregate expenditures must shift upward to achieve full-employment GDP is

(a) an injection

(b) a lump-sum tax

(c) a recessionary gap

(d) an unplanned change in inventories

23. If the MPC in an economy is 0.75, government could eliminate a recessionary gap of $50 billion by decreasing taxes by

(a) $33.3 billion

(b) $50 billion

(c) $66.7 billion

(d) $80 billion

24. To eliminate an inflationary gap of $50 in an economy in which the marginal propensity to save is 0.1, it will be necessary to

(a) decrease the aggregate expenditures schedule by $50

(b) decrease the aggregate expenditures schedule by $5

(c) increase the aggregate expenditures schedule by $50

(d) increase the aggregate expenditures schedule by $5

25. One of the limitations of the aggregate expenditures model is that it

(a) fails to account for demand-pull inflation

(b) has no way of measuring the rate of inflation

(c) explains recessionary gaps but not inflationary gaps

(d) gives more weight to cost-push than demand-pull inflation

■ PROBLEMS

1. Following are two schedules showing several GDPs and the level of investment spending (*I*) at each GDP. (All figures are in billions of dollars.)

Schedule number 1		Schedule number 2	
GDP	I	GDP	I
$1850	$90	$1850	$ 75
1900	90	1900	80
1950	90	1950	85
2000	90	2000	90
2050	90	2050	95
2100	90	2100	100
2150	95	2150	105

a. Each schedule is an _____ schedule.
b. When such a schedule is drawn up, it is assumed

that the real rate of interest is _____.
c. In schedule
(1) number 1, GDP and *I* are (unrelated, directly related)

_____.

(2) number 2, GDP and *I* are _____.
d. Should the real rate of interest rise, investment spending at each GDP would (increase, decrease)

_____ and the curve relating GDP and investment spending would shift (upward, downward)

_____.

2. The following table shows consumption and saving at various levels of real GDP. Assume the price level is constant, the economy is closed to international trade, and there is no government, no business savings, no depreciation, and no net foreign factor income earned in the United States.

Real GDP	C	S	I_g	$C + I_g$	UI
$1300	$1290	$10	$22	$1312	−12
1310	1298	12	22	1320	−10
1320	1306	14	_____	_____	_____
1330	1314	16	_____	_____	_____
1340	1322	18	_____	_____	_____
1350	1330	20	_____	_____	_____
1360	1338	22	_____	_____	_____
1370	1346	24	_____	_____	_____
1380	1354	26	_____	_____	_____
1390	1362	28	22	1384	+6
1400	1370	30	22	1392	+8

a. The next table is an investment demand schedule that shows the amounts investors plan to invest at different rates of interest. Assume the rate of interest is 6%. In the previous table, complete the gross investment, the consumption-plus-investment, and unplanned investment (**UI**) columns, showing unplanned increase in inventories with a + and unplanned decrease in inventories with a −.

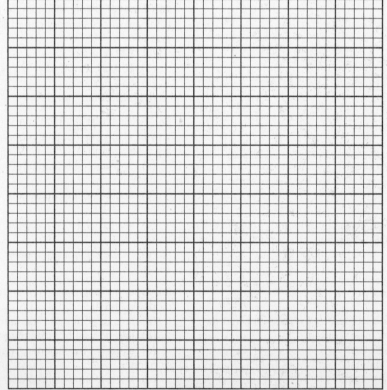

0   **Real GDP**

Interest rate	I_g
10%	$ 0
9	7
8	13
7	18
6	22
5	25

b. The equilibrium real GDP will be $ _____.

c. The value of the marginal propensity to consume in this problem is _____, and the value of the marginal propensity to save is _____.

d. The value of the simple multiplier is _____.

e. If the rate of interest should fall from 6% to 5%, investment would (increase, decrease) _____ by $_____; and the equilibrium real GDP would, as a result, (increase, decrease) _____ by $_____.

f. Suppose the rate of interest were to rise from 6% to 7%. Investment would _____ by $_____, and the equilibrium real GDP would _____ by $_____.

g. Assume the rate of interest is 6%, on the following graph, plot C, $C + I_g$, and the 45-degree line, and indicate the equilibrium real GDP.

3. The second column of the schedule that follows shows what aggregate expenditures (consumption plus investment) would be at various levels of real domestic product in a closed economy.

a. Were this economy to become an open economy, the volume of exports would be a constant $90 billion (column 3), and the volume of imports would be a constant $86 billion (column 4). At each of the seven levels of real GDP (column 1), net exports would be $_____ billion (column 5).

b. Compute aggregate expenditures in this open economy at the seven real GDP levels and enter them in the table (column 6).

c. The equilibrium real GDP in this open economy would be _____ billion.

d. The value of the multiplier in this open economy is equal to _____.

e. A $10 billion increase in

(1) exports would (increase, decrease) _____ the equilibrium real GDP by $_____ billion.

(2) imports would (increase, decrease) _____ the equilibrium real GDP by $_____ billion.

4. Below are consumption schedules.

a. Assume government levies a lump-sum tax of $100. Also assume that imports are $5. Because the marginal propensity to consume in this problem is _____, the imposition of this tax will reduce consumption at all levels of real GDP by $_____. Complete the C_a column to show consumption at each real GDP after this tax has been levied.

Real GDP	C	C_a	$C_a + I_g + X_n + G$
$1500	$1250	$_____	$_____
1600	1340	_____	_____
1700	1430	_____	_____
1800	1520	_____	_____
1900	1610	_____	_____
2000	1700	_____	_____
2100	1790	_____	_____

b. Suppose that investment is $150, exports are $5, and government purchases of goods and services equal $200. Complete the (after-tax) consumption-plus-investment-plus-net-exports-plus-government-purchases column ($C_a + I_g + X_n + G$).

c. The equilibrium real GDP is $ _____.

d. On the following graph, plot C_a, $C_a + I_g + X_n + G$, and the 45-degree line. Show the equilibrium real GDP. (To answer the questions that follow, it is *not* necessary to recompute C_a, or $C_a + I_g + X_n + G$. They can be answered by using the multipliers.)

(1) Possible levels of real GDP (billions)	(2) Aggregate expenditures, closed economy (billions)	(3) Exports (billions)	(4) Imports (billions)	(5) Net exports (billions)	(6) Aggregate expenditures, open economy (billions)
$ 750	$ 776	$90	$86	$_____	$_____
800	816	90	86	_____	_____
850	856	90	86	_____	_____
900	896	90	86	_____	_____
950	936	90	86	_____	_____
1000	976	90	86	_____	_____
1050	1016	90	86	_____	_____

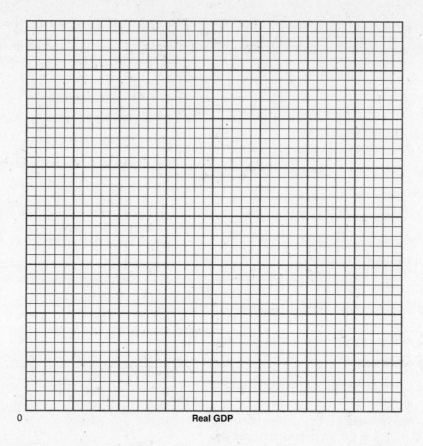

0   **Real GDP**

e. If taxes remained at $100 and government purchases rose by $10, the equilibrium real GDP would (rise, fall) _____ by $ _____.

f. If government purchases remained at $200 and the lump-sum tax increased by $10, the equilibrium real GDP would _____ by $ _____.

g. The combined effect of a $10 increase in government purchases *and* a $10 increase in taxes is to _____ real GDP by $ _____.

5. Here is a consumption schedule for a closed economy. Assume that the level of real GDP at which full employment without inflation is achieved is $590.

Real GDP	C
$550	$520
560	526
570	532
580	538
590	544
600	550
610	556
620	562
630	568

a. The value of the multiplier is _____.

b. If planned investment is $58, the equilibrium nominal GDP is $_____ and exceeds full-employment real GDP by $_____. There is a(n) _____ gap of $_____.

c. If planned investment is $38, the equilibrium real GDP is $_____ and is less than full-employment real GDP by $_____. There is a(n) _____ gap of $_____.

■ **SHORT ANSWER AND ESSAY QUESTIONS**

1. What does it mean that an economy is private and closed?

2. What assumptions are made in this chapter about production capacity, unemployment, and the price level?

3. What is the difference between an investment demand curve and an investment schedule?

4. Why is the equilibrium level of real GDP that level of real GDP at which domestic output equals aggregate expenditures? What will cause real GDP to rise if it is below this level, and what will cause it to fall if it is above this level?

5. Explain what is meant by a leakage and by an injection. Which leakage and which injection are considered in this chapter? Why is the equilibrium real GDP the real GDP at which the leakages equal the injections?

6. Why is it important to distinguish between planned and actual investment in explaining how a private, closed economy achieves its equilibrium level of real GDP?

7. Why does the equilibrium level of real GDP change?

8. How do exports and imports get included in the aggregate expenditures model?

9. What happens to the aggregate expenditures schedule when net exports increase or decrease?

10. Give some examples of international economic linkages affecting the domestic level of GDP.

11. Explain the simplifying assumptions used to include the public sector in the aggregate expenditures model.

12. Describe how government expenditures affect equilibrium GDP.

13. What effect will taxes have on the consumption schedule?

14. Explain why, with government taxing and spending, the equilibrium real GDP is the real GDP at which real GDP equals consumption plus investment plus net exports plus government purchases of goods and services.

15. Use leakages and injections to explain how changes in the different components of aggregate expenditures cause GDP to move to its equilibrium level.

16. Explain what is meant by a recessionary gap.

17. What economic conditions contributed to the recessionary gap in the U.S. economy in 2001?

18. What is an inflationary gap?

19. Why is the U.S. inflation in the late 1980s an example of an inflationary gap?

20. What are the limitations of the demand aggregate expenditures model in terms of the measurement of the price level and treatment of demand-pull and cost-push inflation? Are there other limitations?

ANSWERS

Chapter 10 The Aggregate Expenditures Model

FILL-IN QUESTIONS

1. a closed, private, income, increase
2. investment, investment
3. equal to, equal to, 45-degree
4. a withdrawal from, an addition to, saving, investment
5. less than, decreases, rise
6. greater than, increases, fall
7. equal to, zero
8. increase, an increase, an increase
9. increases, decreases, greater, multiplier
10. minus, plus, plus
11. *a.* −; *b.* +; *c.* +; *d.* −; *e.* +; *f.* −; *g.* +
12. increase, decrease
13. lump-sum
14. consume, save
15. expenditures, output, plus, plus, plus

16. investment, exports, saving, imports
17. less, increase, divided
18. an inflationary, decrease
19. demand-pull, cost-push, inflation
20. demand-pull, beyond, corrects

TRUE−FALSE QUESTIONS

1. T, p. 172	**10.** T, pp. 177−178	**19.** T, pp. 184−185
2. T, p. 172	**11.** F, pp. 177−178	**20.** T, p. 186
3. T, p. 172	**12.** T, p. 178	**21.** F, pp. 186−187
4. T, pp. 175−176	**13.** F, p. 179	**22.** F, p. 186
5. T, pp. 174−175	**14.** T, p. 179	**23.** T, p. 187
6. F, pp. 174−175	**15.** T, p. 179−180	**24.** F, p. 187
7. F, pp. 176−177	**16.** F, p. 181	**25.** F, p. 189
8. T, pp. 176−177	**17.** F, p. 181	
9. T, pp. 176−177	**18.** T, pp. 182−183	

MULTIPLE-CHOICE QUESTIONS

1. b, p. 172	**10.** c, pp. 173−174	**19.** c, pp. 182−183
2. c, p. 172	**11.** b, p. 178	**20.** c, pp. 182−183
3. c, pp. 173−174	**12.** a, p. 179	**21.** b, pp. 182−183
4. b, pp. 174−175	**13.** b, pp. 179−180	**22.** c, p. 186
5. d, pp. 175−176	**14.** c, pp. 179−180	**23.** c, p. 186
6. a, pp. 176−177	**15.** a, p. 181	**24.** a, p. 187
7. c, pp. 176−177	**16.** d, p. 181	**25.** b, p. 187
8. c, pp. 176−177	**17.** d, p. 181	
9. b, pp. 176−177	**18.** c, p. 180	

PROBLEMS

1. *a.* investment; *b.* constant (given); *c.* (1) unrelated, (2) directly related; *d.* decrease, downward

2. *a.* I_g: 22, 22, 22, 22, 22, 22, 22; **C** + I_g: 1,328, 1,336, 1,344, 1,352, 1,360, 1,368, 1,376; *UI*: −8, −6, −4, −2, 0, +2, +4; *b.* 1,360; *c.* 0.8, 0.2; *d.* 5; *e.* increase, 3, increase, 15; *f.* decrease, 4, decrease, 20

3. *a.* $4 (and put $4 in each of the seven net exports values in the table); *b.* $780, 820, 860, 900, 940, 980, 1,020; *c.* $900; *d.* 5; *e.* (1) increase, $50, (2) decrease, $50

4. *a.* 0.9, 90, C_a: 1160, 1250, 1340, 1430, 1520, 1610, 1700; *b.* C_a + I_g + X_n + **G**: 1510, 1600, 1690, 1780, 1870, 1960, 2050; *c.* 1600; *d.* plot graph; *e.* rise, 100; *f.* fall, 90; *g.* raise, 10

5. *a.* 2.5; *b.* 620, 30, inflationary, 12; *c.* 570, 20, recessionary, 8

SHORT ANSWER AND ESSAY QUESTIONS

1. p. 172	**8.** pp. 179−180	**15.** pp. 185−186
2. p. 172	**9.** pp. 179−180	**16.** p. 186
3. p. 173	**10.** p. 181	**17.** pp. 186−187
4. pp. 173−175	**11.** p. 182	**18.** p. 187
5. pp. 176−177	**12.** p. 182	**19.** p. 187
6. pp. 176−177	**13.** p. 183	**20.** pp. 187, 189
7. pp. 177−178	**14.** pp. 182−184	

CHAPTER 11

Aggregate Demand and Aggregate Supply

Chapter 11 introduces another macro model of the economy, one based on aggregate demand and aggregate supply. This model can be used to explain real domestic output and the level of prices at any point in time and to understand what causes output and the price level to change.

The **aggregate demand (AD) curve** is downsloping because of the real balances, interest rate, and foreign purchases effects resulting from changes in the price level. With a downsloping aggregate demand curve, changes in the price level have an inverse effect on the level of spending by domestic consumers, businesses, government, and foreign buyers, and thus on real domestic output, assuming *other things equal*. This change would be equivalent to a movement along an existing aggregate demand curve: A lower price level increases the quantity of real domestic output demanded, and a higher price level decreases the quantity of real domestic output demanded.

The aggregate demand curve can increase or decrease because of a change in one of the nonprice level **determinants of aggregate demand.** The determinants include changes affecting consumer, investment, government, and net export spending. You will learn that underlying each demand determinant are various factors that cause the determinant to change. The size of the change involves two components. For example, if one of these spending determinants increases, then aggregate demand will increase. The change in aggregate demand involves an increase in initial spending plus a multiplier effect that results in a greater change in aggregate demand than the initial change.

The **aggregate supply (AS) curve** shows the relationship between the output of producers and the price level. In the long run, the aggregate supply curve is vertical because the price level does not change production at the full-employment level of output. In the short run, however, the upsloping shape of the aggregate supply curve reflects what happens to per-unit production costs as real domestic output increases or decreases.

You should remember that an assumption has also been made that other things are equal when one moves along an aggregate supply curve. When other things change, the aggregate supply curve can shift. The **determinants of aggregate supply** include changes in input prices, changes in productivity, and changes in the legal and institutional environment for production. As with aggregate demand, you will learn that there are underlying factors that cause these supply determinants to change.

The intersection of the aggregate demand and aggregate supply curves determines **equilibrium real output** and the **equilibrium price level.** Assuming that the determinants of aggregate demand and aggregate supply do not change, there are pressures that will tend to keep the economy at equilibrium. If a determinant changes, then aggregate demand, aggregate supply, or both, can shift.

When **aggregate demand increases,** this will lead to changes in equilibrium real output and the price level. If the economy is operating at full employment, the increase in AD may not have its full multiplier effect on the real GDP of the economy, and it will result in **demand-pull inflation.** There can also be a **decrease in aggregate demand,** but it may reduce output and not the price level. In this case, there can be downward price inflexibility for several reasons, as you will learn in the chapter.

Aggregate supply may increase or decrease. An increase in aggregate supply gives a double bonus for the economy because the price level falls, and output and employment increase. Conversely, a decrease in aggregate supply doubly harms the economy because the price level increases, and output and employment fall, and thus the economy experiences **cost-push inflation.**

The aggregate demand–aggregate supply model is an important framework for determining the equilibrium level of real domestic output and prices in an economy. The model will be used extensively throughout the next eight chapters to analyze how different parts of the economy function.

■ **CHECKLIST**

When you have studied this chapter you should be able to

☐ Define aggregate demand.
☐ Describe the characteristics of the aggregate demand curve.
☐ Use the real-balances, interest-rate, and foreign purchases effects to explain why the aggregate demand curve slopes downward.
☐ Identify the four major spending determinants of aggregate demand.
☐ Give an example of the effect of the multiplier on changes in aggregate demand.
☐ Explain the four factors that can change the consumer spending determinant.

☐ Explain the two factors that can change the investment spending determinant.

☐ Explain what changes the government spending determinant.

☐ Explain the two factors that can cause changes in the net export spending determinant.

☐ Discuss how the four major spending determinants of aggregate demand (and their underlying factors) can increase or decrease aggregate demand.

☐ Define aggregate supply in both the long run and short run.

☐ Explain why the aggregate supply curve in the long run is vertical.

☐ Explain why the aggregate supply curve in the short run is upsloping.

☐ Identify the three major spending determinants of aggregate supply.

☐ Describe three factors that change the input prices determinant.

☐ Explain what changes the productivity determinant.

☐ Identify two factors that change the legal-institutional environment determinant.

☐ Explain how the three major determinants of aggregate supply (and their underlying factors) can increase or decrease aggregate supply.

☐ Explain why in equilibrium the economy will produce a particular combination of real output and the price level rather than another combination.

☐ Show the effects of an increase in aggregate demand on the real output and the price level and relate the changes to demand-pull inflation.

☐ Illustrate the effects of a decrease in aggregate demand on real output and the price level in the economy and relate the changes to recession and unemployment.

☐ Give five reasons for downward inflexibility of changes in the price level when aggregate demand decreases.

☐ Explain the effects of a decrease in aggregate supply on real output and the price level and relate the changes to cost-push inflation.

☐ Describe the effects of an increase in aggregate supply on real output and the price level and relate the changes in productivity.

■ **CHAPTER OUTLINE**

1. This chapter introduces the *aggregate demand–aggregate supply model* (AD–AS model). It explains why real domestic output *and* the price level fluctuate in the economy. The chapter begins by explaining the meaning and characteristics of aggregate demand.

    a. *Aggregate demand* is a curve that shows the total quantity of goods and services (real output) that will be purchased (demanded) at different price levels. With aggregate demand there is an inverse or negative relationship between the amount of real output demanded and the price level, so the curve slopes downward.

    b. Three reasons account for the inverse relationship between real output and the price level, and the downward slope of the aggregate demand curve.

(1) *Real-balances effect:* An increase in the price level decreases the purchasing power of financial assets with a fixed money value, and because those who own such assets are now poorer, they spend less for goods and services. A decrease in the price level has the opposite effects.

(2) *Interest-rate effect:* With the supply of money fixed, an increase in the price level increases the demand for money, increases interest rates, and as a result reduces those expenditures (by consumers and business firms) that are sensitive to increased interest rates. A decrease in the price level has the opposite effects.

(3) *Foreign purchases effect:* An increase in the price level (relative to foreign price levels) will reduce U.S. exports because U.S. products are now more expensive for foreigners, and expand U.S. imports because foreign products are less expensive for U.S. consumers. As a consequence, net exports will decrease, which means there will be a decrease in the quantity of goods and services demanded in the U.S. economy as the price level rises. A decrease in the price level (relative to foreign price levels) will have opposite effects.

2. Spending by domestic consumers, businesses, government, and foreign buyers that is independent of changes in the price level are *determinants of aggregate demand.* The amount of changes in aggregate demand involves two components: the amount of the initial change in one of the determinants, and a multiplier effect that multiplies the initial change. These determinants are also called aggregate demand shifts because a change in one of them, other things equal, will shift the entire aggregate demand curve. Figure 11.2 shows the shifts. What follows is a description of each of the four major determinants and underlying factors.

    a. *Consumer spending* can increase or decrease AD. If the price level is constant, and consumers decide to spend more, then AD will increase; if consumers decide to spend less, then AD will decrease. Four factors increase or decrease consumer spending.

(1) *Consumer wealth:* If the real value of financial asset increases, then consumers will feel wealthier, spend more, and AD increases. If the real value of financial assets falls, consumers will spend less and AD will decrease.

(2) *Consumer expectations:* If consumers become more optimistic about the future, they will likely spend more and AD will increase. If consumers expect the future to be worse, they will decrease their spending and AD will decrease.

(3) *Household indebtedness:* If consumers have a high level of debt relative to normal, they may be forced to reduce their spending, thus decreasing AD. Conversely, if the level of debt falls to a more manageable level, they may be able to borrow more money and increase their spending, thus increasing AD.

(4) *Taxes:* Cuts in taxes increase disposable income and the capacity for consumer spending, thus increasing AD. A rise in taxes decreases disposable income, consumer spending, and AD.

b. *Investment spending* can increase or decrease AD. If the price level is constant, and businesses decide to spend more on investment, then AD will increase. If businesses decide to spend less on investment, then AD will decrease. Three factors increase or decrease investment spending.

(1) *Real interest rates:* A decrease in real interest rates will increase the quantity of investment spending, thus increasing AD. An increase in real interest rates will decrease the quantity of investment spending, thus decreasing AD.

(2) *Expected returns:* If businesses expect higher returns on investments in the future, they will likely increase their investment spending today, so AD will increase. If businesses expect lower returns on investments in the future, they will decrease their investment spending today, and AD will decrease. These expected returns are influenced by expectations about future business conditions, the state of technology, the degree of excess capacity (the amount of unused capital goods), and business taxes.

(a) More positive future expectations, more technological progress, less excess capacity, and lower taxes will increase investment spending and thus increase AD.

(b) Less positive future expectations, less technological progress, more excess capacity, and higher taxes will decrease investment spending and thus decrease AD.

c. *Government spending* has a direct effect on AD, assuming that tax collections and interest rates do not change as a result of the spending. More government spending tends to increase AD and less government spending will decrease AD.

d. *Net export spending* can increase or decrease AD. If the price level is constant and net exports (exports minus imports) should increase, then AD will increase. If net exports are negative, then AD will decrease. Two factors explain the increase or decrease in net export spending.

(1) *National income abroad:* An increase in the national income of other nations will increase the demand for all goods and services, including U.S. exports. If U.S. exports increase relative to U.S. imports, then net exports will increase, and so will AD. A decline in national incomes abroad will tend to reduce U.S. net exports and thus reduces AD.

(2) *Exchange rates:* A depreciation in the value of the U.S. dollar means that U.S. imports should decline because domestic purchases cannot buy as many imports as they used to buy. U.S. exports should increase because foreigners have more purchasing power to buy U.S. products. These events increase net exports, and thus increase AD. An appreciation in the value of the dollar will decrease net exports, and thus decrease AD.

3. *Aggregate supply* is a curve that shows the total quantity of goods and services that will be produced (supplied) at different price levels.

a. In the *long run,* the aggregate supply curve is vertical at the full-employment level of output for the economy because the rise in wages and other inputs will match changes in the price level.

b. In the *short run,* the aggregate supply curve is upsloping because nominal wages and input prices adjust only slowly to changes in the price level. With this curve, an increase in the price level increases real output and a decrease in the price level reduces real output.

4. The *determinants of aggregate supply* that shift the curve include changes in the prices of inputs for production, changes in productivity, and changes in the legal and institutional environment in the economy, as outlined in Figure 11.5.

a. A change in *input prices* for resources used for production will change aggregate supply in the short run. Lower input prices increase AS and higher input prices decrease AS. These input prices are both for domestic and imported resources, and they can be influenced by market power.

(1) *Domestic resource prices* include the prices for labor, capital, and natural resources used for production. If any of these input prices decrease, then AS will decrease because the per-unit cost of production will decrease. When the prices of these domestic factors of production increase, then AS will decrease.

(2) The *prices of imported resources* is the cost of paying for resources imported from other nations. If the value of the dollar appreciates, then it will cost less to pay for imported resources used for production. As a result, per-unit production costs will decrease, and AS will increase. Conversely, if the value of the dollar depreciates, then it will cost more to import resources, so AS will decrease.

(3) A change in the degree of *market power* in resource markets can change resource prices, and thus change AS supply. A more competitive market will tend to decrease resource prices and increase AS. A more monopolistic market will tend to drive up resource prices and decrease AS.

b. As *productivity* improves, per-unit production costs will fall and AS will increase. This outcome occurs because productivity (output divided by input) is the denominator for the formula for per-unit production costs (which is: total input cost divided by productivity). As productivity declines, per-unit production costs will increase, so AS will decrease.

c. Changes in the *legal and institutional environment* for business can affect per-unit production costs and thus AS.

(1) A decrease in *business taxes* is like a reduction in the per-unit cost of production, so it will increase AS. The same effect occurs when there is an increase in *business subsidies.* The raising of taxes or lowering of subsidies for business will increase per-unit production costs and decrease AS.

(2) A decrease in the amount of *government regulation* is similar to a decrease in the per-unit cost of production, so it will increase AS. An increase in government regulation will raise costs, and thus will decrease AS.

5. The *equilibrium domestic output* and the *equilibrium price level* are at the intersection of the aggregate demand and the aggregate supply curves. If the price level were below equilibrium, then producers would supply less real output than was demanded by purchasers. Competition among buyers would bid up the price level and producers would increase their output, until an equilibrium price level and quantity was reached. If the price level were above equilibrium, then producers would supply more real output than was demanded by purchasers. Competition among sellers would lower the price level and producers would reduce their output, until an equilibrium price level and quantity was reached. The aggregate demand and aggregate supply curves can also **shift to change equilibrium.**

    a. An **increase in aggregate demand** would result in an increase in both real domestic output and the price level. An increase in the price level beyond the full-employment level of output is associated with **demand-pull inflation.**

    b. A **decrease in aggregate demand** reduces real output, but it may not decrease the price level. This **price level is inflexible downward** because it is largely influenced by labor costs which account for most of the input prices for the production of many goods and services. There are at least five interrelated reasons for this downward inflexibility of the price level.

    (1) If wages are determined largely by **long-term contracts,** it means that wages cannot be changed in the short run.

    (2) **Morale, effort, and productivity** may be affected by changes in wage rates. Employers may be reluctant to lower wages if they reduce work effort and productivity.

    (3) The **minimum wage** puts a legal floor on the wages for the least skilled workers in the economy.

    (4) Firms are reluctant to change input prices if there are costs related to changing the prices or announcing the change. Such **menu costs** increase the waiting time before businesses make any price changes.

    (5) The fear of starting a **price war** in which firms compete with each other on lowering prices regardless of the cost of production. Such a price war hurts business profits and makes firms reluctant to cut prices for fear of starting one.

    c. A **decrease in aggregate supply** means there will be a decrease in real domestic output (economic growth) and employment along with a rise in the price level, or **cost-push inflation.**

    d. An **increase in aggregate supply** arising from an increase in productivity has the beneficial effects of improving real domestic output and employment while maintaining a stable price level.

■ **HINTS AND TIPS**

1. Aggregate demand and supply are the tools used to explain what determines the economy's real output and price level. These tools, however, are **different from the demand and supply** used in Chapter 3 to explain what determines the output and price of a *particular* product. Instead of thinking about the quantity of a *particular* good or service demanded or supplied, it is necessary to think

about the total or *aggregate* quantity of all final goods and services demanded (purchased) and supplied (produced). You will have no difficulty with the way demand and supply are used in this chapter once you switch from thinking about a *particular* good or service and its price to the *aggregate* of all final goods and services and their average price.

2. Make a chart showing each of the **determinants** of aggregate demand (see Figure 11.2) and aggregate supply (Figure 11.5). In the chart, state the direction of the change in each determinant, and then state the likely resulting change in AD or AS. For example, if consumer wealth *increases,* then AD *increases.* Or, if imported prices for resources *increase,* then AS *decreases.* This simple chart can help you quickly see in one quick glance all the possible changes in determinants and their likely effects on AD or AS. Problem 2 in this study guide will give you an application for this chart.

3. Make sure you know the difference between a **movement** along an existing aggregate demand or supply curve and a **shift** in (increase or decrease in) an aggregate demand or supply curve. Figures 11.7 and 11.9 illustrate the distinction.

■ **IMPORTANT TERMS**

aggregate demand–aggregate supply model	**short-run aggregate supply curve**
aggregate demand (AD)	**determinants of aggregate supply**
real-balances effect	
interest-rate effect	**productivity**
foreign purchases effect	**equilibrium price level**
determinants of aggregate demand	**equilibrium real output**
	efficiency wages
aggregate supply (AS)	**menu costs**
long-run aggregate supply curve	

SELF-TEST

■ **FILL-IN QUESTIONS**

1. Aggregate demand and aggregate supply together determine the equilibrium real domestic (price, output)

_____ and the equilibrium _____
level.

2. The aggregate demand curve shows the quantity of goods and services that will be (supplied, demanded)

_____ or purchased at various price levels. For aggregate demand, the relationship between real output and the price level is (positive, negative)

_____.

3. The aggregate demand curve slopes (upward, downward) _____ because of the (real-balances, consumption) _____ effect, the (profit, interest) _____-rate effect, and the (domestic, foreign) _____ purchases effect.

4. For the aggregate demand curve, an increase in the price level (increases, decreases) _____ the quantity of real domestic output demanded, whereas a decrease in the price level _____ the quantity of real domestic output demanded, assuming other things equal.

5. For the aggregate demand curve, when the price level changes, there is a (movement along, change in) _____ the curve. When the entire aggregate demand curve shifts, there is a change in (the quantity of real output demanded, aggregate demand) _____.

6. List the four factors that may change consumer spending, and thus shift aggregate demand:

a. _____

b. _____

c. _____

d. _____

7. List two major factors that may change investment spending, and thus shift aggregate demand:

a. _____

b. _____

8. If government spending increases, then aggregate demand is likely to (increase, decrease) _____, but if government spending decreases, it is likely to _____.

9. If there is an increase in national income abroad, then net exports spending is most likely to (increase, decrease) _____ and if there is a depreciation of the value of the U.S. dollar, then net exports are likely to _____. When net exports increase, aggregate demand will (increase, decrease) _____.

10. The aggregate supply curve shows the quantity of goods and services that will be (demanded, supplied) _____ or produced at various price levels. As the price level increases, real domestic output (increases, decreases) _____, and as the price level decreases, real domestic output _____. The relationship between the price level and real domestic output supplied is (positive, negative) _____.

11. The basic cause of a decrease in aggregate supply is the (increase, decrease) _____ in per-

unit costs of producing goods and services, and the basic cause of an increase in aggregate supply is the _____ in per-unit costs of production, all other things equal.

12. Aggregate supply shifts may result from:

a. a change in input prices caused by a change in

(1) _____

(2) _____

(3) _____

b. a change in (consumption, productivity) _____

c. a change in the legal and institutional environment caused by a change in

(1) _____

(2) _____

13. The equilibrium real domestic output and price level are found at the (zero values, intersection) _____ of the aggregate demand and the aggregate supply curves. At this price level, the aggregate quantity of goods and services demanded is (greater than, less than, equal to) _____ the aggregate quantity of goods and services supplied. And at this real domestic output, the prices producers are willing to (pay, accept) _____ are equal to the prices buyers are willing to _____.

14. If the price level were below equilibrium, the quantity of real domestic output supplied would be (greater than, less than) _____ the quantity of real domestic output demanded. As a result competition among buyers eliminates the (surplus, shortage) _____ and bids up the price level.

15. If the price level were above equilibrium, the quantity of real domestic output supplied would be (greater than, less than) _____ the quantity of real domestic output demanded. As a result competition among producers eliminates the (surplus, shortage) _____ and lowers the price level.

16. An increase in aggregate demand will (increase, decrease) _____ real domestic output and will _____ the price level. If the economy is initially operating at its full-employment level of output, and aggregate demand increases, it will produce (demand-pull, cost-push) _____ inflation.

17. If aggregate demand decreases, then real domestic output will (increase, decrease) _____. Such a change often produces economic conditions called (inflation, recession) _____ and unemployment (rises, falls) _____.

18. When aggregate demand decreases, the price level is often inflexible (upward, downward) _____.
This inflexibility occurs because of wage (contracts, flexibility) _____, workers are paid (efficiency, inefficiency) _____ wages, there is a (maximum, minimum) _____ wage, businesses experience menu (benefits, costs) _____, and there is fear of (price, wage) _____ wars.

19. A decrease in aggregate supply will (increase, decrease) _____ real output and _____ the price level. Such a change in aggregate supply contributes to (demand-pull, cost-push) _____ inflation.

20. An increase in aggregate supply will (increase, decrease) _____ real domestic output and _____ the price level. If aggregate demand increased, the price level would (increase, decrease) _____, but a simultaneous increase in aggregate supply (reinforces, offsets) _____ this change and helps keep the price level stable.

■ **TRUE–FALSE QUESTIONS**

Circle T if the statement is true, F if it is false.

1. Aggregate demand reflects a positive relationship between the price level and the amount of real output demanded.   **T F**

2. The explanation for why the aggregate demand curve slopes downward is the same as the explanation for why the demand curve for a single product slopes downward.   **T F**

3. A fall in the price level increases the real value of financial assets with fixed money values and, as a result, increases spending by the holders of these assets.   **T F**

4. Given a fixed supply of money, a rise in the price level increases the demand for money in the economy and drives interest rates downward.   **T F**

5. A rise in the price level of an economy (relative to foreign price levels) tends to increase that economy's exports and to reduce its imports of goods and services.   **T F**

6. A movement along a fixed aggregate demand curve is the same as a shift in aggregate demand.   **T F**

7. Changes in aggregate demand involve a change in initial spending from one of the determinants and a multiplier effect on spending.   **T F**

8. A change in aggregate demand is caused by a change in the price level, *other things equal.*   **T F**

9. A fall in excess capacity, or unused existing capital goods, will retard the demand for new capital goods and therefore reduce aggregate demand.   **T F**

10. The real-balances effect is one of the determinants of aggregate demand.   **T F**

11. A high level of household indebtedness will tend to increase consumption spending and aggregate demand.   **T F**

12. Appreciation of the dollar relative to foreign currencies will tend to increase net exports and aggregate demand.   **T F**

13. The aggregate supply curve is vertical in the long run at the full-employment level of output.   **T F**

14. When the determinants of short-run aggregate supply change, they alter the per-unit production cost and thereby aggregate supply.   **T F**

15. A change in the degree of market power or monopoly power held by sellers of resources can affect input prices and aggregate supply.   **T F**

16. Productivity is a measure of real output per unit of input.   **T F**

17. Per-unit production cost is determined by dividing total input cost by units of output.   **T F**

18. At the equilibrium price level, the real domestic output purchased is equal to the real domestic output produced.   **T F**

19. An increase in aggregate demand will increase both the price level and the real domestic output.   **T F**

20. An increase in aggregate demand is associated with cost-push inflation.   **T F**

21. The greater the increase in the price level that results from an increase in aggregate demand, the greater will be the increase in the equilibrium real GDP.   **T F**

22. A significant decrease in aggregate demand can result in recession and cyclical unemployment.   **T F**

23. Fear of price wars tends to make the price level more flexible rather than less flexible.   **T F**

24. A decrease in aggregate supply decreases the equilibrium real domestic output and increases the price level, resulting in cost-push inflation.   **T F**

25. An increase in aggregate supply driven by productivity increases can offset the inflationary pressures from an increase in aggregate demand.   **T F**

■ **MULTIPLE-CHOICE QUESTIONS**

Circle the letter that corresponds to the best answer.

1. The aggregate demand curve is the relationship between the
  (a) price level and what producers will supply
  (b) price level and the real domestic output purchased

(c) price level and the real domestic output produced

(d) real domestic output purchased and the real domestic output produced

2. When the price level rises,
(a) the demand for money and interest rates rises
(b) spending that is sensitive to interest-rate changes increases
(c) holders of financial assets with fixed money values increase their spending
(d) holders of financial assets with fixed money values have more purchasing power

3. One explanation for the downward slope of the aggregate demand curve is that a change in the price level results in
(a) a multiplier effect
(b) an income effect
(c) a substitution effect
(d) a foreign purchases effect

4. A sharp decline in the real value of stock prices, which is independent of a change in the price level, would best be an example of
(a) the interest-rate effect
(b) the foreign purchases effect
(c) a change in household indebtedness
(d) a change in real value of consumer wealth

5. The aggregate demand curve will be increased by
(a) a decrease in the price level
(b) an increase in the price level
(c) a depreciation in the value of the U.S. dollar
(d) an increase in the excess capacity of factories

6. The aggregate supply curve is the relationship between the
(a) price level and the real domestic output purchased
(b) price level and the real domestic output produced
(c) price level that producers are willing to accept and the price level purchasers are willing to pay
(d) real domestic output purchased and the real domestic output produced

7. In the long run, the aggregate supply curve is
(a) upsloping
(b) downsloping
(c) vertical
(d) horizontal

8. The short-run aggregate supply curve assumes that
(a) nominal wages respond to changes in the price level
(b) nominal wages do not respond to changes in the price level
(c) the economy is operating at full-employment output
(d) the economy is operating at less than full-employment output

9. If the prices of imported resources increase, then this event would most likely
(a) decrease aggregate supply
(b) increase aggregate supply
(c) increase aggregate demand
(d) decrease aggregate demand

Suppose that real domestic output in an economy is 50 units, the quantity of inputs is 10, and the price of each input is $2. Answer Questions 10, 11, 12, and 13 on the basis of this information.

10. The level of productivity in this economy is
(a) 5
(b) 4
(c) 3
(d) 2

11. The per-unit cost of production is
(a) $0.40
(b) $0.50
(c) $2.50
(d) $3.50

12. If productivity increased such that 60 units are now produced with the quantity of inputs still equal to 10, then per-unit production costs would
(a) remain unchanged and aggregate supply would remain unchanged
(b) increase and aggregate supply would decrease
(c) decrease and aggregate supply would increase
(d) decrease and aggregate supply would decrease

13. All else equal, if the price of each input increases from $2 to $4, productivity would
(a) decrease from $4 to $2 and aggregate supply would decrease
(b) decrease from $5 to $3 and aggregate supply would decrease
(c) decrease from $4 to $2 and aggregate supply would increase
(d) remain unchanged and aggregate supply would decrease

14. If Congress passed much stricter laws to control the air pollution from businesses, this action would tend to
(a) increase per-unit production costs and shift the aggregate supply curve to the right
(b) increase per-unit production costs and shift the aggregate supply curve to the left
(c) increase per-unit production costs and shift the aggregate demand curve to the left
(d) decrease per-unit production costs and shift the aggregate supply curve to the left

15. An increase in business taxes will tend to
(a) decrease aggregate demand but not change aggregate supply
(b) decrease aggregate supply but not change aggregate demand
(c) decrease aggregate demand and decrease aggregate supply
(d) decrease aggregate supply and increase aggregate demand

16. If at a particular price level, real domestic output from producers is less than real domestic output desired by buyers, there will be a
(a) surplus and the price level will rise
(b) surplus and the price level will fall
(c) shortage and the price level will rise
(d) shortage and the price level will fall

Answer Questions 17, 18, and 19 on the basis of the following aggregate demand–aggregate supply schedule for a hypothetical economy.

Real domestic output demanded (in billions)	Price level	Real domestic output supplied (in billions)
$1500	175	$4500
2000	150	4000
2500	125	3500
3000	100	3000
3500	75	2500
4000	50	2000

17. The equilibrium price level and quantity of real domestic output will be
(a) 100 and $2500
(b) 100 and $3000
(c) 125 and $3500
(d) 150 and $4000

18. If the quantity of real domestic output demanded increased by $2000 at each price level, the new equilibrium price level and quantity of real domestic output would be
(a) 175 and $4000
(b) 150 and $4000
(c) 125 and $3500
(d) 100 and $3000

19. Using the original data from the table, if the quantity of real domestic output demanded *increased* by $1500 and the quantity of real domestic output supplied *increased* by $500 at each price level, the new equilibrium price level and quantity of real domestic output would be
(a) 175 and $4000
(b) 150 and $4500
(c) 125 and $4000
(d) 100 and $3500

20. An increase in aggregate demand will increase
(a) the price level and have no effect on real domestic output
(b) the real domestic output and have no effect on the price level
(c) the price level and decrease the real domestic output
(d) both real output and the price level

21. In the aggregate demand–aggregate supply model, an increase in the price level will
(a) increase the real value of wealth
(b) increase the strength of the multiplier
(c) decrease the strength of the multiplier
(d) have no effect on the strength of the multiplier

22. Aggregate demand decreases and real output falls but the price level remains the same. Which factor most likely contributes to downward price inflexibility?
(a) an increase in aggregate supply
(b) the foreign purchases effect
(c) lower interest rates
(d) efficiency wages

23. Menu costs, wage contracts, and fear of price wars are associated with
(a) a price level that is inflexible upward

(b) a price level that is inflexible downward
(c) a domestic output that cannot be increased
(d) a domestic output that cannot be decreased

24. If there were cost-push inflation,
(a) both the real domestic output and the price level would decrease
(b) the real domestic output would increase and rises in the price level would become smaller
(c) the real domestic output would decrease and the price level would rise
(d) both the real domestic output and rises in the price level would become greater

25. An increase in aggregate supply will
(a) increase the price level and real domestic output
(b) decrease the price level and real domestic output
(c) decrease the price level and increase the real domestic output
(d) decrease the price level and have no effect on real domestic output

■ **PROBLEMS**

1. Following is an aggregate supply schedule.

Price level	Real domestic output supplied
250	2100
225	2000
200	1900
175	1700
150	1400
125	1000
100	900

a. Plot this aggregate supply schedule on the graph on the next page.
b. The following table has three aggregate demand schedules.

Price level (1)	Real domestic output demanded		
	(2)	(3)	(4)
250	1400	1900	500
225	1500	2000	600
200	1600	2100	700
175	1700	2200	800
150	1800	2300	900
125	1900	2400	1000
100	2000	2500	1100

(1) On the graph, plot the aggregate demand curve shown in columns 1 and 2; label this curve **AD₁**. At this level of aggregate demand, the equilibrium real

domestic output is _____ and the equilibrium price level is _____.

(2) On the same graph, plot the aggregate demand curve shown in columns 1 and 3; label this curve **AD₂**.

The equilibrium real domestic output is _____ and

the equilibrium price level is _____.

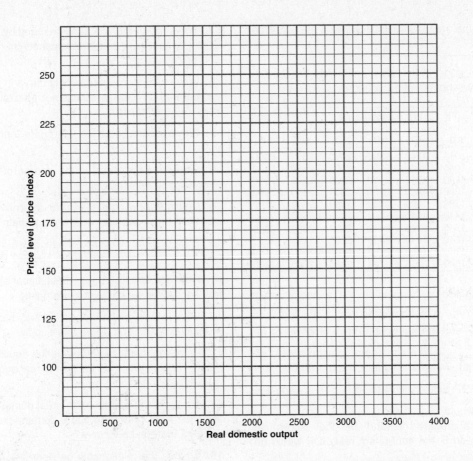

Price level (price index) vs Real domestic output

(3) On the same graph, plot the aggregate demand curve shown in columns 1 and 4; label it **AD₃.** The equilibrium real domestic output is _____

and the equilibrium price level is _____.

2. In the following list, what will most likely happen as a result of each event to (1) aggregate demand (AD); (2) aggregate supply (AS); (3) the equilibrium price level (**P**); and (4) equilibrium real domestic output (**Q**)? Assume that all other things remain constant when the event occurs and that the economy is operating in the intermediate range of the aggregate supply curve. Use the following symbols to indicate the expected effects: **I** = increase, **D** = decrease, **S** = remains the same, and **U** = uncertain.

a. A decrease in labor productivity.

AD_____   AS_____   **P**_____   **Q**_____

b. A fall in the interest rate for business loans.

AD_____   AS_____   **P**_____   **Q**_____

c. Consumer incomes decline as the economy moves into a recession.

AD_____   AS_____   **P**_____   **Q**_____

d. The price of oil on the world market falls to a low level.

AD_____   AS_____   **P**_____   **Q**_____

e. There is an appreciation in the value of the U.S. dollar.

AD_____   AS_____   **P**_____   **Q**_____

3. Following are hypothetical data showing the relationships between the real domestic output and the quantity of input resources needed to produce each level of output.

Output	Input	Productivity		Per-unit cost		
		(1)	(2)	(3)	(4)	(5)
2500	500	____	____	____	____	____
2000	400	____	____	____	____	____
1500	300	____	____	____	____	____

a. In column 1, compute the level of productivity at each level of real domestic output.

b. In column 2, compute the level of productivity if there is a doubling in the quantity of inputs required to produce each level of output.

c. In column 3, compute the per-unit production cost at each level of output if each unit of input costs $15, given the level of productivity in column 1.

d. In column 4, compute the new per-unit production cost at each level of output if each unit of input costs $15, given that there has been a doubling in the required quantity of inputs to produce each level of output as shown in column 2. If this situation occurs, will aggregate supply (decrease, increase, stay the same)?

_____

e. In column 5, compute the new per-unit production cost at each level of output, given that input price is now $10 instead of $15 but the level of productivity stays as it was originally shown in column 1. What will happen to the aggregate supply curve if this situation occurs? _____

4. Columns 1 and 2 in the table that follows are the aggregate supply schedule of an economy.

(1) Price level	(2) Real GDP	(3) AD$_1$	(4) AD$_2$	(5) AD$_3$	(6) AD$_4$	(7) AD$_5$	(8) AD$_6$
260	2540	940	1140	1900	2000	2090	2390
240	2490	1040	1240	2000	2100	2190	2490
220	2430	1140	1340	2100	2200	2290	2590
200	2390	1240	1440	2200	2300	2390	2690
190	2350	1390	1590	2250	2350	2540	2740
180	2300	1440	1640	2300	2400	2590	2890
160	2200	1540	1740	2400	2500	2690	2990
140	2090	1640	1840	2500	2600	2790	3090
120	1940	1740	1940	2600	2700	2890	3190
100	1840	1840	2040	2700	2800	2990	3290

a. If the aggregate demand in the economy were columns 1 and 3, the equilibrium real GDP would be

_____ and the equilibrium price level would be

_____, and if aggregate demand should increase to that shown in columns 1 and 4, the equilibrium real GDP would increase to _____ and the

price level would _____.

b. Should aggregate demand be that shown in columns 1 and 5, the equilibrium real GDP would be

_____ and the equilibrium price would be

_____, and if aggregate demand should increase by 100 units to that shown in columns 1 and 6,

the equilibrium real GDP would increase to _____

and the price level would rise to _____.

c. If aggregate demand were that shown in columns 1 and 7, the equilibrium real GDP would be

_____ and the equilibrium price level would

be _____, but if aggregate demand increased to that shown in columns 1 and 8, the equilibrium real

GDP would _____ and the price level would

rise to _____.

■ SHORT ANSWER AND ESSAY QUESTIONS

1. What is the aggregate demand curve? Draw a graph and explain its features.

2. Use the interest-rate effect, the real-balances effect, and the foreign purchases effect to explain the relationship between the price level and the real domestic output demanded.

3. Explain the wealth effect and its impact on purchasing power. Give an example.

4. What roles do the expectations of consumers and businesses play in influencing aggregate demand?

5. How is aggregate demand changed by changes in net export spending? What factors cause changes in net export spending?

6. Why is the aggregate supply curve in the long run a vertical curve? Why is output not affected by the price level in the long run?

7. Why does the short-run aggregate supply curve slope upward?

8. Why does a change in the degree of market power affect aggregate supply?

9. Describe how changes in the international economy influence aggregate demand or aggregate supply.

10. How does an increase or decrease in per-unit production costs change aggregate supply? Give examples.

11. How does the legal and institutional environment affect aggregate supply? Give examples.

12. Explain how a change in business taxes affects aggregate demand and aggregate supply.

13. What real domestic output is the equilibrium real domestic output? What will happen to real output if the price level is below equilibrium?

14. What are the effects on the real domestic output and the price level when aggregate demand increases along the aggregate supply curve?

15. What is the relationship between the effect of an increase in aggregate demand on real GDP and the rise in the price level that accompanies it? Discuss it in terms of the multiplier effect.

16. If prices were as flexible downward as they are upward, what would be the effects on real domestic output and the price level of a decrease in aggregate demand?

17. Give reasons why prices in the economy tend to be "sticky" or inflexible in a downward direction in the horizontal range of aggregate supply.

18. What are the effects on the real domestic output and the price level of a decrease in aggregate supply?

19. How does an increase in aggregate supply affect the price level and real output?

20. Using the aggregate demand and aggregate supply concepts, explain the difference between demand-pull and cost-push inflation.

ANSWERS

Chapter 11 Aggregate Demand and Aggregate Supply

FILL-IN QUESTIONS

1. output, price
2. demanded, negative
3. downward, real-balances, interest, foreign
4. decreases, increases
5. movement along, aggregate demand

6. *a.* consumer wealth; *b.* consumer expectations; *c.* household indebtedness; *d.* personal taxes (any order for *a–d*)

7. *a.* interest rates; *b.* expected returns on investment (any order for *a–b*)

8. increase, decrease

9. increase, increase, increase

10. supplied, increases, decreases, positive

11. increase, decrease

12. *a.* (1) domestic resource availability, (2) prices of imported resources, (3) market power (any order for *1–3*); *b.* productivity; *c.* (1) business taxes and subsidies, (2) government regulation (any order for *1–2*)

13. intersection, equal to, accept, pay

14. less than, shortage

15. greater than, surplus

16. increase, increase, demand-pull

17. decrease, recession, rises

18. downward, contracts, efficiency, minimum, costs, price

19. decrease, increase, cost-push

20. increase, decrease, increase, offsets

TRUE–FALSE QUESTIONS

1. F, pp. 193–194 **10.** F, p. 195 **19.** T, p. 203

2. F, p. 194 **11.** F, p. 196 **20.** F, p. 203

3. T, p. 194 **12.** F, p. 197 **21.** F, p. 203

4. F, p. 194 **13.** T, pp. 197–198 **22.** T, pp. 203–204

5. F, pp. 194–195 **14.** T, pp. 198–199 **23.** F, p. 205

6. F, p. 195 **15.** T, p. 200 **24.** T, p. 205

7. T, p. 195 **16.** T, pp. 201–202 **25.** T, pp. 205–206

8. F, p. 195 **17.** T, p. 201

9. F, pp. 196–197 **18.** T, pp. 201–202

MULTIPLE-CHOICE QUESTIONS

1. b, p. 193 **10.** a, pp. 200–201 **19.** c, pp. 205–206

2. a, p. 194 **11.** a, pp. 200–201 **20.** d, p. 203

3. d, pp. 194–195 **12.** c, pp. 200–201 **21.** c, p. 203

4. d, p. 196 **13.** d, pp. 200–201 **22.** d, pp. 203–204

5. c, p. 197 **14.** b, p. 201 **23.** b, pp. 204–205

6. b, p. 197 **15.** c, p. 201 **24.** c, p. 205

7. c, pp. 197–198 **16.** c, pp. 201–203 **25.** c, pp. 205–206

8. b, pp. 198–199 **17.** b, p. 202

9. a, p. 200 **18.** b, p. 202

PROBLEMS

1. *b.* (1) 1700, 175, (2) 2000, 225, (3) 1000, 125

2. *a. S, D, I, D; b. I, S, I, I; c. D, S, D, D; d. I, I, U, I; e. D, I, D, U*

3. *a.* 5, 5, 5; *b.* 2.5, 2.5, 2.5; *c.* $3, $3, $3; *d.* $6, $6, $6, decrease; *e.* $2, $2, $2, it will increase

4. *a.* 1840, 100, 1940, 120; *b.* 2300, 180, 2350, 190; *c.* 2390, 200, 2490, 240

SHORT ANSWER AND ESSAY QUESTIONS

1. pp. 193–194 **8.** p. 200 **15.** p. 203

2. pp. 194–195 **9.** pp. 197, 200 **16.** pp. 204–205

3. p. 196 **10.** pp. 200–201 **17.** pp. 204–205

4. pp. 196–197 **11.** p. 201 **18.** p. 205

5. p. 197 **12.** pp. 197, 201 **19.** pp. 205–206

6. pp. 197–198 **13.** pp. 201–203 **20.** pp. 203, 205

7. pp. 198–199 **14.** p. 203

The Relationship of the Aggregate Demand Curve to the Aggregate Expenditure Model

This appendix explains how the aggregate expenditures (AE) model that you learned about in Chapter 10 is related to the aggregate demand (AD) curve that was presented in Chapter 11. There are two short sections to this appendix. The first one focuses on the derivation of the aggregate demand curve from the AE model. The second one explains how shifts in aggregate demand are related to shifts in aggregate expenditures.

Although the aggregate expenditures model is a fixed-price-level model and the aggregate demand–aggregate supply model is a variable-price-level model, there is a close relationship between the two models. The important thing to understand is that prices can be fixed or constant at different levels. The AD curve can be derived from the aggregate expenditures model by letting the price level be constant at different levels. For example, the lower (the higher) the level at which prices are constant in the aggregate expenditures model, the larger (the smaller) will be the equilibrium real GDP in that model of the economy. Various output-price-level combinations can be traced to derive an AD curve that slopes downward, as shown in Figure 1 in the text.

The aggregate demand curve can shift (increase or decrease) because of a change in the nonprice level **determinants of aggregate demand.** The determinants include changes in factors affecting consumer, investment, government, and net export spending. These determinants are similar to the components of the aggregate expenditures model. It is easy to show the relationship between the shifts in the two models. A change in spending will cause a shift (upward or downward) in the aggregate expenditures schedule as shown in Figure 2 in the text. The initial change in spending when multiplied times the multiplier would be equal to the size of the horizontal shift in AD, assuming a constant price level.

■ CHECKLIST

When you have studied this appendix you should be able to

☐ Contrast the aggregate expenditures and the aggregate demand–aggregate supply models by comparing the variability of the price level and real GDP.
☐ Use a graph to derive the aggregate demand curve from the aggregate expenditures model.
☐ Explain the effect of a change in a determinant of aggregate demand on aggregate expenditures.

☐ Use a graph to show the relationship between a shift in aggregate expenditures and a shift in aggregate demand.
☐ Discuss how the initial change in spending and the multiplier effect influence the size of the shift in aggregate demand.

■ CHAPTER OUTLINE

1. This chapter introduces the **aggregate demand–aggregate supply model** of the economy to explain why real domestic output *and* the price level fluctuate. This model has an advantage over the aggregate expenditures model because it allows the price level to vary (rise and fall) rather than be constant or fixed as in the aggregate expenditures model.

2. The aggregate demand curve can be derived from the intersections of the aggregate expenditures curves and the 45-degree curve. As the price level falls, the aggregate expenditures curve shifts upward and the equilibrium real GDP increases, but as the price level rises, the aggregate expenditures curve shifts downward and the equilibrium real GDP decreases. The inverse relationship between the price level and equilibrium real GDP is the aggregate demand curve. Note that for the aggregate expenditures model,

(1) changes in real balances (wealth) increase or decrease the consumption schedule;
(2) changes in the interest rate increase or decrease the investment schedule; and,
(3) changes in imports or exports affect net exports, which can increase or decrease the net export schedule.

3. If the price level is constant, any change in nonprice-level determinants of consumption and planned investment that shifts the aggregate expenditures curve upward will increase the equilibrium real GDP and shift the AD curve to the right by an amount equal to the initial increase in aggregate expenditures times the multiplier. Conversely, any change in nonprice-level determinants of consumption and planned investment that shifts the aggregate expenditures curve downward will decrease the equilibrium real GDP and shift the AD curve to the left by an amount equal to the initial decrease in aggregate expenditures times the multiplier.

■ HINTS AND TIPS

1. Figure 1 is worth extra study to see the relationship between the quantity (real domestic output) and the price level in both models. The upper panel shows the aggregate expenditures model with aggregate expenditures on the vertical axis and quantity on the horizontal axis. The lower panel shows the aggregate demand model with the price level on the vertical axis and quantity on the horizontal axis. Thus the horizontal axes in both graphs are the same and directly related. The connection between the price levels in each graph is more indirect but they are related nevertheless as shown in Figure 1.

2. Figure 2 shows how shifts are accounted for in each model. A shift upward in aggregate expenditures is the same as a shift outward in aggregate demand. The magnitude of the change in quantity will depend on the multiplier effect, but in both models quantity increases by the same amount.

■ IMPORTANT TERMS

aggregate demand (AD)
determinants of
  aggregate demand

aggregate expenditures
  schedule
multiplier

SELF-TEST

■ FILL-IN QUESTIONS

1. In the aggregate demand–aggregate supply model, the price level is (fixed, variable) _____, but in the aggregate expenditures model, the price level is

_____ .

2. In the aggregate expenditures model, a lower price level would (raise, lower) _____ the consumption, investment, and aggregate expenditures curves, and the equilibrium level of real GDP would (rise, fall) _____ .

3. In the aggregate expenditures model, a higher price level would (raise, lower) _____ the consumption, investment, and aggregate expenditures curves, and the equilibrium level of real GDP would (rise, fall) _____ .

4. This relationship between the price level and equilibrium real GDP in the aggregate expenditures model is (direct, inverse) _____ and can be used to derive the aggregate (demand, supply) _____ curve.

5. If the price level were constant, an increase in the aggregate expenditures curve would shift the aggregate demand curve to the (right, left) _____ by an amount equal to the upward shift in aggregate expenditures times the (interest rate, multiplier) _____ . A decrease in the aggregate expenditures curve would shift the aggregate demand curve to the (right, left) _____ by an amount equal to the (upward, downward) _____ shift in aggregate expenditures times the (interest rate, multiplier) _____ .

■ TRUE–FALSE QUESTIONS

Circle T if the statement is true, F if it is false.

1. Both the graph of the aggregate demand curve and the aggregate expenditures model show the price level on the vertical axis. **T F**

2. The higher the price level, the smaller the real balances of consumers and the lower the aggregate expenditures schedule. **T F**

3. An increase in the price level will shift the aggregate expenditures schedule upward. **T F**

4. An increase in investment spending will shift the aggregate expenditures curve upward and the aggregate demand curve leftward. **T F**

5. A shift in the aggregate demand curve is equal to the initial change in spending times the multiplier. **T F**

■ MULTIPLE-CHOICE QUESTIONS

Circle the letter that corresponds to the best answer.

1. If the price level in the aggregate expenditures model were lower, the consumption and aggregate expenditures curves would be
  (a) lower, and the equilibrium real GDP would be smaller
  (b) lower, and the equilibrium real GDP would be larger
  (c) higher, and the equilibrium real GDP would be larger
  (d) higher, and the equilibrium real GDP would be smaller

2. In the aggregate expenditures model, a decrease in the price level, other things held constant, will shift the
  (a) consumption, investment, and net exports curves downward
  (b) consumption, investment, and net exports curves upward
  (c) consumption and investment curves upward, but the net exports curve downward
  (d) consumption and net export curves upward, but the investment curve downward

3. An increase in investment spending will
  (a) increase aggregate expenditures and increase aggregate demand
  (b) decrease aggregate expenditures and decrease aggregate demand

(c) increase aggregate expenditures and decrease aggregate demand

(d) decrease aggregate expenditures and increase aggregate demand

4. A decrease in net export spending will shift the
(a) aggregate expenditures schedule upward and the aggregate demand curve rightward
(b) aggregate expenditures schedule upward and the aggregate demand curve leftward
(c) aggregate expenditures schedule downward and the aggregate demand curve rightward
(d) aggregate expenditures schedule downward and the aggregate demand curve leftward

5. An increase in aggregate expenditures shifts the aggregate demand curve to the
(a) right by the amount of the increase in aggregate expenditures
(b) right by the amount of the increase in aggregate expenditures times the multiplier
(c) left by the amount of the increase in aggregate expenditures
(d) left by the amount of the increase in aggregate expenditures times the multiplier

■ **PROBLEMS**

1. Column 1 of the following table shows the real GDP an economy might produce.

(1) Real GDP	(2) $AE_{1.20}$	(3) $AE_{1.00}$	(4) $AE_{0.80}$
$2100	$2110	$2130	$2150
2200	2200	2220	2240
2300	2290	2310	2330
2400	2380	2400	2420
2500	2470	2490	2510
2600	2560	2580	2600

a. If the price level in this economy were $1.20, the aggregate expenditures (AE) at each real GDP would be those shown in column 2 and the equilibrium real

GDP would be $_____.
b. If the price level were $1.00, the aggregate expenditures at each real GDP would be those shown in column 3 and the equilibrium real GDP would be

$_____.
c. If the price level were $0.80, the aggregate expenditures at each real GDP would be those shown in column 4 and the equilibrium real GDP would be

$_____.
d. Show in the following schedule the equilibrium real GDP at each of the three price levels.

Price level	Equilibrium real GDP
$1.20	$_____
1.00	_____
0.80	_____

(1) This schedule is the aggregate (demand, supply)

_____ schedule.
(2) The equilibrium real GDP is (directly, inversely)

_____ related to the price level.

■ **SHORT ANSWER AND ESSAY QUESTIONS**

1. What do the horizontal axes measure in a graph of the aggregate expenditures model and the aggregate demand curve?

2. Why is there an inverse relationship between aggregate expenditures and the price level? Explain, using real balance, the interest rate, and foreign purchases.

3. Describe how the aggregate demand curve can be derived from the aggregate expenditures model.

4. What is the effect of an increase in aggregate expenditures on the aggregate demand curve? Explain in words and with a graph.

5. What role does the multiplier play in shifting aggregate expenditures and aggregate demand?

ANSWERS

Appendix to Chapter 11 The Relationship of the Aggregate Demand Curve to the Aggregate Expenditures Model

FILL-IN QUESTIONS

1. variable, fixed
2. raise, rise
3. lower, fall
4. inverse, demand
5. right, multiplier, left, downward, multiplier

TRUE–FALSE QUESTIONS

1. F, pp. 211–212
2. T, p. 211
3. F, p. 211
4. F, pp. 211–212
5. T, p. 212

MULTIPLE-CHOICE QUESTIONS

1. c, p. 211
2. b, p. 211
3. a, pp. 211–212
4. d, pp. 211–212
5. b, pp. 211–212

PROBLEMS

1. *a.* 2200; *b.* 2400; *c.* 2600; *d.* 2200, 2400, 2600, (1) aggregate demand, (2) inversely

SHORT ANSWER AND ESSAY QUESTIONS

1. p. 211
2. p. 211
3. pp. 211–212
4. pp. 211–212
5. pp. 211–212

CHAPTER 12

Fiscal Policy

Principles of economics are generalizations about how the economy works. These principles are studied to help devise policies to solve real problems. Over the past 100 years or so, the most serious macroeconomic problems have been those resulting from the swings of the business cycle. Learning what determines the equilibrium level of real output and prices in an economy and what causes them to fluctuate makes it possible to find ways to achieve maximum output, full employment, and stable prices. In short, macroeconomic principles suggest policies to control both recession and inflation in an economy.

As you will discover in Chapter 12, government may use *fiscal policy* to influence the economy's output, employment, and price level. These policies use the Federal government's spending and taxing powers to improve economic conditions. The brief first section of this chapter explains how Congress, in the Employment Act of 1946, committed the Federal government to achieving three goals: economic growth, full employment, and stable prices. This act also established the Council of Economic Advisers (CEA) to advise the president and the Joint Economic Committee (JEC) to advise Congress on national economic policies.

The second section of the chapter discusses *discretionary fiscal policy,* which can be either *expansionary* or *contractionary.* Here you will learn how these fiscal policies affect aggregate demand and the Federal budget. *Expansionary fiscal policy* is used to stimulate the economy and pull it out of a slump or recession. This type of policy can be achieved by increasing government spending, decreasing taxes, or some combination of the two. *Contractionary fiscal policy* is enacted to counter inflationary pressure in the economy. The policy actions taken to dampen inflation include cutting government spending, raising taxes, or a combination of the two. As you will learn, each policy may have a significant effect on aggregate demand and the Federal budget. If the government has a *budget deficit* or *budget surplus,* the way the government finances it may affect the economy's operation as much as the size of the deficit or surplus.

Discretionary fiscal policy requires that Congress take action to change tax rates, transfer payment programs, or purchases of goods and services. *Nondiscretionary fiscal policy* does not require Congress to take any action and is a *built-in stabilizer* for the economy. You should be sure that you understand *why* net taxes increase when the GDP rises and decrease when the GDP falls and *how* this tends to stabilize the economy.

Nondiscretionary fiscal policy by itself may not be able to eliminate any recessionary or inflationary gap that might develop, and discretionary fiscal policy may be necessary if the economy is to produce its full-employment GDP and avoid inflation. The built-in stabilizers make it more difficult to use discretionary fiscal policy to achieve this goal because they create the illusion that the Federal government's policy is expansionary or contractionary when in fact its policy may be just the opposite.

The need to evaluate the direction of fiscal policy has led economists to develop a *full-employment budget* and to distinguish between a *cyclical deficit* and a *full-employment deficit.* This budget analysis enables economists to determine whether Federal fiscal policy is expansionary, contractionary, or neutral, and to determine what policy should be enacted to improve the economy's economic performance. From this budget analysis you will gain insights into the course of U.S. fiscal policy in recent years.

Fiscal policy is not without its problems, criticisms, or complications as you will learn in this section of the chapter. There are timing problems in getting it implemented. There are political considerations in getting it accepted by politicians and voters. If the fiscal policy is temporary rather than permanent it is thought to be less effective. Some economists criticize the borrowing of money by the Federal government for expansionary fiscal policy because they think it will raise interest rates and crowd out investment spending, thus reducing the policy effects. Another complication may arise from aggregate demand shocks from abroad or a net export effect that may increase or decrease the effectiveness of fiscal policy.

The debate over the advisability and effectiveness of discretionary fiscal policy is an ongoing one as will be discussed in the brief concluding section of the chapter. Some economists argue that this policy, with its potential problems and complications, should not be used. Other economists contend that discretionary fiscal policy is a valuable macroeconomic tool for directing economic activity. Perhaps most important in the design of fiscal policy are actions that contribute to the growth of long-run aggregate supply.

■ **CHECKLIST**

When you have studied this chapter you should be able to

☐ State the responsibility imposed on the Federal government by the Employment Act of 1946 and the roles of the CEA and JEC in fulfilling this responsibility.

☐ Distinguish between discretionary and nondiscretionary fiscal policy.

☐ Explain expansionary fiscal policy and the effect of spending and tax policy options on aggregate demand.

☐ Describe contractionary fiscal policy and the effect of spending and tax policy options on aggregate demand.

☐ Explain how the expansionary effect of a budget deficit depends on the method used to finance it.

☐ Describe how the deflationary effect of a budget surplus depends on the method used to finance it.

☐ Assess whether it is preferable to use government spending or taxes to counter recession and reduce inflation.

☐ Define automatic or built-in stabilizers.

☐ Indicate how the built-in stabilizers help to counter recession and inflationary pressures.

☐ Describe the relationship among progressive, proportional, and regressive tax systems and the built-in stability of the economy.

☐ Distinguish between the actual budget and the full-employment budget for evaluating fiscal policy.

☐ Describe recent U.S. fiscal policy using the full-employment budget.

☐ Use the full-employment budget to evaluate the status of discretionary fiscal policy.

☐ Outline three timing problems that may arise with fiscal policy.

☐ Discuss the political considerations affecting fiscal policy.

☐ Explain how policy reversals change the effectiveness of fiscal policy.

☐ Describe how changes in state and local finances may offset fiscal policy at the federal level.

☐ Explain and use a graph to illustrate the crowding-out effect of an expansionary fiscal policy.

☐ State the major criticisms of the crowding-out effect.

☐ Describe two ways that the effectiveness of domestic fiscal policy is complicated by the connection of a national economy with the world economy.

☐ Discuss current thinking on fiscal policy.

■ **CHAPTER OUTLINE**

1. *Fiscal policy* consists of the changes made by the Federal government in its expenditures and tax receipts to expand or contract the economy. In making these changes, the Federal government may seek to either increase the economy's real output (and employment) or control its rate of inflation.

2. *The Employment Act of 1946* set the goals of fiscal policy in the United States and provided for a *Council of Economic Advisers* to the president and the Joint Economic Committee.

3. Fiscal policy is *discretionary* when changes in government spending or taxation by Congress are designed to change the level of real GDP, employment, incomes, or the price level. Specific action needs to be taken by Congress to initiate this discretionary policy, in contrast to nondiscretionary fiscal policy that occurs automatically (see item 4 in the next column).

a. *Expansionary fiscal policy* is generally used to counteract the negative economic effects of a recession or cyclical downturn in the economy (a decline in real GDP and rising unemployment). The purpose of the policy is to stimulate the economy by increasing aggregate demand. The policy will create a *budget deficit* if the budget was in balance before the policy was enacted. The stimulative effect on the economy from the initial increase in spending from the policy change will be increased by the multiplier effect. Three policy options are used:
(1) an increase in government spending;
(2) a reduction in taxes (which increases consumer spending); or
(3) a combination of an increase in government spending and a tax reduction.

b. *Contractionary fiscal policy* is a restrictive form of fiscal policy generally used to control demand-pull inflation. The purpose of this policy is to reduce aggregate demand pressures that increase the price level. If the government budget is balanced before the policy is enacted, it will create a *budget surplus.* The contractionary effect on the economy from the initial reduction in spending from the policy will be reinforced by the multiplier effect. Three policy options are used:
(1) a decrease in government spending;
(2) an increase in taxes (which reduces consumer spending); or
(3) a combination of a reduction in government spending and a tax increase.

c. In addition to the size of the budget deficit or surplus, the manner in which government finances its deficit or disposes of its surplus affects the level of total spending in the economy.
(1) To finance a deficit, the government can either borrow money from the public or issue new money to creditors, with the latter action being more expansionary.
(2) Budget surpluses may be used for debt reduction, or the funds may be impounded, with the latter action being more contractionary.

d. Whether government purchases or taxes should be altered to reduce recession and inflation depends on whether an expansion or a contraction of the public sector is desired.

4. In the U.S. economy there are automatic or *built-in stabilizers.* Net taxes revenues (tax revenues minus government transfer payments) are not a fixed amount or lump sum; they automatically increase as the GDP rises and automatically decrease as the GDP falls.

a. The economic importance of this net tax system is that it serves as a built-in stabilizer of the economy. It reduces purchasing during periods of inflation and expands purchasing during periods of recession.

b. As GDP increases, the average tax rates will increase in a *progressive tax system,* remain constant in a *proportional tax system,* and decrease in a *regressive tax system;* there is more built-in stability for the economy in progressive tax systems. Built-in stabilizers can only reduce and cannot eliminate economic fluctuations, so discretionary fiscal policy may be needed.

5. To evaluate the direction of discretionary fiscal policy, adjustments need to be made to the actual budget deficits or surpluses.

    a. The *full-employment budget* is a better index than the actual budget of the direction of government fiscal policy because it indicates what the Federal budget deficit or surplus would be if the economy were to operate at full employment. In the case of a budget deficit, the full-employment budget

    (1) removes the *cyclical deficit* that is produced by swings in the business cycle, and

    (2) reveals the size of the *full-employment deficit,* indicating how expansionary the fiscal policy was that year.

    b. U.S. data from the past decade show the years in which fiscal policy was expansionary or contractionary. There were full-employment budget deficits in the early 1990s and full-employment budget surpluses in later years. In 2002 the full-employment budget turned to deficit.

6. Certain *problems, criticisms, and complications* arise in enacting and applying fiscal policy.

    a. There will be problems of timing because it requires time to recognize the need for fiscal policy, to take the appropriate steps in Congress, and for the action taken there to affect output, employment, and the rate of inflation in the economy.

    b. There may be political considerations with fiscal policy that counter the economic effects. Elected officials may cause a *political business cycle* if they lower taxes and increase spending before elections and then do the opposite after elections.

    c. Fiscal policy may be less effective if people think that it may be reversed in the future, thus making the policy temporary rather than permanent.

    d. The fiscal policies of state and local governments can run counter to Federal fiscal policy and offset it.

    e. An expansionary fiscal policy may, by raising the level of interest rates in the economy, reduce (or *crowd out*) investment spending and weaken the effect of the policy on real GDP; but this *crowding-out effect* may be small and can be offset by an expansion in the nation's money supply.

    f. The connection of the domestic economy to a world economy means that fiscal policy may be inappropriate or less effective because of aggregate demand shocks from the world economy and from a *net export effect.* The net export effect may offset an expansionary or contractionary fiscal policy.

    (1) An expansionary fiscal policy may lead to a higher domestic interest rate which causes the dollar to appreciate, and thus net exports (and aggregate demand) decline.

    (2) A contractionary fiscal policy may lead to a lower domestic interest rate which causes the dollar to depreciate, and thus net exports (and aggregate demand) increase.

7. Chapter 12 concludes with a brief review of current thinking about discretionary fiscal policy. Some economists think that fiscal policy is ineffective because of all the potential problems and complications. They recommend the use of monetary policy to guide the economy. Other economists think that fiscal policy can be useful for directing the economy and that it can reinforce or support monetary policy. There is general agreement that fiscal policy should be designed so that its incentives and investments strengthen long-term economic growth.

■ **HINTS AND TIPS**

1. Fiscal policy is a broad concept that covers various taxation and spending policies of the Federal government; it is not limited to one policy. You will need to know the distinctions between the several kinds of fiscal policies. The main difference is between discretionary and nondiscretionary fiscal policies. *Discretionary* fiscal policy is *active* and means that Congress has taken specific actions to change taxes or government spending to influence the economy. It can be *expansionary* or *contractionary.* *Nondiscretionary* fiscal policy is *passive,* or *automatic,* because changes in tax revenues will occur without specific actions by Congress.

2. An increase in government spending that is equal to a cut in taxes will not have an equal effect on real GDP. To understand this point, assume that the MPC is .75, the increase in government spending is $8 billion, and the decrease in taxes is $8 billion. The multiplier would be 4 because it equals 1/(1 − .75). The increase in government spending will increase real GDP by $32 billion ($8 billion × 4). Of the $8 billion decrease in taxes, however, one-quarter of it will be saved ($6 billion × .25 = $2 billion) and just three-quarters will be spent ($8 billion × .75 = $6 billion). Thus, the tax cut results in an increase in *initial* spending in the economy of $6 billion, not $8 billion as was the case with the increase in government spending. The tax cut effect on real GDP is $24 billion ($6 billion × 4), not $32 billion.

3. A large part of the chapter deals with the problems, criticisms, and complications of fiscal policy. Do not miss the big picture and get lost in the details of each problem.

■ **IMPORTANT TERMS**

fiscal policy	progressive tax system
Employment Act of 1946	proportional tax system
Council of Economic Advisers (CEA)	regressive tax system
	full-employment budget
expansionary fiscal policy	cyclical deficit
budget deficit	political business cycle
contractionary fiscal policy	crowding-out effect
budget surplus	net export effect
built-in stabilizer	

SELF-TEST

■ **FILL-IN QUESTIONS**

  1. The use of fiscal policy to reduce inflation and recession became national economic policy in the

(Employment, Unemployment) _____ Act of 1946. To assist and advise the president, the act established the (Joint Economic Committee, Council of Economic Advisers) _____, and to aid Congress in investigating economic matters, the act established the _____.

2. Policy actions taken by Congress designed to change government spending or taxation are (discretionary, nondiscretionary) _____ fiscal policy, but when the policy takes effect automatically or independently of Congress, then it is _____ fiscal policy.

3. Expansionary fiscal policy is generally designed to (increase, decrease) _____ aggregate demand and thus _____ real GDP and employment in the economy. Contractionary fiscal policy is generally used to (increase, decrease) _____ aggregate demand and _____ the level of prices.

4. Expansionary fiscal policy can be achieved with an increase in (government spending, taxes) _____, a decrease in _____, or a combination of the two; contractionary fiscal policy can be achieved by a decrease in (government spending, taxes) _____, an increase in _____, or a combination of the two.

5. An increase of government spending of $5 billion from an expansionary fiscal policy for an economy might ultimately produce an increase in real GDP of $20 billion. This magnified effect occurs because of the (multiplier, crowding-out) _____ effect.

6. If the Federal budget is balanced and Congress passes legislation supporting an expansionary fiscal policy, then this action is likely to produce a budget (deficit, surplus) _____, but if Congress passes legislation supporting a contractionary fiscal policy, then the action will result in a budget _____.

7. If fiscal policy is to have a countercyclical effect, it probably will be necessary for the Federal government to incur a budget (surplus, deficit) _____ during a recession and a budget _____ during inflation.

8. Of the two principal means available to the Federal government for financing budget deficits, the one that is more expansionary is (borrowing money from the public, creating new money) _____. Of the two principal means available to the Federal government for using funds from a budget surplus, the one that is more contractionary is (impounding funds, debt reduction) _____.

9. Net taxes equal taxes (plus, minus) _____ transfer payments and are called "taxes" in this chapter. In the United States, as GDP increases, tax revenue will (increase, decrease) _____, and as the GDP decreases, tax revenues will _____.

10. Because tax revenues are (directly, indirectly) _____ related to the GDP, the economy has some (artificial, built-in) _____ stability. If the GDP increases, then tax revenue will increase, and the budget surplus will (increase, decrease) _____, thus (stimulating, restraining) _____ the economy when it is needed. When GDP decreases, tax revenues decrease, and the budget deficit (increases, decreases) _____, thus (stimulating, restraining) _____ the economy when it is needed.

11. As GDP increases, the average tax rates will increase with a (progressive, proportional, regressive) _____ tax system, remain constant with a _____ tax system, and decrease with a _____ tax system. With a progressive tax system, there is (more, less) _____ built-in stability for the economy.

12. If there is a deficit in the full-employment budget, then fiscal policy is (contractionary, expansionary) _____ and when there is a surplus in the full-employment budget, then fiscal policy is _____.

13. A deficit produced by swings in the business cycle is (actual, cyclical) _____. When there is a cyclical deficit, the full-employment budget deficit will be (greater, less) _____ than the actual budget deficit.

14. There is a problem of timing in the use of discretionary fiscal policy because of the time between the beginning of a recession or inflation and awareness of it, or (an administrative, an operational, a recognition) _____ lag; the time needed for Congress to adjust fiscal policy, or _____ lag; and the time needed for fiscal policy to take effect, or _____ lag.

15. Political problems arise in the application of discretionary fiscal policy to stabilize the economy because government has (one, several) _____ economic goals, state and local fiscal policies may (reinforce, counter) _____ Federal fiscal policy, and politicians may use fiscal policies in a way that creates (an international, a political) _____ business cycle.

16. Expectations among households and businesses that fiscal policy will be reversed in the future make fiscal policy (more, less) _____ effective. For example, if taxpayers expect a tax cut to be temporary, they may save (more, less) _____ now to pay for a future increase in the tax rate and spend _____ now. As a result, consumption and aggregate demand (increase, decrease) _____.

17. When the Federal government employs an expansionary fiscal policy to increase real GDP and employment in the economy, it usually has a budget (surplus, deficit) _____ and (lends, borrows) _____ in the money market. These actions will (raise, lower) _____ interest rates in the economy and (contract, expand) _____ investment spending. This change in investment spending is the (net export, crowding-out) _____ effect of the expansionary fiscal policy, and it tends to (weaken, strengthen) _____ the influence of the expansionary fiscal policy on real GDP and employment.

18. Fiscal policy is subject to further complications from (independence from, interdependency with) _____ _____ the world economy. For example, the domestic economy can be influenced by aggregate demand (inflation, shocks) _____ from abroad that alter GDP and might reinforce or offset fiscal policy.

19. International trade can also produce a (crowding-out, net export) _____ effect that influences aggregate demand and partially offsets fiscal policy.
 a. When fiscal policy is expansionary, it tends to (increase, decrease) _____ interest rates, which in turn tends to _____ the value of the dollar, (increase, decrease) _____ net exports, and _____ aggregate demand.
 b. When fiscal policy is contractionary, it tends to (increase, decrease) _____ interest rates, which in turn tends to _____ the value of the dollar, (increase, decrease) _____ net exports, and _____ aggregate demand.

20. Current thinking on the advisability and effectiveness of discretionary fiscal policy shows general (agreement, disagreement) _____ about the value of fiscal policy in the short run, and general _____ about evaluating fiscal policy for its contribution to long-run productivity growth.

■ **TRUE–FALSE QUESTIONS**

Circle T if the statement is true, F if it is false.

1. The Council of Economic Advisers was established to give economic advice to Congress. **T   F**

2. Discretionary fiscal policy is independent of Congress and left to the discretion of state and local governments. **T   F**

3. Expansionary fiscal policy during a recession or depression will create a budget deficit or add to an existing budget deficit. **T   F**

4. A decrease in taxes is one of the options that can be used to pursue a contractionary fiscal policy. **T   F**

5. To increase initial consumption by a specific amount, government must reduce taxes by more than that amount because some of the tax cut will be saved by households. **T   F**

6. A reduction in taxes and an increase in government spending would be characteristic of a contractionary fiscal policy. **T   F**

7. Borrowing from the public is the way a budget surplus is financed. **T   F**

8. The creation of new money is more expansionary than borrowing from the public as a way of financing deficit spending. **T   F**

9. Using a budget surplus to pay off a large public debt may reduce the anti-inflationary impact of the surplus. **T   F**

10. The impounding of a budget surplus means that it is used for tax cuts. **T   F**

11. Built-in stabilizers are not sufficiently strong to prevent recession or inflation, but they can reduce the severity of a recession or inflation. **T   F**

12. The less progressive the tax system, the greater the economy's built-in stability. **T   F**

13. The full-employment budget indicates how much government must spend and tax if there is to be full employment in the economy. **T   F**

14. The key to assessing discretionary fiscal policy is to observe the change in the full-employment budget. **T   F**

15. A full-employment budget surplus is expansionary. **T   F**

16. Recognition, administrative, and operational lags in the timing of Federal fiscal policy make fiscal policies more effective in reducing the rate of inflation and decreasing unemployment in the economy. **T   F**

17. Economists who see evidence of a political business cycle argue that members of Congress tend to increase taxes and reduce expenditures before elections and to reduce taxes and increase expenditures after elections. **T   F**

18. If households expect that a tax cut will be temporary, they are likely to spend more and save less, thus reinforcing the intended effect of the tax cut on aggregate demand. **T F**

19. State and local governments' fiscal policies have tended to assist and reinforce the efforts of the Federal government to counter recession and inflation. **T F**

20. The fiscal policies of state and local governments are frequently procyclical. **T F**

21. The crowding-out effect occurs when an expansionary fiscal policy decreases the interest rate, increases investment spending, and strengthens fiscal policy. **T F**

22. Critics contend that the crowding-out effect will be greatest when the economy is in a recession. **T F**

23. For a domestic economy, there are gains for specialization and trade but also complications from the interdependency with the world economy. **T F**

24. A net export effect may partially offset an expansionary fiscal policy. **T F**

25. A net export effect will help the economy achieve the desired objectives of a contractionary fiscal policy. **T F**

■ **MULTIPLE-CHOICE QUESTIONS**

Circle the letter that corresponds to the best answer.

1. Which of the following was instrumental in assigning to the Federal government the basic responsibility for promoting economic stability in the U.S. economy?
  (a) the Employment Act of 1946
  (b) the Tax Reform Act of 1986
  (c) Say's law
  (d) Okun's law

2. If the government wishes to increase the level of real GDP, it might reduce
  (a) taxes
  (b) transfer payments
  (c) the size of the budget deficit
  (d) its purchases of goods and services

3. If Congress passes legislation to make a substantial increase in government spending to counter the effects of a severe recession, this would be an example of a
  (a) supply-side fiscal policy
  (b) contractionary fiscal policy
  (c) discretionary fiscal policy
  (d) nondiscretionary fiscal policy

4. Which combination of policies would be the most expansionary?
  (a) an increase in government spending and taxes
  (b) a decrease in government spending and taxes
  (c) an increase in government spending and a decrease in taxes
  (d) a decrease in government spending and an increase in taxes

5. An economy is in a recession and the government decides to increase spending by $4 billion. The MPC is .8.

What would be the full increase in real GDP from the change in government spending?
  (a) $3.2 billion
  (b) $4 billion
  (c) $16 billion
  (d) $20 billion

6. Which combination of fiscal policies would be the most contractionary?
  (a) an increase in government spending and taxes
  (b) a decrease in government spending and taxes
  (c) an increase in government spending and a decrease in taxes
  (d) a decrease in government spending and an increase in taxes

7. Which is a more expansionary way for government to finance a budget deficit?
  (a) borrowing money in the money market
  (b) decreasing government spending
  (c) creating new money
  (d) increasing taxes

8. Which would be the most contractionary use of funds from a budget surplus?
  (a) cutting tax rates
  (b) impounding the funds
  (c) using the funds to retire outstanding government debt
  (d) increasing government spending on social programs

9. When government tax revenues change automatically and in a countercyclical direction over the course of the business cycle, this is an example of
  (a) the political business cycle
  (b) nondiscretionary fiscal policy
  (c) the full-employment budget
  (d) crowding out

10. If the economy is to have built-in stability, when real GDP falls,
  (a) tax revenues and government transfer payments both should fall
  (b) tax revenues and government transfer payments both should rise
  (c) tax revenues should fall and government transfer payments should rise
  (d) tax revenues should rise and government transfer payments should fall

Answer Questions 11, 12, and 13 on the basis of the following diagram.

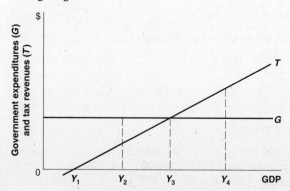

11. If the slope of the line *T* were steeper, there would be
(a) more built-in stability for the economy
(b) less built-in stability for the economy
(c) no change in the built-in stability for the economy
(d) the need for more emphasis on discretionary fiscal policy

12. If the slope of the line *T* were flatter, there would be
(a) larger cyclical deficits produced as GDP moved from Y_3 to Y_2
(b) smaller cyclical deficits produced as GDP moved from Y_3 to Y_2
(c) larger full-employment deficits produced as GDP moved from Y_3 to Y_2
(d) smaller full-employment deficits produced as GDP moved from Y_3 to Y_2

13. Actions by the Federal government to increase the progressivity of the tax system
(a) flatten the slope of line *T* and increase built-in stability
(b) flatten the slope of line *T* and decrease built-in stability
(c) steepen the slope of line *T* and increase built-in stability
(d) steepen the slope of line *T* and decrease built-in stability

14. With a proportional tax system, as the level of income increases in an economy, the average tax rate will
(a) increase
(b) decrease
(c) remain the same
(d) either increase or decrease

Use the following table to answer Question 15. The table shows the full-employment budget deficit or surplus as a percentage of GDP over a five-year period.

Year	Deficit (−) Surplus (+)
1	−2.1%
2	−3.0
3	−1.5
4	+0.5
5	+1.0

15. In which year was the fiscal policy expansionary?
(a) Year 2
(b) Year 3
(c) Year 4
(d) Year 5

16. If the full-employment budget shows a deficit of about $200 billion and the actual budget shows a deficit of about $250 billion over a several-year period, it can be concluded that there is a
(a) cyclical deficit
(b) net export effect
(c) recognition lag
(d) political business deficit

17. When the actual budget deficit is greater than the full-employment deficit, it can be concluded that
(a) discretionary fiscal policy is contractionary

(b) the economy is at less than full employment
(c) the tax system for the economy is regressive
(d) the budget surplus has increased

18. If the full-employment deficit as a percentage of GDP is zero one year, and there is a full-employment budget surplus the next year, it can be concluded that
(a) fiscal policy is expansionary
(b) fiscal policy is contractionary
(c) the federal government is borrowing money
(d) the federal government is lending money

19. The length of time involved for the fiscal action taken by Congress to affect output, employment, or the price level is referred to as the
(a) administrative lag
(b) operational lag
(c) recognition lag
(d) fiscal lag

20. The crowding-out effect of an expansionary (deficit) fiscal policy is the result of government borrowing in the money market which
(a) increases interest rates and net investment spending in the economy
(b) increases interest rates and decreases net investment spending
(c) decreases interest rates and increases net investment spending
(d) decreases interest rates and net investment spending

21. The effect of an expansionary fiscal policy on the real GDP of an economy is
(a) strengthened by the crowding-out effect
(b) weakened by the crowding-out effect
(c) reinforced by raising tax rates
(d) offset by lowering tax rates

22. The crowding-out effect may be
(a) counteracted by decreasing the supply of money to offset a decrease in the demand for money
(b) reinforced by decreasing the supply of money to offset a decrease in the demand for money
(c) reinforced by increasing the supply of money to offset an increase in the demand for money
(d) counteracted by increasing the supply of money to offset an increase in the demand for money

23. Suppose the United States pursued an expansionary fiscal policy to stimulate its economy and eliminate a recession. The net export effect suggests that net exports would
(a) decrease, thus decreasing aggregate demand and partially offsetting the fiscal policy
(b) decrease, thus increasing aggregate demand and partially offsetting the fiscal policy
(c) increase, thus decreasing aggregate demand and partially offsetting the fiscal policy
(d) increase, thus increasing aggregate demand and partially reinforcing the fiscal policy

24. Suppose the United States pursued a contractionary fiscal policy to reduce the level of inflation. The net export effect suggests that net exports would

(a) decrease, thus decreasing aggregate demand and partially reinforcing the fiscal policy
(b) decrease, thus increasing aggregate demand and partially offsetting the fiscal policy
(c) increase, thus decreasing aggregate demand and partially reinforcing the fiscal policy
(d) increase, thus increasing aggregate demand and partially offsetting the fiscal policy

25. Current thinking about discretionary fiscal policy among mainstream economists is that it should be designed to
(a) counteract the effects of monetary policy
(b) contribute to long-run economic growth
(c) "fine-tune" the economy in the short run, but not in the long run
(d) control inflationary pressure, but not be used to fight recession

■ **PROBLEMS**

1. Columns 1 and 2 in the following table are an aggregate supply schedule. Columns 1 and 3 are an aggregate demand schedule.

(1) Price level	(2) Real GDP$_1$	(3) AD$_1$	(4) AD$_2$	(5) Real GDP$_2$
220	$ 2390	$ 2100	$ 2200	$ 2490
200	2390	2200	2340	2490
190	2350	2250	2350	2450
180	2300	2300	2400	2400
160	2200	2400	2500	2300

a. The equilibrium real GDP is $_____ and the price level is _____.
b. Suppose the expansionary fiscal policy increases aggregate demand from that shown in columns 1 and 3 to that shown in columns 1 and 4. The price level will increase to _____, and this rise in the price level will result in real GDP increasing to $_____.
c. If the expansionary fiscal policy that increased aggregate demand also has supply-side effects and increased aggregate supply from that shown in columns 1 and 2 to that shown in columns 1 and 5, the equilibrium real GDP would increase to $_____ and the price level would _____.

2. The following table shows seven real GDPs and the net tax revenues of government at each real GDP.

Real GDP	Net tax revenues	Government purchases	Government deficit/surplus
$ 850	$170	$____	$____
900	180	____	____
950	190	____	____
1000	200	____	____
1050	210	____	____
1100	220	____	____
1150	230		

a. Looking at the two columns on the left side of the table, it can be seen that
(1) when real GDP increases by $50, net tax revenues (increase, decrease) _____ by $_____.
(2) when real GDP decreases by $100, net tax revenues (increase, decrease) _____ by $_____.
(3) the relationship between real GDP and net tax revenues is (direct, inverse) _____.
b. Assume the simple multiplier has a value of 10 and that investment spending in the economy decreases by $10.
(1) *If* net tax revenues remained constant, the equilibrium real GDP would decrease by $_____.
(2) But when real GDP decreases, net tax revenues also decrease; and this decrease in net tax revenues will tend to (increase, decrease) _____ the equilibrium real GDP.
(3) And, therefore, the decrease in real GDP brought about by the $10 decrease in investment spending will be (more, less) _____ than $100.
(4) The direct relationship between net tax revenues and real GDP has (lessened, expanded) _____ the impact of the $10 decrease in investment spending on real GDP.
c. Suppose the simple multiplier is also 10 and government wishes to increase the equilibrium real GDP by $50.
(1) *If* net tax revenues remained constant, government would have to increase its purchases of goods and services by $_____.
(2) But when real GDP rises, net tax revenues also rise, and this rise in net tax revenues will tend to (increase, decrease) _____ the equilibrium real GDP.
(3) The effect, therefore, of the $5 increase in government purchases will also be to increase the equilibrium real GDP by (more, less) _____ than $50.
(4) The direct relationship between net tax revenues and real GDP has (lessened, expanded) _____ the effect of the $5 increase in government purchases, and to raise the equilibrium real GDP by $50, the government will have to increase its purchases by (more, less) _____ than $5.
d. Imagine that the full-employment real GDP of the economy is $1150 and that government purchases of goods and services are $200.
(1) Complete the previous table by entering the government purchases and computing the budget deficit or surplus at each of the real GDPs. (Show a government deficit by placing a minus sign in front of the amount by which expenditures exceed net tax revenues.)

(2) The full-employment surplus equals $_____.

(3) If the economy were in a recession and producing a real GDP of $900, the budget would show a (surplus, deficit) _____ of $_____.

(4) This budget deficit or surplus makes it appear that government is pursuing (an expansionary, a contractionary) _____ fiscal policy, but this deficit or surplus is not the result of a countercyclical fiscal policy but the result of the _____.

(5) If government did not change its net tax *rates,* it could increase the equilibrium real GDP from $900 to the full-employment real GDP of $1150 by increasing its purchases by (approximately) $70. At the full-employment real GDP the budget would show a (surplus, deficit) _____ of $_____.

(6) If government did not change its purchases, it would increase the equilibrium real GDP from $900 to the full-employment real GDP of $1150 by decreasing net tax revenues at all real GDPs by a lump sum of (approximately) $80. The full-employment budget would have a (surplus, deficit) _____ of $_____.

3. a. Complete the table below by computing the average tax rates, given the net tax revenue data in columns 2, 4, and 6. Calculate the average tax rate in percentage to one decimal place (for example, 5.4%).

b. As real GDP increases in column 1, the average tax rate (increases, decreases, remains the same) _____ in column 3, _____ in column 5, and _____ in column 7. The tax system is (progressive, proportional, regressive) _____ in column 2, _____ in column 4, and _____ in column 6.

c. On the graph following the table, plot the real GDP, net tax revenue, and government spending data given in columns 1, 2, 4, 6, and 8. The tax revenue system with the steepest slope is found in column _____, and it is (progressive, proportional, regressive) _____ while the one with the flattest slope is found in column _____, and it is_____.

4. a. Complete the table on the next page by stating whether the direction of discretionary fiscal policy was contractionary (**C**), expansionary (**E**), or neither (**N**) given the hypothetical budget data for an economy.

b. The best gauge of the direction of fiscal policy is the (actual, full-employment) _____ budget deficit or surplus because it removes the (cyclical, actual) _____ component from the discussion of the budget situation.

(1) Real GDP	(2) Net tax revenue	(3) Average tax rate	(4) Net tax revenue	(5) Average tax rate	(6) Net tax revenue	(7) Average tax rate	(8) Government spending
$1000	$100	_____%	$100	_____%	$100	_____%	$120
$1100	120	_____	110	_____	108	_____	120
$1200	145	_____	120	_____	115	_____	120
$1300	175	_____	130	_____	120	_____	120
$1400	210	_____	140	_____	123	_____	120

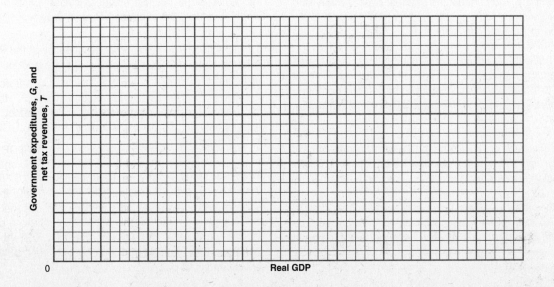

Government expeditures, G, and net tax revenues, T

0   Real GDP

(1) Year	(2) Actual budget deficit (−) or surplus (+)	(3) Full-employment budget deficit (−) or surplus (+)	(4) Direction of fiscal policy
1	−$170 billion	−$130 billion	
2	− 120 billion	− 90 billion	_____
3	+ 40 billion	+ 20 billion	_____
4	− 60 billion	− 50 billion	_____
5	− 120 billion	− 100 billion	_____

c. (1) In what years were there cyclical deficits, and what was the amount of the cyclical deficit in each of those years? _____

_____

(2) In what year was the actual budget surplus greater than the full-employment budget surplus, and by what amount greater? _____

_____

■ **SHORT ANSWER AND ESSAY QUESTIONS**

1. In the Employment Act of 1946, (*a*) what responsibility was given to the Federal government, (*b*) what tasks were assigned to the Council of Economic Advisers and the Joint Economic Committee?

2. What is the difference between discretionary fiscal policy and nondiscretionary fiscal policy?

3. What are the Federal government's three options for conducting expansionary or contractionary fiscal policy?

4. Under what economic conditions would expansionary or contractionary fiscal policy be used? What would be the effect on the Federal budget?

5. Compare and contrast the effect of expansionary and of contractionary fiscal policy on aggregate demand. Draw a graph to illustrate the likely effects.

6. What is the effect of the multiplier on the initial change in spending from fiscal policy? When the government wants to increase initial consumption by a specific amount, why must the government reduce taxes by more than that amount?

7. In the real world, is the purpose of contractionary fiscal policy to restore a previously lower price level? How do "sticky" prices affect events?

8. What are the alternative means of financing deficits and disposing of surpluses available to the Federal government? What is the difference between these methods insofar as their expansionary and contractionary effects are concerned?

9. Explain the fiscal policies that would be advocated during a recession and during a period of inflation by those who (*a*) wish to expand the public sector and (*b*) wish to contract the size of government.

10. What is a built-in stabilizer? How do the built-in stabilizers work to reduce rises and falls in the level of nominal GDP?

11. What is the economic importance of the direct relationship between tax receipts and GDP?

12. Supply definitions of progressive, proportional, and regressive tax systems. What are the implications of each type of tax system for the built-in stability of the economy?

13. What is the full-employment budget? What was the problem that the use of the full-employment budget was designed to solve?

14. Explain the distinction between a cyclical deficit and full-employment deficit. Which type of deficit provides the best indication of the direction of fiscal policy? Why?

15. Explain the three kinds of time lags that make it difficult to use fiscal policy to stabilize the economy.

16. What is the political business cycle? Explain how it works. Evaluate the likelihood of such a cycle.

17. How might the direction of fiscal policy at the Federal level be countered by the actions of state and local governments?

18. How does crowding out reduce the effect of an expansionary (deficit) fiscal policy on real GDP and employment?

19. What complications for fiscal policy arise from interdependency with the world economy? Explain how aggregate demand shocks from abroad and the net export effect influence fiscal policy.

20. What is the current thinking about the advisability and effectiveness of discretionary fiscal policy?

ANSWERS

Chapter 12 Fiscal Policy

FILL-IN QUESTIONS

1. Employment, Council of Economic Advisers, Joint Economic Committee
2. discretionary, nondiscretionary
3. increase, increase, decrease, decrease
4. government spending, taxes, government spending, taxes
5. multiplier
6. deficit, surplus
7. deficit, surplus
8. creating new money, impounding funds
9. minus, increase, decrease
10. directly, built-in, increase, restraining, increases, stimulating
11. progressive, proportional, regressive, more
12. expansionary, contractionary
13. cyclical, less
14. a recognition, an administrative, an operational
15. several, counter, a political
16. less, more, less, decrease
17. deficit, borrows, raise, contract, crowding-out, weaken
18. interdependency with, shocks
19. net export; *a.* increase, increase, decrease, decrease; *b.* decrease, decrease, increase, increase
20. disagreement, agreement

TRUE–FALSE QUESTIONS

1. F, pp. 214–215
2. F, p. 215
3. T, pp. 215–216
4. F, pp. 216–217
5. T, p. 216
6. F, pp. 216–217
7. F, pp. 217–218
8. T, p. 218
9. T, p. 218
10. F, p. 218
11. T, pp. 218–219
12. F, pp. 219–220
13. F, pp. 220–221
14. T, pp. 221–222
15. F, pp. 221–222
16. F, p. 223
17. T, p. 223
18. F, pp. 223–224
19. F, p. 224
20. T, p. 224
21. F, pp. 224–225
22. F, pp. 224–225
23. T, pp. 225–226
24. T, p. 226
25. F, p. 226

MULTIPLE-CHOICE QUESTIONS

1. a, p. 214
2. a, p. 216
3. c, pp. 215–216
4. c, pp. 215–216
5. d, pp. 215–216
6. d, pp. 216–217
7. c, pp. 217–218
8. b, p. 218
9. b, pp. 218–219
10. c, pp. 218–219
11. a, pp. 219–220
12. b, pp. 219–220
13. c, pp. 219–220
14. c, pp. 219–220
15. a, pp. 220–222
16. a, pp. 220–222
17. b, pp. 220–222
18. b, pp. 220–222
19. b, p. 223
20. b, pp. 224–225
21. b, pp. 224–225
22. d, p. 225
23. a, p. 226
24. d, p. 226
25. b, p. 228

PROBLEMS

1. *a.* 2300, 180; *b.* 190, 2350; *c.* 2400, remain constant
2. *a.* increase, $10, (2) decrease, $20, (3) direct; *b.* (1) $100, (2) increase, (3) less, (4) lessened; *c.* (1) $5, (2) decrease, (3) less, (4) lessened, more; *d.* (1) government purchases are $200 at all GDPs, government surplus or deficit: −30, −20, −10, 0, 10, 20, 30, (2) $30, (3) deficit, $20, (4) an expansionary, recession, (5) deficit, $40, (6) deficit, $50
3. *a.* column 3: 10.0, 10.9, 12.1, 13.5, 15.0; column 5: 10.0 at each GDP level; column 7: 10.0, 9.8, 9.6, 9.2, 8.8; *b.* increases, remains the same, decreases; progressive, proportional, regressive; *c.* 2, progressive, 6, regressive
4. *a.* (Year 1–2) contractionary, (Year 2–3) contractionary, (Year 3–4) expansionary, (Year 4–5) expansionary; *b.* full-employment, cyclical; *c.* (1) year 1 ($40 billion), year 2 ($30 billion), year 4 ($10 billion), year 5 ($20 billion), (2) year 3 ($20 billion)

SHORT ANSWER AND ESSAY QUESTIONS

1. pp. 214–215
2. pp. 215, 218
3. pp. 215–217
4. pp. 215–217
5. pp. 215–217
6. pp. 215–216
7. pp. 216–217
8. pp. 217–218
9. p. 218
10. pp. 218–219
11. pp. 219–220
12. pp. 219–220
13. pp. 220–221
14. pp. 220–222
15. p. 223
16. p. 223
17. p. 224
18. pp. 224–225
19. pp. 225–226
20. p. 228

CHAPTER 13

Money and Banking

Chapter 13 explains how the financial system affects the operation of the economy. The chapter is largely descriptive and factual. Pay particular attention to the following: (1) what the money supply is and the function money performs; (2) what gives value to or "backs" money in the United States; (3) how the total demand for money and the money supply together determine the equilibrium rate of interest; and (4) the principal institutions of the U.S. financial system and their functions.

Several points are worth repeating. First, money is whatever performs the three functions of money (*medium of exchange, unit of account, store of value*). In the United States, the supply of money consists largely of the debts (promises to pay) of the Federal Reserve Banks and depository institutions. This money is backed by the willingness to exchange goods and services, *and not by gold*.

Second, the *total demand for money* is made up of a *transactions demand for money* and an *asset demand for money.* Because money is used as a medium of exchange, consumers and business firms wish to hold money for transaction purposes. The quantity of money they demand for this purpose is directly related to the size of the economy's nominal (or money) gross domestic product. This means that when either the price level or the real gross domestic product increases, they will want to have more money on hand to use for transactions.

Money is also used as a store of value that creates an asset demand. Consumers and businesses who own assets may choose to have some of their assets in the form of money (rather than in stocks, bonds, goods, or property). Holding money, however, imposes a cost. This cost is the interest they lose when they own money rather than an interest-earning asset such as a bond. Consumers and businesses will demand less money for asset purposes when the rate of interest (the cost of holding money) is high and demand more money when the rate of interest is low; the quantity of money demanded as an asset is inversely related to the interest rate.

The total demand for money is the sum of the transactions demand and the asset demand. It is affected by both nominal GDP and the rate of interest. The total demand and the supply of money determine interest rates in the *money market.* The inverse relationship between bond prices and interest rates helps this market adjust to shortages or surpluses of money.

Third, the central bank in the United States consists of the 12 *Federal Reserve Banks* and the *Board of Governors* of the *Federal Reserve System* which oversees their operation. These banks, while privately owned by the commercial banks, are operated more or less as agencies of the Federal government. They operate on a not-for-profit basis but are used primarily to regulate the nation's money supply in the best interests of the economy as a whole and secondarily to perform other services for the banks, the government, and the economy. They are able to perform their primary function because they are bankers' banks in which depository institutions (commercial banks and thrifts) can deposit and borrow money. They do not deal directly with the public.

Fourth, these depository institutions accept deposits and make loans, but they also are able to create money by lending checkable deposits. Because they are able to do this, they have a strong influence on the size of the money supply and the value of money. The Federal Reserve Banks exist primarily to regulate the money supply and its value by influencing and controlling the amount of money depository institutions create.

The final section of Chapter 13 discusses recent developments in money and banking, of which three are particularly noteworthy. The relative decline of banks and thrifts and changes in their services have significantly altered the financial services industry. Also, financial markets are now global and more highly integrated than in previous decades. In addition, technological advances have changed the character of money.

■ CHECKLIST

When you have studied this chapter you should be able to

☐ List and explain the three functions of money.
☐ Give an *M*1 definition of money that explains its two major components.
☐ Describe the two major types of institutions offering checkable deposits.
☐ Give an *M*2 definition of money and its components.
☐ Give an *M*3 definition of money and its components.
☐ Distinguish between credit cards and money.
☐ Explain why money is debt in the U.S. economy and who holds that debt.
☐ State three reasons why currency and checkable deposits are money and have value.
☐ Use an equation to explain the relationship between the value of money and the price level, or the purchasing power of money.

☐ Discuss how inflation affects the acceptability of money.

☐ Explain what role government plays in maintaining or stabilizing the value of money.

☐ Give a definition of the transactions demand for money that describes how it varies with nominal GDP.

☐ Give a definition of the asset demand for money that describes how it varies with the rate of interest.

☐ Illustrate graphically how the transactions and asset demands for money combine to form the total demand for money.

☐ Describe the money market and what determines the equilibrium rate of interest.

☐ Explain how changes in nominal GDP and in the money supply affect the interest rate.

☐ Illustrate with an example how disequilibrium in the money market is corrected through changes in bond prices.

☐ Describe the purposes of the Board of Governors and FOMC of the Federal Reserve System.

☐ Explain why the Federal Reserve Banks are central, quasi-public, and bankers' banks.

☐ Discuss the relationship between the Federal Reserve System and commercial banks and thrifts.

☐ List and explain the seven major functions of the Federal Reserve System and indicate which one is most important.

☐ Discuss the reason for the independence of the Federal Reserve System.

☐ Describe five major changes in the financial services industry in the United States in recent years.

■ **CHAPTER OUTLINE**

1. Money is whatever performs the three **basic functions of money.** It is a **medium of exchange** for buying and selling goods and services. It serves as a **unit of account** for measuring the monetary cost of goods and services. It is a **store of value** so money can be used over time.

2. In the U.S. economy, the definition of **money** is whatever is generally used as a medium of exchange and consists of the debts of the Federal government and of commercial banks and other financial institutions.

   a. The narrowly defined money supply is called **M1** and has two principal components.

   (1) The smaller component is currency: coins which are token money and paper money largely in the form of Federal Reserve Notes.

   (2) The larger and more important component is checkable deposits.

   (3) The two major types of financial institutions offering checkable deposits are **commercial banks** and **thrift institutions.**

   (4) Currency and checkable deposits owned by the Federal government, commercial banks and savings institutions, and the Federal Reserve Banks are not included in **M1** or in any of the more broadly defined money supplies.

   b. **M2** is a broader definition of money and includes not only the currency and checkable deposits in **M1**

but such near-monies as noncheckable savings deposits and time deposits in commercial banks and savings institutions. **M2** includes **M1** plus noncheckable savings deposits plus small time deposits (less than $100,000) plus money market deposit accounts (MMDA) plus money market mutual funds (MMMF).

   c. **M3** includes **M2** plus large time deposits ($100,000 or more). There are advantages to each of the different measures of money, but since **M1** is included in all the definitions and the principles that apply to it are applicable to the other measures, that narrow definition is used for the textbook discussion unless noted otherwise.

3. The **money supply gets its "backing"** from the ability of the government to keep the value of money stable.

   a. Money is debt or the promise of a commercial bank, a thrift institution, or a Federal Reserve Bank to pay, but these debts cannot be redeemed for anything tangible.

   b. Money has value only because: It is acceptable for the exchange of desirable goods and services; it is **legal tender** (legally acceptable for payment of debts); and it is relatively scarce.

   c. The value of money is inversely related to the price level. Rapid inflation can erode the value of money and public confidence in it.

   d. Money is backed by the confidence the public has that the value of money will remain stable; the Federal government can use monetary and fiscal policy to keep the value of money relatively stable.

4. Business firms and households wish to hold and, therefore, demand money for two reasons.

   a. Because they use money as a medium of exchange, they have a **transactions demand for money** that is directly related to the nominal gross domestic product of the economy.

   b. Because they also use money as a store of value, they have an **asset demand for money** that is inversely related to the rate of interest.

   c. Their **total demand for money** is the sum of the transactions and asset demands.

5. In the **money market,** the demand for money and the supply of money determine the interest rate. Graphically, the demand for money is a downsloping line and the supply of money is a vertical line, and their intersection determines the interest rate. Disequilibrium in this market is corrected by changes in bond prices and their inverse relationship with interest rates.

   a. If there is a decrease in the money supply, there will be a shortage of money and bonds will be sold. The increase in supply of bonds will drive down bond prices, causing interest rates to rise until the shortage is eliminated.

   b. If there is an increase in the money supply, there will be a surplus of money and bonds will be bought. The increased demand for bonds will drive up bond prices, causing interest rates to fall until the surplus is eliminated.

6. The financial sector of the economy is significantly influenced by the *Federal Reserve System (the Fed)* and the nation's banks and thrift institutions.

   a. The banking system remains centralized and regulated by government because historical problems have led to different kinds of money and the mismanagement of the money supply.

   b. The *Board of Governors* of the Fed exercises control over the supply of money and the banking system. The U.S. president appoints the seven members of the Board of Governors.

   c. Four important bodies help the Board of Governors establish and conduct policy: the *Federal Open Market Committee (FOMC)*, which establishes policy over the buying and selling of government securities; and three Advisory Councils that provide input from commercial banks, thrift institutions, and consumer-related organizations.

   d. The *12 Federal Reserve Banks* of the Fed serve as central banks, quasi-public banks, and bankers' banks.

   e. The U.S. banking system contains thousands of commercial banks and thrift institutions that are directly affected by the Fed's decisions.

   f. The Fed performs seven functions: issuing currency, setting reserve requirements and holding reserves, lending money to banks and thrifts, collecting and processing checks, serving as the fiscal agent for the Federal government, supervising banks, and controlling the money supply. The last function is the most important.

   g. The independence of the Fed protects it from strong political pressure from the U.S. Congress or the president that could lead to poor economic decisions.

7. Three recent developments have affected money and banking and the *financial services industry* in the United States.

   a. The number of banks and thrift institutions has declined, partly as a result of bank and thrift mergers. There has also been a convergence in the services offered by different types of financial institutions (banks, insurance companies, etc.).

   b. Financial markets are now more globalized and integrated because of advances in computer and communications technologies.

   c. The character of money has changed with the shift to the use of *electronic money.*

■ HINTS AND TIPS

1. Most students think of currency as the major component of the money supply, but it is a very small component relative to *checkable deposits.* There are several definitions of the *money supply* that you must know about, from the narrow *M*1 to the broader *M*2 and *M*3.

2. Spend extra time learning how the *total demand for money* is determined (see Figure 13.1 in the text). The total demand for money is composed of the transactions and the asset demands for money. *The transactions demand for money* is influenced by the level of nominal GDP and not affected by the interest rate, so it *is graphed as a vertical line.* The *asset demand for money* is affected by the interest rate, so it *is graphed as a downsloping curve.* The total demand for money is also graphed as a *downsloping curve* because of the influence of the asset demand, but the curve is shifted farther to the right than the asset demand curve because of the influence of the transactions demand.

3. One of the most difficult concepts to understand is the *inverse* relationship between bond prices and interest rates. The simple explanation is that interest yield from a bond is the ratio of the *fixed* annual interest payment to the bond price. The numerator is fixed, but the denominator (bond price) is variable. If the bond price falls, the interest yield on the bond rises because the fixed annual interest payment is being divided by a smaller denominator.

■ IMPORTANT TERMS

medium of exchange	legal tender
unit of account	transactions demand for money
store of value	
*M*1, *M*2, and *M*3	asset demand for money
token money	total demand for money
Federal Reserve Notes	money market
checkable deposits	Federal Reserve System
commercial banks	Board of Governors
thrift institutions	Federal Open Market Committee (FOMC)
near-monies	
savings account	Federal Reserve Banks
money market deposit account (MMDA)	financial services industry
	electronic transactions
time deposits	
money market mutual fund (MMMF)	

SELF-TEST

■ FILL-IN QUESTIONS

1. When money is usable for buying and selling goods and services, it functions as (a unit of account, a store of value, a medium of exchange) _____ _____, but when money serves as a measure of relative worth, it functions as _____, and when money serves as a liquid asset it functions as _____.

2. All coins in circulation in the United States are (paper, token) _____ money, which means that their intrinsic value is (less, greater) _____ than the face value of the coin.

3. Paper money and coins are considered (currency, checkable deposits) _____. One major component of *M*1 is (currency, checkable deposits) _____, and the other major component is _____.

4. *M*2 is equal to (*M*1, *M*3) _____ plus (checkable, noncheckable) _____ savings deposits, (small, large) _____ time deposits, and money market (deposit accounts, mutual funds) _____ and _____.

5. *M*3 is equal to *M*2 plus (small, large) _____ time deposits. These deposits have a face value of (less than $100,000; $100,000 or greater) _____.

6. Credit cards (are, are not) _____ considered money but rather a form of (paper money, loan) _____ from the institution that issued the card.

7. Paper money is the circulating debt of (banks and thrifts, the Federal Reserve Banks) _____ _____, while checkable deposits are the debts of _____. In the United States, currency and checkable deposits (are, are not) _____ backed by gold and silver.

8. Money has value because it is (unacceptable, acceptable) _____ in exchange for products and resources, because it is (legal, illegal) _____ tender, and because it is relatively (abundant, scarce) _____.

9. The value of money varies (directly, inversely) _____ with the price level. To find the value of $1 (multiply, divide) _____ 1 by the price level.

10. Runaway inflation may significantly (increase, decrease) _____ the value of money and _____ its acceptance as a medium of exchange.

11. The transactions demand varies (directly, inversely) _____ with (the rate of interest, nominal GDP) _____, and the asset demand varies (directly, inversely) _____ with (the rate of interest, nominal GDP) _____.

12. The sum of the transactions and asset demands for money is the total (demand, supply) _____ of money, and the intersection of it with the _____ of money determines the equilibrium (interest rate, price level) _____.

13. When the quantity of money demanded exceeds the quantity of money supplied, bond prices (increase, decrease) _____ and interest rates _____. When the quantity of money demanded is less than the quantity of money supplied, bond prices (increase, decrease) _____ and interest rates _____.

14. The Federal Reserve System is composed of the Board of (Control, Governors) _____ that is assisted by the powerful (U.S. Mint, Federal Open Market Committee) _____. There are also (10, 12) _____ Federal Reserve Banks.

15. The Federal Reserve Banks are (private, quasi-public) _____ banks, serve as (consumers', bankers') _____ banks, and are (local, central) _____ banks whose policies are coordinated by the Board of Governors.

16. The workhorses of the U.S. banking system are about 7800 (thrifts, commercial banks) _____ and about 11,800 _____.

17. The seven major functions of the Fed are

a. _____
_____

b. _____
_____

c. _____
_____

d. _____
_____

e. _____
_____

f. _____
_____

g. _____
_____

Of these, the most important function is _____
_____

18. The Congress established the Fed as a(n) (dependent, independent) _____ agency of government. The object was to protect it from political pressure so it could control (taxes, inflation) _____.

19. In the past decade, the number of banks and thrifts (increased, decreased) _____ due to (mergers, inflation) _____ in the financial services industry.

20. Two other recent developments in money and banking are the (localization, globalization) _____ of financial markets and the use of (paper, electronic) _____ transactions.

■ **TRUE–FALSE QUESTIONS**

Circle T if the statement is true, F if it is false.

1. When the price of a product is stated in terms of dollars and cents, then money is functioning as a unit of account. **T F**

2. The money supply designated *M*1 is the sum of currency and noncheckable deposits. **T F**

3. The currency component of *M*1 includes both coins and paper money. **T F**

4. If a coin is token money, its face value is less than its intrinsic value. **T F**

5. Both commercial banks and thrift institutions accept checkable deposits. **T F**

6. The checkable deposits of the Federal government at the Federal Reserve Banks are a component of *M*1. **T F**

7. *M*2 exceeds *M*1 by the amount of noncheckable savings, small time deposits, and money market deposit accounts and money market mutual funds. **T F**

8. A *small* time deposit is one that is less than $100,000. **T F**

9. *M*2 is less than *M*3 by the amount of small time deposits in depository institutions. **T F**

10. Economists and public officials are in general agreement on how to define the money supply in the United States. **T F**

11. The major components of the money supply are debts, or promises to pay. **T F**

12. Currency and checkable deposits are money because they are acceptable to sellers in exchange for goods and services. **T F**

13. If money is to have a fairly stable value, its supply must be limited relative to the demand for it. **T F**

14. There is a transactions demand for money because households and business firms use money as a store of value. **T F**

15. An increase in the price level would increase the transactions demand for money. **T F**

16. An increase in the nominal GDP, other things remaining the same, will increase both the total demand for money and the equilibrium rate of interest in the economy. **T F**

17. Bond prices and interest rates are inversely related. **T F**

18. Members of the Board of Governors of the Federal Reserve System are appointed by the president of the United States and confirmed by the Senate. **T F**

19. The Federal Open Market Committee (FOMC) is responsible for keeping the stock market open and regulated. **T F**

20. The Federal Reserve Banks are owned and operated by the U.S. government. **T F**

21. Federal Reserve Banks are bankers' banks because they make loans to and accept deposits from depository institutions. **T F**

22. At times, the Fed lends money to banks and thrifts, charging them an interest rate called the *bank and thrift rate*. **T F**

23. Congress established the Fed as an independent agency to protect it from political pressure so that it can effectively control the money supply and maintain price stability. **T F**

24. In recent years, banks and thrifts have increased their share of the financial services industry and control of financial assets. **T F**

25. It is expected that electronic transactions such as the use of smart cards will replace all other means of payment. **T F**

■ **MULTIPLE-CHOICE QUESTIONS**

Circle the letter that corresponds to the best answer.

1. Which one is an economic function of money?
  (a) a medium of communications
  (b) a factor of production
  (c) a store of bonds
  (d) a unit of account

2. The largest element of the currency component of *M*1 is
  (a) coins
  (b) gold certificates
  (c) silver certificates
  (d) Federal Reserve Notes

3. Which constitutes the largest element in the *M*1 money supply?
  (a) savings deposits
  (b) small time deposits
  (c) large time deposits
  (d) checkable deposits

4. Checkable deposits are money because they are
  (a) legal tender
  (b) fiat money
  (c) token money
  (d) a medium of exchange

5. The supply of money *M*1 consists almost entirely of the debts of
   (a) the Federal government
   (b) the Federal Reserve Banks
   (c) depository institutions
   (d) the Federal Reserve Banks and depository institutions

Use the following table to answer Questions 6, 7, and 8 about the money supply, given the following hypothetical data for the economy.

Item	Billions of dollars
Checkable deposits	$1775
Small time deposits	345
Currency	56
Large time deposits	1230
Noncheckable savings deposits	945
Money market deposit accounts	256
Money market mutual funds	587

6. The size of the *M*1 money supply is
   (a) $1775
   (b) $1831
   (c) $2176
   (d) $3019

7. The size of the *M*2 money supply is
   (a) $2176
   (b) $3146
   (c) $3964
   (d) $4532

8. The size of the *M*3 money supply is
   (a) $4532
   (b) $5194
   (c) $5339
   (d) $6007

9. Which *best* describes the backing of money in the United States?
   (a) the gold bullion stored in Fort Knox, Kentucky
   (b) the belief of holders of money that it can be exchanged for desirable goods and services
   (c) the willingness of banks and the government to surrender something of value in exchange for money
   (d) the faith and confidence of the public in the ability of government to pay its debts

10. If the price level increases 20%, the value of money decreases
   (a) 14.14%
   (b) 16.67%
   (c) 20%
   (d) 25%

11. To keep the value of money fairly constant, the Federal Reserve
   (a) uses price and wage controls
   (b) controls the money supply
   (c) employs fiscal policy
   (d) buys corporate stock

12. If the dollars held for transactions purposes are, on the average, spent five times a year for final goods and services, then the quantity of money people will wish to hold for transactions is equal to
   (a) five times the nominal GDP
   (b) 20% of the nominal GDP
   (c) five divided by the nominal GDP
   (d) 20% divided by the nominal GDP

13. There is an asset demand for money because money is
   (a) a store of value
   (b) a measure of value
   (c) a medium of exchange
   (d) a standard of deferred payment

14. An increase in the rate of interest would increase
   (a) the opportunity cost of holding money
   (b) the transactions demand for money
   (c) the asset demand for money
   (d) the prices of bonds

Use the table below to answer Questions 15 and 16.

Interest rate	Asset demand (billions)
14%	$100
13	150
12	200
11	250

15. Suppose the transactions demand for money is equal to 10% of the nominal GDP, the supply of money is $450 billion, and the asset demand for money is that shown in the table. If the nominal GDP is $3000 billion, the equilibrium interest rate is
   (a) 14%
   (b) 13%
   (c) 12%
   (d) 11%

16. If the nominal GDP remains constant, an increase in the money supply from $450 billion to $500 billion would cause the equilibrium interest rate to
   (a) rise to 14%
   (b) fall to 11%
   (c) fall to 12%
   (d) remain unchanged

17. The total quantity of money demanded is
   (a) directly related to nominal GDP and the rate of interest
   (b) directly related to nominal GDP and inversely related to the rate of interest
   (c) inversely related to nominal GDP and directly related to the rate of interest
   (d) inversely related to nominal GDP and the rate of interest

18. The stock of money is determined by the Federal Reserve System and does not change when the interest rate changes; therefore the
   (a) supply of money curve is downward sloping
   (b) demand for money curve is downward sloping
   (c) supply of money curve is upward sloping
   (d) supply of money curve is vertical

19. If the legal ceiling on the interest rate was set below equilibrium, the

(a) quantity of money demanded would be greater than the quantity of money supplied

(b) quantity of money demanded would be less than the quantity of money supplied

(c) supply of money would increase and the demand for money would decrease

(d) demand for money would increase and the supply of money would decrease

20. Which one of the following points would be true?

(a) Bond prices and the interest rate are directly related.

(b) A lower interest rate raises the opportunity cost of holding money.

(c) The supply of money is directly related to the interest rate.

(d) The total demand for money is inversely related to the interest rate.

Answer Questions 21 and 22 on the basis of the following information: Bond price = $10,000; bond fixed annual interest payment = $1000; bond annual rate of interest = 10%.

21. If the price of this bond decreases by $2500, the interest rate in effect will

(a) decrease by 1.1 percentage points

(b) decrease by 1.9 percentage points

(c) increase by 2.6 percentage points

(d) increase by 3.3 percentage points

22. If the price of this bond increases by $2000, the interest rate in effect will

(a) decrease by 1.7 percentage points

(b) decrease by 2.4 percentage points

(c) increase by 1.1 percentage points

(d) increase by 2.9 percentage points

23. The Federal Open Market Committee (FOMC) of the Federal Reserve System is primarily responsible for

(a) supervising the operation of banks to make sure they follow regulations and monitoring banks so they do not engage in fraud

(b) handling the Fed's collection of checks and adjusting legal reserves among banks

(c) setting the Fed's monetary policy and directing the buying and selling of government securities

(d) acting as the fiscal agent for the Federal government and issuing currency

24. The most important function of the Federal Reserve System is

(a) issuing currency

(b) controlling the money supply

(c) supervising commercial banks

(d) lending money to banks and thrifts

25. According to the text, which would be a recent development in the banking industry?

(a) an increase in the number of banks and thrifts

(b) increased integration of world financial markets

(c) increased use of coins and currency as a medium of exchange

(d) an increase in the separation of services offered by financial institutions

■ **PROBLEMS**

1. From the figures in the following table it can be concluded that

Item	Billions of dollars
Small time deposits	$630
Large time deposits	645
Money market deposit accounts	575
Money market mutual funds	425
Checkable deposits	448
Noncheckable savings deposits	300
Currency	170

a. *M*1 is equal to the sum of $_____ and $_____, so it totals $_____ billion.

b. *M*2 is equal to *M*1 plus $_____ and $_____ and $_____ and $_____, so it totals $_____ billion.

c. *M*3 is equal to *M*2 plus $_____, so it totals $_____ billion.

2. Complete the following table that shows the relationship between a percentage change in the price level and the percentage change in the value of money. Calculate the percentage change in the value of money to one decimal place.

Change in price level	Change in value of money
a. *rises* by:	
5%	−_____.___%
10%	−_____.___
15%	−_____.___
20%	−_____.___
25%	−_____.___
b. *falls* by:	
5%	+_____.___%
10%	+_____.___
15%	+_____.___

3. The total demand for money is equal to the transactions plus the asset demand for money.

a. Assume each dollar held for transactions purposes is spent (on the average) four times per year to buy final goods and services.

(1) This means that the transactions demand for money will be equal to (what fraction or percent) _____ of the nominal GDP, and,

(2) if the nominal GDP is $2000 billion, the transactions demand will be $_____ billion.

b. The following table shows the number of dollars demanded for asset purposes at each rate of interest.

(1) Given the transactions demand for money in (*a*), complete the table.

Interest rate	Amount of money demanded (billions)	
	For asset purposes	Total
16%	$ 20	$_____
14	40	_____
12	60	_____
10	80	_____
8	100	_____
6	120	_____
4	140	_____

(2) On the following graph plot the total demand for money (D_m) at each rate of interest.

c. Assume the money supply (S_m) is $580 billion.

(1) Plot this money supply on the graph.

(2) Using either the graph or the table, the equilibrium rate of interest is _____ %.

d. Should the money supply

(1) increase to $600 billion, the equilibrium interest rate would (rise, fall) _____ to _____ %.

(2) decrease to $540 billion, the equilibrium interest rate would _____ to _____ %.

e. If the nominal GDP

(1) increased by $80 billion, the total demand for money would (increase, decrease) _____ by $_____ billion at each rate of interest and the equilibrium rate of interest would (rise, fall) _____ by _____ %.

(2) decreased by $120 billion, the total demand for money would _____ by $_____ billion at each rate of interest and the equilibrium interest rate would _____ by _____ %.

4. Suppose a bond with no expiration date pays a fixed $500 annually and sells for its face value of $5000.

a. Complete the following table and calculate the interest rate (to one decimal place) that would be obtained from the bond when the bond price is given or calculate the bond price when the interest rate is given.

Bond price	Interest rate
$4000	_____.___%
$_____	11.0
$5000	_____.___
$5500	_____.___
$_____	8.0

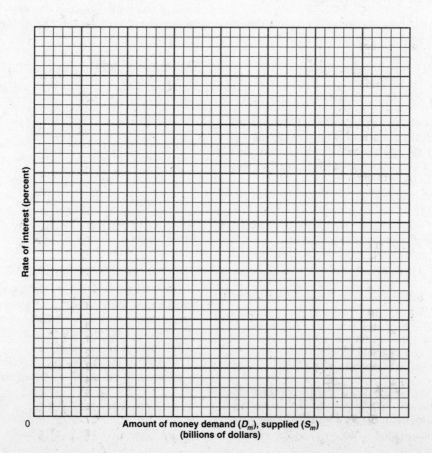

Rate of interest (percent)

0   Amount of money demand (D_m), supplied (S_m)
(billions of dollars)

b. Based on the results of the table, as the price increases on a bond with a fixed annual payment, the interest yield on the bond (decreases, increases)

_____, but when the price of a bond decreases, the interest yield _____. Given this situation in an economy, you can conclude that a higher price for bonds (increases, decreases) _____ interest rates and that a lower price for bonds _____ interest rates.

■ **SHORT ANSWER AND ESSAY QUESTIONS**

1. How would you define money based on its three functions?

2. What are the two components of the *M*1 supply of money in the United States?

3. What are checkable deposits? What are the different types of institutions offering checkable deposits?

4. Are the checkable deposits of government, the Fed, commercial banks, and other financial institutions included in *M*1? Explain.

5. Define *M*2 and *M*3. Explain how they are related.

6. For what reasons are checkable deposits included in the money supply?

7. What backs the money used in the United States? What determines the value of money?

8. Explain the relationship between the value of money and the price level.

9. What must government do if it is to stabilize the value of money?

10. What are the two reasons people wish to hold money? How are these two reasons related to the functions of money?

11. Explain the determinant of each of the two demands for money and how a change in the size of these determinants will affect the amount of money people wish to hold.

12. The rate of interest is a price. Of what good or service is it the price? Explain how demand and supply determine this price.

13. Describe how changes in bond prices correct disequilibrium in the money market. What is the relationship between bond prices and interest rates?

14. Outline the structure of the Federal Reserve System and explain the chief functions of each of the four parts of the system.

15. As briefly as possible, outline the three characteristics of the Federal Reserve Banks and explain the meaning of these characteristics.

16. What are the chief functions the Federal Reserve Banks perform? Explain briefly the meaning of each function. Which of the chief functions is the most important?

17. What are the basic reasons for the independence of the Federal Reserve System?

18. Describe the decline of and consolidation among banks and thrifts in recent years.

19. Discuss the meaning and effects of increased integration of world financial markets.

20. Explain how electronic transactions change the way money is stored and transferred. How do these changes affect banks, thrifts, and the Federal Reserve?

ANSWERS

Chapter 13 Money and Banking

FILL-IN QUESTIONS

1. a medium of exchange, a unit of account, a store of value
2. token, less
3. currency, checkable deposits, currency (either order for the last two)
4. *M*1, noncheckable, small, deposit accounts, mutual funds (either order for the last two)
5. large, $100,000 or greater
6. are not, loan
7. the Federal Reserve Banks, banks and thrifts, are not
8. acceptable, legal, scarce
9. inversely, divide
10. decrease, decrease
11. directly, nominal GDP, inversely, the rate of interest
12. demand, supply, interest rate
13. decrease, increase, increase, decrease
14. Governors, Federal Open Market Committee, 12
15. quasi-public, bankers', central
16. commercial banks, thrifts
17. *a.* issuing currency; *b.* setting reserve requirements and holding reserves; *c.* lending money to banks and thrifts; *d.* collecting and processing checks; *e.* serving as fiscal agent for the Federal government; *f.* bank supervision; *g.* controlling the money supply; controlling the money supply
18. independent, inflation
19. decreased, mergers
20. globalization, electronic

TRUE–FALSE QUESTIONS

1. T, pp. 232–233	**10.** F, p. 235	**19.** F, p. 243
2. F, pp. 233–234	**11.** T, pp. 234–235	**20.** F, pp. 243–244
3. T, pp. 233–234	**12.** T, p. 236	**21.** T, p. 244
4. F, p. 234	**13.** T, p. 237	**22.** F, p. 244
5. T, p. 234	**14.** F, pp. 238–239	**23.** T, p. 245
6. F, p. 234	**15.** T, pp. 238–239	**24.** F, p. 245
7. T, pp. 234–235	**16.** T, p. 240	**25.** F, p. 247
8. T, p. 235	**17.** T, pp. 240–241	
9. F, p. 235	**18.** T, pp. 242–243	

MULTIPLE-CHOICE QUESTIONS

1. d, pp. 232–233	**10.** b, p. 237	**19.** a, pp. 240–241
2. d, pp. 233–234	**11.** b, p. 237	**20.** d, pp. 240–241
3. d, pp. 233–234	**12.** b, pp. 238–239	**21.** d, p. 241
4. d, p. 234	**13.** a, pp. 239–240	**22.** a, p. 241
5. d, p. 236	**14.** a, pp. 239–240	**23.** c, p. 243
6. b, pp. 233–234	**15.** b, pp. 239–240	**24.** b, pp. 244–245
7. c, pp. 234–235	**16.** c, pp. 239–240	**25.** b, p. 247
8. b, p. 235	**17.** b, p. 240	
9. b, p. 236	**18.** d, p. 240	

PROBLEMS

1. *a.* 170, 448 (either order), 618; *b.* 300, 630, 575, 425 (any order), 2548; *c.* 645, 3193

2. *a.* 4.8, 9.1, 13, 16.7, 20; *b.* 5.3, 11.1, 17.6

3. *a.* (1) 1/4 (25%), (2) 500; *b.* (1) 520, 540, 560, 580, 600, 620, 640; *c.* (2) 10; *d.* (1) fall, 8, (2) rise, 14; *e.* (1) increase, 20, rise, 2, (2) decrease, 30, fall, 3

4. *a.* 12.5%, $4545, 10.0%, 9.1%, $6250; *b.* decreases, increases, decreases, increases

SHORT ANSWER AND ESSAY QUESTIONS

1. pp. 232–233	**8.** p. 237	**15.** pp. 243–244
2. pp. 233–234	**9.** p. 237	**16.** pp. 244–245
3. p. 234	**10.** pp. 238–240	**17.** p. 245
4. p. 234	**11.** pp. 238–240	**18.** pp. 245–246
5. pp. 234–235	**12.** pp. 240–241	**19.** p. 247
6. p. 235	**13.** pp. 240–241	**20.** p. 247
7. pp. 236–237	**14.** pp. 242–244	

CHAPTER 14

How Banks and Thrifts Create Money

Chapter 13 explained the institutional structure of banking in the United States today, the functions which banks and the other depository institutions and money perform, and the composition of the money supply. Chapter 14 explains how banks create money—**checkable deposits**—and the factors that determine and limit the money-creating ability of commercial banks. The other depository institutions, such as thrift institutions, also create checkable deposits, but this chapter focuses on the commercial banks to simplify the discussion.

The convenient and simple device used to explain commercial banking operations and money creation is the **balance sheet.** Shown within it are the **assets, liabilities,** and **net worth** of commercial banks. All banking transactions affect this balance sheet. The first step to understanding how money is created is to understand how various simple and typical transactions affect the commercial bank balance sheet.

In reading this chapter you must analyze for yourself the effect of each and every banking transaction discussed on the balance sheet. The important items in the balance sheet are checkable deposits and reserves because **checkable deposits are money.** The ability of a bank to create new checkable deposits is determined by the amount of reserves the bank has. Expansion of the money supply depends on the possession by commercial banks of excess reserves. They do not appear explicitly in the balance sheet but do appear there implicitly because **excess reserves** are the difference between the **actual reserves** and the **required reserves** of commercial banks.

Two cases—the single commercial bank and the banking system—are presented to help you build an understanding of banking and money creation. It is important to understand that the money-creating potential of a single commercial bank differs from the money-creating potential of the entire banking system. It is equally important to understand how the money-creating ability of many single commercial banks is **multiplied** and influences the **money-creating ability** of the banking system as a whole.

Certain assumptions are used throughout most of this chapter to analyze money creation; in certain instances these assumptions may not be completely realistic and may need to be modified. The chapter concludes with a discussion of how the earlier analysis must be modified—but not changed in its essentials—to take into account slightly unrealistic assumptions.

You will also learn that the money-creating actions of banks have a procyclical effect on the economy which needs to be controlled by the Federal Reserve System—a topic discussed in more detail in the next chapter.

■ CHECKLIST

When you have studied this chapter you should be able to

☐ Define the basic items in a bank's balance sheet.

☐ Recount the story of how goldsmiths came to issue paper money and became bankers who created money and held fractional reserves.

☐ Cite two significant characteristics of the fractional reserve banking system today.

☐ Explain the effects of the deposit of currency in a checking account on the composition and size of the money supply.

☐ Define the reserve ratio.

☐ Compute a bank's required and excess reserves when you are given the needed balance-sheet figures.

☐ Explain why a commercial bank is required to maintain a reserve and why a required reserve is not sufficient to protect the depositors from losses.

☐ Indicate how the deposit of a check drawn on one commercial bank and deposited into another will affect the reserves and excess reserves of the two banks.

☐ Show what happens to the money supply when a commercial bank makes a loan (or buys government securities).

☐ Explain what happens to a commercial bank's reserves and checkable deposits after it has made a loan, a check has been written on the newly created checkable deposit and deposited in another commercial bank and cleared, and explain what happens to the reserves and checkable deposits of the commercial bank in which the check was deposited.

☐ Describe what would happen to a commercial bank's reserves if it made loans (or bought government securities) in an amount greater than its excess reserves.

☐ Show what happens to the money supply when a loan is repaid (or a bank sells government securities).

☐ State the money-creating potential of a commercial bank (the amount of money a commercial bank can safely create by lending or buying securities).

☐ Explain how the Federal funds market helps reconcile the goals of profits and liquidity for commercial banks.

☐ State the money-creating potential of the banking system.

☐ Explain how it is possible for the banking system to create an amount of money that is a multiple of its excess reserves when no individual commercial bank ever creates money in an amount greater than its excess reserve.

☐ Compute the size of the monetary multiplier and the money-creating potential of the banking system when you are provided with the necessary data.

☐ Illustrate with an example using the monetary multiplier how money can be destroyed in the banking system.

☐ List the two leakages which reduce the money-creating potential of the banking system.

☐ Explain why there is a need for control of the money supply by the Federal Reserve System.

■ **CHAPTER OUTLINE**

1. The **balance sheet** of the commercial bank is a statement of the **assets, liabilities,** and **net worth** (capital stock) of the bank at a specific time; and in the balance sheet, the bank's assets equal its liabilities plus its net worth.

2. The history of the early goldsmiths illustrates how paper money came into use in the economy. This history also shows how goldsmiths became bankers when they began making loans and issuing money in excess of their gold holdings. The goldsmiths' fractional reserve system is similar to today's fractional banking system, which has two significant characteristics:

a. Banks can create money in such a system.

b. Banks are subject to "panics" or "runs" in a **fractional reserve system** and thus need government regulation.

3. By examining the ways the balance sheet of the commercial bank is affected by various transactions, it is possible to understand how a **single commercial bank** in a multibank system can create money.

a. Once a commercial bank has been founded,

(1) by selling shares of stock and obtaining cash in return;

(2) and acquiring the property and equipment needed to carry on the banking business;

(3) the deposit of cash in the bank does not affect the total money supply; it only changes its composition by substituting checkable deposits for currency in circulation;

(4) three reserve concepts are vital to an understanding of the money-creating potential of a commercial bank.

(a) The **required reserves,** which a bank *must* maintain at its Federal Reserve Bank (or as **vault cash**—which can be ignored), equal the reserve ratio multiplied by the checkable deposit liabilities of the commercial bank. (The **reserve ratio** is the ratio of required reserves to a bank's own checkable deposit liabilities.)

(b) The **actual reserves** of a commercial bank are its deposits at the Federal Reserve Bank (plus the vault cash, which is ignored).

(c) The **excess reserves** are equal to the actual reserves less the required reserve.

(5) The writing of a check on the bank and its deposit in a second bank results in a loss of reserves and deposits for the first bank and a gain in reserves and deposits for the second bank.

b. When a single commercial bank lends or buys government securities, it increases its own deposit liabilities and therefore the supply of money by the amount of the loan or security purchase. But the bank only lends or buys securities in an amount equal to its excess reserves because it fears the loss of reserves to other commercial banks in the economy.

c. When a single commercial bank receives loan repayments or sells government securities, its deposit liabilities and therefore the supply of money are described by the amount of the loan repayments or securities sale.

d. An individual commercial bank balances its desire for profits (which result from the making of loans and the purchase of securities) with its desire for liquidity or safety (which it achieves by having excess reserves or vault cash).

e. The Federal funds market allows banks with excess reserves to lend funds overnight to banks that are short of reserves. The interest rate paid on the overnight loans is the **Federal funds rate.**

4. The ability of a **banking system** composed of many individual commercial banks to lend and to create money is a multiple (greater than 1) of its excess reserves and is equal to the excess reserves of the banking system multiplied by the checkable-deposit (or monetary) multiplier.

a. The banking system as a whole can do this even though no single commercial bank ever lends an amount greater than its excess reserves because the banking system, unlike a single commercial bank, does not lose reserves.

b. The **monetary multiplier** is equal to the reciprocal of the required reserve ratio for checkable deposits, and the maximum expansion of checkable deposits is equal to the excess reserves in the banking system times the monetary multiplier.

c. The potential lending ability of the banking system may not be fully achieved if there are leakages because borrowers choose to hold additional currency or bankers choose to hold excess reserves.

d. If bankers lend as much as they are able during periods of prosperity and less than they are able during recessions, they add to the instability of the economy. To reduce this instability, the Federal Reserve Banks must control the size of the money supply.

■ **HINTS AND TIPS**

1. Note that several terms are used interchangeably in this chapter: "commercial bank" (or "bank") is sometimes called "thrift institution" or "depository institution."

2. A bank's balance sheet must balance. The bank's assets are either claimed by owners (net worth) or by nonowners (liabilities). **Assets = liabilities + net worth.**

3. Make a running balance sheet in writing for yourself as you read about each of the eight transactions in the text for the Wahoo Bank. Then determine if you understand the material by telling yourself (or a friend) the story for each transaction without using the text.

4. The ***maximum amount of checkable-deposit expansion*** is determined by multiplying two factors: the excess reserves by the monetary multiplier. Each factor, however, is affected by the required reserve ratio. The monetary multiplier is calculated by dividing 1 by the required reserve ratio. Excess reserves are determined by multiplying the required reserve ratio by the amount of new deposits. Thus, a change in the required reserve ratio will change the monetary multiplier and the amount of excess reserves. For example, a required reserve ratio of 25% gives a monetary multiplier of 4. For $100 in new money deposited, required reserves are $25 and excess reserves are $75. The maximum checkable-deposit expansion is $300 (4 × $75). If the reserve ratio drops to 20%, the monetary multiplier is 5 and excess reserves are $80, so the maximum checkable-deposit expansion is $400. Both factors have changed.

5. Be aware that the monetary multiplier can result in ***money destruction*** as well as money creation in the banking system. You should know how the monetary multiplier reinforces effects in one direction or the other.

■ **IMPORTANT TERMS**

balance sheet
fractional reserve banking system
vault cash
required reserves
reserve ratio

excess reserves
actual reserves
Federal funds rate
monetary multiplier

───────────────
SELF-TEST
───────────────

■ **FILL-IN QUESTIONS**

1. In this chapter, a commercial bank may also be called a (checkable, thrift) _____ institution and a deposit at a bank may also be called a _____ deposit.

2. The balance sheet of a commercial bank is a statement of the bank's (gold account, assets) _____, the claims of the owners of the bank [called (net worth, liabilities) _____], and claims of the nonowners (called _____). This relationship would be written in equation form as:

_____.

3. The banking system used today is a (total, fractional) _____ reserve system, which means that (100%, less than 100%) _____ of the money deposited in a bank is kept on reserve.

4. There are two significant characteristics to the banking system of today.

a. Banks can create (reserves, money) _____ depending on the amount of _____ they hold.
b. Banks are susceptible to (panics, regulation) _____ or "runs," and to prevent this situation from happening, banks are subject to government _____.

5. The coins and paper money that a bank has in its possession are (petty, vault) _____ cash or (till, capital) _____ money.

6. When a person deposits cash in a commercial bank and receives a checkable deposit in return, the size of the money supply has (increased, decreased, not changed) _____.

7. The legal reserve of a commercial bank (ignoring vault cash) must be kept on deposit at (a branch of the U.S. Treasury, its district Federal Reserve Bank) _____ _____.

8. The reserve ratio is equal to the commercial bank's (required, gold) _____ reserves divided by its checkable deposits (assets, liabilities) _____.

9. The authority to establish and vary the reserve ratio within limits legislated by Congress is given to the (U.S. Treasury, Fed) _____.

10. If commercial banks are allowed to accept (or create) deposits in excess of their reserves, the banking system is operating under a system of (fractional, currency) _____ reserves.

11. The excess reserves of a commercial bank equal its (actual, required) _____ reserves minus its _____ reserves.

12. The basic purpose for having member banks deposit a legal reserve in the Federal Reserve Bank in their district is to provide (liquidity for, control of) _____ the banking system by the Fed.

13. When a commercial bank deposits a legal reserve in its district Federal Reserve Bank, the reserve is (a liability, an asset) _____ to the commercial bank and _____ to the Federal Reserve Bank.

14. When a check is drawn on Bank X, deposited in Bank Y, and cleared, the reserves of Bank X are (increased, decreased, not changed) _____ and the reserves of Bank Y are _____; deposits in Bank X are (increased, decreased, not changed) _____ and deposits in Bank Y are _____.

15. A single commercial bank in a multibank system can safely make loans or buy government securities equal in amount to the (required, excess) _____ reserves of that commercial bank.

16. When a commercial bank makes a new loan of $10,000, the supply of money (increases, decreases) _____ by $_____, but when a loan is repaid, the supply of money (increases, decreases) _____ by $_____.

17. When a commercial bank sells a $10,000 government bond to a securities dealer, the supply of money (increases, decreases) _____ by $_____, but when a commercial bank buys a $10,000 government bond from a securities dealer, the supply of money (increases, decreases) _____ by $_____.

18. A bank ordinarily pursues two conflicting goals; one goal is the desire to make money, or (profits, liquidity) _____, and the other goal is the need for safety, or _____.

19. When a bank lends temporary excess reserves held at its Federal Reserve Bank to other commercial banks that are temporarily short of legal reserves, it is participating in the (government securities, Federal funds) _____ market. The interest rate paid on these overnight loans is called the (government securities, Federal funds) _____ rate.

20. The monetary multiplier is equal to 1 divided by the (excess, required) _____ reserve ratio.

21. The greater the reserve ratio, the (larger, smaller) _____ the monetary multiplier.

22. The banking system can make loans (or buy government securities) and create money in an amount equal to its (required, excess) _____ reserves multiplied by the (required reserve ratio, monetary multiplier) _____.

23. Assume that the required reserve ratio is 16.67% and the banking system is $6 million short of required reserves. If the banking system is unable to increase its reserves, the banking system must (increase, decrease) _____ the money supply by ($6, $36) _____ million.

24. The money-creating potential of the commercial banking system is lessened by the (addition, withdrawal) _____ of currency from banks and by banks not lending (required, excess) _____ reserves.

25. Commercial banks in the past have kept excess reserves during periods of (prosperity, recession) _____ and have kept few or no excess reserves during periods of _____. By acting this way, they have made the economy (more, less) _____ stable, which has given rise to the need for monetary control by the Federal Reserve System.

■ **TRUE–FALSE QUESTIONS**

Circle T if the statement is true, F if it is false.

1. The balance sheet of a commercial bank shows the transactions in which the bank has engaged during a given period of time.   **T F**

2. A commercial bank's assets plus its net worth equal the bank's liabilities.   **T F**

3. Goldsmiths increased the money supply when they accepted deposits of gold and issued paper receipts to the depositors.   **T F**

4. Modern banking systems use gold as the basis for the fractional reserve system.   **T F**

5. Cash held by a bank is sometimes called vault cash.   **T F**

6. A commercial bank may maintain its legal reserve either as a deposit in its Federal Reserve Bank or as government bonds in its own vault.   **T F**

7. The legal reserve that a commercial bank maintains must equal its own deposit liabilities multiplied by the required reserve ratio.   **T F**

8. Legal reserves permit the Board of Governors of the Federal Reserve System to influence the lending ability of commercial banks.   **T F**

9. The actual reserves of a commercial bank equal excess reserves plus required reserves.   **T F**

10. The reserve of a commercial bank in the Federal Reserve Bank is an asset of the Federal Reserve Bank.   **T F**

11. A check for $1000 drawn on Bank X by a depositor and deposited in Bank Y will increase the excess reserves in Bank Y by $1000.   **T F**

12. Mary Lynn, a music star, deposits a $30,000 check in a commercial bank and receives a checkable deposit in return; 1 hour later the Manfred Iron and Coal Company borrows $30,000 from the same bank. The money supply has increased $30,000 as a result of the two transactions.   **T F**

13. A single commercial bank can safely lend an amount equal to its excess reserves multiplied by the monetary multiplier ratio. **T F**

14. When a borrower repays a loan of $500, either in cash or by check, the supply of money is reduced by $500. **T F**

15. The granting of a $5000 loan and the purchase of a $5000 government bond from a securities dealer by a commercial bank have the same effect on the money supply. **T F**

16. The selling of a government bond by a commercial bank will increase the money supply. **T F**

17. A commercial bank seeks both profits and liquidity, but these are conflicting goals. **T F**

18. The Federal funds rate is the interest rate at which the Federal government lends funds to commercial banks. **T F**

19. The reason that the banking system can lend by a multiple of its excess reserves, but each individual bank can only lend "dollar for dollar" with its excess reserves, is that reserves lost by a single bank are not lost to the banking system as a whole. **T F**

20. The monetary multiplier is excess reserves divided by required reserves. **T F**

21. The maximum checkable-deposit expansion is equal to excess reserves divided by the monetary multiplier. **T F**

22. If the banking system has $10 million in excess reserves and if the reserve ratio is 25%, the system can increase its loans by $40 million. **T F**

23. When borrowers from a commercial bank wish to have cash rather than checkable deposits, the money-creating potential of the banking system is increased. **T F**

24. A desire by banks to hold excess reserves may reduce the size of the monetary multiplier. **T F**

25. There is a need for the Federal Reserve System to control the money supply because profit-seeking banks tend to make changes in the money supply that are pro-cyclical. **T F**

■ **MULTIPLE-CHOICE QUESTIONS**

Circle the letter that corresponds to the best answer.

1. The claims of the owners of the bank against the bank's assets is the bank's
  (a) net worth
  (b) liabilities
  (c) balance sheet
  (d) fractional reserves

2. The fractional reserve system of banking started when goldsmiths began
  (a) accepting deposits of gold for safe storage
  (b) issuing receipts for the gold stored with them

  (c) using deposited gold to produce products for sale to others
  (d) issuing paper money in excess of the amount of gold stored with them

3. When cash is deposited in a demand-deposit account in a commercial bank, there is
  (a) a decrease in the money supply
  (b) an increase in the money supply
  (c) no change in the composition of the money supply
  (d) a change in the composition of the money supply

4. A commercial bank has actual reserves of $9000 and liabilities of $30,000, and the required reserve ratio is 20%. The excess reserves of the bank are
  (a) $3000
  (b) $6000
  (c) $7500
  (d) $9000

5. The primary reason commercial banks must keep required reserves on deposit at Federal Reserve Banks is to
  (a) protect the deposits in the commercial bank against losses
  (b) provide the means by which checks drawn on the commercial bank and deposited in other commercial banks can be collected
  (c) add to the liquidity of the commercial bank and protect it against a "run" on the bank
  (d) provide the Fed with a means of controlling the lending ability of the commercial bank

6. A depositor places $750 in cash in a commercial bank, and the reserve ratio is 33.3%; the bank sends the $750 to the Federal Reserve Bank. As a result, the *reserves* and the *excess reserves* of the bank have been increased, respectively, by
  (a) $750 and $250
  (b) $750 and $500
  (c) $750 and $750
  (d) $500 and $500

7. A commercial bank has no excess reserves until a depositor places $600 in cash in the bank. The bank then adds the $600 to its reserves by sending it to the Federal Reserve Bank. The commercial bank then lends $300 to a borrower. As a consequence of these transactions the size of the money supply has
  (a) not been affected
  (b) increased by $300
  (c) increased by $600
  (d) increased by $900

8. A commercial bank has excess reserves of $500 and a required reserve ratio of 20%; it grants a loan of $1000 to a borrower. If the borrower writes a check for $1000 that is deposited in another commercial bank, the first bank will be short of reserves, after the check has been cleared, in the amount of
  (a) $200
  (b) $500
  (c) $700
  (d) $1000

9. The selling of government bonds by commercial banks is most similar to the
(a) making of loans by banks because both actions increase the money supply
(b) making of loans by banks because both actions decrease the money supply
(c) repayment of loans to banks because both actions decrease the money supply
(d) repayment of loans to banks because both actions increase the money supply

10. A commercial bank sells a $1000 government security to a securities dealer. The dealer pays for the bond in cash, which the bank adds to its vault cash. The money supply has
(a) not been affected
(b) decreased by $1000
(c) increased by $1000
(d) increased by $1000 multiplied by the reciprocal of the required reserve ratio

11. A commercial bank has deposit liabilities of $100,000, reserves of $37,000, and a required reserve ratio of 25%. The amount by which a *single commercial bank* and the amount by which the *banking system* can increase loans are, respectively,
(a) $12,000 and $48,000
(b) $17,000 and $68,000
(c) $12,000 and $60,000
(d) $17,000 and $85,000

12. If the required reserve ratio were 12.5%, the value of the monetary multiplier would be
(a) 5
(b) 6
(c) 7
(d) 8

13. The commercial banking system has excess reserves of $700, makes new loans of $2100, and is just meeting its reserve requirements. The required reserve ratio is
(a) 20%
(b) 25%
(c) 30%
(d) 33.33%

14. The commercial banking system, because of a recent change in the required reserve ratio from 20% to 30%, finds that it is $60 million short of reserves. If it is unable to obtain any additional reserves it must decrease the money supply by
(a) $60 million
(b) $180 million
(c) $200 million
(d) $300 million

15. Only one commercial bank in the banking system has an excess reserve, and its excess reserve is $100,000. This bank makes a new loan of $80,000 and keeps an excess reserve of $20,000. If the required reserve ratio for all banks is 20%, the potential expansion of the money supply is
(a) $80,000
(b) $100,000

(c) $400,000
(d) $500,000

16. The money-creating potential of the banking system is reduced when
(a) bankers choose to hold excess reserves
(b) borrowers choose to hold none of the funds they have borrowed in currency
(c) the Federal Reserve lowers the required reserve ratio
(d) bankers borrow from the Federal Reserve

Use the following balance sheet for the First National Bank to answer Questions 17, 18, 19, 20, and 21. Assume the required reserve ratio is 20%.

Assets		Liabilities and Net Worth	
Reserves	$ 50,000	Checkable deposits	$150,000
Loans	70,000	Capital stock	100,000
Securities	30,000		
Property	100,000		

17. This commercial bank has excess reserves of
(a) $10,000
(b) $20,000
(c) $30,000
(d) $40,000

18. This bank can safely expand its loans by a maximum of
(a) $50,000
(b) $40,000
(c) $30,000
(d) $20,000

19. Using the original bank balance sheet, assume that the bank makes a loan of $10,000 and has a check cleared against it for the amount of the loan; its reserves and checkable deposits will now be
(a) $40,000 and $140,000
(b) $40,000 and $150,000
(c) $30,000 and $150,000
(d) $60,000 and $140,000

20. Using the original bank balance sheet, assume that the bank makes a loan of $15,000 and has a check cleared against it for the amount of the loan; it will then have excess reserves of
(a) $5000
(b) $10,000
(c) $15,000
(d) $20,000

21. If the original bank balance sheet was for the commercial banking *system,* rather than a single bank, loans and deposits could have been expanded by a maximum of
(a) $50,000
(b) $100,000
(c) $150,000
(d) $200,000

Answer Questions 22 and 23 on the basis of the following consolidated balance sheet for the commercial banking system. All figures are in billions. Assume that the required reserve ratio is 12.5%.

Assets		Liabilities and Net Worth	
Reserves	$ 40	Checkable deposits	$200
Loans	80	Capital stock	120
Securities	100		
Property	200		

22. If there is a deposit of $20 billion of new currency into checking accounts in the banking system, excess reserves will increase by
(a) $16.5 billion
(b) $17.0 billion
(c) $17.5 billion
(d) $18.5 billion

23. The maximum amount by which this commercial banking system can expand the supply of money by lending is
(a) $120 billion
(b) $240 billion
(c) $350 billion
(d) $440 billion

24. The excess reserves held by banks tend to
(a) rise during periods of prosperity
(b) fall during periods of recession
(c) rise during periods of recession
(d) fall when interest rates in the economy fall

25. Unless controlled, the money supply will
(a) fall during periods of prosperity
(b) rise during periods of recession
(c) change in a procyclical fashion
(d) change in an anticyclical fashion

■ PROBLEMS

1. The following table shows the simplified balance sheet of a commercial bank. Assume that the figures given show the bank's assets and checkable-deposit liabilities *prior to each of the following four transactions.* Draw up the balance sheet as it would appear after each of these transactions is completed and place the balance-sheet figures in the appropriate column. Do *not* use the figures you place in columns **a, b,** and **c** when you work the next part of the problem; start all parts of the problem with the printed figures.

		(a)	(b)	(c)	(d)
Assets:					
Cash	$100	$____	$____	$____	$____
Reserves	200	____	____	____	____
Loans	500	____	____	____	____
Securities	200	____	____	____	____
Liabilities and net worth:					
Checkable deposits	900	____	____	____	____
Capital stock	100	100	100	100	100

a. A check for $50 is drawn by one of the depositors of the bank, given to a person who deposits it in another bank, and cleared (column a).

b. A depositor withdraws $50 in cash from the bank, and the bank restores its vault cash by obtaining $50 in additional cash from its Federal Reserve Bank (column b).

c. A check for $60 drawn on another bank is deposited in this bank and cleared (column c).

d. The bank sells $100 in government bonds to the Federal Reserve Bank in its district (column d).

2. Following are five balance sheets for a single commercial bank (columns 1a–5a). The required reserve ratio is 20%.

a. Compute the required reserves (A), ignoring vault cash, the excess reserves (B) of the bank (if the bank is short of reserves and must reduce its loans or obtain additional reserves, show this by placing a minus sign in front of the amounts by which it is short of reserves), and the amount of new loans it can extend (C).

	(1a)	(2a)	(3a)	(4a)	(5a)
Assets:					
Cash	$ 10	$ 20	$ 20	$ 20	$ 15
Reserves	40	40	25	40	45
Loans	100	100	100	100	150
Securities	50	60	30	70	60
Liabilities and net worth:					
Checkable deposits	175	200	150	180	220
Capital stock	25	20	25	50	50
A. Required reserve	$____	$____	$____	$____	$____
B. Excess reserve	____	____	____	____	____
C. New loans	____	____	____	____	____

b. In the following table, draw up for the individual bank the five balance sheets as they appear after the bank has made the new *loans* that it is capable of making.

	(1b)	(2b)	(3b)	(4b)	(5b)
Assets:					
Cash	$____	$____	$____	$____	$____
Reserves	____	____	____	____	____
Loans	____	____	____	____	____
Securities	____	____	____	____	____
Liabilities and net worth:					
Checkable deposits	____	____	____	____	____
Capital stock	____	____	____	____	____

3. The following table shows several reserve ratios. Compute the monetary multiplier for each reserve ratio and enter the figures in column 2. In column 3 show the maximum amount by which a single commercial bank can increase its loans for each dollar's worth of excess reserves it possesses. In column 4 indicate the maximum amount by which the banking system can increase its loans for each dollar's worth of excess reserves in the system.

(1)	(2)	(3)	(4)
12.5%	$_____	$_____	$_____
16.67	_____	_____	_____
20	_____	_____	_____
25	_____	_____	_____
30	_____	_____	_____
33.33	_____	_____	_____

4. The table at the bottom of the page is the simplified consolidated balance sheet for all commercial banks in the economy. Assume that the figures given show the banks' assets and liabilities *prior to each of the following three transactions* and that the reserve ratio is 20%. Do *not* use the figures you placed in columns 2 and 4 when you begin parts **b** and **c** of the problem; start parts **a, b,** and **c** of the problem with the printed figures.

    a. The public deposits $5 in cash in the banks and the banks send the $5 to the Federal Reserve, where it is added to their reserves. Fill in column 1. If the banking system extends the maximum amount of new loans that it is capable of extending, show in column 2 the balance sheet as it would then appear.

    b. The banking system sells $8 worth of securities to the Federal Reserve. Complete column 3. Assuming the system extends the maximum amount of credit of which it is capable, fill in column 4.

    c. The Federal Reserve lends $10 to the commercial banks; complete column 5. Complete column 6 showing the condition of the banks after the maximum amount of new loans that the banks are capable of making is granted.

■ SHORT ANSWER AND ESSAY QUESTIONS

1. Why does a bank's balance sheet balance?

2. How did the early goldsmiths come to issue paper money and then become bankers?

3. Explain the difference between a 100% and fractional reserve system of banking.

4. What are two significant characteristics of a fractional reserve system of banking?

5. Explain what happens to the money supply when a bank accepts deposits of cash.

6. What are legal reserves? How are they determined? How are legal reserves related to the reserve ratio?

7. Define the meaning of excess reserves. How are they calculated?

8. Explain why bank reserves can be an asset to the depositing commercial bank but a liability to the Federal Reserve Bank receiving them.

9. Do the reserves held by commercial banks satisfactorily protect the bank's depositors? Are the reserves of commercial banks needed? Explain your answers.

10. The owner of a sporting goods store writes a check on his account in a Kent, Ohio, bank and sends it to one of his suppliers who deposits it in his bank in Cleveland, Ohio. How does the Cleveland bank obtain payment from the Kent bank? If the two banks were in Kent and New York City, how would one bank pay the other? How are the excess reserves of the two banks affected?

11. Explain why the granting of a loan by a commercial bank increases the supply of money. Why does the repayment of a loan decrease the supply of money?

12. Why is a single commercial bank able to lend safely only an amount equal to its excess reserves?

13. How does the buying or selling of government securities by commercial banks influence the money supply?

14. Commercial banks seek both profits and safety. Explain how the balance sheet of the commercial banks reflects the desires of bankers for profits and for liquidity.

15. What is the Federal funds rate?

		(1)	(2)	(3)	(4)	(5)	(6)
Assets:							
Cash	$ 50	$_____	$_____	$_____	$_____	$_____	$_____
Reserves	100	_____	_____	_____	_____	_____	_____
Loans	200	_____	_____	_____	_____	_____	_____
Securities	200	_____	_____	_____	_____	_____	_____
Liabilities and net worth:							
Checkable deposits	500	_____	_____	_____	_____	_____	_____
Capital stock	50	50	50	50	50	50	50
Loans for Federal Reserve	0	_____	_____	_____	_____	_____	_____
Excess reserves		_____	_____	_____	_____	_____	_____
Maximum possible expansion of the money supply		_____	_____	_____	_____	_____	_____

16. Discuss how the Federal funds market helps banks reconcile the two goals of profits and liquidity.

17. No one commercial bank ever lends an amount greater than its excess reserves, but the banking system as a whole is able to extend loans and expand the money supply by an amount equal to the system's excess reserves multiplied by the reciprocal of the reserve ratio. Explain why this is possible and how the multiple expansion of deposits and money takes place.

18. What is the monetary multiplier? How does it work?

19. On the basis of a given amount of excess reserves and a given reserve ratio, a certain expansion of the money supply may be possible. What are two reasons why the potential expansion of the money supply may not be fully achieved?

20. Why is there a need for monetary control in the U.S. economy?

ANSWERS

Chapter 14 How Banks and Thrifts Create Money

FILL-IN QUESTIONS

1. thrift, checkable
2. assets, net worth, liabilities, assets = liabilities + net worth
3. fractional, less than 100%
4. *a.* money, reserves; *b.* panics, regulation
5. vault, till
6. not changed
7. its district Federal Reserve Bank
8. required, liabilities
9. Fed
10. fractional
11. actual, required
12. control of
13. an asset, a liability
14. decreased, increased, decreased, increased
15. excess
16. increases, 10,000, decreases, 10,000
17. decreases, 10,000, increases, 10,000
18. profits, liquidity
19. Federal funds, Federal funds
20. required
21. smaller
22. excess, monetary multiplier
23. decrease, $36
24. withdrawal, excess
25. recession, prosperity, less

TRUE–FALSE QUESTIONS

1. F, p. 252	4. F, pp. 252–253	7. T, pp. 254–255
2. F, p. 252	5. T, p. 253	8. T, pp. 255–256
3. F, pp. 252–253	6. F, pp. 254–255	9. T, pp. 254–255
10. F, pp. 256–257	16. F, p. 260	22. T, p. 263
11. F, pp. 256–257	17. T, p. 260	23. F, p. 264
12. T, pp. 258–259	18. F, p. 260	24. T, p. 264
13. F, pp. 258–259	19. T, pp. 260–262	25. T, p. 264
14. T, p. 259	20. F, pp. 262–263	
15. T, pp. 258–260	21. F, p. 263	

MULTIPLE-CHOICE QUESTIONS

1. a, p. 252	10. b, p. 260	19. b, pp. 258–259
2. d, pp. 252–253	11. a, pp. 260–262	20. a, pp. 258–259
3. d, p. 254	12. d, pp. 262–263	21. b, pp. 262–263
4. a, p. 255	13. d, pp. 262–263	22. c, p. 255
5. d, pp. 255–256	14. c, pp. 262–263	23. a, pp. 262–263
6. b, pp. 256–257	15. c, pp. 262–263	24. c, p. 264
7. b, pp. 258–259	16. a, pp. 262–263	25. c, p. 264
8. b, pp. 258–259	17. b, p. 255	
9. c, pp. 259–260	18. d, pp. 258–259	

PROBLEMS

1. Table

	(a)	(b)	(c)	(d)
Assets:				
Cash	$100	$100	$100	$100
Reserves	150	150	260	300
Loans	500	500	500	500
Securities	200	200	200	100
Liabilities and net worth:				
Checkable deposits	850	850	960	900
Capital stock	100	100	100	100

2. *a.* Table

	(1a)	(2a)	(3a)	(4a)	(5a)
A. Required reserve	$35	$40	$30	$36	$44
B. Excess reserve	5	0	−25	4	1
C. New loans	5	0	*	4	1

b. Table

	(1b)	(2b)	(3b)	(4b)	(5b)
Assets:					
Cash	$ 10	$ 20	$ 20	$ 20	$ 15
Reserves	40	40	25	40	45
Loans	105	100	*	104	151
Securities	50	60	30	70	60
Liabilities and net worth:					
Checkable deposits	180	200	*	184	221
Capital stock	25	20	25	50	50

*If an individual bank is $5 short of reserves it must either obtain additional reserves of $5 by selling loans, securities, or its own IOUs to the reserve bank or contract its loans by $25.

3. Table

(1)	(2)	(3)	(4)
12.50%	$8	$1	$8
16.67	6	1	6
20	5	1	5
25	4	1	4
30	3.33	1	3.33
33.33	3	1	3

4. Table

	(1)	(2)	(3)	(4)	(5)	(6)
Assets:						
Cash	$ 50	$ 50	$ 50	$ 50	$ 50	$ 50
Reserves	105	105	108	108	110	110
Loans	200	220	200	240	200	250
Securities	200	200	192	192	200	200
Liabilities and net worth:						
Checkable deposits	505	525	500	540	500	550
Capital stock	50	50	50	50	50	50
Loans from Federal						
Reserve	0	0	0	0	10	10
Excess reserves	4	0	8	0	10	0
Maximum possible expansion						
of the money supply	20	0	40	0	50	0

SHORT ANSWER AND ESSAY QUESTIONS

1. p. 252

2. pp. 252–253

3. pp. 252–253

4. p. 253

5. pp. 254–255

6. pp. 254–255

7. p. 255

8. p. 256

9. pp. 255–256

10. pp. 256–257

11. pp. 258–259

12. pp. 258–259

13. pp. 259–260

14. p. 260

15. p. 260

16. p. 260

17. pp. 260–263

18. pp. 262–263

19. pp. 263–264

20. p. 264

CHAPTER 15

Monetary Policy

Chapter 15 is the third chapter dealing with money and banking. It explains how the Board of Governors of the Federal Reserve System and the Federal Reserve Banks affect output, income, employment, and the price level of the economy. Central bank policy designed to affect these variables is called *monetary policy,* the goal of which is price-level stability, full employment, and economic growth.

The first half of the chapter explains how the Federal Reserve achieves its basic goal. In this discussion, attention should be paid to the following: (1) the important items on the balance sheet of the Federal Reserve Banks; (2) the three major controls available to the Federal Reserve, and how the employment of these controls can affect the reserves, excess reserves, actual money supply, and money-creating potential of the banking system; (3) the actions the Federal Reserve would take if it were pursuing a *tight money policy* to curb inflation, and the actions it would take if it were pursuing an *easy money policy* to increase economic growth and reduce unemployment; and (4) the relative importance of the three major controls.

Following the examination of "The Tools of Monetary Policy," Professors McConnell and Brue explain how changes in the money supply ultimately affect the economy. They achieve this objective by describing how the demand for money and the supply of money determine the interest rate (in the *money market*), and how the interest rate and the investment demand schedule determine the level of equilibrium GDP. The effects of an easy money policy or a tight money policy in this *cause-effect chain* are illustrated with examples and summarized in Table 15.3. Changes in monetary policy shift aggregate demand across the aggregate supply curve, thus changing real output and the price level.

A major section of the chapter discusses the monetary policy in action. The major strengths are related to its speed and flexibility and isolation from political pressures. In current practice, the Federal Reserve changes monetary policy by adjusting its targets for the *Federal fund rates.* These rates in turn have an effect on other interest rates in the economy, such as the prime interest rate. The Federal Reserve has had many successes during the 1990s and the early 2000s in countering recession by lowering the interest rate and controlling inflation by raising the interest rate.

Monetary policy, however, is not without its problems or complications. There can be lags between the time

actions are taken and the time the monetary policy influences economic activity. Changes in the velocity of money can blunt the effectiveness of monetary policy. Monetary policy can also suffer from cyclical asymmetry by being more influential in controlling inflation than in preventing recession. There have been debates about whether there should be more or less discretion in the conduct of monetary policy and the adoption of inflation targeting. Linkages with the international economy further complicate outcomes because change in monetary policy can affect exchange rates and net exports.

The final section on the "Big Picture" is short but important. Figure 15.4 gives you an overview of the economic factors and government policies that affect aggregate demand and aggregate supply. It summarizes much of the economic theory and policy that have been discussed in this chapter and the eight chapters that preceded it.

■ CHECKLIST

When you have studied this chapter you should be able to

☐ State the fundamental goal of monetary policy.

☐ List the important assets and liabilities of the Federal Reserve Banks.

☐ Identify the three tools of monetary policy.

☐ Explain how the Federal Reserve can expand the money supply by buying government securities from commercial banks and from the public.

☐ Explain how the Federal Reserve can contract the money supply by selling government securities to commercial banks and to the public.

☐ Describe how raising or lowering the reserve ratio can increase or decrease the money supply.

☐ Illustrate how raising or lowering the discount rate can increase or decrease the money supply.

☐ Describe three actions the Fed can take to pursue an easy money policy.

☐ Describe three actions the Fed can take to pursue a tight money policy.

☐ Discuss the relative importance of monetary policy tools.

☐ Draw the demand-for-money and the supply-of-money curves and use them to show how a change in the supply of money will affect the interest rate.

☐ Draw an investment demand curve to explain the effects of changes in the interest rate on investment spending.

☐ Construct an aggregate supply and aggregate demand graph to show how aggregate demand and the equilibrium level of GDP are affected by changes in interest rates and investment spending.

☐ Use a cause-effect chain to explain the links between a change in the money supply and a change in the equilibrium level of GDP when there is an easy money policy and a tight money policy.

☐ List several strengths of monetary policy.

☐ Explain how the Federal Reserve uses monetary policy to change the Federal funds rate.

☐ Describe the relationship between the Federal funds rate and the prime interest rate.

☐ Evaluate monetary policy in the 1990s and 2000s.

☐ Describe three limitations or complications of monetary policy.

☐ Debate whether monetary policy should be largely conducted with discretion or whether there should be inflation targeting.

☐ Explain how the effectiveness of an easy money policy or a tight money policy is influenced by net exports and how these policies affect balance-of-trade deficits.

☐ Summarize the key factors and policies affecting aggregate supply and demand, and the level of output, employment, income, and prices in an economy using Figure 15.4.

■ **CHAPTER OUTLINE**

1. The fundamental *objective of monetary policy* is full employment without inflation. The Federal Reserve can accomplish this objective by exercising control over the amount of excess reserves held by commercial banks, and thereby influencing the size of the money supply and the total level of spending in the economy.

2. By examining the consolidated *balance sheet* and the principal assets and liabilities of the Federal Reserve Banks, an understanding of the ways the Federal Reserve can control and influence the reserves of commercial banks and the money supply can be obtained.

    a. The principal *assets* of the Federal Reserve Banks (in order of size) are U.S. government securities and loans to commercial banks.

    b. Their principal *liabilities* are Federal Reserve Notes, the reserve deposits of commercial banks, and U.S. Treasury deposits.

3. The Federal Reserve Banks use three principal tools (techniques or instruments) to control the reserves of banks and the size of the money supply.

    a. The Federal Reserve can *buy* or *sell government securities* in the open market to change the lending ability of the banking system.

    (1) Buying government securities in the open market from either banks or the public increases the excess reserves of banks.

    (2) Selling government securities in the open market to either banks or the public decreases the excess reserves of banks.

    b. It can *raise or lower the reserve ratio.*

    (1) Raising the reserve ratio decreases the excess reserves of banks and the size of the monetary (checkable-deposit) multiplier.

    (2) Lowering the reserve ratio increases the excess reserves of banks and the size of the monetary multiplier.

    c. It can also *raise* or *lower the discount rate.* Raising the discount rate discourages banks from borrowing reserves from the Fed. Lowering the discount rate encourages banks to borrow from the Fed.

    d. Monetary policy can be easy or tight.

    (1) An *easy money policy* can be implemented by actions of the Federal Reserve to buy government securities in the open market, decrease the discount rate, or decrease the reserve ratio.

    (2) A *tight money policy* can be implemented by actions of the Federal Reserve to sell government securities in the open market, increase the discount rate, or increase the reserve ratio.

    e. Open-market operations is the most important of the three monetary tools because it is the most flexible and direct.

4. Monetary policy affects the *equilibrium GDP* in many ways.

    a. In the *money market,* the demand curve for money and the supply curve of money determine the real interest rate. This rate of interest in turn determines investment spending. Investment spending then affects aggregate demand and the equilibrium levels of real output and prices.

    b. If recession or slow economic growth is a major problem, the Federal Reserve can institute an *easy money policy* that increases the money supply, causing the interest rate to fall and investment spending to increase, thereby increasing aggregate demand and increasing real GDP by a multiple of the increase in investment.

    c. If inflation is the problem, the Federal Reserve can adopt a *tight money policy* that decreases the money supply, causing the interest rate to rise and investment spending to decrease, thereby reducing aggregate demand and inflation.

5. Monetary policy is considered more important and valuable for stabilizing the national economy because of its several advantages over fiscal policy: It is quicker and more flexible, and there is more isolation from political pressure.

    a. The *Federal funds rate,* the interest rate that banks charge each other for overnight loans of excess reserves, has been the recent focus of monetary policy.

    (1) The Federal Reserve can influence the Federal funds rate by buying or selling government bonds. When the Federal Reserve buys bonds, it becomes cheaper for banks to borrow excess reserves overnight because the Federal funds rate falls; conversely, when the Federal Reserve sells bonds, the Federal funds rate rises and it becomes more expensive for banks to borrow funds.

    (2) The *prime interest rate* is the benchmark rate that banks use to decide on the interest rate for loans to

businesses and individuals; it rises and falls with the Federal funds rate.

b. Recent monetary policy has been easy and tight in response to concerns about recession and inflation. In the early 1990s, the Federal Reserve increased excess reserves and reduced interest rates to counter a recession. Interest rates were raised in the mid-1990s to control inflation, but then lowered again in 1998 in response to the financial crisis in southeast Asia. They were raised again in 1999 and 2000, but in 2001 and 2002 the Federal Reserve cut rates to counter an economic slowdown and recession.

c. There are some limitations and complications with monetary policy. It is subject to lags between the time the need for the policy is recognized and the time the policy influences economic activity. Changes in the velocity of money can offset changes in monetary policy. There is a cyclical asymmetry with monetary policy: A tight money policy works better than an easy money policy.

d. Debates over the conduct of monetary policy have focused on the use of management discretion or inflation targeting. Although the Federal Reserve has been successful in recent years with its "artful management" of monetary policy, some economists would like it to adopt inflation targeting, in which the Federal Reserve must specify and be accountable for achieving an inflation target within a range.

e. Monetary policy has international linkages and there is a ***net export effect.***

(1) An easy money policy to bring the economy out of recession or slow growth will tend to lower domestic interest rates and cause the dollar to depreciate. In this situation, net exports will increase, thus increasing aggregate demand and reinforcing the effects of the easy money policy.

(2) A tight money policy to reduce inflation will tend to raise domestic interest rates and cause the dollar to appreciate. These events will decrease net exports and reduce aggregate demand, thereby increasing the effects of a tight money policy.

(3) An easy money policy is *compatible* with the goal of correcting a balance-of-trade deficit, but a tight money policy *conflicts* with this economic goal.

6. The ***"big picture" of macroeconomics*** shows that the equilibrium levels of output, employment, income, and prices are determined by the interaction of aggregate supply and aggregate demand.

a. There are four expenditure components of aggregate demand: consumption, investment, government spending, and net export spending.

b. There are three major components of aggregate supply: the prices of inputs or resources, factors affecting the productivity with which resources are used, and the legal and institutional environment.

c. Fiscal, monetary, or other government policies may have an effect on the components of aggregate demand or supply, which in turn will affect the level of output, employment, income, and prices.

■ **HINTS AND TIPS**

1. To acquire a thorough knowledge of how the Federal Reserve transactions affect required reserves, excess reserves, the actual money supply, and the potential money supply, carefully study the ***balance sheets*** that are used to explain these transactions. The items to watch are the reserves and checkable deposits. Be sure that you know why a change is made in each balance sheet, and be able to make the appropriate balance-sheet entries as you trace through the effects of each transaction. Problem 2 in this chapter provides additional practice.

2. You must understand and remember the ***cause-effect chain of monetary policy.*** The best way to learn it is to draw your own chain (graphs) that shows the links for an easy money policy and a tight money policy as in Figure 15.2. Then check each step for how monetary policy can be used to counter recession or limit inflation using Table 15.3 in the text. Draw another chain for describing monetary policy and the net export effect and check your cause-effect chain against Table 15.4.

3. The section on "monetary policy in action" shows how the theory you have learned has been applied in the real world. In particular, you want to pay attention to how the Federal Reserve uses the Federal funds rate to implement monetary policy, and also learn about the policy successes in recent years to counter recession and limit inflation.

4. The single most important figure for a "big picture" of the macroeconomics part of the textbook is ***Figure 15.4.*** It reviews and summarizes the determinants of aggregate supply and demand and identifies the key policy variables that have been discussed in this chapter and in Chapters 7–14.

■ **IMPORTANT TERMS**

monetary policy	tight money policy
open-market operations	Federal funds rate
reserve ratio	prime interest rate
discount rate	inflation targeting
easy money policy	

SELF-TEST

■ **FILL-IN QUESTIONS**

1. The goal of monetary policy in the United States is to achieve and maintain stability in the (price level, tax level) _____, a rate of (full, partial) _____ employment in the economy, and economic growth.

2. The two important assets of the Federal Reserve Banks are (Treasury deposits, government securities) _____ and (reserves of, loans to)

_____ commercial banks. The three major liabilities are (Treasury deposits, government securities) _____, (reserves of, loans to) _____ commercial banks, and (government securities, Federal Reserve Notes) _____ .

3. The three tools the monetary authority uses to control the money supply are (open, closed) _____ market operations, changing the (loan, reserve) _____ ratio, and changing the (prime interest, discount) _____ rate.

4. When the Federal Reserve Banks buy government securities in the open market, the reserves of commercial banks will (increase, decrease) _____ and when they sell government securities in the open market, the reserves of commercial banks will _____ .

5. If the Federal Reserve Banks were to sell $10 million in government bonds to the *public* and the reserve ratio were 25%, the supply of money would immediately be reduced by $_____, the reserves of commercial banks would be reduced by $_____, and the excess reserves of the banks would be reduced by $_____. But if these bonds were sold to the commercial banks, the supply of money would immediately be reduced by $_____, the reserves of the banks would be reduced by $_____, and the excess reserves of the banks would be reduced by $_____.

6. An increase in the reserve ratio will (increase, decrease) _____ the size of the monetary multiplier and _____ the excess reserves held by commercial banks, thus causing the money supply to (increase, decrease) _____. A decrease in the reserve ratio will (increase, decrease) _____ the size of the monetary multiplier and _____ the excess reserves held by commercial banks, thus causing the money supply to (increase, decrease) _____ .

7. If the Federal Reserve Banks were to lower the discount rate, commercial banks would tend to borrow (more, less) _____ from them, and this would (increase, decrease) _____ their excess reserves.

8. To increase the supply of money, the Federal Reserve Banks should (raise, lower) _____ the reserve ratio, (buy, sell) _____ securities in the open market, and/or (increase, decrease) _____ the discount rate.

9. An easy money policy would be characterized by actions of the Federal Reserve to (increase, decrease) _____ the discount rate, _____ reserve ratios, and (buy, sell) _____ government bonds, whereas a tight money policy would include actions taken to (increase, decrease) _____ the discount rate, _____ reserve ratios, and (buy, sell) _____ government bonds.

10. The most effective and most often used tool of monetary policy is a change in (the discount rate, the reserve ratio, open-market operations) _____, and a rarely used tool is a change in _____; an announcement effect is created by a change in _____, but it is relatively weak because banks may not be inclined to borrow even at a lower rate.

11. There is a cause-effect chain of monetary policy.
a. In the money market, the demand for and the supply of money determine the equilibrium rate of (discount, interest) _____ .
b. This rate in turn determines the level of (government, investment) _____ spending based on the _____ demand curve.
c. This spending in turn affects aggregate (demand, supply) _____, and the intersection of aggregate supply and demand determine the equilibrium level of real (interest, GDP) _____ and the (discount, price) _____ level.

12. This cause-effect chain can be illustrated with examples.
a. When there is an *increase* in the money supply curve, the real interest rate will (increase, decrease) _____, investment spending will _____, aggregate demand will (increase, decrease) _____, and real GDP will _____ .
b. When there is a *decrease* in the money supply curve, the real interest rate will (increase, decrease) _____, investment spending will _____, aggregate demand will (increase, decrease) _____, and real GDP will _____ .

13. To eliminate inflationary pressures in the economy, the traditional view holds that the monetary authority should seek to (increase, decrease) _____ the reserves of commercial banks; this would tend to _____ the money supply and to (increase, decrease) _____ the rate of interest, and this in turn would cause investment spending, aggregate demand, and GDP to _____. This action by monetary authorities would be considered (an easy, a tight) _____ money policy.

14. If there were a serious problem with economic growth and unemployment in the economy, the traditional view would be that the Federal Reserve should pursue (an easy, a tight) _____ money policy, in which case the Federal Reserve would (buy, sell) _____ government bonds as a way of (increasing, decreasing) _____ the money supply, and thereby _____ interest rates; these events would have the effect of (increasing, decreasing) _____ investment spending and thus _____ real GDP.

15. An increase in the money supply will shift the aggregate (supply, demand) _____ curve to the (right, left) _____. A decrease in the money supply will shift the aggregate (supply, demand) _____ curve to the (right, left) _____. If the marginal propensity to consume is .75, then the multiplier will be (3, 4) _____, an initial increase in investment of $10 billion will (increase, decrease) _____ aggregate demand by ($30, $40) _____ billion.

16. Monetary policy has strengths. Compared to fiscal policy, monetary policy is speedier and (more, less) _____ flexible, and _____ isolated from political pressure.

17. The interest rate that banks charge one another for overnight loans is the (prime interest, Federal funds) _____ rate, but the rate banks use as a benchmark for setting interest rates on loans is the _____ rate. The (prime interest, Federal funds) _____ rate has been the recent focus of the monetary policy of the Federal Reserve. Since 1990, the Federal Reserve has been successful in countering recession by (raising, lowering) _____ the Federal funds, and it has been successful in limiting inflation by _____ the Federal funds rate.

18. Monetary policy has shortcomings and problems, too.

a. It may be subject to timing (limits, lags) _____ that occur between the time a need is recognized and the policy takes effect.

b. It may be offset when the velocity of money changes in the (same, opposite) _____ direction as the money supply.

c. It may be more effective in counteracting (recession, inflation) _____ than _____.

19. In recent years, there have been calls for the Federal Reserve to focus primarily on the goal of price-level stability and be more accountable for its actions by using (deflation, inflation) _____ targeting. Critics of such a policy contend that the role that it assigns to the Federal Reserve is too (wide, narrow) _____ and that policymakers at the Federal Reserve should have (more, less) _____ discretion over the conduct of monetary policy.

20. An easy money policy (increases, decreases) _____ net exports; a tight money policy _____ net exports. The net export effect from an easy money policy thus (strengthens, weakens) _____ domestic monetary policy, and the net export effect from a tight money policy _____ it. An easy money policy is (compatible, incompatible) _____ with the economic goal of reducing a balance-of-trade deficit, but a tight money policy is _____ with this economic goal.

■ **TRUE–FALSE QUESTIONS**

Circle T if the statement is true, F if it is false.

1. The goal of monetary policy is to lower interest rates.
T F

2. The securities owned by the Federal Reserve Banks are almost entirely U.S. government bonds.
T F

3. If the Federal Reserve Banks buy $15 in government securities from the public in the open market, the effect will be to increase the excess reserves of commercial banks by $15.
T F

4. When the Federal Reserve sells bonds in the open market, the price of these bonds falls.
T F

5. A change in the reserve ratio will affect the multiple by which the banking system can create money, but it will not affect the actual or excess reserves of member banks.
T F

6. If the reserve ratio is lowered, some required reserves are turned into excess reserves.   **T   F**

7. When commercial banks borrow from the Federal Reserve Banks, they increase their excess reserves and their money-creating potential.   **T   F**

8. If the monetary authority wished to follow a tight money policy, it would sell government bonds in the open market.   **T   F**

9. An increase in the required reserve ratio tends to reduce the profits of banks.   **T   F**

10. The least effective and least used tool of monetary policy is the open-market operation, in which government securities are bought and sold.   **T   F**

11. The equilibrium rate of interest is found at the intersection of the money demand and the money supply curves.   **T   F**

12. An increase in the equilibrium GDP will shift the demand-for-money curve to the left and increase the equilibrium interest rate.   **T   F**

13. In the cause-effect chain, an easy money policy increases the money supply, decreases the interest rate, increases investment spending, and increases aggregate demand.   **T   F**

14. A tight money policy is designed to correct a problem of high unemployment and sluggish economic growth.   **T   F**

15. It is generally agreed that fiscal policy is more effective than monetary policy in controlling the business cycle because fiscal policy is more flexible.   **T   F**

16. Monetary policy is subject to more political pressure than fiscal policy.   **T   F**

17. In recent years, the Federal Reserve has announced its changes in monetary policy by changing its targets for the Federal funds rate.   **T   F**

18. The prime interest rate is the rate that banks charge other banks for overnight loans of excess reserves at Federal Reserve banks.   **T   F**

19. To increase the Federal funds interest rate, the Federal Reserve buys bonds in the open market to increase the excess reserves of banks.   **T   F**

20. Monetary policy is limited by a time lag that occurs from when the problem is recognized to when the policy becomes operational.   **T   F**

21. An easy money policy suffers from a "You can lead a horse to water, but you can't make the horse drink" problem.   **T   F**

22. Inflation targeting is largely a monetary policy that permits the Federal Reserve to use substantial discretion in managing the economy.   **T   F**

23. An easy money policy decreases net exports.   **T   F**

24. A tight money policy will tend to cause the dollar to appreciate.   **T   F**

25. A tight money policy is compatible with the goal of correcting a trade deficit.   **T   F**

■ **MULTIPLE-CHOICE QUESTIONS**

Circle the letter that corresponds to the best answer.

1. The organization directly responsible for monetary policy in the United States is the
  (a) Internal Revenue Service
  (b) Federal Reserve
  (c) Congress of the United States
  (d) U.S. Treasury

2. The largest single asset in the Federal Reserve Banks' consolidated balance sheet is
  (a) securities
  (b) the reserves of commercial banks
  (c) Federal Reserve Notes
  (d) loans to commercial banks

3. The largest single liability of the Federal Reserve Banks is
  (a) securities
  (b) the reserves of commercial banks
  (c) Federal Reserve Notes
  (d) loans to commercial banks

4. Assume that there is a 20% reserve ratio and that the Federal Reserve buys $100 million worth of government securities. If the securities are purchased from the public, this action has the potential to increase bank lending by a maximum of
  (a) $500 million, but only by $400 million if the securities are purchased directly from commercial banks
  (b) $400 million, but by $500 million if the securities are purchased directly from commercial banks
  (c) $500 million, and also by $500 million if the securities are purchased directly from commercial banks
  (d) $400 million, and also by $400 million if the securities are purchased directly from commercial banks

5. Assuming that the Federal Reserve Banks sell $20 million in government securities to commercial banks and the reserve ratio is 20%, then the effect will be
  (a) to reduce the actual supply of money by $20 million
  (b) to reduce the actual supply of money by $4 million
  (c) to reduce the potential money supply by $20 million
  (d) to reduce the potential money supply by $100 million

6. Lowering the reserve ratio changes
  (a) required reserves to excess reserves
  (b) increases the amount of excess reserves banks must keep
  (c) increases the discount rate
  (d) decreases the discount rate

7. Commercial bank borrowing from the Federal Reserve
(a) is not permitted because of the Federal Reserve Act
(b) is permitted but only for banks that are bankrupt
(c) decreases the excess reserves of commercial banks and their ability to offer credit
(d) increases the excess reserves of commercial banks and their ability to offer credit

8. The economy is experiencing high unemployment and a low rate of economic growth and the Fed decides to pursue an easy money policy. Which set of actions by the Fed would be most consistent with this policy?
(a) buying government securities and raising the reserve ratio
(b) selling government securities and raising the discount rate
(c) buying government securities and lowering the reserve ratio
(d) selling government securities and lowering the discount rate

9. The economy is experiencing inflation and the Federal Reserve decides to pursue a tight money policy. Which set of actions by the Fed would be most consistent with this policy?
(a) buying government securities and lowering the discount rate
(b) buying government securities and lowering the reserve ratio
(c) selling government securities and raising the discount rate
(d) selling government securities and lowering the discount rate

10. Which is the most important control used by the Federal Reserve to regulate the money supply?
(a) changing the reserve ratio
(b) open-market operations
(c) changing the discount rate
(d) changing the Federal funds rate

11. A newspaper headline reads: "Fed Cuts Discount Rate for Third Time This Year." This headline indicates that the Federal Reserve is most likely trying to
(a) reduce inflationary pressures in the economy
(b) increase the Federal funds rate
(c) reduce the cost of credit and stimulate the economy
(d) increase the value of the dollar

12. In the chain of cause and effect between changes in the excess reserves of commercial banks and the resulting changes in output and employment in the economy,
(a) an increase in excess reserves will decrease the money supply
(b) a decrease in the money supply will increase the rate of interest
(c) an increase in the rate of interest will increase aggregate demand
(d) an increase in aggregate demand will decrease output and employment

13. Which is most likely to be affected by changes in the rate of interest?
(a) tax rates
(b) investment spending
(c) government spending
(d) the imports of the economy

Use the following graph to answer Questions 14, 15, and 16.

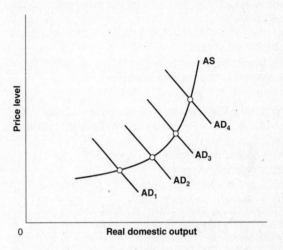

14. A shift from **AD₁** to **AD₂** would be most consistent with
(a) an increase in the prime interest rate by corporations
(b) an increase in the discount rate by the Federal Reserve
(c) the buying of securities by the Federal Reserve
(d) the selling of securities by the Federal Reserve

15. Assume that the Federal Reserve lowers interest rates to increase investment spending. This monetary policy is most likely to shift
(a) **AD₃** to **AD₂**
(b) **AD₃** to **AD₄**
(c) **AD₄** to **AD₃**
(d) **AD₂** to **AD₁**

16. A tight money policy would be most consistent with a shift from
(a) **AD₁** to **AD₂**
(b) **AD₃** to **AD₄**
(c) **AD₄** to **AD₃**
(d) **AD₂** to **AD₃**

17. Assume that monetary policy increases interest rates and results in a decrease in investment spending of $5 billion. If the marginal propensity to consume is .80, then aggregate demand is most likely to
(a) increase by $5 billion
(b) decrease by $25 billion
(c) increase by $25 billion
(d) decrease by $25 billion

18. Which one is considered a *strength* of monetary policy compared to fiscal policy?
(a) cause-effect chain
(b) cyclical asymmetry
(c) isolation from political pressure
(d) effect on changes in the velocity of money

19. The Federal funds rate is the rate that
(a) banks charge for overnight use of excess reserves held at the Federal Reserve banks
(b) banks charge for loans to the most creditworthy customers
(c) the Federal Reserve charges for short-term loans to commercial banks
(d) government bonds are sold in the open-market operations of the Federal Reserve

20. When the Federal Reserve uses open-market operations to reduce the Federal funds rate several times over a year it is pursuing
(a) an easy money policy
(b) a tight money policy
(c) a prime interest rate policy
(d) a discretionary fiscal policy

21. When the Federal Reserve Banks decide to buy government bonds from banks and the public, the supply of reserves in the Federal fund market
(a) increases and the Federal funds rate decreases
(b) decreases and the Federal funds rate decreases
(c) increases and the Federal funds rate increases
(d) decreases and the Federal funds rate increases

22. Assume the Fed creates excess reserves, but the policy does not encourage banks to make loans and thus increase the money supply. This situation is a problem of
(a) tight money
(b) cyclical asymmetry
(c) changes in velocity
(d) targeting the Federal funds rate

23. A tight money policy in the United States is most likely to
(a) increase domestic interest rates and cause the value of the dollar to depreciate
(b) decrease domestic interest rates and cause the value of the dollar to appreciate
(c) increase domestic interest rates and cause the value of the dollar to appreciate
(d) decrease domestic interest rates and cause the value of the dollar to depreciate

24. Which policy combination would tend to reduce net exports?
(a) tight money policy and expansionary fiscal policy
(b) easy money policy and expansionary fiscal policy
(c) tight money policy and contractionary fiscal policy
(d) easy money policy and contractionary fiscal policy

25. A tight money policy that is used to reduce inflation in the domestic economy
(a) is best conducted by reducing the required reserve ratios at commercial banks
(b) increases net exports and the effectiveness of the policy
(c) conflicts with the economic goal of correcting a trade deficit
(d) causes the dollar to depreciate

■ **PROBLEMS**

1. Assume that the following consolidated balance sheet is for all commercial banks. Assume also that the required reserve ratio is 25% and that cash is *not* a part of the commercial banks' legal reserve.

Assets		Liabilities	
Cash	$ 50	Checkable deposits	$400
Reserves	100	Loans from Federal	
Loans	150	Reserve	25
Securities	200	Net worth	75
	$500		$500

a. To *increase* the supply of money by $100, the Fed could (buy, sell) _____ securities worth $_____ in the open market.
b. To *decrease* the supply of money by $50, the Fed could (buy, sell) _____ securities worth $_____ in the open market.

2. Following are the consolidated balance sheets of the Federal Reserve and of the commercial banks. Assume that the reserve ratio for commercial banks is 25%, that cash is *not* a part of a bank's legal reserve, and that the figures in column 1 show the balance sheets of the Federal Reserve and the commercial banks *prior to each of the following five transactions.* Place the new balance sheet figures in the appropriate columns and complete A, B, C, D, and E in these columns. Do *not* use the figures you place in columns 2 through 5 when you work the next part of the problem; start all parts of the problem with the printed figures in column 1.
a. The Federal Reserve Banks sell $3 in securities to the public, which pays by check (column 2).
b. The Federal Reserve Banks buy $4 in securities from the commercial banks (column 3).
c. The Federal Reserve Banks lower the required reserve ratio for commercial banks to 20% (column 4).
d. The U.S. Treasury buys $5 worth of goods from U.S. manufacturers and pays the manufacturers by checks drawn on its accounts at the Federal Reserve Banks (column 5).
e. Because the Federal Reserve Banks have raised the discount rate, commercial banks repay $6 which they owe to the Federal Reserve (column 6).

	(1)	(2)	(3)	(4)	(5)	(6)
Federal Reserve Banks						
Assets:						
Gold certificates	$ 25	$____	$____	$____	$____	$____
Securities	30	____	____	____	____	____
Loans to commercial banks	10	____	____	____	____	____
Liabilities:						
Reserves of commercial banks	50	____	____	____	____	____
Treasury deposits	5	____	____	____	____	____
Federal Reserve Notes	10	____	____	____	____	____
Commercial Banks						
Assets:						
Reserves	$ 50	$____	$____	$____	$____	$____
Securities	70	____	____	____	____	____
Loans	90	____	____	____	____	____
Liabilities:						
Demand deposits	200	____	____	____	____	____
Loans from Federal Reserve	10	____	____	____	____	____
A. Required reserves		____	____	____	____	____
B. Excess reserves		____	____	____	____	____
C. How much has the money supply changed?		____	____	____	____	____
D. How much more can the money supply change?		____	____	____	____	____
E. What is the total of C and D?		____	____	____	____	____

3. On the following graph is the demand-for-money curve that shows the amounts of money consumers and firms wish to hold at various rates of interest (when the nominal GDP in the economy is given).

b. Below is a graph of an investment demand curve which shows the amounts of planned investment at various rates of interest. Given your answer to (2) above, how much will investors plan to spend for capital goods? $_____ billion.

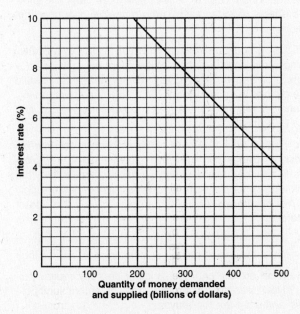

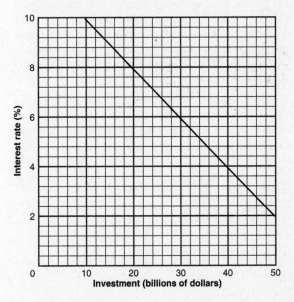

a. Suppose the supply of money is equal to $300 billion. (1) Draw the supply-of-money curve on the above graph. (2) The equilibrium rate of interest in the economy is _____ %.

c. The following figure shows the aggregate supply (**AS**) curve in this economy. On the graph, draw an aggregate demand curve (**AD₁**) so that it crosses the **AS** in the middle of the curve. Label the price level (**P₁**) and output level (**Q₁**) associated with the intersection of **AD₁** and **AS**.

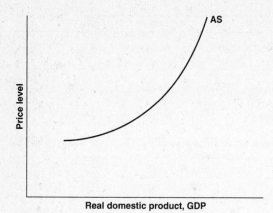

d. Now assume that monetary authorities increase the money supply to $400.

(1) On the money market graph, plot the new money supply curve. The new equilibrium interest rate is

_____ %.

(2) On the investment graph, determine the level of investment spending that is associated with this new

interest rate: $_____ billion. By how much has investment spending increased as a result

of the change in the interest rate? $_____ billion.

(3) Assume that the marginal propensity to consume

is .75. What is the multiplier? _____
By how much will the new investment spending in-

crease aggregate demand? $_____ billion.

(4) On the previous figure, indicate how the change in investment spending affects aggregate demand. Draw a new aggregate demand curve (**AD₂**) so that it crosses the **AS** curve. Also label the new price level (**P₂**) and output level (**Q₂**) associated with the intersection of **AD₂** and **AS.**

4. Columns 1 and 2 of the following table show the aggregate supply schedule. (The price level is a price index, and real domestic output is measured in billions of dollars.)

(1) Price level	(2) Real output	(3) AD₁	(4) AD₂
110	1600	1800	____
120	1700	1700	____
130	1790	1600	____
140	1800	1500	____
150	1940	1400	____
160	2000	1300	____

a. If the aggregate demand schedule were that shown in columns 1 and 3, the equilibrium real domestic

output would be $_____ billion and the price

level would be _____.

b. Now assume that the Federal Reserve took actions to lower the Federal funds rate, and these actions increased investment spending in this economy by $60 billion. Also assume that the marginal propensity to consume in the economy was .8. How much would

aggregate demand increase? $_____ billion

c. In column 4, enter this amount of increase in real domestic output at each price level to define the new **AD** schedule (**AD₂**).

d. What is the new equilibrium real domestic output?

$_____ billion. And the new price level? _____.

■ SHORT ANSWER AND ESSAY QUESTIONS

1. What is the basic goal of monetary policy?

2. What are the important assets and liabilities of the Federal Reserve Banks?

3. Explain how the monetary policy tools of the Federal Reserve Banks would be used to contract the supply of money. How would they be used to expand the supply of money?

4. What is the difference between the effects of the Federal Reserve's buying (selling) government securities in the open market from (to) commercial banks and from (to) the public?

5. Which of the monetary policy tools available to the Federal Reserve is most effective? Why is it more important than other tools?

6. Using three graphs, explain what determines (*a*) the equilibrium interest rate, (*b*) investment spending, and (*c*) the equilibrium GDP. Now use these three graphs to show the effects of a decrease in the money supply upon the equilibrium GDP.

7. Using your answers to Question 6, (*a*) what determines how large the effect of the decrease in the money supply on the equilibrium GDP will be, and (*b*) how would the change in the equilibrium GDP affect the demand-for-money curve, the interest rate, investment spending, and the GDP itself?

8. Explain how the Board of Governors and the Federal Reserve Banks can influence income, output, employment, and the price level. In your explanation, employ the following concepts: reserves, excess reserves, the supply of money, the availability of bank credit, and the rate of interest.

9. Why are changes in the rate of interest likely to affect investment spending more than consumption and saving?

10. What are the characteristics of an easy money policy? How does the Federal Reserve implement such policies and what are the effects?

11. What are the characteristics of a tight money policy? How does the Federal Reserve implement such policies and what are the effects?

12. What policies will the Federal Reserve use to counter inflation, or unemployment and recession? Describe the effects on bank reserves, the money supply, interest rates, investment spending, aggregate demand, and real GDP from each policy.

13. What are the major strengths of monetary policy?

14. What happens to the Federal funds rate when the Federal Reserve expands or contracts the money supply through open-market operations?

15. Discuss how monetary policy has been used to counter recession and limit inflation since the 1990s.

16. Why is monetary policy more effective in controlling inflation than in reducing unemployment?

17. Why might a change in velocity reduce the effectiveness of monetary policy?

18. Should monetary policy be "artful management" or should there be inflation targeting? Discuss the advantages and disadvantages of each approach.

19. Explain how the net export effect influences the effectiveness of a tight or an easy money policy.

20. What type of monetary policy would you recommend to correct a balance-of-trade deficit? Why?

ANSWERS

Chapter 15 Monetary Policy

FILL-IN QUESTIONS

1. price level, full
2. government securities, loans to, Treasury deposits, reserves of, Federal Reserve Notes
3. open, reserve, discount
4. increase, decrease
5. 10 million, 10 million, 7.5 million, 0, 10 million, 10 million
6. decrease, decrease, decrease, increase, increase, increase
7. more, increase
8. lower, buy, decrease
9. decrease, decrease, buy, increase, increase, sell
10. open-market operations, the reserve ratio, the discount rate
11. *a.* interest; *b.* investment, investment; *c.* demand, GDP, price
12. *a.* decrease, increase, increase, increase; *b.* increase, decrease, decrease, decrease
13. decrease, decrease, increase, decrease, a tight
14. an easy, buy, increasing, decreasing, increasing, increasing
15. demand, right, demand, left, 4, increase, $40
16. more, more
17. Federal funds, prime interest, Federal funds, lowering, raising
18. lags, opposite, inflation, recession
19. inflation, narrow, more
20. increases, decreases, strengthens, strengthens, compatible, incompatible

TRUE–FALSE QUESTIONS

1. F, p. 268	**10.** F, p. 275	**19.** F, pp. 280–281
2. T, pp. 268–269	**11.** T, pp. 276–277	**20.** T, p. 281
3. F, pp. 270–271	**12.** F, pp. 276–278	**21.** T, pp. 281–282
4. T, pp. 271–272	**13.** T, pp. 276–278	**22.** F, pp. 282–283
5. F, pp. 273–274	**14.** F, p. 279	**23.** F, pp. 283, 286
6. T, p. 274	**15.** F, pp. 279–280	**24.** T, pp. 283, 286
7. T, pp. 274–275	**16.** F, pp. 279–280	**25.** F, pp. 283, 286
8. T, p. 275	**17.** T, p. 280	
9. T, p. 275	**18.** F, pp. 280–281	

MULTIPLE-CHOICE QUESTIONS

1. b, p. 268	**10.** b, p. 275	**19.** a, p. 280
2. a, pp. 268–269	**11.** c, p. 275	**20.** a, pp. 280–281
3. c, pp. 268–269	**12.** b, pp. 276–278	**21.** a, p. 281
4. b, pp. 270–271	**13.** b, pp. 276–278	**22.** b, p. 282
5. d, pp. 271–273	**14.** c, pp. 276–278	**23.** c, pp. 283, 286
6. a, pp. 273–274	**15.** b, pp. 276–278	**24.** a, pp. 283, 286
7. c, pp. 274–275	**16.** c, pp. 276–278	**25.** c, pp. 283, 286
8. c, p. 275	**17.** d, p. 279	
9. c, p. 275	**18.** c, pp. 279–280	

PROBLEMS

1. *a.* buy, 25; *b.* sell, 12 1/2
2. See below

	(2)	(3)	(4)	(5)	(6)
Federal Reserve Banks					
Assets:					
Gold certificates	$ 25	$ 25	$ 25	$ 25	$ 25
Securities	27	34	30	30	30
Loans to commercial banks	10	10	10	10	4
Liabilities:					
Reserves of commercial banks	47	54	50	55	44
Treasury deposits	5	5	5	0	5
Federal Reserve Notes	10	10	10	10	10
Commercial Banks					
Assets:					
Reserves	$ 47	$ 54	$ 50	$ 55	$ 44
Securities	70	66	70	70	70
Loans	90	90	90	90	90
Liabilities:					
Checkable deposits	197	200	200	205	200
Loans from Federal Reserve	10	10	10	10	4
A. Required reserves	49.25	50	40	51.25	50
B. Excess reserves	−2.25	4	10	3.75	−6
C. How much has the money supply changed?	−3	0	0	+5	0
D. How much more can the money supply change?	−9	+16	+50	+15	−24
E. What is the total of C and D?	−12	+16	+50	+20	−24

3. *a.* (2) 8; *b.* 20; *c.* see Figure 15.2 in text; *d.* (1) 6, (2) 30, 10, (3) 4, 40, (4) see Figure 15.2 in text

4. *a.* 1700, 120; *b.* 300 (multiplier of 5 × $60 billion = $300 billion); *c.* 2100, 2000, 1900, 1800, 1700, 1600; *d.* 1800, 140

7. pp. 276–278	**12.** pp. 278–279	**17.** p. 281
8. pp. 276–278	**13.** pp. 279–280	**18.** pp. 282–283
9. p. 278	**14.** pp. 280–281	**19.** pp. 283, 286
10. pp. 278–279	**15.** p. 281	**20.** pp. 283, 286
11. p. 279	**16.** pp. 281–282	

SHORT ANSWER AND ESSAY QUESTIONS

1. p. 268	**3.** pp. 270–275	**5.** p. 275
2. pp. 268–269	**4.** pp. 270–274	**6.** pp. 276–278

Extending the Analysis of Aggregate Supply

Chapter 16 adds to the aggregate demand–aggregate supply (AD–AS) model first introduced in Chapter 11. This addition will give you the analytical tools to improve your understanding of the short-run and long-run relationships between unemployment and inflation.

The major extension to the AD–AS model is the explanation for the **short-run aggregate supply curve** and the **long-run aggregate supply curve.** In the **short run,** nominal wages do not adjust fully as the price level changes, so an increase in the price level increases business profits and real output. In the **long run,** nominal wages are fully responsive to previous changes in the price level, so business profits and employment return to their original levels. Thus, the long-run aggregate supply curve is vertical at the full-employment level of output.

The distinction between the short-run and long-run aggregate supply curves requires a reinterpretation of demand-pull inflation and cost-push inflation. Although **demand-pull inflation** will increase the price level and real output in the short run, once nominal wages increase, the temporary increase in output is gone, but the price level will be higher at the full-employment level of output. **Cost-push inflation** will increase the price level and decrease real output in the short run, but again, once nominal wages fall, output and the price level will return to their original positions. If government policymakers try to counter cost-push inflation by increasing aggregate demand, they may make matters worse by increasing the price level and causing the short-run aggregate supply curve to decrease, thereby setting off an inflationary spiral.

The relationship between inflation and unemployment has been studied for many years. One influential observation, supported by data from the 1950s and 1960s, was embodied in the **Phillips Curve,** which suggested that there was a stable and predictable tradeoff between the rate of inflation and the unemployment rate. During the 1960s, it was thought that this tradeoff could be used for formulating sound monetary and fiscal policy to manage the economy.

The events of the 1970s and early 1980s, however, called into question the shape and stability of the Phillips Curve because the economy was experiencing both higher rates of inflation and unemployment—**stagflation.** The **aggregate supply shocks** of this period shifted the Phillips Curve rightward. When these shocks dissipated in the 1980s, the Phillips Curve began to shift back to its original position. By the end of the 1990s, points on the Phillips Curve were similar to those of the 1960s.

The conclusion to be drawn from studies of the Phillips Curve is that there is *no long-run tradeoff between inflation and unemployment.* In the long run, the downsloping Phillips Curve is actually a vertical line at the natural rate of unemployment. In the short run, if aggregate demand increases and reduces the unemployment rate below its natural rate, the result is only temporary. Eventually, the unemployment rate will return to its natural rate, but at a higher rate of inflation.

Aggregate supply can also be affected by taxation. **Supply-side economics** contends that aggregate supply is important for determining levels of inflation, unemployment, and economic growth. Tax cuts are proposed by supply-siders as a way to create more incentives to work, save, and invest, thus increasing productivity and aggregate supply. The relationship between marginal tax rates and tax revenues is expressed in the **Laffer Curve,** which suggests that cuts in tax rates can increase tax revenues if tax rates are too high for the economy. Critics contend, however, that the incentive effects are small, potentially inflationary, and can have positive or negative effects on tax revenues.

■ CHECKLIST

When you have studied this chapter you should be able to

☐ Give a definition of the short run and long run in macroeconomics.

☐ Distinguish between a change in real wages and a change in nominal wages.

☐ Draw the short-run aggregate supply curve and describe its characteristics.

☐ Explain how the long-run aggregate supply curve is determined.

☐ Draw a graph that illustrates equilibrium in the extended AD–AS model.

☐ Explain demand-pull inflation using the extended AD–AS model and identify its short-run and long-run outcomes.

☐ Describe cost-push inflation using the extended AD–AS model.

☐ Give two generalizations about the policy dilemma for government in dealing with cost-push inflation.

☐ Explain recession and the process of adjustment using the extended AD–AS model.

☐ Draw a Phillips Curve and explain the basic tradeoff it presents.

☐ Define stagflation.

☐ Explain why adverse aggregate supply shocks shifted the Phillips Curve over time.

☐ List events that contributed to the demise of stagflation.

☐ State a generalization about the inflation-unemployment tradeoff in the long run.

☐ Use short-run and long-run Phillips Curves to explain inflation.

☐ Use short-run and long-run Phillips Curves to explain disinflation.

☐ Describe supply-siders' views of the effects of taxation on incentives to work and to save and invest.

☐ Use the Laffer Curve to explain the hypothesized relationship between marginal tax rates and tax revenues.

☐ State three criticisms of the Laffer Curve.

☐ Offer a rebuttal of the criticisms and an evaluation of supply-side economics in the 1980s and 1990s.

■ **CHAPTER OUTLINE**

1. The aggregate supply curve has short- and long-run characteristics. The short-run curve also shifts because of a change in nominal wages. These factors make the analysis of aggregate supply and demand more complex.

  a. The *short run* is a period in which nominal wages (and other input prices) are unresponsive to changes in the price level. The *long run* is a period in which nominal wages are fully responsive to changes in the price level.

  b. The *short-run aggregate supply curve* is upward sloping: An increase in the price level increases business revenues and profits because nominal wages do not change; in contrast, when the price level decreases, business revenue and profits decline, and so does real output, but nominal wages do not change.

  c. The *long-run aggregate supply curve* is vertical at the potential level of output. Increases in the price level will increase nominal wages and cause a decrease (shift left) in the short-run aggregate supply curve, or declines in the price level will reduce nominal wages and cause an increase (shift right) in the short-run aggregate supply curve. In either case, although the price level changes, output returns to its potential level, and the long-run aggregate supply curve is vertical at the full-employment level of output.

  d. *Equilibrium* in the extended AD–AS model occurs at the price level and output where the aggregate demand curve crosses the long-run aggregate supply curve and also crosses the short-run aggregate supply curve.

2. The extended AD–AS model can be applied to explain conditions of inflation and recession in an economy.

  a. *Demand-pull inflation* will increase (shift right) the aggregate demand curve, which increases the price level and causes a temporary increase in real output. In the long run, workers will realize that their real wages have fallen and will demand an increase in their nominal wages. The short-run aggregate supply curve, which was based on fixed nominal wages, now decreases (shifts left), resulting in an even higher price level with real output returning to its initial level.

  b. *Cost-push inflation* will decrease (shift left) the short-run aggregate supply curve. This situation will increase the price level and temporarily decrease real output, causing a recession. It creates a policy dilemma for government.

  (1) If government takes actions to counter the cost-push inflation and recession by increasing aggregate demand, the price level will move to an even higher level, and the actions may set off an inflationary spiral.

  (2) If government takes no action, the recession will eventually reduce nominal wages, and eventually the short-run aggregate supply curve will shift back to its original position.

  c. If aggregate demand decreases, it will result in a *recession.* If prices and wages are flexible downward, the price level will fall and increase real wages. Eventually, nominal wages will fall to restore the original real wages. This change will increase short-run aggregate supply and end the recession, but not without a long period of high unemployment and lost output.

3. The short- and long-run relationships between inflation and unemployment are important.

  a. If aggregate supply is constant and the economy is operating in the upsloping range of aggregate supply, then the greater the rate of increase in aggregate demand, the higher the rate of inflation (and output) and the lower the rate of unemployment. This inverse relationship between the rate of inflation and unemployment is known as the *Phillips Curve.* In the 1960s, economists thought there was a predictable tradeoff between unemployment and inflation. All society had to do was to choose the combination of inflation and unemployment on the Phillips Curve.

  b. The *aggregate supply shocks* of the 1970s and early 1980s called into question the validity of the Phillips Curve. In that period, the economy experienced *stagflation*—both higher rates of inflation and unemployment. The aggregate supply shocks came from an increase in resource prices (oil), shortages in agricultural production, higher wage demands, and declining productivity. These shocks decreased the short-run aggregate supply curve, which increased the price level and decreased output (and unemployment). These shocks shifted the Phillips Curve to the right or showed there was no dependable tradeoff between inflation and unemployment.

  c. The *demise of stagflation* came in the 1982–1989 period because of such factors as a severe recession in 1981–1982 that reduced wage demands, increased foreign competition that restrained price increases, and a decline in OPEC's monopoly power. The short-run aggregate supply curve increased, and the price level and unemployment rate fell. This meant that the Phillips Curve may have shifted back (left). Recent unemployment–inflation data are now similar to the Phillips Curve of the 1960s.

4. In the *long run,* there is no apparent tradeoff between inflation and unemployment. Any rate of inflation is consistent with the natural rate of unemployment at that time. The long-run Phillips Curve is vertical at the natural rate of unemployment. In the **short run,** there can be a trade-off between inflation and unemployment.

  a. An increase in aggregate demand may temporarily reduce unemployment as the price level increases and profits expand but the actions also set other events into motion.

  (1) The increase in the price level reduces the real wages of workers who demand and obtain higher nominal wages; these actions return unemployment to its original level.

  (2) Back at the original level, there are now higher actual and expected rates of inflation for the economy, so the short-run Phillips Curve has shifted upward.

  (3) The process is repeated if aggregate demand continues to increase. The price level rises as the short-run Phillips Curve shifts upward.

  b. In the long run, the Phillips Curve is stable only as a vertical line at the natural rate of unemployment. After all adjustments in nominal wages to increases and decreases in the rate of inflation, the economy returns to its full-employment level of output and its natural rate of unemployment. There is no tradeoff between unemployment and inflation in the long run.

  c. Disinflation—reductions in the inflation rate from year to year—is also explained by the distinction between the short-run and long-run Phillips Curves.

5. **Supply-side economics** views aggregate supply as active rather than passive in explaining changes in the price level and unemployment.

  a. It argues that higher marginal tax rates reduce incentives to work and high taxes also reduce incentives to save and invest. These policies lead to a misallocation of resources, less productivity, and a decrease in aggregate supply. To counter these effects, supply-side economists call for a cut in marginal tax rates.

  b. The **Laffer Curve** suggests that it is possible to lower tax rates and increase tax revenues, thus avoiding a budget deficit because the policies will result in less tax evasion and avoidance.

  c. Critics of supply-side economics and the Laffer Curve suggest that the policy of cutting tax rates will not work because

  (1) It has only a small and uncertain effect on incentives to work (or on aggregate supply).

  (2) It would increase aggregate demand relative to aggregate supply and thus reinforce inflation when there is full employment.

  (3) The expected tax revenues from tax rate cuts depend on assumptions about the economy's position on the Laffer Curve. If tax cuts reduce tax revenues, it will create budget deficits.

  d. Supply-siders argue that the tax cuts under the Reagan administration in the 1980s worked as would be expected: The cut in tax rates increased tax revenue. Critics contend that the reason was that aggregate demand increased as the economy came out of recession and not that aggregate supply increased. There is now general recognition that changes in marginal tax rates change people's behavior, although there is continuing debate about the size of the effect.

■ HINTS AND TIPS

1. Chapter 16 is a more difficult chapter because the AD–AS model is extended to include both short-run and long-run effects. Spend extra time mastering this material, but do not try to read everything at once. Break the chapter into its logical sections, and practice drawing each graph.

2. Be sure you understand the distinction between the **short-run and long-run aggregate supply curves.** Then use these ideas to explain demand-pull inflation, cost-push inflation, and recession. Doing problem 2 will be especially helpful.

3. Be sure you understand how adverse **aggregate supply shocks** shift and create stability in the Phillips Curve.

4. Use Figure 16.9 in the text to help you understand why there is a difference in the short-run and long-run relationships between unemployment and inflation. Problem 4 will help your understanding of this complicated graph.

5. The rationales for tax cuts and tax increases have been at the forefront of fiscal policy since the 1980s. This chapter offers a detailed explanation of supply-side economics that has been used to justify the tax cut policies during the past twenty-five years. The last section of the chapter will help you understand the arguments for and against such tax policies that have real-world applications.

■ IMPORTANT TERMS

short run	stagflation
long run	aggregate supply shocks
short-run aggregate supply curve	disinflation
long-run aggregate supply curve	supply-side economics
Phillips Curve	Laffer Curve

SELF-TEST

■ FILL-IN QUESTIONS

1. In an AD–AS model with a stable aggregate supply curve, when the economy is producing in the upsloping portion of the aggregate supply curve, an increase in aggregate demand will (increase, decrease) _____ real output and employment, but a decrease in aggregate supply will _____ real output and employment.

2. In the short run, when the price level changes, nominal wages are (responsive, unresponsive) _____, but in the long run nominal wages are _____. In the short run, the aggregate supply curve is (upsloping, vertical) _____, but in the long run the curve is _____.

3. Demand-pull inflation occurs with a shift in the aggregate demand curve to the (right, left) _____, which will (decrease, increase) _____ the price level and temporarily _____ real output. As a consequence, the (short-run, long-run) _____ aggregate supply curve will shift left because of a rise in (real, nominal) _____ wages, producing a (lower, higher) _____ price level at the original level of real output.

4. Cost-push inflation occurs with a shift in the short-run aggregate supply curve to the (right, left) _____; thus the price level will (increase, decrease) _____ and real output will temporarily _____.

5. If government takes no actions to counter the cost-push inflation, the resulting recession will (increase, decrease) _____ nominal wages and shift the short-run aggregate supply curve back to its original position, yet if the government tries to counter the recession with a(n) _____ in aggregate demand, the price level will move even higher.

6. A recession will occur when there is (an increase, a decrease) _____ in aggregate demand. If the controversial assumption is made that prices and wages are flexible downward, then the price level (rises, falls) _____. Real wages will then (increase, decrease) _____, but eventually nominal wages will _____ and the aggregate supply curve will (increase, decrease) _____ and end the recession.

7. Along the upsloping portion of the short-run aggregate supply curve, the greater the increase in aggregate demand, the (greater, smaller) _____ the increase in the rate of inflation, the _____ the increase in real output, and the (greater, smaller) _____ the unemployment rate.

8. The original Phillips Curve indicates that there will be (a direct, an inverse) _____ relationship between the rate of inflation and the unemployment rate. This means that high rates of inflation will be associated with a (high, low) _____ unemployment rate, or that low rates of inflation will be associated with a _____ unemployment rate.

9. The policy tradeoff based on a stable Phillips Curve was that for the economy to reduce the unemployment rate, the rate of inflation must (increase, decrease) _____, and to reduce the rate of inflation, the unemployment rate must _____.

10. During the 1970s and early 1980s, aggregate (demand, supply) _____ shocks made the Phillips Curve (stable, unstable) _____. These shocks produced (demand-pull, cost-push) _____ inflation that resulted in a simultaneous increase in the inflation rate and the unemployment rate, called (disinflation, stagflation) _____.

11. Several factors contributed to stagflation's demise during the 1982–1989 period. They included

   a. the 1981–1982 (inflation, recession) _____ largely caused by (a tight, an easy) _____ money policy. There was also (increased, decreased) _____ foreign competition and the _____ monopoly power of OPEC.

   b. The effect of these factors (increased, decreased) _____ the short-run aggregate supply curve; thus the inflation rate_____ and the unemployment rate _____.

12. The standard explanation for the Phillips Curve is that during the stagflation of the 1970s, the Phillips Curve shifted (right, left) _____, and during the demise of stagflation from 1982–1989, the Phillips Curve shifted _____. In this view, there is a tradeoff between the unemployment rate and the rate of inflation, but changes in (short-run, long-run) _____ aggregate supply can shift the Phillips Curve.

13. In the long run, the tradeoff between the rate of inflation and the rate of unemployment (does, does not) _____ exist, and the economy is stable at its natural rate of (unemployment, inflation) _____.

14. The Phillips Curve may be downsloping in the (short run, long run) _____, but it is vertical in the _____ at the natural rate of unemployment. A shift in aggregate demand that reduces the unemployment rate in the short run results in the long run in (an increase, a decrease) _____ in the rate of inflation and a return to the natural rate of unemployment.

15. When the actual rate of inflation is higher than the expected rate, profits temporarily (fall, rise) _____ and the unemployment rate temporarily (rises, falls) _____. This case would occur during a period of (inflation, disinflation) _____.

16. When the actual rate of inflation is lower than the expected rate, profits temporarily (fall, rise) _____ and the unemployment rate temporarily (rises, falls)

_____. This case would occur during a period of (inflation, disinflation) _____.

17. It is the view of supply-side economists that high marginal tax rates (increase, decrease) _____ incentives to work, save, invest, and take risks. According to supply-side economists a stimulus for the economy would be a substantial (increase, decrease) _____ in marginal tax rates that would _____ economic growth through (an increase, a decrease) _____ in aggregate supply.

18. The Laffer Curve depicts the relationship between tax rates and (inflation, tax revenues) _____. It is useful for showing how a (cut, rise) _____ in marginal tax rates will increase aggregate supply.

19. In theory, the Laffer Curve shows that as the tax rates increase from 0%, tax revenues will (increase, decrease) _____ to some maximum level, after which tax revenues will _____ as the tax rates increase; or as tax rates are reduced from 100%, tax revenues will (increase, decrease) _____ to some maximum level, after which tax revenues will _____ as tax rates decrease.

20. Criticisms of the Laffer Curve are that the effects of a cut in tax rates on incentives to work, save, and invest are (large, small) _____; that the tax cuts generate an increase in aggregate (demand, supply) _____ that outweigh any increase in aggregate _____ and may lead to inflation when at full employment; and that tax cuts can produce a (gain, loss) _____ in tax revenues that will only add to a budget deficit.

■ **TRUE–FALSE QUESTIONS**

Circle T if the statement is true, F if it is false.

1. The short run in macroeconomics is a period in which nominal wages are fully responsive to changes in the price level.   **T F**

2. The short-run aggregate supply curve has a negative slope.   **T F**

3. The long-run aggregate supply curve is vertical because nominal wages eventually change by the same amount as changes in the price level.   **T F**

4. Demand-pull inflation will increase the price level and real output in the short run, but in the long run, only the price level will increase.   **T F**

5. Cost-push inflation results in a simultaneous increase in the price level and real output.   **T F**

6. When the economy is experiencing cost-push inflation, an inflationary spiral is likely to result when the government enacts policies to maintain full employment.   **T F**

7. A recession is the result of an increase in the short-run aggregate supply curve.   **T F**

8. If the economy is in a recession, prices and nominal wages will presumably fall, and the short-run aggregate supply curve will increase, so that real output returns to its full-employment level.   **T F**

9. The Phillips Curve shows an inverse relationship between the rate of inflation and the unemployment rate.   **T F**

10. Stagflation refers to a situation in which both the price level and the unemployment rate are rising.   **T F**

11. Aggregate supply shocks can cause both higher rates of inflation and higher rates of unemployment.   **T F**

12. The data from the 1970s and early 1980s indicated the aggregate supply curve increased.   **T F**

13. One explanation of the stagflation of the 1970s and early 1980s was an increase in aggregate demand.   **T F**

14. Among the factors that contributed to the demise of stagflation during the 1980s was a recession in 1981 and 1982.   **T F**

15. There is no apparent long-run tradeoff between inflation and unemployment.   **T F**

16. When the actual rate of inflation is higher than the expected rate, profits temporarily fall and the unemployment rate temporarily rises.   **T F**

17. The long-run Phillips Curve is essentially a vertical line at the economy's natural rate of unemployment.   **T F**

18. Disinflation is the same as mismeasurement of the inflation rate.   **T F**

19. When the actual rate of inflation is lower than the expected rate of inflation, profits temporarily fall and the unemployment rate temporarily rises.   **T F**

20. Most economists reject the idea of a short-run tradeoff between the unemployment and inflation rates but accept the long-run tradeoff.   **T F**

21. Supply-side economists contend that aggregate demand is the only active factor in determining the price level and real output in an economy.   **T F**

22. One proposition of supply-side economics is that the marginal tax rates on earned income should be reduced to increase the incentives to work.   **T F**

23. Supply-side economists recommend a higher marginal tax rate on interest from saving because no productive work was performed to earn the interest.   **T F**

24. The Laffer Curve suggests that lower tax rates will increase the rate of inflation. **T F**

25. A criticism of supply-side economics is that the incentive effects of tax cuts on working and saving are small and have little influence on aggregate supply. **T F**

■ **MULTIPLE-CHOICE QUESTIONS**

Circle the letter that corresponds to the best answer.

1. For macroeconomics, the short run is a period in which nominal wages
(a) do not fully adjust as the price level stays constant
(b) change as the price level stays constant
(c) do not fully adjust as the price level changes
(d) change as the price level changes

2. Once sufficient time has elapsed for wage contracts to expire and nominal wage adjustments to occur, the economy enters
(a) the short run
(b) the long run
(c) a period of inflation
(d) a period of unemployment

3. A graph of the short-run aggregate supply curve is
(a) downsloping, and a graph of the long-run aggregate supply is upsloping
(b) upsloping, and a graph of the long-run aggregate supply is vertical
(c) upsloping, and a graph of the long-run aggregate supply is downsloping
(d) vertical, and a graph of the long-run aggregate supply is upsloping

4. Assume that initially your nominal wage was $10 an hour and the price index was 100. If the price level increases to 110, then your
(a) real wage has increased to $11.00
(b) real wage has decreased to $9.09
(c) nominal wage has increased to $11.00
(d) nominal wage has decreased to $9.09

5. In the extended AD–AS model, demand-pull inflation occurs because of an increase in aggregate demand that will eventually produce
(a) an increase in real wages, thus a decrease in the short-run aggregate supply curve
(b) an increase in nominal wages, thus an increase in the short-run aggregate supply curve
(c) a decrease in nominal wages, thus a decrease in the short-run aggregate supply curve
(d) an increase in nominal wages, thus a decrease in the short-run aggregate supply curve

6. In the short run, demand-pull inflation increases real
(a) output and decreases the price level
(b) wages and increases nominal wages
(c) output and increases the price level
(d) wages and decreases nominal wages

7. In the long run, demand-pull inflation
(a) decreases real wages
(b) increases the price level
(c) increases the unemployment rate
(d) decreases real output

8. A likely result of the government trying to reduce the unemployment associated with cost-push inflation through stimulative fiscal policy or monetary policy is
(a) an inflationary spiral
(b) stagflation
(c) a recession
(d) disinflation

9. What will occur in the short run if there is cost-push inflation and if the government adopts a hands-off approach to it?
(a) an increase in real output
(b) a fall in unemployment
(c) demand-pull inflation
(d) a recession

10. If prices and wages are flexible, a recession will increase real wages as the price level falls. Eventually, nominal wages will
(a) fall to the previous real wages, and the short-run aggregate supply will increase
(b) rise to the previous real wages, and the short-run aggregate supply will increase
(c) fall to the previous real wages, and the short-run aggregate supply will decrease
(d) rise to the previous real wages, and the short-run aggregate supply will decrease

11. The traditional Phillips Curve is based on the idea that with a constant short-run aggregate supply curve, the greater the increase in aggregate demand
(a) the greater the unemployment rate
(b) the greater the rate of inflation
(c) the greater the increase in real output
(d) the smaller the increase in nominal wages

12. The traditional Phillips Curve shows the
(a) inverse relationship between the rate of inflation and the unemployment rate
(b) inverse relationship between the nominal wage and the real wage
(c) direct relationship between unemployment and demand-pull inflation
(d) tradeoff between the short run and the long run

13. As the unemployment rate falls below its natural rate,
(a) excessive spending produces demand-pull inflation
(b) productivity rises and creates cost-push inflation
(c) the expected rate of inflation equals the actual rate
(d) there is an aggregate supply shock

14. Which would be a factor contributing to stagflation in the 1970s?
(a) a doubling of stock prices
(b) a fivefold increase in productivity
(c) a quadrupling of oil prices by OPEC
(d) a 10% decline in the rate of inflation

15. If there are adverse aggregate supply shocks, with aggregate demand remaining constant, then there will be
  (a) a decrease in the price level
  (b) a decrease in the unemployment rate
  (c) an increase in real output
  (d) an increase in both the price level and the unemployment rate

16. A cause of both higher rates of inflation and higher rates of unemployment would be
  (a) an increase in aggregate demand
  (b) an increase in aggregate supply
  (c) a decrease in aggregate demand
  (d) a decrease in aggregate supply

17. Which would be a factor contributing to the demise of stagflation during the 1982–1989 period?
  (a) a lessening of foreign competition
  (b) a strengthening of the monopoly power of OPEC
  (c) a recession brought on largely by a tight monetary policy
  (d) an increase in regulation of airline and trucking industries

18. The economy is stable only in the
  (a) short run at a high rate of profit
  (b) short run at the natural rate of inflation
  (c) long run at the natural rate of unemployment
  (d) long run at the natural rate of inflation

19. When the actual inflation rate is higher than expected, profits temporarily
  (a) fall and the unemployment rate temporarily falls
  (b) rise and the unemployment rate temporarily falls
  (c) rise and the unemployment rate temporarily rises
  (d) fall and the unemployment rate temporarily rises

20. When the actual rate of inflation is lower than the expected rate, profits temporarily
  (a) fall and the unemployment rate temporarily rises
  (b) rise and the unemployment rate temporarily falls
  (c) rise and the unemployment rate temporarily rises
  (d) fall and the unemployment rate temporarily falls

21. In a disinflation situation, the
  (a) actual rate of inflation is lower than the expected rate, so the unemployment rate will rise to bring the expected and actual rates into balance
  (b) expected rate of inflation is lower than the actual rate, so the unemployment rate will rise to bring the expected and actual rates into balance
  (c) actual rate of inflation is higher than the expected rate, so the unemployment rate will fall to bring the expected and actual rates into balance
  (d) expected rate of inflation is higher than the actual rate, so the unemployment rate will fall to bring the expected and actual rates into balance

22. The long-run Phillips Curve is essentially
  (a) horizontal at the natural rate of unemployment
  (b) vertical at the natural rate of unemployment
  (c) vertical at the natural rate of inflation
  (d) horizontal at the natural rate of inflation

23. Supply-side economists contend that the U.S. system of taxation reduces
  (a) unemployment but causes inflation
  (b) incentives to work, save, and invest
  (c) transfer payments to the poor
  (d) the effects of cost-push inflation

24. Based on the Laffer Curve, a cut in the tax rate from 100% to a point before the maximum level of tax revenue will
  (a) increase the price level
  (b) increase tax revenues
  (c) decrease real output
  (d) decrease the real wages

25. A criticism of tax cuts and supply-side economics made by many economists is that
  (a) the demand-side effects exceed the supply-side effects
  (b) the supply-side effects exceed the demand-side effects
  (c) the demand-side and supply-side effects offset each other
  (d) there are only supply-side effects

■ **PROBLEMS**

1. In columns 1 and 2 of the table on the next page is a portion of a short-run aggregate supply schedule. Column 3 shows the number of full-time workers (in millions) that would have to be employed to produce each of the seven real domestic outputs (in billions) in the short-run aggregate supply schedule. The labor force is 80 million workers and the full-employment output of the economy is

$ _____ .

  a. If the aggregate demand schedule were that shown in columns 1 and 4,

  (1) the price level would be _____ and the real output would be $ _____ .

  (2) the number of workers employed would be _____, the number of workers unemployed would be _____ million, and the unemployment rate would be _____ %.

  b. If aggregate demand were to increase to that shown in columns 1 and 5 and short-run aggregate supply remained constant,

  (1) the price level would rise to _____ and the real output would rise to $ _____ .

  (2) employment would increase by _____ million workers and the unemployment rate would fall to_____ %.

  (3) the price level would increase by _____ and the rate of inflation would be _____ %.

(1) Price level	(2) Real output supplied	(3) Employment (in millions)	(4) Real output demanded	(5) Real output demanded	(6) Real output demanded
130	$ 800	69	$2300	$2600	$1900
140	1300	70	2200	2500	1800
150	1700	72	2100	2400	1700
160	2000	75	2000	2300	1600
170	2200	78	1900	2200	1500
180	2300	80	1800	2100	1400
190	2300	80	1700	2000	1300

c. If aggregate demand were to decrease to that shown in columns 1 and 6 and short-run aggregate supply remained constant,

(1) the price level would fall to _____ and the real output would fall to $_____.

(2) employment would decrease by _____ compared with situation **a,** and workers and the unemployment rate would rise to _____%.

(3) the price level would decrease and the rate of inflation would be (positive, negative) _____.

2. The following is an aggregate demand and aggregate supply model. Assume that the economy is initially in equilibrium at **AD₁** and **AS₁**. The price level will be _____ and the real domestic output will be _____.

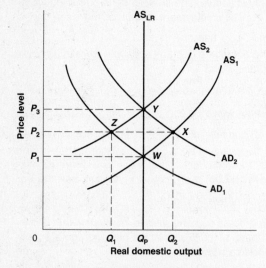

a. If there is demand-pull inflation, then
(1) in the short run, the new equilibrium is at point

_____, with the price level at _____ and real output at _____;
(2) in the long run, nominal wages will rise so the aggregate supply curve will shift from _____ to

_____. The equilibrium will be at point _____ with the price level at _____ and real output at _____, so the increase in aggregate demand has only moved the economy along

its _____ curve.
b. Now assume that the economy is initially in equilibrium at point **W,** where **AD₁** and **AS₁** intersect. If there is cost-push inflation, then
(1) in the short run, the new equilibrium is at point

_____, with the price level at _____ and real output at _____.
(2) if the government tries to counter the cost-push inflation with expansionary monetary and fiscal policy,

then aggregate demand will shift from _____

to _____, with the price level becoming

_____ and real output _____, but this policy has a trap because the price level has shifted

from _____ to _____ and the new

level of inflation might shift _____ leftward.
(3) if government does not counter the cost-push inflation, the price level will eventually move to _____

and real output to _____ as the recession reduces nominal wages and shifts the aggregate supply

curve from _____ to _____.
c. Now assume that the economy is initially in equilibrium at point **Y,** where **AD₂** and **AS₂** intersect. If there is a recession that reduces investment spending, then
(1) aggregate demand decreases and real output

shifts from _____ to _____, and, assuming that prices and wages are flexible down-

ward, the price level shifts from _____ to

_____.
(2) these events cause real wages to (rise, fall)

_____, and eventually nominal wages

_____ to restore the previous real wages.
(3) when this happens, the short-run aggregate supply

curve shifts from _____ to _____

to its new equilibrium at point _____. The

equilibrium price level is _____ and the equilibrium level of output is _____ at the long-run aggregate supply curve _____.

3. The following is a traditional Phillips Curve.

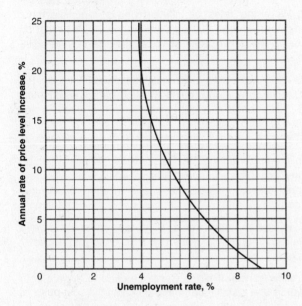

a. At full employment (a 4% unemployment rate) the price level would rise by _____% each year.
b. If the price level were stable (increasing by 0% a year), the unemployment rate would be _____%.
c. Which of the combinations along the Phillips Curve would you choose for the economy? _____

Why would you select this combination? _____

_____

4. Following is a model of short- and long-run Phillips Curves.

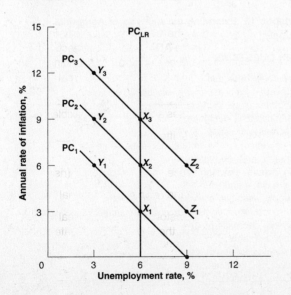

a. Suppose you begin at point **X_1** and an assumption is made that nominal wages are set on the original expectation that a 3% rate of inflation will continue in the economy.

(1) If an increase in aggregate demand reduces the unemployment rate from 6% to 3%, then the actual rate of inflation will move to _____%. The higher product prices will lift profits of firms and they will hire more workers; thus in the short run the economy will temporarily move to point _____.

(2) If workers demand and receive higher wages to compensate for the loss of purchasing power from higher than expected inflation, then business profits will fall from previous levels and firms will reduce employment; therefore, the unemployment rate will move from point _____ to point _____ on the graph.

The short-run Phillips Curve has shifted from _____ to _____ on the graph.

(3) If aggregate demand continues to increase so that the unemployment rate drops from 6% to 3%, then prices will rise before nominal wages, and output and employment will increase, so that there will be a move from point _____ to point _____ on the graph.

(4) But when workers get nominal wage increases, profits fall, and the unemployment rate moves from point _____ at _____% to point _____ at _____%. The short-run Phillips Curve has now shifted from _____ to _____ on the graph.

(5) The long-run Phillips Curve is the line _____.

b. Suppose you begin at point **X_3**, where the expected and actual rate of inflation is 9% and the unemployment rate is 6%.

(1) If there should be a decline in aggregate demand because of a recession and if the actual rate of inflation should fall to 6%, well below the expected rate of 9%, then business profits will fall and the unemployment rate will decrease to 9% as shown by the movement from point **X_3** to point _____.

(2) If firms and workers adjust their expectation to the 6% rate of inflation, the nominal wages will fall, profits will rise, and the economy will move from point _____ to point _____. The short-run Phillips Curve has shifted from _____ to _____.

(3) If this process is repeated, the long-run Phillips Curve will be traced as line _____.

5. The following is a Laffer Curve.

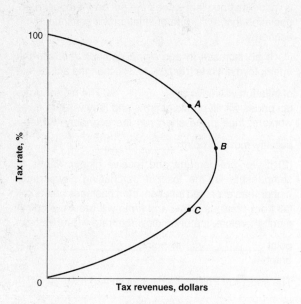

a. The point of maximum tax revenue is _____. As tax rates decrease from 100% to point **B,** tax revenues will (increase, decrease) _____. As tax rates increase from 0% to point **B,** tax revenues will _____.

b. Supply-side economists would contend that it would be beneficial for government to cut tax rates if they are (below, above) _____ point **B,** whereas critics of supply-side economics contend that it would be harmful for government to cut tax rates if they are _____ point **B.**

■ **SHORT ANSWER AND ESSAY QUESTIONS**

1. What distinguishes the short run from the long run in macroeconomics?

2. Identify the basic difference between a short-run and a long-run aggregate supply curve.

3. Explain what happens to aggregate supply when an increase in the price level results in an increase in nominal wages.

4. Explain how to find equilibrium in the extended AD–AS model.

5. Describe the process of demand-pull inflation in the short run and in the long run.

6. How does demand-pull inflation influence the aggregate supply curve?

7. Describe cost-push inflation in the extended AD–AS model.

8. What two generalizations emerge from the analysis of cost-push inflation? Describe the two scenarios that provide the basis for the generalizations.

9. Describe recession in the extended AD–AS model.

10. What is a Phillips Curve? What two rates are related?

11. Explain how a Phillips Curve with a negative slope may be derived by holding aggregate supply constant and mentally increasing aggregate demand.

12. Were the rates of inflation and of unemployment consistent with the Phillips Curve in the 1960s? What do data on these two rates suggest about the curve since then?

13. What were the aggregate supply shocks to the U.S. economy during the 1970s and early 1980s? How did these shocks affect interpretation of the Phillips Curve?

14. Describe the factors that contributed to stagflation's demise during the 1982–1989 period. What do many economists contend happened to the aggregate supply curve, unemployment, and inflation during this period?

15. How can there be a short-run tradeoff between inflation and unemployment, but no long-run tradeoff? Explain.

16. How can the Phillips Curve be used to explain both inflation and disinflation in the economy?

17. What are the characteristics of the long-run Phillips Curve? How is it related to the natural rate of unemployment?

18. Discuss why supply-side economists contend there are tax disincentives in the economy.

19. Draw and explain a Laffer Curve showing the relationship between tax rates and tax revenues.

20. Outline the three criticisms of the ideas expressed in the depiction of the Laffer Curve.

ANSWERS

Chapter 16 Extending the Analysis of Aggregate Supply

FILL-IN QUESTIONS

1. increase, decrease
2. unresponsive, responsive, upsloping, vertical
3. right, increase, increase, short-run, nominal, higher
4. left, increase, decrease
5. decrease, increase
6. a decrease, falls, increase, decrease, increase
7. greater, greater, smaller
8. an inverse, low, high
9. increase, increase
10. supply, unstable, cost-push, stagflation
11. *a.* recession, a tight, increased, decreased; *b.* increased, decreased, decreased
12. right, left, short-run
13. does not, unemployment
14. short run, long run, an increase
15. rise, falls, inflation
16. fall, rises, disinflation

17. decrease, decrease, increase, an increase
18. tax revenues, cut
19. increase, decrease, increase, decrease
20. small, demand, supply, loss

TRUE–FALSE QUESTIONS

1. F, p. 292	**10.** T, p. 299	**19.** T, p. 302
2. F, pp. 293–294	**11.** T, pp. 299–300	**20.** F, pp. 300–302
3. T, p. 294	**12.** F, pp. 299–300	**21.** F, pp. 302–303
4. T, p. 295	**13.** F, pp. 299–300	**22.** T, pp. 302–303
5. F, p. 296	**14.** T, p. 300	**23.** F, p. 303
6. T, p. 296	**15.** T, p. 300	**24.** F, p. 303
7. F, pp. 296–297	**16.** F, p. 301	**25.** T, p. 304
8. T, pp. 296–297	**17.** T, p. 301	
9. T, pp. 297–298	**18.** F, p. 302	

MULTIPLE-CHOICE QUESTIONS

1. c, p. 292	**10.** a, pp. 296–297	**19.** b, p. 301
2. b, p. 293	**11.** b, pp. 297–299	**20.** a, p. 302
3. b, pp. 293–294	**12.** a, pp. 297–299	**21.** a, p. 302
4. b, p. 293	**13.** a, pp. 298–299	**22.** b, pp. 301–302
5. d, p. 295	**14.** c, p. 299	**23.** b, pp. 302–303
6. c, p. 295	**15.** d, p. 299	**24.** b, p. 303
7. b, p. 295	**16.** d, pp. 299–300	**25.** a, p. 304
8. a, p. 296	**17.** c, p. 300	
9. d, p. 296	**18.** c, pp. 300–301	

PROBLEMS

1. 2300; *a.* (1) 160, 2000, (2) 75, 5, 6.25; *b.* (1) 170, 2200, (2) 3, 2.5, (3) 10, 6.25; *c.* (1) 150, 1700, (2) 3, 10, (3) negative

2. P_1, Q_p; *a.* (1) X, P_2, Q_2 (2) AS_1, AS_2, Y, P_3, Q_p, AS_{LR}; *b.* (1) Z, P_2, Q_1, (2) AD_1, AD_2, P_3, Q_p, P_2, P_3, AS_2, (3) P_1, Q_p, AS_2, AS_1; *c.* (1) Q_p, Q_1, P_3, P_2, (2) rise, fall, (3) AS_2, AS_1, W, P_1, Q_p, AS_{LR}

3. *a.* 20; *b.* 9

4. *a.* (1) 6, Y_1, (2) Y_1, X_2, PC_1 PC_2, (3) X_2, Y_2, (4) Y_2, 3, X_3, 6, PC_2, PC_3, (5) PC_{LR}; *b.* (1) Z_2, (2) Z_2, X_2, PC_3, PC_2, (3) PC_{LR}

5. *a.* B, increase, decrease; *b.* above, below

SHORT ANSWER AND ESSAY QUESTIONS

1. pp. 292–293	**8.** p. 296	**15.** pp. 300–301
2. pp. 293–294	**9.** pp. 296–297	**16.** pp. 300–302
3. p. 293	**10.** pp. 297–298	**17.** pp. 300–302
4. p. 294	**11.** pp. 297–299	**18.** pp. 302–303
5. p. 295	**12.** pp. 298–299	**19.** p. 303
6. p. 295	**13.** pp. 299–300	**20.** p. 304
7. p. 296	**14.** p. 300	

CHAPTER 17

Economic Growth

The United States has an impressive record of economic growth in the past half century. The purpose of this chapter is to explain what factors contributed to this economic growth and the implications for the economy.

The chapter begins by discussing the six main ingredients of economic growth. The four **supply factors** increase the output potential of the economy. Whether the economy actually produces its full potential—that is, whether the economy has both full employment and full production—depends upon two other factors: the level of aggregate demand (the **demand factor**) and the efficiency with which the economy allocates resources (the **efficiency factor**).

The next section of the chapter places the factors contributing to economic growth in graphical perspective with the use of two familiar **economic models.** The production possibilities model was originally presented in Chapter 2 and is now used to discuss how the two major supply factors—labor input and labor productivity—shift the production possibilities curve outward. The second model is the aggregate demand–aggregate supply model that was first explained in Chapter 11 and was discussed in more detail in Chapter 16. Here you learn how both the short-run and the long-run shifts in aggregate supply combined with shifts in aggregate demand (and the factors underlying those shifts) affect the output and the price level.

The **growth record** of the United States has been impressive both in terms of increases in real GDP and in real GDP per capita. What accounts for this long-term economic growth of the United States? First, the size of its labor force has grown. Second and more important, the productivity of the labor force in the United States has increased. The increase in the productivity of labor is the result of technological advances, the expansion of the stock of capital goods in the U.S. economy, the improved education and training of its labor force, economies of scale, the reallocation of resources, and the supportive social, cultural, and political environments.

Increases in productivity have a direct effect on real output, real income, and real wages. A major development in recent years was the doubling in the rate of labor productivity from 1995–2002 compared with that in the 1973–1995 period. This change heralded to some observers that the United States has achieved a **New Economy** that is characterized by advances in technology, more entrepreneurship, increasing returns from resource inputs, and greater global competition. The implications for macroeconomics are significant: faster growth with low inflation,

a reduction in the natural rate of unemployment, and an increase in tax revenues. Whether the economy is in fact "new" remains to be seen because the trend may simply be a short-run upturn in labor productivity and not a long-run outcome.

The last section of the chapter raises an important question: Is more economic growth **desirable and sustainable?** This controversy has two sides. The antigrowth view is based on the pollution problems it creates, its effects on human values, and doubts about whether growth can be sustained. The defense of growth is based in part on its contribution to higher standards of living, improvements in worker safety and the environment, and history of sustainability. After reading this section, you will have to evaluate the advantages and disadvantages of economic growth for the economy.

■ CHECKLIST

When you have studied this chapter you should be able to

☐ Identify four supply factors in economic growth.
☐ Explain the demand factor in economic growth.
☐ Describe the efficiency factor in economic growth.
☐ Show graphically how economic growth shifts the production possibilities curve.
☐ Explain the rationale for an equation for real GDP that is based on labor inputs and labor productivity.
☐ Show that a shift outward in the production possibilities curve is equivalent to a rightward shift in the economy's long-run aggregate supply curve.
☐ Illustrate graphically how economic growth shifts the short-run and long-run aggregate supply curves and the aggregate demand curve.
☐ Describe the average annual growth rates of real GDP and real per capita GDP in the U.S. economy since 1950.
☐ Compare the relative importance of the two major means of increasing the real GDP in the United States.
☐ List the sources of growth in the productivity of labor in the United States and state their relative importance.
☐ Describe the other factors that affect an economy's growth rate.
☐ Explain the relationship between productivity growth and the standard of living.
☐ Describe the growth of labor productivity in the United States since 1973.
☐ Identify the major characteristics of the New Economy.

☐ Discuss how the microchip and information technology have contributed to the New Economy.

☐ Describe the sources of increasing returns and economies of scale within the New Economy.

☐ Explain how the New Economy increases global competition.

☐ Describe three macroeconomic implications from the New Economy.

☐ Offer a skeptical perspective on the New Economy.

☐ Present several arguments against more economic growth.

☐ Make a case for more economic growth.

■ **CHAPTER OUTLINE**

1. The *ingredients of growth* depend on supply, demand, and efficiency factors.

a. *Supply factors* include the quantity and quality of resources (natural, human, and capital) and technology.

b. The *demand factor* influences the level of aggregate demand in the economy that is important for sustaining full employment of resources.

c. The *efficiency factor* affects the efficient use of resources to obtain maximum production of goods and services (productive efficiency) and to allocate them to their highest and best use by society (allocative efficiency).

2. Two familiar *economic models* can be used for the analysis of economic growth.

a. In the *production possibilities model*, economic growth shifts the production possibilities curve outward because of improvement in supply factors. Whether the economy operates on the frontier of the curve or inside the curve depends on the demand factor and efficiency factors.

b. Discussions of growth, however, focus primarily on supply factors. From this perspective, economic growth is obtained by increasing the *labor inputs* and by increasing the *productivity of labor*. This relationship can be expressed in equation terms: real GDP = worker-hours × labor productivity.

c. In the *aggregate demand–aggregate supply model*, economic growth is illustrated by long-run and short-run shifts.

(1) A shift outward in the production possibilities curve is equivalent to a shift rightward in the long-run aggregate supply curve for the economy. In either model, changes in the price level are not important because they do not shift either curve.

(2) The extended AD–AS model takes into account the supply, demand, and efficiency factors. Supply factors shift the long-run aggregate supply curve to the right, and supply and efficiency factors make that curve vertical at the economy's potential output. If the price level increased over time, it would indicate that the rise in potential output was accompanied by a greater shift in aggregate demand.

3. Over the past 50 years, the *rate of growth in real GDP* was about 3.5% annually. The growth rate for real per capita GDP in the United States was about 2.3% annually. These rates increased significantly from 1996–2000, declined significantly in the recession of 2001, and are now starting to return to previous levels.

4. Several factors *account for U.S. economic growth*.

a. The two main factors are increases in quantity of labor (hours of work) and increases in labor productivity. From 1990 to 2002, about two-thirds of this growth was the result of the increased *productivity of labor*. About one-third of the growth was the result of the increased *quantity of labor* employed in the economy.

b. *Technological advance* is combining given amounts of resources in new and innovative ways that result in a larger output. It involves the use of new managerial methods and business organizations that improve production. Technological advance is also embodied in new capital investment that adds to the productive capacity of the economy. It accounted for about 40% of the increase in productivity growth.

c. The *quantity of capital* has expanded with the increase in saving and investment spending in capital goods. This private investment has increased the quantity of each worker's tools, equipment, and machinery. There is also public investment in infrastructure in the United States. The increase in the quantity of capital goods explains about 30% of productivity growth.

d. Increased investment in *human capital* (the training and education of workers) has expanded the productivity of workers, and accounted for about 15% of productivity growth.

e. *Improved allocation of resources* (workers shifting to higher-productivity employment) and *economies of scale* (reductions in the per-unit cost to firms achieved from larger-sized markets) have also expanded the productivity of workers. Together, these factors contribute about 15% to explaining productivity growth.

f. Other factors that are difficult to quantify, such as the *social-cultural-political environment* of the United States, have contributed to economic growth. These factors have fostered growth of the market system under a stable political system and developed positive attitudes towards work, investing, and risk taking.

5. Increases in *productivity growth*, even small ones, can have a substantial effect on average real hourly wages and the standard of living in an economy. From 1973–1995, labor productivity grew by an average of 1.4% annually, but from 1995–2000 it grew by 3.1% annually. This increase indicates there may be a *New Economy*.

a. This New Economy has several characteristics.

(1) It is based on a dramatic rise in entrepreneurship and innovation based on the microchip and information technology.

(2) The new start-up firms often experience increasing returns, which means a firm's output increases by a larger percentage than the increase in its resource inputs. These increasing returns have been achieved by more specialized inputs, the spreading of development costs, simultaneous consumption, the effects of networks, and learning by doing.

(3) The new technology and improvements in communication have increased global competition, thus lowering production costs, restraining price increases, and stimulating innovation to remain competitive.

b. The New Economy has implications for **macroeconomics.**

(1) There can be a faster rate of economic growth with low inflation.

(2) It can lower the natural rate of unemployment.

(3) Tax revenues will increase as economic growth and productivity rise to a higher rate.

c. Questions remain about whether there is a New Economy or just a short upturn in the business cycle. Skeptics wonder whether the five-year increase in productivity growth can be sustained over a longer period of time or whether the economy will return to its long-term trend in productivity. Inflationary pressures can increase in economic boom times. More time may be needed to be sure there is a New Economy.

6. There is an ongoing debate about whether economic growth is desirable and sustainable.

a. The antigrowth view sees several problems: Growth pollutes the environment; may produce more goods and services, but does not create a better life; and doubts remain about whether growth is sustainable at the current rate of resource depletion.

b. The defense of economic growth is based on several considerations: Growth produces a higher standard of living and reduces the burden of scarcity; the technology it creates improves people's lives and can reduce pollution; and it is sustainable because market incentives encourage the use of substitute resources.

■ HINTS AND TIPS

1. Chapter 17 contains very little economics that should be new to you. Chapter 2 introduced you to the production possibilities model that is now discussed in more detail. In Chapters 11 and 16 you learned about the aggregate demand–aggregate supply models that are now used to discuss economic growth. You might review these concepts and models from previous chapters before reading this chapter.

2. Table 17.1 is important if you want to understand the factors that influence economic growth in the United States. The figures in the table indicate the relative importance of each major factor. In the past decade, about two-thirds of U.S. economic growth came from factors affecting increases in labor productivity, and about one-third came from increases in the quantity of labor. Five factors affecting the growth of labor productivity include technological advance, quantity of capital, education and training, economies of scale, and resource allocation.

3. The remaining two sections of the chapter focus on major economics issues about which there is some debate. You will want to evaluate the evidence for and against the idea that there is a "New Economy." You will also want to understand the advantages and disadvantages of economic growth.

■ IMPORTANT TERMS

economic growth	human capital
supply factor	economies of scale
demand factor	New Economy
efficiency factor	information technology
labor productivity	start-up firm
labor-force participation rate	increasing returns
growth accounting	network effects
infrastructure	learning by doing

SELF-TEST

■ FILL-IN QUESTIONS

1. Economic growth means that real output in the economy (increases, decreases) _____ and produces a standard of living that is (higher, lower) _____ with (more, less) _____ material abundance.

2. The four supply factors in economic growth are

a. _____

b. _____

c. _____

d. _____

3. To realize its growing production potential, a nation must fully employ its expanding supplies of resources, which is the (efficiency, demand) _____ factor in economic growth, and it must also achieve productive and allocative _____, the other factor contributing to economic growth.

4. In the production possibilities model, economic growth increases primarily because of (demand, supply) _____ factors that shift the production possibilities curve to the (left, right) _____; but if there is less than full employment and production, the economy (may, may not) _____ realize its potential.

5. Real GDP of any economy in any year is equal to the quantity of labor employed (divided, multiplied) _____ by the productivity of labor. The quantity of labor is measured by the number of (businesses, hours of labor) _____. Productivity is equal to real GDP per (capita, worker-hour) _____.

6. The quantity of labor employed in the economy in any year depends on the size of the (unemployed, employed)

_____ labor force and the length of the average workweek. The size element depends on the size of the working-age population and the labor-force (unemployment, participation) _____ rate.

7. In the aggregate demand–aggregate supply framework, economic growth is illustrated by an (increase, decrease) _____ in the long-run aggregate supply curve, which is (vertical, horizontal) _____. When the price level also increases, it indicates that the aggregate demand curve has increased (more, less) _____ rapidly than the long-run aggregate supply.

8. Since 1950, real GDP in the United States increased at an annual rate of about (2.3, 3.5) _____% and real GDP per capita increased at an annual rate of about _____%. From 1996–1999, annual growth in real GDP was significantly (higher, lower) _____ than in previous periods and _____ than those in most other industrial nations. Economic growth since 2000 has been (constant, variable) _____ because of a recession and slow economic recovery.

9. The economic growth record of the United States shows that since 1990, the increase in the quantity of labor accounted for (one-third, two-thirds) _____ of economic growth and increases in labor productivity accounted for _____ of economic growth.

10. Factors contributing to labor productivity include

  a. technological _____

  b. increases in the quantity of _____ and in the quantity available per _____

  c. the improved _____ and _____ of workers

  d. economies of _____

  e. the improved _____ of resources.

11. An increase in the quantity of the capital stock of a nation is the result of saving and (consumption, investment) _____. A key determinant of labor productivity is the amount of capital goods available per (consumer, worker) _____.

12. Infrastructure, such as highways and bridges, is a form of (private, public) _____ investment that complements _____ capital goods.

13. The knowledge and skills that make a productive worker are a form of (physical, human) _____ capital. This type of capital is often obtained through (consumption, education) _____.

14. Reductions in per-unit costs that result from the increase in the size of markets and firms is called (improved resource allocation, economies of scale) _____, but the movement of a worker from a job with lower productivity to one with higher productivity would be an example of _____.

15. Other factors that have led to economic growth in the United States are its social-cultural-political (parties, environment) _____ and (negative, positive) _____ attitudes toward work and risk taking that increase the supply of willing workers and innovative entrepreneurs.

16. An increase in labor productivity will (increase, decrease) _____ real output, real income, and real wages. Assuming an economy has an increase in labor productivity of 1.5%, it will take (28, 47) _____ years for its standard of living to double, but an increase in labor productivity of 2.5% annually will increase its standard of living in _____ years.

17. The characteristics of the New Economy are (advances, declines) _____ in information technology, business firms that experience returns to scale that are (decreasing, increasing) _____, and global competition that is _____.

18. Some implications for macroeconomics in the New Economy include a growth rate that is (faster, slower) _____ with low inflation, a natural rate of unemployment that is (higher, lower) _____, and tax revenues that are _____ because of personal income that is _____.

19. Skeptics of the New Economy argue that the rapid increase in the rate of productivity growth may be a (short-run, long-run) _____ trend that is not sustainable over a _____ period.

20. Critics of economic growth contend that it (cleans up, pollutes) _____ the environment, it (does, does not) _____ solve problems such as poverty and homelessness, and (is, is not) _____ sustainable. Defenders of economic growth say that it creates (less, greater) _____ material abundance, results in a (higher, lower) _____ standard of living, and an efficient and sustainable allocation of resources based on price (discounts, incentives) _____.

■ TRUE–FALSE QUESTIONS

Circle T if the statement is true, F if it is false.

1. Economic growth is measured as either an increase in real GDP or an increase in real per capita GDP.　**T　F**

2. Changes in the physical and technical agents of production are supply factors for economic growth that enable an economy to expand its potential GDP.　**T　F**

3. The demand factor in economic growth refers to the ability of the economy to expand its production as the demand for products grows.　**T　F**

4. An increase in the quantity and quality of natural resources is an efficiency factor for economic growth.　**T　F**

5. A shift outward in the production possibilities curve is the direct result of improvements in supply factors for economic growth.　**T　F**

6. The potential output of an economy will not be completely realized unless there is full employment of resources and their efficient use.　**T　F**

7. The real GDP of an economy in any year is equal to its input of labor divided by the productivity of labor.　**T　F**

8. The hours of labor input depend on the size of the employed labor force and the length of the average workweek.　**T　F**

9. One determinant of labor productivity is the quantity of capital goods available to workers.　**T　F**

10. Supply factors that shift the economy's production possibilities curve outward also cause a leftward shift in its long-run aggregate supply curve.　**T　F**

11. An increase in economic growth will increase the long-run aggregate supply curve and the short-run aggregate supply curve, but will decrease the aggregate demand curve.　**T　F**

12. Since 1950, the U.S. data show that the average annual rate of growth was greater for real GDP per capita than for real GDP.　**T　F**

13. Increased labor productivity has been more important than increased labor inputs in the growth of the U.S. economy since 1990.　**T　F**

14. The largest factor increasing labor productivity in the U.S. economy has been technological advance.　**T　F**

15. Public investment in the form of new infrastructure often complements private capital investment.　**T　F**

16. Education and training contribute to a worker's stock of human capital.　**T　F**

17. Economies of scale are reductions in per-unit cost that result in a decrease in the size of markets and firms.　**T　F**

18. The social, cultural, and political environment in the United States has fostered economic growth.　**T　F**

19. If the rate of growth in labor productivity averages 2.5% a year, it will take about 50 years for the standard of living to double.　**T　F**

20. The idea of a New Economy is based largely on a slower rate of productivity growth and therefore slower economic growth.　**T　F**

21. Productivity growth is the basic source of improvements in real wage rates and the standard of living.　**T　F**

22. More specialized inputs and network effects are two sources of increasing returns and economies of scale in the New Economy.　**T　F**

23. From a macroeconomic perspective, a New Economy is likely to experience a lower natural rate of unemployment.　**T　F**

24. Critics of economic growth say that it adds to environmental problems, increases human stress, and exhausts natural resources.　**T　F**

25. Defenders of economic growth say it is sustainable in the short run, but not in the long run.　**T　F**

■ MULTIPLE-CHOICE QUESTIONS

Circle the letter that corresponds to the best answer.

1. What is one major measure of economic growth?
 (a) the supply of money
 (b) the demand for money
 (c) nominal GDP per capita
 (d) real GDP per capita

2. A supply factor in economic growth would be
 (a) an increase in the efficient use of resources
 (b) a decline in the rate of resource depletion
 (c) an improvement in the quality of labor
 (d) an increase in consumption spending

3. Which is a demand factor in economic growth?
 (a) an increase in the purchasing power of the economy
 (b) an increase in the economy's stock of capital goods
 (c) more natural resources
 (d) technological progress

Use the following graph to answer Questions 4 and 5.

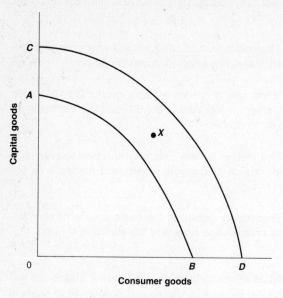

Use the following graph to answer Questions 9 and 10.

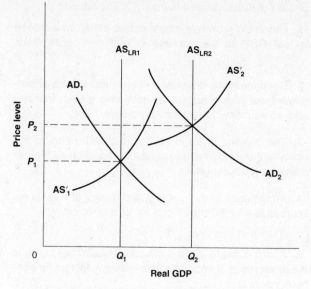

4. If the production possibilities curve of an economy shifts from *AB* to *CD*, it is most likely the result of what factor affecting economic growth?
(a) a supply factor
(b) a demand factor
(c) an efficiency factor
(d) an allocation factor

5. If the production possibilities curve for an economy is at *CD* but the economy is operating at point *X*, the reasons are most likely to be because of
(a) supply and environmental factors
(b) demand and efficiency factors
(c) labor inputs and labor productivity
(d) technological progress

6. Total output or real GDP in any year is equal to
(a) labor inputs divided by resource outputs
(b) labor productivity multiplied by real output
(c) worker-hours multiplied by labor productivity
(d) worker-hours divided by labor productivity

7. Assume that an economy has 1000 workers, each working 2000 hours per year. If the average real output per worker-hour is $9, then total output or real GDP will be
(a) $2 million
(b) $9 million
(c) $18 million
(d) $24 million

8. A shift outward of the production possibilities curve would be equivalent to a shift
(a) upward in aggregate demand
(b) downward in aggregate demand
(c) rightward in long-run aggregate supply
(d) leftward in long-run aggregate supply

9. A shift from Q_1 to Q_2 is caused by a shift in the
(a) level of prices
(b) aggregate demand curve
(c) short-run aggregate supply curve
(d) long-run aggregate supply curve

10. Which combination would best explain a shift in the price level from P_1 to P_2 and an increase in real domestic output from Q_1 to Q_2?
(a) an increase in the long-run aggregate supply (AS_1 to AS_2) and in short-run aggregate supply (AD_1 to AD_2).
(b) an increase in aggregate demand (AD_1 to AD_2) and a decrease in long-run aggregate supply (AS_2 to AS_1).
(c) an increase in the long-run aggregate supply (AS_1 to AS_2), an increase in aggregate demand (AD_1 to AD_2), and an increase in short-run aggregate supply (AS_1' to AS_2').
(d) a decrease in the long-run aggregate supply (AS_2 to AS_1), a decrease in aggregate demand (AD_2 to AD_1), and a decrease in short-run aggregate supply (AS_2' to AS_1').

11. The average annual rate of increase in real GDP since 1950 has been about
(a) 1.7%
(b) 2.3%
(c) 3.5%
(d) 4.5%

12. Real GDP per capita in the United States since 1950 grew by an average annual rate of about
(a) 1.1%
(b) 2.3%
(c) 3.5%
(d) 4.5%

13. What is the other major factor that, when combined with the growth of labor productivity, accounts for long-term economic growth in the United States?
(a) an increase in government spending
(b) an increase in the quantity of labor

(c) a decrease in the interest rate

(d) a decrease in personal taxes

14. The factor accounting for the largest increase in the productivity of labor in the United States has been

(a) economies of scale

(b) technological advance

(c) the quantity of capital

(d) the education and training of workers

15. How does a nation typically acquire more capital goods?

(a) by reducing the workweek and increasing leisure

(b) by saving income and using it for capital investment

(c) by increasing government regulation on the capital stock

(d) by reducing the amount of capital goods available per worker

16. An example of U.S. public investment in infrastructure would be

(a) an airline company

(b) a natural gas pipeline

(c) an auto and truck plant

(d) an interstate highway

17. Economists call the knowledge and skills that make a productive worker

(a) the labor-force participation rate

(b) learning by doing

(c) human capital

(d) infrastructure

18. What economic concept would be most closely associated with a situation where a large manufacturer of food products uses extensive assembly lines with computerization and robotics that serve to reduce per-unit costs of production?

(a) economies of scale

(b) sustainability of growth

(c) network effects

(d) simultaneous consumption

19. The decline of discrimination in education and labor markets increased the overall rate of labor productivity in the economy by giving groups freedom to move from jobs with lower productivity to ones with higher productivity. This development would be an example of a(n)

(a) fall in the labor-force participation rate

(b) rise in the natural rate of unemployment

(c) technological advance

(d) improvement in resource allocation

20. If the annual growth in a nation's productivity is 2% rather than 1%, then the nation's standard of living will double in

(a) 25 years

(b) 35 years

(c) 50 years

(d) 70 years

21. The New Economy is described as one with

(a) more tax revenues and more government spending

(b) a faster rate of inflation and fewer specialized inputs

(c) more experienced workers, but fewer available jobs for them

(d) a faster rate of productivity growth and faster economic growth

22. Increasing returns would be a situation where a firm

(a) triples its workforce and other inputs and its output doubles

(b) doubles its workforce and other inputs and its output triples

(c) doubles its workforce and other inputs and its output doubles

(d) quadruples its workforce and other inputs and its output triples

23. Which would be a source of increasing returns and economies of scale within the New Economy?

(a) social environment

(b) noninflationary growth

(c) simultaneous consumption

(d) less specialized inputs

24. A skeptic of the New Economy would argue that it

(a) is based on learning by doing instead of infrastructure

(b) raises tax revenues collected by government

(c) lowers the natural rate of unemployment

(d) is based on a short-run trend

25. Defenders of rapid economic growth say that it

(a) produces an equitable distribution of income

(b) creates common property resources

(c) leads to higher living standards

(d) spreads costs of development

■ PROBLEMS

1. The table below shows the quantity of labor (measured in hours) and the productivity of labor (measured in real GDP per hour) in a hypothetical economy in three different years.

Year	Quantity of labor	Productivity of labor	Real GDP
1	1000	$100	$ _____
2	1000	105	_____
3	1100	105	_____

a. Compute the economy's real GDP in each of the three years and enter them in the table.

b. Between years 1 and 2, the quantity of labor remained constant, but

(1) the productivity of labor increased by _____%, and

(2) as a consequence, real GDP increased by _____%.

c. Between years 2 and 3, the productivity of labor remained constant, but

(1) the quantity of labor increased by _____%, and

(2) as a consequence, real GDP increased by

_____%.

d. Between years 1 and 3

(1) real GDP increased by _____%, and

(2) this rate of increase is approximately equal to the

sum of the rates of increase in the _____

and the _____ of labor.

2. In the table below, indicate how many years it will take to double the standard of living (Years) in an economy given different annual rates of growth in labor productivity.

Productivity	Years
1.0%	_____
1.4	_____
1.8	_____
2.2	_____
2.6	_____
3.0	_____

What can you conclude about the importance of small changes in the growth rate of productivity on the standard of living?

3. In the first graph below, show an increase in economic growth using a hypothetical production possibilities curve. In the second graph in the next column, show what that increase would mean in terms of the extended aggregate demand and aggregate supply models.

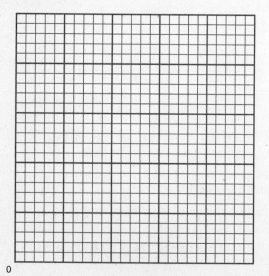

0

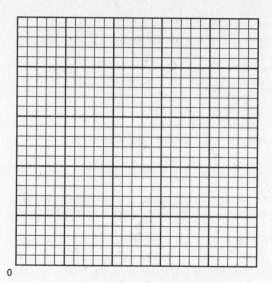

0

■ **SHORT ANSWER AND ESSAY QUESTIONS**

1. What is economic growth and how is it measured?

2. What are the six basic ingredients of economic growth? What are the essential differences between the supply, demand, and efficiency factors?

3. How does economic growth affect production possibilities? What demand and efficiency assumptions are necessary to achieve maximum productive potential?

4. What is the relationship between the real GDP produced in any year and the quantity of labor employed and labor productivity?

5. What determines the number of hours worked each year?

6. Identify and describe the factors that determine labor productivity.

7. Describe how economic growth can be illustrated in an aggregate demand–aggregate supply framework. What has happened to aggregate demand compared to long-run aggregate supply when the price level and real domestic output both increase?

8. What has been the growth record of the U.S. economy over the past half-century?

9. What have been the sources of the growth of the real output in the United States?

10. What changes have occurred in the size of the U.S. population and labor force since 1960? What factor has slowed the rate of growth of the former, and what factor has speeded the growth of the latter?

11. What is technological advance, and why are technological advance and capital formation closely related processes?

12. What is the relationship between investment and the stock of capital? What is the connection between increases in the capital stock and the rate of economic growth?

13. What increases the "quality" or human capital of labor? How is this quality usually measured? What are some of the problems with this path to improving the quality of the labor force?

14. Explain the relationship between productivity growth and the New Economy.

15. Discuss how the microchip and information technology contributed to the New Economy.

16. Describe at least four sources of increasing returns and economies of scale within the New Economy.

17. Identify and explain three macroeconomic implications from the New Economy.

18. Is the New Economy too good to be true? Present the skeptic's case.

19. What arguments are made against economic growth in the United States?

20. How can economic growth be defended? What are the reasons given to support this type of growth?

ANSWERS

Chapter 17 Economic Growth

FILL-IN QUESTIONS

1. increases, higher, more
2. *a.* quantity and quality of natural resources; *b.* quantity and quality of human resources; *c.* the supply or stock of capital goods; *d.* technology (any order for *a–d*)
3. demand, efficiency
4. supply, right, may not
5. multiplied, hours of labor, worker-hour
6. employed, participation
7. increase, vertical, more
8. 3.5, 2.3, higher, higher, variable
9. one-third, two-thirds
10. *a.* advance; *b.* capital, worker; *c.* education, training (either order); *d.* scale; *e.* allocation
11. investment, worker
12. public, private
13. human, education
14. economies of scale, improved resource allocation
15. environment, positive
16. increase, 47, 28
17. advances, increasing, increasing
18. faster, lower, higher, higher
19. short-run, long-run
20. pollutes, does not, is not, greater, higher, incentives

TRUE–FALSE QUESTIONS

1. T, p. 308	10. F, pp. 310–311	19. F, p. 317
2. T, p. 308	11. F, pp. 310–312	20. F, p. 317
3. F, pp. 308–309	12. F, p. 312	21. T, p. 317
4. F, p. 309	13. T, p. 313	22. T, pp. 317–318
5. T, pp. 309–310	14. T, pp. 313–314	23. T, p. 319
6. T, p. 309	15. T, p. 314	24. T, pp. 320–321
7. F, p. 310	16. T, pp. 314–315	25. F, p. 321
8. T, p. 310	17. F, p. 315	
9. T, p. 310	18. T, p. 316	

MULTIPLE-CHOICE QUESTIONS

1. d, p. 308	10. c, pp. 310–312	19. d, p. 316
2. c, p. 308	11. c, p. 312	20. b, p. 317
3. a, pp. 308–309	12. b, p. 312	21. d, p. 317
4. a, p. 309	13. b, p. 313	22. b, pp. 317–318
5. b, p. 309	14. b, p. 313	23. c, pp. 317–318
6. c, p. 310	15. b, p. 314	24. d, p. 319
7. c, p. 310	16. d, p. 314	25. c, p. 321
8. c, pp. 310–311	17. c, pp. 314–315	
9. d, pp. 310–312	18. a, p. 315	

PROBLEMS

1. *a.* 100,000, 105,000, 115,500; *b.* (1) 5, (2) 5; *c.* (1) 10, (2) 10; *d.* (1) 15.5, (2) quantity, productivity
2. 70, 50, 39, 31, 27, 23. Small changes make a large difference in the number of years it takes for the standard of living to double in an economy, especially at very low rates of growth in productivity.
3. See Figure 17.3 and Figure 17.4 in the text.

SHORT ANSWER AND ESSAY QUESTIONS

1. p. 308	8. p. 312	15. p. 317
2. pp. 308–309	9. pp. 312–313	16. pp. 317–318
3. pp. 309–310	10. p. 313	17. p. 319
4. p. 310	11. pp. 313–314	18. pp. 319–320
5. p. 310	12. p. 314	19. pp. 320–321
6. p. 310	13. pp. 314–315	20. p. 321
7. pp. 310–312	14. pp. 316–317	

Deficits, Surpluses, and the Public Debt

Over the years the United States accumulated a public debt that now totals about $6.2 trillion. This debt increased because of annual budget deficits. In recent years, these budget deficits were replaced by budget surpluses. Now budget deficits have returned. This chapter looks at the data and issues affecting these three fiscal concepts and explains their significance for the U.S. economy.

The Federal government can operate with a budget deficit, a budget surplus, or a balanced budget during a year. Any budget surplus or deficit affects the size of the **public debt** (often called the national debt). **Budget deficits** increase the public debt and **budget surpluses** decrease it. After defining these basic terms, the chapter discusses three budget philosophies. Be aware that the budget philosophy the Federal government adopts has a significant effect on the level of the public debt, and also on output, employment, and the price level in the economy.

Three major factors—wars, recessions, and lack of fiscal discipline—have contributed to increases in the public debt since 1940. The size of the public debt is placed into perspective by: (1) comparing it (and interest payments on the debt) to the size of the economy (GDP); (2) looking at the sizes of the public debt in other industrial nations; (3) describing who owns the debt; and (4) explaining how Social Security affects its calculation.

The two middle sections of the chapter examine the economic implications or **consequences of the public debt.** These economic problems do not include bankrupting the Federal government because the government can meet its obligations by refinancing and taxation. Nor does the public debt simply shift the economic burden to future generations because the public debt is a public credit for the many people who hold that debt in the form of U.S. securities. Rather, the public debt and payment of interest on the debt contribute to important problems: increased inequality in income, reduced incentives for work and production, decreased standard of living when part of the debt is paid to foreigners, and less capital investment.

The crowding out of investment in plant and equipment in the United States is probably the most serious of the problems. You should understand how crowding out works and how it may impose a burden on future generations by reducing the growth of the nation's capital stock. Whether it does impose a burden on future generations depends on the uses of government spending. If it is used for public investment that increases the future productive capacity of the economy and complements private in-

vestment spending, then this government spending can reduce the net burden on future generations.

The final section of the chapter discusses the recent historical record of budget deficits and surpluses in the United States. As the economy moved from deficits at the beginning of the 1990s to surpluses at the end of the 1990s, the public debate focused on what to do with these **budget surpluses.** The merits and drawbacks of three options were considered—paying down the public debt, cutting taxes, and increasing government spending for various programs. Now the focus has shifted back to budget deficits. As you will learn, they returned because of an economic downturn, a stock market decline, tax cuts without offsetting cuts in government spending, and increased government spending for the war on terrorism.

■ **CHECKLIST**

When you have studied this chapter you should be able to

☐ Define a budget deficit, budget surplus, and the public debt.

☐ Explain how budget deficits, budget surpluses, and the public debt are related.

☐ Describe three major philosophies about the budget.

☐ Explain how an annually balanced budget works and what its economic effects would be.

☐ State the rationale for a cyclically balanced budget.

☐ Explain how functional finance operates as a budget philosophy.

☐ Identify the three principal causes of the public debt and discuss their relative importance.

☐ Describe the quantitative aspects of the public debt and interest payments since 1940.

☐ Compare the relative size of the public debt of the United States to those of other industrial nations.

☐ State who owns the public debt.

☐ Explain how Social Security affects the size of the federal budget.

☐ Give two reasons why a large public debt will not bankrupt the government.

☐ Discuss whether the public debt imposes a burden on future generations.

☐ List four substantive issues related to the public debt.

☐ State the effect of the public debt on income distribution.

☐ Explain how the public debt affects incentives.

☐ Compare the effects of ownership of the debt by whether it is owned by U.S. or foreign citizens or institutions.

☐ Describe the crowding-out effect from a public debt.

☐ Give two qualifications to the argument for a crowding-out effect.

☐ Describe the transition from budget deficits to budget surpluses to budget deficits since 1990.

☐ Evaluate three policy options for the use of budget surpluses.

☐ Discuss the legislative actions and national events that contributed to a return to budget deficits in recent years.

■ **CHAPTER OUTLINE**

1. A **budget deficit** of the Federal government is the amount by which its expenditures are greater than its revenues in a given year. A **budget surplus** is just the opposite: the amount by which government revenues are greater than government expenditures in a given year. The **public debt** at any time is the sum of the Federal government's previous annual deficits, minus any annual surpluses.

2. If the Federal government uses fiscal policy to combat recession and inflation, its budget is not likely to be balanced in any particular year. The government may adopt one of three **budget philosophies.** Any of these philosophies will affect employment, real output, and the price level of the economy.

   a. Proponents of an **annually balanced budget** would have government expenditures and tax revenues equal in every year. Such a budget is pro- rather than countercyclical; but conservative economists favor it to prevent the expansion of the public sector (and the contraction of the private sector) of the economy without the increased payment of taxes by the public.

   b. Those who advocate a **cyclically balanced budget** propose matching surpluses (in years of prosperity) with deficits (in depression years) to stabilize the economy, but there is no assurance that the surpluses will equal the deficits over the years.

   c. Advocates of **functional finance** contend that deficits, surpluses, and the size of the debt are of minor importance and that the goal of full employment without inflation should be achieved regardless of the effects of the necessary fiscal policies on the budget and the size of the public debt.

3. Any government deficit increases the size of the public debt. The public debt has grown substantially since 1940.

   a. There are three basic **causes of the debt:**

   (1) *Wars* require increased Federal borrowing to finance the war effort.

   (2) *Recessions* result in budget deficits because of the built-in stability of the economy (tax revenues fall and domestic spending rises).

   (3) *Lack of fiscal discipline*, such as a cut in tax rates without offsetting reductions in expenditures or a lack of control over increased government spending, will contribute to budget deficits.

   b. The public debt in 2002 was about $6.2 trillion, an increase of $5.3 trillion from 1980.

   (1) The size of the debt as a percentage of the economy's GDP was much less in 2002 than in 1950 even though the absolute size of the debt rose substantially over that period.

   (2) Many industrial nations have public debts as a percentage of GDP that are similar to or greater than that of the United States.

   (3) Since the 1970s the interest payments on the debt rose significantly because of increases in the size of the debt and higher interest rates. Interest payments as a percentage of the economy's GDP also grew dramatically. This latter percentage reflects the level of taxation required to pay interest on the public debt. It is now about 1.6% of GDP.

   (4) About four-tenths (43%) of the public debt is owed to government agencies and the Federal Reserve Banks. About six-tenths (57%) is owed to others, including 18% owed to foreign citizens, firms, and governments.

   (5) The **Social Security trust fund** currently generates more revenue than expenditures for the federal government. This situation decreases budget deficits and increases budget surpluses.

4. The **false contentions** about a large debt are that it will eventually bankrupt the government and that borrowing to finance expenditures passes the cost on to future generations.

   a. The debt **cannot bankrupt** the government because the government

   (1) need not reduce the debt and can refinance it, and

   (2) has the constitutional authority to levy taxes to pay the debt.

   b. The burden of the debt **cannot be shifted to future generations** because U.S. citizens and institutions hold most of the debt. Repayment of any portion of the principal and the payment of interest on it does not reduce the wealth or purchasing power in the United States because it would be paid to U.S. citizens and institutions.

5. The public debt does create real and potential problems in the economy.

   a. The payment of interest on the debt probably increases the extent of **income inequality.**

   b. The payment of taxes to finance these interest payments may **reduce incentives** to bear risks, to innovate, to invest, and to save, and therefore slow economic growth in the economy.

   c. The portion of the debt that is externally held (by foreign citizens and institutions) requires the repayment of principal and the payment of interest to foreign citizens and institutions. This repayment would **transfer to foreigners** a part of the real output of the U.S. economy.

   d. An increase in government spending may impose a burden on future generations by **crowding out** private investment spending, and thus reducing the future stock of capital goods.

(1) If government spending is financed by increased public debt, the increased borrowing of the Federal government will raise interest rates and reduce private investment spending. Future generations will inherit a smaller stock of capital goods.

(2) The burden imposed on future generations is lessened if the increase in government expenditures is for worthwhile public investment that increases the production capacity of the economy. This public investment can also complement and stimulate private investment spending that increases the future capital stock.

6. The growth or shrinkage in the public debt will depend on the size of budget deficits and budget surpluses in future years.

a. In the 1990s, Federal budget deficits were the focus of fiscal policy because of the large size of these deficits early in the decade. In 1993, the Deficit Reduction Act increased individual and corporate tax rates (and gasoline excise taxes) to increase government revenues, and it required that government spending be held to its 1993 nominal level. Strong economic growth later in the decade also increased tax revenues. By 2000, there were growing surpluses in the Federal budget, a remarkable turnaround.

b. In the early 2000s, debate over the Federal budget turned to what to do with the annual **surpluses.** Three basic options were discussed.

(1) The Federal government could use the surpluses to **reduce the public debt.** The advantage of this option was that it would reduce public borrowing from credit markets and thus lower interest rates. In turn, the lower rates would stimulate more private investment spending, adding to the capital stock and contributing to economic growth (a reverse crowding-out effect). The annual interest saving could also be used to bolster the Social Security trust fund.

(2) **Tax cuts** could be used to reduce budget surpluses. This option returns money to taxpayers who were responsible for creating the surpluses. Tax cuts also help maintain consumer spending and saving for the economy, which can be especially important in times of recession or slow economic growth.

(3) Surpluses could pay for **new government spending** on desired programs in such areas as health care, education, or national defense.

c. In 2002, the budget moved from surplus to deficit because of legislative actions and unexpected events that reduced tax revenues and increased government spending.

(1) In 2001, the Economic Growth and Tax Relief Reconciliation Act that cut marginal tax rates was passed.

(2) A recession in 2001 and the stock market decline in 2002 reduced tax revenues as incomes fell and increased government spending.

(3) The terrorist attacks of September 11, 2001, increased government spending for homeland security and national defense to conduct a war on terror.

(4) More tax cuts were passed in 2003 to help stimulate the sluggish economy.

■ HINTS AND TIPS

1. Make sure you know the difference between the **public debt** and the **budget deficit.** These two negative fiscal terms are often confused.

2. The best way to gauge the public debt and budget deficit is to calculate each one as a **percentage of real GDP.** The absolute size of the public debt or the budget deficit is *not* a good indicator of whether it causes problems for the economy.

3. Try to understand the real rather than the imagined problems caused by the public debt. The debt will not cause the country to go bankrupt, nor will it be a burden on future generations. Carefully read the sections on the false issues and the real issues.

■ IMPORTANT TERMS

public debt	functional finance
U.S. securities	Social Security trust fund
annually balanced budget	external public debt
cyclically balanced budget	public investments

■ FILL-IN QUESTIONS

1. If the Federal government has a budget deficit in any year, then its expenditures are (less, greater) _____ than its revenues, but if it has a budget surplus, then its expenditures are _____ than its revenues in that year.

2. The public debt is equal to the sum of the Federal government's past budget (deficits, surpluses) _____ minus its budget _____.

3. An annually balanced budget is (pro-, counter-) _____ cyclical because governments would have to (raise, lower) _____ taxes and _____ their purchases of goods and services during a recession.

4. A cyclically balanced budget designed to ensure full employment without inflation would mean that during recession, government would incur (deficits, surpluses) _____, and during periods of strong economic growth it would incur _____, with the deficits and surpluses offsetting each other over the business cycle.

5. The budget philosophy that has as its main goal the achievement of full employment without inflation is (external debt, functional finance) _____. It regards budget deficits and increases in the public debt as of (primary, secondary) _____ importance.

6. The principal causes of the public debt are the expense of paying for (wars, inflation) _____, changes in the economy such as (a recession, an expansion) _____, and tax rate (cuts, increases) _____ without offsetting reductions in government expenditures.

7. There are several quantitative aspects to the public debt.

   a. The most meaningful way to measure the public debt is relative to (interest rates, GDP)_____, and in 2002 it was (21, 59) _____ % of this figure.

   b. In 2002 the public debt as a percentage of GDP was (higher, lower) _____ in Japan and Italy and _____ in Finland and Australia.

   c. Of the public debt, Federal government agencies and the Federal Reserve hold about (43, 57) _____%, and commercial banks, financial institutions, state and local governments, and individuals and institutions here and abroad hold about _____ %.

   d. Most of the public debt is (internal, external) _____ because foreigners hold only about (9, 18) _____% of the public debt.

8. In the Social Security trust fund, current tax revenues are (greater, less) _____ than benefit payouts to retirees. This trust fund, therefore, creates a (deficit, surplus) _____ that (adds to, subtracts from) _____ the size of a Federal budget surplus.

9. The possibility that the Federal government will go bankrupt is a false issue. It does not need to reduce its debt; it can retire maturing U.S. securities by (taxing, refinancing) _____ them. The government can also pay its debts by increasing (interest, tax) _____ rates.

10. If the public debt is held domestically, then for U.S. taxpayers it is (a liability, an asset) _____ and for U.S. citizens and institutions owning the U.S. debt securities, it is _____.

11. The public debt and the payment of interest on it may (increase, decrease) _____ income inequality in the economy and _____ the incentives to work, take risks, save, and invest in the economy.

12. The public debt is a burden on an economy if it is held by (foreigners, U.S. citizens) _____.

13. A public debt imposes a burden on future generations if the borrowing done to finance an increase in government expenditures results in (an increase, a decrease) _____ in interest rates, _____ in investment spending, and _____ in the stock of capital goods for future generations.

14. The size of the burden from the crowding out of private investment is lessened if government expenditures are used to finance worthwhile (increases, decreases) _____ in physical and human capital that contribute to the productive capacity of the economy, or if they (encourage, discourage) _____ more private investment that complements the public investment.

15. In the 1990s, Federal budget deficits and the growing public debt were the main focus of (monetary, fiscal) _____ policy. To reduce these deficits, in 1993 personal and corporate tax rates were (increased, decreased) _____ and future government spending was _____ by limiting it to the level of 1993 nominal spending. The robust economic growth later in the decade (increased, decreased) _____ tax revenues and helped create a budget (surplus, deficit) _____ for the first time since 1969.

16. One proposed option for the use of the budget surpluses was to (increase, decrease) _____ the public debt, which would _____ interest rates and _____ private investment spending. The economic benefit of this type of policy is that there would be a (direct, reverse) _____ crowding-out effect.

17. A second option for the use of budget surpluses was for tax rates to be (raised, lowered) _____ so that money could be returned to the public and improve incomes in the event of a recession.

18. Arguments were also made to use the budget surpluses for new programs that would (increase, decrease) _____ government spending. This spending would be used for education, health care, and infrastructure projects that would (help, hurt) _____ society and (weaken, strengthen) _____ the economy over the long term.

19. In 2002, the budget moved from (deficit, surplus) _____ to _____. A factor contributing to this development was cuts in (spending, taxes) _____ in 2001, and in 2003 there were additional cuts in _____.

20. An economic downturn in 2001 and a stock market decline in 2002 contributed to the return of budget (surpluses, deficits) _____. As a result of these events tax revenues (increased, decreased) _____, and government spending _____ to counter the downturn. Also, the costs of more homeland security and the financing of a war on terrorism led to (increased, decreased) _____ government spending.

■ **TRUE–FALSE QUESTIONS**

Circle T if the statement is true, F if it is false.

1. If there is a Federal budget surplus, then government revenues are less than its expenditures.　**T　F**

2. The public debt is the total accumulation of the deficits, minus any surpluses, that the Federal government has incurred over time.　**T　F**

3. An annually balanced budget is economically neutral in its effects on the economy.　**T　F**

4. A cyclically balanced budget is pro-cyclical, not countercyclical.　**T　F**

5. Proponents of functional finance argue that a balanced budget, whether it is balanced annually or over the business cycle, is of minor importance when compared with the objective of full employment without inflation.　**T　F**

6. A major reason for the increase in the public debt since 1940 was the government spending associated with financing wartime expenditures.　**T　F**

7. When national income declines during a recession, tax revenues automatically increase and increase the public debt.　**T　F**

8. An example of lack of fiscal discipline contributing to the public debt would be tax cuts without offsetting cuts in government spending.　**T　F**

9. The public debt as a percentage of GDP is higher in the United States than in most other industrial nations.　**T　F**

10. Interest payments as a percentage of GDP reflect the level of taxation (average tax rate) required to service the public debt.　**T　F**

11. Most of the public debt is held by Federal government agencies and the Federal Reserve.　**T　F**

12. In the Federal budget, surpluses obtained from Social Security are treated as an offset to current government spending.　**T　F**

13. A large public debt will bankrupt the Federal government because it can refinance the debt or increase taxes to pay it.　**T　F**

14. The public debt is also a public credit.　**T　F**

15. The payment of interest on the public debt probably increases income inequality.　**T　F**

16. The additional taxes needed to pay the interest on the public debt increase incentives to work, save, invest, and bear risks.　**T　F**

17. Selling U.S. securities to foreigners to finance increased expenditures by the Federal government imposes a burden on future generations.　**T　F**

18. Citizens and institutions of foreign countries hold about 90 percent of the U.S. public debt.　**T　F**

19. The crowding-out effect is caused by a rise in interest rates resulting from an increase in government borrowing to finance government expenditures.　**T　F**

20. The crowding-out effect increases the investment-demand curve and investment in private capital goods.　**T　F**

21. If government spending is for public investments that increase the capital stock, then this spending can increase the future production capacity of the economy.　**T　F**

22. At the beginning of the 1990s there were budget surpluses, but by the end of the decade there were budget deficits.　**T　F**

23. Advocates for using budget surpluses to pay down the debt say these actions will reduce interest rates, increase private investment, and thus eventually increase economic growth.　**T　F**

24. Those individuals who argue for a cut in tax rates as the best use of the budget surpluses justify this option in part based on its beneficial effect on household incomes and consumption in the economy.　**T　F**

25. The factors contributing to a return to annual budget deficits in 2002 include increases in marginal tax rates and reduction in government spending.　**T　F**

■ **MULTIPLE-CHOICE QUESTIONS**

Circle the letter that corresponds to the best answer.

1. The public debt is the sum of all previous
 (a) expenditures of the Federal government
 (b) budget deficits of the Federal government
 (c) budget deficits minus any budget surpluses of the Federal government
 (d) budget surpluses less the current budget deficit of the Federal government

2. If there is a budget surplus in a given year, it means that
 (a) government expenditures are greater than revenues
 (b) government revenues are greater than expenditures
 (c) the size of the public debt is increasing
 (d) the economy is experiencing a recession

3. Which would involve reducing government expenditures and increasing tax rates during a recession?
 (a) functional finance
 (b) a cyclically balanced budget policy
 (c) an annually balanced budget policy
 (d) a policy employing built-in stability

4. A cyclically balanced budget philosophy is
 (a) pro-cyclical
 (b) countercyclical
 (c) functional finance
 (d) economically neutral

5. What three factors largely explain why the public debt has increased since 1940?
 (a) interest payments on the public debt, spending for Social Security, and depreciation of the dollar
 (b) deficit spending to finance wars, effects of automatic stabilizers on the budget during recessions, and lack of fiscal discipline
 (c) deficit spending caused by depressions, borrowing funds from other nations, and increased government spending to cover health care problems
 (d) interest payments on the public debt, government spending for welfare programs, and the crowding out of investment spending

6. To place the public debt in perspective based on the wealth and productive capacity of the economy, it is more meaningful to
 (a) examine its absolute size
 (b) calculate the interest payments on the debt
 (c) measure it relative to the gross domestic product
 (d) compare it to imports, exports, and the trade deficit

7. According to many economists, the primary burden of the debt is the
 (a) absolute size of the debt for the economy
 (b) annual interest charges from bonds sold to finance the public debt
 (c) deficit arising from a decline in exports and increase in imports
 (d) government spending that the public debt finances for the economy

8. The public debt of the United States as a percentage of its GDP is
 (a) larger than all other industrial nations
 (b) smaller than all other industrial nations
 (c) less than all other industrial nations except Japan
 (d) greater than some industrial nations but less than others

9. In 2002, about what percentage of GDP in the form of taxes did the Federal government have to collect to service the public debt?
 (a) 2%
 (b) 22%
 (c) 55%
 (d) 91%

10. Foreign individuals and institutions held about what percentage of the public debt in 2002?
 (a) 5%
 (b) 9%
 (c) 18%
 (d) 34%

11. If there is a surplus for the Social Security trust fund in a given year, then this Social Security surplus will increase
 (a) a Federal budget deficit that year
 (b) a Federal budget surplus that year
 (c) interest payments on the public debt
 (d) holdings of U.S. securities by foreigners

12. A major reason that a public debt cannot bankrupt the Federal government is because the Federal government has
 (a) an annually balanced budget
 (b) the Social Security trust fund
 (c) the power to levy taxes
 (d) a strong military defense

13. Incurring an internal debt to finance a war does not pass the cost of the war on to future generations because
 (a) the opportunity cost of the war was borne by the generation that fought it
 (b) the government need not pay interest on internally held debts
 (c) there is never a need for government to refinance the debt
 (d) wartime inflation reduces the relative size of the debt

14. Which would be a consequence of the retirement of the internally held (U.S.-owned) portion of the public debt?
 (a) a reduction in the nation's productive capacity
 (b) a reduction in the nation's standard of living
 (c) a redistribution of the nation's wealth among its citizens
 (d) a decrease in aggregate demand in the economy

15. Which is an important consequence of the public debt of the United States?
 (a) It decreases the need for U.S. securities.
 (b) It transfers a portion of the U.S. output to foreign nations.
 (c) It reduces the income inequality in the United States.
 (d) It leads to greater saving at every level of disposable income.

16. Greater interest charges on the public debt can lead to
 (a) fewer purchases of U.S. securities by foreigners
 (b) more private investment spending in the economy
 (c) lower taxes, and thus greater incentives to work and invest
 (d) higher taxes, and thus reduced incentives to work and invest

17. The crowding-out effect of borrowing to finance an increase in government expenditures
 (a) reduces current spending for private investment
 (b) increases the privately owned stock of real capital
 (c) reduces the economic burden on future generations
 (d) increases incentives to innovate

18. The crowding-out effect from government borrowing is reduced when
(a) interest rates are rising
(b) the economy is operating at full employment
(c) government spending improves human capital in the economy
(d) private investment spending can substitute for government spending

19. During the early 1990s, Federal deficits and the growing public debt and the legislative efforts to control them were the main focus of
(a) unemployment policy
(b) inflation policy
(c) monetary policy
(d) fiscal policy

20. Deficits in the early 1990s were primarily increased by
(a) an increase in spending for Social Security
(b) a recession and a bailout of the savings and loan industry
(c) an increased demand by foreigners for government securities
(d) an easy money policy of the Federal Reserve

21. The Deficit Reduction Act of 1993 was legislation passed by Congress and signed by President Clinton. It was designed to
(a) decrease tax rates on personal income, but increase corporate income taxes
(b) increase taxes on personal income and hold all government spending to 1993 nominal levels
(c) use fiscal policy to stimulate the sluggish U.S. economy and reduce the rate of unemployment in 1993
(d) coordinate fiscal policy with the monetary policy of the Federal Reserve to achieve a budget balance by the year 2010

22. One option considered for the use of budget surpluses is to
(a) decrease tax rates
(b) decrease government spending
(c) increase the public debt by borrowing
(d) decrease spending for Social Security

23. The primary economic benefit from using budget surpluses to help pay off the public debt would be
(a) a reverse crowding-out effect
(b) a cyclically balanced budget
(c) an increase in the number of government securities
(d) a decrease in the size of the Social Security trust fund

24. One reason that budget deficits returned to the U.S. economy in 2002 was because of
(a) cost-push inflation
(b) an economic downturn
(c) less government spending
(d) a reduction in interest rates

25. The 2001 and 2003 tax acts passed by the U.S. Congress and signed into law by President Bush had the immediate effect of
(a) increasing marginal tax rates and decreasing tax revenues
(b) decreasing marginal tax rates and increasing tax revenues
(c) increasing marginal tax rates and increasing tax revenues
(d) decreasing marginal tax rates and decreasing tax revenues

■ PROBLEMS

1. The following table gives data on the public debt and the GDP for selected 5-year periods from 1961–2001. Data for the public debt and the GDP are in billions of dollars.

Year	Debt	GDP	Debt/GDP
1961	$ 296.1	$ 545.7	_____%
1966	329.3	789.3	_____
1971	424.1	1128.6	_____
1976	653.5	1823.9	_____
1981	1028.7	3131.3	_____
1986	2125.3	4452.9	_____
1991	3665.3	5986.2	_____
1996	5224.8	7813.2	_____
2001	5807.5	10082.2	_____

a. Calculate the ratio of the public debt to GDP expressed as a percentage of GDP. Enter the numbers into the last column of the table.
b. On the graph below, plot the year on the horizontal axis and plot the public debt as a percentage of GDP on the vertical axis.

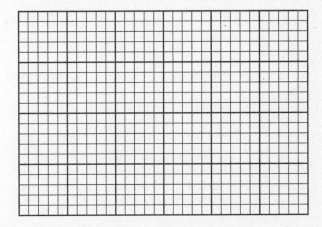

c. Explain what happened to the public debt as a percentage of GDP from 1961–2001.

_____

_____

_____

2. The following table gives data on interest rates and investment demand (in billions of dollars) in a hypothetical economy.

Interest rate	I_{d1}	I_{d2}
10%	$250	$300
8	300	350
6	350	400
4	400	450
2	450	500

a. Use the I_{d1} schedule. Assume that the government needs to finance a budget deficit and this public borrowing increases the interest rate from 4% to 6%. How much crowding out of private investment will occur?

b. Now assume that the deficit is used to improve the capital stock of the economy and that, as a consequence, the investment-demand schedule changes from I_{d1} to I_{d2}. At the same time, the interest rate rises from 4% to 6% as the government borrows money to finance the deficit. How much crowding out of private investment will occur in this case?

c. Graph the two investment-demand schedules on the next graph and show the difference between the two events. Put the interest rate on the vertical axis and the quantity of investment demanded on the horizontal axis.

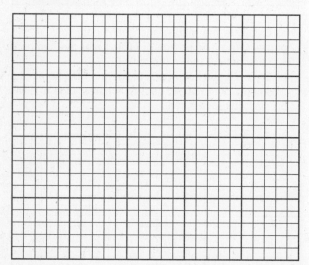

3. Columns 1 and 2 in the following table are investment-demand schedules and show planned investment (I) at different rates of interest (i). Assume the marginal propensity to consume in the economy is 0.8.

(1) i	(2) I	(3) I'
.08	$115	$125
.07	140	150
.06	165	175
.05	190	200
.04	215	225

a. If the Federal government were to spend an additional $20 for goods and services, the equilibrium real GDP would (increase, decrease) _____ by $_____.

b. If the Federal government had obtained the additional $20 by
(1) increasing taxes by $20, the equilibrium real GDP would have (increased, decreased) _____ by a total of $_____;
(2) borrowing $20 in the money market and this borrowing had increased the interest rate from 5% to 6%, (a) planned investment spending would have (increased, decreased) _____ by $_____, (b) the equilibrium real GDP would have _____ by $_____, and (c) the net effect of the increased government spending of the $20 borrowed in the money market would have been to _____ the equilibrium real GDP by $_____.

c. But if the government deficit spending had improved the nation's capital stock and shifted the investment-demand schedule to the one shown in columns 1 and 3 in the preceding table, the total effect of the increased government spending of the $20 borrowed in the money market would have been to (increase, decrease) _____ the equilibrium real GDP by $_____.

■ **SHORT ANSWER AND ESSAY QUESTIONS**

1. What is the difference between the (Federal) budget deficit and surplus?

2. How are budget deficits and surpluses related to the public debt?

3. Explain why an annually balanced budget is not neutral and how it can intensify, rather than reduce, the tendencies for GDP to rise and fall.

4. How does a cyclically balanced budget philosophy differ from the philosophy of functional finance? Why do advocates of functional finance argue that budget deficits and a mounting national debt are of secondary importance?

5. What have been the three basic causes of the public debt since 1940?

6. How big is the public debt of the United States absolutely and relative to the GDP? How large are the interest payments on this debt absolutely and relative to the GDP?

7. What has happened to the relative size of the debt and the interest payments from 1980–1995 and then from 1995–2002? What explains these changes?

8. Who owns the public debt? What percentage is held by the two major groups? What percentage of the public debt is held by foreigners?

9. Why can't the public debt result in the bankruptcy of the Federal government? What two actions can the government take to prevent bankruptcy?

10. If most of the public debt was owned by American citizens and institutions, and the government decided to pay off the debt, what would happen?

11. Was the increase in the cost of the public debt that resulted from World War II a burden borne by the wartime generation or future generations? Explain.

12. How do the public debt and the payment of interest on this debt affect the distribution of income?

13. What effects does the public debt have on incentives to work, to save, or to assume risk in the economy?

14. What are the economic implications of the portion of the public debt held by foreigners?

15. How does the public debt crowd out private investment and impose a burden on future generations?

16. Does it matter to future generations whether increases in government spending are financed by taxation or increased public debt?

17. What two qualifications might lessen the crowding-out effect on the size of the economic burden that has shifted to future generations?

18. What has been the history of budget deficits and surpluses in recent years? What fiscal policies did the government adopt to eliminate the budget deficits?

19. What are three options for the use of budget surpluses? State a rationale for each option.

20. What legislative actions and national events contributed to the return to budget deficits in recent years?

ANSWERS

Chapter 18 Deficits, Surpluses, and the Public Debt

FILL-IN QUESTIONS

1. greater, less
2. deficits, surpluses
3. pro-, raise, lower
4. deficits, surpluses
5. functional finance, secondary
6. wars, a recession, cuts
7. *a.* GDP, 59; *b.* higher, lower; *c.* 43, 57; *d.* internal, 18
8. greater, surplus, adds to
9. refinancing, tax
10. a liability, an asset
11. increase, decrease
12. foreigners
13. an increase, a decrease, a decrease
14. increases, encourage
15. fiscal, increased, decreased, increased, surplus
16. decrease, decrease, increase, reverse
17. lowered
18. increase, help, strengthen
19. surplus, deficit, taxes, taxes
20. deficits, decreased, increased, increased

TRUE–FALSE QUESTIONS

1. F, p. 325	**10.** T, p. 328	**19.** T, p. 331
2. T, p. 325	**11.** F, pp. 328–329	**20.** F, p. 331
3. F, p. 326	**12.** T, p. 329	**21.** T, p. 331
4. F, p. 326	**13.** F, pp. 329–330	**22.** F, p. 332
5. T, p. 326	**14.** T, p. 330	**23.** T, p. 333
6. T, p. 327	**15.** T, p. 330	**24.** T, p. 333
7. F, p. 327	**16.** F, p. 330	**25.** F, pp. 333–335
8. T, p. 327	**17.** T, pp. 330–331	
9. F, p. 328	**18.** F, p. 330	

MULTIPLE-CHOICE QUESTIONS

1. c, p. 325	**10.** c, p. 329	**19.** d, p. 332
2. b, p. 325	**11.** b, p. 329	**20.** b, p. 332
3. c, p. 326	**12.** c, pp. 329–330	**21.** b, p. 332
4. b, p. 326	**13.** a, p. 330	**22.** a, p. 333
5. b, p. 327	**14.** c, p. 330	**23.** a, p. 333
6. c, p. 328	**15.** b, pp. 330–331	**24.** b, pp. 334–335
7. b, p. 328	**16.** d, p. 330	**25.** d, pp. 333–335
8. d, p. 328	**17.** a, p. 331	
9. a, p. 328	**18.** c, p. 331	

PROBLEMS

1. *a.* 54, 42, 38, 37, 33, 48, 61, 69, 58; *b.* graph; *c.* The debt as a percentage of GDP fell from 1961 to 1981 and then rose substantially from 1981 to 1996. It has fallen since 1996.

2. *a.* $50 billion; *b.* none; *c.* graph

3. *a.* increase, 100; *b.* (1) increased, 20, (2) (a) decreased, 25, (b) decreased, 125, (c) decrease, 25; *c.* increase, 25

SHORT ANSWER AND ESSAY QUESTIONS

1. p. 325	**8.** pp. 328–329	**15.** p. 331
2. p. 325	**9.** pp. 329–330	**16.** pp. 330–331
3. p. 326	**10.** p. 330	**17.** p. 331
4. p. 326	**11.** p. 330	**18.** p. 332
5. p. 327	**12.** p. 330	**19.** p. 333
6. pp. 327–328	**13.** p. 330	**20.** pp. 333–335
7. pp. 327–328	**14.** pp. 330–331	

CHAPTER 19

Disputes over Macro Theory and Policy

Now that you understand the basic theory and models of the macro economy, you are ready to learn about different perspectives on how the economy functions and the major disputes in macro theory and policy.

Economics has always been an arena in which conflicting theories and policies oppose each other. This field of intellectual combat, in major engagements, has seen Adam Smith do battle with the defenders of a regulated economy. It witnessed the opposition of Karl Marx to the orthodox economics of his day. In the 1930s, it saw John Maynard Keynes oppose the classical economists. Around the major engagements have been countless minor skirmishes between opposing viewpoints. Out of these major and minor confrontations have emerged not winners and losers, but the advancement of economic theory and the improvement of economic policy.

Chapter 19 sets the foundation for understanding the modern debates by comparing **classical economics** and **Keynesianism** in terms of macroeconomic theory. The now familiar aggregate demand–aggregate supply model is used to illustrate the classical view that aggregate supply is vertical and aggregate demand relatively stable. Keynesians, however, saw aggregate supply as being horizontal (to full-employment output), aggregate demand as being highly unstable, and a need for government intervention to stabilize the macro economy.

The chapter then turns to the first of three major questions: **What causes macro instability in the economy?** Four different perspectives on the issues are given. First, from the Keynesian-based *mainstream* view, this instability arises primarily from volatility in investment that shifts aggregate demand or from occasional shocks to aggregate supply. Second, *monetarists* focus on the money supply and assume that the competitive market economy has a high degree of stability, except when there is inappropriate monetary policy. The monetarist analysis is based on the equation of exchange and the assumption that the velocity of money is stable. Changes in the money supply, therefore, directly affect the level of nominal GDP. Third, *real-business-cycle* theorists see instability as coming from the aggregate supply side of the economy and from real factors that affect the long-term growth rather than monetary factors that affect aggregate demand. Fourth, some economists think that macroeconomic instability is the result of *coordination failures* that do not permit people to act jointly to determine the optimal level of output, and that the equilibrium in the economy changes as expectations change.

The next question the chapter discusses is: **Does the economy self-correct its macro instability?** The view of new classical economics is that internal mechanisms in the economy allow it to self-correct. The two variants of this new classical perspective are based on *monetarism* and the *rational expectations theory (RET)*. Monetarists think the economy will self-correct to its long-run level of output, although there can be short-run changes in the price level and real output. The rational expectations theory suggests that the self-correction process is quick and does not change the price level or real output, except when there are price-level surprises.

By contrast, mainstream economists contend that the downward inflexibility of wages limits the self-correction mechanisms in the economy. Several explanations are offered for this inflexibility. There can be long-term wage contracts that support wages. Firms may also pay an efficiency wage to encourage work effort, reduce turnover, and prevent shirking. Firms may also be concerned about maintaining the support and teamwork of key workers (insiders), so they do not cut wages even when other workers (outsiders) might be willing to accept a lower wage.

The different perspectives on macro instability and self-correction set the stage for discussion of the third and final question: **Should the macro economy be guided by policy rules or discretion?** To restrict monetary policy, monetarists and rational expectations economists call for a monetary rule that would have monetary authorities allow the money supply to grow in proportion to the long-term growth in the productive capacity of the economy. Both monetarists and rational expectations economists also oppose the use of fiscal policy, and a few call for a balanced budget requirement to limit the use of discretionary fiscal policy.

Mainstream economists see value in discretionary monetary and fiscal policies. They suggest that a monetary rule would be ineffective in achieving growth and would destabilize the economy. A balanced-budget requirement would also have a pro-cyclical effect that would reinforce recessionary or inflationary tendencies in the economy. And, since government has taken a more active role in the economy, the historical record shows that discretionary monetary and fiscal actions have reduced macro instability.

As was the case in the past, macroeconomic theory and policy have changed because of the debates among economists. The disputes among mainstream economists, monetarists, rational expectationists, and real-business-cycle theorists have produced new insights about how the macro economy operates. In particular, it is now recognized that "money matters" and that the money supply has a significant effect on the economy. More attention is also being given to the influence of people's expectations on policy and coordination failures in explaining macroeconomic events. The disputes in macroeconomics in the past half-century forced economists to reconsider previous conclusions and led to the incorporation of new ideas about macro theory and policy into mainstream thinking.

■ **CHECKLIST**

When you have studied this chapter you should be able to

☐ Compare and contrast the classical and Keynesian views of the aggregate demand curve and the aggregate supply curve.

☐ Describe the mainstream view of stability in the macro economy and the two potential sources of instability.

☐ Explain the monetarist view of stability in the macro economy.

☐ Write the equation of exchange and define each of the four terms in the equation.

☐ Explain why monetarists think the velocity of money is relatively stable.

☐ Write a brief scenario that explains what monetarists believe will happen to change the nominal GDP and will happen to **V** (velocity of money) when **M** (money supply) is increased.

☐ Discuss the monetary causes of instability in the macro economy.

☐ Describe the real-business-cycle view of stability in the macro economy.

☐ Give noneconomic and macroeconomic examples of the coordination failures view of stability in the macro economy.

☐ Use a graph to explain the new classical view of self-correction in the macro economy.

☐ Discuss the differences between the monetarist and rational expectations views on the speed of adjustment for self-correction in the macro economy.

☐ State the two basic assumptions of the rational expectations theory (RET).

☐ Use a graph to explain how RET views unanticipated and fully anticipated changes in the price level.

☐ Describe the mainstream view of self-correction in the macro economy.

☐ Give two reasons why there may be downward wage inflexibility.

☐ State three reasons why a higher wage might result in greater efficiency.

☐ Use ideas from the insider–outsider theory to explain the downward inflexibility of wages.

☐ State why monetarists think there should be a monetary rule, and illustrate the rationale using aggregate demand and aggregate supply models.

☐ Describe how monetarists and new classical economists view the effectiveness of fiscal policy.

☐ Offer a mainstream defense of a discretionary stabilization policy and a critique of a monetary rule and balanced-budget requirement.

☐ Describe the possible reasons for increased stability in the macro economy in the past half-century.

☐ Summarize the three alternative views on issues affecting the macro economy.

■ **CHAPTER OUTLINE**

1. *Classical economics* and *Keynesian economics* can be compared by examining their aggregate demand–aggregate supply models of the economy.

　a. In the *classical model,*

　(1) the aggregate supply curve is *vertical* at the economy's full-employment output, and a decrease in aggregate demand will lower the equilibrium price level and have no effect on the real output (or employment) in the economy because of Say's law and flexible, responsive prices and wages.

　(2) the aggregate demand curve slopes downward because (with a fixed money supply in the economy) a fall in the price level increases the purchasing power of money and enables consumers and business firms to purchase a larger real output. Aggregate demand will be reasonably stable if the nation's monetary authorities maintain a constant supply of money to accommodate long-term growth.

　b. In the *Keynesian model,*

　(1) the aggregate supply curve is *horizontal* at the current price level, and a decrease in aggregate demand will lower the real output (and employment) in the economy and have no effect on the equilibrium price level because of the downward inflexibility of prices and wages.

　(2) aggregate demand is viewed as being *unstable* over time, even if the supply of money is held constant, partly because of fluctuations in investment spending. A decline in aggregate demand decreases real domestic output but has no effect on the price level, thereby causing output to stay permanently below the full-employment level.

2. There are four different views among economists on *instability* in the macro economy.

　a. The *mainstream view* is Keynesian-based and holds that instability in the economy arises from

　(1) the volatility in investment spending that makes aggregate demand unstable, and

　(2) occasional aggregate supply shocks which cause cost-push inflation and recession.

　b. *Monetarism* focuses on the money supply. Monetarists think markets are highly competitive and that government intervention destabilizes the economy.

　(1) In monetarism, the equation of exchange is $MV = PQ$, where **M** is the money supply, **V** the velocity of money, **P** the price level, and **Q** the quantity of goods and services produced.

　(2) Monetarists think that velocity is relatively stable or that the quantity of money demanded is a stable

percentage of GDP (GDP/**M** is constant). If velocity is stable, there is a predictable relationship between **M** and nominal GDP (= **PQ**). An increase in **M** will leave firms and households with more money than they wish to have, so they will increase spending and boost aggregate demand. This causes nominal GDP and the amount of money they wish to hold to rise until the demand for money is equal to **M** and nominal GDP/**M** = **V**.

(3) Monetarists view macroeconomic instability as a result of inappropriate monetary policy. An increase in the money supply will increase aggregate demand, output, and the price level; it will also reduce unemployment. Eventually, nominal wages rise to restore real wages and real output, and the unemployment rate falls back to its natural level at long-run aggregate supply.

c. **Real-business-cycle theory** sees macroeconomic instability as being caused by real factors influencing aggregate supply instead of monetary factors causing shifts in aggregate demand. Changes in technology and resources will affect productivity and thus the long-run growth rate of aggregate supply.

d. A fourth view of instability in the macro economy attributes the reasons to **coordination failures.** These failures occur when people are not able to coordinate their actions to achieve an optimal equilibrium. A self-fulfilling prophecy can lead to a recession because if households and firms expect it, they individually cut back on spending and employment. If, however, they were to act jointly, they could take actions to counter the recession expectations to achieve an optimal equilibrium.

3. Economists also debate the issue of whether the macro economy self-corrects.

a. **New classical economics,** based on monetarism and a rational expectations theory, says the economy may deviate from full-employment output, but it eventually returns to this output level because there are self-corrective mechanisms in the economy.

(1) Graphically, if aggregate demand increases, it temporarily raises real output and the price level. Nominal wages rise and productivity falls, so short-run aggregate supply decreases, thus bringing the economy back to its long-run output level.

(2) There is disagreement about the speed of adjustment. The monetarists adopt the adaptive expectations view that there will be a slower, temporary change in output but that in the long run it will return to its natural level. Other new classical economists adopt the **rational expectations theory** (*RET*) view that there will be a rapid adjustment with little or no change in output. RET is based on two assumptions: People understand how the economy works so that they quickly anticipate the effect on the economy of an economic event, and all markets in the economy are so competitive that equilibrium prices and quantities quickly adjust to changes in policy.

(3) In RET, unanticipated price-level changes, called price-level surprises, cause short-run changes in real output because they cause misperceptions about the economy among workers and firms.

(4) In RET, fully anticipated price-level changes do not change real output even in the short run because workers and firms anticipate and counteract the effects of the changes.

b. The **mainstream view** of self-correction suggests that price and wages may be inflexible downward in the economy.

(1) Graphically, a decrease in aggregate demand will decrease real output but not the price level because nominal wages will not decline and cause the short-run aggregate supply curve to shift right.

(2) Downward wage inflexibility primarily arises because of wage contracts and the legal minimum wage, but they may also occur from efficiency wages and insider–outsider relationships, according to new Keynesian economics.

(3) An **efficiency wage** minimizes the firm's labor cost per unit of output but may be higher than the market wage. This higher wage may result in greater efficiency because it stimulates greater work effort, requires less supervision costs, and reduces job turnover.

(4) **Insider–outsider relationships** may also produce downward wage inflexibility. During a recession, outsiders (who are less essential to the firm) may try to bid down wages to try to keep their jobs, but the firm may not lower wages because it does not want to alienate insiders (who are more essential to the firm) and disrupt the cooperative environment in the firm needed for production.

4. The debates over macro policy also focus on the need for **policy rules or discretion.**

a. Monetarists and new classical economists argue for policy rules to reduce government intervention in the economy. They believe this intervention causes macroeconomic instability.

(1) In regard to monetary policy, monetarists such as Milton Friedman have proposed a monetary rule that the money supply be increased at the same annual rate as the potential annual rate of increase in the real GDP. A monetary rule would shift aggregate demand rightward to match a shift in the long-run aggregate supply curve that occurs because of economic growth, thus keeping the price level stable over time. More recently economists have advocated inflation targeting as an alternative to a Friedman-type monetary rule.

(2) Monetarists and new classical economists question the value of fiscal policy, and some would like to see a balanced Federal budget over time. An expansionist fiscal policy will tend to crowd out investment and cause only a temporary increase in output. RET economists also think that fiscal policy is ineffective and that people will anticipate it and their acts will counteract its intended effects.

b. Mainstream economists think that discretionary fiscal and monetary policy can be effective and are opposed to a monetary rule and a balanced-budget requirement.

(1) They see the velocity of money as relatively unstable and a loose link between changes in the money supply and aggregate demand. This means that a mon-

etary rule might produce too great a shift in aggregate demand (and demand-pull inflation) or too small a shift (and deflation) to match the shift in aggregate supply. Such a rule would contribute to price instability, not price stability.

(2) They support the use of fiscal policy during a recession or to counter growing inflation. Fiscal policy, however, should be reserved for those situations where monetary policy is relatively ineffective. They also oppose a balanced-budget amendment because its effects would be pro-cyclical rather than countercyclical and would reinforce recessionary or inflationary tendencies.

c. Mainstream economists also note that there has been greater stability in the macro economy since 1946, when discretionary monetary and fiscal policies were more actively used to moderate the effects of the business cycle.

5. The ***disputes in macroeconomics*** have led to the incorporation of several ideas from monetarism and rational expectations theories into the mainstream thinking about macroeconomics. First, monetarists have gotten mainstream economists to recognize that changes in the money supply are important in explaining long-lasting and rapid inflation. Second, mainstream economists now recognize that expectations matter because of arguments from the rational expectations theory and theories about coordination failures in the economy. There will be more price stability, full employment, and economic growth if government can create reliable expectations of those outcomes for households and businesses. In short, macroeconomics continues to develop. Table 19.1 summarizes the three alternative views of macroeconomics.

■ HINTS AND TIPS

1. The chapter may appear complex because many alternative viewpoints are presented. To simplify matters, first focus on the three questions that the chapter addresses: What causes macro instability in the economy? Does the economy self-correct? Should policymakers use rules or discretion? For each question, identify how different types of economists answer each question.

2. Review the discussions of aggregate demand and aggregate supply in Chapters 11 and 16 as preparation for the comparison of alternate views of the macro economy presented in this chapter.

3. Monetarist and mainstream views of the macro economy are two approaches of looking at the same thing. The similarities can best be seen in equations in nominal form. The monetarist equation of exchange is $MV = PQ$. The Keynesian-based mainstream equation is $C_a + I_g + X_n + G = GDP$. The MV term is the monetarist expression for the mainstream equilibrium $C_a + I_g + X_n + G$. The PQ term is the monetarist expression for GDP. Monetarists give more emphasis to the role of money and assume that velocity is relatively stable. Mainstream economists give more emphasis to the instability caused by investment

spending and to influences on GDP from consumption, net exports, and government spending.

■ IMPORTANT TERMS

classical view	rational expectations theory
Keynesian view	new classical economics
monetarism	price-level surprises
equation of exchange	efficiency wage
velocity	insider–outsider theory
real-business-cycle theory	monetary rule
coordination failures	

■ FILL-IN QUESTIONS

1. The aggregate supply curve of the classical economists is (horizontal, vertical) _____, and the aggregate supply curve of the Keynesian economists is

_____ up to the full-employment level of output. Therefore, a decrease in aggregate demand will have no effect on price level and will decrease output and employment in the (classical, Keynesian) _____ model, but a decrease in aggregate demand will decrease the price level and have no effect on output and employ-

ment in the _____ model.

2. In the classical way of thinking, changes in the money supply shift the aggregate (demand, supply) _____ curve. If the money supply increases, then the curve will (increase, decrease)

_____, and if the money supply decreases,

then the curve will _____. If the nation's monetary authorities maintain a constant supply of money, this

curve will be (stable, unstable) _____.

3. From the Keynesian perspective, aggregate demand

is (stable, unstable) _____, even if there are no changes in the supply of money, largely because of the volatility in (investment, government) _____ spending.

4. The mainstream view is that macro instability is caused by changes in investment spending that shift the

aggregate (demand, supply) _____ curve. If it increases too rapidly, then (inflation, recession)

_____ can occur, but if it decreases, then

the economy can experience _____. Occasionally, adverse aggregate (demand, supply)

_____ shocks also cause instability.

5. Monetarists argue that capitalism is inherently (sta-

ble, unstable) _____ because most of its

markets are (competitive, noncompetitive) _____. They believe that government intervention in the economy has contributed to macroeconomic (stability, instability) _____ and has promoted (flexibility, inflexibility) _____ in wages.

6. The basic equation of the monetarists is _____ = _____. Indicate what each of the following four letters in the equation represents:

    a. *M:* _____

    b. *V:* _____

    c. *P:* _____

    d. *Q:* _____

7. Monetarists believe that *V* is relatively (stable, unstable) _____ because people have a _____ desire to hold money relative to holding other financial and real assets or for making purchases. The amount of money people will want to hold will depend on the level of (real, nominal) _____ GDP.

8. An increase in *M,* to the monetarist's way of thinking, will leave the public with (more, less) _____ money than it wishes to have, induce the public to (increase, decrease) _____ its spending for consumer and capital goods, which will result in a(n) _____ in aggregate demand and nominal GDP until nominal GDP equals *MV.*

9. Monetarists believe that the most significant cause of macroeconomic instability has been inappropriate (fiscal, monetary) _____ policy. Too rapid increases in *M* cause (recession, inflation) _____; insufficient growth of *M* causes _____.

10. The theory that changes in resource availability and technology (real factors), which alter productivity, are the main causes of instability in the macro economy is held by (real-business-cycle, rational expectations) _____ economists. In this theory, shifts in the economy's long-run aggregate (demand, supply) _____ curve change real output. As a consequence, money demand and money supply change, shifting the aggregate demand curve in the (opposite, same) _____ direction as the initial change in long-run aggregate supply. Real output thus can change (with, without) _____ a change in the price level.

11. A coordination failure is said to occur when people (do, do not) _____ reach a mutually benefi-

cial equilibrium because they lack some way to jointly coordinate their actions. In this view, there is (are) (one, a number of) _____ equilibrium position(s) in the economy. Macroeconomic instability is the result of changing (the money supply, expectations) _____ that result in changing the equilibrium position(s).

12. Monetarists and rational expectations economists view the economy as (capable, incapable) _____ of self-correction when it deviates from the full-employment level of real output. Monetarists suggest that this adjustment occurs (gradually, rapidly) _____, while rational expectations economists argue that it occurs _____.

13. Rational expectations theory assumes that with sufficient information, people's beliefs about future economic outcomes (are, are not) _____ accurate reflections of the likelihood of the outcomes occurring. It also assumes that markets are highly competitive, meaning that prices and wages are (flexible, inflexible) _____.

14. In the rational expectations theory, changes in aggregate demand that change the price level and real output are (anticipated, unanticipated) _____, while changes in aggregate demand that only change the price level and not real output are _____.

15. The view of mainstream economists is that many prices and wages are (flexible, inflexible) _____ downward for (short, long) _____ periods of time. This situation (increases, decreases) _____ the ability of the economy to automatically self-correct for deviations from full-employment output.

16. A higher wage can result in more efficiency because it results in (greater, less) _____ work effort, supervision costs that are (lower, higher) _____, and (more, less) _____ turnover in jobs. Efficiency wages (increase, decrease) _____ the downward inflexibility of wages because they make firms more reluctant to cut wages when aggregate demand declines.

17. Monetarists and rational expectations economists support a monetary rule because they believe that discretionary monetary policy tends to (stabilize, destabilize) _____ the economy. With this rule the money supply would be increased at a rate (greater than, less than, equal to) _____ the long-run growth of potential GDP; graphically, this can be shown by a shift in aggregate demand that would be _____ the shift in long-run aggregate supply resulting from economic growth.

18. Proponents of the rational expectations theory contend that discretionary monetary policy is (effective, ineffective) _____ and like the monetarists favor (rules, discretion) _____. When considering discretionary fiscal policy, most monetarists and RET economists (do, do not) _____ advocate its use.

19. Mainstream economists (support, oppose) _____ a monetary rule and a balanced-budget requirement. They view discretionary monetary policy as (effective, ineffective) _____, and think discretionary fiscal policy is _____ but should be held in reserve when monetary policy works too slowly. They say the use of discretionary monetary and fiscal policies since 1950 has produced (more, less) _____ stability in the macro economy.

20. Many ideas from alternative views of the macro economy have been absorbed into mainstream thinking about macroeconomics. There is more recognition that excessive growth of the money supply is a major cause of (recession, inflation) _____, and that expectations and coordination failures are (important, unimportant) _____ in the formulation of government policies for price stability, unemployment, and economic growth.

■ **TRUE–FALSE QUESTIONS**

Circle T if the statement is true, F if it is false.

1. The classical view is that the aggregate supply curve is vertical. **T F**

2. Classical economists consider the aggregate demand curve to be unstable. **T F**

3. Keynesians think that the aggregate supply curve is horizontal (to full-employment output). **T F**

4. Keynesians suggest that full employment is the norm in the economy. **T F**

5. The mainstream view is that macro instability is caused by the volatility of investment spending, which shifts the aggregate demand curve. **T F**

6. Monetarists argue that the market system would provide for macroeconomic stability were it not for government interference in the economy. **T F**

7. In the equation of exchange, the left side, **MV**, represents the total amount received by sellers of output, while the right side, **PQ,** represents the total amount spent by purchasers of that output. **T F**

8. Monetarists argue that **V** in the equation of exchange is relatively stable and that a change in **M** will bring about a direct and proportional change in **PQ**. **T F**

9. Most monetarists believe that an increase in the money supply has no effect on real output and employment in the short run. **T F**

10. In the monetarist view, the only cause of the Great Depression was the decline in investment spending. **T F**

11. Real-business-cycle theory views changes in resource availability and technology, which alter productivity, as the main cause of macroeconomic instability. **T F**

12. In the real-business-cycle theory, real output changes only with a change in the price level. **T F**

13. A coordination failure is said to occur when people do not reach a mutually beneficial equilibrium because they lack some way to jointly coordinate their actions to achieve it. **T F**

14. People's expectations have no effect on coordination failures. **T F**

15. New classical economists see the economy as automatically correcting itself when disturbed from its full-employment level of real output. **T F**

16. The rational expectations theory assumes that both product and resource markets are uncompetitive and wages and prices are inflexible. **T F**

17. In the rational expectations theory, a fully anticipated price-level change results in a change in real output. **T F**

18. Mainstream economists contend that many wages and prices are inflexible downward. **T F**

19. An efficiency wage is a below-market wage that spurs greater work effort and gives the firm more profits because of lower wage costs. **T F**

20. Insider–outsider theory offers one explanation for the downward inflexibility of wages in the economy. **T F**

21. Monetarists believe that a monetary rule would reduce instability in the macro economy. **T F**

22. Rational expectations economists argue that monetary policy should be left to the discretion of government. **T F**

23. Monetarists support the use of fiscal policy, especially as a means of controlling inflation. **T F**

24. Mainstream economists believe that discretionary monetary policy is an effective tool for stabilizing the economy. **T F**

25. The mainstream view of the economy since 1950 believes that the economy has become inherently less stable because of the use of fiscal policy. **T F**

■ MULTIPLE-CHOICE QUESTIONS

Circle the letter that corresponds to the best answer.

1. Classical economists suggest that full employment is
   (a) best achieved through government interventions
   (b) not possible in an unstable market economy
   (c) inversely related to the price level
   (d) the norm in a market economy

2. The aggregate supply curve of classical economists
   (a) is vertical
   (b) is horizontal
   (c) slopes upward
   (d) slopes downward

3. Classical theory concludes that the production behavior of firms will not change when the price level decreases because input costs would
   (a) rise along with product prices to leave real profits and output unchanged
   (b) fall along with product prices to leave real profits and output unchanged
   (c) fall, but product prices would rise, offsetting any change in real profits or output
   (d) rise, but product prices would rise, offsetting any change in real profits or output

4. In classical economics, a decrease in aggregate demand results in
   (a) a decrease in both the price level and domestic output
   (b) a decrease in the price level and no change in domestic output
   (c) no change in the price level and a decrease in domestic output
   (d) no change in either the price level or domestic output

5. The aggregate supply curve in the Keynesian model is
   (a) vertical at the full-employment output level
   (b) horizontal to the full-employment output level
   (c) positively sloped to the full-employment output level
   (d) negatively sloped to the full-employment output level

6. In the Keynesian model, a decrease in aggregate demand results in
   (a) a decrease in both the price level and domestic output
   (b) a decrease in the price level and no change in domestic output
   (c) no change in the price level and a decrease in domestic output
   (d) no change in either the price level or domestic output

7. The mainstream view of the economy holds that
   (a) government intervention in the economy is not desirable
   (b) product and labor markets are highly competitive and flexible

   (c) changes in investment spending lead to changes in aggregate demand
   (d) economic growth is best achieved through implementation of a monetary rule

8. In the monetarist perspective
   (a) discretionary monetary policy is the most effective way to moderate swings in the business cycle
   (b) government policies have reduced macroeconomic stability
   (c) macroeconomic stability results from adverse aggregate supply shocks
   (d) markets in a capitalistic economy are largely noncompetitive

9. Which is the equation of exchange?
   (a) $PQ/M + V = GDP$
   (b) $V = M + PQ$
   (c) $MV = PQ$
   (d) $V + I_g + M = GDP$

10. In the equation of exchange, if V is stable, an increase in M will necessarily increase
   (a) the demand for money
   (b) government spending
   (c) nominal GDP
   (d) velocity

11. When nominal gross domestic product (GDP) is divided by the money supply (M), you will obtain the
   (a) velocity of money
   (b) monetary multiplier
   (c) equation of exchange
   (d) monetary rule

12. Monetarists argue that the amount of money the public will want to hold depends primarily on the level of
   (a) nominal GDP
   (b) investment
   (c) taxes
   (d) prices

13. Real-business-cycle theory suggests that
   (a) velocity changes gradually and predictably; thus it is able to accommodate the long-run changes in nominal GDP
   (b) the volatility of investment is the main cause of the economy's instability
   (c) inappropriate monetary policy is the single most important cause of macroeconomic instability
   (d) changes in technology and resources affect productivity, and thus the long-run growth of aggregate supply

14. In the real-business-cycle theory, if the long-run aggregate supply increased, then aggregate demand would increase by
   (a) an equal amount, so real output and the price level would increase
   (b) less than an equal amount, so real output would increase and the price level would decrease
   (c) greater than an equal amount, so real output and the price level would increase
   (d) an equal amount, so real output would increase and the price level would be unchanged

15. If aggregate demand declined and the economy experienced a recession due to a self-fulfilling prophecy, this would be an example of
(a) real-business-cycle theory
(b) insider–outsider theory
(c) a coordination failure
(d) a change in velocity

16. In the new classical view, when the economy diverges from its full-employment output,
(a) internal mechanisms within the economy would automatically return it to its full-employment output
(b) discretionary monetary policy is needed to return it to its full-employment output
(c) discretionary fiscal policy is needed to return it to its full-employment output
(d) the adoption of an efficiency wage in the economy would return it to its full-employment output

17. The views about the speed of adjustment for self-correction in the economy suggest that
(a) monetarists think it would be gradual, and rational expectations economists think it would be quick
(b) monetarists think it would be quick, and rational expectations economists think it would be gradual
(c) monetarists and mainstream economists think it would be quick
(d) real-business-cycle theorists and rational expectations economists think it would be gradual

18. Proponents of the rational expectations theory argue that people
(a) are not as rational as monetarists assume them to be
(b) make forecasts that are based on poor information, causing economic policy to be driven by self-fulfilling prophecy
(c) form beliefs about future economic outcomes that accurately reflect the likelihood that those outcomes will occur
(d) do not respond quickly to changes in wages and prices, causing a misallocation of economic resources in the economy

19. In the rational expectations theory, a temporary change in real output would occur from a
(a) fully anticipated price-level change
(b) downward wage inflexibility
(c) coordination failure
(d) price-level surprise

20. The conclusion mainstream economists draw about the downward price and wage inflexibility is that
(a) the effects can be reversed relatively quickly
(b) efficiency wages do not contribute to the problem
(c) the economy can be mired in recession for long periods
(d) wage and price controls are needed to counteract the situation

21. According to mainstream economists, which of the following contributes to the downward inflexibility of wages?
(a) price-level surprises
(b) insider–outsider relationships
(c) adverse aggregate supply shocks
(d) inadequate investment spending

22. The rule suggested by the monetarists is that the money supply should be increased at the same rate as the
(a) price level
(b) interest rate
(c) velocity of money
(d) potential growth in real GDP

23. To stabilize the economy, monetarist and rational expectations economists advocate
(a) the use of price-level surprises and adoption of an efficiency wage
(b) a monetary rule and a balanced-budget requirement
(c) the use of discretionary fiscal policy instead of discretionary monetary policy
(d) the use of discretionary monetary policy instead of discretionary fiscal policy

24. Mainstream economists support
(a) increasing the money supply at a constant rate
(b) eliminating insider–outsider relationships in business
(c) the use of discretionary monetary and fiscal policies
(d) a balanced-budget requirement and a monetary rule

25. Which of the following would be an idea from monetarism that has been absorbed into mainstream macroeconomics?
(a) how changes in investment spending change aggregate demand
(b) the importance of money and the money supply in the economy
(c) using discretion rather than rules for guiding economic policy
(d) building the macro foundations for microeconomics

■ **PROBLEMS**

1. Assume that you are a monetarist in this problem and that **V** is stable and equal to 4. In the following table is the aggregate supply schedule: the real output **Q** which producers will offer for sale at seven different price levels **P**.

P	Q	PQ	MV
$1.00	100	$____	$____
2.00	110	____	____
3.00	120	____	____
4.00	130	____	____
5.00	140	____	____
6.00	150	____	____
7.00	160	____	____

a. Compute and enter in the table on the previous page the seven values of **PQ**.

b. Assume **M** is $90. Enter the values of **MV** on each of the seven lines in the table. The equilibrium

(1) nominal domestic output (**PQ** or **MV**) is $_____.

(2) price level is $_____.

(3) real domestic output (**Q**) is $_____.

c. When **M** increases to $175, **MV** at each price level

is $_____ and the equilibrium

(1) nominal domestic output is $_____.

(2) price level is $_____.

(3) real domestic output is $_____.

2. Indicate what perspective(s) of economics would be most closely associated with each position. Use the following abbreviations: **MAI** (mainstream economics), **MON** (monetarism), **RET** (rational expectations theory), and **RBC** (real-business-cycle theory).

    a. macro instability from investment spending

    _____

    b. macro instability from inappropriate monetary

    policy   _____

    c. macro instability from changes in resource

    availability and technology   _____

    d. equation of exchange   _____

    e. fiscal policy can be effective   _____

    f. unanticipated price-level changes   _____

    g. downward inflexibility of wages and prices_____

    h. monetary rule   _____

    i. neutral fiscal policy   _____

    j. economy automatically self-corrects   _____

    k. monetary policy is effective   _____

3. Following are price-level (**PL**) and output (**Q**) combinations to describe aggregate demand and aggregate supply curves: (1) **PL** and Q_1 is AD_1; (2) **PL** and Q_2 is AD_2; (3) **PL** and Q_3 is AS_{LR1}; (4) **PL** and Q_4 is AS_{LR2}.

PL	Q_1	Q_2	Q_3	Q_4
250	0	200	400	600
200	200	400	400	600
150	400	600	400	600
100	600	800	400	600
50	800	1,000	400	600

a. Use the following to graph AD_1, AD_2, AS_{LR1}, and AS_{LR2}. Label the vertical axis as the price level and the horizontal axis as real output (**Q**).

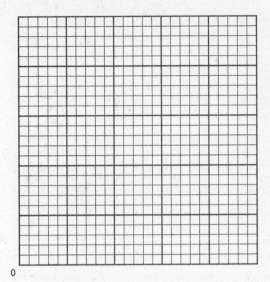

0

b. If the economy is initially in equilibrium where AD_1 and AS_{LR1} intersect, the price level will be _____ and real output will be _____.

c. If, over time, the economy grows from AS_{LR1} to AS_{LR2}, the equilibrium price level will be _____ and real output will be _____.

d. Assume a monetary rule is adopted that increases the money supply proportionate to the increase in aggregate supply. Aggregate demand will increase from AD_1 to AD_2, making the price level_____ and real output _____.

e. Mainstream economists would argue that velocity is unstable, so a constant increase in the money supply might not shift AD_1 all the way to AD_2. In this case, the price level would fall below the target of _____. It might also be the case that the constant increase in the money supply might shift AD_1 beyond AD_2, so the price level would rise above the target of _____.

■ SHORT ANSWER AND ESSAY QUESTIONS

1. What is the difference between the classical and Keynesian aggregate supply curves? Draw a graph showing the difference. What is the justification for each viewpoint?

2. What is the effect of a decrease in aggregate demand on the price level and real domestic output in the classical and Keynesian models? Show the change in a graph.

3. Why did classical economists consider the aggregate demand curve to be stable? What is the response of Keynesians to this position?

4. Why does the classical aggregate demand curve have a negative (downward) slope?

5. Explain the two causes of macroeconomic instability in the view of mainstream economists.

6. What do monetarists see as the cause of economic instability in the economy? Explain, using the equation of exchange, how a change in the money supply will affect nominal GDP.

7. Why do monetarists argue that the velocity of money is stable? If the money supply increases, how will people respond from a monetarist perspective?

8. Compare and contrast the monetarist and mainstream views on the causes of macroeconomic instability. How do monetarists explain the Great Depression?

9. Explain the real-business-cycle view of macroeconomic instability using an aggregate demand and supply graph.

10. Give a macroeconomic example of how coordination failures cause macroeconomic instability.

11. Explain the new classical view of self-correction in the macro economy. Contrast the monetarist perspective with that of rational expectations in terms of the real output, the price level, and the speed of adjustment.

12. Describe the two assumptions on which rational expectations are based. How realistic is it to expect that people will be able to accurately forecast economic outcomes?

13. Use a graph to illustrate and explain the mainstream view of self-correction in the macro economy.

14. Why would an efficiency wage lead to downward inflexibility in prices?

15. Give an example of insider–outsider relationships and explain how it affects wage flexibility.

16. What is the monetary rule? Why do monetarists suggest this rule to replace discretionary monetary policy?

17. What is the perspective of rational expectations economists on a monetary rule and the conduct of monetary policy?

18. What is the position of some monetarist and rational expectations economists on a requirement for a balanced budget? Why do they adopt such a position?

19. How do mainstream economists defend the use of discretionary monetary and fiscal policies? What interpretation do mainstream economists make of the historical evidence on the relationship between macroeconomic policy and instability?

20. What influences have monetarism and the rational expectations theory had on mainstream macroeconomic theory and policy? Give several examples of ideas that have changed mainstream thinking.

ANSWERS

Chapter 19 Disputes over Macro Theory and Policy

FILL-IN QUESTIONS

1. vertical, horizontal, Keynesian, classical
2. demand, increase, decrease, stable
3. unstable, investment
4. demand, inflation, recession, supply
5. stable, competitive, instability, inflexibility
6. $MV = PQ$; a. the money supply; b. the velocity of money; c. the average price of each unit of physical output; d. the physical volume of goods and services produced
7. stable, stable, nominal
8. more, increase, increase
9. monetary, inflation, recession
10. real-business-cycle, supply, same, without
11. do not, a number of, expectations
12. capable, gradually, rapidly
13. are, flexible
14. unanticipated, anticipated
15. inflexible, long, decreases
16. greater, lower, less, increase
17. destabilize, equal to, equal to
18. ineffective, rules, do not
19. oppose, effective, effective, more
20. inflation, important

TRUE–FALSE QUESTIONS

1. T, pp. 338–339	10. F, p. 342	19. F, pp. 346–347
2. F, p. 339	11. T, pp. 342–343	20. T, p. 347
3. T, p. 340	12. F, pp. 342–343	21. T, pp. 347–348
4. F, p. 340	13. T, p. 343	22. F, pp. 347–348
5. T, p. 340	14. F, p. 343	23. F, p. 348
6. T, p. 340	15. T, pp. 344–345	24. T, pp. 349–350
7. F, p. 341	16. F, pp. 345–346	25. F, p. 350
8. T, p. 341	17. F, pp. 345–346	
9. F, p. 341	18. T, p. 346	

MULTIPLE-CHOICE QUESTIONS

1. d, pp. 338–339	10. c, p. 341	19. d, pp. 345–346
2. a, pp. 338–339	11. a, p. 341	20. c, p. 346
3. b, pp. 338–339	12. a, pp. 341–342	21. b, p. 347
4. b, p. 339	13. d, pp. 342–343	22. d, pp. 347–348
5. b, p. 340	14. d, pp. 342–343	23. b, pp. 348–349
6. c, p. 340	15. c, pp. 343–344	24. c, pp. 349–350
7. c, p. 340	16. a, pp. 344–345	25. b, pp. 350–352
8. b, p. 341	17. a, p. 345	
9. c, p. 341	18. c, pp. 345–346	

PROBLEMS

1. a. 100, 220, 360, 520, 700, 900, 1120; b. 360, 360, 360, 360, 360, 360, 360, (1) 360, (2) 3.00, (3) 120; c. 700, (1) 700, (2) 5.00, (3) 140
2. a. MAI; b. MON, RET; c. RBC; d. MON; e. MAI; f. RET; g. MAI; h. MON, RET; i. MON, RET; j. MON, RET; k. MAI
3. a. graph similar to Figure 17.4 in the text; b. 150, 400; c. 100, 600; d. 150, 600; e. 150, 150

SHORT ANSWER AND ESSAY QUESTIONS

1. pp. 338–340	8. pp. 340–342	15. p. 347
2. pp. 338–340	9. pp. 342–343	16. pp. 348–349
3. pp. 339–340	10. p. 343	17. p. 349
4. pp. 338–339	11. pp. 344–345	18. p. 349
5. pp. 340–341	12. pp. 345–346	19. pp. 349–350
6. pp. 341–342	13. pp. 346–347	20. pp. 350–352
7. pp. 341–342	14. pp. 346–347	

CHAPTER 20

Elasticity of Demand and Supply

Chapter 20 is basically a continuation of Chapter 3, as you might have guessed from the chapter title. In the earlier part of the book, you needed only an elementary knowledge of supply and demand. Now the economic principles, problems, and policies to be studied require a more detailed discussion of supply and demand. Therefore, before you start reading Chapter 20, you are urged—you would be commanded if this were possible—to read and study Chapter 3 again. It is absolutely essential that you master Chapter 3 before reading Chapter 20.

The concept of *price elasticity of demand,* to which the major portion of Chapter 20 is devoted, is of great importance for studying the material found in the remainder of the text. You must understand (1) what price elasticity measures; (2) how the price-elasticity formula is applied to measure the price elasticity of demand; (3) the difference between price elastic, price inelastic, and unit elasticity; (4) how total revenue varies by the type of price elasticity of demand; (5) the meaning of perfect price elasticity and of perfect price inelasticity of demand; (6) the four major determinants of price elasticity of demand; and (7) the practical application of the concept to many economic issues.

When you have become thoroughly acquainted with the concept of price elasticity of demand, you will find that you have very little trouble understanding the *price elasticity of supply.* The transition requires no more than the substitution of the words "quantity supplied" for the words "quantity demanded." You should concentrate your attention on the meaning of price elasticity of supply and how it is affected by time. Several examples are provided to show how it affects the prices of many products.

The chapter also introduces you to two other elasticity concepts. The *cross elasticity of demand* measures the sensitivity of a change in the quantity demanded for one product due to a change in the price of another product. This concept is especially important in identifying substitute, complementary, or independent goods. The *income elasticity of demand* assesses the change in the quantity demanded of a product resulting from a change in consumer incomes. It is useful for categorizing products as superior, normal, or inferior.

The concepts of demand and supply, which have been expanded in this chapter to include discussion of elasticity and price ceilings and price floors, are the foundations of the next 10 chapters in the text. If you master the topics in this chapter, you will be prepared to understand the material in the chapters that follow.

■ CHECKLIST

When you have studied this chapter you should be able to

☐ Define price elasticity of demand and compute its coefficient when you are given the demand data.
☐ State two reasons why the formula for price elasticity of demand uses percentages rather than absolute amounts in measuring consumer responsiveness.
☐ Explain the meaning of elastic, inelastic, and unit elasticity as they relate to demand.
☐ Define and illustrate graphically the price elasticity of demand concepts of perfectly elastic and perfectly inelastic.
☐ State the midpoint formula for price elasticity of demand and explain how it refines the original formula for price elasticity.
☐ Describe the relationship between price elasticity of demand and the price range for most demand curves.
☐ Explain why the slope of the demand curve is not a sound basis for judging price elasticity.
☐ Apply the total-revenue test to determine whether demand is elastic, inelastic, or unit elastic.
☐ Illustrate graphically the relationship between price elasticity of demand and total revenue.
☐ List the four major determinants of the price elasticity of demand, and explain how each determinant affects price elasticity.
☐ Describe several applications of the concept of price elasticity of demand.
☐ Define the price elasticity of supply and compute its coefficient when given the relevant data.
☐ Explain the effect of time (short run and long run) on price elasticity of supply.
☐ Describe several applications of price elasticity of supply.
☐ Define cross elasticity of demand and compute its coefficient when given relevant data.
☐ Cite applications of cross elasticity of demand and income elasticity of demand.
☐ Define income elasticity of demand and compute its coefficient when given relevant data.

■ CHAPTER OUTLINE

1. *Price elasticity of demand* is a measure of the responsiveness or sensitivity of quantity demanded to changes in the price of a product. When quantity demanded is relatively responsive to a price change, demand is said to be **elastic.** When quantity demanded is relatively unresponsive to a price change, demand is said to be **inelastic.**

a. The exact degree of elasticity can be measured by using a formula to compute the elasticity coefficient.

(1) The changes in quantity demanded and in price are comparisons of consumer responsiveness to price changes of different products.

(2) Because price and quantity demanded are inversely related to each other, the price elasticity of demand coefficient is a negative number, but economists ignore the minus sign in front of the coefficient and focus their attention on its absolute value.

b. The coefficient of price elasticity has several interpretations.

(1) Demand is **elastic** when the percentage change in quantity is greater than the percentage change in price. The elasticity coefficient is greater than 1.

(2) Demand is **inelastic** when the percentage change in quantity is less than the percentage change in price. The elasticity coefficient is less than 1.

(3) Demand is **unit elastic** when the percentage change in quantity is equal to the percentage change in price. The elasticity coefficient is equal to 1.

(4) **Perfectly inelastic demand** means that a change in price results in no change in quantity demanded of a product, whereas **perfectly elastic demand** means that a small change in price causes buyers to purchase all they desire of a product.

c. A midpoint formula calculates price elasticity across a price and quantity range to overcome the problem of selecting the reference points for price and quantity. In this formula, the average of the two quantities and the average of the two prices are used as reference points.

d. Note several points about the graph of the demand curve and price elasticity of demand.

(1) It is not the same at all prices, and demand is typically elastic at higher and inelastic at lower prices.

(2) It cannot be judged from the slope of the demand curve.

e. **Total revenue** changes when price changes. The **total-revenue test** shows that when demand is:

(1) **elastic,** a decrease in price will increase total revenue and an increase in price will decrease total revenue.

(2) **inelastic,** a decrease in price will decrease total revenue and an increase in price will increase total revenue.

(3) **unit elastic,** an increase or decrease in price will not affect total revenue.

f. The relationship between price elasticity of demand and total revenue can be shown by graphing demand and total revenue, one above the other. In this case, the horizontal axis for each graph uses the same quantity scale. The vertical axis for demand represents price. The vertical axis for the total revenue graph measures total revenue.

(1) When demand is price elastic, as price declines and quantity increases along the demand curve, total revenue increases in the total revenue graph.

(2) Conversely, when demand is price inelastic, as price declines and quantity increases along the demand curve, total revenue decreases.

(3) When demand is unit elastic, as price and quantity change along the demand curve, total revenue remains the same.

g. The price elasticity of demand for a product depends on the number of good substitutes for the product, its relative importance in the consumer's budget, whether it is a necessity or a luxury, and the period of time under consideration.

h. Price elasticity of demand has practical applications to public policy and business decisions. The concept is relevant to bumper crops in agriculture, decriminalization of illegal drugs, and minimum wage laws.

2. **Price elasticity of supply** is a measure of the sensitivity of quantity supplied to changes in the price of a product.

a. There are both a general formula and a midpoint formula that are similar to those for the price elasticity of demand, but "quantity supplied" replaces "quantity demanded." This means that the elasticity of supply is the percentage change in quantity supplied of a product divided by its percentage change in the price of the product. There is a midpoint formula that is an average of quantities and prices and is used for calculating the elasticity of supply across quantity or price ranges. The price elasticity of supply depends primarily on the amount of time sellers have to adjust to a price change. The easier and faster suppliers can respond to changes in price, the greater the price elasticity of supply.

b. In the *market period,* there is too little time for producers to change output in response to a change in price. As a consequence supply is perfectly inelastic. Graphically, this means that the supply curve is vertical at that market level of output.

c. In the *short run*, producers have less flexibility to change output in response to a change in price because they have fixed inputs that they cannot change. They have only a limited control over the range in which they can vary their output. As a consequence, supply is *price inelastic* in the short run.

d. In the *long run*, producers can make adjustments to all inputs to vary production. As a consequence, supply is *price elastic* in the long run. There is no total-revenue test for price elasticity of supply because price and total revenue move in the same direction regardless of the degree of price elasticity of supply.

e. Price elasticity of supply has many practical applications for explaining price volatility. The concept is relevant to the pricing of antiques and gold, for which the supply is perfectly inelastic.

3. Two other elasticity concepts are important.

a. The **cross elasticity of demand** measures the degree to which the quantity demanded of one product is affected by a change in the price of another product; cross elasticities of demand are positive for substitute goods, negative for complementary goods, and essentially zero for independent goods.

b. The *income elasticity of demand* measures the effect of a change in income on the quantity demanded of a product; income elasticities of demand are positive for normal or superior goods, and negative for inferior goods.

■ **HINTS AND TIPS**

1. This chapter is an extension of the material presented in Chapter 3. Be sure you thoroughly review the contents and exercises in Chapter 3 before you do the self-test exercises for this chapter.

2. You should *not judge* the price elasticity of demand based on the slope of the demand curve unless it is horizontal (*perfectly elastic*) or vertical (*perfectly inelastic*). Remember that elasticity varies from elastic to inelastic along a downsloping, linear demand curve. The price elasticity equals 1 at the midpoint of a downsloping linear demand curve.

3. Master the *total-revenue test* for assessing the price elasticity of demand (review Table 20.2). For many problems, the total-revenue test is easier to use than the midpoint formula for identifying the type of elasticity (elastic, inelastic, unit), and the test has many practical applications.

4. Do not just memorize the elasticity formulas in this chapter. Instead, work on understanding what they mean and how they are used for economic decisions. The elasticity formulas simply measure the *responsiveness* of a percentage change in *quantity* to a percentage change in some other characteristic (price or income). The elasticity formulas each have a similar structure: A percentage change in some type of *quantity* (demanded, supplied) is divided by a percentage change in the other variable. The price elasticity of demand measures the responsiveness of a percentage change in *quantity demanded* for a product to a percentage change in its *price*. The cross elasticity of demand measures the percentage change in the *quantity demanded of product X* to a percentage change in the *price of product Y*. The income elasticity of demand is the percentage change in *quantity demanded* for a product to a percentage change in *income*. The price elasticity of supply is the percentage change in the *quantity supplied* of a product to a percentage change in its *price*.

SELF-TEST

■ **IMPORTANT TERMS**

price elasticity of demand	total-revenue test
elastic demand	price elasticity of supply
inelastic demand	market period
unit elasticity	short run
perfectly inelastic demand	long run
perfectly elastic demand	cross elasticity of demand
total revenue	income elasticity of demand

■ **FILL-IN QUESTIONS**

1. The present chapter begins the study of (macro, micro) _____ economics. This requires an analysis of the (revenues, markets) _____ and how (actions, prices) _____ are determined in them.

2. If a relatively large change in price results in a relatively small change in quantity demanded, demand is (elastic, inelastic) _____. If a relatively small change in price results in a relatively large change in quantity demanded, demand is (elastic, inelastic) _____.

3. The price elasticity formula is based on (absolute amounts, percentages) _____ because it avoids the problems caused by the arbitrary choice of units and permits meaningful comparisons of consumer (responsiveness, incomes) _____ to changes in the prices of different products.

4. If a change in price causes no change in quantity demanded, demand is perfectly (elastic, inelastic) _____ and the demand curve is (horizontal, vertical) _____. If an extremely small change in price causes an extremely large change in quantity demanded, demand is perfectly (elastic, inelastic) _____ and the demand curve is (horizontal, vertical) _____.

5. The midpoint formula for the price elasticity of demand uses the (total, average) _____ of the two quantities as a reference point in calculating the percentage change in quantity and the (total, average) _____ of the two prices as a reference point in calculating the percentage change in price.

6. Two characteristics of the price elasticity of a linear demand curve are that elasticity (is constant, varies) _____ over the different price ranges, and that the slope is (a sound, an unsound) _____ basis for judging its elasticity.

7. Assume the price of a product declines.
   a. When demand is inelastic, the loss of revenue due to the lower price is (less, greater) _____ than the gain in revenue due to the greater quantity demanded.
   b. When demand is elastic, the loss of revenue due to the lower price is (less, greater) _____ than the gain in revenue due to the greater quantity demanded.
   c. When demand is unit elastic, the loss of revenue due to the lower price (exceeds, is equal to)

_____ the gain in revenue due to the greater quantity demanded.

8. If demand is elastic, price and total revenue are (directly, inversely) _____ related, but if demand is inelastic, price and total revenue are (directly, inversely) _____ related.

9. Complete the following summary table.

If demand is	The elasticity coefficient is	If price rises, total revenue will	If price falls, total revenue will
Elastic	_____	_____	_____
Inelastic	_____	_____	_____
Unit elastic	_____	_____	_____

10. What are the four most important determinants of the price elasticity of demand?

a._____

b._____

c._____

d._____

11. The demand for most farm products is highly (elastic, inelastic) _____, which means that large crop yields will most likely (increase, decrease) _____ the total revenue of farmers.

12. Governments often tax products such as liquor, gasoline, and cigarettes because the price elasticity of the demand is (elastic, inelastic) _____. A higher tax on such products will (increase, decrease) _____ tax revenue.

13. The price elasticity of supply measures the percentage change in (price, quantity supplied) _____ divided by the percentage change in _____. If the percentage change in quantity was 30 percent and the percentage change in price was 40 percent, then the elasticity of supply would be (.75, 1.33) _____ and supply would be (elastic, inelastic) _____.

14. The most important factor affecting the price elasticity of supply is (revenue, time) _____. It is easier to shift resources to alternative uses when there is (more, less) _____ time.

15. In the immediate market period, the price elasticity of supply will be perfectly (elastic, inelastic) _____ and the supply curve will be (horizontal, vertical) _____.

16. Typically, in the short run the price elasticity of supply is (more, less) _____ elastic but in the long run the price elasticity of supply is _____ elastic.

17. There is a total-revenue test for the elasticity of (demand, supply) _____. There is no total-revenue test for the elasticity of (demand, supply) _____ because regardless of the degree of elasticity, price and total revenue are (directly, indirectly) _____ related.

18. The measure of the sensitivity of the consumption of one product given a change in the price of another product is the (cross, income) _____ elasticity of demand, while the measure of the responsiveness of consumer purchases to changes in income is the _____ elasticity of demand.

19. When the cross elasticity of demand is positive, two products are (complements, substitutes, independent) _____, but when the cross elasticity of demand is negative, they are _____; a zero cross elasticity suggests that two products are _____.

20. If consumers increase purchases of a product as consumer incomes increase, then a good is classified as (inferior, normal or superior) _____, but if consumers decrease purchases of a product as consumer incomes increase, then a good is classified as _____.

■ **TRUE–FALSE QUESTIONS**

Circle T if the statement is true, F if it is false.

1. If the percentage change in price is greater than the percentage change in quantity demanded, the price elasticity coefficient is greater than 1.　**T F**

2. If the quantity demanded for a product increases from 100 to 150 units when the price decreases from $14 to $10 using the midpoint formula, the price elasticity of demand for this product in this price range is 1.2.　**T F**

3. A product with a price elasticity of demand equal to 1.5 is described as price inelastic.　**T F**

4. The flatness or steepness of a demand curve is based on absolute changes in price and quantity, while elasticity is based on relative or percentage changes in price and quantity.　**T F**

5. Demand tends to be inelastic at higher prices and elastic at lower prices.　**T F**

6. Price elasticity of demand and the slope of the demand curve are two different things.　**T F**

7. If the price of a product increases from $5 to $6 and the quantity demanded decreases from 45 to 25, then according to the total-revenue test, the product is price inelastic in this price range.　**T F**

8. Total revenue will not change when price changes if the price elasticity of demand is unitary.　**T F**

9. When the absolute value of the price elasticity coefficient is greater than 1 and the price of the product decreases, then the total revenue will increase.　**T F**

10. In general, the larger the number of substitute goods that are available, the less the price elasticity of demand.　**T F**

11. Other things equal, the higher the price of a good relative to consumers' incomes, the greater the price elasticity of demand.　**T F**

12. Other things equal, the higher the price of a good relative to the longer the time period the purchase is considered, the greater the price elasticity of demand.　**T F**

13. The more that a good is considered to be a "luxury" rather than a "necessity," the less the price elasticity of demand.　**T F**

14. Studies indicate that the short-run demand for gasoline is price elastic, while the long-run response is price inelastic.　**T F**

15. The demand for most agricultural products is price inelastic. Consequently, an increase in supply will reduce the total income of producers of agricultural products.　**T F**

16. A state government seeking to increase its excise-tax revenues is more likely to increase the tax rate on restaurant meals than on gasoline.　**T F**

17. The degree of price elasticity of supply depends on how easily and quickly producers can shift resources between alternative uses.　**T F**

18. If an increase in product price results in no change in the quantity supplied, supply is perfectly elastic.　**T F**

19. The market period is a time so short that producers cannot respond to a change in demand and price.　**T F**

20. The price elasticity of supply will tend to be more elastic in the long run.　**T F**

21. There is a total revenue test for the elasticity of supply.　**T F**

22. For a complementary good, the coefficient of the cross elasticity of demand is positive.　**T F**

23. Cross elasticity of demand is measured by the percentage change in quantity demanded over the percentage change in income.　**T F**

24. A negative cross elasticity of demand for two goods indicates that they are complements.　**T F**

25. Inferior goods have a positive income elasticity of demand.　**T F**

■ MULTIPLE-CHOICE QUESTIONS

Circle the letter that corresponds to the best answer.

1. If, when the price of a product rises from $1.50 to $2, the quantity demanded of the product decreases from 1000 to 900, the price elasticity of demand coefficient, using the midpoint formula, is
(a) 3.00
(b) 2.71
(c) 0.37
(d) 0.33

2. If a 1% fall in the price of a product causes the quantity demanded of the product to increase by 2%, demand is
(a) inelastic
(b) elastic
(c) unit elastic
(d) perfectly elastic

3. In the following diagram, D_1 is a
(a) perfectly elastic demand curve
(b) perfectly inelastic demand curve
(c) unit elastic demand curve
(d) long-run demand curve

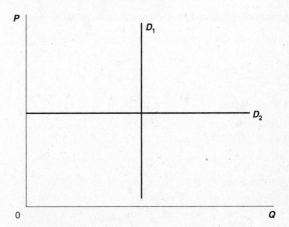

4. Compared to the lower-right portion, the upper-left portion of most demand curves tends to be
(a) more inelastic
(b) more elastic
(c) unit elastic
(d) perfectly inelastic

5. In which range of the demand schedule is demand price inelastic?

Price	Quantity demanded
$11	50
9	100
7	200
5	300
3	400

(a) $11–$9
(b) $9–$7
(c) $7–$5
(d) $5–$3

6. If a business increased the price of its product from $7 to $8 when the price elasticity of demand was inelastic, then
   (a) total revenues decreased
   (b) total revenues increased
   (c) total revenues remain unchanged
   (d) total revenues were perfectly inelastic

7. You are the sales manager for a pizza company and have been informed that the price elasticity of demand for your most popular pizza is greater than 1. To increase total revenues, you should
   (a) increase the price of the pizza
   (b) decrease the price of the pizza
   (c) hold pizza prices constant
   (d) decrease demand for your pizza

8. Assume Amanda Herman finds that her total spending on compact discs remains the same after the price of compact discs falls, other things equal. Which of the following is true about Amanda's demand for compact discs with this price change?
   (a) It is unit price elastic.
   (b) It is perfectly price elastic.
   (c) It is perfectly price inelastic.
   (d) It increased in response to the price change.

Questions 9, 10, and 11 are based on the following graph.

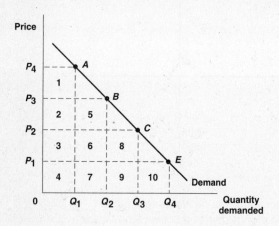

9. If price is P_3, then total revenue is measured by the area
   (a) $0P_3\,CQ_3$
   (b) $0P_3\,BQ_2$
   (c) $0P_3\,BQ_3$
   (d) $0P_3\,CQ_2$

10. If price falls from P_2 to P_1, then in this price range demand is
   (a) relatively inelastic because the loss in total revenue (areas $3 + 6 + 8$) is greater than the gain in total revenue (area 10)
   (b) relatively elastic because the loss in total revenue (areas $3 + 6 + 8$) is greater than the gain in total revenue (area 10)
   (c) relatively inelastic because the loss in total revenue (area 10) is less than the gain in total revenue (areas $3 + 6 + 8$)

(d) relatively inelastic because the loss in total revenue (areas $4 + 7 + 9 + 10$) is greater than the gain in total revenue (areas $3 + 6 + 8$)

11. As price falls from P_4 to P_3, you know that demand is
   (a) elastic because total revenue decreased from $0P_4\,AQ_1$ to $0P_3\,BQ_2$
   (b) inelastic because total revenue decreased from $0P_3\,BQ_2$ to $0P_4\,AQ_1$
   (c) elastic because total revenue increased from $0P_4\,AQ_1$ to $0P_3\,BQ_2$
   (d) inelastic because total revenue decreased from $0P_4\,AQ_1$ to $0P_3\,BQ_2$

12. Which product is most likely to be the most price elastic?
   (a) bread
   (b) clothing
   (c) restaurant meals
   (d) local telephone service

13. Which is characteristic of a product whose demand is elastic?
   (a) The price elasticity coefficient is less than 1.
   (b) Total revenue decreases if price decreases.
   (c) Buyers are relatively insensitive to price changes.
   (d) The percentage change in quantity is greater than the percentage change in price.

14. The demand for Nike basketball shoes is more price elastic than the demand for basketball shoes as a whole. This is best explained by the fact that
   (a) Nike basketball shoes are a luxury good, not a necessity
   (b) Nike basketball shoes are the best made and widely advertised
   (c) there are more complements for Nike basketball shoes than for basketball shoes as a whole
   (d) there are more substitutes for Nike basketball shoes than for basketball shoes as a whole

15. Which is characteristic of a good whose demand is inelastic?
   (a) There are a large number of good substitutes for the good for consumers.
   (b) The buyer spends a small percentage of total income on the good.
   (c) The good is regarded by consumers as a luxury.
   (d) The period of time for which demand is given is relatively long.

16. From a time perspective, the demand for most products is
   (a) less elastic in the short run and unit elastic in the long run
   (b) less elastic in the long run and unit elastic in the short run
   (c) more elastic in the short run than in the long run
   (d) more elastic in the long run than in the short run

17. If a 5% fall in the price of a commodity causes quantity supplied to decrease by 8%, supply is
   (a) inelastic

(b) unit elastic
(c) elastic
(d) perfectly inelastic

18. In the following diagram, what is the price elasticity of supply between points **A** and **C**?
(a) 1.33
(b) 1.67
(c) 1.85
(d) 2.46

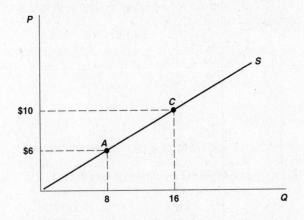

19. If supply is inelastic and demand decreases, the total revenue of sellers will
(a) increase
(b) decrease
(c) decrease only if demand is elastic
(d) increase only if demand is inelastic

20. The chief determinant of the price elasticity of supply of a product is
(a) the number of good substitutes the product has
(b) the length of time sellers have to adjust to a change in price
(c) whether the product is a luxury or a necessity
(d) whether the product is a durable or a nondurable good

21. A study shows that the coefficient of the cross elasticity of Coke and Sprite is negative. This information indicates that Coke and Sprite are
(a) normal goods
(b) complementary goods
(c) substitute goods
(d) independent goods

22. If a 5% increase in the price of one good results in a decrease of 2% in the quantity demanded of another good, then it can be concluded that the two goods are
(a) complements
(b) substitutes
(c) independent
(d) normal

23. Most goods can be classified as *normal* goods rather than inferior goods. The definition of a normal good means that

(a) the percentage change in consumer income is greater than the percentage change in price of the normal good
(b) the percentage change in quantity demanded of the normal good is greater than the percentage change in consumer income
(c) as consumer income increases, consumer purchases of a normal good increase
(d) the income elasticity of demand is negative

24. Based on the information in the table, which product would be an inferior good?

Product	% change in income	% change in quantity demanded
A	−10	+10
B	+10	+10
C	+5	+5
D	−5	−5

(a) Product A
(b) Product B
(c) Product C
(d) Product D

25. For which product is the income elasticity of demand most likely to be negative?
(a) automobiles
(b) bus tickets
(c) computers
(d) tennis rackets

■ **PROBLEMS**

1. Complete the following table, using the demand data given, by computing total revenue at each of the seven prices and the six price elasticity coefficients between each of the seven prices, and indicate whether demand is elastic, inelastic, or unit elastic between each of the seven prices.

Price	Quantity demanded	Total revenue	Elasticity coefficient	Character of demand
$1.00	300	$_____		
.90	400	_____	_____	_____
.80	500	_____	_____	_____
.70	600	_____	_____	_____
.60	700	_____	_____	_____
.50	800	_____	_____	_____
.40	900	_____	_____	_____

2. Use the data from the table for this problem. On the *first* of the two following graphs, plot the demand curve (price and quantity demanded) and indicate the elastic, inelastic, and unit elastic portions of the demand curve. On the *second* graph, plot the total revenue on the vertical axis and the quantity demanded on the horizontal axis. (*Note:* The scale for quantity demanded that you plot on the horizontal axis of each graph should be the same.)

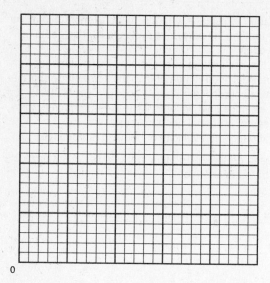

0

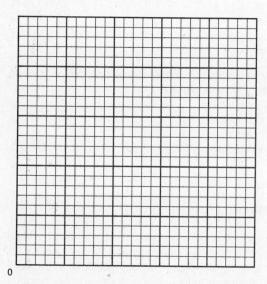

0

a. As price decreases from $1.00 to $0.70, demand is

(elastic, inelastic, unit elastic) _____ and total revenue (increases, decreases, remains the

same) _____.

b. As price decreases from $0.70 to $0.60, demand is

(elastic, inelastic, unit elastic) _____ and total revenue (increases, decreases, remains the

same) _____.

c. As price decreases from $0.60 to $0.40, demand is

(elastic, inelastic, unit elastic) _____ and total revenue (increases, decreases, remains the

same) _____.

3. Using the supply data in the following schedule, complete the table by computing the six price elasticity of supply coefficients between each of the seven prices, and indicate whether supply is elastic, inelastic, or unit elastic.

Price	Quantity demanded	Elasticity coefficient	Character of supply
$1.00	800		
.90	700	_____	_____
.80	600	_____	_____
.70	500	_____	_____
.60	400	_____	_____
.50	300	_____	_____
.40	200	_____	_____

4. The following graph shows three different supply curves (S_1, S_2, and S_3) for a product bought and sold in a competitive market.

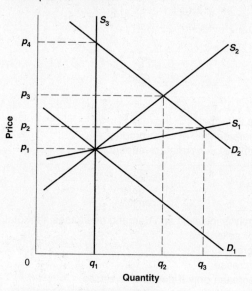

a. The supply curve for the

(1) market period is the one labeled _____.

(2) short run is the one labeled _____.

(3) long run is the one labeled _____.

b. No matter what the period of time under consideration, if the demand for the product were D_1, the equilibrium price of the product would be

_____ and the equilibrium quantity would

be _____.

(1) If demand were to increase to D_2 in the market period the equilibrium price would increase to

_____ and the equilibrium quantity would

be _____.

(2) In the short run the price of the product would increase to _____ and the quantity would

increase to _____.

(3) In the long run the price of the product would be

_____ and the quantity would be

_____.

c. The longer the period of time allowed to sellers to adjust their outputs, the (more, less)

_____ elastic is the supply of the product.

d. The more elastic the supply of a product, the (greater, less) _____ the effect on equilibrium price and the _____ the effect on equilibrium quantity of an increase in demand.

5. For the following three cases, use a midpoint formula to calculate the coefficient for the cross elasticity of demand and identify the relationship between the two goods (complement, substitute, or independent).

a. The quantity demanded for good A increases from 300 to 400 as the price of good B increases from $1 to $2. Coefficient: _____ Relationship: _____

b. The quantity demanded for good J decreases from 2000 to 1500 as the price of good K increases from $10 to $15. Coefficient: _____ Relationship: _____

c. The quantity demanded for good X increases from 100 to 101 units as the price of good Y increases from $8 to $15. Coefficient: _____ Relationship: _____

6. Use the information in the following table to identify the income characteristic of each product A–E using the following labels: **N** = normal (or superior), **I** = inferior.

Product	% change in income	% change in quantity demanded	Income type (N or I)
A	10	10	_____
B	1	15	_____
C	5	−12	_____
D	5	−2	_____
E	10	1	_____

■ **SHORT ANSWER AND ESSAY QUESTIONS**

1. Define and explain the price elasticity of demand in terms of the relationship between the relative (percentage) change in quantity demanded and the relative (percentage) change in price. Use the elasticity coefficient in your explanation.

2. What is meant by perfectly elastic demand? By perfectly inelastic demand? What does the demand curve look like when demand is perfectly elastic and when it is perfectly inelastic?

3. In computing the price elasticity coefficient, it usually makes a considerable difference whether the higher price and lower quantity or the lower price and higher quantity are used as points of reference. What have economists done to eliminate the confusion that would arise if the price elasticity of demand coefficient varied and depended upon whether a price rise or fall were being considered?

4. Demand seldom has the same elasticity at all prices. What is the relationship between the price of most products and the price elasticity of demand for them?

5. Define and explain the price elasticity of demand in terms of the change in total revenue when price changes.

6. What is the relationship—if there is one—between the price elasticity of demand and the slope of the demand curve?

7. When the price of a product declines, the quantity demanded of it increases. When demand is elastic, total revenue is greater at the lower price, but when demand is inelastic, total revenue is smaller. Explain why total revenue will sometimes increase and why it will sometimes decrease.

8. Explain the effect of the number of substitutes on the price elasticity of demand.

9. Why does the price elasticity of demand differ based on the price of a good as a proportion of household income? Give examples.

10. Is the quantity demanded for necessities more or less responsive to a change in price? Explain using examples.

11. What role does time play in affecting the elasticity of demand?

12. How do opponents of the decriminalization of illegal drugs use elasticity to make their arguments?

13. Explain what determines the price elasticity of supply of an economic good or service.

14. Explain the distinction between the intermediate market period, the short run, and the long run.

15. Why is there no total revenue test for the elasticity of supply?

16. Discuss the supply and demand conditions for antiques. Why are antique prices so high?

17. Use the concepts of the elasticity of supply to explain the volatility of gold prices.

18. How can goods be classified as complementary, substitute, or independent? On what basis is this judgment made?

19. Give definitions of a normal good and an inferior good. Illustrate each definition with an example.

20. What are two examples of insights that income elasticity of demand coefficients provide about the economy?

ANSWERS

Chapter 20 Elasticity of Demand and Supply

FILL-IN QUESTIONS

1. micro, markets, prices
2. inelastic, elastic
3. percentages, responsiveness
4. inelastic, vertical, elastic, horizontal
5. average, average
6. varies, an unsound
7. *a.* greater; *b.* less; *c.* is equal to
8. inversely, directly
9. Elastic: greater than 1, decrease, increase; Inelastic: less than 1, increase, decrease; Unit elastic: equal to 1, remain constant, remain constant

10. *a.* The number of good substitute products; *b.* The relative importance of the product in the total budget of the buyer; *c.* Whether the good is a necessity or a luxury; *d.* The period of time in which demand is being considered (any order *a–d*)

11. inelastic, decrease

12. inelastic, increase

13. quantity supplied, price, .75, inelastic

14. time, more

15. inelastic, vertical

16. less, more

17. demand, supply, directly

18. cross, income

19. substitutes, complements, independent

20. normal or superior, inferior

TRUE–FALSE QUESTIONS

1. F, pp. 356–357

2. T, pp. 358–359

3. F, p. 357

4. T, p. 359

5. F, pp. 359–360

6. T, p. 359

7. F, pp. 360–361

8. T, p. 361

9. T, pp. 360–361

10. F, p. 362

11. T, p. 362

12. T, p. 362

13. F, p. 362

14. F, p. 363

15. T, p. 363

16. F, pp. 363–364

17. T, p. 365

18. F, p. 365

19. T, p. 365

20. T, p. 366

21. F, p. 366

22. F, p. 367

23. F, p. 367

24. T, p. 367

25. F, p. 368

MULTIPLE-CHOICE QUESTIONS

1. c, pp. 358–359

2. b, p. 357

3. b, p. 358

4. b, p. 359

5. d, pp. 359–360

6. b, pp. 360–361

7. b, pp. 360–361

8. a, p. 361

9. b, pp. 360–361

10. a, pp. 360–361

11. c, pp. 360–361

12. c, pp. 362–363

13. d, p. 362

14. d, p. 362

15. b, p. 362

16. d, pp. 362–363

17. c, pp. 364–365

18. a, pp. 364–365

19. b, p. 366

20. b, pp. 365–366

21. b, p. 367

22. a, p. 367

23. c, p. 368

24. a, p. 368

25. b, p. 368

PROBLEMS

1. Total revenue: $300, 360, 400, 420, 420, 400, 360; Elasticity coefficient: 2.71, 1.89, 1.36, 1, 0.73, 0.53; Character of demand: elastic, elastic, elastic, unit elastic, inelastic, inelastic

2. *a.* elastic, increases; *b.* unit elastic, remains the same; *c.* inelastic, decreases

3. Elasticity coefficient: 1.27, 1.31, 1.36, 1.44, 1.57, 1.8; Character of supply: elastic, elastic, elastic, elastic, elastic, elastic

4. *a.* (1) S_3; (2) S_2; (3) S_1; *b.* p_1, q_1; (1) p_4, q_1; (2) p_3, q_2; (3) p_2, q_3; *c.* more; *d.* less, greater

5. *a.* 43, substitute; *b.* −.71, complement; *c.* .02, independent

6. N, N, I, I, N

SHORT ANSWER AND ESSAY QUESTIONS

1. pp. 356–357

2. pp. 356–357

3. pp. 358–359

4. p. 359

5. pp. 360–361

6. p. 359

7. pp. 360–361

8. p. 362

9. p. 362

10. p. 362

11. pp. 362–363

12. p. 368

13. p. 365

14. pp. 365–366

15. p. 366

16. p. 366

17. pp. 366–367

18. p. 368

19. p. 369

20. p. 369

CHAPTER 21

Consumer Behavior and Utility Maximization

Previous chapters explained that consumers typically buy more of a product as its price decreases and less of a product as its price increases. Chapter 21 looks behind this law of demand to explain why consumers behave this way.

Two explanations for the law of demand are presented. The first explanation is a general and simple one based on *income effects* and *substitution effects*. From this perspective, a change in the price of a product changes the amount consumed because of a change in the real income and a change in the price of this good relative to other products that could be purchased. The other explanation is more detailed and abstract because it is based on the concept of *marginal utility*. In this view, the additional satisfaction (or marginal utility) that a consumer obtains from the consumption of each additional unit of a product will tend to decline; therefore a consumer will have an incentive to purchase additional units of a product only if its price falls. (A third explanation of consumer demand that is more complete than the first two is based on the use of indifference curves; this more complex topic is discussed in the appendix to the chapter.)

Most of this chapter presents the *marginal-utility* view of consumer behavior. This explanation requires that you first understand the concepts and assumptions on which this theory of consumer behavior rests, and second, do some rigorous reasoning using these concepts and assumptions. It is an exercise in logic, but be sure that you follow the reasoning. To help you, several problems are provided so that you can work things out for yourself.

No one believes that consumers actually perform these mental gymnastics before they spend their incomes or make purchases. But we study the marginal-utility approach to consumer behavior because the consumers behave as if they made their purchases on the basis of very fine calculations. Thus, this approach explains what we do in fact observe and makes it possible for us to predict with a good deal of precision how consumers will react to changes in their incomes and the prices of products.

The final section of the chapter describes how the theory of consumer behavior can be used to explain many economic events in the real world. The five applications discussed are the takeover by compact discs of the market for recorded music, the water-diamond paradox, the value of time in consumption, the reasons for increased consumer purchases of medical care, and the economic effects of cash and noncash gifts. Be sure you understand how consumer theory is used to explain these five phenomena.

■ CHECKLIST

When you have studied this chapter you should be able to

☐ Define and distinguish between the income and the substitution effects of a price change.
☐ Use the income and the substitution effects to explain why a consumer will buy more of a product when its price falls and less of a product when its price rises.
☐ Define utility, marginal utility, and total utility.
☐ Describe the law of diminishing marginal utility.
☐ Explain the relationship of the law of diminishing marginal utility to demand and elasticity.
☐ List four dimensions of the typical consumer's situation.
☐ State the utility-maximizing rule.
☐ When you are given the utility and price data, use the utility-maximizing rule to determine how consumers would spend their fixed incomes.
☐ Explain how a consumer decides between an optimal and an inferior solution to a utility-maximization problem.
☐ Give an algebraic restatement of the utility-maximizing rule based on an example using two products, A and B.
☐ Derive a consumer's demand for a product from utility, income, and price data.
☐ Explain how the income and substitution effects are involved in utility maximization and the deriving of the demand curve for a product.
☐ Give examples of how consumer theory can be used to explain such economic situations as the
  (1) popularity of DVDs and DVD players,
  (2) diamond-water paradox,
  (3) value of time in consumption,
  (4) consumer purchases of medical care, and
  (5) tradeoffs between cash and noncash gifts.

■ CHAPTER OUTLINE

1. The *law of consumer demand* can be explained in two ways.
   a. The first explanation is the income and substitution effects
   (1) The *income effect* is the impact that a change in the price of a product has on a consumer's real income and thus the quantity demanded of that product. Consumers buy more of a product when its price falls because their real income will increase, and thus they can afford to buy more (if the product is a normal good).

(2) The **substitution effect** is the impact that a change in the price of a product has on how expensive it is relative to other products, and thus the quantity demanded of that product. Consumers buy more of a product when its price falls because the product is now less expensive compared to other products.

b. The second explanation is based on the **law of diminishing marginal utility** that describes how consumers will spend their income.

(1) **Utility** is subjective and difficult to quantify. For the purposes of this chapter it will be assumed that utility is the satisfaction or pleasure a person gets from consuming a product. It will be measured in hypothetical units called *utils.*

(2) **Total utility** is the total amount of satisfaction that a consumer obtains from consuming a product. **Marginal utility** is the extra satisfaction that a consumer obtains from consuming an additional or extra unit of a product. The principle that the marginal utility of a product falls as a consumer uses (consumes) additional units of a product is the law of diminishing marginal utility.

(3) Marginal utility, demand, and elasticity are related. If marginal utility falls sharply as additional units of a product are consumed, then demand is *inelastic.* If marginal utility falls slowly as additional units of a product are consumed, then demand is *elastic.*

2. The **law of diminishing marginal utility** is the basis of the theory that explains how consumers will spend their incomes for particular goods and services.

a. It is assumed that the typical consumer is rational, knows marginal-utility schedules for the various goods available, has a limited money income to spend, and must pay a price to acquire each of the goods that yields utility.

b. Given these assumptions, the consumer maximizes the total utility obtained when the marginal utility of the last dollar spent on each product is the same for all products (the **utility-maximizing rule**).

c. A numerical example is used to illustrate the rule using two products, A and B, and assuming that all money income is spent on one of the two products. In making the decision, the rational consumer must compare the extra or marginal utility from each product with its added cost (as measured by its price). Thus, marginal utility is compared on a per-dollar basis.

d. The allocation rule states that consumers will maximize their satisfaction when they allocate their money income so that the last dollar spent on each product yields the same marginal utility. In the two-product case, this can be stated algebraically as

$$\frac{\text{Marginal utility of A}}{\text{Price of A}} = \frac{\text{Marginal utility of B}}{\text{Price of B}}$$

Total utility is a maximum when the marginal utility of the last unit of a product purchased divided by its price is the same for all products.

3. The utility-maximizing rule can be applied to determine the amount of the product the consumer will purchase at different prices with income, tastes, and the prices of other products remaining constant.

a. The numerical example that is used is based on one price for a product. If the price of the product falls, it is possible to use the utility-maximizing rule to determine how much more of the product the consumer will purchase. Based on this exercise it is possible to show the inverse relationship between price and quantity demanded as shown by a demand curve.

b. Utility maximization can also be understood in terms of the income and substitution effects to explain the law of demand. As the price of a product drops, a consumer increases the amounts purchased to restore equilibrium following the utility-maximizing rule. The change can be viewed as the consumer substituting more of the now less-expensive product for another product and having more real income to spend.

4. Five of the many **applications** and **extensions** of consumer theory for the real world are discussed in this chapter.

a. DVDs have gained popularity among consumers relative to videocassettes (VCs) because many consumers have concluded that DVDs have a higher ratio of marginal utility to price than the ratio for VCs.

b. Diamonds are high in price, but of limited usefulness, while water is low in price, but essential for life. This diamond-water paradox is explained by distinguishing between marginal and total utility. Water is low in price because it is generally in plentiful supply and thus has low marginal utility. Diamonds are high in price because they are relatively scarce and thus have high marginal utility. Water, however, is considered more useful than diamonds because it has much greater total utility.

c. The facts that consumption takes time and time is a scarce resource can be included in the marginal-utility theory. The full price of any consumer good or service is equal to its market price plus the value of time taken to consume it (i.e., the income the consumer could have earned had he or she used that time for work).

d. Expenditures on medical care have increased because of its financing through insurance. Under this system, the consumer does not pay the full price of medical care services and thus has an incentive to consume more than would be the case if the consumer paid the full price.

e. Cash gifts tend to be more efficient for consumers because they are more likely to match consumer preferences and increase the total utility compared to noncash gifts that restrict consumer choice.

■ **HINTS AND TIPS**

1. Remember that a change in the price of a good has both an **income effect** and a **substitution effect.** For most products, a price decrease gives consumers more income to spend on that product and other products, so the quantity demanded for that product increases. The three steps in the logic for typical product A are (1) $P_A\downarrow$, (2) income$\uparrow$, and (3) $Q_{dA}\uparrow$. A price decrease also makes product A more attractive to buy relative to its substitutes, so the demand for these substitutes decreases and the quantity demanded for product A increases. Again, there are three steps in the logic: (1) $P_A\downarrow$, (2) demand for substitutes$\downarrow$, and (3) $Q_{dA}\uparrow$. In both cases, the end result is the same: $Q_{dA}\uparrow$. Practice your understanding by showing the logic for an increase in the price of product A.

2. *Utility* is simply an abstraction useful for explaining consumer behavior. Do not become overly concerned with the precise measurement of utility or satisfaction. What you should focus on is the relative comparison of the additional satisfaction (marginal utility) from a dollar spent on one good to the additional satisfaction obtained from a dollar spent on another good. The choice of producing more additional utility satisfaction from one good than the other will maximize consumer satisfaction. Thus, you just need to know which good won the contest, not the final score (how much additional utility was added).

3. Master the difference between marginal utility and total utility. Once you think you understand the difference, use the concepts to explain to someone the diamond-water paradox at the end of the chapter.

■ **IMPORTANT TERMS**

income effect	law of diminishing marginal utility
substitution effect	rational behavior
utility	budget constraint
total utility	utility-maximizing rule
marginal utility	

SELF-TEST

■ **FILL-IN QUESTIONS**

1. The law of demand can be explained in terms of income and (complements, substitution) _____ effects or by the law of (increasing, diminishing) _____ marginal utility.

2. A fall in the price of a product tends to (increase, decrease) _____ a consumer's real income, and a rise in its price tends to _____ real income. This is called the (substitution, income) _____ effect.

3. When the price of a product increases, the product becomes relatively (more, less) _____ expensive than it was and the prices of other products become relatively (higher, lower) _____ than they were; the consumer will therefore buy (less, more) _____ of the product in question and _____ of the other products. This is called the (substitution, income) _____ effect.

4. The overall satisfaction a consumer gets from consuming a good or service is (marginal, total) _____ utility, but the extra or additional satisfaction that a consumer gets from a good or service is (marginal, total) _____ utility. Utility is (an objective, a subjective) _____ concept and (is, is not) _____ the same thing as usefulness.

5. The law of diminishing marginal utility states that marginal utility will (increase, decrease) _____ as a consumer increases the quantity consumed of a product.

6. A graph of total utility and marginal utility shows that when total utility is increasing, marginal utility is (positive, negative) _____, and when total utility is at a maximum, marginal utility is at (a maximum, zero, a minimum) _____.

7. Assuming all other things equal, if the marginal utility of a product decreases rapidly as additional units are consumed, then demand is likely to be (elastic, inelastic) _____, but if marginal utility decreases slowly as consumption increases, then it suggests that demand is _____.

8. The marginal-utility theory of consumer behavior assumes that the consumer is (wealthy, rational) _____ and has certain (preferences, discounts) _____ for various goods.

9. A consumer cannot buy every good and service desired because income is (subsidized, limited) _____ and goods and services are (unlimited, scarce) _____ in relation to the demand for them; thus they have (prices, quantities) _____ attached to them.

10. When the consumer is maximizing the utility the consumer's income will obtain, the ratio of the marginal utility of the (first, last) _____ unit purchased of a product to its price is (the same, greater than) _____ for all the products bought.

11. If the marginal utility of the last dollar spent on one product is greater than the marginal utility of the last dollar spent on another product, the consumer should (increase, decrease) _____ purchases of the first and _____ purchases of the second product.

12. Assume there are only two products, X and Y, that a consumer can purchase with a fixed income. The consumer is maximizing utility algebraically when:

a. _____ = c. _____
b. _____   d. _____

13. In deriving a consumer's demand for a particular product, the two factors (other than the preferences or tastes of the consumer) that are held constant are

a._____

b._____

14. The utility-maximizing rule and the demand curve are logically (consistent, inconsistent) _____. Because marginal utility declines, a lower price is needed to get the consumer to buy (less, more) _____ of a particular product.

15. When consumer preferences changed from video-cassette tapes to DVDs, and the prices of DVD players (increased, decreased) _____ significantly, this led to (increased, decreased) _____ purchases of DVDs.

16. Water is low in price because its (total, marginal) _____ utility is low, while diamonds are high in price because their _____ utility is high. Water, however, is more useful than diamonds because the (total, marginal) _____ utility of water is much greater than the _____ utility of diamonds.

17. The theory of consumer behavior has been generalized to account for (supply, time) _____. This is a valuable economic resource because it is (limited, unlimited) _____. Its value is (greater than, equal to) _____ the income that can be earned with it. The full price to the consumer of any product is, therefore, the market (time, price) _____ plus the value of the consumption _____.

18. With health insurance coverage, the price consumers pay for health care services is less than the "true" value or opportunity (benefit, cost) _____. The lower price to consumers encourages them to consume (more, less) _____ health care services.

19. A comparison of food consumption at an all-you-can-eat buffet with a pay-per-item cafeteria would show that people tend to eat (less, more) _____ at the buffet because the marginal utility of an extra food item is (positive, zero) _____ while its price is _____.

20. Noncash gifts are (less, more) _____ preferred than cash gifts because they yield (less, more) _____ total utility to consumers.

■ **TRUE–FALSE QUESTIONS**

Circle T if the statement is true, F if it is false.

1. An increase in the real income of a consumer will result from an increase in the price of a product the consumer is buying.   **T F**

2. The income and substitution effects will induce the consumer to buy more of normal good Z when the price of Z increases.   **T F**

3. Utility and usefulness are not synonymous.   **T F**

4. Marginal utility is the change in total utility from consuming one more unit of a product.   **T F**

5. Because utility cannot actually be measured, the marginal-utility theory cannot really explain how consumers will behave.   **T F**

6. A consumer's demand curve for a product is downsloping because total utility decreases as more of the product is consumed.   **T F**

7. If total utility is increasing, then marginal utility is positive and may be either increasing or decreasing.   **T F**

8. There is a significant, positive relationship between the rate of decrease in marginal utility and the price elasticity of demand.   **T F**

9. When marginal utility falls slowly as more of a good is consumed, demand will tend to be inelastic.   **T F**

10. The theory of consumer behavior assumes that consumers act rationally to get the most from their money.   **T F**

11. All consumers are subject to budget constraints.   **T F**

12. To find a consumer's demand for a product, the price of the product is varied while tastes, income, and the prices of other products remain unchanged.   **T F**

13. The theory of consumer behavior assumes that consumers attempt to maximize marginal utility.   **T F**

14. If the marginal utility per dollar spent on product A is greater than the marginal utility per dollar spent on product B, then to maximize utility, the consumer should purchase less of A and more of B.   **T F**

15. When consumers are maximizing total utility, the marginal utilities of the last unit of every product they buy are identical.   **T F**

16. The marginal utility of product X is 15 and its price is $5, while the marginal utility of product Y is 10 and its price is $2. The utility-maximizing rule suggests that there should be *less* consumption of product Y.   **T F**

17. In most cases, a change in incomes will cause a change in the portfolio of goods and services purchased by consumers.   **T F**

18. A fall in the price of DVD players will decrease the demand for DVDs.   **T F**

19. The diamond-water paradox is explained by the fact that the total utility derived from water is low while the total utility derived from diamonds is high.   **T F**

20. If a consumer can earn $10 an hour and it takes 2 hours to consume a product, the value of the time required for the consumption of the product is $5.   **T F**

21. Paying $300 to fly from one city to another may be cheaper than paying $50 for a bus trip between the two cities when the economic value of time is taken into account.   **T F**

22. A decrease in the productivity of labor will tend over time to increase the value of time.   **T F**

23. One reason for the increased use of health care services is that consumers pay only part of the full price of the services.   **T F**

24. People tend to eat more at an "all-you-can-eat buffet" because the "price" of additional items is zero but the marginal utility for these items is likely to be positive.
   T F

25. Noncash gifts add more to total utility than cash gifts.
   T F

■ **MULTIPLE-CHOICE QUESTIONS**

Circle the letter that corresponds to the best answer.

1. The reason the substitution effect works to encourage a consumer to buy more of a product when its price decreases is
   (a) the real income of the consumer has been increased
   (b) the real income of the consumer has been decreased
   (c) the product is now relatively less expensive than it was
   (d) other products are now relatively less expensive than they were

2. Kristin Hansen buys only two goods, food and clothing. Both are normal goods for Kristin. Suppose the price of food decreases. Kristin's consumption of clothing will
   (a) decrease due to the income effect
   (b) increase due to the income effect
   (c) increase due to the substitution effect
   (d) not change due to the substitution effect

3. Which best expresses the law of diminishing marginal utility?
   (a) The more a person consumes of a product, the smaller becomes the utility that he receives from its consumption.
   (b) The more a person consumes of a product, the smaller becomes the additional utility that she receives as a result of consuming an additional unit of the product.
   (c) The less a person consumes of a product, the smaller becomes the utility that she receives from its consumption.
   (d) The less a person consumes of a product, the smaller becomes the additional utility that he receives

as a result of consuming an additional unit of the product.

4. Summing the marginal utilities of each unit consumed will determine total
   (a) cost
   (b) revenue
   (c) utility
   (d) consumption

The following table shows a hypothetical total utility schedule for a consumer of chocolate candy bars. Use the table to answer Questions 5, 6, and 7.

Number consumed	Total utility
0	0
1	9
2	19
3	27
4	35
5	42
6	42
7	40

5. This consumer begins to experience diminishing marginal utility when he consumes the
   (a) first candy bar
   (b) second candy bar
   (c) third candy bar
   (d) fourth candy bar

6. Marginal utility becomes negative with the consumption of the
   (a) fourth candy bar
   (b) fifth candy bar
   (c) sixth candy bar
   (d) seventh candy bar

7. Based on the data, you can conclude that the
   (a) marginal utility of the fourth unit is 6
   (b) marginal utility of the second unit is 27
   (c) total utility of 5 units is 42
   (d) total utility of 3 units is 55

8. After eating eight chocolate chip cookies, you are offered a ninth cookie. You turn down the cookie. Your refusal indicates that the
   (a) marginal utility for chocolate chip cookies is negative
   (b) total utility for chocolate chip cookies is negative
   (c) marginal utility is positive for the eighth and negative for the ninth cookie
   (d) total utility was zero because you ate one cookie and refused the other

9. Other things being equal, demand for a product is likely to be *elastic* if the marginal utility
   (a) decreases rapidly as additional units are consumed
   (b) decreases slowly as additional units are consumed
   (c) increases rapidly as additional units are consumed
   (d) increases slowly as additional units are consumed

10. Which is a dimension or assumption of the marginal-utility theory of consumer behavior?
   (a) The consumer has a small income.
   (b) The consumer is rational.

(c) Goods and services are free.

(d) Goods and services yield continually increasing amounts of marginal utility as the consumer buys more of them.

11. A consumer is making purchases of products A and B such that the marginal utility of product A is 20 and the marginal utility of product B is 30. The price of product A is $10 and the price of product B is $20. The utility-maximizing rule suggests that this consumer should

(a) increase consumption of product B and decrease consumption of product A

(b) increase consumption of product B and increase consumption of product A

(c) increase consumption of product A and decrease consumption of product B

(d) make no change in consumption of A or B

12. Suppose that the prices of A and B are $3 and $2, respectively, that the consumer is spending her entire income and buying 4 units of A and 6 units of B, and that the marginal utility of both the fourth unit of A and the sixth unit of B is 6. It can be concluded that the consumer should buy

(a) more of both A and B

(b) more of A and less of B

(c) less of A and more of B

(d) less of both A and B

13. Robert Woods is maximizing his satisfaction consuming two goods, X and Y. If the marginal utility of X is half that of Y, what is the price of X if the price of Y is $1.00?

(a) $0.50

(b) $1.00

(c) $1.50

(d) $2.00

Answer Questions 14, 15, and 16 based on the following table showing the marginal-utility schedules for goods X and Y for a hypothetical consumer. The price of good X is $1 and the price of good Y is $2. The income of the consumer is $9.

Good X		Good Y	
Quantity	MU	Quantity	MU
1	8	1	10
2	7	2	8
3	6	3	6
4	5	4	4
5	4	5	3
6	3	6	2
7	2	7	1

14. To maximize utility, the consumer will buy

(a) 7X and 1Y

(b) 5X and 2Y

(c) 3X and 3Y

(d) 1X and 4Y

15. When the consumer purchases the utility-maximizing combination of goods X and Y, total utility will be

(a) 36

(b) 45

(c) 48

(d) 52

16. Suppose that the consumer's income increased from $9 to $12. What would be the utility-maximizing combination of goods X and Y?

(a) 5X and 2Y

(b) 6X and 3Y

(c) 2X and 5Y

(d) 4X and 4Y

17. A decrease in the price of product Z will

(a) increase the marginal utility per dollar spent on Z

(b) decrease the marginal utility per dollar spent on Z

(c) decrease the total utility per dollar spent on Z

(d) cause no change in the marginal utility per dollar spent on Z

Answer Questions 18, 19, 20, and 21 on the basis of the following total utility data for products A and B. Assume that the prices of A and B are $6 and $8, respectively, and that consumer income is $36.

Units of A	Total utility	Units of B	Total utility
1	18	1	32
2	30	2	56
3	38	3	72
4	42	4	80
5	44	5	84

18. What is the level of total utility for the consumer in equilibrium?

(a) 86

(b) 102

(c) 108

(d) 120

19. How many units of the two products will the consumer buy?

(a) 1 of A and 4 of B

(b) 2 of A and 2 of B

(c) 2 of A and 3 of B

(d) 3 of A and 4 of B

20. If the price of A decreases to $4, then the utility-maximizing combination of the two products is

(a) 2 of A and 2 of B

(b) 2 of A and 3 of B

(c) 3 of A and 3 of B

(d) 4 of A and 4 of B

21. Which of the following represents the demand curve for A?

(a)		(b)		(c)		(d)	
P	Q_d	P	Q_d	P	Q_d	P	Q_d
$6	1	$6	2	$6	2	$6	2
4	4	4	5	4	3	4	4

22. The price of water is substantially less than the price of diamonds because

(a) the marginal utility of a diamond is significantly less than the marginal utility of a gallon of water

(b) the marginal utility of a diamond is significantly greater than the marginal utility of a gallon of water

(c) the total utility of diamonds is greater than the total utility of water

(d) diamonds have a low marginal utility

23. The full price of a product to a consumer is
(a) its market price
(b) its market price plus the value of its consumption time
(c) its market price less the value of its consumption time
(d) the value of its consumption time less its market price

24. A consumer has two basic choices: rent a DVD movie for $4.00 and spend 2 hours of time watching it or spend $15 for dinner at a restaurant that takes 1 hour of time. If the marginal utilities of the movie and the dinner are the same, and the consumer values time at $15 an hour, the rational consumer will most likely
(a) rent more movies and buy fewer restaurant dinners
(b) buy more restaurant dinners and rent fewer movies
(c) buy fewer restaurant dinners and rent fewer movies
(d) make no change in the consumption of both

25. Compared to cash gifts, noncash gifts are preferred
(a) more because they decrease total utility
(b) more because they increase total utility
(c) less because they increase total utility
(d) less because they decrease total utility

■ **PROBLEMS**

1. Suppose that when the price of bread is $2 per loaf, the Robertson family buys six loaves of bread in a week.
a. When the price of bread falls from $2 to $1.60, the Robertson family will increase its bread consumption to seven loaves.
(1) Measured in terms of bread, the fall in the price of bread will _____ their real income by _____ loaves. (*Hint:* How many loaves of bread *could* they now buy without changing the amount they spend on bread?)

(2) Is the Robertsons' demand for bread elastic or inelastic? _____
b. When the price of bread rises from $2 to $2.40 per loaf, the Robertson family will decrease its bread consumption to four loaves.
(1) Measured in terms of bread, this rise in the price of bread will _____ their real income by $_____ loaf.
(2) Is the Robertsons' demand for bread elastic or inelastic? _____

2. Assume that Harriet Palmer finds only three goods, A, B, and C, for sale and that the amounts of utility that their consumption will yield her are as shown in the table below. Compute the marginal utilities for successive units of A, B, and C and enter them in the appropriate columns.

3. Using the marginal-utility data for goods A, B, and C that you obtained in problem 2, assume that the prices of A, B, and C are $5, $1, and $4, respectively, and that Palmer has an income of $37 to spend.
a. Complete the table on the next page by computing the *marginal utility per dollar* for successive units of A, B, and C.
b. Palmer would *not* buy 4 units of A, 1 unit of B, and 4 units of C because _____.
c. Palmer would *not* buy 6 units of A, 7 units of B, and 4 units of C because _____.
d. When Palmer is maximizing her utility, she will buy _____ units of A, _____ units of B, _____ units of C; her total utility will be _____, and the marginal utility of the last dollar spent on each good will be _____.
e. If Palmer's income increased by $1, she would spend it on good _____, assuming she can buy fractions of a unit of a good, because _____.

	Good A			Good B			Good C	
Quantity	Total utility	Marginal utility	Quantity	Total utility	Marginal utility	Quantity	Total utility	Marginal utility
1	21	____	1	7	____	1	23	____
2	41	____	2	13	____	2	40	____
3	59	____	3	18	____	3	52	____
4	74	____	4	22	____	4	60	____
5	85	____	5	25	____	5	65	____
6	91	____	6	27	____	6	68	____
7	91	____	7	28.2	____	7	70	____

	Good A		Good B		Good C
Quantity	Marginal utility per dollar	Quantity	Marginal utility per dollar	Quantity	Marginal utility per dollar
1	——	1	——	1	——
2	——	2	——	2	——
3	——	3	——	3	——
4	——	4	——	4	——
5	——	5	——	5	——
6	——	6	——	6	——
7	——	7	——	7	——

4. Sam Thompson has an income of $36 to spend each week. The only two goods he is interested in purchasing are H and J. The marginal-utility schedules for these two goods are shown in the table at the bottom of the page.

The price of J does not change from week to week and is $4. The marginal utility per dollar from J is also shown in the table. But the price of H varies from one week to the next. The marginal utilities per dollar from H when the prices of H are $6, $4, $3, $2, and $1.50 are shown in the table.

a. Complete the table below to show how much of H Thompson will buy each week at each of the five possible prices of H.

Price of H	Quantity of H demanded
$6.00	——
4.00	——
3.00	——
2.00	——
1.50	——

b. What is the table you completed in part **a** called?

_____

5. Assume that a consumer can purchase only two goods: R (recreation) and M (material goods). The market price of R is $2 and the market price of M is $1. The consumer spends all her income in such a way that the marginal utility of the last unit of R she buys is 12 and the marginal utility of the last unit of M she buys is 6.

a. If we ignore the time it takes to consume R and M, is the consumer maximizing the total utility she obtains from the two goods? _____

b. Suppose it takes 4 hours to consume each unit of R, 1 hour to consume each unit of M, and the consumer can earn $2 an hour when she works.

(1) The full price of a unit of R is $_____.

(2) The full price of a unit of M is $_____.

c. If we take into account the full price of each of the commodities, is the consumer maximizing her total utility? _____ How do you know this?

_____

d. If the consumer is not maximizing her utility, should she increase her consumption of R or of M? _____ Why should she do this?

_____

e. Will she use more or less of her time for consuming R? _____

■ SHORT ANSWER AND ESSAY QUESTIONS

1. Explain, employing the income-effect and substitution-effect concepts, the reasons consumers buy more of a product at a lower price than at a higher price and vice versa.

2. Why is utility a "subjective concept"?

3. How does the subjective nature of utility limit the practical usefulness of the marginal-utility theory of consumer behavior?

4. Define total utility and marginal utility. What is the relationship between total utility and marginal utility?

5. How can the law of diminishing marginal utility be used to explain the law of demand?

	Good H						Good J	
Quantity	MU	MU/$6	MU/$4	MU/$3	MU/$2	MU/$1.50	MU	MU/$4
1	45	7.5	11.25	15	22.5	30	40	10
2	30	5	7.5	20	15	20	36	9
3	20	3.33	5	6.67	10	13.33	32	8
4	15	2.5	3.75	5	7.5	10	28	7
5	12	2	3	4	6	8	24	6
6	10	1.67	2.5	3.33	5	6.67	20	5
7	9	1.5	2.25	3	4.5	6	16	4
8	7.5	1.25	1.88	2.5	3.75	5	12	3

6. What is the relationship of marginal utility to the price elasticity of demand?

7. What essential assumptions are made about consumers and the nature of goods and services in developing the marginal-utility theory of consumer behavior?

8. What is meant by "budget constraint"?

9. When is the consumer in equilibrium and maximizing total utility? Explain why any deviation from this equilibrium will decrease the consumer's total utility.

10. Why must the amounts of extra utility derived from differently priced goods mean that marginal utility must be put on a per-dollar-spent basis? Give an example.

11. How can saving be incorporated into the utility-maximizing analysis?

12. Give and explain an algebraic restatement of the utility-maximizing rule.

13. Using the marginal-utility theory of consumer behavior, explain how an individual's demand schedule for a particular consumer good can be obtained.

14. Why does the demand schedule that is based on the marginal-utility theory almost invariably result in an inverse or negative relationship between price and quantity demanded?

15. What aspects of the theory of consumer behavior explain why consumers started buying DVDs in larger numbers instead of videocassette tapes or long-playing records in the past decade?

16. Why does water have a lower price than diamonds despite the fact that water is more useful than diamonds?

17. Explain how a consumer might determine the value of his or her time. How does the value of time affect the full price the consumer pays for a good or service?

18. What does taking time into account explain that the traditional approach to consumer behavior does not explain?

19. How does the way that we pay for goods and services affect the quantity purchased? Explain by using medical care as an example.

20. Why are noncash gifts less preferred than cash gifts?

ANSWERS

Chapter 21 Consumer Behavior and Utility Maximization

FILL-IN QUESTIONS

1. substitution, diminishing
2. increase, decrease, income
3. more, lower, less, more, substitution
4. total, marginal, a subjective, is not
5. decrease
6. positive, zero
7. inelastic, elastic
8. rational, preferences
9. limited, scarce, prices
10. last, the same
11. increase, decrease
12. *a.* MU of product *X*; *b.* price of *X*; *c.* MU of product *Y*; *d.* price of *Y*
13. *a.* the income of the consumer; *b.* the prices of other products
14. consistent, more
15. decreased, increased
16. marginal, marginal, total, total
17. time, limited, equal to, price, time
18. cost, more
19. more, positive, zero
20. less, less

TRUE–FALSE QUESTIONS

1. F, pp. 372–373	10. T, p. 376	19. F, p. 380
2. F, pp. 372–373	11. T, p. 376	20. F, pp. 380–381
3. T, p. 373	12. T, p. 376	21. T, pp. 380–381
4. T, p. 373	13. F, p. 376	22. F, pp. 380–381
5. F, p. 373	14. F, pp. 376–378	23. T, p. 381
6. F, pp. 373–375	15. F, p. 378	24. T, p. 381
7. T, pp. 373–375	16. F, p. 378	25. F, p. 381
8. F, p. 375	17. T, p. 379	
9. F, p. 375	18. F, pp. 379–380	

MULTIPLE-CHOICE QUESTIONS

1. c, p. 373	10. b, p. 376	19. c, pp. 376–378
2. b, pp. 372–373	11. c, pp. 376–378	20. c, pp. 378–379
3. b, pp. 373–375	12. c, pp. 376–378	21. c, pp. 378–379
4. c, pp. 373–375	13. a, pp. 376–378	22. b, p. 380
5. c, pp. 373–375	14. b, pp. 376–378	23. b, p. 380
6. d, pp. 373–375	15. c, pp. 376–378	24. b, pp. 380–381
7. c, pp. 373–375	16. b, pp. 378–379	25. d, p. 381
8. c, pp. 373–375	17. a, pp. 378–379	
9. b, p. 375	18. b, pp. 376–378	

PROBLEMS

1. *a.* (1) increase, 1 1/2, (2) inelastic; *b.* (1) decrease, 1, (2) elastic

2. marginal utility of good A: 21, 20, 18, 15, 11, 6, 0; marginal utility of good B: 7, 6, 5, 4, 3, 2, 1.2; marginal utility of good C: 23, 17, 12, 8, 5, 3, 2

3. *a.* marginal utility per dollar of good A: 4.2, 4, 3.6, 3, 2.2, 1.2, 0; marginal utility per dollar of good B: 7, 6, 5, 4, 3, 2, 1.2; marginal utility of good C: 5.75, 4.25, 3, 2, 1.25, .75, .5; *b.* the marginal utility per dollar spent on good B (7) is greater than the marginal utility per dollar spent on good A (3), and the latter is greater than the marginal utility per dollar spent on good C (2); *c.* she would be spending more than her $37 income; *d.* 4, 5, 3, 151, 3; *e.* A, she would obtain the greatest marginal utility for her dollar (2.2)

4. *a.* 2, 3, 4, 6, 8; *b.* the demand schedule (for good H)

5. *a.* yes; *b.* (1) 10, (2) 3; *c.* no, the marginal-utility-to-price ratios are not the same for the two goods; *d.* M, because its MU/P ratio is greater; *e.* less

SHORT ANSWER AND ESSAY QUESTIONS

1. pp. 372–373	8. p. 376	15. pp. 379–380
2. p. 373	9. pp. 376–378	16. p. 380
3. p. 373	10. pp. 376–378	17. pp. 380–381
4. pp. 373–375	11. pp. 376–378	18. pp. 380–381
5. pp. 373–375	12. p. 378	19. p. 381
6. p. 375	13. pp. 378–379	20. p. 381
7. p. 376	14. pp. 378–379	

Indifference Curve Analysis

This brief appendix contains the third explanation or approach to the theory of consumer behavior. In it you are introduced first to the **budget line** and then to the **indifference curve.** These two geometrical concepts are then combined to explain when a consumer is purchasing the combination of two products that maximizes the total utility obtainable with his or her income. The last step is to vary the price of one of the products to find the consumer's demand (schedule or curve) for the product.

■ CHECKLIST

When you have studied this appendix you should be able to

☐ Describe the concept of a budget line and its characteristics.
☐ Explain how to measure the slope of a budget line and determine the location of the budget line.
☐ Describe the concept of an indifference curve.
☐ State two characteristics of indifference curves.
☐ Explain the meaning of an indifference map.
☐ Given an indifference map, determine which indifference curves bring more or less total utility to consumers.
☐ Use indifference curves to identify which combination of two products maximizes the total utility of consumers.
☐ Derive a consumer's demand for a product using indifference curve analysis.
☐ Compare and contrast the marginal-utility and the indifference curve analyses of consumer behavior.

■ APPENDIX OUTLINE

1. A **budget line** shows graphically the different combinations of two products a consumer can purchase with a particular money income. A budget line has a negative slope.
   a. An increase in the money income of the consumer will shift the budget line to the right without affecting its slope. A decrease in money income will shift the budget line to the left.
   b. An increase in the prices of both products shifts the budget line to the left. A decrease in the prices of both products shifts the budget line to the right. An increase (decrease) in the price of the product, the quantity of which is measured horizontally (the price of the other product remaining constant), pivots the budget line around a fixed point on the vertical axis in a clockwise (counterclockwise) direction.

2. An **indifference curve** shows graphically the different combinations of two products that bring a consumer the same total utility.
   a. An indifference curve is downsloping. If the utility is to remain the same when the quantity of one product increases, the quantity of the other product must decrease.
   b. An indifference curve is also convex to the origin. The more a consumer has of one product, the smaller the quantity of a second product he or she is willing to give up to obtain an additional unit of the first product. The slope of an indifference curve is the **marginal rate of substitution** (MRS), the rate at which the consumer will substitute one product for another to remain equally satisfied.
   c. The consumer has an indifference curve for every level of total utility. The nearer a curve is to the origin in this indifference map, the smaller is the utility of the combinations on that curve. The further a curve is from the origin, the larger is the utility of the combinations on that curve.

3. The consumer is in an **equilibrium position,** and purchasing the combination of two products that brings the maximum utility to him, when the budget line is tangent to an indifference curve.

4. In the marginal-utility approach to consumer behavior, it is assumed that utility is measurable, but in the indifference curve approach, it need only be assumed that a consumer can say whether a combination of products has more utility than, less utility than, or the same amount of utility as another combination.

5. The demand (schedule or curve) for one of the products is derived by varying the price of that product and shifting the budget line, holding the price of the other product and the consumer's income constant, and finding the quantity of the product the consumer will purchase at each price when in equilibrium.

■ HINTS AND TIPS

1. This appendix simplifies the analysis by limiting consumer choice to just two goods. The **budget line** shows the consumer what it is possible to purchase in the two-good world, given an income. Make sure that you understand what a budget line is. To test your understanding, practice with different income levels and prices. For example, assume you had an income of $100 to spend for two goods (A and B). Good A costs $10 and Good B costs $5. Draw a budget line to show the possible combinations of A and B that you could purchase.

2. **Indifference curves** and the marginal rate of substitution are perhaps the most difficult concepts to understand in this appendix. Remember that the points on the curve show the possible combinations of two goods for which the consumer is *indifferent*, and thus does not care what combination is chosen. The **marginal rate of substitution** is the rate at which the consumer gives up units of one good for units of another along the indifference curve. This rate will change (diminish) as the consumer moves down an indifference curve because the consumer is less willing to *substitute* one good for the other.

■ **IMPORTANT TERMS**

budget line   indifference map

indifference curve   equilibrium position

marginal rate of substitution (MRS)

SELF-TEST

■ **FILL-IN QUESTIONS**

1. A schedule or curve that shows the various combinations of two products a consumer can buy with a specific (income, feature) _____ is called (a budget, an indifference) _____ line.

2. Given two products X and Y, and a graph with the quantities of X measured horizontally and the quantities of Y measured vertically, the budget line has a slope equal to the ratio of the _____ to the _____.

3. When a consumer's income increases, the budget line shifts to the (left, right) _____, while a decrease in income shifts the budget line to the _____.

4. Given two products, A and B, and a budget line graph with the quantities of A measured horizontally and the quantities of B measured vertically, an increase in the price of A will fan the budget line (outward, inward) _____, and a decrease in the price of A will fan the budget line _____ around a fixed point on the (A, B) _____ axis.

5. (A demand, An indifference) _____ curve shows the various combinations of two products that give a consumer the same total satisfaction or total (cost, utility) _____.

6. An indifference curve slopes (upward, downward) _____ and is (concave, convex) _____ to the origin.

7. The slope of the indifference curve at each point measures the (marginal, total) _____ rate of substitution of the combination represented by that point.

8. The more a consumer has of the first product than the second product, the (greater, smaller) _____ is the quantity of the first product the consumer will give up to obtain an additional unit of the second product. As a result, the marginal rate of substitution (MRS) of the first for the second product (increases, decreases) _____ as a consumer moves from left to right (downward) along an indifference curve.

9. A set of indifference curves reflects different levels of (marginal, total) _____ utility and is called an indifference (plan, map) _____.

10. The farther from the origin an indifference curve lies, the (greater, smaller) _____ the total utility obtained from the combinations of products on that curve.

11. A consumer obtains the greatest attainable total utility or satisfaction when he or she purchases that combination of two products at which his or her budget line is (tangent to, greater than) _____ an indifference curve. At this point the consumer's marginal rate of substitution is equal to the (slope, axis) _____ of the budget line.

12. Were a consumer to purchase a combination of two products that lie on her budget line and at which her budget line is steeper than the indifference curve intersecting that point, she could increase her satisfaction by trading (down, up) _____ her budget line.

13. The marginal-utility approach to consumer behavior requires that we assume utility (is, is not) _____ numerically measurable; the indifference curve approach (does, does not) _____ require that we make this assumption.

14. When quantities of product X are measured along the horizontal axis, a decrease in the price of X
   a. fans the budget line (inward, outward) _____ and to the (right, left) _____;
   b. puts the consumer, when in equilibrium, on a (higher, lower) _____ indifference curve; and
   c. normally induces the consumer to purchase (more, less) _____ of product X.

15. Using indifference curves and different budget lines to determine how much of a particular product an individual consumer will purchase at different prices makes it possible to derive that consumer's (supply, demand) _____ curve or schedule for that product.

■ **TRUE–FALSE QUESTIONS**

Circle T if the statement is true, F if it is false.

1. The budget line shows all combinations of two products that the consumer can purchase, given money income and the prices of the products. **T F**

2. The slope of the budget line when quantities of Alpha are measured horizontally and quantities of Beta are measured vertically is equal to the price of Beta divided by the price of Alpha. **T F**

3. A consumer is unable to purchase any of the combinations of two products which lie below (or to the left) of the consumer's budget line. **T F**

4. An increase in the money income of a consumer shifts the budget line to the right. **T F**

5. If a consumer moves from one combination (or point) on an indifference curve to another combination (or point) on the same curve, the total utility obtained by the consumer does not change. **T F**

6. An indifference curve is concave to the origin. **T F**

7. The marginal rate of substitution shows the rate, at the margin, at which the consumer is prepared to substitute one good for the other so as to remain equally satisfied. **T F**

8. The closer to the origin an indifference curve lies, the smaller the total utility a consumer obtains from the combinations of products on that indifference curve. **T F**

9. On an indifference map, the further from the origin, the lower the level of utility associated with each indifference curve. **T F**

10. There can be an intersection of consumer indifference curves. **T F**

11. A consumer maximizes total utility when she or he purchases the combination of the two products at which her or his budget line crosses an indifference curve. **T F**

12. On an indifference map, the consumer's equilibrium position will be where the slope of the highest attainable indifference curve equals the slope of the budget line. **T F**

13. It is assumed in the marginal-utility approach to consumer behavior that utility is numerically measurable. **T F**

14. In both the marginal-utility and indifference curve approaches to consumer behavior, it is assumed that a consumer is able to say whether the total utility obtained from combination A is greater than, equal to, or less than the total utility obtained from combination B. **T F**

15. A decrease in the price of a product normally enables a consumer to reach a higher indifference curve. **T F**

■ **MULTIPLE-CHOICE QUESTIONS**

Circle the letter that corresponds to the best answer.

1. Suppose a consumer has an income of $8, the price of **R** is $1, and the price of **S** is $0.50. Which of the following combinations is on the consumer's budget line?
(a) 8*R* and 1*S*
(b) 7*R* and 1*S*
(c) 6*R* and 6*S*
(d) 5*R* and 6*S*

2. If a consumer has an income of $100, the price of **U** is $10, and the price of **V** is $20, the maximum quantity of **U** the consumer is able to purchase is
(a) 5
(b) 10
(c) 20
(d) 30

3. When the income of a consumer is $20, the price of **T** is $5, the price of **Z** is $2, and the quantity of **T** is measured horizontally, the slope of the budget line is
(a) 0.4
(b) 2.5
(c) 4
(d) 10

4. Assume that everything else remains the same, but there is a decrease in a consumer's money income. The most likely effect is
(a) an inward shift in the indifference curves because the consumer can now satisfy fewer wants
(b) an inward shift in the budget line because the consumer can now purchase less of both products
(c) an increase in the marginal rate of substitution
(d) no change in the equilibrium of the consumer

5. An indifference curve is a curve that shows the different combinations of two products that
(a) give a consumer equal marginal utilities
(b) give a consumer equal total utilities
(c) cost a consumer equal amounts
(d) have the same prices

6. In the following schedule for an indifference curve, how much of **G** is the consumer willing to give up to obtain the third unit of **H**?
(a) 3
(b) 4
(c) 5
(d) 6

Quantity of G	Quantity of H
18	1
12	2
7	3
3	4
0	5

7. The slope of the indifference curve measures the
(a) slope of the budget line
(b) total utility of a good
(c) space on an indifference map
(d) marginal rate of substitution

8. The marginal rate of substitution
(a) may rise or fall, depending on the slope of the budget line
(b) rises as you move downward along an indifference curve
(c) falls as you move downward along an indifference curve
(d) remains the same along a budget line

9. Which of the following is characteristic of indifference curves?
(a) They are concave to the origin.
(b) They are convex to the origin.
(c) Curves closer to the origin have the highest level of total utility.
(d) Curves closer to the origin have the highest level of marginal utility.

10. To derive the demand curve of a product, the price of the product is varied. For the indifference curve analysis, the
(a) budget line is held constant
(b) money income of the consumer changes
(c) tastes and preferences of the consumer are held constant
(d) prices of other products the consumer might purchase change

Questions 11, 12, 13, and 14 are based on the diagram below.

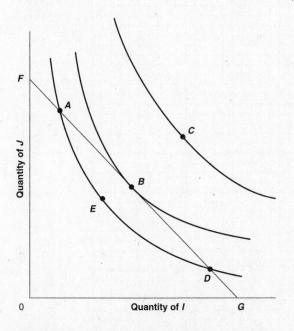

11. The budget line is best represented by line
(a) *AB*
(b) *AD*
(c) *FG*
(d) *DG*

12. Which combination of goods *I* and *J* will the consumer purchase?

(a) *A*
(b) *B*
(c) *C*
(d) *E*

13. Suppose the price of good *I* increases. The budget line will shift
(a) inward around a point on the *J* axis
(b) outward around a point on the *J* axis
(c) inward around a point on the *I* axis
(d) outward around a point on the *I* axis

14. If the consumer chooses the combination of goods *I* and *J* represented by point *E*, then the consumer could
(a) obtain more goods with the available money income
(b) not obtain more goods with the available money income
(c) shift the budget line outward so that it is tangent with point *C*
(d) shift the budget line inward so that it is tangent with point *E*

15. In indifference curve analysis, the consumer will be in equilibrium at the point where the
(a) indifference curve is concave to the origin
(b) budget line crosses the vertical axis
(c) two indifference curves intersect and are tangent to the budget line
(d) budget line is tangent to an indifference curve

16. If a consumer is initially in equilibrium, a decrease in money income will
(a) move the consumer to a new equilibrium on a lower indifference curve
(b) move the consumer to a new equilibrium on a higher indifference curve
(c) make the slope of the consumer's indifference curves steeper
(d) have no effect on the equilibrium position

Questions 17, 18, 19, and 20 are based on the following graph.

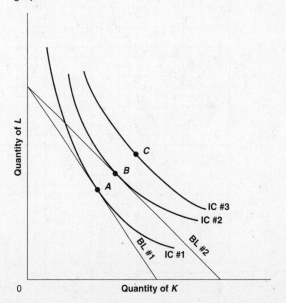

17. If the budget line shifts from **BL #1** to **BL #2**, it is because the price of
  (a) **K** increased
  (b) **K** decreased
  (c) **L** increased
  (d) **L** decreased

18. If the budget line shifts from **BL #2** to **BL #1**, it is because the price of
  (a) **K** increased
  (b) **K** decreased
  (c) **L** increased
  (d) **L** decreased

19. When the budget line shifts from **BL #2** to **BL #1**, the consumer will buy
  (a) more of **K** and **L**
  (b) less of **K** and **L**
  (c) more of **K** and less of **L**
  (d) less of **K** and more of **L**

20. Point **C** on indifference curve **IC #3** can be an attainable combination of products **K** and **L**, if
  (a) the price of **K** increases
  (b) the price of **L** increases
  (c) money income increases
  (d) money income decreases

■ **Problems**

1. Following are the schedules for three indifference curves.

Indifference schedule 1		Indifference schedule 2		Indifference schedule 3	
A	**B**	**A**	**B**	**A**	**B**
0	28	0	36	0	45
1	21	1	28	1	36
2	15	2	21	2	28
3	10	3	15	3	21
4	6	4	11	4	15
5	3	5	7	5	10
6	1	6	4	6	6
7	0	7	1	7	3
		8	0	8	1
				9	0

a. On the graph below, measure quantities of **A** along the horizontal axis (from 0 to 9) and quantities of **B** along the vertical axis (from 0 to 45).
(1) Plot the 8 combinations of **A** and **B** from indifference schedule 1 and draw through the 8 points a curve which is in no place a straight line. Label this curve **IC #1.**
(2) Do the same for the 9 points in indifference schedule 2 and label it **IC #2.**

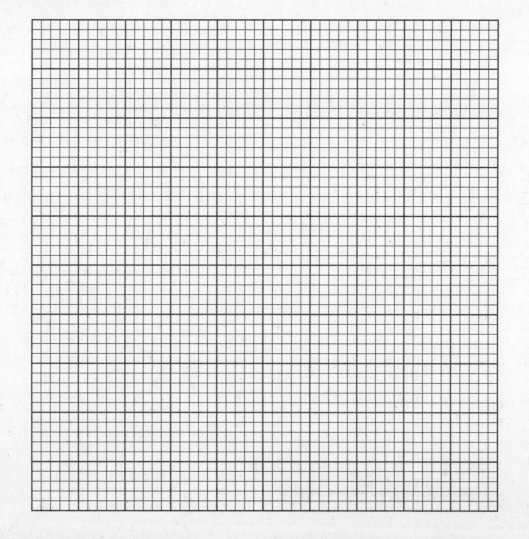

(3) Repeat the process for the 10 points in indifference schedule 3 and label the curve **IC #3.**

b. Assume the price of **A** is $12, the price of **B** is $2.40, and a consumer has an income of $72.

(1) Complete the following table to show the quantities of **A** and **B** this consumer is able to purchase.

A	B
0	___
1	___
2	___
3	___
4	___
5	___
6	___

(2) Plot this budget line on the graph you completed in part **a.**

(3) This budget line has a slope equal to _____.

c. To obtain the greatest satisfaction or utility from his income of $72 this consumer will

(1) purchase _____ units of **A** and _____ of **B;**

(2) and spend $_____ on **A** and $_____ on **B.**

2. Following is a graph with three indifference curves and three budget lines. This consumer has an income of $100, and the price of **Y** remains constant at $5.

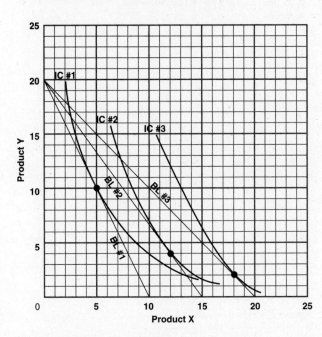

a. When the price of **X** is $10, the consumer's budget line is **BL #1** and the consumer

(1) purchases _____ **X** and _____ **Y;**

(2) and spends $_____ on **X** and $_____ on **Y.**

b. If the price of **X** is $6, 2/3 the budget line is **BL #2** and the consumer

(1) purchases _____ **X** and _____ **Y;**

(2) and spends $_____ for **X** and $_____ for **Y.**

c. And when the price of **X** is $5, the consumer has budget line **BL #3** and

(1) buys _____ **X** and _____ **Y;** and

(2) spends $_____ on **X** and $_____ on **Y.**

d. On the following graph, plot the quantities of **X** demanded at the three prices.

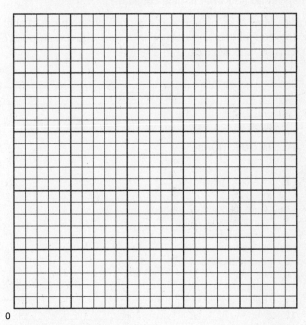

e. Between $10 and $5 this consumer's demand for **X** is (elastic, inelastic) _____, and for him products **X** and **Y** are (substitutes, complements) _____.

■ **SHORT ANSWER AND ESSAY QUESTIONS**

1. Why is the slope of the budget line negative?

2. How will each of the following events affect the budget line?
   (a) a decrease in the money income of the consumer
   (b) an increase in the prices of both products
   (c) a decrease in the price of one of the products

3. Explain why the budget line can be called "objective" and an indifference curve "subjective."

4. What is the relationship between an indifference curve and total utility? Between an indifference map and total utility?

5. Why is the slope of an indifference curve negative and convex to the origin?

6. You are given two products, alpha and beta. Why will the utility-maximizing combination of the two products be the one lying on the highest attainable indifference curve?

7. Suppose a consumer purchases a combination of two products that is on her budget line but the budget line is not tangent to an indifference curve at that point. Of which product should the consumer buy more, and of which should she buy less? Why?

8. What is the important difference between the marginal-utility theory and the indifference-curve theory of consumer demand?

9. Explain how the indifference map of a consumer and the budget line are utilized to derive the consumer's demand for one of the products. In deriving demand, what is varied and what is held constant?

10. How does a change in the price of one product shift the budget line and determine a new equilibrium point? Explain and illustrate with a graph.

ANSWERS

Appendix to Chapter 21 Indifference Curve Analysis

FILL-IN QUESTIONS

1. income, a budget
2. price of X, price of Y
3. right, left
4. inward, outward, B
5. An indifference, utility
6. downward, convex
7. marginal
8. greater, decreases
9. total, map
10. greater
11. tangent, slope
12. up
13. is, does not
14. *a.* outward, right; *b.* higher; *c.* more
15. demand

TRUE–FALSE QUESTIONS

1. T, p. 386	6. F, pp. 387–388	11. F, pp. 388–389
2. F, p. 386	7. T, pp. 387–388	12. T, pp. 388–389
3. F, p. 386	8. T, p. 388	13. T, pp. 389–390
4. T, pp. 386–387	9. F, p. 388	14. T, pp. 389–390
5. T, p. 387	10. F, p. 388	15. T, p. 390

MULTIPLE-CHOICE QUESTIONS

1. d, p. 386	8. c, pp. 387–388	15. d, pp. 388–389
2. b, p. 386	9. b, pp. 387–388	16. a, pp. 386, 388
3. b, p. 386	10. c, p. 387	17. b, pp. 390–391
4. b, p. 386	11. c, p. 386	18. a, pp. 390–391
5. b, p. 387	12. b, pp. 388–389	19. b, pp. 390–391
6. c, pp. 387–388	13. a, p. 386	20. c, pp. 390–391
7. d, pp. 387–388	14. a, pp. 386–387	

PROBLEMS

1. *a.* graph; *b.* (1) 30, 25, 20, 15, 10, 5, 0, (2) graph, (3) −5; *c.* (1) 3, 15, (2) 36, 36
2. *a.* (1) 5, 10, (2) 50, 50; *b.* (1) 12, 4, (2) 80, 20; *c.* (1) 18, 2, (2) 90, 10; *d.* graph; *e.* elastic, substitutes

SHORT ANSWER AND ESSAY QUESTIONS

1. p. 386	5. pp. 387–388	9. pp. 390–391
2. pp. 386–387	6. p. 389	10. pp. 390–391
3. p. 387	7. pp. 388–389	
4. p. 389	8. pp. 388–389	

CHAPTER 22

The Costs of Production

Previous chapters discussed consumer behavior and product demand. This chapter switches to producer behavior and business firms. It explains how a firm's **costs of production** change as the firm's output changes, in the short run and in the long run.

This chapter begins with a definition of cost and profit. You should be somewhat familiar with these terms because they were first introduced in Chapters 2 and 4. The explanation is now more detailed. Several definitions of cost and profit are given in the chapter, so you must know the distinctions if you are to understand the true meaning of **economic cost** and **economic profit.**

The second and third sections of the chapter focus on **short-run** variable relationships and production costs for the firm. You are first introduced to the important **law of diminishing returns,** which defines the relationship between the quantity of resources used by the firm and the output the firm produces in the short run. The chapter discussion then shifts to costs because resource prices are associated with the fixed and variable resources the typical firm uses to produce its output. The three basic types of short-run costs—total, average, and marginal—vary for the firm as the quantity of resources and output changes. The chapter describes the relationship among the various cost curves and how they are shaped by the law of diminishing returns.

The fourth section of the chapter looks at production costs in the **long run.** All resources, and also production costs, are variable in the long run. You will learn that the long-run cost curve for the typical firm is based on the short-run cost curves for firms of different sizes. In the long run, firms can experience **economies of scale** and **diseconomies of scale** that will shape the long-run cost curve for the firm. The chapter concludes with several practical applications of the concept of scale economies.

It is important that you master this material on the costs of production because it sets the foundation for understanding the price and output decisions of a firm operating under different market structures that you will be reading about in the next three chapters.

■ CHECKLIST

When you have studied this chapter you should be able to

☐ Define economic cost in terms of opportunity cost.
☐ Distinguish between an explicit cost and an implicit cost.

☐ Explain the difference between normal profit and economic profit and why the former is a cost and the latter is not a cost.
☐ Distinguish between the short run and the long run in production.
☐ Define total product, marginal product, and average product.
☐ State the law of diminishing returns and explain its rationale.
☐ Compute marginal product and average product to illustrate the law of diminishing returns when you are given the necessary data.
☐ Describe the relationship between marginal product and average product.
☐ Define fixed costs, variable costs, and total cost.
☐ Define average fixed cost, average variable cost, and average total cost.
☐ Explain how average product is related to average variable cost.
☐ Define marginal cost.
☐ Explain how marginal product is related to marginal cost.
☐ Compute and graph average fixed cost, average variable cost, average total cost, and marginal cost when given total-cost data.
☐ Describe the relation of marginal cost to average variable cost and average total cost.
☐ Explain why short-run cost curves shift.
☐ Illustrate the difference between short-run average total cost curves for a firm at different outputs and its long-run average total cost curves.
☐ Describe various possible long-run average total cost curves.
☐ Define and list reasons for the economies and diseconomies of scale.
☐ Explain the concept of minimum efficient scale and its relation to industry structure.
☐ Give examples of short-run costs, economies of scale, and minimum efficient scale in the real world.

■ CHAPTER OUTLINE

1. Resources are scarce and are used to produce many different products. The **economic cost** of using resources to produce a product is an opportunity cost: the value or worth of the resources in its best alternative use.

a. Economic costs can be explicit or implicit. **Explicit costs** are the monetary payments that a firm makes to obtain resources from nonowners of the firm. **Implicit costs** are the monetary payments that would have been paid for self-owned or self-employed resources if they had been used in their next best alternative outside the firm.

b. **Normal profit** is an implicit cost and is the minimum payment that entrepreneurs must receive for performing the entrepreneurial functions for the firm.

c. **Economic,** or pure, **profit** is the revenue a firm receives in excess of all its explicit and implicit economic (opportunity) costs. (The firm's accounting profit is its revenue less only its explicit costs.)

d. A distinction is made between the **short run** and the **long run.** The firm's economic costs vary as the firm's output changes. These costs depend on whether the firm is able to make short-run or long-run changes in its resource use. In the short run, the firm's plant is a fixed resource, but in the long run it is a variable resource. So, in the short run the firm cannot change the size of its plant and can vary its output only by changing the quantities of the variable resources it employs.

2. There are **short-run** relationships between inputs and outputs in the production process.

a. Several product terms need to be defined to show these relationships. **Total product** is the total quantity of output produced. **Marginal product** is the change made in total product from a change in a variable resource input. **Average product,** or productivity, is the total product per unit of resource input.

b. The **law of diminishing returns** determines the manner in which the costs of the firm change as it changes its output in the short run. As more units of a variable resource are added to a fixed resource, beyond some point the marginal product from each additional unit of a variable resource will decline.

(1) There are three phases reflected in a graph of the total product and marginal product curves: increasing, decreasing, and negative marginal returns.

(2) When total product is increasing at an increasing rate, marginal product is rising; when total product is increasing at a decreasing rate, marginal product is falling; and when total product declines, marginal product is negative.

(3) When marginal product is greater than average product, average product rises, and when marginal product is less than average product, average product falls.

3. When input, output, and price information are available, it is possible to calculate **short-run production costs.**

a. The **total cost** is the sum of its fixed costs and variable costs. As output increases,

(1) fixed costs do not change;

(2) at first, the variable costs increase at a decreasing rate, and then increase at an increasing rate;

(3) and at first total costs increase at a decreasing rate and then increase at an increasing rate.

b. **Average costs** consist of **average fixed, average variable,** and **average total costs.** They are equal, respectively, to the firm's fixed, variable, and total costs divided by its output. As output increases,

(1) average fixed cost decreases;

(2) at first, average variable cost decreases and then increases;

(3) and at first, average total cost also decreases and then increases.

c. **Marginal cost** is the extra cost incurred in producing one additional unit of output.

(1) Because the marginal product of the variable resource increases and then decreases (as more of the variable resource is employed to increase output), marginal cost decreases and then increases as output increases.

(2) At the output at which average variable cost is a minimum, average variable cost and marginal cost are equal, and at the output at which average total cost is a minimum, average total cost and marginal cost are equal.

(3) On a graph, marginal cost will always intersect average variable cost at its minimum point and marginal cost will always intersect average total cost at its minimum point. These intersections will always have marginal cost approaching average variable cost and average total cost from below.

d. Changes in either resource prices or technology will cause the cost curves to shift.

4. In the long run, all the resources employed by the firm are variable resources. **Long-run production costs** are all variable costs.

a. As the firm expands its output by increasing the size of its plant, average total cost tends to fall at first because of the **economies of scale,** but as this expansion continues, sooner or later, average total cost begins to rise because of the **diseconomies of scale.**

b. The long-run average total cost curve shows the least average total cost at which any output can be produced after the firm has had time to make all changes in its plant size. Graphically, it is made up of all the points of tangency of the unlimited number of short-run average total cost curves.

c. The economies and diseconomies of scale encountered in the production of different goods are important factors influencing the structure and competitiveness of various industries.

(1) **Economies of scale** (a decline in long-run average total costs) arise because of labor specialization, managerial specialization, efficient capital, and other factors such as spreading the start-up, advertising, or development costs over an increasing level of output.

(2) **Diseconomies of scale** arise primarily from the problems of efficiently managing and coordinating the firm's operations as it becomes a large-scale producer.

(3) **Constant returns to scale** are the range of output where long-run average total cost does not change.

d. Economies and diseconomies of scale can determine the structure in an industry. **Minimum efficient scale (MES)** is the smallest level of output at which a firm can minimize long-run average costs. This concept explains why relatively large and small firms could co-exist in an industry and be viable when there is an extended range of constant returns to scale.

(1) In some industries the long-run average cost curve will decline over a range of output. Given consumer demand, efficient production will be achieved only with a small number of large firms.

(2) If economies of scale extend beyond the market size, the conditions for a **natural monopoly** are produced, which is a rare situation where unit costs are minimized by having a single firm produce a product.

(3) If there are few economies of scale, then there is minimum efficient size at a low level of output and there are many firms in an industry.

5. There are several applications and illustrations of short-run costs, economies of scale, and minimum efficient cost.

a. The rising cost of insurance and security raised short-run average total costs after the terrorists' attacks of September 11, 2001.

b. Economies of scale can be seen in the successful start-up firms such as Intel, Microsoft, or Starbucks.

c. Economies of scale are also exhibited in the Verson stamping machine that makes millions of auto parts per year.

d. A small price can be charged for a newspaper because the fixed costs are spread across a large amount of output, thus achieving economies of scale.

e. Economies of scale are extensive in aircraft production, but modest in concrete mixing, which achieves minimum efficient scale at a low level of output. As a consequence, there are few aircraft factories and many concrete mixing companies.

■ HINTS AND TIPS

1. Many **cost** terms are described in this chapter. Make yourself a glossary so that you can distinguish among them. You need to know what each one means if you are to master the material in the chapter. If you try to learn them in the order in which you encounter them, you will have little difficulty because the later terms build on the earlier ones.

2. Make sure you know the difference between **marginal** and **average** relationships in this chapter. Marginal product (MP) shows the *change* in total output associated with each additional input. Average product (AP) is simply the output per unit of resource input. Marginal cost (MC) shows the change in total cost associated with producing another unit of output. Average cost shows the per-unit cost of producing a level of output.

3. Practice drawing the different sets of **cost curves** used in this chapter: (1) short-run total cost curves, (2) short-run average and marginal cost curves, and (3) long-run cost curves. Also, explain to yourself the relationship between the curves in each set that you draw.

4. In addition to learning *how* the costs of the firm vary as its output varies, be sure to understand *why* the costs vary the way they do. In this connection note that the behavior of short-run costs is the result of the law of diminishing returns and that the behavior of long-run costs is the consequence of economies and diseconomies of scale.

■ IMPORTANT TERMS

economic (opportunity) cost	variable costs
explicit costs	total cost (TC)
implicit costs	average fixed cost (AFC)
normal profit	average variable cost (AVC)
economic profit	average total cost (ATC)
short run	marginal cost (MC)
long run	economies of scale
total product (TP)	diseconomies of scale
marginal product (MP)	constant returns to scale
average product (AP)	minimum efficient scale (MES)
law of diminishing returns	
fixed costs	natural monopoly

SELF-TEST

■ FILL-IN QUESTIONS

1. The value or worth of any resource in its best alternative use is called the (out-of-pocket, opportunity) _____ cost of that resource.

2. The economic cost of producing a product is the amount of money or income the firm must pay or provide to (government, resource suppliers) _____ to attract land, labor, and capital goods away from alternative uses in the economy. The monetary payments, or out-of-pocket payments, are (explicit, implicit) _____ costs, and the costs of self-owned or self-employed resources are _____ costs.

3. Normal profit is a cost because it is the payment that the firm must make to obtain the services of the (workers, entrepreneurs) _____. Accounting profit is equal to the firm's total revenue less its (explicit, implicit) _____ costs. Economic profit is not a cost and is equal to the firm's total (costs, revenues) _____ less its economic _____.

4. In the short run the firm can change its output by changing the quantity of the (fixed, variable) _____ resources it employs, but it cannot change the quantity of the _____ resources. This means that the firm's plant capacity is fixed in the (short, long) _____ run and variable in the _____ run.

5. The law of diminishing returns is that as successive units of a (fixed, variable) _____ resource are added to a _____ resource, beyond some point the (total, marginal) _____ product of the former resource will decrease. The law assumes that all units of input are of (equal, unequal) _____ quality.

6. If the total product increases at an increasing rate, the marginal product is (rising, falling) _____.
If it increases at a decreasing rate, the marginal product is (positive, negative, zero) _____, but (rising, falling) _____.

7. If total product is at a maximum, the marginal product is (positive, negative, zero) _____, but if it decreases, the marginal product is _____.

8. If the marginal product of any input exceeds its average product the average product is (rising, falling) _____, but if it is less than its average product the average product is _____. If the marginal product is equal to its average product the average product is at a (minimum, maximum) _____.

9. Those costs that in total do not vary with changes in output are (fixed, variable) _____ costs, but those costs that in total change with the level of output are _____ costs. The sum of fixed and variable costs at each level of output is (marginal, total) _____ cost.

10. The law of diminishing returns explains why a firm's average variable, average total, and marginal cost may at first tend to (increase, decrease) _____ but ultimately _____ as the output of the firm increases.

11. Marginal cost is the increase in (average, total) _____ variable cost or _____ cost that occurs when the firm increases its output by one unit.

12. If marginal cost is less than average variable cost, average variable cost will be (rising, falling, constant) _____ but if average variable cost is less than marginal cost, average variable cost will be _____.

13. Assume that labor is the only variable input in the short run and that the wage rate paid to labor is constant.
  a. When the marginal product of labor is rising, the marginal cost of producing a product is (rising, falling) _____.

b. When the average variable cost of producing a product is falling, the average product of labor is (rising, falling) _____.
c. At the output at which marginal cost is at a minimum, the marginal product of labor is at a (minimum, maximum) _____.
d. At the output at which the average product of labor is at a maximum, the average variable cost of producing the product is at a (minimum, maximum) _____.
e. At the output at which the average variable cost is at a minimum, average variable cost and (marginal, total) _____ cost are equal and average product and _____ product are equal.

14. Changes in either resource prices or technology will cause cost curves to (shift, remain unchanged) _____. If average fixed costs increase, then the average fixed costs curve will (shift up, shift down, remain unchanged) _____ and the average total cost curve will _____, but the average variable cost curve will _____ and the marginal cost curve will (shift up, shift down, remain unchanged) _____.

15. If average variable costs increase, then the average variable cost curve will (shift up, shift down, remain unchanged) _____ and the average total cost curve will _____, and the marginal cost curve will (shift up, shift down, remain unchanged) _____, but the average fixed cost curve would _____.

16. The short-run costs of a firm are fixed and variable costs, but in the long run all costs are (fixed, variable) _____. The long-run average total cost of producing a product is equal to the lowest of the short-run costs of producing that product after the firm has had all the time it requires to make the appropriate adjustments in the size of its (workforce, plant) _____.

17. List the three important sources of economies of scale:
  a. _____
  b. _____
  c. _____

18. When the firm experiences diseconomies of scale, it has (higher, lower) _____ average total costs as output increases. Where diseconomies of scale are operative, an increase in all inputs will cause a (greater, less) _____-than-proportionate increase in output. The factor that gives rise to large diseconomies of scale is managerial (specialization, difficulties) _____.

19. The smallest level of output at which a firm can minimize long-run average costs is (maximum, minimum) _____ efficient scale. Relatively large and small firms could coexist in an industry and be equally viable when there is an extended range of (increasing, decreasing, constant) _____ returns to scale.

20. In some industries, the long-run average cost curve will (increase, decrease) _____ over a long range of output and efficient production will be achieved with only a few (small, large) _____ firms. The conditions for a natural monopoly are created when (economies, diseconomies) _____ of scale extend beyond the market's size so that unit costs are minimized by having a single firm produce a product.

■ **TRUE–FALSE QUESTIONS**

Circle T if the statement is true, F if it is false.

1. The economic costs of a firm are the payments it must make to resource owners to attract their resources from alternative employments.   **T F**

2. Economic or pure profit is an explicit cost, while normal profit is an implicit cost.   **T F**

3. In the short run the size (or capacity) of a firm's plant is fixed.   **T F**

4. The resources employed by a firm are all variable in the long run and all fixed in the short run.   **T F**

5. The law of diminishing returns states that as successive amounts of a variable resource are added to a fixed resource, beyond some point total output will diminish.   **T F**

6. An assumption of the law of diminishing returns is that all units of variable inputs are of equal quality. **T F**

7. When total product is increasing at a decreasing rate, marginal product is positive and increasing.   **T F**

8. When average product is falling, marginal product is greater than average product.   **T F**

9. When marginal product is negative, total production (or output) is decreasing.   **T F**

10. The larger the output of a firm, the smaller the fixed cost of the firm.   **T F**

11. The law of diminishing returns explains why increases in variable costs associated with each 1-unit increase in output become greater and greater after a certain point.   **T F**

12. Fixed costs can be controlled or altered in the short run.   **T F**

13. Total cost is the sum of fixed and variable costs at each level of output.   **T F**

14. Marginal cost is the change in fixed cost divided by the change in output.   **T F**

15. The marginal-cost curve intersects the average-total-cost (ATC) curve at the ATC curve's minimum point. **T F**

16. If the fixed cost of a firm increases from one year to the next (because the premium it must pay for the insurance on the buildings it owns has been increased) while its variable-cost schedule remains unchanged, its marginal-cost schedule will also remain unchanged.   **T F**

17. Marginal cost is equal to average variable cost at the output at which average variable cost is at a minimum.   **T F**

18. When the marginal product of a variable resource increases, the marginal cost of producing the product will decrease, and when marginal product decreases, marginal cost will increase.   **T F**

19. If the price of a variable input should increase, the average variable cost, average total cost, and marginal cost curves would all shift upward, but the position of the average fixed cost curve would remain unchanged. **T F**

20. One explanation why the long-run average-total-cost curve of a firm rises after some level of output has been reached is the law of diminishing returns.   **T F**

21. If a firm increases all its inputs by 20% and its output increases by 30%, the firm is experiencing economies of scale.   **T F**

22. The primary cause of diseconomies of scale is increased specialization of labor.   **T F**

23. If a firm has constant returns to scale in the long run, the *total* cost of producing its product does not change when it expands or contracts its output.   **T F**

24. Minimum efficient scale occurs at the largest level of output at which a firm can minimize long-run average costs.   **T F**

25. The fundamental reason that newspapers have such low prices is the low production costs from economies of scale.   **T F**

■ **MULTIPLE-CHOICE QUESTIONS**

Circle the letter that corresponds to the best answer.

1. Suppose that a firm produces 100,000 units a year and sells them all for $5 each. The explicit costs of production are $350,000 and the implicit costs of production are $100,000. The firm has an accounting profit of
  (a) $200,000 and an economic profit of $25,000
  (b) $150,000 and an economic profit of $50,000
  (c) $125,000 and an economic profit of $75,000
  (d) $100,000 and an economic profit of $50,000

2. Economic profit for a firm is defined as the total revenues of the firm minus its
  (a) accounting profit

(b) explicit costs of production
(c) implicit costs of production
(d) opportunity cost of all inputs

3. Which would best describe the short run for a firm as defined by economists?
(a) The plant capacity for a firm is variable.
(b) The plant capacity for a firm is fixed.
(c) There are diseconomies of scale.
(d) There are economies of scale.

4. Which is most likely to be a long-run adjustment for a firm that manufactures golf carts on an assembly line basis?
(a) an increase in the amount of steel the firm buys
(b) a reduction in the number of shifts of workers from three to two
(c) a change in the production managers of the assembly line
(d) a change from the production of golf carts to motorcycles

5. The change in total product divided by the change in resource input defines
(a) total cost
(b) average cost
(c) average product
(d) marginal product

Use the following table to answer Questions 6 and 7. Assume that the only variable resource used to produce output is labor.

Amount of labor	Amount of output
1	3
2	8
3	12
4	15
5	17
6	18

6. The marginal product of the fourth unit of labor is
(a) 2 units of output
(b) 3 units of output
(c) 4 units of output
(d) 15 units of output

7. When the firm hires four units of labor the average product of labor is
(a) 3 units of output
(b) 3.75 units of output
(c) 4.25 units of output
(d) 15 units of output

8. Because the marginal product of a variable resource initially increases and later decreases as a firm increases its output,
(a) average variable cost decreases at first and then increases
(b) average fixed cost declines as the output of the firm expands
(c) variable cost at first increases by increasing amounts and then increases by decreasing amounts
(d) marginal cost at first increases and then decreases

9. Because the marginal product of a resource at first increases and then decreases as the output of the firm increases,
(a) average fixed cost declines as the output of the firm increases
(b) average variable cost at first increases and then decreases
(c) variable cost at first increases by increasing amounts and then increases by decreasing amounts
(d) total cost at first increases by decreasing amounts and then increases by increasing amounts

For Questions 10, 11, and 12, use the data given in the following table. The fixed cost of the firm is $500, and the firm's total variable cost is indicated in the table.

Output	Total variable cost
1	$ 200
2	360
3	500
4	700
5	1000
6	1800

10. The average variable cost of the firm when 4 units of output are produced is
(a) $175
(b) $200
(c) $300
(d) $700

11. The average total cost of the firm when 4 units of output are being produced is
(a) $175
(b) $200
(c) $300
(d) $700

12. The marginal cost of the sixth unit of output is
(a) $200
(b) $300
(c) $700
(d) $800

13. Marginal cost and average variable cost are equal at the output at which
(a) marginal cost is a minimum
(b) marginal product is a maximum
(c) average product is a maximum
(d) average variable cost is a maximum

14. Average variable cost may be either increasing or decreasing when
(a) marginal cost is decreasing
(b) marginal product is increasing
(c) average fixed cost is decreasing
(d) average total cost is increasing

15. Why does the short-run marginal-cost curve eventually increase for the typical firm?
(a) diseconomies of scale
(b) minimum efficient scale
(c) the law of diminishing returns
(d) economic profit eventually decreases

16. If the price of labor or some other variable resource increased, the
  (a) AVC curve would shift downward
  (b) AFC curve would shift upward
  (c) AFC curve would shift downward
  (d) MC curve would shift upward

Questions 17, 18, 19, and 20 are based on the following figure.

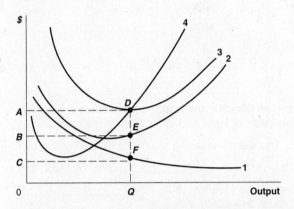

17. In the figure, curves **1, 3,** and **4,** respectively, represent
  (a) average variable cost, marginal cost, and average total cost
  (b) average total cost, average variable cost, and marginal cost
  (c) average fixed cost, average total cost, and marginal cost
  (d) marginal cost, average total cost, and average variable cost

18. At output level **Q,** the average fixed cost is measured by the vertical distance represented by
  (a) *DE*
  (b) *DF*
  (c) *DQ*
  (d) *EF*

19. As output increases beyond the level represented by **Q,**
  (a) marginal product is rising
  (b) marginal product is falling
  (c) total fixed costs are rising
  (d) total costs are falling

20. If the firm is producing at output level **Q,** then the total variable costs of production are represented by area
  (a) 0*QFC*
  (b) 0*QEB*
  (c) 0*QDC*
  (d) *CFEB*

21. At an output of 10,000 units per year, a firm's total variable costs are $50,000 and its average fixed costs are $2. The total costs per year for the firm are
  (a) $50,000
  (b) $60,000
  (c) $70,000
  (d) $80,000

22. A firm has total fixed costs of $4,000 a year. The average variable cost is $3.00 for 2000 units of output. At this level of output, its average total costs are

  (a) $2.50
  (b) $3.00
  (c) $4.50
  (d) $5.00

23. If you know that total fixed cost is $100, total variable cost is $300, and total product is 4 units, then
  (a) marginal cost is $50
  (b) average fixed cost is $45
  (c) average total cost is $125
  (d) average variable cost is $75

24. If the short-run average variable costs of production for a firm are falling, then this indicates that
  (a) average variable costs are above average fixed costs
  (b) marginal costs are below average variable costs
  (c) average fixed costs are constant
  (d) total costs are falling

Answer Questions 25 and 26 using the following table. Three short-run cost schedules are given for three plants of different sizes that a firm might build in the long run.

Plant 1		Plant 2		Plant 3	
Output	ATC	Output	ATC	Output	ATC
10	$10	10	$15	10	$20
20	9	20	10	20	15
30	8	30	7	30	10
40	9	40	10	40	8
50	10	50	14	50	9

25. What is the long-run average cost of producing 40 units of output?
  (a) $7
  (b) $8
  (c) $9
  (d) $10

26. At what output is long-run average cost at a minimum?
  (a) 20
  (b) 30
  (c) 40
  (d) 50

27. If the long-run average total cost curve for a firm is downsloping, then it indicates that there
  (a) is a minimum efficient scale
  (b) are constant returns to scale
  (c) are diseconomies of scale
  (d) are economies of scale

28. Which factor contributes to economies of scale?
  (a) less efficient use of capital goods
  (b) less division of labor and specialization
  (c) greater specialization in management of a firm
  (d) greater difficulty controlling the operations of a firm

29. A firm is encountering constant returns to scale when it increases all of its inputs by 20% and its output increases by
  (a) 10%
  (b) 15%
  (c) 20%
  (d) 25%

30. If economies of scale are limited and diseconomies appear quickly in an industry, then minimum efficient scale occurs at a

(a) high level of output, and there will be a few firms
(b) high level of output, and there will be many firms
(c) low level of output, and there will be few firms
(d) low level of output, and there will be many firms

■ PROBLEMS

1. On the following graph, sketch the way in which the average product and the marginal product of a resource change as the firm increases its employment of that resource.

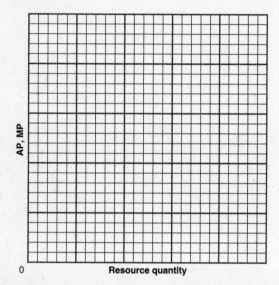

0   **Resource quantity**

AP, MP

2. The table in the next column shows the total production of a firm as the quantity of labor employed increases. The quantities of all other resources employed remain constant.

    a. Compute the marginal products of the first through the eighth units of labor and enter them in the table.

Units of labor	Total production	Marginal product of labor	Average product of labor
0	0		0
1	80	_____	
2	200	_____	_____
3	330	_____	_____
4	400	_____	_____
5	450	_____	_____
6	480	_____	_____
7	490	_____	_____
8	480	_____	_____

b. Now compute the average products of the various quantities of labor and enter them in the table.

c. There are increasing returns to labor from the first through the _____ units of labor and decreasing returns from the _____ through the eighth units.

d. When total production is increasing, marginal product is (positive, negative) _____ and when total production is decreasing, marginal product is _____.

e. When marginal product is greater than average product, then average product will (rise, fall) _____, and when marginal product is less than average product, then average product will _____.

3. On the graph in the first column of the next page, sketch the manner in which fixed cost, variable cost, and total cost change as the output the firm produces in the short run changes.

Quantity of labor employed	Total output	Marginal product of labor	Average product of labor	Total cost	Marginal cost	Average variable cost
0	0	—	—	$_____	—	—
1	5	5	5	_____	$_____	$_____
2	11	6	5.50	_____	_____	_____
3	18	7	6	_____	_____	_____
4	24	6	6	_____	_____	_____
5	29	5	5.80	_____	_____	_____
6	33	4	5.50	_____	_____	_____
7	36	3	5.14	_____	_____	_____
8	38	2	4.75	_____	_____	_____
9	39	1	4.33	_____	_____	_____
10	39	0	3.90			

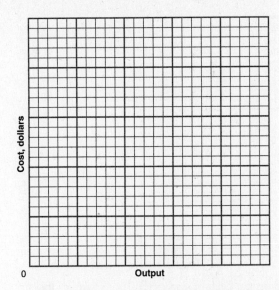

0   **Output**

4. Assume that a firm has a plant of fixed size and that it can vary its output only by varying the amount of labor it employs. The table at the bottom of page 254 shows the relationships between the amount of labor employed, the output of the firm, the marginal product of labor, and the average product of labor.

    a. Assume each unit of labor costs the firm $10. Compute the total cost of labor for each quantity of labor the firm might employ, and enter these figures in the table.

    b. Now determine the marginal cost of the firm's product as the firm increases its output. Divide the increase in total labor cost by the *increase* in total output to find the marginal cost. Enter these figures in the table.

    c. When the marginal product of labor

    (1) increases, the marginal cost of the firm's product

(increases, decreases) _____.

    (2) decreases, the marginal cost of the firm's product

_____.

    d. If labor is the only variable input, the total labor cost and total variable cost are equal. Find the average variable cost of the firm's product (by dividing the total labor cost by total output) and enter these figures in the table.

e. When the average product of labor

    (1) increases, the average variable cost (increases,

decreases) _____.

    (2) decreases, the average variable cost _____.

5. The law of diminishing returns causes a firm's average variable, average total, and marginal cost to decrease at first and then to increase as the output of the firm increases.

    Sketch these three cost curves on the following graph in such a way that their proper relationship to each other is shown.

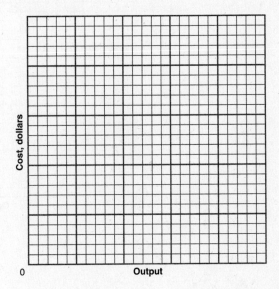

0   **Output**

6. The table that follows is a schedule of a firm's fixed cost and variable cost.

    a. Complete the table by computing total cost, average fixed cost, average total cost, and marginal cost.

    b. On the graph at the top of next page 256, plot and label fixed cost, variable cost, and total cost.

    c. On the graph at the bottom of next page 256, plot average fixed cost, average variable cost, average total cost, and marginal cost. Label the four curves.

Output	Total fixed cost	Total variable cost	Total cost	Average fixed cost	Average variable cost	Average total cost	Marginal cost
$ 0	$200	$ 0	$ ___				
1	200	50	___	$ ___	$50.00	$ ___	$ ___
2	200	90	___	___	45.00	___	___
3	200	120	___	___	40.00	___	___
4	200	160	___	___	40.00	___	___
5	200	220	___	___	44.00	___	___
6	200	300	___	___	50.00	___	___
7	200	400	___	___	57.14	___	___
8	200	520	___	___	65.00	___	___
9	200	670	___	___	74.44	___	___
10	200	900	___	___	90.00	___	___

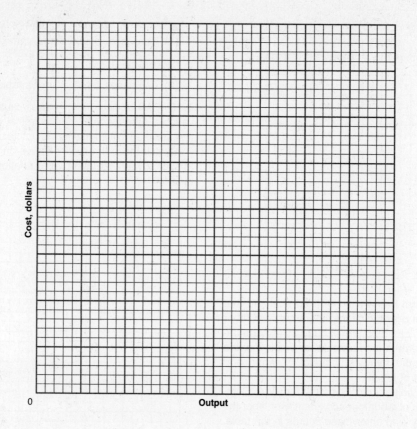

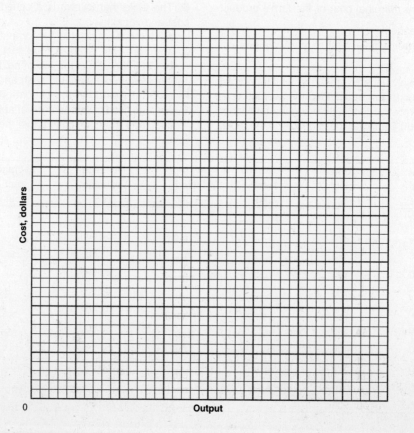

7. Following are the short-run average-cost curves of producing a product with three different sizes of plants, **Plant 1, Plant 2,** and **Plant 3.** Draw the firm's long-run average cost on this graph.

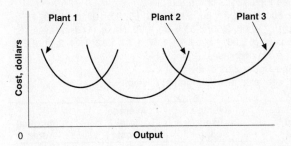

8. Following are the short-run average-total-cost schedules for three plants of different sizes that a firm might build to produce its product. Assume that these are the only possible sizes of plants that the firm might build.

Plant size A		Plant size B		Plant size C	
Output	ATC	Output	ATC	Output	ATC
10	$ 7	10	$17	10	$53
20	6	20	13	20	44
30	5	30	9	30	35
40	4	40	6	40	27
50	5	50	4	50	20
60	7	60	3	60	14
70	10	70	4	70	11
80	14	80	5	80	8
90	19	90	7	90	6
100	25	100	10	100	5
110	32	110	16	110	7
120	40	120	25	120	10

a. Complete the *long-run* average-cost schedule for the firm in the following table.

Output	Average cost	Output	Average cost
10	$_____	70	$_____
20	_____	80	_____
30	_____	90	_____
40	_____	100	_____
50	_____	110	_____
60	_____	120	_____

b. For outputs between

(1) _____ and _____, the firm should build Plant A.

(2) _____ and _____, the firm should build Plant B.

(3) _____ and _____, the firm should build Plant C.

■ **SHORT ANSWER AND ESSAY QUESTIONS**

1. Explain the meaning of the opportunity cost of producing a product and the difference between an explicit cost and an implicit cost. How would you determine the implicit money cost of a resource?

2. What is the difference between normal profit and economic profit? Why is the former an economic cost? How do you define accounting profit?

3. What type of adjustments can a firm make in the long run that it cannot make in the short run? What adjustments can it make in the short run? How long is the short run?

4. Why is the distinction between the short run and the long run important?

5. State precisely the law of diminishing returns. Exactly what is it that diminishes, and why does it diminish?

6. Distinguish between a fixed cost and a variable cost.

7. Why are short-run total costs partly fixed and partly variable costs, and why are long-run costs entirely variable?

8. Why do short-run variable costs increase at first by decreasing amounts and later increase by increasing amounts?

9. How does the behavior of short-run variable costs influence the behavior of short-run total costs?

10. Describe the way in which short-run average fixed cost, average variable cost, average total cost, and marginal cost vary as the output of the firm increases.

11. What are the connections between marginal product and marginal cost, and between average product and average variable cost? How will marginal cost behave as marginal product decreases and increases? How will average variable cost change as average product rises and falls?

12. What are the precise relationships between marginal cost and minimum average variable cost, and between marginal cost and minimum average total cost? Why are these relationships necessarily true?

13. What happens to the average total cost, average variable cost, average fixed cost, and marginal cost curves when the price of a variable input increases or decreases? Describe what other factor can cause short-run cost curves to shift.

14. What does the long-run average-cost curve of a firm show? What relationship is there between long-run average cost and the short-run average-total-cost schedules of the different-sized plants which a firm might build?

15. Why is the long-run average-cost curve of a firm U-shaped?

16. What is meant by economies of scale and by diseconomies of scale?

17. What are factors that contribute to economies of scale?

18. What causes diseconomies of scale?

19. What is minimum efficient scale? How can this concept, combined with economies and diseconomies of scale, be used to describe the number and size of firms in an industry?

20. Describe real examples of short-run costs, economies of scale, and minimum efficient scale.

ANSWERS

Chapter 22   The Costs of Production

FILL-IN QUESTIONS

1. opportunity
2. resource suppliers, explicit, implicit
3. entrepreneurs, explicit, revenues, costs
4. variable, fixed, short, long
5. variable, fixed, marginal, equal
6. rising, positive, falling
7. zero, negative
8. rising, falling, maximum
9. fixed, variable, total
10. decrease, increase
11. total, total
12. falling, rising
13. *a.* falling; *b.* rising; *c.* maximum; *d.* minimum; *e.* marginal, marginal
14. shift, shift up, shift up, remain unchanged, remain unchanged
15. shift up, shift up, shift up, remain unchanged
16. variable, plant
17. *a.* labor specialization; *b.* managerial specialization; *c.* more efficient use
18. higher, less, difficulties
19. minimum, constant
20. decrease, large, economies

TRUE–FALSE QUESTIONS

1. T, pp. 392–393	**10.** F, p. 398	**19.** T, pp. 402–403
2. F, pp. 393–394	**11.** T, pp. 398–399	**20.** F, pp. 403–405
3. T, p. 394	**12.** F, p. 398	**21.** T, pp. 403–404
4. F, p. 394	**13.** T, p. 398	**22.** F, p. 407
5. F, pp. 395–396	**14.** F, p. 400	**23.** F, p. 407
6. T, pp. 395–396	**15.** T, p. 401	**24.** F, pp. 407–408
7. F, pp. 396–398	**16.** T, pp. 400–403	**25.** T, pp. 408–409
8. F, pp. 396–398	**17.** T, pp. 400–403	
9. T, pp. 396–398	**18.** T, pp. 400–403	

MULTIPLE-CHOICE QUESTIONS

1. b, pp. 392–393	**11.** c, pp. 398–400	**21.** c, pp. 398–400
2. d, pp. 393–394	**12.** d, pp. 398–400	**22.** d, pp. 398–400
3. b, p. 394	**13.** c, pp. 399–401	**23.** d, pp. 398–400
4. d, p. 394	**14.** c, pp. 399–401	**24.** b, pp. 399–402
5. d, p. 395	**15.** c, pp. 400–403	**25.** b, pp. 403–405
6. b, pp. 395–396	**16.** d, p. 403	**26.** b, pp. 403–405
7. b, pp. 395–396	**17.** c, pp. 400–401	**27.** d, pp. 404–405
8. a, pp. 395–397	**18.** a, pp. 399–400	**28.** c, pp. 404–406
9. d, pp. 395–397	**19.** b, pp. 401–402	**29.** c, pp. 404–406
10. a, pp. 398–400	**20.** b, pp. 399–401	**30.** d, p. 407

PROBLEMS

1. See Figure 22.2(b) of the text
2. *a.* 80, 120, 130, 70, 50, 30, 10, −10; *b.* 80, 100, 110, 100, 90, 80, 70, 60; *c.* third, fourth; *d.* positive, negative; *e.* rise, fall
3. See Figure 22.3 of the text
4. *a.* $0, 10, 20, 30, 40, 50, 60, 70, 80, 90, 100; *b.* $2.00, 1.67, 1.43, 1.67, 2.00, 2.50, 3.33, 5.00, 1.00, NA; *c.* (1) decreases, (2) increases; *d.* 2.00, 1.82, 1.67, 1.67, 1.72, 1.82, 1.94, 2.11, 2.31, 2.56; *e.* (1) decreases, (2) increases
5. See Figure 22.5 of the text
6. *a.* see table below; *b.* graph; *c.* graph

Total cost	Average fixed cost	Average total cost	Marginal cost
$ 200	—	—	—
250	$200.00	$250.00	$ 50
290	100.00	145.00	40
320	66.67	106.67	30
360	50.00	90.00	40
420	40.00	84.00	60
500	33.33	83.33	80
600	28.57	85.71	100
720	25.00	90.00	120
870	22.22	96.67	150
1100	20.00	110.00	230

7. See Figures 22.7 and 22.8 of the text
8. *a.* $7.00, 6.00, 5.00, 4.00, 4.00, 3.00, 4.00, 5.00, 6.00, 5.00, 7.00, 10.00; *b.* (1) 10, 40, (2) 50, 80, (3) 90, 120

SHORT ANSWER AND ESSAY QUESTIONS

1. pp. 392–393	**8.** pp. 398–402	**15.** pp. 404–405
2. pp. 393–394	**9.** pp. 398–402	**16.** pp. 404–406
3. p. 394	**10.** pp. 398–402	**17.** pp. 404–406
4. p. 394	**11.** pp. 402–403	**18.** p. 407
5. pp. 395–396	**12.** pp. 402–403	**19.** pp. 407–408
6. p. 398	**13.** p. 403	**20.** pp. 408–409
7. pp. 398–400	**14.** pp. 403–404	

CHAPTER 23

Pure Competition

Chapter 23 is the first of three chapters that bring together the previous discussion of demand and production costs. These chapters examine demand and production costs under four different market structures: pure competition, monopoly, oligopoly, and monopolistic competition. This chapter focuses exclusively on the pure competition market structure, which is characterized by (1) a large number of firms, (2) the selling of a standardized product, (3) firms that are price takers rather than price makers, and (4) ease of entry into and exit from the industry.

The main section of the chapter describes profit maximization for the purely competitive firm in the **short run.** Although two approaches to profit maximization are presented, the one given the greatest emphasis is the **marginal revenue–marginal cost** approach. You will learn the rule that a firm maximizes profit or minimizes losses by producing the output level at which marginal revenue equals marginal cost. Finding this equality provides the answers to the three central questions each firm has to answer: (1) Should we produce? (2) If so, how much output? (3) What profit (or loss) will be realized?

Answers to these questions also give insights about the **short-run supply curve** for the individual firm. The firm will find it profitable to produce at any output level where marginal revenue is greater than marginal costs. The firm will also produce in the short run, but it will experience losses if marginal revenue is less than marginal costs and greater than the minimum of average total cost. You will be shown how to construct the short-run supply curve for the purely competitive firm, given price and output data. The market supply curve for the industry is the sum of all supply curves for individual firms.

This chapter also discusses what happens to competitive firms in the **long run** as equilibrium conditions change. Over time, new firms will enter an industry that is making economic profits and existing firms will exit an industry that is experiencing economic losses, and changing price and output in the industry. Here you will learn that the shape of the **long-run supply curve** is directly affected by whether the industry is one characterized by constant costs, increasing costs, or decreasing costs as output increases.

In the long run, pure competition produces almost ideal conditions for **economic efficiency.** These ideal conditions and their qualifications are discussed in detail near the end of the chapter. A pure competition results in products produced in the least costly way, and thus it is *productively efficient.* Pure competition also allocates resources to firms so that they produce the products most wanted by society, and therefore it is *allocatively efficient.* You will find out that these two efficiency conditions can be expressed in the triple equality: Price (and marginal revenue) = marginal cost = minimum of average total cost.

You must understand the purely competitive model because it is the efficiency standard or norm for evaluating different market structures. You will be using it often for comparison with the pure monopoly model in Chapter 24 and with the models for monopolistic and oligopoly competition in Chapter 25.

■ **CHECKLIST**

When you have studied this chapter you should be able to

☐ List the five characteristics of each of the four basic market models.
☐ Give examples of industries that reflect the characteristics of the four basic market models.
☐ Describe the major features of pure competition.
☐ Explain why a purely competitive firm is a price taker.
☐ Describe the demand curve for a purely competitive firm.
☐ Explain the relationship between marginal revenue and price in pure competition.
☐ Compute average, total, and marginal revenues when you are given a demand schedule faced by a purely competitive firm.
☐ Use the total-revenue and total-cost approach to determine the output that a purely competitive firm will produce in the short run in the profit-maximizing case.
☐ Use the marginal-revenue and marginal-cost approaches to determine the output that a purely competitive firm will produce in the short run in the profit-maximizing, loss-minimizing, and shutdown cases.
☐ State three characteristics of the MR = MC rule.
☐ Find the firm's short-run supply curve when you are given the firm's short-run cost schedules.
☐ Explain the links among the law of diminishing returns, production costs, and product supply in the short run.
☐ Graph a shift in the firm's short-run supply curve and cite factors that cause the curve to increase or decrease.
☐ Find the industry's short-run supply curve (or schedule) when you are given the typical firm's short-run cost schedules.

☐ Determine, under short-run conditions, the price at which the product will sell, the output of the industry, and the output of the individual firm.

☐ Describe the basic goal for long-run adjustments in pure competition.

☐ Determine, under long-run conditions, the price at which the product will sell, the output of the firm, and the output of the industry.

☐ Explain the role played by the entry and exit of firms in a purely competitive industry in achieving equilibrium in the long run.

☐ Describe the characteristics and rationale for the long-run supply curve in a constant-cost industry, in an increasing-cost industry, and in a decreasing-cost industry.

☐ Distinguish between productive and allocative efficiency.

☐ Explain the significance of MR (= P) = MC = minimum ATC.

☐ Discuss how pure competition makes dynamic adjustments.

■ CHAPTER OUTLINE

1. The price a firm charges for the good or service it produces and its output of that product depend not only on the demand for and the cost of producing it, but on the characteristics of the market (industry) in which it sells the product. The **four market models** are pure competition, pure monopoly, monopolistic competition, and oligopoly. These models are defined by the number of firms, whether the product is standardized or differentiated, the firm's control over price, the conditions for entry into the industry, and degree of nonprice competition.

2. This chapter examines **pure competition,** in which a large number of independent firms, no one of which is able to influence market price by itself, sell a standardized product in a market where firms are free to enter and to leave in the long run. Although pure competition is rare in practice, it is the standard against which the *efficiency* of the economy and other market models can be compared.

3. **Demand** as seen by the purely competitive firm is unique because a firm selling its product cannot influence the price at which the product sells, and therefore is a **price taker.**

   a. The demand for its product is **perfectly elastic.**

   b. Average revenue (or price) and marginal revenue are equal and constant at the fixed (equilibrium) market price (**AR = P = MR**). Total revenue increases at a constant rate as the firm increases its output.

   c. The demand (average revenue) and marginal revenue curves faced by the firm are horizontal and identical at the market price. The total revenue curve has a constant positive slope.

4. The purely competitive firm operating in the **short run** is a price taker that can maximize profits (or minimize losses) only by changing its level of output. Two approaches can be used to determine the optimal level of output for the firm.

   a. The **total revenue–total cost** approach to profit maximization sets the level of output at that quantity where the difference between total revenue minus total cost is greatest.

   b. The **marginal revenue–marginal cost** approach to profit maximization basically sets the level of output at the quantity where marginal revenue (or price) equals marginal cost. There are three possible cases to consider when using this approach.

   (1) The firm will **maximize profits** when MR = MC at an output level where price is greater than average total cost.

   (2) The firm will **minimize losses** when MR = MC at an output level where price is greater than the minimum average variable cost (but less than average total cost).

   (3) The firm will **shut down** when MR = MC at an output level where price is less than average variable cost.

5. There is a close relationship between **marginal cost and the supply curve** for the purely competitive firm and industry.

   a. The **short-run supply curve for the purely competitive firm** is the portion of the marginal-cost curve that lies above average variable cost.

   b. There are links among the law of diminishing returns, production costs, and product supply. The law of diminishing returns suggests that marginal costs will increase as output expands. The firm must receive more revenue (get higher prices for its products) if it is to expand output.

   c. Changes in variable inputs will change the marginal-cost or supply curve for the purely competitive firm. For example, an improvement in technology that increases productivity will decrease the marginal-cost curve (shift it downward).

   d. The **short-run supply curve of the industry** (which is the sum of the supply curves of the individual firms) and the total demand for the product determine the short-run equilibrium price and equilibrium output of the industry. Firms in the industry may be either prosperous or unprosperous in the short run.

6. In the **long run,** the price of a product produced under conditions of pure competition will equal the minimum average total cost (**P = minimum ATC**). The firms in the industry will neither earn economic profits nor suffer economic losses.

   a. If economic profits are being received in the industry in the short run, firms will enter the industry in the long run (attracted by the profits), increase total supply, and thereby force price down to the minimum average total cost, leaving only a normal profit.

   b. If losses are being suffered in the industry in the short run, firms will leave the industry in the long run (seeking to avoid losses), reduce total supply, and thereby force price up to the minimum average total cost, leaving only a normal profit.

   c. If an industry is a **constant-cost industry,** the entry of new firms will not affect the average-total-cost schedules or curves of firms in the industry.

(1) An increase in demand will result in no increase in the long-run equilibrium price, and the industry will be able to supply larger outputs at a constant price.

(2) Graphically, the long-run supply curve in a constant-cost industry is horizontal at the minimum of the average-total-cost curve, indicating that firms make only normal profits, but not economic profits.

d. If an industry is an ***increasing-cost industry,*** the entry of new firms will raise the average-total-cost schedules or curves of firms in the industry.

(1) An increase in demand will result in an increase in the long-run equilibrium price, and the industry will be able to supply larger outputs only at higher prices.

(2) Graphically, the long-run supply curve in an increasing-cost industry is upsloping at the minimum of the average-total-cost curve, indicating that firms make only normal profits but not economic profits.

e. If an industry is a ***decreasing-cost industry,*** the entry of new firms will lower the average-total-cost schedules or curves of firms in the industry.

(1) An increase in demand will result in a decrease in the long-run equilibrium price, and the industry will be able to supply larger outputs only at lower prices.

(2) Graphically, the long-run supply curve in a decreasing-cost industry is downsloping at the minimum of the average-total-cost curve, indicating that firms make only normal profits, but not economic profits.

7. In the long run, ***competition*** and ***efficiency*** compel the purely competitive firm to produce that output at a price at which marginal revenue, average cost, and marginal cost are equal and average cost is a minimum. An economy in which all industries were purely competitive makes efficient use of its resources.

a. There is ***productive efficiency*** when the average total cost of producing goods is at a minimum; buyers benefit most from this efficiency when they are charged a price just equal to minimum average total cost (***P = minimum ATC***).

b. There is ***allocative efficiency*** when goods are produced in such quantities that the total satisfaction obtained from the economy's resources is at a maximum, or when the price of each good is equal to its marginal cost (***P = MC***).

(1) When price is greater than marginal cost, there is an *underallocation* of resources to the production of a product.

(2) When price is less than marginal cost, there is an *overallocation* of resources to the production of a product.

(3) When price is equal to marginal cost, there is efficient allocation of resources to the production of a product.

(4) The purely competitive economy makes dynamic adjustments to changes in demand or supply that restore equilibrium and efficiency.

(5) The "invisible hand" is at work in a competitive market system by organizing the private interests of producers that will help achieve society's interest in the efficient use of scarce resources.

■ HINTS AND TIPS

1. The purely competitive model is extremely important for you to master even if examples of it in the real world are rare. The model is the standard against which the other market models—pure monopoly, monopolistic competition, and oligopoly—will be compared for effects on economic efficiency. Spend extra time learning the material in this chapter so you can make model comparisons in later chapters.

2. Make sure that you understand why a purely competitive firm is a ***price "taker"*** and not a price "maker." The purely competitive firm has no influence over the price of its product and can only make decisions about the level of output.

3. Construct a table for explaining how the purely competitive firm maximizes profits or minimizes losses in the short run. Ask yourself the three questions in the table: (1) Should the firm produce? (2) What quantity should be produced to maximize profits? (3) Will production result in economic profit? Answer the questions using a marginal-revenue–marginal-cost approach. Check your answers against those presented in the text.

4. The average purely competitive firm in long-run equilibrium will not make economic profits. Find out why by following the graphical analysis in Figures 23.8 and 23.9.

5. The triple equality of MR (= *P*) = MC = minimum ATC is the most important equation in the chapter because it allows you to judge the allocative and productive efficiency of a purely competitive economy. Check your understanding of this triple equality by explaining what happens to productive efficiency when *P* > minimum ATC, or to allocative efficiency when *P* < MC or *P* > MC.

■ IMPORTANT TERMS

pure competition	break-even point
pure monopoly	MC = MR rule
monopolistic competition	short-run supply curve
oligopoly	long-run supply curve
imperfect competition	constant-cost industry
price taker	increasing-cost industry
average revenue	decreasing-cost industry
total revenue	productive efficiency
marginal revenue	allocative efficiency

SELF-TEST

■ FILL-IN QUESTIONS

1. The four market models examined in this and the next two chapters are

a. _____

b. _____

c. _____

d. _____

2. The four market models differ in terms of the (age, number) _____ of firms in the industry, whether the product is (a consumer good, standardized) _____ or (a producer good, differentiated) _____, and how easy or difficult it is for new firms to (enter, leave) _____ the industry.

3. What are the four specific conditions that characterize pure competition?

a. _____

b. _____

c. _____

d. _____

4. The individual firm in a purely competitive industry is a price (maker, taker) _____ and finds that the demand for its product is perfectly (elastic, inelastic) _____.

5. The firm's demand schedule is also a (cost, revenue) _____ schedule. The price per unit to the seller is (marginal, total, average) _____ revenue; price multiplied by the quantity the firm can sell is _____ revenue; and the extra revenue that results from selling one more unit of output is _____ revenue.

6. In pure competition, product price (rises, falls, is constant) _____ as an individual firm's output increases. Marginal revenue is (less than, greater than, equal to) _____ product price.

7. Economic profit is total revenue (plus, minus) _____ total cost. If the firm is making only a normal profit, total revenue is (greater than, equal to) _____ total cost. In the latter case, this output level is called the (profit, break-even) _____ point by economists.

8. If a purely competitive firm produces any output at all, it will produce that output at which its profit is at a (maximum, minimum) _____ or its loss is at a _____. Or, said another way, the output at which marginal cost is (equal to, greater than) _____ marginal revenue.

9. A firm will be willing to produce at an economic loss in the short run if the price which it receives is greater than its average (fixed, variable, total) _____ cost.

10. In the short run, the individual firm's supply curve in pure competition is that portion of the firm's (total, marginal) _____ cost curve which lies (above, below) _____ the average variable cost curve.

11. The short-run market supply curve is the (average, sum) _____ of the (short-run, long-run) _____ supply curves of all firms in the industry.

12. In the short run in a purely competitive industry, the equilibrium price is the price at which quantity demanded is equal to (average cost, quantity supplied) _____, and the equilibrium quantity is the quantity demanded and _____ at the equilibrium price.

13. In a purely competitive industry, in the short run the number of firms in the industry and the sizes of their plants are (fixed, variable) _____, but in the long run they are _____.

14. When a purely competitive industry is in long-run equilibrium, the price that the firm is paid for its product is equal to (total, average) _____ revenue, and to long-run _____ cost. In this case, the long-run average cost is at a (maximum, minimum) _____.

15. An industry will be in long-run equilibrium when firms are earning (normal, economic) _____ profits, but firms tend to enter an industry if the firms in the industry are earning _____ profits. Firms will tend to leave an industry when they are realizing economic (profits, losses) _____.

16. If the entry of new firms into an industry tends to raise the costs of all firms in the industry, the industry is said to be (a constant-, an increasing-, a decreasing-) _____ cost industry. Its long-run supply curve is (horizontal, downsloping, upsloping) _____.

17. If the entry of new firms into an industry tends to lower costs of all firms in the industry, the industry is said to be (a constant-, an increasing-, a decreasing-) _____ cost industry. Its long-run supply curve is (horizontal, downsloping, upsloping) _____.

18. The purely competitive economy achieves productive efficiency in the long run because price and (total, average) _____ cost are equal and the latter is at a (maximum, minimum) _____.

19. In the long run the purely competitive economy is allocatively efficient because price and (total, marginal) _____ cost are equal.

20. One of the attributes of purely competitive markets is their ability to restore (monopoly, efficiency) _____ when disrupted by changes in the economy. The "invisible hand" also operates in a competitive market system because it (maximizes, minimizes) _____ the profits of individual producers and at the same time the system creates a pattern of resource allocation that _____ consumer satisfaction.

■ **TRUE–FALSE QUESTIONS**

Circle T if the statement is true, F if it is false.

1. The structures of the markets in which business firms sell their products in the U.S. economy are very similar. **T   F**

2. A large number of sellers does not necessarily mean that the industry is purely competitive. **T   F**

3. Only in a purely competitive industry do individual firms have no control over the price of their product. **T   F**

4. Imperfectly competitive markets are defined as all markets except those that are purely competitive. **T · F**

5. One reason for studying the pure competition model is that many industries are almost purely competitive. **T   F**

6. The purely competitive firm views an average revenue schedule as identical to its marginal revenue schedule. **T   F**

7. The demand curves for firms in a purely competitive industry are perfectly inelastic. **T   F**

8. Under purely competitive conditions, the product price charged by the firm increases as output increases. **T   F**

9. The purely competitive firm can maximize its economic profit (or minimize its loss) only by adjusting its output. **T   F**

10. Economic profit is the difference between total revenue and average revenue. **T   F**

11. The break-even point means that the firm is realizing normal profits, but not economic profits. **T   F**

12. A purely competitive firm that wishes to produce and not close down will maximize profits or minimize losses at that output at which marginal costs and marginal revenue are equal. **T   F**

13. Assuming that the purely competitive firm chooses to produce and not close down, to maximize profits or minimize losses it should produce at that point where price equals average cost. **T   F**

14. If a purely competitive firm is producing output less than its profit-maximizing output, marginal revenue is greater than marginal cost. **T   F**

15. If, at the profit-maximizing level of output for the purely competitive firm, price exceeds the minimum average variable cost but is less than average total cost, the firm will make a profit. **T   F**

16. A purely competitive firm will produce in the short run the output at which marginal cost and marginal revenue are equal provided that the price of the product is greater than its average variable cost of production. **T   F**

17. The short-run supply curve of a purely competitive firm tends to slope upward from left to right because of the law of diminishing returns. **T   F**

18. If a purely competitive firm is in short-run equilibrium and its marginal cost is greater than its average total cost, firms will leave the industry in the long run. **T   F**

19. When firms in a purely competitive industry are earning profits that are less than normal, the supply of the product will tend to decrease in the long run. **T   F**

20. The long-run supply curve for a competitive, increasing-cost industry is upsloping. **T   F**

21. Pure competition, if it could be achieved in all industries in the economy, would result in the most efficient allocation of resources. **T   F**

22. Under conditions of pure competition, firms are forced to employ the most efficient production methods available to survive. **T   F**

23. The marginal costs of producing a product are society's measure of the marginal worth of alternative products. **T   F**

24. In a purely competitive market, product price measures the marginal benefit, or additional satisfaction, that society obtains from producing additional units of the product. **T   F**

25. The operation of the "invisible hand," in which the pursuit of private interests promotes the public or social interests, is a missing feature of pure competition. **T   F**

■ **MULTIPLE-CHOICE QUESTIONS**

Circle the letter that corresponds to the best answer.

1. For which market model are there a very large number of firms?
(a) monopolistic competition
(b) oligopoly
(c) pure monopoly
(d) pure competition

2. In which market model is the individual seller of a product a price taker?
(a) pure competition
(b) pure monopoly

(c) monopolistic competition
(d) oligopoly

3. Which industry comes *closest* to being purely competitive?
(a) wheat
(b) shoes
(c) electricity
(d) automobile

4. In a purely competitive industry,
(a) each existing firm will engage in various forms of nonprice competition
(b) new firms are free to enter and existing firms are able to leave the industry very easily
(c) individual firms have a price policy
(d) each firm produces a differentiated (nonstandardized) product

5. The demand schedule or curve confronted by the individual purely competitive firm is
(a) perfectly inelastic
(b) inelastic but not perfectly inelastic
(c) perfectly elastic
(d) elastic but not perfectly elastic

6. Total revenue for producing 10 units of output is $6. Total revenue for producing 11 units of output is $8. Given this information, the
(a) average revenue for producing 11 units is $2.
(b) average revenue for producing 11 units is $8.
(c) marginal revenue for producing the 11th unit is $2.
(d) marginal revenue for producing the 11th unit is $8.

7. In pure competition, product price is
(a) greater than marginal revenue
(b) equal to marginal revenue
(c) equal to total revenue
(d) greater than total revenue

8. The individual firm's short-run supply curve is that part of its marginal-cost curve lying above its
(a) average total-cost curve
(b) average variable-cost curve
(c) average fixed-cost curve
(d) average revenue curve

9. Which statement is true of a purely competitive industry in short-run equilibrium?
(a) Price is equal to average total cost.
(b) Total quantity demanded is equal to total quantity supplied.
(c) Profits in the industry are equal to zero.
(d) Output is equal to the output at which average total cost is a minimum.

10. Suppose that when 2000 units of output are produced, the marginal cost of the 2001st unit is $5. This amount is equal to the minimum of average total cost, and marginal cost is rising. If the optimal level of output in the short run is 2500 units, then at that level,
(a) marginal cost is greater than $5 and marginal cost is less than average total cost
(b) marginal cost is greater than $5 and marginal cost is greater than average total cost

(c) marginal cost is less than $5 and marginal cost is greater than average total cost
(d) marginal cost is equal to $5 and marginal cost is equal to average total cost

11. The Zebra, Inc., is selling in a purely competitive market. Its output is 250 units, which sell for $2 each. At this level of output, marginal cost is $2 and average variable cost is $2.25. The firm should
(a) produce zero units of output
(b) decrease output to 200 units
(c) continue to produce 250 units
(d) increase output to maximize profits

Questions 12, 13, 14, and 15 are based on the following graph.

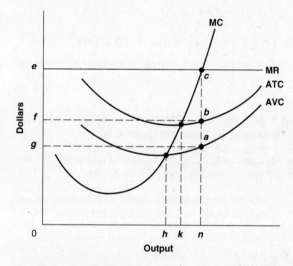

12. If the firm is producing at output level 0**n**, the rectangular area **fecb** is
(a) total variable cost
(b) total fixed costs
(c) total revenue
(d) total economic profit

13. At the profit-maximizing output, average fixed cost is
(a) **ab**
(b) **ac**
(c) **na**
(d) **nb**

14. At the profit-maximizing output, the total variable costs are equal to the area
(a) 0**fbn**
(b) 0**ecn**
(c) 0**gan**
(d) **gfba**

15. The demand curve for this firm is equal to
(a) **MR,** and the supply curve is the portion of the **MC** curve where output is greater than level **n**
(b) **MR,** and the supply curve is the portion of the **MC** curve where output is greater than level **k**
(c) **MR,** and the supply curve is the portion of the **MC** curve where output is greater than level **h**
(d) **MR,** and the supply curve is the portion of the **ATC** curve where output is greater than level **k**

Answer Questions 16, 17, 18, 19, and 20 on the basis of the following cost data for a firm that is selling in a purely competitive market.

Output	AFC	AVC	ATC	MC
1	$300	$100	$400	$100
2	150	75	225	50
3	100	70	170	60
4	75	73	148	80
5	60	80	140	110
6	50	90	140	140
7	43	103	146	180
8	38	119	156	230
9	33	138	171	290
10	30	160	190	360

16. If the market price for the firm's product is $140, the competitive firm will produce
(a) 5 units at an economic loss of $150
(b) 6 units and break even
(c) 7 units and break even
(d) 8 units at an economic profit of $74

17. If the market price for the firm's product is $290, the competitive firm will produce
(a) 7 units at an economic profit of $238
(b) 8 units at an economic profit of $592
(c) 9 units at an economic profit of $1071
(d) 10 units at an economic profit of $1700

18. If the product price is $179, the *per-unit* economic profit at the profit-maximizing output is
(a) $15
(b) $23
(c) $33
(d) $39

19. The total fixed costs are
(a) $100
(b) $200
(c) $300
(d) $400

Assume there are 100 identical firms in this industry and total or market demand is as shown.

Price	Quantity demanded
$360	600
290	700
230	800
180	900
140	1000
110	1100
80	1200

20. The equilibrium price will be
(a) $140
(b) $180
(c) $230
(d) $290

21. Assume that the market for wheat is purely competitive. Currently, firms growing wheat are experiencing economic losses. In the long run, we can expect this market's
(a) supply curve to increase
(b) demand curve to increase
(c) supply curve to decrease
(d) demand curve to decrease

22. The long-run supply curve under pure competition will be
(a) downsloping in an increasing-cost industry and upsloping in a decreasing-cost industry
(b) horizontal in a constant-cost industry and upsloping in a decreasing-cost industry
(c) horizontal in a constant-cost industry and upsloping in an increasing-cost industry
(d) upsloping in an increasing-cost industry and vertical in a constant-cost industry

23. The long-run supply curve in a constant-cost industry will be
(a) perfectly elastic
(b) perfectly inelastic
(c) unit elastic
(d) income elastic

24. In a decreasing-cost industry, the long-run
(a) demand curve would be perfectly inelastic
(b) demand curve would be perfectly elastic
(c) supply curve would be upsloping
(d) supply curve would be downsloping

25. Increasing-cost industries find that their costs rise as a consequence of an increased demand for the product because of
(a) the diseconomies of scale
(b) diminishing returns
(c) higher resource prices
(d) a decreased supply of the product

26. When a purely competitive industry is in long-run equilibrium, which statement is true?
(a) Firms in the industry are earning normal profits.
(b) Price and long-run average total cost are not equal to each other.
(c) Marginal cost is at its minimum level.
(d) Marginal cost is equal to total revenue.

27. Which triple identity results in the most efficient use of resources?
(a) $P = MC =$ minimum ATC
(b) $P = AR = MR$
(c) $P = MR =$ minimum MC
(d) $TR = MC = MR$

28. An economy is producing the goods most wanted by society when, for each and every good, its
(a) price and average cost are equal
(b) price and marginal cost are equal
(c) marginal revenue and marginal cost are equal
(d) price and marginal revenue are equal

29. If there is an increase in demand for a product in a purely competitive industry, it results in an industry
(a) contraction that will end when the price of the product is greater than its marginal cost
(b) contraction that will end when the price of the product is equal to its marginal cost

(c) expansion that will end when the price of the product is greater than its marginal cost

(d) expansion that will end when the price of the product is equal to its marginal cost

30. The idea of the "invisible hand" operating in the competitive market system means that

(a) there is a unity of private and social interests that promotes efficiency

(b) the industries in this system are described as decreasing-cost industries

(c) there is an overallocation of resources to the production of goods and services

(d) productive efficiency is more important than allocative efficiency

■ **PROBLEMS**

1. Using the following set of terms, complete the following table by inserting the appropriate letter or letters in the blanks.

a. one
b. few
c. many
d. a very large number
e. standardized
f. differentiated
g. some

h. considerable
i. very easy
j. blocked
k. fairly easy
l. fairly difficult
m. none
n. unique

Market characteristics	Market model			
	Pure competition	Pure monopoly	Monopolistic competition	Oligopoly
Number of firms	____	____	____	____
Type of product	____	____	____	____
Control over price	____	____	____	____
Conditions of entry	____	____	____	____
Nonprice competition	____	____	____	____

2. Following is the demand schedule facing the individual firm.

Price	Quantity demanded	Average revenue	Total revenue	Marginal revenue
$10	0	$____	$____	---
10	1	____	____	$____
10	2	____	____	____
10	3	____	____	____
10	4	____	____	____
10	5	____	____	____
10	6	____	____	____

a. Complete the table by computing average revenue, total revenue, and marginal revenue.

b. Is this firm operating in a market that is purely competitive? _____ How can you tell?

_____

c. The coefficient of the price elasticity of demand is the same between every pair of quantities demanded.

What is it? _____

d. What relationship exists between average revenue and marginal revenue? _____

_____

e. On the first graph on page 267, plot the demand schedule, average revenue, total revenue, and marginal revenue; label each curve.

f. The demand, average-revenue, and marginal-revenue curves are all _____ lines at a price of $_____ across all quantities.

g. The total-revenue curve is an upsloping line with a _____ slope because marginal revenue is _____.

3. Assume that a purely competitive firm has the following schedule of costs.

Output	TFC	TVC	TC
0	$300	$ 0	$ 300
1	300	100	400
2	300	150	450
3	300	210	510
4	300	290	590
5	300	400	700
6	300	540	840
7	300	720	1020
8	300	950	1250
9	300	1240	1540
10	300	1600	1900

a. Complete the following table to show the total revenue and total profit of the firm at each level of output the firm might produce. Assume the market price is $200.

Output	Market price = $200	
	Revenue	Profit
0	$____	$____
1	____	____
2	____	____
3	____	____
4	____	____
5	____	____
6	____	____
7	____	____
8	____	____
9	____	____
10	____	____

b. At a price of $200, the firm would produce an output of _____ units and earn a profit of $_____.

c. Plot the cost data for total variable cost and total cost on the second graph on page 267. Then plot the total revenue when the price is $200. For this price, indicate the level of output and the economic profit or loss on the graph.

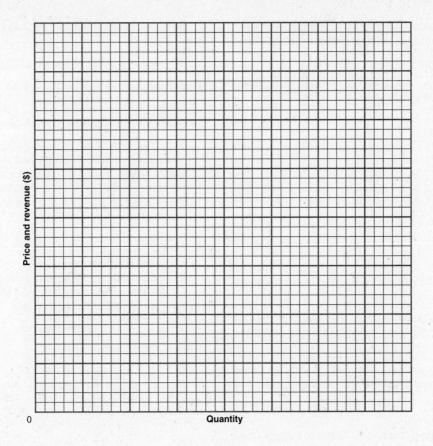

Price and revenue ($)

0   **Quantity**

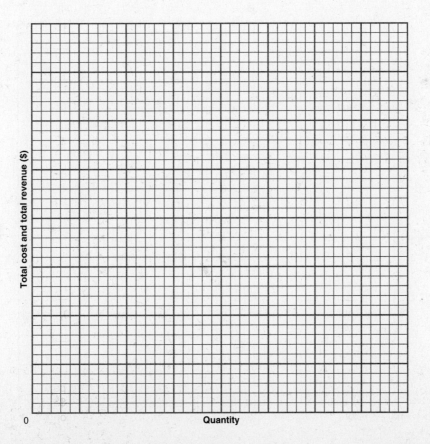

Total cost and total revenue ($)

0   **Quantity**

4. Now assume that the same purely competitive firm has the following schedule of average and marginal costs:

Output	AFC	AVC	ATC	MC
1	$300	$100	$400	$100
2	150	75	225	50
3	100	70	170	60
4	75	73	148	80
5	60	80	140	110
6	50	90	140	140
7	43	103	146	180
8	38	119	156	230
9	33	138	171	290
10	30	160	190	360

a. At a price of $55, the firm would produce

_____ units of output. At a price of $120,

the firm would produce _____ units of output. At a price of $200, the firm would produce

_____ units of output. At the $200 price compare your answers to those you gave in problem 3.
b. The *per-unit* economic profit (or loss) is calculated

by subtracting _____ at a particular level of output from the product price. This *per-unit* economic profit is then multiplied by the number of units of

_____ to determine the economic profit for the competitive firm.
(1) At the product price of $200, the average total

costs are $_____, so *per-unit* economic

profit is $_____. Multiplying this amount

by the number of units of output results in an economic

profit of $_____.
(2) At the product price of $120, the average total

costs are $_____, so *per-unit* economic

losses are $_____. Multiplying this amount by the number of units of output results in an

economic loss of $_____.
c. Plot the data for average and marginal cost in the graph below. Then plot each marginal revenue when the price is $55, $120, and $200. For each price, indicate the level of output and the economic profit or loss on the graph.

5. Use the average and marginal cost data in problem 4 in your work on problem 5.
a. In the following table, complete the supply schedule for the competitive firm and state what the economic profit will be at each price.

Price	Quantity supplied	Profit
$360	_____	$_____
290	_____	_____
230	_____	_____
180	_____	_____
140	_____	_____
110	_____	_____
80	_____	_____
60	_____	_____

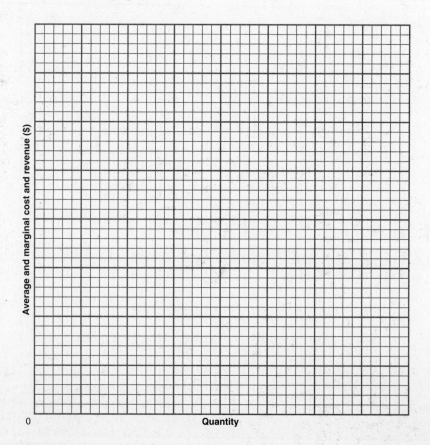

b. If there are 100 firms in the industry and all have the same cost schedule,

(1) complete the market supply schedule in the following table.

Quantity demanded	Price	Quantity supplied
400	$360	____
500	290	____
600	230	____
700	180	____
800	140	____
900	110	____
1000	80	____

(2) Using the demand schedule given in (1):

(a) What will the market price of the product be?

$_____

(b) What quantity will the individual firm produce?

_____

(c) How large will the firm's profit be?

$_____

(d) Will firms tend to enter or leave the industry in the

long run? _____ Why? _____

_____

6. If the average total costs assumed for the individual firm in problem 4 were long-run average total costs and if the industry were a constant-cost industry,

a. what would be the market price of the product in

the long run? $_____

b. what output would each firm produce when the in-

dustry was in long-run equilibrium? _____

c. approximately how many firms would there be in the industry in the long run, given the present demand for the product as shown in the table in **5b**?

_____

d. if the following table were the market demand schedule for the product, how many firms would there

be in the long run in the industry? _____

Price	Quantity demanded
$360	500
290	600
230	700
180	800
140	900
110	1000
80	1100

7. On the following graph, draw a long-run supply curve of

a. a constant-cost industry

b. an increasing-cost industry

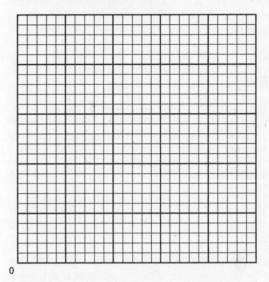

0

■ SHORT ANSWER AND ESSAY QUESTIONS

1. What are the four market models (or situations) that economists employ, and what are the major characteristics of each type of market?

2. Describe in detail four characteristics of pure competition.

3. If pure competition is so rare in practice, why are students of economics asked to study it?

4. Explain how the firm in a purely competitive industry sees the demand for the product it produces in terms of the

   (a) price elasticity of demand,

   (b) relationship of average to marginal revenue, and

   (c) behavior of total, average, and marginal revenues as the output of the firm increases.

5. Describe the total-revenue–total-cost approach to profit maximization.

6. Compare and contrast the total-revenue–total-cost approach with the marginal-revenue–marginal-cost approach to profit maximization. Are the two approaches consistent?

7. Explain the MR = MC rule and its three characteristics.

8. Why does the purely competitive firm want to maximize total profit but not its per-unit profit?

9. Why is a firm willing to produce at a loss in the short run if the loss is no greater than the fixed costs of the firm?

10. Explain how the short-run supply of an individual firm and of the purely competitive industry are each determined.

11. What determines the equilibrium price and output of a purely competitive industry in the short run? Will economic profits in the industry be positive or negative?

12. Why do the MC = MR rule and MC = *P* rule mean the same thing under conditions of pure competition?

13. What are the important distinctions between the short run and the long run and between equilibrium in the short run and in the long run in a competitive industry?

14. When is the purely competitive industry in long-run equilibrium? What forces the purely competitive firm into this position?

15. What is a constant-cost industry? What is an increasing-cost industry? Under what economic conditions is each likely to be found? What will be the nature of the long-run supply curve in each of these industries?

16. Explain the conditions for productive efficiency in an economy.

17. Describe the conditions for allocative efficiency. Why is it said that a purely competitive economy is an efficient economy?

18. How does a purely competitive economy eliminate an overallocation for resources for the production of a product and correct for an underallocation?

19. Explain how dynamic adjustments are made in pure competition as a result of changes in demand for a product or the supply of a resource.

20. What is the relationship between the "invisible hand" of Adam Smith and efficiency in the competitive market system?

ANSWERS

Chapter 23 Pure Competition

FILL-IN QUESTIONS

1. *a.* pure competition; *b.* pure monopoly; *c.* monopolistic competition; *d.* oligopoly (any order *a–d*)
2. number, standardized, differentiated, enter
3. *a.* a large number of sellers; *b.* a standardized product; *c.* firms are price takers; *d.* free entry and exit of firms
4. taker, elastic
5. revenue, average, total, marginal
6. is constant, equal to
7. minus, equal to, break-even
8. maximum, minimum, equal to
9. variable
10. marginal, above
11. sum, short-run
12. quantity supplied, quantity supplied
13. fixed, variable
14. average, average, minimum
15. normal, economic, losses
16. an increasing-, upsloping
17. a decreasing-, downsloping
18. average, minimum
19. marginal
20. efficiency, maximizes, maximizes

TRUE–FALSE QUESTIONS

1. F, pp. 413–414	10. F, p. 417	19. T, pp. 427–429
2. T, pp. 413–414	11. T, p. 417	20. T, p. 430
3. T, pp. 413–414	12. T, p. 419	21. T, pp. 431–433
4. T, pp. 413–414	13. F, p. 419	22. T, pp. 431–433
5. F, p. 415	14. T, pp. 419–422	23. T, pp. 431–433
6. T, p. 415	15. F, pp. 419–422	24. T, pp. 431–433
7. F, pp. 415–416	16. T, pp. 419–422	25. F, p. 433
8. F, pp. 415–416	17. T, pp. 423–424	
9. T, pp. 416–418	18. F, pp. 427–429	

MULTIPLE-CHOICE QUESTIONS

1. d, pp. 413–414	11. a, pp. 418–422	21. c, pp. 427–429
2. a, pp. 413–414	12. d, pp. 418–422	22. c, pp. 427–430
3. a, pp. 413–414	13. a, pp. 418–422	23. a, pp. 429–430
4. b, pp. 413–414	14. c, pp. 418–422	24. d, pp. 430–431
5. c, p. 415	15. c, pp. 418–422	25. c, p. 430
6. c, pp. 415–416	16. b, pp. 418–422	26. a, pp. 431–433
7. b, pp. 415–416	17. c, pp. 418–422	27. a, pp. 431–433
8. b, pp. 423–424	18. d, pp. 418–422	28. b, pp. 431–433
9. b, pp. 425–426	19. c, pp. 418–422	29. d, pp. 431–433
10. b, pp. 418–422	20. c, pp. 425–426	30. a, p. 433

PROBLEMS

1. Number of firms: d, a, c, b; Type of product: e, n, f, e, or f; Control over price: m, h, g, g; Conditions of entry: i, j, k, l; Non-price competition: m, g, h, g, or h

2. *a.* Average revenue: all are $10.00; Total revenue: $0, 10.00, 20.00, 30.00, 40.00, 50.00, 60.00; Marginal revenue: all are $10.00; *b.* yes, because price (average revenue) is constant and equal to marginal revenue; *c.* infinity; *d.* they are equal; *e.* see Figure 23.1 of the text for an example; *f.* horizontal, $10; *g.* constant, constant

3. *a.* See following table; *b.* 7, 380; *c.* see Figure 23.2 of the text for an example

	Market price = $200	
Output	Revenue	Profit
0	$ 0	$−300
1	200	−200
2	400	−50
3	600	90
4	800	210
5	1000	300
6	1200	360
7	1400	380
8	1600	350
9	1800	260
10	2000	100

4. *a.* 0, 5, 7 (last answer is the same as 3b); *b.* average total cost, output; (1) $146, ($200 − $146 = $54), ($54 × 7 = $378), (2) $140, ($120 − $140 = −$20), (−$20 × 5 = −$100); *c.* see Figure 23.3 of the text for an example

5. *a.* see following table; *b.* (1) Quantity supplied: 1000, 900, 800, 700, 600, 500, 400, (2) (a) 180, (b) 7, (c) 238, (d) enter, profits in the industry will attract them into the industry

Price	Quantity supplied	Profit
$360	10	$1700
290	9	1071
230	8	592
180	7	238
140	6	0
110	5	−150
80	4	−272
60	0	−300

6. *a.* 140; *b.* 6; *c.* 133 = 800 [the total quantity demanded at $140 divided by 6 (the output of each firm)]; *d.* 150 = 900 divided by 6

7. *a.* The curve is a horizontal line (see Figure 23.10 in the text); *b.* the curve slopes upward (see Figure 23.11 in the text)

SHORT ANSWER AND ESSAY QUESTIONS

1. pp. 413–414
2. pp. 413–414
3. p. 415
4. pp. 415–416
5. pp. 416–417
6. pp. 416–422
7. pp. 418–419
8. pp. 420–422
9. p. 421
10. pp. 423–426
11. pp. 425–426
12. pp. 423–425
13. pp. 425–428
14. pp. 427–431
15. pp. 429–430
16. pp. 431–433
17. p. 432
18. pp. 432–433
19. p. 433
20. p. 433

CHAPTER 24

Pure Monopoly

This chapter looks at the other end of the spectrum and examines pure monopoly, a market structure in which there is a **single seller**. Like pure competition, pure monopoly is rarely found in the U.S. economy, but it is still important. Many government-owned or government-regulated public utilities (electricity, water, natural gas, or cable television) are close to being pure monopolies, and other business firms are near monopolies because they have a large share of a market. Monopolies play a key role in the allocation of resources and the production of goods and services in the economy.

It is possible for a single seller or pure monopolist to dominate an industry if firms are prevented in some way from entering the industry. Factors that restrict firms from entering an industry are referred to as **barriers to entry**. The second section of this chapter is devoted to a description of the more important types of these barriers, such as economies of scale, patents and licenses, control of essential resources, and strategies for product pricing.

The chapter answers certain questions about the pure monopolist, such as what output will the firm produce, what price it will charge, and the amount of profit for the firm. In answering these questions and in comparing pure competition and pure monopoly, note the following:

1. Both the competitive and monopoly firm try to maximize profits by producing the output at which marginal cost and marginal revenue are equal (**MR = MC**).

2. The individual firm in a perfectly competitive industry sees a perfectly price elastic demand for its product at the going market price because it is but one of many firms in the industry, but the monopolist sees a market demand schedule that is less than perfectly price elastic because the **monopolist is the industry.** The purely competitive firm has *only* an output policy and is a price taker, but the monopolist is able to determine the price at which it will sell its product and is a price maker.

3. When demand is perfectly price elastic, price is equal to marginal revenue and is constant, but when demand is less than perfectly price elastic, marginal revenue is less than price and both decrease as the output of the firm increases.

4. Because entry is blocked in the long run, firms cannot enter a monopolistic industry to compete away profits as they can under conditions of pure competition.

This chapter has three other goals that deserve your study time and careful attention. One goal is to evaluate *economic efficiency* under pure monopoly. Here the purely competitive industry that you read about in Chapter 23 serves as the standard for comparison. You will learn that unlike the purely competitive industry, pure monopoly does not result in allocative efficiency. Although the inefficiencies of monopoly are offset or reduced by economies of scale and technological progress, they are reinforced by the presence of X-inefficiency and rent-seeking behavior.

The second goal is to discuss the possible pricing strategies of the pure monopolist. The monopolist may be able to set multiple prices for the same product even when the price differences are not justified by cost differences, a situation called **price discrimination.** This type of pricing power works only under certain conditions, and when it is effective it results in higher profits for the monopolist and also greater output.

The pricing power and inefficiency of the pure monopoly have made it a target for **regulation.** Therefore, the last section of the chapter explains the economic choices a regulatory agency faces when it must determine the maximum price that a public utility will be allowed to charge for its product. Here you will learn about the **socially optimum price** and the **fair-return price** and their effects on efficiency and profits. You will also discover the difficult economic dilemma regulatory officials face as they decide what prices they should permit a monopolist to charge.

■ **CHECKLIST**

When you have studied this chapter you should be able to

☐ Define pure monopoly based on five characteristics.
☐ Give several examples of monopoly and explain its importance.
☐ List and explain four potential barriers that would prevent or deter the entry of new firms into an industry.
☐ Define a natural monopoly using an average total-cost curve.
☐ Compare the demand curve for the pure monopolist with that of the purely competitive firm.
☐ Compute marginal revenue when you are given the demand for the monopolist's product.
☐ Explain the relationship between the price a monopolist charges and the marginal revenue from the sale of an additional unit of the product.

☐ Explain why the monopolist is a price maker.

☐ Use elasticity to explain the region of the demand curve where the monopolist produces.

☐ State the rule that explains what output the monopolist will produce and the price that will be charged.

☐ Determine the profit-maximizing output and price for the pure monopolist when you are given the demand and cost data.

☐ Explain why there is no supply curve for the pure monopolist.

☐ Counter two popular misconceptions about the price charged and the profit target in pure monopoly.

☐ Explain why monopolists can experience losses.

☐ Compare the economic effects of pure monopoly in terms of price, output, efficiency, and income distribution with a purely competitive industry producing the same product.

☐ Discuss the cost complications caused by economies of scale, X-inefficiency, rent-seeking behavior, and technological advance for pure monopoly and a purely competitive industry.

☐ Describe three general policy options for dealing with the economic inefficiency of monopoly.

☐ Define and give examples of price discrimination.

☐ List three conditions that are necessary for price discrimination.

☐ Explain the economic consequences of price discrimination.

☐ Use graphical analysis to identify the socially optimal price and the fair-return price for the regulated monopoly.

☐ Explain the dilemma of regulation based on a graphical analysis of a regulated monopoly.

■ **CHAPTER OUTLINE**

1. Pure monopoly is a market structure in which a single firm sells a product for which there are no close substitutes. These characteristics make the monopoly firm a **price maker** rather than a price taker, as was the case for the purely competitive firm. Entry into the industry is blocked, and there can be nonprice competition through advertising to influence the demand for the product.

    a. Examples of monopolies typically include regulated public utilities such as firms providing electricity, natural gas, local telephone service, and cable television, but they can also be unregulated, such as the De Beers diamond syndicate.

    b. The study of monopoly is useful for understanding the economic effects of other market structures—oligopoly and monopolistic competition—where there is some degree of monopoly power.

2. Pure monopoly can exist in the long run only if potential competitors find there are *barriers* that prevent their entry into the industry. There are four major **barriers to entry** that can prevent or severely restrict entry into an industry.

    a. *Economies of scale* can reduce production costs in the long run so that one producer can supply a range of output at a minimum total cost. If other producers

try to enter the industry, extensive financing would be required and they may not be able to produce output at a lower cost than the monopolist. The conditions for a **natural monopoly** arise in the extreme case in which the market demand curve cuts the long-run ATC curve where they are still declining. One firm can supply the market demand at a minimum cost.

    b. Government creates legal restrictions through issuing patents and licenses. **Patents** give the inventor the exclusive right to use or allow others to use the invention. **Licenses** give a firm the exclusive right to provide a good or service.

    c. The ownership or control of essential resources can effectively block entry into an industry.

    d. Pricing and other strategic practices, such as price cuts, advertising campaigns, and producing excess capacity, can deter entry into an industry by making entry very costly for a firm.

3. The **demand curve** of the pure monopolist is downsloping because the monopolist is the industry. By contrast, the purely competitive firm has a horizontal (perfectly price-elastic) demand curve because it is only one of many small firms in an industry. There are several implications of the downsloping shape of the monopolist's demand curve.

    a. The monopolist can increase sales only by lowering product price; thus price will exceed marginal revenue ($P > MR$) for every unit of output but the first.

    b. The monopolist will have a pricing policy, and is a *price maker;* the purely competitive firm has no price policy and is a price taker.

    c. The monopolist will avoid setting price in the inelastic segment of its demand curve because total revenue will be decreasing and marginal revenue will be negative; price will be set in the *elastic* portion of the demand curve.

4. The **output and price determination** of the profit-maximizing pure monopolist entails several considerations.

    a. Monopoly power in the sale of a product does not necessarily affect the prices that the monopolist pays for resources or the costs of production; an assumption is made in this chapter that the monopolist hires resources in a competitive market and uses the same technology as competitive firms.

    b. The monopolist produces that output at which marginal cost and marginal revenue are equal ($MR = MC$) and charges a price at which this profit-maximizing output can be sold.

    c. The monopolist has **no supply curve** because there is no unique relationship between price and quantity supplied; price and quantity supplied will change when demand and marginal revenue change. By contrast, a purely competitive firm has a supply curve that is the portion of the marginal cost curve above average variable cost, and there is a unique relationship between price and quantity supplied.

    d. Two popular misconceptions about monopolists are that they charge as high a price as possible and that they seek maximum profit per unit of output.

e. The monopolist is ***not guaranteed a profit*** and can experience losses because of weak demand for a product or high costs of production.

5. Pure monopoly has significant ***economic effects*** on the economy when compared to outcomes that would be produced in a purely competitive market.

   a. The pure monopolist charges a *higher price* and *produces less output* than would be produced by a purely competitive industry. Pure monopoly is **not productively efficient** because price is greater than the minimum of average cost. It is **not allocatively efficient** because price is greater than marginal cost.

   b. Monopoly contributes to income inequality in the economy by transferring income from consumers to stockholders who own the monopoly.

   c. A pure monopolist in an industry may produce output at a lower or higher average cost than would be the case for a purely competitive industry producing the same product. The costs of production may differ between the two industries for four reasons.

   (1) ***Economies of scale*** in the production of the product allow the pure monopolist to produce it at a lower long-run average cost than a large number of small pure competitors. In the extreme, a firm may be a ***natural monopoly*** that can supply the market demand at the lowest average cost. There can also be other factors such as *simultaneous consumption* and *network effects* that create extensive economies of scale for firms, especially those firms involved in information technology.

   (2) If a pure monopolist is more susceptible to ***X-inefficiency*** than firms in a purely competitive industry, then long-run average costs at every level of output are higher than those of purely competitive firms.

   (3) ***Rent-seeking*** expenditures in the form of legal fees, lobbying, and public-relations expenses to obtain or maintain a position as a monopoly add nothing to output, but do increase monopoly costs.

   (4) Monopoly is not likely to contribute to technological advance because there is little incentive for the monopolist to produce a more advanced product. The threat of potential competition, however, may stimulate research and technological advance, but the purpose of this effort is often to restrict or block entry into the industry.

   d. Monopoly causes problems for an economy because of higher prices and restricted output. Monopoly, however, is relatively rare. Technological advance and the development of substitute products can also undermine a monopoly. The policy options for dealing with the economic inefficiency of monopoly include the use of antitrust laws and the breakup of firms, the regulation of price, output, and profits of the monopolist, and simply ignoring the monopoly because its position cannot be sustained.

6. To increase profits a pure monopolist may engage in ***price discrimination*** by charging different prices to different buyers of the same product (when the price differences do not represent differences in the costs of producing the product).

   a. To discriminate, the seller must have some monopoly power, be capable of separating buyers into groups with different price elasticities of demand, and be able to prevent the resale of the product from one group to another group.

   b. Price discrimination is common in the U.S. economy. Airlines charge different fares to different passengers for the same flight. Movie theaters vary prices for the same product based on time of day or age. Discount coupons allow firms to charge different prices to different customers for the purchase of the same product.

   c. There are several consequences from ***perfect price discrimination,*** in which the seller charges each customer the highest price he or she would be willing to pay for the product. It increases the profits, but also increases the output of the monopolist.

7. Monopolies are often ***regulated*** by government to reduce the misallocation of resources and control prices.

   a. A price ceiling determined by the intersection of the marginal-cost and demand schedules is the ***socially optimum price*** and improves the allocation of resources.

   b. This ceiling may force the firm to produce at a loss, and therefore government may set the ceiling at a level determined by the intersection of the average cost and demand schedules to allow the monopolist a ***fair return.***

   c. The dilemma of regulation is that the socially optimum price may cause losses for the monopolist, and a fair-return price may result in a less efficient allocation of resources.

■ **HINTS AND TIPS**

1. Make sure you understand ***how pure monopoly differs from pure competition.*** Here are key distinctions: (a) The monopolist's demand curve is downsloping, not horizontal as in pure competition; (b) the monopolist's marginal revenue is less than price (or average revenue) for each level of output except the first, whereas in pure competition marginal revenue equals price; (c) the monopoly firm is a price maker, not a price taker as in pure competition; (d) *the firm is the industry* in monopoly, but not in pure competition; (e) there is the potential for long-run economic profits in pure monopoly, but purely competitive firms will only break even in the long run; and (f) there is no supply curve for a pure monopoly, but there is one for the purely competitive firm.

2. A key similarity between a profit-maximizing pure monopolist and a purely competitive firm is that both types of firms will produce up to that output level at which marginal revenue equals marginal cost (***MR = MC***).

3. Figure 24.3 helps explain why the profit-maximizing monopolist will always want to select some price and quantity combination in the ***elastic*** and not in the ***inelastic*** portion of the demand. In the inelastic portion, total revenue declines and marginal revenue is negative.

4. Drawing the marginal revenue curve for a monopolist with a linear demand curve is easy if you remember that the marginal revenue curve will always be a straight line that intersects the quantity axis at half of the level of output as the demand curve. (See Figure 24.3.)

5. Spend extra time studying Figure 24.8 and reading the related discussion. It will help you see how *price discrimination* results in more profits, a greater output, and a higher price for some consumers and lower prices for other consumers.

■ **IMPORTANT TERMS**

pure monopoly	price discrimination
barrier to entry	socially optimal price
X-inefficiency	fair-return price
rent-seeking behavior	

SELF-TEST

■ **FILL-IN QUESTIONS**

1. Pure monopoly is an industry in which a single firm is the sole producer of a product for which there are no close (substitutes, complements) _____ and into which entry in the long run is effectively (open, blocked) _____.

2. The closest example of pure monopoly would be government-regulated (nonprofit organizations, public utilities) _____ that provide water, electricity, or natural gas. There are also "near monopolies," such as private businesses that might account for (40, 80) _____% of a particular market, or businesses in a geographic region that are the (multiple, sole) _____ supplier(s) of a good or service.

3. If there are substantial economies of scale in the production of a product, a small-scale firm will find it difficult to enter into and survive in an industry because its average costs will be (greater, less) _____ than those of established firms, and a firm will find it (easy, difficult) _____ to start out on a large scale because it will be nearly impossible to acquire the needed financing.

4. Legal barriers to entry by government include granting an inventor the exclusive right to produce a product for 20 years, or a (license, patent) _____, and limiting entry into an industry or occupation through its issuing of a _____.

5. Other barriers to entry include the ownership of essential (markets, resources) _____ and

strategic changes in product (price, regulation) _____.

6. The demand schedule confronting the pure monopolist is (perfectly elastic, downsloping) _____. This means that marginal revenue is (greater, less) _____ than average revenue (or price) and that both marginal revenue and average revenue (increase, decrease) _____ as output increases.

7. When demand is price elastic, a decrease in price will (increase, decrease) _____ total revenue, but when demand is price inelastic, a decrease in price will _____ total revenue. The demand curve for the purely competitive firm is (horizontal, downsloping) _____, but it is _____ for the monopolist. The profit-maximizing monopolist will want to set price in the price (elastic, inelastic) _____ portion of its demand curve.

8. The supply curve for a purely competitive firm is the portion of the (average-variable-cost, marginal-cost) _____ curve that lies above the _____ curve. The supply curve for the monopolist (is the same, does not exist) _____.

9. When the economic profit of a monopolist is at a maximum, (marginal, average) _____ revenue equals _____ cost and price is (greater, less) _____ than marginal cost.

10. Two common misconceptions about pure monopoly are that it charges the (lowest, highest) _____ price possible and seeks the maximum (normal, per-unit) _____ profit.

11. The pure monopolist (is, is not) _____ guaranteed an economic profit; in fact, the pure monopolist can experience economic losses in the (short run, long run) _____ because of (strong, weak) _____ demand for the monopoly product.

12. The monopolist will typically charge a (lower, higher) _____ price and produce (less, more) _____ output and is (less, more) _____ efficient than if the product was produced in a purely competitive industry.

a. The monopolist is inefficient *productively* because the average (variable, total) _____ cost of producing a product is not at a (maximum, minimum) _____.

b. It is inefficient *allocatively* because (marginal revenue, price) _____ is not equal to (marginal, total) _____ cost.

c. Monopolies seem to result in a greater inequality in the distribution of income because the owners of monopolies are largely in the (upper, lower) _____ income groups.

13. Resources can be said to be more efficiently allocated by pure competition than by pure monopoly only if the purely competitive firms and the monopoly have the same (costs, revenues) _____, and they will not be the same if the monopolist

a. by virtue of being a large firm enjoys (economies, diseconomies) _____ of scale not available to a pure competitor;

b. is more susceptible to X-(efficiency, inefficiency) _____ than pure competitors;

c. may need to make (liability, rent-seeking) _____ expenditures to obtain or maintain monopoly privileges granted by government; and,

d. reduces costs through adopting (higher prices, new technology) _____.

14. The incidence of pure monopoly is relatively (rare, common) _____ because eventually new developments in technology (strengthen, weaken) _____ monopoly power or (substitute, complementary) _____ products are developed.

15. Three general policy options to reduce the economic (losses, inefficiency) _____ of a monopoly are to file charges against it through (liability, antitrust) _____ laws, have government regulate it if it is a (conglomerate, natural monopoly) _____, or ignore it if it is unsustainable.

16. Price discrimination occurs whenever a product is sold at different (markets, prices) _____, and these differences are not equal to the differences in the (revenue from, cost of) _____ producing the product.

17. Price discrimination is possible when the following three conditions exist:

a. _____

b. _____

c. _____

18. The two economic consequences of a monopolist's use of price discrimination are (an increase, a decrease) _____ in profits and _____ in the output.

19. If the monopolist were regulated and a socially optimal price for the product were sought, the price would be set equal to (marginal, average total) _____ cost. Such a legal price would achieve (productive, allocative) _____ efficiency but might result in losses for the monopolist.

20. If a regulated monopolist is allowed to earn a fair return, the ceiling price for the product would be set equal to (marginal, average total) _____ cost. Such a legal price falls short of (allocative, productive) _____ efficiency.

■ **TRUE–FALSE QUESTIONS**

Circle T if the statement is true, F if it is false.

1. The pure monopolist produces a product for which there are no close substitutes. **T F**

2. The weaker the barriers to entry into an industry, the more competition there will be in the industry, other things equal. **T F**

3. In pure monopoly, there are strong barriers to entry. **T F**

4. A monopolist may create an entry barrier by price cutting or substantially increasing the advertising of its product. **T F**

5. The monopolist can increase the sales of its product if it charges a lower price. **T F**

6. As a monopolist increases its output, it finds that its total revenue at first decreases, and that after some output level is reached, its total revenue begins to increase. **T F**

7. A purely competitive firm is a price taker but a monopolist is a price maker. **T F**

8. A monopolist will avoid setting a price in the *inelastic* segment of the demand curve and prefer to set the price in the *elastic* segment. **T F**

9. The monopolist determines the profit-maximizing output by producing that output at which marginal cost and marginal revenue are equal and sets the product price equal to marginal cost and marginal revenue at that output. **T F**

10. The supply curve for a monopolist is the upsloping portion of the marginal cost curve that lies above the average variable cost. **T F**

11. A monopolist will charge the highest price it can get. **T F**

12. A monopolist seeks maximum total profits, not maximum unit profits. **T F**

13. Pure monopoly guarantees economic profits. **T F**

14. Resources are misallocated by monopoly because price is not equal to marginal cost. **T F**

15. One of the economic effects of monopoly is less income inequality.   **T F**

16. When there are substantial economies of scale in the production of a product, the monopolist may charge a price that is lower than the price that would prevail if the product were produced by a purely competitive industry. **T F**

17. The purely competitive firm is more likely to be affected by X-inefficiency than a monopolist.   **T F**

18. Rent-seeking expenditures that monopolists make to obtain or maintain monopoly privilege have no effect on the firm's costs.   **T F**

19. The general view of economists is that a pure monopoly is efficient because it has strong incentives to be technologically progressive.   **T F**

20. One general policy option for a monopoly that creates substantial economic inefficiency and is long lasting is to directly regulate its prices and operation. **T F**

21. Price discrimination occurs when a given product is sold at more than one price and these price differences are not justified by cost differences.   **T F**

22. A discriminating monopolist will produce a larger output than a nondiscriminating monopolist.   **T F**

23. The regulated utility is likely to make an economic profit when price is set to achieve the most efficient allocation of resources ($P = MC$).   **T F**

24. A fair-return price for a regulated utility would have price set to equal average total cost.   **T F**

25. The dilemma of monopoly regulation is that the production by a monopolist of an output that causes no misallocation of resources may force the monopolist to suffer an economic loss.   **T F**

■ **MULTIPLE-CHOICE QUESTIONS**

Circle the letter that corresponds to the best answer.

1. Which would be defining characteristics of pure monopoly?
  (a) The firm does no advertising and it sells a standardized product.
  (b) No close substitutes for the product exist and there is one seller.
  (c) The firm can easily enter into or exit from the industry and profits are guaranteed.
  (d) The firm holds a patent and is technologically progressive.

2. A barrier to entry that significantly contributes to the establishment of a monopoly would be
  (a) economies of scale
  (b) price-taking behavior
  (c) technological progress
  (d) X-inefficiency

3. The demand curve for the pure monopolist is
  (a) perfectly price elastic
  (b) perfectly price inelastic
  (c) downsloping
  (d) upsloping

4. Which is true with respect to the demand data confronting a monopolist?
  (a) Marginal revenue is greater than average revenue.
  (b) Marginal revenue decreases as average revenue decreases.
  (c) Demand is perfectly price elastic.
  (d) Average revenue (or price) increases as the output of the firm increases.

5. When the monopolist is maximizing total profits or minimizing losses,
  (a) total revenue is greater than total cost
  (b) average revenue is greater than average total cost
  (c) average revenue is greater than marginal cost
  (d) average total cost is less than marginal cost

6. At which combination of price and marginal revenue is the price elasticity of demand less than 1?
  (a) Price equals $102, marginal revenue equals $42.
  (b) Price equals $92, marginal revenue equals $22.
  (c) Price equals $82, marginal revenue equals $2.
  (d) Price equals $72, marginal revenue equals −$18.

7. The region of demand in which the monopolist will choose a price-output combination will be the
  (a) elastic one because total revenue will increase as price declines and output increases
  (b) inelastic one because total revenue will increase as price declines and output increases
  (c) elastic one because total revenue will decrease as price declines and output increases
  (d) inelastic one because total revenue will decrease as price declines and output increases

8. At present output a monopolist determines that its marginal cost is $18 and its marginal revenue is $21. The monopolist will maximize profits or minimize losses by
  (a) increasing price while keeping output constant
  (b) decreasing price and increasing output
  (c) decreasing both price and output
  (d) increasing both price and output

Answer Questions 9, 10, 11, and 12 based on the demand and cost data for a pure monopolist given in the following table.

Output	Price	Total cost
0	$1000	$ 500
1	600	520
2	500	580
3	400	700
4	300	1000
5	200	1500

9. How many units of output will the profit-maximizing monopolist produce?
  (a) 1
  (b) 2
  (c) 3
  (d) 4

10. The profit-maximizing monopolist would set its price at
(a) $120
(b) $200
(c) $233
(d) $400

11. If the monopolist could sell each unit of the product at the maximum price the buyer of that unit would be willing to pay for it, and if the monopolist sold 4 units, total revenue would be
(a) $1200
(b) $1800
(c) $2000
(d) $2800

12. If the monopolist were forced to produce the socially optimal output by the imposition of a ceiling price, the ceiling price would have to be
(a) $200
(b) $300
(c) $400
(d) $500

13. The supply curve for a pure monopolist
(a) is the portion of the marginal cost curve that lies above the average variable cost curve
(b) is perfectly price elastic at the market price
(c) is upsloping
(d) does not exist

14. The analysis of monopoly indicates that the monopolist
(a) will charge the highest price it can get
(b) will seek to maximize total profits
(c) is guaranteed an economic profit
(d) is only interested in normal profit

15. When compared with the purely competitive industry with identical costs of production, a monopolist will charge a
(a) higher price and produce more output
(b) lower price and produce more output
(c) lower price and produce less output
(d) higher price and produce less output

16. At an equilibrium level of output, a monopolist is *not* productively efficient because
(a) the average total cost of producing the product is not at a minimum
(b) the marginal cost of producing the last unit is equal to its price
(c) it is earning a profit
(d) average revenue is less than the cost of producing an extra unit of output

17. Which will tend to increase the inefficiencies of the monopoly producer?
(a) price-taking behavior
(b) rent-seeking behavior
(c) economies of scale
(d) technological progress

18. Which is one of the conditions that must be realized before a seller finds that price discrimination is workable?
(a) The demand for the product is perfectly elastic.
(b) The seller must be able to segment the market.

(c) The buyer must be able to resell the product.
(d) The product must be a service.

19. If a monopolist engages in price discrimination rather than charging all buyers the same price, its
(a) profits and its output are greater
(b) profits and its output are smaller
(c) profits are greater and its output is smaller
(d) profits are smaller and its output is greater

Answer Questions 20, 21, 22, and 23 based on the demand and cost data for a pure monopolist given in the following table.

Quantity demanded	Price	Total cost
0	$700	$ 300
1	650	400
2	600	450
3	550	510
4	500	590
5	450	700
6	400	840
7	350	1020
8	300	1250
9	250	1540
10	200	1900

20. The profit-maximizing output and price for this monopolist would be
(a) 5 units and a $450 price
(b) 6 units and a $400 price
(c) 7 units and a $350 price
(d) 8 units and a $300 price

In answering Questions 21, 22, and 23, assume this monopolist is able to engage in price discrimination and sell each unit of the product at a price equal to the maximum price the buyer of that unit would be willing to pay.

21. The marginal revenue that the price-discriminating monopolist obtains from the sale of an additional unit is equal to
(a) total revenue
(b) average cost
(c) unit cost
(d) price

22. The profit-maximizing output for the price-discriminating monopolist would be
(a) 6 units
(b) 7 units
(c) 8 units
(d) 9 units

23. How much greater would the total economic profits be for the discriminating monopolist than the non-discriminating monopolist?
(a) $720
(b) $830
(c) $990
(d) $1070

Question 24 is based on the following graph.

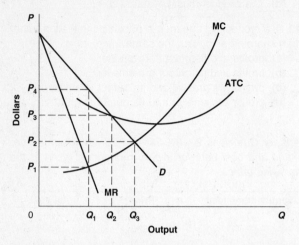

24. The price and output combination for the unregulated profit-maximizing monopoly compared with the socially optimal price and output combination for the regulated monopoly would be, respectively,
(a) P_4 and Q_1 versus P_3 and Q_2
(b) P_4 and Q_1 versus P_2 and Q_3
(c) P_3 and Q_2 versus P_4 and Q_1
(d) P_2 and Q_3 versus P_3 and Q_2

25. A monopolist who is limited by the imposition of a ceiling price to a fair return sells the product at a price equal to
(a) average total cost
(b) average variable cost
(c) marginal cost
(d) average fixed cost

■ **PROBLEMS**

1. The demand schedule for the product produced by a monopolist is given in the following table.

Quantity demanded	Price	Total revenue	Marginal revenue	Price elasticity
0	$700	$_____		
1	650	_____	$_____	_____
2	600	_____	_____	_____
3	550	_____	_____	_____
4	500	_____	_____	_____
5	450	_____	_____	_____
6	400	_____	_____	_____
7	350	_____	_____	_____
8	300	_____	_____	_____
9	250	_____	_____	_____
10	200	_____	_____	_____
11	150	_____	_____	_____
12	100	_____	_____	_____
13	50	_____	_____	_____
14	0	_____	_____	_____

a. Complete the table by computing total revenue, marginal revenue, and the price elasticity of demand (use midpoints formula).
b. The relationships in the table indicate that
(1) total revenue rises from $0 to a maximum of

$_____ as price falls from $700 to

$_____, and as price falls to $0, total rev-

enue falls from its maximum to $_____;
(2) the relationship between price and total revenue suggests that demand is price (elastic, inelastic)

_____ when quantity demanded is
between 0 and 7 units of output, but that demand is

price (elastic, inelastic) _____ when quantity demanded is between 8 units and 14 units;
(3) when demand is price elastic and total revenue rises from $0 to a maximum, marginal revenue is

(negative, positive) _____, but when demand is price inelastic and total revenue falls from

its maximum, marginal revenue is _____.
c. Use the data in the previous table and the graph on page 281 to plot and graph the demand curve and the marginal revenue curve for the monopolist. Indicate the portion of the demand curve that is price elastic and the portion that is price inelastic.

2. The following table shows demand and cost data for a pure monopolist.

Quantity	Price	Total revenue	Marginal revenue	Total cost	Marginal cost
0	$17	$_____		$10	
1	16	_____	$_____	18	$_____
2	15	_____	_____	23	_____
3	14	_____	_____	25	_____
4	13	_____	_____	27	_____
5	12	_____	_____	28	_____
6	11	_____	_____	32	_____
7	10	_____	_____	40	_____
8	9	_____	_____	50	_____
9	8	_____	_____	64	_____
10	7	_____	_____	80	_____

a. Complete the table by filling in the columns for total revenue, marginal revenue, and marginal cost.
b. Answer the next three questions using the data you calculated in the table.

(1) What output will the monopolist produce? _____

(2) What price will the monopolist charge? _____
(3) What total profit will the monopolist receive at the

profit-maximizing level of output? _____

3. Now assume that the pure monopolist in problem 2 is able to engage in price discrimination and sell each unit of the product at a price equal to the maximum price the buyer of that unit of the product would be willing to pay.

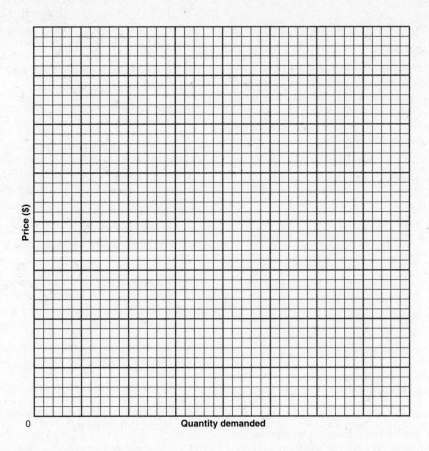

a. Complete the following table by computing total revenue and marginal revenue.

Quantity	Price	Total revenue	Marginal revenue	Total cost	Marginal cost
0	$17	$____		$10	
1	16	____	$____	18	$____
2	15	____	____	23	____
3	14	____	____	25	____
4	13	____	____	27	____
5	12	____	____	28	____
6	11	____	____	32	____
7	10	____	____	40	____
8	9	____	____	50	____
9	8	____	____	64	____
10	7	____	____	80	____

b. From the table it can be seen that
(1) the marginal revenue that the discriminating monopolist obtains from the sale of an additional unit

is equal to the _____;
(2) using the same table of costs, the discriminating monopolist would produce _____ units of the product, charge the buyer of the last unit of product produced a price of $_____, and

obtain a total economic profit of $_____;
(3) If the pure monopolist is able to engage in price discrimination its profits will be (larger, smaller, the

same) _____ and it will produce an output that is (larger, smaller, the same)_____.

4. In the following table are cost and demand data for a pure monopolist.

Quantity demanded	Price	Marginal revenue	Average cost	Marginal cost
0	$17.50			
1	16.00	$16.00	$24.00	$24.00
2	14.50	13.00	15.00	6.00
3	13.00	10.00	11.67	5.00
4	11.50	7.00	10.50	7.00
5	10.00	4.00	10.00	8.00
6	8.50	1.00	9.75	8.50
7	7.00	−2.00	9.64	9.00
8	5.50	−5.00	9.34	9.25
9	4.00	−8.00	9.36	9.50

a. An unregulated monopolist would produce _____

units of this product, sell it at a price of $_____,

and receive a total profit of $_____.
b. If this monopolist were regulated and the maximum price it could charge were set equal to marginal cost,

it would produce _____ units of a product,

sell it at a price of $_____, and receive a

total profit of $_____: Such regulation

would either _____ the firm or require that the regulating government _____ the firm.

c. If the monopolist were not regulated and were allowed to engage in price discrimination by charging the maximum price it could obtain for each unit sold, it would produce 6 units (because the marginal revenue from the 6th unit and the marginal cost of the 6th unit would both be $8.50). Its total revenue would be $_____, its total costs would be $_____, and its total profit would be $_____.

d. If the monopolist were regulated and allowed to charge a fair-return price, it would produce _____ units of product, charge a price of $_____, and receive a profit of $_____.

e. From which situation—**a, b,** or **d**—does the most efficient allocation of resources result? _____ From which situation does the least efficient allocation result? _____ In practice, government would probably select situation _____.

5. Identify whether the following long-run conditions apply to a firm under pure monopoly (**M**), pure competition (**C**), or both. Put the appropriate letter(s) (**M** or **C**) next to the condition.

a. There is the potential for long-run profits because price is greater than or equal to average total cost.

_____

b. The firm's demand curve is perfectly elastic.

_____

c. The firm maximizes profits at the output level where **MC = MR.** _____

d. The firm exhibits productive efficiency because price is equal to the minimum average total cost.

_____

e. Price is greater than marginal revenue for each output level except the first. _____

f. There is an optimal allocation of resources because price is equal to marginal cost. _____

■ **SHORT ANSWER AND ESSAY QUESTIONS**

1. What is pure monopoly? Define its characteristics.

2. Give examples of monopoly. How might a professional sports team be considered a monopoly when there are other such teams in the nation?

3. Why are the economies of scale a barrier to entry?

4. Why are most natural monopolies also public utilities? What does government hope to achieve by granting

exclusive franchises to and regulating such natural monopolies?

5. How do patents and licenses create barriers to entry? Cite examples.

6. How can the monopolist use changes in price and other strategic actions to maintain a monopoly position?

7. Compare the pure monopolist and the individual pure competitor with respect to: (a) the demand schedule; (b) the marginal-revenue schedule; (c) the relationship between marginal revenue and average revenue; (d) price policy, and (e) the ability to administer (or set) price.

8. Explain why marginal revenue is always less than average revenue (price) when demand is less than perfectly elastic.

9. Suppose a pure monopolist discovered it was producing and selling an output at which the demand for its product was inelastic. Explain why a decrease in its output would increase its economic profits.

10. How does the profit-maximizing monopolist determine what output to produce? What price will it charge?

11. Why is there no supply curve for a monopoly?

12. Why does the monopolist not charge the highest possible price for its product?

13. Why does the monopolist not set the price for its product in such a way that average profit is a maximum?

14. Why are some monopolies unprofitable? Explain what will happen to the firm in the short run and the long run in this situation.

15. In what sense is resource allocation and production more efficient under conditions of pure competition than under monopoly conditions?

16. How do monopolies allegedly affect the distribution of income in the economy and why do monopolies seemingly have this effect on income distribution in the U.S. economy?

17. What are some reasons why costs might differ between a monopoly and purely competitive firms operating in the same industry? Give at least four possible reasons.

18. Explain how economies of scale offset some of the economic inefficiencies of a monopoly. Evaluate the importance of this factor in reducing a monopolist's cost.

19. What is X-inefficiency? How does it affect the cost of production for the monopolist?

20. A monopolist will often engage in rent-seeking behavior. Explain what this means and how it changes a monopolist's cost.

21. Evaluate this statement from an economic perspective: "A pure monopoly has great incentive to discover and use new technology."

22. What is meant by price discrimination? What conditions must be realized before it is workable?

23. Explain how a monopolist who perfectly discriminates would determine what price to charge for each unit of the product sold (or to charge each group of buyers).

24. How does price discrimination affect the profits and the output of the monopolist? How does it affect consumers?

25. Explain what public utility regulatory agencies attempt to do to eliminate the misallocation of resources that results from monopoly. Describe the dilemma of regulation for these agencies, and explain why a fair-return policy only reduces but does not eliminate misallocation.

ANSWERS

Chapter 24 Pure Monopoly

FILL-IN QUESTIONS

1. substitutes, blocked
2. public utilities, 80, sole
3. greater, difficult
4. patent, license
5. resources, price
6. downsloping, less, decrease
7. increase, decrease, horizontal, downsloping, elastic
8. marginal-cost, average-variable-cost, does not exist
9. marginal, marginal, greater
10. highest, per-unit
11. is not, short run, weak
12. higher, less, less; *a.* total, minimum; *b.* price, marginal; *c.* upper
13. costs; *a.* economies; *b.* inefficiency; *c.* rent-seeking; *d.* new technology
14. rare, weaken, substitute
15. inefficiency, antitrust, natural monopoly
16. prices, cost of
17. *a.* the seller has some monopoly power; *b.* the seller is able to separate buyers into groups that have different elasticities of demand for the product; *c.* the original buyers cannot resell the product
18. an increase, an increase
19. marginal, allocative
20. average total, allocative

TRUE–FALSE QUESTIONS

1. T, p. 438
2. T, p. 439
3. T, p. 439
4. T, p. 441
5. T, pp. 441–443
6. F, pp. 441–443
7. T, p. 443
8. T, pp. 443–444
9. F, pp. 444–445
10. F, pp. 445–446
11. F, p. 446
12. T, p. 446
13. F, pp. 446–447
14. T, pp. 447–448
15. F, p. 448
16. T, pp. 448–449
17. F, pp. 449–450
18. F, p. 450
19. F, p. 450
20. T, p. 451
21. T, p. 452
22. T, p. 453
23. F, pp. 454–455
24. T, p. 455
25. T, p. 455

MULTIPLE-CHOICE QUESTIONS

1. b, p. 438
2. a, pp. 439–440
3. c, pp. 441–442
4. b, pp. 441–443
5. c, pp. 444–446
6. d, pp. 443–444
7. a, pp. 443–444
8. b, pp. 444–446
9. c, pp. 444–446
10. d, pp. 444–446
11. b, p. 453
12. b, pp. 454–455
13. d, pp. 445–446
14. b, p. 446
15. d, pp. 447–448
16. a, pp. 447–448
17. b, p. 450
18. b, p. 452
19. a, p. 453
20. b, pp. 444–446
21. d, p. 453
22. c, p. 453
23. c, p. 453
24. b, pp. 454–455
25. a, pp. 454–455

PROBLEMS

1. *a.* Total revenue: $0, 650, 1200, 1650, 2000, 2250, 2400, 2450, 2400, 2250, 2000, 1650, 1200, 650, 0; Marginal revenue: $650, 550, 450, 350, 250, 150, 50, −50, −150, −250, −350, −450, −550, −650; Price elasticity: 27, 8.33, 4.60, 3.00, 2.11, 1.55, 1.15, .87, .65, .47, .33, .22, .12, .04; *b.* (1) $2450, $350, 0, (2) elastic, inelastic, (3) positive, negative; *c.* see Figure 24.3a in the text as an example

2. *a.* Total revenue: $0, 16, 30, 42, 52, 60, 66, 70, 72, 72, 70; Marginal revenue: $16, 14, 12, 10, 8, 6, 4, 2, 0, −2; Marginal cost: $8, 5, 2, 2, 1, 4, 8, 10, 14, 16; *b.* (1) 6, (2) $11, (3) $34 (TR of $66 minus TC of $32)

3. *a.* Total revenue: $0, 16, 31, 45, 58, 70, 81, 91, 100, 108, 115; Marginal revenue: $16, 15, 14, 13, 12, 11, 10, 9 , 8 , 7; Marginal cost: $8, 5, 2, 2, 1, 4, 8, 10, 14, 16; *b.* (1) price, (2), 7, 10, 51 (TR of $91 minus TC of $40), (3) larger, larger

4. *a.* 4, 11.50, 4.00; *b.* 6, 8.50, −7.50, bankrupt, subsidize; *c.* 73.50, 58.50, 15.00; *d.* 5, 10.00, zero; *e.* b or c, a, d

5. *a.* M; *b.* C; *c.* C, M; *d.* C; *e.* M; *f.* C

SHORT ANSWER AND ESSAY QUESTIONS

1. pp. 438–439
2. p. 439
3. pp. 439–440
4. pp. 439–440
5. pp. 440–441
6. p. 441
7. pp. 441–442
8. pp. 441–442
9. pp. 443–444
10. pp. 444–446
11. p. 445
12. p. 446
13. p. 446
14. pp. 446–447
15. pp. 447–448
16. p. 448
17. pp. 448–450
18. pp. 448–449
19. pp. 449–450
20. p. 450
21. p. 450
22. pp. 451–452
23. p. 453
24. p. 453
25. pp. 453–455

CHAPTER 25

Monopolistic Competition and Oligopoly

This chapter examines two market structures, monopolistic competition and oligopoly, that fall between the extremes of pure competition and pure monopoly. Both structures are important because they offer descriptions of firms and industries typically found in the U.S. economy.

Monopolistically competitive firms are prevalent because most retail establishments, such as clothing stores and restaurants, fall into the monopolistically competitive category. In such industries, there are a relatively large number of firms, so no one has a large market share, they sell differentiated products, and each has limited pricing power.

The chapter focuses on the **demand curve** for the monopolistically competitive firm. This demand curve differs from those found in pure competition and pure monopoly. As the individual firm changes the character of its product, or changes product promotion, both the costs of the firm and the demand for its product will change.

The **price-output** analysis of the monopolistic competitor is relatively simple. In the short run, this analysis is identical with the analysis of the price-output decision of a pure monopolist. Only in the long run does the competitive element make itself apparent: The entry of firms forces the price a firm charges to fall. This price, however, is not equal either to minimum average cost or to marginal cost; consequently, monopolistic competition can be said to be less efficient than pure competition.

This chapter also discusses **product variety** under monopolistic competition. A part of the competitive effort of individual firms is devoted to product differentiation, product development, and advertising. Each firm has three things to manipulate—price, product, and advertising—in maximizing profits. Although monopolistic competition has been characterized as inefficient, some of the positive benefits of product variety may offset some of the inefficiencies of this market structure.

The concept of **oligopoly** is fairly easy to grasp: a few firms that are mutually interdependent and that dominate the market for a product. The underlying causes of oligopoly are economies of scale and barriers to entry, subjects you read about earlier. Economists use **concentration ratios** and the **Herfindahl index** to measure the degree of firm dominance of an industry, but these processes have shortcomings.

More difficult to grasp is oligopoly behavior. **Game theory** helps explain *what is meant* by mutual interdependence and *why it exists* in an oligopoly. It also explains why specific conclusions cannot be drawn about the price and output decisions of individual firms. Oligopolists are loath to engage in price competition because of **mutual interdependence,** and frequently resort to **collusion** to set prices and sometimes use nonprice competition to determine market share. Collusion, however, does not give firms complete protection from competition because there are incentives to cheat on collusive agreements.

There is no standard model of oligopoly because of the diversity of markets and the uncertainty caused by mutual interdependence among firms. **Three oligopoly models,** however, cover the range of most market situations. The **kinked-demand curve** explains why, in the absence of collusion, oligopolists will not raise or lower their prices even when their costs change. This model does not explain what price oligopolists will set; it only explains why prices will be relatively inflexible.

The second model examines how oligopolists resort to **collusion** to set price. The collusion can be **overt,** as in a cartel agreement, or the collusion can be **covert,** as in a secret agreement. The OPEC oil cartel is a classic example of covert collusion. Obstacles, such as cheating on price, make collusive agreements difficult to establish and maintain.

The third model of oligopoly is **price leadership.** In some industries a dominant firm serves as the *price leader* for other firms. There is no overt collusion, only tacit understandings about price and competition among firms. This model explains why there are infrequent price changes, why the lead firm makes price and output announcements for other firms to follow, and why low pricing is used to prevent new entry. Such covert collusion, however, can be undermined by price wars.

The next-to-last section of the chapter looks at **advertising** in oligopoly. Product development and advertising are often the means of competition in oligopoly. Drawing conclusions about the effects of advertising, however, is difficult. Reasonable arguments can be made that advertising is both beneficial and costly for consumers and about whether advertising helps or hurts economic efficiency.

Compared with pure competition, oligopoly does not result in allocative or productive efficiency. Nevertheless, the qualifications noted at the end of the chapter may offset some of oligopoly's shortcomings.

■ **CHECKLIST**

When you have studied this chapter you should be able to

☐ Describe monopolistic competition in terms of the number of sellers, type of product, entry and exit conditions, and advertising.

☐ Cite three consequences from having relatively large numbers of sellers in monopolistic competition.

☐ Describe five aspects of differentiated products in monopolistic competition.

☐ Describe the entry and exit conditions in monopolistic competition.

☐ State the role of advertising and nonprice competition in monopolistic competition.

☐ Compare the firm's demand curve under monopolistic competition with a firm's demand curves in pure competition and pure monopoly.

☐ Determine the output of and the price charged by a monopolistic competitor in the short run when given cost and demand data.

☐ Explain why the price charged by a monopolistic competitor will in the long run tend to equal average cost and result in only a normal profit.

☐ Cite two real-world complications that may affect the outcome for monopolistically competitive firms in the long run.

☐ Show graphically how the typical firm in monopolistic competition achieves neither productive nor allocative efficiency and how excess capacity occurs.

☐ Discuss the effects of product variety in monopolistic competition.

☐ Explain why monopolistic competition is more complex in practice.

☐ Define oligopoly in terms of the number of producers, type of product, control over price, and interdependence.

☐ Explain how entry barriers and mergers contribute to the existence of oligopolies.

☐ Define a concentration ratio and cite its shortcomings.

☐ Use the Herfindahl index to assess the distribution of market power among dominant firms in an oligopoly.

☐ Use game theory to explain three characteristics of oligopoly behavior.

☐ Cite two reasons why there is no standard model of oligopoly.

☐ Use the kinked-demand theory to explain the tendency for prices to be inflexible in a noncollusive model oligopoly.

☐ Describe the price and output conditions for a cartel or collusive pricing model of oligopoly.

☐ Give real examples of overt and covert collusion.

☐ State six obstacles to collusion.

☐ Describe the price leadership model of oligopoly and its outcomes.

☐ Explain why advertising is often heavily used in oligopoly.

☐ Cite the potential positive and negative effects of advertising.

☐ Compare economic efficiency in oligopoly to other market structures.

■ **CHAPTER OUTLINE**

1. *Monopolistic competition* has several defining characteristics.

   a. The *relatively large number of sellers* means that each has a small market share, there is no collusion, and firms take actions that are independent of each other.

   b. Monopolistic competition exhibits **product differentiation**. This differentiation occurs through: differences in attributes or features of products; services to customers; location and accessibility; brand names and packaging; and some control over price.

   c. *Entry* into the industry or *exit* is relatively easy.

   d. There is **nonprice competition** in the form of product differentiation and advertising.

   e. Monopolistically competitive firms are common, and examples include clothing stores, restaurants, and grocery stores.

2. Given the products produced in a monopolistically competitive industry and the amounts of promotional activity, it is possible to analyze the **price and output decisions** of a firm.

   a. The **demand curve** confronting each firm will be highly but not perfectly price elastic because each firm has many competitors who produce close but not perfect substitutes for the product it produces.

   (1) Comparing the demand curve for the monopolistic competitor to other market structures suggests that it is not perfectly elastic, as is the case with the pure competitor, but it is also more elastic than the demand curve of the pure monopolist.

   (2) The degree of elasticity, however, for each monopolistic competitor will depend on the number of rivals and the extent of product differentiation.

   b. In the **short run** the individual firm will produce the output at which marginal cost and marginal revenue are equal and charge the price at which the output can be sold; either economic profits or losses may result in the short run.

   c. In the **long run** the entry and exodus of firms will tend to change the demand for the product of the individual firm in such a way that economic profits are eliminated and there are only normal profits. (Price and average costs are made equal to each other.)

3. Monopolistic competition among firms producing a given product and engaged in a given amount of promotional activity results in **less economic efficiency and more excess capacity** than does pure competition.

   a. The average cost of each firm is equal in the long run to its price. The industry **does not realize allocative efficiency** because output is smaller than the output at which marginal cost and price are equal. The industry **does not realize productive efficiency** because the output is less than the output at which average cost is a minimum.

   b. **Excess capacity** results because firms produce less output than at the minimum of average total cost. In monopolistic competition, many firms operate below optimal capacity.

4. Each monopolistically competitive firm attempts to differentiate its product and advertise it to increase the firm's profit. These activities give rise to **nonprice competition** among firms.

    a. The benefit of product variety is that firms offer consumers a wide range of types, styles, brands, and quality variants of a product. Products can also be improved. The expanded range of consumer choice from product differentiation and improvement may offset some of the economic inefficiency (excess capacity problem) of monopolistic competition.

    b. Monopolistic competition is more complex than the simple model presented in the chapter because the firm must constantly juggle three factors—price, product characteristics, and advertising—in seeking to maximize profits.

5. **Oligopoly** is frequently encountered in the U.S. economy.

    a. It is composed of a few firms that dominate an industry.

    b. It may produce homogeneous or differentiated products.

    c. Firms have control over price, and thus are price makers. **Mutual interdependence** exists because firms must consider the reaction of rivals to any change in price, output, product characteristic, or advertising.

    d. Barriers to entry, such as economies of scale or ownership, control over raw materials, patents, and pricing strategies, can explain the existence of oligopoly.

    e. Some industries have become oligopolistic not from internal growth but from external factors such as mergers.

    f. The concentration in an industry among a few large producers can be measured in several ways.

    (1) A **concentration ratio** gives the percentage of an industry's total sales provided by the largest firms. If the four largest firms account for 40 percent or more of the industry output, the industry is considered oligopolistic. Shortcomings of this measure include the imprecise definition of the market area and failure to take into account interindustry competition or import competition.

    (2) The **Herfindahl index** measures concentration more accurately because it accounts for the market share of each firm. It is the sum of the squared percentage market shares of all firms in the industry.

6. Insight into the pricing behavior of oligopolists can be gained by thinking of the oligopoly as a game of strategy. This **game theory** approach leads to three conclusions.

    a. Firms in an oligopolistic industry are mutually interdependent and must consider the actions of rivals when they make price decisions.

    b. Oligopoly often leads to overt or covert collusion among the firms to fix prices or to coordinate pricing because competition among oligopolists results in low prices and profits; collusion helps maintain higher prices and profits.

    c. Collusion creates incentives to cheat among oligopolists by lowering prices or increasing production to obtain more profit.

7. Economic analysis of oligopoly is difficult because of the diversity among the firms and complications resulting from mutual interdependence. Nevertheless, two important characteristics of oligopoly are inflexible prices and simultaneous price changes by firms. An analysis of three oligopoly models helps explain the pricing practices of oligopolists.

    a. In the **kinked-demand model** there is no collusion. Each firm believes that if it lowers its price its rivals will lower their prices, but if it raises its price its rivals *will not* increase their prices. Therefore the firm is reluctant to change its price for fear of reducing its profits. The model has two shortcomings: it does not explain how the going price gets set; prices are not as rigid as the model implies.

    b. Mutual interdependence indicates there is *collusion* among oligopoly firms to maintain or increase profits.

    (1) Firms that collude tend to set their prices and joint output at the same level a pure monopolist would set them.

    (2) **Collusion may be overt,** as in a cartel agreement. The OPEC cartel is an example of effective overt collusion.

    (3) **Collusion may be covert** whereby agreements or tacit understandings between firms set price or market share. Examples of such collusion have included bid rigging on milk prices for schools or fixing worldwide prices for a livestock feed additive.

    (4) At least six obstacles make it difficult for firms to collude or maintain collusive arrangements: difference in demand and cost among firms, the number of firms in the arrangement, incentives to cheat, changing economic conditions, potential for entry by other firms, and legal restrictions and penalties.

    c. **Price leadership** is a form of covert collusion in which one firm initiates price changes and the other firms in the industry follow the lead. Three price leadership tactics have been observed.

    (1) Price adjustments tend to be made infrequently, only when cost and demand conditions change to a significant degree.

    (2) The price leader announces the price change in various ways, through speeches, announcements, or other such activities.

    (3) The price set may not maximize short-run profits for the industry, especially if the industry wants to prevent entry by other firms.

    (4) Price leadership can break down and result in a price war. Eventually the wars end, and a price leader reemerges.

8. Oligopolistic firms often avoid price competition but engage in **product development and advertising** for two reasons: Price cuts are easily duplicated, but nonprice competition is more unique; and firms have more financial resources for advertising and product development.

a. The potential positive effects of advertising include providing low-cost information to consumers that reduces search time and monopoly power, thus enhancing economic efficiency.

b. The potential negative effects of advertising include manipulating consumers to pay higher prices, serving as a barrier to entry into an industry, and offsetting campaigns that raise product costs and prices.

9. The *efficiency of oligopoly* is difficult to evaluate.
a. Many economists think that oligopoly price and output characteristics are similar to those of monopoly. Oligopoly firms set output where price exceeds marginal cost and the minimum of average total cost. Oligopoly is allocatively inefficient (*P* > **MC**) and productively inefficient (*P* > **minimum ATC**).
b. This view must be qualified because of increased foreign competition to oligopolistic firms, the use of limit pricing that sets prices at less than the profit-maximizing price, and the technological advances arising from this market structure.

■ **HINTS AND TIPS**

1. Review the four basic market models in Table 23.1 so that you see how monopolistic competition and oligopoly compare with the other market models on five characteristics.

2. The same **MC = MR** rule for maximizing profits or minimizing losses for the firm from previous chapters is now used to determine output and price in monopolistic competition and in certain oligopoly models. If you understood how the rule applied under pure competition and pure monopoly, you should have no trouble applying it here.

3. Make sure you know how to interpret Figure 25.1 because it is an important graph. It illustrates why a representative firm in monopolistic competition just breaks even in the long run, and earns just a normal rather than an economic profit. It also shows how economic inefficiency in monopolistic competition produces excess capacity.

4. Where is the kink in the kinked-demand model? To find out, practice drawing the model. Then use Figure 25.4 to check your answer. Explain to yourself what each line means in the graph.

5. Price and output determinations under collusive oligopoly or a cartel are essentially the same as those for pure monopoly.

■ **IMPORTANT TERMS**

monopolistic competition
product differentiation
nonprice competition
excess capacity

oligopoly
homogeneous oligopoly
differentiated oligopoly
strategic behavior

mutual interdependence
concentration ratio
interindustry competition
import competition
Herfindahl index
game-theory model

collusion
kinked-demand curve
price war
cartel
tacit understandings
price leadership

SELF-TEST

■ **FILL-IN QUESTIONS**

1. In a monopolistically competitive market, there are a relatively (large, small) _____ number of producers who sell (standardized, differentiated) _____ products. Entry into such a market is relatively (difficult, easy) _____. The number of firms means that each one has a (large, small) _____ market share, the firms (do, do not) _____ collude, and they operate in (an independent, a dependent) _____ manner.

2. Identify the different aspects of production differentiation in monopolistic competition:
a. _____
b. _____
c. _____
d. _____
e. _____

3. In the *short run* for a monopolistically competitive firm,
a. the demand curve will be (more, less) _____ elastic than that facing a monopolist and _____ elastic than that facing a pure competitor;
b. the elasticity of this demand curve will depend on
(1) _____ and
(2) _____; and
c. it will produce the output level where marginal cost is (less than, equal to, greater than) _____ marginal revenue.

4. In the long run for a monopolistically competitive industry,
a. the *entry* of new firms will (increase, decrease) _____ the demand for the product produced by each firm in the industry and _____ the elasticity of that demand.
b. the price charged by the individual firm will tend to equal (average, marginal) _____ cost, its economic profits will tend to be (positive, zero)

_____, and its average cost will be (greater, less) _____ than the minimum average cost of producing and promoting the product.

5. Although representative firms in monopolistic competition tend to earn (economic, normal) _____ profits in the long run, there can be complications that may result in firms earning _____ profits in the long run. Some firms may achieve a degree of product differentiation that (can, cannot) _____ be duplicated by other firms. There may be (collusion, barriers to entry) _____ that prevent penetration of the market by other firms.

6. In monopolistic competition, price is (less than, equal to, greater than) _____ marginal cost, and so the market structure (does, does not) _____ yield allocative efficiency. Also, average total cost is (less than, equal to, greater than) _____ the minimum of average total cost, and so the market structure (does, does not) _____ result in (allocative, productive) _____ efficiency.

7. In the long run, the monopolistic competitor tries to earn economic profits by using (price, nonprice) _____ competition in the form of product differentiation and advertising. This results in a tradeoff between a choice of more consumer goods and services and (more, less) _____ economic efficiency.

8. The more complex model of monopolistic competition suggests that in seeking to maximize profits, each firm juggles the factors of (losses, price) _____, changes in (collusion, product) _____, and decisions about (controls, advertising) _____ until the firm feels no further change in the variables will result in greater profit.

9. In an oligopoly (many, a few) _____ large firms produce either a differentiated or a (heterogeneous, homogeneous) _____ product, and entry into such an industry is (easy, difficult) _____. The oligopolistic firm is a price (maker, taker) _____ and there is mutual (independence, interdependence) _____ among firms in an industry. The existence of oligopoly can be explained by (exit, entry) _____ barriers and by (markets, mergers) _____.

10. The percentage of the total industry sales accounted for by the top four firms in an industry is known as a four-firm (Herfindahl index, concentration ratio)

_____, whereas summing the squared percentage market shares of each firm in the industry is the way to calculate the _____.

11. The basics of the pricing behavior of oligopolists can be understood from a (game, advertising) _____ theory perspective. Oligopoly consists of a few firms that are mutually (funded, interdependent) _____. This means that when setting the price of its product, each producer (does, does not) _____ consider the reaction of its rivals. The monopolist (does, does not) _____ face this problem because it has no rivals, and the pure competitor, or monopolistic competitor, _____ face the problem because it has many rivals.

12. It is difficult to use formal economic analysis to explain the prices and outputs of oligopolists because oligopoly encompasses (diverse, similar) _____ market situation(s), and when firms are mutually interdependent, each firm is (certain, uncertain) _____ about how its rivals will react when it changes the price of its product. Despite the analytical problems, oligopoly prices tend to be (flexible, inflexible) _____ and oligopolists tend to change their prices (independently, together) _____.

13. The noncolluding oligopolist has a kinked-demand curve that

a. is highly (elastic, inelastic) _____ at prices above the current or going price and tends to be only slightly _____ or (elastic, inelastic) _____ below that price.
b. is drawn on the assumption that if the oligopolist raises its price its rivals (will, will not) _____ raise their prices or if it lowers its price its rivals _____ lower their prices.
c. has an associated marginal-(cost, revenue) _____ curve with a gap, such that small changes in the marginal-_____ curve do not change the price the oligopolist will charge.

14. A situation in which firms in an industry reach an agreement to fix prices, divide up the market, or otherwise restrict competition among them is called (concentration, collusion) _____. In this case, the prices they set and their combined output tend to be the same as that found with pure (competition, monopoly) _____.

15. A formal written agreement among sellers in which the price and the total output of the product and each seller's share of the market are specified is a (cartel, duopoly) _____. It is a form of (covert, overt) _____ collusion, whereas tacit understandings among firms to divide up a market would be _____ collusion.

16. Six obstacles to collusion among oligopolists are

a. _____

b. _____

c. _____

d. _____

e. _____

f. _____

17. When one firm in an oligopoly is almost always the first to change its price and the other firms change their prices after the first firm has changed its price, the oligopoly model is called the (price war, price leadership) _____ model. The tactics of this model include (infrequent, frequent) _____ price changes, announcements of such price changes, and (limit, no limit) _____ pricing. One event that can undermine this practice is (price leadership, price wars) _____.

18. There tends to be very little (price, nonprice) _____ competition among oligopolists and a great deal of _____ competition such as product development and advertising used to determine each firm's share of the market.

a. The positive view of advertising contends that it is (efficient, inefficient) _____ because it provides important information that (increases, reduces) _____ search costs, and information about competing goods _____ monopoly power.

b. The negative view of advertising suggests that it is (inefficient, efficient) _____ because the advertising campaigns are (offsetting, reinforcing) _____, the creation of brand loyalty serves as a barrier to (entry, exit) _____, and consumers are persuaded to pay (lower, higher) _____ prices than they would have paid otherwise.

19. Although it is difficult to evaluate the economic efficiency of oligopoly, when comparisons are made to pure competition, the conclusion drawn is that oligopoly (is, is not) _____ allocatively efficient and (is, is not) _____ productively efficient. The price and output behavior of the oligopolist is more likely to be

similar to that found under (competition, monopoly) _____.

20. The view that oligopoly is inefficient in the short run needs to be qualified because of the effects of (decreased, increased) _____ foreign competition that make pricing more competitive, policies to restrict entry into an industry that keep consumer prices (high, low) _____, and profits that are used to fund (more, less) _____ research and development that produces improved products.

■ **TRUE–FALSE QUESTIONS**

Circle T if the statement is true, F if it is false.

1. Monopolistic competitors have no control over the price of their products. **T F**

2. The firm's reputation for servicing or exchanging its product is a form of product differentiation under monopolistic competition. **T F**

3. Entry is relatively easy in pure competition, but there are significant barriers to entry in monopolistic competition. **T F**

4. The smaller the number of firms in an industry and the greater the extent of product differentiation, the greater will be the elasticity of the individual seller's demand curve. **T F**

5. The demand curve of the monopolistic competitor is likely to be less elastic than the demand curve of the pure monopolist. **T F**

6. In the short run, firms that are monopolistically competitive may earn economic profits or incur losses. **T F**

7. The long-run equilibrium position in monopolistic competition would be where price is equal to marginal cost. **T F**

8. Representative firms in a monopolistically competitive market earn economic profits in the long run. **T F**

9. One reason why monopolistic competition is economically inefficient is that the average cost of producing the product is greater than the minimum average cost at which the product could be produced. **T F**

10. The more product variety offered to consumers by a monopolistically competitive industry, the less excess capacity there will be in that industry. **T F**

11. Successful product improvement by one firm has little or no effect on other firms under monopolistic competition. **T F**

12. The products produced by the firms in an oligopolistic industry may be either homogeneous or differentiated. **T F**

13. Oligopolistic industries contain a few large firms that act independently of one another. **T F**

14. Concentration ratios include adjustments for interindustry competition in measuring concentration in an industry. **T F**

15. The Herfindahl index is the sum of the market shares of all firms in the industry. **T F**

16. Game theory analysis of oligopolist behavior suggests that oligopolists will not find any benefit in collusion. **T F**

17. One shortcoming of kinked-demand analysis is that it does not explain how the going oligopoly price was established in the first place. **T F**

18. Collusion occurs when firms in an industry reach an overt or covert agreement to fix prices, divide or share the market, and in some way restrict competition among the firms. **T F**

19. A cartel is usually a written agreement among firms which sets the price of the product and determines each firm's share of the market. **T F**

20. Secret price concessions and other forms of cheating will strengthen collusion. **T F**

21. The practice of price leadership is almost always based on a formal written or oral agreement. **T F**

22. Limit pricing is the leadership tactic of limiting price increases to a certain percentage of the basic price of a product. **T F**

23. Those contending that advertising contributes to monopoly power argue that the advertising by established firms creates barriers to the entry of new firms into an industry. **T F**

24. Oligopolies are allocatively and productively efficient when compared with the standard set in pure competition. **T F**

25. Increased competition from foreign firms in oligopolistic industries has stimulated more competitive pricing in those industries. **T F**

■ MULTIPLE-CHOICE QUESTIONS

Circle the letter that corresponds to the best answer.

1. Which would be most characteristic of monopolistic competition?
(a) collusion among firms
(b) firms selling a homogeneous product
(c) a relatively large number of firms
(d) difficult entry into and exit from the industry

2. The concern that monopolistically competitive firms express about product attributes, services to customers, or brand names are aspects of
(a) allocative efficiency in the industry
(b) collusion in the industry
(c) product differentiation
(d) concentration ratios

3. The demand curve a monopolistically competitive firm faces is

(a) perfectly elastic
(b) perfectly inelastic
(c) highly, but not perfectly inelastic
(d) highly, but not perfectly elastic

4. In the short run, a typical monopolistically competitive firm will earn
(a) only a normal profit
(b) only an economic profit
(c) only an economic or normal profit
(d) an economic or normal profit or suffer an economic loss

5. A monopolistically competitive firm is producing at an output level in the short run where average total cost is $3.50, price is $3.00, marginal revenue is $1.50, and marginal cost is $1.50. This firm is operating
(a) with an economic loss in the short run
(b) with an economic profit in the short run
(c) at the break-even level of output in the short run
(d) at an inefficient level of output in the short run

6. If firms enter a monopolistically competitive industry, we would expect the typical firm's demand curve to
(a) increase and the firm's price to increase
(b) decrease and the firm's price to decrease
(c) remain the same but the firm's price to increase
(d) remain the same and the firm's price to remain the same

Answer Questions 7, 8, 9, and 10 on the basis of the following diagram for a monopolistically competitive firm in short-run equilibrium.

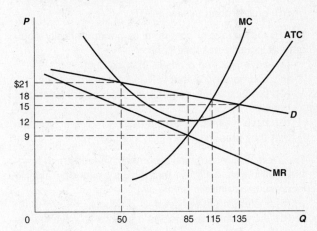

7. The firm's profit-maximizing price will be
(a) $9
(b) $12
(c) $15
(d) $18

8. The equilibrium output for this firm will be
(a) 50
(b) 85
(c) 115
(d) 135

9. This firm will realize an economic profit of
(a) $510

(b) $765
(c) $1021
(d) $1170

10. If firms enter this industry in the long run,
(a) demand will decrease
(b) demand will increase
(c) the marginal revenue curve will shift upward
(d) economic profits will increase

11. Given a representative firm in a typical monopolistically competitive industry, in the long run
(a) the firm will produce that output at which marginal cost and price are equal
(b) the elasticity of demand for the firm's product will be less than it was in the short run
(c) the number of competitors the firm faces will be greater than it was in the short run
(d) the economic profits being earned by the firm will tend to equal zero

12. *Productive* efficiency is not realized in monopolistic competition because production occurs where
(a) MR is greater than MC
(b) MR is less than MC
(c) ATC is greater than minimum ATC
(d) ATC is less than MR and greater than MC

13. The *underallocation* of resources in monopolistic competition means that at the profit-maximizing level of output, price is
(a) greater than MC
(b) less than MC
(c) less than MR
(d) greater than minimum ATC

14. Excess capacity occurs in a monopolistically competitive industry because firms
(a) advertise and promote their product
(b) charge a price that is less than marginal cost
(c) produce at an output level short of the least-cost output
(d) have a perfectly elastic demand for the products that they produce

15. Were a monopolistically competitive industry in long-run equilibrium, a firm in that industry might be able to increase its economic profits by
(a) increasing the price of its product
(b) increasing the amounts it spends to advertise its product
(c) decreasing the price of its product
(d) decreasing the output of its product

16. Which would be most characteristic of oligopoly?
(a) easy entry into the industry
(b) a few large producers
(c) product standardization
(d) no control over price

17. Mutual interdependence means that
(a) each firm produces a product similar but not identical to the products produced by its rivals
(b) each firm produces a product identical to the products produced by its rivals

(c) each firm must consider the reactions of its rivals when it determines its price policy
(d) each firm faces a perfectly elastic demand for its product

18. One major problem with concentration ratios is that they fail to take into account
(a) the national market for products
(b) competition from imported products
(c) excess capacity in production
(d) mutual interdependence

19. Industry A is composed of four large firms that hold market shares of 40, 30, 20, and 10. The Herfindahl index for this industry is
(a) 100
(b) 1000
(c) 3000
(d) 4500

Questions 20, 21, and 22 are based on the following payoff matrix for a duopoly in which the numbers indicate the profit in thousands of dollars for a high-price or a low-price strategy.

		Firm A Strategy	
		High price	Low price
Firm B Strategy	High price	A = $425 B = $425	A = $525 B = $275
	Low price	A = $275 B = $525	A = $300 B = $300

20. If both firms collude to maximize joint profits, the total profits for the two firms will be
(a) $400,000
(b) $800,000
(c) $850,000
(d) $950,000

21. Assume that Firm B adopts a low-price strategy while Firm A maintains a high-price strategy. Compared to the results from a high-price strategy for both firms, Firm B will now
(a) lose $150,000 in profit and Firm A will gain $150,000 in profit
(b) gain $100,000 in profit and Firm A will lose $150,000 in profit
(c) gain $150,000 in profit and Firm A will lose $100,000 in profit
(d) gain $525,000 in profit and Firm A will lose $275,000 in profit

22. If both firms operate independently and do not collude, the most likely profit is
(a) $300,000 for Firm A and $300,000 for Firm B
(b) $525,000 for Firm A and $275,000 for Firm B
(c) $275,000 for Firm A and $525,000 for Firm B
(d) $425,000 for Firm A and $425,000 for Firm B

23. If an individual oligopolist's demand curve is kinked, it is necessarily
(a) perfectly elastic at the going price
(b) less elastic above the going price than below it

(c) more elastic above the going price than below it

(d) of unitary elasticity at the going price

Use the following diagram to answer Question 24.

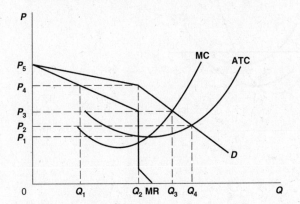

24. The profit-maximizing price and output for this oligopolistic firm is

(a) P_5 and Q_2

(b) P_4 and Q_2

(c) P_3 and Q_3

(d) P_2 and Q_4

25. What is the situation called whenever firms in an industry reach an agreement to fix prices, divide up the market, or otherwise restrict competition?

(a) interindustry competition

(b) incentive to cheat

(c) price leadership

(d) collusion

26. When oligopolists collude the results are generally

(a) greater output and higher price

(b) greater output and lower price

(c) smaller output and lower price

(d) smaller output and higher price

27. To be successful, collusion requires that oligopolists be able to

(a) keep prices and profits as low as possible

(b) block or restrict the entry of new producers

(c) reduce legal obstacles that protect market power

(d) keep the domestic economy from experiencing high inflation

28. Which is a typical tactic that has been used by the price leader in the price leadership model of oligopoly?

(a) limit pricing

(b) frequent price changes

(c) starting a price war with competitors

(d) giving no announcement of a price change

29. Market shares in oligopoly are typically determined on the basis of

(a) product development and advertising

(b) covert collusion and cartels

(c) tacit understandings

(d) joint profit maximization

30. Many economists think that relative to pure competition, oligopoly is

(a) allocatively efficient, but not productively efficient

(b) productively efficient, but not allocatively efficient

(c) both allocatively and productively efficient

(d) neither allocatively nor productively efficient

■ PROBLEMS

1. Assume that the short-run cost and demand data given in the following table confront a monopolistic competitor selling a given product and engaged in a given amount of product promotion.

Output	Total cost	Marginal cost	Quantity demanded	Price	Marginal revenue
0	$ 50		0	$120	
1	80	$____	1	110	$____
2	90	____	2	100	____
3	110	____	3	90	____
4	140	____	4	80	____
5	180	____	5	70	____
6	230	____	6	60	____
7	290	____	7	50	____
8	360	____	8	40	____
9	440	____	9	30	____
10	530		10	20	____

a. Compute the marginal cost and marginal revenue of each unit of output and enter these figures in the table.

b. In the short run the firm will (1) produce

_____ units of output, (2) sell its output at

a price of $_____, and (3) have a total

economic profit of $_____.

c. In the long run, (1) the demand for the firm's product will _____, (2) until the price of the

product equals _____, and (3) the total

economic profits of the firm are _____.

2. Match the descriptions to the six graphs on page 294. Indicate on each graph the area of economic profit or loss or state if the firm is just making normal profits.

a. a purely competitive firm earning economic profits in the short run   Graph _____

b. a purely competitive firm in long-run equilibrium

            Graph _____

c. a natural monopoly   Graph _____

d. a monopolistically competitive firm earning economic profits in the short run   Graph _____

e. a monopolistically competitive firm experiencing economic losses in the short run   Graph _____

f. a monopolistically competitive firm in long-run equilibrium   Graph _____

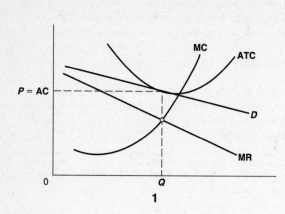

1

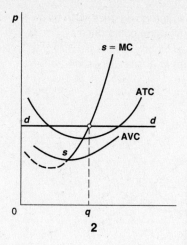

2

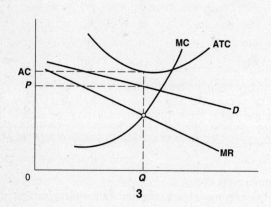

3

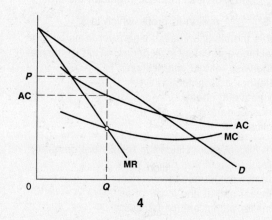

4

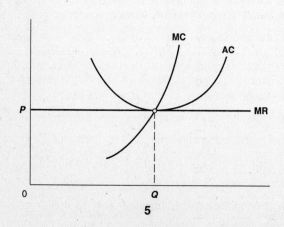

5

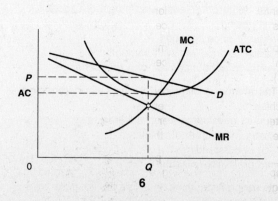

6

3. Consider the following payoff matrix in which the numbers indicate the profit in millions of dollars for a duopoly based on either a high-price or a low-price strategy.

		Firm X Strategy	
		High price	**Low price**
Firm Y Strategy	**High price**	X = $200 Y = $200	X = $250 Y = $ 50
	Low price	X = $ 50 Y = $250	X = $ 50 Y = $ 50

a. *Situation 1:* Each firm chooses a high-price strategy. *Result:* Each firm will earn $_____ million in profit for a total of $_____ million for the two firms.

b. *Situation 2:* Firm X chooses a low-price strategy while Firm Y maintains a high-price strategy. *Result:*

Firm X will earn $_____ million and Firm Y will earn

$_____ million. Compared to Situation 1, Firm X has an incentive to cut prices because it will earn

$_____ million more in profit and Firm Y will earn

$_____ million less in profit. Together, the firms will

earn $_____ million in profit, which is $_____ million less than in Situation 1.

c. *Situation 3:* Firm Y chooses a low-price strategy while Firm X maintains a high-price strategy. *Result:* Compared to Situation 1, Firm Y has an incentive

to cut prices because it will earn $_____ million and

Firm X will earn $_____. Compared to Situation 1,

Firm Y will earn $_____ million more in profit and Firm

X will earn $_____ million less in profit. Together,

the firms will earn $_____ million in profit, which is

$_____ less than in Situation 1.

d. *Situation 4:* Each firm chooses a low-price

strategy. *Result:* Each firm will earn $_____ million

in profit for a total of $_____ million for the two firms.

This total is $_____ less than in Situation 1.

e. *Conclusions:*

(1) The two firms have a strong incentive to collude and adopt the high-price strategy because there is the

potential for $_____ million more in profit for the two

firms than with a low-price strategy (Situation 4), or

the potential for $_____ million more for the two firms than with a mixed-price strategy (Situations 2 or 3).

(2) There is also a strong incentive for each firm to cheat on the agreement and adopt a low-price strategy when the other firm maintains a high-price strategy because this situation will produce

$_____ million more in profit for the cheating firm compared to its honoring a collusive agreement for a high-price strategy.

4. The kinked-demand schedule which an oligopolist believes confronts the firm is presented in the following table.

a. Compute the oligopolist's total revenue at each of the nine prices and enter these figures in the table.

b. Also compute marginal revenue *for each unit* between the nine prices and enter these figures in the table.

Price	Quantity demanded	Total revenue	Marginal revenue per unit
$2.90	100	$_____	
2.80	200	_____	$_____
2.70	300	_____	_____
2.60	400	_____	_____
2.50	500	_____	_____
2.40	525	_____	_____
2.30	550	_____	_____
2.20	575	_____	_____
2.10	600	_____	_____

c. What is the current, or going, price for the oligopolist's product? $_____ How much is it sell-

ing? _____

d. On the graph at the top on page 296, plot the oligopolist's demand curve and marginal-revenue curve. Connect the demand points and the marginal-revenue points with as straight a line as possible. (Be sure to plot the marginal-revenue figures at the average of the two quantities involved, that is, at 150, 250, 350, 450, 512.5, 537.5, 562.5, and 587.5.)

e. Assume that the marginal-cost schedule of the oligopolist is given in columns 1 and 2 of the following table. Plot the marginal-cost curve on the graph on which demand and marginal revenue were plotted.

(1) Output	(2) MC	(3) MC′	(4) MC″
150	$1.40	$1.90	$.40
250	1.30	1.80	.30
350	1.40	1.90	.40
450	1.50	2.00	.50
512.5	1.60	2.10	.60
537.5	1.70	2.20	.70
562.5	1.80	2.30	.80
587.5	1.90	2.40	.90

(1) Given demand and marginal cost, what price should the oligopolist charge to maximize profits?

$_____ How many units of product will it

sell at this price? _____

(2) If the marginal-cost schedule changed from that shown in columns 1 and 2 to that shown in columns 1 and 3, what price should it charge?

$_____ What level of output will it pro-

duce? _____ How have profits changed

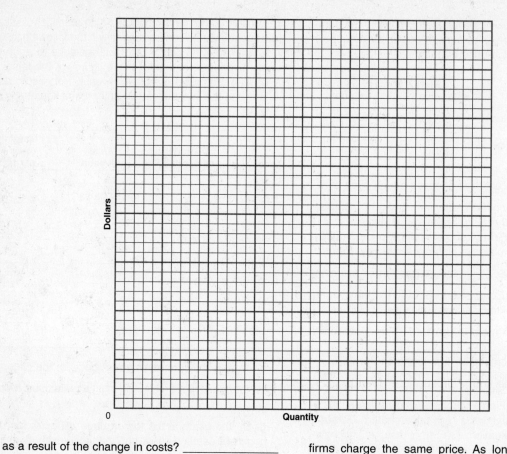

as a result of the change in costs? _____
Plot the new marginal-cost curve on the graph.

(3) If the marginal-cost curve schedule changed from that shown in columns 1 and 2 to that shown in columns 1 and 4, what price should it charge?

$_____ What level of output will it produce? _____ How have profits changed as a result of the change in costs?

_____ Plot the new marginal-cost curve on the graph.

5. An oligopoly producing a homogeneous product is composed of three firms. Assume that these three firms have identical cost schedules. Assume also that if any one of these firms sets a price for the product, the other two firms charge the same price. As long as the firms all charge the same price they will share the market equally, and the quantity demanded of each will be the same.

Following is the total-cost schedule of one of these firms and the demand schedule that confronts it when the other firms charge the same price as this firm.

a. Complete the marginal-cost and marginal-revenue schedules facing the firm.

b. What price would this firm set if it wished to maximize its profits? $ _____

c. How much would

(1) it sell at this price? _____

(2) its profits be at this price? $ _____

d. What would be the industry's

(1) total output at this price? _____

(2) joint profits at this price? $ _____

Output	Total cost	Marginal cost	Price	Quantity demanded	Marginal revenue
0	$ 0		$140	0	
1	30	$_____	130	1	$_____
2	50	_____	120	2	_____
3	80	_____	110	3	_____
4	120	_____	100	4	_____
5	170	_____	90	5	_____
6	230	_____	80	6	_____
7	300	_____	70	7	_____
8	380	_____	60	8	_____

e. Is there any other price this firm can set, assuming that the other two firms charge the same price, that would result in a greater joint profit for them?

_____ If so, what is that price?

$_____

f. If these three firms colluded in order to maximize their joint profit, what price would they charge?

$_____

■ **SHORT ANSWER AND ESSAY QUESTIONS**

1. What are the three characteristics of monopolistic competition?

2. What is meant by product differentiation? By what methods can products be differentiated?

3. How does product differentiation affect the kind of competition and the degree of monopoly in monopolistic competition?

4. Describe the elasticity of the demand curve faced by a monopolistically competitive firm in the short run.

5. Assume that the firm is producing a given product and is engaged in a given amount of promotional activity. What two factors determine how elastic the demand curve will be for a monopolistic competitor?

6. At what level of output will the monopolistic competitor produce in the short run? What price will it charge for its product? Draw a graph to help explain your answer.

7. What determines whether a monopolistically competitive firm will earn economic profits or suffer economic losses in the short run?

8. What will be the level of economic profit that the monopolistic competitor will tend to receive in the long run? What forces economic profits toward this level? Why is this just a _tendency_?

9. What are two complications that would explain why the representative firm may not earn only a normal profit in the long run and may earn economic profits?

10. Use the concepts of allocative and productive efficiency to explain excess capacity and the level of prices under monopolistic competition.

11. Describe the methods, other than price cutting, that a monopolistic competitor can use to protect and increase its economic profits in the long run.

12. Explain how product variety and improvement may offset the economic inefficiency associated with monopolistic competition.

13. What are the essential characteristics of an oligopoly? How does oligopoly differ from pure competition, pure monopoly, and monopolistic competition?

14. Explain how the concentration ratio in a particular industry is computed. What is the relationship between this ratio and fewness? What are the shortcomings of the concentration ratio as a measure of the extent of competition in an industry?

15. What is the Herfindahl index? How can it be used to correct problems with concentration ratios?

16. How can game theory be used to explain strategic behavior under oligopoly? What do mutual interdependence and collusion mean with respect to oligopoly?

17. Why is it difficult to use one standard model to explain the prices charged by and the outputs of oligopolists?

18. How can the kinked-demand curve be used to explain why oligopoly prices are relatively inflexible?

19. Suppose a few firms produce a homogeneous product, have identical cost curves, and charge the same price (act as a cartel). Compare the results in terms of price, combined output, and joint profits with those from a pure monopoly producing the same market output.

20. Why do oligopolists find it advantageous to collude? What are the obstacles to collusion?

21. What is the price leadership model, and what leadership tactics do oligopolistic firms use?

22. Why do oligopolists engage in little price competition and in extensive product development and advertising?

23. How is it possible for consumers to get a lower price on a product with advertising than they would in its absence?

24. Explain how the advertising efforts of firms may be offsetting and lead to higher prices for consumers.

25. Evaluate the economic efficiency of the oligopoly market structure. What qualifications should be noted for the evaluation?

ANSWERS

Chapter 25 Monopolistic Competition and Oligopoly

FILL-IN QUESTIONS

1. large, differentiated, easy, small, do not, an independent
2. _a._ product attributes; _b._ services; _c._ location; _d._ brand names and packaging; _e._ some control over price
3. _a._ more, less; _b._ (1) number of rivals the firm has, (2) the degree of product differentiation; _c._ equal to
4. _a._ decrease, increase; _b._ average, zero, greater
5. normal, economic, cannot, barriers to entry
6. greater than, does not, greater than, does not, productive
7. nonprice, more
8. price, product, advertising
9. a few, homogeneous, difficult, maker, interdependence, entry, mergers
10. concentration ratio, Herfindahl index
11. game, interdependent, does, does not, does not
12. diverse, uncertain, inflexible, together
13. _a._ elastic, elastic, inelastic; _b._ will not, will; _c._ revenue, cost
14. collusion, monopoly
15. cartel, overt, covert

16. *a.* demand and cost differences; *b.* a large number of firms; *c.* cheating (secret price cutting); *d.* a recession; *e.* potential entry; *f.* legal obstacles (antitrust laws) (any order for *a–f*)

17. price leadership, infrequent, limit, price wars

18. price, nonprice; *a.* efficient, reduces, reduces; *b.* inefficient, offsetting, entry, higher

19. is not, is not, monopoly

20. increased, low, more

TRUE–FALSE QUESTIONS

1. F, p. 461	**10.** F, pp. 464–465	**19.** T, p. 475
2. T, p. 461	**11.** F, p. 466	**20.** F, p. 476
3. F, p. 461	**12.** T, p. 467	**21.** F, pp. 476–477
4. F, pp. 462–463	**13.** F, p. 467	**22.** F, p. 477
5. F, pp. 462–463	**14.** F, pp. 468–469	**23.** T, pp. 478–479
6. T, p. 464	**15.** F, p. 469	**24.** F, p. 479
7. F, p. 464	**16.** F, pp. 469–471	**25.** T, p. 479
8. F, p. 464	**17.** T, p. 474	
9. T, pp. 464–465	**18.** T, pp. 474–475	

MULTIPLE-CHOICE QUESTIONS

1. c, p. 460	**11.** d, pp. 463–464	**21.** b, pp. 469–471
2. c, p. 461	**12.** c, p. 465	**22.** a, pp. 469–471
3. d, pp. 462–463	**13.** a, p. 465	**23.** c, pp. 471–472
4. d, pp. 463–464	**14.** c, pp. 465–466	**24.** b, pp. 471–472
5. a, pp. 463–464	**15.** b, p. 466	**25.** d, pp. 474–475
6. b, pp. 463–464	**16.** b, p. 467	**26.** a, pp. 474–475
7. d, pp. 463–464	**17.** c, p. 467	**27.** b, p. 476
8. b, pp. 463–464	**18.** b, pp. 468–469	**28.** a, pp. 476–477
9. a, pp. 463–464	**19.** c, p. 469	**29.** a, pp. 477–478
10. a, pp. 463–464	**20.** c, pp. 469–471	**30.** d, p. 479

PROBLEMS

1. *a.* Marginal cost: $30, 10, 20, 30, 40, 50, 60, 70, 80, 90; Marginal revenue: $110, 90, 70, 50, 30, 10, −10, −30, −50, −70; *b.* (1) 4, (2) $80, (3) $180; *c.* (1) decrease, (2) average cost, (3) equal to zero

2. *a.* 2; *b.* 5; *c.* 4; *d.* 6; *e.* 3; *f.* 1

3. *a.* 200, 400; *b.* 250, 50, 50, 150, 300, 100; *c.* 250, 50, 50, 150, 300, 100; *d.* 50, 100, 300; *e.* (1) 300, 100, (2) 50

4. *a.* Total revenue: 290, 560, 810, 1040, 1250, 1260, 1265, 1265, 1260; *b.* Marginal revenue: 2.70, 2.50, 2.30, 2.10, 0.40, 0.20, 0, −0.20; *c.* 2.50, 500; *d.* graph; *e.* (1) 2.50, 500, (2) 2.50, 500, they have decreased, (3) 2.50, 500, they have increased

5. *a.* Marginal cost: $30, 20, 30, 40, 50, 60, 70, 80; Marginal revenue: $130, 110, 90, 70, 50, 30, 10, −10; *b.* $90; *c.* (1) 5, (2) $280; *d.* (1) 15, (2) $840; *e.* no; *f.* $90

SHORT ANSWER AND ESSAY QUESTIONS

1. pp. 460–461	**10.** pp. 464–465	**19.** pp. 474–475
2. p. 461	**11.** p. 466	**20.** pp. 474–476
3. p. 461	**12.** p. 466	**21.** pp. 476–477
4. pp. 462–464	**13.** pp. 467–468	**22.** pp. 477–478
5. pp. 462–464	**14.** pp. 468–469	**23.** p. 478
6. pp. 463–464	**15.** p. 469	**24.** pp. 478–479
7. pp. 463–464	**16.** pp. 469–471	**25.** p. 479
8. pp. 463–464	**17.** p. 471	
9. p. 464	**18.** pp. 471–473	

CHAPTER 26

Technology, R&D, and Efficiency

A market economy is not static but subject to change over time. One dynamic force affecting an economy and industries is **technological advance.** This advance occurs over a very long time and allows firms to introduce new products and adopt new methods of production.

The chapter begins by discussing the three-step process that constitutes technological advance: **invention, innovation,** and **diffusion.** Here the text describes many real-world examples of how technological change has affected firms and industries. You will also find out that research and development (R&D) expenditures by firms and government play an integral role in directly supporting this technological advance. The traditional view of economists was that technological advance was something external to the economy, but most contemporary economists think that technological advance is integral to capitalism and arises from intense rivalry among firms.

Entrepreneurs and other innovators play a major role in encouraging innovation and technological change. Entrepreneurs typically form small companies—**start-ups**—to create and introduce new products and production techniques. In this activity entrepreneurs assume personal financial risk, but if they are successful, they can be highly rewarded in the marketplace. There are also innovators within existing firms who can use R&D work to develop new products. University and government research can also contribute output that can be useful for fostering technological advance.

A major section of this chapter analyzes how the firm determines the **optimal amount of R&D spending.** The decision is made by equating marginal benefit with marginal cost. The marginal cost is measured by the interest-rate cost of funds that the firm borrows or obtains from other sources to finance its R&D expenditures. The expected rate of return from the last dollar spent on R&D is the measure of marginal benefit. You should remember that the outcomes from R&D spending are only expected, not guaranteed for the firm.

Technological changes can increase a firm's profit in two ways. Recall that profit is simply the difference between total revenue and total cost. **Product innovation** can increase revenues because people buy more products from the innovative firm. These increased revenues will increase profits, assuming that costs stay the same. **Process innovation** can also increase profits by reducing costs. This type of innovation leads to better methods for producing a product and decreases the average total cost for the firm.

One problem with technological advance is that it encourages **imitation.** Successful innovative firms are often emulated by others. This imitation problem can be especially threatening to innovative, smaller firms because the dominant firms in the industry can challenge them. A firm, however, has some advantages in taking the lead in innovation because there are protections and rewards. Legal protections include patents, copyrights, and trademarks; other advantages are early brand-name recognition or the potential for a profitable buyout.

You spent the past three chapters learning about the differences in the four market structures. Now you may be wondering whether one market structure is better suited than another for encouraging technological progress. The answer is clearly mixed because each structure has its strengths and shortcomings. The **inverted-U theory** gives you an even better framework for figuring out the optimal industry structure for R&D.

The chapter ends by returning to the issue of **economic efficiency,** a topic discussed throughout the text. Technological advance has a double benefit because it enhances both productive efficiency and allocative efficiency. Productive efficiency increases from process innovation that reduces production costs. Allocative efficiency increases because product innovation gives consumers more choice and gives society a more desired mix of products. The efficiency results are not automatic, and the outcome may depend on whether innovation strengthens or weakens monopoly power.

■ CHECKLIST

When you have studied this chapter you should be able to

☐ Define technological advance.
☐ Describe each of the three steps in technological advance.
☐ Explain the role of research and development (R&D) in technological advance.
☐ Contrast the traditional with the modern view of technological advance.
☐ Distinguish between entrepreneurs and other innovators and between start-ups and innovation in existing firms.
☐ Explain how innovators are rewarded for anticipating the future.
☐ Describe the role that universities and government play in fostering technological advance.

☐ Identify five means for financing R&D that are available to firms.

☐ Describe and give a rationale for the interest-rate cost-of-funds curve and the expected-rate-of-return curve.

☐ Show graphically with an example how the optimal level of R&D expenditures is determined.

☐ State three important points from the analysis of optimal R&D expenditures.

☐ Explain how product innovation can increase profits by increasing revenues.

☐ Describe how process innovation can increase profits by reducing costs.

☐ Explain the imitation problem for firms.

☐ Identify six protections for or advantages to being the first to develop a new product or process.

☐ Evaluate which of the four market structures is best suited to technological advance.

☐ Explain the inverted-U theory and its implications for technological progress.

☐ Describe how technological advance enhances both productive and allocative efficiency.

☐ Explain how innovation may lead to creative destruction and describe the criticisms of this view.

■ **CHAPTER OUTLINE**

1. ***Technological advance*** involves the development of new and improved products and new and improved ways of producing and distributing the products. It is a three-step process of invention, innovation, and diffusion.

   a. ***Invention*** is the most basic part of technological advance and involves the discovery of a product or process. Governments encourage invention by granting the inventor a patent, which is an exclusive right to sell a product.

   b. ***Innovation*** is the first successful commercial use of a new product or method or the creation of a new form of business. There are two major types: product innovation, which involves new and improved products or services, and process innovation, which involves new and improved production or distribution methods. Innovation is an important factor in competition because it can enable a firm to leapfrog competitors by making their products or methods obsolete.

   c. ***Diffusion*** is the spread of an innovation through imitation or copying. New and existing firms copy or imitate successful innovation of other firms to profit from new opportunities or to protect their profits.

   d. In business, research and development (R&D) includes work and expenditures directed toward invention, innovation, and diffusion. Government also supports R&D through defense expenditures and the funding of other activities.

   e. The traditional view of technological advance was that it was external to the economy. It was viewed as a random force to which the economy adjusted and it depended on the advance of science. The modern view is that it is internal to capitalism. Intense rivalry among individuals and firms motivates them to seek and exploit new or expand existing opportunities for profit.

Entrepreneurs and other innovators are the drivers of technological advance.

2. The ***entrepreneur*** is an initiator, innovator, and risk bearer. Other innovators are key people involved in the pursuit of innovation but who do not bear personal financial risk.

   a. Entrepreneurs often form small new companies called ***start-ups,*** which are firms that create and introduce a new product or production technique.

   b. Innovators are found within existing corporations. R&D work in major corporations has resulted in technological improvements, often by splitting off units to form innovative firms.

   c. Innovators attempt to anticipate future needs. Product innovation and development are creative activities with both nonmonetary and monetary rewards. More resources for further innovation by entrepreneurs often come from past successes. Successful businesses that meet consumer wants are given the opportunity to produce goods and services for the market.

   d. New scientific knowledge is important to technological advance. Entrepreneurs study the scientific results from university and government laboratories to find those with commercial applicability.

3. The ***optimal amount of R&D*** expenditures for the firm depends on the marginal benefit and marginal cost of R&D activity. To earn the greatest profit, the firm will expand an activity until its marginal benefit equals its marginal cost.

   a. Several sources are available for financing firms' R&D activities: bank loans, bonds, retained earnings, venture capital, or personal savings. A firm's marginal cost of these funds is an interest rate i.

   b. A firm's marginal benefit of R&D is its expected profit (or return) from the last dollar spent on R&D.

   c. The optimal amount of R&D in marginal-cost and marginal-benefit analysis is the point where the ***interest-rate cost-of-funds*** (marginal-cost) ***curve*** and the ***expected-rate-of-return*** (marginal-benefit) ***curve*** intersect. This analysis leads to three important points. First, R&D expenditures can be justified only if the expected return equals or exceeds the cost of financing the R&D. Second, the firm expects positive outcomes from R&D, but the results are not guaranteed. Third, firms adjust R&D spending when expected rates of return change on various projects.

4. A firm's profit can be increased through ***innovation*** in two ways.

   a. The firm can increase revenues through ***product innovation.*** From a utility perspective, consumers will purchase a new product only if it increases total utility from their limited incomes. The purchases of the product by consumers increase the firm's revenues. Note three other points.

   (1) Consumer acceptance of a new product depends on both its marginal utility and price.

   (2) Many new products are not successful, so the firm fails to realize the expected return in these instances.

   (3) Most product innovations are small or incremental improvements to existing products, not major changes.

b. *Process innovation,* the introduction of better ways to make products, is another way to increase profit and obtain a positive return on R&D expenditures. It results in a shift upward in the firm's total product curve and a shift downward in the firm's average total cost curve, which increases the firm's profit.

5. The *imitation problem* is that the rivals of a firm may copy or emulate the firm's product or process and thus decrease the profit from the innovator's R&D effort. When a dominant firm quickly imitates the successful new product of smaller competitors with the goal of becoming the second firm to adopt the innovation, it is using a *fast-second strategy.*

    a. Taking the lead in innovation offers the firm several protections and potential advantages from being first to produce a product.

    (1) Patents limit imitation and protect profits over time.

    (2) Copyrights and trademarks reduce direct copying and increase the incentives for product innovation.

    (3) Brand names may provide a major marketing asset.

    (4) Trade secrets and learning by doing give firms advantages.

    (5) The time lags between innovation and diffusion give innovators time to make substantial economic profits.

    (6) There is the potential purchase of the innovating firm by a larger firm at a high price.

6. Certain market structures may foster *technological advance.*

    a. Each *market structure* has strengths and limitations.

    (1) *Pure competition:* Strong competition gives firms the reason to innovate, but the expected rate of return on R&D may be low or negative for a pure competitor.

    (2) *Monopolistic competition:* These firms have a strong profit incentive to develop and differentiate products, but they have limited ability to obtain inexpensive R&D financing. It is also difficult for these firms to extract large profits because the barriers to entry are relatively low.

    (3) *Oligopoly:* Although the size of these firms makes them capable of promoting technological progress, there is little reason for them to introduce costly new technology and new products when they earn large economic profits without doing it.

    (4) *Pure monopoly:* This type of firm has little incentive to engage in R&D because its high profit is protected by high barriers to entry.

    b. *Inverted-U theory* suggests that R&D effort is weak in industries with very low concentration (pure competition) and very high concentration (pure monopoly). The optimal industry structure for R&D is one in which expected returns on R&D spending are high and funds are readily available and inexpensive to finance. This generally occurs in industries with a few firms that are absolutely and relatively large, but the concentration ratio is not so high as to limit strong competition by smaller firms.

    c. General support for the inverted-U theory comes from industry studies. The optimal market structure for technological advance appears to be an industry with a mix of large oligopolistic firms (a 40–60% concentration ratio) and several highly innovative smaller firms. The technical characteristics of an industry, however, may be a more important factor influencing R&D and its structure.

7. Technological advance enhances *economic efficiency.*

    a. *Process innovation* improves productive efficiency by increasing the productivity of inputs and reducing average total costs.

    b. *Product innovation* enhances allocative efficiency by giving society a more preferred mixture of goods and services.

    (1) The efficiency gain from innovation, however, can be reduced if patents and the advantages of being first lead to monopoly power.

    (2) Monopoly power can be reduced or destroyed by innovation because it provides competition where there was none.

    c. Innovation may foster *creative destruction,* whereby the creation of new products and production methods simultaneously destroys the monopoly positions of firms protecting existing products and methods. This view is expressed by Joseph Schumpeter, and there are many examples of it in business history. Another view suggests that creative destruction is not inevitable or automatic. In general, innovation improves economic efficiency, but in some cases it can increase monopoly power.

■ HINTS AND TIPS

1. The section of the chapter on a firm's *optimal amount of R&D* uses marginal-cost and marginal-benefit analysis similar to what you saw in previous chapters. In this case, the interest rate or expected return is graphed on the vertical axis and the amount of R&D spending on the horizontal axis. The only difference from previous MB-MC graphs is that the marginal cost in this example is assumed to be constant at the given interest rate. *It is graphed as a horizontal line.* The expected-rate-of-return curve is downward sloping because there are fewer opportunities for R&D expenditures with higher expected rates of return than at lower expected rates of return.

2. The explanation for how new products gain acceptance by consumers is based on the marginal utility theory that you learned about in Chapter 21. Be sure to review the text discussion of Table 21.1 before reading about the example in Table 26.1.

3. When new processes are developed, they can increase a firm's total product curve and decrease a firm's average total cost curve. Review the section in Chapter 22, "Shifting the Cost Curves," to understand these points.

■ IMPORTANT TERMS

technological advance
very long run
invention
patent
innovation
product innovation
process innovation
diffusion
start-ups

venture capital
interest-rate cost-of-funds curve
expected-rate-of-return curve
optimal amount of R&D
imitation problem
fast-second strategy
inverted-U theory of R&D
creative destruction

SELF-TEST

■ FILL-IN QUESTIONS

1. Technological advance is a three-step process of

a. _____

b. _____

c. _____

2. The first discovery of a product or process is (innovation, invention) _____, whereas the first commercial introduction of a new product or process is_____; patent protection is available for (invention, innovation) _____ but not _____. The spread of an innovation through imitation or copying is (trademarking, diffusion) _____.

3. The development of new or improved products is (process, product) _____ innovation; the development of new or improved production or distribution methods is _____ innovation.

4. The traditional view of technological advance was that it was (internal, external) _____ to the economy, but the modern view is that technological advance is _____. In the modern view, technological advance arises from (scientific progress, rivalry among firms) _____, but the traditional view holds that it arises from _____ that is largely (internal, external) _____ to the market system.

5. The individual who is an initiator, innovator, and risk bearer who combines resources in unique ways to produce new goods and services is called an (entrepreneur, intrapreneur) _____, but an individual who promotes entrepreneurship within existing corporations is called an _____. Entrepreneurs tend

to form (large, small) _____ companies called start-ups, and if they are successful they will receive _____ monetary rewards.

6. Past successes often give entrepreneurs access to (more, less) _____ resources for further innovation because the market economy (punishes, rewards) _____ those businesses that meet consumer wants.

7. To earn the greatest profit from R&D spending, the firm should expand the activity until its marginal benefit is (greater than, less than, equal to) _____ its marginal cost, but a firm should cut back its R&D if its marginal benefit is _____ its marginal cost.

8. Five ways a firm can obtain funding to finance R&D spending are

a. _____

b. _____

c. _____

d. _____

e. _____

9. Product innovation will tend to increase a firm's profit by increasing the (costs, revenues) _____ of the firm; process innovation will tend to increase a firm's profit by reducing the (costs, revenues) _____ of the firm.

10. Consumer acceptance of a new product depends on its marginal utility (and, or) _____ its price. The expected return that motivates product innovation (is, is not) _____ always realized. Most product innovations are (major, minor) _____ improvements to existing products.

11. Process innovation results in a shift (downward, upward) _____ in the firm's total product curve and a shift _____ in the firm's average-total-cost curve, which in turn (increases, decreases) _____ the firm's profit.

12. The imitation problem occurs when the rivals of a firm copy or emulate the firm's product or process and thus (increase, decrease) _____ the innovator's profit from the R&D effort. When a dominant firm quickly imitates the successful new product of smaller competitors with the goal of becoming the second firm to adopt the innovation, it is using a (second-best, fast-second) _____ strategy.

13. An example of legal protection for taking the lead in innovation would be (copyrights, trade secrets)

_____, but a nonlegal advantage might come from (patents, learning by doing) _____.

14. In regard to R&D, purely competitive firms tend to be (less, more) _____ complacent than monopolists, but the expected rate of return for a pure competitor may be (high, low) _____, and they (may, may not) _____ be able to finance R&D.

15. Monopolistically competitive firms have a (weak, strong) _____ profit incentive to develop and differentiate products, but they have (extensive, limited) _____ ability to obtain inexpensive R&D financing, and it is (difficult, easy) _____ for these firms to extract large profits because the barriers to entry are relatively (high, low) _____.

16. The size of oligopolistic firms makes them (capable, incapable) _____ of promoting technological advance, but there is (much, little) _____ reason for them to introduce costly new technology and new products when they earn (small, large) _____ economic profit without doing it.

17. Pure monopoly has a (strong, weak) _____ incentive to engage in R&D because its high profit is protected by (low, high) _____ barriers to entry. This type of firm views R&D spending as (an offensive, a defensive) _____ move to protect the monopoly from new products that would undercut its monopoly position.

18. Inverted-U theory suggests that R&D effort is at best (strong, weak) _____ in industries with very low and very high concentrations. The optimal industry structure for R&D is one in which expected returns on R&D spending are (low, high) _____ and funds are readily available and inexpensive to finance R&D. This generally occurs in industries with (many, a few) _____ firms that are absolutely and relatively large, but the concentration ratio is not so high as to limit strong competition by smaller firms.

19. Technological advance increases the productivity of inputs, and by reducing average total costs it enhances (allocative, productive) _____ efficiency; when it gives society a more preferred mixture of goods and services it enhances _____ efficiency. The efficiency gain from innovation can be (increased, decreased) _____ if patents and the advantages of being first lead to monopoly power, but it can be _____ if innovation provides competition where there was none.

20. Innovation may foster creative destruction, where the (destruction, creation) _____ of new products and production methods simultaneously leads to the _____ of the monopoly positions of firms committed to existing products and methods. Another view, however, suggests that creative destruction (is, is not) _____ automatic. In general, innovation improves economic efficiency, but in some cases it can increase monopoly power.

■ TRUE–FALSE QUESTIONS

Circle T if the statement is true, F if it is false.

1. Technological advance consists of new and improved goods and services and new and improved production or distribution processes.   **T F**

2. In economists' models, technological advance occurs in the short run, not the long run.   **T F**

3. Invention is the first successful commercial introduction of a new product.   **T F**

4. Firms channel a majority of their R&D expenditures to innovation and imitation rather than to basic scientific research.   **T F**

5. Historically, most economists viewed technological advance as a predictable and internal force to which the economy adjusted.   **T F**

6. The modern view of economists is that capitalism is the driving force of technological advance and such advance occurs in response to profit incentives within the economy.   **T F**

7. The entrepreneur is an innovator but not a risk bearer.   **T F**

8. Start-ups are small companies focused on creating and introducing a new product or using a new production or distribution technique.   **T F**

9. The only innovators are entrepreneurs.   **T F**

10. The market entrusts the production of goods and services to businesses that have consistently succeeded in fulfilling consumer wants.   **T F**

11. Research and development rarely occur outside the labs of major corporations.   **T F**

12. When entrepreneurs use personal savings to finance the R&D for a new venture, the marginal cost of financing is zero.   **T F**

13. The optimal amount of R&D spending for the firm occurs where its expected return is greater than its interest-rate cost of funds to finance it.   **T F**

14. Most firms are guaranteed a profitable outcome when making an R&D expenditure because the decisions are carefully evaluated.   **T F**

15. A new product succeeds when it provides consumers with higher marginal utility per dollar spent than do existing products.   **T   F**

16. Most product innovations consist of major changes to existing products and are not incremental improvements.   **T   F**

17. Process innovation increases the firm's total product, lowers its average total cost, and increases its profit.   **T   F**

18. Imitation poses no problems for innovators because there are patent and trademark protections for their innovations.   **T   F**

19. A fast-second strategy involves letting the dominant firm set the price of the product and then smaller firms quickly undercutting that price.   **T   F**

20. Pure competition is the best market structure for encouraging R&D and innovation.   **T   F**

21. One major shortcoming of monopolistic competition in promoting technological progress is its limited ability to secure inexpensive financing for R&D.   **T   F**

22. The inverted-U theory suggests that R&D effort is strongest in very low-concentration industries and weakest in very high-concentration industries.   **T   F**

23. The technical and scientific characteristics of an industry may be more important than its structure in determining R&D spending and innovation.   **T   F**

24. Technological advance enhances productive efficiency but not allocative efficiency.   **T   F**

25. Creative destruction is the process the inventor goes through in developing new products and innovations.   **T   F**

■ **MULTIPLE-CHOICE QUESTIONS**

Circle the letter that corresponds to the best answer.

1. The period in which technology can change and in which firms can introduce entirely new products is the
 (a) short run
 (b) very short run
 (c) long run
 (d) very long run

2. Technological progress is a three-step process of
 (a) creation, pricing, and marketing
 (b) invention, innovation, and diffusion
 (c) manufacturing, venturing, and promotion
 (d) start-ups, imitation, and creative destruction

3. The first discovery of a product or process through the use of imagination, ingenious thinking, and experimentation and the first proof that it will work is
 (a) process innovation
 (b) product innovation
 (c) creative destruction
 (d) invention

4. From the time of application, patents have a uniform duration of

 (a) 10 years
 (b) 15 years
 (c) 20 years
 (d) 25 years

5. Innovation is a major factor in competition because it can
 (a) be patented to protect the investment of the developers
 (b) enable firms to make competitors' products obsolete
 (c) guarantee the monopoly position of innovative firms
 (d) reduce research and development costs for firms

6. What idea is best illustrated by the example of McDonald's successfully introducing the fast-food hamburger and then that idea being adopted by other firms such as Burger King and Wendy's?
 (a) start-ups
 (b) diffusion
 (c) invention
 (d) fast-second strategy

7. About what percentage of GDP in the United States is spent on research and development?
 (a) 2.8%
 (b) 7.6%
 (c) 10.6%
 (d) 21.2%

8. The modern view of technological advance is that it is
 (a) rooted in the independent advancement of science
 (b) best stimulated through government R&D spending
 (c) a result of intense rivalry among individuals and firms
 (d) a random outside force to which the economy adjusts

9. The major difference between entrepreneurs and other innovators is
 (a) innovators work in teams, but entrepreneurs do not
 (b) innovators manage start-ups, but entrepreneurs do not
 (c) entrepreneurs bear personal financial risk, but innovators do not
 (d) entrepreneurs invent new products and processes, but innovators do not

10. Past successes in developing products often mean that entrepreneurs and innovative firms
 (a) have access to more private resources for further innovation
 (b) have access to less private resources for further innovation
 (c) have access to more public support for further innovation
 (d) experience no change in the availability of private or public resources for further innovation

Questions 11, 12, and 13 are based on the following table showing the expected rate of return, R&D spending, and interest-rate cost of funds for a hypothetical firm.

Expected rate of return (%)	R&D (millions of $)	Interest-rate cost of funds (%)
15	20	9
13	40	9
11	60	9
9	80	9
7	100	9

11. In a supply and demand graph, the interest-rate cost-of-funds curve would be a(n)
(a) vertical line at 9%
(b) horizontal line at 9%
(c) upward sloping line over the 15 to 7% range
(d) downward sloping line over the 15 to 7% range

12. The optimal amount of R&D would be
(a) $40 million
(b) $60 million
(c) $80 million
(d) $100 million

13. If the interest-rate cost-of-funds curve rose to 13%, the optimal amount of R&D spending would be
(a) $40 million
(b) $60 million
(c) $80 million
(d) $100 million

14. Product innovation tends to increase the profits of firms primarily by
(a) decreasing the firm's average costs
(b) increasing the firm's total revenue
(c) decreasing marginal utility per dollar spent
(d) increasing the success of R&D spending

15. Consumers will buy a new product only if
(a) it has a lower marginal utility per dollar spent than another product
(b) there is a substantial budget for promotion and marketing
(c) it can be sold at a lower price than that for a competing product
(d) it increases the total utility they obtain from their limited income

16. Process innovation produces a(n)
(a) downward shift in the total-product curve and an upward shift in the average-cost curve
(b) upward shift in the total-product curve and a downward shift in the average-cost curve
(c) upward shift in both the total-product and average-cost curves
(d) downward shift in both the total-product and average-cost curves

17. Some dominant firms in an industry use a fast-second strategy that involves
(a) developing two products to compete with rivals
(b) cutting the development time for the introduction of a new product
(c) moving quickly to buy the second largest firm in the industry to gain larger market share
(d) letting smaller firms initiate new products and then quickly imitating the success

18. One legal protection for taking the lead in innovation is
(a) venture capital
(b) trademarks
(c) trade secrets
(d) mergers

19. One major advantage of being the first to develop a product is the
(a) use of the fast-second strategy
(b) increase in retained earnings
(c) lower interest-rate costs of funds
(d) potential for profitable buyouts

20. Which firm has a strong incentive for product development and differentiation?
(a) a monopolistically competitive firm
(b) a purely competitive firm
(c) an oligopolistic firm
(d) a pure monopoly

21. In which market structure is there the least incentive to engage in R&D?
(a) a monopolistically competitive firm
(b) a purely competitive firm
(c) an oligopolistic firm
(d) a pure monopoly

22. The inverted-U theory suggests that R&D effort is at best weak in
(a) low-concentration industries only
(b) high-concentration industries only
(c) low- and high-concentration industries
(d) low- to middle-concentration industries

23. The optimal market structure for technological advance seems to be an industry in which there
(a) are many purely competitive firms
(b) are monopolists closely regulated by government
(c) is a mix of large oligopolistic firms with several small and highly innovative firms
(d) is a mix of monopolistically competitive firms and a few large monopolists in industries with high capital costs

24. Technological advance as embodied in process innovation typically
(a) decreases allocative efficiency
(b) increases allocative efficiency
(c) decreases productive efficiency
(d) increases productive efficiency

25. Why did Joseph Schumpeter view capitalism as a process of "creative destruction"?
(a) Innovation would lead to monopoly power and thus destroy the economy.
(b) The creation of new products and production methods would destroy the market for existing products.
(c) Invention would create new products, but diffusion would destroy many potentially good ideas.
(d) Firms are being creative with learning by doing, but this spirit is destroyed by the inability of firms to finance R&D expenditures.

■ PROBLEMS

1. Match the terms with the phrase using the appropriate number

1. invention   2. innovation   3. diffusion

a. Imitation of the Chrysler Corporation's Jeep Grand Cherokee with sport utility vehicles developed by other auto companies   _____

b. The first working model of the microchip

_____

c. Computers and word processing software that eliminated the need for typewriters   _____

d. Adoption of Alamo's offer of unlimited mileage by other major car rental companies   _____

e. The creation of the first electric light bulb

_____

f. Development of a new brand of carpet by Du Pont

_____

2. Use the following table that shows the rate of return and R&D spending for a hypothetical firm.

Expected rate of return (%)	R&D (millions of $)
24	3
20	6
16	9
12	12
9	15
6	18
3	21

a. Assume the interest-rate cost of funds is 12%. The optimal amount of R&D expenditures will be $_____ million. At this amount, the marginal cost of R&D spending is _____% and the marginal benefit (the expected rate of return) is _____%.

b. Graph the marginal cost and marginal benefit curves of R&D spending in the graph below. Be sure to label the axes.

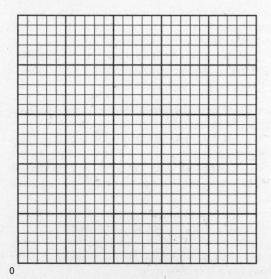

0

c. Now assume that the interest-rate cost of funds falls to 6%. The optimal amount of spending will be $ _____ million. For this amount of R&D spending, the marginal cost of R&D spending is _____% and the marginal benefit (expected rate of return) is _____%.

d. Show on the graph above how the interest-rate cost-of-funds curve changed in the answer that you gave for **b**.

3. Following are two average-total-cost schedules for a firm. The first schedule (ATC₁) shows the cost of producing the product at five levels of output before a new innovation. The second schedule (ATC₂) shows the average total cost at the five output levels after the innovation.

Output	Before ATC_1	After ATC_2
10	$30	$27
20	25	18
30	18	14
40	22	19
50	28	26

a. Plot the average-cost curves for the schedules on the graph on the top of page 307.

b. What was the reduction in average total cost at each of the five levels of output as a result of the innovation? 10 _____, 20 _____, 30 _____, 40 _____, 50 _____.

c. If the product price is $20 per unit and the firm was producing at 30 units of output, the profit for the firm before the innovation was $_____. At this level of output, the profit after the innovation was

$ _____.

■ SHORT ANSWER AND ESSAY QUESTIONS

1. Give a definition of technological advance. According to economists, what role does time play in the definition?

2. Explain and give examples of invention. What does government do to protect it?

3. How does innovation differ from invention and diffusion? How does innovation affect competition among firms?

4. Compare and contrast the modern view of technological advance with the traditional view.

5. In what ways do entrepreneurs differ from other innovators? In what types of business does each tend to work? How have the characteristics of entrepreneurs changed over time?

6. What does it mean that "innovators try to anticipate the future"? What are the economic consequences of this effort?

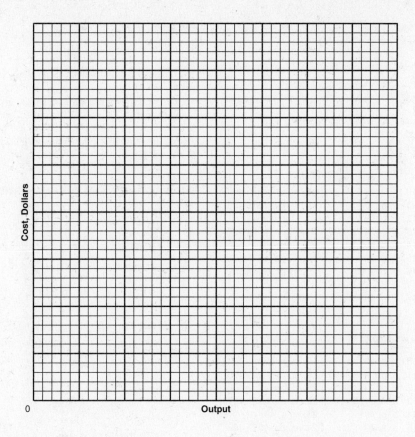

7. Why do entrepreneurs and other innovators actively study the scientific output of universities and government laboratories?

8. What are the many different sources of funding to finance firms' R&D expenditures? If an entrepreneur uses personal funds, is there a cost for financing?

9. Explain how the firm decides on the optimal amount of research and development. Use a marginal-cost and marginal-benefit graph in your explanation.

10. Why might many R&D expenditures be affordable but not worthwhile? Are outcomes from R&D guaranteed?

11. Describe how a firm's revenues and profits are increased through product innovation. Why does consumer acceptance of a new product depend on both its marginal utility and price?

12. Explain how process innovation reduces cost and increases profits. Illustrate the point graphically using a total-product and average-cost curve graph.

13. Describe the fast-second strategy and give an example of it.

14. What is the imitation problem resulting from technological advance?

15. Describe the legal protections and potential advantages of taking the lead in innovation.

16. Compare and contrast the suitability of different market structures for fostering technological advance.

17. Explain the basic conclusions from inverted-U theory. What will be the optimal market structure for technological progress?

18. How does technological advance enhance economic efficiency? Distinguish between its effects on productive efficiency and allocative efficiency.

19. How might innovation create or reduce monopoly power? Why might both effects be possible?

20. Explain the idea of creative destruction as championed by Joseph Schumpeter. What are the objections to that idea?

ANSWERS

Chapter 26 Technology, R&D, and Efficiency

FILL-IN QUESTIONS

  1. *a.* invention; *b.* innovation; *c.* diffusion
  2. invention, innovation, invention, innovation, diffusion
  3. product, process
  4. external, internal, rivalry among firms, scientific progress, external
  5. entrepreneur, intrapreneur, small, large
  6. more, rewards
  7. equal to, less than
  8. *a.* bank loans; *b.* bonds; *c.* retained earnings; *d.* venture capital; *e.* personal savings (any order *a–e*)
  9. revenues, costs
  10. and, is not, minor
  11. upward, downward, increases

12. decrease, fast-second
13. copyrights, learning by doing
14. less, low, may not
15. strong, limited, difficult, low
16. capable, little, large
17. weak, high, a defensive
18. weak, high, a few
19. productive, allocative, decreased, increased
20. creation, destruction, is not

TRUE–FALSE QUESTIONS

1. T, p. 484	**10.** T, p. 487	**19.** F, p. 493
2. F, p. 484	**11.** F, p. 487	**20.** F, pp. 495–496
3. F, p. 485	**12.** F, p. 488	**21.** T, p. 496
4. T, p. 485	**13.** F, pp. 488–490	**22.** F, pp. 496–497
5. F, pp. 485–486	**14.** F, p. 490	**23.** T, p. 497
6. T, p. 486	**15.** T, p. 491	**24.** F, pp. 497–499
7. F, p. 486	**16.** F, p. 492	**25.** F, pp. 499–500
8. T, pp. 486–487	**17.** T, pp. 492–493	
9. F, p. 487	**18.** F, p. 493	

MULTIPLE-CHOICE QUESTIONS

1. d, p. 484	**10.** a, p. 487	**19.** d, p. 494
2. b, p. 484	**11.** b, pp. 488–490	**20.** a, pp. 495–496
3. d, p. 485	**12.** c, pp. 488–490	**21.** d, pp. 495–496
4. c, p. 485	**13.** a, pp. 488–490	**22.** c, pp. 496–497
5. b, p. 485	**14.** b, p. 491	**23.** c, p. 497
6. b, p. 485	**15.** d, p. 491	**24.** d, pp. 497–498
7. a, p. 485	**16.** b, pp. 492–493	**25.** b, pp. 499–500
8. c, pp. 485–486	**17.** d, p. 493	
9. c, p. 486	**18.** b, p. 493	

PROBLEMS

1. *a.* 3; *b.* 1; *c.* 2; *d.* 3; *e.* 1; *f.* 2
2. *a.* 12, 12, 12; *b.* similar to Figure 26.5 in the text; *c.* 18, 6, 6; *d.* horizontal interest-rate cost-of-funds curve will drop from 12 to 6%
3. *a.* Put output on the horizontal axis, and put average cost on the vertical axis. Plot the set of points. Connect the set with lines; *b.* 3, 7, 4, 3, 2; *c.* Before: TR is $600 (30 × $20), TC is $540 (30 x $18), profit is $60; After: TR is $600, TC is $420 (30 × $14), profit is $180

SHORT ANSWER AND ESSAY QUESTIONS

1. p. 484	**8.** p. 488	**15.** pp. 493–494
2. p. 485	**9.** pp. 488–490	**16.** pp. 495–496
3. p. 485	**10.** p. 490	**17.** pp. 496–497
4. pp. 485–486	**11.** p. 491	**18.** pp. 497–499
5. pp. 486–487	**12.** pp. 492–493	**19.** pp. 499–500
6. p. 487	**13.** p. 493	**20.** pp. 499–500
7. p. 487	**14.** p. 493	

CHAPTER 27

The Demand for Resources

This chapter is the first of three that examine the market for resources. In resource markets the demanders are the employers of the resources and the suppliers are the owners of the resources. As you already know, the demand for and the supply of a resource will determine the resource price and the quantities in a competitive market.

Chapter 27 focuses on the demand or employer side of the resource market. It offers a general explanation of what determines demand for any resource. Chapters 28 and 29 discuss the characteristics of the market for particular resources—labor, capital, land, or entrepreneurial ability—and present the supply side of the resource market.

The **resource market is important** for several reasons, as you will learn in the first section of the chapter. Resource prices determine what resource owners (or households) receive in exchange for supplying their resources, and thus it determines the incomes of households. Prices allocate resources to their most efficient uses and encourage the least costly methods of production in our economy. Many public policy issues also involve resource pricing, such as setting a minimum wage.

The next section of the chapter focuses on the **marginal productivity theory of resource demand.** When a firm wishes to maximize its profits, it produces that output at which marginal revenue and marginal cost are equal. But how much of each resource does the firm hire if it wishes to maximize its profits? You will learn that the firm hires that amount of each resource up to the point that the marginal revenue product and the marginal resource cost of that resource are equal (**MRP = MPC**).

There is another similarity between the output and the resource markets for the firm. Recall that the competitive firm's supply curve is a portion of its marginal-cost curve. The purely competitive firm's demand curve for a resource is a portion of its marginal-revenue-product curve. Just as cost is the important determinant of supply, the revenue derived from the use of a resource is the important factor determining the demand for that resource in a competitive market for resources.

The next major section of the chapter presents the **determinants of resource demand.** Three major ones are discussed—changes in product demand, productivity, and the prices of other resources. The last one is the most complicated because you must consider whether the other resources are substitutes or complements and also the underlying factors affecting them.

This chapter has a section on the **elasticity of resource demand,** which is no different from the elasticity concept you learned about in Chapter 20. In this case,

it is the relation of the percentage change in quantity demanded of the resource to a percentage change in the price of the resource. As you will discover, the three factors that affect elasticity are the availability of other substitute resources, the elasticity of product demand, and the ratio of resource cost to total cost.

Most of the chapter examines the situation in which there is only one variable resource. The next-to-last section of the chapter, however, offers a general perspective on the **combination of resources** the firm will choose to use when multiple inputs are used and all inputs are variable. Two rules are presented. The *least-cost rule* states that the firm will minimize costs when the last dollar spent on each resource results in the same marginal product. The *profit-maximizing rule* means that in a competitive market the firm will maximize its profits when each resource is used so that its marginal product is equal to its price. The second rule is equally important because a firm that employs the quantity of resources that maximizes its profits also produces the output that maximizes its profits and is thus producing at the least cost.

The marginal productivity theory of resource demand is not without criticism, as you will learn in the last section of the chapter. If resource prices reflect marginal productivity, then this relationship can produce income inequality in society. In addition, market imperfection may skew the distribution of income.

■ CHECKLIST

When you have studied this chapter you should be able to

☐ Present four reasons for studying resource pricing.

☐ Explain why the demand for an economic resource is a derived demand.

☐ Define the marginal revenue product and relate it to the productivity and price of a resource.

☐ Determine the marginal-revenue-product schedule of a resource for a product sold in a purely competitive market, when given the data.

☐ Define the marginal resource cost.

☐ State the rule used by a profit-maximizing firm to determine how much of a resource it will employ.

☐ Apply the **MRP = MRC** rule to determine the quantity of a resource a firm will hire, when you are given the necessary data.

☐ Explain why the marginal-revenue-product schedule of a resource is the firm's demand for the resource.

☐ Find the marginal-revenue-product schedule of a resource for a product sold in an imperfectly competitive market, when given the data.
☐ Derive the market demand for a resource.
☐ List the three factors which would change a firm's demand for a resource.
☐ Predict the effect on resource demand of an increase or decrease in one of its three determinants.
☐ Give trends on the occupations with the fastest growth in jobs both in percentage terms and in absolute numbers.
☐ State three determinants of the price elasticity of resource demand.
☐ Describe how a change in each determinant would change the price elasticity of demand for a resource.
☐ State the rule used by a firm for determining the least-cost combination of resources.
☐ Use the least-cost rule to find the least-cost combination of resources for production, when given data.
☐ State the rule used by a profit-maximizing firm to determine the quantity of each of several resources to employ.
☐ Apply the profit-maximizing rule to determine the quantity of each resource a firm will hire, when given the data.
☐ Explain the marginal productivity theory of income distribution.
☐ Give two criticisms of the marginal productivity theory of income distribution.

■ **CHAPTER OUTLINE**

1. The study of what determines the prices of resources *is important* because resource prices influence the size of individual incomes and the resulting distribution of income. They allocate scarce resources and affect the way in which firms combine resources in production. Resource pricing also raises ethical questions about income distribution.

2. The *demand* for a single resource depends on (or is derived from) the demand for the goods and services it can produce.
a. Because resource demand is a *derived demand,* it depends on the marginal productivity of the resource and the market price of the good or service it is used to produce.
b. *Marginal revenue product* (MRP) is the change in total revenue divided by a one-unit change in resource quantity. It combines two factors—the marginal product of a resource and the market price of the product it produces—into a single useful tool.
c. *Marginal resource cost* (MRC) is the change in total resource cost divided by a one-unit change in resource quantity. A firm will hire resources until the marginal revenue product of the resource is equal to its marginal resource cost (***MRP = MRC***).
d. The firm's marginal-revenue-product schedule for a resource is that firm's demand schedule for the resource.
e. If a firm sells its output in an ***imperfectly competitive market,*** the more the firm sells, the lower the

price of the product becomes. This causes the firm's marginal-revenue-product (resource demand) schedule to be less elastic than it would be if the firm sold its output in a purely competitive market.
f. The market (or total) demand for a resource is the horizontal summation of the demand schedules of all firms using the resource.

3. The ***determinants of resource demand*** are changes in the demand for the product produced, changes in the productivity of the resource, and changes in the prices of other resources.
a. A change in the demand for a product produced by a resource will change the demand of a firm for labor in the same direction.
b. A change in the productivity of a resource will change the demand of a firm for the resource in the same direction.
c. A change in the price of a
(1) ***substitute resource*** will change the demand for a resource in the same direction if the substitution effect outweighs the output effect and in the opposite direction if the output effect outweighs the substitution effect;
(2) ***complementary resource*** will change the demand for a resource in the opposite direction.
d. Changes in the demand for labor have significant effects on employment growth in occupations, both in percentage and absolute terms. Projections (1998–2008) are reported for the fastest growing occupations (e.g., computer engineers) and the occupations with the greatest absolute job growth (e.g., systems analysts).

4. The ***price elasticity of resource demand*** measures the sensitivity of producers to changes in resource prices.
a. Three factors affect the price elasticity of resource demand:
(1) the ease of substitution of other resources: the more good substitute resources are available, the more elastic the resource demand;
(2) the elasticity of the demand for the product that the resource produces: the more elastic the product demand, the more elastic the resource demand;
(3) the ratio of labor cost to total cost: the greater the ratio of labor cost to total cost, the greater the price elasticity of demand for labor.

5. Firms often employ more than one resource in producing a product.
a. The firm employing resources in purely competitive markets is hiring resources in the least-cost combination when the ratio of the marginal product of a resource to its price is the same for all the resources the firm hires.
b. The firm is hiring resources in the most profitable combination if it hires resources in a purely competitive market when the marginal revenue product of each resource is equal to the price of that resource.
c. A numerical example illustrates the least-cost and profit-maximizing rules for a firm that employs resources in purely competitive markets.

6. The marginal productivity theory of *income distribution* seems to result in an equitable distribution of income because each unit of a resource receives a payment equal to its marginal contribution to the firm's revenue. The theory has at least two serious faults.

   a. The distribution of income will be unequal because resources are unequally distributed among individuals in the economy.

   b. The income of those who supply resources will not be based on their marginal productivities if there is monopsony or monopoly in the resource markets of the economy.

■ HINTS AND TIPS

1. The list of important terms for Chapter 27 is relatively short, but included in the list are two very important concepts—*marginal revenue product* and *marginal resource cost*—which you must grasp if you are to understand how much of a resource a firm will hire. These two concepts are similar to, but not identical with, the marginal-revenue and marginal-cost concepts used in the study of product markets and in the explanation of the quantity of output a firm will produce.

   Marginal revenue and marginal cost are, respectively, the change in the firm's total revenue and the change in the firm's total cost when it produces and sells an additional unit of *output*. Marginal revenue product and marginal resource cost are, respectively, the change in the firm's total revenue and the change in the firm's total cost when it hires an additional unit of *input*. Note that the two new concepts deal with changes in revenue and costs as a consequence of hiring more of a *resource*.

2. The marginal revenue product (MRP) of a resource is simply the marginal product of the resource (MP) times the price of the product that the resource produces (*P*), or MRP = MP × *P*. Under pure competition, MP changes, but *P* is constant as more resources are added to production. Under imperfect competition, both MP and *P* change as more resources are added, and thus each variable (MP and *P*) affects MRP. Compare the data in Tables 27.1 and 27.2 in the textbook to see this difference.

3. Make sure you understand the rule **MRP = MRC.** A firm will hire one more unit of a resource only so long as the resource adds more to the firm's revenues than it does to its costs. If MRP > MRC, the firm will hire more resources. If MRP < MRC, the firm will cut back on resource use.

4. It can be difficult to figure out what outcome will result from a change in the price of a substitute resource (capital) on the demand for another resource (labor). It is easy to understand why the demand for labor might decrease if the price of capital decreases because cheaper capital would be substituted for labor. It is harder to explain why the opposite might be true. That insight requires an understanding of both the **substitution effect** and the **output effect.** Find out how one effect may offset the other.

5. The **profit-maximizing rule** for a combination of resources may seem difficult, but it is relatively simple. Just remember that the price of any resource must be equal to its marginal revenue product, and thus *the ratio must always equal 1.*

■ IMPORTANT TERMS

derived demand	output effect
marginal product	elasticity of resource demand
marginal revenue product (MRP)	least-cost combination of resources
marginal resource cost (MRC)	profit-maximizing combination of resources
MRP = MRC rule	marginal productivity theory of income distribution
substitution effect	

SELF-TEST

■ FILL-IN QUESTIONS

1. Resource prices allocate (revenues, resources) _____ and are one factor that determines household (incomes, costs) _____ and business _____.

2. The demand for a resource is a (constant, derived) _____ demand that depends on the (productivity, cost) _____ of the resource and the (cost, price) _____ of the product made from the resource.

3. A firm will find it profitable to hire units of a resource up to the quantity at which the marginal revenue (cost, product) _____ equals the marginal resource _____.

4. If the firm hires the resource in a purely competitive market, the marginal resource (cost, product) _____ will be (greater than, less than, equal to) _____ the price of the resource.

5. A firm's demand schedule for a resource is the firm's marginal revenue (cost, product) _____ schedule for that resource because both indicate the quantities of the resource the firm will employ at various resource (costs, prices) _____.

6. A producer in an imperfectly competitive market finds that the more of a resource it employs, the (higher, lower) _____ becomes the price at which it can sell its product. As a consequence, the (supply, demand) _____ schedule for the resource is (more, less) _____ elastic than it would be if the output were sold in a purely competitive market.

7. Adding the quantity demanded for the resource at each and every price for each firm using the resource gives the market (supply, demand) _____ curve for the resource.

8. The demand for a resource will change if the (demand, supply) _____ of the product the resource produces changes, if the (productivity, price) _____ of the resource changes, or if the (price, elasticity) _____ of other resources changes.

9. If the demand for a product increases, then the demand for the resource that produces that product will (increase, decrease) _____. Conversely, if the demand for a product decreases, then the demand for the resource that produces that product will _____.

10. When the productivity of a resource falls, the demand for the resource (rises, falls) _____, but when the productivity of a resource rises, the demand for the resource _____.

11. The output of the firm being constant, a decrease in the price of resource A will induce the firm to hire (more, less) _____ of resource A and _____ of other resources; this is called the (substitution, output) _____ effect. But if the decrease in the price of A results in lower total costs and an increase in output, the firm may hire (more, less) _____ of both resources; this is called the (substitution, output) _____ effect.

12. A decrease in the price of a complementary resource will cause the demand for labor to (increase, decrease) _____, but an increase in the price of a complementary resource will cause the demand for labor to _____.

13. The three determinants of the price elasticity of demand for a resource are the ease with which other resources can be (substitutes, complements) _____ for it, the price elasticity of (supply, demand) _____ for the product the resource produces, and the ratio of resource (demand, cost) _____ to total (demand, cost) _____.

14. If the marginal product of labor declines slowly when added to a fixed stock of capital, the demand curve for labor (MRP) will decline (rapidly, slowly) _____ and will tend to be highly (elastic, inelastic) _____.

15. The larger the number of good substitutes available for a resource, the (greater, less) _____ will be the elasticity of demand for a resource.

16. Suppose a firm employs resources in purely competitive markets. If the firm wishes to produce any given amount of its output in the least costly way, the ratio of the marginal (cost, product) _____ of each resource to its (demand, price) _____ must be the same for all resources.

17. A firm that hires resources in purely competitive markets is employing the combination of resources that will result in maximum profits for the firm when the marginal (revenue product, resource cost) _____ of every resource is equal to its (demand, price) _____.

18. If the marginal revenue product of a resource is equal to the price of that resource, the marginal revenue product divided by its price is equal to (1, infinity) _____.

19. In the marginal productivity theory, the distribution of income is an equitable one because each unit of each resource is paid an amount equal to its (total, marginal) _____ contribution to the firm's (revenues, costs) _____.

20. The marginal productivity theory rests on the assumption of (competitive, imperfect) _____ markets. In the real world, there are many labor markets with imperfections because of employer pricing or monopoly power, so wage rates and other resource prices (do, do not) _____ perfectly measure contributions to domestic output.

■ **TRUE–FALSE QUESTIONS**

Circle T if the statement is true, F if it is false.

1. In the resource markets of the economy, resources are demanded by business firms and supplied by households.　**T F**

2. The prices of resources are an important factor in the determination of resource allocation.　**T F**

3. The demand for a resource is a derived demand based on the demand for the product it produces.　**T F**

4. A resource that is highly productive will always be in great demand.　**T F**

5. A firm's demand schedule for a resource is the firm's marginal-revenue-product schedule for the resource.　**T F**

6. It will be profitable for a firm to hire additional units of labor resources up to the point where the marginal revenue product of labor is equal to its marginal resource cost. **T F**

7. A firm with one worker can produce 30 units of a product that sells for $4 a unit, but the same firm with two workers can produce 70 units of that product. The marginal revenue product of the second worker is $400. **T F**

8. The competitive firm's marginal revenue product of labor will fall as output expands because marginal product diminishes and product price falls. **T F**

9. A producer's demand schedule for a resource will be more elastic if the firm sells its product in a purely competitive market than it would be if it sold the product in an imperfectly competitive market. **T F**

10. The market demand for a particular resource is the sum of the individual demands of all firms that employ that resource. **T F**

11. An increase in the price of a resource will cause the demand for the resource to decrease. **T F**

12. The demand curve for labor will increase when the demand for (and price of) the product produced by that labor increases. **T F**

13. There is an inverse relationship between the productivity of labor and the demand for labor. **T F**

14. The demand for a resource will be increased with improvements in its quality. **T F**

15. When two resources are substitutes for each other, both the substitution effect and the output effect of a decrease in the price of one of these resources operate to increase the quantity of the other resource employed by the firm. **T F**

16. The output effect of an increase in the price of a resource increases the quantity demanded of that resource. **T F**

17. If two resources are complementary, an increase in the price of one will reduce the demand for the other. **T F**

18. Price declines for computer equipment have had stronger output effects than substitution effects, increasing the demand for computer software engineers and specialists. **T F**

19. The larger the number of good substitute resources available, the less will be the elasticity of demand for a particular resource. **T F**

20. The greater the elasticity of product demand, the greater the elasticity of resource demand. **T F**

21. The demand for labor will be less elastic when labor is a smaller proportion of the total cost of producing a product. **T F**

Use the following information as the basis for answering Questions 22 and 23. The marginal revenue product and price of resource A are $12 and a constant $2, respectively, and the marginal revenue product and price of resource B are $25 and a constant $5, respectively. The firm sells its product at a constant price of $1.

22. The firm should decrease the amount of A and increase the amount of B it employs if it wishes to decrease its total cost without affecting its total output. **T F**

23. If the firm wishes to maximize its profits, it should increase its employment of both A and B until their marginal revenue products fall to $2 and $5, respectively. **T F**

24. The marginal productivity theory of income distribution results in an equitable distribution if resource markets are competitive. **T F**

25. The marginal productivity theory rests on the assumption of imperfectly competitive markets. **T F**

■ **MULTIPLE-CHOICE QUESTIONS**

Circle the letter that corresponds to the best answer.

1. The prices paid for resources affect
  (a) the money incomes of households in the economy
  (b) the allocation of resources among different firms and industries in the economy
  (c) the quantities of different resources employed to produce a particular product
  (d) all of the above

2. In a competitive resource market, the firm employing a resource such as labor is a
  (a) price maker
  (b) cost maker
  (c) wage taker
  (d) revenue taker

3. The demand for a resource is *derived* from the
  (a) demand for the products it helps produce
  (b) price of the resource
  (c) supply of the resource
  (d) income of the firm selling the resource

4. The law of diminishing returns explains why
  (a) the MRP of an input in a purely competitive market decreases as a firm increases the quantity of an employed resource
  (b) the MRC of an input in a purely competitive market decreases as a firm increases the quantity of an employed resource
  (c) resource demand is a derived demand
  (d) there are substitution and output effects for resources

Answer Questions 5, 6, and 7 on the basis of the information in the following table for a purely competitive market.

Number of workers	Total product	Product price ($)
0	0	4
1	16	4
2	26	4
3	34	4
4	40	4
5	44	4

5. At a wage rate of $15, the firm will choose to employ
   (a) 2 workers
   (b) 3 workers
   (c) 4 workers
   (d) 5 workers

6. At a wage rate of $30, the firm will choose to employ
   (a) 2 workers
   (b) 3 workers
   (c) 4 workers
   (d) 5 workers

7. If the product price increases to a constant $8, then at a wage rate of $30, the firm will choose to employ
   (a) 2 workers
   (b) 3 workers
   (c) 4 workers
   (d) 5 workers

Use the following total-product and marginal-product schedules for a resource to answer Questions 8, 9, 10, and 11. Assume that the quantities of other resources the firm employs remain constant.

Units of resource	Total product	Marginal product
0	0	–
1	8	8
2	14	6
3	18	4
4	21	3
5	23	2

8. If the product the firm produces sells for a constant $3 per unit, the marginal revenue product of the fourth unit of the resource is
   (a) $3
   (b) $6
   (c) $9
   (d) $12

9. If the firm's product sells for a constant $3 per unit and the price of the resource is a constant $15, the firm will employ how many units of the resource?
   (a) 2
   (b) 3
   (c) 4
   (d) 5

10. If the firm can sell 14 units of output at a price of $1 per unit and 18 units of output at a price of $0.90 per unit, the marginal revenue product of the third unit of the resource would be
   (a) $4
   (b) $3.60
   (c) $2.20
   (d) $0.40

11. If the firm can sell 8 units at a price of $1.50, 14 units at a price of $1.00, 18 units at a price of $0.90, 21 units at a price of $0.70, and 23 units at a price of $0.50, then the firm is
   (a) maximizing profits at a product price of $0.50
   (b) minimizing its costs at a product price of $1.00

   (c) selling in an imperfectly competitive market
   (d) selling in a purely competitive market

12. As a firm that sells its product in an imperfectly competitive market increases the quantity of a resource it employs, the marginal revenue product of that resource falls because
   (a) the price paid by the firm for the resource falls
   (b) the marginal product of the resource falls
   (c) the price at which the firm sells its product falls
   (d) both the marginal product and the price at which the firm sells its product fall

13. Which would increase a firm's demand for a particular resource?
   (a) an increase in the prices of complementary resources used by the firm
   (b) a decrease in the demand for the firm's product
   (c) an increase in the productivity of the resource
   (d) an increase in the price of the particular resource

14. The substitution effect indicates that a firm will use
   (a) more of an input whose relative price has decreased
   (b) more of an input whose relative price has increased
   (c) less of an input whose relative price has decreased
   (d) less of an input whose relative price has remained constant

15. Suppose resource A and resource B are substitutes and the price of A increases. If the output effect is greater than the substitution effect,
   (a) the quantity of A employed by the firm will increase and the quantity of B employed will decrease
   (b) the quantities of both A and B employed by the firm will decrease
   (c) the quantities of both A and B employed by the firm will increase
   (d) the quantity of A employed will decrease and the quantity of B employed will increase

16. Two resource inputs, capital and labor, are complementary and used in fixed proportions. A decrease in the price of capital will
   (a) increase the demand for labor
   (b) decrease the demand for labor
   (c) decrease the quantity demanded for labor
   (d) have no effect because the relationship is fixed

17. Which would result in an increase in the elasticity of demand for a particular resource?
   (a) an increase in the demand for the resource
   (b) a decrease in the elasticity of demand for the product that the resource helps to produce
   (c) an increase in the percentage of the firm's total costs accounted for by the resource
   (d) a decrease in the number of other resources that are good substitutes for the particular resource

18. The demand for labor would most likely become more inelastic as a result of
   (a) an increase in the elasticity of the demand for the product that the labor produces

(b) an increase in the time for employers to make technological changes or purchase new equipment
(c) a decrease in the proportion of labor costs to total costs
(d) a decrease in the demand for the product

19. A firm is allocating its expenditures for resources in a way that will result in the least total cost of producing any given output when the
(a) amount the firm spends on each resource is the same
(b) marginal revenue product of each resource is the same
(c) marginal product of each resource is the same
(d) marginal product per dollar spent on the last unit of each resource is the same

20. A business is employing inputs such that the marginal product of labor is 20 and the marginal product of capital is 45. The price of labor is $10 and the price of capital is $15. If the business wants to minimize costs while keeping output constant, then it should
(a) use more labor and less capital
(b) use less labor and less capital
(c) use less labor and more capital
(d) make no change in resource use

21. Assume that a computer disk manufacturer is employing resources so that the MRP of the last unit hired for resource X is $240 and the MRP of the last unit hired for resource Y is $150. The price of resource X is $80 and the price of resource Y is $50. To maximize profit the firm should
(a) hire more of resource X and less of resource Y
(b) hire less of resource X and more of resource Y
(c) hire less of both resource X and resource Y
(d) hire more of both resource X and resource Y

22. Which does not suggest that a firm that hires resources in a purely competitive market is maximizing its profits?
(a) The marginal revenue product of every resource is equal to 1.
(b) The marginal revenue product of every resource is equal to its price.
(c) The ratio of the marginal revenue product of every resource to its price is equal to 1.

(d) The ratio of the price of every resource to its marginal revenue product is equal to 1.

23. Assume that a purely competitive firm uses two resources—labor (L) and capital (C)—to produce a product. In which situation would the firm be maximizing profit?

	MRP_L	MRP_C	P_L	P_C
(a)	10	20	30	40
(b)	10	20	10	20
(c)	15	15	10	10
(d)	30	40	10	5

24. In the marginal productivity theory of income distribution, when all markets are purely competitive, each unit of each resource receives a money payment equal to
(a) its marginal product
(b) its marginal revenue product
(c) the needs of the resource owner
(d) the payments received by each of the units of the other resources in the economy

25. A major criticism of the marginal productivity theory of income distribution is that
(a) labor markets are often subject to imperfect competition
(b) the theory suggests that there eventually will be equality in incomes
(c) purely competitive firms are only interested in profit maximization
(d) the demand for labor resources is price elastic

■ PROBLEMS

1. The table below shows the total production a firm will be able to obtain if it employs varying amounts of resource **A** while the amounts of the other resources the firm employs remain constant.
   a. Compute the marginal product of each of the seven units of resource **A** and enter these figures in the table.
   b. Assume the product the firm produces sells in the market for $1.50 per unit. Compute the total revenue of the firm at each of the eight levels of output and the marginal revenue product of each of the seven units of resource **A.** Enter these figures in the table below.

Quantity of resource A employed	Total product	Marginal product of A	Total revenue	Marginal revenue product of A
0	0		$_____	
1	12	_____	_____	$_____
2	22	_____	_____	_____
3	30	_____	_____	_____
4	36	_____	_____	_____
5	40	_____	_____	_____
6	42	_____	_____	_____
7	43	_____	_____	_____

c. On the basis of your computations, complete the firm's demand schedule for resource **A** by indicating in the following table how many units of resource **A** the firm would employ at the given prices.

Price of A	Quantity of A demanded
$21.00	_____
18.00	_____
15.00	_____
12.00	_____
9.00	_____
6.00	_____
3.00	_____
1.50	_____

2. In the table below are the marginal product data for resource **B**. Assume that the quantities of other resources employed by the firm remain constant.

a. Compute the total product (output) of the firm for each of the seven quantities of resource **B** employed and enter these figures in the table.

b. Assume that the firm sells its output in an imperfectly competitive market and that the prices at which it can sell its product are those given in the table. Compute and enter in the table:

(1) the total revenue for each of the seven quantities of **B** employed.

(2) the marginal revenue product of each of the seven units of resource **B**.

c. How many units of **B** would the firm employ if the market price of **B** were

(1) $25? _____

(2) $20? _____

(3) $15? _____

(4) $9? _____

(5) $5? _____

(6) $1? _____

3. Use the following total-product schedule as a resource to answer questions **a**, **b**, and **c**. Assume that the quantities of other resources the firm employs remain constant.

Units of resource	Total product
0	0
1	15
2	28
3	38
4	43
5	46

a. If the firm's product sells for a constant $2 per unit, what is the marginal revenue product of the second unit of the resource? _____

b. If the firm's product sells for a constant $2 and the price of the resource is $10, how many units of the resource will the firm employ? _____

c. If the firm can sell 15 units of output at a price of $2.00 and 28 units of output at a price of $1.50, what is the marginal revenue product of the second unit of the resource? _____

4. In the space to the right of each of the following changes, indicate whether the change would tend to increase (+) or decrease (−) a firm's demand for a particular resource.

a. An increase in the demand for the firm's product

_____

b. A decrease in the price of the firm's output _____

c. An increase in the productivity of the resource

_____

d. An increase in the price of a substitute resource when the output effect is greater than the substitution effect _____

e. A decrease in the price of a complementary resource _____

f. A decrease in the price of a substitute resource when the substitution effect is greater than the output effect _____

Quantity of resource B employed	Marginal product of B	Total product	Product price	Total revenue	Marginal revenue product of B
0	–	0		$0.00	–
1	22	_____	$1.00	_____	_____
2	21	_____	.90	_____	_____
3	19	_____	.80	_____	_____
4	16	_____	.70	_____	_____
5	12	_____	.60	_____	_____
6	7	_____	.50	_____	_____
7	1	_____	.40	_____	_____

Quantity of resource C employed	Marginal product of C	Marginal revenue product of C	Quantity of resource D employed	Marginal product of D	Marginal revenue product of D
1	10	$5.00	1	21	$10.50
2	8	4.00	2	18	9.00
3	6	3.00	3	15	7.50
4	5	2.50	4	12	6.00
5	4	2.00	5	9	4.50
6	3	1.50	6	6	3.00
7	2	1.00	7	3	1.50

5. The above table shows the marginal-product and marginal-revenue-product schedules for resource **C** and resource **D**. Both resources are variable and are employed in purely competitive markets. The price of **C** is $2 and the price of **D** is $3. (Assume that the productivity of each resource is independent of the quantity of the other.)

a. The least-cost combination of **C** and **D** that would enable the firm to produce

(1) 64 units of its product is _____ **C** and _____ **D.**

(2) 99 units of its product is _____ **C** and _____ **D.**

b. The profit-maximizing combination of **C** and **D** is

_____ **C** and _____ **D.**

c. When the firm employs the profit-maximizing combination of **C** and **D,** it is also employing **C** and **D** in

the least-cost combination because _____

equals _____.

d. Examination of the figures in the table reveals that

the firm sells its product in a _____ com-

petitive market at a price of $ _____.

e. Employing the profit-maximizing combination of **C** and **D,** the firm's

(1) total output is _____.

(2) total revenue is $ _____.

(3) total cost is $ _____.

(4) total profit is $ _____.

■ **SHORT ANSWER AND ESSAY QUESTIONS**

1. Give four reasons why it is important to study resource pricing.

2. How does the demand for a product differ from the demand for a resource? Explain why the demand for a resource is a derived demand.

3. What two factors determine the strength of the demand for a resource?

4. Explain why firms that wish to maximize their profits follow the MRP = MRC rule.

5. What effects do marginal product and marginal price have on a firm's resource demand curve under pure competition and under imperfect competition?

6. Why is the demand schedule for a resource less elastic when the firm sells its product in an imperfectly competitive market than when it sells it in a purely competitive market?

7. How do you derive the market demand for a resource?

8. Identify and describe three factors that will cause the demand for a resource to increase or decrease. Give examples of how each factor influences changes in demand.

9. What is the difference between the substitution effect and the output effect?

10. If the price of capital falls, what will happen to the demand for labor if capital and labor are substitutes in production? Describe what happens when the substitution effect outweighs the output effect and when the output effect outweighs the substitution effect. What can you conclude?

11. Why does a change in the price of a complementary resource cause the demand for labor to change in the opposite direction?

12. Describe trends in occupational employment data. Give examples of jobs with the greatest projected growth in percentage and absolute terms.

13. What are the three factors that determine the elasticity of demand for a resource?

14. Use an example to explain what happens to elasticity when there are many substitute resources compared to when there are few.

15. How can the ratio of labor cost to the total cost influence how producers react to changes in the price of labor?

16. Assume that a firm employs resources in purely competitive markets. How does the firm know that it is spending money on resources in such a way that it can produce a given output for the least total cost?

17. Why is minimizing cost not sufficient for maximizing profit for a firm?

18. When is a firm that employs resources in purely competitive markets using these resources in amounts that will maximize the profits of the firm?

19. What is the marginal productivity theory of income distribution? What ethical proposition must be accepted if this distribution is to be fair and equitable?

20. What are the two major shortcomings of the marginal productivity theory of income distribution?

ANSWERS

Chapter 27 The Demand for Resources

FILL-IN QUESTIONS

1. resources, incomes, costs
2. derived, productivity, price
3. product, cost
4. cost, equal to
5. product, prices
6. lower, demand, less
7. demand
8. demand, productivity, price
9. increase, decrease
10. falls, rises
11. more, less, substitution, more, output
12. increase, decrease
13. substitutes, demand, cost, cost
14. slowly, elastic
15. greater
16. product, price
17. revenue product, price
18. 1
19. marginal, revenues
20. competitive, do not

TRUE–FALSE QUESTIONS

1. T, p. 504
2. T, p. 504
3. T, p. 505
4. F, pp. 505–506
5. T, pp. 506–507
6. T, pp. 506–507
7. F, p. 506
8. F, pp. 507–508
9. T, pp. 507–508
10. T, p. 508
11. F, pp. 509–510
12. T, p. 509
13. F, pp. 509–510
14. T, pp. 509–510
15. F, pp. 510–511
16. F, pp. 510–511
17. T, pp. 510–511
18. T, p. 512
19. F, p. 513
20. T, p. 513
21. T, p. 513
22. F, pp. 514–516
23. T, pp. 514–516
24. F, pp. 516–517
25. F, pp. 516–517

MULTIPLE-CHOICE QUESTIONS

1. d, pp. 504–505
2. c, p. 505
3. a, p. 505
4. a, pp. 505–506
5. d, pp. 506–507
6. b, pp. 506–507
7. d, pp. 506–507
8. c, pp. 506–507
9. a, pp. 506–507
10. c, pp. 507–508
11. c, pp. 507–508
12. d, pp. 507–508
13. c, pp. 509–511
14. a, pp. 510–511
15. b, pp. 510–511
16. a, pp. 510–511
17. c, p. 513
18. c, p. 513
19. d, p. 514
20. c, p. 514
21. d, pp. 515–516
22. a, pp. 515–516
23. b, pp. 515–516
24. b, pp. 516–517
25. a, pp. 516–517

PROBLEMS

1. *a.* Marginal product of A: 12, 10, 8, 6, 4, 2, 1; *b.* Total revenue: 0, 18.00, 33.00, 45.00, 54.00, 60.00, 63.00, 64.50; Marginal revenue product of A: 18.00, 15.00, 12.00, 9.00, 6.00, 3.00, 1.50; *c.* 0, 1, 2, 3, 4, 5, 6, 7

2. *a.* Total product: 22, 43, 62, 78, 90, 97, 98; *b.* (1) Total revenue: 22.00, 38.70, 49.60, 54.60, 54.00, 48.50, 39.20, (2) Marginal revenue product of B: 22.00, 16.70, 10.90, 5.00, −0.60, −5.50, −9.30; *c.* (1) 0, (2) 1, (3) 2, (4) 3, (5) 4, (6) 4

3. *a.* \$26. The second worker increases TP by 13 units (13 × \$2 = \$26); *b.* 4 units. The marginal product of the fourth resource is 5 units of output (5 × \$2 = \$10). Thus MRP = \$10 and MRC = \$10 when the fourth resource is employed; *c.* \$12. The total revenue from 1 unit is \$30.00 (15 × \$2.00). The total revenue with 2 units is \$42 (28 × \$1.50). The difference is the MR of the second unit.

4. *a.* +; *b.* −; *c.* +; *d.* −; *e.* +; *f.* −

5. *a.* (1) 1, 3, (2) 3, 5; *b.* 5, 6; *c.* the marginal product of **C** divided by its price, the marginal product of **D** divided by its price; *d.* purely, \$.50; *e.* (1) 114, (2) 57, (3) 28, (4) 29

SHORT ANSWER AND ESSAY QUESTIONS

1. pp. 504–505
2. pp. 505–506
3. pp. 505–506
4. p. 506
5. pp. 506–508
6. pp. 506–508
7. p. 508
8. pp. 509–511
9. pp. 510–511
10. pp. 510–511
11. pp. 510–511
12. pp. 511–512
13. p. 513
14. p. 513
15. p. 513
16. p. 514
17. pp. 514–515
18. pp. 515–516
19. pp. 516–517
20. pp. 516–517

CHAPTER 28

Wage Determination

The preceding chapter explained the demand for *any* resource in a competitive resource market. Chapter 28 uses demand and supply analysis to describe what determines the quantity of a *particular* resource—*labor*—and the price paid for it—*wages*—in different markets.

The chapter begins by defining terms and briefly discussing the general level of wages in the United States and other advanced economies. You will learn about the role that productivity plays in explaining the long-run growth of real wages and the increased demand for labor over time.

In a product market, the degree of competition significantly influences how prices are determined and what output is produced. In a labor resource market, the degree of competition directly affects the determination of wage rates and the level of employment. The main purpose of the chapter is to explain how wage rates and the quantity of labor are determined in labor markets varying in competitiveness.

Six labor markets are discussed in the chapter: (1) the *purely competitive* market, in which the number of employers is large and labor is nonunionized; (2) the *monopsony* market, in which a single employer hires labor under competitive (nonunion) conditions; (3) a market in which a union controls the supply of labor, the number of employers is large, and the union attempts to increase the total demand for labor; (4) a similar market in which the union attempts to reduce the total supply of labor; (5) another similar market in which the union attempts to obtain a wage rate that is above the competitive-equilibrium level by threatening to strike; and (6) the *bilateral monopoly* market, in which a single employer faces a labor supply controlled by a single union.

What is important for you to learn is how the characteristics of each labor market affect wage rates and employment. In the purely competitive or monopsony labor market, there is no union. The determination of the wage rate and employment will be quite definite, although different for each market. In the next four types of labor markets, *unions* control the supply of labor, and thus the outcomes for wage rates and employment will be less definite. If the demand for labor is competitive, the wage rate and the amount of employment will depend on how successful the union is in increasing the demand for labor, restricting the supply of labor, or setting a wage rate that employers will accept. If there is both a union and one employer (a bilateral monopoly), wages and employment will fall within certain limits, but exactly where will

depend on the bargaining power of the union or the employer.

Three other issues are discussed in the last three sections of the chapter. First, for many years the Federal government has set a legal *minimum wage* for labor. The chapter uses supply and demand analysis to make the case for and against the minimum wage and then discusses its real-world effects. Second, wage rates are not homogeneous and differ across workers and occupations. The chapter presents important reasons why these *wage differentials* exist. Third, there is a *principal–agent problem* in most types of employment that may lead to shirking on the job. Different pay schemes have been devised to tie workers' pay to performance in an effort to overcome this problem. Each of these issues should be of direct interest to you and deepen your understanding about how labor markets work.

■ CHECKLIST

When you have studied this chapter you should be able to

☐ Define wages (or the wage rate).

☐ Distinguish between nominal and real wages.

☐ List five reasons for high productivity in the United States and other advanced economies.

☐ Describe the long-run relationship between real wages and productivity in the United States.

☐ Evaluate the importance of the two factors contributing to the secular growth in U.S. real wages.

☐ Define the three characteristics of a purely competitive labor market.

☐ Use demand and supply graphs to explain wage rates and the equilibrium level of employment in a purely competitive labor market.

☐ Define the three characteristics of a labor market monopsony and compare it with a purely competitive labor market.

☐ Explain why the marginal resource cost exceeds the wage rate in monopsony.

☐ Use demand and supply graphs to explain wage rates and the equilibrium level of employment in the monopsony model.

☐ Give examples of monopsony power.

☐ List three types of union models.

☐ Identify three strategies of labor unions to increase the demand for labor and their effects on wage rates and employment.

☐ Explain and illustrate graphically the effects of actions taken by craft unions to decrease the supply of labor on wages and the employment of workers.

☐ Explain and illustrate graphically how the organization of workers by an industrial union in a previously competitive labor market would affect the wage rate and the employment level.

☐ Describe the effect of unions on wage increases and two factors that might reduce the unemployment effect from wage increases.

☐ Use a graph to explain why the equilibrium wage rate and employment level are indeterminate when a labor market is a bilateral monopoly and to predict the range for the wage rate.

☐ Present the case for and the case against a legally established minimum wage.

☐ Use supply and demand analysis to explain wage differentials.

☐ Connect wage differentials to marginal revenue productivity.

☐ Give two reasons why noncompeting groups of workers earn different wages.

☐ Explain why some wage differentials are due to compensatory differences in the nonmonetary aspects of jobs.

☐ Cite four types of labor market imperfections that contribute to wage differentials.

☐ Describe the principal–agent problem in worker pay and performance issues.

☐ Describe four pay schemes employers use to prevent shirking or to tie worker pay to performance.

☐ Explain the negative side effects of pay-for-performance schemes.

■ **CHAPTER OUTLINE**

1. A *wage* (or the wage rate) is the price paid per unit of time for any type of labor. Earnings are equal to the wage multiplied by the amount of time worked. Wages can be measured either in nominal or real terms. A *real wage* is adjusted for the effects of inflation. It reflects the quantity of goods and services a worker can purchase with a *nominal wage*.

2. The *general level of real wages* in the United States and other advanced economies is high because the demand for labor has been large relative to the supply of labor.

   a. The demand for labor in the United States and advanced economies has been strong because labor is highly productive for several reasons: substantial quantities of capital goods and natural resources; technological advancement; improvements in labor quality; and other intangible factors (management techniques, business environment, and size of the domestic market).

   b. The real hourly wage rate and output per hour of labor are closely and directly related to each other, and real income per worker can increase only at the same rate as output per worker.

   c. Increases in the demand for labor over time have been greater than increases in the supply of labor in the United States, increasing the real wage rate in the long run.

3. In a *purely competitive labor market* many firms compete in hiring a specific type of labor and there are many qualified workers with identical skills who independently supply this labor. Both firms and workers are "wage takers" who do not influence the price of labor.

   a. The market *demand curve* for labor is a horizontal summation of the demand curves for individual firms.

   b. The market *supply curve* slopes upward, indicating that a higher wage will entice more workers to supply their labor.

   c. The *wage rate* for labor in this market is determined by the interaction of the market demand for and the supply of that labor. For the individual firm, the supply of labor is perfectly elastic at this wage rate (so the marginal labor cost is equal to the wage rate). The firm will hire the amount of labor at which its marginal revenue product of labor is equal to its marginal labor cost.

4. In a *monopsony* market for labor, there is only one buyer of a particular kind of labor, the labor is relatively immobile, and the hiring firm is a "wage maker" (the wage rate a firm pays varies with the number of workers it employs).

   a. The supply curve is upsloping and indicates that the firm (the single buyer of labor) must pay higher wages to attract more workers.

   b. A monopsonistic firm's marginal labor costs are greater than the wage rates it must pay to obtain various amounts of labor because once it offers a higher wage to one worker, it must offer the same wage to all workers.

   c. The firm hires the amount of labor at which marginal labor cost and the marginal revenue product of labor are equal. Both the wage rate and the level of employment are less than they would be under purely competitive conditions in labor markets.

   (1) Note that if the firm employs resources in imperfectly competitive markets, it is hiring resources in the least-cost combination when the ratio of the marginal product of a resource to its marginal resource cost is the same for all resources, and

   (2) it is hiring resources in the most profitable combination when the marginal revenue product of each resource is equal to its marginal resource cost.

   d. Monopsony power can be found in such situations as small cities where there are one or two firms that hire most of the workers of a particular type in a region or in professional sports franchises that have exclusive rights to obtain the service of professional athletes.

5. In labor markets in which *labor unions* represent workers, the unions attempt to raise wages in three ways.

   a. The union can increase *the demand for labor* by increasing the demand for the products the union workers produce, by increasing productivity, and by increasing the prices of resources that are substitutes for the labor provided by the members of the union.

b. An *exclusive* or *craft union* will seek to increase wages by reducing the supply of labor. *Occupational licensing* is another means of restricting the supply of a particular type of labor.

c. An *inclusive* or *industrial union* will try to increase wages by forcing employers to pay wages in excess of the equilibrium rate that would prevail in a purely competitive labor market.

d. Labor unions are aware that their actions to increase wage rates may also increase the unemployment of their members, which tends to limit the demands for higher wages. The unemployment effect of higher wages, however, is lessened by increases in, and a relatively inelastic, demand for labor.

6. A *bilateral monopoly* is a labor market with a monopsony (single buyer of labor) and an inclusive union (single seller of labor).

a. In this situation, the wage rate depends, within certain limits, on the relative bargaining power of the union and of the employer.

b. This model may be desirable because the monopoly power on the buy side is offset by the monopoly power on the sell side. The resulting wage rate may be close to levels found in purely competitive markets.

7. The *minimum wage* is a price floor that has been used to set a minimum price for unskilled labor.

a. Critics argue that it increases wage rates and reduces the employment of workers. It is a poor policy for reducing household poverty because the benefits largely go to teenagers who do not need the assistance.

b. Defenders think that in a monopsonistic market, it can increase the wage rate and employment. A minimum wage may also increase productivity, thus increasing the demand for labor and reducing turnover.

c. The evidence is mixed. In theory, a higher wage should reduce employment, but in practice the negative effects on employment may be minor or nil. The minimum wage, however, is not a strong antipoverty policy, despite its popular appeal in this respect.

8. *Wage differentials* are found across many occupations. They are often explained by the forces of demand and supply.

a. The strength of the demand for workers in an occupation, given the supply of workers, is due largely to the productivity of workers and the revenues they generate for the firm (or marginal revenue productivity).

b. One major reason for wage differentials is that workers are not homogeneous and can be thought of as falling into many *noncompeting groups.* The wages for each group differ because of

(1) differences in the abilities or skills possessed by workers, the number of workers in each group, and the demand for those abilities or skills in the labor market, and

(2) *investment in human capital* by workers through education and training.

c. A second reason for wage differentials is that jobs vary in difficulty and attractiveness. Higher wages may be necessary to compensate for less desirable nonmonetary aspects of some jobs.

d. A third reason for wage differentials are market imperfections. These arise from a lack of job information, geographic immobilities, union or government restraints, and discrimination.

9. Wage payments in labor markets are often more complex in practice and are often designed to make a connection between *worker pay and performance.*

a. A principal–agent problem arises when the interests of agents (workers) diverge from the interests of the principals (firms). For example, shirking on the job can occur if workers give less than the desired level of performance for pay received.

b. Firms can try to reduce shirking by monitoring worker activity, but this monitoring is costly; therefore, *incentive pay plans* are adopted by firms to tie worker compensation more closely to performance. Among the various incentive schemes are

(1) piece rate payments, commissions, royalties, bonuses, and profit sharing plans, and

(2) efficiency wages that pay workers above-market wages to get greater effort.

c. Sometimes the "solutions" to principal–agent problems lead to negative results. Commissions may cause employees to pad bills; changes in work rules may demoralize workers.

■ **HINTS AND TIPS**

1. The reason why the market supply curve for labor rises in competitive markets is based on an economic concept from Chapter 2 that you may want to review. To obtain more workers, firms must increase wages to cover the *opportunity cost* of workers' time spent on other alternatives (other employment, household work, or leisure).

2. In monopsony, the marginal resource cost exceeds the wage rate (and the marginal-resource-cost curve lies above the supply curve of labor). The relationship is difficult to understand, so you should pay careful attention to the discussion of Table 28.2 and Figure 28.4.

3. To illustrate the differences in the three union models presented in this chapter, draw supply and demand graphs of each model.

4. The chapter presents the positive economic explanations for the differences in wages between occupations. Remember that whether these wage differentials are "fair" is a normative question. (See Chapter 1 for the positive and normative distinction.)

■ **IMPORTANT TERMS**

wage rate	bilateral monopoly
nominal wages	minimum wage
real wages	wage differentials
purely competitive labor market	marginal revenue productivity
	noncompeting groups
monopsony	investment in human capital
exclusive unionism	compensating differences
occupational licensing	incentive pay plan
inclusive unionism	

SELF-TEST

■ **FILL-IN QUESTIONS**

1. The price paid for labor per unit of time is the (piece, wage) _____ rate. The earnings of labor are equal to the _____ rate (divided, multiplied) _____ by the amount of time worked. The amount of money received per hour or day by a worker is the (nominal, real) _____ wage, while the purchasing power of that money is the _____ wage.

2. The general level of wages is high in the United States and other advanced economies because the demand for labor in these economies is (weak, strong) _____ relative to the supply of labor. United States labor tends to be highly productive, among other reasons, because it has access to relatively large amounts of (consumer, capital) _____ goods, abundant (financial, natural) _____ resources, a high-quality (service sector, labor force) _____, and superior (wages, technology) _____. There is a close (short-run, long-run) _____ relationship between output per labor hour and real hourly wages in the United States.

3. In a purely competitive labor market,
a. the supply curve slopes upward from left to right because it is necessary for employers to pay (higher, lower) _____ wages to attract workers from alternative employment. The market supply curve rises because it is an (average cost, opportunity cost) _____ curve.
b. the demand is the sum of the marginal (revenue product, resource cost) _____ schedules of all firms hiring this type of labor.
c. the wage rate will equal the rate at which the total quantity of labor demanded is (less than, equal to, greater than) _____ the total quantity of labor supplied.

4. Insofar as an individual firm hiring labor in a purely competitive market is concerned, the supply of labor is perfectly (elastic, inelastic) _____ because the individual firm is unable to affect the wage rate it must pay. The firm will hire that quantity of labor at which the wage rate, or marginal labor cost, is (less than, equal to, greater than) _____ the marginal revenue product.

5. A monopsonist employing labor in a market that is competitive on the supply side will hire that amount of labor at which the marginal revenue product is (less than, equal to, greater than) _____ marginal labor cost. In such a market, the marginal labor cost is (less, greater) _____ than the wage rate, so the employer will pay a wage rate that is _____ than both the marginal revenue product of labor and the marginal labor cost.

6. A monopsonist facing a competitive supply of labor
a. is employing the combination of resources that enables it to produce any given output in the least costly way when the marginal product of every resource (divided, multiplied) _____ by its marginal resource cost is the same for all resources.
b. is employing the combination of resources that maximizes its profits when the marginal revenue product of every resource is (equal to, greater than) _____ its marginal resource cost or when the marginal revenue product of each resource (divided, multiplied) _____ by its marginal resource cost is equal to (infinity, 1) _____.

7. When compared with a competitive labor market, a market dominated by a monopsonist results in (higher, lower) _____ wage rates and in (more, less) _____ employment.

8. The basic objective of labor unions is to increase wages, and they attempt to accomplish this goal either by increasing the (demand for, supply of) _____ labor, restricting the _____ labor, or imposing (a below, an above) _____-equilibrium wage rate on employers.

9. Labor unions can increase the demand for the services of their members by increasing the (demand for, supply of) _____ the products they produce, by increasing the (number, productivity) _____ of their members, and by (increasing, decreasing) _____ the prices of resources that are substitutes for the services supplied by their members.

10. Restricting the supply of labor to increase wages is the general policy of (exclusive, inclusive) _____ unionism, and imposing above-equilibrium wage rates is the strategy used in _____ unionism. An example of exclusive unionism is (an industrial, a craft) _____ union, while an example of inclusive unionism would be _____ union.

11. If unions are successful in increasing wages, employment in the industry will (increase, decrease) _____, but this effect on members may lead unions to _____ their wage demands. Unions, however, will not worry too much about the effect on employment from the higher wage rates if the economy is growing or if the demand for labor is relatively (elastic, inelastic) _____.

12. In a labor market that is a bilateral monopoly, the monopsonist will try to pay a wage (less, greater) _____ than the marginal revenue product of labor; the union will ask for some wage _____ than the competitive and monopsonist equilibrium wage. Within these limits, the (wage rate, elasticity) _____ of labor will depend on the relative bargaining strength of the union and the monopsonist.

13. Critics of the minimum wage contend that in purely competitive labor markets, the effect of imposing such a wage is to (increase, decrease) _____ the wage rate and to _____ employment. Defenders of the minimum wage argue that such labor markets are monopsonistic, so the effect is to (increase, decrease) _____ the wage rate and to _____ employment. The evidence suggests that the employment and antipoverty effects from increasing the minimum wage are (positive, uncertain) _____.

14. Actual wage rates received by different workers tend to differ because workers (are, are not) _____ homogeneous, jobs (vary, do not vary) _____ in attractiveness, and labor markets may be (perfect, imperfect) _____.

15. The total labor force is composed of a number of (competing, noncompeting) _____ groups of workers. Wages differ among these groups as a consequence of differences in (ability, wealth) _____ and because of different investments in (the stock market, human capital) _____.

16. Within each of these noncompeting groups, some workers receive higher wages than others to compensate these workers for the less desirable (monetary, nonmonetary) _____ aspects of a job. These wage differentials are called (monopsony, compensating) _____ differences.

17. Workers performing identical jobs often receive different wages due to market imperfections such as lack of information about (investment, job) _____ opportunities, geographic (mobility, immobility) _____, union or government (subsidies, restraints) _____, and (taxes, discrimination) _____.

18. Firms, or parties, who hire others to achieve their objectives may be regarded as (agents, principals) _____, while workers, or parties, who are hired to advance firms' interests can be regarded as the firms' _____. The objective of a firm is to maximize (wages, profits) _____ and workers are hired to help a firm achieve that objective in return for_____, but when the interests of a firm and the workers diverge, a principal–agent problem is created.

19. An example of this type of problem is a situation in which workers provide less than the agreed amount of work effort on the job, which is called (licensure, shirking)_____. To prevent this situation, firms can closely monitor job (pay, performance) _____, but this is costly; therefore, firms offer different incentive _____ plans.

20. Examples of such pay-for-performance schemes include (efficiency, piece) _____ rate payments, commissions and royalties, bonuses and profit sharing, and _____ wages, which means that workers are paid above equilibrium wages to encourage greater work effort. Such plans must be designed with care because of possible (positive, negative) _____ side effects.

■ **TRUE–FALSE QUESTIONS**

Circle T if the statement is true, F if it is false.

1. If you received a 5% increase in your nominal wage and the price level increased by 3%, then your real wage has increased by 8%.   **T F**

2. The general level of wages is high in the United States and other advanced economies because the supply of labor is large relative to the demand for it.   **T F**

3. One reason for the high productivity of labor in the United States and other advanced economies is access to large amounts of capital equipment.　**T　F**

4. Real hourly compensation per worker can increase only at about the same rate as output per worker.　**T　F**

5. In a purely competitive labor market, there are few qualified workers who supply labor and few firms that employ this labor.　**T　F**

6. If an individual firm employs labor in a purely competitive market, it finds that its marginal labor cost is equal to the wage rate in that market.　**T　F**

7. Given a purely competitive employer's demand for labor, a lower wage will result in more workers being hired.　**T　F**

8. Both monopsonists and firms hiring labor in purely competitive markets hire labor up to the quantity at which the marginal revenue product of labor and marginal labor cost are equal.　**T　F**

9. Increasing the productivity of labor will tend to increase the demand for labor.　**T　F**

10. One strategy unions use to bolster the demand for union workers is to lobby against a higher minimum wage for nonunion workers.　**T　F**

11. Restricting the supply of labor is a means of increasing wage rates more commonly used by craft unions than by industrial unions.　**T　F**

12. Occupational licensing is a means of increasing the supply of specific kinds of labor.　**T　F**

13. Unions that seek to organize all available or potential workers in an industry are called craft unions.　**T　F**

14. The imposition of an above-equilibrium wage rate will cause employment to fall off more when the demand for labor is inelastic than it will when the demand is elastic.　**T　F**

15. Union members are paid wage rates that on the average are greater by about 15% than the wage rates paid to nonunion members.　**T　F**

16. The actions of both exclusive and inclusive unions that raise the wage rates paid to them by competitive employers of labor also cause, other things remaining constant, an increase in the employment of their members.　**T　F**

17. In a bilateral monopoly, the negotiated wage will be below the competitive equilibrium wage in that labor market.　**T　F**

18. If a labor market is purely competitive, the imposition of an effective minimum wage will increase the wage rate paid and decrease employment in that market.　**T　F**

19. If an effective minimum wage is imposed on a monopsonist, the wage rate paid by the firm will increase and the number of workers employed by it may also increase.　**T　F**

20. The strength of labor demand differs greatly among occupations due to differences in how much each occupation contributes to its employer's revenue.　**T　F**

21. Actual wage rates received in different labor markets tend to differ because the demands for particular types of labor relative to their supplies differ.　**T　F**

22. Wage differentials that are used to compensate workers for unpleasant aspects of a job are called efficiency wages.　**T　F**

23. Market imperfections that impede workers from moving from lower- to higher-paying jobs help explain wage differentials.　**T　F**

24. Shirking is an example of a principal–agent problem.　**T　F**

25. There are examples of solutions that have been implemented to solve principal–agent problems that produce negative results.　**T　F**

■ **MULTIPLE-CHOICE QUESTIONS**

Circle the letter that corresponds to the best answer.

1. Real wages would decline if the
  (a) prices of goods and services rose more rapidly than nominal-wage rates
  (b) prices of goods and services rose less rapidly than nominal-wage rates
  (c) prices of goods and services and wage rates both rose
  (d) prices of goods and services and wage rates both fell

2. The basic explanation for high real wages in the United States and other industrially advanced economies is that the
  (a) price levels in these nations have increased at a faster rate than nominal wages
  (b) governments in these nations have imposed effective minimum wage laws to improve the conditions of labor
  (c) demand for labor in these nations is quite large relative to the supply of labor
  (d) supply of labor in these nations is quite large relative to the demand for labor

3. A characteristic of a purely competitive labor market would be
  (a) firms hiring different types of labor
  (b) workers supplying labor under a union contract
  (c) wage taker behavior by the firms
  (d) price maker behavior by the firms

4. The supply curve for labor in a purely competitive market is upward sloping because the
  (a) opportunity costs are rising
  (b) the marginal resource cost is constant
  (c) the wage rate paid to workers falls
  (d) the marginal revenue product rises

5. The individual firm that hires labor under purely competitive conditions faces a supply curve for labor that
(a) is perfectly inelastic
(b) is of unitary elasticity
(c) is perfectly elastic
(d) slopes upward from left to right

6. Which is a characteristic of a monopsonist?
(a) The type of labor is relatively mobile.
(b) The supply curve is the marginal resource cost curve.
(c) There are many buyers of a particular kind of labor.
(d) The wage rate it must pay workers varies directly with the number of workers it employs.

7. A monopsonist pays a wage rate that is
(a) greater than the marginal revenue product of labor
(b) equal to the marginal revenue product of labor
(c) equal to the firm's marginal labor cost
(d) less than the marginal revenue product of labor

8. If a firm employs resources in imperfectly competitive markets, to maximize its profits the marginal revenue product of each resource must equal
(a) its marginal product
(b) its marginal resource cost
(c) its price
(d) 1

9. Compared with a purely competitive labor market, a monopsonistic market will result in
(a) higher wage rates and a higher level of employment
(b) higher wage rates and a lower level of employment
(c) lower wage rates and a higher level of employment
(d) lower wage rates and a lower level of employment

10. The monopsonistic labor market for nurses that would be found in a smaller city with two hospitals would lead to
(a) lower starting salaries
(b) higher starting salaries
(c) more employment opportunities
(d) greater demand for nursing services

11. Higher wage rates and a higher level of employment are the usual consequences of
(a) inclusive unionism
(b) exclusive unionism
(c) an above-equilibrium wage rate
(d) an increase in the productivity of labor

12. Which would increase the demand for a particular type of labor?
(a) a decrease in the wages of that type of labor
(b) an increase in the prices of those resources that are substitutes for that type of labor
(c) an increase in the prices of the resources that are complements to that type of labor
(d) a decrease in the demand for the products produced by that type of labor

13. Occupational licensing laws have the economic effect of
(a) increasing the demand for labor
(b) decreasing the supply of labor
(c) strengthening the bargaining position of an industrial union
(d) weakening the bargaining position of a craft union

14. Industrial unions typically attempt to increase wage rates by
(a) imposing an above-equilibrium wage rate on employers
(b) increasing the demand for labor
(c) decreasing the supply of labor
(d) forming a bilateral monopoly

Answer Questions 15, 16, and 17 using the data in the following table.

Wage rate	Quantity of labor supplied	Marginal labor cost	Marginal revenue product of labor
$10	0	—	—
11	100	$11	$17
12	200	13	16
13	300	15	15
14	400	17	14
15	500	19	13
16	600	21	12

15. If the firm employing labor were a monopsonist, the wage rate and the quantity of labor employed would be, respectively,
(a) $14 and 300
(b) $13 and 400
(c) $14 and 400
(d) $13 and 300

16. But if the market for this labor were purely competitive, the wage rate and the quantity of labor employed would be, respectively,
(a) $14 and 300
(b) $13 and 400
(c) $14 and 400
(d) $13 and 300

17. If the firm employing labor were a monopsonist and the workers were represented by an industrial union, the wage rate would be
(a) between $13 and $14
(b) between $13 and $15
(c) between $14 and $15
(d) below $13 or above $15

*Answer Questions 18, 19, 20, and 21 on the basis of the following labor market diagram, where **D** is the demand curve for labor, **S** is the supply curve for labor, and **MRC** is the marginal resource (labor) cost.*

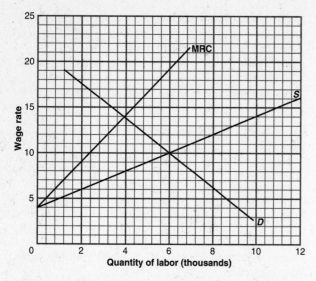

18. If this were a purely competitive labor market, the number of workers hired and the wage rate in equilibrium would be
(a) 4000 and $14
(b) 4000 and $8
(c) 6000 and $10
(d) 8000 and $12

19. If this were a monopsonistic labor market, the number of workers hired and the wage rate in equilibrium would be
(a) 4000 and $14
(b) 4000 and $8
(c) 6000 and $10
(d) 8000 and $12

20. Suppose an inclusive union seeks to maximize the employment of workers with the monopsonist. If successful, the number of workers employed and the wage rate would be
(a) 4000 and $14
(b) 6000 and $12
(c) 6000 and $10
(d) 8000 and $12

21. If the market were characterized as a bilateral monopoly, the number of workers hired and the wage rate in equilibrium would be
(a) 6000 and $10
(b) 4000 and $14
(c) 4000 and $8
(d) indeterminate

22. The major reason that major league baseball players receive an average salary of over $1 million a year and teachers receive an average salary of about $40,000 a year can best be explained in terms of
(a) noncompeting labor groups
(b) compensating differences
(c) lack of job information
(d) discrimination

23. The fact that unskilled construction workers typically receive higher wages than bank clerks is best explained in terms of
(a) noncompeting labor groups
(b) compensating differences
(c) geographic immobilities
(d) union restraints

24. Shirking can be considered to be a principal–agent problem because
(a) work objectives of the principals (the workers) diverge from the profit objectives of the agent (the firm)
(b) profit objectives of the principal (the firm) diverge from the work objectives of the agents (the workers)
(c) the firm is operating in a monopsonistic labor market
(d) the firm pays efficiency wages to workers in a labor market

25. A firm pays an equilibrium wage of $10 an hour and the workers produce 10 units of output an hour. If the firm adopts an efficiency wage and it is successful, then the wage rate for these workers will
(a) rise and output will fall
(b) fall and output will rise
(c) rise and output will rise
(d) fall and output will fall

■ PROBLEMS

1. Suppose a single firm has for a particular type of labor the marginal-revenue-product schedule given in the following table.

Number of units of labor	MRP of labor
1	$15
2	14
3	13
4	12
5	11
6	10
7	9
8	8

a. Assume there are 100 firms with the same marginal-revenue-product schedules for this particular type of labor. Compute the total or market demand for this labor by completing column 1 in the following table.

(1) Quantity of labor demanded	(2) Wage rate	(3) Quantity of labor supplied
———	$15	850
———	14	800
———	13	750
———	12	700
———	11	650
———	10	600
———	9	550
———	8	500

b. Using the supply schedule for labor given in columns 2 and 3,

(1) what will be the equilibrium wage rate? $ _____
(2) what will be the total amount of labor hired in the market?_____

c. The individual firm will

(1) have a marginal labor cost of $ _____.

(2) employ _____ units of labor.

(3) pay a wage of $ _____.

d. On the following graph, plot the market demand and supply curves for labor and indicate the equilibrium wage rate and the total quantity of labor employed.

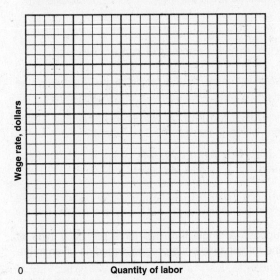

Quantity of labor

e. On the following graph, plot the individual firm's demand curve for labor, the supply curve for labor, and the marginal-labor-cost curve which confronts the individual firm, and indicate the quantity of labor the firm will hire and the wage it will pay.

f. The imposition of a $12 minimum wage rate would change the total amount of labor hired in this market

to _____.

2. In the following table, assume a monopsonist has the marginal-revenue-product schedule for a particular type of labor given in columns 1 and 2 and that the supply schedule for labor is that given in columns 1 and 3.

(1) Number of labor units	(2) MRP of labor	(3) Wage rate	(4) Total labor cost	(5) Marginal labor cost
0		$ 2	$ ____	
1	$36	4	____	$ ____
2	32	6	____	____
3	28	8	____	____
4	24	10	____	____
5	20	12	____	____
6	16	14	____	____
7	12	16	____	____
8	8	18	____	____

a. Compute the firm's total labor costs at each level of employment and the marginal labor cost of each unit of labor, and enter these figures in columns 4 and 5.
b. The firm will

(1) hire _____ units of labor.

(2) pay a wage of $_____.
(3) have a marginal revenue product for labor of

$ _____ for the last unit of labor employed.
c. Plot the marginal revenue product of labor, the supply curve for labor, and the marginal-labor-cost curve on the following graph and indicate the quantity of labor the firm will employ and the wage it will pay.
d. If this firm's labor market were competitive, there

would be at least _____ units hired at a wage of

at least $_____.

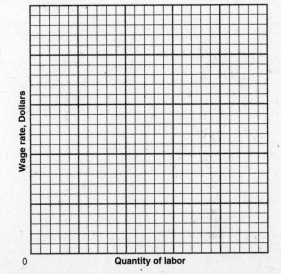

Quantity of labor

3. Assume that the employees of the monopsonist in problem 2 organize a strong industrial union. The union demands a wage rate of $16 for its members, and the monopsonist decides to pay this wage because a strike would be too costly.

a. In the following table, compute the supply schedule for labor that now confronts the monopsonist by completing column 2.

(1) Number of labor units	(2) Wage rate	(3) Total labor cost	(4) Marginal labor cost
0	$ _____	$ _____	
1	_____	_____	$ _____
2	_____	_____	_____
3	_____	_____	_____
4	_____	_____	_____
5	_____	_____	_____
6	_____	_____	_____
7	_____	_____	_____
8	_____	_____	_____

b. Compute the total labor cost and the marginal labor cost at each level of employment and enter these figures in columns 3 and 4.

c. The firm will hire _____ units of labor, pay a wage of $ _____, and pay total wages of $ _____.

d. As a result of unionization, the wage rate has _____, the level of employment has _____, and the earnings of labor have _____.

e. On the graph below plot the firm's marginal revenue product of labor schedule, the labor supply schedule, and the marginal-labor-cost schedule. Indicate also the wage rate the firm will pay and the number of workers it will hire.

Dollars

0   Quantity of labor

4. Match the following descriptions to the one of the six accompanying graphs on page 329.

a. A bilateral monopoly   Graph _____

b. The supply and demand for labor for a purely competitive firm   Graph _____

c. The labor strategy used by a craft union to raise wages   Graph _____

d. A monopsonistic labor market   Graph _____

e. The strategy used by an industrial union to raise wages above a competitive level   Graph _____

f. A strategy used by a union to get people to buy union-made products   Graph _____

■ **SHORT ANSWER AND ESSAY QUESTIONS**

1. What is meant by the term "wages"? What is the difference between real wages and nominal wages?

2. How does the level of wages in the United States compare with that in other foreign nations?

3. Explain why the productivity of the U.S. labor force increased in the past to its present high level.

4. Why has the level of real wages continued to increase even though the supply of labor has continually increased?

5. In the competitive model, what determines the market demand for labor and the wage rate? What kind of supply situation do all firms as a group confront? What kind of supply situation does the individual firm confront? Why?

6. In the monopsony model, what determines employment and the wage rate? What kind of supply situation does the monopsonist face? Why? How does the wage rate paid and the level of employment compare with what would result if the market were competitive?

7. In what sense is a worker who is hired by a monopsonist "exploited" and one who is employed in a competitive labor market "justly" rewarded? Why do monopsonists wish to restrict employment?

8. When supply is less than perfectly elastic, marginal labor cost is greater than the wage rate. Why?

9. What basic methods do labor unions use to try to increase the wages their members receive? If these methods are successful in raising wages, what effect do they have on employment?

10. What three methods might labor use to increase the demand for labor? If these methods are successful, what effects do they have on wage rates and employment?

11. When labor unions attempt to restrict the supply of labor to increase wage rates, what devices do they use

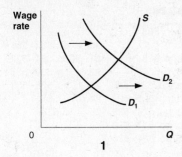

1

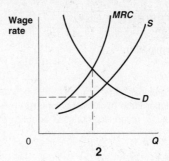

2

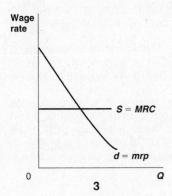

3

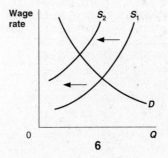

4

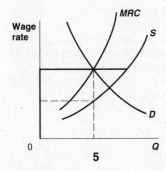

5

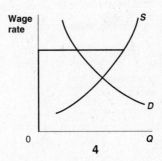

6

to do this for the economy as a whole, and what means do they use to restrict the supply of a given type of worker?

12. How do industrial unions attempt to increase wage rates, and what effect does this method of increasing wages have on employment in the industry affected?

13. Both exclusive and inclusive unions are able to raise the wage rates their members receive. Why might unions limit or temper their demands for higher wages? What two factors determine the extent to which they will or will not reduce their demands for higher wages?

14. What is bilateral monopoly? What determines wage rates in a labor market of this type?

15. Using supply and demand graphs, describe the effect of minimum wage laws on wage rates and employment in (a) purely competitive labor markets and (b) monopsony labor markets.

16. Offer an evaluation of the employment and antipoverty effects of the minimum wage based on past and current evidence.

17. What is meant by the term "noncompeting" groups in a labor market? What two factors tend to explain wage differentials in noncompeting groups?

18. How are wages used to equalize differences in the characteristics of jobs? Give examples.

19. Describe four types of imperfections in labor markets. Discuss how these imperfections contribute to wage differentials.

20. Explain what is meant by the principal–agent problem, and relate it to shirking. What are the different pay incentive plans that correct for shirking on the job? How does profit sharing reduce shirking? What is the reason for efficiency wages?

ANSWERS

Chapter 28 Wage Determination

FILL-IN QUESTIONS

1. wage, wage, multiplied, nominal, real
2. strong, capital, natural, labor force, technology, long-run
3. *a.* higher, opportunity cost; *b.* revenue product; *c.* equal to
4. elastic, equal to
5. equal to, greater, less
6. *a.* divided; *b.* equal to, divided, 1
7. lower, less
8. demand for, supply of, an above
9. demand for, productivity, increasing
10. exclusive, inclusive, a craft, an industrial
11. decrease, decrease, inelastic
12. less, greater, wage rate
13. increase, decrease, increase, increase, uncertain
14. are not, vary, imperfect
15. noncompeting, ability, human capital
16. nonmonetary, compensating
17. job, immobility, restraints, discrimination
18. principals, agents, profits, wages
19. shirking, performance, pay
20. piece, efficiency, negative

TRUE–FALSE QUESTIONS

1. F, pp. 521–522	10. F, p. 529	19. T, pp. 532–533
2. F, p. 522	11. T, p. 529	20. T, p. 534
3. T, p. 522	12. F, p. 530	21. T, p. 534
4. T, p. 523	13. F, pp. 529–530	22. F, pp. 535–536
5. F, p. 524	14. F, p. 531	23. T, pp. 537–538
6. T, p. 524	15. T, p. 531	24. T, p. 537
7. T, pp. 524–525	16. F, pp. 529–531	25. T, p. 539
8. T, pp. 526–527	17. F, pp. 531–532	
9. T, p. 529	18. T, pp. 532–533	

MULTIPLE-CHOICE QUESTIONS

1. a, pp. 521–522	10. a, p. 528	19. b, pp. 526–527
2. c, p. 522	11. d, p. 529	20. c, pp. 530–531
3. c, p. 524	12. b, p. 529	21. d, pp. 531–532
4. a, p. 524	13. b, p. 530	22. a, pp. 534–535
5. c, pp. 524–525	14. a, pp. 524–525	23. b, pp. 535–536
6. d, p. 526	15. d, pp. 526–527	24. b, p. 537
7. d, pp. 526–527	16. c, pp. 524–525	25. c, p. 538
8. b, pp. 526–527	17. b, pp. 531–532	
9. d, pp. 526–527	18. c, pp. 524–525	

PROBLEMS

1. *a.* Quantity of labor demanded: 100, 200, 300, 400, 500, 600, 700, 800; *b.* (1) 10.00, (2) 600; *c.* (1) 10.00, (2) 6, (3) 10.00; *d.* graph; *e.* graph; *f.* 400
2. *a.* Total labor cost: 0, 4.00, 12.00, 24.00, 40.00, 60.00, 84.00, 112.00, 144.00, Marginal labor cost: 4.00, 8.00, 12.00, 16.00, 20.00, 24.00, 28.00, 32.00; *b.* (1) 5, (2) 12.00, (3) 20.00; *c.* graph; *d.* 6, 14.00
3. *a.* Wage rate: 16.00, 16.00, 16.00, 16.00, 16.00, 16.00, 16.00, 16.00, 16.00; *b.* Total labor cost: 0, 16.00, 32.00, 48.00, 64.00, 80.00, 96.00, 112.00, 128.00; Marginal labor cost: 16.00, 16.00, 16.00, 16.00, 16.00, 16.00, 16.00, 16.00; *c.* (1) 6, (2) 16.00, (3) 96.00; *d.* increased, increased, increased; *e.* graph (similar to Figure 28.8)
4. *a.* 5; *b.* 3; *c.* 6; *d.* 2; *e.* 4; *f.* 1

SHORT ANSWER AND ESSAY QUESTIONS

1. pp. 521–522	8. pp. 526–527	15. pp. 532–533
2. pp. 522–523	9. pp. 528–531	16. pp. 532–533
3. pp. 522–523	10. pp. 528–529	17. pp. 534–535
4. p. 523	11. pp. 529–530	18. pp. 535–536
5. pp. 524–526	12. pp. 530–531	19. p. 536
6. pp. 526–527	13. pp. 530–531	20. pp. 537–538
7. pp. 526–527	14. pp. 531–532	

Rent, Interest, and Profit

Chapter 29 concludes the study of the **prices of resources** by examining rent, interest, and profits. There is nothing difficult about this chapter. By now you should understand that the marginal revenue product of a resource determines the demand for that resource. This understanding can be applied to the demand for land and capital. It will be on the supply side of the land market that you will encounter whatever difficulties there are. The **supply of land** is unique because **it is perfectly inelastic:** Changes in rent do not change the quantity of land that will be supplied. Given the quantity of land available, **demand is the sole determinant of economic rent.** Of course land varies in productivity and can be used for different purposes, but these are merely the factors that explain why the rent on all lands is not the same.

Capital, as the economist defines it, means capital goods. Is the rate of interest, then, the price paid for the use of capital goods? No, not quite. Capital is not one kind of good; it is many different kinds. To be able to talk about the price paid for the use of capital goods, there must be a simple way of adding up different kinds of capital goods. The simple way is to measure the quantity of capital goods in terms of money. **Interest** is the price paid for the use of money (or of financial capital) that in turn is used to purchase **capital goods** (factories, machinery, etc.).

The **demand for and supply of loanable funds** in the economy determines the **interest rate.** In a simplified model, businesses are the primary demanders of loanable funds because they want to use this financial capital to buy capital goods (e.g., equipment, machinery, factories). As with the demand for any good or service, the greater the price of using loanable funds (the interest rate), the smaller the amount of loanable funds that firms will be able and willing to borrow. A business will most likely borrow funds and make an investment in capital goods if the expected rate of return on the investment is greater than the interest rate. Therefore, the lower the interest rate, the greater the opportunities for profitable investments and the greater the amount of loanable funds demanded.

On the supply side, households are the typical suppliers of loanable funds. At a higher rate of interest, households are willing to supply more loanable funds than at lower interest rates because of the weighing of present consumption to future consumption. Most consumers prefer present consumption, but they would be willing to forgo this current use of funds and make them available for loan if there is compensation in the form of interest payments. Thus, the greater the interest rate, the more

saving by households, which in turn creates a greater supply of loanable funds.

The intersection of the demand curve and the supply curve for loanable funds determines the equilibrium rate of interest, or the price of loanable funds, and the equilibrium quantity. This relationship is illustrated in Figure 29.2. The demand and supply curves of loanable funds can also shift due to a variety of factors. For example, there could be an increase in the rates of return on investments, which would increase the demand for loanable funds at each and every interest rate; changes in the tax laws could make savings more attractive and this change would increase the supply of loanable funds. Note too that while in the simplified model businesses are the demanders and households the suppliers of loanable funds, in reality these sectors can operate on both sides of the market.

When it comes to **economic profit,** supply and demand analysis fails the economist. Profits are not merely a wage for a particular type of labor; rather, they are rewards for taking risks and the gains of the monopolist. Such things as "the quantity of risks taken" or "the quantity of effort required to establish a monopoly" simply cannot be measured; consequently, it is impossible to talk about the demand for or the supply of them. Nevertheless, profits are important in the economy. They are largely rewards for doing things that have to be done if the economy is to allocate resources efficiently and to progress and develop; they are the lure or the bait that makes entrepreneurs willing to take the risks that result in efficiency and progress.

The final section of Chapter 29 explains what part of the national income goes to workers and what part goes to capitalists—those who provide the economy with land, capital goods, and entrepreneurial ability. You may be surprised to learn that the lion's share—about 80%—of the national income goes to workers today and went to workers at the beginning of the century, and that only about 20% of national income goes to the capitalists today or went to them in 1900.

■ CHECKLIST

When you have studied this chapter you should be able to

☐ Define economic rent.
☐ Explain why supply of land does not affect economic rent.

☐ Illustrate how changes in demand determine economic rent.

☐ Explain why land rent is a surplus payment.

☐ Give the rationale for a single tax on land proposed by Henry George.

☐ State four criticisms of the single tax on land.

☐ Illustrate graphically how productivity differences affect land rent.

☐ Contrast society's and a firm's perspectives on the alternative uses of land and economic rent.

☐ Define interest and state two aspects of it.

☐ Describe the loanable funds theory of interest using supply and demand analysis.

☐ Show how the equilibrium rate of interest is established in the loanable funds market using supply and demand analysis.

☐ Explain why the supply of loanable funds curve has a positive slope.

☐ Explain why the demand for loanable funds curve has a negative slope.

☐ List factors that change the supply or demand for loanable funds.

☐ Distinguish between a change in demand or supply and a change in quantity demanded or supplied as applied to the loanable funds market.

☐ Identify the different sides that participants (households, businesses, or government) take in the demand or supply of loanable funds.

☐ List five reasons why interest rates differ.

☐ Define the pure rate of interest and state how it is measured.

☐ Explain how the interest rate affects investment spending, total output, the allocation of capital, and research and development (R&D) spending.

☐ Distinguish between nominal and real interest rates.

☐ Use graphical analysis to explain the three effects of usury laws.

☐ Distinguish between economic and normal profit.

☐ Describe the return to the entrepreneurial ability in terms of economic and normal profit.

☐ List three sources of economic profit.

☐ Explain the relationship between insurable and uninsurable risks and economic profit.

☐ Describe how innovation affects economic profit.

☐ Discuss the influence of monopoly on economic profit.

☐ Identify two functions of profits for the economy.

☐ Describe the shares of national income going to labor and capital.

■ **CHAPTER OUTLINE**

1. Economic rent is the price paid for the use of land or natural resources whose supply is perfectly inelastic.

a. The **supply of land is perfectly inelastic** because it is virtually fixed in the quantity available. Supply has no influence in determining economic rent.

b. The demand for land is the active determinant of economic rent. As demand increases or decreases, economic rent will increase or decrease given the perfectly inelastic supply of land.

c. **Economic rent serves no incentive function** given the fixed supply of land. It is not necessary to increase economic rent to bring forth more quantity, as is the case with other natural resources. Economists, therefore, consider economic rent a surplus payment.

d. Socialists have argued that land rent is unearned income and that land should be nationalized.

(1) Henry George, in his 1879 book, *Progress and Poverty*, called for a single tax on land as the sole source of government tax revenue. He based his argument on the grounds of equity and efficiency. Such a tax would not alter the supply of land because economic rent serves no incentive function.

(2) Critics of the single tax cite its inadequacy for meeting government needs, the difficulty of identifying the portion of rent in incomes, the conflicting interpretations of unearned income, and adverse equity effects arising from changes in land ownership.

e. Economic rents on different types of land vary because different plots of land vary in productivity or might have location advantages.

f. From society's perspective, economic rent is a surplus payment, but from a firm's perspective, economic rent is a cost. A firm must pay economic rent to bid the land it wants to use for its production away from alternative uses of the land.

2. Interest is the price paid for the use of money. Interest is stated as a percentage. Money is *not* an economic resource because it is not productive. People borrow money at an interest rate and use it to buy capital goods. These capital goods are economic resources that can be used to produce other goods and services.

a. The **loanable funds theory of interest** describes how the interest rate is determined by the demand for and supply of loanable funds. The intersection of the demand for and supply of loanable funds determines the equilibrium interest rate and the quantity of funds loaned.

(1) The **supply of loanable funds** is generally provided by households through savings. There is a positive relationship between the interest rate and the quantity of loanable funds supplied. The supply curve, however, may be relatively inelastic and thus not very responsive to changes in the interest rate.

(2) The **demand for loanable funds** typically comes from businesses for investment in capital goods. There is an inverse relationship between the interest rate and the quantity of loanable funds demanded. Lower interest rates provide more profitable investment opportunities; higher interest rates reduce investments.

b. There are some extensions to the simplified model of the loanable funds market.

(1) Financial institutions serve as intermediaries in the supply and demand market for loanable funds.

(2) The supply of funds can change because of changes in factors that affect the thriftiness of households.

(3) The demand for funds can change because of changes in the rate of return on potential investments.

(4) Households and businesses can operate on both sides of the market—as both demanders and suppli-

ers of loanable funds. Government also participates on both sides of the loanable fund market.

c. There is a range of interest rates, although it is convenient to speak as if there were one interest rate. These rates differ because of differences in five factors: risk, maturity, loan size, taxability, and market imperfections.

d. When economists talk about "the interest rate," they are referring to the **pure rate of interest,** which is best measured by the interest paid on long-term and riskless securities, such as 20-year bonds of the U.S. government.

e. The interest rate plays several roles in the economy.
(1) It affects the total output because of the inverse relationship between the interest rate and investment spending; government often tries to influence the interest rate to achieve its policy goals.
(2) It allocates financial and real capital among competing firms and determines the level and composition of the total output of capital goods.
(3) It changes the level and composition of spending on research and development.
(4) These effects are based on changes in the **real interest rate,** which is the rate expressed in inflation-adjusted dollars, not the **nominal interest rate,** which is the rate expressed in current dollars.

f. **Usury laws** specify a maximum interest rate for loans. They were passed to limit borrowing costs, but they can have other effects. First, they may cause a shortage of credit, which is then given only to the most worthy borrowers. Second, borrowers gain from paying less for credit and borrowers lose from receiving less interest income. Third, it creates inefficiency in the economy because funds get directed to less productive investments.

3. **Economic profit** is what remains of the firm's revenue after all its explicit and implicit opportunity costs have been deducted.

a. Economic profit is a payment for entrepreneurial ability. **Normal profit** is the payment necessary to keep the entrepreneur in current work and is thus a cost. Economic profit is the residual payment to the entrepreneur from total revenues after all other costs have been subtracted.

b. Economic profit comes from three basic sources that reflect the dynamic nature of real-world capitalism:
(1) rewards for assuming **uninsurable risk** that arises from changes in economic conditions, the structure of the economy, and government policy;
(2) a return for assuming the uncertainties in innovation; and
(3) surpluses that firms obtain from monopoly power.

c. The expectation of economic profit serves several functions in the economy. Profits encourage businesses to innovate, and this innovation contributes to economic growth. Profits (and losses) guide businesses to produce products and to use resources in the way desired by society.

4. **National income** is distributed among wages, rent, interest, and profit. Using a broad definition, the share of

national income going to labor is about 80%. The share going to capitalists is about 20%. These percentages have remained relatively stable since 1900.

■ **HINTS AND TIPS**

1. Although this chapter focuses on three resource payments (rent, interest, and profit), the discussion is much simpler and easier to understand than it was for the one resource payment (wages) in the previous chapter. It will help if you think of this chapter as three minichapters.

2. Use a supply and demand graph for land to explain to yourself why **land rent is surplus payment.** Draw a vertical (perfectly inelastic) supply curve and a downsloping demand curve. Identify the price and quantity combination where the two curves intersect. Then draw a new demand curve showing an increase in demand. What happens to price? (It increases.) What happens to quantity? (No change.) Changes in land rent perform no incentive function for the economy because they bring forth no more supply of land. Land rents are unnecessary (surplus) payments for the economy.

3. The **loanable funds theory of interest** will be easy to understand if you think of it as an application of supply and demand analysis. You need to remember, however, who are the suppliers and who are the demanders of loanable funds. In this simplified model, the *suppliers* of loanable funds are *households* who have a different quantity of savings to make available for loans at different interest rates; the higher the interest rate, the greater the quantity of loanable funds supplied. The *demanders* of loanable funds are *businesses* that want to borrow a quantity of money at each interest rate; the higher the interest rate, the smaller the quantity of loanable funds demanded for investment purposes.

4. Remember that it is the **expectation of profit,** not the certainty of it, that drives the entrepreneur. The generation of profit involves risk taking by the entrepreneur. You should distinguish, however, between **insurable risks** and those that are not insurable. A major source of profit for the entrepreneur comes from the **uninsurable risks** that the entrepreneur is willing to assume in an uncertain world.

■ **IMPORTANT TERMS**

economic rent

incentive function

single-tax movement

loanable funds theory of
   interest

pure rate of interest

nominal interest rate

real interest rate

usury laws

explicit costs

implicit costs

economic or pure profit

normal profit

static economy

insurable risks

uninsurable risks

SELF-TEST

■ FILL-IN QUESTIONS

1. Economic rent is the price paid for the use of (labor, land) _____ and (capital, natural) _____ resources which are completely (fixed, variable) _____ in supply.

2. The active determinant of economic rent is (demand, supply) _____ and the passive determinant is _____.

3. Economic rent does not bring forth more supply and serves no (profit, incentive) _____ function. Economists consider economic rent a (tax, surplus) _____ payment that is not necessary to ensure that land is available to the economy.

4. Socialists argue that land rents are (earned, unearned) _____ incomes. Henry George called for a single (price, tax) _____ on land to transfer economic rent to government because it would not affect the amount of land. One criticism of George's proposal is that it would not generate enough (revenue, profit) _____.

5. Rents on different pieces of land are not the same because land differs in (price, productivity) _____.

6. From society's perspective, land rent is a (surplus payment, cost) _____, but from a firm's perspective, land rent is a _____ because land (is a free good, has alternative uses) _____.

7. The price paid for the use of money is (profit, interest) _____. It is typically stated as a (price, percentage) _____ of the amount borrowed. Money (is, is not) _____ an economic resource because money _____ productive.

8. Money or financial capital is obtained in the (mutual, loanable) _____ funds market. At the equilibrium rate of interest, the quantity demanded for loanable funds is (greater than, equal to, less than) _____ the quantity supplied of loanable funds.

9. The quantity supplied of loanable funds is (inversely, directly) _____ related to the interest rate while the quantity demanded for loanable funds is _____ related to the interest rate.

10. With a higher interest rate, there are (greater, fewer) _____ opportunities for profitable investment and hence a (larger, smaller) _____ quantity demanded for loanable funds.

11. An increase in the thriftiness of households will result in (an increase, a decrease) _____ in the (supply, demand) _____ of loanable funds. Anything that increases the rate of return on potential investments will (increase, decrease) _____ the (supply, demand) _____ of loanable funds.

12. State five reasons why there is a range of interest rates:

   a. _____

   b. _____

   c. _____

   d. _____

   e. _____

13. Economists often talk of the (loan, pure) _____ rate of interest. It is approximated by the interest paid on (short-term, long-term) _____ U.S. government bonds.

14. A higher equilibrium interest rate often (increases, decreases) _____ business borrowing for investment and thus _____ total spending in the economy, whereas a lower equilibrium interest rate (increases, decreases) _____ business borrowing and thus _____ total spending in the economy.

15. The rate of interest expressed in purchasing power, or inflation-adjusted dollars, is the (real, nominal) _____ interest rate, while the rate of interest expressed in dollars of current value is the _____ interest rate.

16. Laws that state the maximum interest rate at which loans can be made are called (antitrust, usury) _____ laws. These laws cause (market, nonmarket) _____ rationing of credit that favors creditworthy (lenders, borrowers) _____ and leads to (less, more) _____ economic efficiency in the allocation of credit.

17. The difference between total revenue and total cost is (economic, normal) _____ profit. The minimum payment for the entrepreneur to keep him or her in the current line of business is (economic, normal)

_____ profit. The excess of total revenue above total cost is (economic, normal) _____ profit.

18. Economic profit is a reward for either assuming (insurable, uninsurable) _____ risk or for dealing with the uncertainty of (taxation, innovation) _____.

19. Economic profit over time can also arise from (pure competition, monopoly) _____, and this source of profit is typically based on (increased, decreased) _____ output, _____ prices above competitive levels, and (increased, decreased) _____ economic efficiency.

20. Defining labor income broadly to include both wages and salaries and proprietors' income, labor's share of national income total is about (20%, 50%, 80%) _____, while capitalists' share of income is about _____. The share of income going to capitalists has (increased, decreased, remained stable) _____ since 1900.

■ **TRUE–FALSE QUESTIONS**

Circle T if the statement is true, F if it is false.

1. Rent is the price paid for use of capital resources.　　　　**T　F**

2. The determination of economic rent for land and other natural resources is based on a demand curve that is perfectly inelastic.　　　　**T　F**

3. Rent is a surplus payment because it does not perform an incentive function.　　　　**T　F**

4. Rent is unique because it is not determined by demand and supply.　　　　**T　F**

5. Henry George argued in *Progress and Poverty* that the increasing land rents would produce more unearned income for landowners which could then be taxed by government.　　　　**T　F**

6. Critics of the single tax on land argue that it would bring in too much revenue for the government.　　　　**T　F**

7. For individual producers, rental payments are surplus payments, but for society they are a cost.　　　　**T　F**

8. Money is an economic resource and the interest rate is the price paid for this resource.　　　　**T　F**

9. The quantity of loanable funds demanded is inversely related to the interest rate.　　　　**T　F**

10. The quantity of loanable funds supplied is directly related to the interest rate.　　　　**T　F**

11. An increase in the demand for loanable funds would tend to increase the interest rate.　　　　**T　F**

12. An increase in the rate of return on investments would most likely increase the supply of loanable funds.　　**T　F**

13. Other things equal, long-term loans usually command lower rates of interest than do short-term loans.　　**T　F**

14. The pure rate of interest is best approximated by the interest paid on long-term bonds with very low risk, such as 20-year U.S. Treasury bonds.　　　　**T　F**

15. A higher equilibrium interest rate discourages business borrowing for investment, reducing investment and total spending.　　　　**T　F**

16. The interest rate rations the supply of loanable funds to investment projects whose rate of return will be less than the interest rate.　　　　**T　F**

17. If the nominal rate of interest is 6% and the inflation rate is 3%, the real rate of interest is 9%.　　**T　F**

18. Usury laws result in a shortage of loanable funds and nonmarket rationing in credit markets.　　　　**T　F**

19. Lenders or banks are the main beneficiaries of usury laws.　　　　**T　F**

20. If the economists' definition of profit were used, total profit in the economy would be greater than would be the case if the accountants' definition were used.　　**T　F**

21. A normal profit is the minimum payment the entrepreneur must receive to induce him or her to provide entrepreneurial ability for the production of a certain good.　　　　**T　F**

22. It is the static competitive economy that gives rise to economic profit.　　　　**T　F**

23. Insurable risk is one of the sources of economic profit.　　　　**T　F**

24. Economic profit arising from monopoly is more socially desirable than economic profit arising from uncertainty.　　　　**T　F**

25. Economic profit influences both the level of economic output and the allocation of resources among alternative uses.　　　　**T　F**

■ **MULTIPLE-CHOICE QUESTIONS**

Circle the letter that corresponds to the best answer.

1. The price paid for a natural resource that is completely fixed in supply is
 (a) profit
 (b) interest
 (c) rent
 (d) a risk payment

2. In total, the supply of land is
 (a) perfectly inelastic
 (b) of unitary elasticity
 (c) perfectly elastic
 (d) elastic but not perfectly elastic

3. The economic rent from land will increase, *ceteris paribus*, whenever the
  (a) price of land decreases
  (b) demand for land increases
  (c) demand for land decreases
  (d) supply curve for land increases

4. Which is a characteristic of the tax proposed by Henry George?
  (a) It would be equal to 20% of all land rent.
  (b) It would be the only tax levied by government.
  (c) It would reduce the supply of land.
  (d) It would reduce rents paid by the amount of the tax.

5. A major criticism of the single tax on land is that it would
  (a) bring in more tax revenues than is necessary to finance all current government spending
  (b) not distinguish between payments for the use of land and those for improvements to land
  (c) take into account the history of ownership of the land in determining the tax
  (d) not tax "unearned" income

6. Which is true?
  (a) The greater the demand for land, the greater the supply of land.
  (b) A windfall profits tax on the increases in the profits of petroleum producers was proposed by Henry George.
  (c) Individual users of land have to pay a rent to its owner because that land has alternative uses.
  (d) The less productive a particular piece of land is, the greater will be the rent its owner is able to earn from it.

7. When the supply curve for a plot of land lies entirely to the right of the demand curve,
  (a) landowners will receive an economic rent
  (b) landowners will not receive an economic rent
  (c) the interest rate on loans for land will increase
  (d) the interest rate on loans for land will decrease

8. Which of the following do economists consider a productive economic resource?
  (a) money
  (b) capital goods
  (c) interest
  (d) profit

9. The upsloping supply of loanable funds is best explained by the idea that most people prefer
  (a) current consumption to future consumption
  (b) future consumption to present consumption
  (c) saving over consumption
  (d) investment over saving

10. Why is the demand for loanable funds downsloping?
  (a) At lower interest rates, fewer investment projects will be profitable to businesses, and hence a small quantity of loanable funds will be demanded.
  (b) At lower interest rates, more investment projects will be profitable to businesses, and hence a small quantity of loanable funds will be demanded.
  (c) At higher interest rates, more investment projects will be profitable to businesses, and hence a large quantity of loanable funds will be demanded.
  (d) At higher interest rates, fewer investment projects will be profitable to businesses, and hence a small quantity of loanable funds will be demanded.

11. In the competitive market for loanable funds, when the quantity of funds demanded exceeds the quantity supplied, then the
  (a) interest rate will decrease
  (b) interest rate will increase
  (c) demand curve will increase
  (d) supply curve will decrease

12. A decrease in the productivity of capital goods will, *ceteris paribus*,
  (a) increase the supply of loanable funds
  (b) decrease the supply of loanable funds
  (c) increase the demand for loanable funds
  (d) decrease the demand for loanable funds

13. Which would tend to result in a lower interest rate for a loan?
  (a) the greater the risk involved
  (b) the shorter the length of the loan
  (c) the smaller the amount of the loan
  (d) the greater the monopoly power of the lender

14. What is the most likely reason why a lender would prefer a high-quality municipal bond that pays a 6% rate of interest rather than a high-quality corporate bond paying 8%?
  (a) The municipal bond is tax-exempt.
  (b) The municipal bond is a long-term investment.
  (c) The corporate bond is safer than the municipal bond.
  (d) The municipal bond is easier to purchase than a corporate bond.

15. The pure rate of interest is best approximated by the interest paid on
  (a) consumer credit cards
  (b) tax-exempt municipal bonds
  (c) 90-day Treasury bills
  (d) 20-year Treasury bonds

16. If the annual rate of interest were 18% and the rate of return a firm expects to earn annually by building a new plant were 20%, the firm would
  (a) not build the new plant
  (b) build the new plant
  (c) have to toss a coin to decide whether to build the new plant
  (d) not be able to determine from these figures whether to build the plant

Questions 17 and 18 refer to the following data.

Expected rate of return	Amount of capital goods investment (in billions)
19%	$220
17	250
15	300
13	360
11	430
9	500

17. If the interest rate is 13%,
(a) $300 billion of investment will be undertaken
(b) $360 billion of investment will be undertaken
(c) $430 billion of investment will be undertaken
(d) $500 billion of investment will be undertaken

18. An increase in the interest rate from 15% to 17% would
(a) increase investment by $40 billion
(b) increase investment by $50 billion
(c) decrease investment by $50 billion
(d) decrease investment by $40 billion

19. Which is the definition of a usury law? It is a law that specifies the
(a) alternative uses of surplus government land
(b) tax rate on interest paid for state and municipal bonds
(c) maximum interest rate at which loans can be made
(d) interest paid on long-term, virtually riskless bonds of the U.S. government

20. Which would be a likely economic effect of a usury law?
(a) There would be an increase in economic efficiency.
(b) There would be a decrease in the rationing of credit.
(c) Creditworthy borrowers would lose and lenders would gain.
(d) Creditworthy borrowers would gain and lenders would lose.

21. Which is the minimum return or payment necessary to retain the entrepreneur in some specific line of production?
(a) normal profit
(b) explicit cost
(c) real interest rate
(d) pure rate of interest

22. Which is an economic cost?
(a) uninsurable risk
(b) normal profit
(c) economic profit
(d) monopoly profit

23. One basic reason why there is economic profit is that
(a) risks are insurable
(b) economies are static
(c) there is innovation
(d) there are purely competitive markets

24. Monopoly profit is typically based on
(a) uncertainty and innovation
(b) insurable and uninsurable risk

(c) productivity and economic efficiency
(d) reduced output and above-competitive prices

25. Since 1900, the share of national income
(a) has increased for capitalists, but decreased for labor
(b) has decreased for capitalists, but increased for labor
(c) has increased for capitalists and for labor
(d) has remained relatively constant for capitalists and labor

■ **PROBLEMS**

1. Assume that the quantity of a certain type of land available is 300,000 acres and the demand for this land is that given in the following table.

Pure land rent, per acre	Land demanded, acres
$350	100,000
300	200,000
250	300,000
200	400,000
150	500,000
100	600,000
50	700,000

a. The pure rent on this land will be $ _____ .

b. The total quantity of land rented will be _____ acres.

c. On the following graph, plot the supply and demand curves for this land and indicate the pure rent for land and the quantity of land rented.

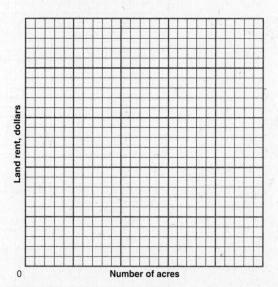

d. If landowners were taxed at a rate of $250 per acre for their land, the pure rent on this land after taxes would be $ _____ but the number of acres rented would be _____ .

2. The following schedule shows interest rates (column 1), the associated quantity demanded of loanable funds (column 2), and the quantity supplied of loanable funds (column 4) in billions of dollars at those interest rates.

Interest rate (1)	Quantity demanded (2)	(3)	Quantity supplied (4)	(5)
12	50	_____	260	_____
10	100	_____	240	_____
8	150	_____	220	_____
6	200	_____	200	_____
4	250	_____	180	_____
2	300	_____	160	_____

a. Plot the demand and supply schedule on the following graph. (The interest rate is measured along the vertical axis and the quantity demanded or supplied is measured on the horizontal axis.)

(1) The equilibrium interest rate is _____%. The quantity demanded is $ _____ billion and the quantity supplied is $ _____ billion.
(2) At an interest rate of 10%, the quantity demanded of loanable funds is $_____ billion and the quantity supplied of loanable funds is $_____ billion. There is an excess of loanable funds of $_____ billion.

(3) At an interest rate of 4%, the quantity demanded of loanable funds is $_____ billion and the quantity supplied of loanable funds is $_____ billion. There is a shortage of loanable funds of $_____ billion.
b. If technology improves and the demand for loanable funds increases by $70 billion at each interest rate, then the new equilibrium interest rate will be _____% and the equilibrium quantity of loanable funds will be $_____ billion. Fill in the new demand schedule in column 3 of the table and plot this new demand curve on the graph.
c. Then, because of changes in the tax laws, households become thriftier by $140 at each interest rate. The new equilibrium interest rate will be _____% and the new equilibrium quantity of loanable funds will be $_____ billion. Fill in the new supply schedule in column 5 of the table, and plot this new supply curve on the graph.

3. Firms make investment decisions based on the rate of return and the interest rate.
a. In each of the following simple cases, calculate the rate of return on an investment.
(1) You invest in a new machine that costs $2000 but which is expected to increase total revenues by $2075 in 1 year. _____

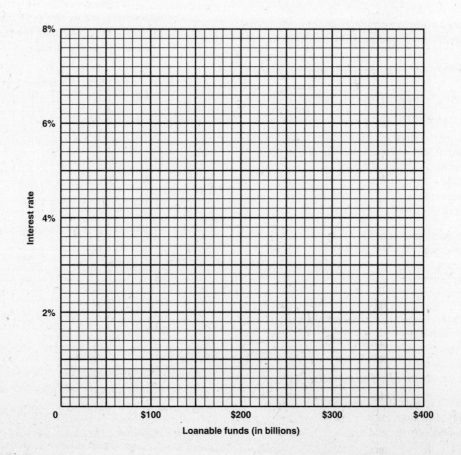

Loanable funds (in billions)

(2) You invest in a new piece of equipment that costs $150,000 but which is expected to increase total revenues in 1 year by $160,000. _____

(3) You invest in a new plant that costs $3 million and which is expected to increase total revenues in 1 year by $3.5 million. _____

b. Given each of the following interest rates, in which situations (1, 2, and 3) would you make an investment?

(1) An interest rate of 5% _____

(2) An interest rate of 8% _____

(3) An interest rate of 15% _____

4. The following table shows estimated wages and salaries, proprietors' income, corporate profits, interest, rent, and the national income of the United States in a recent year.

Wages and salaries	$5,642 billion
Proprietors' income	717 billion
Corporate profits	967 billion
Interest	571 billion
Rent	139 billion
National income	8,036 billion

a. Wages and salaries were _____% of the national income.

b. Labor's share of the national income was _____% and capital's share was _____%.

■ SHORT ANSWER AND ESSAY QUESTIONS

1. Explain what determines the economic rent paid for the use of land. What is unique about the supply of land?

2. Why is land rent a surplus payment?

3. What economic difficulties would be encountered if the government adopted Henry George's single tax proposal as a means of confiscating this surplus? What do the critics think of the concept of a single tax on land?

4. Even though land rent is an economic surplus payment, it is also an economic cost for the individual use of land. Why and how can it be both an economic surplus payment and an economic cost?

5. Explain what determines (a) the amount of loanable funds that households are willing to supply, (b) the amount that businesses wish to demand, and (c) how these desires are resolved in the market for loanable funds.

6. How might a change in productivity affect the interest rate? How might a change in the tax laws affect household savings and the interest rate? What are the implications if the supply curve for loanable funds is highly inelastic?

7. What is the connection between the rate of return on a capital goods investment and the interest rate? Give examples of possible investment situations.

8. Why are there actually many different rates in the economy at any given time?

9. What is the pure rate of interest? How is it approximated?

10. What important functions does the rate of interest perform in the economy?

11. What is the difference between the nominal and the real interest rates? How does each one affect investment spending or decisions about research and development?

12. What are usury laws? Explain in terms of demand and supply analysis.

13. What are the effects of usury laws on allocation of credit, borrowers and lenders, and economic efficiency?

14. What is economic profit? In what way is economic profit a return to entrepreneurial ability?

15. Why would there be no economic profit in a purely competitive and static economy?

16. Why is the distinction between insurable and uninsurable risk important from an economic profit perspective? What are three sources that contribute to uninsurable risk?

17. How does economic profit arise from innovation?

18. "The risks that an entrepreneur assumes arise because of uncertainties that are external to the firm and because of uncertainties that are developed by the initiative of the firm itself." Explain.

19. Explain why profit arising from monopoly is not socially desirable, while profit arising from uncertainty is socially desirable.

20. What part of the U.S. national income is labor's share, and what part is the capitalist's share? Have the shares changed much since 1900?

ANSWERS

Chapter 29 Rent, Interest, and Profit

FILL-IN QUESTIONS

1. land, natural, fixed
2. demand, supply
3. incentive, surplus
4. unearned, tax, revenue
5. productivity
6. surplus payment, cost, has alternative uses
7. interest, percentage, is not, is not
8. loanable, equal to
9. directly, inversely
10. fewer, smaller
11. an increase, supply, increase, demand
12. *a.* risk; *b.* length of loan; *c.* amount of loan; *d.* tax status of loan (or investment); *e.* market imperfections (any order for *a–e*)
13. pure, long-term
14. decreases, decreases, increases, increases
15. real, nominal
16. usury, nonmarket, borrowers, less
17. economic, normal, economic
18. uninsurable, innovation
19. monopoly, decreased, increased, decreased
20. 80%, 20%, remained stable

TRUE–FALSE QUESTIONS

1. F, p. 542	**10.** T, pp. 546–547	**19.** F, p. 550
2. F, p. 543	**11.** T, p. 547	**20.** F, p. 551
3. T, p. 543	**12.** F, pp. 546–547	**21.** T, p. 551
4. F, p. 543	**13.** F, p. 548	**22.** F, pp. 551–552
5. T, p. 544	**14.** T, pp. 548–549	**23.** F, pp. 551–552
6. F, p. 544	**15.** T, p. 549	**24.** F, p. 552
7. F, pp. 544–545	**16.** F, p. 549	**25.** T, p. 552
8. F, p. 545	**17.** F, pp. 549–550	
9. T, pp. 546–547	**18.** T, p. 550	

MULTIPLE-CHOICE QUESTIONS

1. c, p. 542	**10.** d, p. 546	**19.** c, p. 550
2. a, p. 543	**11.** b, p. 546	**20.** d, p. 550
3. b, p. 543	**12.** d, pp. 547–548	**21.** a, p. 551
4. b, p. 544	**13.** b, p. 548	**22.** b, p. 551
5. b, p. 544	**14.** a, p. 548	**23.** c, pp. 551–552
6. c, p. 545	**15.** d, pp. 548–549	**24.** d, p. 552
7. b, pp. 544–545	**16.** b, p. 549	**25.** d, p. 554
8. b, p. 545	**17.** b, p. 549	
9. a, p. 546	**18.** c, p. 549	

PROBLEMS

1. *a.* 250; *b.* 300,000; *c.* graph; *d.* 0, 300,000

2. *a.* (1) 6, 200, 200, (2) 100, 240, 140, (3) 250, 180, 70; *b.* 8, 220; 120, 170, 220, 270, 320, 370; *c.* 4, 320; 400, 380, 360, 340, 320, 300

3. *a.* (1) 3.75; (2) 6.67; (3) 16.67; *b.* (1) 2, 3; (2) 3; (3) 3

4. *a.* 70; *b.* 79, 21

SHORT ANSWER AND ESSAY QUESTIONS

1. pp. 542–543	**8.** p. 548	**15.** pp. 551–552
2. pp. 543–544	**9.** pp. 548–549	**16.** pp. 551–552
3. p. 544	**10.** p. 549	**17.** p. 552
4. pp. 544–545	**11.** pp. 549–550	**18.** pp. 551–552
5. pp. 545–546	**12.** p. 550	**19.** p. 552
6. p. 547	**13.** p. 550	**20.** p. 554
7. p. 547	**14.** p. 551	

CHAPTER 30

Government and Market Failure

This chapter is the first of two on the economic role of government, a topic that was first introduced in Chapter 5. The focus is **market failure** that occurs in our economy. This failure often results in government interventions to provide public goods and services, to address externality problems such as pollution, and to improve the quality and amount of information for buyers and sellers in the private markets.

The chapter first reviews the characteristics of a **public good.** Recall from Chapter 5 that a private good is characterized by rivalry and excludability, but a public good is not. What is new in Chapter 30 is that you are shown how the demand curve and schedule for a public good are constructed and how the optimal allocation of a public good is determined. The demand and supply curves for a public good are related to the collective marginal benefit and cost of providing the good.

Governments sometimes use **cost-benefit analysis** to determine if they should undertake some specific action or project. This analysis requires the government to estimate the marginal costs and the marginal benefits of the project, and it can be used to decide when such projects should be expanded, contracted, or eliminated.

The second topic of the chapter is **externalities,** situations in market transactions that create spillover costs or spillover benefits for parties not involved in the transactions. You learned in Chapter 5 that government can reduce spillover costs to society and increase spillover benefits. This general point is now modified by the **Coase theorem,** which shows that government intervention is not always required because in many cases individual bargaining can settle externality disputes. If this solution is not possible, government action with direct controls or taxes may be used.

Pollution is a prime example of a negative externality. Over the years, the government has developed antipollution policies, but the market-based ones merit your attention in your study of economics. You will discover that the government can create a **market for externality rights,** and that there is a rule for the **optimal reduction of an externality.** You will also learn how supply and demand in the recycling market can reduce landfill demands and the incineration of solid waste.

Another type of market failure you will encounter in the last major section of this chapter is **asymmetric information.** You have probably never thought about the role of information in the functioning of markets, but you will discover how important information is to both buyers and sellers. For example, buyers need some assurance about the measurement standards or quality of products they purchase, be it gasoline or medical care. The government may intervene in some markets to ensure that this information is made available to buyers.

Inadequate information in markets creates problems for sellers, too. In certain markets, such as insurance, sellers experience a **moral hazard problem** because buyers change their behavior and become less careful, and the change in behavior makes the insurance more costly to sellers. There is also an **adverse selection problem** in the insurance market because those buyers most likely to benefit (higher-risk buyers) are more likely to purchase the insurance; therefore this group imposes higher costs on sellers than if the riskers were more widely spread among the population. Actions of sellers to screen buyers would mean that fewer people will be covered by insurance and create situations that may lead to the provision of social insurance by government. Government may provide better information about workplace safety or enforce safety standards to address these information problems.

You should not finish this chapter with the sole thought that all market failures require government intervention and direct control. Some problems do require a specific government action, but other problems may be handled efficiently or in a more optimal way through individual negotiations, lawsuits, or the use of market incentives. What is important for you to understand is the range of solutions to externality and information problems.

■ CHECKLIST

When you have studied this chapter you should be able to

☐ Compare the characteristics of a public good with a private good.

☐ Calculate the demand for a public good when given tabular data.

☐ Explain how marginal benefit is reflected in the demand for a public good.

☐ Describe the relationship between marginal cost and the supply of a public good.

☐ Identify on a graph where there is an overallocation, an underallocation, and an optimal allocation of a public good.

☐ Use cost-benefit analysis to determine the extent to which government should apply resources to a project or program when you are given the cost and benefit data.

☐ Define and give examples of positive and negative externalities (spillovers).

☐ Use supply and demand graphs to illustrate how spillover costs and spillover benefits affect the allocation of resources.

☐ State the conditions that are necessary for individual bargaining with the Coase theorem and give an example.

☐ Explain how liability rules and lawsuits are used to resolve externality problems.

☐ Discuss two means government uses to achieve allocative efficiency when there are spillover costs.

☐ Identify the four major provisions of the Clean Air Act of 1990.

☐ Describe three government options to correct for the underallocation of resources when spillover benefits are large and diffuse.

☐ Define the "tragedy of the commons."

☐ Determine the price a government agency should charge in a market for externality rights (e.g., air pollution), when given the data for analysis.

☐ Compare the advantages of a market for externality rights with the policy of direct controls.

☐ Explain how pollution rights are traded under the Clean Air Act and the policies of the Environmental Protection Agency (EPA).

☐ Explain and illustrate with a graph a rule for determining the optimal reduction of a negative externality.

☐ Describe the solid waste disposal problem and the reason for interest in recycling.

☐ Explain how a market for recyclable input works using a supply and demand analysis.

☐ Discuss the economics issues involved in global warming policies.

☐ Define the terms "information failure" and "asymmetric information."

☐ Explain how inadequate information about sellers can cause market failure and give two examples of government response.

☐ Define the terms "moral hazard" and "adverse selection."

☐ Describe how inadequate information about buyers can create a moral hazard problem, an adverse selection problem, and a workplace problem, and give examples of how government can respond.

☐ Cite examples of how information failures are overcome without government intervention.

■ **CHAPTER OUTLINE**

1. Two characteristics of a **private good** are rivalry and excludability. Rivalry means that consumption of the product by a buyer eliminates the possibility of consumption of that product by another person. Excludability refers to the ability of the seller to exclude a person from consuming the product if the person does not pay for it. A **public good,** such as national defense, is characterized by nonrivalry and nonexcludability. Nonrivalry means that once a public good is consumed by one person, it is still available for consumption by another person. Nonexcludability means that those individuals who do not pay for

the public good can still obtain the benefits from the public good.

    a. The **demand for a public good** is determined by summing the prices that people are willing to pay collectively for the last unit of the public good at each possible quantity demanded, whereas the demand for a private good is determined by summing the quantities demanded at each possible price. The demand curve for a public good is downsloping because of the law of diminishing marginal utility.

    b. The **supply curve of a public good** is upsloping because of the law of diminishing returns; additional units supplied reflect increasing marginal costs.

    c. The **optimal allocation** of a public good is determined by the intersection of the supply and demand curves.

    (1) If the marginal benefit exceeds the marginal cost, there is an underallocation of a public good,

    (2) but if the marginal cost exceeds the marginal benefit there will be an overallocation.

    (3) Only when the marginal benefits equal the marginal costs is there an optimal allocation of public goods.

    d. Government uses **cost-benefit analysis** to decide if it should use resources for a project and to determine the total quantity of resources it should devote to a project. The **marginal cost = marginal benefit rule** is used to make the decision. Additional resources should be devoted to a project only so long as the marginal benefits to society from the project exceed society's marginal costs. In this case, the total benefits minus the total costs are at a maximum.

2. Market failure can arise from **externalities,** or spillovers, whereby a third party bears a portion of the cost associated with the production or consumption of a good or service.

    a. **Spillover costs** (negative externalities) result in an *overallocation* of resources to the production of a product. All the costs associated with the product are not reflected in the supply curve. The producer's supply curve lies to the right of the full-cost supply curve.

    b. **Spillover benefits** (positive externalities) result in an *underallocation* of resources to the production of a product. All the benefits from the product are not reflected in the demand curve. The demand curve lies to the left of the full-benefits demand curve.

    c. Individual bargaining can be used to correct negative externalities or to encourage positive externalities. The **Coase theorem** suggests that private negotiations rather than government intervention should be the course of action if there is clear ownership of the property, the number of people involved is small, and the cost of bargaining is minimal. When these conditions do not hold, however, it may be necessary for government intervention.

    d. The legal system can be used to resolve disputes arising from externalities. This system defines *property rights* and specifies *liability rules* that can be used for *lawsuits* on externality issues. This method has limitations because of the expense, the length of time to resolve the disputes, and the uncertainty of the outcomes.

e. When there is the potential for severe harm to common resources, such as air or water, and when the situation involves a large number of people, two types of government intervention may be necessary.

(1) ***Direct controls*** use legislation to ban or limit the activities that produce a negative externality. These actions reduce the supply of the products that create the negative externalities to levels that are allocatively efficient.

(2) ***Specific taxes*** are also applied to productive activity that creates negative externalities. These taxes increase the cost of production, and thus decrease the supply to levels that are allocatively efficient.

f. With spillover benefits other government actions may be necessary to correct for the underallocation of resources.

(1) The government can give subsidies to buyers to encourage the purchase or consumption of a good or service.

(2) The government can give subsidies to producers to reduce the cost of production and increase output of a good or service.

(3) When spillover benefits are extremely large, government may decide to provide the good or service.

g. There are market-based approaches to spillover problems.

(1) The ***tragedy of the commons*** refers to situations where common resources such as air, water, or oceans are subject to pollution problems because no individual or organization has a monetary incentive to maintain the quality or purity of the resource.

(2) One solution to the problem has been to create a ***market for externality rights*** or to internalize the spillover cost in a market.

(3) For example, the government (a pollution-control agency) might set a limit for the amount of pollution permitted in a region. This limit means that the supply curve is perfectly inelastic (vertical) at some level of pollution. The demand curve would reflect the willingness of polluters to pay for the right to pollute at different prices. The price for pollution rights would be determined by the intersection of the demand and supply curves. Given a fixed supply curve, an increase in demand because of economic growth in the region would increase the price of pollution rights.

(4) This market solution has advantages over direct government controls. It is more efficient and thus reduces society's costs. It puts a price on pollution and thus creates a monetary incentive for businesses to not pollute or to reduce their level of pollution.

(5) Real examples of this approach are found in provisions in the Clean Air Act of 1990 and policies of the Environmental Protection Agency (EPA).

h. In most cases, the ***optimal reduction of an externality*** is not zero from society's perspective.

(1) It occurs where the marginal cost to society from the externality and the marginal benefit of reducing it are equal (**MB = MC**).

(2) Over time, shifts in the marginal-cost and marginal-benefit curves change the optimal level of externality reduction.

i. Solid waste usually has been deposited in garbage dumps or incinerated, but this approach creates negative externalities and is increasingly expensive.

(1) The situation has created a market for recycled items to help reduce this pollution problem.

(2) Government can use either demand or supply incentives to encourage recycling as an alternative to dumps or incineration.

j. Global warming from carbon dioxide and other greenhouse gases may be permanently altering climate patterns and will have economic effects on different regions. In designing government policies, economists stress the use of markets and the need to evaluate the costs and benefits of alternative policies.

3. Economic inefficiency from information failures can occur in markets. These information failures arise from ***asymmetric information***—unequal knowledge that is held by parties to a market transaction.

a. When information involving sellers is incomplete, inaccurate, or very costly, there will be market failures. For example, in the market for gasoline, consumers need accurate information about the amount and quality of gasoline they purchase. In the market for medical services, it is important that consumers have some assurances about the credentials of physicians. Government can respond to these information failures by such actions as establishing measurement standards and by testing and licensing.

b. Inadequate information involving buyers creates market failures.

(1) A market may produce less than the optimal amount of goods and services from society's perspective because of a ***moral hazard problem,*** which results when buyers alter their behavior and increase the costs of sellers. For example, the provision of insurance may cause the insured to be less cautious.

(2) An ***adverse selection problem*** occurs in many markets. In the case of insurance, the buyers most likely to need or benefit from insurance are the ones most likely to purchase it. These higher-risk buyers impose higher costs on sellers. Sellers then screen out the higher-risk buyers, but this action reduces the population covered by insurance in the private market. In some cases, government may establish a social insurance system that is designed to cover a much broader group of the population than would be covered by the private insurers, such as with Social Security.

(3) Market failures occur in resource markets when there is inadequate information for workers about the health hazards or safety of a workplace. Government can act to correct these problems by publishing health and safety information or by forcing businesses to provide more information. The typical approach to this problem has been the enforcement of standards for health and safety on the job.

c. Government does not always need to intervene in the private market to address information problems.

Businesses can adopt policies to correct these problems, and some firms or other organizations can specialize in providing important market information for buyers or sellers.

■ HINTS AND TIPS

1. Review Chapter 5's discussion of public goods and externalities.

2. Make sure you understand the difference between the demand for public and private goods. The *demand for a private good* is determined by adding the quantities demanded at each possible price. The *demand for a public good* is determined by adding the prices people collectively are willing to pay for the last unit of the public good at each possible quantity demanded.

3. Table 30.3 is important because it summarizes the private actions and government policies taken to correct for spillover costs or benefits. The government can influence the allocation of resources in a private market by taking actions that increase or decrease demand or supply.

4. Problems occur because information in a market is sometimes asymmetric, which means that there is *unequal* information for sellers or buyers about product price, quality, or other product conditions. Use the examples in the text to help you distinguish between the different types of information problems created by sellers or buyers.

■ IMPORTANT TERMS

cost-benefit analysis	market for externality rights
marginal cost = marginal benefit rule	optimal reduction of an externality
externalities (spillovers)	asymmetric information
Coase theorem	moral hazard problem
tragedy of the commons	adverse selection problem

SELF-TEST

■ FILL-IN QUESTIONS

1. Rivalry means that when one person buys and consumes a product, it (is, is not) _____ available for purchase and consumption by another person. Excludability means that the seller (can, cannot) _____ keep people who do not pay for the product from obtaining its benefits. Rivalry and excludability apply to (private, public) _____ goods, but these characteristics do not apply to _____ goods.

2. With a private good, to compute the market demand you add together the (prices, quantities demanded) _____ people are willing to pay for at each

possible (price, quantity demanded) _____. With a public good, to compute the collective demand you add together the (prices, quantities demanded) _____ people are willing to pay for the last unit of the public good at each possible (price, quantity demanded) _____.

3. The demand curve for a public good slopes downward because of the law of diminishing marginal (returns, utility) _____; the supply curve for a public good is upsloping because of the law of diminishing _____. The demand curve for a public good is, in essence, a marginal-(benefit, cost) _____ curve; the supply curve for a public good reflects rising marginal _____. The optimal quantity of a public good will be shown by the intersection of the collective demand and supply curves, which means that marginal (benefit, cost) _____ of the last unit equals that unit's marginal _____.

4. In applying cost-benefit analysis, government should use more resources in the production of public goods if the marginal (cost, benefit) _____ from the additional public goods exceeds the marginal _____ that results from having fewer private goods. This rule will determine which plan from a cost-benefit analysis will result in the (maximum, minimum) _____ net benefit to society.

5. One objective of government is to correct for market failures called spillovers or (internalities, externalities) _____. If there is a cost to an individual or group that is a third party to the market transaction, it is a (positive, negative) _____ externality or a spillover (benefit, cost) _____. If there is a benefit to an individual or group that is a third party to a market transaction, it is a (positive, negative) _____ externality or a spillover (benefit, cost) _____.

6. When there are spillover costs in competitive markets, the result is an (over, under) _____ allocation of resources to the production of the good or service. When there are spillover benefits, the result is an (over, under) _____ allocation of resources to the production of the good or service.

7. The (liability, Coase) _____ theorem suggests that when there are negative or positive externalities in situations in which the ownership of property is (undefined, defined) _____, the number of people involved is (large, small) _____, and the costs of bargaining are (major, minor) _____, then government intervention (is, is not) _____ required.

8. The legal system is also important for settling externality disputes between individuals because laws define (political, property) _____ rights and specify (business, liability) _____ rules that can be used for lawsuits. This method, however, has limitations because of its cost, the length of time, and the (certainty, uncertainty) _____ of the results.

9. Government may use direct controls to reduce spillover (benefits, costs) _____ by passing legislation that restricts business activity. In other cases, the government may (subsidize, tax) _____ a producer.

10. The government may correct for the underallocation of resources where spillover (costs, benefits) _____ are large and diffuse. This objective can be achieved by (taxing, subsidizing) _____ buyers or producers and through government (provision, consumption) _____ of a good or service.

11. When no private individual or institution has a monetary incentive to maintain the purity or quality of resources such as air, water, oceans, or lands, it creates an externality problem that is sometime called the tragedy of the (firm, commons) _____. A policy approach to spillover cost problems is to create a (market, government) _____ for externality rights.

12. Consider how such a market for pollution rights would work.

   a. If the regional government agency sets a limit on the amount of air pollution, the supply curve for the air pollution rights would be perfectly (elastic, inelastic) _____.

   b. The demand curve for air pollution rights would be (up, down) _____ sloping and intersect the supply curve to determine the (quantity, price) _____ for the right to pollute the air.

   c. If the demand for air pollution rights increased over time, then the price would (rise, fall, stay the same) _____, but the quantity supplied would _____.

13. Reducing negative externalities comes at a "price" to society, and therefore society must decide how much of a decrease it wants to (buy, sell) "_____." Further abatement of a negative externality increases

economic efficiency if the marginal cost is (greater than, equal to, less than) _____ the marginal benefit, but it is economically inefficient if the marginal benefit is _____ the marginal cost. The optimal reduction of a negative externality occurs where the society's marginal benefit is (greater than, equal to, less than) _____ society's marginal cost.

14. One way the government can increase the recycling of solid waste is to (decrease, increase) _____ the demand for recycled inputs in the production process or _____ the incentives to supply recycled products.

15. One of the most controversial and continuing problems with air pollution abatement is the issue of global (trade, warming) _____. Over the past few decades, there has been a noticeable (increase, decrease) _____ in the temperature of the earth's surface. Economists stress that in designing policies to address this problem, the benefits of reducing greenhouse-gas emissions problems should be (greater than, less than) _____ the costs. They also note that some adjustment to any climate change will occur naturally because of changes in prices and profits in the (environment, market) _____.

16. Markets can produce failures because of (symmetric, asymmetric) _____ information. When information involving sellers is (complete, incomplete) _____ or obtaining such information is (costless, costly) _____, the market will (under, over) _____ allocate resources to the production of that good or service.

17. To correct such problems in the gasoline market, the government establishes quality (prices, standards) _____. In the medical market, the government protects consumers by (taxing, licensing) _____ physicians.

18. Inadequate information involving buyers can lead to two problems. First, if a market situation arises whereby buyers alter their behavior and increase the cost to sellers, (an adverse selection, a moral hazard) _____ problem is created. Second, if buyers withhold information from sellers that would impose a large cost on sellers, _____ problem is created. The moral hazard problem occurs (at the same time, after) _____ a person makes a purchase, but the adverse selection problem occurs _____ the buyer makes a purchase.

19. Another example of information failure occurs in labor markets in which there is incomplete or inadequate information about (productivity, safety) _____. The government will intervene in these situations to enforce (quotas, standards) _____ or provide (health care, information) _____ related to workplace hazards.

20. Private businesses overcome some information problems about the product reliability or quality through (prices, warranties) _____ for products or the (penalizing, franchising) _____ of businesses that make them more uniform. Some businesses and organizations also collect and publish product information that is useful for (sellers, buyers) _____. Despite these actions, there may still be a need for government actions to correct (wage, information) _____ problems and to promote an efficient allocation of society's scarce resources.

◪ TRUE–FALSE QUESTIONS

Circle T if the statement is true, F if it is false.

1. Excludability applies to public goods but not to private goods. **T F**

2. When determining the collective demand for a public good, you add the prices people are willing to pay for the last unit of the public good at each possible quantity demanded. **T F**

3. When the marginal benefit of a public good exceeds the marginal cost, there will be an overallocation of resources to that public good use. **T F**

4. The optimal allocation of a public good is determined by the rule that marginal cost (MC) equals marginal revenue (MR). **T F**

5. "Reducing government spending" means the same as "economy in government." **T F**

6. A spillover is a cost or benefit accruing to an individual or group—a third party—which is external to the market transaction. **T F**

7. In a competitive product market and in the absence of spillover costs, the supply curve or schedule reflects the costs of producing the product. **T F**

8. If demand and supply reflected all the benefits and costs of a product, the equilibrium output of a competitive market would be identical with its optimal output. **T F**

9. There is an underallocation of resources to the production of a commodity when negative externalities are present. **T F**

10. The inclusion of the spillover benefits would increase the demand for a product. **T F**

11. When spillover costs are involved in the production of a product, more resources are allocated to the production of that product and more of the product is produced than is optimal or most efficient. **T F**

12. The Coase theorem suggests that government intervention is required whenever there are negative or positive externalities. **T F**

13. Lawsuits and liability rules create externality problems instead of helping resolve them. **T F**

14. Taxes that are imposed on businesses that create an externality will lower the marginal cost of production and increase supply. **T F**

15. Subsidizing the firms producing goods that provide spillover benefits will usually result in a better allocation of resources. **T F**

16. One solution to the negative externalities caused by pollution is to create a market for pollution rights in which the social costs of pollution are turned into private costs. **T F**

17. In a market for pollution rights, if a government agency sets a fixed level for pollution, the supply curve of pollution rights will be perfectly elastic. **T F**

18. If a society has marginal costs of $10 for pollution abatement and the marginal benefit of pollution abatement is $8, to achieve an optimal amount of the pollution the society should increase the amount of pollution abatement. **T F**

19. If the government requires the use of more recycled paper products, then the demand for recycled paper products will increase. **T F**

20. If the government provides a subsidy to producers of recycled paper products, the supply of recycled paper products will increase. **T F**

21. The economic effects of global warming will be uniform across regions of the world. **T F**

22. Asymmetric information is a market failure that occurs when parties to a market transaction possess unequal knowledge. **T F**

23. The inspection of meat products by the Federal government for quality is justified on the grounds that it reduces the costs of obtaining information in the market for meat. **T F**

24. If the provision of government health insurance encourages people to take more health risks, it has created a moral hazard. **T F**

25. Adverse selection problems primarily result when the government begins enforcing standards for safety in the workplace. **T F**

■ **MULTIPLE-CHOICE QUESTIONS**

Circle the letter that corresponds to the best answer.

1. How do public goods differ from private goods? Public goods are characterized by
- **(a)** rivalry and excludability
- **(b)** rivalry and nonexcludability
- **(c)** nonrivalry and excludability
- **(d)** nonrivalry and nonexcludability

Answer Questions 2, 3, 4, and 5 on the basis of the following information for a public good. P_1 and P_2 represent the prices individuals 1 and 2, the only two people in the society, are willing to pay for the last unit of a public good. P_c represents the price (or collective willingness to pay) for a public good, and Q_s represents the quantity supplied of the public good at those prices.

Q_d	P_1	P_2	P_c	Q_s
1	$4	$5	$9	5
2	3	4	7	4
3	2	3	5	3
4	1	2	3	2
5	0	1	1	1

2. What amount is this society willing to pay for the first unit of the public good?
- **(a)** $10
- **(b)** $9
- **(c)** $8
- **(d)** $7

3. What amount is this society willing to pay for the third unit of the public good?
- **(a)** $5
- **(b)** $6
- **(c)** $7
- **(d)** $8

4. Given the supply curve Q_s, the optimal price and quantity of the public good in this society will be
- **(a)** $9 and 5 units
- **(b)** $5 and 3 units
- **(c)** $5 and 4 units
- **(d)** $3 and 2 units

5. If this good were a private good instead of a public good, the total quantity demanded at the $4 price would be
- **(a)** 3 units
- **(b)** 4 units
- **(c)** 5 units
- **(d)** 6 units

Answer Questions 6, 7, and 8 for a public good on the basis of the following graph.

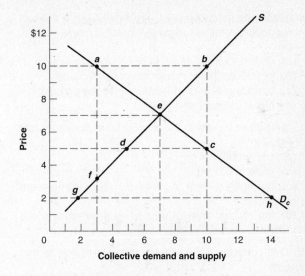

Collective demand and supply

6. Where the marginal benefits equal the collective marginal costs is represented by point
- **(a)** *b*
- **(b)** *c*
- **(c)** *d*
- **(d)** *e*

7. Which line segment would indicate the amount by which the marginal benefit of this public good is less than the marginal cost?
- **(a)** *ab*
- **(b)** *bc*
- **(c)** *fa*
- **(d)** *gh*

8. If 3 units of this public good are produced, the marginal
- **(a)** cost of $10 is greater than the marginal benefit of $3
- **(b)** cost of $10 is greater than the marginal benefit of $5
- **(c)** benefit of $10 is greater than the marginal cost of $5
- **(d)** benefit of $10 is greater than the marginal cost of $3

9. Assume that a government is considering a new antipollution program and may choose to include in this program any number of four different projects. The marginal cost and the marginal benefits of each of the four projects are given in the table below. What total amount should this government spend on the antipollution program?
- **(a)** $2 million
- **(b)** $5 million
- **(c)** $17 million
- **(d)** $37 million

Project	Marginal cost	Marginal benefit
#1	$ 2 million	$ 5 million
#2	5 million	7 million
#3	10 million	9 million
#4	20 million	15 million

10. When the production and consumption of a product entail spillover costs, a competitive product market results in a(n)

(a) underallocation of resources to the product
(b) overallocation of resources to the product
(c) optimal allocation of resources to the product
(d) higher price for the product

11. A spillover benefit in the production of some product will result in

(a) overproduction
(b) underproduction
(c) the optimal level of production if consumers are price takers
(d) the optimal level of production if consumers are utility maximizers

12. One condition for the Coase theorem to hold is that there be

(a) clear ownership of the property rights
(b) a large number of people involved in the dispute
(c) active government intervention to solve the externality problem
(d) a sizable cost for bargaining to settle the dispute between the private parties

13. The Clean Air Act of 1990

(a) permits the exchange of pollution rights within firms and between firms in an area
(b) sets stricter limits on the dumping of garbage in landfills
(c) funds research on applications of asymmetric information and transaction cost
(d) forces companies to clean up toxic waste dumps

Use the following graph which shows the supply and demand for a product to answer Questions 14, 15, and 16.

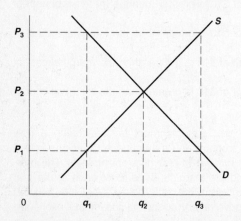

14. If there are neither spillover costs nor spillover benefits, the output that results in the optimal allocation of resources to the production of this product is

(a) q_1
(b) q_2
(c) q_3
(d) 0

15. If the market for a product was in equilibrium at output level q_2 but the optimal level of output for society was at q_1, the government could correct for this

(a) spillover cost with a subsidy to consumers
(b) spillover cost with a subsidy to producers
(c) spillover benefit with a subsidy to producers
(d) spillover cost with a tax on producers

16. If the market for a product was in equilibrium at output level q_2 but the optimal level of output for society was at q_3, the government could correct for this

(a) overallocation of resources by direct controls on consumers
(b) underallocation of resources through taxes on producers
(c) overallocation of resources through a market for externality rights
(d) underallocation of resources through subsidies to producers

17. If government were to sell pollution rights, an increase in the demand for pollution rights would

(a) increase both the quantity of pollutants discharged and the market price of pollution rights
(b) increase the quantity discharged and have no effect on the market price
(c) have no effect on the quantity discharged and increase the market price
(d) have no effect on either the quantity discharged or the market price

Use the following table to answer Questions 18, 19, and 20. The data in the table show the marginal costs and marginal benefits to a city for five different levels of pollution abatement.

Quantity of pollution abatement	Marginal cost	Marginal benefit
500 tons	$500,000	$100,000
400 tons	300,000	150,000
300 tons	200,000	200,000
200 tons	100,000	300,000
100 tons	50,000	400,000

18. If the city seeks an optimal reduction of the externality, it will select how many tons of pollution abatement?

(a) 100
(b) 300
(c) 400
(d) 500

19. If the marginal benefit of pollution abatement increased by $150,000 at each level because of the community's desire to attract more firms, the optimal level of pollution abatement in tons would be

(a) 200
(b) 300
(c) 400
(d) 500

20. What would cause the optimal level of pollution abatement to be 200 tons?

(a) technological improvement in production that decreases marginal costs by $150,000 at each level

(b) an increase in the health risk from this pollution that increases marginal benefits by $200,000 at each level

(c) the need to replace old pollution monitoring equipment with new equipment that increases marginal costs by $200,000 at each level

(d) reduction in the public demand for pollution control that decreases marginal benefits by $100,000 at each level

21. Which would tend to increase the demand for recycled paper?

(a) an increase in the price of regular paper

(b) an increase in taxes on all paper production

(c) a decrease in interest in protecting the environment

(d) a decrease in subsidies for all paper production

22. Inadequate information about sellers and their product can cause market failure in the form of

(a) an increase in the number of market sellers

(b) an increase in the number of market buyers

(c) an overallocation of resources to the product

(d) an underallocation of resources to the product

23. A situation in which one party to a contract alters his or her behavior after signing the contract in ways that can be costly to the other party would be

(a) an adverse selection problem

(b) a moral hazard problem

(c) a tragedy of the commons

(d) a positive externality

24. If Congress adopted an increase in government insurance on bank deposits, this action would create a moral hazard problem because it may

(a) lead to careful screening of depositors and the source of their funds

(b) restrict the amount of deposits made by bank customers

(c) encourage bank officers to make riskier loans

(d) reduce bank investments in real estate

25. Assume that individuals who are most likely to benefit substantially from an insurance policy decide to buy one and the insurance company does not know this information. This situation would be an example of

(a) a free-rider problem

(b) a principal–agent problem

(c) a moral hazard problem

(d) an adverse selection problem

■ PROBLEMS

1. Data on two individuals' preferences for a public good are reflected in the following table. P_1 and P_2 represent the prices individuals 1 and 2, the only two people in the society, are willing to pay for the last unit of the public good.

Quantity	P_1	P_2
1	$6	$6
2	5	5
3	4	4
4	3	3
5	2	2
6	1	1

a. Complete the table below showing the collective demand for the public good in this society.

Q_d	Price	Q_s
1	$ _____	7
2	_____	6
3	_____	5
4	_____	4
5	_____	3
6	_____	2

b. Given the supply schedule for this public good as shown by the Q_s column, the optimal quantity of this public good is _____ units and the optimal price is $ _____.

c. When 3 units of this public good are produced, the perceived marginal benefit is $ _____ and the marginal cost is $ _____; there will be an (overallocation, underallocation) _____ of resources to this public good.

d. When 6 units of this public good are produced, the perceived marginal benefit is $ _____ and the marginal cost is $ _____; there is an (underallocation, overallocation) _____ of resources to this public good.

2. Imagine that a state government is considering constructing a new highway to link its two largest cities. Its estimate of the total costs and the total benefits of building 2-, 4-, 6-, and 8-lane highways between the two cities are shown in the table below. (All figures are in millions of dollars.)

Project	Total cost	Marginal cost	Totalbenefit	Marginal benefit
No highway	$ 0		$ 0	
2-lane highway	500	$ _____	650	$ _____
4-lane highway	680	_____	750	_____
6-lane highway	760	_____	800	_____
8-lane highway	860	_____	825	_____

a. Compute the marginal cost and the marginal benefit of the 2-, 4-, 6-, and 8-lane highways.

b. Will it benefit the state to allocate resources to construct a highway? _____

c. If the state builds a highway,

(1) it should be a _____-lane highway.

(2) the total cost will be $ _____ million.

(3) the total benefit will be $ _____ million.

(4) the *net* benefit will be $ _____ million.

3. The following graph shows the demand and supply curves for a product bought and sold in a competitive market. Assume that there are no spillover benefits or costs.

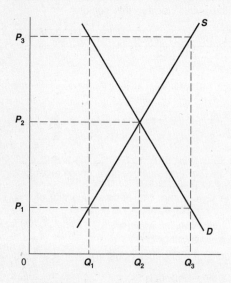

a. Were this market to produce an output of Q_1, there

would be an (optimal, under, over) _____ allocation of resources to the production of this product.

b. Were this market to produce Q_3, there would be an

_____ allocation of resources to this product.

c. The equilibrium output is _____, and

at this output there is an _____ allocation of resources.

4. The two following graphs show product demand and supply curves that do *not* reflect either the spillover costs of producing the product or the spillover benefits obtained from its consumption.

a. On the first graph, draw in another curve that reflects the inclusion of spillover *costs*.

(1) Government might force the (demand for, supply

of) _____ the product to reflect the spillover costs of producing it by (taxing, subsidizing)

_____ the producers.

(2) The inclusion of spillover costs in the total cost of producing the product (increases, decreases)

_____ the output of the product and

_____ its price.

b. On the second graph, draw in a demand curve that reflects the inclusion of spillover *benefits*.

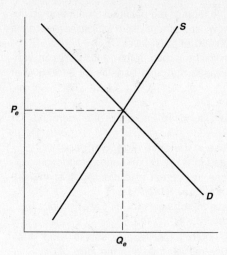

(1) Indicate on the graph the output that is optimal when spillover benefits are included.

(2) To bring about the production of this optimal output, government might (tax, subsidize)

_____ the consumers of this product,

which would (increase, decrease) _____ the demand for the product.

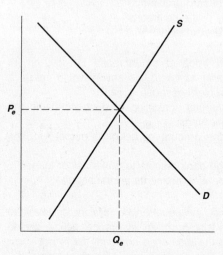

(3) This optimal output is (greater than, less than,

equal to) _____ Q_e; and the price of the

product is (above, below, equal to) _____ P_e.

5. Assume the atmosphere of Cuyahoga County, Ohio (the Cleveland metropolitan area), is able to reabsorb 1500 tons of pollutants per year. The following schedule shows the price polluters would be willing to pay for the right to dispose of 1 ton of pollutants per year and the total quantity of pollutants they would wish to dispose of at each price.

Price (per ton of pollutant rights)	Total quantity of pollutant rights demanded (tons)
$ 0	4000
1000	3500
2000	3000
3000	2500
4000	2000
5000	1500
6000	1000
7000	500

a. If there were no emission fee, polluters would put _____ tons of pollutants in the air each year, and this quantity of pollutants would exceed the ability of nature to reabsorb them by _____ tons.

b. To reduce pollution to the capacity of the atmosphere to recycle pollutants, an emission fee of $_____ per ton should be set.

c. Were this emission fee set, the total emission fees set would be $_____.

d. Were the quantity of pollution rights demanded at each price to increase by 500 tons, the emission fee could be increased by $_____ and total emission fees collected would increase by $_____.

■ **SHORT ANSWER AND ESSAY QUESTIONS**

1. What are the basic characteristics of public goods?

2. How do public goods differ from private goods?

3. Contrast how you construct the demand curve for a public good with the procedure for constructing the demand curve for a private good using individual demand schedules.

4. Explain the relationship between the marginal cost and benefit of a public good when there is an underallocation, an overallocation, and an optimal allocation of resources for the provision of the public good.

5. Describe benefit-cost analysis, and state the rules used to make decisions from marginal and total perspectives.

6. Is "economy in government" the same as "reduced government spending"? Explain the distinction.

7. What are externalities and spillovers? Give examples of positive externalities and negative externalities.

8. Under what conditions might it be worthwhile for the government to intervene or not to intervene to settle a spillover problem?

9. Should the government intervene in an externality dispute between two property owners over the use of one party's land? Should government intervene in the case of acid rain?

10. How do lawsuits and liability rules resolve externality problems? How would these actions be justified?

11. What actions can government take to correct for spillover costs in a market?

12. What is the tragedy of the commons? Give examples of it.

13. How do you create a market for externality rights in the case of pollution? What are some advantages and limitations of this approach to the pollution problem?

14. What rule can society use to determine the optimal level of pollution abatement? What is the problem with this approach?

15. Why is solid-waste disposal of national concern? How is recycling a partial alternative to it? How does a market for recyclable items work?

16. Discuss the economic issues involved in global warming.

17. Describe how inadequate information about sellers creates market problems for buyers. Give examples.

18. Explain what is meant by a "moral hazard problem" and describe how it affects sellers. Give some examples of the application of this problem.

19. How can the market for insurance result in an adverse selection problem? What actions might government take to correct this information problem?

20. In what way does workplace safety become an information problem? How might this problem be resolved by government or businesses?

ANSWERS

Chapter 30 Government and Market Failure

FILL-IN QUESTIONS

1. is not, can, private, public
2. quantities demanded, price, prices, quantity demanded
3. utility, returns, benefit, cost, benefit, cost (*either order for last two*)
4. benefit, cost, maximum
5. externalities, negative, cost, positive, benefit
6. over, under
7. Coase, defined, small, minor, is not
8. property, liability, uncertainty
9. costs, tax
10. benefits, subsidizing, provision
11. commons, market
12. *a.* inelastic; *b.* down, price; *c.* rise, stay the same
13. buy, less than, less than, equal to
14. increase, increase
15. warming, increase, greater than, market
16. asymmetric, incomplete, costly, under
17. standards, licensing
18. a moral hazard, an adverse selection, after, at the same time
19. safety, standards, information
20. warranties, franchising, buyers, information

TRUE–FALSE QUESTIONS

1. F, p. 558	**10.** T, pp. 561–562	**19.** T, pp. 569–570
2. T, pp. 559–560	**11.** T, pp. 561–562	**20.** T, p. 570
3. F, pp. 560–562	**12.** F, p. 563	**21.** F, p. 571
4. F, pp. 560–562	**13.** F, pp. 563–564	**22.** T, p. 572
5. F, p. 561	**14.** F, p. 565	**23.** T, p. 573
6. T, p. 562	**15.** T, p. 565	**24.** T, pp. 573–574
7. T, p. 562	**16.** T, pp. 566–567	**25.** F, p. 574
8. T, pp. 561–562	**17.** F, pp. 566–567	
9. F, pp. 561–562	**18.** F, pp. 568–569	

MULTIPLE-CHOICE QUESTIONS

1. d, p. 558	**10.** b, p. 562	**19.** c, pp. 568–569
2. b, pp. 559–560	**11.** b, pp. 562–563	**20.** c, pp. 568–569
3. a, pp. 559–560	**12.** a, p. 563	**21.** a, pp. 569–570
4. b, pp. 559–560	**13.** a, p. 564	**22.** d, pp. 572–573
5. a, pp. 559–560	**14.** b, pp. 562–563	**23.** b, pp. 573–574
6. d, pp. 559–560	**15.** d, pp. 564–565	**24.** c, pp. 573–574
7. b, pp. 559–560	**16.** d, pp. 564–565	**25.** d, pp. 574–575
8. d, pp. 559–560	**17.** c, pp. 566–567	
9. b, pp. 560–561	**18.** b, pp. 568–569	

PROBLEMS

1. *a.* $12, 10, 8, 6, 4, 2; *b.* 4, 6; *c.* 8, 4, underallocation; *d.* 2, 10, overallocation

2. *a.* Marginal cost: $500, $180, $80, $100; Marginal benefit: $650, $100, $50, $25; *b.* yes; *c.* (1) 2, (2) $500, (3) $650, (4) $150

3. *a.* under; *b.* over; *c.* Q_2, optimal

4. *a.* (1) supply of, taxing, (2) decreases, increases; *b.* (1) graph; (2) subsidize, increase, (3) greater than, above

5. *a.* 4000, 2500; *b.* 5000; *c.* 7,500,000; *d.* 1000, 1,500,000

SHORT ANSWER AND ESSAY QUESTIONS

1. p. 558	**8.** pp. 563–564	**15.** pp. 569–570
2. pp. 558–559	**9.** pp. 563–564	**16.** p. 571
3. pp. 559–560	**10.** pp. 563–564	**17.** pp. 572–573
4. pp. 559–560	**11.** pp. 564–565	**18.** pp. 573–574
5. pp. 560–562	**12.** p. 566	**19.** pp. 574–575
6. pp. 561–562	**13.** pp. 566–567	**20.** pp. 574–575
7. pp. 562–563	**14.** pp. 568–569	

Public Choice Theory and the Economics of Taxation

Although both Chapters 30 and 31 analyze the role of government in the economy, they look at government from opposite perspectives. Chapter 30 discussed market failure issues and what actions government takes to correct these market problems. Chapter 31 now examines government failure, or why government makes inefficient use of the scarce resources. For this explanation, you will first be introduced to **public choice theory,** or the economic analysis of public decision making. Later in the chapter you will learn more about the economics of taxation, which includes such topics as tax principles and the economic effects of specific taxes.

Many public decisions are made by **majority voting,** but this decision-making procedure may distort the true preferences of society. In the first section of the chapter you will find out how majority voting may lead to inefficient outcomes in the provision of public goods. In some choices, the benefits of a public good are greater than the costs, but the majority votes against having it. In other choices, the benefits outweigh the costs, but the provision of the public good is supported by the majority vote. Although actions by interest groups and the use of logrolling may tend to reduce inefficiencies created by majority rule, the final result depends on the circumstances of the decision.

Also note that there is a **paradox of voting** from majority voting. Depending on how a vote or election is arranged, it is possible for majority rule to produce choices that are inconsistent with the ranking of preferences among voters. You should spend time working through the example in the textbook so you understand how opposing outcomes can result from majority rule. You should also learn why the median voters strongly influence the result of a vote or an election when there is majority rule. In fact, the **median-voter model** is very useful for explaining why the middle position on issues is often adopted in public decisions.

The second section of Chapter 31 discusses other reasons for *inefficiencies* by government. Here you will learn that (1) the **special-interest effect** and **rent-seeking** impair public decisions; (2) politicians often have a strong incentive to adopt an economic policy that has clear benefits to voters, but hidden or uncertain costs; (3) public choice is more limited and less flexible than private choice because it entails voting for or accepting a "bundle" of programs, some good and some bad; and (4) bureaucratic inefficiencies in the public sector arise from the lack of the economic incentives and competitive pressures found in the private sector.

Chapter 31 then shifts from public choice theory to taxation. In this third section of the chapter you will learn the economic principles used in levying taxes. You also will learn about the **regressive, progressive,** and **proportional** classifications for taxes and how most U.S. taxes fit into this classification scheme.

The **tax incidence** and **efficiency loss of a tax** are described in the fourth section of the chapter. Incidence means "who ends up paying the tax." As you will discover, the *elasticities* of demand and of supply determine how much of the tax will be paid by buyers and how much of it will be paid by sellers. No matter who pays the tax, however, there is an efficiency loss to society from the tax, the size of which is also affected by the elasticities of demand and of supply. With this knowledge, you are now ready to study the probable incidence of five taxes—personal income, corporate income, sales, excise, and property—that are used to raise most of the tax revenue for government in the United States.

■ **CHECKLIST**

When you have studied this chapter you should be able to

☐ Explain the purpose of public choice theory and the topics it covers.

☐ Illustrate how majority voting procedures can produce inefficient outcomes when the vote is "yes" or the vote is "no."

☐ Describe how interest groups and political logrolling affect the efficiency of outcomes from voting.

☐ Give an example of the paradox of voting.

☐ Describe the median-voter model, its applicability to the real world, and two implications of the model.

☐ Explain the meaning of the phrase "government failure" and cite examples.

☐ Give an example of a special-interest effect and an example of rent-seeking behavior.

☐ Describe the economic problem that arises when a political decision involves clear benefits and hidden costs.

☐ Compare the type of choices consumers make in the private market with the type of choices citizens as voters make.

☐ Contrast the incentives for economic efficiency in private business with those found in public agencies and bureaucracies.

☐ Discuss how government and markets are imperfect in allocating resources.

☐ Distinguish between the ability-to-pay principle of taxation and the benefits-received principle of taxation.

☐ Determine whether a tax is regressive, progressive, or proportional when given the data.

☐ Describe the progressivity or regressivity of the five major taxes used in the United States.

☐ Illustrate the incidence of an excise tax with a supply and demand graph.

☐ Explain how demand and supply elasticities affect tax incidence.

☐ Describe the efficiency loss of a tax with a supply and demand graph.

☐ Explain the effects of demand or supply elasticities on the efficiency loss of a tax.

☐ Evaluate the probable incidence of the personal income, corporate income, sales and excise, and property taxes.

☐ Describe the progressivity of the U.S. tax structure overall and at the Federal, state, and local levels.

■ **CHAPTER OUTLINE**

1. Most decisions about government activity are made collectively through **majority voting,** but the procedure is not without problems.

    a. Voting outcomes may be economically *inefficient* in cases where voters reject a public good whose total benefits exceed total costs or fail to reject a public good whose total costs are greater than the total benefits. These inefficiencies can be resolved sometimes by

    (1) the formation of special-interest groups that work to overcome inefficient outcomes, or

    (2) the use of **logrolling,** in which votes are traded to secure a favorable and efficient decision,

    (3) but logrolling can also lead to inefficient decisions.

    b. The **paradox of voting** suggests that the public may not be able to make consistent choices that reflect its preferences.

    c. Based on the **median-voter model,** it is suggested that the person or groups holding the middle position on an issue will likely determine the outcome from a majority rule election. Public decisions tend to reflect the median view.

2. Public choice theory suggests that there is **government failure** because the process it uses to make decisions is inherently weak and results in an economically inefficient allocation of resources.

    a. The weakness of the decision-making process in the public sector and the resulting inefficient allocation of resources is often the result of pressures exerted on Congress and the bureaucracy by special interests and other groups.

    (1) There can be a **special-interest effect** in which a small number of people obtain a government program or policy giving them large gains at the expense of a large number of people who individually suffer small losses. This special-interest effect is also present in *pork-barrel politics* where a government program will mostly benefit one constituency.

    (2) **Rent-seeking behavior** is reflected in appeals to government for special benefits or treatment at the taxpayers' or someone else's expense. Government can dispense such rents through laws, rules, hiring, and purchases.

    b. Those seeking election to public office frequently favor programs whose benefits are clear and immediate and whose costs are uncertain and deferred, even when the benefits are less than the costs. Conversely, they frequently oppose programs whose costs are clear and immediate and whose benefits are uncertain and deferred, even when the benefits are greater than the costs.

    c. There are limited and bundle choices in political decisions. When citizens must vote for candidates who represent different but complete programs, the voters are unable to select those parts of a program which they favor and reject the other parts of the program.

    d. It is argued that the public sector (unlike the private sector) is inefficient because those employed there are offered no incentive to be efficient; there is no way to measure efficiency in the public sector; and government bureaucrats can join with the special-interest groups to block budget cuts or lobby for increased funding.

    e. Just as the private or market sector of the economy does not allocate resources perfectly, the public sector does not perform its functions perfectly; the imperfections of both sectors make it difficult to determine which sector will be more efficient in providing a good or service.

3. The financing of public goods and services through taxation also raises an important question about how the **tax burden** is allocated among people.

    a. The **benefits-received principle** and the **ability-to-pay principle** are widely used to determine how the tax bill should be apportioned among the economy's citizens.

    (1) The benefits-received principle suggests that those people who benefit most from public goods should pay for them.

    (2) The ability-to-pay principle states that taxes for the support of public goods should be tied to the incomes and wealth of people or their ability to pay.

    b. Taxes can be classified as **progressive, regressive,** or **proportional** according to the way in which the average tax rate changes as incomes change.

    (1) The average tax rate increases as income increases with a progressive tax, it decreases as income increases with a regressive tax, and it remains the same as income increases with a proportional tax.

    (2) In the United States, the personal income tax tends to be mildly progressive, the corporate income tax is proportional (unless the tax is partially passed to consumers, in which case it is partially regressive), and the payroll, sales, and property taxes are regressive.

4. **Tax incidence** and the **efficiency loss of a tax** are also important in discussion of the economics of taxation.

    a. The price elasticities of demand and supply determine the incidence of a sales or excise tax.

    (1) The imposition of such a tax on a product decreases the supply of the product and increases its

price. The amount of the price increase is the portion of the tax paid by the buyer; the seller pays the rest.

(2) The price elasticities of demand and supply for a product affect the portions paid by buyers and sellers: **(a)** the more *elastic* the demand, the greater the portion paid by the seller; **(b)** the more *inelastic* the demand, the smaller the portion paid by the seller; **(c)** the more *elastic* the supply, the greater the portion paid by the buyer; and **(d)** the more *inelastic* the supply, the smaller the portion paid by the buyer.

b. There is an efficiency loss of a tax. This loss occurs because there is a reduction in output, despite the fact that the marginal benefits of that output are greater than the marginal cost. Thus, the consumption and production of the taxed product have been reduced below the optimal level by the tax.

(1) The degree of the efficiency loss of a sales or an excise tax depends on the elasticities of supply and demand. Other things equal, the *greater* the elasticity of supply and demand, the *greater* the efficiency loss of a sales or an excise tax; consequently, the total tax burden to society may not be equal even though two taxes produce equal tax revenue.

(2) Other tax goals, however, may be more important than minimizing efficiency losses from taxes. These goals may include redistributing income or reducing negative externalities.

c. A tax levied on one person or group of persons may be shifted partially or completely to another person or group; and to the extent that a tax can be shifted or passed on through lower prices paid or higher prices received, its incidence is passed on to others. Table 31.2 in the text summarizes the probable shifting and incidence of the personal income tax, corporate income tax, general sales tax, specific excise taxes, and property taxes.

d. The overall U.S. tax structure is only slightly progressive and has little effect on the distribution of income because progressive taxes are generally offset by regressive taxes; however, estimates of the progressivity of the tax system depend on the assumed incidence of various taxes and transfer payments made by governments to reduce income inequality in the United States.

■ HINTS AND TIPS

1. The first part of the chapter presents **public choice theory,** but this theory has many practical applications to politics. As you read about the reasons for inefficient voting outcomes, the influence of special-interest groups, political logrolling, the median-voter model, rent-seeking behavior, limited and bundled choices, and government failures, see if you can apply the ideas to current public issues at the local, state, or Federal level. Also ask your instructor for current examples of the ideas from public choice theory.

2. Remember that what happens to the **average tax rate** as income increases determines whether a tax is progressive, regressive, or proportional. The average tax rate increases for progressive taxes, decreases for

regressive taxes, and remains the same for proportional taxes as income increases.

3. This chapter applies supply, demand, and elasticity concepts to taxation issues. Chapter 20 is worth checking to review your understanding of elasticity. Figure 31.5 and the related discussion in the text are crucially important for understanding the efficiency loss from a tax.

■ IMPORTANT TERMS

public choice theory	benefits-received principle
logrolling	ability-to-pay principle
paradox of voting	progressive tax
median-voter model	regressive tax
government failure	proportional tax
special-interest effect	tax incidence
rent seeking	efficiency loss of a tax

SELF-TEST

■ FILL-IN QUESTIONS

1. Many collective decisions are made on the basis of (minority, majority) _____ voting. One problem with this voting system is that it results in (efficient, inefficient) _____ voting outcomes because it fails to incorporate the strength of (individual, majority) _____ preferences. Voters may defeat a proposal even though the total costs are (less than, greater than) _____ the total benefits, or they might accept a proposal even though the total costs are _____ the total benefits.

2. The voting problem might be resolved or reversed through the influence of (interest, social) _____ groups or through political (primaries, logrolling) _____.

3. Another problem with this voting system occurs in a situation in which the public may not be able to rank its preferences with consistency; this is called the (fallacy, paradox) _____ of voting.

4. There are also insights into majority voting based on the (motor-voter, median-voter) _____ model, whereby the person holding the (lower, middle, upper) _____ position is likely to determine the outcome of an election.

5. When governments use resources to attempt to solve problems and the employment of these resources (does, does not) _____ result in solutions to these problems, there has been (market, government)

_____ failure. This means that there are shortcomings in government that promote economic (efficiency, inefficiency) _____.

6. One reason for this type of failure is that there can be a special-interest effect whereby a (large, small) _____ number of people benefit from a government program at the expense of a _____ number of persons who individually suffer (large, small) _____ losses.

7. Inefficiencies can also be caused by an appeal to government for special benefits at taxpayers' or someone else's expense that is called (revealed preferences, rent-seeking behavior) _____.

8. Another reason for the failure is that the benefits from a government program or project are often (clear, hidden) _____ to citizens or groups, but the costs are frequently _____ when legislation is passed or programs are funded.

9. There can also be inefficiencies in government because voters or elected representatives have to accept political choices that are (limited, unlimited) _____ and (bundled, unbundled) _____, which means government legislation forces voters or elected representatives to take bad programs with the good programs.

10. The incentives for economic efficiency tend to be stronger in the (private, public) _____ sector because there is a profit incentive in the _____ sector but not a similar incentive in the (private, public) _____ sector. As a result, there tends to be (more, less) _____ government bureaucracy and _____ efficient use of scarce resources.

11. Although the public sector can experience (market, government) _____ failure, the private sector can also experience _____ failure, and thus both government and markets can be considered (perfect, imperfect) _____ economic institutions.

12. The tax philosophy that asserts that households and businesses should purchase public goods and services in about the same way as private goods and services are bought is the (ability-to-pay, benefits-received) _____ principle of taxation, but the tax philosophy that the tax burden should be based on a person's wealth or income is the _____ principle of taxation.

13. If the average tax rate remains constant as income increases, the tax is (regressive, progressive, proportional) _____. If the average tax rate decreases as income increases, the tax is _____. If the average tax rate increases as income increases, the tax is (regressive, progressive, proportional) _____.

14. In the United States, the Federal personal income tax is (regressive, progressive, proportional) _____, but sales taxes, property taxes, and payroll taxes are _____. If corporate shareholders bear the burden of the corporate income tax, then it is (regressive, progressive, proportional) _____, but if part of the tax is passed on to consumers in higher prices, then the tax is _____.

15. The person or group who ends up paying a tax is called the tax (avoidance, incidence) _____. When an excise tax is placed on a product, the supply curve will (increase, decrease) _____, or shift to the (right, left) _____. The amount the product price rises as a result of the tax is the portion of the tax burden borne by (buyers, sellers) _____, and the difference between the original price and the after-tax price is the portion of the tax burden borne by _____.

16. The incidence of an excise tax primarily depends on the (price, income) _____ elasticity of demand and of supply. The buyer's portion of the tax is larger the (more, less) _____ elastic the demand and the _____ elastic the supply. The seller's portion of the tax is larger the (more, less) _____ elastic the demand and the _____ elastic the supply.

17. When an excise tax reduces the consumption and production of the taxed product below the level of economic efficiency, there is an efficiency (gain, loss) _____ of the tax. Other things equal, the greater the elasticity of supply and demand, the (greater, less) _____ the efficiency (gain, loss) _____ of the tax.

18. The incidence of the personal income tax is on (individuals, businesses) _____. There is less certainty about the incidence of the corporate income tax because some economists argue that the tax shifts to (businesses, consumers) _____ while other economists argue that it is shifted to _____.

19. The incidence of the sales tax is generally shifted to the (sellers, buyers) _____ of the product, and with excise taxes, if the demand for a product is inelastic, the tax incidence will be shifted to the _____. In the case of the property tax, the incidence of the tax for owner-occupied housing is borne by (owners, government) _____ and with renter-occupied housing it is borne by (owners, renters) _____. In the case of business property, the tax incidence is shifted to (businesses, consumers) _____.

20. The Federal tax system is generally (progressive, regressive, proportional) _____, state and local tax systems are generally _____, and overall the U.S. tax system is slightly _____, but these conditions depend on the incidence of the taxes. The tax system has a relatively (large, small) _____ effect on the distribution of income in the United States, but income inequality is (increased, decreased) _____ by transfer payments made by governments.

■ **TRUE–FALSE QUESTIONS**

Circle T if the statement is true, F if it is false.

1. Majority voting may produce outcomes that are economically inefficient because it fails to take into account the strength of preferences of the individual voter.   **T F**

2. Logrolling will always diminish economic efficiency in government.   **T F**

3. The paradox of voting is that majority voting will result in consistent choices that reflect the preferences of the public.   **T F**

4. The proposition that the person holding the middle position on an issue will likely determine the outcome of an election is suggested by the median-voter model.   **T F**

5. There is a failure in the public sector whenever a governmental program or activity has been expanded to the level at which the marginal social cost exceeds the marginal social benefit.   **T F**

6. Those concerned with public choice theory argue that the special-interest effect tends to reduce government sector failures because the pressures exerted on government by one special-interest group are offset by the pressures brought to bear by other special-interest groups.   **T F**

7. The appeal to government for special benefits at taxpayers' or someone else's expense is called rent seeking.   **T F**

8. When the costs of programs are hidden and the benefits are clear, vote-seeking politicians tend to reject economically justifiable programs.   **T F**

9. The limited choice of citizens refers to the inability of individual voters to select the precise bundle of social goods and services that will best satisfy the citizen's wants when he or she must vote for a candidate and the candidate's entire program.   **T F**

10. Critics of government contend that there is a tendency for government bureaucracy to justify continued employment by finding new problems to solve.   **T F**

11. When comparing government with markets, government is imperfect, whereas markets are perfect in efficiently allocating resources.   **T F**

12. The chief difficulty in applying the benefits-received principle of taxation is determining who receives the benefit of many of the goods and services that government supplies.   **T F**

13. The state and Federal taxes on gasoline are good examples of taxes levied on the benefits-received principle.   **T F**

14. The ability-to-pay principle of taxation states that those with greater incomes should be taxed less, absolutely and relatively, than those with lesser incomes.   **T F**

15. A tax is progressive when the average tax rate decreases as income increases.   **T F**

16. A general sales tax is considered a proportional tax with respect to income.   **T F**

17. A payroll (Social Security) tax is regressive.   **T F**

18. When an excise tax is placed on a product bought and sold in a competitive market, the portion of the tax borne by the seller equals the amount of the tax less the rise in the price of product due to the tax.   **T F**

19. The more elastic the demand for a good, the greater the portion of an excise tax on the good borne by the seller.   **T F**

20. The efficiency loss of an excise tax is the gain in net benefits for the producers from the increase in the price of the product.   **T F**

21. The degrees of efficiency loss from an excise tax vary from market to market and depend on the elasticities of supply and demand.   **T F**

22. The evidence is certain that in the case of the corporate income tax the incidence is borne by the businesses and not consumers.   **T F**

23. The probable incidence of the tax on rented apartment properties is on the landlord, not on the tenant.   **T F**

24. The Federal income tax system is progressive.   **T F**

25. The state and local tax structures are largely regressive.   **T F**

■ MULTIPLE-CHOICE QUESTIONS

Circle the letter that corresponds to the best answer.

1. Deficiencies in the processes used to make collective decisions of government and economic inefficiencies caused by government are the primary focus of
(a) public goods theory
(b) public choice theory
(c) the study of tax incidence
(d) the study of tax shifting

2. The trading of votes to secure favorable outcomes on decisions that otherwise would be adverse is referred to as
(a) logrolling, and it increases economic efficiency
(b) logrolling, and it may increase or decrease economic efficiency
(c) rent-seeking behavior, and it decreases economic efficiency
(d) rent-seeking behavior, and it may increase or decrease economic efficiency

Answer Questions 3, 4, 5, and 6 on the basis of the following table, which shows the rankings of the public goods by three voters: A, B, and C.

Public good	Voter A	Voter B	Voter C
Dam	1	2	3
School	3	1	2
Road	2	3	1

3. In a choice between a dam and the school,
(a) a majority of voters favor the dam
(b) a majority of voters favor the school
(c) a majority of voters favor both the dam and the school
(d) there is no majority of votes for either the dam or the school

4. In a choice between a road and a dam,
(a) a majority of voters favor the dam
(b) a majority of voters favor the road
(c) a majority of voters favor both the dam and the road
(d) there is no majority of votes for either the road or the dam

5. In a choice between a school and a road,
(a) a majority of voters favor the road
(b) a majority of voters favor the school
(c) a majority of voters favor both the road and the school
(d) there is no majority of votes for either the road or the school

6. What do the rankings in the table indicate about choices made under majority rule? Majority voting in this case
(a) reflects irrational preferences
(b) produces inconsistent choices
(c) produces consistent choices in spite of irrational preferences
(d) results in economically efficient outcomes because they have been influenced by special interests

7. The idea that the person holding the middle position will in a sense determine the outcome of an election is suggested by the
(a) rent-seeking behavior
(b) paradox of voting
(c) median-voter model
(d) special-interest effect

8. Actions that groups take to seek government legislation that puts tariffs on foreign products to limit foreign competition or that gives tax breaks to specific corporations would best be an example of
(a) how the median-voter model works
(b) how political choices are bundled
(c) rent-seeking behavior
(d) the paradox of voting

9. It is difficult to determine whether provision for a particular good or service should be assigned to the private or public sector of the economy because the
(a) institutions in both sectors function efficiently
(b) markets function efficiently and the agencies of government perform imperfectly
(c) markets are faulty and government agencies function with much greater efficiency
(d) institutions in both sectors are imperfect

10. Which is true of the ability-to-pay principle as applied in the United States?
(a) It is less widely applied than the benefits-received principle.
(b) Tax incidence is generally taken as the measure of the ability to pay.
(c) Gasoline taxes are based on this principle.
(d) As an individual's income increases, taxes paid increase both absolutely and relatively.

11. Taxing people according to the principle of ability to pay would be most characteristic of
(a) a payroll tax
(b) a value-added tax
(c) a general sales tax
(d) a progressive income tax

12. With a regressive tax, as income
(a) increases, the tax rate remains the same
(b) decreases, the tax rate decreases
(c) increases, the tax rate increases
(d) increases, the tax rate decreases

13. Which tends to be a progressive tax in the United States?
(a) income tax
(b) property tax
(c) sales tax
(d) payroll tax

14. In a competitive market, the portion of an excise tax borne by a buyer is equal to the
(a) amount the price of the product rises as a result of the tax
(b) amount of the tax
(c) amount of the tax less the amount the price of the product rises as a result of the tax

(d) amount of the tax plus the amount the price of the product rises as a result of the tax

15. Which statement is correct?

(a) The more elastic the supply, the greater the portion of an excise tax borne by the seller.

(b) The more elastic the demand, the greater the portion of an excise tax borne by the seller.

(c) The more inelastic the supply, the greater the portion of an excise tax borne by the buyer.

(d) The more inelastic the demand, the greater the portion of an excise tax borne by the seller.

Answer Questions 16, 17, 18, and 19 based on the following graph of an excise tax imposed by government.

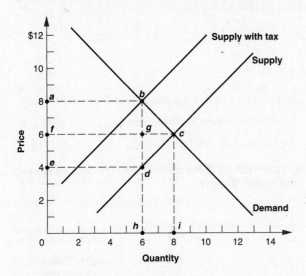

16. What is the amount of the excise tax paid by the seller in terms of price per unit sold?

(a) $1

(b) $2

(c) $3

(d) $4

17. The amount of the excise tax paid by consumers is

(a) $2

(b) $6

(c) $12

(d) $16

18. The tax revenue for government is represented by area

(a) *abde*

(b) *abgf*

(c) *fgde*

(d) *abcde*

19. The efficiency loss of the tax is represented by area

(a) *bgc*

(b) *bdc*

(c) *abcf*

(d) *hbci*

20. The efficiency loss of an excise tax is

(a) greater, the greater the elasticity of supply and demand

(b) greater, the less the elasticity of supply and demand

(c) less, the greater the elasticity of supply and demand

(d) not affected by the elasticity of supply and demand

21. If government imposes a tax on wine to shift the market supply to reduce the amount of resources allocated to wine, then the primary purpose of this tax is to

(a) redistribute income

(b) improve tax progressivity

(c) reduce negative externalities

(d) minimize efficiency losses

22. The probable incidence of a sales tax is borne by

(a) government units that collect the tax

(b) businesses that make the product

(c) businesses that sell the product

(d) consumers who buy the product

23. Which tax is the most difficult to shift to others?

(a) personal income tax

(b) corporate income tax

(c) specific excise taxes

(d) business property taxes

24. Which of the following is most likely to pay the incidence of a property tax on a business property that sells a consumer product?

(a) consumers of the product

(b) the business that produces the product

(c) government that taxes the property

(d) resource suppliers to the business

25. The Federal tax system is

(a) proportional, while state and local tax structures are largely progressive

(b) progressive, while state and local tax structures are largely regressive

(c) regressive, while state and local tax structures are largely proportional

(d) proportional, while state and local tax structures are largely regressive

■ **PROBLEMS**

1. The following table shows the demand and supply schedules for copra in the New Hebrides Islands.

Quantity demanded (pounds)	Price (per pound)	Before-tax quantity supplied (pounds)	After-tax quantity supplied (pounds)
150	$4.60	900	_____
200	4.40	800	_____
250	4.20	700	_____
300	4.00	600	_____
350	3.80	500	_____
400	3.60	400	_____
450	3.40	300	0
500	3.20	200	0
550	3.00	100	0

a. Before a tax is imposed on copra, its equilibrium

price is $_____.

b. The government of New Hebrides now imposes an excise tax of $.60 per pound on copra. Complete the after-tax supply schedule in the right-hand column of the table.

c. After the imposition of the tax, the equilibrium price

of copra is $_____.

d. Of the $.60 tax, the amount borne by

(1) the buyer is $_____ or _____%.

(2) the seller is $_____ or _____%.

2. On the following graph, draw a perfectly elastic demand curve and a normal upsloping supply curve for a product. Now impose an excise tax on the product, and draw the new supply curve that would result.

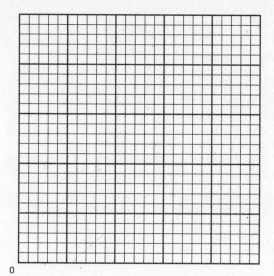

0

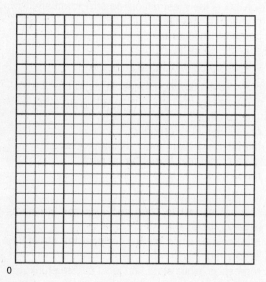

0

a. As a consequence of the tax, the price of the

product has _____.

b. It can be concluded that when demand is perfectly

elastic, the buyer bears _____ of the tax

and the seller bears _____ of the tax.

c. Thus the *more* elastic the demand, the _____ is the portion of the tax borne by the buyer and the

_____ is the portion borne by the seller.

d. But the *less* elastic the demand, the _____ is the portion borne by the buyer and the

_____ is the portion borne by the seller.

3. In the graph at the top of the next column, draw a perfectly elastic supply curve and a normal downsloping demand curve. Impose an excise tax on the product, and draw the new supply curve.

a. As a result of the tax, the price of the product has

_____.

b. From this it can be concluded that when supply

is perfectly elastic, the buyer bears _____ of

the tax and the seller bears _____ of the tax.

c. Thus the *more* elastic the supply, the _____ is the portion of the tax borne by the buyer and the

_____ is the portion borne by the seller.

d. But the less elastic the supply, the _____ is the portion borne by the buyer and the

_____ is the portion borne by the seller.

4. The table at the top of page 361 shows five levels of taxable income and the amount that would be paid at each of the five levels under three tax laws: **A, B,** and **C.** Compute for each of the three tax laws the average rate of taxation at each of the four remaining income levels. Indicate whether the tax is regressive, proportional, progressive, or some combination thereof.

5. Assume a state government levies a 4% sales tax on all consumption expenditures. Consumption expenditures at six income levels are shown in the following table.

Income	Consumption expenditures	Sales tax paid	Average tax rate, %
$ 5000	$5000	$200	4.0
6000	5800	232	3.9
7000	6600	_____	
8000	7400	_____	_____
9000	8200	_____	_____
10,000	9000	_____	_____

a. Compute the sales tax paid at the next four incomes.

b. Compute the average tax rate at these incomes.

c. Using income as the tax base, the sales tax is a

_____ tax.

Income	Tax A		Tax B		Tax C	
	Tax paid	Av. tax rate	Tax paid	Av. tax rate	Tax paid	Av. tax rate
$ 1500	45.00	3%	30.00	2%	135.00	9%
3000	90.00	_____	90.00	_____	240.00	_____
5000	150.00	_____	150.00	_____	350.00	_____
7500	225.00	_____	187.50	_____	450.00	_____
10,000	300.00	_____	200.00	_____	500.00	_____
Type of tax:	_____		_____		_____	

■ SHORT ANSWER AND ESSAY QUESTIONS

1. Why has there been dissatisfaction with government decisions and the economic efficiency in government?

2. What is the relationship between majority voting and the efficiency of outcomes from an election? How do special-interest groups or the use of logrolling influence the efficiency of outcomes?

3. Why is there a paradox with majority voting? Do the outcomes from majority voting suggest that voters are irrational in their preferences?

4. Describe how median voters influence the election results and debates over public issues. What are two important implications of the median voter model?

5. Explain what is meant by "government failure." Is it related to market failure and externalities?

6. Public choice theory suggests that there are a number of reasons for government failures. What are the reasons? Explain how each would tend to result in the inefficient allocation of the economy's resources.

7. It is generally agreed that "national defense must lie in the public sector while wheat production can best be accomplished in the private sector." Why is there no agreement on where many other goods or services should be produced?

8. What are the two basic philosophies for apportioning the tax burden in the United States? Explain each one.

9. What are the difficulties encountered in putting the two basic tax philosophies into practice?

10. Explain the difference among progressive, regressive, and proportional taxes. Which types of taxes fall into each of these categories?

11. Explain the effect the imposition of an excise tax has on the supply of a product that is bought and sold in a competitive market.

12. Illustrate with a supply and demand graph what part of an excise tax is passed on to the buyer and what part is borne by the seller. What determines the division of the tax between the buyer and the seller?

13. What is the relationship between the price elasticity of demand for a commodity and the portion of an excise tax on a commodity borne by the buyer and the seller?

14. What is the relationship between the price elasticity of supply and the incidence of an excise tax?

15. How does an excise tax produce an efficiency loss for society? Explain and illustrate with a supply and demand graph.

16. How is the efficiency loss from an excise tax affected by the elasticity of supply or demand? All else equal, shouldn't the total tax burden be equal for two taxes that produce equal revenues?

17. Describe the probable incidence of the personal income tax, the sales tax, and the excise tax.

18. For whom is the tax shifted, and on whom is the tax incidence for the corporate income tax?

19. Explain whether businesses or consumers are likely to bear the incidence of a corporate income tax or a business property tax.

20. What general conclusion can be drawn about the progressivity or regressivity of the Federal tax system, taxation by state and local governments, and the overall U.S. tax system?

ANSWERS

Chapter 31 Public Choice Theory and the Economics of Taxation

FILL-IN QUESTIONS

1. majority, inefficient, individual, less than, greater than
2. interest, logrolling
3. paradox
4. median-voter, middle
5. does not, government, inefficiency
6. small, large, small
7. rent-seeking behavior
8. clear, hidden
9. limited, bundled
10. private, private, public, more, less
11. government, market, imperfect
12. benefits-received, ability-to-pay
13. proportional, regressive, progressive
14. progressive, regressive, proportional, regressive
15. incidence, decrease, left, buyers, sellers
16. price, less, more, more, less
17. loss, greater, loss
18. individuals, businesses, consumers (*either order for last two*)
19. buyers, buyers, owners, renters, consumers
20. progressive, regressive, progressive, small, decreased

TRUE–FALSE QUESTIONS

1. T, pp. 580–582
2. F, p. 582
3. F, pp. 582–583
4. T, p. 583
5. T, pp. 584–585
6. F, p. 584
7. T, pp. 584–585
8. F, p. 585
9. T, p. 585
10. T, pp. 585–586
11. F, p. 586
12. T, p. 587
13. T, p. 587
14. F, p. 587
15. F, p. 588
16. T, p. 588
17. T, p. 588
18. T, pp. 589–591
19. T, pp. 589–591
20. F, pp. 590–591
21. T, pp. 590–591
22. F, p. 592
23. F, pp. 592–593
24. T, p. 593
25. T, p. 594

MULTIPLE-CHOICE QUESTIONS

1. b, p. 580
2. b, p. 582
3. b, pp. 582–583
4. a, pp. 582–583
5. a, pp. 582–583
6. b, p. 583
7. c, p. 583
8. c, pp. 584–585
9. d, p. 586
10. d, p. 587
11. d, p. 587
12. d, p. 588
13. a, pp. 588–589
14. a, pp. 589–590
15. b, pp. 589–590
16. b, pp. 589–590
17. c, pp. 589–590
18. a, pp. 589–590
19. b, pp. 590–591
20. a, pp. 590–591
21. c, pp. 591–592
22. d, p. 592
23. a, pp. 592–593
24. a, pp. 592–593
25. b, pp. 593–594

PROBLEMS

1. *a.* $3.60; *b.* (reading down) 600, 500, 400, 300, 200, 100; *c.* $4.00; *d.* (1) $.40, 67, (2) $.20, 33
2. *a.* not changed; *b.* none, all; *c.* smaller, larger; *d.* larger, smaller
3. *a.* increased by the amount of the tax; *b.* all, none; *c.* larger, smaller; *d.* smaller, larger
4. Tax A: 3, 3, 3, 3, proportional; Tax B: 3, 3, 2.5, 2, combination; Tax C: 8, 7, 6, 5, regressive
5. *a.* $264, 296, 328, 360; *b.* 3.8, 3.7, 3.64, 3.6; *c.* regressive

SHORT ANSWER AND ESSAY QUESTIONS

1. p. 580
2. pp. 580–582
3. pp. 582–583
4. pp. 583–584
5. pp. 584–585
6. pp. 584–585
7. pp. 585–586
8. p. 587
9. pp. 587–588
10. pp. 588–589
11. pp. 589–590
12. pp. 589–590
13. pp. 589–590
14. pp. 589–590
15. pp. 590–591
16. pp. 590–591
17. p. 592
18. p. 592
19. pp. 592–593
20. pp. 593–594

Antitrust Policy and Regulation

Chapter 32 examines issues related to antitrust policy and the regulation of markets and society. These issues are important for you to study because they affect prices, economic efficiency, and economic welfare.

Over the years the Federal government has taken action to curb or limit the growth of monopolies in the United States through the passage of **antitrust laws** and the establishment of regulatory agencies. The *Sherman Act* of 1890 was the first major antitrust law. It was followed by other antitrust legislation and the creation of regulatory agencies and commissions.

The chapter discusses major antitrust issues and evaluates the effectiveness of **antitrust policy.** Several issues of interpretation address whether businesses should be judged for antitrust violations on the basis of monopoly behavior or structure and what should be the definition of the market. You will learn about the two conflicting perspectives on the enforcement of antitrust laws—activist and laissez-faire. The effectiveness of antitrust policy is also evaluated in the chapter based on such factors as the degree of the monopoly control, mergers, price fixing, price discrimination, and tying contracts.

Industrial regulation focuses on the control of natural monopolies so that they produce economic outcomes that benefit society. It is based on the public interest theory of regulation. This regulation by agencies and commissions has several problems of which you should be aware. One problem is that some of the regulated industries may not be natural monopolies at all and would be competitive industries if they were left unregulated. From this problem comes the legal cartel theory of regulation: Many industries want to be regulated so that competition among the firms will be reduced and the profits will increase.

Beginning in the 1970s, many industries in the United States underwent **deregulation.** These included the airline, trucking, banking, railroad, natural gas, television broadcasting, and telecommunications industries. The results generally show that this deregulation was beneficial for consumers and the efficiency of the economy. A more recent experience with deregulation occurred in the market for electricity. The outcomes from this experiment in deregulation have been less certain because of pricing problems in California.

Beginning in the early 1960s, new agencies and commissions began to engage in **social regulation** that differed from the regulation of the prices, services, and output provided by specific industries. This regulation focused on production conditions, product attributes, and production effects on society. This regulation increases product prices and indirectly reduces worker productivity, but supporters argue that the social benefits over time will exceed the costs. Critics contend that it is costly, often poorly conceived, and has negative secondary effects. The debate over the optimal level of social regulation is not easily resolved because the costs and benefits are difficult to measure. You should spend time understanding both sides of the issue.

■ **CHECKLIST**

When you have studied this chapter you should be able to

☐ State the purpose of antitrust policy.

☐ Discuss the historical background and rationale for antitrust laws and regulatory agencies.

☐ Describe the purpose and major provisions of the Sherman Act, Clayton Act, Federal Trade Commission Act, Wheeler-Lea Act, and Celler-Kefauver Act.

☐ Contrast the monopoly behavior view of the antitrust laws with the monopoly structure view using two landmark Supreme Court decisions.

☐ Explain the importance of market definition in the interpretation of antitrust laws.

☐ Compare and contrast the active antitrust perspective with the laissez-faire perspective.

☐ Describe the application of antitrust laws to monopoly.

☐ Distinguish among a horizontal, vertical, and conglomerate merger.

☐ Explain the concept of the Herfindahl index and its application to merger guidelines.

☐ Describe antitrust policy toward price fixing and price discrimination.

☐ Discuss the antitrust issue in tying contracts.

☐ Define a natural monopoly and cite two ways government controls natural monopolies.

☐ Explain the public interest theory of regulation.

☐ Describe two problems with industrial regulation by government agencies and commissions.

☐ Explain the legal cartel theory of regulation.

☐ Discuss the outcomes from deregulation of selected U.S. industries since the 1970s.

☐ State three distinguishing features of social regulation.

☐ Make a case for social regulation in terms of benefits and costs.

☐ Present a case against social regulation in terms of benefits and costs.

☐ Offer two economic reminders about social regulation.

■ CHAPTER OUTLINE

1. The basic purposes of *antitrust policy* are to restrict monopoly power, promote competition, and achieve allocative efficiency.

a. Following the Civil War, the expansion of the U.S. economy brought with it the creation of trusts (or monopolies) in many industries. The economic problem with monopolies is that they produce less output and charge higher prices than would be the case if their industries were more competitive. To control them, government has passed antitrust laws and created regulatory agencies.

b. The *Sherman Act* of 1890 was the first antitrust legislation. It made restraint of trade and monopolization criminal offenses.

c. The *Clayton Act* of 1914 outlawed price discrimination not based on cost, *tying contracts,* mergers that lessened competition, and *interlocking directorates.*

d. The *Federal Trade Commission Act* of 1914 established the *Federal Trade Commission (FTC)* to investigate unfair practices that might lead to the development of monopoly power. In 1938 this act was amended by the *Wheeler-Lea Act* to prohibit deceptive practices (including false and misleading advertising and misrepresentation of products).

e. The *Celler-Kefauver Act* of 1950 plugged a loophole in the Clayton Act and prohibited mergers that might lead to a substantial reduction in competition.

2. The effectiveness of antitrust laws in preventing monopoly and maintaining competition has depended on judicial interpretation of the laws and enforcement of these laws by Federal agencies.

a. Two issues arise in the judicial interpretation of the antitrust laws.

(1) Should a firm be judged on the basis of its monopoly structure or behavior? The *U.S. Steel case* of 1920, which came before the Supreme Court, applied the *rule of reason* and said that a firm should be judged on the basis of its behavior. The *Alcoa case* of 1945 judged a firm on the basis of its structure (large control of a market). The courts and most economists now use the rule of reason that bases antitrust action on market behavior, not structure.

(2) Should a broad or narrow definition of the market in which firms sell their products be used to judge monopoly power? In the 1956 *DuPont cellophane case,* the Court ruled that DuPont did not monopolize the industry because there were other types of packaging materials that could be used.

b. There are differences in political philosophies about whether antitrust enforcement should be more or less strictly enforced. The active antitrust perspective calls for enforcement of antitrust laws to stop illegal business activity, prevent anticompetitive mergers, and counter monopoly practices. The laissez-faire perspective contends that enforcement is largely unnecessary because market forces will control monopoly behavior and undermine monopoly positions.

c. A question can be raised about whether the antitrust laws have been effective regarding monopoly, mergers, price fixing, price discrimination, and tying contracts.

(1) For existing market structures, enforcement of antitrust laws has been lenient in general if the expansion of market share by a firm is reasonable. The Sherman Act, however, has still been invoked in several high profile cases in which anticompetitive practices were alleged (1982 AT&T and 2000 Microsoft cases).

(2) For *horizontal, vertical,* or *conglomerate mergers,* the application of the laws usually varies by the type of merger and the particulars of a case. Merger guidelines are based on the Herfindahl index (the sum of the squared values of market shares within an industry), but other factors, such as economies of scale, degree of foreign competition, and ease of entry, are considered.

(3) Prohibitions against price fixing are strictly enforced. These activities are viewed as *per se violations,* so even the attempt, and not the actual outcome, will bring legal action and penalties.

(4) Price discrimination is rarely challenged on antitrust grounds because in most cases it benefits consumers, but the practice can be challenged if the purpose is to reduce competition or block entry into a business.

(5) The laws against tying contracts that require a buyer to purchase other products or take certain actions as a condition of a sale have been strictly enforced.

(6) Overall, antitrust laws have not been very effective in breaking up monopolies or in preventing the growth of large oligopolies that have developed legally and because of market conditions. The laws have been effective against abusive or predatory monopolies. They have also been effective in blocking anticompetitive mergers, preventing price fixing, and restricting the use of tying contracts.

3. *Industrial regulation* occurs in some industries for economic reasons.

a. A *natural monopoly* exists if a single producer can provide a good or service for the entire market at a lower average cost (because of economies of scale) than several producers, making competition uneconomical. To achieve better economic outcomes from this situation, government may opt for public ownership of the business or public (industrial) regulation. The latter option is based on the *public interest theory of regulation* that calls for controlling the economic decisions of the monopoly producers to achieve lower costs and greater output benefits for the public.

b. The effectiveness of the regulation of business firms by regulatory agencies has been criticized for two main reasons.

(1) Regulation increases costs and leads to an inefficient allocation of resources and higher prices.

(2) Regulated monopolies get perpetuated over time and would be more competitive firms if they were not

regulated. Regulatory agencies contribute to the problem by protecting these industries, and these actions hurt the public and consumers.

c. The *legal cartel theory of regulation* holds that potentially competitive industries often want and support the regulation of their industries to increase their profits by limiting competition among firms. The government regulatory agency in essence creates a government-sponsored cartel in an industry.

4. Since the 1970s there has been *deregulation* of many industries in the United States: airline, trucking, banking, railroad, natural gas, electricity, television broadcasting, and communications. The overall evidence, however, shows that deregulation has been clearly positive because it has resulted in lower prices, lower costs of production, and increased output. It has also allowed for greater technological advances in many industries. There is less certainty about the positive outcomes from deregulation in electricity markets because of pricing problems in California and illegal manipulations of electricity supplies by some business firms.

5. *Social regulation* has developed since the 1960s and resulted in the creation of additional regulatory agencies that focus on production conditions, product qualities, and production effects on society.

a. Social regulation differs in three ways from industrial regulation: broader coverage of industries; more intrusion into the day-to-day production process; and rapid expansion into many areas.

b. Discussions about social regulation involve deciding whether there is an optimal level of such regulation. The costs and benefits are difficult to measure, so ideology often influences the debate over the proper amount of this regulation.

c. Supporters of social regulation contend it is needed to fight serious problems such as job and auto safety, environment pollution, product defects, and discrimination. Although such regulation is costly, the social benefits would exceed the costs over time, if they could be easily measured. Defenders point to many specific benefits resulting from such regulation.

d. Critics argue that this social regulation is inefficient because the regulations are poorly drawn and targeted. The rules and regulations are also often made based on limited and inadequate information. In addition, there are unintended secondary effects from the regulation that boost product costs. Regulatory agencies tend to attract "overzealous" workers who dislike the market system and advocate government intervention as the only solution.

e. Two reminders are needed in the debate over social regulation.

(1) Supporters need to remember that there is no "free lunch," and that social regulation increases product prices, may slow product innovation, and may lessen competition.

(2) Defenders need to remember that the market system has flaws that sometimes need to be addressed by government through social regulation

and that by doing so, government creates continuing support of the operation of the market system.

■ HINTS AND TIPS

1. The first section of the chapter discusses several Federal antitrust laws. After looking at this section, many students ask, "Am I expected to know these laws?" Yes, you should have an understanding of these laws. A related question asked is, "Why should I know them?" To examine a current economic issue, you need to know how the problem arose, what actions have been taken over time to solve it, and what the outcomes are. Many of these major antitrust laws are enforced to some degree today and may affect a business for which you may work.

2. The *Herfindahl index* was first introduced in Chapter 25. Reread that material if you cannot remember what the index is. In Chapter 32 you will learn how the index is used for merger guidelines.

3. This chapter discusses controversies about many topics—antitrust policy, industrial regulation, deregulation, and social regulation. To help understand these controversies, make a table showing the pro and con positions for each issue. See problem 4 for an example.

■ IMPORTANT TERMS

antitrust policy	rule of reason
industrial regulation	Alcoa case
social regulation	DuPont cellophane case
Sherman Act	horizontal merger
Clayton Act	vertical merger
tying contracts	conglomerate merger
interlocking directorate	per se violations
Federal Trade Commission Act	natural monopoly
cease-and-desist order	public interest theory of regulation
Wheeler-Lea Act	legal cartel theory of regulation
Celler-Kefauver Act	
U.S. Steel case	

SELF-TEST

■ FILL-IN QUESTIONS

1. Laws and government actions designed to prevent monopoly and promote competition are referred to as (industrial regulation, antitrust policy) _____.
Actions taken to control a firm's prices within selected industries are referred to as (social, industrial)

_____ regulation whereas establishing the conditions under which goods are produced, monitoring the physical characteristics of products, and reducing the negative effects of production fall under the category of

_____ regulation.

2. The two techniques of Federal control that have been adopted as substitutes for, or to maintain competition in, markets are

   a. _____

   b. _____

3. Antitrust legislation in 1890 that made it illegal to monopolize or restrain trade between the states or between nations was the (Clayton, Sherman) _____ Act. Legislation passed in 1914 that prohibited such practices as price discrimination, acquisition of the stock of corporations to reduce competition, tying contracts, and interlocking directorates was the (Clayton, Sherman) _____ Act.

4. The 1914 act that had set up an agency to investigate unfair competitive practices, hold public hearings on such complaints, and issue cease-and-desist orders was the (Clayton, Federal Trade Commission) _____ Act.

5. The 1938 antitrust act that had the effect of prohibiting false and misleading advertising was the (Celler-Kefauver, Wheeler-Lea) _____ Act, while the act that plugged a loophole in the Clayton Act by banning the acquisition of assets of one firm by another when it would lessen competition was the _____ Act.

6. When the judicial courts used the rule of reason to evaluate industrial concentration by U.S. Steel in 1920, they were judging the firm on the basis of its market (behavior, structure) _____, but when the courts made a decision to break up Alcoa in 1945, they were judging the firm on the basis of its market _____. Since 1945, the courts have returned to evaluating a firm on the basis of its market (behavior, structure) _____.

7. One major issue of interpretation in antitrust law is the definition of a market. The firm's market share will appear small if the courts define a market (narrowly, broadly) _____, but the firm's market share will appear large if the courts define a market share _____. In 1956, the courts ruled that although DuPont sold nearly all the cellophane produced in the United States, it (did, did not) _____ dominate the market for flexible packaging materials.

8. The active antitrust perspective is that antitrust laws need to be (strictly, loosely) _____ enforced to promote (monopoly, competition) _____ in business. The laissez-faire perspective contends that enforcement is largely (necessary, unnecessary) _____ because monopoly power and control can be countered by (government, markets) _____.

9. A merger between two competitors selling similar products in the same market is a (vertical, horizontal, conglomerate) _____ merger; a _____ merger occurs among firms at different stages in the production process of the same industry; a _____ merger results when a firm in one industry is purchased by a firm in an unrelated industry.

10. The (Sherman, Herfindahl) _____ index is used as a guideline for mergers. An industry of only four firms, each with a 25 percent market share, has an index score of (2500, 10,000) _____ but if the industry was a pure monopoly with only one firm its index score would be _____.

11. If a firm attempts to fix prices, even if the attempt were not effective, it would be an example of a (tying contract, per se violation) _____ under antitrust laws; if a producer will only sell a desired product on condition that the buyer acquire other products, it would be an example of a _____ under antitrust laws. In both cases, the laws are (loosely, strictly) _____ enforced.

12. Most economists conclude that, overall, U.S. antitrust policy (has, has not) _____ been effective in achieving its goal of promoting competition and efficiency and that the application of antitrust laws _____ been effective against predatory and abusive monopoly.

13. A natural monopoly exists when a single firm is able to supply the entire market at a (higher, lower) _____ average cost than a number of competing firms. In the United States, many of these natural monopolies are controlled by (business cartels, regulatory commissions) _____.

14. The two major criticisms of regulation of industries by a government agency or commission are
   a. The regulated firms have no incentive to lower their costs because the commission will then require them to (raise, lower) _____ their prices, and because the prices they are allowed to charge are based on the value of their capital equipment, firms tend to make uneconomical substitutions of (labor, capital) _____ for _____.
   b. Regulation has been applied to industries that (are, are not) _____ natural monopolies, which in the absence of regulation would be more competitive.

15. The public interest theory of regulation assumes that the objective of regulating an industry is to (encourage, discourage) _____ the abuses of monopoly power. An alternative theory assumes firms wish to be regulated because it enables them to form, and the regulatory commission helps them to create, a profitable and legal (conglomerate, cartel) _____.

16. The available evidence indicates that deregulation of many industries that began in the 1970s generally resulted in (decreased, increased) _____ prices because _____ competition among firms led to _____ costs and _____ output.

17. The Food and Drug Administration would be an example of a Federal regulatory commission engaged in (social, industrial) _____ regulation and the Federal Communications Commission would be an example of an agency engaged in _____ regulation.

18. Compared with industrial regulation, social regulation applies to (more, fewer) _____ firms, affects day-to-day production to a (greater, lesser) _____ extent, and has expanded more (rapidly, slowly) _____.

19. It should be remembered by supporters of social regulation that there is "no free lunch" because it can (increase, decrease) _____ product prices and _____ worker productivity, and it also may _____ the rate of innovation.

20. It should be remembered by critics of social regulation that it can be (anti-, pro-) _____ capitalist because when social problems in the market are addressed, the public support for the market system is (increased, decreased) _____.

■ **TRUE–FALSE QUESTIONS**

Circle T if the statement is true, F if it is false.

1. The basic purposes of antitrust policy are to prevent monopolization, promote competition, and achieve allocative efficiency. **T F**

2. The issue of antitrust arose from the emergence of trusts and monopolies in the U.S. economy in the two decades *before* the U.S. Civil War. **T F**

3. The economic problem with monopolists is that they charge a lower price and produce more output than if their industries were competitive. **T F**

4. The Clayton Act declares that price discrimination, tying contracts, stock acquisitions between corporations, and interlocking directorates are illegal when their effect is to reduce competition. **T F**

5. The Federal Trade Commission is in charge of stimulating more international trade between domestic and foreign producers. **T F**

6. The Celler-Kefauver Act of 1950 prohibits one firm from acquiring the assets of another firm when the result is to lessen competition. **T F**

7. In 1920 the courts applied the rule of reason to the U.S. Steel Corporation and decided that the corporation possessed monopoly power and had unreasonably restrained trade. **T F**

8. Those who believe an industry should be judged on the basis of its structure contend that any industry with a monopolistic structure must behave like a monopolist. **T F**

9. The courts broadly defined the market for cellophane in the DuPont cellophane case of 1956. **T F**

10. There is only one perspective on the enforcement of antitrust laws, and it calls for strict enforcement of all laws. **T F**

11. A horizontal merger is a merger between firms at different stages of the production process. **T F**

12. The Herfindahl index is the sum of the squared values of the market shares within an industry. **T F**

13. To gain a conviction under *per se violations,* the party making the charge must show that the conspiracy to fix prices actually succeeded or caused damage. **T F**

14. There is substantial evidence that antitrust policy has *not* been effective in identifying and prosecuting price fixing by businesses. **T F**

15. Industrial regulation consists of regulation of the conditions under which products are made, the impact of products on society, and the physical qualities of the products. **T F**

16. Public ownership rather than public regulation has been the primary means used in the United States to ensure that the behavior of natural monopolists is socially acceptable. **T F**

17. The rationale underlying the public interest theory of regulation of natural monopolies is to allow the consumers of their goods or services to benefit from the economies of scale. **T F**

18. Regulated firms, because the prices they are allowed to charge enable them to earn a "fair" return over their costs, have a strong incentive to reduce their costs. **T F**

19. From the perspective of the legal cartel theory of regulation, some industries want to be regulated by government. **T F**

20. Deregulation of industries since the 1970s has resulted in large gains in economic efficiency for the U.S. economy. **T F**

21. The marginal costs and benefits of social regulation are easy to measure for determining the optimal level of such regulation. **T F**

22. Those who favor social regulation believe that the expenditures on it are needed to obtain a hospitable, sustainable, and just society. **T F**

23. Critics of social regulation argue that its marginal costs exceed its marginal benefits. **T F**

24. The likely effect of social regulation is that it lowers product prices, raises worker productivity, and increases product innovation. **T F**

25. Social regulation can contribute to public support for a market system by addressing production and consumption problems arising from the system. **T F**

■ MULTIPLE-CHOICE QUESTIONS

Circle the letter that corresponds to the best answer.

1. Which term describes the laws and government actions designed to prevent monopoly and promote competition?
(a) industrial regulation
(b) social regulation
(c) legal cartel policy
(d) antitrust policy

2. Which law stated that contracts and conspiracies in restraint of trade, monopolies, attempts to monopolize, and conspiracies to monopolize are illegal?
(a) Sherman Act
(b) Clayton Act
(c) Federal Trade Commission Act
(d) Wheeler-Lea Act

3. Which act specifically outlawed tying contracts and interlocking directorates?
(a) Sherman Act
(b) Clayton Act
(c) Federal Trade Commission Act
(d) Wheeler-Lea Act

4. Which act has given the Federal Trade Commission the task of preventing false and misleading advertising and the misrepresentation of products?
(a) Sherman Act
(b) Clayton Act
(c) Federal Trade Commission Act
(d) Wheeler-Lea Act

5. Which act banned the acquisition of a firm's assets by a competing firm when the acquisition would tend to reduce competition?
(a) Celler-Kefauver Act
(b) Wheeler-Lea Act
(c) Clayton Act
(d) Federal Trade Commission Act

6. The argument that an industry that is highly concentrated will behave like a monopolist and the Alcoa court case of 1945 would both be support for the case that the application of antitrust laws should be based on industry
(a) behavior
(b) structure
(c) efficiency
(d) rule of reason

7. If the market is defined broadly to include a wide range of somewhat similar products, then
(a) firms in the industry will be able to behave as monopolists
(b) firms in the industry will follow the rule of reason
(c) a firm's market share will appear large
(d) a firm's market share will appear small

8. Which perspective holds that the enforcement of antitrust laws is largely unnecessary, especially as related to monopoly, because market forces will counter monopoly?
(a) concentration perspective
(b) active antitrust perspective
(c) relevant market perspective
(d) laissez-faire perspective

9. The merger of a firm in one industry with a firm in an unrelated industry is called a
(a) horizontal merger
(b) vertical merger
(c) secondary merger
(d) conglomerate merger

10. Which is most likely to be the focus of antitrust law scrutiny and enforcement?
(a) a publicly regulated utility
(b) a conglomerate merger
(c) a vertical merger
(d) a horizontal merger

11. An industry has four firms, each with a market share of 25%. There is no foreign competition, entry into the industry is difficult, and no firm is on the verge of bankruptcy. If two of the firms in the industry sought to merge, this action would most likely be opposed by the government because the new Herfindahl index for the industry would be
(a) 2000 and the merger would increase the index by 1000
(b) 2500 and the merger would increase the index by 1000
(c) 3750 and the merger would increase the index by 1250
(d) 5000 and the merger would increase the index by 1250

12. When the government or another party making a charge can show that there was a conspiracy to fix prices, even if the conspiracy did not succeed, this would be an example of
(a) a tying contract
(b) a per se violation
(c) the rule of reason
(d) the legal cartel theory

13. Antitrust laws have been most effective in
(a) breaking up monopolies
(b) prosecuting price fixing in business
(c) expanding industrial concentration
(d) blocking entry of foreign competition in domestic markets

14. If a movie distributor forced theaters to "buy" projection rights to a full package of films as a condition of

showing a blockbuster movie, then this would be an example of
- **(a)** price fixing
- **(b)** a tying contract
- **(c)** a per se violation
- **(d)** an interlocking directorate

15. An example of a government organization involved primarily in industrial regulation would be the
- **(a)** Federal Communications Commission
- **(b)** Food and Drug Administration
- **(c)** Occupational Safety and Health Administration
- **(d)** Environmental Protection Agency

16. Legislation designed to regulate natural monopolies would be based on which theory of regulation?
- **(a)** cartel
- **(b)** public interest
- **(c)** rule of reason
- **(d)** public ownership

17. Those who oppose the regulation of industry by regulatory agencies contend that
- **(a)** many of the regulated industries are natural monopolies
- **(b)** the regulatory agencies may favor industry because they are often staffed by former industry executives
- **(c)** regulation contributes to an increase in the number of mergers in industries
- **(d)** regulation helps moderate costs and improves efficiency in the production of a good or service produced by the regulated industry

18. The legal cartel theory of regulation
- **(a)** would allow the forces of demand and supply to determine the rates (prices) of the good or service
- **(b)** would attempt to protect the public from abuses of monopoly power
- **(c)** assumes that the regulated industry wishes to be regulated
- **(d)** assumes that both the demand for and supply of the good or service produced by the regulated industry are perfectly inelastic

19. Deregulation of previously regulated industries in the United States has resulted in
- **(a)** higher prices, higher costs, and decreased output
- **(b)** higher prices and costs, but increased output
- **(c)** lower prices and costs, but decreased output
- **(d)** lower prices, lower costs, and increased output

20. Which is a concern of social regulation?
- **(a)** the prices charged for goods
- **(b)** the service provided to the public
- **(c)** the conditions under which goods are manufactured
- **(d)** the impact on business profits from the production of goods

21. A major difference between industrial regulation and social regulation is that social regulation
- **(a)** covers fewer industries across the economy

- **(b)** has expanded slowly and waned in recent years
- **(c)** is targeted at the prices charged, the costs of production, and amount of profit
- **(d)** focuses on product design, employment conditions, and the production process

22. Which government organization is primarily engaged in social regulation?
- **(a)** the Federal Trade Commission
- **(b)** the Interstate Commerce Commission
- **(c)** the Environmental Protection Agency
- **(d)** the Federal Energy Regulatory Commission

23. Supporters of social regulation contend that
- **(a)** there is a pressing need to reduce the number of mergers in U.S. business
- **(b)** the presence of natural monopoly requires strong regulatory action by government
- **(c)** the social benefits will exceed the social costs
- **(d)** there are no social costs associated with it

24. A criticism of social regulation by its opponents is that it
- **(a)** is a strong procapitalist force
- **(b)** will decrease the rate of innovation in the economy
- **(c)** will increase the amount of price fixing among businesses
- **(d)** will require too long a time to achieve its objectives

25. The captions for two reminders for proponents and opponents of social regulation are
- **(a)** "there is no free lunch" and "less government is not always better than more"
- **(b)** "the rule of reason will prevail" and "restraint of trade will not be tolerated by government"
- **(c)** "the public interest will win over the powerful" and the "legal cartel will be broken by government"
- **(d)** "demand the lowest price" and "protect the greatest number"

■ **PROBLEMS**

1. Following is a list of Federal laws. Next is a series of provisions found in Federal laws. Match each law with the appropriate provision by placing the appropriate capital letter after each provision.
- **A.** Sherman Act
- **B.** Clayton Act
- **C.** Federal Trade Commission Act
- **D.** Wheeler-Lea Act
- **E.** Celler-Kefauver Act

a. Established a commission to investigate and prevent unfair methods of competition _____
b. Made monopoly and restraint of trade illegal and criminal _____
c. Prohibited the acquisition of the assets of a firm by another firm when such an acquisition would lessen competition _____

d. Had the effect of prohibiting false and misleading advertising and the misrepresentation of products

_____

e. Clarified the Sherman Act and outlawed specific techniques or devices used to create monopolies and restrain trade

_____

2. Indicate with the letter **L** for leniently and the letter **S** for strictly how the antitrust laws tend to be applied to each of the following.

a. Vertical mergers in which each of the merging firms sells a small portion of the total output of its industry

_____

b. Price fixing by a firm in an industry _____

c. Conglomerate mergers _____

d. Existing market structures in which no firm sells 60% or more of the total output of its industry _____

e. Horizontal mergers in which the merged firms would sell a large portion of the total output of their industry and no firm is on the verge of bankruptcy _____

f. Action by firms in an industry to divide up sales

_____

g. Horizontal mergers where one of the firms is on the verge of bankruptcy

_____

3. The following table contains data on five different industries and the market shares for each firm in the industry. Assume that there is no foreign competition, entry into the industry is difficult, and that no firm in each industry is on the verge of bankruptcy.

Industry	Market share of firms in industry						Herfindahl index
	1	2	3	4	5	6	
A	35	25	15	11	10	4	_____
B	30	25	25	20	—	—	_____
C	20	20	20	15	15	10	_____
D	60	25	15	—	—	—	_____
E	22	21	20	18	12	7	_____

a. In the last column, calculate the Herfindahl index.

b. The industry with the most concentration is Industry _____, and the industry with the least monopoly power is Industry _____.

c. If the *sixth* firm in Industry A sought to merge with the *fifth* firm in that industry, then the government (would, would not) _____ be likely to challenge the merger. The Herfindahl index for this industry is _____, which is higher than the merger guideline of _____ points used by the government, but the merger increases the index by only _____ points.

d. If the *fourth* firm in Industry B sought to merge with the *third* firm in that industry, then the government (would, would not) _____ be likely to challenge the merger. The Herfindahl index for this industry is _____, which is higher than the merger guideline of the government, and the merger increases the index by _____ points.

e. A *conglomerate* merger between the *fourth* firm in Industry C and the *fourth* firm in Industry E (would, would not) _____ likely be challenged by the government. The Herfindahl index would (increase, remain the same) _____ with this merger.

f. If a *vertical* merger between the *first* firm in Industry B with the *first* firm in Industry D lessened competition in each industry, then the merger (would, would not) _____ likely be challenged by the government, but the merger _____ likely be challenged if it did not lessen competition in each industry.

4. Social regulation has had its critics and defenders. In the blank spaces in the following table, indicate the effect that critics and defenders thought social regulation would have on each characteristic. Mark an **I** for increase and **D** for decrease. If the text states nothing about this effect, mark an **N**.

	Critics	Defenders
a. Prices	_____	_____
b. Output	_____	_____
c. Competition	_____	_____
d. Product innovation	_____	_____
e. Net benefits to society	_____	_____

■ **SHORT ANSWER AND ESSAY QUESTIONS**

1. Explain the basic differences between antitrust policy, industrial regulation, and social regulation.

2. What are the historical background to and the main provisions of the Sherman Act?

3. The Clayton Act and the Federal Trade Commission Act amended or elaborated on the provisions of the Sherman Act, and both aimed at preventing rather than punishing monopoly. What were the chief provisions of each act, and how did they attempt to prevent monopoly? In what two ways is the FTC Act important?

4. What loophole in the Clayton Act did the Celler-Kefauver Act plug in 1950, and how did it alter the coverage of the antitrust laws with respect to mergers?

5. Contrast the two different approaches to court interpretation of antitrust laws that are illustrated by the decisions of the courts in the U.S. Steel and Alcoa cases.

6. Why is defining the market an important issue in the application of the antitrust laws? How did the courts define the market in the case brought against DuPont for monopolizing the market for cellophane?

7. Discuss two perspectives on strict enforcement of antitrust laws.

8. How have the antitrust laws been applied in the past and in recent years to monopoly? Give examples.

9. Explain the difference between horizontal, vertical, and conglomerate mergers. Give an example of each type.

10. What is the Herfindahl index and how is it used as a guideline for mergers?

11. What are per se violations? Give examples of recent price-fixing investigations and court cases.

12. What is a natural monopoly? What two alternative ways can a natural monopoly be used to ensure that it behaves in a socially acceptable fashion?

13. Explain how public interest regulation can lead to increased costs and economic inefficiency as it is practiced by U.S. commissions and agencies.

14. Discuss the issue involved in regulation that perpetuates a natural monopoly after the conditions for it have evaporated. Give examples.

15. What is the legal cartel theory of regulation? Contrast it with the public interest theory of regulation.

16. Why were a number of industries in the U.S. economy deregulated beginning in the 1970s? What have been the economic effects of deregulation?

17. How does social regulation differ from industrial (or public) regulation? Describe three major differences.

18. Can the optimal level of social regulation be determined? Explain.

19. What are the major arguments for social regulation?

20. What are the major criticisms of social regulation?

ANSWERS

Chapter 32 Antitrust Policy and Regulation

FILL-IN QUESTIONS

1. antitrust policy, industrial, social
2. *a.* establishing regulatory agencies; *b.* passing antitrust laws (either order for *a* and *b*)
3. Sherman, Clayton
4. Federal Trade Commission
5. Wheeler-Lea, Celler-Kefauver
6. behavior, structure, behavior
7. broadly, narrowly, did not
8. strictly, competition, unnecessary, markets
9. horizontal, vertical, conglomerate
10. Herfindahl, 2500, 10,000
11. per se violation, tying contract, strictly
12. has, has
13. lower, regulatory commissions
14. *a.* lower, capital, labor; *b.* are not
15. discourage, cartel
16. decreased, increased, decreased, increased
17. social, industrial
18. more, greater, rapidly
19. increase, decrease, decrease
20. pro-, increased

TRUE–FALSE QUESTIONS

1. T, p. 598	**10.** F, p. 601	**19.** T, p. 606
2. F, p. 598	**11.** F, p. 603	**20.** T, p. 607
3. F, pp. 598–599	**12.** T, p. 603	**21.** F, p. 608
4. T, p. 599	**13.** F, p. 603	**22.** T, pp. 608–609
5. F, p. 600	**14.** F, p. 604	**23.** T, p. 609
6. T, p. 600	**15.** F, pp. 604–605	**24.** F, pp. 609–610
7. F, p. 600	**16.** F, p. 605	**25.** T, pp. 609–610
8. T, pp. 600–601	**17.** T, p. 605	
9. T, p. 601	**18.** F, pp. 605–606	

MULTIPLE-CHOICE QUESTIONS

1. d, pp. 598–599	**10.** d, p. 603	**19.** d, p. 607
2. a, p. 599	**11.** c, p. 603	**20.** c, pp. 607–608
3. b, p. 599	**12.** b, p. 603	**21.** d, pp. 607–608
4. d, p. 600	**13.** b, pp. 603–604	**22.** c, p. 608
5. a, p. 600	**14.** b, p. 604	**23.** c, pp. 608–609
6. b, pp. 600–601	**15.** a, p. 605	**24.** b, p. 609
7. d, p. 601	**16.** b, p. 605	**25.** a, pp. 609–610
8. d, p. 601	**17.** b, pp. 605–606	
9. d, p. 603	**18.** c, p. 606	

PROBLEMS

1. *a.* C; *b.* A; *c.* E; *d.* D; *e.* B
2. *a.* L; *b.* S; *c.* L; *d.* L; *e.* S; *f.* S; *g.* L
3. *a.* 2312, 2550, 1750, 4450, 1842; *b.* D, C; *c.* would not, 2312, 1800, 80; *d.* would, 2550, 1000; *e.* would not, remain the same; *f.* would, would not
4. *a.* I, N; *b.* D, N; *c.* D, N; *d.* D, N; *e.* D, I

SHORT ANSWER AND ESSAY QUESTIONS

1. pp. 598–599	**8.** p. 602	**15.** p. 606
2. pp. 598–599	**9.** pp. 602–603	**16.** pp. 606–607
3. pp. 599–600	**10.** p. 603	**17.** pp. 607–608
4. pp. 599–600	**11.** p. 603	**18.** p. 608
5. pp. 600–601	**12.** pp. 604–605	**19.** pp. 608–609
6. p. 601	**13.** p. 605	**20.** p. 609
7. pp. 601–602	**14.** pp. 605–606	

CHAPTER 33

Agriculture: Economics and Policy

Agriculture is a large and vital part of the U.S. and world economies, and so it merits the special attention it receives in Chapter 33. As you will learn, the economics of agriculture and farm policies of the Federal government are of concern not only to those directly engaged in farming, but also to U.S. consumers and businesses who purchase farm products and to U.S. taxpayers who subsidize farm incomes. Agriculture is also important in the world economy because each nation must find a way to feed its population, and domestic farm policies designed to enhance farm incomes often lead to distortions in world trade and economic inefficiency in world agricultural production.

The chapter begins by examining both the **short-run farm problem** and the **long-run farm problem** in U.S. agriculture. The short-run problem is that farm prices and incomes have fluctuated sharply from year to year. The long-run problem is that agriculture is a declining industry, and as a consequence, farm incomes have fallen over time. To understand the causes of each problem, you will have to use the concept of inelastic demand and your knowledge of how demand and supply determine price in a competitive market. The effort you have put into the study of these tools in previous chapters will now pay a dividend: an understanding of the causes of a real-world problem and the policies designed to solve the problem.

The agricultural policies of the Federal government have been directed at enhancing and stabilizing farm incomes by supporting farm prices. In connection with the support of farm prices, you are introduced to the **parity concept**. Once you understand parity and recognize that the parity price in the past has been above what the competitive price would have been, you will come to some important conclusions. Consumers paid higher prices for and consumed smaller quantities of the various farm products, and at the prices supported by the Federal government, there were surpluses of these products. The Federal government bought these surpluses to keep the price above the competitive market price. The purchases of the surpluses were financed by U.S. taxpayers. To eliminate these surpluses, government looked for ways to increase the demand for or to decrease the supply of these commodities. Programs to increase demand and decrease supply were put into effect, but they failed to eliminate the annual surpluses.

Over the past 60 years, farm policies have not worked well and the price-support system has been criticized for several reasons. First, the policies confuse the *symptoms* of the problem (low farm prices and incomes) with the *causes* of the problem (resource allocation). Second, the costly farm subsidies are also misguided because they tend to benefit the high-income instead of the low-income farmer. Third, some policies of the Federal government contradict or offset other policies to help farmers.

The politics of farm policy can also be studied from the public choice perspective first presented in Chapter 31. In this chapter you will learn how the special-interest effect and rent-seeking behavior related to farm policies result in costly programs that have been supported by political leaders and subsidized by the Federal government for so many years. Nevertheless, the political backing for farm price supports is declining because of a reduction in the farm population. There is also international pressure to reduce farm price supports in all nations to eliminate distortions in world trade and improve worldwide economic efficiency.

The chapter concludes with a discussion of the recent reform of agricultural policy in the United States. The **Freedom to Farm Act** of 1996 was an attempt to eliminate price supports and acreage allotments for many major agricultural products. In return, U.S. farmers were to receive income payments through 2002 to help them make the transition to working in a more competitive market. The deterioration in economic conditions before the end of the act led to emergency aid payments to farmers. The **Farm Act of 2002** was passed by Congress to help stabilize crop prices and incomes for farmers, but as you will learn, this new legislation continued the policy of providing expensive price-support subsidies to agriculture.

■ **CHECKLIST**

When you have studied this chapter you should be able to

☐ Give several reasons why it is important to study the economics of U.S. agriculture.

☐ List three causes of the short-run problem in agriculture.

☐ Explain why the demand for agricultural products is price inelastic.

☐ Cite a reason for the fluctuations in agricultural output.

☐ Discuss the fluctuations in domestic demand for agricultural products.

☐ Describe the stability of foreign demand for agricultural products.

☐ Identify the two major factors contributing to the long-run problem in U.S. agriculture.

☐ Describe how technological change affects the long-run supply of agricultural products.

☐ Give two reasons why increases in demand lag increases in supply over time in U.S. agriculture.

☐ Use a supply and demand graph to illustrate the long-run problem in U.S. agriculture.

☐ Explain the consequences of the long-run problem in agriculture for industry structure, crop prices, and income.

☐ List the six features of the "farm program."

☐ Give cost estimates of the size of U.S. farm subsidies in recent years.

☐ Present several arguments in support of Federal assistance to agriculture.

☐ Define the parity ratio and explain its significance to agricultural policy.

☐ Use a supply and demand graph to identify the economic effects of price supports for agricultural products on output, farm income, consumer and taxpayer expenditures, economic efficiency, the environment, and international trade.

☐ Give examples of how the Federal government restricts supply and bolsters demand for farm products.

☐ Present three criticisms of the price-support system in agriculture.

☐ Use insights from public choice theory to discuss the politics of agricultural legislation and expenditures by the Federal government for farm programs.

☐ Give two reasons, one domestic and one international, to explain the change in the politics of farm subsidies.

☐ Describe the major features of the Freedom to Farm Act of 1996.

☐ Explain the elements of the Farm Act of 2002 and how it affects crop prices, farm incomes, and subsidies in agriculture.

■ **CHAPTER OUTLINE**

1. The economic analysis of U.S. agriculture is important for several reasons: It is one of the nation's largest industries and is a real-world example of the purely competitive model; it illustrates the economic effects of government intervention in markets; it illustrates the special-interest effect and rent-seeking behavior; and it reflects changes in global markets.

2. There is both a **short-run** and a **long-run farm problem:** The short-run problem is the frequent sharp changes in the incomes of farmers from one year to the next; the long-run problem is the tendency for farm prices and incomes to lag behind the upward trend of prices and incomes in the rest of the economy.

    a. The causes of the **short-run problem** (income instability) are the inelastic demand for farm products, fluctuations in the output of agricultural products, fluctuations in the demand, both domestic and foreign. These factors result in relatively large changes in agricultural prices and farm incomes.

    b. The causes of the **long-run problem** (low farm incomes and farm prices) stem from two basic factors:

(1) the supply of agricultural products increased significantly over most of this century because of technological advances in agriculture, and

(2) the demand for agricultural products failed to match the large increase in supply even though there were large increases in income (and population) because the demand for agricultural products is *income* inelastic (that is, increases in income lead to less than proportionate increases in expenditures on farm products).

3. Since the 1930s, farmers have been able to obtain various forms of public aid, but the primary purposes of the Federal **government subsidies** have been to enhance and stabilize farm prices and incomes.

    a. Several arguments are used to justify these expenditures, such as the poor incomes of farmers, the importance of the family farm, the hazards of farming, and market power problems.

    b. The cornerstone of the Federal policy to raise farm prices is the concept of **parity** (or the parity price), which would give the farmer year after year the same real income per unit of output.

    c. Historically, farm policy supported farm prices at some percentage of the parity price. But because the supported price was almost always above the market price, government had to support the price by purchasing and accumulating surpluses of agricultural products; while farmers gained from this policy, there were losses for consumers and society, and problems were created in the environment and international sectors.

    d. To reduce the annual and accumulated surpluses, government attempted to

(1) reduce the output (or supply) of farm products by acreage allotment and soil bank programs and

(2) expand the demand for farm products by finding new uses for farm products, expanding domestic demand, and increasing the foreign demand for agricultural commodities.

4. Agricultural policies designed to stabilize farm incomes and prices have not worked well over the past 60 years. The policies have been subject to **criticisms** *and* **political debate.**

    a. There are three basic criticisms of **price-support programs.**

(1) Price-support programs have confused the *symptoms* of the problem (low farm products and low farm incomes) with the *causes* of the problem (resource allocation) and have encouraged people to stay in agriculture.

(2) The major benefits from price-support programs are *misguided* because low-income farmers often receive small government subsidies while high-income farmers often receive large government subsidies; price supports also affect land values and become a subsidy for owners of farmland who rent their land and do not farm.

(3) The various farm programs of the Federal government have often *offset* or contradicted each other.

Price-support programs have tried to stabilize prices, while other programs have increased supply, thus putting downward pressure on prices.

b. The *politics of agricultural policy* explain why costly and extensive subsidies have persisted in the United States.

(1) Four insights from public choice theory serve to explain this development: rent-seeking behavior by farm groups, the special-interest effect that impairs public decision making, political logrolling to turn negative outcomes into positive outcomes, and the clear benefits and hidden costs of farm programs.

(2) Changing politics also explains why there has been a reduction in the political support for agricultural subsidies. There has been a decline in the farm population and its political power. The United States also is committed to reducing agricultural subsidies worldwide because they distort world trade. This U.S. support for freer trade makes it harder to support domestic farm subsidies.

5. Since the mid-1990s there have been several attempts to reform farm policy to make the farm sector more market-oriented and less dependent on government subsidies, but they have met with mixed success.

a. The *Freedom to Farm Act* of 1996 tried to change 60 years of U.S. farm policy. The law ended price supports and acreage allotments for eight agricultural commodities. In return for accepting more risk, income payments were made to farmers through the year 2002 to help them make the transition to operating in a more competitive market. The change was expected to increase agricultural output, crop diversity, and risk management by farmers. The decline in several farm commodity prices in recent years created pressure to change the Freedom to Farm Act. The U.S. government responded to the problem by increasing subsidies to farmers with emergency aid, but it was only a temporary solution to both a short-run and a long-run farm problem.

b. The *Farm Act of 2002* is a six-year bill costing some $118 billion. It continues the policy of giving farmers freedom to plant and provides constant direct payments to farmers based on past crop production levels. There are also countercyclical payments that cover any gap if the market price of a commodity falls below the target price. In addition, marketing loans can provide additional subsidies. The legislation makes it clear that agriculture will continue to receive large government subsidies in spite of the excess production and market distortion arising from these subsidies.

■ HINTS AND TIPS

1. This chapter applies several economic ideas—supply and demand, elasticity, price controls, and public choice theory—that you learned about in previous chapters. If your understanding of these ideas is weak, review supply and demand in Chapter 3, elasticity and price controls in Chapter 20, and public choice theory in Chapter 31.

2. There are short-run and long-run problems in agriculture. Make sure you understand the distinction. The short-run problem involves the year-to-year changes in the prices of farm products and farm incomes. The long-run problem is that changes in supply and demand over time have made agriculture a declining industry in the U.S. economy.

3. Figure 33.7 and the related discussion are very important to your study. The figure illustrates the economic effects that agricultural price supports have on different groups and the overall economy.

■ IMPORTANT TERMS

short-run farm problem	acreage allotments
long-run farm problem	Freedom to Farm Act
agribusiness	Farm Act of 2002
parity concept	direct payments
parity ratio	countercyclical payments (CCP)
price supports	

SELF-TEST

■ FILL-IN QUESTIONS

1. It is important to study the economics of U.S. agriculture for many reasons; it is one of the (largest, smallest) _____ industries in the nation; it provides a real-world example of pure (monopoly, competition) _____; it demonstrates the intended and unintended effects of (consumer, government) _____ policies that interfere with forces of supply and demand; it reflects the (decreased, increased) _____ globalization of agricultural markets; and it illustrates aspects of (public, private) _____ choice theory.

2. The basic cause of the short-run problems in agriculture is the (elastic, inelastic) _____ demand for farm products. This demand occurs because farm products have few good (complements, substitutes) _____ and because of rapidly diminishing marginal (product, utility) _____.

3. The elasticity of demand for farm products contributes to unstable farm prices and incomes because relatively (large, small) _____ changes in the output of farm products result in relatively _____ changes in prices and incomes and because relatively _____ changes in domestic or foreign demand result in relatively _____ changes in prices and incomes.

4. From a long-run perspective, the (demand for, supply of) _____ agricultural products increased rapidly over the past 60 years because of technological progress, but the _____ agricultural products did not increase as fast, in large part because food demand is income (elastic, inelastic) _____ and because the rate of population increase has not matched the increase in production.

5. Four arguments used to justify expenditures for farm subsidies are: the (inelastic, low) _____ income of farmers, the (cost, value) _____ of the family farm as a U.S. institution; the (rent-seeking, hazards) _____ of farming from many natural disasters, and the fact that the farmers sell their output in (purely, imperfectly) _____ competitive markets and purchase their inputs in _____ competitive markets.

6. If farmers were to receive a parity price for a product, year after year a given output would enable them to acquire a (fixed, increased) _____ amount of goods and services.

7. If the government supports farm prices at an above-equilibrium level, the results will be (shortages, surpluses) _____ that the government must (buy, sell) _____ to maintain prices at their support level.

8. With price-support programs, farmers (benefit, are hurt) _____ and consumers _____. The incomes of farmers (increase, decrease) _____, while the prices consumers pay for products _____ and the quantities of the agricultural product that they purchase _____.

9. Society also is hurt by farm price support programs because they encourage economic (efficiency, inefficiency) _____, an (over, under) _____ allocation of resources to agriculture, and a (small, large) _____ government bureaucracy for agriculture.

10. Agricultural price supports have (increased, decreased) _____ domestic agricultural production and _____ the use of inputs such as pesticides and fertilizers, resulting in (positive, negative) _____ effects on the environment.

11. The above-equilibrium price supports make U.S. agricultural markets (more, less) _____ attractive to foreign producers who try to sell _____ of their agricultural products in the United States. This activity is likely to (increase, decrease)

_____ trade barriers, and _____ the efficiency of U.S. agriculture. The trade barriers will have a (negative, positive) _____ effect on developing nations, which are often dependent on worldwide agricultural markets.

12. To bring the equilibrium level of prices in the market up to their support level, government has attempted to (increase, decrease) _____ the demand for and to _____ the supply of farm products.

13. To decrease supply, the Federal government has used (acreage allotment, rent-seeking) _____ programs. To increase demand, the Federal government has encouraged (new, old) _____ uses for agricultural products and sought to increase domestic and foreign (supply, demand) _____ for agricultural products through the domestic food stamps program or the foreign Food for Peace program.

14. The policies of government to support agricultural prices and income (have, have not) _____ worked well over the past 60 years because they have confused the symptoms of the farm problem, which are (high, low) _____ prices and incomes, with the root cause of the problem, which is (efficient, inefficient) _____ allocation of resources.

15. There are two other criticisms. Much of the benefits from farm price supports go to (high, low) _____-income farmers instead of _____-income farmers. The effects of price-support programs of the Federal government are (reinforced, offset) _____ by other government programs.

16. Despite these criticisms, farm policies have received strong support in Congress over the years; the result of this can be explained by insights from (monopoly, public choice) _____ theory. When farm groups lobby for Federal programs that transfer income to them, they are exhibiting (parity, rent-seeking) _____ behavior. There is also a special-interest effect because the costs to individual taxpayers are (large, small) _____ but the benefits to farmers are _____ from farm programs.

17. In addition, when agricultural groups or farm-state politicians trade votes to turn negative into positive outcomes, they are using political (allotments, logrolling) _____. Another public choice problem with farm subsidies is that the benefits of farm programs are (clear, hidden) _____, while much of the costs are _____ in the form of higher consumer prices for agricultural products.

18. There are also world (aid, trade) _____ considerations from agricultural subsidies. The effects of supports for the prices of agricultural products in the United States and European Union (EU) have been to (increase, decrease) _____ domestic production in these nations, _____ export subsidies for farm products in these nations, and _____ world prices for agricultural products, thus distorting worldwide trade in agricultural products.

19. Calls for reforms of farm policy in the United States led in 1996 to the Freedom to (Trade, Farm) _____ Act that sought to (expand, eliminate) _____ price supports for eight farm crops in return for giving farmers freedom to (plant, export) _____ crops. To make the transition from price-supported agriculture to market-oriented agriculture, farmers received transition (licenses, payments) _____, but the fall in several crop prices later in the decade led to emergency measures to (increase, decrease) _____ farm subsidies.

20. The Farm Act of 2002 continues the policy of freedom to (export, plant) _____, and provides income support for farmers in the form of direct (insurance, payments) _____. In addition, there are price-support subsidies in the form of countercyclical (insurance, payments) _____ and marketing (campaigns, loans) _____. As a result of the act, the government's subsidy for agriculture has (increased, decreased) _____, which in turn contributes to _____ crop production and low crop price. This resulting condition then leads to demands for (more, less) _____ farm subsidies.

■ **TRUE–FALSE QUESTIONS**

Circle T if the statement is true, F if it is false.

1. The short-run farm problem is the sharp year-to-year fluctuations in farm prices and farm incomes that frequently occur. **T F**

2. The demand for farm products is price elastic. **T F**

3. The quantities of agricultural commodities produced tend to be fairly *insensitive* to changes in agricultural prices because a large percentage of farmers' total costs are variable. **T F**

4. The foreign demand for farm products is relatively stable. **T F**

5. Appreciation of the dollar will tend to increase the demand for farm products. **T F**

6. The supply of agricultural products has tended to increase more rapidly than the demand for these products in the United States. **T F**

7. Most of the recent technological advances in agriculture have been initiated by farmers. **T F**

8. The demand for farm products is income elastic. **T F**

9. The long-run farm problem is that the incomes of farmers have been low relative to incomes in the economy as a whole. **T F**

10. The consequences over time of supply and demand conditions in agriculture are that minimum efficient scale has increased. **T F**

11. The size of the farm population in the United States has declined in both relative and absolute terms since about 1930. **T F**

12. The major aim of agricultural policy in the United States for the past 70 years was to support agricultural prices and incomes. **T F**

13. If the prices paid by farmers were 500% higher than in the base year and the price received by farmers were 400% higher than in the base year, the parity ratio would be 125%. **T F**

14. Application of the parity concept to farm prices causes farm prices to decline and results in agricultural surpluses. **T F**

15. When government supports farm prices at above-equilibrium levels, it can reduce the annual surpluses of agricultural commodities either by increasing the supply or by decreasing the demand for them. **T F**

16. The acreage allotment program was designed to decrease the supply of farm products. **T F**

17. Restricting the number of acres that farmers use to grow agricultural products has been only a partially successful method of reducing surpluses because farmers tend to cultivate their land more intensively when the acreage is reduced. **T F**

18. Public policy has been effective in alleviating the resource allocation problem in U.S. agriculture, not just the symptoms. **T F**

19. The price-income support programs for agriculture have given the most benefit to those farmers with the least need for the government assistance. **T F**

20. A political action committee organized by a group of sugar beet farmers to lobby Congress for subsidies for sugar beets is an example of political logrolling. **T F**

21. The reason that farmers, who are a small proportion of the population, can impose a large cost to taxpayers in the form of agricultural subsidies is because the cost imposed on each individual taxpayer is small and not given much attention by each taxpayer. **T F**

22. One hidden cost of agricultural price support programs is the higher prices that consumers pay for the product.   **T F**

23. The decline in farm population and in the related political representation in rural areas is one reason why political support for farm subsidies has increased.   **T F**

24. Domestic farm subsidies distort world trade and contribute to the inefficiencies in the international allocation of agricultural resources.   **T F**

25. Although the Farm Act of 2002 helped reduce the risk for farmers and raised farm incomes, it continues the Federal government policy of subsidizing agricultural production.   **T F**

■ **MULTIPLE-CHOICE QUESTIONS**

Circle the letter that corresponds to the best answer.

1. The inelasticity of demand for agricultural products can be explained by
   (a) the parity ratio
   (b) economies of scale
   (c) rent-seeking behavior
   (d) diminishing marginal utility

2. The inelastic demand for agricultural products means that a relatively small increase in output will result in a relatively
   (a) small increase in farm prices and incomes
   (b) large decrease in farm prices and incomes
   (c) small decrease in farm prices and a relatively large increase in farm incomes
   (d) large increase in farm prices and a relatively small decrease in farm incomes

3. The reason that large declines in farm prices do not significantly reduce farm production in the short run is that farmers'
   (a) fixed costs are high relative to their variable costs
   (b) variable costs are high relative to their fixed costs
   (c) prices received are greater than prices paid for agricultural products
   (d) prices paid are greater than prices received for agricultural products

4. One reason for the year-to-year instability of agricultural product prices is
   (a) stable production of domestic agricultural products
   (b) stable production of foreign agricultural products
   (c) fluctuations in incomes received for agricultural products
   (d) fluctuations in the foreign demand for agricultural products

5. If, over time, the increases in the supply of an agricultural product are much greater than the increases in demand for it, the supply and demand model would suggest that the product price
   (a) and quantity will both increase
   (b) and quantity will both decrease
   (c) will increase, but the quantity will decrease
   (d) will decrease, but the quantity will increase

6. Which is a significant reason why increases in demand for agricultural products have been small relative to increases in supply?
   (a) Increases in the population of the United States have been greater than increases in the productivity of agriculture.
   (b) Increases in the population of the United States have been greater than decreases in the productivity of agriculture.
   (c) Increases in the incomes of U.S. consumers result in less than proportionate increases in their spending on agricultural products.
   (d) Increases in the incomes of U.S. consumers result in more than proportionate increases in their spending on agricultural products.

7. Given an inelastic demand for farm products, a more rapid increase in the
   (a) demand for such products relative to the supply creates a persistent downward pressure on farm incomes
   (b) supply for such products relative to the demand creates a persistent upward pressure on farm incomes
   (c) supply for such products relative to the demand creates a persistent downward pressure on farm incomes
   (d) demand for such products relative to the supply creates a persistent downward pressure on agricultural product prices

8. As a consequence of the migration out of farming over the years, agricultural income per farm household
   (a) has decreased relative to nonfarm incomes
   (b) has increased relative to nonfarm incomes
   (c) is now significantly greater than nonfarm income
   (d) is now significantly less than nonfarm income

9. The consequences of the long-run supply and demand conditions in agriculture are that minimum efficient scale has
   (a) increased and crop prices have decreased
   (b) increased and crop prices have increased
   (c) decreased and crop prices have increased
   (d) decreased and crop prices have decreased

10. Which is a major rationale for public aid for agriculture in the United States?
   (a) Farmers are more affected by competition from foreign producers than other parts of the economy.
   (b) Farmers sell their products in highly competitive markets and buy resources in highly imperfect markets.
   (c) Technological progress in farming has greatly increased the demand for farm products.
   (d) The demand for farm products is income elastic.

11. Farm parity means that over time,
   (a) the real income of the farmer remains constant
   (b) a given output will furnish the farmer with a constant amount of real income
   (c) the purchasing power of the farmer's nominal income remains constant
   (d) the nominal income of the farmer will buy a constant amount of goods and services

12. If the index of prices paid by farmers were 1000 and the prices received by farmers were 600, then the parity ratio would be
(a) 2.1 (or 210%)
(b) 1.7 (or 170%)
(c) 0.6 (or 60%)
(d) 0.4 (or 40%)

13. The necessary consequence of the government's support of agricultural prices at an above-equilibrium level is
(a) a surplus of agricultural products
(b) increased consumption of agricultural products
(c) reduced production of agricultural products
(d) the destruction of agricultural products

14. Another consequence of having government support farm prices at an above-equilibrium level is that consumers pay higher prices for farm products and
(a) consume more of these products and pay higher taxes
(b) consume less of these products and pay higher taxes
(c) consume more of these products and pay lower taxes
(d) consume less of these products and pay lower taxes

Use the graph below to answer Questions 15, 16, and 17.
D is the demand for and S is the supply of a certain product.

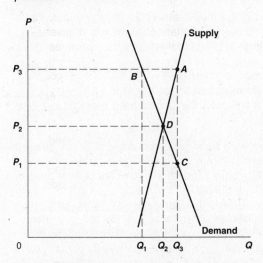

15. If the Federal government supported the price of this product at P_3, the total amount it would have to spend to purchase the surplus of the product would be
(a) $0Q_3AP_3$
(b) Q_1Q_3AB
(c) P_1CAP_3
(d) $0Q_1BP_3$

16. With a support price of P_3, the total income of producers of the product will be
(a) $0Q_3AP_3$
(b) $0Q_1BP_3$
(c) $0Q_3CP_1$
(d) $0Q_2DP_2$

17. With a support price of P_3, the amount spent by consumers will be
(a) $0Q_3AP_3$
(b) $0Q_1BP_3$
(c) $0Q_2DP_2$
(d) Q_1Q_3AB

Answer Questions 18, 19, and 20 on the basis of the demand and supply schedules for agricultural product Z as shown below.

Pounds of Z demanded	Price	Pounds of Z supplied
850	$1.30	1150
900	1.20	1100
950	1.10	1050
1000	1.00	1000
1050	.90	950
1100	.80	900
1150	.70	850

18. If the Federal government supports the price of Z at $1.30 a pound, then at this price, there is
(a) a surplus of 200 pounds of Z
(b) a surplus of 300 pounds of Z
(c) a surplus of 400 pounds of Z
(d) a shortage of 400 pounds of Z

19. With a Federal price support of $1.30 a pound, consumers spend
(a) $1040, the Federal government spends $410, and farmers receive income from product Z of $1450
(b) $1105, the Federal government spends $390, and farmers receive income from product Z of $1495
(c) $1296, the Federal government spends $240, and farmers receive income from product Z of $1320
(d) $1045, the Federal government spends $110, and farmers receive income from product Z of $1155

20. If, instead of supporting the price, the Federal government took actions to increase demand by 150 units at each price and to decrease supply by 150 units at each price, then the equilibrium price would be
(a) $1.00 and the income of farmers would be $1000
(b) $1.10 and the income of farmers would be $1320
(c) $1.20 and the income of farmers would be $1260
(d) $1.30 and the income of farmers would be $1300

21. To help eliminate the agricultural surpluses created by farm subsidies, the Federal government has tried to
(a) increase supply and demand
(b) decrease supply and demand
(c) increase supply and decrease demand
(d) decrease supply and increase demand

22. Which is a major criticism of agricultural price supports?
(a) Restricting agricultural output increases farm prices but reduces farm incomes when demand is inelastic.
(b) The principal beneficiaries of these supports have been farmers with low incomes who would be better off in another type of work.

(c) They fail to treat the underlying problem of the misallocation of resources between agriculture and the rest of the economy.

(d) They duplicate other economic policies that are designed to increase the prices for agricultural products.

23. When farmers and farm organizations lobby Congress for a larger appropriation for agricultural price and income programs, according to public choice theory this action would be an example of

(a) confusing symptoms with causes

(b) misguided subsidies

(c) rent-seeking behavior

(d) political logrolling

24. Which has been a consequence of protective trade barriers for agricultural products established by the European Union (EU)?

(a) higher prices for U.S. agricultural products

(b) restriction of exports of EU agricultural products

(c) lower worldwide prices for agricultural products

(d) more sales of U.S. agricultural products to the EU

25. A consistent feature in both the Freedom to Farm Act of 1996 and the Farm Act of 2002 was

(a) decreasing crop price-support subsidies for farmers

(b) giving farmers the freedom to plant various agriculture crops

(c) bolstering of the domestic and foreign demand for U.S. agricultural products

(d) improving of the parity ratio so that the prices farmers paid for their inputs were similar to the prices they received for their output

■ PROBLEMS

1. The following table is a demand schedule for agricultural product **X**.

(1) Price	(2) Bushels of X demanded	(3) Bushels of X demanded
$2.00	600	580
1.80	620	600
1.60	640	620
1.40	660	640
1.20	680	660
1.00	700	680
.80	720	700
.60	740	720

a. Based on columns 1 and 2, is demand elastic or inelastic in the price range given?

_____

b. Based on columns 1 and 2, if the amount of **X** produced should increase from 600 to 700 bushels, the income of producers of **X** would

_____ from $_____ to

$_____; an increase of _____ %

in the amount of **X** produced would cause income to

_____ by _____ %.

c. If the amount of **X** produced were 700 bushels and the demand for **X** decreased from that shown in columns 1 and 2 to that shown in columns 1 and 3,

the price of **X** would _____ from $_____

to $_____; the income of farmers would

_____ from $_____ to $_____.

d. Assume that the government supports a price of $1.80, that the demand for **X** is that shown in columns 1 and 2, and that farmers grow 720 bushels of **X**.

(1) At the supported price there will be a surplus of

_____ bushels of **X**.

(2) If the government buys this surplus at the support price the cost to the taxpayers of purchasing the surplus is $_____.

(3) The total income of the farmers producing product **X** when they receive the support price of $1.80 per bushel for their entire crop of 720 bushels is

$_____.

(4) Had farmers sold the crop of 720 bushels at the free-market price, the price of **X** would be only

$_____ per bushel, and the total income of

these farmers would be $_____.

(5) The gain to farmers producing **X** from the price-support program is therefore $_____.

(6) In addition to the cost to taxpayers of purchasing the surplus, consumers pay a price that is

$_____ greater than the free-market price

and receive a quantity of **X** that is _____ bushels less than they would have received in a free market.

2. The following table gives the index of prices farmers paid in three different years. The price farmers received in year 1, the base year, for a certain agricultural product was $3.50 per bushel.

Year	Index of prices paid	Parity price	Price received	Parity ratio
1	100	$3.50	$3.50	100%
2	120	_____	3.78	_____%
3	200	_____	5.25	_____%

a. Compute the parity price of the product in years 2 and 3 and enter them in the table.

b. The prices received for the product in each year are also shown in the table. Complete the table by computing the parity *ratio* in years 2 and 3. (*Hint:* It is *not* necessary to construct an index of prices received in order to compute the parity ratio. This ratio can be computed by dividing the price received by the parity price.)

3. The demand schedule for agricultural product **Y** is given in columns 1 and 2 of the following table.

(1) Price	(2) Bales of Y demanded	(3) Bales of Y demanded
$5.00	40,000	41,000
4.75	40,200	41,200
4.50	40,400	41,400
4.25	40,600	41,600
4.00	40,800	41,800
3.75	41,000	42,000
3.50	41,200	42,200

a. If farmers were persuaded by the government to reduce the size of their crop from 41,000 to 40,000 bales, the income of farmers would _____ from $_____ to $_____.

b. If the crop remained constant at 41,000 bales and the demand for **Y** increased to that shown in columns 1 and 3, the income of farmers would _____ from $_____ to $_____.

4. Suppose the demand for sow jowls during a certain period of time was that shown in the table below and the Federal government wished to support the price of sow jowls at $.70 a pound.

Price (per pound)	Quantity demanded (pounds)
$1.00	1000
.90	1020
.80	1040
.70	1060
.60	1080
.50	1100
.40	1120

a. If the output of sow jowls were 1100 pounds during that period of time, the market price of sow jowls would be $_____ and the Federal government would (buy, sell) _____ (how many) _____ pounds of sow jowls.

b. But if the output were 1000 pounds during that period of time, the market price of sow jowls would be $_____ and the Federal government would not have to intervene.

■ SHORT ANSWER AND ESSAY QUESTIONS

1. Why are the economics of agriculture and agricultural policy important topics for study?

2. What is the short-run farm problem and what are its causes?

3. Why does the demand for agricultural products tend to be inelastic? What are the implications for agriculture?

4. What have been the specific causes of the large increases in the supply of agricultural products over time?

5. Why has the demand for agricultural products failed to increase at the same rate as the supply of these products?

6. What have been the consequences of long-run supply and demand conditions in agriculture?

7. What is meant by "the farm program"? What particular aspect of the farm program has traditionally received the major attention of farmers and their representatives in Congress?

8. Why do agricultural interests claim that farmers have a special right to aid from the Federal government?

9. Explain the concept of parity and the parity ratio.

10. Why is the result of government-supported prices invariably a surplus of farm commodities?

11. What are the effects of farm price-support programs on farmers, consumers, and resource allocation in the economy?

12. Identify and describe three ways that society at large loses from farm price-support programs.

13. Explain how U.S. farm policy may cause environmental problems.

14. Discuss the effects of farm price-support programs on international trade and developing nations.

15. What programs has the government used to try to restrict farm production? Why have these programs been relatively unsuccessful in limiting agricultural production?

16. How has the Federal government tried to increase the demand for farm products?

17. Explain the three major criticisms of agricultural price supports.

18. How can public choice theory explain the persistence of Federal government support for farm subsidies for so many decades? Discuss the application of rent-seeking behavior, the special-interest effect, political logrolling, and hidden costs to subsidies for agriculture.

19. What domestic and international factors are contributing to the reduction in political support for agricultural subsidies?

20. What are the key features of the Freedom to Farm Act of 1996 and the Farm Act of 2002? In what ways are the two acts similar and how are they different in terms of government intervention in agriculture, the provision of agricultural price supports, and income payments to farmers?

ANSWERS

Chapter 33 Agriculture: Economics and Policy

FILL-IN QUESTIONS

1. largest, competition, government, increased, public
2. inelastic, substitutes, utility
3. small, large, small, large

4. supply of, demand for, inelastic
5. low, value, hazards, purely, imperfectly
6. fixed
7. surpluses, buy
8. benefit, are hurt, increase, increase, decrease
9. inefficiency, over, large
10. increased, increased, negative
11. more, more, increase, decrease, negative
12. increase, decrease
13. acreage-allotment, new, demand
14. have not, low, inefficient
15. high, low, offset
16. public choice, rent-seeking, small, large
17. logrolling, clear, hidden
18. trade, increase, increase, decrease
19. Farm, eliminate, plant, payments, increase
20. plant, payments, payments, loans, increased, increased, more

TRUE–FALSE QUESTIONS

1. T, pp. 614–615
2. F, pp. 614–615
3. F, p. 616
4. F, p. 617
5. F, p. 617
6. T, pp. 617–618
7. F, p. 618
8. F, p. 618
9. T, p. 618
10. T, p. 618
11. T, p. 619
12. T, p. 620
13. F, pp. 620–621
14. F, pp. 620–621
15. F, p. 622
16. T, p. 623
17. T, p. 623
18. F, p. 624
19. T, p. 624
20. F, p. 625
21. T, p. 625
22. T, p. 625
23. F, pp. 625–626
24. T, p. 626
25. T, pp. 626–627

MULTIPLE-CHOICE QUESTIONS

1. d, p. 615
2. b, pp. 615–616
3. a, p. 616
4. d, pp. 616–617
5. d, pp. 617–619
6. c, p. 618
7. c, pp. 618–619
8. b, p. 619
9. a, pp. 618–619
10. b, p. 620
11. b, pp. 620–621
12. c, pp. 620–621
13. a, p. 622
14. b, p. 622
15. b, p. 622
16. a, p. 622
17. b, p. 622
18. b, p. 622
19. b, p. 622
20. d, pp. 622–624
21. d, pp. 622–624
22. c, p. 624
23. c, p. 625
24. c, p. 626
25. b, pp. 626–627

PROBLEMS

1. *a.* inelastic; *b.* decrease, 1200.00, 700.00, 16.67, decrease, 41.67; *c.* fall, 1.00, 0.80, fall, 700.00, 560.00; *d.* (1) 100, (2) 180, (3) 1296, (4) 0.80, 576, (5) 720, (6) 1.00, 100
2. *a.* 4.20, 7.00; *b.* 90, 75
3. *a.* increase, 153,750.00, 200,000.00; *b.* increase, 153,750.00, 205,000.00
4. *a.* .50, buy, 40; *b.* 1.00

SHORT ANSWER AND ESSAY QUESTIONS

1. p. 614
2. pp. 614–615
3. pp. 614–616
4. p. 618
5. pp. 617–618
6. pp. 618–619
7. p. 620
8. p. 620
9. pp. 620–621
10. p. 622
11. p. 622
12. pp. 622–623
13. p. 623
14. p. 623
15. pp. 623–624
16. pp. 623–624
17. pp. 624–625
18. p. 625
19. p. 626
20. pp. 626–627

CHAPTER 34

Income Inequality and Poverty

Chapter 34 examines another current problem in the economy of the United States: the unequal distribution of income and poverty. Recall from Chapter 5 that the market system does not produce an equal distribution of income, so one economic function of government is to redistribute income. Now you will learn about the income distribution problem and specific actions government takes to address it.

The chapter begins with a look at the facts of *income inequality.* You will discover that there is substantial income inequality in the United States and learn how it is measured with the *Lorenz curve* and *Gini ratio.* You should also note that the degree of income inequality for individuals and families will be less over time because of income mobility and because government taxes and transfer payments will also reduce the amount of income inequality.

The chapter discusses the multiple factors that contribute to income inequality. The seven causes that are described should indicate to you that there is no simple explanation for why some people have more income than others. It is not the result of some grand conspiracy; it can be attributed to ability differences, education and training, discrimination, preferences for jobs and risk, wealth, market power, and luck.

Over time there have been changes in the relative distribution of income that indicate income inequality in the United States is increasing. In this section of the chapter you will learn about the probable reasons for this growing income inequality that include shifts in the demand for skilled labor, changes in the demographics of the workforce, and other factors.

A case can be made for both income equality and income inequality. Few people, however, would advocate that there should be an absolutely equal distribution of income. The question to be decided is not one of inequality or equality but of how much or how little inequality there should be. A major insight from the chapter is that there is a fundamental *tradeoff between equality and efficiency* in the economy. If the society wants more equality, it will have to give up some economic efficiency in the form of less output and employment.

The reason for the focus on income distribution is ultimately the concern about *poverty.* In the later sections of the chapter you will learn about the extent of the poverty problem, whom poverty affects, and the actions government has taken to alleviate it. Poverty and other income problems are addressed through the Federal government's income-maintenance system. This system consists of *social insurance programs,* such as Social Security, and *public assistance programs,* or welfare. You will discover how these programs are designed to meet the needs of different groups, either those who are poor or those who require more stability in their incomes.

The reform of the public assistance programs in the United States has been a major topic of debate. You will learn that it is not possible to design a perfect program because of conflicting goals. Criticism of the welfare system led to the passage of the Personal Responsibility Act of 1996. Here the Federal government ended its long-standing policy of guaranteeing cash assistance for the poor and established Temporary Assistance to Needy Families (TANF) funds. The years of eligibility for these funds were limited and people were required to work after receiving benefits for a period of time. As you might expect, this reform has been subject to both praise and criticism in the nation's ongoing debate on public assistance.

■ **CHECKLIST**

When you have studied this chapter you should be able to

☐ Describe income inequality in the United States based on the percentage of families in a series of income categories.

☐ Discuss income inequality in the United States based on the percentage of personal income received by families in income quintiles.

☐ Explain the Lorenz curve by defining each axis, the diagonal line, and the meaning of the curve.

☐ Use a Lorenz curve to describe the degree of income inequality in the United States.

☐ Use a Gini ratio to measure income inequality.

☐ Explain the effects of time on income mobility and the distribution of U.S. income.

☐ Discuss the effects of government redistribution on income equality in the United States and illustrate the effects using a Lorenz curve.

☐ Explain the seven causes of income inequality in the United States.

☐ Describe the changes in the relative distribution of personal income in the United States over time based on three time periods since 1929.

☐ Identify three probable causes of growing income inequality in the United States over the past three decades.

☐ Present a case for income inequality based on the maximization of total utility.

☐ Make the case for income inequality based on incentives and efficiency.

☐ Explain the tradeoff between equality and efficiency in the debate over how much income inequality there should be.

☐ Give a definition of poverty based on U.S. government standards.

☐ Identify the demographic groups affected by poverty in the United States.

☐ Describe the trends in the poverty rate in the United States since 1960.

☐ Give three reasons why poverty tends to be invisible.

☐ Identify the two basic kinds of programs in the U.S. system for income maintenance.

☐ Describe the characteristics of major social insurance programs.

☐ Explain the purposes of the major public assistance programs.

☐ Discuss the common features and conflicts in three hypothetical plans for public assistance.

☐ State the major criticisms that led to reform of the welfare system.

☐ Describe the major features and offer an economic assessment of Temporary Assistance to Needy Families (TANF).

■ **CHAPTER OUTLINE**

1. There is considerable *income inequality* in the United States.

   a. One way to show this inequality is with a table showing the personal distribution of income of families. In 2001, about 21% of all families had annual before-tax incomes of less than $25,000, but 18% had annual incomes of $100,000 or more.

   b. A table of the personal distribution of income by families in quintiles is a second way to show the inequality. In 2001, the 20% of families with the lowest incomes accounted for 4.2% of personal income while the 20% of families with the highest incomes accounted for 47.7% of personal income.

   c. The degree of income inequality can be shown with a *Lorenz curve.* The percentage of families is plotted on the horizontal axis and the percentage of income is plotted on the vertical axis. The diagonal line between the two axes represents a perfectly equal distribution of income. A Lorenz curve that is bowed to the right from the diagonal shows income inequality. If the actual income distribution were perfectly equal, the Lorenz curve and the diagonal would coincide. The visual measurement of income inequality described by the Lorenz curve can be converted to a *Gini ratio,* which is the area between the Lorenz curve and the diagonal divided by the total area below the diagonal. As the income inequality increases, the Gini ratio will increase.

   d. Looking at income data over a longer time period rather than in a single year shows that there is considerably *less* income inequality. In fact, there is significant *income mobility* for individuals and fami-

lies in income over time. The longer the time period considered for individuals and families, the more equal the distribution of income.

   e. Government redistribution has had a significant effect on income distribution. The distribution of income can be examined after taxes and transfer payments. When this adjustment is made, the distribution of income is more equal. Transfer payments account for most of the reduction in income inequality. The change can be shown by a shift in the Lorenz curve toward more equality.

2. The market system is impersonal and does not necessarily result in a fair distribution of income. At least seven factors explain *why income inequality exists:*

   a. The distribution of abilities and skills differs greatly among people that influences what work they can do and their pay.

   b. There are differences in education and training that affect wages and salaries.

   c. Discrimination in education, hiring, training, and promotion will affect incomes.

   d. People have different preferences for certain types of jobs, for their willingness to accept risk on the job, and also for the amount of leisure that will be earned through their work.

   e. Wealth can provide a source of income in the form of rents, interest, and dividends, and since there are inequalities in the distribution of wealth, it will contribute to income inequalities.

   f. Some individuals have a degree of market power in either resource or product markets that create higher incomes.

   g. Other factors, such as luck, personal connections, and misfortunes, can play a role in contributing to income inequality.

3. Income inequality in the United States has changed over time.

   a. From 1929–1947, the relative distribution of personal income showed a decrease in income inequality. From 1947–1969 there was a slight increase in income inequality. From 1969–2001, the distribution of income became more unequal.

   b. Among the factors that explain the growing income inequality in the United States over the past three decades are:

   (1) increases in the demand for highly skilled workers compared with the demand for less-skilled workers;

   (2) changes in labor demographics from the influx of less-skilled baby boomers into the labor force, the increase in dual incomes among high-wage households, and more single-parent households earning less income; and

   (3) decreases in wages for less-skilled workers and less job security because of more import competition, the influx of less-skilled immigrants into the labor force, and a decline in unionism.

4. An important question to answer for an economy is not whether there will be income inequality, but what is an acceptable amount of inequality.

a. Those who argue for *equality* contend that it leads to the maximum satisfaction of consumer wants (utility) in the economy.

b. Those who argue for *inequality* contend that equality would reduce the incentives to work, save, invest, and take risks, and that these incentives are needed if the economy is to be efficient to produce as large an output (and income) as it is possible for it to produce from its available resources.

c. In the United States there is a *tradeoff between economic equality and efficiency.* A more nearly equal distribution of income results in less economic efficiency (a smaller domestic output) and greater economic efficiency leads to a more unequal distribution of income. The debate over the right amount of inequality depends on how much output society is willing to sacrifice to reduce income inequality.

5. Aside from inequality in the distribution of income, there is a great concern today with the problem of *poverty* in the United States.

a. Using the generally accepted definition of poverty, 11.7% of the population in the United States lived in poverty in 2001.

b. The poor tend to be concentrated among certain groups, such as blacks, Hispanics, female-headed families, and children.

c. The poverty rate has varied over time, as shown in Figure 34.4 of the text. It fell significantly from 1959–1969 and has ranged from about 11% to 15% since 1969.

d. Poverty in the United States tends to be invisible because the pool of poor people changes, the poor are isolated in large cities, and the poor do not have a political voice.

6. The *income-maintenance system* of the United States is intended to reduce poverty and includes both social insurance and public assistance (welfare) programs.

a. The principal *social insurance programs* are OASDHI (Old Age, Survivors and Disability Health Insurance, also known as Social Security) and Medicare. They are financed by taxes levied on employers and employees. The unemployment insurance programs, maintained by the states and financed by taxes on employers, are also a social insurance program in the United States.

b. The *public assistance programs* include SSI (Supplemental Security Income), TANF (Temporary Assistance for Needy Families), food stamps, and Medicaid. The EITC (earned income tax credit) is for low-income working families, with or without children. Other public assistance programs provide noncash transfers for education, job training, and housing assistance.

7. The *ideal public assistance program* has three basic goals: getting people out of poverty, providing incentives to work, and having a reasonable cost. These goals can conflict as illustrated by three hypothetical public assistance plans.

a. In any plan, a family would be guaranteed a minimum income and the subsidy to a family would decrease as its earned income increased. But a comparison of three alternative plans reveals that the guaranteed income, the (benefit-reduction) rate at which the subsidy declines as earned income increases, and the (break-even) income at which the subsidy is no longer paid, may differ.

b. The comparison of the plans also indicates there is a conflict among the goals of taking families out of poverty, maintaining incentives to work, and keeping the costs of the plan at a reasonable level, and that a tradeoff among the three goals is necessary because no one plan can achieve all three goals.

8. The public assistance system has been reformed in recent years under the Personal Responsibility Act of 1996. The reform arose in large part because of problems with the Aid to Families with Dependent Children (AFDC) program: administrative inefficiency, a negative effect on work incentives, and fostering a dependency on welfare.

a. The reform eliminated the Federal government's guarantee of cash assistance for poor families. In its place, states operated their own programs using lump-sum payments called TANF (Temporary Assistance for Needy Families). The reform limited the number of years (5) that a person could receive TANF benefits, and required able-bodied adults to work after 2 years of help. Other work requirements and restrictive provisions were added for those receiving public assistance. New legal immigrants could receive public assistance only after a 5-year waiting period.

b. Supporters contend that the law ended the "culture of poverty." The percentage of the population on welfare rolls dropped from 4.8% of the population in 1996 to 2% of the population in 2002, which was partly due to the reform. Critics argue that the reforms hurt children and penalize the poor. The true test of the reforms may come from an economic downturn that increases the number of people seeking public assistance.

■ **HINTS AND TIPS**

1. The distribution of income often raises issues of *normative economics.* For example, some people may say that "no person should be allowed to make that much money" when a high salary is reported in the media for a sports star or business executive. This chapter focuses on *positive economics* and offers explanations for why there are wide differences in the distribution of income and why there is poverty.

2. The *Lorenz curve* looks more complicated than it really is. The curve shows how the cumulative percentage of income is distributed across the percentage of families. The easiest way to learn about the curve is to use income and family data to construct one. Problem 1 in this chapter will help you with that objective.

3. Public assistance plans differ in two ways because there are two variables that affect the outcomes: the size of the minimum annual income and the difference in the benefit-reduction rate. Problem 2 in this chapter illustrates how those two variables affect the outcomes.

■ **IMPORTANT TERMS**

income inequality

Lorenz curve

Gini ratio

income mobility

noncash transfers

tradeoff between equality and efficiency

poverty rate

entitlement programs

social insurance programs

Old Age, Survivors, and Disability Health Insurance (OASDHI)

Medicare

poverty

unemployment compensation

public assistance programs

Supplemental Security Income (SSI)

Temporary Assistance for Needy Families (TANF)

food stamp program

Medicaid

earned income tax credit (EITC)

SELF-TEST

■ **FILL-IN QUESTIONS**

1. The data on the distribution of personal income by families suggest that there is considerable income (equality, inequality) _____ in the United States. The data show that families with annual incomes of less than $25,000 are about (21, 18) _____% of all families, and families with $100,000 or more in income are about _____% of all families.

2. Income inequality can be portrayed graphically by drawing a (Phillips, Lorenz) _____ curve.
   a. When such a curve is plotted, the cumulative percentage of (income, families) _____ is measured along the horizontal axis, and the cumulative percentage of _____ is measured along the vertical axis.
   b. The curve that would show a completely (perfectly) equal distribution of income is a diagonal line that would run from the (lower, upper) _____ left to the _____ right corner of the graph.
   c. The extent or degree of income inequality is measured by the area that lies between the line of complete equality and the (horizontal axis, Lorenz curve) _____.
   d. The Gini ratio measures the area between the line of equality and the Lorenz curve (multiplied, divided) _____ by the total area below the line of equality.

3. One major limitation with census data on the distribution of income in the United States is that the income-

accounting period is too (short, long) _____. There appears to be significant income (mobility, loss) _____ over time. Also, the longer the time period considered, the (more, less) _____ equal is the distribution of income.

4. The tax system and the transfer programs in the U.S. economy significantly (reduce, expand) _____ the degree of inequality in the distribution of income. The distribution of household income is substantially less equal (before, after) _____ taxes and transfers are taken into account and substantially more equal _____ taxes and transfers are taken into account.

5. The important factors that explain (or cause) income inequality are differences in _____, education and _____, labor market _____, differences in job tastes and _____, the unequal distribution of _____, market _____, and _____, connections, and misfortune.

6. From 1929 to 1947, the percentage of total before-tax income received by the top quintile of families (increased, decreased) _____, and the percentages received by the other four quintiles _____. Since 1969, the distribution of income by quintiles has become (more, less) _____ unequal.

7. The causes of the growing inequality of incomes are due to (more, less) _____ demand for highly skilled workers, entrance into the 1970s and 1980s labor force of _____-experienced baby boomers, and _____ families headed by single-wage earners. Other factors include (more, less) _____ international competition that reduced the average wage of low-skilled workers, _____ immigration that increased the number of low-income families, and _____ unionism.

8. Those who argue for the equal distribution of income contend that it results in the maximization of total (income, utility) _____ in the economy, while those who argue for the unequal distribution of income believe it results in a greater total _____.

9. The fundamental tradeoff is between equality and (welfare, efficiency) _____. This means that less income equality leads to a (greater, smaller)

_____ total output, and a larger total output requires (more, less) _____ income inequality.

10. The economic problem for a society that wants more equality is how to (minimize, maximize) _____ the adverse effects on economic efficiency.

11. Using the more or less official definition of poverty for 1999, the poor included any family of four with an income of less than ($18,104; $31,389) _____ and any individual with an income of less than ($9039; $16,354) _____ a year. In 2001, about (4, 12) _____% of the population, or about (33, 54) _____ million people, were poor.

12. Poverty tends to be concentrated among the (young, elderly) _____, among (whites, blacks) _____, and in families headed by (men, women) _____.

13. In the affluent economy of the United States, much of the poverty in the country is (visible, invisible) _____ because the poverty pool (stays the same, changes) _____ from year to year, the poor are often isolated in (small, large) _____ cities, and the poor do not have a political voice.

14. One part of the income-maintenance system in the United States consists of social insurance programs such as (OASDHI, AFDC) _____, (Medicare, Medicaid) _____, and (employment, unemployment) _____ compensation.

15. The other part of the income-maintenance system consists of public assistance or welfare programs such as (OASDHI, SSI) _____, (AFDC, SEC) _____, (Medicare, Medicaid) _____, and the food stamp program.

16. Public assistance programs include state-administered ones such as cash assistance for families with children, (EITC, TANF) _____ and a tax credit program for low-income working families, _____. Other public assistance programs also provide help in the form of (cash, noncash) _____ transfers, such as rent subsidies for housing and education assistance such as Head Start.

17. An ideal public assistance program would try to achieve three goals at the same time: The plan should get individuals and families off or out of (Medicare, poverty) _____, provide work (insurance, incentives) _____, and ensure that the program (benefits, costs) _____ are reasonable. In reality, these goals are (complementary, conflicting) _____.

18. The two common elements of a public assistance plan are a (maximum, minimum) _____ annual income provided by the government if the family earned no income and a (cost-benefit, benefit-reduction) _____ rate that specifies the rate at which the transfer payment would be cut if earned income increases.

19. The criticisms of past welfare programs, such as Aid to Families with Dependent Children, were that it provided little (insurance, improvement) _____ and created a culture of welfare (equality for, dependency on) _____ government.

20. In 1996, the Congress passed a major welfare reform, the (Family Support, Personal Responsibility) _____ Act. It set a lifetime limit of (5, 10) _____ years for receiving TANF payments and required able-bodied adults to work after (2, 4) _____ years of receiving assistance. Supporters of the law contend that it will end the culture of (compensation, welfare) _____, whereas critics think that it places the (responsibility, blame) _____ for poverty on its victims.

■ **TRUE–FALSE QUESTIONS**

Circle T if the statement is true, F if it is false.

1. If you knew the average income in the United States, you would know a great deal about income inequality in the United States. **T F**

2. The data on the distribution of personal income by families in the United States indicates that there is considerable income inequality. **T F**

3. In a Lorenz curve, the percentage of families in each income class is measured along the horizontal axis and the percentage of total income received by those families is measured on the vertical axis. **T F**

4. Income mobility is the movement of individuals or families from one income quintile to another over time. **T F**

5. Income is less equally distributed over a longer time period than a shorter time period. **T F**

6. The distribution of income in the United States _after_ taxes and transfers are taken into account is more equal than it is _before_ taxes and transfers are taken into account. **T F**

7. Differences in preferences for market work relative to nonmarket activities are one reason for income differences in the United States. **T F**

8. The ownership of wealth is fairly equally distributed across households in the United States. **T F**

9. Luck or misfortune are not factors contributing to income inequality in the United States. **T F**

10. From 1969 to 2001, there was an increase in income inequality in the United States. **T F**

11. A significant contributor to the growing income inequality of the past three decades was the greater demand for highly skilled and highly educated workers. **T F**

12. Growing income inequality means that the "rich are getting richer" in terms of absolute income. **T F**

13. The basic argument for an equal distribution of income is that income equality is necessary if consumer satisfaction (utility) is to be maximized. **T F**

14. Those who favor equality in the distribution of income contend that it will lead to stronger incentives to work, save, and invest and thus to a greater national income and output. **T F**

15. In the tradeoff between equality and economic efficiency, an increase in equality will lead to an increase in efficiency. **T F**

16. Using the government definition of poverty, approximately 12% of the population was poor in 2001. **T F**

17. The incidence of poverty is very high among female-headed families. **T F**

18. OASDHI, Medicare, and unemployment compensation are public assistance or welfare programs. **T F**

19. Social insurance programs provide benefits for those who are unable to earn income because of permanent handicaps or who have no or very low income and also have dependent children. **T F**

20. The benefit-reduction rate is the rate at which government benefits decrease as the earned income of a family increases. **T F**

21. The lower the benefit-reduction rate, the smaller the incentives to earn additional income. **T F**

22. In comparing welfare plans, it is possible to achieve simultaneously the three goals of eliminating poverty, maintaining work incentives, and holding down program costs. **T F**

23. Those who have been critical of welfare contend that it creates dependency on government and reduces the motivation to work. **T F**

24. The Personal Responsibility Act of 1996 was designed to reduce the dependence of the elderly on social security. **T F**

25. The Temporary Assistance for Needy Families (TANF) has among its provisions work requirements for those receiving welfare and a specified limit on the number of years for receiving welfare benefits. **T F**

■ **MULTIPLE-CHOICE QUESTIONS**

Circle the letter that corresponds to the best answer.

1. Recent data on the personal distribution of income in the United States indicate that
   (a) average incomes are falling
   (b) average incomes are constant
   (c) there is considerable income equality
   (d) there is considerable income inequality

2. When a Lorenz curve is drawn, the degree of income inequality in an economy is measured by the
   (a) slope of the diagonal that runs from the southwest to the northeast corner of the diagram
   (b) slope of the Lorenz curve
   (c) area between the Lorenz curve and the axes of the graph
   (d) area between the Lorenz curve and the southwest–northeast diagonal

Use the following graph to answer Questions 3, 4, 5, and 6. The graph shows four different Lorenz curves (1, 2, 3, and 4).

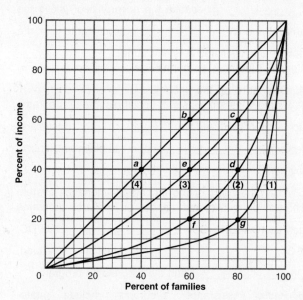

3. The greatest increase in income equality would occur with a shift in a Lorenz curve from
   (a) 1 to 2
   (b) 1 to 4
   (c) 4 to 1
   (d) 3 to 1

4. What point indicates that 80% of the families receive only 40% of the income?
   (a) *c*
   (b) *d*
   (c) *e*
   (d) *g*

5. The movement from point **b** to point **f** in the graph would indicate that

(a) 60% of families now receive 40% of income instead of 60% of income

(b) 60% of income goes to 20% of families instead of 60% of families

(c) 20% of income goes to 20% of families instead of 60% of families

(d) 60% of families now receive 20% of income instead of 60% of income

6. Which change would indicate that there has been an increase in income inequality and an increase in the Gini ratio? A movement from point

(a) **b** to **a**

(b) **g** to **d**

(c) **g** to **f**

(d) **e** to **d**

7. Suppose that Laura earns $5000 in year 1 and $50,000 in year 2, while Kristin earns $50,000 in year 1 and only $5000 in year 2. Is there income inequality for the two individuals?

(a) Both the annual and the 2-year data indicate equality.

(b) Both the annual and the 2-year data indicate inequality.

(c) The annual data indicate inequality, but the 2-year data indicate equality.

(d) The annual data indicate equality, but the 2-year data indicate inequality.

8. The empirical data indicate that the tax system and the transfer programs of the government

(a) significantly reduce the degree of inequality in the distribution of income

(b) produce only a slight reduction in the degree of inequality in the distribution of income

(c) significantly increase the degree of inequality in the distribution of income

(d) produce only a slight increase in the degree of inequality in the distribution of income

9. Most of the contribution to government redistribution of income comes from

(a) taxes

(b) transfers

(c) income mobility

(d) unemployment insurance

10. Which is one cause of unequal income distribution in the United States?

(a) an equitable distribution of wealth and property

(b) differences in education and training

(c) the high levels of noncash transfers

(d) the low benefit-reduction rate

11. The fact that some individuals are willing to take riskier jobs or assume more risk in their businesses is one major reason why there are differences in

(a) social insurance programs

(b) entitlement programs

(c) welfare

(d) income

12. Inequality in the distribution of wealth contributes to

(a) the same percentage of income received by the highest and lowest percentages of families

(b) a smaller percentage of income received by the highest 20 percentage of families

(c) a greater percentage of income received by the highest 20 percentage of families

(d) a greater percentage of income received by the lowest 20 percentage of families

13. Which would be evidence of a decrease in income inequality over time in the United States?

(a) a decrease in the percentage of total personal income received by the lowest quintile

(b) an increase in the percentage of total personal income received by the highest quintile

(c) an increase in the percentage of total personal income received by the four lowest quintiles

(d) a decrease in the percentage of total personal income received by the four lowest quintiles

14. A factor contributing to the increase in income inequality for the past three decades has been:

(a) less international competition from imports

(b) less demand for highly skilled workers in the labor force

(c) more marriages among men and women with high income potential

(d) more power by unions to obtain wage increases for union workers

15. Suppose Ms. Anne obtains 5 units of utility from the last dollar of income received by her, and Mr. Charles obtains 8 units of utility from the last dollar of his income. Those who favor an equal distribution of income would

(a) advocate redistributing income from Charles to Anne

(b) advocate redistributing income from Anne to Charles

(c) be content with this distribution of income between Anne and Charles

(d) argue that any redistribution of income between them would increase total utility

16. The case for income inequality is primarily made on the basis that income inequality

(a) is reduced by the transfer payment programs for the poor

(b) is necessary to maintain incentives to work and produce output

(c) depends on luck and chance, which cannot be corrected by government action

(d) is created by education and training programs that distort the distribution of income

17. The debate over income redistribution focuses on the tradeoff between equality and

(a) efficiency

(b) unemployment

(c) inflation

(d) economic freedom

18. The pizza slice analogy is used to describe the
(a) welfare reform mess
(b) trends in the poverty rate
(c) economic loss from income redistribution programs
(d) piecemeal approach toward income maintenance programs

19. What was the approximate poverty rate for the U.S. population in 2001?
(a) 2%
(b) 6%
(c) 12%
(d) 25%

20. In 2001, which group had the *smallest* percentage in poverty?
(a) Hispanics
(b) families headed by women
(c) children under 18 years of age
(d) the elderly (65 years and older)

21. An example of a social insurance program would be
(a) Medicare
(b) Medicaid
(c) food stamps
(d) Head Start

22. Which is designed to provide a nationwide minimum income for the aged, the blind, and the disabled?
(a) SSI
(b) FFS
(c) AFDC
(d) OASDHI

23. The purpose of the earned income tax credit (EITC) is to
(a) give a tax credit for spending on education and job training for welfare recipients
(b) give a tax break to businesses if they have low-income workers
(c) substitute the payment of cash for food stamps if people are willing to go to work
(d) offset Social Security taxes paid by low-wage earners so they are not "taxed into poverty"

24. The goals of welfare plans often conflict because it is difficult to construct a plan that
(a) provides reasonable income levels and incentives to work for the poor, but is not too costly
(b) is not subject to substantial administrative costs and bureaucratic red tape
(c) does not discriminate against those individuals with similar circumstances, but who have similar needs
(d) promotes family unity and does not create a "culture of poverty" among the participants in the program

25. The Temporary Assistance for Needy Families (TANF) program is administered by
(a) states and puts a lifetime limit of five years on receiving welfare payments
(b) religious institutions and places people in temporary jobs
(c) businesses and develops skills through education assistance
(d) the Federal government and provides food stamps for the needy

■ **PROBLEMS**

1. The distribution of personal income among families in a hypothetical economy is shown in the table below.
a. Complete the table by computing the
(1) percentage of all families in each income class and all lower classes; enter these figures in column 4.
(2) percentage of total income received by each income class and all lower classes; enter these figures in column 5.
b. From the distribution of income data in columns 4 and 5, it can be seen that
(1) families with less than $15,000 a year income

constitute the lowest _____% of all families

and receive _____% of the total income.
(2) families with incomes of $50,000 a year or more

constitute the highest _____% of all families

and receive _____% of the total income.

(1) Personal income class	(2) Percentage of all families in this class	(3) Percentage of total income received by this class	(4) Percentage of all families in this and all lower classes	(5) Percentage of total income received by this and all lower classes
Under $10,000	18	4	_____	_____
$10,000 – $14,999	12	6	_____	_____
$15,000 – $24,999	14	12	_____	_____
$25,000 – $34,999	17	14	_____	_____
$35,000 – $49,999	19	15	_____	_____
$50,000 – $74,999	11	20	_____	_____
$75,000 and over	9	29	_____	_____

c. Use the figures you entered in columns 4 and 5 to draw a Lorenz curve on the above graph. (Plot the seven points and the zero-zero point and connect them with a smooth curve.) Be sure to label the axes.
(1) Draw a diagonal line that would indicate complete equality in the distribution of income.
(2) Shade the area of the graph that shows the degree of income inequality.

2. The following table contains different possible earned incomes for a family of a certain size.

Earned income	Transfer payment	Total income
$ 0	$ 5000	$ 5000
5000	_____	_____
10,000	_____	_____
15,000	_____	_____
20,000	_____	_____
25,000	_____	_____

a. Assume that $5000 is the minimum annual income provided by government for a family of this size and that the benefit-reduction rate is 20%. Enter the transfer payment and the total income at each of the five remaining earned-income levels. (Hint: 20% of $5000 is $1000.)

(1) This program retains strong incentives to work because whenever the family earns an additional $5000 its total income increases by

$_____.
(2) But this program is costly because the family receives a subsidy until its earned income, the break-even income, is $_____.

b. To reduce the break-even income, the benefit reduction rate is raised to 50%. Complete the following table.

Earned income	Transfer payment	Total income
$ 0	$ 5000	$ 5000
2500	_____	_____
5000	_____	_____
7500	_____	_____
10,000	_____	_____

(1) This program is less costly than the previous one because the family only receives a subsidy until it earns

the break-even income of $_____,

(2) but the incentives to work are less because whenever the family earns an additional $5000 its total income increases by only $_____.

c. Both the previous two welfare programs had a minimum annual income of only $5000. Assume that the minimum annual income is raised to $7500 and the benefit-reduction rate is kept at 50%. Complete the following table.

Earned income	Transfer payment	Total income
$ 0	$ 7500	$ 7500
3000	____	____
6000	____	____
9000	____	____
12,000	____	____
15,000	____	____

(1) This program is more costly than the previous one because the break-even income has risen to $_____.

(2) The incentives to earn additional income are no better in this program than in the previous one. But to improve these incentives by reducing the benefit-reduction rate to 40% would raise the break-even income to (divide the minimum annual income by the benefit-reduction rate) $_____.

d. To summarize:

(1) Given the minimum annual income provided by government, the lower the benefit-reduction rate the (greater, less) _____ are the incentives to earn additional income and the (greater, less) _____ are the break-even income and the cost of the welfare program,

(2) and given the benefit-reduction rate, the greater the minimum annual income, the (greater, less) _____ are the break-even income and the cost of the program,

(3) but to reduce the break-even income and the cost of the program requires either (an increase, a decrease) _____ in the benefit-reduction rate or _____ in the minimum annual income.

3. Match the terms with the phrase using the appropriate number.

1. entitlement programs   3. public assistance programs

2. noncash transfers   4. social insurance programs

a. Government programs such as social insurance, food stamps, Medicare, and Medicaid that guarantee particular levels of transfer payments to all who fit the programs' criteria. _____

b. Government programs that pay benefits to those who are unable to earn income (because of permanent handicaps or because they have very low incomes and dependent children). _____

c. Government transfer payments in the form of goods and services rather than money. _____

d. Government programs that replace earnings lost when people retire or are temporarily unemployed. _____

■ **SHORT ANSWER AND ESSAY QUESTIONS**

1. How much income inequality is there in the U.S. economy? Cite figures to support your conclusion.

2. What is measured along each of the two axes when a Lorenz curve is drawn?

(a) If the distribution of income were completely equal, what would the Lorenz curve look like?

(b) If one family received all of the income of the economy, what would the Lorenz curve look like?

(c) After the Lorenz curve for an economy has been drawn, how is the degree of income inequality in that economy measured?

(d) What is the difference between the Lorenz curve and the Gini ratio?

3. Explain how time affects the distribution of income and interpretations of income trends.

4. What effect do taxes and transfers have on the distribution of income in the United States? How much of this change in the distribution of income is the result of the transfer payments made by government?

5. What seven factors contribute to income inequality in the United States?

6. How has the distribution of income changed in the United States since 1929? What has been the trend in income distribution since 1969?

7. What are three probable explanations for the increase in income inequality in the United States over the past three decades?

8. State the case for equal distribution of income.

9. Explain the advantage to the nation from an unequal distribution of income.

10. What is the fundamental tradeoff involving income inequality? Explain the leaky bucket analogy.

11. What is poverty? What is the minimum income level below which the Federal government defines a person or family as "in poverty"? How many people and what percentage of the U.S. population are "in poverty" using this definition?

12. What characteristics—other than the small amounts of money they have to spend—do the greatest concentrations of the poor families of the nation *tend* to have?

13. What have been the trends in the poverty rate since 1960? What were the trends in the 1980s and 1990s?

14. Why does poverty in the United States tend to be invisible or hidden?

15. Explain the difference between social insurance and public assistance. Which do you think is more important?

16. List and briefly describe three social insurance programs of the income-maintenance system of the United States.

17. Explain the major public assistance programs of the income-maintenance system of the United States.

18. What are the three goals of an ideal welfare program? Explain why there is a conflict among these goals—why all three goals cannot be achieved simultaneously.

19. Explain how poverty and the unequal distribution of income would be reduced by three hypothetical welfare plans. Be sure to include in your explanation the definition of the minimum annual income that would be provided by government, the benefit-reduction rate, and the break-even income.

20. Discuss the Temporary Assistance to Needy Families (TANF) program and explain what supporters and critics say about it.

ANSWERS

Chapter 34 Income Inequality and Poverty

FILL-IN QUESTIONS

1. inequality, 21, 18
2. Lorenz; *a.* families, income; *b.* lower, upper; *c.* Lorenz curve; *d.* divided
3. short, mobility, more
4. reduce, before, after
5. ability, training, discrimination, risks, wealth, power, luck
6. decreased, increased, more
7. more, less, more, more, less
8. utility, income
9. efficiency, greater, more
10. minimize
11. $18,104, $9039, 12, 33
12. young, blacks, women
13. invisible, changes, large
14. OASDHI, Medicare, unemployment
15. SSI, AFDC, Medicaid
16. TANF, EITC, noncash
17. poverty, incentives, costs, conflicting
18. minimum, benefit-reduction
19. improvement, dependency on
20. Personal Responsibility, 5, 2, welfare, blame

TRUE–FALSE QUESTIONS

1. F, p. 631	10. T, p. 636	19. F, pp. 642–643
2. T, pp. 631–632	11. T, pp. 636–637	20. T, pp. 644–645
3. T, pp. 632–633	12. F, p. 638	21. F, pp. 644–645
4. T, p. 633	13. T, p. 638	22. F, p. 645
5. F, p. 633	14. F, pp. 638–639	23. T, p. 645
6. T, p. 634	15. F, pp. 639–640	24. F, p. 645
7. T, p. 635	16. T, p. 640	25. T, p. 645
8. F, p. 635	17. T, pp. 640–641	
9. F, p. 636	18. F, pp. 642–643	

MULTIPLE-CHOICE QUESTIONS

1. d, pp. 631–632	10. b, p. 635	19. c, p. 640
2. d, pp. 632–633	11. d, p. 635	20. d, pp. 640–641
3. b, pp. 632–633	12. c, pp. 636–637	21. a, pp. 642–643
4. b, pp. 632–633	13. c, pp. 636–637	22. a, pp. 642–643
5. d, pp. 632–633	14. c, p. 637	23. d, pp. 642–643
6. d, pp. 632–633	15. b, p. 638	24. a, p. 645
7. c, p. 633	16. b, pp. 638–639	25. a, p. 645
8. a, p. 634	17. a, pp. 639–640	
9. b, p. 634	18. c, pp. 639–640	

PROBLEMS

1. *a.* (1) column 4: 18, 30, 44, 61, 80, 91, 100, (2) column 5: 4, 10, 22, 36, 51, 71, 100; *b.* (1) 30, 10, (2) 20, 49 *c.* graph
2. *a.* Transfer payment: 4000, 3000, 2000, 1000, 0; Total income: 9000, 13,000, 17,000, 21,000, 25,000, (1) 4000, (2) 25,000; *b.* Transfer payment: 3750, 2500, 1250, 0; Total income: 6250, 7500, 8750, 10,000, (1) 10,000, (2) 2500; *c.* Transfer payment: 6000, 4500, 3000, 1500, 0; Total income: 9000, 10,500, 12,000, 13,500, 15,000, (1) 15,000, (2) 18,750; *d.* (1) greater, greater, (2) greater, (3) an increase, a decrease
3. *a.* 1; *b.* 3; *c.* 2; *d.* 4

SHORT ANSWER AND ESSAY QUESTIONS

1. pp. 631–632	8. p. 638	15. pp. 642–643
2. pp. 632–633	9. pp. 638–639	16. pp. 642–643
3. p. 633	10. pp. 639–640	17. pp. 642–644
4. p. 634	11. pp. 640–641	18. pp. 644–645
5. pp. 634–636	12. pp. 640–641	19. pp. 644–645
6. pp. 636–637	13. p. 641	20. p. 645
7. pp. 636–638	14. pp. 641–642	

CHAPTER 35

Labor Market Institutions and Issues: Unionism, Discrimination, Immigration

This chapter completes the examination of government and current economic problems by looking at three major issues in labor markets: unionism, discrimination, and immigration. Unions and labor-management relations are frequently in the news because of strikes, new labor legislation, or other issues. Discrimination was cited as a factor contributing to poverty in Chapter 34, but now Chapter 35 extends the discussion by analyzing discrimination in labor markets. Immigration is important because it allows labor resources to move between nations and has economic effects on both the sending and receiving nations.

The **labor union** is an important economic institution in the U.S. economy. Some 16 million workers covering about 13% of the labor force belong to unions. Unions typically focus on specific economic objectives such as improving pay, hours, and working conditions. Union members are more likely to work in government or to be employed in transportation, construction, manufacturing, and mining industries. In spite of its importance, unionism has been on the decline since the mid-1950s, and the explanation for this decline is given in the chapter.

In Chapter 28 you learned how unions directly and indirectly seek to influence wage rates. The impact of the union on its own membership, on employers, and on the economy is more than just a matter of wages; it involves a contract between a union and an employer. This chapter discusses collective bargaining to give you some insights about the union goals and other issues over which employers and employees bargain. Another important idea discussed is that labor-management relations involve more than the periodic signing of a contract; they also involve the day-to-day relations between the union and the employer and the new issues not settled in the contract but which must be resolved under the general provisions of the contract.

The chapter elaborates on the economic effects of unions on the economy. Unions affect their members' wage rates relative to nonunionized workers' wage rates. Unions may also improve the productivity of labor and therefore economic efficiency in the economy. Just how unions affect these economic variables is largely uncertain and debatable. The authors of the text present both sides of the issues and draw conclusions from the empirical evidence.

Discrimination has always been present in labor markets in the form of wage, employment, occupational, or human capital discrimination. This discrimination causes significant costs for individuals who earn lower wages or have fewer work opportunities than would otherwise be the case. There are also costs to society because valuable labor resources are being inefficiently used.

The economic analysis of labor-market discrimination gives you several insights into this significant problem. The taste-for-discrimination model explains the hiring practices of prejudiced employers and the effects on the wages and employment of nonpreferred groups. You will also learn how statistical discrimination, which bases decisions on average characteristics, may disadvantage individuals. The crowding model of occupational discrimination described in the chapter also explains how occupational segregation affects pay and output in an economy.

The government has taken actions and adopted policies to counter discrimination in labor markets. Perhaps the most controversial form of government intervention has been *affirmative action.* You will examine the current debate over affirmative action and learn what supporters and critics have to say about it. You will also learn about recent legal and political developments related to this controversy.

The final major part of the chapter discusses the economics of *immigration,* which moves labor resources from one nation to another. The migration of workers from a poorer nation (such as Mexico) to a richer nation (such as the United States) economically affects wage rates, unemployment, output, and business incomes in the two nations. The method used to analyze the effects of this immigration is similar to the analysis of unions and discrimination you studied earlier in the chapter. The conclusions drawn about immigration using the supply and demand analysis are definite, but as you discover at the end of the chapter, the real world is more complicated, so any conclusions will be modified.

■ CHECKLIST

When you have studied this chapter you should be able to

☐ Identify the number and percentage of union members and the major union organizations.
☐ Explain the meaning of business unionism.
☐ Describe the characteristics of workers belonging to unions.
☐ State how unions have declined since the mid-1950s.
☐ Present two hypotheses to explain unionism's decline.

☐ Explain the four basic areas covered by work agreements in collective bargaining.

☐ Describe the bargaining process and major labor relations law.

☐ Draw conclusions about the effects of unions on the wages of workers.

☐ Identify three negative effects unions might have on productivity and efficiency.

☐ Use a supply and demand model to show how a union might lead to a misallocation of labor resources and reduced output.

☐ List three positive effects unions might have on productivity and efficiency.

☐ Describe four types of labor market discrimination.

☐ Illustrate the cost of discrimination with a production possibilities curve.

☐ Use a wage equation to explain the taste-for-discrimination model in labor markets.

☐ Use a supply and demand graph to illustrate the taste-for-discrimination model in labor markets.

☐ Explain and give an example of statistical discrimination.

☐ Use the crowding model of occupational discrimination to explain differences in wages among groups and efficiency effects.

☐ Identify three types of antidiscrimination policies.

☐ Discuss the arguments for and against affirmative action.

☐ Describe recent legal and political developments in affirmative action.

☐ Give estimates of the number of legal and illegal immigrants entering the United States in recent years.

☐ Use a supply and demand model to explain the effects of worker migration from a poor to a rich nation on wage rates, output, and incomes in both nations.

☐ Explain how four complicating factors modify the effects of migration on the two economies.

☐ Describe two contrasting views of the effects of immigration on the United States.

■ **CHAPTER OUTLINE**

1. About 16 million workers in the United States belong to *unions,* and they account for only about 13% of wage and salary workers. Most union workers are members of the *American Federation of Labor and Congress of Industrial Organizations* (AFL-CIO).

    a. Most unions have adopted a philosophy of *business unionism* that focuses on the economic objectives of higher pay, shorter work hours, and improved working conditions.

    b. Occupation and industry are important factors that explain who belongs to unions. The rate of unionization is high in government and in the transportation, construction, manufacturing, and mining industries. Men, blacks, and those living in urban areas are more likely to be union members.

    c. Union membership has declined since the mid-1950s, when about 25% of the workforce was union-

ized. Two complementary hypotheses explain the decline.

    (1) The *structural-change hypothesis* is that changes in the structure of the economy and the labor force have limited the expansion of union membership.

    (2) The *managerial-opposition hypothesis* is that the opposition of management to unions increased because union firms were thought to be less profitable than nonunion firms. The policies management used against unions decreased union membership.

2. *Collective bargaining* between labor and management results in work agreements.

    a. These agreements take many different forms, but usually cover four basic areas: union status *(open, closed, or agency shops)* and managerial prerogatives; wages and hours; seniority and job protection; and grievance procedures.

    b. This bargaining process on a new contract typically occurs in the 60-day period before the end of the existing contract. After the deadline, a union can strike, or there can be a lockout by the firm. Most contract agreements are compromises; strikes, lockouts, and violence are rare. The *National Labor Relations Act* specifies legal and illegal practices in collective bargaining, and the *National Labor Relations Board* is authorized to investigate unfair labor practices.

3. Labor unions have *economic effects.*

    a. While unions have increased the wages of their members relative to the wages of nonunion members, they have had little or no effect on the average level of real wages in the economy.

    b. Whether unions result in more or less efficiency and an increase or a decrease in the productivity of labor is a two-sided question.

    (1) The negative view is that unions decrease efficiency by featherbedding and establishing work rules, engaging in strikes, and fostering a misallocation of labor resources.

    (2) The positive view is that unions increase efficiency by having a shock effect on management performance, reducing worker turnover, and by informally transferring skills from the more- to the less-skilled workers fostered by the seniority system.

    (3) The empirical evidence is mixed, showing that unions have increased labor productivity in some industries but decreased it in others. There is no generally accepted conclusion as to the effect of unions on the productivity of labor in the economy.

4. *Discrimination* in labor markets occurs when equivalent labor resources that make equally productive contributions are given different pay or treatment. Discrimination affects the earnings of women and minorities in the labor market.

    a. Labor market discrimination against a group can occur in four ways: lower wages; inferior employment treatment in hiring, promotions, assignments, and working conditions; restrictions or prohibitions that limit entry or mobility in occupations; and less access to opportunities for investments in education and training or other forms of human capital.

b. Discrimination has private and social costs. It transfers income and benefits from one group to another. It also reduces the output and income of the economy by operating as an artificial barrier to competition.

5. The economic analysis of discrimination provides some insights even though the issue is complex and multifaceted.

a. The *taste-for-discrimination model* explains prejudice using demand theory. The model assumes that a prejudiced employer is willing to pay a "price" to avoid interactions with a nonpreferred group.

(1) The *discrimination coefficient* measures in monetary units the cost of the employer's prejudice. An employer will hire nonpreferred workers only if their wage rates are below those of the preferred workers by an amount at least equal to the discrimination coefficient.

(2) In the supply and demand model for nonpreferred workers, an increase in the prejudice of employers will decrease the demand for this labor, the number of workers, and their wage rate. A decrease in the prejudice of employers will increase the demand for this labor, the number employed, and the wage rate.

(3) The taste-for-discrimination model suggests that in the very long run, competition will reduce discrimination, but critics question this conclusion, given the insufficient progress in reducing discrimination over time in the United States.

b. *Statistical discrimination* involves judging people based on the average characteristics of the group to which they belong instead of productivity or personal characteristics. In labor markets, employers may stereotype workers by applying the average characteristics of the group in work assessments of individual members of that group. The practice may be profitable and on average it may produce correct decisions, but it fails to take into account the individual skills and capabilities and limits opportunities for workers.

c. The practice of *occupational segregation* suggests that women and minorities are crowded into a small number of occupations. In this crowding model, the supply of these workers is large relative to the demand for them, and thus their wage rates and incomes are lower in these crowded occupations. Eliminating occupational segregation would raise wage rates and incomes for these workers and also increase the economy's output.

6. The government can try to correct the discrimination problem by promoting a growing economy, improving the education and training of women and minorities, and creating policies that restrict or eliminate discriminatory practices.

a. *Affirmative action* involves special efforts by employers to increase employment and promotion opportunities for groups that have experienced and continue to experience discrimination.

(1) Arguments for affirmative action include the need to close the pay and socioeconomic gap for women and minorities and the need to counter long-lasting prejudice and discriminatory employment practices. Eliminating discrimination will also improve economic efficiency and economic growth.

(2) The opposing view is that economic efficiency is reduced because employers are forced to hire less qualified workers. Hiring quotas and preferential treatment are considered a form of reverse discrimination. Some opponents suggest that affirmative action increases hostility and resentment in the workplace and mistakenly leads people to attribute work success not to their personal contributions but to their protected status.

b. Affirmative action has been subject to legal and political attacks in recent years. The Supreme Court declared some affirmative action programs illegal because they promote reverse discrimination. The courts have also limited the application of race-based preferences in Federal programs. Congress has debated the issue, and the Clinton administration halted some minority programs that gave contracting preferences to minorities.

7. The *immigration* of workers into the United States is a controversial issue because this international movement of labor has had economic effects on the U.S. economy.

a. During the 1990s, about 850,000 *legal immigrants* and 100,000 *illegal immigrants* entered the United States each year. About one-third of the recent population growth is from immigration.

b. The economic effects of immigration can be shown in a two-nation model, one poorer and one richer.

(1) The movement of workers from a poorer economy raises the average wages of workers in the poorer nation and lowers the average wage rates in the richer nation. Domestic output in the poorer nation will decline and domestic output in the richer nation will expand, but the net effect from a world perspective is an increase in output and economic efficiency.

(2) The incomes of businesses in the richer nation will increase but decrease in the poorer nation; the richer nation gains "cheap" labor and the poorer nation loses "cheap" labor.

c. These conclusions must be modified to take into account other factors.

(1) There is a cost to migration for workers that will reduce the world gain in output.

(2) Remittances reduce the gains for the richer nation. If immigrant workers remit some of their increased wages to relatives in the poorer nation, then some gain for the domestic economy is lost. The return of immigrants to the poorer nation (backflows) alters gains and losses.

(3) The model assumes full employment in both nations. If there is unemployment or underemployment in the poorer nation, it can increase domestic output when the surplus workers emigrate.

(4) Immigration can affect tax revenues and government spending. If immigrants take advantage of welfare benefits in the richer nation, it imposes an additional cost on the richer nation.

d. The positive view of immigration considers it a source of economic progress for a nation, but the negative view is that it causes socioeconomic problems that hinder a nation.

■ HINTS AND TIPS

1. This chapter deals with three issues—unions, discrimination, and immigration—that can provoke emotional reactions. Make sure you remember the distinction between *positive* and *normative* economics made in Chapter 1. The purpose of the chapter is to analyze and explain the economics of unions, discrimination, and immigration (*what is*), and not the ideal world (*what ought to be*).

2. The effects of discrimination are illustrated by the production possibilities curve you first learned about in Chapter 2. In this model discrimination is similar to unemployment in the economy.

3. Although three different issues are discussed in this chapter, the supply and demand graphs comparing the gains and losses of different groups are quite similar (Figures 35.2, 35.5, and 35.6). In each graph, the wage rate is plotted on the vertical axis and the quantity of labor is on the horizontal axis. Each graph shows how segmentation of a labor market affects the wage rate, employment, and domestic output. Problems 3, 4, and 5 in this chapter will help you master this material.

■ IMPORTANT TERMS

American Federation of Labor-Congress of Industrial Organizations (AFL-CIO)	National Labor Relations Act (NLRA)
independent unions	National Labor Relations Board (NLRB)
business unionism	exit mechanism
structural-change hypothesis	voice mechanism
managerial-opposition hypothesis	labor market discrimination
collective bargaining	wage discrimination
closed shop	employment discrimination
union shop	occupational discrimination
agency shop	human-capital discrimination
right-to-work laws	taste-for-discrimination model
open shop	discrimination coefficient
cost-of-living adjustment (COLA)	statistical discrimination
strike	occupational segregation
lockout	affirmative action
	reverse discrimination
	legal immigrants
	illegal immigrants

■ SELF-TEST

■ FILL-IN QUESTIONS

1. About (16, 32) _____ million workers belong to labor unions in the United States. This number represents about (13, 28) _____% of wage and salary workers.

2. The rate of unionization is relatively (low, high) _____ among workers in government, transportation, construction, and manufacturing, and it is _____ among protective service workers, machine operators, and craft workers. Men are (more, less) _____ likely to be union members than women; blacks are _____ likely to be union members than whites; and those in urban areas are _____ likely to be union members than those workers in other locations.

3. Since the mid-1950s, union membership as a percentage of the labor force has (increased, decreased) _____ and, since 1980, the number of unionized workers has _____.

4. Two complementary hypotheses can be used to explain the changes in the size of union membership. The (structural-change, managerial-opposition) _____ hypothesis suggests that conditions unfavorable to the expansion of unions have occurred in the economy and labor; the _____ hypothesis suggests that union growth has been deterred by the policies of firms to limit or dissuade workers from joining unions.

5. A typical work agreement between a union and an employer covers the following four basic areas:

a. _____

b. _____

c. _____

d. _____

6. Unionization of workers in the U.S. economy has tended to (increase, decrease, have no effect on) _____ the wage rates of union members, _____ the wage rates of nonunion workers, and _____ the average level of real wage rates received by all workers.

7. Unions have a negative effect on productivity and efficiency in the economy to the extent that they engage in (collective bargaining, featherbedding) _____ and impose (a shock effect, work rules) _____ on their employers, participate in (training with, strikes against) _____ their employers, or impose (above, below) _____- equilibrium wage rates on employers that lead to misallocation of labor resources.

8. Unions have a positive effect on productivity and efficiency in the economy when the increased wage rate can have (an income, a shock) _____ effect that induces employers to substitute capital for labor and hasten their search for technologies that (increase, decrease) _____ the costs of production. Unions can also (increase, decrease) _____ labor turnover, and the seniority system can _____ informal training of younger workers by older workers.

9. Discrimination relating to the labor market occurs when women or minorities having (the same, inferior) _____ abilities, education, training, and experience as men or white workers are given _____ treatment with respect to hiring, occupational choice, education and training, promotion, and wage rates. Studies of the differences in earnings between men and women and blacks and whites find that (half, three-fourths) _____ can be explained by factors such as age, education, and training, but about _____ (one-fourth, half) are unexplained and due largely to discrimination.

10. The four principal kinds of economic discrimination are

a. _____

b. _____

c. _____

d. _____

11. Discrimination (increases, decreases) _____ the wages of workers in the nonpreferred group and _____ the wages of workers in the preferred group; it _____ economic efficiency and _____ total output in the economy.

12. In the taste-for-discrimination model, the discrimination coefficient *d* measures the (utility, disutility) _____ that prejudiced employers experience when they must interact with those they are biased against. This coefficient is measured in monetary units and becomes part of the (benefit, cost) _____ of hiring nonpreferred workers. The prejudiced employer will hire nonpreferred workers only if their wage rate is (above, below) _____ that of the preferred workers by at least the amount of the discrimination coefficient.

13. An increase in the prejudice of employers against nonpreferred workers will (increase, decrease) _____ their wage rate and the number employed; a decrease in the prejudice of employers against nonpreferred workers will (increase, decrease) _____ their wage rate and the number employed.

14. When employers base employment decisions about individuals on the average characteristics of groups of workers, this is (reverse, statistical) _____ discrimination. The decisions that firms make based on this type of discrimination may be (irrational, rational) _____ and profitable, on average, but hurt individuals to whom the averages (do, do not) _____ apply.

15. The occupational discrimination that pushes women and blacks into a small number of occupations in which the supply of labor is large relative to the demand is explained by the (managerial-opposition, crowding) _____ model. Because supply is large relative to demand, wages and incomes in these occupations are (high, low) _____. The reduction or elimination of this occupational discrimination would result in a (more, less) _____ efficient allocation of the labor resources of the economy and (an expansion, a contraction) _____ in the domestic output.

16. Those who support affirmative action say that (equal, preferential) _____ treatment is needed to help women and minorities compensate for decades of discrimination. They also argue that affirmative action (increases, decreases) _____ economic efficiency, but opponents argue that it _____ economic efficiency and causes (statistical, reverse) _____ discrimination.

17. The annual number of legal immigrants to the United States in the 1990s was about (450, 850) _____ thousand. About one-(tenth, third) _____ of the population growth in the United States can be attributed to immigration.

18. In the rich nation, the movement of workers from a poor nation to the rich nation tends to (increase, decrease) _____ domestic output, to _____ wage rates, and to (increase, decrease) _____ business incomes; in the poor nation it tends to _____ domestic output, to (increase, decrease) _____ wage rates, and to _____ business incomes; in the world it tends to (increase, decrease) _____ the real output of goods and services.

19. List the four complications that may modify the conclusions reached in question 18.

a. _____

b. _____

c. _____

d. _____

20. Supporters of immigration argue that immigrant workers (increase, decrease) _____ the supply of products with their labor and _____ the demand for products with their incomes, but opponents of immigration contend that immigrants (increase, decrease) _____ the burden of welfare and _____ the wages of domestic workers. These views, however, are too (complex, simplistic) _____ because assessing the net benefits of immigration depends on the number of immigrants, their education, skills, work ethics, and other factors.

■ TRUE–FALSE QUESTIONS

Circle T if the statement is true, F if it is false.

1. Most union members in the United States belong to independent unions not affiliated with the AFL-CIO. **T F**

2. The rate of unionization is high in transportation, construction, and manufacturing industries. **T F**

3. Union membership as a percentage of the labor force has been rising since the 1950s. **T F**

4. The managerial-opposition hypothesis argues that structural changes in the economy have limited management opposition to unions. **T F**

5. Collective bargaining between labor and management means no more than deciding on the wage rates employees will receive during the life of the contract. **T F**

6. The wages of union members exceed the wages of nonunion members on the average by more than 40%. **T F**

7. Strikes in the U.S. economy result in little lost work time and reductions in total output. **T F**

8. The loss of output in the U.S. economy resulting from increases in wage rates imposed by unions on employers is relatively large. **T F**

9. The seniority system, its advocates argue, expands the informal training of less-skilled, younger workers and improves the productivity of a firm's workforce. **T F**

10. It is generally agreed that unions decrease the productivity of labor in the U.S. economy. **T F**

11. Labor market discrimination occurs when equivalent labor resources are paid or treated differently even though their productive contributions are equal. **T F**

12. Almost all the differences in the earnings between men and women and blacks and whites can be explained by discrimination. **T F**

13. Sexual and racial harassment would be considered part of human-capital discrimination. **T F**

14. Discrimination redistributes income and reduces the economy's output. **T F**

15. In the taste-for-discrimination model, employer preference for discrimination is measured in dollars by discrimination coefficient *d*. These employers will hire nonpreferred workers only if their wages are at least *d* dollars below the wages of preferred workers. **T F**

16. In the taste-for-discrimination model, a decline in the prejudice of employers will decrease the demand for black workers and lower the black wage rate and the ratio of black to white wages. **T F**

17. Statistical discrimination occurs when employers base employment decisions about individuals on the average characteristics of groups of workers. **T F**

18. The crowding model of occupational segregation shows how white males earn higher earnings at the expense of women and minorities, who are restricted to a limited number of occupations. **T F**

19. Tight labor markets tend to increase discrimination and stereotyping rather than reduce them. **T F**

20. More than 10 million immigrants enter the United States each year, about half of whom are legal and the other half illegal. **T F**

21. Supply and demand analysis suggests that the movement of workers from a poor to a rich country decreases domestic output in the rich country and increases domestic output in the poor country. **T F**

22. An increase in the mobility of labor from one nation to other nations tends to increase the world's output of goods and services. **T F**

23. Mexican workers who have migrated to the United States and send remittances to their families in Mexico increase the gain to domestic output in the United States and reduce it in Mexico. **T F**

24. When unemployed or underemployed laborers from a poor nation migrate to a rich nation, the poor nation suffers a loss in domestic output because it loses workers. **T F**

25. Immigration will always harm a nation because it reduces the wages of workers in the domestic economy and thus reduces national income. **T F**

■ **MULTIPLE-CHOICE QUESTIONS**

Circle the letter that corresponds to the best answer.

1. About what percent of employed wage and salary workers in the United States belong to unions?
 (a) 7%
 (b) 13%
 (c) 21%
 (d) 35%

2. The rate of unionization is highest in
 (a) services
 (b) retail trade
 (c) government
 (d) manufacturing

3. The decline in union membership in the United States in recent years can be explained by the
 (a) managerial-growth hypothesis
 (b) structural-change hypothesis
 (c) relative-income hypothesis
 (d) complementary-expansion hypothesis

4. If workers at the time they are hired have a choice of joining the union and paying dues or of not joining the union and paying no dues, there exists
 (a) a union shop
 (b) an open shop
 (c) a nonunion shop
 (d) a closed shop

5. A major responsibility of the National Labor Relations Board is to
 (a) enforce right-to-work laws
 (b) keep unions from becoming politically active
 (c) investigate unfair labor practices under labor law
 (d) maintain labor peace between the AFL and CIO

6. Unionization has tended to
 (a) increase the wages of union workers and decrease the wages of some nonunion workers
 (b) increase the wages of some nonunion workers and decrease the wages of union workers
 (c) increase the wages of both union and nonunion workers
 (d) increase the average level of real wages in the economy

7. The higher wages imposed on employers in a unionized labor market tend to result in
 (a) lower wage rates in nonunionized labor markets and a decline in domestic output
 (b) lower wage rates in nonunionized labor markets and an expansion in domestic output
 (c) higher wage rates in nonunionized labor markets and a decline in domestic output
 (d) higher wage rates in nonunionized labor markets and an expansion in domestic output

8. Which tends to decrease (to have a negative effect on) productivity and efficiency in the economy?
 (a) the seniority system
 (b) reduced labor turnover
 (c) featherbedding and union-imposed work rules
 (d) the shock effect of higher union-imposed wage rates

9. The reallocation of a unit of labor from employment where its MRP is $50,000 to employment where its MRP is $40,000 will
 (a) increase the output of the economy by $10,000
 (b) increase the output of the economy by $90,000
 (c) decrease the output of the economy by $10,000
 (d) decrease the output of the economy by $90,000

10. Which tends to increase (have a positive effect on) productivity and efficiency in the economy?
 (a) strikes
 (b) reduced labor turnover
 (c) featherbedding and union-imposed work rules
 (d) a decrease in the training programs for workers

11. A wage increase imposed by unions on employers has a shock effect if it induces employers to
 (a) decrease the substitution of capital for labor
 (b) slow their search for productivity-increasing technologies
 (c) speed their employment of productive techniques that reduce their costs
 (d) lockout workers to encourage bargaining

12. Unions tend to reduce labor turnover by providing workers with all but one of the following. Which one?
 (a) an exit mechanism
 (b) a voice mechanism
 (c) a collective voice
 (d) a wage advantage

13. What form of discrimination is indicated by a report from the U.S. Department of Labor that states the unemployment rate for blacks is double that for whites?
 (a) occupational discrimination
 (b) employment discrimination
 (c) human-capital discrimination
 (d) wage discrimination

14. A study by a labor economist finds that 12% of blacks and 22% of whites have completed 4 or more years of college. These data are evidence of
 (a) occupational discrimination
 (b) employment discrimination
 (c) human-capital discrimination
 (d) wage discrimination

15. In the production possibilities model, the effect of discrimination can be illustrated by a
 (a) point outside the frontier
 (b) point inside the frontier
 (c) point on the frontier
 (d) shift out from the frontier

16. In a supply and demand model of the labor market for nonpreferred workers, an increase in employer prejudice will
 (a) increase supply, raise the wage rate, and decrease the employment of these workers

(b) decrease supply, lower the wage rate, and decrease employment of these workers

(c) decrease demand, lower the wage rate, and decrease the employment of these workers

(d) increase demand, raise the wage rate, and increase the employment of these workers

17. Suppose the market wage rate for a preferred worker is $12 and the monetary value of disutility the employer attaches to hiring a nonpreferred worker is $3. The employer will be indifferent between either type of worker when the wage rate for nonpreferred workers is

(a) $15

(b) $12

(c) $9

(d) $3

18. When people are judged on the basis of the average characteristics of the group to which they belong rather than on their own personal characteristics or productivity, this is

(a) human-capital discrimination

(b) occupational discrimination

(c) employment discrimination

(d) statistical discrimination

19. The crowding of women and minorities into certain occupations results in

(a) higher wages and more efficient allocation of labor resources

(b) lower wages and less efficient allocation of labor resources

(c) lower wages, but more efficient allocation of labor resources

(d) lower wages, but no effect on the efficient allocation of labor resources

20. Supporters of affirmative action believe that

(a) improved social equity is worth the price society must pay in the form of a lowered domestic output

(b) preferential treatment is necessary to eliminate bias and is a good strategy for increasing economic efficiency

(c) it decreases human-capital discrimination but increases statistical discrimination

(d) it decreases occupational discrimination but increases wage discrimination

21. About what percentage of recent population growth in the United States can be attributed to immigration?

(a) 10%

(b) 33%

(c) 67%

(d) 90%

22. The elimination of barriers to the international flow of labor tends to

(a) lower the wage rates for all labor

(b) raise the wage rates for all labor

(c) increase worldwide efficiency

(d) decrease worldwide efficiency

23. If there is full employment in both nations, the effect of the migration of workers from a poor to a rich nation is to increase the

(a) average wage rate in the rich nation

(b) domestic output in the rich nation

(c) business incomes in the poor nation

(d) domestic output in the poor nation

24. Which would increase the gains realized in the world from the migration of workers?

(a) the explicit and implicit costs of migration

(b) the remittances of workers to their native countries

(c) the migration of unemployed workers to nations in which they find employment

(d) the migration of employed workers to nations in which the taxes they pay are less than the welfare benefits they receive

25. From a strictly economic perspective, nations seeking to maximize net benefits from immigration should

(a) expand immigration because it benefits society with a greater supply of products and increased demand for them

(b) contract immigration because the benefits are minor and it reduces the wage rates of domestic workers

(c) expand immigration until its marginal benefits equal its marginal costs

(d) contract immigration until the extra welfare cost for taxpayers is zero

■ **PROBLEMS**

1. Match the union term with the phrase using the appropriate number.

1. lockout	**5.** open shop
2. union shop	**6.** agency shop
3. closed shop	**7.** National Labor Relations Act
4. right-to-work laws	**8.** collective bargaining

a. Employer can hire union or nonunion workers.

_____

b. Acts by states to make compulsory union membership, or the union shop, illegal. _____

c. A worker must be a member of the union before he or she is eligible for employment in the firm. _____

d. First passed as the Wagner Act of 1935 and sets forth the dos and don'ts of union and management-labor practices. _____

e. Requires a worker to pay union dues or donate an equivalent amount to charity. _____

f. A firm forbids its workers from returning to work until a new contract is signed. _____

g. Permits the employer to hire nonunion workers, but provides that these workers must join the union within a specified period or relinquish their jobs. _____

h. The negotiations of labor contracts. _____

2. Suppose there are two identical labor markets in the economy. The supply of workers and the demand for workers in each of these markets are shown in the following table.

Quantity of labor demanded	Wage rate (MRP of labor)	Quantity of labor supplied
1	$100	7
2	90	6
3	80	5
4	70	4
5	60	3
6	50	2
7	40	1

a. In each of the two labor markets the equilibrium wage rate in a competitive labor market would be

$_____ and employment would be

_____ workers.

b. Now suppose that in the first of these labor markets workers form a union and the union imposes an above-equilibrium wage rate of $90 on employers.

(1) Employment in the unionized labor market will

(rise, fall) _____ to _____ workers; and

(2) the output produced by workers employed by the firms in the unionized labor market will (expand,

contract) _____ by $_____.

c. If the workers displaced by the unionization of the first labor market all enter and find employment in the second labor market, which remains nonunionized and competitive,

(1) the wage rate in the second labor market will (rise,

fall) _____ to $_____.

(2) the output produced by the workers employed by firms in the second labor market will (expand, contract)

_____ by $_____.

d. While the total employment of labor in the two labor markets has remained constant, the total output produced by the employers in the two labor markets

has (expanded, contracted) _____ by

$_____.

3. Match the discrimination terms with the phrase using the appropriate number.

1. statistical discrimination	**5.** reverse discrimination
2. human-capital discrimination	**6.** wage discrimination
3. employment discrimination	**7.** occupational discrimination
4. affirmative action	**8.** occupational segregation

a. The crowding of women, blacks, and certain ethnic groups into less desirable, lower-paying occupations.

_____

b. The payment of a lower wage to members of particular groups than to white males for the same work.

_____

c. Inferior treatment in hiring, promotions, and work

assignments for a particular group of workers. _____

d. Judging an individual on the basis of the average characteristics of the group to which the individual belongs rather than the individual's characteristics.

_____

e. The view that preferential treatment associated with affirmative action efforts constitutes discrimination

against other groups.   _____

f. The denial of equal access to productivity-enhancing education and training to members of particular

groups.   _____

g. Policies and programs that establish targets of increased employment and promotion for women and

minorities.   _____

h. The arbitrary restriction of particular groups from entering more desirable higher-paying occupations.

_____

4. Suppose there are only three labor markets in the economy and each market is perfectly competitive. The following table contains the demand (or marginal-revenue-product) schedule for labor in each of these three markets.

Wage rate (marginal revenue product of labor per hour)	Quantity of labor (millions per hour)
$11	4
10	5
9	6
8	7
7	8
6	9
5	10
4	11
3	12

a. Assume there are 24 million homogeneous workers in the economy and that 12 million of these workers are male and 12 million are female.

(1) If the 12 million female workers can be employed only in the labor market Z, for them all to find employment the hourly wage rate must be

$_____.

(2) If of the 12 million male workers 6 million are employed in labor market X and 6 million are employed in labor market Y, the hourly wage rate in labor mar-

kets X and Y will be $_____.

b. Imagine now that the impediment to the employment of females in labor markets X and Y is removed and that as a result (and because the demand and marginal revenue product of labor is the same in all three markets) 8 million workers find employment in each labor market.

(1) In labor market Z (in which only females had previously been employed)

(a) the hourly wage rate will rise to $_____.

(b) the *decrease* in national output that results from the decrease in employment from 12 million to 8 million workers is equal to the loss of the marginal revenue products of the workers no longer employed, and it

totals $_____ .

(2) In labor market X and in labor market Y (in each of which only males had previously been employed)

(a) the hourly wage rate will fall to $_____ .
(b) the *increase* in national output that results from the increase in employment from 6 million to 8 million workers is equal to the marginal revenue products of the additional workers employed; the gain in each of these

markets is $_____ million, and the total

gain in the two markets is $_____ .
(c) the *net* gain to society from the reallocation of

female workers is $_____ million.

5. The following two tables show the demands for labor and the levels of domestic output that can be produced at each level of employment in two countries, **A** and **B.**

Country A		
Wage rate	Quantity of labor demanded	Real output
$20	95	$1900
18	100	1990
16	105	2070
14	110	2140
12	115	2200
10	120	2250
8	125	2290

Country B		
Wage rate	Quantity of labor demanded	Real output
$20	10	$200
18	15	290
16	20	370
14	25	440
12	30	500
10	35	550
8	40	590

a. If there were full employment in both countries and if
(1) the labor force in Country **A** were 110, the wage

rate in Country **A** would be $_____ .
(2) the labor force in Country **B** were 40, the wage

rate in Country **B** would be $_____ .
b. With these labor forces and wage rates

(1) total wages paid in **A** would be $_____
and the incomes of businesses (capitalists) in **A** would

be $_____ . (*Hint:* Subtract total wages paid from the real output.)

(2) total wages paid in **B** would be $_____

and business incomes in **B** would be $_____ .
c. Assume the difference between the wage rates in the two countries induces 5 workers to migrate from **B** to

A. So long as both countries maintain full employment,
(1) the wage rate in **A** would (rise, fall) _____

to $_____ ,
(2) and the wage rate in **B** would _____ to

$_____ .

d. The movement of workers from **B** to **A** would

(1) (increase, decrease) _____ the output of

A by $_____ ,

(2) (increase, decrease) _____ the output of

B by $_____ , and

(3) (increase, decrease) _____ their combined (and the world's) output by $_____ .

e. This movement of workers from **B** to **A** also (increased, decreased) _____ business

incomes in **A** by $_____ and (increased,

decreased) _____ business incomes in

B by $_____ .

■ **SHORT ANSWER AND ESSAY QUESTIONS**

1. Describe the current status of unions in the United States and the major union organization.

2. What is the philosophy of business unionism in the United States? How does it differ from the European approach to unions?

3. Who belongs to unions? Answer in terms of the types of industries and occupations and the personal characteristics of workers.

4. What evidence is there that the labor movement in the United States has declined? What are two possible causes of this decline?

5. What are the four basic areas usually covered in collective-bargaining agreements between management and labor?

6. What four arguments does labor (management) use in demanding (resisting) higher wages? Why are these arguments two-edged?

7. How large is the union wage advantage in the United States? How has the unionization of many labor markets affected the average level of real wages in the U.S. economy?

8. By what basic means do unions have a positive and a negative effect on economic efficiency in the economy? What appears to have been the overall effect of unions on economic efficiency in the U.S. economy?

9. What effect does the unionization of a particular labor market have on the wage rate in that market, wage rates in other labor markets, and the total output of the economy?

10. Explain how unions reduce labor turnover and improve the skills of younger workers.

11. Define labor market discrimination. How much of the differences in the earning of workers is explained by discrimination?

12. Describe the four types of labor market discrimination, and give an example of each type.

13. Describe the cost of discrimination to society. Illustrate the cost using a production possibilities curve.

14. How can discrimination be viewed as resulting from a preference or taste for which the prejudiced employer is willing to pay? What will determine whether the prejudiced employer hires nonpreferred workers in this model?

15. How do changes in employer prejudice affect wage rates for nonpreferred workers and the ratio of wages between preferred and nonpreferred workers?

16. Explain the concept of statistical discrimination and give an example of it. How can it lead to discrimination even in the absence of prejudice?

17. Describe the economic effects of occupational segregation on the wages of women and minorities. How does this type of segregation affect the domestic output of the economy?

18. What three types of antidiscrimination policies have been used in the United States? Distinguish between direct and indirect policies.

19. Explain the arguments for and against affirmative action. Does affirmative action increase or decrease economic efficiency?

20. How has the Supreme Court viewed affirmative action in recent years? What views have been expressed by Congress and the president?

21. Describe the number of legal and illegal immigrants who entered the United States annually during the 1990s. What has been the effect of this immigration on population growth?

22. Construct a supply and demand model to explain the effects of the migration of labor from a poorer nation to a richer nation. Give your answer in terms of the effects on wage rate, domestic output, and business incomes in the two nations.

23. What four complications make it necessary to modify the conclusions that you reached in question 22? Explain how each of these complications alters your conclusion.

24. Why would the elimination of international barriers to the mobility of labor increase worldwide efficiency?

25. Contrast the positive view with the negative view of immigration. Why are these two views too simplistic?

ANSWERS

Chapter 35 Labor Market Institutions and Issues: Unionism, Discrimination, Immigration

FILL-IN QUESTIONS

1. 16, 13
2. high, high, more, more, more
3. decreased, decreased
4. structural-change, managerial-opposition
5. *a.* the degree of recognition and status accorded the union and the prerogatives of management; *b.* wages and hours; *c.* seniority and job opportunities; *d.* a procedure for settling grievances (any order for *a–d*)
6. increase, decrease, have no effect on
7. featherbedding, work rules, strikes against, above
8. a shock, decrease, decrease, increase
9. the same, inferior, half, half
10. *a.* wage discrimination; *b.* employment discrimination; *c.* human-capital discrimination; *d.* occupational discrimination (any order for *a–d*)
11. decreases, increases, decreases, decreases
12. disutility, cost, below
13. decrease, increase
14. statistical, rational, do not
15. crowding, low, more, an expansion
16. preferential, increases, decreases, reverse
17. 850, third
18. increase, decrease, increase, decrease, increase, decrease, increase
19. *a.* including the costs of migration; *b.* remittances and backflows; *c.* the amounts of unemployment in the two nations; *d.* the fiscal aspects of welfare in the country receiving the immigrants (any order *a–d*)
20. increase, increase, increase, decrease, simplistic

TRUE–FALSE QUESTIONS

1. F, p. 650	**10.** F, p. 657	**19.** F, p. 663
2. T, p. 651	**11.** T, p. 657	**20.** F, p. 665
3. F, pp. 651–652	**12.** F, pp. 657–659	**21.** F, pp. 665–666
4. F, p. 652	**13.** F, pp. 657–658	**22.** T, p. 666
5. F, pp. 652–653	**14.** T, p. 659	**23.** F, pp. 666–667
6. F, p. 654	**15.** T, pp. 659–660	**24.** F, p. 667
7. T, p. 655	**16.** F, pp. 659–660	**25.** F, p. 667
8. F, pp. 655–656	**17.** T, p. 661	
9. T, p. 657	**18.** T, pp. 661–662	

MULTIPLE-CHOICE QUESTIONS

1. b, p. 650	**10.** b, pp. 656–657	**19.** b, pp. 661–662
2. c, p. 651	**11.** c, p. 656	**20.** b, p. 664
3. b, pp. 651–652	**12.** a, p. 656	**21.** b, p. 665
4. b, p. 653	**13.** b, pp. 657–658	**22.** c, pp. 665–667
5. c, p. 654	**14.** c, pp. 657–658	**23.** b, pp. 665–667
6. a, p. 654	**15.** b, p. 659	**24.** c, pp. 665–667
7. a, p. 654	**16.** c, pp. 659–660	**25.** c, p. 667
8. c, pp. 654–655	**17.** c, pp. 659–660	
9. c, pp. 655–656	**18.** d, p. 661	

PROBLEMS

1. *a.* 5; *b.* 4; *c.* 3; *d.* 7; *e.* 6; *f.* 1; *g.* 2; *h.* 8

2. *a.* 70, 4; *b.* (1) fall, 2, (2) contract, 150; *c.* (1) fall, 50, (2) expand, 110; *d.* contracted, 40

3. *a.* 8; *b.* 6; *c.* 3; *d.* 1; *e.* 5; *f.* 2; *g.* 4; *h.* 7

4. *a.* (1) 3, (2) 9; *b.* (1) (*a*) 7, (*b*) 18, (2) (*a*) 7, (*b*) 15, 30, (*c*) 12

5. *a.* (1) 14, (2) 8; *b.* (1) 1540, 600, (2) 320, 270; *c.* (1) fall, 12, (2) rise, 10; *d.* (1) increase, 60, (2) decrease, 40, (3) increase, 20; *e.* increased, 220, decreased, 70

SHORT ANSWER AND ESSAY QUESTIONS

1. p. 650
2. pp. 650–651
3. p. 651
4. pp. 651–652
5. pp. 652–653
6. pp. 653–654
7. p. 654
8. pp. 654–657
9. pp. 655–656
10. pp. 656–657
11. p. 657
12. pp. 657–658
13. p. 659
14. pp. 659–660
15. pp. 660–661
16. p. 661
17. pp. 661–662
18. p. 663
19. p. 664
20. p. 664
21. p. 665
22. pp. 665–666
23. pp. 666–667
24. pp. 665–667
25. p. 667

CHAPTER 36

The Economics of Health Care

Health care has been a topic of major national debate. One reason is that health care costs have risen. Another reason is that fewer people in the United States are being covered by the health care system or many have only limited access to health care. The first four sections of the chapter discuss the rising costs and limited access problems of the U.S. health care system. The economics you learned in previous chapters will now be put to good use in analyzing these twin problems of health care.

The explanations for the first problem—the rapid rise in *cost*—rely on your prior knowledge of supply and demand. Before you can appreciate the demand and supply factors that influence health care costs, however, you need to recognize the *peculiar features* of the market for health care that make it different from the other markets with which you are familiar. Society is reluctant to ration health care based solely on price or income, as is the case with most products. The market is also subject to asymmetric information between the buyer (patient) and seller (health care provider), with the seller making most of the decisions about the amount of services to be consumed and the prices to be paid. Medical care generates spillover benefits that may lead to underproduction in the private market and require some government intervention to achieve efficient allocation of resources. The system of third-party payments reduces the price to buyers and distorts the traditional price signals of the marketplace.

With this background in mind, you are ready to read about the *demand* for health care. The demand factors have significantly increased the cost of health care. Health care is relatively price insensitive, so increases in price result in little reduction in the quantity consumed. The demand for health care has increased as per capita incomes increased because health care is a normal good. Adding to the demand pressures are an aging population, unhealthy lifestyles, and the practices of physicians that are influenced by medical ethics and a fee-for-payment system. The medical insurance system also contributes to increased demand by reducing the costs to the consumer, as does the Federal government with its tax subsidy of employer-financed health insurance.

Supply has not increased at the same rate as demand in health care. Although the supply of physicians has increased, it has had little effect on reducing health care costs. Health care is also an area of slow productivity growth because of the personal attention required for services. Also, the development and use of new medical technology have increased cost pressures in health care rather than reduced them.

The *reforms* for the health care system that you will read about in the last section of the chapter focus on achieving universal coverage and cost containment. A number of schemes have been proposed to increase coverage. These include play-or-pay insurance programs for businesses, tax credits and vouchers, and a national health insurance system. Suggestions for cost containment call for increased uses of incentives, such as increased deductibles and copayments for medical services, the adoption of more managed care such as is found in health maintenance organizations, and tighter controls over Medicare payments based on specific classifications of treatments. The reform section concludes with a brief discussion of recent health care legislation.

■ CHECKLIST

When you have studied this chapter you should be able to

☐ Describe the major characteristics of the health care industry.

☐ State the twin problems with the health care system.

☐ Cite data on the dimensions of cost increases in health in absolute and relative terms.

☐ Discuss the quality of medical care in the United States.

☐ Give three economic implications of rising health care expenditures.

☐ Explain the basic problem with rising health care expenditures.

☐ Identify the reasons why people are medically uninsured and the consequences of this limited access.

☐ List four peculiarities of the market for health care.

☐ Discuss the demand factors that have increased health care costs over time.

☐ Explain how health insurance affects health care costs.

☐ Use supply and demand analysis to explain the rapid rise in health care expenditures.

☐ Identify the supply factors affecting the costs of health care.

☐ Evaluate the relative importance of the demand and supply factors affecting health care.

☐ Discuss proposals to reform the health care system so that there can be universal access.

☐ Cite arguments for and against national health insurance.

☐ Explain how incentives can be used to help contain health care costs.

☐ Describe six recent health care laws or proposals.

■ **CHAPTER OUTLINE**

1. The **health care industry** in the United States covers a broad range of services provided by doctors, hospitals, dentists, nursing homes, and medical laboratories. It employs about 9 million people, about 700,000 of whom are physicians. There are about 5800 hospitals. Americans make some 824 million visits to physicians each year.

2. Two major problems face the health care system. The **costs** of health care are high and growing rapidly. Some U.S. citizens do not have **access** to health care or adequate coverage by the system.

3. **Health care costs** are rising for many reasons.
   a. Costs have risen in absolute and relative terms.
   (1) Total health care spending pays for many items and is obtained from many sources, as shown in text Figure 36.1.
   (2) Expenditures were about 14% of domestic output in 2001 and may rise to about 16% by the year 2008.
   (3) The highest per capita health care expenditures in the world are in the United States.
   b. There is general agreement that medical care in the United States is probably the best in the world, which is a consequence of its high expenditures for health care. That does not mean, however, that the United States is the healthiest nation. In fact, it ranks low internationally on many health indicators.
   c. Rising health care expenditures and costs have negative economic effects that include
   (1) reduced access and coverage for workers and others;
   (2) labor market problems in the form of slower wage growth, less labor mobility, and more use of part-time or temporary workers; and
   (3) added demands to budgets at all levels of government.
   d. The basic problem is that there is an *overallocation* of resources to health care and *less* economic efficiency in the use of the nation's resources.

4. A problem with health care is **limited access.** A large percentage of the population (about 15% in 2001) has no medical coverage. Those medically uninsured are generally the poor, although some young adults with good health choose not to buy insurance. Low-income workers and those employed in smaller businesses are less likely to be covered, or have limited coverage, because of the higher costs of health care for smaller firms.

5. There are many reasons for the **rapid rise in health care costs.**
   a. The market for health care is different from other markets because of ethical and equity considerations, asymmetric information, spillover benefits, and third-party insurance.
   b. Several demand factors have increased health care costs over time.
   (1) Health care is a normal good with an income elasticity of about +1.0, so that spending on it will rise in proportion to per capita income. Health care is also

price *inelastic,* which means that total health care spending will increase even as the price of health care rises.
   (2) The aging population of the United States increases the demand for health care.
   (3) Unhealthy lifestyles because of alcohol, tobacco, or drug abuse increase the demand for and spending on health care.
   (4) Doctors can add to costs because there is asymmetric information—the provider knows more than the buyer—and thus there is supplier-induced demand. Doctors have no strong incentive to reduce costs for the buyer and perhaps an economic interest in increasing them because they are paid on a **fee-for-service** basis. Two other doctor practices may contribute to increased costs: **defensive medicine** may be used to prevent possible lawsuits, and medical ethics require the best (and often the most expensive) procedures.
   c. Although health insurance plays a positive role in giving people protection against health risks, it contributes to increased costs and demand for health care.
   (1) It creates a moral hazard problem by encouraging some people to be less careful about their health and gives some people incentives to overconsume health care than would be the case without insurance.
   (2) Health insurance financed by employers is exempt from both Federal income and payroll taxation. This **tax subsidy** increases the demand for health care.
   (3) From a supply and demand perspective, health insurance reduces the price to the buyer below the no-insurance equilibrium price. This lower price induces more health care consumption and creates an efficiency or welfare loss for society.
   d. Supply factors affect health care costs.
   (1) Physicians have high incomes that add to medical costs, although it is difficult to identify what specific factors determine the high income levels.
   (2) The productivity growth in health care has been slow.
   (3) Most new medical technology has increased costs, despite the fact that some technological advances in medicine have decreased costs.
   e. Only a relatively minor portion of the increase in health care costs can be attributed to increasing incomes, the aging of the population, or defensive medicine. The most likely explanations for the rise in health care costs are the use of new medical technology and a third-party system of insurance payments with little incentive to control costs.

6. **Reforms** for the health care system call for increased access to health care and cost containment.
   a. There are three basic proposals for increasing universal access.
   (1) **"Play-or-pay"** schemes would require all employers either to fund a basic health insurance program (play) or finance health care through a special payroll tax (pay).
   (2) **Tax credits** and **vouchers** are another option designed to make health insurance more affordable for the poor.

(3) A *national health insurance (NHI)* program would provide universal coverage at no cost or at a low cost and would be financed out of tax revenues. The basic arguments for NHI are its simplicity, its allowing patients their choice of physician, the reduction in administrative costs, the improvement in labor market mobility, and increased government bargaining power to contain costs. Arguments against NHI are the ineffectiveness of price controls, increased waiting for doctors and tests, the inefficiency of the Federal government, and income redistribution problems.

b. To contain health care costs, alternatives that use incentives have been adopted.

(1) Insurance companies have increased deductibles and copayments to provide more incentives for consumers to reduce health expenditures.

(2) Managed care organizations are being more widely used to control health care costs and are of two types. *Preferred provider organizations (PPOs)* offer discounts to insurance companies and consumers who use them. *Health maintenance organizations (HMOs)* are prepaid health plans that closely monitor health care costs because they operate with fixed budgets.

(3) The *diagnosis-related-group (DRG) system* has been used to classify treatments and fix fees in an effort to reduce the costs of Medicare payments, although the DRG systems may also reduce the quality of care.

c. A status report on health care reform shows several recent laws and proposals, and the continuing national debate over the direction of health care policy.

(1) In 1996, the U.S. Congress passed health legislation that allows workers to maintain health insurance when changing jobs or becoming self-employed.

(2) Congress also authorized in the 1996 legislation the trial use of medical savings accounts as a tax-deductible way for selected groups to pay for medical expenses.

(3) Congress has considered a "patients' bill of rights" to regulate HMOs and give legal protection to patients.

(4) There have been congressional efforts to limit the size of medical malpractice awards to contain health care costs.

(5) Congress has debated the coverage of prescription drugs as part of Medicare because of the significant and rising cost of this form of treatment for seniors.

(6) Recent proposals have been made to reform Medicare.

■ HINTS AND TIPS

1. This chapter contains many health care terms (e.g., preferred provider organization) with which you may not be familiar. Make sure you review the meaning of each important term before reading the text chapter and taking the self-test in this chapter.

2. The two economic ideas that are the most difficult to comprehend are asymmetric information and moral hazard. The buyer and seller information problems were discussed extensively in Chapter 30. To remember the meaning of these ideas, associate them with examples from the text or ones that you construct.

3. This chapter uses the concepts of income elasticity and price elasticity of demand to explain the demand for health care. Reread the text discussion of these concepts in Chapter 20 if you cannot recall how these elasticities are defined.

4. The graphical presentation of a market with and without health insurance (Figure 36.3) is a relatively straightforward application of supply and demand. The one difficult concept is efficiency loss. This concept was originally discussed in Chapter 31 as it related to taxation; you will now see it applied to health care.

■ IMPORTANT TERMS

deductibles	national health insurance (NHI)
copayments	preferred provider organization (PPO)
fee for service	
defensive medicine	health maintenance organization (HMO)
tax subsidy	
"play or pay"	diagnosis-related-group (DRG) system

SELF-TEST

■ FILL-IN QUESTIONS

1. The health care industry in the United States employs about (2, 9) _____ million people, about (300, 700) _____ thousand of whom are physicians. There are about (2200, 5800) _____ hospitals.

2. The twin problems facing the health care system are high and rapidly growing (benefits, costs) _____ and the fact that many U.S. citizens (do, do not) _____ have access to health care or adequate coverage by the system.

3. In 1960, health care spending was about (5, 14) _____% of domestic output, but in 2001 it was _____% of domestic output. Compared to other industrialized nations, the United States has the (lowest, highest) _____ level of per capita health care expenditures.

4. The economic effects of rising health care costs are (more, less) _____ access to health care and _____ coverage for workers. There are labor market problems, such as (more, less) _____ wage growth, _____ labor mobility, and (more, less) _____ use of temporary or part-time workers. Health care costs also create _____ demands on the budgets of governments at the Federal, state, and local levels.

5. The basic problem with growing health care expenditures is that there is an (underallocation, overallocation) _____ of resources to health care. The large expenditures for health care mean that at the margin, health care is worth (more, less) _____ than alternative products that could have been produced with the resources.

6. The uninsured represent about (15, 30) _____% of the population. They are concentrated among the poor, many of whom work at (low-wage, high-wage) _____ jobs, (do, do not) _____ qualify for Medicaid, and may work for (small, large) _____ businesses. Others who are uninsured include (older, younger) _____ adults in excellent health and people with (minor, major) _____ health problems.

7. The market for health care is different from other markets because of (technology, ethical–equity) _____ considerations, (symmetric, asymmetric) _____ information, spillover (costs, benefits) _____, and (first-party, third-party) _____ payments.

8. Health care is (an inferior, a normal, a superior) _____ good with an income elasticity of about (0, 1) _____. In this case, a 10% increase in incomes will result in a (1, 10) _____% increase in health care expenditures.

9. Health care is price (inelastic, elastic) _____, with a coefficient estimated to be (0.2, 1.5) _____. The price elasticity of demand for health care means that a 10% increase in price would decrease health care spending by (2, 15) _____%.

10. Other factors increasing the demand for health care include an (older, younger) _____ population and lifestyles that are often (entertaining, unhealthy) _____.

11. The demand for health care is affected by the problem of asymmetric information in the practice of medicine, which means that the (demander, supplier) _____ will decide the types and amount of

health care to be consumed. Physicians (have, do not have) _____ an incentive to reduce costs for the buyer and perhaps an economic interest in increasing them because they are paid on a (play-or-pay, fee-for-service) _____ basis.

12. Increased demand and costs can arise from the practice of (offensive, defensive) _____ medicine to limit the possibility of a lawsuit or from medical (insurance, ethics) _____ that require the use of the best medical techniques by doctors.

13. Health insurance increases demand because it creates a moral (dilemma, hazard) _____ problem. It makes people be (more, less) _____ careful about their health and gives people incentives to (underconsume, overconsume) _____ health care more than they otherwise would without health insurance.

14. Health insurance financed by employers is (taxed, tax-exempt) _____ at the Federal level. This (tax, tax subsidy) _____ (increases, decreases) _____ the demand for health care.

15. In a supply and demand analysis, health insurance (raises, lowers) _____ the price to the buyer below the no-insurance equilibrium price. This (higher, lower) _____ price induces (less, more) _____ health care consumption and creates an efficiency (benefit, loss) _____ for society.

16. The supply factors that affect health care costs include the (high, low) _____ cost of physician services, (fast, slow) _____ growth in productivity in health care, and the use of (new, old) _____ medical technology.

17. Increasing access to health care could be achieved by a (fee-for-service, play-or-pay) _____ requirement for all employers either to fund a basic health insurance program or pay a special payroll tax to finance health care for workers. Another option would be the use of tax (levies, credits) _____ and vouchers to make health insurance more affordable for the poor.

18. A program that would provide universal coverage at no cost or at a low cost and would be financed out of tax revenues is (managed care, national health insurance) _____.

a. Some of its advantages are that it is a simple and (direct, indirect) _____ way to provide universal coverage, it allows patients to choose their

own (insurance, physician) _____, it (increases, decreases) _____ administrative costs, it _____ labor market mobility, and (increases, decreases) _____ government bargaining power with medical care providers.
b. One argument against it is the ineffectiveness of price (ceilings, floors) _____ on physician services. It may also (increase, decrease) _____ waiting for doctors and tests, _____ the inefficiency of the Federal government, and (increase, decrease) _____ redistribution of income.

19. Actions have been taken to contain health care costs. Insurance companies have (increased, decreased) _____ deductibles and copayments to provide incentives for consumers to reduce expenditures, and there has been _____ use of preferred provider organizations (PPOs) to get consumers to use lower-cost health care providers. Businesses and other organizations have formed health maintenance organizations (HMOs) that have prepaid health plans and use a (fee-for-service, managed care) _____ approach to control health costs. Medical treatments have been classified according to a diagnosis-related-group (DRG) system and the government has (fixed, variable) _____ fee payments for each treatment.

20. In recent years, the U.S. Congress has passed laws and considered several types of health care legislation. For example, in 1996 Congress passed a law so that workers with group health insurance can continue their coverage when they change (titles, jobs) _____. Congress also authorized, on a trial basis, the use of (personal, medical) _____ savings. The cost of prescription drug coverage has been considered for inclusion in (managed care, Medicare) _____, and there has been discussion of financial limits to be placed on awards for medical (research, malpractice) _____.

■ TRUE–FALSE QUESTIONS

Circle T if the statement is true, F if it is false.

1. The twin problems of health care are the rapidly rising cost of health care and the general decline in the quality of health care.　　**T　F**

2. Medicaid is the nationwide Federal health care program available to Social Security beneficiaries and the disabled.　　**T　F**

3. Per capita expenditures on health care are high in the United States but even higher in Japan and Britain.　　**T　F**

4. Rising health care costs reduce workers' access to health care.　　**T　F**

5. Increasing health care expenditures cause problems for the budgets of Federal, state, and local governments.　　**T　F**

6. Aggregate consumption of health care is so great that at the margin it is worth more than the alternative goods and services these resources could otherwise have produced.　　**T　F**

7. About 40% of the population of the United States had no health insurance for the entire year.　　**T　F**

8. Minimum-wage workers have health insurance because their insurance premiums are covered by the Federal government.　　**T　F**

9. There is asymmetric information in the market for health care because the supplier (doctor) acts as the agent for the buyer (patient) and tells the buyer what health care services should be consumed.　　**T　F**

10. The market for health care is characterized by spillover costs.　　**T　F**

11. Third-party payments are a factor in the health care market because about three-fourths of all health care expenses are paid through public or private insurance.　　**T　F**

12. The demand for health care is price elastic.　　**T　F**

13. There is a strong incentive to underconsume health care because consumers have little information about the costs of medical treatments and doctors are paid on a fee-for-service basis.　　**T　F**

14. "Defensive medicine" refers to the medical practice of physicians using preventive medicine to reduce illness and disease in patients.　　**T　F**

15. Health care insurance is a means by which one pays a relatively small known cost for protection against an uncertain and much larger cost in the future.　　**T　F**

16. A moral hazard problem arises from health insurance because those covered tend to take fewer health risks and consume less health care than would be the case without insurance.　　**T　F**

17. The demand for health care is increased by a Federal tax policy that exempts employer-financed health insurance from taxation.　　**T　F**

18. There is overwhelming evidence that the American Medical Association has purposely kept admissions to medical school artificially low to restrict the supply of doctors.　　**T　F**

19. Productivity growth has been slow in the health care industry.　　**T　F**

20. The development and use of new technology in health care has been a major factor in increasing the costs of health care.　　**T　F**

21. The basic intent of reform proposals calling for tax credits and vouchers to pay for health insurance is to reduce or contain costs.   **T F**

22. Proposals for national health insurance would provide a basic package of health care for each citizen at no direct charge or at a low-cost rate and would be financed out of tax revenues rather than health insurance premiums.   **T F**

23. A problem with a government-imposed ceiling on the prices for physician services is that physicians can protect their incomes from fixed prices by altering the quantity and quality of care they give a patient.   **T F**

24. The diagnostic-related-group (DRG) system is a health maintenance organization that specializes in the diagnoses of illnesses to reduce costs.   **T F**

25. The growth of managed care organizations has transformed the medical industry into one dominated by large insurance and health care firms.   **T F**

■ **MULTIPLE-CHOICE QUESTIONS**

Circle the letter that corresponds to the best answer.

1. The two major problems facing the health care system of the United States are
   (a) the formation of health alliances and preferred provider organizations
   (b) a decline in innovation and the rate of technological changes
   (c) increasing supply and decreasing demand for health care
   (d) access to health care and rapidly increasing costs

2. The health care industry employs about how many physicians?
   (a) 50,000
   (b) 100,000
   (c) 700,000
   (d) 1 million

3. What was total spending for health care as a percentage of GDP in 1960 and in 2001?

	1960	2001
(a)	1	4
(b)	2	6
(c)	5	14
(d)	9	18

4. The contradiction about health care in the United States is that the country's
   (a) medical care is the best in the world, but the nation ranks low on many health indicators
   (b) expenditures for health care are modest, but its medical care is the best in the world
   (c) expenditures for health care are the highest in the world, but its quality of medical care is the worst of all industrial nations
   (d) advances in medicine have fallen at a time when its need for better medicine has risen

5. Which is a labor market effect from rapidly rising health care costs?
   (a) a decrease in the number of health care workers
   (b) an increase in the rate of growth of real wages
   (c) an increase in the use of part-time workers
   (d) a decrease in the skill of the labor force

6. Which person is most likely to be uninsured or ineligible for health insurance?
   (a) a college professor working at a state university
   (b) a full-time worker at a big manufacturing plant
   (c) an accountant employed by a large corporation
   (d) a dishwasher working for minimum wage at a restaurant

7. Which would be considered a peculiarity of the market for health care?
   (a) third-party payments
   (b) employer mandates
   (c) tax credits and vouchers
   (d) fee-for-service payments

8. The demand for health care is
   (a) price elastic
   (b) price inelastic
   (c) income elastic
   (d) income inelastic

9. From an income perspective, health care is considered
   (a) an inferior good
   (b) a normal good
   (c) a superior good
   (d) a supply-induced good

10. Which is a demand factor in the market for health care?
   (a) asymmetric information
   (b) advance in new medical technology
   (c) slow productivity growth in the health care industry
   (d) the number of physicians graduating from medical school

11. Asymmetric information causes problems in the health care market because
   (a) the buyer, not the supplier, of health care services makes most of the decisions about the amount and type of health care to be provided
   (b) the supplier, not the buyer, of health care services makes most of the decisions about the amount and type of health care to be provided
   (c) government has less information than the health care providers and can inflate fees
   (d) insurance companies, not the health care consumer, control deductibles and copayment policies

12. Most experts attribute a major portion of the relative rise in health care spending to
   (a) rising incomes
   (b) an aging population
   (c) advances in medical technology
   (d) an increase in the number of physicians

13. Unhealthy lifestyles may be encouraged by medical insurance because people figure that health insurance

will cover illnesses or accidents. This attitude is characteristic of
(a) asymmetric information
(b) the play-or-pay problem
(c) a moral hazard problem
(d) a reduced access problem

Answer Questions 14, 15, 16, and 17 based on the following demand and supply graph of the market for health care.

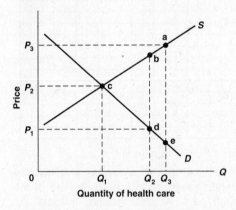

Quantity of health care

14. If there were no health insurance, the equilibrium price and quantity of health care would be
(a) P_1 and Q_2
(b) P_2 and Q_1
(c) P_2 and Q_2
(d) P_3 and Q_3

15. Assume that health insurance pays half the cost of health care. For the consumer, the price and quantity of health care consumed would be
(a) P_1 and Q_2
(b) P_2 and Q_2
(c) P_2 and Q_1
(d) P_3 and Q_3

16. With health insurance paying half the cost of health care, there is allocative
(a) efficiency because at Q_1 the marginal cost to society equals the marginal benefit
(b) efficiency because at Q_2 the marginal cost to society is less than the marginal benefit by the difference between points *b* and *d*
(c) inefficiency because at Q_2 the marginal cost to society exceeds the marginal benefit by the difference between points *b* and *d*
(d) inefficiency because at Q_3 the marginal cost to society exceeds the marginal benefit by the difference between points *a* and *e*

17. The efficiency loss caused by the availability of health insurance is shown by area
(a) Q_1caQ_3
(b) Q_1cbQ_2
(c) *cae*
(d) *cbd*

18. Which is a supply factor in the health care market?
(a) medical technology
(b) an aging population
(c) defensive medicine
(d) growing incomes

19. The play-or-pay proposal for health care reform is intended to
(a) increase access to health care through the use of tax credits and vouchers as part of a national health insurance system
(b) expand health care coverage by requiring all employers to offer a health insurance program for workers or pay a special payroll tax for health care
(c) make states become bigger players in health care reform by having the Federal government match state expenditures for health care and Medicaid
(d) reduce consumption of health care by increasing deductibles and copayments for health insurance

20. Which is primarily designed to increase access to health care rather than contain costs?
(a) national health insurance
(b) diagnosis-related-group system
(c) health maintenance organizations
(d) preferred provider organizations

21. A substantive criticism of national health insurance is that
(a) the Federal government provision of tax credits and vouchers for health care would be inefficient
(b) it would establish a diagnosis-related-group system for the payment of health provider services that is unnecessary and inefficient
(c) it would increase deductibles and copayments that are borne by individuals, making health care more costly
(d) the Federal government does not have a good record of containing the costs of health care programs

22. Insurance companies often have policies that require the insured to pay the fixed portion (e.g., $500) of each year's health costs and a fixed percentage (e.g., 20%) of all additional costs. The expenditures by the insured are
(a) credits and vouchers
(b) deductibles and copayments
(c) fee-for-service payments
(d) diagnosis-related-group expenditures

23. An organization that requires hospitals and physicians to provide discounted prices for their services as a condition for inclusion in the insurance plan is a
(a) health maintenance organization
(b) preferred provider organization
(c) fee-for-service organization
(d) health alliance

24. A portability and accountability act related to health care that the U.S. Congress passed in 1996 was designed to
(a) expand the use of the fee-for-payment system to increase the accountability of health care consumers
(b) make the participation of the employer voluntary in most new health care plans, but employees were required to join

(c) ensure that workers with a group health plan can continue to buy health insurance when they change jobs or become self-employed

(d) limit the number of preferred provider organizations to make health care groups more accountable for costs

25. With medical savings accounts for small business owners, the self-employed, and the uninsured, consumers

(a) make tax-deductible contributions to the accounts and then use the funds to pay for health care expenditures

(b) contract with health maintenance organizations and use the accounts to get medical services at the lowest possible rate

(c) obtain discounted prices for health care services that are provided by the diagnosis-related-group system

(d) deposit money in a bank and receive a certificate of deposit that is indexed to the inflation rate for health care

■ **PROBLEMS**

1. Following is a table showing a supply and demand schedule for health care. In the left column is the price of health care. The middle column shows the quantity demanded (Q_d) for health care. The right column shows the quantity supplied (Q_s) of health care.

Price ($)	Q_d	Q_s
3000	100	500
2500	200	400
2000	300	300
1500	400	200
1000	500	100

a. Assume that there is no health insurance in this market. At a price of $2000, the quantity demanded

will be _____ units of health care and the

quantity supplied will be _____ units. There will be (a surplus, a shortage, equilibrium)

_____ in this market for health care at

_____ units.

b. Now assume that health insurance cuts the price of health care in half for the consumer. The new price to

the consumer will be $_____ and the

quantity consumed will be _____ units. At this level of quantity, the marginal cost to society of

a unit of health care is $_____ while the

marginal benefit is_____.

c. Draw a supply and demand graph in the following graph based on the data in the preceding table. Make sure to label the axes and identify prices and quantities.
(1) Show the equilibrium point in a market without health insurance and label it as point *a*.

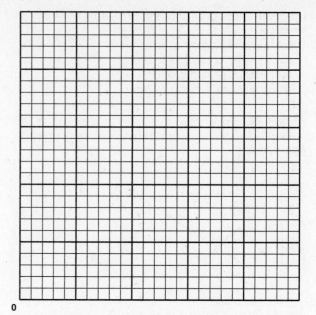

0

(2) Show the price to the consumer and quantity consumed when health insurance covers half of the cost of health care. At this quantity, indicate the marginal cost to society of this unit of health care and label it as point *b*. Also, indicate the marginal benefit to society of this unit of health care and label it as point *c*.

(3) Indicate the area of efficiency loss when health insurance covers half of the cost of health care.

2. In the situations that follow indicate whether the events primarily affect the demand (**D**) for health care or the supply (**S**) of health care. Also, indicate whether it would increase (+) or decrease (−) the demand for or supply of health care.

	D or S	+ or −
a. An aging population	_____	_____
b. More use of defensive medicine	_____	_____
c. Healthier lifestyles	_____	_____
d. Less health insurance coverage	_____	_____
e. Increased productivity in health care	_____	_____
f. Newer and more costly medical technology	_____	_____
g. A sharp reduction in the number of physicians	_____	_____
h. A tax subsidy to consumers to cover health care	_____	_____
i. Rising per capita incomes	_____	_____
j. More use of a fee-for-service payment system	_____	_____

3. Match the terms with the phrase using the appropriate number.

1. copayments	4. preferred provider organization
2. play-or-pay	5. health maintenance organization
3. diagnosis-related-group system	6. deductibles

a. A unit set up by insurance companies that requires hospitals and physicians to provide discounted prices for their services as a condition for being included in the insurance plan   _____

b. The percentage of cost that an insured individual pays while the insurer pays the remainder   _____

c. A health care organization that contracts with employers, insurance companies, and other groups to provide health care for their workers or others who are insured   _____

d. The dollar sum of costs that an insured individual must pay before the insurer begins to pay   _____

e. An arrangement that gives the hospital a fixed payment for treating each patient with the payments based on hundreds of detailed health categories for patient conditions and needs   _____

f. A way to expand health coverage by requiring employers to either provide insurance for their workers or be assessed a special payroll tax to finance insurance for uncovered workers   _____

■ SHORT ANSWER AND ESSAY QUESTIONS

1. Define and describe the major features of the health care industry.

2. Explain the relationship between the cost of and access to health care.

3. What are the dimensions of the cost increases in health care in absolute and relative terms?

4. How do health care expenditures in the United States compare with those in other industrialized nations?

5. What are the economic implications of rising health care costs?

6. Why is the aggregate consumption of health care in the United States a basic problem?

7. Who are the uninsured in the United States? What are the characteristics of the uninsured?

8. What are four peculiarities of the market for health care?

9. How does income and price elasticity affect the demand for health care?

10. In what ways do an aging population and unhealthy lifestyles influence and shape the demand for health care?

11. Why is there asymmetric information in health care? How does it affect consumption and the cost of health care?

12. What role does health insurance play in affecting health care costs? Explain the advantages and disadvantages of health insurance.

13. Why might physicians' high incomes have nothing to do with supply restrictions?

14. How have changes in medical technology affected health care costs?

15. What is the relative importance of demand and supply factors in affecting the rise in health care costs?

16. How would play-or-pay or tax credit and voucher reforms be used to achieve universal access to health care?

17. Discuss the arguments for and against national health insurance.

18. What actions have insurance companies and the Federal government taken to reduce or contain health care costs?

19. In 1996 Congress passed two health care reforms. Describe and comment on each reform.

20. What is the issue of prescription drug coverage? How does the way it would be provided affect its cost and Medicare reform?

ANSWERS

Chapter 36   The Economics of Health Care

FILL-IN QUESTIONS

1. 9, 700, 5800
2. costs, do not
3. 5, 14, highest
4. less, less, less, less, more, more
5. overallocation, less
6. 15, low-wage, do not, small, younger, major
7. ethical–equity, asymmetric, benefits, third-party
8. a normal, 1, 10
9. inelastic, 0.2, 2
10. older, unhealthy
11. supplier, do not have, fee-for-service
12. defensive, ethics
13. hazard, less, overconsume
14. tax-exempt, tax subsidy, increases
15. lowers, lower, more, loss
16. high, slow, new
17. play-or-pay, credits
18. national health insurance; *a.* direct, physician, decreases, increases, increases; *b.* ceilings, increase, increase, increase
19. increased, increased, managed care, fixed
20. jobs, medical, Medicare, malpractice

TRUE–FALSE QUESTIONS

1. F, pp. 672–673	10. F, p. 677	19. T, p. 681
2. F, p. 674	11. T, p. 677	20. T, p. 681
3. F, p. 674	12. F, p. 677	21. F, p. 683
4. T, p. 675	13. F, pp. 677, 679	22. T, p. 683
5. T, p. 675	14. F, p. 678	23. T, p. 684
6. F, pp. 675–676	15. T, pp. 678–679	24. F, p. 685
7. F, p. 676	16. F, p. 679	25. T, p. 684
8. F, p. 676	17. T, p. 679	
9. T, p. 677	18. F, pp. 680–681	

MULTIPLE-CHOICE QUESTIONS

1. d, pp. 672–673
2. c, p. 672
3. c, p. 674
4. a, pp. 674–675
5. c, p. 675
6. d, p. 676
7. a, p. 677
8. b, p. 677
9. b, p. 677

10. a, p. 677
11. b, pp. 677–678
12. c, pp. 677–678
13. c, p. 678
14. b, pp. 679–680
15. a, pp. 679–680
16. c, pp. 679–680
17. d, pp. 679–680
18. a, p. 681

19. b, p. 683
20. a, p. 683
21. d, p. 683
22. b, p. 684
23. b, p. 684
24. c, p. 685
25. a, p. 685

PROBLEMS

1. *a.* 300, 300, equilibrium, 300; *b.* 1000, 500, 3000, 1000; *c.* (1) the intersection of price of $2000 and quantity of 300, (2) point *b* is the intersection of $3000 and quantity of 500 units, and point *c* is the intersection of $1000 and quantity of 500 units, (3) the area of efficiency loss is the area in the triangle outlined by points *a, b,* and *c*

2. *a.* D, +; *b.* D, +; *c.* D, −; *d.* D, −; *e.* S, +; *f.* S, −; *g.* S, −; *h.* D, +; *i.* D, +; *j.* D, +

3. *a.* 4; *b.* 1; *c.* 5; *d.* 6; *e.* 3; *f.* 2

SHORT ANSWER AND ESSAY QUESTIONS

1. p. 672
2. pp. 672–673
3. pp. 673–674
4. p. 674
5. pp. 674–675
6. pp. 675–676
7. p. 676

8. p. 677
9. p. 677
10. pp. 677–678
11. pp. 677–678
12. pp. 678–679
13. pp. 680–681
14. p. 681

15. pp. 681–682
16. p. 683
17. pp. 683–684
18. pp. 684–685
19. p. 685
20. p. 685

CHAPTER 37

International Trade

In Chapter 6 you learned about the role of the United States in the global economy and the basic principles of international trade. Chapter 37 extends that analysis by giving you a more advanced understanding of comparative advantage. It also uses the tools of supply and demand to explain the equilibrium prices and quantities of imports and exports and the economic effects of tariffs and quotas. It examines the fallacious arguments for trade protectionism and the global efforts to liberalize trade.

After a brief review of the facts of international trade presented in Chapter 6, the text uses graphical analysis to explain why nations trade: to take advantage of the benefits of specialization. Nations specialize in and export those goods and services in the production of which they have a *comparative advantage.* A comparative advantage means that the opportunity cost of producing a particular good or service is lower in that nation than in another nation. These nations will avoid producing and will import the goods and services that other nations have a comparative advantage in producing. In this way all nations are able to obtain products that are produced as inexpensively as possible. Put another way, when nations specialize in those products in which they have a comparative advantage, the world as a whole can obtain more goods and services from its resources; each nation of the world can enjoy a standard of living higher than it would have if it did not specialize and export and import.

The principle of comparative advantage tells us why nations trade, but what determines the equilibrium prices and quantities of the imports and exports resulting from trade? To answer this question, the text uses the *supply and demand analysis,* originally presented in Chapter 3, to explain equilibrium in the world market for a product. A simplified two-nation and one-product model of trade is used to construct export supply curves and import demand curves for each nation. Equilibrium occurs where one nation's export supply curve intersects another nation's import demand curve.

Regardless of the advantages of specialization and trade among nations, people in the United States and throughout the world for well over 200 years have debated whether *free trade or protection* was the better policy for their nation. Economists took part in this debate and, with few exceptions, argued for free trade and against protection. Those who favor free trade contend that free trade benefits both the nation and the world as a whole. "Free traders" argue that tariffs, import quotas, and other barriers to international trade prevent or reduce specialization and decrease both a nation's and the world's production and standard of living.

Despite the case for trade, nations have erected and continue to erect *trade barriers* against other nations. The latter part of this chapter focuses attention on (1) what motivates nations to impose tariffs and to limit the quantities of goods imported from abroad; (2) the economic effects of protection on a nation's own prosperity and on the prosperity of the world economy; (3) the kinds of arguments those who favor protection use to support their position (on what grounds do they base their contention that their nation will benefit from the erection of barriers that reduce imports from foreign nations); and (4) how the nations of the world have responded to trade liberalization through the *World Trade Organization* (WTO).

Whether the direction of the international trade policy in the United States will be toward freer trade or more protectionism is a question that gets debated as each new trade issue is presented to the U.S. public. The decision on each issue may well depend on your understanding of the advantages of free trade and the problems with trade protection for the nation and the world economy.

■ **CHECKLIST**

When you have studied this chapter you should be able to

☐ Cite some key facts about international trade.
☐ State the three economic circumstances that make it desirable for nations to specialize and trade.
☐ Compute the costs of producing two commodities when given the data in a two-nation example.
☐ Determine which nation has the comparative advantage in the production of each commodity using the cost data you computed for the two-nation example.
☐ Calculate the range in which the terms of trade will occur in the two-nation example.
☐ Explain how nations gain from trade and specialization based on the two-nation example.
☐ Discuss how increasing costs affect specialization in the two-nation example.
☐ Restate the case for free trade.
☐ Construct domestic supply and demand curves for two nations that trade a product.
☐ Construct export supply and import demand curves for two nations that trade a product.

☐ Use supply and demand analysis to explain how the equilibrium prices and quantities of exports and imports are determined for two nations that trade a product.

☐ Identify the four principal types of artificial barriers to international trade and the motives for erecting these barriers.

☐ Explain the economic effects of a protective tariff on resource allocation, the price of the commodity, the total production of the commodity, and the outputs of foreign and domestic producers of the commodity.

☐ Analyze the economic effects of an import quota and compare them with the economic effects of a tariff.

☐ Enumerate six arguments used to support the case for protection and find the problems with each argument.

☐ Offer a summation of the arguments for and against trade protection.

☐ Describe the formation, purpose, and issues of the World Trade Organization.

■ **CHAPTER OUTLINE**

1. Some facts on international trade from Chapter 6 are worth reviewing.

   a. About 11% of the total output (GDP) of the United States is accounted for by exports of goods and services, a percentage that has doubled since 1975. The percentage of exports is much higher in other industrially advanced nations (e.g., 62% in the Netherlands, 41% in Canada), but the size of the U.S. economy means that it has the largest volume of imports and exports in the world.

   b. The United States has a trade deficit in goods, a trade surplus in services, and a trade deficit in goods and services.

   c. The major exports of the United States are computers, chemicals, semiconductors, and consumer durables. The major imports are petroleum, automobiles, computers, and household appliances. Most of the trade occurs with other industrially advanced nations. Canada is the largest trading partner for the United States.

   d. The major participants in international trade are the United States, Japan, and the nations of Western Europe. Newer participants include the Asian economies of South Korea, Singapore and Taiwan. Russia, the nations of Eastern Europe, and China have increased their international trade.

   e. International trade and finance is also a focus of economic policy as shown by issues faced by the World Trade Organization (WTO) and International Monetary Fund (IMF).

2. The ***economic basis for trade*** is based on several circumstances. Specialization and trade among nations is advantageous because the world's resources are not evenly distributed and efficient production of different commodities requires different technologies and combinations of resources. Also, products differ in quality and other attributes, so people might prefer imported to domestic goods in some cases.

3. The ***principle of comparative advantage,*** first presented in Chapter 6 to explain the gains from trade, can now be reexamined with the aid of graphical analysis.

   a. Suppose the world is composed of only two nations, each of which is capable of producing two different commodities and in which the production possibilities curves are different straight lines (the nations' opportunity cost ratios are constant but different).

   b. With different domestic opportunity cost ratios, each nation will have a comparative (cost) advantage in the production of one of the two commodities, and if the world is to use its resources economically, each nation must specialize in the commodity in the production of which it has a comparative advantage.

   c. The ratio at which one product is traded for another—the terms of trade—lies between the opportunity cost ratios of the two nations.

   d. Each nation gains from this trade because specialization permits a greater total output from the same resources and a better allocation of the world's resources.

   e. If opportunity cost ratios in the two nations are not constant (if there is increasing cost), specialization may not be complete.

   f. The basic argument for free trade among nations is that it leads to a better allocation of resources and a higher standard of living in the world. Several side benefits from trade are that it increases competition and deters monopoly, and offers consumers a wider array of choices. It also links the interests of nations and can reduce the threat of hostilities or war.

4. ***Supply and demand analysis of exports and imports*** can be used to explain how the equilibrium price and quantity for a product (e.g., aluminum) are determined when there is trade between two nations (e.g., the United States and Canada).

   a. For the United States, there will be *domestic* supply and demand as well as *export* supply and import demand for aluminum.

   (1) The price and quantity of aluminum are determined by the intersection of the domestic demand and supply curves in a world without trade.

   (2) In a world with trade, the export supply curve for the United States shows the amount of aluminum that U.S. producers will export at each world price above the domestic equilibrium price. U.S. exports will increase when the world price rises relative to the domestic price.

   (3) The import demand curve for the United States shows the amount of aluminum that U.S. citizens will import at each world price below the domestic equilibrium price. U.S. imports will increase when world prices fall relative to the domestic price.

   b. For Canada, there will be domestic supply and demand as well as export supply and import demand for aluminum. The description of these supply and demand curves is similar to the account of those of the United States previously described in point **a.**

   c. The equilibrium world price and equilibrium world levels of exports and imports can be determined with further supply and demand analysis. The export supply curves of the two nations can be plotted on one graph. The import demand curves of both nations can be plotted on the same graph. In this two-nation model, equilibrium will be achieved when one nation's import demand curve intersects another nation's export supply curve.

5. Nations limit international trade by erecting **trade barriers.** Tariffs, import quotas, a variety of nontariff barriers, and voluntary export restrictions are the principal barriers to trade.

   a. The imposition of a **tariff** on a good imported from abroad has both direct and indirect effects on an economy.

   (1) The tariff increases the domestic price of the good, reduces its domestic consumption, expands its domestic production, decreases its foreign production, and transfers income from domestic consumers to government.

   (2) It also reduces the income of foreign producers and the ability of foreign nations to purchase goods and services in the nation imposing the tariff, causes the contraction of relatively efficient industries in that nation, decreases world trade, and lowers the real output of goods and services.

   b. The imposition of a **quota** on an imported product has the same direct and indirect effects as that of a tariff on that product, with the exception that a tariff generates revenue for government use whereas an import quota transfers that revenue to foreign producers.

   c. Special-interest groups benefit from protection and persuade their nations to erect trade barriers, but the costs to consumers of this protection exceed the benefits to the economy.

   d. Tariffs and quotas affect the distribution of income. They act like sales or excise taxes on a product, so they are highly regressive for low-income consumers.

6. The arguments for **protectionism** are many, but often of questionable validity.

   a. The military self-sufficiency argument can be challenged because it is difficult to determine which industry is "vital" to national defense and must be protected; it would be more efficient economically to provide a direct subsidy to military producers rather than impose a tariff.

   b. Trade barriers do not necessarily increase domestic employment because

   (1) imports may eliminate some jobs, but create others, so imports may change only the composition of employment, not the overall level of employment;

   (2) the exports of one nation become the imports of another, so tariff barriers can be viewed as "beggar thy neighbor" policies;

   (3) other nations are likely to retaliate against the imposition of trade barriers that will reduce domestic output and employment; and

   (4) in the long run, barriers create a less efficient allocation of resources by shielding protected domestic industries from the rigors of competition.

   c. Using tariff barriers to permit diversification for stability in the economy is not necessary for advanced economies such as the United States, and there may be great economic costs to diversification in developing nations.

   d. It is alleged that infant industries need protection until they are sufficiently large to compete, but the argument may not apply in developed economies: It is difficult to select which industries will prosper; protectionism tends to persist long after it is needed; and direct subsidies may be more economically efficient. For advanced nations, a variant of this argument is **strategic trade policy.** It justifies barriers that protect the investment in high-risk, growth industries for a nation, but the policies often lead to retaliation and similar policies from other trading nations.

   e. Sometimes protection is sought against the "dumping" of excess foreign goods on U.S. markets. Dumping is a legitimate concern and is restricted under U.S. trade law, but to use dumping as an excuse for widespread tariff protection is unjustified, and the number of documented cases is few. If foreign companies are more efficient (low-cost) producers, what may appear to be dumping may actually be comparative advantage at work.

   f. Protection is sometimes sought because of the cheap foreign labor argument; it should be realized that nations gain from trade based on comparative advantage, and without trade, living standards will be lower.

   g. In summary, most protectionist arguments are fallacious or based on half-truths. The only points that have some validity, under certain conditions, are the infant industry and military-sufficiency arguments, but both are subject to abuse. The historical evidence suggests that free trade promotes and protectionism deters prosperity and economic growth in the world.

7. The **World Trade Organization** (WTO) is an international agency with about 145 participating nations that is charged with overseeing a 1994 trade agreement among nations. This agreement sought trade liberalization by: reducing tariffs worldwide; implementing new rules to promote trade in services; cutting domestic subsidies for agricultural products; protecting intellectual property; and phasing out quotas on textiles and apparel. The WTO oversees provisions of the agreement, rules on disputes, and meets on occasion to consider other trade policies. The work of the WTO is not without controversy. Critics wildly claim that it promotes global capitalism at the expense of labor and the environment. Economists argue that trade liberalization increases economic efficiency and output worldwide, and that these benefits can then be used to address domestic concerns.

■ **HINTS AND TIPS**

1. In the discussion of **comparative advantage,** the assumption of a constant-cost ratio means the production possibilities "curves" for each nation can be drawn as straight lines. The slope of the line in each nation is the opportunity cost of one product (wheat) in terms of the

other product (coffee). The reciprocal of the slope of each line is the opportunity cost of the other product (coffee) in terms of the first product (wheat).

2. The ***export supply and import demand curves*** in Figures 37.3 and 37.4 in the text look different from the typical supply and demand curves that you have seen so far, so you should understand how they are constructed. The export supply and import demand curves for a nation do not intersect. Each curve meets at the price point on the *Y* axis showing the equilibrium price for domestic supply and demand. At this point there are no exports or imports.

a. The export supply curve is upsloping from that point because as world prices rise above the domestic equilibrium price, there will be increasing domestic surpluses produced by a nation that can be exported. The export supply curve reflects the positive relationship between rising world prices (above the domestic equilibrium price) and the increasing quantity of exports.

b. The import demand curve is downsloping from the domestic equilibrium price because as world prices fall below the domestic equilibrium price, there will be increasing domestic shortages that need to be covered by increasing imports. The import demand curve reflects the inverse relationship between falling world prices (below the domestic price) and the increasing quantity of imports.

3. One of the most interesting sections of the chapter discusses the arguments for and against trade protection. You have probably heard people give one or more of the arguments for trade protection, but now you have a chance to use your economic reasoning to expose the weaknesses in these arguments. Most are half-truths and special pleadings.

■ IMPORTANT TERMS

labor-intensive goods	equilibrium world price
land-intensive goods	tariff
capital-intensive goods	revenue tariff
cost ratio	protective tariff
principle of comparative advantage	import quota
	nontariff barrier (NTB)
terms of trade	voluntary export restriction (VER)
trading possibilities line	
gains from trade	strategic trade policy
world price	dumping
domestic price	World Trade Organization (WTO)
export supply curve	
import demand curve	

SELF-TEST

■ FILL-IN QUESTIONS

1. Exports of goods and services account for about (11, 22) _____% of total output in the United States and since 1975 this percentage has (doubled, quadrupled)_____.

2. Other industrially advanced nations such as the Netherlands and Canada have a (larger, smaller) _____ percentage of exports than the United States. The United States' volume of exports and imports makes it the world's (largest, smallest) _____ trading nation.

3. Nations tend to trade among themselves because the distribution of economic resources among them is (even, uneven) _____, the efficient production of various goods and services necessitates (the same, different) _____ technologies or combinations of resources, and people prefer (more, less) _____ choices in products.

4. The principle of comparative advantage means total world output will be greatest when each good is produced by that nation having the (highest, lowest) _____ opportunity cost. The nations of the world tend to specialize in the production of those goods in which they (have, do not have) _____ a comparative advantage and then export them, and they import those goods in which they _____ a comparative advantage in production.

5. If the cost ratio in country X is 4 Panama hats equal 1 pound of bananas, while in country Y 3 Panama hats equal 1 pound of bananas, then

a. in country X hats are relatively (expensive, inexpensive) _____ and bananas relatively _____,

b. in country Y hats are relatively (expensive, inexpensive) _____ and bananas relatively _____,

c. X has a comparative advantage and should specialize in the production of (bananas, hats) _____, and Y has a comparative advantage and should specialize in the production of _____.

d. when X and Y specialize and trade, the terms of trade will be somewhere between (1, 2, 3, 4) _____ and _____ hats for each pound of bananas and will depend on world demand and supply for hats and bananas.

e. When the actual terms of trade turn out to be 3 1/2 hats for 1 pound of bananas, the cost of obtaining (1) 1 Panama hat has been decreased from (2/7, 1/3) _____ to _____ pounds of bananas in Y.

(2) 1 pound of bananas has been decreased from (3 1/2, 4) _____ to _____ Panama hats in X.

f. International specialization will not be complete if the opportunity cost of producing either good (rises, falls) _____ as a nation produces more of it.

6. The basic argument for free trade based on the principle of (bilateral negotiations, comparative advantage) _____ is that it results in a (more, less) _____ efficient allocation of resources and a (lower, higher) _____ standard of living.

7. The world equilibrium price is determined by the interaction of (domestic, world) _____ supply and demand, while the domestic equilibrium price is determined by _____ supply and demand.

8. When the world price of a good falls relative to the domestic price in a nation, the nation will (increase, decrease)_____ its imports, and when the world price rises relative to the domestic price, the nation will _____ its exports.

9. In a two-nation model for a product, the equilibrium price and quantity of imports and exports occur where one nation's import demand intersects another nation's export (supply, demand) _____ curve. In a highly competitive world market, there can be (multiple, only one) _____ price(s) for a standardized product.

10. Excise taxes on imported products are (quotas, tariffs) _____, whereas limits on the maximum amount of a product that can be imported are import _____. Tariffs applied to a product not produced domestically are (protective, revenue) _____ tariffs, but tariffs designed to shield domestic producers from foreign competition are _____ tariffs.

11. There are other types of trade barriers. Imports that are restricted through the use of a licensing requirement or bureaucratic red tape are (tariff, nontariff) _____ barriers. When foreign firms voluntarily limit their exports to another country, it would represent a voluntary (import, export) _____ restraint.

12. Nations erect barriers to international trade to benefit the economic positions of (consumers, domestic producers) _____ even though these barriers (increase, decrease) _____ economic efficiency and trade among nations and the benefits to that nation are (greater, less) _____ than the costs to it.

13. When the United States imposes a tariff on a good that is imported from abroad, the price of that good in the United States will (increase, decrease) _____, the total purchases of the good in the United States will _____, the output of U.S. producers of the good will (increase, decrease) _____, and the output of foreign producers will _____. The ability of foreigners to buy goods and services in the United States will (increase, decrease) _____ and, as a result, output and employment in U.S. industries that sell goods and services abroad will _____.

14. When comparing the effects of a tariff with the effects of a quota to restrict the U.S. imports of a product, the basic difference is that with a (tariff, quota) _____ the U.S. government will receive revenue, but with a _____ foreign producers will receive the revenue.

15. List the six arguments that protectionists use to justify trade barriers.

a. _____

b. _____

c. _____

d. _____

e. _____

f. _____

16. The military self-sufficiency argument can be challenged because it is difficult to determine which industry is (essential, unessential) _____ for national defense and must be protected. Rather than impose a tariff, a direct subsidy to producers would be (more, less) _____ efficient in this case.

17. Trade barriers do not necessarily increase domestic employment because: imports may change only the (level, composition) _____ of employment; trade barriers can be viewed as "beggar thy (customer, neighbor) _____" policies; other nations can (protest, retaliate) _____ against the trade barriers; and in the long run, the barriers create an allocation of resources that is (more, less) _____ efficient by shielding protected domestic industries from competition.

18. Using trade barriers to permit diversification for stability in an economy is not necessary for (advanced, developing) _____ economies such as in the United States, and there may be great economic costs to forcing diversification in _____ nations; it is also alleged that infant industries need protection until they are sufficiently large to compete, an argument that has been modified to strategic trade policy in

_____ economies.

19. In sum, most arguments for protectionism are (strong, weak) _____ and are designed to benefit (consumers, domestic producers) _____. If these protectionism arguments were followed, it would create (losses, gains) _____ for protected industries and their workers at the expense of

_____ for the economy.

20. The World Trade Organization is charged with overseeing trade (specialization, liberalization) _____. This approach to trade seeks to (increase, decrease) _____ tariffs, _____ agriculture subsidies distorting global trade, and _____ quotas on textiles and apparel. Other areas considered in this agenda are new rules to promote trade in (steel, services) _____ and (more, less) _____ protection of intellectual property rights.

■ **TRUE–FALSE QUESTIONS**

Circle T if the statement is true, F if it is false.

1. The bulk of U.S. export and import trade is with other industrially advanced nations.   **T** F

2. A factor that serves as the economic basis for world trade is the even distribution of resources among nations.   T **F**

3. People trade because they seek products of different quality and other nonprice attributes.   **T** F

4. Examples of capital-intensive goods would be automobiles, machinery, and chemicals.   **T** F

5. The relative efficiency with which a nation can produce specific goods is fixed over time.   T **F**

6. Mutually advantageous specialization and trade are possible between any two nations if they have the same domestic opportunity-cost ratios for any two products.   T **F**

7. The principle of comparative advantage is that total output will be greatest when each good is produced by that nation which has the higher domestic opportunity cost.   T **F**

8. By specializing based on comparative advantage, nations can obtain larger outputs with fixed amounts of resources.   **T** F

9. The terms of trade determine how the increase in world output resulting from comparative advantage is shared by trading nations.   **T** F

10. Increasing opportunity costs tend to prevent specialization among trading nations from being complete.   **T** F

11. Trade among nations tends to bring about a more efficient use of the world's resources and a higher level of material well-being.   **T** F

12. Free trade among nations tends to increase monopoly and lessen competition in these nations.   T **F**

13. A nation will export a particular product if the world price is less than the domestic price.   T **F**

14. In a two-country model, equilibrium in world prices and quantities of exports and imports will occur where one nation's export supply curve intersects the other nation's import demand curve.   **T** F

15. A tariff on coffee in the United States is an example of a protective tariff.   T **F**

16. The imposition of a tariff on a good imported from abroad will reduce the amount of the imported good that is bought.   **T** F

17. A cost of tariffs and quotas imposed by the United States is higher prices that U.S. consumers must pay for the protected product.   **T** F

18. The major difference between a tariff and a quota on an imported product is that a quota produces revenue for the government.   T **F**

19. To advocate tariffs that would protect domestic producers of goods and materials essential to national defense is to substitute a political-military objective for the economic objectives of efficiently allocating resources.   **T** F

20. Tariffs and import quotas meant to increase domestic full employment achieve short-run domestic goals by making trading partners poorer.   **T** F

21. One-crop economies may be able to make themselves more stable and diversified by imposing tariffs on goods imported from abroad, but these tariffs are also apt to lower the standard of living in these economies.   **T** F

22. Protection against the "dumping" of foreign goods at low prices on the U.S. market is one good reason for widespread, permanent tariffs.   T **F**

23. Most arguments for trade protection are special-interest pleas that, if followed, would create gains for protected industries and their workers at the expense of greater losses for the economy.   **T** F

24. The only argument for tariffs that has, in the appropriate circumstances, any economic justification is the increase-domestic-employment argument.   T **F**

25. The World Trade Organization was established by the United Nations to encourage purchases of products from developing nations.   T **F**

☒ MULTIPLE-CHOICE QUESTIONS

Circle the letter that corresponds to the best answer.

1. Which nation leads the world in the volume of exports and imports?
(a) Japan
(b) Germany
(c) United States
(d) United Kingdom

2. Which group of nations dominates world trade?
(a) Saudi Arabia and other OPEC nations
(b) Singapore, South Korea, and Taiwan
(c) United States, Japan, and the nations of Western Europe
(d) China, Russia, and the nations of Eastern Europe

3. Nations engage in trade because
(a) world resources are evenly distributed among nations
(b) world resources are unevenly distributed among nations
(c) all products are produced from the same technology
(d) all products are produced from the same combinations of resources

Use the following tables to answer Questions 4, 5, 6, and 7.

NEPAL PRODUCTION POSSIBILITIES TABLE

Product	A	B	C	D	E	F
			Production alternatives			
Yak fat	0	4	8	12	16	20
Camel hides	40	32	24	16	8	0

KASHMIR PRODUCTION POSSIBILITIES TABLE

Product	A	B	C	D	E	F
			Production alternatives			
Yak fat	0	3	6	9	12	15
Camel hides	60	48	36	24	12	0

4. The data in the tables show that production in
(a) both Nepal and Kashmir are subject to increasing opportunity costs
(b) both Nepal and Kashmir are subject to constant opportunity costs
(c) Nepal is subject to increasing opportunity costs and Kashmir to constant opportunity costs
(d) Kashmir is subject to increasing opportunity costs and Nepal to constant opportunity costs

5. If Nepal and Kashmir engage in trade, the terms of trade will be
(a) between 2 and 4 camel hides for 1 unit of yak fat
(b) between 1/3 and 1/2 units of yak fat for 1 camel hide
(c) between 3 and 4 units of yak fat for 1 camel hide
(d) between 2 and 4 units of yak fat for 1 camel hide

6. Assume that prior to specialization and trade Nepal and Kashmir both choose production possibility C. Now if each specializes according to its comparative advantage, the resulting gains from specialization and trade will be
(a) 6 units of yak fat
(b) 8 units of yak fat
(c) 6 units of yak fat and 8 camel hides
(d) 8 units of yak fat and 6 camel hides

7. Each nation produced only one product in accordance with its comparative advantage, and the terms of trade were set at 3 camel hides for 1 unit of yak fat. In this case, Nepal could obtain a maximum combination of 8 units of yak fat and
(a) 12 camel hides
(b) 24 camel hides
(c) 36 camel hides
(d) 48 camel hides

8. What happens to a nation's imports or exports of a product when the world price of the product rises above the domestic price?
(a) Imports of the product increase.
(b) Imports of the product stay the same.
(c) Exports of the product increase.
(d) Exports of the product decrease.

9. What happens to a nation's imports or exports of a product when the world price of the product falls below the domestic price?
(a) Imports of the product increase.
(b) Imports of the product decrease.
(c) Exports of the product increase.
(d) Exports of the product stay the same.

10. Which one of the following is characteristic of tariffs?
(a) They prevent the importation of goods from abroad.
(b) They specify the maximum amounts of specific commodities that may be imported during a given period of time.
(c) They often protect domestic producers from foreign competition.
(d) They enable nations to reduce their exports and increase their imports during periods of recession.

11. The motive for barriers to the importation of goods and services from abroad is to
(a) improve economic efficiency in that nation
(b) protect and benefit domestic producers of those goods and services
(c) reduce the prices of the goods and services produced in that nation
(d) expand the export of goods and services to foreign nations

12. When a tariff is imposed on a good imported from abroad,
(a) the demand for the good increases
(b) the demand for the good decreases
(c) the supply of the good increases
(d) the supply of the good decreases

Answer Questions 13, 14, 15, 16, and 17 on the basis of the following diagram, where S_d and D_d are the domestic supply and demand for a product and P_w is the world price of that product.

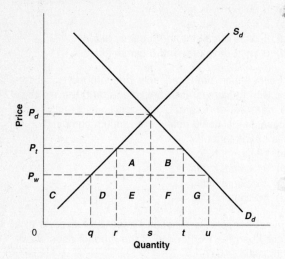

13. In a closed economy (without international trade), the equilibrium price would be
(a) P_d, but in an open economy, the equilibrium price would be P_t
(b) P_d, but in an open economy, the equilibrium price would be P_w
(c) P_w, but in an open economy, the equilibrium price would be P_d
(d) P_w, but in an open economy, the equilibrium price would be P_t

14. If there is free trade in this economy and no tariffs, the total revenue going to the foreign producers is represented by
(a) area C
(b) areas A and B combined
(c) areas A, B, E, and F combined
(d) areas D, E, F, and G combined

15. If a per-unit tariff was imposed in the amount of P_wP_t, then domestic producers would supply
(a) q units and foreign producers would supply qu units
(b) s units and foreign producers would supply su units
(c) r units and foreign producers would supply rt units
(d) t units and foreign producers would supply tu units

16. Given a per-unit tariff in the amount of P_wP_t, the amount of the tariff revenue paid by consumers of this product is represented by
(a) area A
(b) area B
(c) areas A and B combined
(d) areas D, E, F, and G combined

17. Assume that an import quota of rt units is imposed on the foreign nation producing this product. The amount of *total* revenue going to foreign producers is represented by areas

(a) $A + B$
(b) $E + F$
(c) $A + B + E + F$
(d) $D + E + F + G$

18. Tariffs lead to
(a) the contraction of relatively efficient industries
(b) an overallocation of resources to relatively efficient industries
(c) an increase in the foreign demand for domestically produced goods
(d) an underallocation of resources to relatively inefficient industries

19. Tariffs and quotas are costly to consumers because
(a) the price of the imported good rises
(b) the supply of the imported good increases
(c) import competition increases for domestically produced goods
(d) consumers shift purchases away from domestically produced goods

20. Which is a likely result of imposing tariffs to increase domestic employment?
(a) a short-run increase in domestic employment in import industries
(b) a decrease in the tariff rates of foreign nations
(c) a long-run reallocation of workers from export industries to protected domestic industries
(d) a decrease in consumer prices

21. The infant industry argument for tariffs
(a) is especially pertinent for the European Union
(b) generally results in tariffs that are removed after the infant industry has matured
(c) makes it rather easy to determine which infant industries will become mature industries with comparative advantages in producing their goods
(d) might better be replaced by an argument for outright subsidies for infant industries

22. Strategic trade policy is a modified form for advanced economies of which protectionist argument?
(a) the increase-domestic-employment argument
(b) the military self-sufficiency argument
(c) the cheap foreign labor argument
(d) the infant industry argument

23. "The nation needs to protect itself from foreign countries that sell their products in our domestic markets at less than the cost of production." This quotation would be most closely associated with which protectionist argument?
(a) diversification for stability
(b) increase domestic employment
(c) protection against dumping
(d) cheap foreign labor

24. Which is the likely result of the United States using tariffs to protect its high wages and standard of living from cheap foreign labor?
(a) an increase in U.S. exports
(b) a rise in the U.S. real GDP

(c) a decrease in the average productivity of U.S. workers

(d) a decrease in the quantity of labor employed by industries producing the goods on which tariffs have been levied

25. What international agency is charged with overseeing trade liberalization and with resolving disputes among nations?

(a) World Bank
(b) United Nations
(c) World Trade Organization
(d) International Monetary Fund

■ **PROBLEMS**

1. Shown below are the production possibilities curves for two nations: the United States and Chile. Suppose these two nations do not currently engage in international trade or specialization, and suppose that points **A** and **a** show the combinations of wheat and copper they now produce and consume.

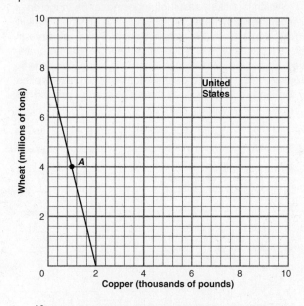

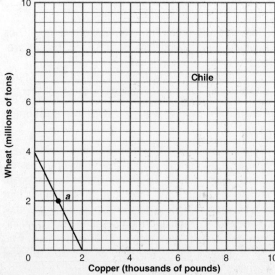

a. The straightness of the two curves indicates that the cost ratios in the two nations are (changing, constant) _____.

b. Examination of the two curves reveals that the cost ratio in

(1) the United States is _____ million tons of wheat for _____ thousand pounds of copper.

(2) Chile is _____ million tons of wheat for _____ thousand pounds of copper.

c. If these two nations were to specialize and trade wheat for copper,

(1) The United States would specialize in the production of wheat because _____

_____.

(2) Chile would specialize in the production of copper because _____

_____.

d. The terms of trade, if specialization and trade occur, will be greater than 2 and less than 4 million tons of wheat for 1000 pounds of copper because _____

_____.

e. Assume the terms of trade turn out to be 3 million tons of wheat for 1000 pounds of copper. Draw in the trading possibilities curve for the United States and Chile.

f. With these trading possibilities curves, suppose the United States decides to consume 5 million tons of wheat and 1000 pounds of copper while Chile decides to consume 3 million tons of wheat and 1000 pounds of copper. The gains from trade to

(1) the United States are _____ million tons of wheat and _____ thousand pounds of copper.

(2) Chile are _____ million tons of wheat and _____ thousand pounds of copper.

2. Following are tables showing the domestic supply and demand schedules and the export supply and import demand schedules for two nations (**A** and **B**).

NATION A

Price	Q_{dd}	Q_{sd}	Q_{di}	Q_{se}
$3.00	100	300	0	200
2.50	150	250	0	100
2.00	200	200	0	0
1.50	250	150	100	0
1.00	300	100	200	0

a. For nation **A,** the first column of the table is the price of a product. The second column is the quantity demanded domestically (Q_{dd}). The third column is the quantity supplied domestically (Q_{sd}). The fourth column is the quantity demanded for imports (Q_{di}). The fifth column is the quantity of exports supplied (Q_{se}).

(1) At a price of $2.00, there (will, will not)

_____ be a surplus or shortage and there

_____ be exports or imports.

(2) At a price of $3.00, there will be a domestic (short-age, surplus) _____ of _____

units. This domestic _____ will be elimi-nated by (exports, imports) _____ of

_____ units.

(3) At a price of $1.00, there will be a domestic (short-age, surplus) _____ of _____

units. This domestic _____ will be elimi-nated by (exports, imports) _____ of

_____ units.

NATION B

Price	Q_{dd}	Q_{sd}	Q_{di}	Q_{se}
$2.50	100	300	0	200
2.00	150	250	0	100
1.50	200	200	0	0
1.00	250	150	100	0

b. For nation **B**, the first column is the price of a prod-uct. The second column is the quantity demanded domestically (Q_{dd}). The third column is the quantity supplied domestically (Q_{sd}). The fourth column is the quantity demanded for imports (Q_{di}). The fifth column is the quantity of exports supplied (Q_{se}).

(1) At a price of $1.50, there (will, will not)

_____ be a surplus or shortage and there

_____ be exports or imports.

(2) At a price of $2.50, there will be a domestic (short-age, surplus) _____ of _____

units. This domestic _____ will be elimi-nated by (exports, imports) _____ of

_____ units.

(3) At a price of $1.00, there will be a domestic (short-age, surplus) _____ of _____

units. This domestic _____ will be elimi-nated by (exports, imports) _____ of

_____ units.

c. The following table shows a schedule of the import demand in Nation **A** and the export supply in Nation **B** at various prices. The first column is the price of the product. The second column is the quantity demanded for imports (Q_{diA}) in Nation **A**. The third column is the quantity of exports supplied (Q_{seB}) in Nation **B**.

Price	Q_{diA}	Q_{seB}
$2.00	0	100
1.75	50	50
1.50	100	0

(1) If the world price is $2.00, then Nation (**A, B**)

_____ will want to import _____

units and Nation _____ will want to export

_____ units of the product.

(2) If the world price is $1.75, then Nation (**A, B**)

_____ will want to import _____

units and Nation _____ will want to export

_____ units of the product.

(3) If the world price is $1.50, then Nation (**A, B**)

_____ will want to import _____

units and Nation _____ will want to export

_____ units of the product.

3. The following table shows the quantities of woolen gloves demanded (**D**) in the United States at several different prices (**P**). Also shown in the table are the quan-tities of woolen gloves that would be supplied by U.S. producers (**S_a**) and the quantities that would be supplied by foreign producers (**S_f**) at the nine different prices.

P	D	S_a	S_f	S_t	S'_f	S'_t
$2.60	450	275	475	_____	_____	_____
2.40	500	250	450	_____	_____	_____
2.20	550	225	425	_____	_____	_____
2.00	600	200	400	_____	_____	_____
1.80	650	175	375	_____	_____	_____
1.60	700	150	350	_____	_____	_____
1.40	750	125	325	_____	_____	_____
1.20	800	0	300	_____	_____	_____
1.00	850	0	0	_____	_____	_____

a. Compute and enter in the table the total quantities that would be supplied (**S_t**) by U.S. and foreign pro-ducers at each of the prices.

b. If the market for woolen gloves in the United States is a competitive one the equilibrium price for woolen

gloves is $_____ and the equilibrium

quantity is _____.

c. Suppose now that the United States government imposes an 80 cent ($.80) tariff per pair of gloves on all gloves imported into the United States from abroad. Compute and enter into the table the quantities that would be supplied (**S'_f**) by foreign producers at the nine different prices. [*Hint:* If foreign producers were willing to supply 300 pairs at a price of $1.20 when there was no tariff, they are now willing to supply 300 pairs at

$2.00 (the $.80 per pair tariff plus the $1.20 they will receive for themselves). The quantities supplied at each of the other prices may be found in a similar fashion.]

d. Compute and enter into the table the total quantities that would be supplied (S'_t) by U.S. and foreign producers at each of the nine prices.

e. As a result of the imposition of the tariff the equilibrium price has risen to $_____ and the equilibrium quantity has fallen to _____.

f. The number of pairs sold by

(1) U.S. producers has (increased, decreased) _____ by _____.

(2) foreign producers has (increased, decreased) _____ by _____.

g. The total revenues (after the payment of the tariff) of

(1) U.S. producers—who do not pay the tariff—have (increased, decreased) _____ by $_____.

(2) foreign producers—who do pay the tariff—have (increased, decreased) _____ by $_____.

h. The total amount spent by U.S. buyers of woolen gloves has _____ by $_____.

i. The total number of dollars earned by foreigners has _____ by $_____, and, as a result, the total foreign demand for goods and services produced in the United States has _____ by $_____.

j. The tariff revenue of the United States government has _____ by $_____.

k. If an import quota were imposed that had the same effect as the tariff on price and output, the amount of the tariff revenue, $_____, would now be received as revenue by _____ producers.

■ **SHORT ANSWER AND ESSAY QUESTIONS**

1. Describe the quantity of imports and exports for the United States in absolute and relative terms. How has the quantity of imports and exports changed over time?

2. What are the major imports and exports of the United States? With which nations does the United States trade?

3. What role does the United States play in international trade? Who are the other major players in international trade?

4. What three factors—one dealing with the resource distribution, the second with production, and the third with

the variety of product—are the basis of a rationale for trade among nations?

5. Explain
(a) the theory or principle of comparative advantage;
(b) what is meant by and what determines the terms of trade; and
(c) the gains from trade.

6. What is the case for free trade?

7. Explain how the equilibrium prices and quantities of exports and imports are determined.

8. Why will exports in a nation increase when world prices rise relative to domestic prices?

9. What motivates nations to erect barriers to the importation of goods from abroad, and what types of barriers do they erect?

10. Suppose the United States increases the tariff on automobiles imported from Germany (and other foreign countries). What is the effect of this tariff-rate increase on
(a) the price of automobiles in the United States;
(b) the total number of cars sold in the United States during a year;
(c) the number of cars produced by and employment in the German automobile industry;
(d) production by and employment in the U.S. automobile industry;
(e) German income obtained by selling cars in the United States;
(f) the German demand for goods produced in the United States;
(g) the production of and employment in those U.S. industries that now export goods to Germany;
(h) the standards of living in the United States and in Germany;
(i) the allocation of resources in the U.S. economy; and
(j) the allocation of the world's resources?

11. Explain the economic effects of a tariff and show them in a supply and demand graph.

12. Compare and contrast the economic effects of a tariff with the economic effects of an import quota on a product.

13. Critically evaluate the military self-sufficiency argument for protectionism. What industries should be protected?

14. What are four shortcomings of using tariffs or quotas to increase domestic employment in the United States?

15. What is the basis for the infant industry arguments (including strategic trade policy) for protectionism? How can it be countered?

16. Can a strong case for protectionism be made on the basis of defending against the "dumping" of products? How do you determine if a nation is dumping a product? What are the economic effects of dumping on consumers?

17. Does the economy need to shield domestic workers from competition from "cheap" foreign labor? Explain using the ideas of comparative advantage and standards of living.

18. Offer a summary of the case for protectionism. What does the historical evidence indicate? Give examples.

19. What are the trade liberalization issues that are the focus of the World Trade Organization?

20. What do critics of the World Trade Organization say about its effects on domestic economies and the global economy and what is the response from economists?

ANSWERS

Chapter 37 International Trade

FILL-IN QUESTIONS

1. 11, doubled
2. larger, largest
3. uneven, different, more
4. lowest, have, do not have
5. *a.* inexpensive, expensive; *b.* expensive, inexpensive; *c.* hats, bananas; *d.* 3, 4; *e.* (1) 1/3, 2/7, (2) 4, 3 1/2; *f.* rises
6. comparative advantage, more, higher
7. world, domestic
8. increase, increase
9. supply, only one
10. tariffs, quotas, revenue, protective
11. nontariff, export
12. domestic producers, decrease, less
13. increase, decrease, increase, decrease, decrease, decrease
14. tariff, quota
15. *a.* military self-sufficiency; *b.* support of infant industry; *c.* increase domestic employment; *d.* diversification for stability; *e.* protection against dumping; *f.* cheap foreign labor (any order for *a–f*)
16. essential, more
17. composition, neighbor, retaliate, less
18. advanced, developing, advanced
19. weak, domestic producers, gains, losses
20. liberalization, decrease, decrease, decrease, services, more

TRUE–FALSE QUESTIONS

1. T, p. 690	**10.** T p. 696	**19.** T, p. 703
2. F, p. 691	**11.** T, pp. 696–697	**20.** T, p. 703
3. T, pp. 691–692	**12.** F, p. 697	**21.** T, p. 704
4. T, p. 691	**13.** F, p. 697	**22.** F, p. 705
5. F, p. 692	**14.** T, pp. 699–700	**23.** T, p. 706
6. F, pp. 692–693	**15.** F, p. 700	**24.** F, p. 706
7. F, p. 693	**16.** T, pp. 701–702	**25.** F, p. 707
8. T, pp. 693–694	**17.** T, p. 702	
9. T, p. 694	**18.** F, p. 702	

MULTIPLE-CHOICE QUESTIONS

1. c, p. 690	**10.** c, p. 700	**19.** a, p. 702
2. c, p. 691	**11.** b, pp. 700–702	**20.** c, p. 703
3. b, p. 691	**12.** d, pp. 701–702	**21.** d, p. 704
4. b, p. 692	**13.** b, pp. 701–702	**22.** d, pp. 704–705
5. a, pp. 693–695	**14.** d, pp. 701–702	**23.** c, p. 705
6. a, pp. 693–695	**15.** c, pp. 701–702	**24.** c, p. 705
7. c, pp. 693–695	**16.** c, pp. 701–702	**25.** c, p. 707
8. c, pp. 697–700	**17.** c, p. 702	
9. a, pp. 697–700	**18.** a, p. 702	

PROBLEMS

1. *a.* constant; *b.* (1) 8, 2, (2) 4, 2; *c.* (1) it has a comparative advantage in producing wheat (its cost of producing wheat is less than Chile's), (2) it has a comparative advantage in producing copper (its cost of producing copper is less than the United States'); *d.* one of the two nations would be unwilling to trade if the terms of trade are outside this range; *f.* (1) 1, 0, (2) 1, 0

2. *a.* (1) will not, will not, (2) surplus, 200, surplus, exports, 200, (3) shortage, 200, shortage, imports, 200; *b.* (1) will not, will not, (2) surplus, 200, surplus, exports, 200, (3) shortage, 100, shortage, imports, 100; *c.* (1) A, 0, B, 100, (2) A, 50, B, 50, (3) A, 100, B, 0

3. *a.* 750, 700, 650, 600, 550, 500, 450, 300, 0; *b.* $2.00, 600; *c.* 375, 350, 325, 300, 0, 0, 0, 0, 0; *d.* 650, 600, 550, 500, 175, 150, 125, 0, 0; *e.* $2.20, 550; *f.* (1) increased, 25, (2) decreased, 75; *g.* (1) increased, $95, (2) decreased, $345; *h.* increased, $10; *i.* decreased, $345, decreased, $345; *j.* increased, $260; *k.* $260, foreign

SHORT ANSWER AND ESSAY QUESTIONS

1. pp. 690–691	**8.** pp. 697–700	**15.** pp. 704–705
2. pp. 690–691	**9.** pp. 700–701	**16.** p. 705
3. pp. 690–691	**10.** pp. 701–702	**17.** p. 705
4. p. 691	**11.** pp. 701–702	**18.** p. 706
5. pp. 692–696	**12.** pp. 701–702	**19.** pp. 707–708
6. pp. 696–697	**13.** p. 703	**20.** p. 707
7. pp. 697–700	**14.** p. 703	

CHAPTER 38

Exchange Rates, the Balance of Payments, and Trade Deficits

In the last chapter you learned *why* nations engage in international trade and *why* they erect barriers to trade with other nations. In Chapter 38 you will learn *how* nations using different currencies are able to trade.

The means nations use to overcome the difficulties that result from the use of different currencies are fairly simple. When the residents of a nation (its consumers, business firms, or governments) wish to buy goods or services or real or financial assets from, make loans or gifts to, or pay interest and dividends to the residents of other nations, they *buy* some of the currency used in that nation. They pay for the foreign money with some of their own currency. In other words, they exchange their own currency for foreign currency.

When the residents of a nation sell goods or services or real or financial assets to, receive loans or gifts from, or are paid dividends or interest by the residents of foreign nations and obtain foreign currencies, they *sell* this foreign currency—often called foreign exchange—in return for some of their own currency. That is, they *exchange* foreign currency for their own currency.

The market in which one currency is sold and is paid for with another currency is called the **foreign exchange market.** The price that is paid (in one currency) for a unit of another currency is called the **foreign exchange rate.** And like most prices, the foreign exchange rate for any foreign currency is determined by the demand for and the supply of that foreign currency.

As you know from Chapter 37, nations buy and sell large quantities of goods and services across national boundaries. But the residents of these nations also buy and sell such financial assets as stocks and bonds and such real assets as land and capital goods in other nations, and the governments and individuals in one nation make gifts (remittances) to other nations. At the end of a year, nations summarize their foreign transactions with the rest of the world. This summary is called the nation's **balance of payments:** a record of how it obtained foreign currency during the year and what it did with this foreign currency.

Of course, all foreign currency obtained was used for some purpose—it did not evaporate—consequently the balance of payments *always* balances. The balance of payments is an extremely important and useful device for understanding the amounts and kinds of international transactions in which the residents of a nation engage. It also allows us to understand the meaning of a balance-of-payments deficit or surplus, the causes of these imbalances, and how to deal with them.

Several difficult sections of this chapter are concerned with how **flexible and fixed exchange-rate systems** handle balance-of-payments deficits and surpluses. A balance-of-payments deficit occurs when the foreign currency receipts are less than foreign currency payments and the nation must reduce its official reserves to balance its payments. Conversely, a balance-of-payments surplus occurs when foreign currency receipts are greater than foreign currency payments, and the nation must expand its official reserves to balance its payments. In these sections pay particular attention to the ways in which a flexible or floating exchange-rate system and a fixed exchange-rate system will correct balance-of-payments deficits and surpluses and the advantages and disadvantages of these two alternative systems for eliminating imbalances in international accounts.

As examples of these two types of exchange-rate systems, the next section of the chapter examines the **gold standard,** the **Bretton Woods system,** and the **managed floating exchange-rate system.** In the first two systems exchange rates are fixed, and in the third system exchange rates are fixed in the short run (to obtain the advantages of fixed exchange rates) and flexible in the long run (to enable nations to correct balance-of-payments deficits and surpluses).

The final section of the chapter examines the U.S. **trade deficits.** As you will learn, these deficits were the result of several factors—differences in national growth rates and a declining saving rate—that contributed to imports rising faster than exports. They also have several implications—increased current consumption at the expense of future consumption and increased U.S. indebtedness to foreigners.

■ CHECKLIST

When you have studied this chapter you should be able to

☐ Explain how U.S. exports create a foreign demand for dollars that in turn generates a supply of foreign currencies.

☐ Describe how U.S. imports create a domestic demand for foreign currencies that in turn generates a supply of dollars.

☐ Give a definition of a nation's balance of payments.

☐ Use the items in the current account to calculate the balance on goods, balance on goods and services, and balance on the current account when given the data.

☐ Describe how balance is achieved in the capital account.

☐ Explain the relationship between the current account, capital account, and official reserves account.

☐ Indicate how the official reserves account is used to determine whether there is a balance-of-payments deficit or surplus.

☐ Use a supply and demand graph to illustrate how a flexible exchange-rate system works to establish the price and quantity of a currency.

☐ Describe the depreciation and appreciation of a nation's currency under a flexible exchange-rate system.

☐ Identify the five principal determinants of the demand for and supply of a particular foreign currency and explain how they alter exchange rates.

☐ Explain how flexible exchange rates eventually eliminate balance-of-payments deficits or surpluses.

☐ List three disadvantages of flexible exchange rates.

☐ Use a supply and demand graph to illustrate how a fixed exchange-rate system functions.

☐ Discuss the objectives and limitations of using official reserves, trade policies, exchange controls, and domestic macroeconomic adjustments to maintain a fixed exchange rate.

☐ Identify three different exchange-rate systems used by the world's nations in recent years.

☐ List three conditions a nation had to fulfill if it was to be on the gold standard.

☐ Explain how the gold standard worked to maintain fixed exchange rates.

☐ Give reasons for the collapse of the gold standard.

☐ Explain how the Bretton Woods system attempted to stabilize exchange rates and to establish orderly changes in exchange rates for correcting balance-of-payments deficits.

☐ State reasons for the demise of the Bretton Woods system.

☐ Describe the current system of managed floating exchange rates.

☐ Discuss the pros and cons of the system of managed floating exchange rates.

☐ Describe the causes of recent trade deficits in the United States.

☐ Explain the economic implications of recent trade deficits in the United States.

■ CHAPTER OUTLINE

1. Trade between two nations differs from domestic trade because the nations use different currencies. This problem is resolved by the existence of *foreign exchange markets,* in which the currency used by one nation can be purchased and paid for with the currency of the other nation.

 a. U.S. exports create a foreign demand for dollars, and the satisfaction of this demand increases the supply of foreign currencies in the foreign exchange market.

 b. U.S. imports create a domestic demand for foreign currencies, and meeting this demand decreases the supplies of foreign currencies in the foreign exchange market.

2. The *balance of payments* for a nation is an annual record of all its transactions with the other nations in the world; it records all the payments received from and made to the rest of the world.

 a. The *current account* section of a nation's balance of payments records its trade in currently produced goods and services. Within this section

 (1) the *balance on goods* of the nation is equal to its exports of goods less its imports of goods;

 (2) the *balance on goods and services* is equal to its exports of goods and services less its imports of goods and services; and

 (3) the *balance on the current account* is equal to its balance on goods and services plus its net investment income (dividends and interest) from other nations and its net private and public transfers to other nations. This balance may be either a surplus or a deficit.

 b. The *capital account* of a nation's balance of payments records foreign purchases of real and financial assets in the United States. This item earns the United States some foreign currencies, so it is entered as a plus (+) in the capital account. U.S. purchases of real and financial assets abroad draw down U.S. holdings of foreign currencies, so this item is entered as a minus (−) in the capital account. The nation has a surplus in its capital account if foreign purchases of U.S. assets are greater than U.S. purchases of assets abroad. The nation has a deficit in its capital account if foreign purchases of U.S. assets are less than U.S. purchases of assets abroad.

 c. The *official reserves* account consists of the foreign currencies owned by the central bank. These reserves *decrease* when they are used to finance a net deficit on the combined current and capital accounts. In this case, the official reserves show as a plus (+) in the balance-of-payments account. The reserves *increase* when a nation has a net surplus on its current and capital account. In this case, they show as a minus (−) in the balance-of-payments account. The three components of the balance of payments—the current account, the capital account, and the official reserves account—must equal zero.

 d. A nation has a *balance-of-payments deficit* when imbalances in the combined current and capital accounts lead to a decrease in official reserves. A *balance-of-payments surplus* arises when imbalances in the combined current and capital accounts result in an increase in official reserves.

3. There are both a flexible or floating exchange system and a fixed exchange-rate system that nations use to correct imbalances in the balance of payments. If nations use a *flexible or floating exchange system,* the demand for and the supply of foreign currencies determine foreign exchange rates. The exchange rate for any foreign currency is the rate at which the quantity of that currency demanded is equal to the quantity of it supplied.

a. A change in the demand for or the supply of a foreign currency will cause a change in the exchange rate for that currency. When there is an increase in the price paid in dollars for a foreign currency, the dollar has *depreciated* and the foreign currency has *appreciated* in value. Conversely, when there is a decrease in the price paid in dollars for a foreign currency, the dollar has *appreciated* and the foreign currency has *depreciated* in value.

b. Changes in the demand for or supply of a foreign currency are largely the result of changes in tastes, relative incomes, relative price levels, relative interest rates, and speculation.

c. Flexible exchange rates can be used to eliminate a balance-of-payments deficit or surplus.

(1) When a nation has a payment deficit, foreign exchange rates will increase, thus making foreign goods and services more expensive and decreasing imports. These events will make a nation's goods and services less expensive for foreigners to buy, thus increasing exports.

(2) With a payment surplus, the exchange rates will increase, thus making foreign goods and services less expensive and increasing imports. This situation makes a nation's goods and services more expensive for foreigners to buy, thus decreasing exports.

d. Flexible exchange rates have disadvantages because they increase the uncertainties exporters, importers, and investors face, thus reducing international trade. This system also changes the terms of trade and creates instability in domestic economies.

4. If nations use a *fixed exchange-rate system,* the nations fix (or peg) foreign exchange rates. The governments of these nations must intervene in the foreign exchange markets to prevent shortages and surpluses caused by shifts in demand and supply.

a. One way a nation can stabilize foreign exchange rates is for its government to sell its reserves of a foreign currency in exchange for its own currency (or gold) when there is a shortage of the foreign currency. Conversely, a government would buy a foreign currency in exchange for its own currency (or gold) when there is a surplus of the foreign currency; however, currency reserves may be limited and inadequate for handling large and persistent deficits or surpluses, so it may use other means to maintain fixed exchange rates.

b. A nation might adopt trade policies that discourage imports and encourage exports.

c. A nation might impose exchange-rate controls and rationing, but these policies tend to distort trade, lead to government favoritism, restrict consumer choice, and create black markets.

d. Another way a nation can stabilize foreign exchange rates is to use monetary and fiscal policy to reduce its national income and price level and raise interest rates relative to those in other nations. These events would

lead to a decrease in demand for and increase in the supply of different foreign currencies.

5. In their recent history, the nations of the world have used three different exchange-rate systems.

a. Under the **gold standard,** each nation must define its currency in terms of a quantity of gold, maintain a fixed relationship between its gold and its money supply, and allow gold to be imported or exported without restrictions.

(1) The potential gold flows between nations would ensure that exchange rates remained fixed.

(2) Payment deficits and surpluses would be eliminated through macroeconomic adjustments. For example, if a nation had a balance-of-payments deficit and gold flowing out of the country, its money supply would decrease. This event would increase interest rates and decrease total spending, output, employment, and the price level. The opposite would happen in the other country because it would have a payments surplus. The changes in both nations would eliminate any payments deficit or surplus.

(3) During the worldwide depression of the 1930s nations felt that remaining on the gold standard threatened their recoveries, and the policy of devaluating their currencies to boost exports led to the breakdown and abandonment of the gold standard.

b. From the end of World War II until 1971, under the **Bretton Woods system,** nations were committed to the adjustable-peg system of exchange rates. The **International Monetary Fund (IMF)** was created to keep this exchange-rate system feasible and flexible.

(1) The adjustable-peg system required the United States to sell gold to other member nations at a fixed price and the other members of the IMF to define their monetary units in terms of either gold or dollars (which established fixed exchange rates among the currencies of all member nations) and required the other member nations to keep the exchange rates for their currencies from rising by selling foreign currencies, selling gold, or borrowing on a short-term basis from the IMF.

(2) The system also provided for orderly changes in exchange rates to correct a fundamental imbalance (persistent and sizable balance-of-payments deficits) by allowing a nation to devalue its currency (increase its defined gold or dollar equivalent).

(3) The other nations of the world used gold and dollars as their international monetary reserves in the Bretton Woods system. For these reserves to grow, the United States had to continue to have balance-of-payments deficits, but to continue the convertibility of dollars into gold it had to reduce the deficits, and, faced with this dilemma, in 1971 the United States suspended the convertibility of the dollar, brought an end to the Bretton Woods system, and allowed the exchange rates for the dollar and the other currencies to float.

c. Exchange rates today are allowed to float in the long term to correct balance-of-payments deficits and surpluses, but there can be short-term interventions by governments to stabilize and manage currencies. This new system of **managed floating exchange rates** is favored by some and criticized by others.

(1) Its proponents contend that this system has *not* led to any decrease in world trade, and has enabled the world to adjust to severe economic shocks throughout its history.

(2) Its critics argue that it has resulted in volatile exchange rates that can hurt those developing nations that are dependent on exports, has *not* reduced balance-of-payments deficits and surpluses, and is a "nonsystem" that a nation may use to achieve its own domestic economic goals.

6. The United States had large and persistent **trade deficits** in the past decade, and they are likely to continue.

a. These trade deficits were the result of several factors:

(1) more rapid growth in the domestic economy than in the economies of several major trading partners, which caused imports to rise more than exports;

(2) the emergence of large trade deficits with China;

(3) a decline in the rate of saving and a capital account surplus, which allowed U.S. citizens to consume more imported goods.

b. The trade deficits of the United States have had two principal effects: They increased current domestic consumption (allowing the nation to operate outside its production possibilities frontier), and they increased the indebtedness of U.S. citizens to foreigners. A possible negative implication of these persistent trade deficits is that they will lead to permanent debt and more foreign ownership of domestic assets, or lead to large sacrifices of future domestic consumption. But, if the foreign lending increases the U.S. capital stock, then it can contribute to long-term U.S. economic growth.

■ HINTS AND TIPS

1. The chapter is filled with many new terms, some of which are just special words used in international economics to mean things with which you are already familiar. Other terms are new to you, so you must spend time learning them if you are to understand the chapter.

2. The terms *depreciation* and *appreciation* can be confusing when applied to foreign exchange markets.

a. First, know the related terms. "Depreciate" means decrease or fall, whereas "appreciate" means increase or rise.

b. Second, think of depreciation or appreciation in terms of quantities:

(1) what *decreases* when the currency of Country A *depreciates* is the *quantity* of Country B's currency that can be purchased for *1 unit* of Country A's currency;

(2) what *increases* when the currency of Country A *appreciates* is the *quantity* of Country B's currency that can be purchased for *1 unit* of Country A's currency.

c. Third, consider the effect of changes in **exchange rates:**

(1) when the exchange rate for Country B's currency *rises*, this means that Country A's currency has

depreciated in value because 1 unit of Country A's currency will now purchase a smaller quantity of Country B's currency;

(2) when the exchange rate for Country B's currency *falls*, this means that Country A's currency has *appreciated* in value because 1 unit of Country A's currency will now purchase a larger quantity of Country B's currency.

3. The meaning of the balance of payments can also be confusing because of the number of accounts in the balance sheet. Remember that the balance of payments must always balance and sum to zero because one account in the balance of payments can be in surplus, but it will be offset by a deficit in another account. However, when people talk about a balance-of-payments surplus or deficit, they are referring to the sum of the current and capital account balances. If the total is positive, there is a balance-of-payments surplus, but if it is negative, there is a balance-of-payments deficit.

■ IMPORTANT TERMS

balance of payments	fixed exchange-rate system
current account	purchasing-power-parity theory
balance on goods and services	currency interventions
trade deficit	exchange controls
trade surplus	gold standard
balance on current account	devaluation
capital account	Bretton Woods system
balance on the capital account	International Monetary Fund (IMF)
official reserves	managed floating exchange rate
balance-of-payments deficit	
balance-of-payments surplus	
flexible or floating exchange-rate system	

SELF-TEST

■ FILL-IN QUESTIONS

1. The rate of exchange for the European euro is the amount in (euros, dollars) _____ that a U.S. citizen must pay to obtain 1 (euro, dollar) _____. The rate of exchange for the U.S. dollar is the amount in (euros, dollars) _____ that a citizen in the euro zone must pay to obtain 1 (euro, dollar) _____. If the rate of exchange for the euro is (1.05 euros, $0.95) _____, the rate of exchange for the U.S. dollar is _____.

2. U.S. exports create a foreign (demand for, supply of) _____ dollars and generate a

_____ foreign currencies owned by U.S. banks and available to domestic buyers; U.S. imports create a domestic (demand for, supply of) _____ foreign currencies and reduce the _____ foreign currencies held by U.S. banks and available for domestic consumers.

3. The balance of payments of a nation records all payments (domestic, foreign) _____ residents make to and receive from _____ residents. Any transaction that *earns* foreign exchange for that nation is a (debit, credit) _____, and any transaction that *uses up* foreign exchange is a _____. A debit is shown with a $(+, -)$ _____ sign, and a credit is shown with a _____ sign.

4. If a nation has a deficit in its balance of goods, its exports of goods are (greater, less) _____ than its imports of goods, and if it has a deficit in its balance on goods and services, its exports of these items are _____ than its imports of them. The current account is equal to the balance on goods and services (plus, minus) _____ net investment income and _____ net transfers.

5. The capital account records the flow of payments from the sale or purchase of real or financial assets. Foreign purchases of real and financial assets in the United States earn foreign currencies, so they are entered as a (plus, minus) _____ in the U.S. capital account, but U.S. purchases of real and financial assets abroad draw down U.S. holding of foreign currencies, so this item is entered as a _____. If foreign purchases of U.S. assets are greater than U.S. purchases of assets abroad, the nation has a (surplus, deficit) _____ in its capital account, but if foreign purchases of U.S. assets are less than U.S. purchases of assets abroad, it has a _____.

6. A nation may finance a current account deficit by (buying, selling) _____ assets or by (borrowing, lending) _____ abroad and may use a current account surplus to (buy, sell) _____ assets or to (borrow, lend) _____ abroad.

7. The official reserves of a nation are the quantities of (foreign currencies, its own money) _____ owned by its central bank. If that nation has a deficit on the current and capital accounts, its official reserves (increase, decrease) _____, but with a surplus on the current and capital accounts, its official

reserves _____. The sum of the current, capital, and official reserves accounts must equal $(0, 1)$ _____.

8. A nation has a balance-of-payments deficit if the sum of its current and capital accounts balances is (positive, negative) _____ and its official reserves (increase, decrease) _____. A nation has a payments surplus when the sum of its current and capital accounts balances is (positive, negative) _____ and its official reserves (increase, decrease) _____.

9. If foreign exchange rates float freely and a nation has a balance-of-payments *deficit*, that nation's currency in the foreign exchange markets will (appreciate, depreciate) _____ and foreign currencies will _____ compared to it. As a result of these changes in foreign exchange rates, the nation's imports will (increase, decrease) _____, its exports will _____, and the size of its deficit will (increase, decrease) _____.

10. What effect would each of the following have—the appreciation (**A**) or depreciation (**D**) of the euro compared to the U.S. dollar in the foreign exchange market, *ceteris paribus?*

a. The increased preference in the United States for domestic wines over wines produced in Europe:

_____

b. A rise in the U.S. national income: _____

c. An increase in the price level in Europe: _____

d. A rise in real interest rates in the United States:

_____

e. The belief of speculators in Europe that the dollar will appreciate in the foreign exchange market:

_____

11. There are three disadvantages of freely floating foreign exchange rates: the risks and uncertainties associated with flexible rates tend to (expand, diminish) _____ trade between nations; when a nation's currency depreciates, its terms of trade with other nations are (worsened, improved) _____; and fluctuating exports and imports can (stabilize, destabilize) _____ an economy.

12. To fix or peg the rate of exchange for the Mexican peso when the exchange rate for the peso is rising, the United States would (buy, sell) _____ pesos in exchange for dollars, and when the exchange rate for the peso is falling, the United States would _____ pesos in exchange for dollars.

13. Under a fixed exchange-rate system, a nation with a balance-of-payments deficit might attempt to eliminate the deficit by (taxing, subsidizing) _____ imports or by _____ exports. The nation might use exchange controls and ration foreign exchange among those who wish to (export, import) _____ goods and services and require all those who _____ goods and services to sell the foreign exchange they earn to the (businesses, government) _____.

14. If the United States has a payments deficit with Japan and the exchange rate for the Japanese yen is rising, under a fixed exchange-rate system the United States might adopt (expansionary, contractionary) _____ fiscal and monetary policies to reduce the demand for the yen, but this would bring about (inflation, recession) _____ in the United States.

15. When the nations of the world were on the gold standard exchange, rates were relatively (stable, unstable) _____. When a nation had a payments deficit, gold flowed (into, out of) _____ the nation, its money supply (increased, decreased) _____, its interest rates _____, and output, employment, income, and perhaps prices (increased, decreased) _____; thus its payments deficit _____.

16. The Bretton Woods system was established to bring about (flexible, fixed) _____ exchange rates. Under the Bretton Woods system, a member nation defined its monetary unit in terms of (oil, gold) _____ or dollars. Each member nation stabilized the exchange rate for its currency and prevented it from depreciating by (supplying, saving) _____ its official reserves of foreign currency, by (buying, selling) _____ gold, or by (borrowing from, lending to) _____ the International Monetary Fund. A nation with a deeply rooted payments deficit could (devalue, revalue) _____ its currency. The system was designed so that in the short run exchange rates would be (stable, flexible) _____ enough to promote international trade and in the long run they would be _____ enough to correct balance-of-payments imbalances.

17. The role of the dollar as a component of international monetary reserves under Bretton Woods produced a dilemma. For the dollar to remain an acceptable international monetary reserve, the U.S. payments deficits had to be (eliminated, continued) _____, but for international monetary reserves to grow to accommodate world trade, the U.S. payments deficits had to be _____. These deficits caused an acceptability problem because they resulted in (a decrease, an increase) _____ in the foreign holding of U.S. dollars and _____ in the U.S. reserves of gold, which contributed to (a decrease, an increase) _____ in the ability of the United States to convert dollars into gold and the willingness of foreigners to hold dollars as if they were as good as gold. In 1971, the United States essentially ended this system when it (adopted, suspended) _____ the convertibility of dollars into gold and allowed the value of the dollar to be determined by markets.

18. Since then the international monetary system has moved to a system of managed (fixed, floating) _____ exchange rates. This means that exchange rates of nations are (restricted from, free to) _____ find their equilibrium market levels, but nations may occasionally (leave, intervene in) _____ the foreign exchange markets to stabilize or alter market exchange rates.

19. The advantages of the current system are that the growth of trade (was, was not) _____ accommodated and that it has survived much economic (stability, turbulence) _____. Its disadvantages are its (equilibrium, volatility) _____ and the lack of guidelines for nations that make it a (bureaucracy, nonsystem) _____.

20. In recent years, the United States had large trade and current account (surpluses, deficits) _____ that were brought about by the sharp increases in its (exports, imports) _____ and the small increases in its _____. One cause was (stronger, weaker) _____ economic growth in the United States relative to _____ economic growth in Europe and Japan. Another contributing factor was a (rising, falling) _____ saving rate. One effect of the trade deficits of the United States has been (decreased, increased) _____ current domestic consumption that allows the nation to operate outside its production possibility frontier, and another effect was a (rise, fall) _____ in the indebtedness of U.S. citizens to foreigners.

■ **TRUE–FALSE QUESTIONS**

Circle T if the statement is true, F if it is false.

1. The imports of goods and services by U.S. citizens from abroad create a supply of dollars in the foreign exchange market. **T** F

2. The balance of payments of the United States records all the payments its residents receive from and make to the residents of foreign nations.   **T   F**

3. Exports are a debit item and are shown with a minus sign (−), and imports are a credit item and are shown with a plus sign (+) in the balance of payments of a nation.   **T   F**

4. The United States would have a balance-of-payments surplus if the balances on its current and capital accounts were positive.   **T   F**

5. Any nation with a balance-of-payments deficit in its current and capital accounts must reduce its official reserves.   **T   F**

6. The sum of a nation's current account balance, its capital account balance, and the change in its official reserves in any year is always equal to zero.   **T   F**

7. The purchasing-power-parity theory basically explains why there is an inverse relationship between the price of dollars and the quantity demanded.   **T   F**

8. The expectations of speculators in the United States that the exchange rate for Japanese yen will fall in the future will increase the supply of yen in the foreign exchange market and decrease the exchange rate for the yen.   **T   F**

9. If a nation has a balance-of-payments deficit and exchange rates are flexible, the price of that nation's currency in the foreign exchange markets will fall; this will reduce its imports and increase its exports.   **T   F**

10. Were the United States' terms of trade with Nigeria to worsen, Nigeria would obtain a greater quantity of U.S. goods and services for every barrel of oil it exported to the United States.   **T   F**

11. If a nation wishes to fix (or peg) the foreign exchange rate for the Swiss franc, it must buy Swiss francs with its own currency when the rate of exchange for the Swiss franc rises.   **T   F**

12. If exchange rates are stable or fixed and a nation has a payments surplus, prices and currency incomes in that nation will tend to rise.   **T   F**

13. A nation using exchange controls to eliminate a balance-of-payments surplus might depreciate its currency.   **T   F**

14. If country A defined its currency as worth 100 grains of gold and country B defined its currency as worth 20 grains of gold, then, ignoring packing, insuring, and shipping charges, 5 units of country A's currency would be worth 1 unit of country B's currency.   **T   F**

15. Under the gold standard, the potential free flow of gold among nations would result in exchange rates that are fixed.   **T   F**

16. In the Bretton Woods system, a nation could not devalue its currency by more than 10% without the permission of the International Monetary Fund.   **T   F**

17. In the Bretton Woods system, a nation with persistent balance-of-payments surpluses had an undervalued currency and should have increased the pegged value of its currency.   **T   F**

18. To accommodate expanding world trade in the Bretton Woods system, the U.S. dollar served as a reserve medium of exchange and the United States ran persistent balance-of-payments deficits.   **T   F**

19. A basic shortcoming of the Bretton Woods system was its inability to bring about the changes in exchange rates needed to correct persistent payments deficits and surpluses.   **T   F**

20. Using the managed floating system of exchange rates, a nation with a persistent balance-of-payments surplus should allow the value of its currency in foreign exchange markets to decrease.   **T   F**

21. Two criticisms of the current managed floating exchange-rate system are its potential for volatility and its lack of clear policy rules or guidelines for nations to manage exchange rates.   **T   F**

22. The trade deficits of the United States in recent years were caused by sharp increases in U.S. exports and slight increases in U.S. imports.   **T   F**

23. Improved economic growth in the major economies of the major trading partners of the United States would tend to worsen the trade deficit.   **T   F**

24. The decline in the saving rate in the United States contributed to the persistent trade deficit of the past decade.   **T   F**

25. The negative net exports of the United States have increased the indebtedness of U.S. citizens to foreigners.   **T   F**

■ MULTIPLE-CHOICE QUESTIONS

Circle the letter that corresponds to the best answer.

1. If a U.S. citizen could buy £25,000 for $100,000, the rate of exchange for the pound would be
 (a) $40
 (b) $25
 (c) $4
 (d) $.25

2. U.S. residents demand foreign currencies to
 (a) produce goods and services exported to foreign countries
 (b) pay for goods and services imported from foreign countries
 (c) receive interest payments on investments in the United States
 (d) have foreigners make real and financial investments in the United States

3. Which of the following would be a credit in the current account?
 (a) U.S. imports of goods
 (b) U.S. exports of services

(c) U.S. purchases of assets abroad

(d) U.S. interest payments for foreign capital invested in the United States

4. A nation's balance on the current account is equal to its exports less its imports of

(a) goods and services

(b) goods and services, plus U.S. purchases of assets abroad

(c) goods and services, plus net investment income and net transfers

(d) goods and services, minus foreign purchases of assets in the United States

5. The net investment income of the United States in its international balance of payments is the

(a) interest income it receives from foreign residents

(b) dividends it receives from foreign residents

(c) excess of interest and dividends it receives from foreign residents over what it paid to them

(d) excess of public and private transfer payments it receives from foreign residents over what it paid to them

6. In a flexible- or floating-exchange-rate system, when the U.S. dollar price of a British pound rises, this means that the dollar has

(a) appreciated relative to the pound and the pound has appreciated relative to the dollar

(b) appreciated relative to the pound and the pound has depreciated relative to the dollar

(c) depreciated relative to the pound and the pound has appreciated relative to the dollar

(d) depreciated relative to the pound and the pound has depreciated relative to the dollar

7. Which statement is correct about a factor that causes a nation's currency to appreciate or depreciate in value?

(a) if the supply of a nation's currency decreases, all else equal, that currency will depreciate

(b) if the supply of a nation's currency increases, all else equal, that currency will depreciate

(c) if the demand for a nation's currency increases, all else equal, that currency will depreciate

(d) if the demand for a nation's currency decreases, all else equal, that currency will appreciate

8. Assuming exchange rates are flexible, which of the following should increase the dollar price of the Swedish krona?

(a) a rate of inflation greater in Sweden than in the United States

(b) real interest rate increases greater in Sweden than in the United States

(c) national income increases greater in Sweden than in the United States

(d) the increased preference of Swedish citizens for U.S. automobiles over Swedish automobiles

9. Under a flexible exchange-rate system a nation may be able to correct or eliminate a persistent (long-term) balance-of-payments deficit by

(a) lowering the barriers on imported goods

(b) reducing the international value of its currency

(c) expanding its national income

(d) reducing its official reserves

10. If a nation had a balance-of-payments surplus and exchange rates floated freely, the foreign exchange rate for its currency would

(a) rise, its exports would increase, and its imports would decrease

(b) rise, its exports would decrease, and its imports would increase

(c) fall, its exports would increase, and its imports would decrease

(d) fall, its exports would decrease, and its imports would increase

11. Which would be a result associated with the use of freely floating foreign exchange rates to correct a nation's balance-of-payments surplus?

(a) The nation's terms of trade with other nations would be worsened.

(b) Importers in the nation who had made contracts for the future delivery of goods would find that they had to pay a higher price than expected for the goods.

(c) If the nation were at full employment, the decrease in exports and the increase in imports would be inflationary.

(d) Exporters in the nation would find their sales abroad had decreased.

12. The use of exchange controls to eliminate a nation's balance-of-payments deficit results in decreasing the nation's

(a) imports

(b) exports

(c) price level

(d) income

13. Which of these conditions did a nation have to fulfill if it was to be under the gold standard?

(a) use only gold as a medium of exchange

(b) maintain a flexible relationship between its gold stock and its currency supply

(c) allow gold to be freely exported from and imported into the nation

(d) define its monetary unit in terms of a fixed quantity of dollars

14. If the nations of the world were on the gold standard and one nation had a balance-of-payments surplus,

(a) foreign exchange rates in that nation would rise

(b) gold would tend to be imported into that country

(c) the level of prices in that country would fall

(d) employment and output in that country would fall

15. Which was the principal disadvantage of the gold standard?

(a) unstable foreign exchange rates

(b) persistent payments imbalances

(c) the uncertainties and decreased trade that resulted from the depreciation of gold

(d) the domestic macroeconomic adjustments experienced by a nation with a payments deficit or surplus

16. The objective of the adjustable-peg or Bretton Woods system was exchange rates that were

(a) adjustable in the short run and fixed in the long run

(b) adjustable in both the short and the long run

(c) fixed in both the short and the long run

(d) fixed in the short run and adjustable in the long run

17. Which is the best definition of international monetary reserves in the Bretton Woods system?

(a) gold

(b) dollars

(c) gold and dollars

(d) gold, dollars, and British pounds

18. The major dilemma created by the persistent U.S. payments deficits under the Bretton Woods system was that in order to maintain the status of the dollar as an acceptable international monetary reserve, the deficits had to

(a) decrease, but to expand reserves to accommodate world trade, the deficits had to continue

(b) continue, but to expand reserves to accommodate world trade, the deficits had to be eliminated

(c) increase, but to expand reserves to accommodate world trade, the deficits had to be reduced

(d) decrease, but to expand reserves to accommodate world trade, the deficits had to be eliminated

19. "Floating" the dollar means

(a) the value of the dollar is determined by the demand for and the supply of the dollar

(b) the dollar price of gold has been increased

(c) the price of the dollar has been allowed to crawl upward at the rate of one-fourth of 1% a month

(d) the IMF decreased the value of the dollar by 10%

20. A system of managed floating exchange rates

(a) allows nations to stabilize exchange rates in the short term

(b) requires nations to stabilize exchange rates in the long term

(c) entails stable exchange rates in both the short and long term

(d) fixes exchange rates at market levels

21. Floating exchange rates

(a) tend to correct balance-of-payments imbalances

(b) reduce the uncertainties and risks associated with international trade

(c) increase the world's need for international monetary reserves

(d) tend to have no effect on the volume of trade

22. The trade problem that faced the United States in recent years was a

(a) deficit in its capital account

(b) surplus in its balance on goods

(c) deficit in its current account

(d) surplus in its current account

23. Which was a cause of the growth of U.S. trade deficits in recent years?

(a) protective tariffs imposed by the United States

(b) slower economic growth in the United States

(c) direct foreign investment in the United States

(d) a declining saving rate in the United States

24. What would be the effect on U.S. imports and exports when the United States experiences strong economic growth but its major trading partners experience sluggish economic growth?

(a) U.S. imports will increase more than U.S. exports

(b) U.S. exports will increase more than U.S. imports

(c) U.S. imports will decrease but U.S. exports will increase

(d) there will be no effect on U.S. imports and exports

25. Two major outcomes from the trade deficits of recent years were

(a) decreased domestic consumption and U.S. indebtedness

(b) increased domestic consumption and U.S. indebtedness

(c) increased domestic consumption but decreased U.S. indebtedness

(d) decreased domestic consumption but increased U.S. indebtedness

■ PROBLEMS

1. Assume a U.S. exporter sells $3 million worth of wheat to an importer in Colombia. If the rate of exchange for the Colombian peso is $.02 (2 cents), the wheat has a total value of 150 million pesos.

a. There are two ways the importer in Colombia may pay for the wheat. It might write a check for 150 million pesos drawn on its bank in Bogotá and send it to the U.S. exporter.

(1) The American exporter would then sell the check to its bank in New Orleans and its demand deposit there would increase by $_____ million.

(2) This New Orleans bank now sells the check for 150 million pesos to a correspondent bank (a U.S. commercial bank that keeps an account in the Bogotá bank).

(a) The New Orleans bank's account in the correspondent bank increases by _____ million (dollars, pesos) _____; and

(b) the correspondent bank's account in the Bogotá bank increases by _____ million (pesos, dollars) _____.

b. The second way for the importer to pay for the wheat is to buy from its bank in Bogotá a draft on a U.S. bank for $3 million, pay for this draft by writing a check for 150 million pesos drawn on the Bogotá bank, and send the draft to the U.S. exporter.

(1) The U.S. exporter would then deposit the draft in its account in the New Orleans bank and its demand deposit account there would increase by $_____ million.

(2) The New Orleans bank collects the amount of the draft from the U.S. bank on which it is drawn through the Federal Reserve Banks.

(a) Its account at the Fed increases by $_____ million; and

(b) the account of the bank on which the draft was drawn decreases by $ _____ million.

c. Regardless of the way used by the Colombian importer to pay for the wheat,

(1) the export of the wheat created a (demand for, supply of) _____ dollars and a

_____ pesos.

(2) The number of dollars owned by the U.S. exporter has (increased, decreased) _____ and the number of pesos owned by the Colombian importer

has _____ .

2. The following table contains hypothetical balance-of-payments data for the United States. All figures are in billions.

Current account

(1) U.S. goods exports	$+150	
(2) U.S. goods imports	−200	
(3) *Balance on goods*		_____
(4) U.S. exports of services	+75	
(5) U.S. imports of services	−60	
(6) *Balance on services*		_____
(7) *Balance on goods and services*		_____
(8) Net investment income	+12	
(9) Net transfers	−7	
(10) **Balance on current account**		_____

Capital account

(11) Foreign purchases of assets in the U.S.	+80	
(12) U.S. purchases of assets abroad	−55	
(13) **Balance on capital account**		_____
(14) *Current and capital account balance*		_____
(15) **Official reserves**		_____
		$ 0

a. Compute with the appropriate sign (+ or −) and enter in the table the seven missing items.
b. The United States had a payments (deficit, surplus)

_____ of $ _____ .

3. The following table shows supply and demand schedules for the British pound.

Quantity of pounds supplied	Price	Quantity of pounds demanded
400	$5.00	100
360	4.50	200
300	4.00	300
286	3.50	400
267	3.00	500
240	2.50	620
200	2.00	788

a. If the exchange rates are flexible
(1) what will be the rate of exchange for the pound?

$_____

(2) what will be the rate of exchange for the dollar?

£_____

(3) how many pounds will be purchased in the market?

_____

(4) how many dollars will be purchased in the market?

_____

b. If the U.S. government wished to fix or peg the price of the pound at $5.00, it would have to (buy, sell)

_____ (how many) _____

pounds for $_____ .
c. And if the British government wished to fix the price of the dollar at £ 2/5, it would have to (buy, sell)

_____ (how many) _____

pounds for $_____ .

■ SHORT ANSWER AND ESSAY QUESTIONS

1. What is the foreign exchange rate? Who are the demanders and suppliers of a particular foreign exchange, say, the British pound? Why is a buyer (demander) in the foreign exchange markets also always a seller (supplier)?

2. What is meant when it is said that "A nation's exports pay for its imports"? Do nations pay for all their imports with exports?

3. What is a balance of payments? What are the principal sections in a nation's balance of payments, and what are the principal "balances" to be found in it?

4. How can a nation finance a current account deficit, and what can it do with a current account surplus?

5. How does a nation finance a balance-of-payments deficit, and what does it do with a balance-of-payments surplus?

6. What types of events cause the exchange rate for a foreign currency to appreciate or to depreciate? How will each event affect the exchange rate for a foreign currency and for a nation's own currency?

7. How can flexible foreign exchange rates eliminate balance-of-payments deficits and surpluses? What are the problems associated with this method of correcting payments imbalances?

8. How may a nation use its international monetary reserves to fix or peg foreign exchange rates? Be precise. How does a nation obtain or acquire these monetary reserves?

9. What kinds of trade policies may nations with payments deficits use to eliminate their deficits?

10. How can foreign exchange controls be used to restore international equilibrium? Why do such exchange controls necessarily involve the rationing of foreign exchange? What effect do these controls have on prices, output, and employment in nations that use them?

11. If foreign exchange rates are fixed, what kind of domestic macroeconomic adjustments are required to eliminate a payments deficit? To eliminate a payments surplus?

12. What is the gold standard? How did the international gold standard correct payments imbalances?

13. What were the disadvantages of the gold standard for eliminating payments deficits and surpluses?

14. What did nations use as international monetary reserves under the Bretton Woods system? Why was the dollar used by nations as international money, and how could they acquire additional dollars?

15. Explain the dilemma created by the need for expanding international monetary reserves and for maintaining the status of the dollar under the Bretton Woods system.

16. Why and how did the United States shatter the Bretton Woods system in 1971?

17. Explain what is meant by a managed floating system of foreign exchange rates. When are exchange rates managed and when are they allowed to float?

18. Explain the arguments of the proponents and the critics of the managed floating system.

19. What were the causes of the trade deficits of the United States in recent years?

20. What were the effects of the trade deficits of recent years on the U.S. economy?

ANSWERS

Chapter 38 Exchange Rates, the Balance of Payments, and Trade Deficits

FILL-IN QUESTIONS

1. dollars, euro, euros, dollar, $0.95, 1.05 euros
2. demand for, supply of, demand for, supply of
3. domestic, foreign, credit, debit, −, +
4. less, less, plus, plus
5. plus, minus, surplus, deficit
6. selling, borrowing, buy, lend
7. foreign currencies, decrease, increase, zero
8. negative, decrease, positive, increase
9. depreciate, appreciate, decrease, increase, decrease
10. *a.* D; *b.* A; *c.* D; *d.* D; *e.* D

11. diminish, worsened, destabilize
12. sell, buy
13. taxing, subsidizing, import, export, government
14. contractionary, recession
15. stable, out of, decreased, increased, decreased, decreased
16. fixed, gold, supplying, selling, borrowing from, devalue, stable, flexible
17. eliminated, continued, an increase, a decrease, a decrease, suspended
18. floating, free to, intervene in
19. was, turbulence, volatility, nonsystem
20. deficits, imports, exports, stronger, weaker, falling, increased, rise

TRUE–FALSE QUESTIONS

1. T, p. 712	**10.** T, p. 720	**19.** T, p. 724
2. T, p. 712	**11.** F, pp. 720–721	**20.** F, pp. 724–725
3. F, pp. 712–713	**12.** T, pp. 721–722	**21.** T, p. 725
4. T, pp. 712–713	**13.** F, p. 721	**22.** F, p. 726
5. T, p. 714	**14.** F, p. 722	**23.** F, p. 726
6. T, p. 714	**15.** T, pp. 722–723	**24.** T, p. 726
7. F, p. 717	**16.** T, pp. 723–724	**25.** T, p. 727
8. T, p. 718	**17.** T, pp. 723–724	
9. T, pp. 718–719	**18.** T, pp. 723–724	

MULTIPLE-CHOICE QUESTIONS

1. c, pp. 711–712	**10.** b, p. 719	**19.** a, p. 724
2. b, pp. 711–712	**11.** d, p. 720	**20.** a, pp. 724–725
3. b, pp. 712–713	**12.** a, p. 721	**21.** a, pp. 718–719, 725
4. c, pp. 712–713	**13.** c, p. 722	**22.** c, p. 726
5. c, p. 713	**14.** b, pp. 722–723	**23.** d, p. 726
6. c, p. 715	**15.** d, p. 723	**24.** a, p. 726
7. b, pp. 716–717	**16.** d, pp. 723–724	**25.** b, p. 727
8. b, p. 718	**17.** c, pp. 723–724	
9. b, pp. 718–719	**18.** a, p. 724	

PROBLEMS

1. *a.* (1) 3, (2) (a) 3, dollars, (b) 150, pesos; *b.* (1) 3, (2) (a) 3, (b) 3; *c.* (1) demand for, supply of, (2) increased, decreased
2. *a.* −50, +15, −35, −30, +25, −5, +5; *b.* deficit, 5
3. *a.* (1) 4.00, (2) 1/4, (3) 300, (4) 1200; *b.* buy, 300, 1500; *c.* sell, 380, 950

SHORT ANSWER AND ESSAY QUESTIONS

1. pp. 711–712	**8.** pp. 720–721	**15.** p. 724
2. pp. 711–712	**9.** p. 721	**16.** p. 724
3. pp. 712–714	**10.** p. 721	**17.** pp. 724–725
4. pp. 712–714	**11.** pp. 721–722	**18.** p. 725
5. pp. 712–715	**12.** pp. 722–723	**19.** p. 726
6. pp. 716–718	**13.** p. 723	**20.** p. 727
7. pp. 718–720	**14.** pp. 723–724	

The Economics of Developing Countries

Note: The bonus web chapter is available at: www.mcconnell16.com.

This chapter looks at the critical problem of raising the standards of living in *developing countries* (DVCs) of the world. The development problems in these nations, especially the poorest ones, are extensive: low literacy rates, low levels of industrialization, high dependence on agriculture, rapid rates of population growth, and widespread poverty.

There is also a growing income gap between DVCs and *industrially advanced nations* (IACs). To close this gap, there needs to be more economic growth in DVCs. To achieve that growth requires that the economic resource bases be expanded and these resources be used efficiently. As you will discover from the chapter, DVCs trying to apply these principles face *obstacles* quite different from those that limit growth in the United States and other IACs. DVCs have many problems with natural, human, and capital resources and with technology, all of which combine to hinder economic growth. Certain social, cultural, and institutional factors also create a poor environment for economic development.

These obstacles do not mean that it is impossible to increase the living standards of these DVCs. What they do indicate is that to encourage growth, the DVCs must do things that do not need to be done in the United States or other IACs. Population pressures need to be managed, and there needs to be better use of labor resources. Steps must be taken to encourage capital investment. Governments must take an active role in promoting economic growth and limiting the public sector problems for economic development. Dramatic changes in social practices and institutions are required. If these and other actions are not taken, it may not be possible to reduce the major obstacles to growth and break the *vicious circle of poverty* in the DVCs.

No matter how successful the DVCs are in overcoming these obstacles, they still will not be able to grow rapidly without more aid from IACs. This assistance can come in the form of lower trade barriers in IACs that would increase sales of products from DVCs to IACs. There can be more foreign aid in the form of government grants and loans to IACs. The banks, corporations, and other businesses in IACs can provide private capital in the form of loans or direct foreign investment in the building of new factories and businesses.

The final section of the chapter is a fitting ending to the discussion of economic problems in developing nations. It focuses on specific policies to promote economic growth in the DVCs and examines the issue from two sides. One side offers a set of policies from the perspective of DVCs, and the other side lists things IACs can do to foster economic growth in developing nations. You will have to decide after reading the chapter if any of these actions would be worthwhile.

■ CHECKLIST

When you have studied this chapter you should be able to

☐ Describe the extent of income inequality among nations.

☐ Classify nations based on three levels of income.

☐ Compare the effects of differences in economic growth in IACs and DVCs.

☐ Discuss the human realities of poverty in DVCs.

☐ Identify two basic avenues for economic growth in IACs and DVCs.

☐ Describe natural resource problems in DVCs.

☐ Identify the three problems related to human resources that plague the poorest DVCs.

☐ Explain the difficulties for economic growth that are created by population growth in DVCs.

☐ Compare the traditional and demographic transition views of population and economic growth in DVCs.

☐ Describe the conditions of unemployment and underemployment in DVCs.

☐ State reasons for low labor productivity in DVCs.

☐ Give three reasons for the emphasis on capital formation in the DVCs.

☐ Identify obstacles to domestic capital formation through saving.

☐ List obstacles to domestic capital formation through investment.

☐ Explain why transferring the technologies from IACs to DVCs may not be a realistic method of improving the technology in DVCs.

☐ Identify three sociocultural factors that can potentially inhibit economic growth.

☐ Describe the institutional obstacles to growth.

☐ Explain why poverty in the poor nations is a vicious circle.

☐ List five ways that governments in the DVCs can play a positive role in breaking the vicious circle of poverty.

☐ Describe the problems with the public sector in fostering economic development.

☐ Identify the three ways IACs can help the DVCs foster economic growth.

☐ Explain how reducing international trade barriers in IACs would help DVCs.

☐ Describe the two sources of foreign aid for DVCs.

☐ Give three criticisms of foreign aid to DVCs.

☐ Explain why foreign aid to DVCs has declined.

☐ Describe what groups in IACs provide private capital to DVCs.

☐ Discuss nine DVC policies for promoting economic growth.

☐ Explain five actions that IACs can take to encourage growth in DVCs.

■ **CHAPTER OUTLINE**

1. There is considerable *income inequality among nations.* The richest 20% of the world's population receives more than 80% of the world's income.

    a. Countries can also be classified into two main groups.

    (1) *Industrially advanced countries* (IACs) are characterized by well-developed market economies based on large stocks of capital goods, advanced technology for production, and well-educated workers. Among the *high-income* nations are the United States, Canada, Japan, Australia, New Zealand, and most of the nations of Western Europe. These countries averaged $26,710 per capita income in 2001.

    (2) *Developing countries* (DVCs) are a diverse group of middle-income and low-income nations. *Middle-income* nations (e.g., Brazil, Poland, Russia, South Africa, and Thailand) have per capita incomes that range from $745 to $9206, and average incomes of about $1850. There are also *low-income* nations with per capita incomes of $745 or less, and average incomes of $430. This latter group is dominated by India, Indonesia, and most of the sub-Saharan nations of Africa. These nations are not highly industrialized, are dependent on agriculture, and often have high rates of population growth and low rates of literacy. The low-income nations comprise about 41% of the world's population.

    b. There are disparities in the growth rates of nations, resulting in sizable income gaps. Some DVC have been able to improve their economic conditions over time and become IACs. Other DVCs are now showing high rates of economic growth, but still other DVCs have experienced a decline in economic growth and standards of living. If growth rates were the same for high- and low-income nations, the gap in per capita income would widen because the income base is higher in high-income nations.

    c. The human realities of extreme poverty are important. Compared with IACs, persons in DVCs have not only lower per capita incomes but also lower life expectancies, and DVCs have higher infant mortality, lower literacy rates, more of the labor force in agriculture, and fewer nonhuman sources of energy.

2. *Economic growth* requires that DVCs use their existing resources more efficiently and that they expand their available supplies of resources. The physical, human, and socioeconomic conditions in these nations are the reasons why DVCs experience different rates of economic growth.

    a. Many DVCs possess inadequate *natural resources.* This limited resource base is an obstacle to growth. The agricultural products that DVCs typically export are also subject to significant price variations on the world market, creating variations in national income.

    b. There are problems with *human resources* in DVCs.

    (1) DVCs tend to be overpopulated and have high rates of population growth. These growing populations reduce the DVCs' capacity to save, invest, and increase productivity. They also overuse land and natural resources, and the migration of rural workers to cities creates urban problems.

    (2) DVCs often experience both unemployment and underemployment, which wastes labor resources.

    (3) DVCs have low levels of labor productivity because of insufficient physical capital and lack of investment in human capital.

    c. DVCs have inadequate amounts of *capital goods,* and so find it difficult to accumulate capital. Domestic capital formation occurs through saving and investing. The potential for saving is low in many DVCs because the nations are too poor to save. There is also *capital flight* of saving from DVCs to more stable IACs. The investment obstacles include a lack of investors and entrepreneurs and a lack of incentives to invest in DVC economies. The infrastructure is poor in many DVCs.

    d. *Technological advance* is slow in DVCs. Although these nations might adopt the technologies of industrial nations, these technologies are not always appropriate for the resource endowments of the DVCs, so they must learn to develop and use their own technologies.

    e. It is difficult for DVCs to alter the *social, cultural, and institutional factors* to create a good environment for achieving economic growth.

3. In summary, DVCs face a *vicious circle of poverty.* They save little and therefore invest little in real and human capital because they are poor, and because they do not invest, their outputs per capita remain low and they remain poor. Even if the vicious circle were to be broken, a rapid increase in population would leave the standard of living unchanged.

4. There are differing views about the *role of government* in fostering economic growth in DVCs.

    a. The positive view holds that in the initial stages of economic development, government action is needed to help overcome such obstacles as the lack of law and order, of entrepreneurship, and of infrastructure. Government policies may also assist capital formation and help resolve social and institutional problems.

    b. Problems and disadvantages with the public sector in promoting growth include bureaucratic impediments, corruption, maladministration, and the importance of political objectives over economic goals. Central planning does not work because it restricts competition and individual incentives, which are important ingredients in the growth process.

5. There are several ways **IACs can help DVCs.**

a. They can lower the **trade barriers** that prevent the DVCs from selling their products in the developed countries.

b. **Loans and grants** from governments and international organizations such as the **World Bank** would also enable the DVCs to accumulate capital. This foreign aid, however, has been criticized because it increases dependency, bureaucracy, and corruption. For these reasons, and because of the end of the cold war, foreign aid to DVCs has declined.

c. DVCs can also receive flows of private capital from IACs. **Direct foreign investment** in new factories and businesses can come from banks, corporations, and financial investment companies, but such investment tends to be highly selective among nations.

6. There are several **policies for promoting growth** that DVCs and IACs might undertake. Both DVC and IAC perspectives are offered.

a. **DVC policies** for promoting growth include establishing the rule of law, opening economies to international trade, controlling population growth, encouraging direct foreign investment, building human capital, making peace with neighbors, establishing independent central banks, making realistic exchange-rate policies, and privatizing state industries.

b. **IAC policies** for encouraging economic growth in DVCs are directing foreign aid to the poorest of the DVCs, reducing tariffs and import quotas, providing debt relief to DVCs, allowing more low-skilled immigration and discouraging brain drains, and limiting arms sales to DVCs.

■ HINTS AND TIPS

1. This chapter offers a comprehensive look at the various factors affecting growth and economic development. Keep in mind that **no one factor** explains why some nations prosper and others remain poor. The chapter should give you insights into how natural, human, and capital resources together with government policies may influence a nation's economic development.

2. Several economic and demographic statistics for comparing rich and poor nations appear in the chapter's tables. You need not memorize the numbers, but you should try to get a sense of the magnitude of the differences between IACs and DVCs on several key indicators. To do this, ask yourself questions calling for **relative comparisons.** For example, how many times larger is average per capita income in IACs than in low-income DVCs? Answer: 62 times greater ($26,710/$430 = 62).

3. The chapter ends with **policy suggestions** for increasing economic growth in DVCs. Be sure to look at these policies from the perspective of both DVCs and

IACs. Identify those that you think are most important, and explain your reasoning.

■ IMPORTANT TERMS

industrially advanced
   countries (IACs)

developing countries (DVCs)

demographic transition view

underemployment

brain drain

capital flight

infrastructure

capital-saving technology

capital-using technology

the will to develop

capricious universe view

land reform

vicious circle of poverty

corruption

World Bank

direct foreign investment

SELF-TEST

■ FILL-IN QUESTIONS

1. There is considerable income inequality among nations. The richest 20% of the world's population receives more than (40, 80) _____% of world income, while the poorest 20% of the world's population receives less than (2, 10) _____% of world income. The poorest 60% of nations receives less than (6, 30) _____% of the world's income.

2. High-income nations can be classified as (industrially advanced, developing) _____ countries, or (IACs, DVCs) _____, and the middle- or low-income nations as _____ countries, or (DVCs, IACs) _____.

3. IACs have a (higher, lower) _____ starting base for per capita income than DVCs, so the same percentage growth rate for both IACs and DVCs means (an increase, a decrease) _____ in the absolute income gap.

4. Low per capita income in DVCs means that there are (lower, higher) _____ life expectancies, _____ adult literacy, (lower, higher) _____ daily calorie supply, _____ energy consumption, and (lower, higher) _____ infant mortality.

5. The process for economic growth is the same for IACs and DVCs. It involves (less, more) _____ efficient use of existing resources and obtaining _____ productive resources.

6. The distribution of natural resources among DVCs is (even, uneven) _____; many DVCs lack vital natural resources. Although oil resources have been used for economic growth in (OPEC nations, DVCs)

_____, IACs own or control much of the natural resources in _____. Also, exports of products from DVCs are subject to (small, large) _____ price fluctuations in the world market, and that tends to make DVC incomes (more, less) _____ stable.

7. In terms of human resources,

a. many DVCs are (under, over) _____ populated and have (higher, lower) _____ population growth rates than IACs. Rapid population growth can cause per capita income to (increase, decrease) _____.

b. In DVCs, many people are unable to find jobs, so there is (underemployment, unemployment) _____, and many people are employed for fewer hours than they desire or work at odd jobs, so there is _____.

c. In DVCs, labor productivity is very (high, low) _____, partly because these countries have not been able to invest in (stocks and bonds, human capital) _____; when the best-trained workers leave DVCs to work in IACs, there is a (demographic transition, brain drain) _____ that contributes to the decline in skill level and productivity.

8. Capital accumulation is critical to the development of DVCs. If there were more capital goods, this would improve (natural resources, labor productivity) _____ and help boost per capita output. An increase in capital goods is necessary because the (demand for, supply of) _____ arable land is limited. The process of capital formation is cumulative, investment increases the (output, natural resources) _____ of the economy, and this in turn makes it possible for the economy to save more and invest more in capital goods.

9. The formation of domestic capital requires that a nation save and invest.

a. Saving is difficult in DVCs because of (high, low) _____ per capita income, and investment is difficult because of (many, few) _____ investors or entrepreneurs, and (strong, weak) _____ incentives to invest. There is also the problem of private savings being transferred to IACs; this transfer is called (brain drain, capital flight) _____.

b. Many DVCs do not have the infrastructure or (private, public) _____ capital goods that are necessary for productive _____ investment by businesses.

c. Nonfinancial (or in-kind) investment involves the transfer of surplus labor from (agriculture, industry) _____ to the improvement of agricultural facilities or the infrastructure.

10. The technologies used in the advanced industrial countries might be borrowed by and used in the DVCs, but

a. the technologies used in the advanced countries are based on a labor force that is (skilled, unskilled) _____, labor that is relatively (abundant, scarce) _____, and capital that is relatively _____, and their technologies tend to be (labor, capital) _____-using, while

b. the technologies required in developing countries must be based on a labor force that is (skilled, unskilled) _____, labor that is relatively (abundant, scarce) _____, and capital that is relatively _____, and their technologies tend to be (labor, capital) _____-using.

c. If technological advances make it possible to replace a worn-out plow, costing $10 when new, with a new $5 plow, the technological advance is capital (saving, using) _____.

11. Other obstacles to economic growth in DVCs include those dealing with problems of national unity, religion, and customs, or (institutional, sociocultural) _____ problems, and those dealing with such issues as political corruption, poor school systems, and land reform, or _____ problems.

12. In most DVCs, there is a vicious circle of poverty. Saving is low because the income per capita is (high, low) _____, and because saving is low, investment in real and human capital is _____. For this reason the productivity of labor and output (income) per capita remain (high, low) _____.

13. List five ways that government can serve a positive role in fostering economic growth in DVCs, especially during the early phases of growth:

a. _____

b. _____

c. _____

d. _____

e. _____

14. Government involvement in the economy of DVCs can create public sector problems because government bureaucracy can (foster, impede) _____ social and economic change, government planners can give too much emphasis to (political, economic)

_____ objectives, and there can be (good, poor) _____ administration and corruption.

15. Three major ways that IACs can assist in the economic development in DVCs is by (increasing, decreasing) _____ international trade barriers, _____ foreign aid, and _____ the flow of private capital investment.

16. Direct foreign aid for DVCs generally comes from individual nations in the form of (private, public) _____ loans, grants, and programs. It can also come from the (Bank of America, World Bank), _____ which is supported by member nations. This organization is a (first, last) _____ resort lending agency for DVCs and provides (military, technical) _____ assistance for DVCs.

17. Foreign aid has been criticized in recent years because it may (increase, decrease) _____ dependency in a nation instead of creating self-sustained growth, may _____ government bureaucracy and control over a nation's economy, and may _____ the misuse of funds or corruption. These criticisms and the end of the cold war have led to a(n) _____ in the amount of foreign aid to DVCs.

18. There can also be private capital flows to DVCs in the form of direct foreign (aid, investment) _____ from IAC firms, individuals, and commercial banks, and it has increased in recent years. The reason for this change is that many DVCs have reformed their economies and adopted policies that (limit, encourage) _____ economic growth and _____ direct foreign investment. Nevertheless, the flow of private capital to DVCs is (selective, widespread) _____ among nations.

19. DVCs can adopt policies to encourage economic growth. They can (open, close) _____ economies to international trade, (encourage, discourage) _____ direct foreign investment and the development of human capital, and (expand, control) _____ population growth.

20. IACs can also adopt policies to help DVCs. They can (raise, lower) _____ trade barriers, (encourage, discourage) _____ immigration of the brightest and best-educated, and direct foreign aid to the (middle-income, low-income) _____ DVCs.

■ TRUE–FALSE QUESTIONS

Circle T if the statement is true, F if it is false.

1. The richest 20% of the world's population receives about 50% of the world's income while the poorest 20% receives only about 20% of the world's income.   **T F**

2. Developing countries generally have high unemployment, low literacy rates, rapid population growth, and a labor force committed to agricultural production.   **T F**

3. The United States has about 5% of the world's population and produces about 31% of the world's output.
T F

4. The absolute income gap between DVCs and industrially advanced countries has decreased over the past 30 years.   **T F**

5. Economic growth in both IACs and DVCs requires using economic resources more efficiently and increasing the supplies of some of these resources.   **T F**

6. It is impossible to achieve a high standard of living with a small supply of natural resources.   **T F**

7. DVCs have low population densities and low population growth relative to IACs.   **T F**

8. The demographic transition view of population growth is that rising incomes must first be achieved, and only then will slower population growth follow.   **T F**

9. A major factor contributing to the high unemployment rates in urban areas of DVCs is the fact that the migration from rural areas to cities has greatly exceeded the growth of urban job opportunities.   **T F**

10. Saving in DVCs is a smaller percentage of domestic output than in IACs, and this is the chief reason total saving in DVCs is small.   **T F**

11. Before private investment can be increased in DVCs, it is necessary to reduce the amount of investment in infrastructure.   **T F**

12. Technological advances in DVCs will be made rapidly because the advances do not require pushing forward the frontiers of technological knowledge, and the technologies used in IACs can be easily transferred to all DVCs.   **T F**

13. When technological advances are capital saving, it is possible for an economy to increase its productivity without any *net* investment in capital goods.   **T F**

14. A critical, but intangible, ingredient in economic development is the "will to develop."   **T F**

15. The capricious universe view is that there is a strong correlation between individual effort and results.   **T F**

16. Land reform is one of the institutional obstacles to economic growth in many developing countries.   **T F**

17. The situation in which poor nations stay poor because they are poor is a description of the vicious circle of poverty.   **T F**

18. The creation of an adequate infrastructure in a nation is primarily the responsibility of the private sector.   **T   F**

19. Governments always play a positive role in fostering the economic growth of DVCs.   **T   F**

20. One effective way that IACs can help DVCs is to raise trade barriers so that DVCs become more self-sufficient.   **T   F**

21. The World Bank is the organization to which DVCs turn for the majority of foreign aid, loans, and grants.   **T   F**

22. Two reasons why foreign aid is viewed as harmful are that it tends to promote dependency and generate government bureaucracy.   **T   F**

23. An example of direct foreign investment would be the building of an automobile factory by General Motors in Brazil.   **T   F**

24. In recent years, a smaller proportion of private capital flows to DVCs has been direct foreign investment rather than loans to DVC governments.   **T   F**

25. One policy suggested for promoting economic growth in DVCs is the establishment of independent central banks (where they do not already exist) to keep inflation in check and control the money supply.   **T . F**

■ **MULTIPLE-CHOICE QUESTIONS**

Circle the letter that corresponds to the best answer.

1. Data on per capita income from the nations of the world indicate that there is considerable
  (a) income equality
  (b) income inequality
  (c) stability in the income growth
  (d) deterioration in incomes for most developing nations

2. Which nation would be considered a developing nation?
  (a) India
  (b) Italy
  (c) Japan
  (d) New Zealand

3. If the per capita income is $600 a year in a DVC and $12,000 in an IAC, then a 2% growth rate in each nation will increase the absolute income gap by
  (a) $120
  (b) $228
  (c) $240
  (d) $252

4. The poorest DVCs would probably exhibit high levels of
  (a) literacy
  (b) life expectancy
  (c) infant mortality
  (d) per capita energy consumption

5. The essential paths for economic growth in any nation are expanding the
  (a) size of the population and improving agriculture

(b) role of government and providing jobs for the unemployed
(c) supplies of resources and using existing resources more efficiently
(d) amount of tax subsidies to businesses and tax credits for business investment

6. Based on the rule of 70, if the United States has an annual rate of population increase of 1% and a DVC has one of 2%, how many years will it take for the population to double in each nation?
  (a) 140 years for the United States and 70 years for the DVC
  (b) 35 years for the United States and 70 years for the DVC
  (c) 70 years for the United States and 35 years for the DVC
  (d) 70 years for the United States and 140 years for the DVC

7. Assume the total real output of a developing country increases from $100 billion to $115.5 billion while its population expands from 200 to 210 million people. Real per capital income has increased by
  (a) $50
  (b) $100
  (c) $150
  (d) $200

8. An increase in the total output of consumer goods in a DVC may not increase the average standard of living because it may increase
  (a) capital flight
  (b) population growth
  (c) disguised unemployment
  (d) the quality of the labor force

9. Which best describes the unemployment found in DVCs?
  (a) the cyclical fluctuations in the nation's economy
  (b) the migration of agricultural workers from rural areas to seek jobs in urban areas
  (c) workers being laid off by large domestic or multi-national corporations during periods of economic instability
  (d) the education and training of workers in the wrong types of jobs and for which there is little demand

10. Which is an obstacle to economic growth in DVCs?
  (a) the low demand for natural resources
  (b) the low supply of capital goods
  (c) the decline in demographic transition
  (d) a fall in population growth

11. Which is a reason for placing special emphasis on capital accumulation in DVCs?
  (a) the flexible supply of arable land in DVCs
  (b) the high productivity of workers in DVCs
  (c) the high marginal benefits of capital goods
  (d) the greater opportunities for capital flight

12. Which is a factor limiting saving in DVCs?
  (a) The output of the economy is too low to permit a large volume of saving.

(b) Those who do save make their savings available only to their families.

(c) Governments control the banking system and set low interest rates.

(d) There is an equal distribution of income in most nations.

13. When citizens of developing countries transfer savings to or invest savings in industrially advanced countries, this is referred to as
(a) brain drain
(b) capital flight
(c) savings potential
(d) in-kind investment

14. Which is a major obstacle to capital formation in DVCs?
(a) lack of oil resources
(b) lack of entrepreneurs
(c) lack of government price supports for products
(d) an excess of opportunities for financial investments

15. If it is cheaper to use a new fertilizer that is better adapted to a nation's topography, this is an example of
(a) a capital-using technology
(b) a capital-saving technology
(c) capital consumption
(d) private capital flows

16. Which is an example of infrastructure?
(a) a farm
(b) a steel plant
(c) an electric power plant
(d) a deposit in a financial institution

17. Which seems to be the most acute *institutional* problem that needs to be resolved by many DVCs?
(a) development of strong labor unions
(b) an increase in natural resources
(c) the adoption of birth control
(d) land reform

18. Which is a major positive role for government in the early stage of economic development?
(a) providing an adequate infrastructure
(b) conducting central economic planning
(c) improving the efficiency of tax collection
(d) creating marketing boards for export products

19. In recent years, many DVCs have come to realize that
(a) there are few disadvantages from government involvement in economic development
(b) competition and economic incentives for individuals are necessary for economic growth
(c) the World Bank is an institutional barrier to economic growth
(d) private capital is not essential for economic growth

20. Industrially advanced countries can best help DVCs by
(a) letting them raise tariffs and quotas to protect domestic markets
(b) reducing foreign grant aid but increasing loan aid
(c) increasing the flows of private capital
(d) increasing control over their capital markets

21. The major objective of the World Bank is to
(a) maximize its profits for its worldwide shareholders
(b) assist developing countries in achieving economic growth
(c) provide financial backing for the operation of the United Nations
(d) maintain stable exchange rates in the currencies of developing countries

22. A major criticism of foreign aid to developing nations is that it
(a) provides incentives for capital flight
(b) is capital using rather than capital saving
(c) encourages growth in government bureaucracy
(d) gives too much power and control to the World Bank

23. Which would be an example of direct foreign investment in DVCs?
(a) a low-interest loan from the U.S. government to Nigeria
(b) a grant from the World Bank to build a dam in Thailand
(c) the purchase of a computer business in Honduras by a U.S. firm
(d) a payment from a worker in the U.S. to a family in Iran

24. A suggested policy for DVCs to implement that promotes economic growth is
(a) reducing the control of monetary policy by central banks
(b) obtaining more low-interest loans from the World Bank
(c) encouraging more direct foreign investment
(d) expanding state industries

25. Which is a suggested policy for industrially advanced countries to adopt to foster economic growth in DVCs?
(a) increased appreciation of currencies in DVCs
(b) increased debt relief in DVCs
(c) elimination of the International Monetary Fund
(d) elimination of the OPEC oil cartel

■ **PROBLEMS**

1. Suppose that the real per capita income in the average industrially advanced country is $8000 per year and in the average DVC $500 per year.

a. The gap between their standards of living is

$_____ per year.

b. If GDP per capita were to grow at a rate of 5% during a year in both the industrially advanced country and the DVC,

(1) the standard of living in the IAC would rise to

$_____ in a year;

(2) the standard of living in the DVC would rise to

$_____ in a year; and

(3) the gap between their standards of living would

(narrow, widen) _____ to $_____ in a year.

2. While economic conditions are not identical in all DVCs, certain conditions are common to or typical of most of them. In the space after each of the following characteristics, indicate briefly the nature of this characteristic in many low-income DVCs.

　a. Standard of living (per capita income): _____

　b. Average life expectancy: _____

　c. Extent of unemployment: _____

　d. Literacy: _____

　e. Technology: _____

　f. Percentage of the population engaged in agriculture: _____

　g. Size of the population relative to the land and capital available: _____

　h. The birthrates and death rates: _____

　i. Quality of the labor force: _____

　j. Amount of capital equipment relative to the labor force: _____

　k. Level of saving: _____

　l. Incentive to invest: _____

　m. Amount of infrastructure: _____

　n. Extent of industrialization: _____

　o. Size and quality of the entrepreneurial class and the supervisory class: _____

　p. Per capita public expenditures for education and per capita energy consumption: _____

　q. Per capita consumption of food: _____

　r. Disease and malnutrition: _____

3. Suppose it takes a minimum of 5 units of food to keep a person alive for a year, the population can double itself every 10 years, and the food supply can increase every 10 years by an amount equal to what it was in the beginning (year 0).

　a. Assume that both the population and the food supply grow at these rates. Complete the following table by computing the size of the population and the food supply in years 10 through 60.

Year	Food supply	Population
0	200	20
10	_____	_____
20	_____	_____
30	_____	_____
40	_____	_____
50	_____	_____
60	_____	_____

　b. What happens to the relationship between the food supply and the population in the 30th year? _____

_____

　c. What would actually prevent the population from growing at this rate following the 30th year? _____

_____

　d. Assuming that the actual population growth in the years following the 30th does not outrun the food supply, what would be the size of the population in

　(1)　Year 40: _____?

　(2)　Year 50: _____?

　(3)　Year 60: _____?

　e. Explain why the standard of living failed to increase in the years following the 30th even though the food supply increased by 75% between years 30 and 60.

_____

■　**SHORT ANSWER AND ESSAY QUESTIONS**

　1. What is the degree of income inequality among nations of the world?

　2. How do the overall levels of economic growth per capita and the rates of economic growth compare among rich nations and poor countries? Why does the income gap widen?

　3. What are the human realities of poverty found in DVCs? (Use the socioeconomic indicators in Table 39W.1 of the text to contrast the quality of life in IACs and in DVCs.)

　4. Describe the basic paths of economic growth. Do these avenues differ for IACs and DVCs?

　5. How would you describe the natural resource situation for DVCs? In what ways do price fluctuations affect DVC exports? Is a weak natural resource base an obstacle to economic growth?

　6. Describe the implications of the high rate of growth in populations and its effects on the standard of living. Can the standard of living be raised merely by increasing the output of consumer goods in DVCs? What is the meaning of the cliché "the rich get richer and the poor get children," and how does it apply to DVCs?

　7. Compare and contrast the traditional view of population and economic growth with the demographic transition view.

　8. What is the distinction between unemployment and underemployment? How do these concepts apply to DVCs?

　9. What are the reasons for the low level of labor productivity in DVCs?

10. How does the brain drain affect DVCs?

11. What are the reasons for placing special emphasis on capital accumulation as a means of promoting economic growth in DVCs?

12. Why is domestic capital accumulation difficult in DVCs? Answer in terms of both the saving side and the investment side of capital accumulation. Is there capital flight from DVCs?

13. In addition to the obstacles that limit domestic investment, what other obstacles tend to limit the flow of foreign capital into DVCs? What role does infrastructure play in capital formation?

14. How might the DVCs improve their technology without engaging in slow and expensive research? Why might this be an inappropriate method of improving the technology used in the DVCs?

15. What is meant by the "will to develop"? How is it related to social and institutional change in DVCs?

16. Explain the vicious circle of poverty in the DVCs. How does population growth make an escape from this vicious circle difficult?

17. Why is the role of government expected to be a positive one in the early phases of development in DVCs? What have been the problems with the involvement of government in economic development?

18. What are three ways that IACs help DVCs?

19. How is it possible for the United States to assist DVCs without spending a penny on foreign aid? Is this type of aid sufficient to ensure rapid and substantial development in DVCs?

20. Discuss the World Bank in terms of its purposes, characteristics, sources of funds, promotion of private capital flows, and success. What are its affiliates and their purposes?

21. Discuss three criticisms of foreign aid to DVCs.

22. Describe the types of private capital flows to encourage economic growth in DVCs.

23. How have DVCs changed to accommodate encouragement of direct foreign investment? What is the problem with the selectivity of this type of investment?

24. Describe the variety of suggested policies that DVCs can adopt to promote economic growth.

25. Explain what IACs can do to assist DVCs in fostering economic growth.

ANSWERS

Chapter 39 The Economics of Developing Countries

FILL-IN QUESTIONS

1. 80, 2, 6
2. industrially advanced, IACs, developing, DVCs
3. higher, an increase
4. lower, lower, lower, lower, higher
5. more, more
6. uneven, OPEC nations, DVCs, large, less
7. *a.* over, higher, decrease; *b.* unemployment, underemployment; *c.* low, human capital, brain drain

8. labor productivity, supply of, output
9. *a.* low, few, weak, capital flight; *b.* public, private; *c.* agriculture
10. *a.* skilled, scarce, abundant, capital; *b.* unskilled, abundant, scarce, labor; *c.* saving
11. sociocultural, institutional
12. low, low, low
13. *a.* establishing effective law and order; *b.* encouraging entrepreneurship; *c.* improving the infrastructure; *d.* promoting saving and investment; *e.* dealing with the social-institutional obstacles (any order for *a–e*)
14. impede, political, poor
15. decreasing, increasing, increasing
16. public, World Bank, last, technical
17. increase, increase, increase, decrease
18. investment, encourage, encourage, selective
19. open, encourage, control
20. lower, discourage, low-income

Note: Page numbers for True–False, Multiple Choice, and Short Answer and Essay Questions refer to Bonus Web Chapter 39.

TRUE–FALSE QUESTIONS

1. F, p. 1	**10.** F, p. 8	**19.** F, p. 12
2. T, p. 3	**11.** F, pp. 8–9	**20.** F, pp. 12–13
3. T, p. 3	**12.** F, p. 9	**21.** F, pp. 13–14
4. F, p. 3	**13.** T, p. 9	**22.** T, p. 14
5. T, pp. 3–4	**14.** T, p. 9	**23.** T, p. 15
6. F, p. 4	**15.** F, p. 10	**24.** F, p. 15
7. F, pp. 4–5	**16.** T, p. 10	**25.** T, pp. 15–17
8. T, p. 6	**17.** T, pp. 10–11	
9. T, p. 7	**18.** F, p. 11	

MULTIPLE-CHOICE QUESTIONS

1. b, p. 1	**10.** b, p. 7	**19.** b, p. 12
2. a, p. 1	**11.** c, pp. 7–8	**20.** c, pp. 12, 15
3. b, p. 3	**12.** a, p. 8	**21.** b, pp. 13–14
4. c, pp. 3–4	**13.** b, p. 8	**22.** c, p. 14
5. c, pp. 3–4	**14.** b, pp. 8–9	**23.** c, p. 15
6. c, p. 5	**15.** b, p. 9	**24.** c, pp. 15–17
7. a, pp. 5–6	**16.** c, p. 9	**25.** b, pp. 17–18
8. b, p. 5	**17.** d, p. 10	
9. b, p. 7	**18.** a, pp. 11–12	

PROBLEMS

1. *a.* 7500; *b.* (1) 8400, (2) 525, (3) widen, 7875
2. *a.* low; *b.* short; *c.* widespread; *d.* low; *e.* primitive; *f.* large; *g.* large; *h.* high; *i.* poor; *j.* small; *k.* low; *l.* absent; *m.* small; *n.* small; *o.* small and poor; *p.* small; *q.* low; *r.* common
3. *a.* Food supply: 400, 600, 800, 1000, 1200, 1400; Population: 40, 80, 160, 320, 640, 1280; *b.* the food supply is just able to support the population; *c.* the inability of the food supply to support a population growing at this rate; *d.* (1) 200, (2) 240, (3) 280; *e.* the population increased as rapidly as the food supply

SHORT ANSWER AND ESSAY QUESTIONS

1. pp. 1–2	**10.** p. 7	**19.** pp. 12–13
2. p. 3	**11.** pp. 7–8	**20.** pp. 13–14
3. pp. 3–4	**12.** pp. 7–8	**21.** p. 14
4. pp. 3–4	**13.** pp. 8–9	**22.** p. 15
5. p. 4	**14.** p. 9	**23.** p. 15
6. pp. 4–6	**15.** p. 9	**24.** pp. 15–17
7. p. 6	**16.** pp. 10–11	**25.** pp. 17–18
8. p. 7	**17.** pp. 11–12	
9. p. 7	**18.** p. 12	

Transition Economies: Russia and China

Note: The bonus web chapter is available at: www.mcconnell16.com.

In the years following the Russian Revolution of 1917, many people in the United States were convinced that the economic system of the Soviet Union was unworkable and that it would break down sooner or later—proof that Marx and Lenin were unrealistic dreamers—and that the reconversion of the Soviet economy to a market system would follow. Now, some 85 years after the revolution, the Russian economy is being transformed into a market economy and a democracy.

China is also undergoing a rapid transition from a centrally planned economy to a market-based economy, but its experience differs from that of Russia. The transition in China has been longer and more gradual. The economic outcomes have also been very positive, with strong economic growth, rising productivity, and a significantly increased standard of living; however, problems remain because the Communist party retains dictatorial political control and economic development is uneven throughout the country.

This chapter provides insights into the profound turn of events in both Russia and China. The first two sections of the chapter explain the basic ideas behind **Marxian ideology,** which gave rise to these command economies. They also discuss two basic institutional features of the former Soviet Union and prereform China: These economies operated under a system of state ownership of property resources; central planning was used to set prices, restrict consumption, and direct investment to heavy industry and the military.

Although central planning served as a powerful form of economic decision making in the former Soviet Union and prereform China, it had two serious problems, as you will discover in the third section. The first problem was one of **coordination,** which resulted in production bottlenecks and managers and bureaucrats missing production targets. Central planning also created an **incentive problem** because it sent out incorrect and inadequate signals for directing the efficient allocation of an economy's resources and gave workers little reason to work hard. The lack of incentives killed entrepreneurship and stifled innovation and technological advance.

The slowing of economic growth in the Soviet economy in the 1970s and 1980s set the stage for the failure of communism and the **collapse of its command economy.** Certainly other factors contributed to the economy's deterioration, as you will discover in the fourth section of the chapter. Production was of poor quality, and there were inadequate or limited consumer goods to meet consumer demands. The economy was overly burdened by government leaders' desire to support a large military. Agricultural inefficiencies were a drain on resources and restricted investment for other sectors of the economy.

The fifth section of the chapter explains the **five elements of market reform in the Russian economy** and its problems and prospects. The transition has led to the privatization of property resources, the promotion of competition, the decontrol of prices, and better connections to the international economy. The hyperinflation problem was solved by the establishment of a Russian central bank and the adoption of an anti-inflation monetary policy. Other problems continue to plague the economy. Real output, as well as living standards, fell significantly during the transition. Income inequality has grown, and government instability and social unrest have given organized crime the opportunity to flourish. In spite of these problems, Russia is likely to succeed in becoming an advanced market economy, but much work remains to be done.

The **market reform in China** is the focus of the sixth section of the chapter. As already noted, China's reform efforts differed significantly from those of Russia because they started earlier and have been more gradual and experimental. Partial decontrol of land and prices in agriculture unleashed the rural economy and made it more market oriented. State-owned enterprises are being consolidated and forced to become more competitive and operate like corporations. The formation of private businesses has been encouraged. New foreign investment is encouraged to help capital formation and to gain access to advanced technology.

The results from Chinese economic reforms have been impressive, as described in the final section of the chapter. The economy has grown at a 9% annual rate since 1978. The standard of living has risen fourfold and at a much faster rate than population growth. Nevertheless, China's transition to a market economy continues to face significant problems. Property rights are ill-defined. The economy has experienced periods of high inflation and is not well-integrated into the world economy. Economic development across the nation is uneven, and the average income remains low by DVC standards.

The transformations of Russian and Chinese economies into market economies are among the most important economic events of recent decades. The sweeping changes in these economies from centrally planned economies to market economies should deepen your understanding of the principles of economics and how the market system works. These dramatic developments are a fitting topic to conclude your study of economics.

■ CHECKLIST

When you have studied this chapter you should be able to

☐ Outline the key elements of Marxian ideology.

☐ Identify two institutional characteristics of the former Soviet Union (prior to collapse) and China (prior to its market reforms).

☐ Make seven generalizations about the central planning goals and techniques in the former Soviet Union and China.

☐ Compare how a market economy coordinates economic activity with how this works in a centrally planned economy.

☐ Explain how a market economy provides incentives and the problems with incentives in a centrally planned economy.

☐ Identify five factors that contributed to the collapse of the Soviet economy.

☐ List five factors that are important for the transition of Russia's economy to a market economy.

☐ Explain the effects of privatization in Russia.

☐ Use a supply and demand graph to discuss the difficulties that price reforms pose in the Russian transition.

☐ Describe the promotion of competition in Russia.

☐ Explain the importance of Russia joining the world economy by making the ruble fully convertible.

☐ Describe the need for price-level stabilization in Russia.

☐ Explain three other major problems the Russian economy has experienced during the transition.

☐ Evaluate the future prospects for Russia's transition to a market economy.

☐ Contrast China's path to market reforms with that of Russia.

☐ Describe agricultural and price reforms in China.

☐ Discuss the reform of urban industries and the use of special economic zones in China.

☐ Describe how the Chinese government has built supporting institutions and transformed state-owned enterprises.

☐ State the positive outcomes from the reform of the Chinese economy.

☐ Identify four significant problems in the Chinese transition to a market economy.

■ CHAPTER OUTLINE

1. The centrally planned economies of the former Soviet Union and prereform China were based on **Marxian ideology.** The government was viewed as a dictatorship of the proletariat (or working class) and the peasantry. Especially important was the Marxian concept of a **labor theory of value,** which held that only labor creates value in production and that profits are a **surplus value** expropriated from workers by capitalists who, because of the institution of private property, were able to control the means of production (capital goods). The purpose of communism was to overthrow capitalism and end this exploitation of workers (and peasants) by eliminating private property and creating a classless society.

2. The two major institutional features of the precollapse Soviet and prereform Chinese economies were **state-owned enterprises** of all property resources and **central economic planning.** The command economy based most economic decisions on bureaucrats' choices rather than relying on market forces to direct economic activity.

 a. The central planning functioned differently in the former Soviet Union and prereform China.

 (1) The former Soviet Union attached great importance to rapid industrialization and military strength, whereas China emphasized rural development.

 (2) Each economy overcommitted its available resources, and often missed planning targets.

 (3) Each economy mobilized resources by increasing the quantity of resources rather than using given resources more productively.

 (4) Directives were used rather than markets and prices to allocate inputs for production in each economy.

 (5) Each government fixed and controlled prices.

 (6) Each economy emphasized self-sufficiency of the nation, viewed capitalist nations as hostile, and restricted trade.

 (7) Each economy passively used monetary and fiscal policies; unemployment was limited or disguised; the price level was controlled through government price fixing.

3. There were two basic problems with a centrally planned economy.

 a. The **coordination problem** involved the difficulty of coordinating the economy's many interdependent segments and avoiding the chain reaction that would result from a bottleneck in any one of the segments. This coordination problem became even more difficult as the economy grew larger and more complex, and more economic decisions had to be made in the production process. There were also inadequate measures of economic performance to determine the degree of success or failure of enterprises or to give clear signals to the economy.

 b. The **incentive problem** arose because in a command economy incentives are ineffective for encouraging economic initiatives and work and for directing the most efficient use of productive resources. In a market economy, profits and losses signal what firms should produce, how they should produce, and how productive resources should be allocated to best meet the wants of a nation. Central planning in the two economies also lacked entrepreneurship and stifled innovation, both of which are important forces for achieving long-term economic growth. Individual workers lacked much motivation to work hard because pay was limited and there were either few consumer goods to buy or they were of low quality.

4. The **collapse of the Soviet economy** stemmed largely from the failure of central economic planning.

  a. Economic growth declined in the 1970s and 1980s. Real output also fell sharply in the few years before the country's breakup.

  b. Technology in manufacturing lagged by western standards, and consumer goods were of poor quality.

  c. Consumers received few material benefits from years of sacrifice for rapid industrialization and the military, and consumer goods were in short supply.

  d. The large financial burden for military expenditures diverted valuable resources from the production of consumer and capital goods to military production.

  e. Agriculture acted as a drag on economic growth and hurt productivity in other sectors of the economy.

5. The **transition** of the former Soviet Union, particularly Russia, from a centrally planned to a market economy is occurring in several ways.

  a. A market economy relies on private property rights and limited government control of business. Private property rights were established to encourage entrepreneurship, and much government property was transferred to private ownership. This privatization was initially achieved through government distribution of vouchers that could be used to purchase businesses; it is now done through the direct sale of state enterprises. This change stimulated foreign investment and the flow of foreign capital to Russia; however, market reforms in agriculture have been limited.

  b. Soviet government controls on prices led to a serious misallocation of resources and poor economic incentives. Most price controls were eliminated, about 90% in 1992, so prices for goods and services were free to change and reflect relative scarcities.

  c. For a market economy to work properly, competition must be promoted by splitting up or restructuring large state-owned enterprises to reduce the potential for monopoly power from having one privatized business in an industry. Progress in this area was slow, but joint ventures and foreign investment stimulated more business competition in the Russian economy.

  d. The Soviet economy was restricted from actively participating in international trade. Action was taken to open the economy to international trade and finance by making the ruble a convertible currency.

  e. The transition to a market economy brought hyperinflation. Contributing factors included price decontrols, the ruble overhang (excess currency saved when there were few consumer goods to purchase), large government budget deficits, and the printing of money to finance the deficits. A Russian central bank was created, and an anti-inflation money policy was adopted to eliminate hyperinflation and keep prices relatively stable.

  f. Several other major problems continued to affect the transition, especially during the early years.

  (1) Real output and living standards fell during the reforms, although the decline bottomed out in 1992. Inflation, reduced international trade, bankruptcy and the closing of state enterprises, and the massive reallocation of resources and reductions in government and military spending precipitated the decline in output.

  (2) Economic inequality and social costs increased during the transition. Market reforms enriched some groups and hurt others. Economic insecurity and instability resulting from the transition raised tensions among workers and other groups, reduced the quality of life and life expectancy, and stimulated the rise of organized crime and "crony" capitalism.

  (3) The government has been weak in its enforcement of property rights and laws. It has also been unable or unwilling to collect the taxes necessary to finance basic government services.

  g. Russia has "muddled through" its first decade of a transition to a market economy. The fall in real output ended by the late 1990s and economic growth has been robust since 1999. The rate of inflation has fallen to more manageable levels. The government has turned its large budget deficits into budget surpluses, and is providing the economic institutions necessary for an effective market economy. Market reforms have taken hold and the economy is prospering.

6. The path of **market economic reforms in China** differed significantly from that in Russia. China's market reforms began earlier and were more gradual and experimental. The Communist Party in China retained dictatorial control, while in Russia the party was replaced with democratic leadership. Russia has privatized much of the economy and sold off state enterprises, whereas China has protected its state enterprises while encouraging competing private enterprises. Russia experienced a significant decline in real output; China's output has continued to grow at high rates.

  a. Agricultural reform in China began in 1978 with the leasing of land to individual farmers and permission to sell the output of the farms at competitive rather than government-controlled prices. This decollectivization and price reform provided a market basis for Chinese agriculture and the economy and released labor resources to private rural manufacturing firms (township and village enterprises).

  b. Market reforms were also established in urban industries to give **state-owned enterprises** (SOEs) more control over production and employment. Enterprises could retain profits and sell more of their output at market prices rather than government-set prices. Urban collectives were formed that operated as private firms jointly owned by managers and workers. The collectives competed strongly with state enterprises and stimulated productivity in the economy.

  c. **Special enterprise zones** were established that were open to foreign investment, private ownership, and international trade. They attracted foreign capital and increased Chinese exports. These areas undercut the support for central planning.

  d. Supporting institutions have been developed to facilitate the transition to a market economy. The Chinese central bank was established to regulate the banking system and control the money supply. The enterprise tax system replaced the profit transfer from state enterprises. Foreign exchange can be swapped as needed between enterprises. A stock market has been established.

e. State-owned enterprises have been transformed; they operate more like corporations and respond to market needs rather than to social directives. The major SOEs have been consolidated into 1000 enterprises. Government plans call for stock to be issued and for the SOEs to become shareholder owned and operate like corporations, with the government retaining control. Other SOEs will be sold or permitted to go bankrupt.

7. There are positive outcomes from China's market-based reforms, but the transition to a market economy is still incomplete.

a. China has an impressive record of growth. It has averaged 9% growth annually since 1978, among the highest percentages on record for such a period. Real output and incomes have quadrupled in less than two decades. Capital formation increased productivity, and labor resources shifted from lower areas of productivity (agriculture) to higher areas of productivity (manufacturing). International trade expanded exports and the imports of critical consumer and capital goods. Foreign investment resulted in access to new technology that can be used to further increase productivity.

b. There are continuing economic problems in China's development.

(1) Property rights are incomplete because the privatization of farmland is opposed by the Communist Party, and such a policy leads to less investment in agriculture.

(2) There have been macroeconomic problems. Until the mid-1990s, China experienced high inflation during the years of rapid economic growth because the financial and monetary control system was weak. (The central bank has been given more control over interest rates and it now has inflation under control.) The financial and banking system is weak because substantial sums are owed by state-owned enterprises to banks. There is considerable unemployment and underemployment, especially in interior regions.

(3) Economic growth is geographically uneven throughout China. Hong Kong is now part of China and has high per capita income. Although people living in enterprise zones and the coastal areas near Hong Kong have experienced substantial growth in incomes and living standards, people in poorer regions still have low incomes. Overall, China is still considered a low-income developing country.

■ HINTS AND TIPS

1. This chapter applies your knowledge of economics to explain the transformation of Russia and China from centrally planned to market-oriented economies. Throughout this chapter you will be comparing a market economy with a command economy. Review Chapter 4 before you read this chapter to make sure you have a good understanding of how capitalism works and its major characteristics.

2. View the chapter as a culminating exercise in your study of economics that gives you a chance to *review, apply,* and *integrate* many of the economic concepts and ideas you learned from the text. Only a few terms and concepts will be new to you in this chapter (they apply to Marxian ideology or the reforms in China or Russia).

3. Supply and demand analysis is used to explain price controls in Figure 40W.1 in the text. The figure differs from those you saw in a previous chapter (Chapter 3) because there are two supply curves. One is vertical (perfectly inelastic) because it assumes fixed government control of production and no effect on quantity supplied as price controls are lifted. The upsloping supply curve shows an increase in quantity supplied as price controls are lifted.

■ IMPORTANT TERMS

labor theory of value

surplus value

state ownership

central economic planning

coordination problem

incentive problem

township and village enterprises

state-owned enterprises (SOEs)

urban collectives

special economic zones (SEZs)

SELF-TEST

■ FILL-IN QUESTIONS

1. The ideology behind the central planning in the former Soviet Union and prereform China was that the value of any commodity is determined by the amount of

(capital, labor) _____ required to produce it. In capitalist economies, capital was (privately, publicly)

_____ owned, and capitalists exploited workers by paying them a wage that was (greater than, less

than) _____ the value of their production and obtained (shortage, surplus) _____ value at the expense of workers.

2. In a communist economy, capital and other property resources would be (publicly, privately)

_____ owned and society would be (segre-

gated, classless) _____. The Communist Party would serve as the representative of the (capital-

ists, proletariat) _____ and peasantry and would redistribute the surplus value of workers in the form

of (tax cuts, subsidies) _____ for public and quasi-public goods. In reality, the Communist Party was

(democratic, a dictatorship) _____.

3. One major institution of the former Soviet Union and prereform China was the ownership of property resources by (the state, property owners) _____. Another institutional feature was (central, decentralized) _____ economic planning.

4. Economic planning in the former Soviet Union and prereform China functioned in several ways. In the former Soviet Union, plans sought to achieve rapid (population growth, industrialization) _____ and provision of (civilian, military) _____ goods. In China, emphasis was on (urban, rural) _____ development. In both nations, the planning policies created an (over, under) _____-commitment of the economy's resources and resulted in an _____-production of goods for consumers.

5. Economic growth was achieved by (importing, mobilizing) _____ resources and by reallocating surplus labor from (industry, agriculture) _____ to _____. The government allocated inputs among industries by (prices, directives) _____, and the government set fixed _____ for goods and services and inputs.

6. Each nation also viewed itself as a (capitalist, socialist) _____ nation surrounded by hostile _____ nations, and central plans were designed to achieve economic (freedom, self-sufficiency) _____. Macroeconomic policies were (active, passive) _____.

7. Coordination and decision making in a market economy are (centralized, decentralized) _____, but in the Soviet and prereform Chinese economies it was _____. The market system tends to produce a reasonably (efficient, inefficient) _____ allocation of resources, but in centrally planned economies it was _____ and resulted in production bottlenecks and failures to meet many production targets. Central planning became (more, less) _____ complex and difficult as each economy grew and changed over time. Indicators of economic performance were (adequate, inadequate) _____ for determining the success or failure of economic activities.

8. Another problem with central planning was that economic incentives were (effective, ineffective) _____ for encouraging work or for giving signals to planners for efficient allocation of resources in the economy. The centrally planned system also lacked the (production

targets, entrepreneurship) _____ so important to technological advance. Innovation (fostered, lagged) _____ because there was no competition.

9. A number of factors contributed to the collapse of the Soviet economy. The economy experienced a (rise, decline) _____ in economic growth in the 1970s and 1980s. Consumer goods were of (good, poor) _____ quality, and there were widespread (shortages, surpluses) _____. There was a large (consumer, military) _____ burden on the economy that diverted resources from the production of (consumer, investment) _____ goods. Agriculture was (efficient, inefficient) _____ and (helped, hurt) _____ economic growth and productivity in other sectors of the economy.

10. The Russian transition to a market economy has resulted in major reforms. Property rights have been (revoked, established) _____, and government property has been transferred to (foreign, private) _____ ownership. In Soviet Russia, the prices of goods and services were kept at low levels through price (competition, controls) _____, so the marginal cost of a product (was, was not) _____ equal to its marginal benefit. This pricing policy led to (efficient, inefficient) _____ use of resources to make products and to (surpluses, shortages) _____ of many consumer goods. Today, most prices in Russia are (still fixed, free to vary) _____.

11. Russia is also promoting competition by (forming, dismantling) _____ state-owned enterprises to reduce the potential for (rivalry, monopoly) _____. Russia has (opened, closed) _____ the economy to international trade and finance. One example of this policy is making the ruble a (fixed, convertible) _____ currency on international markets.

12. The Russian transition to a market economy was accompanied by (inflation, deflation) _____. It occurred because of price (controls, decontrols) _____, a ruble (under, over) _____ hang, and government budget (surpluses, deficits) _____. In response to this problem, the nation created an independent central (account, bank) _____ to provide control over (fiscal, monetary) _____ policy.

13. Major problems affected Russia's transition, especially in the early years. There was a (falling, rising) _____ level of real output and a _____ standard of living. Economic inequality also (increased, decreased) _____ and led to _____ economic security and (increased, decreased) _____ corruption and crime. Government provided (strong, weak) _____ enforcement of laws and was _____ in its actions to collect taxes. But in recent years the Russian economy has revived with (strong, weak) _____ levels of economic growth, (higher, lower) _____ levels of inflation, and a more effective government.

14. Compared with Russia, China's market reforms began (later, earlier) _____ and were more (rapid, gradual) _____. China asserts that communist dictatorship and markets are (incompatible, compatible) _____, while Russia views them as _____. China instituted its market reforms and experienced (growth, depression) _____, while Russia experienced _____ in its transition to a market economy. Russia (sold, protected) _____ state enterprises, while China _____ them but encouraged competing private enterprises.

15. Agricultural reform in China began in 1978 with the (selling, leasing) _____ of land to individual farmers and permission for _____ the agriculture products at (market, government) _____ prices. The reform released (capital, labor) _____ resources to private rural manufacturing firms called township and village enterprises.

16. Market reforms were also established in Chinese urban industries to give state-owned enterprises (less, more) _____ decision making about production and employment. Urban (cartels, collectives) _____ were formed that operated as private firms jointly owned by managers and workers. The competition of state and nonstate enterprises (increased, decreased) _____ productivity and innovation in the economy.

17. China created special economic zones that were (open, closed) _____ to foreign investment, private ownership, and international trade. A Chinese central bank was established to regulate the (trading, banking) _____ system and control the (import, money) _____ supply. Profit transfers from state enterprises to the central government were replaced with an enterprise (spending, tax) _____ system. Foreign exchange can be (hoarded, swapped) _____ as needed between enterprises.

18. There has been a transformation of Chinese state-owned enterprises (SOEs). They operate more like (bureaucracies, corporations) _____ and respond to (social directive, the market) _____. Plans call for the major 100 SOEs to issue (money, stock) _____ and operate more like corporations under government control. Other smaller SOEs will be (bought, sold) _____ by the government or permitted to go bankrupt.

19. The transition to a market economy in China shows positive outcomes. Economic growth in China averaged (2, 9) _____% annually since 1978. Real output and income have (doubled, quadrupled) _____ in less than two decades. China's real GDP and real income have grown much (more, less) _____ rapidly than its population.

20. Problems remain with China's transition. Privatization of farmland is (supported, opposed) _____ by the Communist Party, and this policy leads to (more, less) _____ investment in agriculture. Substantial sums are (paid, owed) _____ by state-owned enterprises to the banking system. China (is, is not) _____ fully integrated into the world economy. Economic growth is (even, uneven) _____, and China is still considered a (low, middle) _____-income developing country.

■ **TRUE–FALSE QUESTIONS**

Circle T if the statement is true, F if it is false.

1. The labor theory of value is the Marxian idea that the value of any good is determined solely by the amount of labor required for its production.　　**T F**

2. Surplus value in Marxian ideology is the value or price of a commodity at equilibrium in a competitive market.　　**T F**

3. The economies of the former Soviet Union and pre-reform China were characterized by state ownership of resources and authoritarian central planning.　　**T F**

4. The former Soviet Union was dedicated to the task of rapid industrialization and building economic self-sufficiency.　　**T F**

5. Prereform China emphasized rural economic development.   **T F**

6. Economic resources tended to be undercommitted in both the former Soviet Union and prereform China. **T F**

7. Both the former Soviet Union and prereform China actively used monetary and fiscal policies to manipulate levels of employment, output, and prices.   **T F**

8. A centrally planned economy is significantly affected by missed production targets and bottlenecks.   **T F**

9. The problems of central planning become easier and less complex as an economy grows over time.   **T F**

10. Profit is the key indicator of success and failure in a centrally planned economy.   **T F**

11. Central planning provided weak or inaccurate incentives for allocating resources to achieve economic efficiency and encourage hard work.   **T F**

12. Centrally planned economies encourage entrepreneurship and technological advance under the directive of the Communist Party.   **T F**

13. In the former Soviet Union, greater productivity and technological progress in the civilian sector were often sacrificed or limited by the demands to support a large military.   **T F**

14. As part of the transition to a market economy, Russia has taken major steps to privatize its economy and establish property rights.   **T F**

15. Price decontrol was a minor problem in the conversion of the Russian economy to capitalism because the prices the Soviet government established over the years were very similar to the economic values established in a competitive market.   **T F**

16. The transition to a market economy in Russia has required the breakup of large industries and coordinated actions to promote competition.   **T F**

17. A major accomplishment during the Russian transition to a market economy was limited inflation because of balanced budgets and a tight control of the money supply.   **T F**

18. Two major problems Russia experienced during its transition to capitalism were a decline in the standard of living and increased economic inequality.   **T F**

19. The Chinese economy used a "shock" approach to economic reform to make its transition to a market economy.   **T F**

20. Collectivization and price controls were instrumental in strengthening production incentives and moving the Chinese economy toward a market-based agriculture.   **T F**

21. The Chinese government has encouraged the formation of nonstate enterprises, called urban collectives, which are jointly owned by workers and managers. **T F**

22. China has created special economic zones that are open to foreign investment, private ownership, and international trade.   **T F**

23. A major limitation of Chinese economic reform is the failure to create a stock market for the exchange of shares of newly created corporations.   **T F**

24. China's economic growth has declined over the past two decades because of the instability caused by its economic reforms.   **T F**

25. One continuing economic problem in China is the uneven regional economic development.   **T F**

■ **MULTIPLE-CHOICE QUESTIONS**

Circle the letter that corresponds to the best answer.

1. Which was an element in Marxian ideology?
  (a) the creation of surplus value by government
  (b) dictatorship over the business class
  (c) the private ownership of property
  (d) the labor theory of value

2. Marxian ideology was highly critical of capitalist societies because in those societies capitalists
  (a) reduced the productivity of workers by not investing their profits in new capital goods
  (b) paid workers a wage that was less than the value of their production
  (c) shared surplus value with the government
  (d) were not taxed as much as the workers

3. The institution that was most characteristic of the former Soviet Union and prereform China was
  (a) private ownership of property
  (b) authoritarian central planning
  (c) a system of markets and prices
  (d) consumer sovereignty

4. Industrialization, rapid economic growth, and military strength in the former Soviet Union and prereform China were primarily achieved by
  (a) mobilizing larger quantities of resources
  (b) joining the international economy
  (c) making currencies convertible
  (d) using an easy-money policy

5. Both the former Soviet Union and prereform China viewed themselves as socialist nations surrounded by hostile capitalist nations, and as a consequence central planning stressed the need for
  (a) hoarding gold
  (b) flexible prices
  (c) consumer sovereignty
  (d) economic self-sufficiency

6. In the former Soviet Union and prereform China, monetary policy
  (a) was active and fiscal policy was passive
  (b) was passive and fiscal policy was active
  (c) and fiscal policy were both passive
  (d) and fiscal policy were both active

7. In the system of central planning, the outputs of some industries became the inputs for other industries, but a failure of one industry to meet its production target would cause
(a) widespread unemployment
(b) inflation in wholesale and retail prices
(c) profit declines and potential bankruptcy of firms
(d) a chain reaction of production problems and bottlenecks

8. What was the major success indicator for Soviet and Chinese state enterprises?
(a) profits
(b) the level of prices
(c) production targets
(d) the enterprise tax

9. The centrally planned system in the former Soviet Union and prereform China lacked
(a) price controls
(b) entrepreneurship
(c) economic growth
(d) allocation by directives

10. In the last year or two before the Soviet economic system collapsed, real output
(a) increased slightly
(b) decreased significantly
(c) remained relatively constant
(d) increased faster than the rate of population growth

11. Which was evidence of the Soviet economy's economic failure?
(a) a tight monetary policy
(b) an oversupply of most products
(c) the poor quality of consumer goods
(d) higher productivity in agriculture than industry

12. What was the size of expenditures for the military as a percentage of domestic output in the former Soviet Union (**SU**) and the United States (**U.S.**)?

	SU %	U.S. %
(a)	26 – 30	18
(b)	21 – 25	12
(c)	15 – 20	6
(d)	10 – 14	3

13. Which was a cause of low productivity in agriculture in the former Soviet Union?
(a) inability to fertilize and weed the abundance of good farmland in the country
(b) failure to construct an effective incentive system for agriculture
(c) increase in the length of the growing season
(d) overuse of certain chemical fertilizers on crops

14. Which helped Russia make a transition to a market economy?
(a) ruble overhang
(b) price controls
(c) privatization
(d) hyperinflation

15. The effect of price controls on most consumer goods in the former Soviet Union was that
(a) surpluses developed because the quantity consumers demanded was greater than the quantity supplied at the price set by government
(b) prices fell because the quantity consumers demanded was greater than the quantity supplied
(c) prices rose because the quantity consumers demanded was less than the quantity supplied
(d) shortages developed because the quantity consumers demanded was greater than the quantity supplied at the price set by government

16. Which set of factors most likely contributed to hyper-inflation as Russia made its transition to a market economy?
(a) the breakup of state monopolies, land reform, and the poor quality of consumer goods
(b) increased military spending, investment in new technology, and the convertibility of the ruble
(c) central planning, production targets, and production bottlenecks
(d) government deficits, the ruble overhang, and price decontrols

17. Which two significant problems did Russia encounter in its transition to a market system?
(a) rising taxes and increasing life expectancies
(b) a loose monetary policy and a strict fiscal policy
(c) falling real output and declining living standards
(d) greater military spending and more environmental pollution

18. Compared with Russia, market reforms in China
(a) occurred over a longer time and were more gradual
(b) focused primarily on industry rather than agriculture
(c) relied more on monetary policy than fiscal policy
(d) were less successful and more disruptive

19. The key elements of the 1978–1984 rural economic reforms in China were
(a) passive macroeconomic policies
(b) formations of special economic zones
(c) foreign investment and loans to state-owned enterprises
(d) decollectivization and creation of a two-track price system

20. Privately owned rural manufacturing firms in China are called
(a) township and village enterprises
(b) special economic zones
(c) incentive collectives
(d) farm cooperatives

21. Chinese enterprises in urban areas that are jointly owned by their managers and workers are
(a) industrial unions
(b) urban collectives
(c) business operating units
(d) manufacturing cooperatives

22. Which would be a supporting institution for market reform in China?
  (a) a price control authority
  (b) a profit transfer system
  (c) a farm collective
  (d) a central bank

23. Since market reforms began, real output and real income in China have
  (a) doubled
  (b) tripled
  (c) quadrupled
  (d) quintupled

24. The shift of employment from agriculture toward rural and urban manufacturing in China has increased
  (a) inflation
  (b) productivity
  (c) bankruptcies
  (d) unemployment

25. One significant problem China faces in its transition to a market economy is
  (a) establishing a stock market
  (b) establishing a central bank
  (c) incomplete privatization of land
  (d) creation of special economic zones

■ PROBLEMS

1. In the following table are several major institutions and characteristics of a capitalistic economy, such as that in the United States, and a centrally planned economy, such as that in the former Soviet Union or prereform China. In the appropriate space, name the corresponding institution or characteristic of the other economy.

Capitalist institution or characteristic	Socialist institution or characteristic
a. _____	labor theory of value
b. _____	surplus value
c. private ownership of economic resources	_____
d. a market economy	_____
e. _____	state-owned enterprises
f. privately owned farms	_____
g. _____	government price controls
h. _____	passive macroeconomic policies
i. representative democracy	_____

2. Answer the following set of questions based on the table in the next column. The columns show the price, quantity demanded Q_d by consumers, and a fixed quantity supplied by government Q_{s1} for a product in the former Soviet Union. The column for Q_{s2} shows the supply curve

for the product after privatization in the industry producing the product.

Price (in rubles)	Q_d	Q_{s1}	Q_{s2}
90	25	25	55
80	30	25	50
70	35	25	45
60	40	25	40
50	45	25	35
40	50	25	30
30	55	25	25

a. When only the government supplies the product as shown in the Q_{s1} schedule, the equilibrium price will be _____ rubles and the equilibrium quantity will be _____ units.

b. If the government tries to make the product more accessible to lower-income consumers by setting the price at 30 rubles, then the quantity demanded will be _____ units and the quantity supplied will be _____ units, producing a shortage of _____ units.

c. If the government decontrolled prices but did not privatize industry, then prices would rise to _____ rubles and the government would still produce _____ units.

d. With privatization, there will be a new quantity supplied schedule (Q_{s2}). The equilibrium price will be _____ rubles and the equilibrium quantity will be _____ units. The equilibrium price has risen by _____ rubles and the equilibrium quantity by _____ units.

3. Match the terms from China's economic reform with the phrase using the appropriate number.

1. special economic zone   4. town and village enterprises
2. urban collective   5. enterprise tax system
3. two-track price system   6. state-owned enterprise

a. Privately-owned rural manufacturing firms _____

b. Replaced the system of profit transfers from state enterprises to the central government _____

c. Areas in coastal regions that are open to foreign investment, private ownership, and international trade

_____

d. Nonstate enterprises jointly owned by managers and their work forces in urban areas _____

e. Gives farmers ability to sell output at market-determined prices _____

f. Enterprises that are controlled by the government

_____

■ SHORT ANSWER AND ESSAY QUESTIONS

1. What are the essential features of Marxian ideology on which the Soviet Union's command economy was based?

2. What were the two principal economic institutions of the prereform and precollapse economies of China and Russia? How do these institutions compare with those in the United States?

3. Describe how central planning functioned in the former Soviet Union and prereform China. What generalizations can you make about resource use, directives, prices, self-sufficiency, and macroeconomic policies?

4. Why does central planning result in a coordination problem? Compare the operation of central planning with the use of markets and prices for economic decision making.

5. How does central economic planning produce a significant incentive problem? What types of economic incentives for business, workers, and consumers exist in a market economy? How are those incentives different in a centrally planned economy?

6. Discuss the five factors that help explain or contributed to the collapse of the Soviet economy.

7. What action has Russia taken to privatize the economy?

8. Why was there a need for price reform in Russia in its transition to a market economy? What has been the *general* effect of this change? Use a supply and demand graph to explain the effect of the price decontrol on a specific product.

9. Discuss what is being done in Russia to promote competition. To what extent are public monopolies a problem?

10. What major problem is confronting Russia as it seeks to join the world economy?

11. How have high rates of inflation affected Russia's transition to a market economy? What has been the shift in macroeconomic policy?

12. What other major problems has Russia encountered in its transition to a market economy?

13. Evaluate the prospects for the transformation of Russia into a market economy.

14. How did China's approach to market reforms differ from that in Russia?

15. Describe how China has tried to transform agriculture and rural production.

16. What market-based changes has the Chinese government made in urban industries?

17. What actions has the Chinese government taken to encourage foreign investment and establish institutions that support a market-based economy?

18. Describe the economic transformation of state-owned enterprises in China.

19. What are the positive outcomes of China's economic reform?

20. Discuss four significant economic problems that China continues to face in its transition to a market economy.

ANSWERS

Chapter 40 Web: Transition Economies: Russia and China

FILL-IN QUESTIONS

1. labor, privately, less than, surplus
2. publicly, classless, proletariat, subsidies, a dictatorship
3. the state, central
4. industrialization, military, rural, over, under
5. mobilizing, agriculture, industry, directives, prices
6. socialist, capitalist, self-sufficiency, passive
7. decentralized, centralized, efficient, inefficient, more, inadequate
8. ineffective, entrepreneurship, lagged
9. decline, poor, shortages, military, consumer, inefficient, hurt
10. established, private, controls, was not, inefficient, shortages, free to vary
11. dismantling, monopoly, opened, convertible
12. inflation, decontrols, over, deficits, bank, monetary
13. falling, falling, increased, decreased, increased, weak, weak, strong, lower
14. earlier, gradual, compatible, incompatible, growth, depression, sold, protected
15. leasing, selling, market, labor
16. more, collectives, increased
17. open, banking, money, tax, swapped
18. corporations, the market, stock, sold
19. 9, quadrupled, more
20. opposed, less, owed, is not, uneven, low

Note: Page numbers for True–False, Multiple Choice, and Short Answer and Essay Questions refer to Bonus Web Chapter 40.

TRUE–FALSE QUESTIONS

1. T, pp. 1–2	**10.** F, pp. 4–5	**19.** F, p. 10
2. F, p. 2	**11.** T, pp. 4–5	**20.** F, pp. 10–11
3. T, p. 2	**12.** F, p. 5	**21.** T, p. 11
4. T, pp. 2–3	**13.** T, p. 6	**22.** T, p. 11
5. T, pp. 2–3	**14.** T, pp. 6–7	**23.** F, pp. 12–13
6. F, p. 3	**15.** F, p. 7	**24.** F, p. 12
7. F, p. 3	**16.** T, p. 8	**25.** T, p. 13
8. T, p. 4	**17.** F, p. 8	
9. F, p. 4	**18.** T, p. 9	

MULTIPLE-CHOICE QUESTIONS

1. d, p. 2	**10.** b, p. 6	**19.** d, pp. 10–11
2. b, p. 2	**11.** c, p. 6	**20.** a, p. 10
3. b, p. 2	**12.** c, p. 6	**21.** b, pp. 10–11
4. a, p. 3	**13.** b, p. 6	**22.** d, p. 11
5. d, p. 3	**14.** c, pp. 6–7	**23.** c, p. 12
6. c, p. 3	**15.** d, p. 7	**24.** b, p. 12
7. d, p. 4	**16.** d, p. 8	**25.** c, pp. 12–13
8. c, pp. 4–5	**17.** c, p. 9	
9. b, pp. 4–5	**18.** a, p. 10	

PROBLEMS

1. *a.* supply and demand; *b.* profit; *c.* state ownership of resources; *d.* command or centrally planned economy; *e.* corporations; *f.* collective farms or agricultural cooperatives; *g.* competitive markets and flexible prices; *h.* active or discretionary macroeconomic policies; *i.* dictatorship by the Communist Party
2. *a.* 90, 25; *b.* 55, 25, 30; *c.* 90, 25; *d.* 60, 40, 30, 15
3. *a.* 4; *b.* 5; *c.* 1; *d.* 2; *e.* 3; *f.* 6

SHORT ANSWER AND ESSAY QUESTIONS

1. pp. 1–2
2. p. 2
3. pp. 2–3
4. p. 4
5. pp. 4–5
6. pp. 5–6
7. pp. 6–7
8. pp. 7–8
9. p. 8
10. p. 8
11. p. 8
12. p. 9
13. pp. 9–12
14. p. 10
15. pp. 10–11
16. pp. 10–11
17. p. 11
18. p. 11
19. pp. 11–12
20. pp. 12–13

Glossary

Note: Terms set in *italic* type are defined separately in this glossary.

ability-to-pay principle The idea that those who have greater *income* (or *wealth*) should pay a greater proportion of it as taxes than those who have less income (or wealth).

abstraction Elimination of irrelevant and noneconomic facts to obtain an *economic principle*.

acreage allotment program A pre-1996 government program that determined the total number of acres to be used in producing (reduced amounts of) various food and fiber products and allocated these acres among individual farmers. These farmers had to limit their plantings to the allotted number of acres to obtain *price supports* for their crops.

actual investment The amount that *firms* do invest; equal to *planned investment* plus *unplanned investment*.

actual reserves The funds that a bank has on deposit at the *Federal Reserve Bank* of its district (plus its *vault cash*).

adjustable pegs The device used in the *Bretton Woods system* to alter *exchange rates* in an orderly way to eliminate persistent payments deficits and surpluses. Each nation defined its monetary unit in terms of (pegged it to) gold or the dollar, kept the *rate of exchange* for its money stable in the short run, and adjusted its rate in the long run when faced with international payments disequilibrium.

adverse selection problem A problem arising when information known to one party to a contract or agreement is not known to the other party, causing the latter to incur major costs. Example: Individuals who have the poorest health are most likely to buy health insurance.

advertising A seller's activities in communicating its message about its product to potential buyers.

affirmative action Policies and programs that establish targets of increased employment and promotion for women and minorities.

AFL-CIO An acronym for the American Federation of Labor–Congress of Industrial Organizations; the largest federation of *labor unions* in the United States.

agency shop A place of employment where the employer may hire either *labor union* members or nonmembers but where those who do not join the union must either pay union dues or donate an equivalent amount of money to a charity.

aggregate demand A schedule or curve that shows the total quantity of goods and services demanded (purchased) at different *price levels*.

aggregate demand–aggregate supply model The macroeconomic model that uses *aggregate demand* and *aggregate supply* to determine and explain the *price level* and the real *domestic output*.

aggregate expenditures The total amount spent for final goods and services in an economy.

aggregate expenditures–domestic output approach Determination of the equilibrium *gross domestic product* by finding the real GDP at which *aggregate expenditures* equal *domestic output*.

aggregate expenditures schedule A schedule or curve showing the total amount spent for final goods and services at different levels of *real GDP*.

aggregate supply A schedule or curve showing the total quantity of goods and services supplied (produced) at different *price levels*.

aggregate supply shocks Sudden, large changes in resource costs that shift an economy's aggregate supply curve.

aggregation The combining of individual units or data into one unit or number. For example, all prices of individual goods and services are combined into a *price level* or all units of output are aggregated into *real gross domestic product*.

Alcoa case A 1945 case in which the courts ruled that the possession of monopoly power, no matter how reasonably that power had been used, was a violation of the antitrust laws; temporarily overturned the *rule of reason* applied in the *U.S. Steel case*.

allocative efficiency The apportionment of resources among firms and industries to obtain the production of the products most wanted by society (consumers); the output of each product at which its *marginal cost* and *price* or *marginal benefit* are equal.

annually balanced budget A budget in which government expenditures and tax collections are equal each year.

anticipated inflation Increases in the price level (*inflation*) that occur at the expected rate.

antitrust laws Legislation (including the *Sherman Act* and *Clayton Act*) that prohibits anticompetitive business activities such as *price fixing*, bid rigging, monopolization, and *tying contracts*.

antitrust policy The use of the *antitrust laws* to promote *competition* and economic efficiency.

appreciation (of the dollar) An increase in the value of the dollar relative to the currency of another nation, so a dollar buys a larger amount of the foreign currency and thus of foreign goods.

asset Anything of monetary value owned by a firm or individual.

asset demand for money The amount of *money* people want to hold as a *store of value;* this amount varies inversely with the *interest rate*.

asymmetric information A situation where one party to a market transaction has much more information about a product or service than the other. The result may be an under- or overallocation of resources.

average fixed cost A firm's total *fixed cost* divided by output (the quantity of product produced).

average product The total output produced per unit of a *resource* employed (*total product* divided by the quantity of that employed resource).

average propensity to consume Fraction (or percentage) of *disposable income* that households plan to spend for consumer goods and services; consumption divided by *disposable income*.

average propensity to save Fraction (or percentage) of *disposable income* that households save; *saving* divided by *disposable income*.

average revenue Total revenue from the sale of a product divided by the quantity of the product sold (demanded); equal to the price at which the product is sold when all units of the product are sold at the same price.

average tax rate Total tax paid divided by total (taxable) income, as a percentage.

average total cost A firm's *total cost* divided by output (the quantity of product produced); equal to *average fixed cost* plus *average variable cost*.

average variable cost A firm's total *variable cost* divided by output (the quantity of product produced).

backflows The return of workers to the countries from which they originally migrated.

balance of payments (See *international balance of payments.*)

balance-of-payments deficit The amount by which the sum of the *balance on current account* and the *balance on capital account* is negative in a year.

balance-of-payments surplus The amount by which the sum of the *balance on current account* and the *balance on capital account* is positive in a year.

balance on capital account The foreign purchases of assets in the United States less American purchases of assets abroad in a year.

balance on current account The exports of goods and services of a nation less its imports of goods and services plus its *net investment income* and *net transfers* in a year.

balance on goods and services The exports of goods and services of a nation less its imports of goods and services in a year.

balance sheet A statement of the *assets, liabilities,* and *net worth* of a firm or individual at some given time.

bank deposits The deposits that individuals or firms have at banks (or thrifts) or that banks have at the *Federal Reserve Banks*.

bank reserves The deposits of commercial banks and thrifts at *Federal Reserve Banks* plus bank and thrift *vault cash*.

bankers' bank A bank that accepts the deposits of and makes loans to *depository institutions;* in the United States, a *Federal Reserve Bank*.

barrier to entry Anything that artificially prevents the entry of firms into an industry.

barter The exchange of one good or service for another good or service.

base year The year with which other years are compared when an index is constructed; for example, the base year for a *price index*.

benefit-reduction rate The percentage by which subsidy benefits in a *public assistance program* are reduced as earned income rises.

benefits-received principle The idea that those who receive the benefits of goods and services provided by government should pay the taxes required to finance them.

bilateral monopoly A market in which there is a single seller *(monopoly)* and a single buyer *(monopsony).*

Board of Governors The seven-member group that supervises and controls the money and banking system of the United States; the Board of Governors of the Federal Reserve System; the Federal Reserve Board.

bond A financial device through which a borrower (a firm or government) is obligated to pay the principal and interest on a loan at a specific date in the future.

brain drain (Web chapter 39) The emigration of highly educated, highly skilled workers from a country.

break-even income The level of *disposable income* at which *households* plan to consume (spend) all their income and to save none of it; also, in an income transfer program, the level of earned income at which subsidy payments become zero.

break-even output Any output at which a (competitive) firm's *total cost* and *total revenue* are equal; an output at which a firm has neither an *economic profit* nor a loss, at which it earns only a normal profit.

Bretton Woods system The international monetary system developed after the Second World War in which *adjustable pegs* were employed, the *International Monetary Fund* helped stabilize foreign exchange rates, and gold and the dollar were used as *international monetary reserves*.

budget constraint The limit that the size of a consumer's income (and the prices that must be paid for goods and services) imposes on the ability of that consumer to obtain goods and services.

budget deficit The amount by which the expenditures of the Federal government exceed its revenues in any year.

budget line A line that shows the different combinations of two products a consumer can purchase with a specific money income, given the products' prices.

budget surplus The amount by which the revenues of the Federal government exceed its expenditures in any year.

built-in stabilizer A mechanism that increases government's budget deficit (or reduces its surplus) during a recession and increases government's budget surplus (or reduces its deficit) during inflation without any action by policymakers. The tax system is one such mechanism.

Bureau of Economic Analysis (BEA) An agency of the U.S. Department of Commerce that compiles the national income and product accounts.

business cycle Recurring increases and decreases in the level of economic activity over periods of years; consists of peak, recession, trough, and recovery phases.

business firm (See *firm*.)

business unionism Labor unionism that concerns itself with such practical and short-run objectives as higher wages, shorter hours, and improved working conditions.

capital Human-made resources (buildings, machinery, and equipment) used to produce goods and services; goods that do not directly satisfy human wants; also called capital goods.

capital account The section of a nation's *international balance-of-payments* statement that records the foreign purchases of assets in the United States (creating monetary inflows) and U.S. purchases of assets abroad (creating monetary outflows).

capital account deficit A negative *balance on capital account*.

capital account surplus A positive *balance on capital account*.

capital flight (Web chapter 39) The transfer of savings from *developing countries* to industrially advanced countries to avoid government expropriation, taxation, and high rates of inflation or to realize better investment opportunities.

capital gain The gain realized when securities or properties are sold for a price greater than the price paid for them.

capital goods (See *capital*.)

capital-intensive commodity A product that requires a relatively large amount of *capital* to be produced.

capitalism An economic system in which property resources are privately owned and markets and prices are used to direct and coordinate economic activities.

capital-saving technological advance (Web chapter 39) An improvement in *technology* that permits a greater quantity of a product to be produced with a specific amount of *capital* (or permits the same amount of the product to be produced with a smaller amount of capital).

capital stock The total available *capital* in a nation.

capital-using technological advance (Web chapter 39) An improvement in *technology* that requires the use of a greater amount of *capital* to produce a specific quantity of a product.

cartel A formal agreement among firms (or countries) in an industry to set the price of a product and establish the outputs of the individual firms (or countries) or to divide the market for the product geographically.

causation A relationship in which the occurrence of one or more events brings about another event.

CEA (See *Council of Economic Advisers*.)

cease-and-desist order An order from a court or government agency to a corporation or individual to stop engaging in a specified practice.

ceiling price (See *price ceiling*.)

Celler-Kefauver Act The Federal act of 1950 that amended the *Clayton Act* by prohibiting the acquisition of the assets of one firm by another firm when the effect would be less competition.

central bank A bank whose chief function is the control of the nation's *money supply;* in the United States, the Federal Reserve System.

central economic planning Government determination of the objectives of the economy and how resources will be directed to attain those goals.

ceteris paribus assumption (See *other-things-equal assumption*.)

change in demand A change in the *quantity demanded* of a good or service at every price; a shift of the *demand curve* to the left or right.

change in supply A change in the *quantity supplied* of a good or service at every price; a shift of the *supply curve* to the left or right.

check clearing The process by which funds are transferred from the checking accounts of the writers of checks to the checking accounts of the recipients of the checks.

checkable deposit Any deposit in a *commercial bank* or *thrift institution* against which a check may be written.

checkable-deposit multiplier (See *monetary multiplier*.)

checking account A *checkable deposit* in a *commercial bank* or *thrift institution*.

circular flow model The flow of resources from *households* to *firms* and of products from firms to households. These flows are accompanied by reverse flows of money from firms to households and from households to firms.

Civil Rights Act of 1964 Federal law that, in Title VII, outlaws *discrimination* based on race, color, religion, gender, or national origin in hiring, promoting, and compensating workers.

classical economics The macroeconomic generalizations accepted by most economists before the 1930s that led to the conclusion that a capitalistic economy was self-regulating and therefore would usually employ its resources fully.

Clayton Act The Federal antitrust act of 1914 that strengthened the *Sherman Act* by making it illegal for firms to engage in certain specified practices.

closed economy An economy that neither exports nor imports goods and services.

closed shop A place of employment where only workers who are already members of a labor union may be hired.

Coase theorem The idea, first stated by economist Ronald Coase, that *spillover* problems may be resolved through private negotiations of the affected parties.

coincidence of wants A situation in which the good or service that one trader desires to obtain is the same as that which another trader desires to give up and an item that the second trader wishes to acquire is the same as that which the first trader desires to surrender.

COLA (See *cost-of-living adjustment*.)

collective bargaining The negotiation of labor contracts between *labor unions* and *firms* or government entities.

collective voice The function a *labor union* performs for its members as a group when it communicates their problems and grievances to management and presses management for a satisfactory resolution.

collusion A situation in which firms act together and in agreement (collude) to fix prices, divide a market, or otherwise restrict competition.

command system A method of organizing an economy in which property resources are publicly owned and government uses *central economic planning* to direct and coordinate economic activities; command economy.

commercial bank A firm that engages in the business of banking (accepts deposits, offers checking accounts, and makes loans).

commercial banking system All *commercial banks* and *thrift institutions* as a group.

communism (See *command system.*)

comparative advantage A lower relative or comparative cost than that of another producer.

compensating differences Differences in the *wages* received by workers in different jobs to compensate for nonmonetary differences in the jobs.

compensation to employees *Wages* and salaries plus wage and salary supplements paid by employers to workers.

competition The presence in a market of independent buyers and sellers competing with one another and the freedom of buyers and sellers to enter and leave the market.

competitive industry's short-run supply curve The horizontal summation of the short-run supply curves of the *firms* in a purely competitive industry (see *pure competition*); a curve that shows the total quantities offered for sale at various prices by the firms in an industry in the short run.

competitive labor market A resource market in which a large number of (noncolluding) firms demand a particular type of labor supplied by a large number of nonunion workers.

complementary goods Products and services that are used together. When the price of one falls, the demand for the other increases (and conversely).

concentration ratio The percentage of the total sales of an industry made by the four (or some other number) largest sellers in the industry.

conglomerate merger The merger of a *firm* in one *industry* with a firm in another industry (with a firm that is neither a supplier, customer, nor competitor).

conglomerates Firms that produce goods and services in two or more separate industries.

constant-cost industry An industry in which expansion by the entry of new firms has no effect on the prices firms in the industry must pay for resources and thus no effect on production costs.

consumer goods Products and services that satisfy human wants directly.

Consumer Price Index (CPI) An index that measures the prices of a fixed "market basket" of some 300 goods and services bought by a "typical" consumer.

consumer sovereignty Determination by consumers of the types and quantities of goods and services that will be produced with the scarce resources of the economy; consumers' direction of production through their dollar votes.

consumer surplus The difference between the maximum price a consumer is (or consumers are) willing to pay for an additional unit of a product and its market price; the triangular area below the demand curve and above the market price.

consumption of fixed capital An estimate of the amount of *capital* worn out or used up (consumed) in producing the *gross domestic product;* also called depreciation.

consumption schedule A schedule showing the amounts *households* plan to spend for *consumer goods* at different levels of *disposable income.*

contractionary fiscal policy A decrease in *government purchases* for goods and services, an increase *in net taxes,* or some combination of the two, for the purpose of decreasing *aggregate demand* and thus controlling inflation.

coordination failure A situation in which people do not reach a mutually beneficial outcome because they lack some way to jointly coordinate their actions; a possible cause of macroeconomic instability.

copayment The percentage of (say, health care) costs that an insured individual pays while the insurer pays the remainder.

copyright A legal protection provided to developers and publishers of books, computer software, videos, and musical compositions against the copying of their works by others.

corporate income tax A tax levied on the net income (accounting profit) of corporations.

corporation A legal entity ("person") chartered by a state or the Federal government that is distinct and separate from the individuals who own it.

correlation A systematic and dependable association between two sets of data (two kinds of events); does not necessarily indicate causation.

cost-benefit analysis A comparison of the *marginal costs* of a government project or program with the *marginal benefits* to decide whether or not to employ resources in that project or program and to what extent.

cost-of-living adjustment (COLA) An automatic increase in the incomes (wages) of workers when inflation occurs; guaranteed by a collective bargaining contract between firms and workers.

cost-push inflation Increases in the price level (inflation) resulting from an increase in resource costs (for example, raw-material prices) and hence in *per-unit production costs;* inflation caused by reductions in *aggregate supply.*

cost ratio An equality showing the number of units of two products that can be produced with the same resources; the cost ratio 1 corn ≡ 3 olives shows that the resources required to produce 3 units of olives must be shifted to corn production to produce a unit of corn.

Council of Economic Advisers (CEA) A group of three persons that advises and assists the president of the United States on economic matters (including the preparation of the annual *Economic Report of the President*).

countercyclical payments   Cash *subsidies* paid to farmers when market prices for certain crops drop below targeted prices. Payments are based on previous production and are received regardless of the current crop grown.

craft union   A labor union that limits its membership to workers with a particular skill (craft).

creative destruction   The hypothesis that the creation of new products and production methods simultaneously destroys the market power of existing monopolies.

credit   An accounting item that increases the value of an asset (such as the foreign money owned by the residents of a nation).

credit union   An association of persons who have a common tie (such as being employees of the same firm or members of the same labor union) that sells shares to (accepts deposits from) its members and makes loans to them.

cross elasticity of demand   The ratio of the percentage change in *quantity demanded* of one good to the percentage change in the price of some other good. A positive coefficient indicates the two products are *substitute goods;* a negative coefficient indicates they are *complementary goods.*

crowding model of occupational discrimination   A model of labor markets suggesting that *occupational discrimination* has kept many women and minorities out of high-paying occupations and forced them into a limited number of low-paying occupations.

crowding-out effect   A rise in interest rates and a resulting decrease in *planned investment* caused by the Federal government's increased borrowing in the money market.

currency   Coins and paper money.

currency appreciation   (See *exchange-rate appreciation.*)

currency depreciation   (See *exchange-rate depreciation.*)

currency intervention   A government's buying and selling of its own currency or foreign currencies to alter international exchange rates.

current account   The section in a nation's *international balance of payments* that records its exports and imports of goods and services, its net *investment income,* and its *net transfers.*

cyclical deficit   A Federal *budget deficit* that is caused by a recession and the consequent decline in tax revenues.

cyclical unemployment   A type of *unemployment* caused by insufficient total spending (or by insufficient *aggregate demand*).

cyclically balanced budget   The equality of government expenditures and net tax collections over the course of a *business cycle;* deficits incurred during periods of recession are offset by surpluses obtained during periods of prosperity (inflation).

debit   An accounting item that decreases the value of an asset (such as the foreign money owned by the residents of a nation).

declining industry   An industry in which *economic profits* are negative (losses are incurred) and that will, therefore, decrease its output as firms leave it.

decreasing-cost industry   An industry in which expansion through the entry of firms lowers the prices that firms in the industry must pay for resources and therefore decreases their production costs.

deductible   The dollar sum of (for example, health care) costs that an insured individual must pay before the insurer begins to pay.

deflating   Finding the *real gross domestic product* by decreasing the dollar value of the GDP for a year in which prices were higher than in the *base year.*

deflation   A decline in the economy's *price level.*

demand   A schedule showing the amounts of a good or service that buyers (or a buyer) wish to purchase at various prices during some time period.

demand curve   A curve illustrating *demand.*

demand factor (in growth)   The increase in the level of *aggregate demand* that brings about the *economic growth* made possible by an increase in the production potential of the economy.

demand management   The use of *fiscal policy* and *monetary policy* to increase or decrease *aggregate demand.*

demand-pull inflation   Increases in the price level (inflation) resulting from an excess of demand over output at the existing price level, caused by an increase in *aggregate demand.*

dependent variable   A variable that changes as a consequence of a change in some other (independent) variable; the "effect" or outcome.

depository institutions   Firms that accept deposits of *money* from the public (businesses and persons); *commercial banks, savings and loan associations, mutual savings banks,* and *credit unions.*

depreciation   (See *consumption of fixed capital.*)

depreciation (of the dollar)   A decrease in the value of the dollar relative to another currency, so a dollar buys a smaller amount of the foreign currency and therefore of foreign goods.

derived demand   The demand for a resource that depends on the demand for the products it helps to produce.

determinants of aggregate demand   Factors such as consumption spending, *investment,* government spending, and *net exports* that, if they change, shift the aggregate demand curve.

determinants of aggregate supply   Factors such as input prices, *productivity,* and the legal-institutional environment that, if they change, shift the aggregate supply curve.

determinants of demand   Factors other than price that determine the quantities demanded of a good or service.

determinants of supply   Factors other than price that determine the quantities supplied of a good or service.

devaluation   A decrease in the governmentally defined value of a currency.

developing countries   Many countries of Africa, Asia, and Latin America that are characterized by lack of capital goods, use of nonadvanced technologies, low literacy rates, high unemployment, rapid population growth, and labor forces heavily committed to agriculture.

differentiated oligopoly   An *oligopoly* in which the firms produce a *differentiated product.*

differentiated product   A product that differs physically or in some other way from the similar products produced by other firms; a product such that buyers are not indifferent to the seller when the price charged by all sellers is the same.

diffusion   The spread of an *innovation* through its widespread imitation.

dilemma of regulation   The tradeoff faced by a *regulatory agency* in setting the maximum legal price a monopolist may charge: The *socially optimal price* is below *average total cost* (and either bankrupts the *firm* or requires that it be subsidized), while the higher, *fair-return price* does not produce *allocative efficiency*.

diminishing marginal returns   (See *law of diminishing returns*.)

direct foreign investment   (Web chapter 39) The building of new factories (or the purchase of existing capital) in a particular nation by corporations of other nations.

direct payments   Cash subsidies paid to farmers based on past production levels; unaffected by current crop prices and current production.

direct relationship   The relationship between two variables that change in the same direction, for example, product price and quantity supplied.

discount rate   The interest rate that the *Federal Reserve Banks* charge on the loans they make to *commercial banks* and *thrift institutions*.

discouraged workers   Employees who have left the *labor force* because they have not been able to find employment.

discretionary fiscal policy   Deliberate changes in taxes (tax rates) and government spending by Congress to promote full employment, price stability, and economic growth.

discrimination   The practice of according individuals or groups inferior treatment in hiring, occupational access, education and training, promotion, wage rates, or working conditions even though they have the same abilities, education and skills, and work experience as other workers.

discrimination coefficient   A measure of the cost or disutility of prejudice; the monetary amount an employer is willing to pay to hire a preferred worker rather than a nonpreferred worker.

diseconomies of scale   Increases in the *average total cost* of producing a product as the *firm* expands the size of its *plant* (its output) in the *long run*.

disinflation   A reduction in the rate of *inflation*.

disposable income   *Personal income* less personal taxes; income available for *personal consumption expenditures* and *personal saving*.

dissaving   Spending for consumer goods and services in excess of *disposable income;* the amount by which *personal consumption expenditures* exceed disposable income.

dividends   Payments by a corporation of all or part of its profit to its stockholders (the corporate owners).

division of labor   The separation of the work required to produce a product into a number of different tasks that are performed by different workers; *specialization* of workers.

Doha Round   The latest, uncompleted (as of 2003) sequence of trade negotiations by members of the *World Trade Organization;* named after Doha, Qatar, where the set of negotiations began.

dollar votes   The "votes" that consumers and entrepreneurs cast for the production of consumer and capital goods, respectively, when they purchase those goods in product and resource markets.

domestic capital formation   The process of adding to a nation's stock of *capital* by saving and investing part of its own domestic output.

domestic output   *Gross* (or net) *domestic product;* the total output of final goods and services produced in the economy.

domestic price   The price of a good or service within a country, determined by domestic demand and supply.

double taxation   The taxation of both corporate net income (profits) and the *dividends* paid from this net income when they become the personal income of households.

dumping   The sale of products below cost in a foreign country or below the prices charged at home.

DuPont cellophane case   The antitrust case brought against DuPont in which the U.S. Supreme Court ruled (in 1956) that while DuPont had a monopoly in the narrowly defined market for cellophane, it did not monopolize the more broadly defined market for flexible packaging materials. It was thus not guilty of violating the *Sherman Act*.

durable good   A consumer good with an expected life (use) of 3 or more years.

earned-income tax credit   A refundable Federal tax credit for low-income working people designed to reduce poverty and encourage labor-force participation.

earnings   The money income received by a worker; equal to the *wage* (rate) multiplied by the amount of time worked.

easy money policy   Federal Reserve System actions to increase the *money supply* to lower interest rates and expand *real GDP*.

economic analysis   The process of deriving *economic principles* from relevant economic facts.

economic concentration   A description or measure of the degree to which an industry is dominated by one or a handful of firms or is characterized by many firms. (See *concentration ratio*.)

economic cost   A payment that must be made to obtain and retain the services of a *resource;* the income a firm must provide to a resource supplier to attract the resource away from an alternative use; equal to the quantity of other products that cannot be produced when resources are instead used to make a particular product.

economic efficiency   The use of the minimum necessary resources to obtain the socially optimal amounts of goods and services; entails both *productive efficiency* and *allocative efficiency*.

economic growth   (1) An outward shift in the *production possibilities curve* that results from an increase in resource supplies or quality or an improvement in *technology;* (2) an increase of real output *(gross domestic product)* or real output per capita.

economic law An *economic principle* that has been tested and retested and has stood the test of time.

economic model A simplified picture of economic reality; an abstract generalization.

economic perspective A viewpoint that envisions individuals and institutions making rational decisions by comparing the marginal benefits and marginal costs associated with their actions.

economic policy A course of action intended to correct or avoid a problem.

economic principle A widely accepted generalization about the economic behavior of individuals or institutions.

economic profit The *total revenue* of a firm less its *economic costs* (which include both *explicit costs* and *implicit costs*); also called "pure profit" and "above-normal profit."

economic regulation (See *industrial regulation* and *social regulation*.)

economic rent The price paid for the use of land and other natural resources, the supply of which is fixed *(perfectly inelastic)*.

economic resources The *land, labor, capital,* and *entrepreneurial ability* that are used in the production of goods and services; productive agents; factors of production.

economic system A particular set of institutional arrangements and a coordinating mechanism for solving the economizing problem; a method of organizing an economy, of which the *market system* and the *command system* are the two general types.

economic theory A statement of a cause-effect relationship; when accepted by all economists, an *economic principle.*

economics The social science dealing with the use of scarce resources to obtain the maximum satisfaction of society's virtually unlimited economic wants.

economies of scale Reductions in the *average total cost* of producing a product as the firm expands the size of plant (its output) in the *long run;* the economies of mass production.

economizing problem The choices necessitated because society's economic wants for goods and services are unlimited but the resources available to satisfy these wants are limited (scarce).

efficiency factors (in growth) The capacity of an economy to combine resources effectively to achieve growth of real output that the *supply factors* (of growth) make possible.

efficiency loss (Web chapter 3) Reductions in combined consumer and producer surplus caused by an underallocation or overallocation of resources to the production of a good or service.

efficiency loss of a tax The loss of net benefits to society because a tax reduces the production and consumption of a taxed good below the level of allocative efficiency.

efficiency wage A wage that minimizes wage costs per unit of output by encouraging greater effort or reducing turnover.

efficient allocation of resources That allocation of an economy's resources among the production of different products that leads to the maximum satisfaction of consumers' wants, thus producing the socially optimal mix of output with society's scarce resources.

elastic demand Product or resource demand whose *price elasticity* is greater than 1. This means the resulting change in *quantity demanded* is greater than the percentage change in *price*.

elastic supply Product or resource supply whose price elasticity is greater than 1. This means the resulting change in quantity supplied is greater than the percentage change in price.

elasticity coefficient The number obtained when the percentage change in *quantity demanded* (or supplied) is divided by the percentage change in the *price* of the commodity.

elasticity formula (See *price elasticity of demand.*)

Employment Act of 1946 Federal legislation that committed the Federal government to the maintenance of economic stability (a high level of employment, a stable price level, and economic growth); established the *Council of Economic Advisers* and the *Joint Economic Committee;* and required an annual economic report by the president to Congress.

employment discrimination Inferior treatment in hiring, promotions, work assignments, and such for a particular group of employees.

employment rate The percentage of the *labor force* employed at any time.

entitlement programs Government programs such as *social insurance, food stamps, Medicare,* and *Medicaid* that guarantee particular levels of transfer payments or noncash benefits to all who fit the programs' criteria.

entrepreneurial ability The human resource that combines the other resources to produce a product, makes nonroutine decisions, innovates, and bears risks.

Equal Pay Act of 1963 Federal government legislation making it illegal to pay men and women different wage rates if they do equal work on jobs that require equal skill, effort, and responsibility and that are performed under similar working conditions.

equality-versus-efficiency tradeoff The decrease in *economic efficiency* that may accompany a decrease in *income inequality;* the presumption that some income inequality is required to achieve economic efficiency.

equation of exchange $MV = PQ$, in which M is the supply of money, V is the *velocity* of money, P is the *price level,* and Q is the physical volume of *final goods and services* produced.

equilibrium price The *price* in a competitive market at which the *quantity demanded* and the *quantity supplied* are equal, there is neither a shortage nor a surplus, and there is no tendency for price to rise or fall.

equilibrium price level The price level at which the aggregate demand curve intersects the aggregate supply curve.

equilibrium quantity (1) The quantity demanded and supplied at the equilibrium price in a competitive market; (2) the profit-maximizing output of a firm.

equilibrium real domestic output The *gross domestic product* at which the total quantity of final goods and services purchased *(aggregate expenditures)* is equal to the total quantity of final goods and services produced (the real domestic output); the real domestic output at which the aggregate demand curve intersects the aggregate supply curve.

euro The common currency unit used by 12 European nations (as of 2003) in the Euro zone, which consists of Austria, Belgium, Finland, France, Germany, Greece, Ireland, Italy, Luxembourg, the Netherlands, Portugal, and Spain.

European Union (EU) An association of 25 European nations including 10 nations to be added in 2004 that has eliminated tariffs and quotas among them, established common tariffs for imported goods from outside the member nations, eliminated barriers to the free movement of capital, and created other common economic policies.

excess capacity Plant resources that are underused when imperfectly competitive firms produce less output than that associated with achieving minimum average total cost.

excess reserves The amount by which a bank's or thrift's *actual reserves* exceed its *required reserves;* actual reserves minus required reserves.

exchange control (See *foreign exchange control.*)

exchange rate The *rate of exchange* of one nation's currency for another nation's currency.

exchange-rate appreciation An increase in the value of a nation's currency in foreign exchange markets; an increase in the *rate of exchange* for foreign currencies.

exchange-rate depreciation A decrease in the value of a nation's currency in foreign exchange markets; a decrease in the *rate of exchange* for foreign currencies.

exchange-rate determinant Any factor other than the *rate of exchange* that determines a currency's demand and supply in the *foreign exchange market.*

excise tax A tax levied on the production of a specific product or on the quantity of the product purchased.

exclusive unionism The practice of a *labor union* of restricting the supply of skilled union labor to increase the wages received by union members; the policies typically employed by a *craft union.*

exhaustive expenditure An expenditure by government resulting directly in the employment of *economic resources* and in the absorption by government of the goods and services those resources produce; a *government purchase.*

exit mechanism The process of leaving a job and searching for another one as a means of improving one's working conditions.

expanding industry An industry whose firms earn *economic profits* and for which an increase in output occurs as new firms enter the industry.

expansionary fiscal policy An increase in *government purchases* of goods and services, a decrease in *net taxes,* or some combination of the two for the purpose of increasing *aggregate demand* and expanding real output.

expectations The anticipations of consumers, firms, and others about future economic conditions.

expected rate of return The increase in profit a firm anticipates it will obtain by purchasing capital (or engaging in research and development); expressed as a percentage of the total cost of the investment (or R&D) activity.

expenditures approach The method that adds all expenditures made for *final goods and services* to measure the *gross domestic product.*

expenditures-output approach (See *aggregate expenditures–domestic output approach.*)

explicit cost The monetary payment a *firm* must make to an outsider to obtain a *resource.*

export subsidies Government payments to domestic producers to enable them to reduce the *price* of a good or service to foreign buyers.

export supply curve An upward-sloping curve that shows the amount of a product that domestic firms will export at each *world price* that is above the *domestic price.*

export transaction A sale of a good or service that increases the amount of foreign currency flowing to a nation's citizens, firms, and government.

exports Goods and services produced in a nation and sold to buyers in other nations.

external benefit (See *spillover benefit.*)

external cost (See *spillover cost.*)

external debt Private or public debt owed to foreign citizens, firms, and institutions.

externality (See *spillover.*)

face value The dollar or cents value placed on a U.S. coin or piece of paper money.

factors of production *Economic resources: land, capital, labor,* and *entrepreneurial ability.*

fair-return price The price of a product that enables its producer to obtain a *normal profit* and that is equal to the *average total cost* of producing it.

fallacy of composition The false notion that what is true for the individual (or part) is necessarily true for the group (or whole).

Farm Act of 2002 Farm legislation that continued the "freedom to plant" and direct subsidies of the *Freedom to Farm Act* of 1996 but added an automatic, countercyclical system of emergency farm aid.

farm problem The fact that technological advance, coupled with a price-inelastic and relatively constant demand, has made agriculture a *declining industry;* also, the tendency for farm income to fluctuate sharply from year to year.

FDIC (See *Federal Deposit Insurance Corporation.*)

Federal Deposit Insurance Corporation (FDIC) The federally chartered corporation that insures deposit liabilities (up to $100,000 per account) of *commercial banks* and *thrift institutions* (excluding *credit unions,* whose deposits are insured by the *National Credit Union Administration*).

Federal funds rate The interest rate banks and other depository institutions charge one another on overnight loans made out of their *excess reserves.*

Federal government The government of the United States, as distinct from the state and local governments.

Federal Open Market Committee (FOMC) The 12-member group that determines the purchase and sale policies of the *Federal Reserve Banks* in the market for U.S. government securities.

Federal Reserve Banks The 12 banks chartered by the U.S. government to control the *money supply* and perform other functions. (See *central bank, quasi-public bank,* and *bankers' bank*.)

Federal Reserve Note Paper money issued by the *Federal Reserve Banks*.

Federal Trade Commission (FTC) The commission of five members established by the *Federal Trade Commission Act* of 1914 to investigate unfair competitive practices of firms, to hold hearings on the complaints of such practices, and to issue *cease-and-desist orders* when firms were found to engage in such practices.

Federal Trade Commission Act The Federal act of 1914 that established the *Federal Trade Commission*.

fiat money Anything that is *money* because government has decreed it to be money.

final goods and services Goods and services that have been purchased for final use and not for resale or further processing or manufacturing.

financial capital (See *money capital*.)

firm An organization that employs resources to produce a good or service for profit and owns and operates one or more *plants*.

fiscal policy Changes in government spending and tax collections designed to achieve a full-employment and noninflationary domestic output; also called *discretionary fiscal policy*.

fixed cost Any cost that in total does not change when the *firm* changes its output; the cost of *fixed resources*.

fixed exchange rate A *rate of exchange* that is set in some way and therefore prevented from rising or falling with changes in currency supply and demand.

fixed resource Any resource whose quantity cannot be changed by a firm in the *short run*.

flexible exchange rate A *rate of exchange* determined by the international demand for and supply of a nation's money; a rate free to rise or fall (to float).

floating exchange rate (See *flexible exchange rate*.)

food-stamp program A program permitting low-income persons to purchase for less than their retail value, or to obtain without cost, coupons that can be exchanged for food items at retail stores.

foreign competition (See *import competition*.)

foreign exchange control The control a government may exercise over the quantity of foreign currency demanded by its citizens and firms and over the *rates of exchange* in order to limit its *outpayments* to its *inpayments* (to eliminate a *payments deficit*).

foreign exchange market A market in which the money (currency) of one nation can be used to purchase (can be exchanged for) the money of another nation.

foreign exchange rate (See *rate of exchange*.)

foreign purchase effect The inverse relationship between the *net exports* of an economy and its price level relative to foreign price levels.

45° line A line along which the value of *GDP* (measured horizontally) is equal to the value of *aggregate expenditures* (measured vertically).

Four Fundamental Questions (of economics) The four questions that every economy must answer: what to produce, how to produce it, how to divide the total output, and how to ensure economic flexibility.

fractional reserve A *reserve requirement* that is less than 100 percent of the checkable-deposit liabilities of a *commercial bank* or *thrift institution*.

freedom of choice The freedom of owners of property resources to employ or dispose of them as they see fit, of workers to enter any line of work for which they are qualified, and of consumers to spend their incomes in a manner that they think is appropriate.

freedom of enterprise The freedom of *firms* to obtain economic resources, to use those resources to produce products of the firm's own choosing, and to sell their products in markets of their choice.

Freedom to Farm Act A law passed in 1996 that revamped 60 years of U.S. farm policy by ending *price supports* and *acreage allotments* for wheat, corn, barley, oats, sorghum, rye, cotton, and rice.

free-rider problem The inability of potential providers of an economically desirable good or service to obtain payment from those who benefit, because of *nonexcludability*.

free trade The absence of artificial (government-imposed) barriers to trade among individuals and firms in different nations.

frictional unemployment A type of unemployment caused by workers voluntarily changing jobs and by temporary layoffs; unemployed workers between jobs.

fringe benefits The rewards other than *wages* that employees receive from their employers and that include pensions, medical and dental insurance, paid vacations, and sick leaves.

full employment (1) The use of all available resources to produce want-satisfying goods and services; (2) the situation in which the *unemployment rate* is equal to the *full-employment unemployment rate* and there is *frictional* and *structural* but no *cyclical unemployment* (and the *real GDP* of the economy equals *potential output*).

full-employment budget A comparison of the government expenditures and tax collections that would occur if the economy operated at *full employment* throughout the year.

full-employment unemployment rate The *unemployment rate* at which there is no *cyclical unemployment* of the *labor force;* equal to between 4 and 5 percent in the United States because some *frictional* and *structural unemployment* is unavoidable.

full production Employment of available resources so that the maximum amount of (or total value of) goods and services is produced; occurs when both *productive efficiency* and *allocative efficiency* are realized.

functional distribution of income The manner in which *national income* is divided among the functions performed to earn it (or the kinds of resources provided to earn it); the division of national income into wages and salaries, proprietors' income, corporate profits, interest, and rent.

functional finance The use of *fiscal policy* to achieve a noninflationary full-employment *gross domestic product* without regard to the effect on the *public debt*.

gains from trade The extra output that trading partners obtain through specialization of production and exchange of goods and services.

game theory A means of analyzing the pricing behavior of oligopolists that uses the theory of strategy associated with games such as chess and bridge.

GDP (See *gross domestic product.*)

GDP gap Actual *gross domestic product* minus potential output; may be either a positive amount (a *positive GDP gap*) or a negative amount (a *negative GDP gap*).

GDP price index A *price index* for all the goods and services that make up the *gross domestic product;* the price index used to adjust *nominal gross domestic product* to *real gross domestic product.*

G8 nations A group of eight major nations (Canada, France, Germany, Italy, Japan, Russia, United Kingdom, and United States) whose leaders meet regularly to discuss common economic problems and try to coordinate economic policies.

General Agreement on Tariffs and Trade (GATT) The international agreement reached in 1947 in which 23 nations agreed to give equal and nondiscriminatory treatment to one another, to reduce tariff rates by multinational negotiations, and to eliminate *import quotas.* It now includes most nations and has become the *World Trade Organization.*

generalization Statement of the nature of the relationship between two or more sets of facts.

Gini ratio A numerical measure of the overall dispersion of income among households, families, or individuals; found graphically by dividing the area between the diagonal line and the *Lorenz curve* by the entire area below the diagonal line.

gold standard A historical system of fixed exchange rates in which nations defined their currencies in terms of gold, maintained a fixed relationship between their stocks of gold and their money supplies, and allowed gold to be freely exported and imported.

government failure Inefficiencies in resource allocation caused by problems in the operation of the public sector (government), specifically, rent-seeking pressure by special-interest groups, shortsighted political behavior, limited and bundled choices, and bureaucratic inefficiencies.

government purchases Expenditures by government for goods and services that government consumes in providing public goods and for public (or social) capital that has a long lifetime; the expenditures of all governments in the economy for those *final goods and services.*

government transfer payment The disbursement of money (or goods and services) by government for which government receives no currently produced good or service in return.

grievance procedure The method used by a *labor union* and a *firm* to settle disputes that arise during the life of the collective bargaining agreement between them.

gross domestic product (GDP) The total market value of all *final goods and services* produced annually within the boundaries of the United States, whether by U.S. or foreign-supplied resources.

gross private domestic investment Expenditures for newly produced *capital goods* (such as machinery, equipment, tools, and buildings) and for additions to inventories.

guiding function of prices The ability of price changes to bring about changes in the quantities of products and resources demanded and supplied.

health maintenance organizations (HMOs) Health care providers that contract with employers, insurance companies, labor unions, or government units to provide health care for their workers or others who are insured.

Herfindahl index A measure of the concentration and competitiveness of an industry; calculated as the sum of the squared percentage market shares of the individual firms in the industry.

homogeneous oligopoly An *oligopoly* in which the firms produce a *standardized product.*

horizontal merger The merger into a single *firm* of two firms producing the same product and selling it in the same geographic market.

household An economic unit (of one or more persons) that provides the economy with resources and uses the income received to purchase goods and services that satisfy economic wants.

human capital The accumulation of prior investments in education, training, health, and other factors that increase productivity.

human capital discrimination The denial of equal access to productivity-enhancing education and training to members of particular groups.

human capital investment Any expenditure undertaken to improve the education, skills, health, or mobility of workers, with an expectation of greater productivity and thus a positive return on the investment.

hyperinflation A very rapid rise in the price level; an extremely high rate of inflation.

hypothesis A tentative explanation of cause and effect that requires testing.

illegal immigrant A person who enters a country unlawfully for the purpose of residing there.

IMF (See *International Monetary Fund.*)

immobility The inability or unwillingness of a worker to move from one geographic area or occupation to another or from a lower-paying job to a higher-paying job.

imperfect competition All market structures except *pure competition;* includes *monopoly, monopolistic competition,* and *oligopoly.*

implicit cost The monetary income a *firm* sacrifices when it uses a resource it owns rather than supplying the resource in the market; equal to what the resource could have earned in the best-paying alternative employment; includes a *normal profit.*

import competition The competition that domestic firms encounter from the products and services of foreign producers.

import demand curve A downsloping curve showing the amount of a product that an economy will import at each *world price* below the *domestic price.*

import quota A limit imposed by a nation on the quantity (or total value) of a good that may be imported during some period of time.

import transaction The purchase of a good or service that decreases the amount of foreign money held by citizens, firms, and governments of a nation.

imports Spending by individuals, *firms,* and governments for goods and services produced in foreign nations.

incentive function of price The inducement that an increase in the price of a commodity gives to sellers to make more of it available (and conversely for a decrease in price), and the inducement that an increase in price offers to buyers to purchase smaller quantities (and conversely for a decrease in price).

incentive pay plan A compensation structure that ties worker pay directly to performance. Such plans include piece rates, bonuses, *stock options,* commissions, and *profit sharing.*

inclusive unionism The practice of a labor union of including as members all workers employed in an industry.

income A flow of dollars (or purchasing power) per unit of time derived from the use of human or property resources.

income approach The method that adds all the income generated by the production of *final goods and services* to measure the *gross domestic product.*

income effect A change in the quantity demanded of a product that results from the change in *real income (purchasing power)* caused by a change in the product's price.

income elasticity of demand The ratio of the percentage change in the *quantity demanded* of a good to a percentage change in consumer income; measures the responsiveness of consumer purchases to income changes.

income inequality The unequal distribution of an economy's total income among households or families.

income-maintenance system A group of government programs designed to eliminate poverty and reduce inequality in the distribution of income.

increase in demand An increase in the *quantity demanded* of a good or service at every price; a shift of the *demand curve* to the right.

increase in supply An increase in the *quantity supplied* of a good or service at every price; a shift of the *supply curve* to the right.

increasing-cost industry An *industry* in which expansion through the entry of new firms raises the prices *firms* in the industry must pay for resources and therefore increases their production costs.

increasing marginal returns An increase in the *marginal product* of a resource as successive units of the resource are employed.

increasing returns An increase in a firm's output by a larger percentage than the percentage increase in its inputs.

independent goods Products or services for which there is little or no relationship between the price of one and the demand for the other. When the price of one rises or falls, the demand for the other tends to remain constant.

independent unions U.S. unions that are not affiliated with the *AFL-CIO.*

independent variable The variable causing a change in some other (dependent) variable.

indifference curve A curve showing the different combinations of two products that yield the same satisfaction or *utility* to a consumer.

indifference map A set of *indifference curves,* each representing a different level of *utility,* that together show the preferences of a consumer.

indirect business taxes Such taxes as *sales, excise,* and business *property taxes,* license fees, and *tariffs* that firms treat as costs of producing a product and pass on (in whole or in part) to buyers by charging higher prices.

individual demand The demand schedule or *demand curve* of a single buyer.

individual supply The supply schedule or *supply curve* of a single seller.

industrial regulation The older and more traditional type of regulation in which government is concerned with the prices charged and the services provided to the public in specific industries, in contrast to *social regulation.*

industrial union A *labor union* that accepts as members all workers employed in a particular industry (or by a particular firm).

industrially advanced countries High-income countries such as the United States, Canada, Japan, and the nations of western Europe that have highly developed *market economies* based on large stocks of technologically advanced capital goods and skilled labor forces.

industry A group of (one or more) *firms* that produce identical or similar products.

inelastic demand Product or resource demand for which the *elasticity coefficient* for price is less than 1. This means the resulting percentage change in *quantity demanded* is less than the percentage change in *price.*

inelastic supply Product or resource supply for which the price elasticity coefficient is less than 1. The percentage change in *quantity supplied* is less than the percentage change in *price.*

inferior good A good or service whose consumption declines as income rises (and conversely), price remaining constant.

inflating Determining *real gross domestic product* by increasing the dollar value of the *nominal gross domestic product* produced in a year in which prices are lower than those in a *base year.*

inflation A rise in the general level of prices in an economy.

inflationary expectations The belief of workers, firms, and consumers that substantial inflation will occur in the future.

inflationary gap The amount by which the *aggregate expenditures schedule* must shift downward to decrease the *nominal GDP* to its full-employment noninflationary level.

inflation premium The component of the *nominal interest rate* that reflects anticipated inflation.

information technology New and more efficient methods of delivering and receiving information through use of computers, fax machines, wireless phones, and the Internet.

infrastructure The capital goods usually provided by the *public sector* for the use of its citizens and firms (for example, highways, bridges, transit systems, wastewater treatment facilities, municipal water systems, and airports).

injection An addition of spending to the income-expenditure stream: *investment, government purchases,* and *net exports.*

injunction A court order directing a person or organization not to perform a certain act because the act would do irreparable damage to some other person or persons; a restraining order.

in-kind transfer The distribution by government of goods and services to individuals for which the government receives no currently produced good or service in return; a *government transfer payment* made in goods or services rather than in money; also called a noncash transfer.

innovation The first commercially successful introduction of a new product, the use of a new method of production, or the creation of a new form of business organization.

inpayments The receipts of domestic or foreign money that individuals, firms, and governments of one nation obtain from the sale of goods and services abroad, as investment income and remittances, and from foreign purchases of its assets.

insider-outsider theory The hypothesis that nominal wages are inflexible downward because firms are aware that workers ("insiders") who retain employment during recession may refuse to work cooperatively with previously unemployed workers ("outsiders") who offer to work for less than the current wage.

insurable risk An event that would result in a loss but whose frequency of occurrence can be estimated with considerable accuracy. Insurance companies are willing to sell insurance against such losses.

interest The payment made for the use of money (of borrowed funds).

interest income Payments of income to those who supply the economy with *capital.*

interest rate The annual rate at which interest is paid; a percentage of the borrowed amount.

interest-rate effect The tendency for increases in the *price level* to increase the demand for money, raise interest rates, and, as a result, reduce total spending and real output in the economy (and the reverse for price-level decreases).

interindustry competition The competition for sales between the products of one industry and the products of another industry.

interlocking directorate A situation where one or more members of the board of directors of a *corporation* are also on the board of directors of a competing corporation; illegal under the *Clayton Act.*

intermediate goods Products that are purchased for resale or further processing or manufacturing.

internally held public debt *Public debt* owed to citizens, firms, and institutions of the same nation that issued the debt.

international balance of payments A summary of all the transactions that took place between the individuals, firms, and government units of one nation and those of all other nations during a year.

international balance-of-payments deficit (See *balance-of-payments deficit.*)

international balance-of-payments surplus (See *balance-of-payments surplus.*)

international gold standard (See *gold standard.*)

International Monetary Fund (IMF) The international association of nations that was formed after the Second World War to make loans of foreign monies to nations with temporary *payments deficits* and, until the early 1970s, to administer the *adjustable pegs.* It now mainly makes loans to nations facing possible defaults on private and government loans.

international monetary reserves The foreign currencies and other assets such as gold that a nation can use to settle a *balance-of-payments deficit.*

international value of the dollar The price that must be paid in foreign currency (money) to obtain one U.S. dollar.

intrinsic value The market value of the metal within a coin.

invention The first discovery of a product or process through the use of imagination, ingenious thinking, and experimentation and the first proof that it will work.

inventories Goods that have been produced but remain unsold.

inverse relationship The relationship between two variables that change in opposite directions, for example, product price and quantity demanded.

inverted-U theory A theory saying that, other things equal, *R&D* expenditures as a percentage of sales rise with industry concentration, reach a peak at a four-firm *concentration ratio* of about 50 percent, and then fall as concentration further increases.

investment Spending for the production and accumulation of *capital* and additions to inventories.

investment demand curve A curve that shows the amounts of *investment* demanded by an economy at a series of *real interest rates.*

investment goods Same as *capital* or capital goods.

investment in human capital (See *human capital investment.*)

investment schedule A curve or schedule that shows the amounts firms plan to invest at various possible values of *real gross domestic product.*

invisible hand The tendency of firms and resource suppliers that seek to further their own self-interests in competitive markets to also promote the interest of society.

Joint Economic Committee (JEC) Committee of senators and representatives that investigates economic problems of national interest.

Keynesian economics The macroeconomic generalizations that lead to the conclusion that a capitalistic economy is characterized by macroeconomic instability and that *fiscal policy* and *monetary policy* can be used to promote *full employment, price-level stability,* and *economic growth.*

Keynesianism The philosophical, ideological, and analytical views pertaining to *Keynesian economics.*

kinked-demand curve The demand curve for a noncollusive oligopolist, which is based on the assumption that rivals will match a price decrease and will ignore a price increase.

labor People's physical and mental talents and efforts that are used to help produce goods and services.

labor force Persons 16 years of age and older who are not in institutions and who are employed or are unemployed and seeking work.

labor-force participation rate The percentage of the working-age population that is actually in the *labor force*.

labor-intensive commodity A product requiring a relatively large amount of *labor* to be produced.

labor productivity Total output divided by the quantity of labor employed to produce it; the *average product* of labor or output per hour of work.

labor theory of value (Web chapter 40) The Marxian idea that the economic value of any commodity is determined solely by the amount of labor that is required to produce it.

labor union A group of workers organized to advance the interests of the group (to increase wages, shorten the hours worked, improve working conditions, and so on).

Laffer Curve A curve relating government tax rates and tax revenues and on which a particular tax rate (between zero and 100 percent) maximizes tax revenues.

laissez-faire capitalism (See *capitalism*.)

land Natural resources ("free gifts of nature") used to produce goods and services.

land-intensive commodity A product requiring a relatively large amount of *land* to be produced.

law of demand The principle that, other things equal, an increase in a product's price will reduce the quantity of it demanded, and conversely for a decrease in price.

law of diminishing marginal utility The principle that as a consumer increases the consumption of a good or service, the *marginal utility* obtained from each additional unit of the good or service decreases.

law of diminishing returns The principle that as successive increments of a variable resource are added to a fixed resource, the *marginal product* of the variable resource will eventually decrease.

law of increasing opportunity costs The principle that as the production of a good increases, the *opportunity cost* of producing an additional unit rises.

law of supply The principle that, other things equal, an increase in the price of a product will increase the quantity of it supplied, and conversely for a price decrease.

leakage (1) A withdrawal of potential spending from the income-expenditures stream via *saving,* tax payments, or *imports;* (2) a withdrawal that reduces the lending potential of the banking system.

learning by doing Achieving greater *productivity* and lower *average total cost* through gains in knowledge and skill that accompany repetition of a task; a source of *economies of scale*.

least-cost combination of resources The quantity of each resource a firm must employ in order to produce a particular output at the lowest total cost; the combination at which the ratio of the *marginal product* of a resource to its *marginal resource cost* (to its *price* if the resource is employed in a competitive market) is the same for the last dollar spent on each of the resources employed.

legal cartel theory of regulation The hypothesis that some industries seek regulation or want to maintain regulation so that they may form or maintain a legal *cartel*.

legal immigrant A person who lawfully enters a country for the purpose of residing there.

legal tender A legal designation of a nation's official currency (bills and coins). Payment of debts must be accepted in this monetary unit, but creditors can specify the form of payment, for example, "cash only" or "check or credit card only."

lending potential of an individual commercial bank The amount by which a single bank can safely increase the *money supply* by making new loans to (or buying securities from) the public; equal to the bank's excess reserves.

lending potential of the banking system The amount by which the banking system can increase the *money supply* by making new loans to (or buying securities from) the public; equal to the *excess reserves* of the banking system multiplied by the *monetary multiplier*.

liability A debt with a monetary value; an amount owed by a firm or an individual.

limited liability Restriction of the maximum loss to a predetermined amount for the owners (stockholders) of a *corporation*. The maximum loss is the amount they paid for their shares of stock.

limited-liability company An unincorporated business whose owners are protected by *limited liability*.

liquidity The ease with which an asset can be converted quickly into cash with little or no loss of purchasing power. Money is said to be perfectly liquid, whereas other assets have a lesser degree of liquidity.

loanable funds *Money* available for lending and borrowing.

loanable funds theory of interest The concept that the supply of and demand for *loanable funds* determine the equilibrium rate of interest.

lockout An action by a firm that forbids workers to return to work until a new collective bargaining contract is signed; a means of imposing costs (lost wages) on union workers in a collective bargaining dispute.

logrolling The trading of votes by legislators to secure favorable outcomes on decisions concerning the provision of *public goods* and *quasi-public goods*.

long run (1) In *microeconomics,* a period of time long enough to enable producers of a product to change the quantities of all the resources they employ; period in which all resources and costs are variable and no resources or costs are fixed. (2) In *macroeconomics,* a period sufficiently long for *nominal wages* and other input prices to change in response to a change in the nation's *price level*.

long-run aggregate supply curve The aggregate supply curve associated with a time period in which input prices (especially *nominal wages*) are fully responsive to changes in the *price level*.

long-run competitive equilibrium The price at which firms in *pure competition* neither obtain *economic profit* nor suffer losses in the *long run* and the total quantity demanded and supplied are equal; a price equal to the minimum long-run *average total cost* of producing the product.

long-run farm problem   The tendency for agriculture to be a declining industry as technological progress increases supply relative to an inelastic and slowly increasing demand.

long-run supply   A schedule or curve showing the prices at which a purely competitive industry will make various quantities of the product available in the *long run*.

Lorenz curve   A curve showing the distribution of income in an economy. The cumulated percentage of families (income receivers) is measured along the horizontal axis and cumulated percentage of income is measured along the vertical axis.

lump-sum tax   A tax that is a constant amount (the tax revenue of government is the same) at all levels of GDP.

M1   The most narrowly defined *money supply,* equal to *currency* in the hands of the public and the *checkable deposits* of commercial banks and thrift institutions.

M2   A more broadly defined *money supply,* equal to *M1* plus *noncheckable savings accounts* (including *money market deposit accounts*), small *time deposits* (deposits of less than $100,000), and individual *money market mutual fund* balances.

M3   A very broadly defined *money supply,* equal to *M2* plus large *time deposits* (deposits of $100,000 or more).

macroeconomics   The part of economics concerned with the economy as a whole; with such major aggregates as the household, business, and government sectors; and with measures of the total economy.

managed floating exchange rate   An *exchange rate* that is allowed to change (float) as a result of changes in currency supply and demand but at times is altered (managed) by governments via their buying and selling of particular currencies.

managerial-opposition hypothesis   An explanation that attributes the relative decline of unionism in the United States to the increased and more aggressive opposition of management to unions.

managerial prerogatives   The decisions that management of the firm has the sole right to make; often enumerated in the labor contract (work agreement) between a *labor union* and a *firm*.

marginal analysis   The comparison of marginal ("extra" or "additional") benefits and marginal costs, usually for decision making.

marginal benefit   The extra (additional) benefit of consuming 1 more unit of some good or service; the change in total benefit when 1 more unit is consumed.

marginal cost   The extra (additional) cost of producing 1 more unit of output; equal to the change in *total cost* divided by the change in output (and, in the short run, to the change in total *variable cost* divided by the change in output).

marginal product   The additional output produced when 1 additional unit of a resource is employed (the quantity of all other resources employed remaining constant); equal to the change in total product divided by the change in the quantity of a resource employed.

marginal productivity theory of income distribution   The contention that the distribution of income is equitable when each unit of each resource receives a money payment equal to its marginal contribution to the firm's revenue (its *marginal revenue product*).

marginal propensity to consume   The fraction of any change in *disposable income* spent for *consumer goods;* equal to the change in consumption divided by the change in disposable income.

marginal propensity to save   The fraction of any change in *disposable income* that households save; equal to the change in *saving* divided by the change in disposable income.

marginal rate of substitution   The rate at which a consumer is prepared to substitute one good for another (from a given combination of goods) and remain equally satisfied (have the same *total utility*); equal to the slope of a consumer's *indifference curve* at each point on the curve.

marginal resource cost   The amount the total cost of employing a *resource* increases when a firm employs 1 additional unit of the resource (the quantity of all other resources employed remaining constant); equal to the change in the *total cost* of the resource divided by the change in the quantity of the resource employed.

marginal revenue   The change in *total revenue* that results from the sale of 1 additional unit of a firm's product; equal to the change in total revenue divided by the change in the quantity of the product sold.

marginal-revenue–marginal-cost approach   A method of determining the total output where *economic profit* is a maximum (or losses are a minimum) by comparing the *marginal revenue* and the *marginal cost* of each additional unit of output.

marginal revenue product   The change in a firm's *total revenue* when it employs 1 additional unit of a resource (the quantity of all other resources employed remaining constant); equal to the change in total revenue divided by the change in the quantity of the resource employed.

marginal tax rate   The tax rate paid on each additional dollar of income.

marginal utility   The extra *utility* a consumer obtains from the consumption of 1 additional unit of a good or service; equal to the change in total utility divided by the change in the quantity consumed.

market   Any institution or mechanism that brings together buyers (demanders) and sellers (suppliers) of a particular good or service.

market demand   (See *total demand.*)

market economy   An economy in which only the private decisions of consumers, resource suppliers, and firms determine how resources are allocated; the *market system*.

market failure   The inability of a market to bring about the allocation of resources that best satisfies the wants of society; in particular, the overallocation or underallocation of resources to the production of a particular good or service because of *spillovers* or informational problems or because markets do not provide desired *public goods*.

market for externality rights   A market in which firms can buy rights to discharge pollutants. The price of such rights is determined by the demand for the right to discharge pollutants and a *perfectly inelastic supply* of such rights (the latter determined by the quantity of discharges that the environment can assimilate).

market period A period in which producers of a product are unable to change the quantity produced in response to a change in its price and in which there is a *perfectly inelastic supply*.

market system All the product and resource markets of a *market economy* and the relationships among them; a method that allows the prices determined in those markets to allocate the economy's scarce resources and to communicate and coordinate the decisions made by consumers, firms, and resource suppliers.

median-voter model The theory that under majority rule the median (middle) voter will be in the dominant position to determine the outcome of an election.

Medicaid A Federal program that helps finance the medical expenses of individuals covered by the *Supplemental Security Income (SSI)* and *Temporary Assistance for Needy Families (TANF)* programs.

Medicare A Federal program that is financed by *payroll taxes* and provides for (1) compulsory hospital insurance for senior citizens and (2) low-cost voluntary insurance to help older Americans pay physicians' fees.

medium of exchange Any item sellers generally accept and buyers generally use to pay for a good or service; *money;* a convenient means of exchanging goods and services without engaging in *barter*.

merger The combination of two (or more) firms into a single firm.

microeconomics The part of economics concerned with such individual units as *industries, firms,* and *households* and with individual markets, specific goods and services, and product and resource prices.

Microsoft case A 2002 antitrust case in which Microsoft was found guilty of violating the *Sherman Act* by engaging in a series of unlawful activities designed to maintain its monopoly in operating systems for personal computers; as a remedy the company was prohibited from engaging in a set of specific anticompetitive business practices.

minimum efficient scale The lowest level of output at which a firm can minimize long-run *average total cost*.

minimum wage The lowest *wage* employers may legally pay for an hour of work.

monetarism The macroeconomic view that the main cause of changes in aggregate output and the price level is fluctuations in the *money supply;* espoused by advocates of a *monetary rule*.

monetary multiplier The multiple of its *excess reserves* by which the banking system can expand *checkable deposits* and thus the *money supply* by making new loans (or buying securities); equal to 1 divided by the *reserve requirement*.

monetary policy A central bank's changing of the *money supply* to influence interest rates and assist the economy in achieving price stability, full employment, and economic growth.

monetary rule The rule suggested by *monetarism*. As traditionally formulated, the rule says that the *money supply* should be expanded each year at the same annual rate as the potential rate of growth of the *real gross domestic product;* the supply of money should be increased steadily between 3 and 5 percent per year. (Also see *Taylor rule*.)

money Any item that is generally acceptable to sellers in exchange for goods and services.

money capital Money available to purchase *capital;* simply *money,* as defined by economists.

money income (See *nominal income*.)

money market The market in which the demand for and the supply of money determine the *interest rate* (or the level of interest rates) in the economy.

money market deposit accounts (MMDAs) Interest-earning accounts at banks and *thrift institutions,* which pool the funds of depositors to buy various short-term securities.

money market mutual funds (MMMFs) Interest-bearing accounts offered by investment companies, which pool depositors' funds for the purchase of short-term securities. Depositors may write checks in minimum amounts or more against their accounts.

money supply Narrowly defined, *M*1; more broadly defined, *M*2 and *M*3.

monopolistic competition A market structure in which many firms sell a *differentiated product,* into which entry is relatively easy, in which the firm has some control over its product price, and in which there is considerable *nonprice competition*.

monopoly A market structure in which the number of sellers is so small that each seller is able to influence the total supply and the price of the good or service. (Also see *pure monopoly*.)

monopsony A market structure in which there is only a single buyer of a good, service, or resource.

moral hazard problem The possibility that individuals or institutions will change their behavior as the result of a contract or agreement. Example: A bank whose deposits are insured against loss may make riskier loans and investments.

most-favored-nation (MFN) status An agreement by the United States to allow some other nation's *exports* into the United States at the lowest tariff level levied by the United States, then or at any later time.

MR = MC rule The principle that a firm will maximize its profit (or minimize its losses) by producing the output at which *marginal revenue* and *marginal cost* are equal, provided product price is equal to or greater than *average variable cost*.

MRP = MRC rule The principle that to maximize profit (or minimize losses), a firm should employ the quantity of a resource at which its *marginal revenue product* (MRP) is equal to its *marginal resource cost* (MRC), the latter being the wage rate in pure competition.

multinational corporations Firms that own production facilities in two or more countries and produce and sell their products globally.

multiple counting Wrongly including the value of *intermediate goods* in the *gross domestic product;* counting the same good or service more than once.

multiplier The ratio of a change in the equilibrium GDP to the change in *investment* or in any other component of *aggregate expenditures* or *aggregate demand;* the number by which a change in any component of aggregate expenditures or aggregate demand must be multiplied to find the resulting change in the equilibrium GDP.

multiplier effect The effect on equilibrium GDP of a change in *aggregate expenditures* or *aggregate demand* (caused by a change in the *consumption schedule, investment,* government expenditures, or *net exports*).

mutual interdependence A situation in which a change in price strategy (or in some other strategy) by one firm will affect the sales and profits of another firm (or other firms). Any firm that makes such a change can expect the other rivals to react to the change.

national bank A *commercial bank* authorized to operate by the U.S. government.

National Credit Union Administration (NCUA) The federally chartered agency that insures deposit liabilities (up to $100,000 per account) in *credit unions*.

national health insurance (NHI) A proposed program in which the Federal government would provide a basic package of health care to all citizens at no direct charge or at a low cost-sharing level. Financing would be out of general tax revenues.

national income Total income earned by resource suppliers for their contributions to *gross domestic product;* equal to the gross domestic product minus *nonincome charges,* minus *net foreign factor income.*

national income accounting The techniques used to measure the overall production of the economy and other related variables for the nation as a whole.

National Labor Relations Act (Wagner Act of 1935) As amended, the basic labor-relations law in the United States; defines the legal rights of unions and management and identifies unfair union and management labor practices; established the *National Labor Relations Board.*

National Labor Relations Board (NLRB) The board established by the *National Labor Relations Act* of 1935 to investigate unfair labor practices, issue *cease-and-desist orders,* and conduct elections among employees to determine if they wish to be represented by a *labor union.*

natural monopoly An industry in which *economies of scale* are so great that a single firm can produce the product at a lower average total cost than would be possible if more than one firm produced the product.

natural rate of unemployment The *full-employment unemployment rate;* the unemployment rate occurring when there is no cyclical unemployment and the economy is achieving its potential output; the unemployment rate at which actual inflation equals expected inflation.

near-money Financial assets, the most important of which are *noncheckable savings accounts, time deposits,* and U.S. short-term securities and savings bonds, which are not a medium of exchange but can be readily converted into money.

negative GDP gap A situation in which actual *gross domestic product* is less than *potential output.*

negative relationship (See *inverse relationship.*)

net domestic product *Gross domestic product* less the part of the year's output that is needed to replace the *capital goods* worn out in producing the output; the nation's total output available for consumption or additions to the *capital stock.*

net export effect The idea that the impact of a change in *monetary policy* or *fiscal policy* will be strengthened or weakened by the consequent change in *net exports.* The change in net exports occurs because of changes in real interest rates, which affect exchange rates.

net exports *Exports* minus *imports.*

net foreign factor income Payments by a nation of resource income to the rest of the world minus receipts of resource income from the rest of the world.

net investment income The interest and dividend income received by the residents of a nation from residents of other nations less the interest and dividend payments made by the residents of that nation to the residents of other nations.

net private domestic investment *Gross private domestic investment* less *consumption of fixed capital;* the addition to the nation's stock of *capital* during a year.

net taxes The taxes collected by government less *government transfer payments.*

net transfers The personal and government transfer payments made by one nation to residents of foreign nations less the personal and government transfer payments received from residents of foreign nations.

net worth The total *assets* less the total *liabilities* of a firm or an individual; for a firm, the claims of the owners against the firm's total assets; for an individual, his or her wealth.

network effects Increases in the value of a product to each user, including existing users, as the total number of users rises.

new classical economics The theory that, although unanticipated price-level changes may create macroeconomic instability in the short run, the economy is stable at the full-employment level of domestic output in the long run because prices and wages adjust automatically to correct movements away from the full-employment, noninflationary output.

New Economy The label attached by some economists and the popular press to the U.S. economy since 1995. The main characteristics are accelerated *productivity growth* and *economic growth,* caused by rapid technological advance and the emergence of the global economy.

NLRB (See *National Labor Relations Board.*)

nominal gross domestic product (GDP) The *GDP* measured in terms of the price level at the time of measurement (unadjusted for *inflation*).

nominal income The number of dollars received by an individual or group for its resources during some period of time.

nominal interest rate The interest rate expressed in terms of annual amounts currently charged for interest and not adjusted for inflation.

nominal wage The amount of money received by a worker per unit of time (hour, day, etc.); money wage.

noncash transfer A *government transfer payment* in the form of goods and services rather than money, for example, food stamps, housing assistance, and job training; also called in-kind transfers.

noncollusive oligopoly An *oligopoly* in which the firms do not act together and in agreement to determine the price of the product and the output that each firm will produce.

noncompeting groups Collections of workers in the economy who do not compete with each other for employment because the skill and training of the workers in one group are substantially different from those of the workers in other groups.

nondiscretionary fiscal policy (See *built-in stabilizer.*)

nondurable good A *consumer good* with an expected life (use) of less than 3 years.

nonexcludability The inability to keep nonpayers (free riders) from obtaining benefits from a certain good; a *public good* characteristic.

nonexhaustive expenditure An expenditure by government that does not result directly in the employment of economic resources or the production of goods and services; see *government transfer payment.*

nonincome charges *Consumption of fixed capital* and *indirect business taxes;* amounts subtracted from *GDP* (along with *net foreign factor income*) in determining *national income.*

nonincome determinants of consumption and saving All influences on consumption and saving other than the level of *GDP.*

noninterest determinants of investment All influences on the level of investment spending other than the *interest rate.*

noninvestment transaction An expenditure for stocks, bonds, or secondhand *capital goods.*

nonmarket transactions The production of goods and services excluded in the measurement of the *gross domestic product* because they are not bought and sold.

nonprice competition Competition based on distinguishing one's product by means of *product differentiation* and then *advertising* the distinguished product to consumers.

nonpriced goods (Web chapter 3) Goods or resources that are not priced in markets because they are owned in common by society and available for the taking on public lands.

nonproduction transaction The purchase and sale of any item that is not a currently produced good or service.

nonrivalry The idea that one person's benefit from a certain good does not reduce the benefit available to others; a *public good* characteristic.

nontariff barriers All barriers other than *protective tariffs* that nations erect to impede international trade, including *import quotas,* licensing requirements, unreasonable product-quality standards, unnecessary bureaucratic detail in customs procedures, and so on.

normal good A good or service whose consumption increases when income increases and falls when income decreases, price remaining constant.

normal profit The payment made by a firm to obtain and retain *entrepreneurial ability;* the minimum income entrepreneurial ability must receive to induce it to perform entrepreneurial functions for a firm.

normative economics The part of economics involving value judgments about what the economy should be like; focused on which economic goals and policies should be implemented; policy economics.

North American Free Trade Agreement (NAFTA) A 1993 agreement establishing, over a 15-year period, a free-trade zone composed of Canada, Mexico, and the United States.

OASDHI (See *Old Age, Survivors, and Disability Health Insurance.*)

occupational discrimination The arbitrary restriction of particular groups from entering the more desirable, higher-paying occupations.

occupational licensure The laws of state or local governments that require that a worker satisfy certain specified requirements and obtain a license from a licensing board before engaging in a particular occupation.

occupational segregation The crowding of women or minorities into less desirable, lower-paying occupations.

official reserves Foreign currencies owned by the central bank of a nation.

Okun's law The generalization that any 1-percentage-point rise in the *unemployment rate* above the *full-employment unemployment rate* will increase the GDP gap by 2 percent of the *potential output* (GDP) of the economy.

Old Age, Survivors, and Disability Health Insurance (OASDHI) The social program in the United States financed by Federal *payroll taxes* on employers and employees and designed to replace the *earnings* lost when workers retire, die, or become unable to work.

oligopoly A market structure in which a few firms sell either a *standardized* or *differentiated product,* into which entry is difficult, in which the firm has limited control over product price because of *mutual interdependence* (except when there is collusion among firms), and in which there is typically *nonprice competition.*

OPEC (See *Organization of Petroleum Exporting Countries.*)

open economy An economy that exports and imports goods and services.

open-market operations The buying and selling of U.S. government securities by the *Federal Reserve Banks* for purposes of carrying out *monetary policy.*

open shop A place of employment in which the employer may hire nonunion workers and the workers need not become members of a *labor union.*

opportunity cost The amount of other products that must be forgone or sacrificed to produce a unit of a product.

Organization of Petroleum Exporting Countries (OPEC) A cartel of 11 oil-producing countries (Algeria, Indonesia, Iran, Iraq, Kuwait, Libya, Nigeria, Qatar, Saudi Arabia, Venezuela, and the UAE) that controls the quantity and price of crude oil exported by its members and that accounts for 60 percent of the world's export of oil.

other-things-equal assumption The assumption that factors other than those being considered are held constant.

outpayments The expenditures of domestic or foreign currency that the individuals, firms, and governments of one nation make to purchase goods and services, for remittances, to pay investment income, and for purchases of foreign assets.

output effect The situation in which an increase in the price of one input will increase a firm's production costs and reduce its level of output, thus reducing the demand for other inputs; conversely for a decrease in the price of the input.

paper money Pieces of paper used as a *medium of exchange;* in the United States, *Federal Reserve Notes.*

paradox of voting A situation where paired-choice voting by majority rule fails to provide a consistent ranking of society's preferences for *public goods* or services.

parity concept The idea that year after year a specific output of a farm product should enable a farmer to acquire a constant amount of nonagricultural goods and services.

parity ratio The ratio of the price received by farmers from the sale of an agricultural commodity to the prices of other goods paid by them; usually expressed as a percentage; used as a rationale for *price supports.*

partnership An unincorporated firm owned and operated by two or more persons.

patent An exclusive right given to inventors to produce and sell a new product or machine for 20 years from the time of patent application.

payments deficit (See *balance-of-payments deficit.*)

payments surplus (See *balance-of-payments surplus.*)

payroll tax A tax levied on employers of labor equal to a percentage of all or part of the wages and salaries paid by them and on employees equal to a percentage of all or part of the wages and salaries received by them.

P = MC rule The principle that a purely competitive firm will maximize its profit or minimize its loss by producing that output at which the *price* of the product is equal to *marginal cost,* provided that price is equal to or greater than *average variable cost* in the short run and equal to or greater than *average total cost* in the long run.

per capita GDP *Gross domestic product* (GDP) per person; the average GDP of a population.

per capita income A nation's total income per person; the average income of a population.

perfectly elastic demand Product or resource demand in which *quantity demanded* can be of any amount at a particular product *price;* graphs as a horizontal *demand curve.*

perfectly elastic supply Product or resource supply in which *quantity supplied* can be of any amount at a particular product or resource *price;* graphs as a horizontal *supply curve.*

perfectly inelastic demand Product or resource demand in which *price* can be of any amount at a particular quantity of the product or resource demanded; *quantity demanded* does not respond to a change in price; graphs as a vertical *demand curve.*

perfectly inelastic supply Product or resource supply in which *price* can be of any amount at a particular quantity of the product or resource demanded; *quantity supplied* does not respond to a change in price; graphs as a vertical *supply curve.*

per se violations Collusive actions, such as attempts by firms to fix prices or divide a market, that are violations of the *antitrust laws,* even if the actions themselves are unsuccessful.

personal consumption expenditures The expenditures of *households* for *durable* and *nondurable consumer goods* and *services.*

personal distribution of income The manner in which the economy's *personal* or *disposable income* is divided among different income classes or different households or families.

personal income The earned and unearned income available to resource suppliers and others before the payment of personal taxes.

personal income tax A tax levied on the taxable income of individuals, households, and unincorporated firms.

Personal Responsibility Act A 1996 law that eliminated the Federal government's six-decade-long guarantee of cash assistance for poor families, whether adults in the family work or not; sets a limit of 5 years on receiving *Temporary Assistance for Needy Families (TANF)* benefits and requires that able-bodied adults work after 2 years to continue to receive public assistance.

personal saving The *personal income* of households less personal taxes and *personal consumption expenditures; disposable income* not spent for *consumer goods.*

per-unit production cost The average production cost of a particular level of output; total input cost divided by units of output.

Phillips Curve A curve showing the relationship between the *unemployment rate* (on the horizontal axis) and the annual rate of increase in the *price level* (on the vertical axis).

planned investment The amount that *firms* plan or intend to invest.

plant A physical establishment that performs one or more functions in the production, fabrication, and distribution of goods and services.

"play or pay" A means of expanding health insurance coverage by requiring that employers either provide insurance for their workers or pay a special *payroll tax* to finance insurance for noncovered workers.

policy economics The formulation of courses of action to bring about desired economic outcomes or to prevent undesired occurrences.

political business cycle The alleged tendency of Congress to destabilize the economy by reducing taxes and increasing government expenditures before elections and to raise taxes and lower expenditures after elections.

positive economics The analysis of facts or data to establish scientific generalizations about economic behavior.

positive GDP gap A situation in which actual *gross domestic product* exceeds *potential output.*

positive relationship A direct relationship between two variables.

post hoc, ergo propter hoc fallacy The false belief that when one event precedes another, the first event must have caused the second event.

potential competition The new competitors that may be induced to enter an industry if firms now in that industry are receiving large *economic profits.*

potential output The real output *(GDP)* an economy can produce when it fully employs its available resources.

poverty A situation in which the basic needs of an individual or family exceed the means to satisfy them.

poverty rate The percentage of the population with incomes below the official poverty income levels that are established by the Federal government.

preferred provider organization (PPO) An arrangement in which doctors and hospitals agree to provide health care to insured individuals at rates negotiated with an insurer.

price The amount of money needed to buy a particular good, service, or resource.

price ceiling A legally established maximum price for a good or service.

price discrimination The selling of a product to different buyers at different prices when the price differences are not justified by differences in cost.

price elasticity of demand The ratio of the percentage change in *quantity demanded* of a product or resource to the percentage change in its *price;* a measure of the responsiveness of buyers to a change in the price of a product or resource.

price elasticity of supply The ratio of the percentage change in *quantity supplied* of a product or resource to the percentage change in its *price;* a measure of the responsiveness of producers to a change in the price of a product or resource.

price fixing The conspiring by two or more firms to set the price of their products; an illegal practice under the *Sherman Act.*

price floor A legally determined price above the *equilibrium price.*

price index An index number that shows how the weighted-average price of a "market basket" of goods changes over time.

price leadership An informal method that firms in an *oligopoly* may employ to set the price of their product: One firm (the leader) is the first to announce a change in price, and the other firms (the followers) soon announce identical or similar changes.

price level The weighted average of the prices of all the final goods and services produced in an economy.

price-level stability A steadiness of the price level from one period to the next; zero or low annual inflation; also called "price stability."

price-level surprises Unanticipated changes in the price level.

price maker A seller (or buyer) of a product or resource that is able to affect the product or resource price by changing the amount it sells (or buys).

price support A minimum price that government allows sellers to receive for a good or service; a legally established or maintained minimum price.

price taker A seller (or buyer) of a product or resource that is unable to affect the price at which a product or resource sells by changing the amount it sells (or buys).

price war Successive and continued decreases in the prices charged by firms in an oligopolistic industry. Each firm lowers its price below rivals' prices, hoping to increase its sales and revenues at its rivals' expense.

prime interest rate The benchmark *interest rate* that banks use as a reference point for a wide range of loans to businesses and individuals.

principal-agent problem A conflict of interest that occurs when agents (workers or managers) pursue their own objectives to the detriment of the principals' (stockholders') goals.

private good A good or service that is individually consumed and that can be profitably provided by privately owned firms because they can exclude nonpayers from receiving the benefits.

private property The right of private persons and firms to obtain, own, control, employ, dispose of, and bequeath *land, capital,* and other property.

private sector The *households* and business *firms* of the economy.

process innovation The development and use of new or improved production or distribution methods.

producer surplus (Web chapter 3) The difference between the actual price a producer receives (or producers receive) and the minimum acceptable price; the triangular area above the supply curve and below the market price.

product differentiation A strategy in which one firm's product is distinguished from competing products by means of its design, related services, quality, location, or other attributes (except price).

product innovation The development and sale of a new or improved product (or service).

product market A market in which products are sold by *firms* and bought by *households.*

production possibilities curve A curve showing the different combinations of two goods or services that can be produced in a *full-employment, full-production* economy where the available supplies of resources and technology are fixed.

productive efficiency The production of a good in the least costly way; occurs when production takes place at the output at which *average total cost* is a minimum and *marginal product* per dollar's worth of input is the same for all inputs.

productivity A measure of average output or real output per unit of input. For example, the productivity of labor is determined by dividing real output by hours of work.

productivity growth The percentage change in *productivity* from one period to another.

profit The return to the resource *entrepreneurial ability* (see *normal profit*); *total revenue* minus *total cost* (see *economic profit*).

profit-maximizing combination of resources The quantity of each resource a firm must employ to maximize its profit or minimize its loss; the combination in which the *marginal revenue product* of each resource is equal to its *marginal resource cost* (to its *price* if the resource is employed in a competitive market).

profit-sharing plan A compensation device through which workers receive part of their pay in the form of a share of their employer's profit (if any).

progressive tax A tax whose *average tax rate* increases as the taxpayer's income increases and decreases as the taxpayer's income decreases.

property tax A tax on the value of property (*capital, land, stocks* and *bonds,* and other *assets*) owned by *firms* and *households.*

proportional tax A tax whose *average tax rate* remains constant as the taxpayer's income increases or decreases.

proprietor's income The net income of the owners of unincorporated firms (proprietorships and partnerships).

protective tariff A *tariff* designed to shield domestic producers of a good or service from the competition of foreign producers.

public assistance programs Government programs that pay benefits to those who are unable to earn income (because of permanent disabilities or because they have very low income and dependent children); financed by general tax revenues and viewed as public charity (rather than earned rights).

public choice theory The economic analysis of government decision making, politics, and elections.

public debt The total amount owed by the Federal government to the owners of government securities; equal to the sum of past government *budget deficits* less government *budget surpluses*.

public good A good or service that is characterized by *nonrivalry* and *nonexcludability;* a good or service with these characteristics provided by government.

public interest theory of regulation The presumption that the purpose of the regulation of an *industry* is to protect the public (consumers) from abuse of the power possessed by *natural monopolies*.

public investments Government expenditures on public capital (such as roads, highways, bridges, mass-transit systems, and electric power facilities) and on *human capital* (such as education, training, and health).

public sector The part of the economy that contains all government entities; government.

public utility A firm that produces an essential good or service, has obtained from a government the right to be the sole supplier of the good or service in the area, and is regulated by that government to prevent the abuse of its monopoly power.

purchasing power The amount of goods and services that a monetary unit of income can buy.

purchasing power parity The idea that exchange rates between nations equate the purchasing power of various currencies. Exchange rates between any two nations adjust to reflect the price-level differences between the countries.

pure competition A market structure in which a very large number of firms sells a *standardized product,* into which entry is very easy, in which the individual seller has no control over the product price, and in which there is no nonprice competition; a market characterized by a very large number of buyers and sellers.

pure monopoly A market structure in which one firm sells a unique product, into which entry is blocked, in which the single firm has considerable control over product price, and in which *nonprice competition* may or may not be found.

pure profit (See *economic profit*.)

pure rate of interest An essentially risk-free, long-term interest rate that is free of the influence of market imperfections.

quantity demanded The amount of a good or service that buyers (or a buyer) desire to purchase at a particular price during some period.

quantity supplied The amount of a good or service that producers (or a producer) offer to sell at a particular price during some period.

quasi-public bank A bank that is privately owned but governmentally (publicly) controlled; each of the U.S. *Federal Reserve Banks*.

quasi-public good A good or service to which excludability could apply but that has such a large *spillover benefit* that government sponsors its production to prevent an underallocation of resources.

R&D Research and development activities undertaken to bring about *technological advance*.

rate of exchange The price paid in one's own money to acquire 1 unit of a foreign currency; the rate at which the money of one nation is exchanged for the money of another nation.

rate of return The gain in net revenue divided by the cost of an investment or an *R&D* expenditure; expressed as a percentage.

rational behavior Human behavior based on comparison of marginal costs and marginal benefits; behavior designed to maximize total utility.

rational expectations theory The hypothesis that firms and households expect monetary and fiscal policies to have certain effects on the economy and (in pursuit of their own self-interests) take actions that make these policies ineffective.

rationing function of prices The ability of market forces in competitive markets to equalize *quantity demanded* and *quantity supplied* and to eliminate shortages and surpluses via changes in prices.

real-balances effect The tendency for increases in the *price level* to lower the real value (or purchasing power) of financial assets with fixed money value and, as a result, to reduce total spending and real output, and conversely for decreases in the price level.

real-business-cycle theory A theory that *business cycles* result from changes in technology and resource availability, which affect *productivity* and thus increase or decrease long-run aggregate supply.

real capital (See *capital*.)

real GDP (See *real gross domestic product*.)

real gross domestic product (GDP) *Gross domestic product* adjusted for inflation; gross domestic product in a year divided by the GDP *price index* for that year, the index expressed as a decimal.

real income The amount of goods and services that can be purchased with *nominal income* during some period of time; nominal income adjusted for inflation.

real interest rate The interest rate expressed in dollars of constant value (adjusted for *inflation*) and equal to the *nominal interest rate* less the expected rate of inflation.

real wage The amount of goods and services a worker can purchase with his or her *nominal wage;* the purchasing power of the nominal wage.

recession A period of declining real GDP, accompanied by lower real income and higher unemployment.

recessionary gap The amount by which the *aggregate expenditures schedule* must shift upward to increase the real *GDP* to its full-employment, noninflationary level.

Reciprocal Trade Agreements Act A 1934 Federal law that authorized the president to negotiate up to 50 percent lower tariffs with foreign nations that agreed to reduce their tariffs on U.S. goods. (Such agreements incorporated the *most-favored-nation* clause.)

refinancing the public debt Paying owners of maturing government securities with money obtained by selling new securities or with new securities.

regressive tax A tax whose *average tax rate* decreases as the taxpayer's income increases and increases as the taxpayer's income decreases.

regulatory agency An agency, commission, or board established by the Federal government or a state government to control the prices charged and the services offered by a *natural monopoly*.

rental income The payments (income) received by those who supply *land* to the economy.

rent-seeking behavior The actions by persons, firms, or unions to gain special benefits from government at the taxpayers' or someone else's expense.

required reserves The funds that banks and thrifts must deposit with the *Federal Reserve Bank* (or hold as *vault cash*) to meet the legal *reserve requirement;* a fixed percentage of the bank's or thrift's checkable deposits.

reserve requirement The specified minimum percentage of its checkable deposits that a bank or thrift must keep on deposit at the Federal Reserve Bank in its district or hold as *vault cash*.

resource A natural, human, or manufactured item that helps produce goods and services; a productive agent or factor of production.

resource market A market in which *households* sell and *firms* buy resources or the services of resources.

retiring the public debt Reducing the size of the *public debt* by purchasing U.S. government securities or by not reissuing maturing securities.

revenue tariff A *tariff* designed to produce income for the Federal government.

reverse discrimination The view that the preferential treatment associated with *affirmative action* efforts constitutes discrimination against other groups.

right-to-work law A state law (in about 22 states) that makes it illegal to require that a worker join a *labor union* in order to retain his or her job; laws that make *union shops* and *agency shops* illegal.

roundabout production The construction and use of *capital* to aid in the production of *consumer goods*.

rule of reason The rule stated and applied in the *U.S. Steel case* that only combinations and contracts unreasonably restraining trade are subject to actions under the antitrust laws and that size and possession of monopoly power are not illegal.

rule of 70 A method for determining the number of years it will take for some measure to double, given its annual percentage increase. Example: To determine the number of years it will take for the *price level* to double, divide 70 by the annual rate of *inflation*.

sales tax A tax levied on the cost (at retail) of a broad group of products.

saving Disposable income not spent for consumer goods; equal to *disposable income* minus *personal consumption expenditures*.

saving schedule A schedule that shows the amounts *households* plan to save (plan not to spend for *consumer goods*), at different levels of *disposable income*.

savings and loan association (S&L) A firm that accepts deposits primarily from small individual savers and lends primarily to individuals to finance purchases such as autos and homes; now nearly indistinguishable from a *commercial bank*.

savings deposit A deposit that is interest-bearing and that the depositor can normally withdraw at any time.

savings institution (See *thrift institution*.)

Say's law The largely discredited macroeconomic generalization that the production of goods and services (supply) creates an equal *demand* for those goods and services.

scarce resources The limited quantities of *land, capital, labor,* and *entrepreneurial ability* that are never sufficient to satisfy people's virtually unlimited economic wants.

scientific method The procedure for the systematic pursuit of knowledge involving the observation of facts and the formulation and testing of hypotheses to obtain theories, principles, and laws.

seasonal variations Increases and decreases in the level of economic activity within a single year, caused by a change in the season.

secular trend A long-term tendency; a change in some variable over a very long period of years.

self-interest That which each firm, property owner, worker, and consumer believes is best for itself and seeks to obtain.

seniority The length of time a worker has been employed absolutely or relative to other workers; may be used to determine which workers will be laid off when there is insufficient work for them all and who will be rehired when more work becomes available.

separation of ownership and control The fact that different groups of people own a *corporation* (the stockholders) and manage it (the directors and officers).

service An (intangible) act or use for which a consumer, firm, or government is willing to pay.

Sherman Act The Federal antitrust act of 1890 that makes monopoly and conspiracies to restrain trade criminal offenses.

shirking Workers' neglecting or evading work to increase their *utility* or well-being.

shortage The amount by which the *quantity demanded* of a product exceeds the *quantity supplied* at a particular (below-equilibrium) price.

short run (1) In microeconomics, a period of time in which producers are able to change the quantities of some but not all of the resources they employ; a period in which some resources (usually plant) are fixed and some are variable. (2) In macroeconomics, a period in which nominal wages and other input prices do not change in response to a change in the price level.

short-run aggregate supply curve An aggregate supply curve relevant to a time period in which input prices (particularly *nominal wages*) do not change in response to changes in the *price level*.

short-run competitive equilibrium The price at which the total quantity of a product supplied in the *short run* in a purely competitive industry equals the total quantity of the product demanded and that is equal to or greater than *average variable cost.*

short-run farm problem The sharp year-to-year changes in the prices of agricultural products and in the incomes of farmers.

short-run supply curve A supply curve that shows the quantity of a product a firm in a purely competitive industry will offer to sell at various prices in the *short run;* the portion of the firm's short-run marginal cost curve that lies above its *average-variable-cost* curve.

shutdown case The circumstance in which a firm would experience a loss greater than its total *fixed cost* if it were to produce any output greater than zero; alternatively, a situation in which a firm would cease to operate when the *price* at which it can sell its product is less than its *average variable cost.*

simple multiplier The *multiplier* in any economy in which government collects no *net taxes,* there are no *imports,* and *investment* is independent of the level of income; equal to 1 divided by the *marginal propensity to save.*

slope of a line The ratio of the vertical change (the rise or fall) to the horizontal change (the run) between any two points on a line. The slope of an upward-sloping line is positive, reflecting a direct relationship between two variables; the slope of a downward-sloping line is negative, reflecting an inverse relationship between two variables.

Smoot-Hawley Tariff Act Legislation passed in 1930 that established very high tariffs. Its objective was to reduce imports and stimulate the domestic economy, but it resulted only in retaliatory tariffs by other nations.

social insurance programs Programs that replace the earnings lost when people retire or are temporarily unemployed, that are financed by payroll taxes, and that are viewed as earned rights (rather than charity).

social regulation Regulation in which government is concerned with the conditions under which goods and services are produced, their physical characteristics, and the impact of their production on society; in contrast to *industrial regulation.*

Social Security program (See *Old Age, Survivors, and Disability Health Insurance.*)

Social Security trust fund A Federal fund that saves excessive Social Security tax revenues received in one year to meet Social Security benefit obligations that exceed Social Security tax revenues in some subsequent year.

socially optimal price The price of a product that results in the most efficient allocation of an economy's resources and that is equal to the *marginal cost* of the product.

sole proprietorship An unincorporated *firm* owned and operated by one person.

special economic zones (Web chapter 40) Regions of China open to foreign investment, private ownership, and relatively free international trade.

special-interest effect Any result of government promotion of the interests (goals) of a small group at the expense of a much larger group.

specialization The use of the resources of an individual, a firm, a region, or a nation to concentrate production on one or a small number of goods and services.

speculation The activity of buying or selling with the motive of later reselling or rebuying for profit.

spillover A benefit or cost from production or consumption, accruing without compensation to nonbuyers and nonsellers of the product (see *spillover benefit* and *spillover cost*).

spillover benefit A benefit obtained without compensation by third parties from the production or consumption of sellers or buyers. Example: A beekeeper benefits when a neighboring farmer plants clover.

spillover cost A cost imposed without compensation on third parties by the production or consumption of sellers or buyers. Example: A manufacturer dumps toxic chemicals into a river, killing the fish sought by sport fishers.

SSI (See *Supplemental Security Income.*)

stagflation Inflation accompanied by stagnation in the rate of growth of output and an increase in unemployment in the economy; simultaneous increases in the *price level* and the *unemployment rate.*

Standard Oil case A 1911 antitrust case in which Standard Oil was found guilty of violating the *Sherman Act* by illegally monopolizing the petroleum industry. As a remedy the company was divided into several competing firms.

standardized product A product whose buyers are indifferent to the seller from whom they purchase it as long as the price charged by all sellers is the same; a product all units of which are identical and thus are perfect substitutes for each other.

startup (firm) A new firm focused on creating and introducing a particular new product or employing a specific new production or distribution method.

state bank A *commercial bank* authorized by a state government to engage in the business of banking.

state-owned enterprises (Web chapter 40) Businesses that are owned by the government; the major type of enterprises in Russia and China before their transitions to the market system.

statistical discrimination The practice of judging an individual on the basis of the average characteristic of the group to which he or she belongs rather than on his or her own personal characteristics.

stock (corporate) An ownership share in a corporation.

stock options Contracts that enable executives or other key employees to buy shares of their employers' stock at fixed, lower prices when the stock prices rise.

store of value An *asset* set aside for future use; one of the three functions of *money.*

strategic behavior Self-interested economic actions that take into account the expected reactions of others.

strategic trade policy The use of trade barriers to reduce the risk inherent in product development by domestic firms, particularly that involving advanced technology.

strike The withholding of labor services by an organized group of workers (a *labor union*).

structural-change hypothesis The explanation that ascribes the decline of unionism in the United States to changes in the structure of the economy and of the labor force.

structural unemployment Unemployment of workers whose skills are not demanded by employers, who lack sufficient skill to obtain employment, or who cannot easily move to locations where jobs are available.

subsidy   A payment of funds (or goods and services) by a government, firm, or household for which it receives no good or service in return. When made by a government, it is a *government transfer payment*.

substitute goods   Products or services that can be used in place of each other. When the price of one falls, the demand for the other product falls; conversely, when the price of one product rises, the demand for the other product rises.

substitution effect   (1) A change in the quantity demanded of a *consumer good* that results from a change in its relative expensiveness caused by a change in the product's price; (2) the effect of a change in the price of a *resource* on the quantity of the resource employed by a firm, assuming no change in its output.

sunk cost   A cost that has been incurred and cannot be recovered.

Supplemental Security Income (SSI)   A federally financed and administered program that provides a uniform nationwide minimum income for the aged, blind, and disabled who do not qualify for benefits under the *Old Age, Survivors, and Disability Health Insurance* or *unemployment insurance* program in the United States.

supply   A schedule showing the amounts of a good or service that sellers (or a seller) will offer at various prices during some period.

supply curve   A curve illustrating *supply*.

supply factor (in growth)   An increase in the availability of a resource, an improvement in its quality, or an expansion of technological knowledge that makes it possible for an economy to produce a greater output of goods and services.

supply-side economics   A view of macroeconomics that emphasizes the role of costs and *aggregate supply* in explaining *inflation, unemployment,* and *economic growth*.

surplus   The amount by which the *quantity supplied* of a product exceeds the *quantity demanded* at a specific (above-equilibrium) price.

surplus payment   A payment to a resource that is not required to ensure its availability in the production process; for example, land rent.

surplus value   (Web chapter 40) The amount by which a worker's daily output in dollar terms exceeds his or her daily wage; the amount of the worker's output appropriated by capitalists as profit; a Marxian term.

tacit collusion   Any method used by an oligopolist to set prices and outputs that does not involve outright (or overt) *collusion. Price leadership* is a frequent example.

TANF   (See *Temporary Assistance for Needy Families*.)

tariff   A tax imposed by a nation on an imported good.

taste-for-discrimination model   A theory that views discrimination as a preference for which an employer is willing to pay.

tax   An involuntary payment of money (or goods and services) to a government by a *household* or *firm* for which the household or firm receives no good or service directly in return.

tax incidence   The person or group that ends up paying a tax.

tax subsidy   A grant in the form of reduced taxes through favorable tax treatment. For example, employer-paid health insurance is exempt from Federal income and payroll taxes.

tax-transfer disincentives   Decreases in the incentives to work, save, invest, innovate, and take risks that allegedly result from high *marginal tax rates* and *transfer payments*.

Taylor rule   A modern monetary rule proposed by economist John Taylor that would stipulate exactly how much the Federal Reserve should change interest rates in response to divergences of real GDP from potential GDP and divergences of actual rates of inflation from a target rate of inflation.

technological advance   New and better goods and services and new and better ways of producing or distributing them.

technology   The body of knowledge and techniques that can be used to combine *economic resources* to produce goods and services.

Temporary Assistance for Needy Families (TANF)   A state-administered and partly federally funded program in the United States that provides financial aid to poor families; the basic welfare program for low-income families in the United States; contains time limits and work requirements.

terms of trade   The rate at which units of one product can be exchanged for units of another product; the price of a good or service; the amount of one good or service that must be given up to obtain 1 unit of another good or service.

theoretical economics   The process of deriving and applying economic theories and principles.

theory of human capital   The generalization that *wage differentials* are the result of differences in the amount of *human capital investment* and that the incomes of lower-paid workers are raised by increasing the amount of such investment.

thrift institution   A *savings and loan association, mutual savings bank,* or *credit union*.

tight money policy   Federal Reserve System actions that contract, or restrict, the growth of the nation's *money supply* for the purpose of reducing or eliminating inflation.

till money   (See *vault cash*.)

time deposit   An interest-earning deposit in a *commercial bank* or *thrift institution* that the depositor can withdraw without penalty after the end of a specified period.

token money   Coins having a *face value* greater than their *intrinsic value*.

total cost   The sum of *fixed cost* and *variable cost*.

total demand   The demand schedule or the *demand curve* of all buyers of a good or service; also called market demand.

total demand for money   The sum of the *transactions demand for money* and the *asset demand for money*.

total product   The total output of a particular good or service produced by a firm (or a group of firms or the entire economy).

total revenue   The total number of dollars received by a firm (or firms) from the sale of a product; equal to the total expenditures for the product produced by the firm (or firms); equal to the quantity sold (demanded) multiplied by the price at which it is sold.

total-revenue test   A test to determine elasticity of *demand* between any two prices: Demand is elastic if *total revenue* moves in the opposite direction from price; it is inelastic when it moves in the same direction as price; and it is of unitary elasticity when it does not change when price changes.

total spending   The total amount that buyers of goods and services spend or plan to spend; also called *aggregate expenditures*.

total supply   The supply schedule or the *supply curve* of all sellers of a good or service; also called market supply.

total utility   The total amount of satisfaction derived from the consumption of a single product or a combination of products.

township and village enterprises   (Web chapter 40) Privately owned rural manufacturing firms in China.

trade balance   The export of goods (or goods and services) of a nation less its imports of goods (or goods and services).

trade bloc   A group of nations that lower or abolish trade barriers among members. Examples include the *European Union* and the nations of the *North American Free Trade Agreement*.

trade controls   *Tariffs, export subsidies, import quotas,* and other means a nation may employ to reduce *imports* and expand *exports*.

trade deficit   The amount by which a nation's *imports* of goods (or goods and services) exceed its *exports* of goods (or goods and services).

trade surplus   The amount by which a nation's *exports* of goods (or goods and services) exceed its *imports* of goods (or goods and services).

trademark   A legal protection that gives the originators of a product an exclusive right to use the brand name.

tradeoff   The sacrifice of some or all of one economic goal, good, or service to achieve some other goal, good, or service.

trading possibilities line   A line that shows the different combinations of two products that an economy is able to obtain (consume) when it specializes in the production of one product and trades (exports) it to obtain the other product.

transactions demand for money   The amount of money people want to hold for use as a *medium of exchange* (to make payments); varies directly with the *nominal GDP*.

transfer payment   A payment of *money* (or goods and services) by a government to a *household* or *firm* for which the payer receives no good or service directly in return.

tying contract   A requirement imposed by a seller that a buyer purchase another (or other) of its products as a condition for buying a desired product; a practice forbidden by the *Clayton Act*.

unanticipated inflation   Increases in the price level (*inflation*) at a rate greater than expected.

underemployment   (1) The failure to produce the maximum amount of goods and services that can be produced from the resources employed; the failure to achieve *full production;* (2) a situation in which workers are employed in positions requiring less education and skill than they have.

undistributed corporate profits   After-tax corporate profits not distributed as dividends to stockholders; corporate or business saving; also called retained earnings.

unemployment   The failure to use all available *economic resources* to produce desired goods and services; the failure of the economy to fully employ its *labor force*.

unemployment compensation   (See *unemployment insurance*).

unemployment insurance   The social insurance program that in the United States is financed by state *payroll taxes* on employers and makes income available to workers who become unemployed and are unable to find jobs.

unemployment rate   The percentage of the *labor force* unemployed at any time.

uninsurable risk   An event that would result in a loss and whose occurrence is uncontrollable and unpredictable. Insurance companies are not willing to sell insurance against such a loss.

union shop   A place of employment where the employer may hire either *labor union* members or nonmembers but where nonmembers must become members within a specified period of time or lose their jobs.

unit elasticity   Demand or supply for which the *elasticity coefficient* is equal to 1; means that the percentage change in the quantity demanded or supplied is equal to the percentage change in price.

unit labor cost   Labor cost per unit of output; total labor cost divided by total output; also equal to the *nominal wage* rate divided by the *average product* of labor.

unit of account   A standard unit in which prices can be stated and the value of goods and services can be compared; one of the three functions of *money*.

unlimited liability   Absence of any limits on the maximum amount that an individual (usually a business owner) may become legally required to pay.

unlimited wants   The insatiable desire of consumers for goods and services that will give them satisfaction or *utility*.

unplanned changes in inventories   Changes in inventories that firms did not anticipate; changes in inventories that occur because of unexpected increases or decreases of aggregate spending (of *aggregate expenditures*).

unplanned investment   Actual investment less *planned investment;* increases or decreases in the *inventories* of firms resulting from production greater than sales.

urban collectives   (Web chapter 40) Chinese enterprises jointly owned by their managers and their workforces and located in urban areas.

Uruguay Round   A 1995 trade agreement (to be fully implemented by 2005) that established the *World Trade Organization (WTO),* liberalized trade in goods and services, provided added protection to intellectual property (for example, *patents* and *copyrights*), and reduced farm subsidies.

U.S. Steel case   The antitrust action brought by the Federal government against the U.S. Steel Corporation in which the courts ruled (in 1920) that only unreasonable restraints of trade were illegal and that size and the possession of monopoly power were not violations of the antitrust laws.

usury laws   State laws that specify the maximum legal interest rate at which loans can be made.

utility   The want-satisfying power of a good or service; the satisfaction or pleasure a consumer obtains from the consumption of a good or service (or from the consumption of a collection of goods and services).

utility-maximizing rule   The principle that to obtain the greatest *utility*, the consumer should allocate *money income* so that the last dollar spent on each good or service yields the same marginal utility.

value added   The value of the product sold by a *firm* less the value of the products (materials) purchased and used by the firm to produce the product.

value-added tax   A tax imposed on the difference between the value of the product sold by a firm and the value of the goods purchased from other firms to produce the product; used in several European countries.

value judgment   Opinion of what is desirable or undesirable; belief regarding what ought or ought not to be (regarding what is right or just and wrong or unjust).

value of money   The quantity of goods and services for which a unit of money (a dollar) can be exchanged; the purchasing power of a unit of money; the reciprocal of the *price level*.

variable cost   A cost that in total increases when the firm increases its output and decreases when the firm reduces its output.

VAT   (See *value-added tax*.)

vault cash   The *currency* a bank has in its vault and cash drawers.

velocity   The number of times per year that the average dollar in the *money supply* is spent for *final goods and services;* nominal GDP divided by the money supply.

vertical integration   A group of *plants* engaged in different stages of the production of a final product and owned by a single *firm*.

vertical intercept   The point at which a line meets the vertical axis of a graph.

vertical merger   The merger of one or more *firms* engaged in different stages of the production of a final product.

very long run   A period in which *technology* can change and in which *firms* can introduce new products.

vicious circle of poverty   (Web chapter 39) A problem common in some *developing countries* in which their low per capita incomes are an obstacle to realizing the levels of saving and investment requisite to acceptable rates of economic growth.

voice mechanism   Communication by workers through their union to resolve grievances with an employer.

voluntary export restrictions   Voluntary limitations by countries or firms of their exports to a particular foreign nation to avoid enactment of formal trade barriers by that nation.

wage   The price paid for the use or services of *labor* per unit of time (per hour, per day, and so on).

wage differential   The difference between the *wage* received by one worker or group of workers and that received by another worker or group of workers.

wage discrimination   The payment of a lower wage to members of a less preferred group than that paid to members of a more preferred group for the same work.

wage rate   (See *wage*.)

wages   The income of those who supply the economy with *labor*.

wealth   Anything that has value because it produces income or could produce income. Wealth is a stock; income is a flow. Assets less liabilities; net worth.

wealth effect   The tendency for people to increase their consumption spending when the value of their financial and real assets rises and to decrease their consumption spending when the value of those assets falls.

welfare programs   (See *public assistance programs*.)

Wheeler-Lea Act   The Federal act of 1938 that amended the *Federal Trade Commission Act* by prohibiting and giving the commission power to investigate unfair and deceptive acts or practices of commerce (such as false and misleading advertising and the misrepresentation of products).

"will to develop"   (Web chapter 39) The state of wanting economic growth strongly enough to change from old to new ways of doing things.

World Bank   (Web chapter 39) A bank that lends (and guarantees loans) to developing nations to assist them in increasing their *capital stock* and thus in achieving *economic growth;* formally, the International Bank for Reconstruction and Development.

world price   The international market price of a good or service, determined by world demand and supply.

World Trade Organization (WTO)   An organization of 145 nations (as of 2003) that oversees the provisions of the current world trade agreement, resolves trade disputes stemming from it, and holds forums for further rounds of trade negotiations.

WTO   (See *World Trade Organization*.)

X-inefficiency   The failure to produce any specific output at the lowest average (and total) cost possible.

Answers to Key Questions

CHAPTER 1

1-4 Use the economic perspective to explain why someone who is normally a light eater at a standard restaurant may become somewhat of a glutton at a buffet-style restaurant which charges a single price for all you can eat.

This behavior can be explained in terms of marginal costs and marginal benefits. At a standard restaurant, items are priced individually—they have a positive marginal cost. If you order more, it will cost you more. You order until the marginal benefit from the extra food no longer exceeds the marginal cost. At a buffet you pay a flat fee no matter how much you eat. Once the fee is paid, additional food items have a zero marginal cost. You therefore continue to eat until your marginal benefit becomes zero.

1-8 Explain in detail the interrelationships between economic facts, theory, and policy. Critically evaluate this statement: "The trouble with economic theory is that it is not practical. It is detached from the real world."

Economic theory consists of factually supported generalizations about economic behavior that can be used to formulate economic policies. Economic theory enables policymakers to formulate economic policies that are relevant to real-world goals and problems that are based upon carefully observed facts.

1-10 Indicate whether each of the following statements applies to microeconomics or macroeconomics:

(a), (d), and (f) are macro; (b), (c), and (e) are micro.

1-11 Identify each of the following as either a positive or a normative statement:
  a. The high temperature today was 89 degrees.
  b. It was too hot today.
  c. Other things being equal, higher interest rates reduce the total amount of borrowing.
  d. Interest rates are too high.

(a) and (c) are positive; (b) and (d) are normative.

1-12 Explain and give an illustration of (a) the fallacy of composition; and (b) the "after this, therefore because of this" fallacy. Why are cause-and-effect relationships difficult to isolate in the social sciences?

(a) The fallacy of composition is the mistake of believing that something true for an individual part is necessarily true for the whole. Example: A single auto producer can increase its profits by lowering its price and taking business away from its competitors. But matched price cuts by all auto manufacturers will not necessarily yield higher industry profits.
(b) The "after this, therefore because of this" fallacy is incorrectly reasoning that when one event precedes another, the first event necessarily caused the second. Example: Interest rates rise, followed by an increase in the rate of inflation, leading to the erroneous conclusion that the rise in interest rates caused the inflation. Actually higher interest rates slow inflation.

Cause-and-effect relationships are difficult to isolate because "other things" are continually changing.

CHAPTER 1 APPENDIX

1-2 Indicate how each of the following might affect the data shown in Table 2 and Figure 2 of this appendix:
  a. GSU's athletic director schedules higher-quality opponents.
  b. An NBA team locates in the city where GSU plays.
  c. GSU contracts to have all its home games televised.

(a) More tickets are bought at each price; the line shifts to the right.
(b) Fewer tickets are bought at each price; the line shifts to the left.
(c) Fewer tickets are bought at each price; the line shifts to the left.

1-3 The following table contains data on the relationship between saving and income. Rearrange these data into a meaningful order and graph them on the accompanying grid. What is the slope of the line? The vertical intercept? Interpret the meaning of both the slope and the intercept. Write the equation that represents this line. What would you predict saving to be at the $12,500 level of income?

Income (per year)	Saving (per year)
$15,000	$1,000
0	−500
10,000	500
5,000	0
20,000	1,500

Income column: $0; $5,000; $10,000, $15,000; $20,000. Saving column: $−500; 0; $500; $1,000; $1,500. Slope = 0.1 (= $1,000 − $500)/($15,000 − $10,000). Vertical intercept = $−500. The slope shows the amount of saving will increase for every $1 increase in income; the intercept shows the amount of saving (dissaving) occurring when income is zero. Equation: $S = \$-500 + 0.1Y$ (where S is saving and Y is income). Saving will be $750 at the $12,500 income level.

1-7 The accompanying graph shows curve XX and tangents at points A, B, and C. Calculate the slope of the curve at these three points.

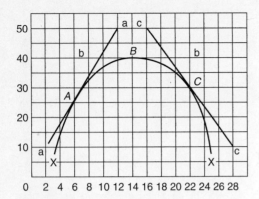

Slopes: at A = +4; at B = 0; at C = −4.

CHAPTER 2

2–4 Classify the following Microsoft resources as land, labor, capital, or entrepreneurial ability: code writers for software, Bill Gates, production facility for Windows CD-ROMs, "campus" on which Microsoft buildings sit, grounds crews at Microsoft campus, Microsoft corporate jet.

Land—campus where Microsoft buildings sit. *Labor*—code writers, grounds crews. *Capital*—production facility, corporate jet. *Entrepreneurial ability*—Bill Gates

2–5 Distinguish between full employment and full production as they relate to production possibilities analysis. Distinguish between productive efficiency and allocative efficiency. Give an illustration of achieving productive efficiency, but not allocative efficiency.

Full employment occurs when all available resources are utilized; full production means that all employed resources are used to provide the maximum possible satisfaction of material wants. Both are required for an economy to be producing on the production possibilities curve. An economy that is employing all available resources but which allocates labor to unproductive tasks will operate inside the curve. Likewise, putting resources to their most productive uses but failing to employ all resources will result in an economy producing inside the curve.

Allocative efficiency means that resources are being used to produce the goods and services most wanted by society. The economy is then located at the optimal point on its production possibilities curve where marginal benefit equals marginal cost for each good. Productive efficiency means the least costly production techniques are being used to produce wanted goods and services. Examples: manual typewriters produced using the least-cost techniques but for which there is no demand; cigarettes produced using least-cost techniques but for which there are "bads" created that are not accounted for by the market.

2–6 Here is a production possibilities table for war goods and civilian goods:

Type of production	Production alternatives				
	A	**B**	**C**	**D**	**E**
Automobiles	0	2	4	6	8
Missiles	30	27	21	12	0

a. Show these data graphically. Upon what specific assumptions is this production possibilities curve based?
b. If the economy is at point C, what is the cost of one more automobile? One more missile? Explain how this curve reflects increasing opportunity costs.

c. What must the economy do to operate at some point on the production possibilities curve?

(a) See curve EDCBA. The assumptions are full employment and productive efficiency, fixed supplies of resources, and fixed technology.

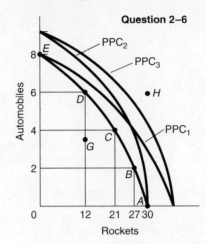

Question 2–6

(b) 4.5 rockets; .33 automobiles, as determined from the table. Increasing opportunity costs are reflected in the concave-from-the-origin shape of the curve. This means the economy must give up larger and larger amounts of rockets to get constant added amounts of automobiles—and vice versa.
(c) It must obtain full employment and productive efficiency.

2–11 Referring again to question 6, suppose improvement occurs in the technology of producing missiles but not in the production of automobiles. Draw the new production possibilities curve. Now assume that a technological advance occurs in producing automobiles but not in producing missiles. Draw the new production possibilities curve. Now draw a production possibilities curve that reflects technological improvement in the production of both products.

See the graph for question 2–6. PPC₁ shows improved missile technology. PPC₂ shows improved auto technology. PPC₃ shows improved technology in producing both products.

CHAPTER 3

3–2 What effect will each of the following have on the demand for product B?
 a. Product B becomes more fashionable.
 b. The price of substitute product C falls.
 c. Income declines and product B is an inferior good.
 d. Consumers anticipate the price of B will be lower in the near future.
 e. The price of complementary product D falls.

Demand increases in (a), (c), and (e); decreases in (b) and (d).

3–5 What effect will each of the following have on the supply of product B?
 a. A technological advance in the methods of producing B.
 b. A decline in the number of firms in industry B.
 c. An increase in the price of resources required in the production of B.
 d. The expectation that the equilibrium price of B will be lower in the future than it is currently.
 e. A decline in the price of product A, a good whose production requires substantially the same techniques as does the production of B.
 f. The levying of a specific sales tax upon B.

g. The granting of a 50-cent per unit subsidy for each unit of B produced.

Supply increases in (a), (d), (e), and (g); decreases in (b), (c), and (f).

3-7 Suppose the total demand for wheat and the total supply of wheat per month in the Kansas City grain market are as follows:

Thousands of bushels demanded	Price per bushel	Thousand of bushels supplied	Surplus (+) or shortage (−)
85	$3.40	72	_____
80	3.70	73	_____
75	4.00	75	_____
70	4.30	77	_____
65	4.60	79	_____
60	4.90	81	_____

a. What will be the market or equilibrium price? What is the equilibrium quantity? Fill in the surplus–shortage column and use it to explain why your answers are correct.
b. Graph the demand for wheat and the supply of wheat. Be sure to label the axes of your graph correctly. Label the equilibrium price "P" and the equilibrium quantity "Q."
c. Why will $3.40 not be the equilibrium price in this market? Why not $4.90? "Surpluses drive prices up; shortages drive them down." Do you agree?

Data from top to bottom: −13; −7; 0; +7; +14; and +21.

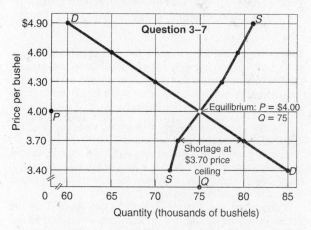

(a) P_e = $4.00; Q_e = 75,000. Equilibrium occurs where there is neither a shortage nor surplus of wheat. At the immediately lower price of $3.70, there is a shortage of 7,000 bushels. At the immediately higher price of $4.30, there is a surplus of 7,000 bushels. (See graph above.)
(b) Quantity (thousands) of bushels.
(c) Because at $3.40 there will be a 13,000 bushel shortage which will drive the price up. Because at $4.90 there will be a 21,000 bushel surplus which will drive the price down. Quotation is incorrect; just the opposite is true.

3-8 How will each of the following changes in demand and/or supply affect equilibrium price and equilibrium quantity in a competitive market; that is, do price and quantity rise, fall, remain unchanged, or are the answers indeterminate because they depend on the magnitudes of the shifts? Use supply and demand diagrams to verify your answers.
a. Supply decreases and demand is constant.
b. Demand decreases and supply is constant.
c. Supply increases and demand is constant.

d. Demand increases and supply increases.
e. Demand increases and supply is constant.
f. Supply increases and demand decreases.
g. Demand increases and supply decreases.
h. Demand decreases and supply decreases.

(a) Price up; quantity down;
(b) Price down; quantity down;
(c) Price down; quantity up;
(d) Price indeterminate; quantity up;
(e) Price up; quantity up;
(f) Price down; quantity indeterminate;
(g) Price up, quantity indeterminate;
(h) Price indeterminate and quantity down.

3-13 Refer to the table in question 7. Suppose that the government establishes a price ceiling of $3.70 for wheat. What might prompt the government to establish this price ceiling? Explain carefully the main effects. Demonstrate your answer graphically. Next, suppose that the government establishes a price floor of $4.60 for wheat. What will be the main effects of this price floor? Demonstrate your answer graphically.

At a price of $3.70, buyers will wish to purchase 80,000 bushels, but sellers will only offer 73,000 bushels to the market. The result is a shortage of 7,000 bushels. The ceiling prevents the price from rising to encourage greater production, discourage consumption, and relieve the shortage. See the graph below.

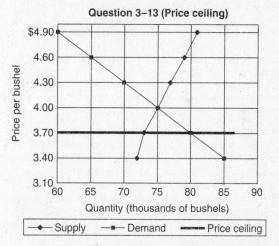

At a price of $4.60, buyers only want to purchase 65,000 bushels, but sellers want to sell 79,000 bushels, resulting in a surplus of 14,000 bushels. The floor prevents the price from falling to eliminate the surplus. See the graph below.

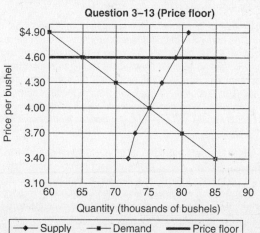

CHAPTER 4

4–7 Assume that a business firm finds that its profits will be at a maximum when it produces $40 worth of product A. Suppose also that each of the three techniques shown in the following table will produce the desired output.

Resource	Price per unit of resource	Technique No. 1	Technique No. 2	Technique No. 3
		Resource Units Required		
Labor	$3	5	2	3
Land	4	2	4	2
Capital	2	2	4	5
Entrepreneurial ability	2	4	2	4

a. With the resource prices shown, which technique will the firm choose? Why? Will production entail profits or losses? Will the industry expand or contract? When is a new equilibrium output achieved?

b. Assume now that a new technique, technique No. 4, is developed. It entails the use of 2 units of labor, 2 of land, 6 of capital, and 3 of entrepreneurial ability. Given the resource prices in the table, will the firm adopt the new technique? Explain your answers.

c. Suppose now that an increase in labor supply causes the price of labor to fall to $1.50 per unit, all other resource prices being unchanged. Which technique will the producer now choose? Explain.

d. "The market system causes the economy to conserve most in the use of those resources which are particularly scarce in supply. Resources that are scarcest relative to the demand for them have the highest prices. As a result, producers use these resources as sparingly as is possible." Evaluate this statement. Does your answer to part c, above, bear out this contention? Explain.

(a) Technique 2 because it produces the output with least cost ($34 compared to $35 each for the other two). Economic profit will be $6 (= 40 − $34), which will cause the industry to expand. Expansion will continue until prices decline to where total revenue is $34 (equal to total cost).

(b) Adopt technique 4 because its cost is now lowest at $32.

(c) Technique 1 because its cost is now lowest at $27.50.

(d) The statement is logical. Increasing scarcity causes prices to rise. Firms ignoring higher resource prices will become high-cost producers and be competed out of business by firms switching to the less expensive inputs. The market system forces producers to conserve on the use of highly scarce resources. Question 8c confirms this: Technique 1 was adopted because labor had become less expensive.

4–10 Some large hardware stores such as Home Depot boast of carrying as many as 20,000 different products in each store. What motivated the producers of those products—everything from screwdrivers to ladders to water heaters—to make them and offer them for sale? How did producers decide on the best combinations of resources to use? Who made these resources available, and why? Who decides whether these particular hardware products should continue to get produced and offered for sale?

The quest for profit led firms to produce these goods. Producers looked for and found the least-cost combination of resources in producing their output. Resource suppliers, seeking income, made these resources available. Consumers, through their dollar votes, ultimately decide on what will continue to be produced.

CHAPTER 5

5–2 Assume that the five residents of Econoville receive incomes of $50, $75, $125, $250, and $500. Present the resulting personal distribution of income as a graph similar to Figure 5.2. Compare the incomes of the lowest and highest fifth of the income receivers.

The distribution of income is quite unequal. The highest 20 percent of the residents receive 10 times more income than the lowest 20 percent.

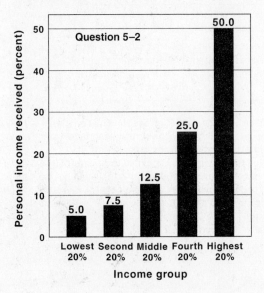

5–4 What are the three major legal forms of business organization? Which form is the most prevalent in terms of numbers? Why do you think that is so? Which form is dominant in terms of total profits? What major advantages of this form of business organization gave rise to its dominance?

The three legal forms of business organizations are: sole proprietorship, partnership, and corporation.

Proprietorships are the most prevalent. They are easy to start (relatively low cost), often don't require a large customer base to be profitable, and provide maximum freedom for the proprietor to do what she/he thinks best.

Corporations are dominant in terms of total profits. They can access large amounts of money by issuing stocks and bonds; their limited liability is attractive to potential owners; their size and broader ownership base help ensure continuity that helps to build a large customer base and gain cost advantages (a preview for economies of scale).

5–9 What are the two characteristics of public goods? Explain the significance of each for public provision as opposed to private provision. What is the free-rider problem as it relates to public goods? Is the U.S. border patrol a public good or a private good? Why? How about satellite TV? Explain.

Public goods are nonrival (one person's consumption does not prevent consumption by another) and nonexcludable (once the goods are produced nobody—including free riders—can be excluded from the goods' benefits). If goods are nonrival, there is less incentive for private firms to produce them—those purchasing the good could simply allow others to use it without compensation. Similarly, if goods are nonexcludable, private firms are unlikely to produce them as the potential for profit is low. The free-rider problem occurs when people benefit from the public good without contributing to the cost (tax revenue proportionate to the benefit received). The U.S. border patrol is a public good—my use and benefit does not prevent yours. Satellite TV is a private good—if the dish, receiver, and service go to my residence it can't go to my neighbors. The fact that I could invite my neighbor over to watch does not change its status from being a private good.

5-10 Draw a production possibilities curve with public goods on the vertical axis and private goods on the horizontal axis. Assuming the economy is initially operating *on the curve,* indicate how the production of public goods might be increased. How might the output of public goods be increased if the economy is initially operating at a point *inside the curve?*

On the curve, the only way to obtain more public goods is to reduce the production of private goods (from *C* to *B*).

An economy operating inside the curve can expand the production of public goods without sacrificing private goods (say, from *A* to *B*) by making use of unemployed resources.

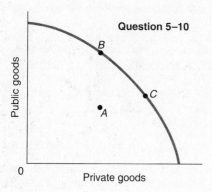

Question 5-10

Public goods (vertical axis) / *Private goods* (horizontal axis)

5-15 Suppose in Fiscalville there is no tax on the first $10,000 of income, but a 20 percent tax on earnings between $10,000 and $20,000 and a 30 percent tax on income between $20,000 and $30,000. Any income above $30,000 is taxed at 40 percent. If your income is $50,000, how much in taxes will you pay? Determine your marginal and average tax rates. Is it a progressive tax? Explain.

Total tax = $13,000; marginal tax rate = 40%; average tax rate = 26%. This is a progressive tax; the average tax rate rises as income goes up.

CHAPTER 6

6-4 The following are production possibilities tables for South Korea and the United States. Assume that before specialization and trade the optimal product-mix for South Korea is alternative B and for the United States alternative U.

Product	South Korea's production possibilities					
	A	**B**	**C**	**D**	**E**	**F**
Radios (in 1000s)	30	24	18	12	6	0
Chemicals (in tons)	0	6	12	18	24	30
	U.S. production possibilities					
Product	**R**	**S**	**T**	**U**	**V**	**W**
Radios (in 1000s)	10	8	6	4	2	0
Chemicals (in tons)	0	4	8	12	16	20

a. Are comparative cost conditions such that the two areas should specialize? If so, what product should each produce?
b. What is the total gain in radio and chemical output that results from this specialization?
c. What are the limits of the terms of trade? Suppose actual terms of trade are 1 unit of radios for 1-1/2 units of chemicals and that 4 units of radios are exchanged for 6 units of chemicals. What are the gains from specialization and trade for each area?
d. Can you conclude from this illustration that specialization according to comparative advantage results in more efficient use of world resources? Explain.

(a) Yes, because the opportunity cost of radios is less (1R = 1C) in South Korea than in the United States (1R = 2C). South Korea should produce radios and the United States should produce chemicals.

(b) If they specialize, the United States can produce 20 tons of chemicals and South Korea can produce 30,000 radios. Before specialization South Korea produced alternative B and the United States alternative U for a total of 28,000 radios (24,000 + 4,000) and 18 tons of chemicals (6 tons + 12 tons). The gain is 2,000 radios and 2 tons of chemicals.

(c) The limits of the terms of trade are determined by the comparative cost conditions in each country before trade: 1R = 1C in South Korea and 1R = 2C in the United States. The terms of trade must be somewhere between these two ratios for trade to occur.

If the terms of trade are 1R = 1-1/2C, South Korea would end up with 26,000 radios (= 30,000 − 4,000) and 6 tons of chemicals. The United States would have 4,000 radios and 14 tons of chemicals (= 20 − 6). South Korea has gained 2,000 radios. The United States has gained 2 tons of chemicals.

(d) Yes, the world is obtaining more output from its fixed resources.

6-6 True or false? "U.S. exports create a demand for foreign currencies; foreign imports of U.S. goods generate supplies of foreign currencies." Explain. Would a decline in U.S. consumer income or a weakening of U.S. preferences for foreign products cause the dollar to depreciate or appreciate? Other things equal, what would be the effects of that depreciation or appreciation on U.S. exports and imports?

The first part of this statement is incorrect. U.S. exports create a domestic *supply* of foreign currencies, not a domestic demand for them. The second part of the statement is accurate. The foreign demand for dollars (from U.S. exports) generates a supply of foreign currencies to the United States.

A decline in U.S. incomes or a weakening of U.S. preferences for foreign goods would reduce U.S. imports, reducing U.S. demand for foreign currencies. These currencies would depreciate (the dollar would appreciate). Dollar appreciation means U.S. exports would decline and U.S. imports would increase.

6-10 Identify and state the significance of each of the following: (a) WTO; (b) EU; (c) euro; and (d) NAFTA. What commonality do they share?

(a) The WTO oversees trade agreements reached by member nations and arbitrates trade disputes among them. (b) The EU is a trading bloc of 25 European countries who have agreed to abolish tariffs and import quotas on most products and have liberalized the movements of labor and capital within the EU. (c) The euro is the common currency that is used by 12 of the original 15 EU countries. (d) NAFTA is a trade bloc made up of the United States, Canada, and Mexico whose purpose is to reduce tariffs and other trade barriers among the three countries.

All of the above have the goals of increasing international trade and a better allocation of the world's resources.

CHAPTER 7

7–3 Why do national income accountants include only final goods in measuring GDP for a particular year? Why don't they include the value of stocks and bonds sold? Why don't they include the value of used furniture bought and sold?

The dollar value of final goods includes the dollar value of intermediate goods. If intermediate goods were counted, then multiple counting would occur. The value of steel (intermediate good) used in autos is included in the price of the auto (the final product).

The value of stocks and bonds sold is not included in GDP because such sales and purchases simply transfer the ownership of existing assets; such sales and purchases are not themselves (economic) investment and thus should not be counted as production of final goods and services.

Used furniture was produced in some previous year; it was counted as GDP then. Its resale does not measure new production.

7–8 Below is a list of domestic output and national income figures for a given year. All figures are in billions. The questions that follow ask you to determine the major national income measures by both the expenditure and income methods. The results you obtain with the different methods should be the same.

Personal consumption expenditures	$245
Net foreign factor income earned	4
Transfer payments	12
Rents	14
Consumption of fixed capital (depreciation)	27
Social Security contributions	20
Interest	13
Proprietors' income	33
Net exports	11
Dividends	16
Compensation of employees	223
Indirect business taxes	18
Undistributed corporate profits	21
Personal taxes	26
Corporate income taxes	19
Corporate profits	56
Government purchases	72
Net private domestic investment	33
Personal saving	20

a. Using the above data, determine GDP by both the expenditure and income approaches. Then determine NDP.
b. Now determine NI: first, by making the required additions and subtractions from GDP; and second, by adding up the types of income that make up NI.
c. Adjust NI (from part b) as required to obtain PI.
d. Adjust PI (from part c) as required to obtain DI.

(a) GDP = $388, NDP = $361
(b) NI = $339
(c) PI = $291
(d) DI = $265

7–11 Suppose that in 1984 the total output in a single-good economy was 7,000 buckets of chicken. Also suppose that in 1984 each bucket of chicken was priced at $10. Finally, assume that in 1996 the price per bucket of chicken was $16 and that 22,000 buckets were purchased. Determine the GDP price index for 1984, using 1996 as the base year. By what percentage did the price level, as measured by this index, rise between 1984 and 1996? Use the two methods listed in Table 7.6 to determine real GDP for 1984 and 1996.

$X/100 = \$10/\$16 = .625$ or 62.5 when put in percentage or index form $(.625 \times 100)$

$$\frac{100 - 62.5}{62.5} = .60 \text{ or } 60\% \text{ (Easily calculated } \frac{16 - 10}{10} =$$

$$\frac{6}{10} = .6 = 60\%)$$

Method 1: 1996 = (22,000 × $16) ÷ 1.0 = $352,000
            1984 = (7,000 × $10) ÷ .625 = $112,000
Method 2: 1996 = 22,000 × $16 = $352,000
            1984 = 7,000 × $16 = $112,000

7–12 The following table shows nominal GDP and an appropriate price index for a group of selected years. Compute real GDP. Indicate in each calculation whether you are inflating or deflating the nominal GDP data.

Year	Nominal GDP, billions	Price index (1996 = 100)	Real GDP, billions
1960	$ 527.4	22.19	$_____
1968	911.5	26.29	$_____
1978	2295.9	48.22	$_____
1988	4742.5	80.22	$_____
1998	8790.2	103.22	$_____

Values for real GDP, top to bottom of the column: $2,376.7 (inflating); $3,467.1 (inflating); $4,761.3 (inflating); $5,911.9 (inflating); $8,516 (deflating).

CHAPTER 8

8–2 Suppose an economy's real GDP is $30,000 in year 1 and $31,200 in year 2. What is the growth rate of its real GDP? Assume that population was 100 in year 1 and 102 in year 2. What is the growth rate of GDP per capita?

Growth rate of real GDP = 4 percent [(= $31,200 − $30,000)/ $30,000]. GDP per capita in year 1 = $300 (= $30,000/100). GDP per capita in year 2 = $305.88 (= $31,200/102). Growth rate of GDP per capita is 1.96 percent = [($305.88 − $300)/300].

8–4 What are the four phases of the business cycle? How long do business cycles last? How do seasonal variations and secular trends complicate measurement of the business cycle? Why does the business cycle affect output and employment in capital goods and consumer durable goods industries more severely than in industries producing nondurables?

The four phases of a typical business cycle, starting at the bottom, are trough, recovery, peak, and recession. As seen in Table 8.2, the length of a complete cycle varies from about 2 to 3 years to as long as 15 years.

There is a pre-Christmas spurt in production and sales and a January slackening. This normal seasonal variation does not signal boom or recession. From decade to decade, the long-term trend (the secular trend) of the U.S. economy has been upward. A period of no GDP growth thus does not mean all is normal, but that the economy is operating below its trend growth of output.

Because capital goods and durable goods last, purchases can be postponed. This may happen when a recession is forecast. Capital and durable goods industries therefore suffer large output declines during recessions. In contrast, consumers cannot long postpone the buying of nondurables such as food; therefore recessions only slightly reduce nondurable output. Also, capital and durable goods expenditures tend to be "lumpy." Usually, a large expenditure is needed to purchase them, and this shrinks to zero after purchase is made.

8-6 Use the following data to calculate (a) the size of the labor force and (b) the official unemployment rate: total population, 500; population under 16 years of age or institutionalized, 120; not in labor force, 150; unemployed, 23; part-time workers looking for full-time jobs, 10.

Labor force = #230 [= 500 − (120 + 150)]; official unemployment rate = 10% [(23/230) × 100].

8-8 Assume that in a particular year the natural rate of unemployment is 5 percent and the actual rate of unemployment is 9 percent. Use Okun's law to determine the size of the GDP gap in percentage-point terms. If the nominal GDP is $500 billion in that year, how much output is being forgone because of cyclical unemployment?

GDP gap = 8 percent [= (9 − 5)] × 2; forgone output estimated at $40 billion (= 8% of $500 billion).

8-11 If the price index was 110 last year and is 121 this year, what is this year's rate of inflation? What is the "rule of 70"? How long would it take for the price level to double if inflation persisted at (a) 2, (b) 5, and (c) 10 percent per year?

This year's rate of inflation is 10% or [(121 − 110)/110] × 100.
Dividing 70 by the annual percentage rate of increase of any variable (for instance, the rate of inflation or population growth) will give the approximate number of years for doubling of the variable.
(a) 35 years (= 70/2); (b) 14 years (= 70/5); (c) 7 years (= 70/10).

CHAPTER 9

9-5 Complete the accompanying table.

Level of output and income (GDP = DI)	Consumption	Saving	APC	APS	MPC	MPS
$240	$____	$ −4	____	____	____	____
260	$____	0	____	____	____	____
280	$____	4	____	____	____	____
300	$____	8	____	____	____	____
320	$____	12	____	____	____	____
340	$____	16	____	____	____	____
360	$____	20	____	____	____	____
380	$____	24	____	____	____	____
400	$____	28	____	____	____	____

Data for completing the table (top to bottom). Consumption: $244; $260; $276; $292; $308; $324; $340; $356; $372. APC: 1.02; 1.00; .99; .97; .96; .95; .94; .94; .93. APS: −.02; .00; .01; .03; .04; .05; .06; .06; .07. MPC: 80 throughout. MPS: 20 throughout.
  a. Show the consumption and saving schedules graphically.
  b. Find the break-even level of income. How is it possible for households to dissave at very low income levels?

c. If the proportion of total income consumed (APC) decreases and the proportion saved (APS) increases as income rises, explain both verbally and graphically how the MPC and MPS can be constant at various levels of income.

(a) See the graphs.

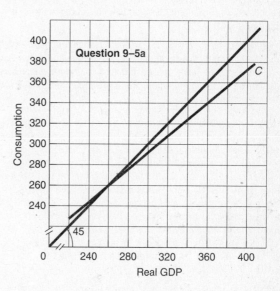

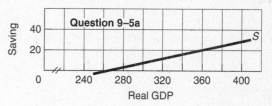

(b) Break-even income = $260. Households dissave borrowing or using past savings.
(c) Technically, the APC diminishes and the APS increases because the consumption and saving schedules have positive and negative vertical intercepts, respectively (Appendix to Chapter 1). MPC and MPS measure *changes* in consumption and saving as income changes; they are the *slopes* of the consumption and saving schedules. For straight-line consumption and saving schedules, these slopes do not change as the level of income changes; the slopes and thus the MPC and MPS remain constant.

9-7 Suppose a handbill publisher can buy a new duplicating machine for $500 and the duplicator has a 1-year life. The machine is expected to contribute $550 to the year's net revenue. What is the expected rate of return? If the real interest rate at which funds can be borrowed to purchase the machine is 8 percent, will the publisher choose to invest in the machine? Explain.

The expected rate of return is 10 percent ($50 expected profit/$500 cost of machine). The $50 expected profit comes from the net revenue of $550 less the $500 cost of the machine.
If the real interest rate is 8 percent, the publisher will invest in the machine as the expected profit (marginal benefit) from the investment exceeds the cost of borrowing the funds (marginal cost).

9-8 Assume there are no investment projects in the economy that yield an expected rate of return of 25 percent or more. But suppose there are $10 billion of investment projects yielding an expected rate of return of between 20 and 25 percent; another $10 billion yielding between 15 and 20 percent; another $10 billion between 10 and 15 percent; and so forth. Cumulate these data and present them graphically, putting the expected rate of net return on the vertical axis and the amount of investment on the horizontal axis. What will be the equilibrium level of aggregate investment if the real interest rate is (a) 15 percent, (b) 10 percent, and (c) 5 percent? Explain why this curve is the investment-demand curve.

See the graph that follows. Aggregate investment: (a) $20 billion; (b) $30 billion; (c) $40 billion. This is the investment-demand curve because we have applied the rule of undertaking all investment up to the point where the expected rate of return, r, equals the interest rate, i.

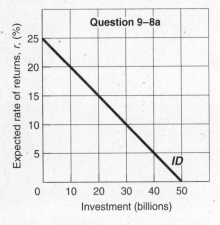

Question 9–8a

9–9 What is the multiplier effect? What relationship does the MPC bear to the size of the multiplier? The MPS? What will the multiplier be when the MPS is 0, .4, .6, and 1? What will it be when the MPC is 1, .9, .67, .5, and 0? How much of a change in GDP will result if firms increase their level of investment by $8 billion and the MPC is .80? If the MPC is .67?

The multiplier effect describes how an initial change in spending ripples through the economy to generate a larger change in real GDP. It occurs because of the interconnectedness of the economy, where a change in Lasslett's spending will generate

more income for Gavidia, who will in turn spend more, generating additional income for Grimes.

The MPC is directly (positively) related to the size of the multiplier. The MPS is inversely (negatively) related to the size of the multiplier.

The multiplier values for the MPS values: undefined, 2.5, 1.67, 0.

The multiplier values for the MPC values: undefined, 10, 3 (approx. actually 3.03), 2, 0.

If MPC is .80, change in GDP is $40 billion (5 × $8 = $40)

If MPC is .67, change in GDP is $24 billion (approximately) (3 × $8 = $24)

CHAPTER 10

10–2 Assuming the level of investment is $16 billion and independent of the level of total output, complete the following table and determine the equilibrium levels of output and employment in this private closed economy. What are the sizes of the MPC and MPS?

Possible levels of employment (millions)	Real domestic output (GDP = DI) (billions)	Consumption (billions)	Saving (billions)
40	$240	$244	$___
45	260	260	$___
50	280	276	$___
55	300	292	$___
60	320	308	$___
65	340	324	$___
70	360	340	$___
75	380	356	$___
80	400	372	$___

Saving data for completing the table (top to bottom): $ − 4; $0; $4; $8; $12; $16; $20; $24; $28.

Equilibrium GDP = $340 billion, determined where (1) aggregate expenditures equal GDP (C of $324 billion + I of $16 billion = GDP of $340 billion); or (2) where planned I = S (I of $16 billion = S of $16 billion). Equilibrium level of employment = 65 million; MPC = .8; MPS = .2.

10–9 The data in columns 1 and 2 of the table below are for a private closed economy.

(1) Real domestic output (GDP = DI) billions	(2) Aggregate expenditures private closed economy, billions	(3) Exports, billions	(4) Imports, billions	(5) Net exports, private economy	(6) Aggregate expenditures, open economy, billions
$200	$240	$20	$30	$___	$___
$250	$280	$20	$30	$___	$___
$300	$320	$20	$30	$___	$___
$350	$360	$20	$30	$___	$___
$400	$400	$20	$30	$___	$___
$450	$440	$20	$30	$___	$___
$500	$480	$20	$30	$___	$___
$550	$520	$20	$30	$___	$___

a. Use columns 1 and 2 to determine the equilibrium GDP for this hypothetical economy.
b. Now open up this economy to international trade by including the export and import figures of columns 3 and 4. Fill in columns 5 and 6 to determine the equilibrium GDP for the open economy. Explain why this equilibrium GDP differs from that of the closed economy.
c. Given the original $20 billion level of exports, what would be the equilibrium GDP if imports were $10 billion greater at each level of GDP?
d. What is the multiplier in this example?

(a) Equilibrium GDP for closed economy = $400 billion.
(b) Net export data for column 5 (top to bottom): $-10 billion in each space. Aggregate expenditure data for column 6 (top to bottom): $230; $270; $310; $350; $390; $430; $470; $510. Equilibrium GDP for the open economy is $350 billion, $50 billion below the $400 billion equilibrium GDP for the closed economy. The $-10 billion of net exports is a leakage that reduces equilibrium GDP by $50 billion.
(c) Imports = $40 billion: Aggregate expenditures in the private open economy would fall by $10 billion at each GDP level and the new equilibrium GDP would be $300 billion.
(d) Since every rise of $50 billion in GDP increases aggregate expenditures by $40 billion, the MPC is .8 and so the multiplier is 5.

10–12 Refer to columns 1 and 6 of the tabular data for question 9. Incorporate government into the table by assuming that it plans to tax and spend $20 billion at each possible level of GDP. Also assume that all taxes are personal taxes and that government spending does not induce a shift in the private aggregate expenditures schedule. Compute and explain the changes in equilibrium GDP caused by the addition of government.

Before G is added, open private sector equilibrium will be at $350. The addition of government expenditures of G to our analysis raises the aggregate expenditures $(C + I_g + X_n + G)$ schedule and increases the equilibrium level of GDP as would an increase in C, I_g, or X_n. Note that changes in government spending are subject to the multiplier effect. Government spending supplements private investment and export spending $(I_g + X + G)$, increasing the equilibrium GDP to $450.

The addition of $20 billion of government expenditures and $20 billion of personal taxes increases equilibrium GDP from $350 to $370 billion. The $20 billion increase in G raises equilibrium GDP by $100 billion (= $20 billion × the multiplier of 5); the $20 billion increase in T reduces consumption by $16 billion at every level (= $20 billion × the MPC of .8). This $16 billion decline in turn reduces equilibrium GDP by $80 billion ($16 billion × multiplier of 5). The net change from including balanced government spending and taxes is $20 billion (= $100 billion − $80 billion).

10–13 Refer to the table below in answering the questions that follow:

(1) Possible levels of employment, millions	(2) Real domestic output, billions	(3) Aggregate expenditures $(C_a + I_g + X_n + G)$, billions
90	$500	$520
100	550	560
110	600	600
120	650	640
130	700	680

a. If full employment in this economy is 130 million, will there be an inflationary gap or a recessionary gap? What will be the consequence of this gap? By how much would aggregate expenditures in column 3 have to change at each level of GDP to eliminate the inflationary or recessionary gap? Explain. What is the multiplier in this example?
b. Will there be an inflationary or recessionary gap if the full-employment level of output is $500 billion? Explain the consequences. By how much would aggregate expenditures in column 3 have to change at each level of GDP to eliminate the gap? Explain. What is the multiplier in this example?
c. Assuming that investment, net exports, and government expenditures do not change with changes in real GDP, what are the sizes of the MPC, the MPS, and the multiplier?

(a) A recessionary gap. Equilibrium GDP is $600 billion, while full employment GDP is $700 billion. Employment will be 20 million less than at full employment. Aggregate expenditures would have to increase by $20 billion (= $700 billion − $680 billion) at each level of GDP to eliminate the recessionary gap. The MPC is .8, so the multiplier is 5.
(b) An inflationary gap. Aggregate expenditures will be excessive, causing demand-pull inflation. Aggregate expenditures would have to *fall* by $20 billion (= $520 billion − $500 billion) at each level of GDP to eliminate the inflationary gap. The multiplier is still 5—the level of full employment GDP does not affect the multiplier.
(c) MPC = .8 (= $40 billion/$50 billion); MPS = .2 (= 1 − .8); multiplier = 5 (= 1/.2).

CHAPTER 11

11–4 Suppose that aggregate demand and supply for a hypothetical economy are as shown:

Amount of real domestic output demanded, billions	Price level (price index)	Amount of real domestic output supplied, billions
$100	300	$450
200	250	400
300	200	300
400	150	200
500	100	100

a. Use these sets of data to graph the aggregate demand and aggregate supply curves. What is the equilibrium price level and the equilibrium level of real output in this hypothetical economy? Is the equilibrium real output also necessarily the full-capacity real output? Explain.
b. Why will a price level of 150 not be an equilibrium price level in this economy? Why not 250?
c. Suppose that buyers desire to purchase $200 billion of extra real domestic output at each price level. Sketch in the new aggregate demand curve as AD_1. What factors might cause this change in aggregate demand? What is the new equilibrium price level and level of real output?

(a) See the graph. Equilibrium price level = 200. Equilibrium real output = $300 billion. No, the full-capacity level of GDP is more likely at $400 billion, where the AS curve starts to become steeper.
(b) At a price level of 150, real GDP supplied is a maximum of $200 billion, less than the real GDP demanded of $400 billion. The shortage of real output will drive the price level up.

At a price level of 250, real GDP supplied is $400 billion, which is more than the real GDP demanded of $200 billion. The surplus of real output will drive down the price level. Equilibrium occurs at the price level at which AS and AD intersect.

(c) See the graph. Increases in consumer, investment, government, or net export spending might shift the AD curve rightward. New equilibrium price level = 250. New equilibrium GDP = $400 billion.

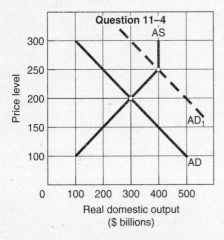

11–5 Suppose that a hypothetical economy has the following relationship between its real output and the input quantities necessary for producing that level of output:

a. What is productivity in this economy?

b. What is the per-unit cost of production if the price of each input is $2?

c. Assume that the input price increases from $2 to $3 with no accompanying change in productivity. What is the new per-unit cost of production? In what direction did the $1 increase in input price push the economy's aggregate supply curve? What effect would this shift in aggregate supply have upon the price level and the level of real output?

d. Suppose that the increase in input price does not occur but instead that productivity increases by 100 percent. What would be the new per-unit cost of production? What effect would this change in per-unit production cost have on the aggregate supply curve? What effect would this shift in aggregate supply have on the price level and the level of real output?

Input quantity	Real domestic output
150.0	400
112.5	300
75.0	200

(a) Productivity = 2.67 (= 400/150; = 300/112.5; = 200/75.0)

(b) Per-unit cost of production = $.75 (= $2 × 112.5/300)

(c) New per-unit production cost = $1.13 (= $3 × 75/200). The AS curve would shift leftward. The price level would rise and real output would decrease.

(d) New per-unit cost of production = $0.375 (= $2 × 112.5/600). AS curve shifts to the right; price level declines, and real output increases.

11–6 What effects would each of the following have on aggregate demand or aggregate supply? In each case use a diagram to show the expected effects on the equilibrium price level and level of real output. Assume that all other things remain constant.

a. A widespread fear of depression on the part of consumers.

b. A $2 increase in the excise tax on a pack of cigarettes.

c. A reduction in interest rates at each price level.

d. A major increase in Federal spending for health care.

e. The expectation of rapid inflation.

f. The complete disintegration of OPEC, causing oil prices to fall by one-half.

g. A 10 percent reduction in personal income tax rates.

h. A sizable increase in labor productivity (with no change in nominal wages).

i. A 12 percent increase in nominal wages (with no change in productivity).

j. Depreciation in the international value of the dollar.

(a) AD curve left, output down, and price level down (assuming no ratchet effect).

(b) AS curve left, output down, and price level up.

(c) AD curve right, output and price level up.

(d) AD curve right, output and price level up (any real improvements in health care resulting from the spending would eventually increase productivity and shift AS right).

(e) AD curve right, output and price level up.

(f) AS curve right, output up, and price level down.

(g) AD curve right, output and price level up.

(h) AS curve right, output up, and price level down.

(i) AS curve left, output down, and price level up.

(j) AD curve right (increased net exports); AS curve left (higher input prices).

11–7 Other things equal, what effect will each of the following have on the equilibrium price level and level of real output?

a. An increase in aggregate demand in the steep portion of the aggregate supply curve.

b. An increase in aggregate supply with no change in aggregate demand (assume that prices and wages are flexible upward and downward).

c. Equal increases in aggregate demand and aggregate supply.

d. A reduction in aggregate demand in the flat portion of the aggregate supply curve.

e. An increase in aggregate demand and a decrease in aggregate supply.

(a) Price level rises rapidly and little change in real output.

(b) Price level drops and real output increases.

(c) Price level falls slowly and real output falls rapidly.

(d) Price level does not change, but real output declines.

(e) Price level increases, but the change in real output is indeterminate.

CHAPTER 12

12–2 Assume that a hypothetical economy with an MPC of .8 is experiencing severe recession. By how much would government spending have to increase to shift the aggregate demand curve rightward by $25 billion? How large a tax cut would be needed to achieve this same increase in aggregate demand? Why the difference? Determine one possible combination of government spending increases and tax decreases that would accomplish this same goal.

In this problem, the multiplier is 1/.2 or 5, so the increase in government spending = $5 billion.

For the tax cut question, initial spending of $5 billion is still required, but only .8 (= MPC) of a tax cut will be spent. So .8 × tax cut = $5 billion or tax cut = $6.25 billion. Part of the tax reduction ($1.25 billion) is saved, not spent.

One combination: a $1 billion increase in government spending and a $5 billion tax cut.

12–3 What are government's fiscal policy options for ending severe demand-pull inflation? Use the aggregate demand-aggregate supply model to show the impact of these policies on the price level. Which of these fiscal policy options do you think might be favored by a person who wants to preserve the size of government? A person who thinks the public sector is too large?

Options are to reduce government spending, increase taxes, or some combination of both. See Figure 12.2. If the price level is flexible downward, it will fall. In the real world, the goal is to reduce inflation—to keep prices from rising so rapidly—not to reduce the price level. A person wanting to preserve the size of government might favor a tax hike and would want to preserve government spending programs. Someone who thinks that the public sector is too large might favor cuts in government spending since this would reduce the size of government.

12–7 Define the "full-employment budget," explain its significance, and state why it may differ from the "actual budget." Suppose the full-employment, noninflationary level of real output is GDP_3 (not GDP_2) in the economy depicted in Figure 12.3. If the economy is operating at GDP_2 instead of GDP_3, what is the status of its full-employment budget? Of its current fiscal policy? What change in fiscal policy would you recommend? How would you accomplish that in terms of the G and T lines in the figure?

The full-employment budget (also call standardized) measures what the Federal deficit or surplus would be if the economy reached full-employment level of GDP with existing tax and spending policies. If the full-employment budget is balanced, then the government is engaging in neither expansionary nor contractionary policy, even if, for example, a deficit automatically results when GDP declines. The "actual" budget is the deficit or surplus that results when revenues and expenditures occur over a year if the economy is not operating at full-employment.

Looking at Figure 12.3, if the full-employment GDP level was GDP_3, then the full-employment budget is contractionary since a surplus would exist. Even though the "actual" budget has no deficit at GDP_2, fiscal policy is contractionary. To move the economy to full employment, government should cut taxes or increase spending. You would raise the G line or lower the T line or a combination of each until they intersect at GDP_3.

12–10 Briefly state and evaluate the problem of time lags in enacting and applying fiscal policy. Explain the notion of a political business cycle. How might expectations of a near-term policy reversal weaken fiscal policy based on changes in tax rates? What is the crowding-out effect and why is it relevant to fiscal policy? In what respect is the net export effect similar to the crowding-out effect?

It takes time to ascertain the direction in which the economy is moving (recognition lag), to get a fiscal policy enacted into law (administrative lag), and for the policy to have its full effect on the economy (operational lag). Meanwhile, other factors may change, rendering inappropriate a particular fiscal policy. Nevertheless, discretionary fiscal policy is a valuable tool in preventing severe recession or severe demand-pull inflation.

A political business cycle is the concept that politicians are more interested in reelection than in stabilizing the economy. Before the election, they enact tax cuts and spending increases to please voters even though this may fuel inflation. After the election, they apply the brakes to restrain inflation; the economy will slow and unemployment will rise. In this view the political process creates economic instability.

A decrease in tax rates might be enacted to stimulate consumer spending. If households receive the tax cut but expect it to be reversed in the near future, they may hesitate to increase their spending. Believing that tax rates will rise again (and possibly concerned that they will rise to rates higher than before the tax cut), households may instead save their additional after-tax income in anticipation of needing to pay taxes in the future.

The crowding-out effect is the reduction in investment spending caused by the increase in interest rates arising from an increase in government spending, financed by borrowing. The increase in G was designed to increase AD but the resulting increase in interest rates may decrease I. Thus the impact of the expansionary fiscal policy may be reduced.

The net export effect also arises from the higher interest rates accompanying expansionary fiscal policy. The higher interest rates make U.S. bonds more attractive to foreign buyers. The inflow of foreign currency to buy dollars to purchase the bonds drives up the international value of the dollar, making imports less expensive for the United States, and U.S. exports more expensive for people abroad. Net exports in the United States decline, and like the crowding-out effect, diminish the expansionary fiscal policy.

CHAPTER 13

13–4 What are the components of the $M1$ money supply? What is the largest component? Which of the components is legal tender? Why is the face value of a coin greater than its intrinsic value? What near-monies are included in the $M2$ money supply? What distinguishes the $M2$ and $M3$ money supplies?

$M1$ = currency (in circulation) + checkable deposits. The largest component of $M1$ is currency (52 percent), and it is the only part that is legal tender. If the face value of a coin were not greater than its intrinsic (metallic) value, people would remove coins from circulation and sell them for their metallic content. $M2$ = $M1$ + noncheckable savings deposits + money market deposit accounts + small time deposits + money market mutual fund balances. $M3$ = $M2$ + large time deposits (those of $100,000 or more). Near-monies are components of $M2$ and $M3$ not included in $M1$. $M3$ is distinguished from $M2$ by large time deposits (certificates of deposit).

13–6 Suppose the price level and value of the dollar in year 1 are 1.0 and $1.00, respectively. If the price level rises to 1.25 in year 2, what is the new value of the dollar? If instead the price level had fallen to .50, what would have been the value of the dollar? What generalization can you draw from your answer?

In the first case, the value of the dollar (in year 2, relative to year 1) is $.80 (= 1/1.25); in the second case the value is $2 (= 1/.50). Generalization: The price level and the value of the dollar are inversely related.

13–7 What is the basic determinant of (a) the transactions demand and (b) the asset demand for money? Explain how these two demands can be combined graphically to determine total money demand. How is the equilibrium interest rate in the money market determined? How might (a) the expanded use of credit cards, (b) a shortening of worker pay periods, and (c) an increase in nominal GDP each independently affect the transactions demand for money and the equilibrium interest rate?

(a) The level of nominal GDP. The higher this level, the greater the amount of money demanded for transactions. (b) The interest rate. The higher the interest rate, the smaller the amount of money demanded as an asset.

On a graph measuring the interest rate vertically and the amount of money demanded horizontally, the two demands for the money curves can be summed horizontally to get the total demand for money. This total demand shows the total amount of money demanded at each interest rate. The equilibrium interest rate is determined at the intersection of the total demand for money curve and the supply of money curve.

(a) Expanded use of credit cards: transaction demand for money declines; total demand for money declines; interest rate falls. (b) Shortening of worker pay periods: transaction demand for money declines; total demand for money declines; interest rate falls. (c) Increase in nominal GDP: transaction demand for money increases; total demand for money increases; interest rate rises.

CHAPTER 14

14–2 Why are commercial banks required to have reserves? Explain why reserves are an asset to commercial banks but a liability to the Federal Reserve Banks. What are excess reserves? How do you calculate the amount of excess reserves held by a bank? What is the significance of excess reserves?

Reserves provide the Fed a means of controlling the money supply. It is through increasing and decreasing excess reserves that the Fed is able to achieve a money supply of the size it thinks best for the economy.

Reserves are assets of commercial banks because these funds are cash belonging to them; they are a claim the commercial banks have against the Federal Reserve Bank. Reserves deposited at the Fed are a liability to the Fed because they are funds it owes; they are claims that commercial banks have against it.

Excess reserves are the amount by which actual reserves exceed required reserves: Excess reserves = actual reserves − required reserves. Commercial banks can safely lend excess reserves, thereby increasing the money supply.

14–4 "When a commercial bank makes loans, it creates money; when loans are repaid, money is destroyed." Explain.

Banks add to checking account balances when they make loans; these checkable deposits are part of the money supply. People pay off loans by writing checks; checkable deposits fall, meaning the money supply drops. Money is "destroyed."

14–8 Suppose that Continental Bank has the simplified balance sheet shown below and that the reserve ratio is 20 percent:

	Assets			Liabilities and net worth	
		(1)	(2)		(1)	(2)
Reserves	$22,000	____	____	Checkable deposits $100,000	____	____
Securities	38,000	____	____			
Loans	40,000	____	____			

a. What is the maximum amount of new loans that this bank can make? Show in column 1 how the bank's balance sheet will appear after the bank has lent this additional amount.
b. By how much has the supply of money changed? Explain.
c. How will the bank's balance sheet appear after checks drawn for the entire amount of the new loans have been cleared against this bank? Show this new balance sheet in column 2.
d. Answer questions a, b, and c on the assumption that the reserve ratio is 15 percent.

(a) $2,000. Column 1 of Assets (top to bottom): $22,000; $38,000; $42,000. Column 1 of Liabilities: $102,000.
(b) $2,000. The bank has lent out its excess reserves, creating $2,000 of new demand-deposit money.

(c) Column 2 of Assets (top to bottom): $20,000; $38,000; $42,000. Column 2 of Liabilities; $100,000.
(d) (a) $7,000. Column 1 of Assets (top to bottom): $22,000; $38,000; $47,000. Column 1 of Liabilities: $107,000.
(b) $7,000
(c) Column 2 of Assets (top to bottom): $15,000; $38,000; $47,000. Column 1 of Liabilities: $100,000.

14–13 Suppose the simplified consolidated balance sheet shown below is for the entire commercial banking system. All figures are in billions. The reserve ratio is 25 percent.

Assets		(1)	Liabilities and Net Worth		(2)
Reserves	$ 52	____	Checkable deposits	$200	____
Securities	48	____			
Loans	100	____			

a. What amount of excess reserves does the commercial banking system have? What is the maximum amount the banking system might lend? Show in column 1 how the consolidated balance sheet would look after this amount has been lent. What is the monetary multiplier?
b. Answer question 13a assuming that the reserve ratio is 20 percent. Explain the resulting difference in the lending ability of the commercial banking system.

(a) Required reserves = $50 billion (= 25% of $200 billion); so excess reserves = $2 billion (= $52 billion − $50 billion). Maximum amount banking system can lend = $8 billion (= 1/.25 ∞ $2 billion). Column (1) of Assets data (top to bottom): $52 billion; $48 billion; $108 billion. Column (1) of Liabilities data: $208 billion. Monetary multiplier = 4 (= 1/.25).
(b) Required reserves = $40 billion (= 20% of $200 billion); so excess reserves = $12 billion (= $52 billion − $40 billion). Maximum amount banking system can lend = $60 billion (= 1/.20 ∞ $12 billion). Column (1) data for assets after loans (top to bottom); $52 billion; $48 billion; $160 billion. Column (1) data for liabilities after loans: $260 billion. Monetary multiplier = 5 (= 1/.20). The decrease in the reserve ratio increases the banking system's excess reserves from $2 billion to $12 billion and increases the size of the monetary multiplier from 4 to 5. Lending capacity becomes 5 ∞ $12 = $609 billion.

CHAPTER 15

15–2 In the table below you will find simplified consolidated balance sheets for the commercial banking system and the 12 Federal Reserve Banks. Use columns 1 through 3 to indicate how the balance sheets would read after each of transactions a to c is completed. Do not cumulate your answers; that is, analyze each transaction separately, starting in each case from the figures provided. All accounts are in billions of dollars.

Consolidated Balance Sheet: All Commercial Banks			
		(1)	(2)	(3)
Assets:				
Reserves	$ 33	____	____	____
Securities	60	____	____	____
Loans	60	____	____	____
Liabilities and net worth:				
Checkable deposits	150	____	____	____
Loans from the Federal Reserve Banks	3	____	____	____

Consolidated Balance Sheet: Twelve Federal Reserve Banks			
	(1)	(2)	(3)
Assets:			
Securities	$60	___	___ ___
Loans to commercial banks	3	___	___ ___
Liabilities and net worth:			
Reserves of commercial banks	$33	___	___ ___
Treasury deposits	3	___	___ ___
Federal Reserve Notes	27	___	___ ___

a. A decline in the discount rate prompts commercial banks to borrow an additional $1 billion from the Federal Reserve Banks. Show the new balance-sheet figures in column 1 of each table.

b. The Federal Reserve Banks sell $3 billion in securities to members of the public, who pay for the bonds with checks. Show the new balance-sheet figures in column 2 of each table.

c. The Federal Reserve Banks buy $2 billion of securities from commercial banks. Show the new balance sheet figures in column 3 of each table.

d. Now review each of the above three transactions, asking yourself these three questions: (1) What change, if any, took place in the money supply as a direct and immediate result of each transaction? (2) What increase or decrease in commercial banks' reserves took place in each transaction? (3) Assuming a reserve ratio of 20 percent, what change in the money-creating potential of the commercial banking system occurred as a result of each transaction?

(a) Column (1) data, top to bottom: Bank Assets: $34, 60, 60; Liabilities: $150, 4; Fed Assets: $60, 4; Liabilities: $34, 3, 27.
(b) Column (2) data: Bank Assets: $30, 60, 60; Liabilities: $147, 3; Fed Assets: $57, 3, 30, 3, 27.
(c) Column (3) data (top to bottom): $35; $58; $60; $150; $3; (Fed banks) $62; $3; $35; $3; $27.
(d) (1) Money supply (checkable deposits) directly changes only in (b), where it decreases by $3 billion; (2) See balance sheets; (3) Money-creating potential of the banking system increases by $5 billion in (a); decreases by $12 billion in (b) (not by $15 billion—the writing of $3 billion of checks by the public to buy bonds reduces demand deposits by $3 billion, thus freeing $0.6 billion of reserves. Three billion dollars minus $0.6 billion equals $2.4 billion of reduced reserves, and this multiplied by the monetary multiplier of 5 equals $12 billion); and increases by $10 billion in (c).

15–3 Suppose that you are a member of the Board of Governors of the Federal Reserve System. The economy is experiencing a sharp and prolonged inflationary trend. What changes in **(a)** the reserve ratio, **(b)** the discount rate, and **(c)** open-market operations would you recommend? Explain in each case how the change you advocate would affect commercial bank reserves, the money supply, interest rates, and aggregate demand.

(a) Increase the reserve ratio. This would increase the size of required reserves. If the commercial banks were fully loaned up, they would have to call in loans. The money supply would decrease, interest rates would rise, and aggregate demand would decline.
(b) Increase the discount rate. This would decrease commercial bank borrowing from the Fed. Actual reserves of the commercial banks would fall, as would excess reserves and lending. The money supply would drop, interest rates would rise, and aggregate demand would decline.

(c) Sell government securities in the open market. Buyers of the bonds would write checks to the Fed on their demand deposits. When these checks cleared, reserves would flow from the banking system to the Fed. The decline in reserves would reduce the money supply, which would increase interest rates and reduce aggregate demand.

15–6 Distinguish between the Federal funds rate and the prime interest rate. In what way is the Federal funds rate a measure of the tightness or looseness of monetary policy? In 2001 the Fed used open-market operations to significantly reduce the Federal funds rate. What was the logic of those actions? What was the effect on the prime interest rate?

The Federal funds interest rate is the interest rate banks charge one another on overnight loans needed to meet the reserve requirement. The prime interest rate is the interest rate banks charge on loans to their most creditworthy customers. The tighter the monetary policy, the less the supply of excess reserves in the banking system and the higher the Federal funds rate. The reverse is true of a loose or easy monetary policy, which expands excess reserves, and the federal funds rate falls.

The Fed wanted to increase excess reserves, increase money supply growth, and lower real interest rates. In 2001 the U.S. economy was in the midst of recession, with spending in decline and stock prices falling. The terrorist attacks of September 11, 2001, added further uncertainty to the already weak economic outlook, and an easy money policy was seen as a way to boost confidence. The prime interest rate fell as a result of these actions.

15–8 Suppose the Federal Reserve decides to engage in a tight money policy as a way to reduce demand-pull inflation. Use the aggregate demand–aggregate supply model to show what this policy is intended to accomplish in a closed economy. Now introduce the open economy and explain how changes in the international value of the dollar might affect the location of your aggregate demand curve.

The intent of a tight money policy would be shown as a leftward shift of the aggregate demand curve and a decline in the price level (or, in the real world, a reduction in the rate of inflation). In an open economy, the interest rate hike resulting from the tight money policy would entice people abroad to buy U.S. securities. Because they would need U.S. dollars to buy these securities, the international demand for dollars would rise, causing the dollar to appreciate. Net exports would fall, pushing the aggregate demand curve farther leftward than in the closed economy.

CHAPTER 16

16–3 Suppose the full-employment level of real output (Q) for a hypothetical economy is $250 and the price level (P) initially is 100. Use the short-run aggregate supply schedules below to answer the questions that follow:

AS(P_{100})		AS(P_{125})		AS(P_{75})	
P	Q	P	Q	P	Q
125	280	125	250	125	310
100	250	100	220	100	280
75	220	75	190	75	250

a. What will be the level of real output in the *short run* if the price level unexpectedly rises from 100 to 125 because of an increase in aggregate demand? What if the price level falls unexpectedly from 100 to 75 because of a decrease in aggregate demand? Explain each situation, using numbers from the table.

b. What will be the level of real output in the long run when the price level rises from 100 to 125? When it falls from 100 to 75? Explain each situation.

c. Show the circumstances described in parts a and b on graph paper, and derive the long-run aggregate supply curve.

(a) $280; $220. When the price level rises from 100 to 125 [in aggregate supply schedule $AS(P_{100})$], producers experience higher prices for their products. Because nominal wages are constant, profits rise and producers increase output to $Q = \$280$. When the price level decreases from 100 to 75, profits decline and producers adjust their output to $Q = \$75$. These are short-run responses to changes in the price level.
(b) $250; $250. In the long run a rise in the price level to 125 leads to nominal wage increases. The $AS(P_{100})$ schedule changes to $AS(P_{125})$ and Q returns to $250, now at a price level of 125. In the long run a decrease in price level to 75 leads to lower nominal wages, yielding aggregate supply schedule $AS(P_{75})$. Equilibrium Q returns to $250, now at a price level of 75.
(c) Graphically, the explanation is identical to Figure 16.1b. Short-run AS: $P_1 = 100$; $P_2 = 125$; $P_3 = 75$; and $Q_1 = \$250$; $Q_2 = \$280$; and $Q_3 = \$220$. Long-run aggregate supply = $Q_1 = \$250$ at each of the three price levels.

16-4 Use graphical analysis to show how each of the following would affect the economy first in the short run and then in the long run. Assume that the United States is initially operating at its full-employment level of output, that prices and wages are eventually flexible both upward and downward, and that there is no counteracting fiscal or monetary policy.

a. Because of a war abroad, the oil supply to the United States is disrupted, sending oil prices rocketing upward.

b. Construction spending on new homes rises dramatically, greatly increasing total U.S. investment spending.

c. Economic recession occurs abroad, significantly reducing foreign purchases of U.S. exports.

(a) See Figure 16.4 in the chapter, less AD₂. Short run: The aggregate supply curve shifts to the left, the price level rises, and real output declines. Long run: The aggregate supply curve shifts back rightward (due to declining nominal wages), the price level falls, and real output increases.
(b) See Figure 16.3. Short run: The aggregate demand curve shifts to the right, and both the price level and real output increase. Long run: The aggregate supply curve shifts to the left (due to higher nominal wages), the price level rises, and real output declines.
(c) See Figure 16.5. Short run: The aggregate demand curve shifts to the left, both the price level and real output decline. Long run: The aggregate supply curve shifts to the right, the price level falls further, and real output increases.

16-6 Suppose the government misjudges the natural rate of unemployment to be much lower than it actually is, and thus undertakes expansionary fiscal and monetary policy to try to achieve the lower rate. Use the concept of the short-run Phillips Curve to explain why these policies might at first succeed. Use the concept of the long-run Phillips Curve to explain the long-run outcome of these policies.

In the short run there is probably a tradeoff between unemployment and inflation. The government's expansionary policy should reduce unemployment as aggregate demand increases. However, the government has misjudged the natural rate and will continue its expansionary policy beyond the point of the natural level of unemployment. As aggregate demand continues to rise,

prices begin to rise. In the long run, workers demand higher wages to compensate for these higher prices. Aggregate supply will decrease (shift leftward) toward the natural rate of unemployment.

In other words, any reduction of unemployment below the natural rate is only temporary and involves a short-run rise in inflation. This, in turn, causes long-run costs to rise and a decrease in aggregate supply. The end result should be an equilibrium at the natural rate of unemployment and a higher price level than the beginning level. The long-run Phillips Curve is thus a vertical line connecting the price levels possible at the natural rate of unemployment found on the horizontal axis. (See Figure 16.9.)

16-7 What is the Laffer Curve, and how does it relate to supply-side economics? Why is determining the location where the economy is on the curve so important in assessing tax policy?

Economist Arthur Laffer observed that tax revenues would obviously be zero when the tax rate was either at 0 percent or 100 percent. In between these two extremes would have to be an optimal rate where aggregate output and income produced the maximum tax revenues. This idea is presented as the Laffer Curve shown in Figure 16.10.

The difficult decision involves the analysis to determine what is the optimum tax rate for producing maximum tax revenue and the related maximum economic output level. Laffer argued that low tax rates would actually increase revenues because low rates improved productivity, saving, and investment incentives. The expansion in output and employment, and thus revenue, would more than compensate for the lower rates.

CHAPTER 17

17-1 What are the four supply factors of economic growth? What is the demand factor? What is the efficiency factor? Illustrate these factors in terms of the production possibilities curve.

The four supply factors are the quantity and quality of natural resources; the quantity and quality of human resources; the stock of capital goods; and the level of technology. The demand factor is the level of purchases needed to maintain full employment. The efficiency factor refers to both productive and allocative efficiency. Figure 17.1 illustrates these growth factors by showing movement from curve AB to curve CD.

17-5 Between 1990 and 2002 the U.S. price level rose by about 38 percent while its real output increased by about 41 percent. Use the aggregate demand–aggregate supply model to illustrate these outcomes graphically.

In the graph shown, both AD and AS expanded over the 1990–2002 period. Because aggregate supply increased as well

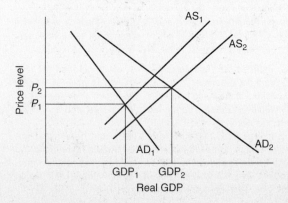

as aggregate demand, the new equilibrium output rose at a faster pace than did the price level. P_2 is 38 percent above P_1 and GDP$_2$ is 41 percent greater than GDP$_1$.

17–6 To what extent have increases in U.S. real GDP resulted from more labor inputs? From higher labor productivity? Rearrange the following contributors to the growth of real GDP in order of their quantitative importance: economies of scale, quantity of capital, improved resource allocation, education and training, technological advance.

The U.S. labor force grew by an average of about 1.7 million workers per year for each of the past 25 years, and this explains much of the growth in real GDP. From 1990–2002, higher labor productivity accounted for 68 percent of the 3 percent average annual growth. Other factors have also been important. Refer to Table 17.1. Factor importance in descending order: (1) Technological advance—the discovery of new knowledge that results in the combining of resources in more productive ways. (2) The quantity of capital. (3) Education and training. (4) Economies of scale. and (5) Improved resource allocation.

17–8 Relate each of the following to the New Economy:
   a. The rate of productivity growth
   b. Information technology
   c. Increasing returns
   d. Network effects
   e. Global competition

Each of the above is a characteristic of the New Economy. The rate of productivity growth has grown substantially due to innovations using microchips, computers, new telecommunications devices, and the Internet. All of these innovations describe features of what we call information technology, which connects information in all parts of the world with information seekers. New information products are often digital in nature and can be easily replicated once they have been developed. The start-up cost of new firms and new technology is high, but expanding production has a very low marginal cost, which leads to economies of scale—firms' outputs grow faster than their inputs. Network effects refer to a type of economy of scale whereby certain information products become more valuable to each user as the number of buyers grows. For example, a fax machine is more useful to you when lots of other people and firms have one; the same is true for compatible word-processing programs. Global competition is a feature of the New Economy because both transportation and communication can be accomplished at much lower cost and faster speed than previously, which expands market possibilities for both consumers and producers who are not very limited by national boundaries today.

CHAPTER 18

18–1 Assess the leeway for using fiscal policy as a stabilization tool under **(a)** an annually balanced budget, **(b)** a cyclically balanced budget, and **(c)** functional finance.

(a) There is practically no potential for using fiscal policy as a stabilization tool under an annually balanced budget. In an economic downturn, tax revenues fall. To keep the budget in balance, fiscal policy would require the government to reduce its spending or increase its tax rates, adding to the deficiency in spending and accelerating the downturn. If the economy were booming and tax revenues were mounting, to keep the budget balanced fiscal policy would have to increase government spending or reduce taxes, thus adding to the already excessive demand and accelerating the inflationary pres-

sures. An annually balanced budget would intensify cyclical ups and downs.

(b) A cyclically balanced budget would be countercyclical, as it should be, since it would bolster demand by lowering taxes and increasing government spending during a recession and restrain demand by raising taxes and reducing government spending during an inflationary boom. However, because boom and bust are not always of equal intensity and duration, budget surpluses during the upswing need not automatically match budget deficits during the downswing. Requiring the budget to be balanced over the cycle may necessitate inappropriate changes in tax rates or levels of government expenditures.

(c) Functional finance pays no attention to the balance of deficits and surpluses annually or over the cycle. What counts is the maintenance of a noninflationary full-employment level of spending. Balancing the economy is what counts, not the budget.

18–3 What are the two main ways the size of the public debt is measured? Distinguish between refinancing the debt and retiring the debt. How does an internally held public debt differ from an externally held public debt? Contrast the effects of retiring an internally held debt and retiring an externally held debt.

Two ways of measuring the public debt: (1) measure its absolute dollar size; (2) measure its size as a percentage of GDP.

Refinancing the public debt simply means rolling over outstanding debt—selling "new" bonds to retire maturing bonds. Retiring the debt means purchasing bonds back from those who hold them or paying the bonds off at maturity.

An internally held debt is one in which the bondholders live in the nation having the debt; an externally held debt is one in which the bondholders are citizens of other nations. Paying off an internally held debt would involve buying back government bonds. This could present a problem of income distribution because holders of the government bonds generally have higher incomes than the average taxpayer. But paying off an internally held debt would not burden the economy as a whole—the money used to pay off the debt would stay within the domestic economy. In paying off an externally held debt, people abroad could use the proceeds of the bonds sales to buy products or other assets from the United States. However, the dollars gained could be simply exchanged for foreign currency and brought back to their home country. This would reduce U.S. foreign reserves holdings and may lower the dollar exchange rate.

18–7 Trace the cause-and-effect chain through which financing and refinancing of the public debt might affect real interest rates, private investment, the stock of capital, and economic growth. How might investment in public capital and complementarities between public and private capital alter the outcome of the cause-effect chain?

Cause and effect chain: Government borrowing to finance the debt competes with private borrowing and drives up the interest rate; the higher interest rate causes a decline in private capital and economic growth slows.

However, if public investment complements private investment, private borrowers may be willing to pay higher rates for positive growth opportunities. Productivity and economic growth could rise.

CHAPTER 19

19–1 Use the aggregate demand–aggregate supply model to compare the "old" classical and Keynesian interpretations of **(a)** the aggregate supply curve and **(b)** the stability of the aggregate demand curve. Which of these interpretations seems more consistent with the realities of the Great Depression?

(a) Classical economists envisioned the AS curve as being perfectly vertical. When prices fall, real profits do not decrease because wage rates fall in the same proportion. With constant real profits, firms have no reason to change the quantities of output they supply. Keynesians viewed the AS curve as being horizontal at outputs less than the full-employment output and vertical only at full employment. Declines in aggregate demand do not change the price level because wages and prices are assumed to be inflexible downward.

(b) Classical economists viewed AD as stable so long as the monetary authorities hold the money supply constant. Therefore inflation and deflation are unlikely. Keynesians viewed the AD curve as unstable—even if the money supply is constant—since investment spending is volatile. Decreases in AD can cause a recession; rapid increases in AD can cause demand-pull inflation.

(c) The Keynesian view seems more consistent with the facts of the Great Depression; in that period, real output declined by nearly 40 percent in the United States and remained low for a decade.

19–4 Suppose that the money supply and the nominal GDP for a hypothetical economy are $96 billion and $336 billion, respectively. What is the velocity of money? How will households and businesses react if the central bank reduces the money supply by $20 billion? By how much will nominal GDP have to fall to restore equilibrium according to the monetarist perspective?

Velocity = 3.5 or 336/96. They will cut back on their spending to try to restore their desired ratio of money to other items of wealth. Nominal GDP will fall to $266 billion (= $76 billion remaining money supply $\times$ 3.5) to restore equilibrium.

19–7 Use an AD-AS graph to demonstrate and explain the price-level and real-output outcome of an anticipated decline in aggregate demand, as viewed by RET economists. (Assume that the economy initially is operating at its full-employment level of output.) Then, demonstrate and explain on the same graph the outcome, as viewed by mainstream economists.

See the graph and the decline in aggregate demand from AD_1 to AD_2. RET view: The economy anticipates the decline in the price level and immediately moves from a to d. Mainstream view: The economy first moves from a to b and then to c. In the long run AS will shift right (as nominal wages fall), intersecting AD_2 at point d. In view of historical evidence, the mainstream view seems more plausible to us than the RET view.

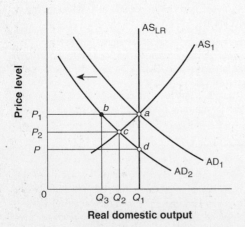

19–13 Place "MON," "RET," or "MAIN" beside the statements that most closely reflect monetarist, rational expectations, or mainstream views, respectively.

a. Anticipated changes in aggregate demand affect only the price level; they have no effect on real output.

b. Downward wage inflexibility means that declines in aggregate demand can cause long-lasting recession.

c. Changes in the money supply M increase PQ; at first only Q rises because nominal wages are fixed, but once workers adapt their expectations to new realities, P rises and Q returns to its former level.

d. Fiscal and monetary policy smooth out the business cycle.

e. The Fed should increase the money supply at a fixed annual rate.

(a) RET
(b) MAIN
(c) MON
(d) MAIN
(e) MON

CHAPTER 20

20–2 Graph the accompanying demand data, and then use the midpoint formula for E_d to determine price elasticity of demand for each of the four possible $1 price changes. What can you conclude about the relationship between the slope of a curve and its elasticity? Explain in a nontechnical way why demand is elastic in the northwest segment of the demand curve and inelastic in the southeast segment.

Product price	Quantity demanded
$5	1
4	2
3	3
2	4
1	5

See the graph accompanying the answer to 20–4. Elasticities, top to bottom: 3; 1.4; .714; .333. Slope does not measure elasticity. This demand curve has a constant slope of -1 (= $-1/1$), but elasticity declines as we move down the curve. When the initial price is high and initial quantity is low, a unit change in price is a *low* percentage while a unit change in quantity is a *high* percentage change. The percentage change in quantity exceeds the percentage change in price, making demand elastic. When the initial price is low and initial quantity is high, a unit change in price is a *high* percentage change while a unit change in quantity is a *low* percentage change. The percentage change in quantity is less than the percentage change in price, making demand inelastic.

20–4 Calculate total-revenue data from the demand schedule in question 20–2. Graph total revenue below your demand curve. Generalize about the relationship between price elasticity and total revenue.

See the graph. Total revenue data, top to bottom: $5; $8; $9; $8; $5. When demand is elastic, price and total revenue move in the opposite direction. When demand is inelastic, price and total revenue move in the same direction.

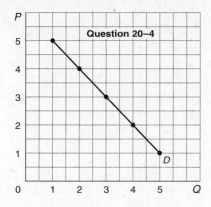

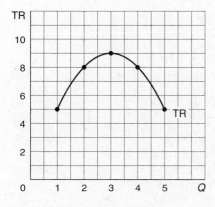

If more than one picture were available (all but one having to be a copy), the demand would likely decrease enormously.

20–12 Suppose the cross elasticity of demand for products A and B is +3.6 and for products C and D is −5.4. What can you conclude about how products A and B are related? Products C and D?

A and B are substitutes; C and D are complements.

20–13 The income elasticities of demand for movies, dental services, and clothing have been estimated to be +3.4, +1.0, and +0.5, respectively. Interpret these coefficients. What does it mean if the income elasticity coefficient is negative?

All are normal goods—income and quantity demanded move in the same direction. These coefficients reveal that a 1 percent increase in income will increase the quantity of movies demanded by 3.4 percent, of dental services by 1.0 percent, and of clothing by 0.5 percent. A negative coefficient indicates an inferior good—income and quantity demanded move in the opposite direction.

20–5 How would the following changes in price affect total revenue? That is, would total revenue increase, decline, or remain unchanged?
  a. Price falls and demand is inelastic.
  b. Price rises and demand is elastic.
  c. Price rises and supply is elastic.
  d. Price rises and supply is inelastic.
  e. Price rises and demand is inelastic.
  f. Price falls and demand is elastic.
  g. Price falls and demand is of unit elasticity.

Total revenue would increase in (c), (d), (e), and (f); decrease in (a) and (b); and remain the same in (g).

20–6 What are the major determinants of price elasticity of demand? Use those determinants and your own reasoning in judging whether demand for each of the following products is elastic or inelastic:
  (a) bottled water; **(b)** toothpaste; **(c)** Crest toothpaste; **(d)** ketchup; **(e)** diamond bracelets; **(f)** Microsoft Windows operating system.

Substitutability, proportion of income; luxury versus necessity, and time. Elastic: (a), (c), (e). Inelastic: (b), (d), and (f).

20–10 In November 1998, Vincent van Gogh's self-portrait sold at auction for $71.5 million. Portray this sale in a demand and supply diagram and comment on the elasticity of supply. Comedian George Carlin once mused, "If a painting can be forged well enough to fool some experts, why is the original so valuable?" Provide an answer.

The supply is perfectly inelastic—vertical—at a quantity of 1 unit. The $71.5 million price is determined where the downward sloping demand curve intersected this supply curve.

CHAPTER 21

21–2 Complete the following table and answer the questions below:

Units consumed	Total utility	Marginal utility
0	0	—
1	10	10
2	—	8
3	25	—
4	30	—
5	—	3
6	34	—

  a. At which rate is total utility increasing: a constant rate, a decreasing rate, or an increasing rate? How do you know?
  b. "A rational consumer will purchase only 1 unit of the product represented by these data, since that amount maximizes marginal utility." Do you agree? Explain why or why not.
  c. "It is possible that a rational consumer will not purchase any units of the product represented by these data." Do you agree? Explain why or why not.

Missing total utility data top to bottom: 18; 33. Missing marginal utility data, top to bottom: 7; 5; 1.
(a) A decreasing rate; because marginal utility is declining.
(b) Disagree. The marginal utility of a unit beyond the first may be sufficiently great (relative to product price) to make it a worthwhile purchase. Consumers are interested in maximizing *total* utility, not marginal utility.
(c) Agree. This product's price could be so high relative to the first unit's marginal utility that the consumer would buy none of it.

21–4 Columns 1 through 4 of the accompanying table show the marginal utility, measured in utils, that Ricardo would get by purchasing various amounts of products A, B, C, and D. Column 5 shows the marginal utility Ricardo gets from saving. Assume that the prices of A, B, C, and D are $18, $6, $4, and $24, respectively, and that Ricardo has an income of $106.

Column 1		Column 2		Column 3		Column 4		Column 5	
Units of A	MU	Units of B	MU	Units of C	MU	Units of D	MU	No. of $ saved	MU
1	72	1	24	1	15	1	36	1	5
2	54	2	15	2	12	2	30	2	4
3	45	3	12	3	8	3	24	3	3
4	36	4	9	4	7	4	18	4	2
5	27	5	7	5	5	5	13	5	1
6	18	6	5	6	4	6	7	6	1/2
7	15	7	2	7	3.5	7	4	7	1/4
8	12	8	1	8	3	8	2	8	1/8

a. What quantities of A, B, C, and D will Ricardo purchase in maximizing his utility?

b. How many dollars will Ricardo choose to save?

c. Check your answers by substituting them into the algebraic statement of the utility-maximizing rule.

(a) 4 units of A; 3 units of B; 3 units of C; and 0 units of D.

(b) Save $4.

(c) 36/$18 = 12/$6 = 8/$4 = 2/$1. The marginal utility per dollar of the last unit of each product purchased is 2.

21-5 You are choosing between two goods, X and Y, and your marginal utility from each is as shown below. If your income is $9 and the prices of X and Y are $2 and $1, respectively, what quantities of each will you purchase to maximize utility? What total utility will you realize? Assume that, other things remaining unchanged, the price of X falls to $1. What quantities of X and Y will you now purchase? Using the two prices and quantities for X, derive a demand schedule (price-quantity-demanded table) for X.

Units of X	MU_x	Units of Y	MU_y
1	10	1	8
2	8	2	7
3	6	3	6
4	4	4	5
5	3	5	4
6	2	6	3

Buy 2 units of X and 5 units of Y. Marginal utility of last dollar spent will be equal at 4 (= 8/$2 for X and 4/$1 for Y) and the $9 income will be spent. Total utility = 48 (= 10 + 8 for X plus 8 + 7 + 6 + 5 + 4 for Y). When the price of X falls to $1, the quantity of X demanded increases from 2 to 4 (income effect). Total utility is now 58 (= 10 + 8 + 6 + 4 for X plus 8 + 7 + 6 + 5 + 4 for Y).

Demand schedule for X: P = $2; Q = 2. P = $1; Q = 4.

CHAPTER 21 APPENDIX

21A-3 Using Figure 4, explain why the point of tangency of the budget line with an indifference curve is the consumer's equilibrium position. Explain why any point where the budget line intersects an indifference curve will not be equilibrium. Explain: "The consumer is in equilibrium where MRS = P_B/P_A."

The tangency point places the consumer on the highest attainable indifference curve; it identifies the combination of goods yielding the highest total utility. All intersection points place the consumer on a lower indifference curve. MRS is the slope of the indifference curve; PB/PA is the slope of the budget line. Only at the tangency point are these two slopes equal. If MRS > P_B/P_A or MRS < P_B/P_A, adjustments in the combination of products can be made to increase total utility (get to a higher indifference curve).

CHAPTER 22

22-2 Gomez runs a small pottery firm. He hires one helper at $12,000 per year, pays annual rent of $5,000 for his shop, and spends $20,000 per year on materials. He has $40,000 of his own funds invested in equipment (pottery wheels, kilns, and so forth) that could earn him $4,000 per year if alternatively invested. He has been offered $15,000 per year to work as a potter for a competitor. He estimates his entrepreneurial talents are worth $3,000 per year. Total annual revenue from pottery sales is $72,000. Calculate accounting profits and economic profits for Gomez's pottery.

Explicit costs: $37,000 (= $12,000 for the helper + $5,000 of rent + $20,000 of materials). Implicit costs: $22,000 (= $4,000 of forgone interest + $15,000 of forgone salary + $3,000 of entreprenuership).

Accounting profit = $35,000 (= $72,000 of revenue − $37,000 of explicit costs); Economic profit = $13,000 (= $72,000 − $37,000 of explicit costs − $22,000 of implicit costs).

22-4 Complete the following table by calculating marginal product and average product from the data given. Plot total, marginal, and average product and explain in detail the relationship between each pair of curves. Explain why marginal product first rises, then declines, and ultimately becomes negative. What bearing does the law of diminishing returns have on short-run costs? Be specific. "When marginal product is rising, marginal cost is falling. And when marginal product is diminishing, marginal cost is rising." Illustrate and explain graphically.

Inputs of labor	Total product	Marginal product	Average product
0	0	___	___
1	15	___	___
2	34	___	___
3	51	___	___
4	65	___	___
5	74	___	___
6	80	___	___
7	83	___	___
8	82	___	___

Marginal product data, top to bottom: 15; 19; 17; 14; 9; 6; 3; −1. Average product data, top to bottom: 15; 17; 17; 16.25; 14.8; 13.33; 11.86; 10.25. Your diagram should have the same general characteristics as text Figure 22.2.

MP is the slope—the rate of change—of the TP curve. When TP is rising at an increasing rate, MP is positive and rising. When TP is rising at a diminishing rate, MP is positive but falling. When TP is falling, MP is negative and falling. AP rises when MP is above it; AP falls when MP is below it.

MP first rises because the fixed capital gets used more productively as added workers are employed. Each added worker contributes more to output than the previous worker because the firm is better able to use its fixed plant and equipment. As still more labor is added, the law of diminishing returns takes hold. Labor becomes so abundant relative to the fixed capital that congestion occurs and marginal product falls. At the extreme, the addition of labor so overcrowds the plant that the marginal product of still more labor is negative—total output falls.

Illustrated by Figure 22.6. Because labor is the only variable input and its price (its wage rate) is constant, MC is found by dividing the wage rate by MP. When MP is rising, MC is falling; when MP reaches its maximum, MC is at its minimum; when MP is falling, MC is rising.

Total product	Total fixed cost	Total variable cost	Total cost	Average fixed cost	Average variable cost	Average total cost	Marginal cost
0	$____	$ 0	$____	$____	$____	$____	$____
1	____	45	____	____	____	____	____
2	____	85	____	____	____	____	____
3	____	120	____	____	____	____	____
4	____	150	____	____	____	____	____
5	____	185	____	____	____	____	____
6	____	225	____	____	____	____	____
7	____	270	____	____	____	____	____
8	____	325	____	____	____	____	____
9	____	390	____	____	____	____	____
10	____	465	____	____	____	____	____

22–7 A firm has fixed costs of $60 and variable costs as indicated in the table above. Complete the table. When finished, check your calculations by referring to question 4 at the end of Chapter 23.

a. Graph total fixed cost, total variable cost, and total cost. Explain how the law of diminishing returns influences the shapes of the total-variable-cost and total-cost curves.

b. Graph AFC, AVC, ATC, and MC. Explain the derivation and shape of each of these four curves and their relationships to one another. Specifically, explain in nontechnical terms why the MC curve intersects both the AVC and ATC curves at their minimum points.

c. Explain how the locations of each of the four curves graphed in question 7b would be altered if (1) total fixed cost had been $100 rather than $60, and (2) total variable cost had been $10 less at each level of output.

The total fixed costs are all $60. The total costs are all $60 more than the total variable cost. The other columns are shown in Question 4 in Chapter 23.

(a) See the graph. Over the 0 to 4 range of output, the TVC and TC curves slope upward at a decreasing rate because of increasing marginal returns. The slopes of the curves then increase at an increasing rate as diminishing marginal returns occur.

(b) See the graph. AFC (= TFC/Q) falls continuously since a fixed amount of capital cost is spread over more units of output. The MC (= change in TC/change in Q), AVC (= TVC/Q), and ATC (= TC/Q) curves are U-shaped, reflecting the influence of first increasing and then diminishing returns. The ATC curve sums AFC and AVC vertically. The ATC curve falls when the MC curve is below it; the ATC curve rises when the MC curve is above it. This means the MC curve must intersect the ATC curve at its lowest point. The same logic holds for the minimum point of the AVC curve.

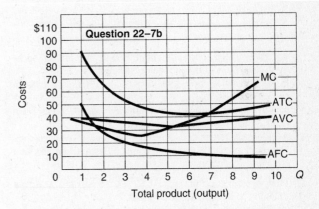

(c1) If TFC had been $100 instead of $60, the AFC and ATC curves would be higher—by an amount equal to $40 divided by the specific output. Example: at 4 units, AVC = $25.00 [= ($60 + $40)/4]; and ATC = $62.50 [= ($210 + $40)/4]. The AVC and MC curves are not affected by changes in fixed costs.

(c2) If TVC had been $10 less at each output, MC would be $10 lower for the first unit of output but remain the same for the remaining output. The AVC and ATC curves would also be lower—by an amount equal to $10 divided by the specific output. Example: at 4 units of output, AVC = $35.00 [= ($150 − $10)/4], ATC = $50 [= ($210 − $10)/4]. The AFC curve would not be affected by the change in variable costs.

22–10 Use the concepts of economies and diseconomies of scale to explain the shape of a firm's long-run ATC curve. What is the concept of minimum efficient scale? What bearing may the exact shape of the long-run ATC curve have on the structure of an industry?

The long-run ATC curve is U-shaped. At first, long-run ATC falls as the firm expands and realizes economies of scale from labor and managerial specialization and the use of more efficient capital. The long-run ATC curve later turns upward when the enlarged firm experiences diseconomies of scale, usually resulting from managerial inefficiencies.

The MES (minimum efficient scale) is the smallest level of output needed to attain all economies of scale and minimum long-run ATC.

If long-run ATC drops quickly to its minimum cost, which then extends over a long range of output, the industry will likely be composed of both large and small firms. If long-run ATC descends slowly to its minimum cost over a long range of output, the

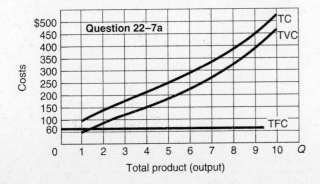

industry will likely be composed of a few large firms. If long-run ATC drops quickly to its minimum point and then rises abruptly, the industry will likely be composed of many small firms.

CHAPTER 23

23-3 Use the following demand schedule to determine total and marginal revenues for each possible level of sales:

Product price ($)	Quantity demanded	Total revenue ($)	Marginal revenue ($)
2	0	——	——
2	1	——	——
2	2	——	——
2	3	——	——
2	4	——	——
2	5	——	——

a. What can you conclude about the structure of the industry in which this firm is operating? Explain.
b. Graph the demand, total-revenue, and marginal-revenue curves for this firm.
c. Why do the demand and marginal-revenue curves coincide?
d. "Marginal revenue is the change in total revenue associated with additional units of output." Explain verbally and graphically, using the data in the table.

Total revenue, top to bottom: 0; $2; $4; $6; $8; $10. Marginal revenue, top to bottom: $2, throughout.
(a) The industry is purely competitive—this firm is a "price taker." The firm is so small relative to the size of the market that it can change its level of output without affecting the market price.
(b) See graph.
(c) The firm's demand curve is perfectly elastic; MR is constant and equal to P.

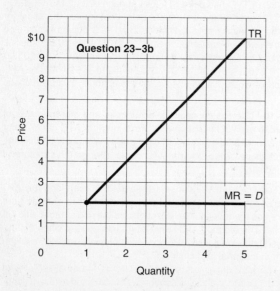

(d) True. Table: When output (quantity demanded) increases by 1 unit, total revenue increases by $2. This $2 increase is the marginal revenue. Figure: The change in TR is measured by the slope of the TR line, 2 (= $2/1 unit).

23-4 Assume the following cost data are for a purely competitive producer:

Total product	Average fixed cost	Average variable cost	Average total cost	Marginal cost
0				
1	$60.00	$45.00	$105.00	$45
2	30.00	42.50	72.50	40
3	20.00	40.00	60.00	35
4	15.00	37.50	52.50	30
5	12.00	37.00	49.00	35
6	10.00	37.50	47.50	40
7	8.57	38.57	47.14	45
8	7.50	40.63	48.13	55
9	6.67	43.33	50.00	65
10	6.00	46.50	52.50	75

a. At a product price of $56, will this firm produce in the short run? Why or why not? If it is preferable to produce, what will be the profit-maximizing or loss-minimizing output? Explain. What economic profit or loss will the firm realize per unit of output?
b. Answer the relevant questions of 4a assuming product price is $41.
c. Answer the relevant questions of 4a assuming product price is $32.
d. In the table below, complete the short-run supply schedule for the firm (columns 1 and 2) and indicate the profit or loss incurred at each output (column 3).

(1) Price	(2) Quantity supplied, single firm	(3) Profit (+) or loss (l)	(4) Quantity supplied, 1500 firms
$26	——	$ ——	——
32	——	——	——
38	——	——	——
41	——	——	——
46	——	——	——
56	——	——	——
66	——	——	——

e. Explain: "That segment of a competitive firm's marginal-cost curve which lies above its average-variable-cost curve constitutes the short-run supply curve for the firm." Illustrate graphically.
f. Now assume there are 1500 identical firms in this competitive industry; that is, there are 1500 firms, each of which has the same cost data as shown here. Calculate the industry supply schedule (column 4).
g. Suppose the market demand data for the product are as follows:

Price	Total quantity demanded
$26	17,000
32	15,000
38	13,500
41	12,000
46	10,500
56	9,500
66	8,000

What will be the equilibrium price? What will be the equilibrium output for the industry? For each firm? What will profit or loss be per unit? Per firm? Will this industry expand or contract in the long run?

(a) Yes, $56 exceeds AVC (and ATC) at the profit-maximizing output. Using the MR = MC rule it will produce 8 units. Profits per unit = $7.87 (= $56 − $48.13); total profit = $62.96.
(b) Yes, $41 exceeds AVC at the loss—minimizing output. Using the MR = MC rule it will produce 6 units. Loss per unit of output is $6.50 (= $41 − $47.50). Total loss = $39 (=6 ∞ $6.50), which is less than its total fixed cost of $60.
(c) No, because $32 is always less than AVC. If it did produce according to the MR = MC rule, its output would be 4—found by expanding output until MR no longer exceeds MC. By producing 4 units, it would lose $82 [= 4 ($32 − $52.50)]. By not producing, it would lose only its total fixed cost of $60.
(d) Column (2) data, top to bottom: 0; 0; 5; 6; 7; 8; 9, Column (3) data, top to bottom in dollars: −60; −60; −55; −39; −8; +63; +144.
(e) The firm will not produce if P < AVC. When P > AVC, the firm will produce in the short run at the quantity where P (= MR) is equal to its increasing MC. Therefore, the MC curve above the AVC curve is the firm's short-run supply curve; it shows the quantity of output the firm will supply at each price level. See Figure 23.6 for a graphical illustration.
(f) Column (4) data, top to bottom: 0; 0; 7,500; 9,000; 10,500; 12,000; 13,500.
(g) Equilibrium price = $46; equilibrium output = 10,500. Each firm will produce 7 units. Loss per unit = $1.14, or $8 per firm. The industry will contract in the long run.

23–6 Using diagrams for both the industry and a representative firm, illustrate competitive long-run equilibrium. Assuming constant costs, employ these diagrams to show how (a) an increase and (b) a decrease in market demand will upset that long-run equilibrium. Trace graphically and describe verbally the adjustment processes by which long-run equilibrium is restored. Now rework your analysis for increasing- and decreasing-cost industries and compare the three long-run supply curves.

See Figures 23.8 and 23.9 and their legends. See Figure 23.11 for the supply curve for an increasing cost industry. The supply curve for a decreasing cost industry is below.

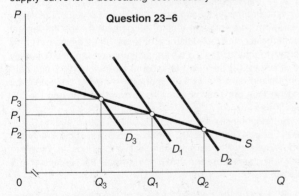

Question 23–6

23–7 In long-run equilibrium, P = minimum ATC = MC. Of what significance for economic efficiency is the equality of P and minimum ATC? The equality of P and MC? Distinguish between productive efficiency and allocative efficiency in your answer.

The equality of P and minimum ATC means the firm is achieving *productive efficiency;* it is using the most efficient technology and employing the least costly combination of resources. The equality of P and MC means the firm is achieving *allocative efficiency;* the industry is producing the right product in the right amount based on society's valuation of that product and other products.

CHAPTER 24

24–4 Use the demand schedule that follows to calculate total revenue and marginal revenue at each quantity. Plot the demand, total-revenue, and marginal-revenue curves and explain the relationships between them. Explain why the marginal revenue of the fourth unit of output is $3.50, even though its price is $5.00. Use Chapter 20's total-revenue test for price elasticity to designate the elastic and inelastic segments of your graphed demand curve. What generalization can you make regarding the relationship between marginal revenue and elasticity of demand? Suppose the marginal cost of successive units of output were zero. What output would the profit-seeking firm produce? Finally, use your analysis to explain why a monopolist would never produce in the inelastic region of demand.

Price	Quantity demanded	Price	Quantity demanded
$7.00	0	$4.50	5
6.50	1	4.00	6
6.00	2	3.50	7
5.50	3	3.00	8
5.00	4	2.50	9

Total revenue, in order from Q = 0: 0; $6.50; $12.00; $16.50; $20.00; $22.50; $24.00; $24.50; $24.00; $22.50. Marginal revenue in order from Q = 1: $6.50; $5.50; $4.50; $3.50; $2.50; $1.50; $.50; −$1.50. See the accompanying graph. Because TR is increasing at a diminishing rate, MR is declining. When TR turns downward, MR becomes negative. Marginal revenue is below D because to sell an extra unit, the monopolist must lower the price on the marginal unit as well as on each of the preceding units sold. Four units sell for $5.00 each, but three of these four could have been sold for $5.50 had the monopolist been satisfied to sell only three. Having decided to sell four, the monopolist had to lower the price of the first three from $5.50 to $5.00, sacrificing $.50 on each for a total of $1.50. This "loss" of $1.50 explains the difference between the $5.00 price obtained on the fourth unit of output and its marginal revenue of $3.50. Demand is elastic from P = $6.50 to P = $3.50, a range where TR is rising. The curve is of unitary elasticity at P = $3.50, where TR is at its maximum. The curve is inelastic from then on as the price continues to decrease and TR is falling. When MR is positive, demand is elastic. When MR is zero, demand is of unitary elasticity. When MR is negative, demand is inelastic. If MC is zero, the monopolist should produce 7 units where MR is also zero. It would never produce where demand is inelastic because MR is negative there while MC is positive.

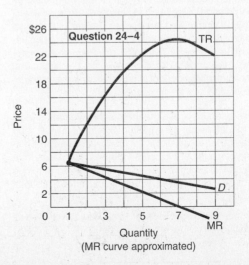

Question 24–4

(MR curve approximated)

24–5 Suppose a pure monopolist is faced with the demand schedule shown below and the same cost data as the competitive producer discussed in question 4 at the end of Chapter 23. Calculate the missing total- and marginal-revenue amounts, and determine the profit-maximizing price and profit-earning output for this monopolist. What is the monopolist's profit? Verify your answer graphically and by comparing total revenue and total cost.

Price	Quantity demanded	Total revenue	Marginal revenue
$115	0	$____	$____
100	1	$____	$____
83	2	$____	$____
71	3	$____	$____
63	4	$____	$____
55	5	$____	$____
48	6	$____	$____
42	7	$____	$____
37	8	$____	$____
33	9	$____	$____
29	10	$____	$____

Total revenue data, top to bottom, in dollars: 0: 100; 166; 213; 252; 275; 288; 294; 296; 297; 290. Marginal revenue data, top to bottom, in dollars: 100; 66; 47; 39; 23; 13; 6; 2; 1; −7.

Price = $63; output = 4; profit = $42 [= 4($63 − 52.50)]. Your graph should have the same general appearance as Figure 24.4. At $Q = 4$, TR = $252 and TC = $210 [= 4($52.50)].

24–6 If the firm described in question 5 could engage in perfect price discrimination, what would be the level of output? Of profits? Draw a diagram showing the relevant demand, marginal-revenue, average-total-cost, and marginal-cost curves and the equilibrium price and output for a nondiscriminating monopolist. Use the same diagram to show the equilibrium position of a monopolist that is able to practice perfect price discrimination. Compare equilibrium outputs, total revenues, economic profits, and consumer prices in the two cases. Comment on the economic desirability of price discrimination.

Perfect price discrimination: Output = 6. TR would be $420 (= $100 + $83 + $71 + $63 + $55 + $48). TC would be $285 [= 6(47.50)]. Profit would be $135 (= $420 − $285).

Your single diagram should combine Figures 24.8a and 24.8b in the chapter. The discriminating monopolist faces a demand curve that is also its MR curve. It will sell the first unit at f in Figure 24.8b and then sell each successive unit at lower prices (as shown on the demand curve) as it moves to Q_2 units, where D (= MR) = MC. Discriminating monopolist: Greater output, total revenue, and profits. Some consumers will pay a higher price under discriminating monopoly than with nondiscriminating monopoly; others, a lower price. Good features: greater output and improved allocative efficiency. Bad feature: More income is transferred from consumers to the monopolist.

24–12 It has been proposed that natural monopolists should be allowed to determine their profit-maximizing outputs and prices and then government should tax their profits away and distribute them to consumers in proportion to their purchases from the monopoly. Is this proposal as socially desirable as requiring monopolists to equate price with marginal cost or average total cost?

No, the proposal does not consider that the output of the natural monopolist would still be at the suboptimal level where $P >$ MC. Too little would be produced and there would be an underallocation of resources. Theoretically, it would be more desirable to force the natural monopolist to charge a price equal to marginal cost and subsidize any losses. Even setting price equal to ATC would be an improvement over this proposal. This fair-return pricing would allow for a normal profit and ensure greater production than the proposal would.

CHAPTER 25

25–2 Compare the elasticity of the monopolistic competitor's demand curve with that of a pure competitor and a pure monopolist. Assuming identical long-run costs, compare graphically the prices and output that would result in the long run under pure competition and under monopolistic competition. Contrast the two market structures in terms of productive and allocative efficiency. Explain: "Monopolistically competitive industries are characterized by too many firms, each of which produces too little."

The monopolistic competitor's demand curve is less elastic than a pure competitor's and more elastic than a pure monopolist's. Your graphs should look like Figures 23.12 and 25.1 in the chapters. Price is higher and output lower for the monopolistic competitor. Pure competition: P = MC (allocative efficiency); P = minimum ATC (productive efficiency). Monopolistic competition: $P >$ MC (allocative efficiency) and $P >$ minimum ATC (productive inefficiency). Monopolistic competitors have excess capacity, meaning that fewer firms operating at capacity (where P = minimum ATC) could supply the industry output.

25–7 Answer the following questions, which relate to measures of concentration.
a. What is the meaning of a four-firm concentration ratio of 60 percent? 90 percent? What are the shortcomings of concentration ratios as measures of monopoly power?
b. Suppose that the five firms in industry A have annual sales of 30, 30, 20, 10, and 10 percent of total industry sales. For the five firms in industry B, the figures are 60, 25, 5, 5, and 5 percent. Calculate the Herfindahl index for each industry and compare their likely competitiveness.

A four-firm concentration ratio of 60 percent means the largest four firms in the industry account for 60 percent of sales; a four-firm concentration ratio of 90 percent means the largest four firms account for 90 percent of sales. Shortcomings: (1) they pertain to the nation as a whole, although relevant markets may be localized; (2) they do not account for interindustry competition; (3) the data are for U.S. products—imports are excluded; and (4) they don't reveal the dispersion of size among the top four firms.

Herfindahl index for A: 2,400 (= 900 + 900 + 400 + 100 + 100). For B: 4,300 (= 3,600 + 625 + 25 + 25 + 25). We would expect industry A to be more competitive than Industry B, where one firm dominates and two firms control 85 percent of the market.

25–8 Explain the general meaning of the following profit payoff matrix for oligopolists C and D. All profit figures are in thousands.
a. Use the payoff matrix to explain the mutual interdependence that characterizes oligopolistic industries.
b. Assuming no collusion between C and D, what is the likely pricing outcome?
c. In view of your answer to 8b, explain why price collusion is mutually profitable. Why might there be a temptation to cheat on the collusive agreement?

C's possible prices

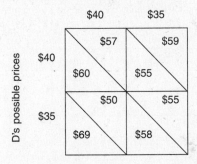

The matrix shows the four possible profit outcomes for each of two firms, depending on which of the two price strategies each follows. Example: If C sets its price at $35 and D at $40, C's profits will be $59,000 and D's $55,000.

(a) C and D are interdependent because their profits depend not just on their own price, but also on the other firm's price.

(b) Likely outcome: Both firms will set their price at $35. If either charged $40, it would be concerned the other would undercut the price and its profit by charging $35. At $35 for both: C's profit is $55,000, D's, $58,000.

(c) Through price collusion—agreeing to charge $40—each firm would achieve higher profits (C = $57,000; D = $60,000). But once both firms agree on $40, each sees it can increase its profit even more by secretly charging $35 while its rival charges $40.

25–9 What assumptions about a rival's response to price changes underlie the kinked-demand curve for oligopolists? Why is there a gap in the oligopolist's marginal-revenue curve? How does the kinked-demand curve explain price rigidity in oligopoly? What are the shortcomings of the kinked-demand model?

Assumptions: (1) Rivals will match price cuts. (2) Rivals will ignore price increases. The gap in the MR curve results from the abrupt change in the slope of the demand curve at the going price. Firms will not change their price because they fear that if they do their total revenue and profits will fall. Shortcomings of the model: (1) It does not explain how the going price evolved in the first place; (2) it does not allow for price leadership and other forms of collusion.

25–11 Why is there so much advertising in monopolistic competition and oligopoly? How does such advertising help consumers and promote efficiency? Why might it be excessive at times?

Two ways for monopolistically competitive firms to maintain economic profits are through product development and advertising. Also, advertising will increase the demand for the firm's product. The oligopolist would rather not compete on a basis of price. Oligopolists can increase their market share through advertising that is financed with economic profits from past advertising campaigns. Advertising can operate as a barrier to entry.

Advertising provides information about new products and product improvements to the consumer. Advertising may result in an increase in competition by promoting new products and product improvements. It may also result in increased output for a firm, pushing it down its ATC curve closer to productive efficiency (P = minimum ATC).

Advertising may result in manipulation and persuasion rather than information. An increase in brand loyalty through advertising will increase the producer's monopoly power. Excessive advertising may create barriers to entry into the industry.

CHAPTER 26

26–4 Suppose a firm expects that a $20 million expenditure on R&D will result in a new product that will increase its revenue by a total of $30 million 1 year from now. The firm estimates that the production cost of the new product will be $29 million.

    a. What is the expected rate of return on this R&D expenditure?

    b. Suppose the firm can get a bank loan at 6 percent interest to finance its $20 million R&D project. Will the firm undertake the project? Explain why or why not.

    c. Now suppose the interest-rate cost of borrowing, in effect, falls to 4 percent because the firm decides to use its own retained earnings to finance the R&D. Will this lower interest rate change the firm's R&D decision? Explain.

(a) 5 percent;

(b) No, because the 5 percent rate of return is less than the 6 percent interest rate;

(c) Yes, because the 5 percent rate of return is now greater than the 4 percent interest rate.

26–5 Answer the lettered questions below on the basis of the information in this table:

Amount of R&D, millions	Expected rate of return on R&D, %
$10	16
20	14
30	12
40	10
50	8
60	6

    a. If the interest-rate cost of funds is 8 percent, what will be the optimal amount of R&D spending for this firm?

    b. Explain why $20 million of R&D spending will not be optimal.

    c. Why won't $60 million be optimal either?

(a) $50 million, where the interest-rate cost of funds (*i*) equals the expected rate of return (*r*);

(b) at $20 million in R&D, *r* of 14 percent exceeds *i* of 8 percent; thus there would be an underallocation of R&D funds;

(c) at $60 million, *r* of 6 percent is less than *i* of 8 percent; thus there would be an overallocation of R&D funds.

26–6 Refer to Table 26.1 and suppose the price of new product C is $2 instead of $4. How does this affect the optimal combination of products A, B, and C for the person represented by the data? Explain: "The success of a new product depends not only on its marginal utility but also on its price."

(a) The person would now buy 5 units of product C and zero units of A and B;

(b) The MU/price ratio is what counts; a new product can be successful by having a high MU, a low price, or both relative to existing products.

26–8 Answer the following questions on the basis of this information for a single firm: Total cost of capital = $1,000; price paid for labor = $12 per labor unit; price paid for raw materials = $4 per raw-material unit.

    a. Suppose the firm can produce 5,000 units of output by combining its fixed capital with 100 units of labor and 450 units of raw materials. What are the total cost and average total cost of producing the 5,000 units of output?

b. Now assume the firm improves its production process so that it can produce 6,000 units of output by combining its fixed capital with 100 units of labor and 450 units of raw materials. What are the total cost and average cost of producing the 6,000 units of output?

c. Refer to your answers to 8a and 8b and explain how process innovation can improve economic efficiency.

(a) Total cost = $4,000; average total cost = $.80 (= $4,000/5,000 units);

(b) Total cost = $4,000; average total cost = $.667 (= $4,000/6,000 units);

(c) Process innovation can lower the average total cost of producing a particular output, meaning that society uses fewer resources to produce a given amount of output. Resources are freed from this production to produce more of other desirable goods. Society realizes extra output through a gain in efficiency.

CHAPTER 27

27–2 Complete the following labor demand table for a firm that is hiring labor competitively and selling its product in a competitive market.

Units of labor	Total product	Marginal product	Product price	Total revenue	Marginal revenue product
0	0	____	$2	$____	$____
1	17	____	2	____	____
2	31	____	2	____	____
3	43	____	2	____	____
4	53	____	2	____	____
5	60	____	2	____	____
6	65	____	2	____	____

a. How many workers will the firm hire if the going wage rate is $27.95? $19.95? Explain why the firm will not hire a larger or smaller number of units of labor at each of these wage rates.

b. Show in schedule form and graphically the labor demand curve of this firm.

c. Now again determine the firm's demand curve for labor, assuming that it is selling in an imperfectly competitive market and that, although it can sell 17 units at $2.20 per unit, it must lower product price by 5 cents in order to sell the marginal product of each successive labor unit. Compare this demand curve with that derived in question 2b. Which curve is more elastic? Explain.

Marginal product data, top to bottom: 17; 14; 12; 10; 7; 5. Total revenue data, top to bottom: $0, $34; $62; $86; $106; $120; $130. Marginal revenue product data, top to bottom: $34; $28; $24; $20; $14; $10.

(a) Two workers at $27.95 because the MRP of the first worker is $34 and the MRP of the second worker is $28, both exceeding the $27.95 wage. Four workers at $19.95 because workers 1 through 4 have MRPs exceeding the $19.95 wage. The fifth worker's MRP is only $14 so he or she will not be hired.

(b) The demand schedule consists of the first and last columns of the table at the top of the next column.

(c) Reconstruct the table. New product price data, top to bottom: $2.20; $2.15; $2.10; $2.05; $2.00; $1.95. New total revenue data, top to bottom: $0; $37.40; $66.65; $90.30; $108.65; $120.00; $126.75. New marginal revenue product data, top to bottom: $37.40; $29.25; $23.65; $18.35; $11.35; $6.75. The new labor demand is less elastic. Here, MRP falls because of diminishing returns *and* because product price declines as

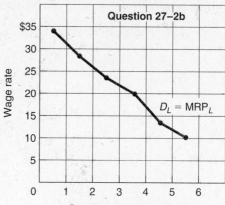

Question 27–2b

y-axis: Wage rate — $35, 30, 25, 20, 15, 10, 5

x-axis: Quantity of labor demanded (plotted at the halfway points along the horizontal axis) — 0, 1, 2, 3, 4, 5, 6

$D_L = MRP_L$

output increases. A decrease in the wage rate will produce less of an increase in the quantity of labor demanded, because the output from the added labor will reduce product price and thus MRP.

27–5 What factors determine the elasticity of resource demand? What effect will each of the following have on the elasticity or location of the demand for resource C, which is being used to produce commodity X? Where there is any uncertainty as to the outcome, specify the causes of the uncertainty.

a. An increase in the demand for product X.
b. An increase in the price of substitute resource D.
c. An increase in the number of resources substitutable for C in producing X.
d. A technological improvement in the capital equipment with which resource C is combined.
e. A fall in the price of complementary resource E.
f. A decline in the elasticity of demand for product X due to a decline in the competitiveness of the product market.

Elasticity of demand for a resource is determined by: (1) ease of resource substitutability; (2) elasticity of product demand; and (3) ratio of resource costs to total costs.

(a) Increase in the demand for resource C.
(b) Uncertainty relative to the change in demand for resource C; answer depends upon which is larger—the substitution effect or the output effect.
(c) Increase in the elasticity of resource C.
(d) Increase in the demand for resource C.
(e) Increase in the demand for resource C.
(f) Decrease in the elasticity of resource C.

27–6 Suppose the productivity of labor and capital are as shown in the accompanying table. The output of these resources sells in a purely competitive market for $1 per unit. Both capital and labor are hired under purely competitive conditions at $3 and $1, respectively.

Units of capital	MP of capital	Units of labor	MP of labor
1	24	1	11
2	21	2	9
3	18	3	8
4	15	4	7
5	9	5	6
6	6	6	4
7	3	7	1
8	1	8	1/2

a. What is the least-cost combination of labor and capital to employ in producing 80 units of output? Explain.
b. What is the profit-maximizing combination of labor and capital the firm should use? Explain. What is the resulting level of output? What is the economic profit? Is this the least costly way of producing the profit-maximizing output?

(a) 2 capital; 4 labor. $MP_L/P_L = 7/1$; $MP_C/P_C = 21/3 = 7/1$. The least-cost combination is found by equating the ratios of the marginal products of each input to their prices.
(b) 7 capital and 7 labor. $MRP_L/P_L = 1$ (= 1/1) = $MRP_C/P_C = 1$(= 3/3). Output is 142 (= 96 from capital + 46 from labor). Economic profit is $114 (= $142 − $28). Yes, least-cost production is part of maximizing profits. The profit-maximizing rule includes the least-cost rule.

27-7 In each of the following four cases, MRP_L and MRP_C refer to the marginal revenue products of labor and capital, respectively, and P_L and P_C refer to their prices. Indicate in each case whether the conditions are consistent with maximum profits for the firm. If not, state which resource(s) should be used in larger amounts and which resource(s) should be used in smaller amounts.
a. $MRP_L = 8; $P_L = 4; $MRP_C = 8; $P_C = 4
b. $MRP_L = 10; $P_L = 12; $MRP_C = 14; $P_C = 9.
c. $MRP_L = 6; $P_L = 6; $MRP_C = 12; $P_C = 12.
d. $MRP_L = 22; $P_L = 26; $MRP_C = 16; $P_C = 19.

(a) Use more of both;
(b) Use less labor and more capital;
(c) Maximum profits obtained;
(d) Use less of both.

CHAPTER 28

28-3 Describe wage determination in a labor market in which workers are unorganized and many firms actively compete for the services of labor. Show this situation graphically, using W_1 to indicate the equilibrium wage rate and Q_1 to show the number of workers hired by the firms as a group. Show the labor supply curve of the individual firm, and compare it with that of the total market. Why the differences? In the diagram representing the firm, identify total revenue, total wage cost, and revenue available for the payment of nonlabor resources.

The labor market is made up of many firms desiring to purchase a particular labor service and of many workers with that labor service. The market demand curve is downward sloping because of diminishing returns and the market supply curve is upward sloping because a higher wage will be necessary to attract additional workers into the market. Whereas the individual firm's supply curve is perfectly elastic because it can hire any number of workers at the going wage, the market supply curve is upward sloping.

For the graphs, see Figure 28.3 and its legend.

28-4 Complete the following labor supply table for a firm hiring labor competitively.

Units of labor	Wage rate	Total labor cost (wage bill)	Marginal resource (labor) cost
0	$14	$____	$____
1	14	____	____
2	14	____	____
3	14	____	____
4	14	____	____
5	14	____	____
6	14	____	____

a. Show graphically the labor supply and marginal resource (labor) cost curves for this firm. Explain the relationships of these curves to one another.
b. Plot the labor demand data of question 2 in Chapter 27 on the graph in part a above. What are the equilibrium wage rate and level of employment? Explain.

Total labor cost data, top to bottom: $0; $14; $28; $42; $56; $70; $84. Marginal resource cost data: $14, throughout.
(a) The labor supply curve and MRC curve coincide as a single horizontal line at the market wage rate of $14. The firm can employ as much labor as it wants, each unit costing $14; wage rate = MRC because the wage rate is constant to the firm.

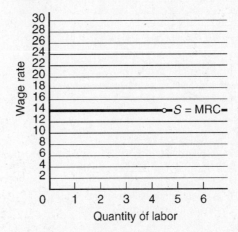

(b) Graph: equilibrium is at the intersection of the MRP and MRC curves. Equilibrium wage rate = $14; equilibrium level of employment = 4 units of labor. Explanation: From the tables: MRP exceeds MRC for each of the first four units of labor, but MRP is less than MRC for the fifth unit.

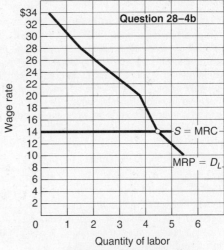

Question 28–4b

Quantity of labor
(MRP is plotted at the halfway
points on the horizontal axis)

28-6 Assume a firm is a monopsonist that can hire its first worker for $6 but must increase the wage rate by $3 to attract each successive worker. Draw the firm's labor supply and marginal resource cost curves and explain their relationships to one another. On the same graph, plot the labor demand data of question 2 in Chapter 27. What are the equilibrium wage rate and level of employment? What will be the equilibrium wage rate and the level of employment? Why do these differ from your answer to question 4?

The monopsonist faces the market labor supply curve S—it is the only firm hiring this labor. MRC lies above S and rises more rapidly than S because all workers get the higher wage rate that is needed to attract each added worker. Equilibrium wage/rate = $12; equilibrium employment = 3 (where MRP = MRC). The monopsonist can pay a below-competitive wage rate by restricting its employment.

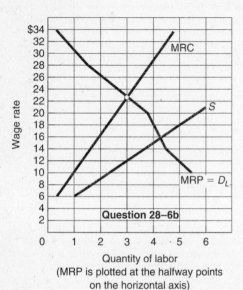

Quantity of labor
(MRP is plotted at the halfway points
on the horizontal axis)

28–7 Assume a monopsonistic employer is paying a wage rate of W_m and hiring Q_m workers, as indicated in Figure 28.8. Now suppose that an industrial union is formed and that it forces the employer to accept a wage rate of W_c. Explain verbally and graphically why in this instance the higher wage rate will be accompanied by an increase in the number of workers hired.

The union wage rate W_c becomes the firm's MRC, which would be shown as a horizontal line to the left of the labor supply curve. Each unit of labor now adds only its own wage rate to the firm's costs. The firm will employ Q_c workers, the quantity of labor where MRP = MRC (= W_c); Q_c is greater than the Q_m workers it would employ if there were no union and if the employer did not have any monopsonistic power, i.e., more workers are willing to offer their labor services when the wage is W_c than W_m.

CHAPTER 29

29–2 Explain why economic rent is a surplus payment when viewed by the economy as a whole but a cost of production from the standpoint of individual firms and industries. Explain: "Rent performs no 'incentive function' for the overall economy."

Land is completely fixed in total supply. As population expands and the demand for land increases, rent first appears and then grows. From society's perspective this rent is a surplus payment unnecessary for ensuring that the land is available to the economy as a whole. If rent declined or disappeared, the same amount of land would be available. If it increased, no more land would be forthcoming. Thus, rent does not function as an incentive for adding land to the economy.

But land does have alternative uses. To get it to its most productive use, individuals and firms compete and the winners are those who pay the highest rent. To the high bidders, rent is a cost

of production that must be covered by the revenue gained through the sale of the commodities produced on that land.

29–6 Why is the supply of loanable funds upward sloping? Why is the demand for loanable funds downward sloping? Explain the equilibrium interest rate. List some factors that might cause it to change.

(a) The supply of loanable funds is upward sloping because savers will make more funds available at higher interest rates than lower interest rates.

(b) The demand for loanable funds is downward sloping because there are few investment and R&D projects that yield a high rate of return and many more that will yield a lower rate of return.

(c) The equilibrium interest rate is determined where the interest rate (cost of borrowing the funds) is equal to the expected rate of return (the expected benefit from borrowing the funds and engaging in the investment or R&D project). The supply of loanable funds may change because of a change in households' attitudes about saving (tax policies, macroeconomic conditions) or changes in Federal Reserve policies relative to the money supply. The demand for loanable funds could change as a result of a change in technology or a change in the demand for the final product. If there is either a change in supply of or demand for loanable funds, the interest rate will change.

29–8 Distinguish between nominal and real interest rates. Which is more relevant in making investment and R&D decisions? If the nominal interest rate is 12 percent and the inflation rate is 8 percent, what is the real rate of interest?

The nominal interest rate is the interest rate stated in dollars of current value (unadjusted for inflation). The real interest rate is the nominal interest rate adjusted for inflation (or deflation). The real interest rate is more relevant for making investment decisions—it reflects the true cost of borrowing money. It is compared to the expected return on the investment in the decision process. Real interest rate = 4 percent (= 12 percent − 8 percent).

29–10 How do the concepts of accounting profit and economic profit differ? Why is economic profit smaller than accounting profit? What are the three basic sources of economic profit? Classify each of the following according to those sources:

a. A firm's profit from developing and patenting a new medication that greatly reduces cholesterol and thus diminishes the likelihood of heart disease and stroke.

b. A restaurant's profit that results from construction of a new highway past its door.

c. The profit received by a firm benefiting from an unanticipated change in consumer tastes.

Accounting profit is what remains of a firm's total revenues after it has paid for all the factors of production employed by the firm (its explicit costs) but not for the use of the resources owned by the business itself. Economists also take into consideration implicit costs—the payment the owners could have received by using the resources they own in some other way. The economist adds these implicit costs to the accountant's explicit costs to arrive at total cost. Subtracting the total cost from total revenue results in a smaller profit (the economic profit) than the accountant's profit.

Sources of economic profit: (1) uninsurable risks; (2) innovations; and (3) monopoly.

(a) Profit from assuming the uncertainties of innovation, as well as monopoly profit from the patent.

(b) Monopoly profit arising from its locational advantage.

(c) Profit from bearing the uninsurable risk of a change in demand (the change could have been unfavorable).

CHAPTER 30

30–1 On the basis of the three individual demand schedules below, and assuming these three people are the only ones in the society, determine (a) the market demand schedule on the assumption that the good is a private good, and (b) the collective demand schedule on the assumption that the good is a public good. Explain the differences, if any, in your schedules.

Individual #1		Individual #2		Individual #3	
Price	Q_d	Price	Q_d	Price	Q_d
$8	0	$8	1	$8	0
7	0	7	2	7	0
6	0	6	3	6	1
5	1	5	4	5	2
4	2	4	5	4	3
3	3	3	6	3	4
2	4	2	7	2	5
1	5	1	8	1	6

(a) Private good, top to bottom: $P = \$8$, $Q = 1$; $P = \$7$, $Q = 2$; $P = \$6$, $Q = 4$; $P = \$5$, $Q = 7$; $P = \$4$, $Q = 10$; $P = \$3$, $Q = 13$; $P = \$2$, $Q = 16$; $P = \$1$, $Q = 19$. (b) Public good, top to bottom; $P = \$19$, $Q = 1$; $P = \$16$, $Q = 2$; $P = \$13$, $Q = 3$; $P = \$10$, $Q = 4$; $P = \$7$, $Q = 5$; $P = \$4$, $Q = 6$; $P = \$2$, $Q = 7$; $P = \$1$, $Q = 8$. The first schedule represents a horizontal summation of the individual demand curves; the second schedule represents a vertical summation of these curves. The market demand curve for the private good will determine—in combination with market supply—an actual price-quantity outcome in the marketplace. Because potential buyers of public goods do not reveal their individual preferences in the market, the collective demand curve for the public good is hypothetical or needs to be determined through "willingness to pay" studies.

30–2 Use your demand schedule for a public good determined in question 1 and the following supply schedule to ascertain the optimal quantity of this public good. Why is this the optimal quantity?

Optimal quantity = 4. It is optimal because at 4 units the collective willingness to pay for the final unit of the good (= $10) matches the marginal cost of production (= $10).

P	Q_S
$19	10
16	8
13	6
10	4
7	2
4	0

30–3 The following table shows the total costs and total benefits in billions for four different antipollution programs of increasing scope. Which program should be undertaken? Why?

Program	Total cost	Total benefit
A	$ 3	$ 7
B	7	12
C	12	16
D	18	19

Program B, since the marginal benefit no longer exceeds marginal cost for programs that are larger in scope. Plan B is where net benefits—the excess of total benefits over total costs—are maximized.

30–4 Why are spillover costs and spillover benefits also called negative and positive externalities? Show graphically how a tax can correct for a spillover cost and a subsidy to producers can correct for a spillover benefit. How does a subsidy to consumers differ from a subsidy to producers in correcting for a spillover benefit?

Spillover costs are called negative externalities because they are *external* to the participants in the transaction and *reduce* the utility of affected third parties (thus "negative"). Spillover benefits are called positive externalities because they are *external* to the participants in the transaction and *increase* the utility of affected third parties (thus "positive"). See Figures 30.3 and 30.4. Compare (b) and (c) in Figure 30.4.

30–7 Explain the following statement, using the MB curve in Figure 30.6 to illustrate: "The optimal amount of pollution abatement for some substances, say, water from storm drains, is very low; the optimal amount of abatement for other substances, say, cyanide poison, is close to 100 percent."

Reducing water flow from storm drains has a low marginal benefit, meaning the MB curve would be located far to the left of where it is in the text diagram. It will intersect the MC curve at a low amount of pollution abatement, indicating the optimal amount of pollution abatement (where MB = MC) is low. Any cyanide in public water sources could be deadly. Therefore, the marginal benefit of reducing cyanide is extremely high and the MB curve in the figure would be located to the extreme right where it would intersect the MC curve at or near 100 percent.

30–13 Place an "M" beside items in the following list that describe a moral hazard problem and an "A" beside those that describe an adverse selection problem.

a. A person with a terminal illness buys several life insurance policies through the mail.
b. A person drives carelessly because he or she has automobile insurance.
c. A person who intends to "torch" his warehouse takes out a large fire insurance policy.
d. A professional athlete who has a guaranteed contract fails to stay in shape during the off-season.
e. A woman anticipating having a large family takes a job with a firm that offers exceptional child-care benefits.

Moral hazard problem: (b) and (d). Adverse selection problem: (a), (c), and (e).

CHAPTER 31

31–2 Explain the paradox of voting through reference to the accompanying table, which shows the ranking of three public goods by voters Jay, Dave, and Conan.

Public good	Jay	Dave	Conan
Courthouse	2d choice	1st choice	3d choice
School	3d choice	2d choice	1st choice
Park	1st choice	3d choice	2d choice

The paradox is that majority voting does not always provide a clear and consistent picture of the public's preferences. Here the courthouse is preferred to the school and the park is preferred to the courthouse, so we would surmise that the park is preferred to the school. But paired-choice voting would show that the school is preferred to the park.

31–3 Suppose that there are only five people in a society and that each favors one of the five highway construction options shown in Table 30.2 (include no highway construction as one of the options). Explain which of these highway options will be selected using a majority paired-choice vote. Will this option be the optimal size of the project from an economic perspective?

Project B (New 2-lane highway wins) using a paired-choice vote. There is no "paradox of voting" problem here and B is the preference of the median voter. The two voters favoring No new construction and Widening, respectively, will prefer New 2-lane highways—project B—to New 4- or 6-lane highways. The two voters preferring New 4- and 6-lane highways will prefer a New 2-lane highway to Widening or No new construction. The median voter's preference for B will prevail. However, the optimal size of the project from an economic perspective is C—it would provide a greater net benefit to society than B.

31–4 How does the problem of limited and bundled choice in the public sector relate to economic efficiency? Why are public bureaucracies alleged to be less efficient than private enterprises?

The electorate is faced with a small number of candidates, each of whom offers a broad range or "bundle" of proposed policies. Voters are then forced to choose the individual candidate whose bundle of policies most resembles their own. The chances of a perfect identity between a particular candidate's preferences and those of any voter are quite slim. As a result, the voter must purchase some unwanted public goods and services. This represents an inefficient allocation of resources.

Government bureaucracies do not function on the basis of profit, so the incentive for holding down costs is less than in the private sector. Also, because there is no profit-and-loss test of efficiency, it is difficult to determine whether public agencies are operating efficiently. Nor is there entry of competing entities to stimulate efficiency and develop improved public goods and services. Furthermore, wasteful expenditures can be maintained through the self-seeking lobbying of bureaucrats themselves, and the public budgetary process can reward rather than penalize inefficiency.

31–7 Suppose a tax is such that an individual with an income of $10,000 pays $2,000 of tax, a person with an income of $20,000 pays $3,000 of tax, a person with an income of $30,000 pays $4,000 of tax, and so forth. What is each person's average tax rate? Is this tax regressive, proportional, or progressive?

Average tax rates: 20; 15; and 13.3 percent. Regressive.

31–9 What is the incidence of an excise tax when demand is highly inelastic? Elastic? What effect does the elasticity of supply have on the incidence of an excise tax? What is the efficiency loss of a tax, and how does it relate to elasticity of demand and supply?

The incidence of an excise tax is likely to be primarily on consumers when demand is highly inelastic and primarily on producers when demand is elastic. The more elastic the supply, the greater the incidence of an excise tax on consumers and the less on producers.

The efficiency loss of a sales or excise tax is the net benefit society sacrifices because consumption and production of the taxed product are reduced below the level of allocative efficiency which would occur without the tax. Other things equal, the greater the elasticities of demand and supply, the greater the efficiency loss of a particular tax.

CHAPTER 32

32–2 Describe the major provisions of the Sherman and Clayton Acts. What government entities are responsible for enforcing those laws? Are firms permitted to initiate antitrust suits on their own against other firms?

Sherman Act: Section 1 prohibits conspiracies to restrain trade; Section 2 outlaws monopolization. Clayton Act (as amended by Celler-Kefauver Act of 1950): Section 2 outlaws price discrimination; Section 3 forbids tying contracts; Section 7 prohibits mergers which substantially lessen competition; Section 8 prohibits interlocking directorates. The acts are enforced by the Department of Justice, Federal Trade Commission, and state attorneys general. Private firms can bring suit against other firms under these laws.

32–5 How would you expect antitrust authorities to react to (a) a proposed merger of Ford and General Motors; (b) evidence of secret meetings by contractors to rig bids for highway construction projects; (c) a proposed merger of a large shoe manufacturer and a chain of retail shoe stores; (d) a proposed merger of a small life insurance company and a regional candy manufacturer; and (e) an automobile rental firm that charges higher rates for last-minute rentals than for rentals reserved weeks in advance?

(a) They would block this horizontal merger (violation of Section 7 of the Clayton Act). (b) They would charge these firms with price fixing (violation of Section 1 of the Sherman Act). (c) They would allow this vertical merger, unless both firms had very large market shares and the resultant merger substantially lessens competition. (d) They would allow this conglomerate merger. (e) They would not interfere with this price discrimination.

32–10 What types of industries, if any, should be subjected to industrial regulation? What specific problems does industrial regulation entail?

Industries composed of firms with natural monopoly conditions are most likely to be subjected to industrial regulation. Regulation based on "fair-return" prices creates disincentives for firms to minimize costs since cost reductions lead regulators to force firms to charge a lower price. Regulated firms may also use "creative" accounting to boost costs and hide profits. Because regulatory commissions depend on information provided by the firms themselves, and commission members are often recruited from the industry, the agencies may in effect be controlled by the firms they are supposed to oversee. Also, industrial regulation sometimes is applied to industries that are not, or no longer are, natural monopolies. Regulation may lead to the conditions of a cartel, conditions that are illegal in an unregulated industry.

32–12 How does social regulation differ from industrial regulation? What types of benefits and costs are associated with social regulation?

Industrial regulation is concerned with prices, output, and profits in specific industries, whereas social regulation deals with the broader impact of business on consumers, workers, and third parties. Benefits: increased worker and product safety, less environmental damage, reduced economic discrimination. Two types of costs: administrative costs, because regulations must be administered by costly government agencies; compliance costs, because firms must increase spending to comply with regulations.

CHAPTER 33

33–1 Carefully evaluate: "The supply and demand for agricultural products are such that small changes in agricultural supply will result in drastic changes in prices. However, large changes in farm prices have modest effects on agricultural output." (*Hint:* A brief review of the distinction between supply and quantity supplied may be of assistance.) Do exports increase or reduce the instability of demand for farm products? Explain.

First sentence: Shifts in the supply curve of agricultural goods (*changes in supply*) relative to fixed inelastic demand curves produce large changes in equilibrium prices. Second sentence: But these drastic changes in prices produce only small changes in equilibrium outputs (where *quantities demanded* equals *quantities supplied*) because demands are inelastic.

Because exports are volatile from one year to the next, they increase the instability of demand for farm products.

33–3 Explain how each of the following contributes to the farm problem: **(a)** the inelasticity of the demand for farm products, **(b)** the rapid technological progress in farming, **(c)** the modest long-run growth in the demand for farm commodities, and **(d)** the volatility of export demand.

(a) Because the demand for most farm products is inelastic, the frequent fluctuations in supply brought about by weather and other factors have relatively small effects on quantity demanded, but large effects on equilibrium prices of farm products. Farmers' sales revenues and incomes therefore are unstable. (b) Technological innovations have decreased production costs, increased long-run supply for most agricultural goods, and reduced the prices of farm output. These declines in prices have put a downward pressure on farm income. (c) The modest long-run growth in the demand for farm products has not been sufficient to offset the expansion of supply, resulting in stagnant farm income. (d) Foreign demand has been unpredictable. Any change in demand will affect farm prices but farmers cannot easily adjust production.

33–8 Explain the economic effects of price supports. Explicitly include environmental and global impacts in your answer. On what grounds do economists contend that price supports cause a misallocation of resources?

Price supports benefit farmers, harm consumers, impose costs on society, and contribute to problems in world agriculture. Farmers benefit because the prices they receive and the output they produce both increase, expanding their gross incomes. Consumers lose because the prices they pay for farm products rise and quantities purchased decline. Society as a whole bears several costs. Surpluses of farm products will have to be bought and stored, leading to a greater burden on taxpayers. Domestic economic efficiency is lessened as the artificially high prices of farm products lead to an overallocation of resources to agriculture. The environment suffers: The greater use of pesticides and fertilizers contributes to water pollution; farm policies discourage crop rotation; and price supports encourage farming of environmentally sensitive land. The efficient use of world resources is also distorted because of the import tariffs or quotas that such programs often require. Finally, domestic overproduction leads to supply increases in international markets, decreasing prices and causing a decline in the gross incomes of foreign producers.

CHAPTER 34

34–2 Assume Al, Beth, Carol, David, and Ed receive incomes of $500, $250, $125, $75, and $50, respectively. Construct and interpret a Lorenz curve for this five-person economy. What percentage of total income is received by the richest and by the poorest quintiles?

See the following figure. In this simple economy each person represents a complete income quintile—20 percent of the total population. The richest quintile (Al) receives 50 percent of total income; the poorest quintile (Ed) receives 5 percent.

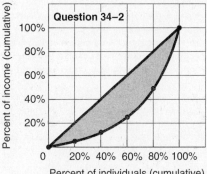

34–5 Briefly discuss the major causes of income inequality. With respect to income inequality, is there any difference between inheriting property and inheriting a high IQ? Explain.

The reasons for income inequality are: differences in abilities and talents among individuals, differences in the amount of education and training an individual obtains, labor market discrimination, differences in tastes and preferences toward work and job attributes, inequality in the distribution of wealth, the ability to use market power to transfer income to oneself, luck, connections, and misfortune.

A high IQ normally does not lead to high income unless it is combined with personal initiative and favorable social circumstances. Inherited property—as long as it is competently managed—provides income irrespective of one's character and personal attributes. Both factors are largely a matter of the luck of being born into a family with good ability genes and/or wealth. What one does with the genes or wealth is up to the recipient.

CHAPTER 35

35–4 What is the estimated size of the union wage advantage? How might this advantage diminish the efficiency with which labor resources are allocated?

Fifteen percent. The higher wages that unions achieve reduce employment, displace workers, and increase the marginal revenue product in the union sector. Labor supply increases in the nonunionized sector, reducing wages and decreasing marginal revenue product there. Because of the lower nonunion marginal revenue product, the workers added in the nonunion sector contribute less to GDP than they would have in the unionized sector. The gain of GDP in the nonunionized sector does not offset the loss of GDP in the unionized sector so there is an overall efficiency loss.

35–7 The labor demand and supply data in the following table relate to a single occupation. Use them to answer the questions that follow. Base your answers on the taste-for-discrimination model.

Quantity of Hispanic labor demanded, thousands	Hispanic wage rate	Quantity of Hispanic labor supplied, thousands
24	$16	52
30	14	44
35	12	35
42	10	28
48	8	20

a. Plot the labor demand and supply curves for Hispanic workers in this occupation.
b. What are the equilibrium Hispanic wage rate and quantity of Hispanic employment?
c. Suppose the white wage rate in this occupation is $16. What is the Hispanic-to-white wage ratio?
d. Suppose a particular employer has a discrimination coefficient, d, of $5 per hour. Will that employer hire Hispanic or white workers at the Hispanic-white wage ratio indicated by part c? Explain.
e. Suppose employers as a group become less prejudiced against Hispanics and demand 14 more units of Hispanic labor at each Hispanic wage rate in the table. What are the new equilibrium Hispanic wage rate and level of Hispanic employment? Does the Hispanic-white wage ratio rise or fall? Explain.
f. Suppose Hispanics as a group increase their labor services in this occupation, collectively offering 14 more units of labor at each Hispanic wage rate. Disregarding the changes indicated in part e, what are the new equilibrium Hispanic wage rate and level of Hispanic employment? Does the Hispanic-white wage ratio rise, or does it fall?

(a)

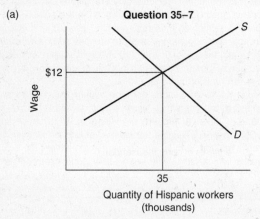

Question 35–7

(b) The equilibrium Hispanic wage rate is $12; the equilibrium quantity of Hispanic employment is 36,000 workers.
(c) The Hispanic-to-white wage ratio is .75 (= $12/$16).
(d) The employer will hire only white workers because the $5 discrimination coefficient exceeds the $4 difference between the wage rates of whites and Hispanics.
(e) The new equilibrium Hispanic wage rate is $14 and the new equilibrium quantity of Hispanic employment is 44,000 workers. The Hispanic-white wage ratio rises to .875 (= $14/$16) because of the increased demand for Hispanic labor in relation to the unchanging supply of Hispanic labor.
(f) The new equilibrium Hispanic wage rate is $10 and the new equilibrium quantity of Hispanic employment is 20,000. This Hispanic-white wage ratio falls to .625 (= $10/$16).

35–9 Use a demand and supply model to explain the impact of occupational segregation or "crowding" on the relative wage rates and earnings of men and women. Who gains and who loses from the elimination of occupational segregation? Is there a net gain or net loss to society? Explain.

See Figure 35.5. Discrimination against women in two of the three occupations will crowd women into the third occupation. Labor supply in the "men's occupations" (X and Y) decreases, making them high-wage occupations. Labor supply in the "women's occupation" (Z) increases, creating a low-wage occupation.

Eliminating occupational segregation would entice women into the high-wage occupations, increasing labor supply there

and reducing it in the low-wage occupation. The wage rates in the three occupations would converge to B. Women would gain, men would lose. Society would gain because the increase in output in the expanding occupations would exceed the loss of output in the contracting occupation.

35–12 Use graphical analysis to show the gains and losses resulting from the migration of population from a low-income country to a high-income country. Explain how your conclusions are affected by (a) unemployment, (b) remittances to the home country, (c) backflows of migrants to their home country, and (d) the personal characteristics of the migrants. If the migrants are highly skilled workers, is there any justification for the sending country to levy a "brain drain" tax on emigrants?

See Figure 35.6. Migration of labor from the low- to high-income country increases the labor supply in the high-income country and decreases it in the low-income country. Wages are equalized at W_e. Output and business income increases in the receiving country, declines in the sending country. World output increases: The output gain in the receiving country exceeds the output loss in the sending country.
(a) The gains to the receiving country will not materialize if the migrants are unemployed after they arrive; there may be gains in the low-income country if the immigrant had been unemployed prior to moving. (b) Remittances to the home country will decrease the income gain in the receiving country and reduce the income loss in the sending country. (c) If migrants who return to their home country have enhanced their skills, their temporary departure might be to the long-run advantage of the home country. (d) Young, skilled migrants will increase output and likely be the net taxpayers in the receiving country, but the sending country will experience a "brain drain." Older or less skilled workers who are not so easily assimilated could be net recipients of government services.
In view of the sometimes-large investments which sending countries have made in providing education and skills, there is a justification for levying a departure tax on such migrants. But if this tax were too high, it would infringe on a basic human right: the right to emigrate.

CHAPTER 36

36–2 What are the "twin problems" of the health care industry? How are they related?

The "twin problems" are rising prices for all and limited access (lack of insurance) for about 16 percent of the population (41 million). The problems are related since rising costs make insurance unaffordable for many individuals and families, and make it difficult for some businesses to insure their workers.

36–7 What are the estimated income and price elasticities of demand for health care? How does each relate to rising health care costs?

Income elasticity is 1.0, suggesting that health care spending will rise proportionately with income. Some studies indicate that it might be 1.5 in the United States. Price elasticity is only 0.2, meaning higher prices for health care services will increase total health care spending.

36–10 Using the concepts in Chapter 21's discussion of consumer behavior, explain how health care insurance results in an overallocation of resources to the health care industry. Use a demand and supply diagram to specify the resulting efficiency loss.

Health care insurance removes or greatly lessens a person's budget restraint at the time health care is purchased, raising health care utility per dollar spent and causing an overconsumption of health care. In Figure 36.3b, insurance reduces the price of health care at the time of purchase from P_u to P_i, increasing the quantity consumed from Q_u to Q_i. At Q_i the marginal cost of health care is represented by point b and exceeds the marginal benefit represented by c, indicating an overallocation of resources. The efficiency loss is area cab.

CHAPTER 37

37–4 Below are the hypothetical production possibilities tables for New Zealand and Spain.

New Zealand's production possibilities table (millions of bushels)

Product	Production alternatives			
	A	B	C	D
Apples	0	20	40	60
Plums	15	10	5	0

Spain's production possibilities table (millions of bushels)

Product	Production alternatives			
	R	S	T	U
Apples	0	20	40	60
Plums	60	40	20	0

Plot the production possibilities data for each of the two countries separately. Referring to your graphs, answer the following: (a) What is each country's cost ratio of producing plums and apples? (b) Which nation should specialize in which product? (c) Show the trading possibilities lines for each nation if the actual terms of trade are 1 plum for 2 apples. (Plot these lines on your graph.) (d) Suppose the optimum product mixes before specialization and trade were alternative B in New Zealand and S in Spain. What would be gains from specialization and trade?

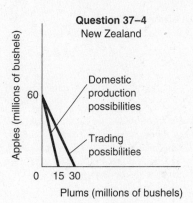

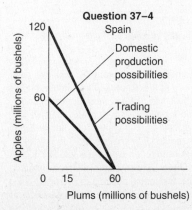

(a) New Zealand's cost ratio is 1 plum = 4 apples (or 1 apple = 1/4 plum). Spain's cost ratio is 1 plum = 1 apple (or 1 apple = 1 plum). See the graphs.
(b) New Zealand should specialize in apples, Spain in plums.
(c) See the graphs.
(d) Total production before specialization and trade: 40 apples (20 + 20) and 50 plums (10 + 40). After specialization and trade: 60 apples and 60 plums. Gain = 20 apples and 10 plums.

37–6 Refer to Figure 3.5, p. 49 (Chapter 3). Assume that the graph depicts the U.S. domestic market for corn. How many bushels of corn, if any, will the United States export or import at a world price of $1, $2, $3, $4, and $5? Use this information to construct the U.S. export supply curve and import demand curve for corn. Suppose the only other corn-producing nation is France, where the domestic price is $4. Which country will export corn; which will import it?

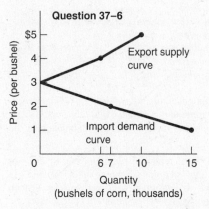

At $1: import 15,000. At $2: import 7,000. At $3: no imports or exports. At $4: export 6,000. At $5: export 10,000.
The United States will export corn; France will import it.

37–7 Draw a domestic supply and demand diagram for a product in which the United States does not have a comparative advantage. What impact do foreign imports have on domestic price and quantity? On your diagram show a protective tariff that eliminates approximately one-half the assumed imports. What are the price-quantity effects of this tariff on (a) domestic consumers, (b) domestic producers, and (c) foreign exporters? How would the effects of a quota that creates the same amount of imports differ?

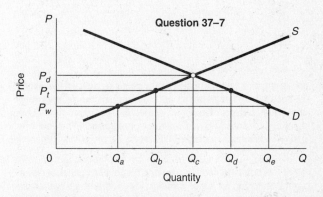

See the graph. The United States does not have a comparative advantage in this product so the world price P_w is below the U.S. domestic price of P_d. Imports will reduce the domestic price, increasing consumption from nontrade Q_c to Q_e, and decreasing domestic production from Q_c to Q_a. See the graph. A tariff of P_wP_t (a) harms domestic consumers by increasing price from P_w to P_t and decreasing consumption from Q_e to Q_d; (b) aids domestic producers through the increase in price from P_w to P_t and the expansion of domestic production from Q_a to Q_b; (c) harms foreign exporters by decreasing exports from Q_aQ_e to Q_bQ_d.

An import quota of Q_bQ_d would have the same effects as the tariff, but there would be no tariff revenues to government from these imports; this revenue would effectively go to foreign producers.

CHAPTER 38

38-2 Indicate whether each of the following creates a demand for, or a supply of, European euros in foreign exchange markets:

  a. A U.S. airline firm purchases several Airbus planes assembled in France.

  b. A German automobile firm decides to build an assembly plant in South Carolina.

  c. A U.S. college student decides to spend a year studying at the Sorbonne in Paris.

  d. An Italian manufacturer ships machinery from one Italian port to another on a Liberian freighter.

  e. The United States' economy grows faster than the French economy.

  f. A United States government bond held by a Spanish citizen matures, and the loan is paid back to that person.

  g. It is widely believed that the euro will depreciate in the near future.

A demand for euros is created in (a),(c),(e), and (f), but see note below for e. A supply of euros is created in (b), (d), and (g).

Note: Answer for (e) assumes U.S. demand for French goods will grow faster than French imports of U.S. goods.

38-3 Alpha's balance-of-payments data for 2003 are shown below. All figures are in billions of dollars. What are (a) the balance of trade, (b) the balance on goods and services, (c) the balance on current account, and (d) the balance on capital account? Does Alpha have a balance-of-payments deficit or surplus? Explain.

Goods exports	+$40	Net transfers	+$10
Goods imports	− 30	Foreign purchases of	+ 10
Service exports	+ 15	U.S. assets	
Service imports	− 10	U.S. purchases of	− 40
Net investment income	− 5	foreign assets	
		Official reserves	+ 10

Balance of trade = $10 billion surplus (= exports of goods of $40 billion minus imports of goods of $30 billion). *Note:* This is goods balance only—uses narrow definition of trade balance. Balance on goods and services = $15 billion surplus (= $55 billion of exports of goods and services minus $40 billion of imports of goods and services). Balance on current account = $20 billion surplus (= credits of $65 billion minus debits of $45 billion). Balance on capital account = $30 billion deficit (= foreign purchases of assets in the United States of $10 billion minus U.S. purchases of assets abroad of $40 billion). Balance of payments = $10 billion deficit. Therefore, U.S. must export official reserves equal to $10 billion.

38-6 Explain why the U.S. demand for Mexican pesos is downward sloping and the supply of pesos to Americans is upward sloping. Assuming a system of flexible exchange rates between Mexico and the United States, indicate whether each of the following would cause the Mexican peso to appreciate or depreciate:

  a. The United States unilaterally reduces tariffs on Mexican products.

  b. Mexico encounters severe inflation.

  c. Deteriorating political relations reduce American tourism in Mexico.

  d. The U.S. economy moves into a severe recession.

  e. The United States engages in a high interest rate monetary policy.

  f. Mexican products become more fashionable to U.S. consumers.

  g. The Mexican government encourages U.S. firms to invest in Mexican oil fields.

  h. The rate of productivity growth in the United States diminishes sharply.

The U.S. demand for pesos is downward sloping: When the peso depreciates in value (relative to the dollar) the United States finds that Mexican goods and services are less expensive in dollar terms and purchases more of them, demanding a greater quantity of pesos in the process. The supply of pesos to the United States is upward sloping: As the peso appreciates in value (relative to the dollar), U.S. goods and services become cheaper to Mexicans in peso terms. Mexicans buy more dollars to obtain more U.S. goods, supplying a larger quantity of pesos.

The peso appreciates in (a), (f), (g), and (h) and depreciates in (b), (c), (d), and (e).

38-9 Diagram a market in which the equilibrium dollar price of one unit of fictitious currency zee (Z) is $5 (the exchange rate is $5 = Z1). Then show on your diagram a decline in the demand for zees.

  a. Referring to your diagram, discuss the adjustment options the United States would have in maintaining the exchange rate at $5 = Z1 under a fixed exchange-rate system.

  b. How would the U.S. balance-of-payments surplus that is created (by the decline in demand) get resolved under a system of flexible exchange rates?

See the graph illustrating the market for zees.

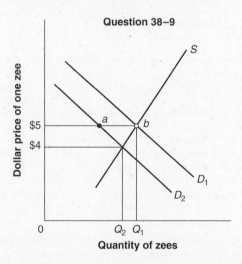

Question 38-9

(a) The decrease in demand for zees from D_1 to D_2 will create a surplus (*ab*) of zees at the $5 price. To maintain the $5 to Z1 exchange rate, the United States must undertake policies to shift the demand-for-zees curve rightward or shift the supply-of-zees curve leftward. To increase the demand for zees, the United States could use dollars or gold to buy zees in the foreign exchange market; employ trade policies to increase imports to the United States from Zeeonia; or enact expansionary fiscal and monetary policies to increase U.S. domestic output and income, thus increasing imports from

Zeeonia and elsewhere. Expansionary monetary policy could also reduce the *supply* of zees: Zeeons could respond to the lower U.S. interest rates by reducing their investing in the United States. Therefore, they would not supply as many zees to the foreign exchange market.

(b) Under a system of flexible exchange rates, the *ab* surplus of zees (the U.S. balance-of-payments surplus) will cause the zee to depreciate and the dollar to appreciate until the surplus is eliminated (at the $4 = Z1 exchange rate shown in the figure) because the United States would import more from Zeeonia and they would buy less from the United States since zees had lost value.

CHAPTER 39W

39W-3 Assume a DVC and an IAC presently have real per capita outputs of $500 and $5,000, respectively. If both nations have a 3 percent increase in their real per capita outputs, by how much will the per capita output gap change?

Rise in per capital output gap = $135 (= 3% × $5,000 − 3% × $500).

39W-5 Contrast the demographic transition view of population growth with the traditional view that slower population growth is a prerequisite for rising living standards in the DVCs.

Demographic transition view: Expanded output and income in developing countries will result in lower birthrates and slower growth of population. As incomes of primary family members expand, they will begin to see the marginal cost of a larger family exceeding the marginal benefit. The policy emphasis should therefore be on economic growth. Traditional view: Developing nations should reduce population growth as a first priority. Slow population growth enables the growth of per capita income.

39W-6 Because real capital is supposed to earn a higher return where it is scarce, how do you explain the fact that most international investment flows to the IACs (where capital is relatively abundant) rather than to the DVCs (where capital is very scarce)?

Capital earns a higher return where it is scarce, *other things equal*. However, when comparing investment opportunities between IACs and DVCs, other things are not equal. Advanced factories filled with specialized equipment require a productive workforce. IACs have an abundance of educated, experienced workers; these workers are scarce in DVCs. Also, IACs have extensive public infrastructures that increase the returns on private capital. Example: a network of highways makes it more profitable to produce goods that need to be widely transported. Finally, investment returns must be adjusted for risk. IACs have stable governments and "law and order," reducing the risk of capital being "nationalized" or pilfered by organized crime.

39W-12 Use Figure 39W.2 (changing the box labels as necessary) to explain rapid economic growth in a country such as South Korea or Chile. What factors other than those contained in the figure might contribute to that growth?

To describe countries such as South Korea and Chile, we would need to change labels on three boxes, leading to a change in the "results" boxes. "Rapid" population growth would change to "low" rate of population growth; "low" level of saving would change to "high" level of saving; "low" levels of investment in physical and human capital would change to "high" levels of invest-ment in physical and human capital. These three changes would result in higher productivity and higher per capita income, which would produce a rising level of demand. Other factors: stable national government; homogeneous population; extensive investment in infrastructure; "will to develop"; strong private incentives.

CHAPTER 40W

40W-5 Use a supply and demand diagram to explain why persistent shortages of many consumer goods occurred under central planning in the Soviet Union and in prereform China. Why were black markets common in each country?

See Figure 40W.1. Because Russia and China set prices and did not allow them to change as supply or demand shifted, prices were below the equilibrium price for most goods and services. When the fixed price, P_f, is below the equilibrium price, P_e, there will be a shortage since the quantity demanded will exceed the quantity supplied.

Black markets are common where prices are fixed below equilibrium levels. People can buy goods at the fixed government prices (or pay off clerks to save such goods to sell to them), and because of the shortages at the low fixed price, resell these goods at a much higher price to those unable to find the goods in government stores at the controlled prices. This reselling is said to occur on the black market.

40W-6 What have been the major components of economic reform in Russia? What is meant when these reforms are described as "shock therapy"? How successful has Russia been thus far in its reforms?

Privatization of state-owned businesses; market-determined prices; promotion of competition; integration with the world economy; and price-level stabilization. These reforms are referred to as shock therapy because they were dramatic and quick rather than phased in over many years. Russia's reform has nominally privatized much of the economy (but property rights are still not clearly defined), establishing market-determined prices, and setting the stage for future prosperity. But the transition has resulted in declining living standards for many and increasing income inequality. Also, the government still does not have a successful program for collecting taxes.

40W-8 Relate each of the following items to the success of market reform in China: (a) leasing farmland, (b) price reform, (c) private rural and urban enterprises, (d) special economic zones, and (e) corporatization of state-owned enterprises.

(a) Leasing of land resulted in individually operated rather than collectivized farms; this greatly increased production incentives and boosted farm output.
(b) Price reform established market-based prices. These higher-than-government prices provided incentives for enterprises to expand output; they also enabled market-determined allocation of resources to replace inefficient central planning.
(c) Private rural and urban enterprises absorbed workers released by greater productivity in China's agricultural sector and established competition for China's state-owned enterprises.
(d) The special economic zones—with their private corporations, free trade, and foreign investment—established the workability and benefits of "near-capitalism."
(e) Corporatization focused the goals of state-owned enterprises on providing high-quality, minimum per-unit cost goods desired by consumers.